AUSTRALIAN MEDICAL LAW

Exploring the patterns in the rich tapestry of medical law, this text is the most up-to-date work of its kind. After an introduction to bio-ethical principles, *Australian Medical Law* discusses the interplay of different areas of law as they impact on medical practice. The text considers the impact of contract, crime and tort law. Particular attention is given to competency and the thorny issue of consent to treatment. Other areas canvassed include confidentiality, access to medical records, complaints and transplants.

The latest case law is included, as well as commentary on the Civil Liability Act. Clearly expressed and accessible, this text is relevant to all students and practitioners involved in the burgeoning field of medical law.

John Devereux is Professor of Common Law at the TC Beirne School of Law, University of Queensland.

AUSTRALIAN MEDICAL LAW

THIRD EDITION

J. A. Devereux

With contribution by
Rachel Moore

Routledge·Cavendish
Taylor & Francis Group
LONDON AND NEW YORK

First edition published 1997 by Cavendish Publishing Limited
Second edition published 2002 by Cavendish Publishing Limited
Third edition published 2007
by Routledge-Cavendish
2 Park Square, Milton Park, Abingdon, Oxon OX14 4RN, UK

Simultaneously published in the USA and Canada
by Routledge-Cavendish
711 Third Avenue, New York, NY 10017

Routledge-Cavendish is an imprint of the Taylor & Francis Group, an informa business

Typeset in Times by
RefineCatch Limited, Bungay, Suffolk

British Library Cataloguing in Publication Data
A catalogue record for this book is available from the British Library

Library of Congress Cataloging in Publication Data
A catalog record for this book has been requested

ISBN10: 1–876905–38–7 (pbk)
ISBN13: 978–1–876905–38–5 (pbk)

CONTENTS

PREFACE

Much has changed since Ian Kennedy was able to state:

> Medical Law used to be fun. All you had to do was read lots of strange American cases, the odd Commonwealth decision, and maybe some English 19th century cases on crime. Then you could reflect that none of these was relevant and get on with the fun of inventing answers [Kennedy, I, 'The Patient on the Clapham Omnibus' (1984) 47 MLR 454].

Australian law is gradually weaving its distinctive, rich tapestry of medical law. This book attempts to explain some (though by no means all) of the intricate patterns inherent in the tapestry. This manuscript does not attempt to be a definitive guide to the law, a function which is more properly the province of a textbook. Rather, this work aims to provide a sourcebook of readings, cases and commentary on medical law topics. (Nor, as it is customary to note these days, is this book a substitute for professional legal advice in the event of a particular medico-legal problem.)

It proved to be as much a challenge to decide what topics and materials to leave out of this work as it was to decide which materials to include. In the end, it was decided to divide the topics into two parts. In the first part, doctor-patient interactions are characterised in terms of the legal obligations which arise. In this part are to be found chapters on the constitutional limitations on the delivery of health care, the application of criminal and civil battery to the doctor-patient interaction and the use of the negligence action by aggrieved patients. The duty of confidence is also explored.

In the second part, particular medical law problems are addressed. The final chapter of the book makes brief reference to complaints schemes which are currently operable in all jurisdictions in Australia.

The book is targeted at people who wish to know more about the way the law views doctor-patient interactions. It is likely to be of most assistance to law students. The book may also be of some interest to students of nursing or medicine. With the latter in mind, as far as possible, each chapter has been written so that it may be read as a separate entity.

In light of the potentially diverse readership, some licence has been taken with respect to referencing style. Footnotes of extracts have been omitted to avoid cluttering the text with extrinsic matters. The legal citation style of 'page number x at y' which is apt to cause confusion to non-legal readers has been abandoned, and in its place the use of the notation pp substituted to indicate which pages of a text are extracted (where not all of a particular piece is extracted).

I should like to thank those students at the University of Queensland, University of Tasmania, Griffith University and the Northern Territory University who, by their enthusiasm and good will, have made teaching medical law a delight. Some of the research for this book was conducted while on sabbatical leave from the University of Queensland. I would like to thank the faculty and staff of the National University of Singapore, Boston University and Harvard University for their generosity and assistance while I was abroad. Special thanks go to Professor Fran and Dr Hugh Miller, whose superbly equipped and wonderfully warm house was the perfect home in which to write during a chilly New England winter.

My thanks go to Jo Reddy at Cavendish for her ready acceptance of a text, cases and materials book on medical law; and to Sonny Leong for his patience and support. Thanks also to Zoe Botterill, Sanjeevi Perera and Madeleine Langford at Cavendish for their assistance and encouragement through the gestation of this book. Special thanks go to Rosalie Sheldrick who assisted in resolving (the inevitable) formatting problems with the text. The law is stated as available to me as at January 2006.

This book is respectfully dedicated to my parents.

John Devereux
Australia Day 2006

ACKNOWLEDGMENTS

Grateful acknowledgment is made for the following:

Buetow, S, 'Formal complaints and disciplinary proceedings involving medical practitioners' (1995) 14 *Medicine and Law*

Cica, N, 'The inadequacies of Australian abortion law' (1991) 5 *Australian Journal of Family Law* 45–52

Creyke, R, *Who Can Decide? Legal Decision Making for Others*, 1995, Australian Government Publishing Service

Dalpont, G and Chalmers, D, *An Introduction to Equity in Australia and New Zealand*, 1996, Lawbook Co Ltd

Devereux, J, 'Competency to consent to treatment: an introduction', in Freckelton, I and Petersen, K, *Controversies in Health*, 2000, Sydney: Law Federation Press

Dickens, B, 'Medical law: speciality or generality?', from *Medicine and the Law*, 1993, Dartmouth Publishing Co

Godwin, J, Hamblin, J, Patterson, D and Buchanan, D, *Australian HIV/AIDS Legal Guide*, 2nd edn, 1993, Sydney: Federation Press

Grubb, A and Pearl, D, 'Blood testing, AIDS and DNA profiling' [1990] Family Law, Jordan Publishing Limited

Human Rights and Equal Opportunity Commission, *Human Rights and Mental Illness*, 1993, Australian Government Publishing Service

Jones, A. *Personal Injuries Queensland* Butterworths, looseleaf service.

Jones, M, *Medical Negligence*, 1991, London: Sweet & Maxwell. See now 2nd edn, 1995

Kennedy, I and Grubb, A, *Medical Law; Text with Materials*, 2nd edn, 1994, London: Butterworths. See now 3rd edn, 2000

Macher, AM, 'HIV Disease/AIDS: medical background', in Webber, D (ed), AIDS and the Law, 1992, New York: John Wiley and Sons, pp 3–5. See now 3rd edn, 1997

Mason, JK and McCall-Smith, RA, *Law and Medical Ethics*, 1994, London: Butterworths. See now McCall-Smith, 5th edn, 1999

National Health and Medical Research Council, *An Australian Code of Practice for Transplantation of Cadaveric Organs and Tissues*, 1991, Australian Government Publishing Service

Petersen, K, 'Criminal abortion laws: an impediment to reproductive health?', in

Freckelton, I and Petersen, K, *Controversies in Health*, 2000, Sydney: Law Federation Press

Review of Professional Indemnity Arrangements for Health Care Professionals, *Compensation and Professional Indemnity in Health Care*, 1994, Australian Government Publishing Service

Somerville, MA, 'Structuring the issues in informed consent' (1981) 26 McGill Law Journal 740, pp 742–52

Sommerville, A, 'Are advance directives really the answer? And what was the question?', in McLean, SAM, *Death, Dying and the Law*, 1996, Dartmouth Publishing Co

Veatch, RM (ed), *Cross Cultural Perspectives in Medical Ethics*, 1989, Jones and Bartlett Publishers, Sudbury, MA, www.jbpub.com. See now 2nd edn, 2000

Wallace, M, *Health Care and the Law*, 2nd edn, 1995, Lawbook Co Ltd

Wheelwright, K, 'Commonwealth and State powers in health – a constitutional diagnosis' (1995) 21 Monash University Law Review 53

Grateful acknowledgment is made for permission to reprint copyright material, and in particular to the following to reprint material from the sources indicated.

'Australian Medical Association - Code of Ethics', 2004, Australian Medical Association. The AMA wishes it to be known that the Code is a living document and that this is a snapshot of the Code as at a particular date.

'Draft Statement on Ethical Conduct in Human Research', National Health and Medical Research Council, copyright Commonwealth of Australia reproduced by permission. This statement is a draft and it is not endorsed by the NHMRC.

'Consent to treatment for transgender and intersex chidren', (2004) 9 (2) *Deakin Law Review* 375–397, Deakin Law Review.

J.A. Devereux 'Actions for Wrongful Birth', (2004) XXXIII No 3 INSAF, Malaysian Bar Council.

M. Fordham, 'Blessing or Burden? Recent Developments In Actions for Wrongful Conception and Wrongful Birth in the UK and Australia' (2004) *Singapore Journal of Legal Studies*, 462.

The publishers have made every effort to contact the owners of copyright for material reprinted in *Australian Medical Law,* 3rd Edition, however, this has not been possible in every case. We would welcome information from any rights holders that have not been acknowledged here and will endeavour to make any corrections in subsequent editions.

TABLE OF CASES

TABLE OF LEGISLATION

1

PRINCIPLES OF MEDICAL LAW

Hope, RA, 'The birth of medical law' (1991) 11 No 2 OJLS 247

After an extensive and somewhat uncertain gestation period, a new subject has been born; its name is Medical Law and its birthweight is well above average. The question is: who are its parents and was the birth assisted?

From the evidence of many recently published books the parents are, on the one hand, the rapid advances which have taken place in medical technology and, on the other, social changes putting increasing value on patient autonomy. The importance of these developments and the role they are playing are openly discussed. The birth, however, has been assisted, although this is not talked about in public, by that age-old conflict: the battle of the professions. Doctors and lawyers are fighting over territory and each claims to have the same 'god' on its side: the good of the patients.

Dickens, B, 'Medical law: speciality or generality?', in *Medicine and The Law*, 1993, Aldershot: Dartmouth, pp xv–xvii

It must be enquired whether medical law, sometimes flattering its intellectual pretensions through the description 'medical jurisprudence', is a truly discrete and coherent body of legal knowledge, or whether it is a somewhat arbitrarily drawn collection of principles of the law of torts, contracts, crime, family relations, property and, for instance, products liability, that is applied to areas of medical origin or health care concern ...

What distinguishes medical lawyers from others is not so much their command of general law, but their familiarity with medical practice, research and developments, how hospitals are run and their different employees interact, and how health care services are organised, delivered and funded. In addition, they are frequently familiar with bioethical language, priorities and sensitivities.

Medical lawyers act at the interface of medicine and law, interpreting medical issues to other lawyers and the law to physicians, related health professionals, health facility administrators and government officials. [In

> addition to advising on statutes and relevant court judgments] medical lawyers are . . . required to offer explanations of the role of law in society that transcend individual judgments or legislated provisions – that is, that transcend separate 'laws' – and address 'the law' in philosophical or jurisprudential terms. Medical lawyers are not necessarily more jurisprudential than others, but are perhaps more likely than many others who deal with non-lawyers to face intelligent, well-informed questions from professionally engaged, sceptical and occasionally resentful questioners who probe the theoretical foundations underlying particular details or manifestations of legal power or direction.

Medical law in Australia is a morass of statutory enactments and judge-made law. It may only readily be understood when placed in its context. In this chapter we will examine that context.

If we were to establish a system of medical laws afresh, we would need some guiding principles. Some of these principles would be relatively straightforward. For example, we might note that any system of laws which sought to regulate the interaction of health care practitioners should do so in a way that did not unduly restrict the application of medical knowledge when an application of the doctor's expertise would benefit a patient. We might like to suggest that the law should apply equally to all practitioners and all patients. The law should respect, in the case of there being a number of different treatment options, the rights of patients to choose their preferred treatments. It should allow patients harmed at the hands of incompetent practitioners some recompense. Expressed in this way, the underlying principles guiding the framing of medical laws seem clear.

It is equally clear, though, that medical laws must be more complex than this. They must somehow deal with differences of opinion between practitioner and practitioner, as well as between practitioner and patient. They must 'fit in' with the increasingly complex nature of Australia's Federal State and with an age of rapid technological advance and differing moral standards. Should the law allow doctors to engage in 'physician-assisted suicide' (euthanasia)? Should the law permit doctors to prescribe the contraceptive pill for a 14 year old girl, without first seeking the permission of the girl's parents? Should the law permit a lesbian woman to join an *in vitro* fertilisation program or a 50 year old mother to bear her infertile daughter's baby for her daughter? All of these questions confront the modern medical lawyer.

Although Hope and Dickens might differ in their definition of medical law, both emphasise the importance of placing medical law in its context (especially the philosophical aspects of such context).

Underpinning the operation of various laws regulating medical practice in Australia are competing principles of the philosophy of health care referred to as bioethics. Once competing bioethical principles are brought into focus, it becomes easier to understand both the role of the law, and the likely outcome of any dispute between a health care practitioner and a patient.

At the same time, medical law (like any other branch of the law) operates within the federal structure of the Australian State. Each level of government in Australia (whether local, State or Federal) has legislative responsibility for different types of health care.

It is beyond the scope of this work to explore either the detailed principles of bioethics or of Australian constitutional law. (Whole books have been devoted to each!)

In Part I of this chapter, we will look at the important conflicting bioethical principles which operate in the health care arena. Though there are many bioethical principles, this work will concentrate on two of the current dominant bioethical principles in Anglo-Australia. It should be remembered, though, that Australia is increasingly a multicultural nation. Part II examines bioethical principles operable in the Codes of Medical Practice emanating from China, Japan, India and Islamic countries.

In Part III, an examination of the constitutional division of powers over health will be undertaken. Once the scope of Commonwealth and State power in respect of health care is defined, the broad nature of each level's legislative activity will be outlined.

The aim of this chapter is not to provide an exhaustive treatise as to bioethics or constitutional law. Rather, it is to place Australian medical law in its 'natural setting'.

PART I: BIOETHICS

> There would be no moral dilemmas if moral principles worked in straight lines and never crossed each other [Tom Stoppard in *Professional Foul*].
>
> It would not be correct to say that every moral obligation involves a legal duty; but every legal duty is founded on a moral obligation [*R v Instan* [1893] 1 QB 453].

Generations of authors have expressed different opinions concerning the underlying philosophical bases of Western medical practice. Justice, non-maleficence ('do no harm'), beneficence and autonomy all have featured. Two principles consistently are referred to. These are the principles of autonomy and beneficence.

Autonomy

Subsequent chapters of this book will be devoted to the patient's right to choose to have (or not to have) certain health care treatments. In law, this is referred to as 'the doctrine of consent'. Underpinning this doctrine is a respect for an individual patient's autonomy. Understanding autonomy is thus critical to understanding the realm of health care decision making.

Autonomy adopts several guises. Beauchamp, TL and Childress, JF, in their seminal work *Principles of Biomedical Ethics*, 5th edn, 2001, New York: Oxford University Press, note that the term may refer to a person him or herself, a person's will or a person's actions in society. There are two classical notions of autonomy which deserve mention, those views on autonomy expressed by Immanuel Kant and John Stuart Mill. Kantian and Millean notions of autonomy are important because they not only explain what autonomy is, but why people should respect each others' autonomy. It should be noted at the outset that the writings of Immanuel Kant are very complex. Books have been written on the differing interpretations of Kant. In reading the extracts below, keep in mind the dominant thesis of Kant's reasoning – that every person is an end in herself and deserves to be treated as an end in herself. Every person is to be treated as a separate person, able to govern herself.

Devereux, JA, 1993, 'Competence to consent to medical treatment', D Phil thesis, Oxford University

(i) Kantian autonomy

Kant's idea of autonomy can be seen most clearly in his writing on morality and human beings as moral agents. Kant focused on the idea of the will. To will was stated to be to decide on a particular course of action. Such a decision would be morally good only where the maxim (the underlying reason for acting) was not only to act in accordance with duty, but for the sake of duty. Determining whether a person was acting for the sake of duty cannot be achieved simply by examining the actor's intentions or purposes. Kant noted:

> Clearly an action designed to bring about a certain state of affairs may have been done for the sake of duty, but again it may not.

Kant pointed out that although everything in nature acts in accordance with laws, only rational beings such as humans have the ability to act in accordance with principles or maxims. Accordingly, only beings who are capable of adopting maxims can be moral or immoral.

A maxim was said to be moral only if it accorded with the moral law. How then was the moral law to be understood? The morality of an action, Kant concluded, was nothing more than conformity to law in general. A person's actions were said to be moral if, and only if, that person willed that his maxim should become a universal law. This last principle has become known as the categorical imperative.

Kant postulated that 'rational nature exists as an end in itself'. Since man possesses a rational nature, he is thus an end in himself. It follows that the law to the effect that a person should act in such a way that he treats each man as an end in himself and not as a means to an end. This principle was said to be binding on every rational will. It is important to note that these principles are deduced using the rational nature of human beings. As such, the categorical imperative is not only binding on man, it is rationally deducted by man and self-imposed. The essence of Kant's autonomy is clearly the freedom of the will. The property the will has of being a law to itself (independently of every property belonging to the objects of volition).

Thus, to Kant:

> ... to be autonomous is to govern oneself, including making one's own choices, in accordance with universal moral principles [Beauchamp and Childress, above].

Kant contrasted his idea of autonomy with what he described as heteronomy. This was the rule of self by others. This control by others could be externally or even internally induced. Thus, heteronomy encompassed the situation where a person acted in a certain way due to fear.

For present purposes, the idea of respecting individuals as ends in themselves, as being able rationally to govern themselves, is relevant.

(ii) Millean autonomy

Mill's conception of autonomy was somewhat different to (and easier to understand!) than Kant's.

Mill did not refer to the idea of autonomy directly. His concern was with liberty. The focus was on a person's thoughts or actions rather than the moral autonomy of his will. Restrictions upon a person's freedom of action were to be tolerated only where the limitations were to prevent one person's freedom impinging upon another's. Consistent with Mill's utilitarian 'bent', it was felt that allowing every person the freedom to pursue own goals would maximise the benefits of all. This was due to the fact that:

> Conformity to established patterns reduces individual productivity and creativity that, if developed, could benefit society [Beauchamp and Childress, above, pp 60, 61].

Thus, Mill argued that:

> Europe is in my judgment wholly indebted to the plurality of paths for its progressive and many-sided development.

To Mill, the autonomous individual was the person with 'true character'. The person without character was controlled by influences such as family, State or church.

'Autonomy may thus be thought of as freedom of actions or will. The concept of autonomy is only worthwhile to the extent that people respect one another's autonomy. In some respects, this respect flows implicitly from the idea that there are separate persons. Thus, to acknowledge another is to acknowledge the possibility of other centres of choice and intention.' If an individual is perceived as a self-governing moral agent, it follows as a matter of logic that no interference with physical integrity may be tolerated without his permission.

It is in the health arena that the idea of autonomy becomes crucial. Health by definition means freedom from mental and physical sickness. More importantly, good health allows an individual to plan his present and future affairs. Achieving full health or making the best of poor health, can therefore, have flow-on effects in respect of other areas of a person's plans. Not surprisingly then, it has been noted that:

> ... given the importance of health to individuals, it is of central

> importance to them that they have the capacity and the opportunity for choice in respect of medical intervention [McLean, SAM, 'The right to consent to medical treatment', in Campbell, T, Goldberg, D, McLean, SAM and Mullen, T (eds), *Human Rights: From Rhetoric to Reality*, 1986, 148 at p 149, Oxford: Blackwell].

If, as is suggested above, autonomy is a central notion in the concept of health care, how should the law treat those who are unable to exercise autonomy?

Which version of autonomy, that provided by Mill or that provided by Kant, do you find more persuasive?

Beneficence

Devereux, JA, 'Competence to consent to medical treatment' (above)

> The countervailing principle to autonomy is often beneficence. The moral duty of beneficence requires medical practitioners to act so as to produce the best medical result for their patient. That is to say, they must act so as to promote the wellbeing of the patient. Beneficence may also involve the prevention of harm; the removal of harm; benevolence or compassion. The idea of beneficence is the *raison d'être* of the medical profession. A medical practitioner is trained to treat, to attempt to cure the patient.
>
> When clinical questions are asked, the correct response will include the optimum course of treatment, that is, that which produces the best medical result, even though there may be an alternative which an individual patient may elect to follow and which differs from that which is scientifically indicated. In this way, the student at an early stage in his professional development, loses touch with the human element (Bromberger, B, 'Patient Participation in Decision Making: Are Courts the Answer?' (1983) 6 UNSWLJ 1 at 18).
>
> This trend has gone so far that it is now claimed that 'the medical practitioner no longer ministers to the sick but rather treats the sickness' (Bromberger, at 19).
>
> What precisely does it mean to say that a practitioner should promote wellbeing and prevent harm? In order more fully to answer this question, resort will be made to three theorists.
>
> **(i) Hippocrates**
>
> Hippocrates, an Ancient Greek philosopher, formulated a series of principles for medical practitioners which was designed to characterise those practitioners as a group of committed men set apart from and above others in society. Hippocrates saw medicine as having a moral purpose:
>
> > I will apply diatetic measures to the benefit of the sick according to my ability and judgment; I will keep them from harm and injustice.
>
> This moral purpose is further expanded upon in Hippocrates' other

writings. Thus, in 'The Art', Hippocrates defines what he understands by the term medicine:

> In general terms, it is to do away with the sufferings of the sick, to lessen the violence of their diseases and to refuse to treat those who are overmastered by their diseases, realising that in such cases medicine is powerless.

Then in 'Epidemics', he notes, 'As to disease, make a habit of two things – to help, or at least do no harm.'

Thus, Hippocrates' model of beneficence builds its account of the moral responsibilities of the physician in terms of the moral ends of medicine. On this basis, meaning is ascribed to the key terms of harm and good. This principle is applied to demonstrate that the *prima facie* duty of the medical practitioner is to benefit the patient, with the prevention of harm serving as a limiting factor to this principle.

(ii) Gregory

Another account of beneficence was offered by Dr John Gregory. Dr Gregory was Professor of Medicine at the Medical School at the University of Edinburgh. He defined medicine as being 'the art of preserving health, of prolonging life and of curing diseases'. Clearly, Gregory was focusing on the wellbeing of patients. In order to 'tie in' the idea of acting in the patient's best interest with the specific obligations and virtues, Gregory utilised Hume's concept of 'sympathy'. David Hume had held that moral judgments do not rest ultimately on reason but rather on sympathy:

> Were I present at any of the more terrible operations of surgery, the heating of the instruments, the laying of the bandages in order, the heating of the irons, with all the signs of anxiety and concern in the patient and assistants would have a great effect upon my mind and excite the strongest sentiments of pity and terror.

Sympathy manifested itself through various virtues and obligations, such as telling the truth to a terminally ill patient and keeping a patient's confidences.

Gregory's theory, like Hippocrates', rests on a moral view of medicine but is able, using the medium of sympathy, to generate specific instances of beneficence.

(iii) Beauchamp and McCulloch – a modern formulation

Drawing upon writings (including those of Gregory and Hippocrates), Beauchamp, TL and McCulloch, LB in their work *Medical Ethics: The Moral Responsibility of Physicians*, 1984, Prentice Hall, Englewood Cliffs, at p 18 have formulated a list of goods to be striven for and harms to be avoided.

How useful are Beauchamp and McCulloch's list of goods versus harms? Would all doctors in Australia agree that prolonging the life of someone who is terminally ill and in great pain be something that 'should be striven for'?

The conflict between autonomy and beneficence

It is possible that the notions of autonomy and beneficence can co-exist. Thus, a patient may present at a surgery, have a diagnosis of illness suggested by a doctor and exercise an autonomous choice to have that doctor treat her. The doctor may exercise her clinical skills to try to ensure the wellbeing of the patient (in accordance with the principles of beneficence).

Problems may arise, however, if the patient, in exercising her autonomy, declines treatment and the doctor feels (in accordance with beneficence) that treatment should be given.

Which principle should be the dominant one?

Generally speaking, where the patient is of full age and mentally competent to agree or refuse treatment, the patient's interest in having his or her autonomy respected is paramount.

Examine the Australian Medical Association's Code of Ethics reprinted below. Determine which paragraphs are a reflection of respect for patient autonomy, and which are reflections of the desire to ensure the best possible medical outcome (beneficence). If there are other values being enunciated, try to enumerate them.

AMA CODE OF ETHICS – 2004

Members are advised of the importance of seeking the advice of colleagues should they be facing difficult ethical situations.

Preamble

The AMA Code of Ethics articulates and promotes a body of ethical principles to guide doctors' conduct in their relationships with patients, colleagues and society.

This Code has grown out of other similar ethical codes stretching back into history including the Hippocratic Oath.

Because of their special knowledge and expertise, doctors have a responsibility to improve and maintain the health of their patients who, either in a vulnerable state of illness or for the maintenance of their health, entrust themselves to medical care.

The doctor-patient relationship is itself a partnership based on mutual respect and collaboration. Within the partnership, both the doctor and the patient have rights as well as responsibilities.

Changes in society, science and the law constantly raise new ethical issues and may challenge existing ethical perspectives.

The AMA accepts the responsibility for setting the standards of ethical behaviour expected of doctors.

The doctor and the patient

1.1 Patient care

(a) Consider first the well-being of your patient.
(b) Treat your patient with compassion and respect.
(c) Approach health care as a collaboration between doctor and patient.
(d) Practise the science and art of medicine to the best of your ability.
(e) Continue lifelong self-education to improve your standard of medical care.
(f) Maintain accurate contemporaneous clinical records.
(g) Ensure that doctors and other health professionals upon whom you call to assist in the care of your patients are appropriately qualified.
(h) Make sure that you do not exploit your patient for any reason.
(i) Avoid engaging in sexual activity with your patient.
(j) Refrain from denying treatment to your patient because of a judgement based on discrimination.
(k) Respect your patient's right to choose their doctor freely, to accept or reject advice and to make their own decisions about treatment or procedures.
(l) Maintain your patient's confidentiality. Exceptions to this must be taken very seriously. They may include where there is a serious risk to the patient or another person, where required by law, where part of approved research, or where there are overwhelming societal interests.
(m) Upon request by your patient, make available to another doctor a report of your findings and treatment.
(n) Recognise that an established therapeutic relationship between doctor and patient must be respected.
(o) Having initiated care in an emergency setting, continue to provide that care until your services are no longer required.
(p) When a personal moral judgement or religious belief alone prevents you from recommending some form of therapy, inform your patient so that they may seek care elsewhere.
(q) Recognise that you may decline to enter into a therapeutic relationship where an alternative health care provider is available, and the situation is not an emergency one.
(r) Recognise that you may decline to continue a therapeutic relationship. Under such circumstances, you can discontinue the relationship only if an alternative health care provider is available and the situation is not an emergency one. You must inform your patient so that they may seek care elsewhere.
(s) Recognise your professional limitations and be prepared to refer as appropriate.
(t) Place an appropriate value on your services when determining any fee. Consider the time, skill, and experience involved in the performance of those services together with any special circumstances.

(u) Ensure that your patient is aware of your fees where possible. Encourage open discussion of health care costs.
(v) When referring your patient to institutions or services in which you have a direct financial interest, provide full disclosure of such interest.
(w) If you work in a practice or institution, place your professional duties and responsibilities to your patients above the commercial interests of the owners or others who work within these practices.
(x) Ensure security of storage, access and utilisation of patient information.
(y) Protect the right of doctors to prescribe, and any patient to receive, any new treatment, the demonstrated safety and efficacy of which offer hope of saving life, re-establishing health or alleviating suffering. In all such cases, fully inform the patient about the treatment, including the new or unorthodox nature of the treatment, where applicable.

1.2 Clinical research

(a) Accept responsibility to advance medical progress by participating in properly developed research involving human participants.
(b) Ensure that responsible human research committees appraise the scientific merit and the ethical implications of the research.
(c) Recognise that considerations relating to the well-being of individual participants in research take precedence over the interests of science or society.
(d) Make sure that all research participants or their agents are fully informed and have consented to participate in the study. Refrain from using coercion or unconscionable inducements as a means of obtaining consent.
(e) Inform treating doctors of the involvement of their patients in any research project, the nature of the project and its ethical basis.
(f) Respect the participant's right to withdraw from a study at any time without prejudice to medical treatment.
(g) Make sure that the patient's decision not to participate in a study does not compromise the doctor-patient relationship or appropriate treatment and care.
(h) Ensure that research results are reviewed by an appropriate peer group before public release.

1.3 Clinical teaching

(a) Honour your obligation to pass on your professional knowledge and skills to colleagues and students.
(b) Before embarking on any clinical teaching involving patients, ensure that patients are fully informed and have consented to participate.
(c) Respect the patient's right to refuse or withdraw from participating

in clinical teaching at any time without compromising the doctor-patient relationship or appropriate treatment and care.

(d) Avoid compromising patient care in any teaching exercise. Ensure that your patient is managed according to the best-proven diagnostic and therapeutic methods and that your patient's comfort and dignity are maintained at all times.

(e) Where relevant to clinical care, ensure that it is the treating doctor who imparts feedback to the patient.

(f) Refrain from exploiting students or colleagues under your supervision in any way.

1.4 The dying patient

(a) Remember the obligation to preserve life, but, where death is deemed to be imminent and where curative or life-prolonging treatment appears to be futile, try to ensure that death occurs with dignity and comfort.

(b) Respect the patient's autonomy regarding the management of their medical condition including the refusal of treatment.

(c) Respect the right of a severely and terminally ill patient to receive treatment for pain and suffering, even when such therapy may shorten a patient's life.

(d) Recognise the need for physical, psychological, emotional, and spiritual support for the patient, the family and other carers not only during the life of the patient, but also after their death.

1.5 Transplantation

(a) Recognise that a potential donor is entitled to the same standard of care as any other patient.

(b) Inform the donor and family fully of the proposal to transplant organs, the purpose and the risks of the procedure.

(c) Exercise sensitivity and compassion when discussing the option to donate organs with the potential donor and family.

(d) Refrain from using coercion when obtaining consent to all organ donations.

(e) Explain brain death to potential donor families. Similarly explain that continued artificial organ support is necessary to enable subsequent organ transplantation.

(f) Ensure that the determination of the death of any donor is made by doctors who are neither involved with the transplant procedure nor caring for the proposed recipient.

(g) Recognise the important contribution donor families make in difficult circumstances. Ensure that they are given the opportunity to receive counselling and support.

2 The doctor and the profession

2.1 Professional conduct

(a) Build a professional reputation based on integrity and ability.
(b) Recognise that your personal conduct may affect your reputation and that of your profession.
(c) Refrain from making comments which may needlessly damage the reputation of a colleague.
(d) Report suspected unethical or unprofessional conduct by a colleague to the appropriate peer review body.
(e) Where a patient alleges unethical or unprofessional conduct by another doctor, respect the patient's right to complain and assist them in resolving the issue.
(f) Accept responsibility for your psychological and physical well-being as it may affect your professional ability.
(g) Keep yourself up to date on relevant medical knowledge, codes of practice and legal responsibilities.

2.2 Advertising

(a) Confine advertising of professional services to the presentation of information reasonably needed by patients or colleagues to make an informed decision about the availability and appropriateness of your medical services.
(b) Make sure that any announcement or advertisement directed towards patients or colleagues is demonstrably true in all respects. Advertising should not bring the profession into disrepute.
(c) Do not publicly endorse therapeutic goods as defined under the *Therapeutic Goods Act 1989 (C'th)*, contrary to the *Therapeutic Goods Advertising Code.*[1]
(d) Exercise caution in publicly endorsing any particular commercial product or service not covered by the *Therapeutic Goods Advertising Code.*
(e) Ensure that any therapeutic or diagnostic advance is described and examined through professional channels, and, if proven beneficial, is made available to the profession at large.

1 Clause 4.41(c) of the *Therapeutic Goods Advertising Code* relevantly reads in relation to therapeutic goods 'Advertisements must not contain or imply endorsement by:
(a) ...
(b) ...
(c) Individual healthcare professionals, other than where the emphasis is on the availability, which may include the price of therapeutic goods through his/her retail business.

2.3 Referral to colleagues

(a) Obtain the opinion of an appropriate colleague acceptable to your patient if diagnosis or treatment is difficult or obscure, or in response to a reasonable request by your patient.
(b) When referring a patient, make available to your colleague, with the patient's knowledge and consent, all relevant information and indicate whether or not they are to assume the continuing care of your patient during their illness.
(c) When an opinion has been requested by a colleague, report in detail your findings and recommendations to that doctor.
(d) Should a consultant or specialist find a condition which requires referral of the patient to a consultant in another field, only make the referral following discussion with the patient's general practitioner – except in an emergency situation.

3 Professional independence

(a) In order to provide high quality healthcare, you must safeguard clinical independence and professional integrity from increased demands from society, third parties, individual patients and governments.
(b) Protect clinical independence as it is essential when choosing the best treatment for patients and defending their health needs against all who would deny or restrict necessary care.
(c) Refrain from entering into any contract with a colleague or organisation which may conflict with professional integrity, clinical independence or your primary obligation to the patient.
(d) Recognise your right to refuse to carry out services which you consider to be professionally unethical, against your moral convictions, imposed on you for either administrative reasons or for financial gain or which you consider are not in the best interest of the patient.

4 The doctor and society

(a) Endeavour to improve the standards and quality of, and access to, medical services in the community.
(b) Accept a share of the profession's responsibility to society in matters relating to the health and safety of the public, health education and legislation affecting the health of the community.
(c) Use your special knowledge and skills to minimise wastage of resources, but remember that your primary duty is to provide your patient with the best available care.
(d) Make available your special knowledge and skills to assist those responsible for allocating healthcare resources.
(e) Recognise your responsibility to give expert evidence to assist the courts or tribunals.
(f) When providing scientific information to the public, recognise a

responsibility to give the generally held opinions of the profession in a form that is readily understood. When presenting any personal opinion which is contrary to the generally held opinion of the profession, indicate that this is the case.

(g) Regardless of society's attitudes, ensure that you do not countenance, condone or participate in the practice of torture or other forms of cruel, inhuman, or degrading procedures, whatever the offence of which the victim of such procedures is suspected, accused or convicted.

References

Canadian Medical Association (1996) *Code of Ethics of the Canadian Medical Association.*

World Medical Association International Code of Medical Ethics, as amended by the 35th World Medical Assembly, Venice, Italy, October 1983.

World Medical Association Declaration on the Rights of the Patient, as amended by the 47th WMA General Assembly, Bali, Indonesia, September 1995.

World Medical Association Declaration of Helsinki, as amended by the 52nd WMA General Assembly, Edinburgh, Scotland, October 2000.

World Medical Association Statement on Human Organ & Tissue Donation and Transplantation, adopted by the 52nd WMA General Assembly in Edinburgh, Scotland, October 2000.

World Medical Association Declaration with Guidelines for Continuous Quality Improvement in Health Care, as adopted by the 49th World Medical Assembly, Hamburg, Germany, November 1997.

Now examine the nurse's statement of ethics and try to establish which principles embody respect for patient autonomy, and which embody medical paternalism.

Australian Nursing Council Code of Ethics

1 Background introduction

Background

This Code of Ethics has been developed for nursing in the Australian context and is relevant to all nurses in all practice settings.

The impetus for its development came at the Australasian Nurse Registering Authorities Conference (ANRAC) of 1990, when the research arising from the ANRAC Nursing Competencies Assessment Project indicated that there was not a clear focus on the ethical standards expected and required of nurses practising in the cultural context of Australia.

The Code of Ethics for Nurses in Australia was first developed in 1993 under the auspices of the Australian Nursing Council Inc., Royal

College of Nursing, Australia and the Australian Nursing Federation. In 2000 these peak organisations agreed to undertake a joint project to review the Code of Ethics. It is recognised that the Code of Ethics could not have been realised without the participation of nurses and nursing organisations in Australia, whose many submissions and comments are acknowledged and appreciated.

The Code of Ethics outlines the nursing profession's intention to accept the rights of individuals and to uphold these rights in practice. The Code of Ethics is complementary to the International Council of Nurses (ICN) Code of Ethics for Nurses (2000).

Thus, the purpose of this Code of Ethics is to:

- identify the fundamental moral commitments of the profession,
- provide nurses with a basis for professional and self reflection on ethical conduct,
- act as a guide to ethical practice, and
- indicate to the community the moral values which nurses can be expected to hold.

Introduction

The nurse's primary professional responsibility is to people requiring nursing care. In fulfilling this responsibility nurses provide care and support before and during birth and throughout life, and alleviate pain and suffering during the dying process.

Nurses enable individuals, families and groups to maintain, restore or improve their health status, or to be cared for and comforted when deterioration of health has become irreversible.

A traditional ideal of nursing is the concern for the care and nurture of human beings giving just and due consideration to their ethnicity, culture, gender, spiritual values, sexuality, disability, age, economic, social or health status, or any other grounds.

Nurses respect and uphold the rights of Australian indigenous peoples. The profession also acknowledges the cultural diversity in contemporary Australian society. Nursing care is based on the development of a therapeutic relationship and the implementation and evaluation of therapeutic processes. Therapeutic processes include health promotion and education, counselling, nursing interventions and empowerment of individuals, families or groups to exercise maximum choice in relation to their health care.

Nursing practice is undertaken in a variety of settings. Any particular setting will be affected to some degree by processes which are not within a nurse's control or influence.

The processes affecting nursing practice can include government policies, laws, resource constraints, institutional policies, management decisions, and the practice of other health care providers. Nurses also recognise the potential for conflict between one person's needs and those of another, or of a group or community.

Such factors may affect the degree to which nurses are able to fulfil their moral obligations and/or the number and type of ethical problems they may face.

The Code contains six broad value statements. Nurses are encouraged to use these statements as a guide in reflecting on the degree to which their practice demonstrates those values. As a means of assisting in interpretation of the six values, a number of explanatory statements are provided. These explanatory statements are not intended to cover all the aspects a nurse should consider, but can be used to assist further exploration and consideration of ethical concerns in nursing practice.

Nurses are also encouraged to undertake discussion and educational opportunities in ethics in order to clarify for themselves issues related to the fulfilment of their moral obligations. This Code of Ethics is not intended to provide a formula for the resolution of ethical problems, nor can it adequately address the definitions and exploration of terms and concepts which are part of the study of ethics.

Nurses are autonomous moral agents and sometimes may adopt a personal moral stance that would make participation in certain procedures morally unacceptable to them. Nurses have a right to refuse (conscientious objection) to participate in procedures, which they judge on strongly held moral beliefs to be unacceptable. In exercising their conscientious objection nurses must take all reasonable steps to ensure that quality of care and patient safety is not compromised.

Nurses accepting employment positions where they foresee they may be called on to be involved in situations at variance with their sincerely held beliefs, have a responsibility to acquaint their employer or prospective employer with this fact within a reasonable time. Nurses, however, should consider seriously whether it is appropriate for them to accept employment positions where they see these situations may arise, particularly if this is likely to be more than a rare occurrence. Employers and colleagues have a responsibility to ensure that such nurses are not overtly or covertly discriminated against in their workplace. The Code of Ethics is supported by the Code of Professional Conduct for Nurses in Australia. While the Code of Ethics focuses on the ethics and ideals of the profession, the Code of Professional Conduct identifies the minimum requirements for practice in the profession, and focuses on the clarification of professional misconduct and unprofessional conduct. The two Codes, together with published practice standards, provide a framework for nursing.

Interpretation of terms

Accountability: the state of being answerable for one's decisions and actions. It cannot be delegated (ANRAC 1990).

Individual/individuals: refers to a person/persons receiving nursing care.

Moral agent: a person who acts morally/ethically on his or her own authority.

Responsibility: the obligation that an individual assumes when undertaking to carry out planned/delegated functions. The individual who authorises the delegated function retains accountability (ANRAC 1990).

Ethics: the moral practices, beliefs, and standards of an individual/s and/or a group.

Ethical problem: a situation that requires ethical consideration or ethical decision making, or a conflict of moral values.

Code of Ethics

Value Statement 1

Nurses respect individuals' needs, values, culture and vulnerability in the provision of nursing care.

EXPLANATORY STATEMENTS

1. Nurses acknowledge the diversity in contemporary Australian society. Nursing care for any individual or group should not be compromised because of ethnicity, culture, aboriginality, gender, spiritual values, sexuality, disability, age, economic, social or health status, or any other ground.
2. Respect for an individual's needs includes recognition of the person's place in a family and community. Nurses should, therefore, facilitate the participation of significant others in the care of the individual if, and as, the person and the significant others wish.
3. Respect for individual needs, beliefs and values includes culturally informed and appropriate care, and the provision of as much comfort, dignity, privacy and alleviation of pain and anxiety as possible.
4. Respect includes the development of confidence and trust in the relationship between nurses and the people for whom they care.
5. Nurses acknowledge that there is a power imbalance in the relationship between a person or group receiving nursing care and a health care provider. To promote a trusting and professional relationship, and to prevent any exploitation of individuals, nurses have an ethical responsibility always to maintain appropriate professional boundaries between themselves and persons to whom they provide care.

Value Statement 2

Nurses accept the rights of individuals to make informed choices in relation to their care.

EXPLANATORY STATEMENTS

1. Individuals have the right to make decisions related to their own health care, based on accurate and complete information given by health care providers. Nurses must be satisfied that they have the person's consent for any care or treatment they are providing. If individuals are not able to provide consent for themselves, nurses have a role in ensuring that valid consent is obtained from the appropriate substitute decision maker.
2. Nurses have a responsibility to inform people about the nursing care that is available to them, and people are entitled morally to accept or reject such care. Nurses have a responsibility to respect the decisions made by each individual.
3. Illness and/or other factors may compromise a person's capacity for self determination. Where able, nurses should ensure such persons continue to have adequate and relevant information to enable them to make informed choices about their care and treatment and to maintain an optimum degree of self-direction and self-determination.

Value Statement 3

Nurses promote and uphold the provision of quality nursing care for all people.

EXPLANATORY STATEMENTS

1. Quality nursing care includes competent care provided by appropriately prepared nurses.
2. Promotion of quality nursing care includes valuing life-long learning and engaging in continuing education as a means of maintaining and increasing knowledge and skills. Continuing education refers to all formal and informal opportunities for education.
3. Nurses research and evaluate nursing practice in order to raise standards of care, and to ensure that such standards are ethical.
4. Research should be conducted in a manner that is ethically responsible and justified. Nurses should not participate in any research or experimental treatment on human subjects, which has not been approved by an institutional ethics committee, and which is not conducted in a manner consistent with the requirements of the National Health and Medical Research Council's national statements relating to ethical conduct in research involving humans.
5. Nurses contribute to the development and implementation of policy to make the best use of available resources and to promote quality care for individuals.

Value Statement 4

Nurses hold in confidence any information obtained in a professional capacity, use professional judgement where there is a need to share information for the therapeutic benefit and safety of a person and ensure that privacy is safeguarded.

EXPLANATORY STATEMENTS

1. The nurse respects a person's rights to determine who will be provided with their personal information and in what detail. Exceptions may be necessary in circumstances where the life of the individual may be placed in danger or where disclosure is required by law.
2. When personal information is required for teaching, research or quality assurance purposes, care must be taken to protect the person's autonomy, anonymity and privacy. Consent must always be obtained from the person or their lawful advocate.
3. Nurses protect persons in their care against breaches of privacy by confining their verbal communications to appropriate personnel and settings, and for professional purposes.
4. Nurses have an obligation to adhere to legislative guidelines limiting access to personal records (whether paper or electronic).

Value Statement 5

Nurses fulfil the accountability and responsibility inherent in their roles.

EXPLANATORY STATEMENTS

1. As morally autonomous professionals, nurses are accountable for their clinical decision making and have moral and legal obligations for the provision of safe and competent nursing care.
2. Nurses contribute with other health care providers in the provision of comprehensive health care, recognising and respecting the perspective and expertise of each team member.
3. Nurses have a right to refuse to participate in procedures, which would violate their reasoned moral conscience (i.e. conscientious objection). In doing so, they must take all reasonable steps to ensure that quality of care and patient safety is not compromised.
4. Nurses have an ethical responsibility to report instances of unsafe and unethical practice. Nurses should support colleagues who appropriately and professionally notify instances of unsafe and unethical practice.

Value Statement 6

Nurses value environmental ethics and a social, economic and ecologically sustainable environment that promotes health and well being.

EXPLANATORY STATEMENTS

1. Nursing includes involvement in the detection of the ill effects of the environment on the health of persons, the ill effects of human activities on the natural environment, and assisting communities in their actions on environmental health problems aimed at minimising these effects.
2. Nurses value participation in the development, implementation and monitoring of policies and procedures, which promote safe and efficient use of resources.
3. Nurses acknowledge that the social environment in which a person resides has an impact on their health, and in collaboration with other health professionals and consumers, initiate and support action to meet the health and social needs of the public.

Special ethical considerations apply in respect of research involving humans: see generally NHMRC National Statement on Ethical Conduct in Research Involving Humans.

Note that this document is now under review and revision by the NHRMC and the AVCC. The draft of the second consultation paper, dated 6 January 2006, is reproduced below.

Draft of the National Statement on Ethical conduct in human research

Second consultation[2]

Developed jointly by National Health and Medical Research Council
Australian Research Council
Australian Vice-Chancellors' Committee
January 2006

Contents

2 Review of the *National Statement on Ethical Conduct in Research Involving Humans* – second consultation draft.

Preamble

This Statement sets national standards for the ethical design, review and conduct of human research. It identifies responsibilities of institutions, researchers, Human Research Ethics Committees (HRECs) and others conducting ethical review of research. The Statement reflects the outcome of wide consultation with Australian communities who participate in, design, conduct, fund and manage human research. The responsibilities set out in the Statement are intended to be consistent with the international human rights instruments that Australia has ratified. Conducting human research is important for Australia and its people. Their willing participation and their justified trust in research are indispensable, and are promoted and maintained only when research meets ethical standards. This Statement will help research to meet such standards.

Historical context

Since earliest times, human societies have reflected on the nature of good behaviour and have sought answers to ethical questions in the writings of philosophers, in the teaching of religions and in everyday individual reflection. The idea that ethical conduct in research might be a distinct sub-field within ethics arose most sharply after the Second World War in the discussion of the role of the so-called 'Nazi doctors' in unethical human experimentation in detention and concentration camps. The judgment recording their conviction included ten principles since referred to as the Nuremberg Code. Discussion of these principles led to the World Medical Assembly in 1964 adopting what came to be known as the Helsinki Declaration. This declaration, amended most recently in 2004, sets out a number of principles and procedures intended to provide guidance to physicians and others involved in medical research. Against this background, this Statement contributes to a global effort to develop ethical guidelines for all research. In extending its scope beyond medical research, the Statement has sought to avoid treating medical research as a paradigm for all research. The Statement acknowledges the independent development of ethical codes in other disciplines, especially in the social sciences and humanities. It reflects not only the great diversity of research techniques employed within institutions but also the fact that many of these techniques have closer analogies in everyday life than in medical research practice. Research, like everyday life, often generates ethical dilemmas in which it may be impossible to find agreement on what is right or wrong.[3] In such circumstances, it is important that researchers bring a heightened ethical awareness to their decision making. The Statement is intended to contribute to the development of such awareness. Various codes of conduct developed by research professionals in different fields also have an important role to play in this process.

Research governance

The Statement should be seen in the broader context of overall governance of research.

While the Statement provides guidelines for researchers, HRECs and others conducting an ethical review of research, it also emphasises the responsibilities of institutions for the quality, safety and ethical acceptability of the research they sponsor or permit to be carried out under their auspices. Responsibility for the ethical design, review and conduct of human research is in fact exercised at many levels by:

- researchers (and where relevant their supervisors);
- HRECs and others conducting ethical review of research;
- institutions which set up the processes of ethical review, and whose employees, resources and facilities are involved in research;
- funding organizations;
- agencies that set standards; and governments.

It should be emphasised that while the processes of ethical review are

3 In this Statement, 'institutions' refers to any institution, organisation or body by which, or in which, human research is carried out. Review of the *National Statement on Ethical Conduct in Research Involving Humans* – second consultation draft vi.

important in this structure, individual researchers and the institutions within which they work have primary responsibility for seeing that the research they conduct and facilitate is ethically acceptable. In addition to this Statement, the *Australian code for the responsible conduct of research* has an essential role in promoting good research governance. That Code sets down the broad principles of responsible and accountable research practice, and identifies the responsibilities of institutions and researchers in areas such as data and record management, publication of findings, authorship, conflict of interest, supervision of students and research trainees, and the handling of allegations of research misconduct.

Authors of this Statement

This Statement has been jointly developed by the National Health and Medical Research Council (NHMRC), the Australian Research Council (ARC) and the Australian Vice-Chancellors' Committee (AVCC). While the previous (1999) version of this document was endorsed by the Australian Vice Chancellors' Committee, the Australian Research Council, the Australian Academy of the Humanities, the Australian Academy of Sciences and the Academy of Social Sciences in Australia, and was supported by the Academy of Technological Sciences and Engineering, it was issued by the NHMRC. The need for ethical[4] guidelines that are genuinely applicable to all human research is now reflected in the agreement between the NHMRC, the ARC and the AVCC to develop this Statement as an agreed set of guidelines. The *National Health and Medical Research Council Act* 1992 (NHMRC Act) establishes the NHMRC as a statutory body and sets out its functions, powers and obligations. Section 8(1) of the Act requires the NHMRC to issue guidelines for the conduct of medical research involving humans, and those guidelines are to be issued precisely as developed by the Australian Health Ethics Committee (AHEC). AHEC is established by the NHMRC Act as a Principal Committee of the NHMRC. All the guidelines in this Statement that are applicable to the conduct of medical research involving humans are issued by the NHMRC in fulfilment of this statutory obligation. The *Australian Research Council Act* 2001 (ARC Act) establishes the ARC to provide the responsible Minister with advice and recommendations about research, including which research programs should receive financial assistance. The functions of the ARC also include administering the regimes of financial assistance for research and providing for the funding of research programs. The AVCC is the council of Australia's University Vice Chancellors (or Presidents). Its purpose is to advance higher education through voluntary, cooperative and

4 This is the proposed revision of the *Joint NHMRC/AVCC Statement and Guidelines on Research Practice* (1997). Review of the *National Statement on Ethical Conduct in Research Involving Humans* – second consultation draft vii.

coordinated action, and to serve the best interests of Australia's universities and, through them, the nation. The AVCC acts as a consultative and advisory body for all university affairs, making submissions to public inquiries of interest to the university sector, and preparing statements on major issues.[5]

Introduction

Purpose

The purpose of this Statement is to promote ethical conduct in all aspects of human research. Fulfilling this purpose involves according participants the respect and protection that is due to them. It also involves the facilitation of research that is of benefit to the community. In order to achieve its purpose, the Statement is designed to clarify the responsibilities of institutions, researchers, Human Research Ethics Committees (HRECs) and others conducting ethical review of research. The Statement will help them to meet their responsibilities: to identify issues of ethics that arise in the design, review and conduct of human research, to deliberate about those ethical issues and to justify decisions about them.

Use of this Statement

This Statement must be used for all ethical review and conduct of human research that is funded by, or takes place under the auspices of, any of the bodies that have developed this Statement. In addition, as a reliable and informative guide to the ethical considerations relevant to the design, review and conduct of that research, this Statement sets national standards for use by any individual, institution or organisation conducting human research. This includes human research undertaken by government, industry, private individuals, organisations, or networks of organisations.

Defining research

Research is to be understood as including investigation undertaken in order to gain knowledge and understanding or in order to train researchers, and the use of existing knowledge in experimental development to produce new or substantially improved materials, devices, products and processes. It does not include routine testing and routine analysis of materials, components and processes as distinct from the development of new analytical techniques. However, some of these activities, such as quality assurance, may sometimes warrant ethical

5 Review of the *National Statement on Ethical Conduct in Research Involving Humans* – second consultation draft 1.

review, even though they are not research (see *When does quality assurance in health care require independent ethical review?* NHMRC 2003).[6]

When is research human research?

Human research is research involving human participants, who may participate by:

- taking part in surveys, interviews or focus groups;
- undergoing psychological, physiological or medical testing or treatment;
- being observed by researchers;
- researchers having access to their personal documents or other materials;
- the collection and use of their body organs, tissues or fluids (e.g. skin, blood, urine, saliva, hair, bones, tumour and other biopsy specimens);
- their information (in individually identifiable, re-identifiable or non-identifiable form) being accessed as part of an existing published or unpublished source or database.

In addition, often the conduct of human research has an impact on the lives of others who are not participants. Reasonably foreseeable impacts on other human beings can be relevant ethical considerations for researchers and those conducting ethical review.

Ethical conduct and review of human research

The primary responsibilities for the ethical design, conduct and dissemination of results of human research lie with researchers and their institutions. Institutions also have the responsibility to establish procedures for the ethical review of human research. That review must be based on the values and principles of this Statement, and can be undertaken at various levels and by means of various processes described in Section 5. The differences in these levels and processes of review should reflect the principle that the necessary degree of ethical review is proportional to the risks involved in the research. Research with more than a low level of risk must be reviewed by an HREC. A determination, after research has been reviewed at the appropriate level, that the research proposal meets the requirements of this Statement and is ethically acceptable must be made before research is commenced and before full funding for the proposal is released. This Statement does not exhaust the ethical discussion of human research. Provided they are consistent with this Statement, other guidelines and codes of practice pertaining to specific areas of research can be used to supplement it, and should

6 Review of the *National Statement on Ethical Conduct in Research Involving Humans* – second consultation draft 2.

be so used where this is considered necessary for ethical review of research.[7]

Ethics and law in human research

Human research is governed by Australian law that establishes rights for participants and imposes general and specific responsibilities on researchers and institutions. Australian common law obligations arise from the relationships between institutions, researchers and participants, while contractual arrangements may impose obligations on research funders and institutions. This Statement of ethical principles and considerations does not discuss any legal rights or obligations. Some human research is subject to specific statutory regulation, at Commonwealth and State and Territory levels. For example, Commonwealth laws regulate certain research on pharmaceutical drugs and medical devices, and the protection of privacy and intellectual property in research. Some examples of such specific Commonwealth legislation or regulation are listed in relevant chapters of the Statement. However, examples of State and Territory laws, such as those that regulate access to, and use of, information held by State or Territory authorities, consumer protection and illegal and professional conduct are not listed. It is the responsibility of institutions and researchers to be aware of both general and specific legal requirements, wherever relevant.

Structure of the Statement

The Statement has five sections. Sections 2–5 have multiple chapters. The five sections are:

1. *Values and principles of ethical conduct* sets out values and principles that apply to all human research.
2. *Themes in ethical review: risk and consent* discusses the concept of risk in research and the role of participants' consent.
3. *Ethical considerations specific to research methods or fields* provides more detailed guidance on ethical considerations specific to different research methods and fields.
4. *Ethical considerations specific to participants* provides more detailed guidance on ethical considerations specific to different categories of participants.
5. *Processes of research governance and ethical review* sets out the requirements on institutions in establishing HRECs and other processes for the ethical review of research; and specifies procedures for the accountability of researchers, those conducting ethical review of research and institutions.[8]

7 Review of the *National Statement on Ethical Conduct in Research Involving Humans* – second consultation draft 3.

8 Review of the *National Statement on Ethical Conduct in Research Involving Humans* – second consultation draft 4.

Section 1 Values and principles of ethical conduct

Introduction

The ethical responsibilities of those conducting human research depend on basic values of respect for human beings, research merit and integrity, justice, and beneficence. While these values have a long history in western culture, they are not the only values that could inform a document of this kind. Others include, for instance, altruism, contributing to societal or community goals, equality, and respect for cultural diversity, along with the values that inform *Values and Ethics: Guidelines for Ethical Conduct in Aboriginal and Torres Strait Islander Health Research* (NHMRC 2003). However, the values of respect, research merit and integrity, justice, and beneficence have become prominent in the ethics of human research in the past six decades, and they provide a substantial and flexible framework for principles to guide the design, review and conduct of such research. This Statement is organised around these values, and the principles set out in paragraphs 1.1–1.10 give practical expression to them. Among those four values, respect is the most fundamental. It centrally involves recognising that each human being has a value in himself or herself, and that this value must govern all interaction between humans. Such respect includes recognising the value of human autonomy – the capacity to determine one's own life and make one's own decisions. But respect goes further than this. It also involves giving particular protection to those with diminished or no autonomy, and protecting and helping people wherever it would be unjust not to do so. In each section of the statement, however, the values are discussed in the following order: research merit and integrity, justice, beneficence and respect. This order of discussion reflects the order in which ethical considerations commonly arise in human research, and its repetition is a constant reminder of the need for ethical reflection at all stages of human research to be informed by these values. Research merit and integrity are discussed first. Unless proposed research has merit, and the researchers who are to carry out the research have integrity, the involvement of human participants in the research cannot be ethically justifiable. Justice is the next consideration. Aspects of justice include distributive justice (the fair distribution of benefits and burdens), and procedural justice ('fair treatment' and accountability in the conduct of research). While benefit to humankind is an important result of research, it is not sufficient in itself. Benefits of research are ethically acceptable only if they have been achieved through just means, are distributed fairly, and involve no unjust burdens.[9]

The third value is beneficence. Researchers exercise beneficence in several ways: in assessing and taking account of the risks of harm and the

9 Review of the *National Statement on Ethical Conduct in Research Involving Humans* – second consultation draft 5.

potential benefits of research to participants and to the wider community; in being sensitive to the rights and interests of people involved in their research; and in reflecting on the social and cultural implications of their work. The final and most important value is respect for human beings. While specific concerns arise under the heading of respect, this value is also the common thread through all the discussions of ethical values. Turning to it as the final value is a reminder that it draws together all of the ethical deliberation that has preceded it. The design, review and conduct of research must reflect each of these values.

Research merit and integrity

1.1 Research that has merit is:

(a) justifiable by its potential benefit to humankind, whether through its contribution to knowledge or other benefit. Justification of some research may require consultation with relevant communities;
(b) designed or developed using methods appropriate for the achievement of the aims of the proposal;
(c) based on a thorough study of the current literature, as well as previous studies. This does not exclude the possibility of novel research for which there is little or no literature available;
(d) designed to ensure that respect for the participants is not compromised by the aims of the research, by the way it is carried out, or by the results;
(e) conducted or supervised by persons or teams with experience, qualifications and competence appropriate to the research;
(f) conducted using facilities and resources appropriate to the research.

1.2 Research that is conducted with integrity is carried out by researchers with a commitment to:

(a) searching for knowledge;
(b) following recognised principles of research conduct;
(c) conducting research honestly and ethically;
(d) disseminating and communicating results, whether favourable or unfavourable, in ways that permit scrutiny and contribute to public knowledge.[10]

Justice

1.3 In research that is just:

(a) the processes of research are transparent and fair;
(b) the selection, exclusion and inclusion of categories of research

10 Review of the *National Statement on Ethical Conduct in Research Involving Humans* – second consultation draft 6.

participants is – taking into account the scope and objectives of the proposed research – fair, and accurately described in the results of the research;
(c) the process of recruiting participants is fair;
(d) there is no unfair burden of participation in research on particular groups;
(e) there is fair distribution of the benefits of participation in research; and
(f) there is fair access to the benefits of research.

1.4 Research outcomes should be made available to research participants in ways that are accessible, timely and clear.

Beneficence

1.5 The risks of harm or discomfort to participants in research should be minimised.
1.6 Any risks of harm or discomfort must be justified by the likely benefit to be gained. The likely benefit may be either to the participants or to the wider community, or to both. Where there are no likely benefits to participants, possible harm to participants should be less serious and the risk of those harms lower. However, respect for participants requires taking into account their views about what is an acceptable level of risk.
1.7 Where the risks to participants are no longer justified by the potential benefits of the research, the research must be suspended to allow time to consider whether it should be discontinued or proceed in a modified form. In making these decisions the researcher may need to consult with participants, the Human Research Ethics Committee (HREC) or other review body or the institution. The HREC or other review body must be notified promptly of such suspension, and of any decisions following it.

Respect

1.8 The fundamental ethical value of research is respect for human beings. This includes abiding by the preceding values of research merit and integrity, justice and beneficence. Respect also requires having due regard for the welfare,[11] beliefs, perceptions, customs and cultural heritage, both individual and collective, of those involved in research.
1.9 Researchers and their institutions should respect the privacy, confidentiality and cultural sensitivities of the participants, and where relevant of their communities. Any specific agreements made with the participants or the community are to be fulfilled.

11 Review of the *National Statement on Ethical Conduct in Research Involving Humans* – second consultation draft 7.

1.10 Respect for human beings involves giving due scope to the capacity of human beings to make their own decisions, as well as protecting those who either are unable or have diminished capacity to do so.

Application of these values and principles

Ethical guidelines such as these are not simply a set of rules. The application of the guidelines should not be mechanical. It always requires deliberation on the values and principles, the exercise of judgement, and an appreciation of context.[12]

Section 2 Themes in ethical review: risk and consent

Chapter 2.1 Risk

Introduction

Application of the values in Section 1, in particular the value of beneficence, requires the assessment of risks to participants, and sometimes to others. This involves assessment of what the risks are, of the extent to which they can be minimised, and of whether they are justified by the potential benefits of the research. This chapter provides information and guidance about this assessment. A risk is a potential for harm. In some types of medical research, potential harms, which may include permanent disability or even death, are readily perceived and agreed upon. In other fields of human research there is less agreement about what might constitute potential harm, and about the magnitude, significance and likelihood of any risks.

Harm, including discomfort, and some categories of harm

Physical harm and discomfort are familiar concepts in some types of health and medical research. In social, behavioural and humanities research, potential harm or discomfort are commonly of other kinds. They can be more difficult to measure and to predict. Such harms are often, but not always, minor or unlikely. There are various kinds of potential harm in research. One helpful classification[13] is physical, psychological, social, economic and legal harms, and devaluation of personal worth. Physical harm includes injury, illness, pain, suffering and discomfort. Psychological harm includes emotional suffering, negative self-perception or aberrations in thought or behaviour, distress, anger or

12 Review of the *National Statement on Ethical Conduct in Research Involving Humans* – second consultation draft 8.

13 Adapted from National Bioethics Advisory Commission, *Ethical and Policy Issues in Research Involving Human Participants*, Bethesda, 2001 pp. 71–72 Review of the *National Statement on Ethical Conduct in Research Involving Humans* – second consultation draft 9.

guilt related to disclosure of sensitive or embarrassing information, and distress or fear at the prospect of research revealing a likelihood of developing an untreatable disease. Social harms include negative effects on one's interactions or relationships with others, examples being discrimination in access to benefits or services, or in employment or insurance, social stigmatization and findings of previously unknown paternity status. Economic harms include imposition of direct or indirect costs on participants; and legal harm includes lawsuits or laying of criminal charges if research brings attention to criminal conduct.

Devaluation of personal worth includes being humiliated, manipulated or in other ways treated disrespectfully. There can be harm to people other than participants. Examples include the effects of an unauthorised biography on close friends, the potential emotional distress when a family member is identified with a serious genetic disorder, and infectious disease risks to the community. A standard dictionary definition of discomfort is 'uneasiness of body or mind'. In some fields of research, discomfort such as the anxiety which may be induced by an interview probing personal beliefs and feelings, fits this definition. In health research, discomforts are commonly physical discomforts, usually temporary and not serious. These include unpleasant accompaniments of invasive procedures, such as the momentary pain of blood-taking, the claustrophobia experienced by some people undergoing scanning, and minor side-effects of medication. Potential harms involved in research depend not only on the research methods and activities themselves but also on the social and political context of the research and the categories of participants. Research into participants' reading habits or sexual preferences may carry relatively few risks in some contexts but may be highly risky for participants in other contexts. Apparently straightforward clinical research may carry social, psychological, economic or legal risks for various categories of participants, including, for example, prisoners or those with genetic abnormalities or intellectual disability.

Risk

Risk, implying the chance or hazard of harm, encompasses two different concepts:

(a) the probability or likelihood that a harm (or discomfort) will occur; and
(b) the magnitude of the harm, including its consequences.

The expression 'low risk' could, logically, therefore refer either to the low probability of a harmful event occurring or to the small size of the harm that will occur, or to a combination of these two features. However, human research with a low probability of serious harm has been regarded, and should continue to be regarded, as not low-risk research. Research of the lowest risk involves a low probability of slight, if any, harm.

Quantifying risk

Individuals' experience of some risks is often very similar. The risk of death or of permanent disability, or the risk of humiliation, will generally be regarded very seriously by people. But people also vary in the significance they attach to different kinds of risk. One person might be greatly distressed by a telephone questionnaire which covers very sensitive topics, but happy to participate in potentially physically dangerous research,[14] while another person's priorities might be the opposite. Another questionnaire may pose no issue for a younger person but raise issues of self-esteem for older people – or vice versa. Other aspects of circumstance and situation can also come into play. In medical research, for example, side effects of an anti-cancer drug may be intolerable to a relatively well person but may be accepted as of lesser import by a seriously ill patient.

Minimising risk

The value of beneficence includes the obligation on researchers in designing research to minimise the risk to participants. Both researchers and those reviewing research will have regard to the aims of the research, their importance, and the methods by which those aims can be achieved, to whether the participants will be adults with unimpaired capacity to consent, and to the participants' experience and opinions as to the level of risk they are prepared to accept. In fields other than human research, minimised risk is often understood as risk that is as low as reasonably practicable or achievable. In human research, a useful criterion for the minimisation of risk may be risk as low as ethically achievable, having taken into account the matters identified in the previous paragraph as well as the ways of quantifying risk described above.

Benefits and risks

Benefits of research refer to gains in knowledge, insight and understanding, and to improved social welfare and individual well-being. A further factor to be considered is whether the research carries the prospect of direct benefit to the research participants themselves, their families or their groups. Where this is the case, participants may be ready to assume a higher risk than in research that carries no prospect of such direct benefit. There are also indirect benefits such as training researchers in research methods. Prospectively, most research design cannot guarantee that there will be actual benefit from research. The benefits to be considered are *potential* benefits. Potential benefits can accrue to those who are not participants – some or all members of their families or communities, or in some instances, the institutions. Human research depends

14 Review of the *National Statement on Ethical Conduct in Research Involving Humans* – second consultation draft 10.

on the willing support of members of the community. Research that involves higher risks to participants than are acceptable to the general community may risk eroding that support. An assessment of the general community's views as to levels of acceptable risk remains a relevant consideration for researchers and for those reviewing research.[15]

Guidelines for assessing risk

2.1.1 Risks to which participants in research would be exposed are ethically acceptable only if they can be justified by the potential benefits of the research.

2.1.2 Steps to arriving at this judgement should include:

(a) identifying the risks;
(b) establishing the means for minimising the risks;
(c) identifying whom, in addition to the participants, the risks may affect;
(d) identifying the potential benefits; and
(e) identifying to whom benefits are intended, and likely, to accrue.

2.1.3 Researchers and those ethically reviewing research should take care neither to assume nor to over-generalise the existence, likelihood and significance of risks.

2.1.4 In determining the existence, likelihood and significance of risks, those reviewing research should consider seeking advice from those with experience in the conduct of research of the kind to be reviewed.

2.1.5 In judging whether the potential benefits justify the risks of research, those reviewing the research should take account of the participants' perspective on the risks involved and assess the significance of risks in research against the experience and opinions of the participants.

2.1.6 In research with the prospect of direct benefit to participants or to their families or communities, those judging the acceptability of risk should be prepared to give weight to any readiness in participants to assume a higher risk than they would be ready to assume in research lacking the prospect of such direct benefit.

2.1.7 Those reviewing research should be satisfied that risks to participants do not exceed those that are as low as is ethically achievable in each research project, having regard to:

(a) the aims and methods of the research;
(b) the potential benefits of the research;
(c) whether the participants will benefit directly from the research;[16]

15 Review of the *National Statement on Ethical Conduct in Research Involving Humans* – second consultation draft 11.

16 Review of the *National Statement on Ethical Conduct in Research Involving Humans* – second consultation draft 12.

(d) whether the benefits will accrue to people other than the participants;
(e) the opinions and experience of the participants; and
(f) the interests of the broader community and their support of human research.[17]

Chapter 2.2 Consent

Introduction

Respect for human beings involves giving due scope to the capacity of human beings to make their own decisions. In the research context, respect for human beings therefore normally requires that participation in research be the result of a choice made by participants. This is commonly known as 'the requirement for consent'. Exceptions to this requirement are set out at paragraphs 2.2.18–2.2.23 below. Where there are exceptions, respect for human beings must be shown in the alternative arrangements under which it will be decided whether potential participants may enter the research. What is needed to satisfy the 'requirement for consent' will vary. It will depend on the nature of the project and may be affected by the requirements of the codes, laws, ethics and cultural sensitivities of the community in which the research is to be conducted.

General requirements for consent

2.2.1 The process through which the opportunity for choice about participation is offered, and the choice is made, can vary. The guiding principle for researchers is that a person's decision to participate is to be voluntary, and based on sufficient information and adequate understanding. For exceptions to this principle, see paragraphs 2.2.18–2.2.23.

2.2.2 Researchers should seek and verify consent in ways appropriate to the participants' culture and circumstances.

2.2.3 Apart from exceptions set out in paragraphs 2.2.10 and 2.2.19–2.2.22, researchers are responsible for communicating to each potential participant the following information, whether orally, in writing, or by some other means, and in ways suitable for that participant:

(a) the purpose of the research;
(b) how it will be conducted;
(c) demands on participants, including any expected costs to participants;
(d) inconveniences and discomforts;
(e) risks and harms;

17 Review of the *National Statement on Ethical Conduct in Research Involving Humans* – second consultation draft 13.

(f) the participant's right to withdraw from further participation at any stage, along with any implications of withdrawal, and whether it will be possible to withdraw data;[18]
(g) financial or other relevant declarations of interests of researchers, sponsors or institutions;
(h) possible outcomes of the research (including the likelihood and form of dissemination, including publication, of research results);
(i) any expected benefits of the research to participants and to the wider community;
(j) how the conduct of the research will be monitored;
(k) the contact details of a person to receive complaints; and
(l) any other relevant information.

2.2.4 The process of communicating such information should not become a matter of merely satisfying a formal requirement. The aim is mutual understanding between researchers and participants. This aim requires an opportunity for participants to ask questions and to discuss the information and their decision with others if they wish.

2.2.5 Where the research process is dynamic and continuous, consent may need to be renegotiated or confirmed, especially in the case of complex, long-running projects or with participants who are vulnerable. Research participants should be told if there are changes to the terms to which they originally agreed, and given the opportunity to continue their participation or withdraw.

2.2.6 The processes of seeking and obtaining consent will vary in complexity and detail according to the nature and level of risk in the research.

2.2.7 The consent of a person to participate in research should not be subject to coercion or pressure. Researchers should also be aware that a participant's consent might be an expression of deference or compliance in the face of the researcher's actual or perceived position of power.

2.2.8 Payment of research participants in money or kind is not in itself unethical. The decision to participate may be voluntary even if a person would not have participated without a payment. No payment that is likely to encourage participants to take undue risks is acceptable.

2.2.9 In most circumstances, it is appropriate to reimburse the costs to participants of taking part in research. These costs include material costs such as travel, but in some circumstances can also justifiably include the cost of participants' time. Further decisions about payment of research participants or benefit in kind to participants or their

18 Review of the *National Statement on Ethical Conduct in Research Involving Humans* – second consultation draft 14.

community should take into account the customs and practices of the community in which the research is to be conducted.[19]

2.2.10 Where a potential participant lacks the capacity to consent, a person or appropriate statutory body with lawful authority to decide for the participant should be provided with relevant information and may exercise that choice.

2.2.11 The most suitable way for participants to demonstrate their consent will vary according to the nature of the research and the kind and level of risk it involves. Whatever method is chosen, research should be designed so that each participant's voluntary participation is clearly established. Different methods include return of a survey, conduct implying consent, a signed form, or other sufficient means.

2.2.12 In some circumstances and within some communities, participation in research is not only a matter of individual decision, but also involves other properly interested parties, such as formally constituted bodies of various kinds, institutions, families, or community elders. In such cases, researchers need to engage with all properly interested parties before beginning the research.

Consent to future use of data and tissue in research

2.2.13 In many circumstances, consent is limited to the specific project under consideration ('specific consent'). Under certain conditions, however, consent may extend to the use of data in future research projects which are an extension of, or closely related to, the original research project, or even in future projects which are in the same general area of research, for example, genealogical, ethnographical, epidemiological, chronic illness research, etc. ('extended consent'). In some circumstances this 'extended consent' may include permission to enter the original data into a databank. Any restrictions on the use of participants' data should be recorded and the record kept with the collected data so that it is always accessible to researchers who want to access those data for research.

2.2.14 Participants may give their consent for the use of their data in future unspecified research that may not be related to the original project ('unspecified consent'). Information about the nature and extent of this research will inevitably be limited. It is important to ensure at the time of agreement that the terms of the unspecified consent are clearly explained and recorded. Research proposals that rely on unspecified consent to the use of data may still require approval from a Human Research Ethics Committee (HREC), except where alternative processes of approval set out in paragraphs 5.1.7–5.1.9 apply to the research. Research proposals should include a record of the unspecified consent given by participants.

19 Review of the *National Statement on Ethical Conduct in Research Involving Humans* – second consultation draft 15.

2.2.15 Data additional to that covered by the original extended or unspecified consent will sometimes be needed for research. Additional consent for access to such data may need to be sought from potential participants.[20]

Declining to consent and withdrawing consent

2.2.16 People who elect not to participate in a research project need not give any reason for that decision. Researchers should take care to do whatever they can to see that people who decline to participate will suffer no disadvantage as a result of that decision.

2.2.17 Participants are entitled to withdraw from the research at any stage. Before consent to involvement in research is given, participants should be informed about any consequences of such withdrawal (see paragraph 2.2.3).

Qualifying or waiving consent requirements

2.2.18 In some circumstances and in some fields of research, significant qualifications on the obligation to provide information before participation may be justified.

2.2.19 An HREC may approve a research proposal that does not include or alters some or all of the requirements set out in paragraphs 2.2.1–2.2.12 or waive the requirement that consent be given for participation.

2.2.20 Before approving the omission or alteration of any of the elements of the consent process, the HREC should be satisfied that:

(a) participation in the research involves no more than low risk to participants;
(b) the omission or alteration is unlikely to adversely affect participants;
(c) the research could not practicably be carried out without the omission or alteration; and
(d) whenever possible and appropriate, after their participation has ended:
    (i) participants will be provided with information about the aims of the research and an explanation of why the omission or alteration was necessary and
    (ii) participants will be offered the opportunity to withdraw any data or tissue provided by them.

2.2.21 In thinking about whether to waive the requirement of consent for participation in proposed research, an HREC should consider the following matters:

20 Review of the *National Statement on Ethical Conduct in Research Involving Humans* – second consultation draft 16.

(a) the scope of any existing consent relating to the collection or storage of data or tissue to be used in the research;
(b) whether there is any reason to think participants would not have consented if they had been asked;[21]
(c) in protecting the privacy of participants, the extent to which it is possible to re-identify or potentially identify the data or tissue or for the identity of the participants to become known;
(d) the extent to which there is an adequate plan to protect the confidentiality of data;
(e) the extent of any interaction between investigators and participants, such as in projects using existing identifiable or re-identifiable data or tissue; and
(f) the possibility of commercial exploitation of derivatives of the data or tissue.

2.2.22 Before taking the decision to waive the requirement that consent be given for participation in proposed research, an HREC must be satisfied that:

(a) participation in the research involves no more than low risk to participants;
(b) it is impracticable to obtain consent;
(c) there is a sufficient justification for the waiver;
(d) the research could not practicably be carried out without the waiver;
(e) any risks to the privacy of participants will be minimised;
(f) there is an adequate plan for contacting participants with information derived from the research, should the need arise;
(g) whenever appropriate, the participants will be provided with additional pertinent information after participating;
(h) the benefits from the knowledge to be gained from the research justify any risks of harm associated with not seeking consent; and that
(i) the waiver is not otherwise prohibited by State, federal, or international law.

2.2.23 When an HREC waives the requirement for consent under paragraph 2.2.22, it should report details of that decision to the institution. The institution should make details of all such decisions publicly accessible.[22]

Section 3 Ethical considerations specific to research methods or fields

This section discusses various methodologies that may be used in different types of research. The section is a result of the further expansion of

21 Review of the *National Statement on Ethical Conduct in Research Involving Humans* – second consultation draft 17.

22 Review of the *National Statement on Ethical Conduct in Research Involving Humans* – second consultation draft 18.

the revised National Statement beyond health and medical research. The discussion focuses on general principles and is not intended to be exhaustive. It reflects the interdisciplinary nature of many types of research, and that some researchers might employ a number of research methods. Human research may be conducted only with ethical approval. Section 5 describes the processes that institutions may use to provide that approval. Those processes include ethical review by Human Research Ethics Committees (HRECs) or other ethical review bodies, according to the risks of the research (see paragraphs 5.1.4, 5.1.7 and 5.1.8). Research involving more than low risk must be ethically reviewed and approved by an HREC (see paragraph 5.1.15). Research covered by Chapter 3.2 *Limited disclosure*, 3.4 *Therapies and interventions, including clinical and non-clinical trials, and innovations*, 3.5 *Human genetics* and 3.7 *Human stem cells* must also be ethically reviewed and approved by an HREC.[23]

Chapter 3.1 Qualitative methods

Introduction

The information in this introduction is intended for users of the Statement who may not be familiar with the purposes and main methods of qualitative research. It has been included because this is the first time the Statement has dealt explicitly with qualitative research. Qualitative research involves disciplined inquiry that examines people's lives, experiences and behaviours, and the stories and meanings individuals ascribe to them.[24] Qualitative research can also investigate organisational functioning, relationships between individuals and groups, and social environments. This approach to research involves the studied use and collection of a variety of empirical materials – such as case studies, personal experience, life stories, interviews, observations, and cultural texts – that describe routine and problematic moments and meanings in the lives of individuals. Qualitative research can provide in-depth information that may bring new insights into the experiences of individuals or groups, leading to a better understanding of the subject matter that is being investigated.

Qualitative research may also have quantitative elements or aspects. Qualitative research contributes to the development of new knowledge by:

(a) enabling researchers to better understand complex concepts;
(b) investigating how communities and individuals interpret and make sense of their experiences;

23 Review of the *National Statement on Ethical Conduct in Research Involving Humans* – second consultation draft 19.

24 Denzin NK & Lincoln YS (eds.) 2000 Handbook of Qualitative Research, Sage: California Review of the *National Statement on Ethical Conduct in Research Involving Humans* – second consultation draft 20.

(c) eliciting contextual data in order to improve validity of quantitative tools, such as surveys.

Commonly used approaches to data collection in qualitative research

A number of approaches can be used in qualitative research to collect data. Common approaches to data collection include (but are not limited to) the following methods.

- **Interviews** involve researchers talking to one or more participants, where the category of responses is focused but not necessarily predetermined. Interviews are usually recorded by tape, video or notes. These records may be transcribed but are adequate as research data in themselves. Interviews are usually conducted in a location of the participants' choice. Interviews can take many forms, including:
  - *structured interviews*, which follow a set list of questions;
  - *semi-structured interviews*, which use an interview guide listing a set of issues to be explored;
  - *unstructured interviews*, which involve spontaneous generation of questions in the natural flow of interaction, and where the interview is driven by the interviewee rather than the interviewer;
  - *key informant interviews*, which are conducted with individuals or groups with special expertise or knowledge about the issue being investigated.
- **Life story or oral history** is based on both structured and semi-structured interviews and is a form of research commonly undertaken in the humanities.
- **Focus groups** of participants draw together a range of responses to a set of research questions. This may entail the researcher acting as a moderator for the discussion.
- **Observation** involves the researcher observing participant(s) in their own environment, or in the environment being studied. Data collection through observation can be structured or unstructured, with the observer as a collaborative participant (participant observation) or external to the environment.
- **Archival research** refers to materials that are usually but not necessarily deposited in libraries.
- **On-line research** includes conducting on-line real-time group discussions using web-based chat-room technology (also known as E-groups) through the use of electronic bulletin boards and moderated email groups. On-line recruitment of participants provides the opportunity for extensive global participation in research. Data collection and dissemination can also be utilised on-line.
- **Action research** is often community-based and carried out by a practitioner in the field. This approach involves testing ideas in practice as a means of improving social conditions and increasing knowledge. Action research proceeds in a spiral of steps consisting

of planning, action, and evaluation. It provides a basis for further planning of critically informed action.[25]

Decisions about the design, review and conduct of human research must clearly reflect the values, principles and themes set out in Section 1 *Values and principles of ethical conduct* and Section 2 *Themes in ethical review: risk and consent*. When these values, principles and themes are applied to research involving qualitative methods, the following additional matters must be considered.

Research merit and integrity

3.1.1 In their relationships with participants, researchers are expected to maintain their role as researchers and not to engage in activities outside of the research or for which they are not qualified.

3.1.2 Qualitative research emphasises the significance of particular contexts and settings, and aims to provide a sufficiently detailed account and/or analysis to enable others to determine whether the findings are applicable to other circumstances. It is not necessary to be able to apply the results of qualitative research more generally.

3.1.3 The most common sampling strategy is purposeful sampling, which is aimed at the selection of information-rich cases relevant to the research question. While random and representative sampling are not precluded in qualitative studies, most sampling frames are based on other types of logic.

3.1.4 The rigour of a qualitative study should not be judged on sample size. When sampling is appropriate, the objectives and theoretical basis of the research should determine the size of the sample and the sampling strategy. For example, some qualitative methods use a principle of 'saturation', where sampling occurs until no new information is being obtained. This is only one of several criteria for assessing sample size (see paragraph 3.1.7).

3.1.5 Research proposals should clearly describe the recruitment strategy and criteria for selecting participants when sampling is proposed.

3.1.6 The rigour of qualitative research should be assessed primarily by criteria of quality and credibility of data collection and analysis, as well as justice for research participants, and not by matters of validity and reliability as defined in research designs that employ quantitative methods.

Justice

3.1.7 In qualitative research, the criteria for inclusion and exclusion of participants are often complex. For this reason, researchers should state clearly and be able to justify the criteria by which participants are to be

25 Review of the *National Statement on Ethical Conduct in Research Involving Humans* – second consultation draft 21.

included or excluded from a study using qualitative methods (see paragraph 3.1.4).[26]

Beneficence

3.1.8 In qualitative research, participants are often easily identifiable, for example, as members of small communities or groups, or as key informants, and the information they provide may be sensitive. For these reasons, care should be taken that participants are not identified by the information they provide, unless they have consented to be identified. Special care should be taken to protect the identity of participants when disseminating information and storing material.

3.1.9 Participants should be informed about any potential to be identified in the results of research even if identifiers, such as name and address, are removed.

3.1.10 Qualitative research that explores sensitive topics in depth may involve emotional and other risks to both participant and researcher. There should be clear protocols for dealing with distress experienced by participants. Researchers should have sufficient training, and should outline courses of action, such as a referral process, to deal with these effects.

3.1.11 Qualitative research may involve methods of data collection that require the development of personal relationships with participants. Researchers should be aware of the impact that they may have on the participants and vice versa, and as far as possible, describe in the research proposal any anticipated such impact.

Respect

3.1.12 Qualitative research by its nature allows for the interpretive analysis of data. Researchers should try to avoid the risk that their own values will distort their understanding either of the information provided by participants or of its relevance to the research.

3.1.13 While consent is usually expressed in writing in qualitative research, there are justifiable exceptions (see paragraph 2.2.11). Sometimes oral consent is more appropriate, for example, when the research topic is particularly sensitive or the participant feels vulnerable or out of respect for participants' culture or circumstances. In some circumstances, consent may be implied by participation. In other circumstances, for example when observing, photographing or filming people in public places, consent cannot be given by some or all 'participants'.[27]

26 Review of the *National Statement on Ethical Conduct in Research Involving Humans* – second consultation draft 22.

27 Review of the *National Statement on Ethical Conduct in Research Involving Humans* – second consultation draft 23.

Chapter 3.2 Limited disclosure

Introduction

Some research involves limited disclosure of the methods or purposes of research, and can be ethically justified where the following requirements are satisfied.

Decisions about the design, review and conduct of human research must clearly reflect the values, principles and themes set out in Section 1 *Values and principles of ethical conduct* and Section 2 *Themes in ethical review: risk and consent*. When these values, principles and themes are applied to research involving limited disclosure, the following additional matters must be considered. Research to which this chapter applies must be reviewed and approved by a Human Research Ethics Committee (HREC) rather than by one of the other processes of ethical review described in paragraphs 5.1.7 and 5.1.8.

Research merit and integrity

3.2.1 For research that involves limited disclosure, researchers should demonstrate that:

(a) the research is warranted, even though disclosure is limited;
(b) there are no suitable alternatives involving full disclosure by which the aims of the research can be achieved;
(c) the precise extent of the limited disclosure is defined;
(d) participants will eventually be fully informed;
(e) it can reasonably be anticipated that, following debriefing, the research participants will regard the research as justified and acceptable conduct;
(f) the participants are not likely to be harmed by their participation.

Beneficence

3.2.2 Participants must not be exposed to an increased risk of harm as a result of the limited disclosure.

3.2.3 The potential benefits of the research should be sufficient to justify any risk that the research might corrupt the relationship between the community and researchers and research in general.[28]

Respect

3.2.4 An HREC must be satisfied that alterations to the elements for consent meet the requirements set out in paragraph 2.2.20.[29]

28 Review of the *National Statement on Ethical Conduct in Research Involving Humans* – second consultation draft 24.

29 Review of the *National Statement on Ethical Conduct in Research Involving Humans* – second consultation draft 25.

Chapter 3.3 Databanks[30]

Introduction

Data are pieces of information. Data may arise through either a specific donation or response by a person, or the actions of others. Examples of data derived through donations include what people say in interviews, focus groups, questionnaires, personal histories and biographies, and may also arise from the donation of human tissue such as blood, bone, muscle and urine. Examples of data derived by the actions of others include information or observations about a person, such as those in a photograph, or information or observations made during studies where drugs and/or treatment programs, clinical devices or psychological stimuli are tested. Data are collected, stored or disclosed, as identifiable data, re-identifiable or potentially identifiable data, or non-identifiable data (which includes a subset, anonymous data).

These three categories of data, described below, are mutually exclusive:

(a) individually identifiable: data from which the identity of a specific individual can reasonably be ascertained. Examples of identifiers may include the individual's name, image, date of birth or address;
(b) re-identifiable or potentially re-identifiable: data from which identifiers have been removed and replaced by a code, but from which it remains possible to reidentify a specific individual, for example, by using the code or by linking different data sets;
(c) non-identifiable: data that have never been labelled with individual identifiers or from which identifiers have been permanently removed, and by means of which no specific individual can be identified. This includes a subset, anonymous: data which can be linked with other data so it can be known that they are about the same data subject, while the identity of that specific individual remains unknown. The term 'de-identified data' sometimes refers to a record that cannot be linked to an individual (non-identifiable), and at other times refers to a record in which identifying information has been removed but for which the means exist to re-identify the individual (re-identifiable or potentially re-identifiable).

Because of this ambiguity, the terms above are preferred. When the term 'de-identified data' is used, researchers and those reviewing research need to establish precisely which of these possible meanings it has. It should be noted that with advances in genetic knowledge and data linkage, and the proliferation of tissue banks of identified material, human tissue samples may always be regarded as, in principle, potentially re-identifiable. This increased ability to link data has greatly enhanced the contribution the accumulation of data can make to research. It allows researchers to match individuals in different data sets without being able to identify the person. Technology has also enabled a wide range of

30 In the National Statement, the term 'databank' includes databases. Review of the *National Statement on Ethical Conduct in Research Involving Humans* – second consultation draft 26.

routine data to be employed as research data. For example, in epidemiological research, which is concerned with the study of populations, information about individuals and groups may be collected so that features of groups of people can be investigated. These data may, or may not, have originally been obtained for research purposes. In the majority of instances, data are collected, aggregated and stored for a single purpose or activity. In some other cases, however, permission may be sought from participants to 'bank' their data for possible use in future research projects. Data can also be stored in a data warehouse that aggregates data over time, similar to an archive or library. For example, the Australian Social Science Data Archive collects and preserves computer-readable data relating to social, political and economic affairs and makes the data available for further analysis. Data stored in the archives can usually be made available for secondary analysis, depending on whether the depositor(s) imposed restrictions on access to the data. The values and principles of this Statement apply to data collection not only by researchers but also by others whom they authorise to collect data or to whom they outsource the collection. These ethical principles for the use of databanks should be reflected and applied in the guidelines and procedures established by institutions for the setting up of data collections.

Decisions about the design, review and conduct of human research must clearly reflect the values, principles and themes set out in Section 1 *Values and principles of ethical conduct* and Section 2 *Themes in ethical review: risk and consent*. When these values, principles and themes are applied to research involving databanks, the following additional matters must be considered.

Research merit and integrity

3.3.1 When planning a databank, researchers should clearly describe how their research data will be collected, stored, used and disclosed, outlining how that process conforms to this Statement.[31]

Justice

3.3.2 In order to treat participants and their contributions fairly and to promote access to the benefits of research, data should be collected, stored and accessible in such a way that they can be used in future research projects.

Beneficence

3.3.3 Researchers may only use data from databanks as identifiable data, reidentifiable or potentially re-identifiable data, or, characteristically,

31 Review of the *National Statement on Ethical Conduct in Research Involving Humans* – second consultation draft 27.

nonidentifiable data, according to the conditions specified by the providers of data (see paragraphs 2.2.13–2.2.15).

3.3.4 Where research involves linkage of data sets, the use of identified data to ensure that the linkage is accurate may be approved even if consent has not been given for the use of identified data in research. Once linkage has been completed, identifiers from the data to be used in the research should be removed.

3.3.5 It is the duty of the custodian to ensure that the data are used responsibly, respectfully, and so as to safeguard the privacy of participants.

3.3.6 Whenever research using re-identifiable data reveals information that, in conformity with paragraph 1.4, ought to be made available to participants, the custodian should be in a position to re-identify the person to whom the original data related.

3.3.7 In most situations, the custodian of data will be the individual researcher or agency who collected the information, or an intermediary such as a data warehouse that manages data coming from a number of sources. In some cases, an independent custodian may be necessary. For example, when coded data are stored in a databank, a custodian who is independent of the collectors of the data and the researchers proposing to use the data may be appointed to enable research participants to access identified results or data.

Respect

3.3.8 When collecting data for deposit in a databank, researchers should provide clear and comprehensive information about the type of data that will be stored, and about the purposes for which the data will be used and/or disclosed. This will include whether specific, extended or unspecified consent for future research will be sought, or whether permission will be sought from an HREC to waive the need for consent (see paragraphs 2.2.21–2.2.23).

3.3.9 Identifiable, re-identifiable and potentially re-identifiable data may be included in a repository to which other researchers have access only with the consent of the participant. In preserving and using data, any confidentiality agreement with the participant should be observed, and the researcher should take every precaution to prevent the data becoming available for uses for which participants did not consent.[32]

3.3.10 When depositing identified research data in a databank or archive, researchers should consider restricting uses of the data that might be detrimental to the welfare of people to whom the data relates. For example, access to the data could be precluded for a period of time,

32 Review of the *National Statement on Ethical Conduct in Research Involving Humans* – second consultation draft 28.

whether before or even after the death of the people to whom the data relates.[33]

Chapter 3.4 Therapies and interventions, including clinical and non-clinical trials, and innovations

Introduction

Clinical research

Clinical research involves the use of clinical procedures and is designed to derive information that can be applied in a clinical setting and to improve the provision of care to individuals. Commonly, this takes the form of a clinical trial (see below), especially of new therapies. It also includes assessment of other interventions in many different fields and may be conducted by a range of different health professionals studying a wide range of matters, including disease prevention and causation, diagnostic methods, treatments, and effects of and responses to illness. Such research can occur in a number of settings, including public and private hospitals and clinics, other institutions or organisations, community settings, and general or specialist medical practices. This chapter focuses especially on randomised clinical trials, but it should be noted that clinical trials are not always randomised. Further, as noted below, randomisation may be used in other areas of human research (for example, education research) and therefore the ethical issues outlined here will be relevant to such research. At times, it may be difficult to distinguish clinical and related research from quality improvement and clinical audit. In such situations, guidance is available from the NHMRC publication *When does quality assurance need review by a Human Research Ethics Committee?* (NHMRC 2003).

Innovative therapy or intervention

Innovations in clinical practice and complementary medicine include new diagnostic or therapeutic methods which aim at improving health outcomes beyond those of existing methods but which have not yet been fully assessed for safety and/or efficacy. It should always be made clear to potential participants that the proposed intervention is innovative. The spectrum of innovations ranges widely from minor variations of existing methods, or the extension of existing methods, to new indications, through to completely novel technologies. Whether a change in an individual's investigation or treatment represents an innovation or constitutes clinical research is generally a matter for the responsible clinician's judgement, guided by the relevant institutional policies.[34]

33 Review of the *National Statement on Ethical Conduct in Research Involving Humans* – second consultation draft 29.

34 Review of the *National Statement on Ethical Conduct in Research Involving Humans* – second consultation draft 30.

Clinical and other trials

A clinical trial is a form of clinical research designed to find out whether an intervention, including a treatment or diagnostic procedure, which it is believed may improve a person's health, actually does so. A clinical trial can involve testing a drug, a surgical procedure, other therapeutic procedures and devices, a preventive procedure, or a diagnostic device or procedure. Characteristically, such trials seek to test a hypothesis and uses appropriate methods to test it. Clinical trials of new therapeutic substances are typically categorised into Phase I, II or III trials. Phase I and II studies involve the initial evaluation of a new drug, compound or device for safety, tolerability and suitable dosage in healthy volunteers, while Phase III trials usually involve comparison with existing treatments, using randomisation and 'blinding' or other strategies to ensure freedom from bias. Many disciplines conduct research using similar methodology including randomisation. Such research raises similar ethical considerations to those raised in this chapter. Clinical research also includes Phase IV studies which most often constitute postregistration surveillance research designed to document safety in a broader and larger population than that involved in Phase III trials. The design, review and conduct of Phase IV trials should satisfy the principles outlined in this chapter. In pharmaceutical and medical device trials there are established codes of good clinical research practice that define clearly what is meant by a clinical trial for those purposes. This chapter has principal application to biomedical clinical trials but also applies to any other intervention claiming therapeutic benefit, wherever provided or conducted. Trials involving experimentation with therapeutic goods, whether drugs or devices, that are not yet registered or listed on the Australian Therapeutic Goods Register (ATGR) are subject to notification to and oversight by the Therapeutic Goods Administration (TGA).

Application of randomised trial methods to other areas of human research

Research methods intended to avoid or reduce bias include randomisation and 'blinding' participants and researchers to the identity of agents being compared. First applied to the study of new therapies, these research methods are now used in various other fields, including, for example, psychology and education. Researchers in any fields who propose to use such methods should be aware of the ethical issues which may arise in the design and conduct of such research. In particular, paragraphs 3.4.3 and 3.4.6 will apply in all situations, while other paragraphs may be relevant depending on the nature of the research and the relationship between the researcher and potential participants.

Decisions about the design, review and conduct of human research must clearly reflect the values, principles and themes set out in Section 1 *Values and principles of ethical conduct* and Section 2 *Themes in ethical review: risk and consent*. When these values, principles and themes are applied to

research involving therapies[35] and interventions, including clinical and non-clinical trials, and innovations, the following additional matters must be considered. Research to which this chapter applies must be reviewed and approved by a Human Research Ethics Committee (HREC) rather than by one of the other processes of ethical review described in paragraphs 5.1.7 and 5.1.8.

Research merit and integrity

3.4.1 Health care and medical institutions should develop and implement policies about the use of innovative interventions and treatments. These policies should include criteria for deciding when innovations should be subjected to systematic investigation to determine their safety and efficacy.

3.4.2 When, in the light of those policies, an innovative diagnostic or therapeutic method should be subject to systematic investigation to determine its efficacy and safety, it should be treated as clinical research requiring formal consideration by a Human Research Ethics Committee (HREC).

3.4.3 Researchers should show that:

(a) the research is directed to answering a specific question or questions;
(b) there is a scientifically valid hypothesis being tested which offers a realistic possibility that the interventions being studied will be at least as effective as standard treatment;
(c) the size and profile of the sample to be recruited is adequate to answering the specific research question; and
(d) where relevant, the research meets the requirements of the *CPMP/ICH Note for Guidance on Good Clinical Practice* (CPMP/ICH–135/95), ISO 14155 *Clinical Investigation of Medical Devices* and the TGA.

3.4.4 Researchers should inform the HREC of any business, financial or other similar association between a researcher and the supplier of a drug or surgical or other device to be used in the trial, and of any other possible conflicts of interest.

3.4.5 In any clinical research, especially clinical trials, an HREC should be satisfied that:

(a) funding is sufficient to conduct and complete the trial as designed; and
(b) any payment in money or kind, whether to institutions, researchers

35 Review of the *National Statement on Ethical Conduct in Research Involving Humans* – second consultation draft 31.

or participants, will not adversely influence the design, conduct, findings or publication of the research.[36]

Justice

3.4.6 The research methodology should provide a rationale for the selection of appropriate participants and an appropriate method of recruitment (see paragraph 1.3).

Beneficence

3.4.7 The proportion of risks to potential benefits will vary for different research participants. In research without likely benefit to participants, the risks to participants should be low. In clinical research where patient care is combined with intent to contribute to knowledge, any higher risks of participation should be justified by likely benefits for the participants.

3.4.8 The prospect of benefit from research participation should not be exaggerated, either to justify to an HREC a higher risk than that involved in the participant's current treatment or to persuade a participant to accept that higher risk.

3.4.9 The use of a placebo alone or the incorporation of a non-treatment control group is ethically unacceptable in a controlled trial where:

(a) other available treatment has already been clearly shown to be effective; and
(b) there is risk of significant harm in the absence of treatment. If there is genuine uncertainty as to whether currently available treatment has a net clinical benefit, a placebo controlled trial or a trial with a no-treatment arm may be considered.

3.4.10 Data should be accurately recorded in a durable and appropriately referenced form that complies with established legislation, policies and guidelines. Where materials of biological origin, or other materials of which there is limited experience of long-term use, are being used in a trial, records should be preserved for such periods as will enable participants to be traced in the event that evidence of late or long-term effects emerges.

Respect

3.4.11 Due to the potential complexity of information to be provided to participants in seeking consent, the requirements of paragraph 2.2.3 should be carefully considered and followed. In particular, in clinical

36 Review of the *National Statement on Ethical Conduct in Research Involving Humans* – second consultation draft 32.

trials, written information should not be unduly long or complex. Adequate time should be allowed for prospective participants to read and take in what is proposed.[37]

3.4.12 Particular care should be taken in clinical trials to make it clear to participants whether there is intended to be any therapeutic benefit to them from the trial.

3.4.13 In clinical research, where patient care is combined wih an intent to contribute to knowledge, the following matters should be carefully weighed:

(a) the seriousness of the condition being treated;
(b) the risks involved in the proposed research; and
(c) the possible effects of an unequal or dependent relationship between the treating health professional or researcher and the potential participant.

3.4.14 Where the researcher is also the treating health professional, it may be appropriate for an independent person to seek the consent of potential participants.

3.4.15 An HREC should examine the budgets and other financial aspects of clinical research, especially clinical trials, to be satisfied that:

(a) payment in money or incentives of any kind, whether to researchers or participants, does not result in pressure on individuals to consent to participate;
(b) research participants are informed of the funding arrangements of the research and given the option of knowing the details of any capitation payments to researchers; and
(c) it has been made clear to participants whether they will have continued access after the trial to treatments they have received during the trial and on the same terms.

Monitoring of approved clinical research

3.4.16 The ultimate responsibilities of institutions for monitoring the conduct of approved research are described in Chapter 5.5 *Monitoring approved research*. In clinical research, and especially clinical trials, research sponsors have complementary responsibilities.

3.4.17 Institutions responsible for the conduct of clinical research should require that:

(a) for each project, there are mechanisms by which adverse events will be reported;

37 Review of the *National Statement on Ethical Conduct in Research Involving Humans* – second consultation draft.

(b) for each large multi-centre trial, a Data Safety and Monitoring Board (DSMB) will be used;[38]
(c) there is a mechanism for informing the HREC of any relevant emerging data from the DSMB and from reports of local adverse events; and
(d) for local trials, there is an identified person or committee with responsibility for collecting and storing data on adverse events and for notifying the HREC of adverse events related to research approved by that HREC.

3.4.18 HRECs should consider information provided to them about adverse events and review the project in light of this new information.

3.4.19 In addition to the requirements outlined in Chapter 5.5 *Monitoring approved research*, the granting and continuation of ethical approval of clinical research must be on the condition that the researcher:

(a) conducts the trial in compliance with the approved protocol;
(b) provides reports of the progress of the trial to the HREC at a frequency directed by the HREC that is related to the degree of risk to participants, but at least annually;
(c) informs the HREC, and seeks its approval, of amendments to the protocol including any:
    (i) proposed or undertaken in order to eliminate immediate hazards to participants,
    (ii) that may increase the risks to participants, or
    (iii) that significantly affect the conduct of the trial;
(d) informs the HREC, the DSMB or person identified by the institution, and the TGA of all adverse events that occur during the trial and may affect the conduct of the trial, the safety of the participants or their willingness to continue participating. This information should be accompanied by an explanation of the significance of these events;
(e) informs the HREC as soon as possible of any new information from other published or unpublished studies which may have an impact on the continued ethical acceptability of the trial or which may indicate the need for amendments to the trial protocol;
(f) informs the HREC, giving reasons, if the trial is discontinued before the expected date of completion; and
(g) in relation to trials with implantable medical devices, confirms the existence of or establishes a system for tracking the participant, with consent, for the lifetime of the device, and for reporting any device incidents to the TGA.[39]

38 Review of the *National Statement on Ethical Conduct in Research Involving Humans* – second consultation draft 34.

39 Review of the *National Statement on Ethical Conduct in Research Involving Humans* – second consultation draft.

3.4.20 It may be unethical for a researcher to continue a trial if:

(a) there are or have been substantial deviations from the trial protocol;
(b) side effects of unexpected type, severity, or frequency are encountered; or
(c) as the trial progresses, one of several treatments or procedures being compared proves to be so much better, or worse, than other(s) that continuation of the trial would disadvantage some of the participants.

3.4.21 Research sponsors and institutions must ensure that arrangements that meet accepted standards are established to provide compensation to participants for harm suffered as a result of their participation in clinical research.[40]

Chapter 3.5 Human genetics

Introduction

Genetic research involves the study of how genes influence the health of individuals and populations with the aim of generating knowledge that has the potential to improve individual and community health. Genes are being studied increasingly in clinical, epidemiological and social research, as well as in basic research. Genetic research may involve study of:

(a) one or thousands of genes, depending on the research aims and the technology used;
(b) inherited (genomic) gene sequences, both normal and variant;
(c) both inherited (genomic) gene sequences and acquired (somatic) variation in gene sequence at the same time, for example, in cancer tissue;
(d) gene expression, which reflects the activity of inherited genes as well as genes that have been altered by somatic mutation, and also reflects the action of environmental factors on these genes; and
(e) the genes of individuals, families or populations.

When genetic research is conducted using stored data, see also Chapter 3.3 *Databanks* and when conducted using human tissue samples, see also Chapter 3.6 *Human tissue samples*.

In addition to ethical considerations which apply to all human research there are ethical issues specific to genetic research. These arise from the nature of genes and genetic information which, though personal, are also shared with other family members and with unrelated individuals in the population. Where research is conducted on inherited (genomic) gene sequences, the familial character of the genetic information involved raises ethical issues of greater consequence for individuals and

40 Review of the *National Statement on Ethical Conduct in Research Involving Humans* – second consultation draft.

families than those raised by research on acquired (somatic) variations in gene sequences. Genetic research can reveal information about research participants' predispositions to disease. Although they may neither have nor develop the disease, the information may have implications for their access to employment and education and to benefits or services, including financial services such as banking, insurance and superannuation. The information may also have similar implications for relatives. When identified genetic variation is associated with large increases or decreases in the chance of future disease, such information may be of concern, interest or benefit to research participants, especially if preventive strategies exist for those at increased risk.[41]

When genetic variation is associated with only small increases or decreases in the chance of future disease and the chance can be influenced by the function of other genes and environmental factors, information gained from the research is likely to be of little value to individual research participants. Research results and genetic material and information collected for genetic research may be significant for close genetic relatives, commonly called 'blood relatives', of research participants. These family members may have an interest in their relatives' genetic material, or in information which the research generates, because testing that material or acquiring that information may create new options for life decisions, including those with potential to improve health. However, some family members may prefer not to be given such information, or even not to know of its existence. In addition, other family members who are not blood relatives, such as partners and spouses, may have an interest because of concerns about the health of offspring. Genetic research can also reveal information about previously unknown paternity or maternity.

Decisions about the design, review and conduct of human research must clearly reflect the values, principles and themes set out in Section 1 *Values and principles of ethical conduct* and Section 2 *Themes in ethical review: risk and consent*. When these values, principles and themes are applied to human genetic research, the following additional matters must be considered. Research to which this chapter applies must be reviewed and approved by a Human Research Ethics Committee (HREC) rather than by one of the other processes of ethical review described in paragraphs 5.1.7 and 5.1.8.

Research merit and integrity

3.5.1 Where research may discover or generate information of potential importance to the future health of participants, their offspring or blood relatives, researchers should prepare and follow an ethically defensible plan for handling that information. The plan should include procedures

41 Review of the *National Statement on Ethical Conduct in Research Involving Humans* – second consultation draft.

to enable participants or relatives to decide whether or not they wish to receive the information, and to whom the information may be conveyed. Those procedures should take into account the clinical relevance of the information and the quality of the genetic tests in the research and of their results. The procedures should also include measures to protect the degree of confidentiality that participants wish to maintain. Where participants decide to be notified of or given genetic information that is important for their own health, the plan should provide access to clinical advice and counselling from health professionals with appropriate training, qualifications and experience, or make a clear recommendation to participants to seek such services.[42]

Justice

3.5.2 Researchers should consider the potential psychological, social and cultural significance of their research, particularly in the areas of complex socially significant characteristics and the genetic characteristics of communities. When such characteristics are the subject of research, researchers should adopt measures designed to prevent mis-use or misrepresentation of the results of research. These measures are particularly important where results might otherwise lead to prejudice, disrespect or other harm to the participants or communities to which they belong.

3.5.3 Before deciding to store information and material in non-identifiable form, researchers should consider carefully the consequences for future research and for communication of personal research results to participants.

Beneficence

3.5.4 Genetic research may potentially reveal information of importance to the future health of an identified or a re-identifiable participant or of a participant's offspring or blood relatives, although that potential may not be clear until after interim analysis of research information. Both at the commencement of the research and also when the potential is clear, participants should be given the option of whether they wish to be notified of the existence of that information. They should also be given the further option of receiving the information. In accordance with the plan referred to in paragraph 3.5.1, they should be clearly informed of any need for advice or counselling about the implications of these decisions. This advice needs to include a clear explanation of the difference between research and clinical testing, and to clarify any need for clinical testing of research results.

42 Review of the *National Statement on Ethical Conduct in Research Involving Humans* – second consultation draft.

3.5.5 Researchers should not transfer genetic material and related information to a researcher in another research group, unless:

(a) the transferring and receiving researchers are conducting research which has been ethically approved in Australia or through an equivalent process in another country;
(b) either
    (i) the genetic material and information provided is in practice nonidentifiable (even though, as with all genetic information, it may be in principle re-identifiable), or
    (ii) the transfer is approved by an HREC;[43] and
(c) the other research group undertakes to hold the material and information in such a manner that there is no reduction in the protection of the privacy of the participants or of the confidentiality of the information.

3.5.6 There is potential for harm to participants arising from the use of genetic information, including stigmatisation or unfair discrimination. Researchers should take special care to protect the privacy and confidentiality of this information. Statutory or contractual duties of disclosure may require participants to disclose the results of genetic tests, particularly those which provide information about future health, to third parties such as insurance companies, employers and financial and educational institutions. As far as possible, participation in genetic research should be designed to minimise any risk, arising from such disclosures, that participants are deprived of benefits that are available to other members of the community.

Respect

3.5.7 Consent from participants should be obtained for human genetic research unless an HREC is satisfied that the research meets the requirements of paragraphs 2.2.21–2.2.23 and waives the requirement for consent.

3.5.8 Stored genetic material or genetic information should be used only for research falling within the scope of the consent originally provided for its use.

3.5.9 In addition to being given information required by paragraph 2.2.3, individuals whose consent is being sought for collection of genetic material and data for use in research should be informed:

(a) that they are free to decline to consent without giving reasons. Researchers should be aware that for some genetic research, an individual's participation may be requested by, and may primarily

43 Review of the *National Statement on Ethical Conduct in Research Involving Humans* – second consultation draft.

serve the interests of, other family members and that the individual may agree to participate out of a sense of obligation;

(b) about arrangements to ensure the privacy and confidentiality of their genetic information with regard both to other family members and to persons who are not family members. Participants should be informed whether their genetic material and data will be used in an identified, reidentifiable or non-identifiable form. If their material or data is to be used in a non-identifiable form, they should also be informed that it will not be possible to provide them with personal research results;

(c) if the research may reveal information of potential importance to the future health of an identified or re-identifiable participant or of the participant's offspring and their blood relatives;[44]

(d) that the researchers will endeavour to provide information about the outcome of the research. Participants should be advised whether feedback will relate to individual participants or to participants as a group. If it is not intended to provide feedback, participants should be told why. If relevant, participants should be asked whether they wish to be notified of research results which relate to them as individuals. A decision not to be notified should normally be respected. Participants should be informed, however, that an HREC may consider overriding this decision if research reveals unforeseen information with serious implications for their health unless preventive measures that are available are taken;

(e) that if the research generates information about participants which may be of relevance to the health of other family members, the written consent of participants will be sought before offering to disclose such information to the family members concerned. If, however, the research discloses that a family member may be at risk of a life threatening or serious illness for which treatment is available or pending, this information may be given to the family member, even if the research participant does not consent to this;

(f) if information from or about family members, in addition to that provided by participants, is required for the research;

(g) that if it is proposed to approach relatives, consent to do so will first be obtained from the participant;

(h) if the research has the potential to detect non-paternity or non-maternity, or non-blood relationship to siblings;

(i) if the research has potential to generate information that a participant may be legally required to disclose to a third party for the purposes of insurance, employment, finance or education;

(j) that genetic material and data may have uses unrelated to research. Participants should be advised that their material and data will not

44 Review of the *National Statement on Ethical Conduct in Research Involving Humans* – second consultation draft.

be released for such uses without their consent, unless required by law;

(k) about any proposal, subject to participants' consent, to store their genetic material and data because it might be useful for as yet unspecified future research conducted in accordance with paragraph 3.5.16 below;

(l) that if consent is not given, the genetic material and data will be disposed of at the end of the research, once the sample storage and record keeping requirements of good research practice have been met;

(m) that any wishes about the method of disposal will be recorded at the start of the research and taken into account at the time of disposal;[45]

(n) that they are free to withdraw from the research at any time. Participants should be informed of any consequences of such withdrawal, including that they may request that their genetic material and data be then disposed of if the samples can be identified. They should also be clearly informed of any practical limitations on the granting of this request; and

(o) that when research involves the study of large numbers of genes simultaneously, it is not necessary for researchers to provide participants with the names of all the individual genes to be studied.

3.5.10 In considering whether to approach relatives, researchers need to consider the privacy and any known sensitivities of the relatives, accepted habits of communication within the family, and the balance of potential benefits and harms which might result from the relatives' participation in the research.

3.5.11 Where a participant has given consent to approach relatives, the initial contact should be made by the participant or another relative.

3.5.12 When researchers propose to collect genetic material and information from individuals chosen because of their membership of a particular community, consent should be sought from appropriate community representatives as well as from the individuals concerned (see paragraph 2.2.12).

3.5.13 Researchers should ensure the confidentiality and privacy of stored genetic information or research results relating to identified or re-identifiable participants. Such information or research results should not be added to a participant's clinical record(s).

3.5.14 Researchers should keep information provided by participants about family members confidential. Such confidential information should not be revealed either to family members who are not participants or to anyone else. Identifying genetic information about family members should not be released to anyone, including those family members themselves, without the written consent of the participant who

45 Review of the *National Statement on Ethical Conduct in Research Involving Humans* – second consultation draft.

provided the information or of a person or institution legally authorised to consent for that participant.

3.5.15 The research proposal should specify whether genetic information or genetic material, and any information derived from studying the genetic material, will be stored in identified, potentially re-identifiable, or non-identifiable form (see 3.3 Introduction). Researchers should be aware that the rarity of some genetic disorders might allow certain families to be identified by other researchers, and in some cases by members of the community, even if information is communicated to others in non-identifiable form. Where genetic data is stored, it might sometimes be appropriate to place an embargo on the release of data (see paragraph 3.3.9).

3.5.16 Institutions wishing to conduct research on genetic material and information collected for non-research purposes, should develop and disseminate a general[46] policy informing patients of the terms and conditions on which that material and information may be used for future approved research. These policies should reflect the values and principles of this Statement. Patients of such institutions should be informed that this policy exists and be given the opportunity to decline to consent to use of their material and information for future research.

3.5.17 If asked to consent to the use of their genetic material and information for future research, participants should be provided with information about the likely implications of that use. They should also be advised to consider the need for counselling about these implications.

3.5.18 Where genetic material and information will be used for future research in nonidentifiable form feedback will not be practically possible. However, researchers may use the genetic material and information in potentially reidentifiable form. In such cases, participants' wishes about the feedback of information of potential significance to their own or their relatives' future health should be established, recorded and respected. If feedback is requested, the participant should be informed, either at the time of consent or prior to the feedback, about the implications of the feedback, and advised to consider the need for counselling about those implications.[47]

Chapter 3.6 Human tissue samples

Introduction

Samples of tissue, including blood and other body fluids, are collected from people in hospitals and other health care institutions. Samples collected for diagnostic purposes in the course of treatment have also

46 Review of the *National Statement on Ethical Conduct in Research Involving Humans* – second consultation draft.

47 Review of the *National Statement on Ethical Conduct in Research Involving Humans* – second consultation draft.

traditionally been used for teaching or quality assurance activities and for research. Hospitals and pathology laboratories are required by law to retain archival samples for diagnostic or forensic purposes. Accordingly, most hospitals have collections of stored samples whose use in research may lead to important advances in the understanding and treatment of disease.

Research involving the use of gametes or embryos is governed by *Ethical guidelines on the use of assisted reproductive technology in clinical practice and research* (NHMRC 2004). Decisions about the design, review and conduct of human research must clearly reflect the values, principles and themes set out in Section 1 *Values and principles of ethical conduct* and Section 2 *Themes in ethical review: risk and consent*. When these values, principles and themes are applied to research using human tissue samples, the following additional matters must be considered.

Research merit and integrity

3.6.1 Institutions should develop policies to guide researchers and those reviewing research about the conduct and ethical approval of research using human tissue. These policies should conform to relevant legislation and be consistent with this Statement. In the development of policies, relevant considerations include:

(a) the source, nature and cultural or religious sensitivity of the tissue;
(b) the original reason for its collection;
(c) when consent should be sought for the use of tissue in research and when a waiver of the requirement for consent may be considered; and
(d) the purpose of the research.

3.6.2 Where tissue is imported from overseas for use in Australia, researchers should try to establish whether there are ethical and professional policies in that country governing the collection of tissue for use in research.

(a) If there are such policies, researchers should seek assurance that the tissue was collected in accordance with them. Where this assurance is provided, but there is no indication of whether consent was obtained for the use of[48] the tissue in research, an HREC may decide to waive consent in accordance with paragraphs 2.2.21–2.2.23.
(b) Where such policies exist, and reasonable enquiry as to whether the tissue was collected in accordance with them is inconclusive but reveals no positive reason to believe it was not so collected, an HREC may also decide to waive consent.
(c) Where it cannot be established that such policies exist, or where

48 Review of the *National Statement on Ethical Conduct in Research Involving Humans* – second consultation draft.

they exist but enquiry reveals reason to believe the tissue was not collected in accordance with them, the tissue should not be used in research in Australia. (For specific conditions on the research use of imported stem cell lines, see paragraph 3.7.4. See also Chapter 4.8 *People in other countries.*)

Justice

3.6.3 Wherever human tissue samples or related information are gathered in the course of a professional relationship, confidentiality must be observed. Identification of samples must be limited to the minimum necessary to achieve the stated objectives of the research. If the research may produce information relevant to the health and well being of the person from whom it was derived, procedures to allow participants to be identified for appropriate follow-up should, wherever possible, be included in the research proposal.

Beneficence

3.6.4 Researchers should demonstrate that:

(a) tissue to be used will be professionally removed;
(b) tissue will be appropriately and securely stored;
(c) data will be recorded, stored and released in ways that ensure confidentiality and privacy; and
(d) tissue will be managed and used in accountable ways.

Respect

3.6.5 Consent for the use of tissue in research should be sought from donors. Consent may be specific, extended or unspecified (see paragraphs 2.2.13–2.2.15).

3.6.6 Where it is proposed to use tissue samples which have been:[49]

(a) collected for, or held in storage following or in association with, clinical investigations;
(b) held in archives or banks; or
(c) removed in the course of a clinical procedure and not required for any clinical purpose, and the use of these samples may lead to harm, benefit or injustice to the donors, they should be informed of those possibilities and specific consent then sought for use of the samples.

3.6.7 An HREC may sometimes waive, with or without conditions, the need for consent when the requirements of paragraphs 2.2.21–2.2.23 are met.

49 Review of the *National Statement on Ethical Conduct in Research Involving Humans* – second consultation draft.

3.6.8 Human tissue samples that have been collected and stored with consent only for use in a specific research project should not be used for a different research project unless further consent for that project is given or an HREC has waived the need for further consent.

3.6.9 Where it is proposed to use tissue from a cadaver, whether removed at autopsy or not, it should first be ascertained whether the deceased person expressed any wish about the issue of his or her post-mortem tissue for research. If so, that wish should be respected. If no such wish is discovered, consent for the use of the tissue should be sought from the senior available next-of-kin.

3.6.10 At the time of seeking consent, it should be agreed with the next of kin how the tissue is to be disposed of when the research has been completed. Researchers should try to accommodate any reasonable wishes of the next of kin about the means of disposal.[50]

Chapter 3.7 Human stem cells

Introduction

Stem cells have the capacity to divide to generate 'progenitor' cells that retain the properties of the stem cell, or to produce 'daughters' that begin to differentiate into a more specialised cell type, or to produce one daughter cell of each type. Stem cells are thus central to normal human growth and development, and are also a potential source of new cells for the regeneration of diseased or damaged tissue. Stem cells are present at all stages of development, and in many (possibly most) tissues of the adult. At present, there are three recognised classes of stem cells: embryonic stem cells, embryonic germ cells, and somatic stem cells.

Legislation

The *Research Involving Human Embryos Act 2002* (the RIHE Act) and corresponding State and Territory legislation establishes a regulatory framework for the use of these excess assisted reproductive technology (ART) embryos. This legislation does not regulate research activity using stem cells or stem cell lines after they have been derived from an excess ART embryo. The RIHE Act refers to *Ethical guidelines on the use of assisted reproductive technology in clinical practice and research* (NHMRC 2004), known as the 'ART guidelines'. At paragraphs 17.10–17.18, these guidelines provide guidance for the design, ethical review and conduct of research involving excess ART embryos.

50 Review of the *National Statement on Ethical Conduct in Research Involving Humans* – second consultation draft.

Stem cell research

Stem cell research involves studies designed to improve biological knowledge of cellular disease processes, such as studies on the pluripotentiality of stem cells, and attempts to improve understanding of specific diseases or studies related to drug metabolism and therapeutics. Research also includes clinical trials and innovative therapy involving stem cells or their products. The following guidelines[51] relate to research using derived human stem cells or stem cell lines, whether embryonic stem cells or non-embryonic stem cells. For the purpose of these guidelines, these cells are regarded as human tissue, so that Chapter 3.6 *Human tissue samples*, also applies. Where research is proposed using stem cells derived from human umbilical cord or placental tissue, Chapter 4.1 *Women who are pregnant and the human fetus*, also applies. Where clinical research is proposed using stem cells, reference may be needed to the requirements of the Therapeutic Goods Administration (TGA) and the *Australian Code of Good Manufacturing Practice for Medicinal Products*.

Decisions about the design, review and conduct of human research must clearly reflect the values, principles and themes set out in Section 1 *Values and principles of ethical conduct* and Section 2 *Themes in research: risk and consent*. When these values, principles and themes are applied to research involving human stem cells, the following additional matters must be considered. Research to which this chapter applies must be reviewed and approved by a Human Research Ethics Committee (HREC) rather than by one of the other processes of ethical review described in paragraphs 5.1.7 and 5.1.8.

Research merit and integrity

3.7.1 To inform the ethical review of clinical research involving stem cells, whether embryonic or non-embryonic, researchers and HRECs should seek advice from the NHMRC's Gene and related Therapies Research Advisory Panel (GTRAP).

3.7.2 Research on human embryonic stem cell lines, embryonic germ cell lines or other cell lines of a pluripotent nature created in Australia should only be conducted where those cell lines were derived and made available for research in accordance with this Statement and relevant legislation.

3.7.3 Research is conducted on human embryonic stem cell lines, embryonic germ cell lines or other cell lines of a pluripotent nature, for example, those derived from fetal tissue. Where these cell lines were created in another country, research should only be conducted on them

51 The guidelines have been adapted from the Updated Guidelines for Human Pluripotent Stem Cell Research, June 7, 2005, Canadian Institutes of Health Research. Review of the *National Statement on Ethical Conduct in Research Involving Humans* – second consultation draft 47.

where there is reason to believe that the manner in which the stem cell lines were created and made available for research does not vary significantly from the requirements of Australian legislation, the ART guidelines and this Statement. There must be reason to believe that the stem cell lines were derived and made available for research under laws and policies of that country which require that:

(a) the human embryos from which cell lines were derived were created for reproductive purposes;
(b) embryo donors consented to the use of their embryos for stem cell research;[52]
(c) the human embryos from which the stem cell lines were derived were created by the fertilization of a genetically unaltered ovum by a genetically unaltered sperm;
(d) the pregnant woman from whom fetal tissue was obtained for deriving cell lines made the decision to donate that tissue in a manner similar to that required by Chapter 4.1 *Women who are pregnant and the human fetus*;
(e) the pregnant woman from whom fetal tissue was obtained consented to the use of that tissue for research in the manner similar to that required by Chapter 4.1 *Women who are pregnant and the human fetus*; and
(f) the embryos used to create stem cell lines were not obtained through commercial transactions.

3.7.4 Research involving the grafting of human stem cells or other human cells that are likely to be pluripotent into humans should only be conducted where:

(a) there is overwhelming evidence, from pre-clinical models, of safety and efficacy;
(b) the research is carried out in well-designed clinical trials; and
(c) consent by research participants meets the requirements of this Statement.

3.7.5 Research using human or non-human stem cells that are likely to be pluripotent is ethically unacceptable if those cells are:

(a) combined with a human embryo;
(b) grafted to a human fetus; or
(c) grafted to a non-human fetus.

Justice

3.7.6 Stem cell research should not involve the directed donation of stem cell lines or other human cells or cell lines of a pluripotent nature, to particular individuals, except for autologous donation.

52 Review of the *National Statement on Ethical Conduct in Research Involving Humans* – second consultation draft 48.

3.7.7 Human stem cell lines, other human cells or cell lines of a pluripotent nature from human embryos, fetuses or adults, should be anonymised for use in research, unless the research involves autologous donation.[53]

Beneficence

3.7.8 Health professionals with clinical care responsibilities for a woman whose consent is to be sought for involvement in research using embryonic stem cells to be derived from her embryo or fetus should not be members of the research team conducting that research (see paragraph 4.1.1 and the ART guidelines).

3.7.9 Human stem cells are human tissue and there should be no element of commerce involved in the transfer of human stem cells, except for the reimbursement of reasonable expenses.

Respect

3.7.10 Research to derive and study human stem cell lines, human embryonic germ cell lines or other cells of a pluripotent nature from the umbilical cord, placenta, human fetal tissue or amniotic fluid should be conducted only where the requirements of Chapter 4.1 *Women who are pregnant and the human fetus* are satisfied.

3.7.11 Research to derive and study human stem cell lines of a pluripotent nature from human somatic tissues should only be conducted where the requirements of Chapter 3.6 *Human tissue samples* are satisfied.

3.7.12 In addition to the information to be given under paragraph 2.2.3, researchers should give to those from whose tissue stem cells will be derived:

(a) an explanation of the research for which the stem cells are to be used, and, where extended consent is sought, sufficient information to meet the requirements of paragraphs 2.2.13 and 2.2.14;
(b) an explanation that the cell line(s) will be anonymised unless the research involves autologous donation;
(c) an assurance that research participants are free not to participate and have the right to withdraw at any time before an anonymised cell line is created;
(d) an explanation that the research could result in the production of a stem cell line that could be maintained for many years, distributed to other parts of the world, and used for various research purposes; and
(e) an explanation that the research participants will not benefit

53 Review of the *National Statement on Ethical Conduct in Research Involving Humans* – second consultation draft 49.

financially from any future commercialization of cell lines, and that there will not be any authority over any cell lines created unless the research involves autologous donation.[54]

Section 4 Ethical considerations specific to participants

Introduction

In addition to the ethical considerations pertaining to all research participants, specific issues arise in the design, conduct and review of research involving the categories of participants identified in this section. The Introduction to this Statement contains a definition of participants and notes that the impact of research on wider populations is an important ethical consideration in the design, review and conduct of human research. Human research may be conducted only with ethical approval. Section 5 describes the processes that institutions may use to provide that approval. Those processes include ethical review by Human Research Ethics Committees (HRECs) or other ethical review bodies, according to the risks of the research (see paragraphs 5.1.4, 5.1.7 and 5.1.8). Research involving more than low risk must be ethically reviewed and approved by an HREC (see paragraph 5.1.15). Research covered by Chapter 4.1 *Women who are pregnant and the human fetus,* 4.4 *People highly dependent on medical care,* 4.5 *People with a cognitive impairment, an intellectual disability, or a mental illness,* 4.6 *People who may be involved in illegal activities,* 4.7 *Aboriginal and Torres Strait Islander Peoples* and 4.8 *People in other countries* must also be ethically reviewed and approved by an HREC.[55]

Chapter 4.1 Women who are pregnant and the human fetus

Introduction

This chapter provides guidelines for the ethical conduct of research involving women who are pregnant, the human fetus ex utero, and human fetal tissue after the separation of the fetus from the woman. For the purpose of this chapter, the term *fetus* applies to the whole of the developing human being from implantation to delivery, and whether alive or dead at delivery. Australian legislation and the *Ethical guidelines on the use of assisted reproductive technology in clinical practice and research* govern research on embryos created using assisted reproductive technology that have been declared to be excess to the needs of those for whom they were created. For this reason the guidelines in this chapter do not apply to that research. *Fetal tissue* includes membranes, placenta,

54 Review of the *National Statement on Ethical Conduct in Research Involving Humans* – second consultation draft.

55 Review of the *National Statement on Ethical Conduct in Research Involving Humans* – second consultation draft.

umbilical cord, amniotic fluid and tissue that contains the genome of a fetus. Fetal tissue is regarded as part of the fetus prior to separation of the fetus from the woman. After separation, the following chapters of this Statement may also be relevant in designing and conducting research: Chapter 3.4 *Therapies and interventions, including clinical and non-clinical trials, and innovations;* Chapter 3.6 *Human tissue samples;* and Chapter 3.7 *Human stem cells.*

Decisions about the design, conduct and review of human research must clearly reflect the values and principles and themes set out in Section 1 *Values and principles of ethical conduct* and Section 2 *Themes in ethical review: risk and consent.* When these values, principles and themes are applied to research involving women who are pregnant and the human fetus, the following additional matters must be considered. Research to which this chapter applies must be reviewed and approved by a Human Research Ethics Committee (HREC) rather than by one of the other processes of ethical review described in paragraphs 5.1.7 and 5.1.8. Paragraphs 4.1.1–4.1.8 should be considered for all research involving women who are pregnant, the human fetus or human fetal tissue. Paragraphs 4.1.9–4.1.22 address additional issues specific to some of that research.[56]

Research merit and integrity

4.1.1 Research involving the human fetus ex utero or fetal tissue should be conducted by people with no involvement in the clinical care of the women from whom the fetus or fetal tissue was derived, and no financial or legal relationships with those who are so involved. Such research should be conducted in separate locations from those in which the clinical care of those women is provided.

4.1.2 Researchers should demonstrate that there are no suitable alternatives by which the aims of the research can be achieved.

4.1.3 There should be no commercial element in the transfer of human fetal tissue from the woman who originally gave the tissue except for the reimbursement of reasonable expenses.

Justice

4.1.4 Those who conscientiously object to being engaged in research projects involving fetuses or fetal tissue should not be obliged to participate in those projects, nor should they be put at a disadvantage because of their objection.

56 Review of the *National Statement on Ethical Conduct in Research Involving Humans* – second consultation draft 52.

Beneficence

4.1.5 Research involving the fetus or fetal tissue, however derived, should include arrangements for access to counselling and support for the woman who consents to the research.

Respect

4.1.6 The well-being and care of the woman who is pregnant and involved in research always takes precedence over research considerations or use of fetal tissue. Her consent should always be obtained for any research involving her fetus or fetal tissue. Where research involves a fetus ex utero or fetal tissue, the interests of others who have parental responsibilities may also be relevant, and seeking their consent may be necessary. Processes for seeking and obtaining consent should also take into account the guidelines in Chapter 2.2 *Consent*.

4.1.7 Proposals for research other than therapeutic innovative therapy should separate the process of providing information and obtaining consent for involvement in the research from clinical care. Information sheets for research projects should be completely separate from, and able to be understood independently of, written information about routine clinical care.[57]

Women who are pregnant

4.1.8 Research involving a woman who is pregnant may affect both the woman and the unborn child. The risks and benefits to each should be carefully considered in every case.

4.1.9 Research of therapeutic benefit to the woman may affect the fetus, and research of therapeutic benefit to the fetus does affect the woman. In both cases the research should:

(a) comply with the standards of disclosure and consent that apply to the woman as a participant; and
(b) involve a second process of disclosure and consent in relation to the effect of the research on the fetus in utero, including consideration of fetal stress, and on the child who may subsequently be born.

4.1.10 It may be ethical to conduct research on the fetus in utero if doing so is consistent with promoting the life and health of the fetus, for example, research aiming to provide the woman with information about the health of the fetus.

4.1.11 Research should be designed so as to minimise pain or distress for the fetus, and should include steps for monitoring for signs of

57 Review of the *National Statement on Ethical Conduct in Research Involving Humans* – second consultation draft.

fetal pain or distress and for suspending or ceasing the research if necessary.

4.1.12 The procedures involved in some innovative therapy including fetal surgery, transfusion of cells into the fetal vascular system, gene transfer, and fetal vaccination, should continue to be regarded as innovative treatment to which relevant paragraphs of Chapter 3.4 *Therapies and interventions, including clinical trials and non-clinical trials and innovations* apply.

4.1.13 It is ethically unacceptable to conduct non-therapeutic research that involves administering drugs or carrying out a procedure on the woman or her fetus with the intention of establishing the safety or efficacy of these for the fetus, whether in anticipation of an induced termination or otherwise.

4.1.14 A fetus or fetal tissue may become available for research as the result of induced termination. The process by which the woman is approached, informed about, and her consent sought for research on that fetus should be separate from the process by which she decides whether to terminate her pregnancy and should not begin until that decision has been made. Consenting to the research does not compromise the woman's freedom to change her decision to terminate her pregnancy.

4.1.15 Where it is contemplated that fetal tissues derived after induced termination are to be used for research, the research methods proposed, including the process of seeking the woman's consent for the research, should be designed and[58] conducted so as not to influence the woman's decision about when to terminate the pregnancy or the method of termination used.

4.1.16 Consideration of a woman's wishes and her physical, psychological and emotional welfare should inform a decision whether to approach her about proposed research involving her, her fetus or fetal tissue. If she is approached, those same considerations should be taken into account in the way information is provided about research on the fetus or fetal tissue, and in the process by which her consent is sought.

4.1.17 In addition to information required to be disclosed under paragraph 2.2.3 of this Statement, the woman should also be informed of:

(a) the need for consent from any other person to the proposed research (see paragraph 4.1.6);
(b) the feasibility of storing the fetus or fetal tissues before commencing research; and
(c) her freedom to withdraw her consent to the research at any time, whether before or after a termination.

58 Review of the *National Statement on Ethical Conduct in Research Involving Humans* – second consultation draft

Live fetus

4.1.18 A fetus delivered alive should, for all purposes including research, be treated as a child and receive the care that is due to a child, including life-sustaining treatment if the fetus is viable and the prospects for recovery warrant it.

Deceased fetus

4.1.19 Organs and tissues may be removed from a fetus delivered dead and used for research only if:

(a) consent has been given by the woman, and where relevant such others as described in 4.1.6, to the removal and the research;
(b) the fetus is available for research only as a result of separation by natural processes or by lawful means;
(c) death of the fetus has been determined by a registered medical practitioner who has no part in the research; and
(d) research procedures are performed in separate locations from those in which clinical procedures are carried out.[59]

Separated fetal tissue

4.1.20 Those conducting research involving the use of tissue from a fetus should have no part in the management of either the woman or her fetus, nor in deciding whether death of the fetus has occurred.

4.1.21 If, for research purposes, fetal cells are to be derived from the fetal tissue and stored or propagated in tissue culture, or tissues or cells are to be transplanted into a human recipient, consent of the woman, and where practicable such others as are described in paragraph 4.1.6, is required.

4.1.22 Women whose consent is being sought for involvement of their fetus or fetal tissue in research should be given the following information in addition to that required by paragraph 2.2.3:

(a) whether there is potential for commercial application of outcomes of the research, including the development of cell lines;
(b) that they will not be entitled to a share in the profits of any commercial applications; and
(c) whether fetal organs, tissues or stem cells lines developed from them will be exported.[60]

59 Review of the *National Statement on Ethical Conduct in Research Involving Humans* – second consultation draft.

60 Review of the *National Statement on Ethical Conduct in Research Involving Humans* – second consultation draft.

Chapter 4.2 Children and young people

Introduction

Research involving children is essential to advance knowledge about children's and young people's welfare. In such research, ethical considerations arise additional to those in research with only adult participants. These additional considerations include the capacity of a young person to give sufficiently informed consent, the possibility of coercion by parents, peers or researchers to participate in research, and conflicting values and interests of parents and children. These considerations apply to all research involving children and young people but assume special prominence in educational and health research. In the latter context there are particular tensions between not placing children at risk in studies of new interventions and the need for knowledge about how they are best used for children.

Decisions about the design, review and conduct of human research must clearly reflect the values, principles and themes set out in Section 1 *Values and principles of ethical conduct* and Section 2 *Themes in ethical review: risk and consent*. When these values, principles and themes are applied to research involving children and young people, the following additional matters must be considered.

Research merit and integrity

4.2.1 The research and its methods should be appropriate for children or young people.

Justice

4.2.2 Involving children and young people in research is justifiable when:

(a) it is likely to advance knowledge about the health or welfare of, or other matters relevant to, children and young people; or
(b) children's or young people's participation is indispensable to the conduct of the research.

Beneficence

4.2.3 The circumstances in which the research is conducted should provide for the physical, emotional and psychological safety of the child or young person.[61]

61 Review of the *National Statement on Ethical Conduct in Research Involving Humans* – second consultation draft.

Respect

4.2.4 Except in circumstances described in paragraphs 4.2.5–4.2.9, consent to a child's or young person's participation in research should be obtained from:

(a) the child or young person whenever he or she has the capacity to make this decision; and
(b) either:
  (i) one parent, except when, in the opinion of the Human Research Ethics Committee (HREC) or others reviewing research, the risks involved in a child's participation require the consent of both parents, or where applicable,
  (ii) the guardian or other primary care giver, or any organisation or person required by law.

4.2.5 An HREC may approve research to which only the child or young person consents when:

(a) the child or young person has the capacity to consent to participation in the specific project; and
(b) (i) the research involves no more than low risk, or
  (ii) the child or young person is estranged or separated from his or her parents or guardian, or
  (iii) it would be contrary to the best interest of the child or young person to seek consent from the parents.

4.2.6 In any of the circumstances in paragraph 4.2.5, researchers should specify how they will judge the capacity of the child to consent to participation in research, and should demonstrate that the requirements of this chapter will be satisfied.

4.2.7 The justification for a decision that a child or young person does not have the capacity to consent should always be explicitly stated, even if it is as obvious as the fact that the child is an infant.

4.2.8 Schools may arrange for standing parental consent to be given for a child's participation in research that is:

(a) for the benefit of children;
(b) not undertaken for profit;[62] and
(c) comprises no more than overt observation in school classrooms or anonymous or coded (potentially identifiable) questionnaires or surveys on subject matters not involving sensitive personal information or personal or family relationships. Parental consent for each specific project of this kind is not needed; notification to parents of each project is enough.

62 Review of the *National Statement on Ethical Conduct in Research Involving Humans* – second consultation draft.

4.2.9 A child or young person should not be included as a participant in research where there is reason to believe that such participation is contrary to that child's or young person's best interest.

4.2.10 A child or young person's refusal to participate in research should be respected, except:

(a) where there is standing parental consent for research, refusal to participate should be respected only if there is reason to believe participation in the research is contrary to the child's best interest; or
(b) where in the case of very young children, the child's refusal may be overridden by the parents' judgement as to what is in the child's best interest.[63]

Chapter 4.3 People in dependent or unequal relationships

Introduction

In some situations, pre-existing or continuing relationships between researchers and participants competent to make their own decisions may impair the voluntary character of consent. Those relationships typically involve unequal status, in which one party, almost always the researcher, has or had a position of influence or authority. Examples include relationships where the researcher and potential participants are, or have been:

(a) carers and persons with chronic conditions or disabilities, including long-term hospital patients or residents in nursing homes;
(b) health care professionals and their patients or clients;
(c) teachers and their students;
(d) prison authorities and prisoners;
(e) governmental authorities and refugees;
(f) employers or supervisors and their employees (including members of the police force and Defence forces);
(g) federal, State or local government service-providers and the communities to whom the service is provided.

Decisions about the design, review and conduct of human research must clearly reflect the values, principles and themes set out in Section 1 *Values and principles of ethical conduct* and Section 2 *Themes in ethical review: risk and consent*. When these values, principles and themes are applied to research involving people in dependent or unequal relationships, the following additional matters must be considered.

Research merit and integrity

4.3.1 The influence of dependent or unequal relationships on the consent process may lead to decisions or responses that participants would

63 Review of the *National Statement on Ethical Conduct in Research Involving Humans* – second consultation draft.

not otherwise have made. This does not necessarily invalidate the decision or response. However, it always constitutes a reason to pay particular attention to the process through which consent is negotiated.[64]

Justice

4.3.2 Where the research is designed to improve understanding of dependent or unequal relationships, research proposals involving people in such relationships as participants may be approved.

4.3.3 Where the dependence or unequal nature of the relationship is incidental to the purpose of the research, researchers should make a specific case for including people in dependent or unequal relationships as participants.

Beneficence

4.3.4 Participants in dependent relationships with researchers do not necessarily act under undue influence. However, any potentially detrimental effects of these relationships on research participants should be identified and minimised. Such effects might include the researcher engaging in punitive behaviour in the nonresearch relationship as a result of what has happened in the research, or participants feeling unable to withdraw consent for fear that doing so will lead to hostility or withdrawal of services.

4.3.5 A person declining to participate in, or deciding to withdraw from, research should not suffer any negative consequences, such as discrimination, reduction in the level of care, or any other disadvantage.

Respect

4.3.6 The design of research involving those in dependent relationships should not compromise respect for them.

4.3.7 Where the researcher is in a pre-existing or continuing relationship with potential participants, it may be appropriate for their consent to be sought by an independent person.

4.3.8 Researchers should take special care to maintain confidentiality of all information they receive, particularly in settings where privacy may be compromised, such as shared work places, rooms in hospitals or nursing homes.[65]

64 Review of the *National Statement on Ethical Conduct in Research Involving Humans* – second consultation draft 60.

65 Review of the *National Statement on Ethical Conduct in Research Involving Humans* – second consultation draft 61.

Chapter 4.4 People highly dependent on medical care

Introduction

Medical care increasingly offers interventions or treatment for people at times of serious risk to their lives. These risks may be temporary or permanent. People can become highly dependent on those interventions and treatments and are often incapable of comprehending or communicating about their situation. At the same time, research on the use of those interventions and treatments is necessary to assess and improve their efficacy. The purpose of this chapter is to describe conditions under which researchers may seek to proceed where participants' dependence on medical care impedes their capacity to give consent. A process is described, under the heading *Respect*, through which a Human Research Ethics Committee (HREC) may authorise participation before consent is possible. Each of the following types of research raises significant ethical concerns:

(a) emergency care research;
(b) intensive care research;
(c) neonatal intensive care research;
(d) terminal care research; and
(e) research involving unconscious people.

Decisions about the design, review and conduct of human research must clearly reflect the values, principles and themes set out in Section 1 *Values and principles of ethical conduct* and Section 2 *Themes in ethical review: risk and consent*. When these values, principles and themes are applied to research involving people highly dependent on medical care, the following additional matters must be considered. Research to which this chapter applies must be reviewed and approved by a Human Research Ethics Committee (HREC) rather than by one of the other processes of ethical review described in paragraphs 5.1.7 and 5.1.8.

Research merit and integrity

4.4.1 Research on the use and efficacy of medical interventions to address, arrest, alleviate or overcome severe threats to the life of humans may be approved where:[66]

(a) it is likely that the research will lead to improvement of those interventions; and
(b) either:
    (i) in the particular case, the overall level of risk of the participant's present condition combined with the risk of the proposed intervention is justified by the potential benefits of the intervention to this participant, or

66 Review of the *National Statement on Ethical Conduct in Research Involving Humans* – second consultation draft.

(ii) where participants have capacity to consent, that overall level of risk is acceptable to participants and is justified by the potential benefits of the research.

Justice

4.4.2 People highly dependent on medical care may be exposed to severe threats to their lives, so that recruiting them into research might seem unfair. However, those people are entitled to participate in research; and when the conditions of paragraph 4.4.1 are met, and their participation is indispensable to the conduct of the research, their involvement is not unfair.

Beneficence

4.4.3 The distinguishing features of *neonatal intensive care research* are the small size and unique developmental vulnerability of the participants and the potential for very long-range impact on their growth, development and health. In neonatal intensive care research, risks and potential benefits should be assessed with particular care by individuals or groups with relevant expertise.

4.4.4 The distinguishing features of *terminal care research* are the short remaining life expectancy of participants and their potential vulnerability to unrealistic expectations of benefits. Terminal care research should be designed so that:

(a) the benefits of research to individual participants or groups of participants, or to others in the same circumstances, justify any discomfort or inconvenience to the participants;
(b) the prospect of benefit from research participation is not exaggerated;
(c) the needs and wishes of participants to spend time as they choose, particularly with family members, are respected; and
(d) the entitlement of those receiving palliative care to participate is recognised.[67]

Respect

4.4.5 People involved in research to which this chapter applies may have impaired capacity for verbal or written communication. Provision should be made for them to receive information and to express their wishes in other ways.

4.4.6 In *emergency care research*, recruitment into a project usually has to be achieved rapidly, when participants and their families are likely to

67 Review of the *National Statement on Ethical Conduct in Research Involving Humans* – second consultation draft.

be vulnerable. It may not be possible to obtain consent for recruitment from the participants without so delaying the initiation of treatment that there is risk of reducing potential benefits.

4.4.7 In *intensive care research*, communicating with participants receiving ventilatory assistance is difficult and heavy sedation may impair their cognition. Whenever possible, consent to intensive care research, based on adequate information, should be sought from or on behalf of potential participants before admission to that level of treatment.

4.4.8 In *research involving unconscious people*, the participants, because of their incapacity for cognition and communication, cannot be informed about the research and their wishes cannot be determined. Those who are unconscious should be included only in minimally invasive research or in research designed both to be therapeutic for them and to improve the method of treatment for the condition from which they suffer.

Process to be followed

4.4.9 Consent should be sought from people highly dependent on medical care wherever they are capable of giving consent and it is practicable to approach them.

4.4.10 Wherever it is not practicable to approach a person highly dependent on medical care, or the person is not capable of making such a decision, consent should be sought from the participant's guardian, or organisation or person authorised by law, before inclusion in the research. Such consent needs to be based upon receipt of all the information set out in paragraph 2.2.3.

4.4.11 When consent is to be given, either by the participant or another on his or her behalf, steps should be taken to minimise the likelihood that:

(a) stress or emotional factors impair the understanding of the research or the decision to participate; and
(b) the dependency of participants and their relatives on the medical personnel providing treatment compromises the freedom of a decision to participate.[68]

4.4.12 Where the researcher is also the treating health professional, it may be appropriate for an independent person to obtain consent to participation from potential participants or from others on their behalf.

4.4.13 When neither the participant nor another on his or her behalf can consider the proposal and give consent, an HREC may approve a research project without prior consent provided that:

68 Review of the *National Statement on Ethical Conduct in Research Involving Humans* – second consultation draft.

(a) the research is valid;
(b) there is a reasonable belief that were the participant or the participant's representative to be informed of the proposal, he or she would be willing to consent;
(c) the research is so designed that the risks of harm to individuals, families or groups linked to the participant, or to their financial or social interests, are minimised;
(d) the project is not of a controversial nature and does not involve significant moral or cultural sensitivities in the community; and, where the research is interventional, also provided that:
(e) the research supports a reasonable possibility of benefit over standard care;
(f) inclusion in the research project is not contrary to the interests of the participant and does not impose an unfair burden of participation on him or her;
(g) the overall level of risk of the participant's present condition combined with the risk of the proposed intervention is justified by the potential benefits of the intervention to this participant.

4.4.14 As soon as reasonably possible, the participant and/or the participant's relatives and authorised representative should be informed of the participant's inclusion in the research and of the option to withdraw from the research without any reduction in quality of care.[69]

Chapter 4.5 People with a cognitive impairment, an intellectual disability, or a mental illness

Introduction

While the three kinds of condition discussed in this chapter are different, the participation in research of people with any of these conditions raises similar ethical issues. People with a cognitive impairment, intellectual disability or mental illness are entitled to participate in research. While research involving these people need not be limited to their particular impairment or illness, their distinctive vulnerability as research participants should be taken into account. The capacity of a person with any of these conditions to consent to research, and the ability to participate in it, can vary because of factors such as the person's medication or treatment, or discomfort or distress, and the complexity of the research project. In addition, while intellectual disability is usually permanent, cognitive impairment and mental illness are often temporary or episodic. This is a further cause of variability in the capacity to consent and to participate in research. Even when capable of giving consent and participating, people with these conditions may be more-than-usually vulnerable to various forms of discomfort and stress.

69 Review of the *National Statement on Ethical Conduct in Research Involving Humans* – second consultation draft 65.

Decisions about the design, review and conduct of human research must clearly reflect the values, principles and themes set out in Section 1 *Values and principles of ethical conduct* and Section 2 *Themes in ethical review: risk and consent*. When these values, principles and themes are applied to research involving people with a cognitive impairment, an intellectual disability or a mental illness, the following additional matters must be considered. Research to which this chapter applies must be reviewed and approved by a Human Research Ethics Committee (HREC) rather than by one of the other processes of ethical review described in paragraphs 5.1.7 and 5.1.8.

Research merit and integrity

4.5.1 The research design should take into account factors that may affect the capacity to consent to the research and the ability to participate in it. These factors may be permanent or variable.

4.5.2 Special care should be taken to determine whether participants' cognitive impairment, intellectual disability or mental illness makes them more susceptible than other participants to various forms of discomfort or distress. If so,[70] ways of trying to minimise the effects of this susceptibility should be described in the research proposal.

Justice

4.5.3 People with a cognitive impairment, intellectual disability or mental illness are entitled to participate in research. However, because of their distinctive vulnerability, it should be clearly established that involving people with these conditions in research is justifiable because either:

(a) it is likely to significantly advance knowledge about the health or welfare of, or other matters relevant to, people with these conditions; or
(b) the participation of people with these conditions is indispensable to the conduct of the research.

Beneficence

4.5.4 Because of the distinctive vulnerability of participants with a cognitive impairment, intellectual disability or mental illness, special care should be taken to ensure that the risks and any burden involved in the proposed research are justified by the potential benefits of the research.

4.5.5 A person with a cognitive impairment, intellectual disability or mental illness should not be included as a participant in research where there is reason to believe that such participation is contrary to that person's best interest.

70 Review of the *National Statement on Ethical Conduct in Research Involving Humans* – second consultation draft 66.

Respect

4.5.6 Consent to participation in research by a person with a cognitive impairment, intellectual disability or mental illness should be sought from either:

(a) the person with the impairment, disability or illness if he or she has the capacity to consent and, where the impairment, disability or illness is temporary or episodic, at a time when the condition does not prevent the person from giving or refusing consent; or

(b) where at the time consent is initially sought the person lacks the capacity to consent, the person's guardian, or any organisation or person required by law.

4.5.7 The process of seeking consent from a person with a cognitive impairment, intellectual disability or mental illness should include discussion of any possibility that the person's capacity to consent or to participate in the research may vary or be lost altogether.[71] The participant's wishes about what should happen in that circumstance should be followed.

4.5.8 Where consent has been given under paragraph 4.5.6(b) a researcher should, as far as possible, still explain his or her presence to the participant and explain what participation in the research involves. If at any time the participant recovers the capacity to give or withdraw consent, the researcher should offer him or her the opportunity to decide whether to remain in the research under the terms of paragraph 4.5.7, or to withdraw from the research.

4.5.9 Researchers should inform HRECs how they propose to determine the capacity of a person with a cognitive impairment, intellectual disability or mental illness to consent to the research. This information should include how the decision about the person's capacity will be made, who will make it, the criteria that will be used in making it, and the process for reviewing during the research the participant's capacity to consent and to participate in the research.

4.5.10 Refusal or reluctance to participate in a research project by a person with a cognitive impairment, intellectual disability or mental illness should be respected.[72]

Chapter 4.6 People who may be involved in illegal activities

Introduction

In the conduct of human research, researchers may inadvertently learn of activity that may be illegal, whether of participants in the research or

71 Review of the *National Statement on Ethical Conduct in Research Involving Humans* – second consultation draft.

72 Review of the *National Statement on Ethical Conduct in Research Involving Humans* – second consultation draft.

others. Research may also involve gathering information from participants recruited because they are or have been involved in illegal activity, or may aim to discover and expose illegal activity by identifiable individuals. The mere collection of some information may subject a researcher to a statutory obligation to disclose some or all of it while the nature of other information collected may attract legal orders that compel disclosure. This chapter does not contain information or guidance about legal obligations of researchers arising from their conduct of such research. Further, it is not the role of a Human Research Ethics Committee (HREC) or others conducting ethical review to provide legal advice on the existence or performance of any of those obligations.

Decisions about the design, review and conduct of human research must clearly reflect the values, principles and themes set out in Section 1 *Values and principles of ethical conduct* and Section 2 *Themes in research: risk and consent*. When these values, principles and themes are applied to research involving illegal activities, the following additional matters must be considered. Research to which this chapter applies must be reviewed and approved by a Human Research Ethics Committee (HREC) rather than by one of the other processes of ethical review described in paragraphs 5.1.7 and 5.1.8.

Research merit and integrity

4.6.1 It should be clearly established that the risks to participants of research that may involve discovery of illegal activity by them are justified by the benefits of the research. This is especially the case in research which aims to discover and expose illegal activity by identifiable people.

4.6.2 The possibility that research designed to expose unlawful conduct may have an adverse impact on those whose conduct is exposed is not a reason for regarding the research as ethically unacceptable.

Justice

4.6.3 Where research may foreseeably discover information about illegal activity by participants or others, researchers and institutions may become subject to orders[73] to disclose that information to courts or to law enforcement authorities. Institutions should develop policies to inform their and researchers' responses to such orders. Those policies should have regard to values and principles set out in this Statement and to scholarly values of academic freedom and inquiry.

Beneficence

4.6.4 In research that may reveal illegal activity, including research designed to do so, consideration should be given to whether the risks to

73 Review of the *National Statement on Ethical Conduct in Research Involving Humans* – second consultation draft.

those whose illegal activity may be revealed can and should be minimised by using pseudonyms, or removing links between names and data.

Respect

4.6.5 Where researchers in research that may reveal illegal activity by participants have contact with those participants in other professional roles, they should ensure that participants understand when a contact or intervention is part of research and when it is not. Researchers who have contact in other roles should ensure that contact in a research role will not compromise contact in those other roles.

4.6.6 Even when research is not intended to reveal illegal activity by participants or others, it nevertheless may foreseeably do so. In such cases researchers should, in addition to the information required by paragraph 2.2.3, provide participants with as clear an explanation as possible of:

(a) the likelihood of such revelation and of any obligation of disclosure they may incur from the revelation; and
(b) the extent to which the researcher will maintain confidentiality of information about illegal activity by participants or others, and the response the researcher will make to a legally enforceable order to disclose such information.

4.6.7 Where research is not intended to reveal illegal activity by participants or others but may foreseeably do so, researchers should take particular care that decisions to participate by those who have been or may be subject to criminal justice processes are voluntary.[74]

Chapter 4.7 Aboriginal and Torres Strait Islander Peoples

Introduction

Research with Aboriginal and Torres Strait Islander Peoples spans many research methodologies and disciplines. It is recognised that the extent to which Aboriginal and Torres Strait Islander individuals, communities or groups are integrated as key players in the research process, varies greatly. Research proposals involving a number of Aboriginal and Torres Strait Islander Peoples as research participants should address appropriate methodological, ethical and cultural issues. Depending on the field and complexity of the research proposal there might be numerous ways that these issues are addressed. A fundamental tenet of research with Aboriginal and Torres Islander Peoples is the development of ethical relationships that respect and value cultural diversity. Health researchers intending to involve Aboriginal and Torres Strait Islander

74 Review of the *National Statement on Ethical Conduct in Research Involving Humans* – second consultation draft.

individuals, communities or groups in proposed research must consult the NHMRC *Values and Ethics: Guidelines for Ethical Conduct in Aboriginal and Torres Strait Islander Health Research* (2003) (*Values and Ethics*) for guidance on ways to develop and adapt their research methods. Human Research Ethics Committees (HRECs) are also required to apply the *Values and Ethics* guidelines as the basis for ethically assessing proposals for health research involving Aboriginal and Torres Strait Islander participation. In applying Section 1 of this Statement, researchers from other disciplines may also find the *Values and Ethics* guidelines informative. The ethical principles outlined in the *Values and Ethics* guidelines are based on six core values identified as being important to Aboriginal and Torres Strait Islander Peoples and described as:

Spirit and integrity[75]

This is an overarching value that binds all others into a coherent whole. It has two components. The first is about the continuity between past, current and future generations. The second is about behaviour which maintains the coherence of Aboriginal and Torres Strait Islander values and cultures. Any behaviour that diminishes any of the following other values could not be described as having integrity.

Reciprocity[76]

A mutual obligation exists among members of Aboriginal and Torres Strait Islander families and communities to achieve an equitable distribution of resources, responsibility and capacity and to achieve cohesion and survival of the social order. This mutual obligation extends to the land, animals and other natural elements and features. In contemporary settings the value of reciprocity continues in various forms, and may vary between locations. Examples include the redistribution of income, benefits from the air, land and sea, and the sharing of other resources such as housing.

Respect[77]

Respect for human dignity and worth, as a characteristic of relationships between people, and in the way individuals behave, is fundamental to a functioning and moral society. Within Aboriginal and Torres Strait

75 NHMRC (2003) *Values and Ethics: Guidelines for Ethical Conduct in Aboriginal and Torres Strait Islander Health Research*, Commonwealth of Australia, Canberra, p. 19. Review of the *National Statement on Ethical Conduct in Research Involving Humans* – second consultation draft.

76 *Ibid* p. 10.

77 *Ibid* p. 11.

Islander cultures respect is reinforced by and in turn strengthens dignity. A respectful relationship induces trust and co-operation. Strong culture is a personal and collective framework built on respect and trust that promotes dignity and recognition.

Equality[78]

One of the values expressed by Aboriginal and Torres Strait Islander Peoples and cultures is the equal value of people. One of the ways this is reflected is a commitment to distributive fairness and justice. Equality affirms Aboriginal and Torres Strait Islander Peoples' right to be different.

Survival and protection[79]

Aboriginal and Torres Strait Islander Peoples continue to act to protect their cultures and identity from erosion by colonisation and marginalisation. A particular feature of Aboriginal and Torres Strait Islander cultures and these efforts has been the importance of a collective identity. This collective bond reflects and draws strength from the values-base of Aboriginal and Torres Strait Islander Peoples and cultures.

Responsibility[80]

Central to Aboriginal and Torres Strait Islander societies and cultures is the recognition of core responsibilities. These responsibilities include those to country, kinship bonds, caring for others and the maintenance of harmony and balance within and between the physical and spiritual realms. A key responsibility within this framework is to do no harm, including avoiding impacting adversely on others' abilities to comply with their responsibilities. As well, one person's responsibilities may be shared with others so that they will also be held accountable. The message for researchers is that there is a great diversity across the many Aboriginal and Torres Strait Islander cultures and societies. Each community has the right to express how these common values and their own unique values should be addressed in research.

Decisions about the design, review and conduct of human research must clearly reflect the values, principles and themes set out in Chapter 1 *Values and principles of ethical conduct* and Chapter 2 *Themes of ethical review: risk and consent*. When these values, principles and themes are applied to research involving Aboriginal and Torres Strait Islander Peoples, the following additional matters must be considered. Research to which this chapter applies must be reviewed and approved by a Human Research Ethics

78 *Ibid* p. 14.
79 *Ibid* p. 18.
80 *Ibid* p. 16.

Committee (HREC) advised by people who have knowledge of research with Aboriginal and Torres Strait Islander peoples and who are familiar with the culture and practices of the Aboriginal and Torres Strait Islander people with whom participation in the research will be discussed.

Research merit and integrity

4.7.1 The research methodology should provide for mechanisms for such matters as ongoing feedback, agreement about final reporting, appropriate recruitment techniques, and appropriate informed consent processes.

4.7.2 The methodology should be sensitive to the social and cultural protocols and there should be evidence of support for the research project from appropriate Aboriginal and Torres Strait Islander communities or groups involved.

4.7.3 The methodology should respect and acknowledge the cultural distinctiveness of any Aboriginal and Torres Strait Islander community or group involved.

Justice

4.7.4 The research processes should provide opportunities to develop trust and a sense of equal research partnerships.

4.7.5 The research team should recognise any potential consequences from proposed research outcomes and, if negative, provide processes to monitor and take appropriate action to ameliorate any negative impact.[81]

Beneficence

4.7.6 The realisable benefits from the research processes, outcomes and outputs should be reasonably equally proportioned among the research stakeholders.

4.7.7 The described benefits from research should have been discussed with and agreed to by the Aboriginal or Torres Strait Islander research stakeholders.

4.7.8 The benefits should include the enhancement or establishment of capacities, opportunities or outcomes that advance the interests of Aboriginal and Torres Strait Islander Peoples.

Respect

4.7.9 The research proposal should demonstrate evidence of respectful engagement with Aboriginal and Torres Strait Islander Peoples.

81 Review of the *National Statement on Ethical Conduct in Research Involving Humans* – second consultation draft.

4.7.10 The research processes should foster respectful, ethical research relationships that affirm the right of people to have different values, norms and aspirations.

4.7.11 The research methodology should value and create opportunities for Aboriginal and Torres Strait Islander Peoples to provide advice on processes and interpretation of the research data, drawing on their knowledge and wisdom.[82]

Chapter 4.8 People in other countries

Introduction

When a researcher from an Australian institution proposes to conduct research in another country, additional ethical considerations may arise. In some situations, regard for the beliefs, customs and cultural heritage of participants will require recognition of values other than those of this Statement. Sometimes these values will be in tension with one or more of the ethical values of this Statement. Sometimes the legal, regulatory or ethical review processes of another country may also demand conduct that is in tension with the ethical values of this Statement. Institutions, Human Research Ethics Committees (HRECs) and researchers may also need to consider whether proposed research that, on its own, may meet relevant ethical standards ought nonetheless be considered against a global background.

Decisions about the design, review and conduct of human research must clearly reflect the values, principles and themes set out in Section 1 *Values and principles of ethical conduct* and Section 2 *Themes of ethical review: risk and consent*. When these values, principles and themes are applied to research involving participants in other countries, the following additional matters must be considered. Research to which this chapter applies must be reviewed and approved by a Human Research Ethics Committee (HREC) rather than by one of the other processes of ethical review described in paragraphs 5.1.7 and 5.1.8.

Research merit and integrity

4.8.1 Researchers should inform HRECs whether there are ethics approval processes in the overseas country in which they intend to do research, and if so, whether they are mandatory or voluntary in relation to the proposed research, how they function, on what values and principles they rely, and whether they require reporting of the Australian HREC's approval.

4.8.2 While local cultural values should always be acknowledged in the design and conduct of the research, it should also be clearly established

82 Review of the *National Statement on Ethical Conduct in Research Involving Humans* – second consultation draft.

that such acknowledgement will result in participants being accorded no less respect and protection than this Statement requires.

4.8.3 Where there are no ethics approval processes in the overseas country, this Statement then provides the only applicable process for ethical approval. In this case, the HREC should take account of the available resources and means to conduct the research and avoid imposing unrealistic requirements, providing always that research participants are accorded no less respect and protection than this Statement requires.[83]

4.8.4 Some funding or national requirements will mean that researchers and HRECs have to conform to the ethics guidelines of local institutions or to recognised international guidelines or instruments. Research conducted under those guidelines or instruments should be approved only if participants will be accorded no less respect and protection than this Statement requires.

4.8.5 Researchers should have enough experience or access to expertise to enable them to engage with participants in ways that accord them due respect and protection.

4.8.6 When research is to be conducted overseas by a researcher who is subject to academic supervision, researchers should inform an HREC of how that supervision is to be effected so that due respect and protection will be accorded to participants.

4.8.7 When co-researchers are to be recruited in an overseas country, researchers should inform an HREC of how the capacity and expertise to conduct that part of the research assigned to the co-researchers will be established.

Justice

4.8.8 When it is proposed to conduct research in another country, the balance between burdens and benefits of the research, for the participants and in some instances the broader community, should be fair and the research should be neither opportunistic nor exploitative.

4.8.9 The assessment of the fairness of the research should take into account the opinions and expectations of participants and their communities about the effect of any limits of resources on the way the research will be conducted, on the participants' post-research welfare and on the implementation of the results of the research.

4.8.10 Proposed research that on its own may meet ethical standards might, even so, perpetuate injustice, discrimination or economic or social disadvantage. Where there is good reason for believing that a particular research project will have this effect, it should not be approved.

83 Review of the *National Statement on Ethical Conduct in Research Involving Humans* – second consultation draft.

4.8.11 Institutions share with researchers a responsibility for finding out whether what they are planning to do in another country is lawful in that country.[84]

Beneficence

4.8.12 Researchers need to inform HRECs about situations in which participants will be in dependent relationships with researchers, whether through previous or proposed arrangements.

4.8.13 Researchers need to know enough about the communities, and how to engage with them, to be able to assess the burdens and benefits of their research to the communities. Political and social factors that may jeopardise the safety of participants need to be taken into account. Researchers should inform HRECs about these likely burdens and benefits.

4.8.14 Whenever possible, research participants should have a local, readily accessible contact point independent of the researcher for responses, questions or complaints about the research.

4.8.15 In proposing mechanisms for monitoring research, researchers should take account of local circumstances.

4.8.16 Conducting research in other countries can expose researchers to risks of harm. Institutions and researchers should try to identify and evaluate any such risks, and also make provision for dealing with them, for instance by establishing local academic or institutional affiliations.

Respect

4.8.17 The value of respect requires having due regard for the beliefs, customs and cultural heritage of participants in other countries.

4.8.18 Local beliefs and practices regarding recruitment, consent, and remuneration to participants or contributions to communities for participating in research should be taken into account in the ethical review process. It should be clearly established that arrangements about these matters do not compromise the freedom of the participants' choice to participate.

4.8.19 Social or educational factors in the other country that may compromise the freedom or capacity of participants to choose whether to participate should be taken into account in the review process.

4.8.20 It should be clearly established that the processes to be followed in recruiting participants and through which they choose whether to be

84 Review of the *National Statement on Ethical Conduct in Research Involving Humans* – second consultation draft.

involved are respectful of their different cultural context and likely to lead to participation that is freely chosen and adequately informed.[85]

Section 5 Processes of research governance and ethical review

Human research encompasses a wide range of activities with an equally wide range of risks and potential benefits. In some research the apparent risk is negligible, such as research using publicly available material or epidemiological studies using only previously collected non-identifiable data. In other research the risk is widely recognised as high, such as physiological studies involving strenuous exercise activities or studies of treatments for life threatening conditions.

The Statement allows for a range of processes of ethical review of research, reflecting the difference in degree of risk involved in different kinds of research. This Section sets out this range of processes, and among them describes the operations of Human Research Ethics Committees in some detail. Equally important, but described in less detail because more fully set out in the *Australian code for the responsible conduct of research*, are the processes of research governance which must be in place if the ethical review of research is to be undertaken well.[86]

Chapter 5.1 Institutional responsibilities

Research governance

5.1.1 Institutions have responsibilities to ensure that human research that they conduct or for which they are responsible is designed and conducted in accordance with the *Australian code for the responsible conduct of research* and is reviewed and monitored in accordance with this Statement.

5.1.2 Towards meeting these responsibilities, institutions should formulate and implement policies and procedures for:

(a) establishing that human research meets relevant scholarly or scientific standard;
(b) establishing that those conducting human research are:
    (i) adequately experienced and qualified, or supervised,
    (ii) informed of the need to assess risks to their own safety, and
    (iii) free to withdraw from research on conscientious grounds;
(c) ethical review of research (Chapters 5.1, 5.2, 5.3);
(d) managing conflicts of interest (Chapter 5.4);
(e) monitoring research (Chapter 5.5);

85 Review of the *National Statement on Ethical Conduct in Research Involving Humans* – second consultation draft.

86 Review of the *National Statement on Ethical Conduct in Research Involving Humans* – second consultation draft.

(f) handling complaints (Chapter 5.6); and
(g) ensuring accountability (Chapter 5.7).

Processes for ethical review

5.1.3 Institutions must establish and implement processes of ethical review appropriate for the types of human research they conduct and in accordance with this Statement.

5.1.4 Where different processes of ethical review are to be used for different kinds of human research, those processes should be established according to the principle that the level of review of research is proportional to any risks of the kind of research.

5.1.5 Institutions must develop and publish the criteria by which the risks of research are identified and the different processes for peer and ethical review established.[87] Research that, according to such criteria, involves more than low risk must be reviewed by a Human Research Ethics Committee (HREC).

5.1.6 Institutions should regularly assess all their ethical review processes to ensure that those processes continue to enable the institution to meet its responsibilities under this Statement.

Research involving no more than low risk

5.1.7 Institutions may establish processes for review of research involving no more than low risk to participants in ways that meet institutional responsibilities described in this section. These processes must:

(a) have due regard to Section 1, and to Sections 3 and 4 which relate to different kinds of research and different categories of research participants;
(b) involve peer review;
(c) adequately address the research methodology and the relevant expertise of researcher or supervisor;
(d) allow for interdisciplinary or multi-disciplinary research and make provision for the different scholarly standards of different disciplines;
(e) consider whether the research provides sufficient protection of participants; and
(f) ensure that scholarly standards are not confused with ethical considerations arising from this Statement or other sources (see Introduction, *Ethical conduct and review of human research*).

5.1.8 The processes referred to in paragraph 5.1.7 may include, but need not be limited to:

87 Review of the *National Statement on Ethical Conduct in Research Involving Humans* – second consultation draft.

(a) review or assessment at the departmental level by the head of department;
(b) review or assessment by a departmental committee of peers (with or without external or independent members);
(c) delegated review with reporting to an HREC; or
(d) ethical review by a subcommittee of an HREC.[88]

Research that can be exempted from review

5.1.9 Research in which the only involvement of subjects is in any of the following categories may be exempted by institutions from ethical review because it involves such low levels of risk:

(a) the collection or study of existing data, documents or records, that are all publicly available;
(b) the use of existing collections of data or records that contain only nonidentifiable data about human beings;
(c) the observation of public behaviour that involves no interaction with those observed, provided the information obtained is recorded in such a manner that those observed cannot be identified in any way; or
(d) research making use of standard educational practices and conducted in established educational settings, provided there is no interaction with those participating in these activities other than giving and receiving test materials. Institutions must recognise that in allowing exempt research they are thereby determining that the research meets the requirements of this Statement and is ethically acceptable. If they are not prepared to recognise this, they must subject the research to ethical review.

Continuing oversight of review procedures

5.1.10 Where human research is ethically reviewed and approved by a process other than HREC review, institutions must ensure, as an element of good research governance, that adequate records of the decisions made using any such processes are maintained.

5.1.11 Whatever review processes are established for different kinds of human research, institutions have a responsibility to remain alert to ethical issues in any area of human research which may warrant referral to a different level of review, including referral from exemption to low level review.

5.1.12 The ethical values and principles in this Statement should be the basis on which institutions establish review processes, allocate kinds of research to them and review those allocations.

88 Review of the *National Statement on Ethical Conduct in Research Involving Humans* – second consultation draft.

5.1.13 Institutions must monitor the processes of ethical review of research involving low risk to ensure that they continue to provide sufficient protection for participants.[89]

5.1.14 Institutions must regularly review, and where found necessary revise, the criteria for allocation of kinds of research to the various processes of review. Where possible the review of the criteria should be informed by the documented experience of research participants or by involving participants or the wider community in this review.

Research involving more than low risk

5.1.15 Institutions that conduct human research involving more than low risk have a responsibility to arrange for the review and approval of such research by an HREC constituted and functioning in accordance with this Statement or to establish such an HREC to review and approve that research.

5.1.16 Institutions that establish HRECs have a responsibility to ensure that those HRECs are established and continue to operate in conformity with this Statement.

5.1.17 Institutions which, either individually or jointly, establish HRECs should adequately resource and maintain them. Resourcing should be sufficient to make it possible for HRECs to satisfy the requirements for good ethical review, and for communicating well with researchers, that are set out in this Section.

5.1.18 An institution, when establishing an HREC, should set out its terms of reference including:

(a) the scope of its responsibilities for ethical review;
(b) its relationship to other processes of research review;
(c) its relationship to non-affiliated researchers and external organisations;
(d) its institutional accountability;
(e) its mechanisms of reporting; and
(f) remuneration, if any, for members.

5.1.19 Where an institution has established an HREC, the institution should see that mechanisms have been put in place to ensure that:

(a) members have relevant experience and/or expertise;
(b) members undertake appropriate induction, including mentoring by a current HREC member, and ongoing training;[90]

89 Review of the *National Statement on Ethical Conduct in Research Involving Humans* – second consultation draft.

90 Where the context is the establishment and maintenance of an HREC, 'institutions' also includes any body or agency that establishes an HREC but does not conduct human research (see Preamble footnote 1). Review of the *National Statement on Ethical Conduct in Research Involving Humans* – second consultation draft.

(c) review of research proposals is thorough;
(d) processes and procedures of review are expeditious;
(e) decisions are transparent and consistent and promptly communicated;
(f) actual and potential conflicts of interest that may affect research are identified and managed;
(g) membership of HRECs is promulgated within institutions who submit research for review and is made public in annual reports or by other routine processes;
(h) good communication between the institution(s), the HREC and researchers is promoted;
(i) the workload of the HREC does not compromise the quality and timeliness of ethical review; and
(j) the institution can be assured that the HREC is operating in conformity with this Statement.

5.1.20 An institution is legally responsible for HREC decisions and approvals in relation to research and should indemnify its HREC members.

Composition of HRECs

5.1.21 The minimum membership of an HREC is eight members. As far as possible there should be equal numbers of men and women on the committee, and at least one third of the members should be from outside the institution for which the HREC is reviewing research. This minimum membership is:

(a) a chairperson;
(b) at least two members who are lay people, one man and one woman, who have no affiliation with the institution and are not currently involved in medical, scientific or legal work;
(c) at least one member with knowledge of, and current experience in, the professional care, counselling or treatment of people, for example, a nurse, or a social worker;
(d) at least one member who performs a pastoral care role in a community, for example, a minister of religion or an Aboriginal elder;
(e) at least one member who is a lawyer, but not a lawyer engaged to advise the institution;[91] and
(f) at least two members with current research experience relevant to research proposals to be considered at the meetings they attend. These two members may be selected, according to need, from a pool of further members. No member may be appointed in more than one of the foregoing categories, but in each category alternating members may be appointed.

91 Review of the *National Statement on Ethical Conduct in Research Involving Humans* – second consultation draft.

5.1.22 The institution should ensure that the membership of the HREC includes a member or members with experience in the application of this Statement.

5.1.23 The institution should establish procedures to ensure that the HREC has access to the expertise necessary to enable it to address the ethical considerations arising from the categories of research it is likely to consider. This may necessitate going outside the HREC membership.

Appointment of members of HRECs

5.1.24 The chair should be a person with suitable experience, whose other responsibilities will not impair the HREC's capacity to carry out its obligations under this Statement.

5.1.25 Members should be appointed to an HREC using open and transparent processes. Institutions should consider reviewing appointments to the HREC at least every three years.

5.1.26 Members are to be appointed as individuals for their knowledge, qualities and experience and not as representatives of any organization, community or opinion.

5.1.27 An institution that establishes an HREC should provide each member with a formal notice of appointment and an assurance of legal protection in respect of liabilities that may arise in the course of bona fide conduct of their duties as HREC members.[92]

Chapter 5.2 Responsibilities of Human Research Ethics Committees

Procedures

5.2.1 An institution that establishes an HREC should ensure that the HREC establishes, implements and documents working procedures to promote good ethical review, including procedures for:

(a) frequency of meetings;
(b) attendance at meetings;
(c) conduct and structure of meetings and deliberations;
(d) preparation of agendas and minutes;
(e) timely distribution of papers prior to meetings;
(f) presentation of applications for ethical review;
(g) timely consideration and review of applications;
(h) managing conflicts of interest (see paragraphs 5.4.1–5.4.6);
(i) communicating with researchers, including face to face, by telephone and in writing (see paragraphs 5.2.40–5.2.42);
(j) reporting on its activities to the institution;
(k) methods of decision making;

92 Review of the *National Statement on Ethical Conduct in Research Involving Humans* – second consultation draft.

(l) prompt notification of decisions;
(m) record keeping;
(n) monitoring of approved research (see paragraphs 5.5.1–5.5.11);
(o) reporting and handling adverse occurrences;
(p) receiving and handling of complaints (see paragraphs 5.6.1–5.6.6);
(q) advising the institution(s) of decisions to withdraw ethical approval of a research project;
(r) accommodating observers at meetings;[93]
(s) fees, if any, to be charged; and
(t) appropriate confidentiality of the content of applications.

Meetings

5.2.2 As far as possible each meeting of an HREC should be arranged to allow relevant members of each category the opportunity to attend and to be fully informed by prior receipt of papers.

5.2.3 Where there is less than full attendance at a meeting, the Chairperson should be satisfied, before a decision is reached, that the minimum membership listed in paragraph 5.1.21 have received all papers and have had an opportunity to contribute their views and that these have been recorded and considered.

5.2.4 An HREC should endeavour to reach decisions by general agreement. This need not involve unanimity.

Attendance of researchers or experts

5.2.5 An HREC may invite researcher(s) to be present for discussions of their proposed research and may request amendments to the proposal.

5.2.6 An HREC may seek advice from experts to assist with consideration of a research proposal. Such experts are to be bound by the same confidentiality requirements as the HREC members. Any conflicts of interest that such experts have in relation to the research proposal under consideration should be disclosed and appropriately managed (see paragraphs 5.4.1–5.4.6).

Participants' interests

5.2.7 An HREC should consider whether to consult an advocate for any participant or group of participants to inform the HREC about how best to enable informed decision making and understanding by these participants.

5.2.8 Where a significant proportion of potential participants in research are unfamiliar with the language in which the research is to be

93 Review of the *National Statement on Ethical Conduct in Research Involving Humans* – second consultation draft.

conducted, an HREC should be satisfied that all information relevant to participation has been reliably translated into the participants' language. This applies whether or not the information is provided in writing.

5.2.9 An HREC should be satisfied that someone able to interpret for participants unfamiliar with the language in which the research is to be conducted, is present during discussions with them about the project.[94]

5.2.10 HRECs should be satisfied that information relevant to participants with a vision or hearing impairment is made available to them in a way that takes their impairment in to account.

5.2.11 An HREC should consider how much of the information provided by the researcher about amounts and sources of funding, financial interests or affiliations, should be disclosed to research participants.

5.2.12 An HREC should not communicate directly with a research sponsor on matters relating to the proposal or to the ethics of a project, but the institution and the sponsor may have direct communication on administrative matters.

Making and communicating decisions

5.2.13 An HREC may approve, request amendment of, or reject a research proposal on ethical grounds.

5.2.14 An HREC should clearly communicate its decisions about a research proposal to the researcher, including its requests for amendments, providing reasons for those decisions and requests. A final decision to approve or reject a proposal should be communicated to the researcher in writing. Where the proposal is approved, approval should state explicitly that the proposal meets the requirements of this Statement. Where the proposal is rejected, reasons linked to this Statement should be provided.

Documents and records

5.2.15 All documents and other material used in recruiting potential research participants should be approved by the HREC, including information sheets, consent forms, advertisements and letters of invitation.

5.2.16 An HREC may approve, request amendment of, or reject a research proposal on ethical grounds.

5.2.17 An HREC should maintain a record of all research proposals received and reviewed including at least the:

(a) name of the institution(s) for which the research approval is being sought;

94 Review of the *National Statement on Ethical Conduct in Research Involving Humans* – second consultation draft.

(b) project identification number(s);
(c) name of principal researcher(s);
(d) title of the project;
(e) correspondence between the HREC and the researcher relating to the review;[95]
(f) acceptance or rejection of any changes to the proposal;
(g) proposed date of completion of the proposal;
(h) formal advice of final ethical approval or non-approval, with date;
(i) terms and conditions, if any, of approval of any proposal;
(j) duration of the approval;
(k) name of any other HREC whose opinion was considered;
(l) mechanisms to be used to monitor the conduct of the research; and
(m) relevance, if any, of the Commonwealth, State or Territory legislation or guidelines relating to privacy of personal or health information.

5.2.18 An HREC should record decisions about approval, amendment or rejection of proposals in written or electronic form, with reasons for those decisions, linking those reasons to this Statement.

5.2.19 For research proposals reviewed by more than one HREC, each HREC undertaking the review should also record, as far as information available allows (see paragraph 5.3.3):

(a) details of other HREC(s) involved;
(b) the decision(s) of each other HREC; and
(c) details of any amendments required by each other HREC.

5.2.20 An HREC should retain on file a copy of each research proposal and application for HREC approval, including any information sheets, consent forms or relevant correspondence, in the form in which they are approved.

HREC member responsibilities

5.2.21 Each member of an HREC has the responsibility to decide whether, in his of her judgement, a proposal submitted to the HREC for review meets the requirements of this Statement and is ethically acceptable.

5.2.22 To fulfil the responsibility in paragraph 5.2.21, each member of an HREC should:

(a) become familiar with this Statement and where relevant other guidelines which the Statement requires to be considered in the review of a research proposal;[96]

95 Review of the *National Statement on Ethical Conduct in Research Involving Humans* – second consultation draft.

96 Review of the *National Statement on Ethical Conduct in Research Involving Humans* – second consultation draft.

(b) prepare for and attend scheduled meetings of the HREC, or, if unavailable, provide opinions on the ethical acceptability of research proposals before meetings, subject to institutional policies as to absences; and
(c) attend continuing education or training programs in research ethics at least every two years.

Researcher responsibilities

5.2.23 In each research proposal, researchers should show that the proposal, by meeting paragraph 1.1 of this Statement, has research merit. Researchers should also describe how the proposal reflects the ethical values of justice, beneficence and respect for humans.

5.2.24 Researchers should meet deadlines for the submission of their applications. Applications should contain clear and comprehensive information, in lay language, so that the HREC or other review body (see paragraphs 5.1.7 and 5.1.8) can decide whether the application meets the requirements of this Statement.

5.2.25 A researcher should disclose to the HREC or other review body the amount and sources or potential sources of funding for the research.

Good communication between HRECs and researchers

5.2.26 Without open communication between HRECs and researchers good ethical review is unlikely. The ethical review process should not be adversarial and needs a shared commitment to the process by researchers and HRECs. Institutions should encourage that commitment by promoting awareness of this Statement among researchers, and ready accessibility of HRECs and their staff to researchers.

5.2.27 Misunderstandings often arise when written communication alone is relied upon. From the outset HRECs should encourage informal communication from researchers, and during the review process should consider meeting face to face with researchers to resolve issues about research proposals that have not been resolved by written or telephone communication.

5.2.28 Open communication of these kinds has implications for the resourcing of HRECs (see paragraph 5.1.17).[97]

Chapter 5.3 Minimising duplication of ethical review

Introduction

Research projects which may require multiple ethical review in Australia include:

97 Review of the *National Statement on Ethical Conduct in Research Involving Humans* – second consultation draft.

(a) a research project conducted at more than one institution either by the same or different researchers;
(b) a research project conducted jointly by researchers affiliated with different institutions;
(c) a research project conducted at one institution by a researcher affiliated with another institution, for example, a university-based researcher conducting research at a hospital; and
(d) any other research for which more than one institution has responsibility for ethical review and approval.

This chapter applies both to HRECs and to other ethical review bodies described in paragraphs 5.1.7 and 5.1.8.

Guidelines for minimising duplication of ethical review

5.3.1 Wherever more than one institution has a responsibility to ensure that a human research project is subject to ethical review and approval, whether by an HREC or other review body, they have the further responsibility to reduce or eliminate any duplication of ethical review.

5.3.2 Institutions with responsibilities for the conduct of human research must establish and publish policies for deciding when to accept the outcome of ethical review by other review bodies established at State, regional or institutional level and functioning in compliance with this Statement.

5.3.3 Those institutional policies must:

(a) identify any circumstances local to the institution that are relevant to the ethical review of human research conducted at the institution, and provide both for their disclosure to the review body reviewing that research and for their management;
(b) require communication, and the exchange of information or advice, with any other review body;[98]
(c) permit acceptance of a scientific/technical/methodological assessment of the research by another institution or suitably qualified body, person or persons;
(d) authorise acceptance of a review body's ethical review and approval or disapproval as meeting the institution's responsibility for ethical review of that human research;
(e) specify exceptional circumstances in which the institution may request a review body that it has established to conduct further ethical review, for example, where an institution adopts research begun and ethically approved at another institution;
(f) identify the ways the conduct of the research may be monitored and what roles the institution and the review body will have in the monitoring;

98 Review of the *National Statement on Ethical Conduct in Research Involving Humans* – second consultation draft.

(g) identify mechanisms for informing participants of an early discontinuance of research; and
(h) adopt any other administrative procedures to avoid unnecessary duplication and promote timely ethical review and approval of human research.

5.3.4 A researcher developing or designing a research proposal involving two or more institutions should inform them at an early stage in this process. Those institutions should agree as early as possible about which review body will accept the role of reviewing the proposal.

5.3.5 Where a human research project is to be conducted by different researchers at more than one institution, those researchers should jointly determine, in the light of institutional policies, which institution(s) or suitably qualified other body or bodies should be asked to conduct the ethical and scientific/technical/methodological review of the project.

5.3.6 Researchers involved in human research to which paragraphs 5.3.1 to 5.3.5 apply, should make arrangements to ensure that:

(a) each institution with responsibility for the research is informed of all other Australian sites at which the research is being proposed or conducted, and of the name and location of the body that will conduct the ethical review of the research; and
(b) the review body is informed of any previous decisions made about the research by review bodies in overseas countries.[99]

Chapter 5.4 Conflicts of interest

Introduction

A conflict of interest exists where a divergence between a person's individual interests and institutional role or professional obligation raises the question whether those individual interests influence the person's carrying out of that role or obligation. Similar conflicts can arise where there is a divergence between the interests of an institution and the commitment it has, for example, to doing good research. A conflict of interest can compromise the validity of the research process by leading to judgments being made on the basis of factors external to the requirements of the research, or can compromise the institutional processes governing research. While financial conflicts of interest are foremost in the public mind, other conflicting interests can include private benefits significantly dependent on research outcomes or significant personal or professional advantage. A perception that a conflict of interest exists can be as serious as an actual conflict, raising concerns about the integrity of individuals or the management practices of an institution.

This chapter applies both to HRECs and to other ethical review bodies described in paragraphs 5.1.7 and 5.1.8.

99 Review of the *National Statement on Ethical Conduct in Research Involving Humans* – second consultation draft.

Guidelines for identifying and managing conflicts of interest

5.4.1 Institutions should establish processes to identify and manage actual or potential conflicts of interest. Where a potential conflict of interest involves an institution, the institution should inform the body reviewing the research to which the conflict relates, of the sources and nature of the conflict.

5.4.2 A researcher should disclose to the review body any actual or potential sources of conflict of interest and, when proposing and reporting the research, any affiliation or financial or other interest in the research and/or its outcomes.

5.4.3 When information provided by a researcher to a review body indicates that there is likely to be a conflict of interest that may affect the ethical conduct of the research, the review body should adopt measures to manage that conflict. These measures may include requiring that the information be disclosed to research participants, that a person other than the researcher negotiate consent with participants or that the information be disclosed in any report of the research.[100]

5.4.4 Where information provided by a researcher indicates to a review body that there may be a conflict of interest involving the institution, the review body should notify the institution.

5.4.5 A review body should require its members to disclose any actual or potential conflict of interest in any research to be reviewed, including any personal involvement or participation in the research, any financial interest in the outcome, or any involvement in competing research. The review body should adopt measures to manage such conflicts of interest. Measures may include either exclusion or absence from some or all of the committee's discussion and/or decision.

5.4.6 A review body may seek advice from experts to assist with consideration of a research proposal. A review body should require those experts to disclose any actual or potential conflicts of interest arising from any personal involvement or participation in the research, and any financial interest in the outcome or any involvement in competing research. The review body should adopt measures to manage such conflicts of interest. Measures may include requiring that expert to provide only written advice, as well as either exclusion or absence from some or all of the committee's discussion and/or decision.[101]

100 Review of the *National Statement on Ethical Conduct in Research Involving Humans* – second consultation draft.

101 Review of the *National Statement on Ethical Conduct in Research Involving Humans* – second consultation draft.

Chapter 5.5 Monitoring approved research

Introduction

Monitoring approved research is the responsibility of the institution in which the research is conducted. Monitoring includes any process or mechanism put in place to check that the conduct of the research conforms to the approved proposal. It contributes to the safety of research participants and the maintenance of community confidence in human research. Mechanisms of monitoring can include:

(a) reports from researchers;
(b) reports from independent agencies (such as a data and safety monitoring board);
(c) review of adverse event reports;
(d) random inspections of research sites, data or consent documentation; and
(e) interviews with research participants or other forms of feedback from them.

This chapter applies both to HRECs and to other ethical review bodies described in paragraphs 5.1.7 and 5.1.8.

Guidelines for monitoring approved research

5.5.1 Institutions have the ultimate responsibility for ensuring via their research governance arrangements that the conduct of all approved research is monitored.

5.5.2 The frequency and type of monitoring should reflect the degree of risk to participants in that research.

5.5.3 Researchers have a significant responsibility in monitoring, as they are in the best position to observe any adverse events or unexpected outcomes and to take prompt steps to deal with any unexpected risks.

5.5.4 Researcher integrity, as demonstrated by the capacity to self-monitor research in progress, should be emphasised in educating researchers in research ethics.[102]

5.5.5 Researchers are responsible for notifying the review body that mechanisms for monitoring are in place, and for satisfying the review body that the mechanisms are appropriate to the research.

5.5.6 At regular periods, at least annually and at the completion of the project, researchers should provide reports to institutions, which include information on at least the following matters:

(a) progress to date, or outcome in the case of completed research;
(b) maintenance and security of records;
(c) compliance with the approved proposal; and
(d) compliance with any conditions of approval.

102 Review of the *National Statement on Ethical Conduct in Research Involving Humans* – second consultation draft.

5.5.7 Researchers should report to the review body events that might affect continued ethical acceptability of the project, including:

(a) serious or unexpected adverse effects on participants; and
(b) proposed significant changes in the conduct, the participant profile or the risks of the proposed research.

Suspension or cessation of research

5.5.8 Researchers should inform the institution, the review body that approved the research and wherever possible research participants, if the research project is to be discontinued before the expected date of completion, and why. In the case of research at more than one site, or research where there has been multiple ethical review, it must be clearly established, before the research begins, how this information will be communicated.

5.5.9 Where an institution or a review body is satisfied that a research project cannot continue to be conducted in accordance with the approved proposal, and that as a result the welfare of participants will not be protected, ethical approval for the research should be withdrawn. The researcher, the institution and where possible the participants should be informed of this withdrawal. The researcher should promptly suspend the research and make arrangements to meet the needs of participants. The research may not be resumed unless it is modified to provide sufficient protection for participants, and the modification is ethically reviewed and the research again approved.

5.5.10 In the light of reports received under paragraph 5.5.7, review bodies may require researchers to amend research procedures to protect participants. Where they are satisfied that such amendments will not achieve that end, review bodies should notify the institution of the report.[103]

Chapter 5.6 Handling complaints

Introduction

Institutions may expect to receive complaints relating to research from:

(a) participants or others about researchers or the conduct of research; and
(b) participants, researchers or others about the conduct of the Human Research Ethics Committee (HREC) or other review body. Processes of ethical review of research should be transparent and accountable to the research participants they are intended to

103 Review of the *National Statement on Ethical Conduct in Research Involving Humans* – second consultation draft.

protect, and to the researchers whose applications are reviewed. Accessible, prompt and effective handling of complaints demonstrates this transparency and accountability. The conclusions of ethical review bodies as to whether applications meet the requirements of this Statement involve substantive ethical judgments on which there can be justifiable differences of opinion. For this reason, this chapter does not provide for appeals to other bodies or authorities by researchers against a final decision to reject a proposal, but deals only with complaints about other decisions or requirements made during the review process.

This chapter applies both to HRECs and to other ethical review bodies described in paragraphs 5.1.7 and 5.1.8.

Guidelines for handling complaints

5.6.1 Where complaints raise the possibility of serious research misconduct the matter should be handled in accordance with other institutional processes established to deal with these issues (see the *Australian Code for the responsible conduct of research*).

5.6.2 Procedures referred to in paragraph 5.2.1(p) should include written procedures for receiving and promptly handling complaints or concerns about the conduct of an approved research project and about the review of research proposals.

5.6.3 Complaints handling procedures should provide two paths, corresponding to the two categories of complaints described in the Introduction to this chapter.

5.6.4 Institutions should:

(a) establish procedures for receiving, handling and resolving complaints from research participants and others about researchers or the conduct of research; and
(b) identify a person to receive these complaints.[104]

5.6.5 Institutions should also:

(a) establish procedures for receiving, handling and resolving complaints from

    (i) researchers about the conduct of ethical review bodies in reviewing research proposals, and
    (ii) participants or others about the conduct of ethical review bodies in handling complaints; and

(b) appoint a person or persons independent of all ethical review bodies to receive, handle and resolve these complaints.

104 Review of the *National Statement on Ethical Conduct in Research Involving Humans* – second consultation draft.

5.6.6 Institutions should identify a person or agency external to the institution to whom a person can take a complaint that has not been resolved by the institution.

5.6.7 Institutions should publicise their complaints handling procedures.[105]

Chapter 5.7 Accountability

Introduction

Responsibility for the ethical design, review and conduct of research involving humans is exercised at all levels, from the detail of research conduct to the more general oversight of review and funding. Accordingly, responsibility is exercised at different levels by: researchers (and where relevant their supervisors); Human Research Ethics Committees (HRECs) and others conducting ethical review of research; institutions whose employees, resources or facilities are involved; funding organisations; agencies that set standards; and governments. These responsibilities are arranged in a hierarchy from the more detailed to the more general: from researchers to institutions and HRECs or other review bodies, from those bodies and institutions to funders and other agencies, from agencies to government and from government to the Australian public. In this Statement, accountability means the measures by which any of those involved can demonstrate that their responsibilities have been, or are being, fulfilled. Typical accountability measures involve reporting from one level of the hierarchy to another higher (or more general) level.

This chapter applies both to HRECs and to other ethical review bodies described in paragraphs 5.1.7 and 5.1.8.

Guidelines for accountability

5.7.1 Researchers have responsibilities for the ethical design and conduct of research. The measures of accountability by which researchers demonstrate, to institutions and to ethical review bodies, fulfilment of those responsibilities appear in Chapter 5.1 *Institutional responsibilities* and Chapter 5.5 *Monitoring approved research.*

5.7.2 HRECs have responsibilities for the ethical review of research. The measures of accountability by which HRECs demonstrate, to institutions, fulfilment of those responsibilities appear in Chapter 5.2 *Responsibilities of Human Research Ethics Committees.*

5.7.3 Institutions have responsibilities for the conduct of research and to ensure that ethical review of research occurs. The former responsibilities, that include ensuring that research is both sound and lawful, and

105 Review of the *National Statement on Ethical Conduct in Research Involving Humans* – second consultation draft.

is conducted by educated and experienced researchers, are set out in the *Australian code for the responsible conduct of research.* The latter responsibilities are set out in Chapter 5.1 *Institutional responsibilities.*[106]

5.7.4 In addition to providing information annually, institutions shall provide other information about their ethical review processes to the NHMRC on reasonable request.

5.7.5 Institutions in which health and medical human research is undertaken, and which are in receipt of NHMRC research funding or intend to remain eligible for it, must be registered with the NHMRC. Registration will include information about any HREC(s) or other review bodies which the institution has decided to use, or has established, to provide ethical review of human research.

5.7.6 As provided for in the deed of agreement attached to any NHMRC funding, it will be a requirement that institutions attest annually to the NHMRC in writing that the research governance and ethical oversight processes in place remain compliant with this Statement and with the *Australian code for the responsible conduct of research. [From a date to be determined, such attestation must be accompanied by evidence that the research governance processes of the institution have been subjected to external review or accreditation by a relevant agency within the previous four years.]*

PART II: NON-WESTERN MEDICAL PHILOSOPHIES

A common assumption of Anglophiles is that the British Empire brought civilisation to all parts of the world. Such a gross oversimplification belies the fact that many other civilisations possess highly developed ethical theories, especially in respect of the healing professions.

As Australia becomes more multicultural, exposure to these non-Western views of medical ethics become increasingly important, especially as some of these views may one day reflect Australian medical ethics.

What follows is a series of brief extracts outlining bioethical principles which have emerged in Islamic countries, in India, China and Japan. In reading the extracts, try to focus your attention on three matters:

1 Which foreign bioethical principles mirror those found in Australian bioethics?
2 Which foreign bioethical principles strike you as being somehow different?
3 Which principles of foreign bioethics would be likely to cause difficulty, in the event that an Australian medical practitioner were to treat someone more familiar with foreign bioethics (or if a foreign medical practitioner were to treat someone used to Australian bioethics)?

106 Review of the *National Statement on Ethical Conduct in Research Involving Humans* – second consultation draft.

Veatch, RM (ed), *Cross Cultural Perspectives in Medical Ethics*, 1989, p 120, Boston: Jones and Bartlett

Islam offers another alternative to Hippocratic medical ethics or the liberal ethics of western political philosophy. The style of contemporary Muslim writings on medical ethics is quite different from the secular medical ethical literature of either the East or West. It is much more explicitly religious in tone. Much more so even than the medical ethical writings of most contemporary religious commentators on medical ethical issues. It works very closely with the Quranic texts that it considers relevant to medical decision-making. In doing so, it makes clear how different the moral reasoning is of one in the Muslim tradition from secular and Judeo-Christian medical ethical discussions. The following text is representative. It was originally written for an international conference on Islamic Medicine in Kuwait in 1989. It concludes with a reprinting of the oath of the Islamic Medical Association of the United States and Canada.

Amine, ARC and Elkadi, A, 'Islamic Code of Medical Professional Ethics', in Veatch, RM (ed) (above), pp 120–23

Medicine was defined by Muslim physicians such as Al-Razi (841–926 AD) and Ibn Sina (Avicenna, 980–1036 AD) as the art concerned with the preservation of good health, combating of diseases and restoration of health to the sick. For several centuries, the world has witnessed and benefited from the great advances made by Muslim physicians in the area of health sciences. These advances were not just based on technical skill or intellectual superiority. They were equally well founded on a clear understanding of the role of the Muslim physician as derived from Islamic teachings and philosophy. For thousands of years, ethics have been recognised as an essential requirement in the making of a physician. Although the ancient codes of ethics have to some extent stressed this requirement, they were still deficient and contained grave errors. Contemporary codes of ethics tend to be more liberal and less restrictive. The Quranic ethics, on the other hand, stand out as a perfect model for all mankind, all professions and all time.

The medical ethical requirements proposed in this paper are primarily based on Quranic ethics. They include guidelines for the physician's behaviour and attitude, both at the personal and professional levels. The same standard of moral and ethical values should guide the physician in his private life and while conducting his professional business as well. A person who lacks moral values in private life cannot be trusted in professional activities, even with the highest professional and technical standards.

It is impossible for a person to have two different ethical standards. Truthful is God the Almighty when He says:

> God has not made for any man two hearts in his body.

The following verses from the Quran are most suited as a guide for the personal characteristics of the physician:

> Luqman admonished his son: 'My son,' he said, 'serve no God besides God, for idolatry is an abominable injustice.' We have enjoined man to show kindness to his parents, for with much pain does his mother bear him and he is not weaned before he is two years of age. We said: Give thanks to Me and to your parents; to Me shall all things return. But if they press you to serve besides Me what you know nothing of, do not obey them, be kind to them in this world and follow the path of those who submit to Me: to Me you shall all return and I will declare to you all that you have done. 'My son, God will know about all things, be they as small as a grain of mustard seed, be they hidden inside a rock or in heaven or on earth, God is wise and all-knowing. My son, establish regular prayer, enjoin what is just and forbid what is wrong, endure with fortitude whatever befalls you, for this is firmness of purpose in the conduct of affairs. Do not treat men with scorn nor walk proudly on the earth; God does not love the arrogant boaster. Rather, let your gait be modest and your voice low; the harshest of voices is the braying of the ass.'
> . . . and those who restrain anger and forgive other men, verily God loves those who do good.

God further states:

> It was the mercy of God that you have dealt with them gently and if you were severe and harsh-hearted they would have broken away from about you. Therefore, forgive them, pray for their forgiveness and consult them in the conduct of affairs; then, when you have decided to proceed, depend on God for support: verily God loves those who depend on Him.

Based on the above, the Muslim physician must believe in God and in Islamic teachings and practice, both in private and public life. He must be grateful to his parents, teachers and elders. He must be humble, modest, kind, merciful, patient and tolerant. He must follow the path of the righteous and always seek God's support. The physician equipped with the above-listed virtues is capable of complying with the needed professional requirements. The professional requirement is to acquire and maintain proper knowledge. God makes it clear in the Quran: '. . . Say: Are those equal, those who know and those who do not know?' . . . God also states:

> . . . Verily, those who fear God among His servants are those who have knowledge . . .

This implies that anything forbidden by God must be bad or harmful; anything proven to be bad or harmful must be forbidden.

The humanitarian aspect of the medical profession must never be neglected nor overlooked. The physician must render the needed help regardless of the financial ability or ethnic origin of the patient. A beautiful hint is found in the following Quranic verses:

> And they feed, for the love of God, the indigent, the orphan, and the captive, (saying) 'We feed you for the sake of God alone: no reward do we desire from you, nor thanks.'

When entrusted with the care of a patient, the physician must offer the needed advice with consideration for both the patient's body and mind, always remembering his basic obligation to enjoin what is just and forbid what is wrong.

The physician must protect the patient's confidentiality, reflecting God's description of the believers:

> Those who faithfully keep their trusts and their covenants.

The physician must adopt an appropriate manner of communication and be reminded of the ethics of speech referred to in the Quranic verses quoted earlier in this paper. God also describes the good believers in the Quran and says: 'For they have been guided to the purest of speeches.'

Situations requiring the physician to examine patients of the opposite sex are always a test of his moral character and his strength. A basic instruction is found in the following Quranic verses:

> Say to the believing men that they should lower their gaze and guard their modesty; that will make for greater purity for them, for God is well acquainted with all that they do. And say to the believing women that they should lower their gaze and guard their modesty . . .

God further says:

> God does wish to lighten your burden, for man was created weak.

It is, therefore, advisable that the physician examine patients of the opposite sex in the presence of a third person whenever feasible. This will be an added protection for the physician and the patient.

The physician must not criticise another physician in the presence of patients or health personnel, remembering the wise Quranic advice:

> O you who believe, let not some men among you make fun of others; it may be that they are better than them; nor let some women make fun of others; it may be that they are better than them; not defame, nor be sarcastic to each other, nor call each other by offensive nicknames . . .

God further says:

> God does not love that evil be voiced in public speech, except where the person has suffered injustice . . .

Veatch, RM (ed) (above), p 132

Chinese medical ethics are as closely integrated with ancient Confucian, Buddhist, and Taoist teaching as Indian medicine is with Hindu texts. In China, however, there are no definitive religious texts as there are in Hindu and Muslim thought. Instead there exists compendia of codes or rules of conduct compiled by many Confucian medical scholars and critics of the classical Confucian position.

Lee, T, 'Medical ethics in Ancient China', in Veatch, RM (ed) (above), pp 132–39

The real foundation for medical ethics as understood in the West is laid in the grand Hippocratic Oath in 5th century BC. The Egyptian papyri of the second millennium BC also mentioned medical ethics. Medical ethics in China, however, were not established until the 7th century. Sun Ssu-miao (581–673 AD), the father of medicine in China, first discussed the duties of a physician to his patients and to the public in his book, *The Thousand Golden Remedies*. In content this is similar in certain respects to the Hippocratic Oath. The essential points may be translated as follows:

> Medicine is an art which is difficult to master. If one does not receive a divine guidance from God, he will not be able to understand the mysterious points. A foolish fellow, after reading medical formularies for three years, will believe that all diseases can be cured. But, after practising for another three years, he will realise that most formulae are not effective. A physician should, therefore, be a scholar, mastering all the medical literature and working carefully and tirelessly.
>
> A great doctor, when treating a patient, should make himself quiet and determined. He should not have covetous desire. He should have bowels of mercy on the sick and pledge himself to relieve suffering among all classes. Aristocrat or commoner, poor or rich, aged or young, beautiful or ugly, enemy or friend, native or foreigner, and educated or uneducated, all are to be treated equally. He should look upon the misery of the patient as if it were his own and be anxious to relieve the distress, disregarding his own inconveniences, such as night-call, bad weather, hunger, tiredness, etc. Even foul cases, such as ulcer, abscess, diarrhoea, etc, should be treated without the slightest antipathy. One who follows this principle is a great doctor, otherwise, he is a great thief.
>
> A physician should be respectable and not talkative. It is a great mistake to boast of himself and slander other physicians.

Lao Tze, the father of Taoism, said:

> Open acts of kindness will be rewarded by man while secret acts of evil will be punished by God. Retribution is very definite. A physician should not utilise his profession as a means for lusting. What he does to relieve distress will be duly rewarded by Providence.

> He should not prescribe dear and rare drugs just because the patient is rich or of high rank, nor is it honest and just to do so for boasting.

Another important work on medical ethics is *The Medical Talks* written by Chang Kao in 1189. In a special chapter he collected twelve stories of retribution in order to warn physicians against professional faults. Gratuitous service was especially commended. Lusting after women and riches was considered to be immoral. The inducing of artificial abortion was severely denounced. The following story is cited as an example of gratuitous service:

> Mr Hsu Shu-wei in his youth prayed to the Gods that he might attain literary rank. One night he dreamed of a God who told him to perform some secret deeds of virtue in order to attain his ambition. Hsu was so poor that he could not help others financially. The only thing he could do was to become a doctor and then help the sick. He decided therefore to study medicine and soon mastered the art. He gave free treatment to all patients and responded readily to any request for his assistance without consideration whether the patient was of high or low rank. When he sat in the next examination, he passed with honours.

A story is told concerning artificial abortion as follows:

> A woman called Pai Mu-tan, lived by selling drugs for artificial abortion. One day she suffered suddenly from headache and her head became swollen. Physicians were unable to cure her. After many days an ulcer appeared with an offensive odour. Her crying at night could be heard by all the neighbours. One day she asked her son to burn all the prescriptions for abortion, and warned him not to engage in such a vocation as hers. Her son asked her why she would not hand down the prescriptions to him. She answered, 'I dreamed of hundreds of infants striking at my head every night. My illness is entirely due to my selling drugs for abortion.' After saying this, she died.

Ancient Chinese laid great emphasis on the virtue of chastity. The following story from the same book is a good example:

> During the period of Hsuan-ho (1119–25) a scholar was sick for many years. His wife requested the great doctor, Ho-cheng, to come to her boudoir and said to him, 'My husband has been sick for a long time; everything we possess has been sold to pay the expenses of medical care. We have no more money. If you will kindly cure my husband, I will place my body at your disposal.' The doctor rejected her offer sternly and said to her: 'Don't insult me. I will cure your husband. If your suggestion should be spread abroad by any chance, my career would be spoiled and I would be condemned by man and by the spirits.' Soon her husband was cured. One night the physician dreamed of a man taking him to a temple where a judge said to him, 'You have the virtue of the medical profession. You did not lust after woman in time of danger. God grant you 50,000 strings of cash and

> an official rank.' A few months later a prince of the Imperial family was sick. The court medical official could not cure him. An Imperial decree was then issued to summon the physicians in the country. Ho-cheng presented himself and cured the prince. The court thereupon granted him 3,000 strings of cash and an official rank.

In the Ming Dynasty, the question of medical ethics was discussed by many physicians. Hsu Chun-fu in 1556 compiled a section on this subject under a special title, 'The Medical Way'. At the same time, Kung Hsin wrote a maxim for reputable physicians. The maxim, which was instructive and concise, has been used as a motto in the baccalaureate service of the Peiping Union Medical College since 1939. It reads:

> The good physician of the present day cherishes kindness and righteousness. He reads widely and is highly skilled in the arts of his profession. He has in his mind adequate methods of treatment, which he adapts to different conditions. He cares not for vainglory, but is intent upon relieving suffering among all classes. He revives the dying and restores them to health: his beneficence is equal to that of Providence. Such a good physician will be remembered through endless generations.

Kung Ting-hsien, son of Kung Hsin, set 10 requirements for physicians in 1588, in content very similar to the maxim given above. About 30 years later Chen Shih-kung in his book *An Orthodox Manual of Surgery*, stated five commandments and 10 requirements for physicians. These included the duties of a physician to his patients, such as professional secrecy, responsibility, deportment and compensation. Attention was also given to the obligations of a physician to other physicians. The importance of advancement of medical knowledge was pointed out and rules for social intercourse were also suggested. This is really the most comprehensive statement on medical ethics in China. It reads as follows:

Five Commandments

1 Physicians should be ever ready to respond to any calls of patients, high or low, rich or poor. They should treat them equally and care not for financial reward. Thus the profession will become prosperous naturally day by day and conscience will remain intact.
2 Physicians may visit a lady, widow or nun only in the presence of an attendant but not alone. The secret diseases of female patients should be examined with a right attitude, and should not be revealed to anybody, not even to the physician's own wife.
3 Physicians should not ask patients to send pearl, amber or other valuable substances to the home for preparing medicament. If necessary, patients should be instructed how to mix the prescriptions themselves in order to avoid suspicion. It is also not proper to admire things which patients possess.
4 Physicians should not leave the office for excursion and drinking.

Patients should be examined punctually and personally. Prescriptions should be made according to the medical formulary, otherwise a dispute may arise.

5 Prostitutes should be treated just like patients from a good family and gratuitous services should not be given to the poor ones. Mocking should not be indulged for this brings loss of dignity. After examination physicians should leave the house immediately. If the case improves, drugs may be sent but physicians should not visit them again for lewd reward.

Ten Requirements

1 A physician or surgeon must first know the principles of the learned. He must study all the ancient standard medical books ceaselessly day and night, and understand them thoroughly so that the principles enlighten his eyes and are impressed on his heart. Then he will not make any mistake in the clinic.

2 Drugs must be carefully selected and prepared according to the refining process of Lei Kung. Remedies should be prepared according to the pharmaceutical formulae but may be altered to suit the patient's condition. Powders should be freely made. Pills and distilled medicine should be prepared in advance. The older the plaster is the more effective it will be. Tampons become more effective on standing. Don't spare valuable drugs; their use is eventually advantageous.

3 A physician should not be arrogant and insult other physicians in the same district. He should be modest and careful towards his colleagues; respect his seniors, help his juniors, learn from his superiors and yield to the arrogant. Thus there will be no slander and hatred. Harmony will be esteemed by all.

4 The managing of a family is just like the curing of a disease. If the constitution of a man is not well cared for and becomes overexhausted, diseases will attack him. Mild ones will weaken his physique, while serious ones may result in death. Similarly, if the foundation of the family is not firmly established and extravagance be indulged in, reserves will gradually drain away and poverty will come.

5 Man receives his fate from Heaven. He should not be ungrateful to the Heavenly decree. Professional gains should be approved by the conscience and conform to the Heavenly will. If the gain is made according to the Heavenly will, natural affinity takes place. If not, offspring will be condemned. Is it not better to make light of professional gain in order to avoid the evil retribution?

6 Gifts, except in the case of weddings, funerals and for the consolation of the sick, should be simple. One dish of fish and one of vegetable will suffice for a meal. This is not only to reduce expenses but also to save provisions. The virtue of a man lies not in grasping but rather in economy.

7 Medicine should be given free to the poor. Extra financial help should be extended to the destitute patients, if possible. Without food, medicine alone cannot relieve the distress of a patient.
8 Savings should be invested in real estate but not in curios and unnecessary luxuries. The physician should also not join the drinking club and the gambling house which would hinder his practice. Hatred and slander can thus be avoided.
9 Office and dispensary should be fully equipped with necessary apparatus. The physician should improve his knowledge by studying medical books, old and new, and reading current publications. This really is the fundamental duty of a physician.
10 A physician should be ready to respond to the call of government officials with respect and sincerity. He should inform them the cause of the disease and prescribe accordingly. After healing, he should not seek for a complimentary tablet or plead excuse for another's difficulty. A person who respects the law should not associate with officials.

In 1695, Chang-Lu wrote *Chang-shih-iitung*, a book on general medicine, with 10 commandments for physicians in the first chapter. The physician's self-control and his duties to his patients and to the public are emphasised. The essential features are to abstain from the following:

1 acquiring evil habits;
2 over self-confidence;
3 strong prejudice;
4 imitation or lack of initiative;
5 making careless diagnosis;
6 practising magic healing;
7 treating the nobility and commoners similarly;
8 neglecting poor patients;
9 extorting high compensation from critical cases;
10 criticising or slandering other physicians.

In the early 19th century, Huai Yuan also stated six maxims for physicians in his book. They are very much the same as those above cited, and will not be quoted here.

Comment

Medical ethics is a body of rules compounded from idealism and practicality which physicians accept as their moral standard. Its purpose is to promote the prime object of the medical profession, service to humanity, and also to assist the regulation of medical practice by the government. The standard of medical ethics varies according to races, habits, customs and times. An action considered moral by one people may not be so considered by others. On the other hand, conduct once regarded as a great fault may not be so in our times. Medical ethics has no permanent single standard. From the Chinese medical literature cited above, we may recognise several differences in the ideals of oriental and western peoples on medical ethics. Several points should be noted.

1 Treatment of female patients

Mencius said, 'Men and women, in giving and receiving, must not touch each other.' The influence of this proverb on the medical profession is very great. As the female patient could not expose any part of her body to the male physician, a model, the so-called 'medicine lady' was used for illustration during the medical examination. For the same reason, palpation was not considered proper for women. The examination of the female sex organs was a great offence to the ancient Chinese custom. It was also not proper for a physician to lay his fingers on a woman's wrists to examine her pulse. This last inconvenience was ingeniously avoided by physicians in the Imperial family of the Ming Dynasty. A long string was tied to the patient's wrists while another person held the other end. The doctor then laid his fingers in the middle of the string to examine the pulse, a method based on the principle of the transmission of waves through the string. But since the transmission was too weak to be effective, this fantastic method was not generally adopted.

2 Gratuitous service

Most of the prominent physicians in Chinese medical history were either retired government officials or scholars who had failed in the Imperial examination. They disliked to think of the practice of medicine as their profession. They all endeavoured to encourage gratuitous services and looked on the practice of medicine as a philanthropic undertaking or a benevolent act. As a result, a good tradition has come down among physicians. All, with few exceptions, are pledged to serve the community by the alleviation of suffering without caring much for financial return.

3 Retribution

The idea of retribution played an important part in medical ethics. Most Chinese believed that disease and distress were retribution for past sins while health and happiness were rewards for past virtues. This is probably attributable to Buddhist influence in China. The practice of medicine was considered a benevolent act – observance of professional ethics would be rewarded with rich harvest of blessing. For this reason, ancient Chinese physicians dared not to do anything unethical or unprofessional.

4 Complimentary tablets

Chinese patients used to present wooden boards with complimentary inscriptions to doctors who had cured them, as an expression of appreciation. This was also intended to announce the skill of the doctor to others who might suffer from the same disease. This good custom can be traced back to ancient times. Later, however, it was abused as a means of propaganda. Physicians began to ask patients to present tablets. Some even made tablets themselves and claimed that they were presented by their patients. The wrong use of this good custom made Chen Shih-kung consider it vainglory and he warned physicians against it in his 10 requirements in the early 17th century.

5 Relationship between social problems and medical problems

Many patients cannot be cured of their illness unless their financial pressure or other social problems are also relieved. Therefore, a social service has been established in many modern hospitals. Chen Shih-kung, in the early seventeenth century, noticed the close connection between medicine and social problems and made the utmost effort to provide relief work for the poor.

6 Difference between the physique of the nobility and commoners

Chang Lu believed that the physique of a noble was delicate while that of a commoner was tough and they should be treated differently. He also classified physicians into two groups, one specialised in curing those of high rank, and the other, the common people. Although this idea, very similar to the four temperaments in Greek medicine, overestimates the difference between individual constitutions, it is not altogether without scientific basis.

7 Secret prescriptions

The dispensing of secret prescriptions was never considered to be unethical in China. Some even deemed it an honour for a physician to know a secret formula. Even today secret remedies still prevail. The public generally believes that such prescriptions will become ineffective if popularly used. This attitude is probably due to the lack of formal medical organisation before the introduction of western medicine.

Conclusion

The important writings on medical ethics in ancient China have been briefly mentioned and commented upon. One of the good features of Chinese medical ethics is the encouragement of gratuitous service to the poor. This custom is well established in China and should continue to be followed by modern physicians. Fortunately the Chinese Medical Code promulgated by the Chinese Medical Association in 1932 already has given a great emphasis to this point.

The chief weakness in Chinese medical ethics is the lack of opposition to patients and secret remedies. This is probably due to there being no medical guilds in China. Another shortcoming is that no reference is made to the teaching of medicine such as that found in the second sentence of the Hippocratic Oath, where the pledge is given to teach without fee or stipulation to all who are bound by a stipulation and Oath according to the law of medicine. This places all medical knowledge at the disposal of all physicians. The Chinese adhere rather to the Hippocratic injunction to restrict the teaching of medicine to the sons of physicians and to disciples bound by a stipulation and Oath.

Veatch, RM (ed) (above), pp 140–41, 'Japanese medical ethics'

Traditional Japanese medical ethics draws both on Buddhist thought and indigenous Shinto tradition. One example comes from the 16th century when an approach to disease commonly known as the Ri-shu school was widely practised. A code known as the 17 Rules of Enjuin was drawn up by practitioners of this medical art. Note that similar to the Hippocratic Oath, there is a notion that medical knowledge can be very dangerous. It is disseminated only to members of the school and to no others. These rules even go so far as to require that if a practitioner dies or ceases to practice, he must return his books to the school so that they will not fall into the hands of untrained persons. The view of knowledge, quite consistent with the Hippocratic tradition, stands in dramatic contrast with the ethics of Protestantism, which places great emphasis on entrusting the texts to the lay person, and with secular liberalism, which insists that lay persons should be reasonably informed about the nature of treatments and the consequences.

The 17 Rules of Enjuin

(For Disciples in Our School)

Each person should follow the path designated by Heaven (Buddha, the Gods).

You should always be kind to people. You should always be devoted and loving.

The teaching of Medicine should be restricted to selected persons.

You should not tell others what you are taught, regarding treatments, without permission.

You should not establish association with doctors who do not belong to this school.

All the successors and descendants of the disciples of this school shall follow the teachers' ways.

If any disciples cease the practice of Medicine, or, if successors are not found at the death of the disciple, all the medical books of this school should be returned to the SCHOOL OF ENJUIN.

You should not kill living creatures, nor should you admire hunting or fishing. In our school, teaching about poisons is prohibited, nor should you receive instructions about poisons from other physicians. Moreover, you should not give abortives to the people.

> You should rescue even such patients as you dislike or hate. You should do virtuous acts, but in such a way that they do not become known to people. To do good deeds secretly is a mark of virtue.
>
> You should not exhibit avarice and you must not strain to become famous. You should not rebuke or reprove a patient, even if he does not present you with money or goods in gratitude.
>
> You should be delighted if, after treating a patient without success, the patient receives medicine from another physician, and is cured.
>
> You should not speak ill of other physicians.
>
> You should not tell what you have learned from the time you enter a woman's room, and, moreover, you should not have obscene or immoral feelings when examining a woman.
>
> Proper or not, you should not tell others what you have learned in lectures, or what you have learned about prescribing medicine.
>
> You should not like undue extravagance. If you like such living, your avarice will increase, and you will lose the ability to be kind to others. If you do not keep the rules and regulations of this school, then you will be cancelled as a disciple. In more severe cases, the punishment will be greater.

PART III: CONSTITUTIONAL LIMITATIONS ON THE DELIVERY OF HEALTH CARE IN AUSTRALIA

The laws which govern all aspects of life in Australia are enacted by Parliaments (State or Commonwealth) according to the distribution of legislative powers in the Commonwealth Constitution. In addition to statutes, there exist in Australia (as in other Commonwealth countries) 'judge-made' or 'common law'. The common law is a series of principles formulated by judges over hundreds of years. So, for example, much of the law regulating contracts in Australia is to be found in the common law, rather than in the statutes passed by the legislatures. Common law principles can, it is important to note, be altered or abolished by legislative enactment.

In Chapter 2, the relevant principles of contract governing medical scenarios will be addressed. In Chapter 3, the principles of the law of torts (civil wrongs) will be canvassed. At this stage, it is important to isolate the relevant jurisdiction (State or Federal) whose parliament may pass laws regulating health care.

Wheelwright, K, 'Commonwealth and State powers in health – a constitutional diagnosis' (1995) 21 Monash University Law Review 53

> One of the fundamental influences on the way Australian health care services are structured, funded and delivered is Australia's constitutional system . . . Many of the difficulties that exist in health service planning and delivery result from the complex mix of Commonwealth, State, local government and private sector involvement in the health sector. At its best, the involvement of different levels of government and

> sectors of the community can produce well resourced and planned services responsive to community needs. At worst, there is a lack of integration of planning, difficulties over funding and gaps and inconsistencies in regulation which are exacerbated by the constitutional division in power and responsibility between the States and the Commonwealth.
>
> The fact that both high quality health programs and programs fraught with difficulties grow from the same constitutional system indicates that factors other than constitutional ones fundamentally influence health programs . . .
>
> The Australian health system is a product of a diverse range of economic, technical, social, legal, constitutional and political factors, some of which are unique to Australia. The system is also a product of the historical evolution from the provision of care based on private philanthropy to a system which is largely government funded and controlled. The way health services are organised, funded and delivered is affected particularly by the existence of federalism as a major organising principle for the distribution of political power in Australia. This is complicated further by the philosophies of governments of different political persuasions about the role of the State in health service provision and funding and the appropriate balance between public and private service provision. Governments in turn are influenced to varying degrees by powerful interest groups in the health sector including the organised medical profession, pharmaceutical manufacturers, and the private health insurance industry. These political factors and influences cannot be overestimated because they have a profound influence on the preparedness of governments, in particular the Commonwealth Government, to test their potential legal powers . . .
>
> The political complexion of Commonwealth and State Governments and their relative positions on the State/Federal balance of power are no doubt important . . . When political tensions between State and Commonwealth Governments are high, the divisions between their constitutional powers and their relative resources are highlighted. In this context, the constitutional framework for health service delivery becomes a substantial obstacle to implementing an integrated health system based on best practice care.

When the Commonwealth of Australia was formed in 1901, the new Commonwealth (or Federal) Parliament was assigned powers in respect of only certain areas. The balance of powers not explicitly referred to in the Federal Constitution were to be exercised by the State Parliaments. Over time, some States have chosen to delegate some of their responsibilities to local government authorities, or to refer the power to the Commonwealth. In order to understand the regulation of the delivery of health care services in Australia then, recourse must first be had to the Constitution.

The Constitution gives no explicit power over health to the Commonwealth Parliament. Some powers over other matters, however, inferentially lead to the

Commonwealth Parliament having control over health-related matters. This is because s 51(xxxix) of the Constitution allows the Commonwealth Parliament to pass legislation concerning matters ancillary to areas of Federal legislative competence.

Examples of these powers as at 1901 are to be found in s 51(ix) of the Constitution (the Quarantine Power), s 51(xiv) ('Insurance, other than State insurance; also State insurance extending beyond the limits of the State concerned') and s 51(xxiii) ('Invalid and old age pensions'). The first-mentioned power allowed the Federal Government to pass the Quarantine Act of 1908. This Act controls the importation of people, animals or goods including making orders in respect of 'sanitary regulation and disinfection'. The insurance power will be dealt with in the discussion of Medicare, below.

Despite the absence of a clear legislative authority residing in the Constitution, the Federal Government attempted in 1943 to introduce a scheme of pharmaceutical benefits. The Federal Act provided for the gratuitous provision to the public of certain medicines, prescribed in a formulary. The Act also imposed duties on medical practitioners and chemists in relation to the prescription and supply of medicines. In passing the Act, the Federal Government relied upon s 81 of the Constitution which permits the Commonwealth to make appropriations 'for the purposes of the Commonwealth'.

The Federal Government claimed that the provision of pharmaceutical benefits to the people of Australia was a legitimate purpose of the Federal Parliament. It argued that the purposes of the Commonwealth were those decided by the Commonwealth Parliament from time to time. The State of Victoria (who opposed the legislation) claimed that s 81 should be construed as only meaning purposes for which the Commonwealth Parliament has power to make laws under the various subsections of s 51 of the Constitution.

The Act establishing this scheme, the Pharmaceutical Benefits Act 1944, was challenged in the High Court of Australia (the body which, under the Constitution is empowered to determine the constitutional validity of any legislation). The High Court's judgment has become known as the *Pharmaceutical Benefits* case. (Its full name is *Attorney General for Victoria (ex rel Dale and Others) v The Commonwealth and Others* (1945) 71 CLR 237.)

In upholding Victoria's opposition to the scheme, the Judges of the High Court distinguished the Australian Constitution from the United States Constitution. In the US Constitution, the Federal Congress was given power to make legislation 'for the welfare of' the people of the United States. No such broad grant of power was made by the Australian Constitution. Furthermore, Mr Justice Dixon held that:

> The Pharmaceutical Benefits Act emerges as a statute which must be held completely invalid upon the simple ground that it is not relevant to any power which the Constitution confers upon the [Federal] Parliament (at 267).

Mr Justice Starke, after noting that the phrase 'the purposes of the Commonwealth' included not only the express grant of powers in s 51, but also 'such matters arising from the existence of the Commonwealth and its status as a

Federal Government', such as payment of Members of Parliament, agreed with Mr Justice Dixon. He noted:

> . . . the Pharmaceutical Benefits Act 1944 is beyond any purpose of the Commonwealth. No legislative, executive or judicial function of the Commonwealth can be found which supports it, and it cannot be justified because of the existence of the Commonwealth or its status as a Federal Government (at 266).

Mr Justice Williams was perhaps clearest in his condemnation of the Federal Government's interference with health issues:

> [The Pharmaceutical Benefits Act] contains provisions affecting the relationship, contractual or under the laws of the States, of medical practitioners and patients, of customers and chemists, and many other provisions which can only be described as legislation upon the subject matter of public health. There is no express power in the Constitution for the Parliament of the Commonwealth to legislate upon this subject matter except to make laws with respect to quarantine and as incidental to the execution of any powers vested in the Commonwealth by the Constitution (at 280).

He noted that:

> The Parliament of the Commonwealth is empowered by s 51(xxiii) to make laws with respect to invalid and old age pensions, and it can, therefore, appropriate moneys out of the Consolidated Revenue Fund for this purpose, but it has no general power to legislate for social services. This power is left to the States . . . The Pharmaceutical Benefits Act cannot, therefore, be supported under s 81 because it purports to appropriate money for a purpose which is not a purpose of the Commonwealth (at 282).

The scope of the Social Security power in the Constitution was enlarged by way of Constitutional Referendum in 1946. The new s 51(xxiiiA) gave the Commonwealth Parliament power to legislate with respect to:

> The provision of maternity allowances, widows' pensions, child endowment, unemployment, pharmaceutical, sickness and hospital benefits, medical and dental services (but not so as to authorise any form of civil conscription), benefits to students and family allowances.

The Federal Government again enacted a Pharmaceutical Benefits Act (the Pharmaceutical Benefits Act 1947–49) in terms similar to the Pharmaceutical Benefits Act 1944, but with the addition of the gratuitous provision to the public of appliances specified in an addendum. Also different to the operation of the earlier act was the inclusion, in 1949, of s 7A of the Act. This section provided that a medical practitioner could not provide medicines or appliances specified (respectively) in the formulary or addendum except by using a form prescribed by the Commonwealth. A penalty was provided for non-compliance. The British Medical Association in Australia challenged the legislation on the basis that forcing doctors to use a particular type of form amounted to civil conscription and was thus invalid as contravening the express words of s 51(xxiiiA) of the Constitution.

Federal Council of the British Medical Association in Australia and Others v The Commonwealth and Others (1949) 79 CLR 201

Williams J:

The reason for the insertion of the new paragraph (xxxiiiA) in the Constitution is common ground. In *Attorney General (Vic) v The Commonwealth*, the Pharmaceutical Benefits Act 1944, the predecessor with an important difference of (sic) the present Act, was declared to be invalid by Latham CJ, Rich J, Starke J, Dixon J and myself, McTiernan J dissenting. The power relied upon to support the constitutional validity of this Act was the power of appropriation in s 81 of the Constitution . . . The reasons for Judgment in *Attorney General (Vic) v The Commonwealth* disclosed a division of opinion as to the meaning of the words 'for the purposes of the Commonwealth' in s 81 of the Constitution. Latham CJ and McTiernan J thought that the purposes could be any purposes determined by the Commonwealth Parliament. Starke J thought that the purposes could only be the purposes of the Commonwealth as 'an organised political body, with legislative, executive and judicial functions, whatever is incidental thereto, and the status of the Commonwealth as a Federal Government'. I was substantially of the same opinion. Dixon J did not find it necessary finally to decide judicially between these two views, but indicated that in the past he had not entertained the view that s 81 of the Constitution empowered the Parliament to expend money for any purpose that was for the benefit of the people of the Commonwealth. Rich J was in substantial agreement with the reasons of Dixon J from which it would appear that he also had not in the past entertained this view.

It was therefore likely, if the point arose for decision, that the majority of the court would hold that the only form of social services upon which the Commonwealth could lawfully expend its moneys were those expressly authorised by the Constitution, that is invalid and old age pensions which are authorised by s 51 para (xxiii), and that the Acts authorising payments for maternity allowances, child endowment and widows' pensions were invalid.

Accordingly, the main purpose of the alteration of the Constitution now embodied in s 51, para (xxiiiA) was to empower the Commonwealth Parliament to legislate to spend its moneys on a wider range of social services than those authorised by s 51, para (xxiii). The new paragraph is of course plenary in its fullest sense and must, like every other legislative power in the Constitution, be given a wide and liberal interpretation. It contains 11 separate heads of legislative power. These heads may to some extent overlap, but there is no reason why the paragraph, because it is part of the Constitution, should not be construed so as to make it a consistent enactment and to give a meaning if possible to every part of it (*Bank of New South Wales v The Commonwealth*). It is important to discover at the outset the heads to which the expression in parenthesis 'but not so as to authorise any form of civil conscription' applies. There is a comma after the words 'hospital benefits' and a further comma after the words 'civil conscription' so that the punctuation tends to confine the expression to the words 'medical and dental services', and this is in my opinion the true intent of the paragraph. If the expression was meant to apply to all the preceding words, it would only be natural to expect that it would also be made to apply to the succeeding words 'benefits to students and family allowance', because medical and dental services could be provided as part of such benefits and allowances just as readily as they could be provided as part of the preceding allowances and benefits. It would appear therefore that the other heads of legislative power in the new paragraph are not subject to the expression. This may well have been thought to be unnecessary because a legislative power to provide allowances, pensions, endowments, and benefits points strongly to a power which is intended to be exercised by the Commonwealth itself providing such allowances and such in cash or in kind, and not a power to make or compel a State or some private individual to provide the benefit. But it is unnecessary to express a final opinion because the express inclusion of medical and dental services in the paragraph clearly indicates to my mind that whenever such services are provided, whether as services exclusively or in the course of providing some other benefit, the law must not authorise any form of civil conscription of such services.

The expression is a prohibition upon the exercise of the legislative powers of the Commonwealth under para (xxiiiA) of the same character as the prohibition contained in ss 92 and 116 of the Constitution. It invalidates all legislation to which it applies. The words 'civil conscription' have no ordinary meaning in the English language. The ordinary meaning of conscription is the compulsory enrolment of men (and now women) for service in the military or naval (and now in the air) forces . . . It would no doubt be a form of industrial conscription to compel persons by law to work in industries whether the industries were carried on by the Commonwealth or its authorities or by the States or their authorities or by private individuals. It would equally be a form of civil conscription of medical or dental services to compel medical practitioners or dentists by law to make their professional services as civilians available to the Commonwealth or its authorities or the States or their authorities or to carry on their professions in particular localities. Conscription as a word of general application would seem to signify compulsory as opposed to voluntary service, so that the words 'industrial conscription' would seem naturally to connote compulsory as opposed to voluntary employment in industry, and the expression 'civil conscription of medical and dental services' naturally to connote the compulsory as opposed to the voluntary exercise of such services in civil life. Accordingly, in my opinion, the expression invalidates all legislation which compels medical practitioners or dentists to provide any form of medical or dental service.

The crucial question is whether s 7A of the Pharmaceutical Benefits Act 1947–49 is such a law. The Acts of 1944 and 1947 did not seek to compel medical practitioners to write prescriptions on Commonwealth forms. They were supplied with copies of the formulary and with forms and requested to use the forms when a pharmaceutical benefit was prescribed. We were told by the Attorney General that the Government believed that medical practitioners would co-operate voluntarily and that it would not be necessary to use compulsion. It may have been thought that patients would exercise a practical compulsion by urging practitioners to use the forms so that they might become entitled to receive the pharmaceutical benefits. But neither event happened and s 7A was inserted in the principal Act by Acts Nos 8 and 26 of 1949 to make the use of the Commonwealth forms compulsory. When a statute inflicts a penalty for not doing an act, the penalty implies that there is a legal compulsion to do the act in question. Section 7A therefore compels a medical practitioner, who cannot obtain a request to the contrary from the person in respect of whom or at whose request the prescription is written, to write the prescription on the forms supplied by the Commonwealth. The Attorney General submitted that the section does not compel a medical practitioner to render any medical service, and that its whole effect is to compel a medical practitioner to write the prescription on a particular piece of paper if he decides, in the unfettered exercise of his discretion, that the patient requires treatment which is included in the formulary. It was submitted that the subject matter of the legislation is not the medical service of treating the patient, but merely the question of the use of a document for the particular purpose of enabling the patient to obtain the pharmaceutical benefits at or from the premises of an approved chemist without payment. But this is not in my opinion the true effect of the section. The scheme of the Act is to make the provision of a pharmaceutical benefit conditional upon a medical practitioner prescribing particular treatment, so that in prescribing that treatment the medical practitioner is rendering medical service to the Commonwealth. He is in effect certifying to the Commonwealth that the patient requires a pharmaceutical benefit within the meaning of the Act. Section 16 of the Act provides that: 'The Minister may, on behalf of the Commonwealth, enter into an agreement (on such terms as to remuneration, allowances and otherwise as he thinks fit) with a medical practitioner providing that the services of the medical practitioner shall be available without charge to members of the public for the purpose of furnishing prescriptions for the purposes of this Act.' This section describes as a medical service, the service which a practitioner provides when he is compelled by s 7A to write a prescription on a Commonwealth form. He is compelled to render that service in the course of rendering a contractual service to his patient. But it is a service which forms no part of the implied contract for services created by a patient seeking the advice and treatment of a medical practitioner and the medical practitioner examining the patient with a view to giving him advice and treatment. It is a compulsory service to the Commonwealth for the purposes of the Act which is super-imposed upon the contract of the parties. It is a compulsory service whether the obligation is absolute or absolute unless performance is excused by the person in respect of whom or at whose request the prescription is written . . . When analysed, the submission of the defendants appears to imply that a law only authorises a form of civil conscription of medical services when it operates directly to compel medical practitioners to work for some civil authority or in some particular locality or for some particular class of patients, and that a law which merely compels medical practitioners to act in some particular manner in the course of or as incidental to the carrying on of their profession does not authorise any form of civil conscription. This submission, if accepted, would mean that medical practitioners could be compelled in the course of their practice to perform all sorts of medical duties as, for instance, to give certificates, keep records, and give information, confidential or otherwise, about the health of their patients provided the certificates, etc were reasonably incidental to the execution of a law with respect to the provision of any of the allowances or benefits specified in the paragraph. In my opinion, such a submission unduly narrows the effect of the wide words 'any form of' in the expression in parenthesis . . .

Webb J:

The two most important questions that arise are as to (1) the meaning of para (xxiiiA) of s 51 of the Commonwealth Constitution; and (2) the validity of s 7A of the Pharmaceutical Benefits Act 1947–49 . . .

As to (1): in my opinion, para (xxiiiA) does not empower the Commonwealth Parliament to do more than legislate for the provision by the Commonwealth itself of the allowances, pensions, endowment, benefits and services to which it refers, and the provision may be of money, goods or services, even in the case of 'benefits'; but, as regards medical and dental services at least, it does not authorise any form of civil conscription. As the paragraph is punctuated the words in brackets excluding civil conscription qualify only 'services' and not 'benefits'. However, the Chief Justice gives strong reasons why the punctuation should be disregarded and the words in brackets held to qualify 'benefits'; but I find it unnecessary to decide, and so I do not decide, that they do so. So far as medical services are incidental to the provision of pharmaceutical benefits, there is no power to conscript such services, as the incidental power to legislate under para (xxxix) of s 51 cannot be held to exceed the express power given by para (xxiiiA). The Constitution states that medical and dental services shall not be conscripted, and that is conclusive for all purposes . . .

Then as to the meaning of the words in brackets, it was not submitted that civil conscription meant the enlistment of persons for full-time service. During World War I, 'conscription' was employed to designate compulsory military service anywhere, including service overseas; but during World War II, it was used in Commonwealth legislation to describe any compulsory service in the armed forces or in industry. As to 'civil conscription', I cannot remember hearing or seeing the term used until I saw it in the proposed law in the terms of para (xxiiiA) passed by Parliament and subsequently submitted to the electors under s 128 of the Commonwealth Constitution. I think the electors would have taken the proposed law to emphasise, in the use of the words 'any form', that legislation for the provision of benefit or services of the kind referred to could not authorise compulsory service of any kind, at least in the provision of medical or dental services, either independently or as incidental to pharmaceutical or other benefits, and that compulsion, to any extent or of any nature, whether legal by the imposition of penalties, or practical, by any other means, direct or indirect, could not be authorised. To require a person to do something which he may lawfully decline to do but only at the sacrifice of the whole or a substantial part of the means of his livelihood would, I think, be to subject him to practical compulsion amounting to conscription in the case of services required by Parliament to be rendered to the people. If Parliament cannot lawfully do this directly by legal means, it cannot lawfully do it indirectly by creating a situation, as distinct from merely taking advantage of one, in which the individual is left no real choice but compliance.

As to (2), the validity of s 7A: in the Pharmaceutical Benefits Act as enacted after the para (xxiiiA) became part of the Constitution and before July 1949, there was no compulsion of any kind in respect of medical or dental services; but in July 1949, after the doctors had declined to use the Commonwealth form in writing their prescriptions, and so prevented their patients from obtaining the pharmaceutical benefits, the Act was amended to require, in a new s 7A, that a doctor should use the Commonwealth form if he prescribed anything in the Commonwealth Pharmaceutical Formulary or the addendum thereto, unless the patient requested otherwise. The penalty for non-compliance was fixed at 50 pounds. In this way, it was sought to compel the doctors to do something which they were not prepared to do voluntarily. But the learned Attorney General submitted that a doctor, in putting the prescription on the Commonwealth form instead of on his own paper, would not be performing a medical service; that the medical service would be complete when the doctor made up his mind what to prescribe; and that s 7A operated on him only as from the time when he proceeded to write the prescription. However, I think that 'medical service' in para (xxiiiA) is not limited to the exercise of the professional skill required to arrive at a conclusion as to what should be prescribed, but extends to the writing of the prescription, whether on the doctor's paper or on the Commonwealth form. Ordinarily, the writing of a prescription is a medical service. Taking the allegations in the statement of claim to be true for the purposes of this demurrer, the position appears to be that, as every person residing in Australia who is not a patient occupying a bed in a public hospital is entitled to the benefits provided by the Act, and the great majority of the people of Australia are likely to want these benefits, the doctors must treat them or lose a considerable part of their practice, if not the whole of it; but if a doctor treats patients to retain his practice, then s 7A requires him to sign the Commonwealth form and renders him liable to a penalty of 50 pounds if he fails to do so. This, in my opinion, imposes on doctors a compulsory medical service and is a form of civil conscription within the meaning of para (xxiiiA). It may well appear that at present the doctor is compelled to do very little in being required to use the Commonwealth form, but, if it is conceded that he may be compelled to do this on the ground that it is not the performance of a medical service but merely a method of rendering it, he may also be compelled to do many other things on the same ground, such as attending at certain places during certain hours to write prescriptions for the convenience of patients not confined to their homes. It is for Parliament to stipulate the conditions attaching to its grant of benefits, but not by compelling the doctors, under penalty as for an offence, to sign the required forms or be deprived of practice; otherwise by fines or deprivation of practice the doctors could be controlled to any extent as to their movements and time. Of course, patients may be forced by the attitude of the doctors to request that the Commonwealth form be not used; but the compulsion on the doctors remains, although for the time being it is countered by a measure which, however undesirable it may appear, is not unlawful.

To reiterate: if s 7A had not been enacted, a patient requesting a doctor to write a prescription on the Commonwealth form, which involves consulting and consideration of the Commonwealth Pharmaceutical Formulary or its addendum or both, would request a service which only a doctor can render, and which therefore is properly described as a medical service. But when this service is made compulsory by a fine, or loss of practice to avoid the fine, in the case of any patient, with few exceptions, who does not request that the Commonwealth form be not used, then, having regard not only to the extent of the professional work involved but to the almost unlimited number of persons entitled to insist on the service at any time, it becomes, I think, not merely a compulsory service but a form of civil conscription within any meaning that can be given to that expression which, if not quite clear, was certainly intended to be comprehensive. It is civil conscription of doctors as doctors. When Parliament comes between patient and doctor and makes the lawful continuance of their relationship as such depend upon a condition, enforceable by fine, that the doctor shall render the patient a special service, unless that service is waived by the patient, it creates a situation that amounts to a form of civil conscription. This civil conscription can be avoided, without any breach of the law, to the extent that the doctor vacates the field of medicine, which, however, would involve in many, if not most cases, a considerable loss of practice and of income. But it is still civil conscription. Military conscription would not cease to be such

> because those liable to it might avoid it by a change of occupation. To amount to civil conscription, it is not necessary that the service be a full-time service, or be rendered as a member of a corps created for the purpose.

Does the requirement that a doctor use a particular form, if her patient wishes to claim a benefit, really amount to a type of civil conscription? Would the fact that a university student was required to fill in a form in order to claim AUSTUDY amount to the university staff member who supplied the form being conscripted by the Commonwealth?

The question of the scope of s 51(xxiiiA) was again considered by the High Court in *General Practitioners Society of Australia v Commonwealth* (1980) 145 CLR 532. That case concerned certain provisions of The Health Insurance Act 1973 inserted by The Health Insurance Amendment Act 1977. These sections placed conditions on the entitlement of a medical practitioner to claim benefits in respect of pathology services performed. The General Practitioners Society objected to such provisions on the ground that they amounted to a form of civil conscription.

General Practitioners Society of Australia v Commonwealth (1980) 145 CLR 532

> **Gibbs J:**
>
> The argument that the sections and regulations now challenged, considered together with the undertaking and code of conduct, impose a form of civil conscription upon medical practitioners, was advanced in two ways. First, it was said that the laws positively require a practitioner to perform services of a medical kind. Secondly, it was said that the laws, by prohibiting practitioners from carrying on practice in what was formerly the normal way, compel them to carry out practice in a different way. It had to be conceded that the challenged provisions have no application to a medical practitioner who is prepared to render pathology services for which no benefit will be payable. No one is under any legal compulsion to seek to become an approved pathology practitioner or to give the undertaking which is required of a person who wishes to become an approved pathology practitioner. However, it was argued for the plaintiffs that few practitioners would be able to attract patients, or to make a living from their profession, if medical benefits were not payable in respect of their services . . .
>
> The question whether a law imposes civil conscription cannot be answered in the negative simply because the law does not create any legal liability to perform any medical or dental service; the effect of the law in the economic and other circumstances must be considered, and practical compulsion is enough . . . In my opinion, the circumstance that no medical practitioner is legally obliged to become an approved pathology practitioner is not decisive of the question whether the provisions in question impose a form of civil conscription within s 51(xxiiiA) . . .

The word 'conscription', in the sense that seems to be most apposite for present purposes, means the compulsory enlistment of men (or women) for military service. [His Honour then summarised the findings of the High Court in *BMA v Commonwealth*.]

With the greatest respect, I am unable to agree with those observations by Latham CJ and Williams and Webb JJ as to the meaning and effect of the expression 'any form of civil conscription'. That expression, used in its natural meaning, and applied, as the context of p 1 (xxiiiA) requires, to medical and dental services, refers to any sort of compulsion to engage in practice as a doctor or a dentist or to perform particular medical or dental services. However, in its natural meaning it does not refer to compulsion to do, in a particular way, some act in the course of carrying on practice or performing a service, when there is no compulsion to carry on the practice or perform the service. It would be an abuse of language to say that a soldier who has voluntarily enlisted in the army becomes a conscript because he is obliged to obey orders as to the manner in which he performs his military duties. Similarly, it could not properly be said that it would be a form of civil conscription to require a person who had voluntarily engaged in civilian employment to perform the duties of that employment in accordance with the instructions given to him by his employers. For example, a clerk who was instructed to write out orders for goods or services only on a specified form could not be said to be thereby subjected to a form of civil conscription. There is nothing in the Constitution that would indicate that the expression 'any form of civil conscription' where it appears in s 51(xxiiiA) should be given an enlarged meaning which its words do not naturally bear. The words 'any form of' do not, in my opinion, extend the meaning of 'conscription', and that word connotes compulsion to serve rather than regulation of the manner in which a service is performed. Of course, no express power is conferred on the Parliament to make laws to regulate the manner of performance of medical or dental services, but it appears clearly necessary to the effective exercise of the power conferred by s 51(xxiiiA) that the Parliament should be able to make laws as to the way in which medical and dental services provided by the Commonwealth under the authority of that paragraph are performed, and laws annexing conditions to the entitlement to any of the benefits provided under that authority even if those conditions may have the result that a medical or dental service must be rendered in a particular way if the benefit is to be obtained. I find it impossible to discern in the words in parenthesis in p 1 (xxiiiA) any intention to prevent the Parliament from making laws of that kind, provided that no compulsion to serve is imposed. I respectfully agree with the opinion expressed by Dixon J in *British Medical Association v Commonwealth*, at p 278, that 'a wide distinction exists between on the one hand a regulation of the manner in which an incident of medical practice is carried out, if and when it is done, and on the other hand the compulsion to serve medically or to render medical services', the latter is within the prohibition but the former is not. If the incident of practice which is regulated is not medical or dental, but financial and administrative, it is clearly outside the prohibition.

Latham CJ and Webb J were influenced in reaching this conclusion by the opinion that if the bracketed words of p l (xxiiiA) did not have the effect which they attributed to them, the Parliament would be able to legislate so as to bring about a complete control of medical and dental practices: see at pp 251, 294. Williams J (at p 290) expressed a similar opinion, although the examples he gave suggest that he thought that the sort of control which might be exerted would be rather more limited. No doubt their Honours had in mind the principle of interpretation under which a statutory provision, if ambiguous, may be construed so as to avoid inconvenience and injustice. However, it would seem to me impermissible to give to the words of a constitutional prohibition a meaning wider than that which they naturally convey out of an apprehension that the legislative powers, if not heavily fettered, might be used to effect a wide control of professional activities. In any case, it does not in my opinion necessarily follow, as Latham CJ and Webb J feared, that if the construction which those Justices adopted is rejected, it would be possible for the Parliament, without infringing the prohibition of civil conscription, to provide that a doctor or dentist should carry on his practice at a particular place, or at a particular time, or only for a particular class of patients. In some circumstances, at least, provisions having that result might well be regarded as imposing a form of civil conscription. It is necessary in every case to consider the true meaning and effect of the challenged provisions, in order to determine whether they do compel doctors or dentists to perform services generally as such, or to perform particular medical or dental services; if so, they will be invalid . . .

The provisions in question in these proceedings do compel medical practitioners to perform certain duties in the course of carrying out their medical practices, but they do not go beyond regulating the manner in which some of the incidents of those practices are carried out, and they do not compel any medical practitioner to perform any medical services. Most of the duties imposed relate only to things done incidentally in the course of practice, rather than to a medical service itself. The only possible exception is s 16A(1), which requires that a request by a medical practitioner to an approved pathology practitioner to render a pathology service shall be made or confirmed in writing as prescribed. A request of that kind may be regarded as a medical service. However, s 16A(1) does not compel any medical practitioner to make such a request. What it requires is that the request, if made, be made or confirmed by a written instrument which satisfies Regulation 5. There is nothing in that regulation which affects in the slightest the performance by a medical practitioner of his medical duties and functions. The statutory requirements may impose on him more administrative work. In particular, he is required to specify, in his own handwriting, the services to which the instrument relates, and cannot simply mark a form on

> which is printed a list of possible services. The reason why a condition of this kind is attached to the entitlement to medical benefits is no doubt that the use of the printed form might reasonably be regarded as likely to contribute to laxity and to facilitate fraud. However that may be, to require a practitioner to write out particulars of the service which he has decided to request another practitioner to perform is not to compel the practitioner making the request to perform a medical service. Even more clearly, the requirements of s 16A(2) with regard to accounts and receipts, and those of s 16A(3) with regard to the retention and production of any written request or confirmation, do not compel any medical practitioner to perform any medical service. Clause 3(b) of the undertaking, which obliges a practitioner to exercise some supervision over his servants and agents, and which requires a medical practitioner to furnish such information as is reasonably requested with regard to the requesting or rendering of pathology in respect of which medical benefits are payable, are also no more than a regulation of the incidents of medical practice and do not compel a medical practitioner to perform any medical service.
>
> For these reasons, none of the provisions in question imposes any form of conscription contrary to s 51(xxiiiA) of the Constitution.

The question of whether legislation regulating nursing homes infringes section 51(xxiiiA) of the Constitution was considered by the High Court in *Alexandra Private Geriatric Hospital Pty Ltd* v *The Commonwealth* (1987) 162 CLR 271

Considering the above cases, consider which, if any, of the following proposals would be constitutionally permitted:

A. The Federal Government introduces a scheme requiring newly admitted doctors, before they may be eligible to be assigned a Medicare provider number, to:

(a) Undertake two years military service as a doctor.
(b) Undertake two years service in remote or rural Australia.
(c) Provide 24 hour coverage for patients registered with their surgery, such that one doctor in the practice must be 'on call' at all times.

Over what health matters, then, does the Commonwealth legislate?

The Commonwealth's legislation with respect to Quarantine has already been mentioned. Similarly, the Commonwealth has legislated in the Customs Act with respect to the importation of various substances (including drugs). The two most important pieces of Commonwealth legislation in the health care field are The National Health Act 1953 and the Health Insurance Act 1973. These pieces of legislation are extremely complex and constantly changing. The effect of the two Acts is discussed in the extract below.

***Australian Health and Medical Law Reporter*, CCH, Sydney, para 3–120**

> The National Health Act, in addition to allowing for the provision of a wide range of health services, provides conditions for receipt of benefits for health care in nursing homes, regulates the establishment and business of organisations providing medical and hospital benefits [private health insurance] and provides for and regulates the payment of benefits for pharmaceuticals prescribed by medical practitioners. [There are sections which] set up committees to enquire into the payment of benefits and, consequently, into professional conduct of medical practitioners.
>
> The Health Insurance Act provides for the payment of medical and hospital benefits. Those benefits are payments for, or repayments of, costs of medical or hospital services, most of which have been provided by, or at the direction of, a medical practitioner [The Medicare Scheme]. [There are sections which are] designed to monitor these uses of public money by establishing committees. Their function is to enquire, where necessary, into payment of benefits and, consequently, into the professional conduct of medical practitioners.

Medicare

Pursuant to ss 51(xxiiiA) and 96 of the Constitution, the Commonwealth introduced in 1984 a universal scheme of health insurance referred to as Medicare. This scheme was the successor to the earlier Medibank program. Funding for Medicare and other health care projects is negotiated between the Commonwealth and the States under the States (Tax Sharing and Health Grants) Act 1981 (Cth). Agreements between the Commonwealth and the States are incorporated in the Health Insurance Act 1973 (in Schedule 2).

Each eligible person (which, under s 3 of the Health Insurance Act 1973 basically means Australian resident or resident of a country with which Australia has reciprocal agreements) may claim against Medicare the cost of 85% of the 'scheduled fee' of a service provided outside of hospital, or 75% of a service provided in hospital. Each service is assigned a benefit number by a schedule to the Health Insurance Act 1973. This benefit number is quoted on the relevant claim form.

The following services are currently included in Medicare: medical services (general practitioner and specialist consultations); hospital services (including surgical, psychiatric, obstetric and anaesthetic services); pathology services; optometry services; radiology services; and 'day surgery' services. Benefits are not payable by virtue of the Health Insurance Act 1973 in the following circumstances:

> Where the patient is being examined for the purposes of assessing his eligibility to join an insurance scheme, superannuation scheme or a friendly society;
>
> Where the patient has an entitlement to compensation or damages from another source;

Where payment has already been made to a hospital for provision of the service and the patient therefore incurred no expense;

Where the patient is vaccinated as part of a mass immunisation program;

Where medical expenses were paid by another;

Where the patient was being screened for a disease (except as otherwise provided).

The impact of the Medicare scheme on the utilisation of medical services should not be underestimated. The CCH *Australian Health and Medical Law Reporter* (at para 60–210) notes:

> In 1989/90, the average number of services processed by Medicare was 8.301 per person Australia-wide . . . Hospital admissions in Australia are amongst the highest in the OECD. In 1987, there were 216 hospital admissions per 1,000 population. Australians have high expectations of the quality and availability of care and treatment without considering the cost of hospitalisation. In countries like the United States, where hospital services are paid for privately, hospital admissions are 50% lower than in Australia.

The scheme itself is partly funded through a Medicare levy imposed on taxpayers. Those individuals who earn only a small amount of money pay no levy. Again, the impact of the scheme on Australia's finances should not be underestimated. The CCH *Australian Health and Medical Law Reporter* (at para 60–150) notes:

> The total expenditure on Medicare for 1993/1994 was $10.2 billion, comprising $4.44 billion for hospitals and $5.77 billion for medical services. The amount of money spent on Medicare has risen steadily since the scheme's inception. An increased demand for services cannot be held solely responsible for increased costs. Contributing factors to increased expenditure have been an expanding population rate, the use of high-technology diagnostic techniques and the inclusion of new items in the medical benefits scheme which did not formerly attract a benefit. Annual adjustments to rebates for professional services to compensate for increases in medical practice costs has been the single most important factor contributing to the growth in Medicare outlays.

Services provided to a patient in a public hospital are, by virtue of the Australian Health Care Agreements, in some circumstances, free.

On 5 January 2006, following a perceived 'health crisis' in the State of Queensland, that State announced plans to consider co-payments for the provision of formerly free medical services, or to impose means tests on the provision of formerly free public health services. Consideration of such approach was recommended by the Forster I Queensland Health Systems Review.

That review recommended consideration of:

- making the level of indexation to existing fees and charges more comparable to other states and territories, and better reflecting the soaring costs of medical equipment and facilities;
- means testing or co-payments for the Spectacle Subsidy Scheme;
- means testing or co-payments for adults accessing dental health services with an annual cap per person;
- means testing or co-payments for non-urgent surgery;
- means testing or co-payments for specialist outpatient services for non-concession card holders;
- means testing or co-payments for the secondary safety net for pharmaceuticals.

If such changes are introduced, they herald the 'beginning of the end' of free public health services in Australian hospitals.

Private health insurance

The Federal Government also regulates, through the Health Insurance Act 1973, companies which provide private health insurance. The primary restriction on such companies is that the premium charged to subscribers is uniform, ie, the premium an individual pays does not depend on the age, health or other factors of the individual. Coverage typically includes those treatments which Medicare does not cover (such as dentistry or physiotherapy services) or allows an individual his choice of specialist or private hospital. Until recently, restrictions on health insurance companies were quite strict. Companies had to have a separate registered office in each State in which they offered coverage, and no company could offer 'gap insurance' to pay for the difference between the Medicare rebate (a proportion of the scheduled fee) and the full fee charged by the doctor.

Amendments in 1995 outlined below significantly alter this position.

Devereux, JA, 'New health insurance legislation' (1995) 3 No 1 Journal of Law and Medicine, pp 11–13

The level of Australians' participation in private health insurance and the extent of its coverage has been a source of concern to the federal government since 1993. Although 59% of Australians had private health insurance in February 1984 (prior to the introduction of the Medicare scheme), by December 1993 this figure had dropped to 38.4%: Australian Institute of Health and Welfare, 4th Biennial Report (1994), p 136. Figures released by the federal government on 19 May 1995 indicate that only 35.6% of Australians had private health coverage as of March 1995 – a drop of 2% over a 12-month period. Of as much significance as the fall in the participation rates has been the increase in the drop-out rate of young people. In 1992–1993, the number of people 65 years or older with private health insurance increased by 12,000 whereas the number of people 64 years old or less decreased by 208,000: Private Health Insurance Administration Council, Annual Report (1993). These two factors have led to a 'vicious circle': healthy young people drop out of health insurance; health insurance premiums continue to rise as the proportion of aged people in the health insurance schemes rises (aged people are more likely to need health care); more young people drop out of health insurance schemes as a result of rising premiums; premiums rise again: P Mackey, 'Medicare, Private Health Insurance and Proposals for Change', Department of the Parliamentary Library (1994).

The first response to the perceived crisis in private health insurance was the Richardson Discussion Paper of December 1993. The discussion paper claimed that the major causes of falling participation rates were rising premiums and out-of-pocket expenses. It proposed dual changes. The first was the reform of the private health insurance industry so as to permit the insurance organisations to lower premiums. This was to be done by allowing schemes to operate on a national basis, reducing administrative inefficiencies; establishing processes by which holders of private health insurance could seek redress through an independent body; and increasing the powers of the Private Health Insurance Advisory Council. The second was the reform of payment options to ensure some measure of cost control by encouraging negotiation between health insurance schemes, hospitals and doctors to eliminate out-of-pocket expenses.

Cabinet referred the proposals outlined above to a Caucus-ACTU working group which reported in June 1994. The working group was critical of the Richardson proposals. Notwithstanding the working group report, the Federal Government (with new Health Minister, Carmen Lawrence) has proceeded to implement the reforms recommended by the Richardson Report, albeit in a modified form.

The Act, the Health Insurance (Private Health Insurance Reform) Amendment Act 1994 (Cth), which passed through the Senate on 11 May 1995, amends the National Health Act 1953 (Cth), the Health Insurance Act 1973 (Cth) and the Health Insurance Commission Act 1973 (Cth). The amendments to the last Act remove the necessity that health insurance funds conduct a separate fund in each State. The move to larger funds should result in administrative efficiencies and increased bargaining power which should relieve pressure on premiums. Amendments to the National Health Act will allow health insurance organisations to enter into agreements with hospitals and day-care facilities, and hospitals to enter into agreements with medical practitioners, in respect of payments for care provided. The Health Minister noted that the aims of requiring agreements are threefold:

(i) to generate competition between health insurance organisations and hospitals, resulting in improved efficiency;
(ii) to link hospital funding to appropriate quality assurance and accreditation procedures; and
(iii) to reduce restrictions on products offered, thereby allowing health organisations to operate according to market demand for different products.

The Caucus-ACTU working group sounded a note of caution in respect of such an idea. They argued that insurance organisations, hospitals and medical practitioners would be unwilling and unable to negotiate such agreements effectively and without dispute. On 30 April 1995, 220 specialists in Sydney voted to boycott entering into any such agreements, giving some credence to the concerns raised by the Caucus-ACTU working group. It is also interesting to note that the Opposition was successful in moving an amendment to the Act to provide that nothing in the Act was meant to derogate from the right of a 'natural person' to enter into an agreement for themselves (or those who are dependent upon them) directly with a medical practitioner.

Importantly, the Health Insurance Amendment Act 1995 (Cth) introduces a case-payment system to the private sector called episodic casemix payments. Casemix is a system developed over 20 years ago in the United States where it is used to regulate public funding of health care for the poor (Medicaid) and the elderly (Medicare). The casemix of any particular hospital is the mix of categories of patients and cases which the hospital treats. Diagnosis-related groups classify illnesses and weights are calculated for each diagnosis-related group. Under casemix, funding is provided to the hospital on the basis of the mix of cases which it treats. (See generally Parliamentary Research Service Bill (No 14 of 1995).)

The casemix system has been the source of some criticism. Some commentators argue that no diagnosis-related group can adequately indicate the severity of illness. Critics have also claimed that diagnosis-related groups do not properly reflect some clinical situations, for example, post acute care, psychiatric care, rehabilitation: M Draper, 'The Casemix maze' (1992) 23 Health Forum 16. Diagnosis-related groups are also thought to be insensitive to the special funding needs of small or rural hospitals or hospitals engaged in teaching or research: B Nelson, 'Casemix – an AMA perspective' (1994) 161 Medical Journal of Australia, Supplement 4. It has also been suggested that under a casemix system, hospitals have a greater financial incentive to accelerate patients through hospital, which might result in some patients not being properly treated: Parliamentary Research Service Bill (No 14 of 1995), p 5. The Caucus-ACTU working group was particularly critical of the use of casemix as the basis for payments of individual episodes of hospital treatment. It saw casemix as being more a system for comparison between hospitals rather than a measure of individual care.

Amendments to the Health Insurance Act 1973 (Cth) made by the Health Insurance Amendment Act will facilitate the assignment of the Medicare rebate direct to private health insurance organisations who enter into agreements with hospitals.

By virtue of the Health Insurance Amendment Act 1995 (Cth), health insurance organisations will be permitted to offer cover eliminating the gap between scheduled fee and Medicare rebate (so-called 'gap insurance').

The Act also provides for the establishment of an independent Private Health Insurance Complaints Commissioner who will have investigatory, recommendatory and conciliatory powers to resolve complaints about private health insurance. Costs which may be incurred by the Complaints Commissioner are to be offset by a levy to be imposed on health insurance companies by the Private Health Insurance Complaints Levy Act 1995 (Cth). Of some concern here, though, is the fact that information about patients may now be provided to health insurance organisations by a hospital and that s 73G of the National Health Act 1953 (Cth) will be amended by the Act such that no action for breach of confidence will lie provided that such disclosure of information is reasonably necessary in deciding whether or not to make a payment or 'any other matter relating to the operation of an applicable benefits arrangement'. The latter seems an unduly wide imposition on a keystone of medical care – confidentiality. Similar provision is made in the Act for disclosure of patient information (admittedly in a 'patient de-identified state') to a data bureau to be established by statute no later than 1 January 1996. The role of such a bureau is to be defined by statute 'after appropriate consultations with registered organisations, hospitals and medical practitioners'.

Amendments to the Health Insurance Amendment Act 1995 (Cth) agreed to by the Government require a Private Health Insurance Administration Council to distribute copies of a Private Patient Hospital Charter to insurance organisations and the public. The Charter is designed to inform patients what they may legitimately expect from health insurance organisations, hospitals and medical practitioners. The Act further provides for the Health Minister to make a statement in the Gazette about the Charter and for the Private Health Insurance Complaints Commission and health insurance organisations to make copies of the Charter available at all their offices. An aggregate Advisory Billing Division has also been established by the Act, to advise the Health Minister by 1 January 1997 as to the most appropriate method of instituting aggregate billing so as to include all hospital services and related services. The Australian Democrats indicated on 21 March 1995 that they would support passage of the Health Insurance Amendment Act in the Senate. The Democrats co-sponsored with the Government a number of amendments to the Act. These amendments include provisions that insurance organisations cannot refuse to enter into a hospital-provider agreement solely by reason of the number of beds in the hospital, the range of hospital services provided or the ownership of the hospital. Under the Act, all health care insurance policies must insure patients against the costs of psychiatric care, rehabilitation and palliative care.

It is hard to assess the outcome of the Government's reforms. The Australian Medical Association has estimated that the combined costs of Casemix, the development of contracts and covering gap insurance, far from reducing the cost of premiums, are likely to cause premiums to rise by 11.5%. The AMA is also concerned that the reforms will allow insurance companies to interfere with hospital treatment and shorten hospital stays. Comparisons are already being drawn with the United States health management organisations (HMO). In the United States, people who are members of a HMO may only be treated (and have their costs covered) by doctors who have agreements with the HMO. The HMO is able to regulate the brand of prescription drugs provided to patients (in some instances, for example, opting for cheaper drugs). Medibank Private, probably the first health insurance organisation to take advantage of the Government's reforms, has negotiated agreements with hospitals. Interestingly though, those members of Medibank Private who choose to have medical treatment with a hospital with which Medibank Private does not have an agreement are not left 'out in the cold'. Patients are still free to choose another hospital but, if they do so, their benefits will be determined by a table of benefits. It remains to be seen whether other health funds are as flexible.

Presumably the Trade Practices Act 1974 (Cth) is supposed to prevent any uncompetitive practices from developing among providers of health care or insurers. It might have been better to place such limitations explicitly in the relevant health legislation. The Caucus-ACTU working group suggested that the whole idea of private health insurance reforms would cause 'a great deal of upheaval for dubious returns'. Its preferred option was to strengthen Medicare's ability to meet the present and future health demands of Australians. The Government's announcement in the 1995 budget that it would increase the Medicare levy may, according to the Opposition, put further pressure on people to abandon private health insurance.

State regulation of health care

As is suggested by the above analysis of Commonwealth regulatory powers in respect of health care, the balance of powers repose in the State Governments in Australia. Under s 96 of the Commonwealth Constitution, the Federal Government is empowered to make grants to the States 'on such terms as it sees fit'. In practice, since the Federal Government collects all income tax in Australia, this gives the Federal Government enormous leverage power in determining the scope of health care. This can be done, for example, by the Federal Government funding the provision of hospitals in the States in return for certain undertakings by the States (eg, the Medicare agreements).

Australian States have regulated, by means of legislation, various aspects of health including public health, professional registration requirements, access to patient records and patient complaint mechanisms. Some of these statutes will be explored in subsequent chapters. For a detailed discussion of the registration requirements of the various health care professions in Australia, see *Australian Health and Medical Law Reporter*, paras 3–040 to 7–230.

2

CONSENT TO TREATMENT I – BATTERY

In Chapter 1, we saw that the Commonwealth and States share the responsibility for the regulation of health care. While Commonwealth and State statutes may control the amount or type of service offered, or who it is offered by, they do not alter the fundamental nature of the relationship between medical practitioner and patient.

In this chapter and the next, the legal responsibilities which arise out of the relationship between medical practitioner and patient will be explored. Three responsibilities will be emphasised as being particularly relevant. These are:

1 the relationship between medical practitioner and patient which may give rise to an action for breach of contract;
2 the relationship between medical practitioner and patient which may give rise to an action for battery; and
3 the relationship between medical practitioner and patient which may give rise to an action in negligence.

This chapter will explore the first two responsibilities, while the third will be canvassed in the next chapter.

PART I: CONTRACT

When a patient presents with a problem, and the medical practitioner agrees to diagnose the illness and treat the problem, a contract for services is created between the parties. The three formalities required of a contract are agreement, consideration and an intention to be legally bound. A patient's request for treatment may be regarded as an offer. Acceptance is signified by the medical practitioner's acceptance of caring for the patient. Consideration may be the promise of payment for services (Picard, EI, *Legal Liabilities of Doctors and Patients in Canada*, 2nd edn, 1984, p 20, Toronto: Carswell).

It has been noted that this contract arises even in the absence of any express agreement as to treatment, fee or duration of attendance (Thomson, BJ, 'Claims arising out of the relationship between doctor and patient', in *Special Lectures of the Law Society of Canada*, 1963, p 185, Toronto; Meredith, CJ, *Malpractice Liability of Doctors and Hospitals*, 1956, p (i), Toronto: Carswell). In one English case, *Sidaway v Board of Governors of Bethlem Royal Hospital* [1985] AC 871 at 904, Lord Templeman noted:

> The relationship between doctor and patient is contractual in origin, the doctor performing services in consideration for fees payable by the patient.

What then of the patient who is unable to offer the consideration of fees? Older cases suggest that, where the patient has no money to offer to pay to the medical practitioner, consideration is provided by the patient's submission to treatment (*Coggs v Bernard* (1703) 92 ER 107; *Banbury v Bank of Montreal* [1918] AC 626).

Whichever view of consideration is adopted, it is clear that Medicare has not altered the contractual nature of medical services in Australia.

What is the scope of such a contract between medical practitioner and patient? This question may be analysed in two parts. Firstly, express terms. Secondly, implied terms.

Express terms

Kennedy, I and Grubb, A, *Medical Law: Cases and Materials*, 3rd edn, 2000, London: Butterworths

> This is entirely a matter of what the parties agree amongst themselves, for example, as to payment or who may carry out a particular procedure. A consent form is an example of an agreement containing express terms.
>
> There are, of course, limits to what the parties may purport to agree through express terms. They cannot, for example, agree to do that which would be regarded as contrary to public policy, for example, selling an organ nor to waive those obligations implied by law.

Implied terms

Most actions in which a patient sues for breach of contract arise in circumstances where the patient alleges that the medical practitioner has breached a term of the contract which was implied into the contract by virtue of the operation of law.

Will the law imply a term of the contract, that the medical practitioner will effect a cure of the patient's condition?

Eyre v Measday [1986] 1 All ER 488 *per* Slade LJ, pp 488, 492–494

A woman consulted a gynaecologist to arrange a sterilisation operation. The gynaecologist stressed to the woman and her husband that such an operation was irreversible. At no time did he warn the woman of the 1% risk of the operation proving unsuccessful, exposing the woman to the risk of having more children. The woman underwent the operation. After resuming sexual relations with her husband, the woman conceived a child. A healthy child was subsequently born. The woman sued, alleging breach of a contractual term (the term being a promise to render the woman sterile). The trial judge dismissed the woman's claim, whereupon she appealed to the Court of Appeal.

The outstanding issues raised by the proceedings and by this appeal seem to me to resolve themselves essentially to two: (1) Was the nature of the contract between the plaintiff and the defendant one by which the defendant contracted to render the plaintiff 100% sterile? (2) If it was not, did the contract contain a warranty by the defendant, express or implied, to the effect that the operation which he was to perform on her would have this effect? . . .

It is, I think, common ground that the relevant contract between the parties in the present case was embodied as to part in the oral conversations which took place between the plaintiff and her husband and the defendant at the defendant's consulting rooms, and as to the other part in the written form of consent signed by the plaintiff, which referred to the explanation of the operation which had been given in that conversation. It is also common ground, I think, that in order to ascertain what was the nature and what were the terms of the contract, this court has to apply an objective rather than a subjective test. The test thus does not depend on what either the plaintiff or the defendant thought were the terms of the contract in her or his own mind. It depends on what the court objectively considers that the words used by the respective parties must be reasonably taken to have meant. It would, therefore, be of no assistance to the defendant to say that he did not intend to enter into a contract which absolutely guaranteed the plaintiff's future sterility. It would likewise be of no assistance to the plaintiff to say that she firmly believed that she was being offered a contract of this nature.

I now turn to the first of the two principal issues which I have indicated. At the start of his argument for the plaintiff, counsel indicated that his primary ground of appeal would be that the effect of the contract between the plaintiff and the defendant was one by which the defendant contracted to render the plaintiff absolutely sterile . . . on the facts of this case, I, for my part, find this contention quite impossible to sustain. It seems to me quite clear from the evidence which we have as to the conversation which took place between the plaintiff and her husband and the defendant at the defendant's consulting rooms that he explained to them that the operation which he would propose to perform on the plaintiff was an operation by way of laparoscopic sterilisation and that that was the method he intended to adopt and no other. Equally, that was the nature of the operation to which the plaintiff herself agreed, as is shown by the form of consent which she signed. The contract was, to my mind, plainly a contract by the defendant to perform that particular operation.

The matter may be tested in this way. Suppose that when the plaintiff had been under anaesthetic the defendant had formed the view that an even more effective way of sterilising her would be to perform a hysterectomy and had carried out that operation, the plaintiff would, of course, have had the strongest grounds for complaint. She could have said:

I did not give you a general discretion to perform such operation as you saw fit for the purpose of sterilising me. I gave my consent to one particular form of operation. That was the operation I asked you to do and that was the operation you agreed to do.

In the end, as I understood him, counsel for the plaintiff did not feel able to press his argument on the first issue very strongly. The nature of the contract was, in my view, indubitably one to perform a laparoscopic sterilisation.

That, however, is by no means the end of the matter. The question still arises: did the defendant give either an express warranty or an implied warranty to the effect that the result of the operation when performed would be to leave the plaintiff absolutely sterile? In response to our inquiry, counsel for the plaintiff helpfully listed the two particular passages in the evidence on which he relied for the purpose of asserting that there was an express warranty. The first was a passage where, in the course of examination by her counsel, the plaintiff said:

> We went to the consulting rooms and we saw Mr Measday and we discussed sterilisation. He told us the method that he used for sterilising was the clip. He told us once I had had it done it was irreversible.

Counsel for the plaintiff also relied on a passage in which the plaintiff was asked in chief:

> Q: Did he show you a clip?
>
> A: He showed us a clip and he also showed us the diagram and told us where the clips would go on the tubes. He said once I had the operation done there was no turning back, I could not have it reversed.

Counsel for the plaintiff referred us to para 2 of the defence in the action which reads as follows:

> On the 30th October 1978 the plaintiff consulted the defendant about an operation of sterilisation. The defendant examined her and agreed to carry out the operation and advised her that it must be regarded as a permanent procedure. He did nor warn the plaintiff of the slight risk of failure, nor did he guarantee success.

There was thus a specific admission in the defence that the defendant advised the plaintiff that it must be 'regarded as a permanent procedure'.

In the light of these various representations or statements by the defendant, counsel for the plaintiff submitted that it was being expressly represented to the plaintiff that the effect of the operation would be to render her sterile absolutely and for ever. I, for my part, cannot accept that submission. There has been some discussion in the course of argument on the meaning of the phrase 'irreversible' and as to the relevance of the statement, undoubtedly made by the defendant to the plaintiff, that the proposed operation must be regarded as being irreversible.

However, I take the reference to irreversibility as simply meaning that the operative procedure in question is incapable of being reversed, that what is about to be done cannot be undone. I do not think it can reasonably be construed as a representation that the operation is bound to achieve its acknowledged object, which is a different matter altogether. For my part, I cannot spell out any such express warranty as is asserted from the particular passages in the evidence and in the pleadings relied on by counsel for the plaintiff to support it, or from any other parts of the evidence.

In the alternative, however, counsel for the plaintiff relies on an implied warranty. In this context he relies particularly on what, if I may say so, seems to me to have been a skilful piece of cross-examination by himself of the defendant and on the answers given by the defendant in the course of that cross-examination. It is very short and I think I should read it in full:

> Q: There is no doubt Mrs Eyre wanted to be sterilised; that is right, is it not?
> A: Yes.
> Q: She did not want there to be any question at all of her being pregnant again, that for her had come to an end?
> A: Yes.
> Q: Did you say anything at all at the consultation which might have left her with the impression that she was capable of becoming pregnant again?
> A: No, I think not.
> Q: Would it have been reasonable for her to have gone away from your consulting rooms thinking that she would be sterilised and that would be the end of the matter?
> A: Yes, it would.
> Q: And equally for Mr Eyre?
> A: Yes.
> Q: Indeed, your own defence in para 2 indicates that you advised her it must be regarded as a permanent procedure. Is that the effect of the advice which you gave her?
> A: Yes.
> Q: When you wrote to Doctor Dearing on 30 October and said, 'Everybody is very happy with it and realises it will be a permanent procedure,' that was your anticipation and reasonably hers?
> A: Yes.
> Q: The consent form, exhibit P3, indicates that the effect and nature of the operation had been explained to her, and the effect of the operation was to render her almost certainly sterile rather than sterile, was it not?
> A: Yes.
> Q: But in fact that particular effect was never explained to her?
> A: No, I think not.

The test to be applied by the court in considering whether a term can or cannot properly be implied in a contract is that embodied in what is frequently called the doctrine of *The Moorcock* (1889) 14 PD 64; [1886–90] All ER Rep 530. It is conveniently set out in 9 *Halsbury's Laws* (4th edn) para 355:

> A term can only be implied if it is necessary in the business sense to give efficacy to the contract; that is if it is such a term that it can confidently be said that if at the time the contract was being negotiated someone had said to the parties, 'What will happen in such a case?', they would both have replied, 'Of course, so and so will happen; we did not trouble to say that; it is too clear.'

Counsel for the plaintiff, in the light of the passage in cross-examination which I have just read and in the light of all the other background of the case to which I have referred, submitted that if someone had said to the parties, 'Is it intended that the defendant should warrant that the operation will render the plaintiff absolutely sterile?', the answer of both parties must have been, 'Yes.' This, he submitted, is really the only possible inference from what had been said on both sides in the defendant's consulting rooms. He particularly drew attention to the question that he had put to the defendant, 'Would it have been reasonable for her to have gone away from your consulting rooms thinking that she would be sterilised and that would be the end of the matter?', to which the defendant had replied, 'Yes, it would.' Counsel for the plaintiff submitted that the defendant himself was thus acknowledging that the reasonable inference would have been as he suggested.

Applying *The Moorcock* principles, I think there is no doubt that the plaintiff would have been entitled reasonably to assume that the defendant was warranting that the operation would be performed with reasonable care and skill. That, I think, would have been the inevitable inference to be drawn, from an objective standpoint, from the relevant discussion between the parties. The contract did, in my opinion, include an implied warranty of that nature. However, that inference on its own does not enable the plaintiff to succeed in the present case. She has to go further. She has to suggest, and it is suggested on her behalf, that the defendant, by necessary implication, committed himself to an unqualified guarantee as to the success of the particular operation proposed, in achieving its purpose of sterilising her, even though he were to exercise all due care and skill in performing it. The suggestion is that the guarantee went beyond due care and skill and extended to an unqualified warranty that the plaintiff would be absolutely sterile.

On the facts of the present case, I do not think that any intelligent lay bystander (let alone another medical man), on hearing the discussion which took place between the defendant and the other two parties, could have reasonably drawn the inference that the defendant was intending to give any warranty of this nature. It is true that in cross-examination he admitted that it would have been reasonable for the plaintiff to have gone away from his consulting rooms thinking that she would be sterilised. He did not, however, admit that it would have been reasonable for her to have left his consulting rooms thinking that he had given her a guarantee that after the operation she would be absolutely sterile; this, I think, is the really relevant point. She has to say that this would have been the reasonable inference from what he said to her and from what she and her husband said to him. But, in my opinion, in the absence of any express warranty, the court should be slow to imply against a medical man an unqualified warranty as to the results of an intended operation, for the very simple reason that, objectively speaking, it is most unlikely that a responsible medical man would intend to give a warranty of this nature. Of course, objectively speaking, it is likely that he would give a guarantee that he would do what he had undertaken to do with reasonable care and skill; but it is quite another matter to say that he has committed himself to the extent suggested in the present case.

For these reasons, which are much the same as those given by the judge, more succinctly, at the end of his judgment, I think that he reached the right conclusion . . .

[Purchas LJ delivered a judgment in which he agreed with the findings of Slade LJ. Cummin-Bruce LJ concurred.]

Thake and Another v Maurice [1986] 1 QB 644

The facts of this case were similar to those in *Eyre v Measday*, except that here, the sterilisation operation was performed on a man. No warning was given as to the possibility of the vas 're-canalising', meaning that the male would no longer be infertile. When the man's wife gave birth to a healthy child, the man and his wife sued for distress on discovering the pregnancy as well as for the costs of birth and maintenance of the child until the child reached adulthood. The wife sued for pain and discomfort associated with labour, and for loss of earnings. The action was based on breach of contract or breach of collateral warranty. At trial, judgment was entered for the man and his wife. The surgeon appealed.

The question then is whether the defendant contracted to carry out a vasectomy or to render Mr Thake permanently sterile. The latter alternative necessarily involved a guarantee; in other words, a warranty that there was not the remotest chance, not one in a thousand, that the operation would not succeed. Peter Pain J held, in my view correctly, that the contract was contained partly in the words used between the parties and partly in the words of the consent form. The object of the operation, as stated in the form, was to render Mr Thake sterile and incapable of parenthood. The contract contains an implied warranty that, in carrying out the operation, the defendant would exercise the ordinary skill and care of a competent surgeon. It did not contain an implied warranty that, come what may, the objective would be achieved: see *Greaves & Co (Contractors) Ltd v Baynham Meikle & Partners* [1975] 1 WLR 1095, at 1100 *per* Denning MR. The only question is whether it contained an express warranty to that effect. Would the words and visual demonstrations of the defendant have led a reasonable person standing in the position of the plaintiffs to understand that, come what may, Mr Thake was to be rendered sterile and incapable of parenthood?

The function of the court in ascertaining, objectively, the meaning of words used by contracting parties is one of everyday occurrence. But it is often exceedingly difficult to discharge it where the subjective understandings and intentions of the parties are clear and opposed. Here the plaintiffs understood that Mr Thake would be permanently sterile. The defendant himself recognised that they would have left with that impression. On the other hand, he did not intend, on the state of his knowledge he could not have intended, to guarantee that that would be the case. Both the understanding and the intention appear, as individuals, to have been entirely reasonable, but an objective interpretation must choose between them. In the end the question seems to be reduced to one of determining the extent of the knowledge which is to be attributed to the reasonable person standing in the position of the plaintiffs. Would he have known that the success of the operation was uncertain, either because it depended on healing of human tissue, or because in medical science all things or nearly all things, are uncertain. If he would, the defendant's words could only have been reasonably understood as forecasts of an almost certain, but nevertheless uncertain, outcome and his visual demonstrations as no more than explanations of how the operation would be done. He could not be taken to have given a guarantee of its success.

I do not suppose that a reasonable person standing in the position of the plaintiffs would have known that a vasectomy is an operation whose success depends on a healing of human tissue which cannot be guaranteed. To suppose that would be to credit him with omniscience beyond all reason. But it does seem to me to be reasonable to credit him with the more general knowledge that in medical science all things, or nearly all things, are uncertain. That knowledge is part of the general experience of mankind, and in my view it makes no difference whether what has to be considered is some form of medical or surgical treatment or the excision, apparently final, of a section of the vas. Doubtless the general experience of mankind will acknowledge the certainty that a limb, once amputated, has gone forever. Such has been the observation from time immemorial of a species to whom the spectacle of war and suffering is a commonplace. But where an operation is of a modern origin, its effects untried over several generations, would a reasonable person confronted even with the words and demonstrations of the defendant in this case, believe that there was not one chance in 10,000 that the object would not be achieved? I do not think that he would.

[In *Eyre v Measdale*, it was said at p 15 of the transcript:]

> But, in my opinion, in the absence of any express warranty, the court should be slow to imply against a medical man an unqualified warranty as to the results of an intended operation, for the very

> simple reason that, objectively speaking, it is most unlikely that a responsible medical man would intend to give a warranty of this nature. Of course, objectively speaking, it is likely that he would give a guarantee that he would do what he had undertaken to do with reasonable care and skill; but it is quite another matter to say that he has committed himself to the extent suggested in the present case.

The second is at p 16:

> I am afraid that, in my view, if they had wanted a guarantee of the nature which they now assert, they should have specifically asked for it.

The particular concern of this court in *Eyre v Measday* was to decide whether there had been an implied guarantee that the operation would succeed. But the approach of Slade LJ, in testing that question objectively, is of equal value in a case where it is said that there has been an express guarantee. Valuable too are the observations of Lord Denning MR in *Greaves & Co (Contractors) Ltd v Baynham Meikle & Partners* [1975] 1 WLR 1095, at 1100 which I now quote in full:

> Apply this to the employment of a professional man. The law does not usually imply a warranty that he will achieve the desired result, but only a term that he will use reasonable care and skill. The surgeon does not warrant that he will cure the patient. Nor does the solicitor warrant that he will win the case.

Lord Denning thought, and I respectfully agree with him, that a professional man is not usually regarded as warranting that he will achieve the desired result. Indeed, it seems that that would not fit well with the universal warranty of reasonable care and skill, which tends to affirm the inexactness of the science which is professed. I do not intend to go beyond the case of a doctor. Of all sciences medicine is one of the least exact. In my view, a doctor cannot be objectively regarded as guaranteeing the success of any operation or treatment unless he says as much in clear and unequivocal terms. The defendant did not do that in the present case.

For these reasons, I am of the opinion that the defendant did not contract to render Mr Thake permanently sterile.

[Neill LJ delivered a judgment agreeing with Nourse LJ. Kerr LJ dissented.]

PART II: BATTERY

It is a long established principle that the least touching of another, if unconsented to, gives rise to an action called battery (*Cole v Turner* (1704) 6 Mod 149 *per* Holt CJ). It was originally thought that hostility was an essential element of proving a battery. As most medical treatments are unlikely to be regarded as being hostile, this suggested that no battery action would lie in the case of a medical treatment in circumstances where no consent was given. This hostility element has now been dispensed with. Thus, in *In Re F* [1990] 2 AC 1, at 73, Lord Goff noted that:

> It has recently been said that the touching must be hostile – see *Wilson v Pringle*. I respectfully doubt whether this is correct. A prank that gets out of hand, an over-friendly slap on the back, surgical treatment by a surgeon who mistakenly thinks that the patient has consented to it – all these things may transcend the bounds of lawfulness without being characterised as hostile.

Note also the statement of Lord Donaldson MR in the same case:

> In the absence of consent all, or almost all, medical treatment and all surgical treatment of an adult is unlawful, however beneficial such treatment might be. This is incontestable (at 12).

Consent is thus a key issue in determining whether treatment amounts to battery or not. There are clear linkages between the importance of consent, and the bioethical principles explored in Chapter 1.

Jones, M, *Medical Negligence*, 1991, London: Sweet & Maxwell, p 200

> Consent to treatment is widely regarded as the cornerstone of the doctor-patient relationship. As a general rule, patients cannot be required to accept treatment that they do not want, no matter how painless, beneficial and risk-free the treatment may be and no matter how dire the consequences of refusal of treatment. This proposition is recognised as both an ethical principle and a legal rule, and is founded, ultimately, on the principle of respect for the patient's autonomy, or, expressed in more compelling terms, on the patient's right to 'self-determination'. Thus, the legal requirement for consent expresses respect for the patient's autonomy. In the famous words of Cardozo J:
>
>> Every human being of adult years and sound mind has a right to determine what shall be done with his own body; and a surgeon who performs an operation without his patient's consent commits an assault ... [*Schloendorff v Society of New York Hospital* (1914) 211 NY 125, at 126].

What are the elements of a valid consent?

Jones (above) identifies three elements of a valid consent:

1 Volition – the decision to consent must be a free one.
2 Information – the patient must have explained to him information about the procedure.
3 Capacity – the patient must possess sufficient age and intelligence.

Volition

It is clear that a patient's consent to treatment has to be freely given. Early cases adopted a cavalier approach to the concept of voluntariness. Thus, in *Latter v Braddell* (1881) 50 LJQB 448, a 'domestic servant' was thought by her employer to be pregnant. He forced the servant to undergo a pregnancy test. The court held that the medical examination did not amount to a battery.

More recent cases are, however, more guarded about such an approach.

Beausoleil v Sisters of Charity (1964) 53 DLR (2d) 65

Casey J:

A few weeks prior to August 24 1955, the appellant who was then 29 years old, unmarried and gainfully employed, consulted Dr Andre Cusson, orthopaedic surgeon attached to the Hospital du Sacre Coeur. She complained of backaches but was otherwise in good health. Dr Cusson came to the conclusion that a disc operation was indicated and the appellant was hospitalised.

Prior to the operation she discussed with Dr Cusson the type of anaesthetic that would be given. She stated that she wanted a general anaesthetic and not a spinal and since Dr Cusson was prepared to operate with his patient under the one or other he agreed and told his patient that she should so advise the anaesthetist.

On the day fixed, the appellant was given sedation and then taken to the operating room where she told Dr Piuze, a staff anaesthetist, that she did not want a spinal. The chief anaesthetist, Dr Forest, then appeared and talked the appellant into submitting to the spinal which was administered. Shortly after, the surgeon, Dr Cusson, came to the operating room and when he asked the anaesthetist to proceed with the giving of the general he was told that the spinal had already been administered. The operation was performed and the appellant ended up being paralysed from the waist down. This action, which was dismissed by judgment *a quo*, is in recovery of the damages resulting from this condition which may now be regarded as permanent . . .

If a delict has been committed the responsibility of the doctor is clear. It is equally clear that if an emergency arises and the doctor, in the exercise of professional judgment, does something from which unfortunate consequences result, it may be that he will not be responsible, even though he has acted without the consent of his patient.

But when in cases in which there is no urgency the doctor for one reason or another is unwilling to render the services agreed upon by the patient the only course of action open to him is to withdraw. He may not overrule his patient and submit him to risks that he is unwilling and in fact has refused to accept. And if he does so and damages result, he will be responsible without proof of negligence or want of skill. In these circumstances, it is not a defence to say that the technique employed was above reproach or that what happened was a pure accident.

This case is of the last type. Dr Forest gave the spinal contrary to the instructions and against the will of his patient. In so doing, he violated her person and submitted her to a risk that she had refused to assume.

In answer to this, Dr Forest attacks the factual premise. He says that appellant consented to the change from general to spinal, thereby setting up a new contract. He adds that since the obligation so created was one of means and since the appellant has failed to establish malpractice her action was properly dismissed.

The vital question is whether or not appellant gave a full and free consent to the change. This requires an examination of the evidence; and in reading the record one must bear in mind that the burden of proof rests on Dr Forest.

It will be recalled that Dr Forest was the Hospital's chief anaesthetist and that he intervened because the appellant presented a problem to his assistant, Dr Piuze. It seems that it was the practice at this Hospital to give spinals for these operations and when Dr Piuze found himself with a patient whose pre-anaesthetic examination called for a general anaesthetic he had his chief take over.

Dr Forest appeared some 30 minutes before the operation, saw the pre-anaesthetic report and heard the patient repeat her wishes. Despite the fact that he had never examined her and notwithstanding his knowledge that she had been given a sedative shortly before, he proceeded to convince her that she should accept a change . . .

On the question of sedation and of his failure to have gone into the matter earlier with appellant, it is interesting to read this extract from Dr Forest's testimony:

> Q: When you spoke with Mademoiselle Beausoleil, this was a short time before the operation?
> A: Fifteen or 20 minutes or a half hour before.
> Q: She was already under sedation?
> A: Yes.
> Q: I think you will agree with me that that could have affected her from the point of view of her manifesting her consent?
> A: Yes, that could have affected her in one way as well as the other.
> Q: Do you think that it would have been preferable to have discussions with her when she was not under sedation?
> A: That would have been rather difficult, she was under sedation during the entire time that she was at the hospital.
> Q: She was under sedation during the entire time that she was at the hospital?
> A: Yes, we got the file (dossier) out this morning. If one admits that that can change one's opinion. Because she received sedatives and sybalgines all the time she was at the hospital.

Present with the patient was her special nurse, Miss Fugere. After having said (p 183) that the patient had 'refused categoriquement' she goes on to say this:

Q: You say Dr Forest came later?
A: Yes, Dr Forest.
Q: What happened then?
A: Then, the patient refused and finally she consented, meaning, she could no longer help herself, you know, she said: 'No, no, no,' and then at one point she said: 'Since you wish.' She put herself in their hands.
Q: You say, 'Since you wish'. Did you hear those very words?
A: Yes, I recall something like that, to the effect that 'Since there is nothing else to do' or something like that.

Then there is the evidence of the appellant. She repeats the story of her having refused a spinal and has no recollection of having consented to any change.

On this evidence, I am of the opinion that Dr Forest did not discharge the burden that he assumed by taking the position that the appellant had consented to the change from the general to the spinal anaesthetic . . .

Note that it is not enough that a patient is in a vulnerable position vis à vis the medical practitioner such that his consent might not be voluntary. It must actually be the case that his freedom to consent or refuse was overborne.

Freeman v The Home Office (No 2) [1984] 1 QB 524, pp 549–53

Stephen-Brown LJ:

In July 1972, Dr Xavier took over the psychiatric care of the plaintiff. The first record in the plaintiff's case papers of Dr Xavier having dealt with him appears on 3 August 1972. On 10 August 1972, Dr Xavier is recorded as having prescribed Stelazin to be taken orally. The plaintiff refused to take it. There are also entries in the case papers relating to 17, 24 and 30 August 1972 which record that the plaintiff refused oral medication prescribed by Dr Xavier. On 31 August 1972, Dr Xavier is recorded as having prescribed Stelazin again. The records show that the plaintiff refused to take the Stelazin and on 31 August 1972, there is an entry by a Prison Officer Copley to the effect that the plaintiff 'states he does not want anything to do with Dr Xavier'.

The case papers show that on 1 September 1972 the plaintiff still refused to take medication orally and on that day Dr Xavier is recorded as having prescribed Serenace to be injected intra-muscularly and the plaintiff was injected on that day. It is not disputed that injections of Serenace were also given on 2 and on 3 September 1972. The plaintiff's claim was that these injections were administered by force against his will.

Subsequently, on 3 and 20 November and 4 December 1972, he was injected with Modecate prescribed by Dr Xavier. Again the plaintiff's contention was that these injections were administered against his will and were administered by force. The plaintiff's evidence was that he first remembered meeting Dr Xavier on 10 August 1972 for two minutes or so in the Chief Hospital Officer's room at the prison and that Dr Xavier asked him to try his mixture, saying, 'It will make a new man of you.' The plaintiff said that he replied, 'No, I don't want it. I feel better. I don't need the drugs,' and that that was all that happened on that occasion. He then saw Dr Xavier each week whilst he was attending the workshop and again he was asked by the doctor if he would have his mixture, and that each time he refused.

On 31 August 1972, he had a brief meeting with Dr Xavier when he was again asked to accept his mixture. On no occasion did the doctor tell him what the mixture was and he did not ask him. The plaintiff said that he told the doctor that he wanted nothing to do with him or his treatment. On 1 September 1972, the plaintiff said that he was working normally in the workshop between 10 am and 11 am when he was called out by an officer and taken back to the prison hospital and to his cell. He said he was not told why and he did not ask and then he was locked in his cell.

He told the court:

> A few minutes after, at least four or five prison hospital officers unlocked my cell and came in. No doctor was present. I particularly remember the officer holding the syringe, a Mr Clark, the younger of the two officers called Clark. Mr Copley may have been present. I can't remember the identity of any of the others. They were with me no more than five minutes, if that. The officers entered. Mr Clark was holding the syringe with the needle upwards. With his other arm he held a wad of cotton wool over the needle. There was a strong smell of surgical spirit. Clark said, 'Drop your trousers and lie down.' I said, 'I don't want any drugs.' One of them said, 'It's on doctor's orders. You can have it the easy way or the hard way.' I continued to protest and put my back to the wall and said, 'I'm not having it.' At least four or five men seized me and manhandled me to the bed. They held me down and wrenched my trousers off. I thrashed about on the bed and shouted. Clark said, 'If you don't keep still, when this needle goes in it could snap off in your arse and be very painful.' I was terrified. When I felt the needle going in my buttocks I stopped struggling. I surmise it was my left buttock from the position of my bed. They continued to hold me down until the needle was withdrawn. Then they released me and went out of the cell. Nothing more was said to me. I was left locked in. I cannot remember which officer next unlocked my cell. I said nothing to him. I knew it was dinner time. In the afternoon I went to the workshop. I became very ill and returned to the hospital. I became very agitated and had a pain in my head. I felt very debilitated.

He gave a full account of the injections on the two succeeding days and also alleged that he was injected on 4 September, although there was no record in the case papers of such an event. Thereafter oral administrations of drugs were prescribed and given, but the plaintiff said that he spat out all the drugs, retaining them in his mouth until he was able to do so.

The judge also heard the evidence of one of the prison hospital officers, Clifford Copley, that if a prisoner was going to be difficult the senior medical officer would have to be informed and he would come up. He said:

> If a prisoner objected, we would not just go ahead and inject him; we would call the medical officer. A prisoner can refuse. If he is struggling, he does not want it. If the man refused the injection, we would tell the MO, and if he said we had to give it nonetheless, we would give it using the minimum force. I do not remember ever using force in any case, not just in the case of Mr Freeman. If it had ever happened that a doctor had insisted on our injecting a prisoner, despite the fact that he refused it, and we would have had to do it with minimum force, there would have been an entry to that effect in the occurrence book.

The judge said that having seen Mr Copley he impressed him as an honest and decent prison officer, and the judge went on to say:

> I accept his evidence, including that part of it dealing with where the oral drugs were usually given. I do not accept the plaintiff's evidence that he never swallowed the Stelazin or Tryptizol.

The judge in fact rejected the plaintiff's evidence; he did not believe it and said so in straightforward terms. After a careful and thorough review of the evidence, the judge said above, p 535A:

> There is in fact no evidence that the plaintiff's capacity to consent was overborne or inhibited in any way. He gave no such evidence. He does not suggest for a moment that he was not man enough to say 'No' and, had that been his evidence, having seen him I would not have believed him. On the contrary, his evidence is that he said 'No' to the drugs in plain terms, and no lack of information or fear of the consequences would have persuaded him to say 'Yes' had he not been overborne by physical force. There is, moreover, no evidence from any other source that he was overborne by the prison situation. He refused electro-convulsive therapy and that was respected; he refused to have a tooth out and that was respected. I am satisfied that if this man had not been consenting, it would have been necessary for him physically to be held down and injected by superior force. I have no doubt that did not happen. Therefore, I conclude that he consented.

The judge therefore made a clear finding of fact that the plaintiff had in fact consented to the injections of the drugs on the material occasions.

Before this court Mr Blom-Cooper on behalf of the plaintiff accepts that the judge totally rejected the plaintiff's evidence and he does not seek to challenge the judge's decision so to do. He says that he accepts that the plaintiff must be taken to have 'permitted' the injections . . . [but he submitted that] it is impossible within the prison context as between a prisoner and a prison medical officer for free and voluntary consent to exist at least, he added, in the absence of any written consent form. The prison medical officer is not merely a doctor, he is, submits Mr Blom-Cooper, a prison officer within the meaning of the Prison Rules and accordingly is a person who can influence a prisoner's life and his prospect of release on licence. There must inevitably be an atmosphere of constraint upon an inmate in such circumstances. He cited the well-known passage from the judgment of Scott LJ in *Bowater v Rowley Regis Corporation* [1944] KB 476 at 479:

> With regard to the doctrine *volenti non fit injuria* I would add one reflection of a general kind. That general maxim has to be applied with specially careful regard to the varying facts of human affairs and human nature in any particular case just because it is concerned with the intangible factors of mind and will. For the purpose of the rule, if it be a rule, a man cannot be said to be truly 'willing' unless he is in a position to choose freely, and freedom of choice predicates, not only full knowledge of the circumstances on which the exercise of choice is conditioned, so that he may be able to choose wisely, but the absence from his mind of any feeling of constraint so that nothing shall interfere with the freedom of his will.

He also cited the American case of *Kaimowitz v Michigan Department of Mental Health* (unreported) (1973), Cir Ct, Wayne Co, Mich, the decision of a circuit court in the County of Michigan in 1973 which is the subject of a learned article by Brooks, A, 'Law, psychiatry and the mental health system', 1974, p 902. The judgment appears in the course of the article. The case concerned an inmate of a State hospital who had been committed to that institution as a criminal sexual psychopath and had signed what was termed an 'informed consent form' to become an experimental subject for experimental surgery and he later withdrew his consent. The court had to consider the nature of a legally adequate 'informed consent'. Although Mr Blom-Cooper recognised that having regard to recent authority 'informed consent' as such does not apply to the law of this country, he nevertheless placed reliance upon a passage of the judgment which appears at p 914 of the article:

> We turn now to the third element of an informed consent, that of voluntariness. It is obvious that the most important thing to a large number of involuntarily detained mental patients incarcerated for an unknown length of time, is freedom.

The Nuremberg standards require that the experimental subjects be so situated as to exercise free power of choice without the intervention of any element of force, fraud, deceit, duress, overreaching, or other ulterior form of constraint or coercion. It is impossible for an involuntarily detained mental patient to be free of ulterior forms of restraint or coercion when his very release from the institution may depend upon his cooperating with the institutional authorities and giving consent to experimental surgery.

At p 915:

> Involuntarily confined mental patients live in an inherently coercive institutional environment. Indirect and subtle psychological coercion has profound effect upon the patient population. Involuntarily confined patients cannot reason as equals with the doctors and administrators over whether they should undergo psychosurgery. They are not able to voluntarily give informed consent because of the inherent inequality in their position.

Mr Blom-Cooper seeks to apply those considerations and that reasoning to the position of the plaintiff in this present case, and he argues that in fact a valid free and voluntary consent cannot be given by a person such as the plaintiff, who is in prison, to a prison medical officer who is an officer of the prison having a disciplinary role in relation to him. Although the circumstances and the facts giving rise to the allegations made in this action afford an opportunity for interesting matters of principle and policy to be raised and considered, nevertheless, I find myself in complete agreement with the trial judge that the sole issue raised at the trial, that is to say whether the plaintiff had consented to the administration of the drugs injected into his body, was essentially one of fact. The judge considered with care all the evidence, both oral and documentary, and it is clear from his careful judgment that he took into account the various submissions which Mr Blom-Cooper made as to the nature and effect of the documentary evidence and the setting in which the events occurred. The judge said, above, pp 542H–43A:

> The right approach, in my judgment, is to say that where, in a prison setting, a doctor has the power to influence a prisoner's situation and prospects a court must be alive to the risk that what may appear, on the face of it, to be real consent is not in fact so. I have borne that in mind throughout the case.

Essentially, however, the matter is one of fact. The judge made the positive finding that the plaintiff consented. He rejected Mr Blom-Cooper's submission that the plaintiff was entitled to judgment because he was incapable in law of giving his consent to the treatment by Dr Xavier in question. In my judgment he was right so to do. There was ample evidence to justify his finding of fact and accordingly the decision to which he came. It is not for this court to consider and decide this appeal upon the basis of an alternative and hypothetical set of facts and circumstances. I would dismiss this appeal.

[Donaldson MR delivered a judgment in which he agreed with Stephen-Brown LJ. Fox LJ concurred.]

Information

In order to decide whether or not to consent to a particular treatment, a patient needs to have explained to him or her certain information (and understand that information). But exactly what information is relevant?

Chatterton v Gerson [1981] QB 432, pp 443–44

Bristow J:

A woman who suffered chronic pain in the region surrounding a scar was referred to Dr Gerson for treatment. Dr Gerson recommended a treatment known as an intrathecal block which was designed to 'block' the pain messages which ran along the nerves. He mentioned a possible side-effect of the procedure, but not the one which she subsequently suffered (loss of sensation in her right leg and pain so bad in the area of the scar that she could not bear having clothing in contact with it). She sued Dr Gerson alleging that the failure to warn of the risk sounded in damages for battery and negligence.

Trespass to the person and consent

It is clear law that in any context in which consent of the injured party is a defence to what would otherwise be a crime or a civil wrong, the consent must be real. Where, for example, a woman's consent to sexual intercourse is obtained by fraud, her apparent consent is no defence to a charge of rape. It is not difficult to state the principle or to appreciate its good sense. As so often, the problem lies in its application.

No English authority was cited before me of the application of the principle in the context of consent to the interference with bodily integrity by medical or surgical treatment. In *Reibl v Hughes* (1978) 89 DLR (3d) 112, which was an action based on negligence, by failure to inform the patient of the risk in surgery involving the carotid artery, the Ontario Court of Appeal said that the trial judge was wrong in injecting the issue, 'Was it a battery?' into the case pleaded and presented in negligence. The majority of the court, having referred to the United States cases on what is there called the 'doctrine of informed consent', decided that the action of 'battery' seemed quite inappropriate to cases in which the doctor has acted in good faith, and in the interests of the patient, but in doing so has been negligent in failing to disclose a risk inherent in the recommended treatment. They reversed the finding of battery. I am told that that decision is now under appeal.

In *Stogberg v Elliott* [1923] CPD 148, Watermeyer J, in his summing up to the jury in an action of assault in this context, directed them that consent to such surgical and medical treatment as the doctors might think necessary is not to be implied simply from the fact of going to hospital. There it was admitted that express consent to the operation should have been obtained, but was not, due to oversight.

In my judgment, what the court has to do in each case is to look at all the circumstances and say 'Was there a real consent?' I think justice requires that, in order to vitiate the reality of consent there must be a greater failure of communication between doctor and patient than that involved in a breach of duty if the claim is based on negligence. When the claim is based on negligence, the plaintiff must prove not only the breach of duty

> to inform, but that had the duty not been broken she would not have chosen to have the operation.
>
> In my judgment once the patient is informed in broad terms of the nature of the procedure which is intended, and gives her consent, that consent is real, and the cause of the action on which to base a claim for failure to go into risks and implications is negligence, not trespass. Of course, if information is withheld in bad faith, the consent will be vitiated by fraud. Of course, if by some accident, as in a case in the 1940s in the Salford Hundred Court, where a boy was admitted to hospital for tonsillectomy and due to administrative error was circumcised instead, trespass would be the appropriate cause of action against the doctor, though he was as much the victim of the error as the boy. But, in my judgment, it would be very much against the interests of justice if actions which are really based on a failure by the doctor to perform his duty adequately to inform were pleaded in trespass.
>
> In this case in my judgment, even taking the plaintiff's evidence at its face value, she was under no illusion as to the general nature of what an intrathecal injection of phenol solution nerve block would be, and in the case of each injection her consent was not unreal. I should add that getting the patient to sign a *pro forma* expressing consent to undergo the operation ' the effect and nature of which have been explained to me', as was done here in each case, should be a valuable reminder to everyone of the need for explanation and consent. But it would be no defence to an action based on trespass to the person if no explanation had in fact been given. The consent would have been expressed in form only, not in reality.

The reference to an explanation 'in broad terms' of the nature of a procedure posits a deceptively simple test. What seems clear is that the test is meant to distinguish between the physical intrusions involved in treatment and the attendant risks of undertaking that treatment. The first are within the nature of the treatment, the latter are more properly the concern of an action for negligence in failing to advise. This latter action, the negligence action, will be explored in the next chapter. The High Court of Australia in *Rogers v Whitaker* (1992) 175 CLR 479 approved the following statement made by Cole J in *Ellis v Wallsend District Hospital* (1989) 17 NSWLR 553, Supreme Court of NSW:

> Notwithstanding the failure to warn the plaintiff of the risks of paralysis and of the low prospect of success of long-term pain relief, I am satisfied the plaintiff gave consent to the operation sufficient to defeat the count in trespass. It is well established in major common law jurisdictions that failure to fully inform of risks does not vitiate consent provided that the patient is informed in broad terms of the procedure intended. Actions for failure to warn of risks lie in negligence, not trespass.

The dividing line between risks that are incidental (thus not forming part of the nature of the treatment) and those side effects which are so serious as to alter the nature of the treatment is a fine one. Consider the case of *D v S* (1981) LS (SA) JS 405. In that case, the plaintiff had undergone a hysterectomy. Following the hysterectomy, she took oestrogen tablets which had the effect of increasing her bust size. She consulted the defendant complaining of neck and back pain. The defendant said that he could relieve her pain by surgery called a 'reduction mammoplasty'.

D v S (1981) LS (SA) JS 405

Matheson J:

The plaintiff took pride in her dress, in her appearance and in her figure. She and her husband used to swim in the nude in their pool. She used to go to health studios and to Maslin's Beach with her daughters and friends. On such occasions and at home, she never had any concern about displaying her body naked.

On 9 November 1976, the defendant told her he could reduce the size of her bust with surgery and that this would relieve her neck and headaches. She particularly asked him about what scarring would be left. The plaintiff said that the defendant drew a diagram showing that there would be a v-shaped incision under each nipple, the apex of the v being just under each nipple, and that she would have one faint hairline scar starting from the base of the breast up to the base of the nipple area and down, and that would fade in time . . . She said that she expressed concerns to the doctor, and he said that there would not be any problems. He told her that he had done a lot of them, and had assisted in a lot of them and that there would be no problem . . . she believed that there was going to be a plastic surgeon present, although she was under the impression that it was to be a very minor operation . . .

The defendant did not tell her at any time before the operation that there would be any incision around her nipples, nor that her nipples would be moved up, nor that drips and drains would be involved.

When she woke up after the operation her husband was sitting with her. She had two drips, blood from one and 'intravenous feed' from another. Her breasts were aching and terribly painful. When the sheet fell down she saw what she described as 'horrible big black stitches' around each nipple, and that her nipples had been moved, and drains hanging out of her wounds. She became upset and hysterical.

[The judge found that the plaintiff's nipples had been unevenly relocated, that she had experienced great pain and scarring which was 'very prominent, red and grossly disfiguring' and that one of her breasts was now larger in size than the other. The plaintiff developed a drinking problem and left home on a number of occasions.]

Since the plaintiff has been home her drinking has improved. She said that she and her husband are 'first class friends', but they are not sleeping in the same room and there is no sexual contact. She said that she was still attracted to him, but did not know what the long-term outcome of the relationship would be . . . [she is seeing a counsellor] and has been taking anti-depressant tablets, tranquillisers and sleeping pills . . . At times her scars itch and ache, and that makes her irritable. She has been to a health studio only once since the operation and she wore bathers. She has not been to the beach at all. She wears bathers when she uses the swimming pool at home . . .

From time to time, some of the plaintiff's scars break down and weep, particularly when she is hot and scratches them. When this happens she does not wear brassieres because they irritate the relevant scar. She has to bathe the scar and put on cream. She told me that she could not cover it straightaway and when it is not covered it tends to weep through enough to be seen through a frock or a blouse . . . I was asked to look at the plaintiff's scars on 30 April, not only to assess the cosmetic damage but also to note that on that date, a portion of the scarring was weeping. She told me that that had resulted from irritation from a seat belt.

[The plaintiff brought actions in negligence and in assault and battery, the latter on the basis that 'any consent she gave resulted from false representations to her by the defendant (and from the failure of the plaintiff to warn her) any consent was a nullity and of no effect at all . . .']

[After referring to *Chatterton v Gerson*, Matheson J held:]

I think the defendant should have told the plaintiff that there would be incisions around the circumference of the areolae, that the incisions would require stitching, that there could be a loss of sensation in the nipples and the areolae, that there would be some permanent scars, that upon waking up from the operation she would see drips and drains, and that for some time she would have substantial pain. I find that the defendant told her none of these things, and that his failure was a breach of his duty . . . I am satisfied that if she had been told all these things she would not have consented to the operation and, moreover, that in all the circumstances her consent was not a true consent . . . It follows from my findings that the plaintiff succeeds both on the claim in negligence and on the claim for assault and battery, and that she is entitled to be compensated for all the scarring and all the suffering that the operation caused.

The difference between matters which are part of the nature of the treatment, and those which are collateral has been explored in some detail by Margaret Somerville.

Somerville, MA, 'Structuring the issues in informed consent' (1981)

26 McGill Law Journal 740

Common law courts in Canada have taken the traditional approach that the consent that is both necessary and sufficient for avoiding a cause of action in battery in medical cases is consent to 'the basic nature and character of the operation or the procedure'. The difficulty in applying this rule is determining which factors form part of the basic nature and character of an act and which do not. Such determinations have been made by judges on a case-by-case basis, with no more definite guidelines than the rule itself. But some judges have tried to formulate a clearer, more objective rule, which would help determine when non-disclosure of information or failure to obtain consent should give rise to a cause of action in battery.

The situation facing the judges can be represented diagrammatically [as an outer square encompassing a smaller, inner square. The inner square has 'basic nature of the act' written in it. The outer square has 'collateral features of the act' written on it] . . .

The outer square represents all the consequences or risks to which the patient must consent if liability in tort (battery or negligence) for failure to obtain consent is to be avoided. The inner square represents the factors that make up the basic nature and character of the act of touching. Failure to obtain consent to these factors will give rise to a cause of action in battery. Thus, whether or not battery lies depends on where the inner line is drawn.

That judges will vary in drawing this line can be seen by comparing the decisions of the majority [in a number of] criminal assault (battery) cases, as the rules governing consent in criminal law and in the tort of battery not only have common origins but are directly comparable. Such cases demonstrate that because criminal assault (or battery) will not lie if there is consent as to the basic nature and character of the act, liability will depend on whether or not the feature to which consent has not been obtained forms part of the act's basic nature and character. Thus, to the extent that there is discretion involved in determining whether or not a particular feature forms part of the basic nature and character of the act ('basic features'), there is discretion as to the imposition of liability. The two possible alternative analyses of any given fact situation that gives rise to this discretion may be represented as:

Analysis I:
CONSENT to Act (which consists of 'basic features' ABC) + NO CONSENT to 'collateral features' XYZ
= NO BATTERY

Analysis II:
CONSENT to Act (which consists of 'basic features' ABC X) + NO CONSENT to 'collateral features' YZ
= BATTERY

From this . . . it can be seen that, depending on whether or not X is held to be a 'collateral feature' or a 'basic feature' of the act alleged to constitute criminal assault or the tort of battery, the necessary consent will or will not be present, respectively, and liability will be determined accordingly.

There is another way in which a holding as to whether or not battery-avoiding consent is present can be varied. This does not require altering the characterisation of a feature of the act from 'basic' to 'collateral' or vice versa, but rather makes consent to the act conditional upon the collateral features being as represented. Using the same model this can be represented as follows:

NO CONSENT to 'collateral features' XYZ, therefore, NO CONSENT to Act which consists of 'basic features' ABC (to which there was consent).

Pursuant to this analysis, it is irrelevant whether X is characterised as a 'basic' or 'collateral' feature, as even if X is a 'collateral' feature, if X is not as represented the consent will fail to 'flow through' as a valid consent to the act. *R v Williams* [1923] 1 KB 340, in which the accused, a choirmaster, persuaded a young woman that sexual intercourse was therapy for her voice, is probably an example of a court taking such an approach. Depending on the circumstances, whether an act is therapeutic for the patient could be regarded as a 'collateral' feature of the act or could relate to the basic nature of the act. However, accepting that in the particular circumstances characterisation of an act as therapy is a collateral feature, battery could still lie when there is fraud or misrepresentation in this respect. For instance, if, as in the *Williams* case, a collateral feature of an act was not as represented (that is the act of sexual intercourse was not voice therapy) then despite the consent to the act itself (having sexual intercourse), that consent would be invalid, as the court held, because consent to the act was conditional on the collateral feature (that the act was therapy) being as represented. Although this example may seem very far removed from a normal medical context, it may have important applications. For instance, if a patient were misled to the effect that a particular procedure was therapeutic when in fact it was performed for the purposes of non-therapeutic research, battery-avoiding consent could similarly be vitiated.

How has the law outlined above been applied in the medical relationship? The requirement that there be consent to the basic nature and character of the operation or procedure means that a physician must disclose all inevitable consequences of a proposed procedure in order to obtain battery-avoiding consent. Consequently, all courts faced with the issue have held that there will be a cause of action in battery when a physician does something to which the patient has not consented at all, or which the patient has expressly requested not be done or has refused. Battery could also be established where the physician's act was essentially different in nature from that to which the patient consented. For instance, if the patient was told that the purpose of the operation was to relieve pain, but not told that the consequences would include sterility, any consent given would be invalidated and a cause of action in battery would be available.

Some courts have also held that knowledge of certain risks could be so material to understanding of the basic nature and character of an operation that failure to disclose them would vitiate battery-avoiding consent. In other words, it has been held that not only non-disclosure of inevitable results of a procedure can vitiate battery-avoiding consent, but also non-disclosure of risks of which knowledge was 'essential to an informed decision to undergo the operation'. It is with respect to failures to disclose a risk, as compared with an inevitable consequence, that the Supreme Court of Canada has probably restricted the availability of an action in battery.

It is not easy to decide, from a policy point of view, whether or not a cause of action in battery should be allowed for non-disclosure of certain risks. The argument that it should be allowed is that some risks are so serious that they necessarily relate to the basic nature and character of an operation and, therefore, their non-disclosure should give rise to a battery action. The difficulty is that as only some risks have this effect, how is the line to be drawn between those that do and those that do not? The alternative solution, which may be the position adopted by the Supreme Court of Canada in *Reibl v Hughes* (1980) 114 DLR (3d) is that any liability for non-disclosure of a risk can only lie in negligence and not in battery:

> [Actions of battery, in respect of surgical or other medical treatment should be confined to cases where surgery or treatment has been performed or given to which there has been no consent at all or where, emergency situations aside, surgery or treatment has been performed or given beyond that to which there was consent . . .] Unless there has been misrepresentation or fraud to secure consent to the treatment, a failure to disclose the attendant risks, however serious, should go to negligence rather than to battery. Although such a failure relates to an informed choice of submitting to or refusing recommended and appropriate treatment, it arises as the breach of an anterior duty of due care, comparable in legal obligation to the duty of due care in carrying out the particular treatment to which the patient has consented. It is not a test of the validity of the consent.

That is, non-disclosure of a risk will not give rise to a cause of action in battery except when there has been a 'misrepresentation or fraud to secure consent to . . . treatment'. But what can constitute misrepresentation within this rule, and why does such misrepresentation allow non-disclosure of a risk to give rise to an action in battery whereas without such misrepresentation it does not? In exploring these issues, it is necessary to determine the basis of the holding of the Supreme Court referred to above. Is it, first, that non-disclosure of a risk does not amount to misrepresentation (although that of an inevitable consequence can); or, second, that information about risks can never relate to the basic nature and character of an operation and thus cannot vitiate battery-avoiding consent; or both propositions; or neither? Presumably, the court has established the second proposition rather than the first, as it is difficult to draw a distinction between one type of non-disclosure (non-disclosure of inevitable consequences) constituting misrepresentation, and the other (non-disclosure of risks) not doing so. It may be argued that because there is a pre-existing duty to disclose inevitable consequences, but not risks, non-disclosure of inevitable consequences constitutes a misrepresentation, while that of risks does not. But this pre-empts the question to which an answer is sought, that is, just what information is there a duty to disclose so as to avoid an action in battery? Moreover, reliance on a rule that total non-disclosure of a risk does not give rise to a cause of action in battery, because a total non-disclosure cannot constitute misrepresentation, would not exclude a partial disclosure. But an approach that recognises partial but not total non-disclosure of risks as misrepresentation would be artificial and could give rise to fortuitous results. Further, the distinction between nonfeasance and misfeasance has no place when there is a pre-existing duty relationship, as there is between physician and patient.

If the court has not relied on a rule that a non-disclosure is unable to constitute misrepresentation, has it held that the risks of a procedure cannot relate to its basic nature and character? This question can be explored by asking what the situation would be where a significant and serious risk was grossly misrepresented, rather than undisclosed. This could, arguably, give rise to a cause of action in battery within the court's ruling. However, the fact that misrepresentation of a risk could give rise to a cause of action in battery means, by definition, that the misrepresentation must relate to the basic nature and character of the act. If this is true, it shows that the action in battery is not excluded because of the nature of the misrepresentation, that is, because the misrepresentation related to a risk and a risk cannot relate to the basic nature and character of a procedure, but that battery is excluded on some other basis.

If the above analysis is accepted, the basis of the Supreme Court's holding is not that total non-disclosure of risks cannot constitute misrepresentation, nor that risks cannot relate to the basic nature and character of a medical procedure. This leaves the question which reveals the key to the basis of the Supreme Court's ruling still unanswered. Why does 'misrepresentation or fraud to secure consent to the treatment' cause non-disclosure of a risk to give rise to a cause of action in battery, where it would not do so if the elements in misrepresentation or fraud were not present?

The true test of whether or not a cause of action in battery will lie for non-disclosure of a risk, provided the risk is serious and sufficiently likely of occurrence to relate to the basic nature and character of the act carried out, depends on the nature of the physician's conduct with respect to the non-disclosure. Not only the nature of the undisclosed information is significant, but also the nature of the failure to disclose. It is not proposed that, if the physician negligently (ie, unintentionally) fails to disclose or misrepresents a risk, he will be liable in negligence. If he intentionally does either of these things, the action will also lie in battery, provided that the risk which is not disclosed or is misrepresented is fundamental enough to relate to the basic nature and character of the procedure. Thus, the presence or absence of intention with respect to the non-disclosure of a risk which relates to the basic nature and character of an intervention will determine the cause of action available for failure to obtain consent to that risk. By contrast, when the non-disclosure relates to an inevitable consequence of an intervention, intention or lack of it in relation to the non-disclosure is irrelevant to establishing a cause of action in battery. This is true because the intention necessary to support a cause of action for battery arising from an intentional, nonconsensual touching of the kind which occurs is present in carrying out the act which has those inevitable consequences, regardless of the presence or absence of intention with respect to the non-disclosure.

Hence what is being suggested is that the intention necessary to support an intentional tort will be found in relation to a different element of the tortious act (that is, either the touching or the non-disclosure) depending on whether the failure in obtaining consent relates to failure to inform of risks or of inevitable consequences, but in both cases, the necessary intention may be present.

In relation to determining whether the touching itself was intentional, there is a key concept: the question which must be asked is not simply whether there was consent to a touching, which in most cases there will be, but whether there was consent to touching of that kind or in that manner. Likewise, it is relevant to ask not only whether there was intention to touch, but whether there was intention to touch in that manner. The concept of intention 'to touch in that manner' is broader and more precise than the concept of just touching. It includes the inevitable consequences and purposes of an intervention, as well as the touching itself. Because risks, by definition, may not occur, it is not possible to find the required intention to touch in the manner which results from risks occurring simply by demonstrating their crystallisation. Any proof of intention relates, rather, to the act of non-disclosure of these risks. By contrast, when what occurs is an inevitable consequence of an intervention, it can be presumed that this was intended, as in tort a reasonable person is presumed to intend the inevitable consequences of his acts. Consequently, in the latter case, the necessary intention to support intentional touching in that manner and a *prima facie* tort of battery is established by proving the touching, and the only question is whether or not there was sufficient consent.

An objection could be raised here that two different entities are being compared: in one case, the question asked is whether or not there is intentional non-disclosure of information to which the patient is entitled: that is, is there intentional failure to obtain consent? In the other case, the question is whether there is intentional touching in a situation where the failure to obtain consent to that touching may have been intentional or unintentional. It is submitted that there is no contradiction between these two approaches. Battery is an intentional tort, which may be established through the intention 'to touch in that manner' or the intentional failure to obtain the necessary consent. It is just that demonstrating the latter is superfluous when it can be shown that there was an intention to touch in a certain manner to which there was no consent.

There is one further problem with the Supreme Court's approach to actions in battery for failure to obtain adequate consent. Some risks are so important that most people would regard them as an essential part of any description of the basic nature and character of a procedure. For instance, the fact that an operation carries a substantial risk of death would cause most persons to characterise that operation as being of a serious nature. Further, can any real distinction be drawn between failure to disclose, for instance, that as a result of an operation a person will certainly be rendered sterile, and failure to disclose that there is a substantial risk of this occurring? It is submitted that the law should not try to draw distinctions that do not accord with generally held views as to what factors constitute the basic nature and character of an act, no matter how conceptually pleasing and easy of application the resulting rule may be.

Thus, with all respect, it is submitted that to the extent that the Supreme Court has limited the availability of an action in battery by stating the law to be that risks do not relate to the basic nature and character of an act and, consequently, their non-disclosure cannot vitiate battery-avoiding consent, the ruling may not be desirable. However, as shown above, the effect of the Supreme Court's ruling on the availability of a battery action will vary depending on how it is analysed. The analysis suggested accepts the Supreme Court's ruling but minimises its effect of making unavailable a battery action that otherwise would have been available under Canadian common law.

The approach suggested may be summarised as follows: in all cases where lack of consent is alleged, one is arguing either that there was no consent at all to the touching or to touching in that manner. The first question is whether the touching itself and in that manner was intentional. It is highly unlikely that the touching itself will be unintentional, but this is not true of the manner of the touching. The manner of the touching includes two types of consequences, inevitable consequences and risks which eventuate. When the feature of the touching to which it is alleged there was no consent is an inevitable consequence, then there will necessarily have been an intention to touch in that manner. When, on the other hand, the touching is of that manner because of the crystallisation of a risk, touching in that manner is unintentional (unless, possibly, the risk which eventuates was of very high probability, but this case will not be considered here). In the second case, it may initially seem that battery should not lie for non-disclosure of a risk, as the act of which the plaintiff complains – that he was touched in a manner to which he did not consent – was unintentional. However, a second question is relevant: whether the failure to obtain consent was intentional. It is suggested that where it is intentional, and provided the non-disclosure is of a

> sufficiently serious and probable risk that the risk can be said to form part of the basic nature and character of the intervention, the necessary intention for a cause of action in battery will exist. Such an approach would allow non-disclosure of certain risks because of misrepresentation or fraud to give rise to a cause of action in battery, as the Supreme Court suggests. It would include within the notion of misrepresentation some total non-disclosure; that is, intentional concealment of certain risks would suffice. Thus, only the unintentional non-disclosure of a risk that relates to the basic nature and character of an act would not be actionable in battery. The suggested approach and the correlation of the variables it includes can be demonstrated in the following way:

	Non-disclosure of inevitable consequence of	'sufficiently serious and probable risk'
INTENTIONAL	Battery	Battery
UNINTENTIONAL	Battery	Negligence

> Defects in consent which do not give rise to a cause of action in battery will be either actionable in negligence (or possibly in contract) or will not be actionable at all. The dividing line between those that are actionable in negligence and those that are not actionable at all is determined by whether or not the physician has breached the standard of care required of him by the law relating to negligence with respect to obtaining the patient's consent . . .
>
> Finally, it is appropriate here to note that some confusion may be caused because two doctrines, 'consent' and 'informed consent', are not distinguished. It is suggested that the word 'consent' be reserved to refer to the substantive entity which must be present to avoid liability in battery and similarly for the term 'informed consent' in relation to negligence. It is proposed that with respect to the substantive content of consent the traditional notion should be retained. This means that consent will be present when there is consent to the basic nature and character of the act. Informed consent is a more extensive concept that also comprehends consent to certain consequences or risks of consequences. But, as further discussion will show, there has not always been consensus as to its requirements. It necessarily includes all elements of the consent doctrine, but the reverse is not true. Thus, a physician may have obtained sufficient consent to avoid liability in battery, but not in negligence.

The test as to what amounts to the nature of treatment is derived from the test used in criminal law in order to determine whether someone has consented to a battery (or, in the case of rape, a sexual battery). Perhaps some guidance may be drawn from the criminal cases.

In *R v Williams* [1923] 1 KB 340, it was held that a 16 year old girl did not give consent to intercourse and that the appellant was therefore guilty of rape. This was so because the appellant had fraudulently represented the nature of sexual intercourse to the 16 year old as a medical procedure which would help her breathing.

In *R v Rosinski* (1824) 1 Lew CC 11, a man held himself out as being able to cure disorders. He was approached by a woman who wanted to be cured of her fits. Rosinski took the woman's clothes off and rubbed her with some liquid from a bottle. This was done not to cure the girl, but for the defendant's 'own lewd gratification'. It was held that the woman had not consented to the nature of the procedure.

These older cases have their modern parallels. What is the situation where a practitioner correctly explains the physical nature of what is being done, but is not himself medically qualified or is performing a medical procedure for a collateral purpose? Has a patient consented to the nature of the treatment in this circumstance?

R v Maurantonia [1968] 1 OR 145

The appellant was convicted of six counts of indecent assault. The charges arose out of the attendance of six female patients at the appellant's 'clinic' in Toronto. The appellant had made the following admissions:

1 That he was not a medical doctor and did not have any formal education or training and was not entitled to practise medicine;
2 That he represented to the public and specifically to the complainants that he was a doctor of medicine and licensed to practise medicine; and
3 That the complainants consented to be treated or examined by him only because they believed he was licensed to practise medicine.

It is urged by counsel for the appellant that the words 'nature and quality of the act' as used in [the Canadian Criminal Code] have reference only to the physical touching, that such contact was known to the complainants to be part of the alleged treatment or examination and that each complainant did, in fact, consent to what took place. The admittedly false representation of the appellant that he was a licensed and duly qualified medical practitioner then becomes only fraud in the inducement and not fraud in the factum. That is, although the appellant may have fraudulently induced them to submit to the examination or treatment upon the false representation that he was a physician, nevertheless there was no misrepresentation as to the nature and quality of the act to be performed. Therefore, each complainant having consented to the actual physical contact involved, the appellant, despite the admitted fraudulent misrepresentation as to his state, could not be convicted under [the Canadian Criminal Code].

Although superficially appealing, this argument cannot prevail. In my opinion, the words 'nature and quality of the act' as used in [the Canadian Criminal Code] should not be so narrowly construed as to include only the physical action but rather must be interpreted to encompass those concomitant circumstances which give meaning to the particular physical activity in question. Here the physical touching was essentially bound up with, and consented to, as part of the medical treatment or examination. It was only to a medical examination or medical treatment, including the reasonable intimate physical contact necessary thereto, that each complainant consented. If that to which they were subjected was not in fact of the nature of a *bona fide* medical examination or treatment then it was something entirely different from that to which they consented. The physical contact in issue here being of an equivocal nature in the circumstances, the question whether or not the complainants received *bona fide* medical attention was dependent upon the intent with which it was carried out and, as such, became a question of fact to be determined on all the evidence by the trial tribunal. On the six counts upon which convictions were registered, that issue was found adversely to the appellant by the trial judge and there is ample evidence to support that finding.

The fraudulent misrepresentation of the appellant that he was a duly qualified and licensed physician was not what induced the complainants to submit to the physical acts entailing the touching of their persons. The false representation which led to consent was that what the appellant was about to do was to conduct a medical examination or administer medical treatment. Since the representation went to the very nature and quality of the act to be performed, the consent of each of the complainants, even if given in the full understanding of what physical acts the appellant was about to perform, 'was obtained by false and fraudulent representations as to the nature and quality of the act'. The question is not whether the appellant was a duly qualified and licensed physician but rather an issue of fact as to whether or not the physical touching was a necessary part of a *bona fide* medical examination or treatment, because it was to that and that alone that consent was given. In deciding this issue of fact, the trial tribunal would, of course, be entitled to consider the lack of professional qualifications. The weight to be given to this and other relevant facts would depend on the circumstances of a particular case . . .

R v Mobilio [1991] 1 VR 339, pp 340–52

Crockett, McGarvie and Beach JJ:

It is necessary now to say something of the facts disclosed by the evidence called for the prosecution in relation to each of the counts in respect of which the appellant was convicted.

Count 2 relates to an ultrasound examination conducted by the applicant on Miss B. In April 1989, Miss B attended her doctor, Dr Houghton, complaining of vaginal bleeding. Dr Houghton referred her to the Heritage Clinic [where the applicant worked] for an ultrasound examination. On 7 April 1989, Miss B attended at the clinic where she was referred to the applicant. Once in the examination room he told her to take off all her clothes below her waist. She asked why that was necessary whereupon he told her just to 'drop them to your knees'. The applicant then conducted an external ultrasound examination on Miss

B's lower stomach. During that examination the applicant pulled her underpants down to the area of her mid-thigh and at times rested his arm on her thigh area. He also asked her when she had last had sexual intercourse. He then told her that he needed to do a transvaginal interior ultrasound examination to get a proper view. Miss B asked if a female radiographer could do it but the applicant told her that there were no female radiographers available. The applicant then pulled Miss B's underpants further down to her knees and inserted the transducer about an inch into her vagina. He then moved it sideways, inserting it and withdrawing it on more than one occasion for about five minutes. Whilst the applicant was moving the transducer sideways, he was studying the screen of the ultrasound equipment. At the conclusion of the examination, he showed Miss B the ultrasound images which had been recorded on film. Shortly after the examination, Miss B made a complaint about it to Dr Houghton. Dr Houghton swore that at no time had she asked for a transvaginal interior ultrasound examination to be carried out. If she had wished such an examination to be carried out, she would have written it on the request for the ultrasound.

Count 7 relates to Miss P. In April 1989, Miss P consulted her doctor, Dr Mitchell, complaining of stomach pains. Dr Mitchell referred her to the Heritage Clinic for an ultrasound examination. On 21 April, Miss P attended at the clinic and was referred to the applicant. The applicant took her to an examination room, told her to remove her tracksuit pants and to get up on to the examination table. Miss P did as she was told. The applicant then pulled her underpants [down] to what she described as the mid-pubic line. The applicant then commenced to conduct an external ultrasound examination. After a while he told her that she had not had enough to drink as her bladder was not full. Standard practice required that the patient have a full bladder at the time of examination. The applicant told Miss P to put her tracksuit pants and shoes back on, go to the toilet, and drink some more water. She complied with the applicant's instructions and later returned again to the examination room. Once more he told her to remove her tracksuit pants and get up on the examination table. Miss P did what he told her. The applicant again pulled her underpants down to the mid-pubic region and conducted an external ultrasound examination. He then pulled Miss P's underpants down to her knees and told her to bend her knees. Before Miss P had time to do so, the applicant raised one of her knees. At the same time she lifted up her other knee. The applicant then got a bottle of gel and squirted some of it on to Miss P's vagina. The applicant then inserted the end of the transducer a distance of about one centimetre into Miss P's vagina, saying as he did so that he might get a better picture. The applicant then asked Miss P when was the last time she had had sex. The applicant kept the transducer in Miss P's vagina for a couple of minutes and then removed it. During the time the transducer was in Miss P's vagina, the applicant was studying the screen on the ultrasound equipment. At the end of the examination, the applicant showed her the images which had been recorded on film. According to

Miss P, at no time did the applicant tell her what he proposed to do or ask her permission to insert the transducer in her vagina. There was medical evidence at the trial to the effect that to insert the transducer only one centimetre into the vagina was of little or no value as the transducer had to be inserted at least two to three centimetres to obtain a satisfactory picture. After Miss P left the clinic she returned to her place of employment and complained to a friend about what the applicant had done.

Count 8 on the presentment relates to Miss H. In May 1989, Miss H consulted her doctor, Dr Pye, complaining of abdominal pains. Dr Pye made an appointment for Miss H to have an ultrasound examination carried out at the Heritage Clinic. On 12 May, Miss H attended at the clinic and was referred to the applicant. The applicant showed her into an examination room and told her to take her clothes off. She undressed down to her polo top, bra and underpants. The applicant then told her to take off her polo top which she did. As she was getting up on to the examination table the applicant told her to remove her bra which she also did. The applicant then proceeded to make an external ultrasound examination of Miss H's abdomen. As he did so he moved her underpants further down her abdomen.

Whilst the applicant was conducting the ultrasound examination, he asked Miss H a number of questions including whether she had a boyfriend and when she had last had sex.

The applicant then told Miss H that he would have to do an internal examination. The only explanation he gave her for the internal examination was that that way he would be able to see more. The applicant then removed her underpants, leaving her completely naked. The applicant parted Miss H's legs and put some gel on her vagina. He then inserted the transducer into her vagina. She said that as he did so he was 'sort of feeling the outside of my vagina with his hand'. At first, the applicant inserted the transducer into Miss H's vagina slowly and then moved it around in a circular motion. However, when he reinserted it on later occasions 'it got more vigorous'. In all, the internal examination took some 15–20 minutes. During the course of the examination, the applicant told Miss H on a number of occasions to watch the ultrasound monitor or screen. The applicant was himself watching the screen during most of the examination. Having completed the examination, the applicant wiped the gel from Miss H's vagina with a tissue. She then put on her underpants, bra and top. He then asked her to come towards him. When she did he placed his hand on her abdomen and palpated it. As he did so he asked Miss H whereabouts her pains were coming from. When the applicant concluded the examination he examined the images the films had recorded and told Miss H that he could not see anything abnormal in the photos. Miss H then dressed and went to walk out the door. However, the door was locked. She unlocked the door and left the clinic. She later contacted Dr Pye and told him what had happened.

Each referring doctor was called to give evidence in respect of the counts on which the applicant was convicted. They all gave evidence to the effect that they had not requested or anticipated that a transvaginal ultrasound examination of their patient would be carried out . . .

Having set out the basic facts which the evidence placed before the jury, we turn to the law.

The Crimes (Sexual Offences) Act 1980 introduced to the Crimes Act 1958 an amendment which defined rape as including conduct which would not have amounted to rape at common law. Section 2A of the Crimes Act now contains the following definition:

> 'Rape' includes the introduction (to any extent) in circumstances where the introduction of the penis of a person into the vagina of another would be rape, of:
>
> (b) an object (not being part of the body) manipulated by a person (whether male or female) into the vagina or anus of another person (whether male or female) . . .

In this case, proof of a crime of rape required it to be established that the applicant introduced the ultrasound transducer into the vagina of the woman in circumstances where the introduction of the penis would have amounted to rape.

It was undisputed that the applicant, by manipulating the transducer, introduced it into the vagina of each woman. The case put against the applicant was that he had intentionally introduced the transducer into the woman's vagina knowing that he did so without her consent. Each of the women had given her apparent consent expressly or by her conduct. The issue was whether the woman's apparent consent was, to the knowledge of the applicant, not a real consent.

It was contended for the prosecution at the trial and before this court that the apparent consents were vitiated and not real consents because each woman consented to the introduction of the transducer only for medical diagnostic purposes but the applicant introduced it solely for the purpose of his own sexual gratification.

We first consider what deprives a woman's consent of reality when it is a penis which is introduced to her vagina.

The common law as to rape is relatively simple and practical. It is designed to deter only one form of conduct. It is designed to deter a man from having any sexual intercourse with a woman – any introduction of his penis into her vagina – without her consent. For this act to amount to rape, the man must intend to have intercourse without her consent. He has this intention if he intends to have intercourse and is aware that the woman is not consenting or realises that she might not be. If, with that state of mind, a man has any intercourse with a woman who is not consenting, the crime is committed. It makes no difference whether his ultimate or ulterior purpose, motive or reason for intercourse is his own sexual gratification, his self-aggrandisement, the hurting or humiliation of the woman, her psychological or bodily betterment, or some combination of those.

Because the common law of rape prohibits only acts of sexual intercourse without consent, it is the absence of consent to an act of intercourse which the prosecution must prove. If the woman consented to an act of intercourse, there is no rape. The man's act does not amount to rape if the woman consented to an act of intercourse even though she believed that he had one ultimate or ulterior purpose, motive or reason for intercourse but in fact he had another.

Difficulties have arisen where the woman consented to what was in fact sexual intercourse but later discovered that her consent was given due to her having made a mistake. In some cases, she was mistaken because she did not know at the time that the act was one of sexual intercourse but thought it to be another act altogether. In other cases, while she knew the act was one of sexual intercourse, she believed the man had a purpose which would have rendered the intercourse moral, ethical and socially acceptable but later discovered he had a different purpose which rendered it immoral, unethical or socially unacceptable.

In our opinion, it is established in Australia by the High Court that if the woman consented to the act knowing it to be an act of sexual intercourse, no mistake as to the man's purpose deprives her consent of reality. The consent is real even though the act of intercourse, having been done for the purpose the man actually had, may wear a different moral complexion from that it would have worn if done for the purpose the woman believed he had.

In the situations mentioned above, the woman's consent is deprived of reality only if she was mistaken so that she did not know that the proposed act to which she consented was an act of sexual intercourse, but believed that she was consenting to an act of an essentially different nature and character. For the man to be guilty of rape, he must have known that the woman was only consenting to an act essentially different in nature and character from sexual intercourse, or have realised that she might only be consenting to an essentially different act.

Whether a woman's apparent consent lacked reality so that the penetration of her vagina was done without her consent and amounted to rape was considered by the High Court in *Papadimitropoulos v R* (1957) 98 CLR 249. In that case, a woman consented to sexual intercourse with a man because she mistakenly believed his untrue statement that they had been married on a visit they made to a registrar of marriages.

The man was convicted of rape and an application to this court for leave to appeal against conviction was dismissed by a majority . . . The High Court held that the woman's consent to sexual intercourse was a real consent and the man was not guilty of rape. Her consent was a real consent because her mistake was not a mistake as to the nature and character of the act of intercourse but a mistake as to the existence of a valid marriage which had induced her to consent. The court identified

... the essential inquiry, namely, whether the consent is no consent because it is not directed to the nature and character of the act.

The court continued that:

> The identity of the man and the character of the physical act that is done or proposed seem now clearly to be regarded as forming part of the nature and character of the act to which the woman's consent is directed. That accords with the principles governing mistake vitiating apparent manifestations of will in other chapters of the law.

In the present case, the decision of the majority of the Full Court extends this conception beyond the identity of the physical act and the immediate conditions affecting its nature to an antecedent inducing cause – the existence of a valid marriage.

After reference to some historical aspects it was said:

> Rape, as a capital felony, was defined with exactness, and although there has been some extension over the centuries in the ambit of the crime, it is quite wrong to bring within its operation forms of evil conduct because they wear some analogy to aspects of the crime and deserve punishment. The judgment of the majority of the Full Court of the Supreme Court goes upon the moral differences between marital intercourse and sexual relations without marriage. The difference is indeed so radical that it is apt to draw the mind away from the real question which is carnal knowledge without consent. It may well be true that the woman in the present case never intended to consent to the latter relationship. But . . . the key to such a case as the present lies in remembering that it is the penetration of the woman's body without her consent to such penetration that makes the felony. The capital felony was not directed to fraudulent conduct inducing her consent. Frauds of that kind must be punished under other heads of the criminal law or not at all: they are not rape. To say that in the present case the facts which the jury must be taken to have found amount to wicked and heartless conduct on the part of the applicant is not enough to establish that he committed rape. To say that in having intercourse with him she supposed that she was concerned in a perfectly moral act is not to say that the intercourse was without her consent. To return to the central point; rape is carnal knowledge of a woman without her consent: carnal knowledge is the physical fact of penetration; it is the consent to that which is in question; such a consent demands a perception as to what is about to take place, as to the identity of the man and the character of what he is doing. But once the consent is comprehending and actual the inducing causes cannot destroy its reality and leave the man guilty of rape.

The basic issue in this case is whether on the evidence it was open in law to the jury to be satisfied that while each woman had given apparent consent it was not real consent. If that was open to them, it was open to them to be satisfied that the applicant was aware that the women had not given real consent. We consider that on the evidence it was open to the jury to be satisfied that the women consented to the transducer being inserted solely for a diagnostic purpose but that the applicant inserted it solely for his own sexual gratification. The parties are in contest as to whether on such a finding it was open to the jury to find there was no real consent by the individual woman to the introduction of the transducer into her vagina. This depends on whether it could be found that the woman consented to an act of an essentially different nature and character from the act actually done by the applicant.

The argument of the prosecution receives support from the decision of the Saskatchewan Court of Appeal in *R v Harms* (1944) 2 DLR 61. A young woman of 20, complaining of pain in the chest and irregular menstrual periods, consulted the appellant who made his living from massage and was known as 'Dr Harms'. He gave her medicine and had her lie on a bed. He removed her undergarments and inserted two pills in her vagina. He then attempted to excite her so as to have intercourse with her, saying that he was doing so to make the pills operative and produce an effective cure. She objected and pushed him away and eventually he desisted saying she would have to take the consequences. Ultimately, she yielded and he had complete intercourse with her. He was convicted of rape and appealed against the conviction.

In cross-examination at the trial, the young woman admitted she knew that intercourse could lead to pregnancy, and that she had discussed with the appellant the possibility of pregnancy and he had recommended the pills. She said that she knew she had sexual intercourse with him but thought that because of the pills it would be all right. In fact she became pregnant.

In that case, the prosecution relied on a provision in the Criminal Code which provided that the act of a man having carnal knowledge of a woman who was not his wife, with consent obtained by false and fraudulent representations as to the nature and quality of the act, was rape.

Mackenzie JA who delivered the judgment of the court said, at p 65:

> . . . the question of the complainant's knowledge of the nature and quality of the prisoner's act is not necessarily to be determined by a mere consideration of her understanding of the intimate incidents preceding it, or by its usually natural consequences but by the purpose which rendered her submissive to it and by the effect she was moved by the prisoner to believe would result therefrom.

Later he said, at p 654:

> . . . in this case while it may be conceded that the complainant knew the meaning of carnal knowledge as a sexual act, yet it is quite clear that she was so well aware of its possible ill consequences that she was definitely indisposed to run the risk of incurring the same for the sorry satisfaction of indulging in sexual intercourse with a man

> like the prisoner. It is, moreover, obvious that she did not yield to him under the expectation of receiving any money or other material reward. There still remains open the possible conclusion that she did it because he led her by false and fraudulent misrepresentations to believe that it was part of a treatment which by their sexual cooperation would correct her physical disorder. Hence, in my opinion, the jury may well have decided that the nature and the quality of the act so far as she was concerned (that is subjectively) was pathological and not carnal. After examining English decisions the learned judge concluded, at p 68: In the present case, counsel for the prisoner contended that running all through these cases was the doctrine that a man cannot be convicted of rape if it appears that the woman actually knew that the act he sought to accomplish involved sexual intercourse. I find myself unable to agree with him. It seems to me that the principle they are seeking to enunciate is rather that a man shall be deemed guilty of rape if he has succeeded by fraud no less than by force in overcoming her permanent will to virtue.

The appeal was dismissed.

In *Papadimitropoulos*, the court . . . regarded the decision in *Harms* as wrong . . .

In *Bolduc v R* (1967) 63 DLR (2d) 82, decided by the Supreme Court of Canada, the majority referred to *Harms* as a case where the girl's consent to the intercourse had been obtained by false and fraudulent misrepresentations as to the nature and quality of the act. However, having referred to the full review by the High Court in *Papadimitropoulos* of the relevant law and cases, including *Harms*, the majority quoted the law as stated by the High Court. There was no reference to the High Court's disapproval of *Harms* nor was any preference expressed as between the two views, it not being necessary.

Another case which on its face supports the argument put by the prosecution is *R v Rosinski* (1824) 1 Lew CC 11; 168 ER 941. A girl attended a medical man for treatment, her parents understanding before she went that the treatment would involve her being stripped naked. Her evidence was that the medical man himself took her clothes off and laid her on a table. Then he put his private part into hers. She made such resistance as she could but did not call out. Bayley J told the jury: In my opinion, if a medical man falsely pretends that it is necessary for a female to strip herself naked in his presence, for the purpose of applying his medical skill, and the jury think it unnecessary, and done for his own lewd gratification, it is a question well worthy the grave consideration of the judges, whether it be not a misdemeanour. The jury convicted, apparently of common assault, and the judge postponed sentencing until he had taken the opinion of the judges. The judges were of the opinion that in the circumstances the prisoner was properly convicted of common assault.

The editorial note in the report of *Harms*, at p 61, treats *Rosinski* as a case in a separate category where the act committed is of an equivocal nature depending upon the intent with which it was done so that it can be said that the complainant consented to one act whereas the accused did another and quite different act. While the report of *Rosinski's* case referred to in the editorial note suffers from a paucity of information, the case does not seem to have any feature which distinguishes it from many similar medical cases in which the test for reality of consent is whether the woman was mistaken as to the nature and character of the act. That test was not referred to in *Rosinski.*

There are statements in some of the early cases which would give support to the prosecution's argument here. However, in view of the High Court's examination and interpretation of those cases and statement of the law in *Papadimitropoulos*, we regard it as unnecessary to go to the earlier cases . . .

What then is involved in knowing the nature and character of an act and in directing consent to an act of a different nature and character from the act done? The *Macquarie Dictionary* gives as a meaning of 'nature' the particular combination of qualities belonging to a person or thing by birth or constitution; native or inherent character. It gives as a meaning of 'character' the aggregate of qualities that distinguishes one person or thing from others.

In a number of cases, where a woman has apparently consented to a man inserting his penis into her vagina, the test for determining whether her consent was not a real consent because it was not directed to an act of that nature and character has been considered.

In *R v Morgan* [1970] VR 337, the applicants' convictions for rape were based on evidence that although the 19 year old woman with whom they had had intercourse had apparently consented, to their knowledge she was mentally retarded to a marked degree, lacked capacity to consent and had given no real consent.

The trial judge told the jury that to show there was no consent it had to be shown that because of lack of knowledge and understanding she was not capable of real consent. He gave the direction that to have the knowledge and understanding to give a real consent the woman would need more than an understanding that the act consisted of the insertion of a male penis into her vagina: she must also have a rudimentary understanding of a number of what he called 'rudimentary concepts': the concept of virginity and the effect of intercourse upon the hymen; that intercourse may cause pregnancy; that most of the community draw a distinction in quality between the act of intercourse and other acts of intimacy; and that to consent or not involves a moral judgment. The applicants were convicted of rape and sought leave to appeal to this court.

In allowing the appeals, the court quoted passages from *R v Lambert* [1919] VLR 205 and *Papadimitropoulos* and said, at pp 341–42:

> It appears to us to follow from these statements of authority that where capacity to consent is in issue in order to establish that a girl does not have that capacity – and there is accordingly no consent – it must be proved that she has not sufficient knowledge or understanding to comprehend (a) that what is proposed to be done is the physical fact of penetration of her body by the male organ or, if that is not proved, (b) that the act of penetration proposed is one of sexual connection as distinct from an act of a totally different character.
>
> The Crown may prove both (a) and (b), but if it fails to satisfy the burden as to (a) it may still establish incapacity to consent by proving she had not sufficient knowledge or understanding to comprehend (b).

Equally so, we are of opinion that capacity to consent does not involve, as a matter of law, knowledge or understanding of any of the ingredients referred to as 'rudimentary concepts' by the learned trial judge.

Accordingly, if the prosecutrix has knowledge or understanding of what the act comprises, ie the fact of penetration, and of its character in the sense above mentioned, then she has all that the law requires for capacity to consent. That knowledge or understanding need not, of course, be a complete or sophisticated one. It is enough that she has sufficient 'rudimentary knowledge' of what the act comprises and of its character to enable her to decide whether to give or withhold consent.

It follows that the charge of the learned judge, as we understand it, in directing the jury that absence of one or more of the 'rudimentary concepts' established incapacity, constituted a misdirection and that as it went to the heart of the crime charged, the verdicts based upon it cannot stand.

Nothing that we have said is, of course, intended to suggest that considerations of the nature referred to by the learned judge in his charge are outside the purview of the jury, as the tribunal of fact, in arriving at a conclusion as to the state of the girl's knowledge or understanding in the relevant sense at the material time.

Convictions of rape have been upheld in cases where, through deception, the woman did not know that the insertion of the man's penis into her vagina was a sexual act, but believed it to be an act of medical treatment or bodily improvement. Such cases are to be understood on the background of a degree of ignorance and naivety by some women as to sexual matters in earlier days that seems incredible today. If cases such as *R v Case* (1850) 1 Den 580; 169 ER 381; *R v Flattery* (1877) 2 QBD 410 and *R v Williams* [1923] 1 KB 340 are to be regarded as consistent with the law stated in *Papadimitropoulos*, they must be regarded as decided on the basis mentioned above: Glanville Williams, *Textbook of Criminal Law*, 2nd edn, pp 561–62.

There are cases in modern times where a woman, undergoing medical examination and unable to see what was being done, consented to what she believed to be the examiner's finger or a medical instrument being inserted into her vagina but later realised that the examiner had inserted his penis and was having sexual intercourse. Situations of that type are discussed in the Californian cases of *Boro v Superior Court* (1985) 163 Cal App 3d 1224; 210 Cal Rptr 122 and *People v Ogunmola* (1987) 192 Cal App 3d 277; 238 Cal Rptr 300. Under a provision of the Californian Penal Code defining rape as an act of sexual intercourse with a person at the time unconscious of the nature of the act, and this being known to the accused, the courts have treated the women as unconscious of the nature of the act and the examiners as guilty of rape.

By contrast, in the first of those cases, *Boro*, a man claiming to be a doctor, persuaded a woman that she had a dangerous and perhaps fatal disease and the cheapest treatment was for her to have sexual intercourse with an anonymous donor who had been injected with a serum which would cure the disease. The man then pretended to be the anonymous donor and the woman consented to, and had, intercourse with him, believing that otherwise she would die. The Court of Appeal held that as the woman had understood the nature of the act the man was not guilty of rape.

In our opinion, it is established that for a woman to have the knowledge of a man's proposed act of inserting his penis in her vagina, sufficient to render her consent a real one, she must understand more than that what is proposed is the physical act of penetration by the penis. She must have some further perception of what is about to take place including the immediate conditions affecting the nature of the act and the character of what he proposes to do: *R v Lambert* [1919] VLR 205, at p 212 and *Papadimitropoulos*, at p 61. She needs to understand that the act is one of sexual connection as distinct from an act of a totally different character: *R v Morgan* [1970] VR 337, at p 341.

The decision in *Morgan* makes it clear that a complete and detailed knowledge of all aspects of the proposed act is unnecessary. Persons know what a proposed act is if they have an understanding which would in ordinary language be described as knowing what it is. Thus, a person has sufficient knowledge to give effective consent to a complex surgical operation without a complete knowledge of all that is involved. No doubt the knowledge of the nature and character of an act requires some knowledge of its possible or probable immediate effects or future consequences.

Is a knowledge of the purpose with which a man proposes to perform an act of intercourse part of the woman's knowledge of the nature and character of the proposed act? Our reading of the High Court judgment in *Papadimitropoulos* leads us to conclude that it is not. The disagreement of the High Court with the decision in *Harms* indicates that if a woman understands that a proposed act is an act of sexual intercourse she knows its nature and character. This knowledge is not affected by a mistake as to the purpose for which the man proposes to perform that act of known nature and character.

In relation to the crime of rape, there is nothing artificial in treating a mistake by the woman as to the purpose for which the man proposes to have intercourse as not detracting from her knowledge of the nature and character of the proposed act. The actual act to which she consents, the act of sexual intercourse, is not different and has no different effect on her body if the man has one ulterior purpose rather than another. It is otherwise in other areas of law where one person having consented to another performing an act for a limited purpose is held not to have consented to the person performing the act for a different purpose. In those cases, if the other person performed the act for the different purpose, its effect on the person who gave the limited consent would be harmful, or more harmful, than if it were performed for the limited purpose. Examples of such cases are provided by *Barker v R* (1983) 153 CLR 338; 47 ALR 1; 57 ALJR 426 and *Pallante v Stadiums Pty Ltd (No 1)* [1976] VR 331.

What was said by this court in *Morgan* in the last paragraph of the passage quoted above, indicates that whether or not a woman was able to appreciate the morality of the act is one of the considerations which could be taken into account in deciding whether she had the intellectual capacity to give a real consent to sexual intercourse. Situations encountered in the cases show that a woman's appreciation of the morality of a proposed act will sometimes turn on her knowledge of the man's purpose in proposing an act of intercourse. Although that statement by the court was not strictly necessary to the decision and was on a subject which does not appear to have been argued, it was made by way of guidance to trial judges and carries its own persuasive weight.

In our opinion, the passage quoted from the judgment of this court in *Morgan* is to be understood on the background that the law requires that a woman must understand the nature and character of sexual intercourse before she can be capable of consenting to it, but the fact that she does understand that does not necessarily establish her capacity to consent. In addition to her knowledge of the nature and character of the act, her capacity to make a decision may be relevant. A jury might think that a woman whose intellect was insufficient to enable her to make a refusal of consent or to know that she had a right to refuse consent, lacked the capacity to consent despite her understanding of the nature and character of sexual intercourse: see *R v Lang* (1975) 62 Cr App R 50, at p 52 and Howard's *Criminal Law*, 5th edn (edn Fisse), p 180; cf *R v Roden* (1981) 4 A Crim R 166. In deciding whether a woman who knew the nature and character of an act of sexual intercourse had the capacity to give a real consent to it, a jury could have regard to such things as her capacity to appreciate that most of the community draw a distinction in quality between the act of intercourse and other acts of intimacy and that a decision to consent or not involves questions of the morality or social acceptability of the conduct. We think the court is to be understood as meaning that in saying that those things are not outside the purview of the jury.

Where the consent in issue is that of a woman possessing normal intellect, the reality of her consent turns only on whether she knew, or was mistaken as to, the nature and character of the act to which she directed her consent. As Howard's *Criminal Law*, 5th edn (edn Fisse), p 181 says of the position: 'If V [victim] understands the physical significance of sexual intercourse and freely consents to it, any harm she suffers through deception is outside the relatively simple concept of physical protection embodied in rape' and 'If V consents to intercourse because she is told that intercourse is part of a treatment, understanding what is being done to her but being misled as to the reason why it is being done, D [defendant] is not guilty of rape.'

For the consent of a woman of normal intellect to an act to be deprived of reality through difference between the nature and character of the act consented to and that actually done, the difference must be essential. In *Papadimitropoulos*, while the High Court disagreed with the test applied in this court by the majority, there was no disagreement with the approach of both majority and minority that their respective tests were applied so as to determine whether the act which took place was essentially different from that to which the woman thought she was consenting: see 98 CLR, pp 954–55. This necessary degree of difference is conveyed by the reference in the passage quoted from *Morgan*, to 'an act of a totally different character'.

In referring to mistake as to the nature and character of the act, the High Court was clearly referring to essential mistake. It said that the test of inquiring whether the woman's consent was directed to the nature and character of the act accords with the principles governing mistake vitiating apparent manifestations of will in other chapters of the law. The mistake which has that effect in other areas of the law is mistake as to that which is essential: see, for example, Salmond and Williams on *Contracts*, 2nd edn (edn Williams), pp 219–25. That passage contains valuable discussions and illustrations of the distinction between difference of kind or essence and differences of quality or the inessential.

In applying the law with regard to rape by the penis to the statutory concept of rape by a manipulated object, it is important to free the mind of incorrect assumptions which can arise from a feature almost invariably present in cases where the reality of a woman's consent to the introduction of a penis was the issue. In cases of rape by the penis, it would be extraordinary for the man's conduct not to be driven, at least to some extent, by his sexual impulse and urge. In the case of vaginal rape by manipulated object, the man or woman might not be driven by any sexual impulse, but insert the object into the vagina of a woman without her consent in order to hurt, injure, degrade or humiliate her.

The statutory crime of vaginal rape by a manipulated object is based on the same policy and legal principles as common law rape. It is designed to deter the introduction by a man or woman of a manipulated object into a woman's vagina without her consent. The consent which must be proved to be absent, in order to establish the crime, is consent to the introduction of the object. If the woman consented to the person introducing the object by the act which he or she did, the crime of rape is not committed whatever was, or was believed by the consenting woman to be, the ulterior purpose of the person for doing that act. On the other hand, if the woman consented to the introduction of an object by an act of one nature and character and the person introduced an object by an act of an essentially different nature and character, the woman's consent would lack reality and the object would be introduced without her consent.

In this case, each of the women consented to the applicant introducing the transducer into her vagina in the performance of the act of conducting a transvaginal ultrasound examination. That is precisely what the applicant did. For the reasons earlier discussed, the woman's consent to the proposed act, which she knew to be of the nature and character of the act which was done, was not deprived of reality if she believed the applicant proposed to do the act solely for a medical diagnostic purpose and if he actually did it solely for his own sexual gratification. The applicant did no act which was essentially different from the act which the women knew he proposed to do, and to which they consented.

We have discussed this case on the basis that the jury could have found that the applicant inserted the transducer solely for his own sexual gratification. The position would be the same if the jury found that he inserted the transducer partly for a medical diagnostic purpose and partly for his sexual gratification.

R v Richardson (1998) 43 BMLR 21

OTTON LJ:

The facts can be briefly stated. The appellant was a registered dental practitioner until 30 August 1996 but was suspended from practice by the General Dental Council. Whilst still suspended, she carried out dentistry on a number of patients in September 1996. The mother of two of those patients complained to the police, not because of the suspension, but because she thought that the appellant appeared to be under the influence of drink or drugs. The appellant denied having taken drink, and said that the only drugs that she had taken had been prescribed by a doctor for psychiatric reasons. The police discovered that the appellant had been practising whilst disqualified, resulting in the charges.

Before the trial judge, defence counsel submitted: (1) that the indictment was an abuse of process and should be quashed. There was a statutory offence of practising or holding oneself out to practise when not qualified contrary to s 38 of the Dentists Act 1934. Such an offence was statute-barred. She was charged on indictment because of public concern; (2) the hostile intent requisite for assault was not present; (3) the patients consented to the treatment, even though they did not know that the appellant was disqualified from practice.

The judge ruled against the appellant on each ground. This appeal is concerned only with the last two grounds. On the third ground the judge accepted the argument for the Crown that there was fraud here which vitiated the apparent consent. He said:

> It would not be unlawful if there was consent to the act, that is real consent, not one induced by fraud relating to a fundamental fact, that is, as put here, the identity of the person who claims to have acted by consent. The prosecution say here there was such fraud because the apparent consent was on the basis of the identity of a person who was qualified to act and, indeed, a person who was not qualified to act. In my judgment, identity in those circumstances means not merely facial features or other features, bodily features and dress or whatever of a person, identity encompasses other matters, the whole identity and that includes, in this particular case a qualification to practise. The identity presented to the patients – 'Mrs Diane Richardson able and presently lawfully dealing with your teeth' which was, in fact, a fraudulent claim and, in my judgment, a fundamental one, it was not merely not having a piece of paper it was a fraudulent total identity.

Following these rulings the defendant pleaded guilty to all offences in the indictment.

The agreed basis upon which the plea of guilty was tendered was that the appellant had practised while suspended, that the treatment was of a reasonable standard and was carried out on willing patients who had presented themselves for such treatment, and that all of the complainants had been treated by her before her suspension, without complaint.

Miss Caroline Bradley on behalf of the appellant now concentrates her argument on the issue of consent. She acknowledges that, without consent, the surgical procedures carried out were capable of amounting to an assault in law.

The general proposition which underlies this area of the law is that the human body is inviolate, but there are circumstances which the law recognises where consent may operate to prevent conduct which would otherwise be classified as an assault from being so treated. Reasonable surgical interference is clearly such an exception. Counsel relies upon the dicta of Lord Lane CJ in *A-G's Reference* (*No 6 of 1980*) [1981] 2 All ER 1057, [1981] QB 715, where it was held that an assailant was not guilty of assault if the victim consented to it but that an exception to that principle existed where the public interest required. Lord Lane said ([1981] 2 All ER 1057 at 1059, [1981] QB 715 at 719):

> Nothing which we have said is intended to cast doubt upon the accepted legality of . . . lawful chastisement . . . reasonable surgical interference . . . etc. These apparent exceptions can be justified as involving the exercise of a legal right, in the case of chastisement . . . or as needed in the public interest, in other cases.

Thus it can be accepted that a person may give lawful consent to the infliction of actual bodily harm upon himself and is justifiable as being in the public interest where reasonable surgical treatment is concerned. But the question then arises, what is the effect on the validity of consent, if any, if the complainant has had concealed from them the true nature of the status of the person who, in the guise of performing a reasonable surgical procedure, subsequently inflicts bodily harm.

In *Smith and Hogan Criminal Law* (8th edn, 1996) Professor JC Smith QC states at p 420: 'Fraud does not necessarily negative consent. It does so only if it deceives P as to the identity of the person or the nature of the act.'

This statement of principle is derived from *R v Clarence* (1888) 22 QBD 23, [1886–90] All ER 113, where the victim consented to sexual intercourse with the accused and although she would not have consented had she been aware of the disease from which D knew he was suffering, this was no assault. Wills J stated ((1888) 22 QBD 23 at 27, [1886–90] All ER Rep 133 at 135): 'That consent obtained by fraud is no consent at all is not true as a general proposition either in fact or in law.'

Stephen J stated ((1888) 22 QBD 23 at 44, [1886–90] ALL ER Rep 133 at 144):

> . . . the only sorts of fraud which so far destroy the effect of a woman's consent as to convert a connection consented to in fact into a rape are frauds as to the nature of the act itself, or as to the identity of the person who does the act.

There is a clear line of authority concerning fraud and the nature of the act. In *R v Williams* [1923] 1 KB 340, [1922] All ER Rep 433, the appellant, a choir master, had sexual intercourse with a girl of 16 years of age under the pretence that her breathing was not quite right and that he had to perform an operation to enable her to produce her voice properly. The girl submitted to what was done under the belief, wilfully and fraudulently induced by the appellant, that she was being medically and surgically treated by the appellant and not with any intention that she should have intercourse with him. The Court of Criminal Appeal held that the appellant was properly convicted of rape. Lord Hewart CJ referred to *R v Case* (1850) 4 Cox CC 220, where a medical practitioner had sexual connection with a girl of 14 years of age upon the pretence that he was treating her medically and the girl made no resistance owing to a bona fide belief that she was being medically treated. It was held that he was properly convicted of an assault and might have been convicted of rape. Lord Hewart CJ also referred with approval to the dicta of Branson J in *R v Williams*:

> The law has laid it down that where a girl's consent is procured by the means which the girl says this prisoner adopted, that is to say, where she is persuaded that what is being done to her is not the ordinary act of sexual intercourse but is some medical or surgical operation in order to give her relief from some disability from which

> she is suffering, then that is rape although the actual thing that was done was done with her consent, because she never consented to the act of sexual intercourse. She was persuaded to consent to what he did because she thought it was not sexual intercourse and because she thought it was a surgical operation. (See [1923] 1 KB 340 at 347.)

In *R v Harms* (1944) 2 DLR 61, the Supreme Court of Canada considered s 298 of the Canadian Criminal Code, which established that, in order to vitiate consent, the false or fraudulent misrepresentation had to be as to the nature and quality of the act. Harms had falsely represented himself to be a medical doctor. Although the complainant knew that he was proposing sexual intercourse, she consented thereto because of his representations that the intercourse was in the nature of a medical treatment necessitated by a condition which he said he had diagnosed. Harms was not a medical man at all. The court held that a jury was entitled to conclude that the nature and quality of the act as far as the complainant was concerned was therapeutic and not carnal. In other words, the complainant had consented to a therapeutic act, which it was not, and had not consented to a carnal act, which it was. The consent induced by the fraudulent representation was held to have been vitiated.

The later case of *Bolduc and Bird v The Queen* (1967) 63 DLR 82 (2d) was held to be on the other side of the line. The Supreme Court of Canada considered the case of a doctor who falsely represented that his colleague was a medical student and obtained the complainant's consent to the colleague's presence at a vaginal examination. It was held that there was no indecent assault because the fraud was not as to the nature and quality of what was to be done. It was observed that the defendant's conduct was 'unethical and reprehensible, but did not have the effect of vitiating the consent'.

In *Papadimitropoulos v The Queen* (1957) 98 CLR 249, the High Court of Australia considered the case of a complainant who had sexual relations with a man whom she believed to be her husband. Unknown to her no valid marriage ceremony had ever taken place. The complainant had consented to sexual intercourse under the belief, fraudulently induced, that she had contracted a valid marriage to the man whom she believed to be her husband. It was held that in these circumstances this did not support a conviction for rape. The court stated ((1957) 98 CLR 249 at 261):

> Rape, as a capital felony, was defined with exactness, and although there has been some extension over the centuries in the ambit of the crime, it is quite wrong to bring within its operation forms of evil conduct because they wear some analogy to aspects of the crime and deserved punishment . . . the key to such a case as the present lies in remembering that it is the penetration of the woman's body without her consent to such penetration that makes the felony. The capital felony was not directed to fraudulent conduct inducing her

> consent. Frauds of that kind must be punished under other heads of the criminal law or not at all: they are not rape . . . To return to the central point; rape is carnal knowledge of a woman without her consent: carnal knowledge is the physical fact of penetration; it is the consent to that which is in question; such a consent demands a perception as to what is about to take place, as to the identity of the man and the character of what he is doing. But once the consent is comprehending and actual the inducing causes cannot destroy its reality and leave the man guilty of rape.

And earlier (at 260):

> It must be noted that in considering whether an apparent consent is unreal it is the mistake or misapprehension that makes it so. It is not the fraud producing the mistake which is material so much as the mistake itself . . . tends to distract the attention from the essential inquiry, namely, whether the consent is no consent because it is not directed to the nature and character of the act. The identity of the man and the character of the physical act that is done or proposed seem now clearly to be regarded as forming part of the nature and character of the act to which the woman's consent is directed. That accords with the principles governing mistake vitiating apparent manifestations within other chapters of the law. (My emphasis.)

This result is not altogether surprising, for otherwise every bigamist would be guilty of rape.

The Law Commission in their Consultation Paper No 139 Consent in the Criminal Law, having considered fraud and consent generally proposed a lesser offence of obtaining consent by deception and stated (at para 6.27) that:

> consent should not in general be nullified by deception as to any circumstances other than the nature of the act and the identity of the person doing it, but that deception as to other circumstances should give rise to liability for a lesser offence than that of non-consensual conduct. Where the defendant is aware that the other person is or may be mistaken about the nature of the act or the defendant's identity, we think that the other person's consent should be nullified as if the mistake were induced by fraud . . . If a deception as to circumstances in question would give rise to liability only for our proposed offence of obtaining consent by deception, as distinct from the more serious offence of acting without any consent at all, liability for taking advantage of a self-induced mistake as to that circumstance could at most be for the lesser offence.

It is, thus, unremarkable that neither counsel has been able to cite any authority in which the complainant in a sexual case has been deceived as to the identity of the assailant and her apparent consent has held to have been vitiated by fraud. It is to be noted that s 1(3) of the Sexual Offences Act 1956 provides that a man can be guilty of rape if he induces a married woman to have sexual intercourse with him by impersonating her husband. However, this only covers the type of case where the woman is legally married and for some reason believes that the person with whom she is having sexual relations is her husband when in fact he is not.

Miss Bradley, who argued the case, ably contends that the complainants were deceived neither as to the nature or quality of the act nor as to the identity of the person carrying out the act. The statutory offence was created to punish such conduct as took place here.

Both before the judge and before this court the respondent expressly disavowed reliance upon the nature or quality of the act. Mr Walmsley for the Crown succinctly submitted that the patients were deceived into consenting to treatment by the representation that the defendant was a qualified and practising dentist and not one who had been disqualified. He further submitted that the evidence of the patients was unequivocal: had they known that the defendant had been suspended, they would not have consented to any treatment. If the treatment had been given by a person impersonating a dentist, it would have been an assault. There was no distinction to be drawn between the unqualified dentist and one who is suspended. On this basis, there was a mistake as to the true identity of the defendant.

We are unable to accept that argument. There is no basis for the proposition that the rules which determine the circumstances in which consent is vitiated can be different according to whether the case is one of sexual assault or one where the assault is non-sexual. The common element in both these cases is that they involve an assault, and the question is whether consent has been negatived. It is nowhere suggested that the common law draws such a distinction. The common law is not concerned with the question whether the mistaken consent has been induced by fraud on the part of the accused or has been self-induced. It is the nature of the mistake that is relevant, and not the reason why the mistake has been made. In summary, either there is consent to actions on the part of a person in the mistaken belief that he or they are other than they truly are, in which case it is assault or, short of this, there is no assault.

In essence, the Crown contended that the concept of the 'identity of the person' should be extended to cover the qualifications or attributes of the dentist on the basis that the patients consented to treatment by a qualified dentist and not a suspended one. We must reject that submission. In all the charges brought against the appellant, the complainants were fully aware of the identity of the appellant. To accede to the submission would be to strain or distort the everyday meaning of the word 'identity', the dictionary definition of which is 'the condition of being the same'.

It was suggested in argument that we might be assisted by the civil law of consent, where such expressions as 'real' or 'informed' consent prevail. In this regard, the criminal and the civil law do not run along the same track. The concept of informed consent has no place in the criminal law. It would also be a mistake, in our view, to introduce the concept of a duty to communicate information to a patient about the risk of an activity before consent to an act can be treated as valid. The gravamen of the appellant's conduct in the instant case was that the complainants consented to treatment from her although their consent had been procured by her failure to inform them that she was no longer qualified to practise. This was clearly reprehensible and may well found the basis of a civil claim for damages. But we are quite satisfied that it is not a basis for finding criminal liability in the field of offences against the person.

We have arrived at this conclusion without any real difficulty. It is our considered view that the common law has developed as far as it can without the intervention of the legislature. For the better part of a century, the common law concept of consent in the criminal law has been certain and clearly delineated. It is not for this court to attempt to unwrite the law which has been settled for so long. This is an area in which it is to be hoped that the proposals of the Law Commission will be given an early opportunity for implementation.

Finally, we feel obliged to observe that we are left with a state of unease at the procedure which was adopted in this case. We are concerned about the wisdom of the Crown being prepared to accept 'reasonable surgical intervention' as the factual basis of the plea. If the allegations of assault occasioning actual bodily harm had been persisted in and proved in accordance with the committal statements, there would have been little or no room for the defence of consent. The nature of the dental treatment (if proved) would have gone far beyond the treatment that was either contemplated or consented to by the patients or their parents.

Accordingly, we must allow the appeal and quash the convictions.

R v Naveed Tabassum [2000] 2 Cr App R 328

ROSE LJ (Vice President):

On November 30, 1999 at Preston Crown Court, following a trial before Judge Livesey QC, the appellant was convicted on three counts of indecent assault, on three different female complainants. Counts 1, 3 and 4 related to those offences. No evidence was offered on count 2 which also alleged indecent assault, and the appellant was acquitted on that count on the direction of the judge.

The appellant had been previously tried but the jury had been discharged from giving verdicts at the close of the prosecution case. Following an adjournment for reports, on February 21, 2000, the appellant was sentenced to nine months' imprisonment on each count concurrently. He appeals against conviction by leave of the single judge who referred to the full court his application for leave to appeal against sentence.

In outline, the prosecution case was that the appellant had asked several women to take part in what he said was a breast cancer survey to enable him to prepare a database software package for sale to doctors. The three complainant women agreed to the appellant showing them how to examine their own breasts. That involved the appellant, himself, feeling the breasts of two of the women and using a stethoscope beneath the bra of the third woman. Each of the three women said that they had only consented because they thought the appellant had either medical qualifications or relevant training. He had neither. There was no evidence of any sexual motive.

The defence case was that the appellant was collecting information for the database and he did no more than each of the complainants consented to. He touched their breasts, to show them how to examine themselves and they each consented to that. He had no medical qualifications, but he did have experience in the field of breast cancer.

Somewhat unusually, at the outset of the trial, a submission was made by Mr Macdonald QC, then, as now, appearing for the defendant, that the judge should stay the case on the basis that the prosecution could not prove the absence of consent and therefore no assaults had taken place. The submission was made then, because this was the same judge who had presided at the first trial and he had, of course, during the first trial, heard the evidence of the complainant women. It is unnecessary to analyse further the propriety or wisdom of making a submission at the outset of the case in this way, because, in due course, the submission was formally repeated at the close of the prosecution case. The question at the heart of this appeal is whether or not the submission, whenever made, was well-founded.

The grounds of the submission are repeated in this Court and to those we shall shortly return. First, we refer, in summary form, to some of the evidence. The complainant in relation to count 1 had first met the appellant at the beginning of 1996, when she did a computer course on which the appellant was a lecturer. He told her that he had worked at Christie's, the well-known cancer hospital in Manchester and that he was a breast cancer specialist. She thought he was a doctor, who was doing his lecturing in the evenings. She understood that he had medical training in the breast cancer field.

After she had completed her course, she and her husband employed the appellant to carry out some computer work for them. In connection with this, he attended their home.

The time came when he told her that he was going to do a study on breast cancer; he was compiling a questionnaire and would market his research to doctors. She thought it was a good cause; she trusted him.

A meeting occurred between the two of them at which, on July 18, 1997, she completed and signed the questionnaire. The appellant took her blood pressure and pulse. He referred to the desirability of using a chest height mirror. He had a bag, looking like a doctor's bag, from which he took a stethoscope. He examined her chest. He asked her to remove her bra, in order for him to show her the right way to examine her breasts. She did so. He applied his fingertips on the outside of her breast and worked towards the centre. He pressed her nipples between his thumb and index finger and told her to look out for a discharge. The examination took three or four minutes. She told the jury she would not have allowed the appellant to touch her if she had known he had no relevant qualifications. They discussed medical matters. He expressed his opinion on the treatment of her children's ailments.

A little later, in order, as it was said, to assist the appellant with his database, he asked her some questions, including her bust size and told her that she would have to take her top off again. She said no, she had done that once and made it obvious that she wanted him to leave. He went quiet, as she put it, and that was the last time she saw him. He had never told her that he was a doctor, but she was under the impression that he was and he had said he was a breast cancer specialist. There was no sign of any sexual excitement on the defendant's behalf. None of the actual qualifications which he did have would have led her to consent to him touching her breasts.

The complainant on count 3 knew the appellant. In September 1997 he came to her house and said that he was doing a survey on breast cancer. He seemed very knowledgeable. He left her with the impression that he had medical experience. She agreed to take part in the survey, knowing it involved an examination. For that purpose the appellant came on the evening of October 3, 1997 to see her. She filled in a questionnaire, and signed the consent form. He took her pulse and blood pressure. He took a stethoscope from his black bag and asked her to remove her top and bra. He thoroughly examined her breasts, pushing them with his hands and squeezing her nipples. He said it would be better if she lay down. She lay on a chair. He examined her again and the examination took 20 minutes. She would not have allowed him to touch her if she had known he had no medical training, which he had led her to believe he had.

The complainant on count 4 met the appellant on a college course where he lectured. She did not know either of the two other women. In October 1997 he gave her a form about breast cancer and said that he was building up a database. She filled in the questionnaire. She asked if he was a doctor and he said no, but he was helping doctors with the database. He came to her house on October 10, 1997. He checked her blood pressure, pulse and heart. She again asked him if he was a doctor and he said he was not but he had done a lot of work for Christie's cancer hospital. He asked if he could examine her. She refused. He checked her blood pressure and heart again and went beneath her bra with his stethoscope. He then asked again if he could examine her. Again she refused and he left after about an hour. She would not have let him touch her if she had known that he did not work at Christie's hospital, where she thought he had been training.

A Miss Hamlyn, a director of a company called Bristol Myers, gave evidence of that company having employed the appellant in July 1995, as a hospital representative, to call on doctors and tell them about the availability of drugs. He had received training on drugs and treatable diseases. In February 1996 he had scored 86 per cent in an examination relating largely to breast cancer but, the following May, he failed a test on cancer by a very substantial margin and that led to the termination of his employment due to his lack of technical knowledge. Her company produced hand-outs on how to examine breasts, for use by doctors, to give to their patients.

A highly experienced breast care nurse at Christie's, with a Master's degree in medical ethics, gave evidence that a number of the questions on the appellant's questionnaire, for example, as to the duration of periods and the size of busts, were not relevant to breast cancer, nor were blood pressure or pulse readings, nor was the use of a stethoscope to examine the chest or back.

The appellant was arrested on October 12, 1997. At his house the police found copies of the questionnaires, a pulse monitor, a stethoscope and leaflets and slides showing breast diseases. In interview, he admitted knowing the three complainants but denied telling them that he had any medical knowledge. He said he had told them about the questionnaire which was part of a project for a database for general practitioners. He would examine the woman's breasts, in order to show the woman how to do it herself. He had taken blood pressure and examined their chest and back.

So far as the complainant on count 1 was concerned, she had agreed to the examination. He denied telling her to take her top off. She had done it of her own initiative. He denied squeezing her nipples. He agreed he had no medical qualifications and had never been trained to examine breasts, but he had learned about diseases through his work. He denied that he had handled the breasts for sexual gratification. He denied, so far as the second complainant was concerned, having examined her breasts twice, but he said he might have touched her nipples. He only examined women if they wanted him to show them the procedure. He wanted them to know they were doing it properly and it was not for sexual gratification on his part. He had never deliberately misled them. He had not, at the time of his arrest, actually started the database, because he did not have enough details.

When he was charged, he said he had not acted or pretended to be a doctor or committed the assault. He gave evidence before the jury. He was a man who not only had no previous convictions, but had both a Chemistry degree and Master of Science degree. He had worked as a medical representative, selling drugs to doctors and hospitals, and he also had done a Master's degree in business administration, based on the use of information technology (IT) in training doctors. He had started lecturing in IT in 1996. He had, he said, worked for Bristol Myers as an oncology hospital specialist and he had gained knowledge about breast cancer and seen there was a need for a database. He had himself prepared a leaflet for self-examination of the breast.

He did not dispute the evidence which the first complainant gave. He said that at no stage did he not have her consent to do what he did. He denied asking her to take her top off a second time. The second complainant had consented to him showing her the procedure which involved him feeling her breasts. The third complainant had consented to being examined with a stethoscope and she had asked him if he was a doctor and he said no. He agreed with the evidence which she gave. He agreed, in cross-examination, that he had no medical qualifications. He thought he was right to describe himself as having had medical training, but his knowledge had all been gained from his employment as a medical representative. No one had ever trained him to examine a breast for breast cancer.

The safety of the appellant's conviction is challenged by Mr Macdonald on two grounds. First, he submits that the judge was wrong to reject the submission made to him and to rule that, in the light of the evidence which the complainants were to give and did give, the case was capable of proceeding before the jury on the issue of consent.

Mr Macdonald drew attention to the way in which the judge, in his summing-up, ultimately directed the jury. At p 4F, in the course of directing the jury as to the elements of indecent assault, he said this:

> Was it unlawful? That is, was it done without the consent of these women or any of them? That, members of the jury, is the vital question for you to decide in this case.
>
> Now, of course, it is right and correct to say that what these women consented to certainly in two of the three cases was to take off their clothes and to allow this man to feel their breasts. But if you are satisfied to the extent that I have indicated as a matter of fact that they only did so because they believed that this man had medical qualifications, then their consent has been negated and so it is not a true consent.
>
> So, if you find that one or more of these women only consented to what occurred on the basis that this man had medical qualifications, then I must tell you that their consent is not a true consent because what they agreed to was an examination by a person who had medical qualifications which we know that this defendant does not have and if that is right, then the assaults would have been unlawful.
>
> During his first interview which is Exhibit 11 on page 5, he was describing the training that he had with these various drug companies and he was asked:
>
> Q. As any part of that training, were you given the opportunity to physically examine women patients?
> A. No.
> Q. Why do you think that was?
> A. Because we're not medically qualified.
>
> [The first complainant] told you 'I would not have allowed him to touch me if I had known he had no qualifications.' [The second complainant] told you 'I would not have allowed him to touch me if

> he had had no medical training.' [The third complainant] told you 'I would not have let him touch me if I had known that he did not work at Christie's.'
>
> Mr Macdonald says, rightly, that in that passage the judge did not refer to the nature and quality of the act, which was a matter to which the submissions before him, when he was invited to rule on the matter, had been directed. In the course of his ruling, the judge at p 2F said this, in rehearsing the submissions of counsel for the Crown:
>
> What they consented to was a medical examination by a person with medical qualifications and not a sexual act.
>
> Mr Macdonald's reply to such a submission is that the nature and quality of the act is the same and it does not change.

The judge went on to refer to a passage in the judgment of Stephen J, in *Clarence* (1888) 22 QBD 23 at p 44, which we shall cite at a later stage. The judge went on at p 3E to say this:

> I accept the submissions made on behalf of the Crown and have come to the conclusion that what these women consented to was a medical examination to be carried out by a person with medical qualifications and not to a sexual act and, therefore, the nature and quality of the act has changed from that to which they consented.

In challenging that ruling, and the way in which in due course the learned judge left the matter to the jury on this aspect of the case, Mr Macdonald referred to a number of authorities. In *Linekar* [1995] 2 Cr App R 49, [1995] QB 250, Morland J, giving the judgment of the Court, having referred to *Flattery* (1877) 2 QBD 410 and *Williams* (1924) 17 Cr App R 56, [1923] 1 KB 340, said this at pp 53 and 255:

> . . . it is the non-consent to sexual intercourse rather that the fraud of the doctor or choir master that makes the offence rape.

At pp 57 and 259c, Morland J quoted, among other passages, that passage from the judgment of Stephen J in Clarence which the judge himself rehearsed in the course of his ruling:

> There is an abundant authority to show that such frauds as these vitiate consent both in the case of rape and in the case of indecent assault. I should myself prefer to say that consent in such cases does not exist at all, because the act consented to is not the act done . . .
>
> Consent to a surgical operation or examination is not a consent to sexual connection or indecent behaviour.

Mr Macdonald accepts that there will be no genuine consent if, in the present circumstances, a woman is misled either as to the identity of the man who does the acts complained of, or as to the nature and quality of the act done. But, he submits, the nature and quality of the act, albeit not merely related to the act itself, but including the immediate conditions affecting its nature, does not, as he put it, 'extend back' to the qualifications of the defendant.

Mr Macdonald referred to *Richardson (Diane)* [1998] 2 Cr App R 200, [1999] QB 444, in which the patient believed that she was receiving dental treatment which otherwise would have given rise to an assault occasioning actual bodily harm, from a dentist who had in fact been struck off the register. The Court in that case held that the identity of the defendant was not a feature which, in that case, precluded the giving of consent by the patient. Mr Macdonald submits that, because the identity of the defendant was different from that which the patient believed it to be, that changed the nature and quality of the act, yet, in that case, Richardson, the conviction was quashed.

He submits that to impose criminal liability in the circumstances of the present case would be to extend the criminal law beyond its existing boundaries. In his written submissions, he submitted that the case law establishes that, where an undoubted consent is given, it can only be negatived by deception or mistake and if the victim has been deceived or is mistaken as to the identity of the perpetrator, or the nature and quality of the act is different from that for which consent was given. Consent is not negatived merely because the victim would not have agreed to the act if he or she had known all the facts. In *Clarence*, the wife would not have consented to sexual intercourse with her husband if she had known that he had a venereal disease. In *Richardson*, the patients would not have consented to dentistry if they had known the dentist had been struck off. In *Linekar*, the prostitute's consent to sex was not negated by cheating over payment.

On behalf of the Crown, Mr Grout-Smith, who prosecuted in the court below, in helpful written submissions, submits that the judge was right to rule that consent to an act that is different in nature from the act performed is not a consent to the act performed. He relies on *Clarence*, and a decision of the Saskatchewan Court of Appeal in *Harms* (1944) 2 DLR 61.

The judge correctly ruled, he submits, that the complainants, if their evidence was accepted, consented to a medical act and not a sexual act. As the defendant had no medical qualifications, he could not have been touching the complainants' breasts for a proper medical purpose. The judge was correct to rule that sexual motive was irrelevant – as to which see *Court* (1988) 87 Cr App R 144, [1989] AC 28 and *C* [1992] Crim LR 642.

The direction to the jury that they could only convict on any count if they were sure that the complainant only allowed the appellant to touch her breasts because she thought he was medically qualified, was sufficient to ensure that they would only convict if they were sure that the complainants consented to acts medical in nature.

The second criticism which Mr Macdonald advances is that the judge failed adequately to direct the jury as to the necessary element of *mens rea* on the part of the defendant. What the judge said, at p 7C, was this:

> Did he intend to assault these three women? Or did he believe that he had their consent when, in fact, he did not? Well, members of the jury, if you accept that what he told these ladies was half truths and perhaps lies, then clearly it is not far of a step to come to the conclusion that he must have known that he did not have their consent and he must have intended to indecently assault them.

Then at p 47B, the judge said this:

> The defence say to you that what this man did was no more than what each of these women consented to. He touched their breasts and they consented to that and, say the defence, the prosecution must also prove that the defendant knew that he did not have their consent. Well, members of the jury, of course we cannot look into his mind as to what he knew or did not know but if you come to the conclusion that he told lies or half truths when addressing these women, then you may have no difficulty in concluding that he knew perfectly well that they did not consent and would not have done so had he not said this. But that, of course, is entirely a matter for you. It is a matter of fact.

Mr Macdonald referred the Court to *Kimber* (1984) 77 Cr App R 225, [1983] 1 WLR 1118. There, it was held that the prosecution has to prove that the defendant intended to lay hands on the victim without her consent and, if he did not intend to do this, he is entitled to be found not guilty. If he did not so intend because he believed she was consenting, the prosecution would have failed to prove the charge, see pp 229 and 1122:

> It is the defendant's belief, not the grounds on which it was based, which goes to negative consent.

Mr Macdonald submits, in his written submission, that the judge failed to give the jury any direction as to the reasonableness of the defendant's belief in the complainant's consent.

In our judgment, the pertinent authorities, in relation to Mr Macdonald's first submission, can properly be analysed in this way. The wife in *Clarence*, and the prostitute in *Linekar*, each consented to sexual intercourse knowing both the nature and the quality of that act. The additional unexpected consequences, of infection in the one case and non-payment in the other, were irrelevant to and did not detract from the women's consent to sexual intercourse.

In *Richardson*, the case proceeded solely by reference to the point on identity. As is apparent from pp 205F and 449 of the judgment, the prosecution in that case did not at trial or on appeal rely on the nature or quality of the act. In our judgment, the learned judge was entitled to follow the passage in the judgment of Stephen J in *Clarence*, which he cited in the course of his ruling. In the present case the motive and intent of the defendant were irrelevant (see *C*, to which reference has already been made). The nature and quality of the defendant's acts in touching the breasts of women to whom, in sexual terms he was a stranger, was unlawful and an indecent assault unless the complainants consented to that touching.

On the evidence, if the jury accepted it, consent was given because they mistakenly believed that the defendant was medically qualified or, in the case of the third complainant, trained at Christie's and that, in consequence, the touching was for a medical purpose. As this was not so, there was no true consent. They were consenting to touching for medical purposes not to indecent behaviour, that is, there was consent to the nature of the act but not its quality. *Flattery* and *Harms*, which we have earlier cited, are entirely consistent with that view because, in each of those cases, the woman's consent to sexual intercourse was to a therapeutic, not a carnal, act. A similar principle underlies the decision in *Rosinski* (1824) 1 Mood 18, 168 Eng Rep 1168. It follows that, in our judgment, the judge's ruling was correct.

As to the criticisms of the judge's directions on *mens rea*, there was, as it seems to us, no need for the judge to direct the jury as to the absence of evidence that the defendant's conduct was intended to be sexual. The touching was *prima facie* indecent, as we have said. Whether the defendant had any sexual motive or intent was irrelevant. The only issues were consent and whether the defendant may have believed that the complainants were consenting.

As to that, the directions which we have quoted were, as it seems to us, entirely adequate. The reasonableness or otherwise of any such behaviour on the defendant's part called for no direction, in our judgment: for the issue was not whether any belief which the defendant had was reasonable, but whether there may have been, on his part, any belief at all that the victims were consenting. Unlike the trial judge in *Kimber*, this trial judge gave, as it seems to us, an appropriate direction on this aspect of the matter. It follows that the appeal against conviction is dismissed.

As to sentence, Mr Macdonald submits that nine months was, as he put it, manifestly too long: he stresses that this was an unique case, in the sense that there was no evidence of sexual motivation so, in consequence, the conduct here equated with common assault. Because of the unique nature of the circumstances it would not have been appropriate for the judge to impose a deterrent sentence because such conduct is not, nor could be, expected to be of particular prevalence.

Mr Macdonald recognises that there would, so far as each of these complainants is concerned, be an element of shock and humiliation when they discovered the quality of the act which had been done to them. As against that, the appellant is of positive good character, who has always had an ambition to become a doctor and this lay behind his wish to establish the database to which earlier we referred.

> Mr Macdonald stresses that, in the family context, the appellant took responsibility for his brothers and sisters, following a serious accident involving their parents. Mr Macdonald submits that, if the custody threshold was passed in this case, the sentence imposed should be as short as possible.
>
> To all of these matters we pay regard. In our judgment, on the interpretation of these facts most favourable to the accused, he was playing at being a doctor. Conduct of the present kind emanating from such role-playing is such as to require a custodial sentence. Women's confidence in examinations of this kind is likely otherwise to be gravely undermined. . . .

Capacity

In order for a patient to be able validly to consent to treatment, the patient must be competent to consent to treatment. There is a presumption that every adult is competent to consent to his or her own treatment. Problems, however, arise in the case of children, mentally handicapped or mentally ill patients.

Devereux, J, 'Competency to consent to treatment: an introduction', in Freckelton, I and Petersen, K, *Controversies in Health*, 2000, Sydney: Law Federation Press

The role of competency

> A study of the role that something plays often betrays the nature of something. Thus, the role of a teacher is to impart knowledge to students. The nature of a teacher is an information importer. What is the role of competency?
>
> Broadly speaking, competency operates as a 'gatekeeper'. Competency tells us which bioethical principle, respect for autonomy or beneficence, should take precedence in any particular patient's case. Respect for autonomy is the idea that every rational person should be able to decide matters for him or herself. Thus respect for autonomy decrees that a person should be free to decide how to spend his or her own money (on clothes, on gambling or on a loved one). In medical circles, respect for autonomy means allowing patients to make their own choices whether to undergo a certain treatment or not.
>
> The countervailing principle to autonomy is beneficence: the idea of promoting the well-being of another, or, at the very least, not doing them any harm. It has been suggested that beneficence is the *raison d'être* of the medical profession. Things may, of course, go too far.
>
> When clinical questions are asked, the correct response will include the optimum course of treatment, that is, that which produces the best medical result, even though there may be an alternative which an individual patient may elect to follow and which differs from that which is

scientifically indicated. In this way, the student at an early stage in his or her professional development loses touch with the human element.

Some authors have even suggested that, on occasion, 'the medical practitioner no longer ministers to the sick, but rather treats the sickness'.

Autonomy and beneficence may often happily co-exist. If a patient consults a doctor, receives medical advice and decides to undergo treatment recommended by the doctor, the principles of respect for autonomy and beneficence operate together in harmony. The doctor's preference for promoting the well-being of his or her patient (beneficence) is not in conflict with the patient's free choice in adopting the treatment (autonomy).

Problems may arise when a doctor prefers a certain treatment option in order to promote the health or well-being of a patient, whereas the patient prefers not to undergo treatment. Beneficence suggests the patient undergo treatment; respect for autonomy decrees that the patient be allowed not to undergo treatment.

Competency solves the impasse. Competent patients will have their wishes respected. A competent patient will have his or her autonomy respected. Incompetent patients will have treatment which is in their best interests, imposed upon them. As Lord Donaldson, Master of the Rolls, put it, 'The right to decide one's own fate presupposes a capacity to do so'. Incompetent patients will find that beneficence overrides respect for autonomy.

The legal function of competency

At a legal level, competency again functions as a gatekeeper. It is trite learning to state that any person who has force applied to him or her by another, in circumstances where that first person has not given consent for such intervention, will have an action in battery. This applies equally in the case of bar brawls, unsolicited kisses or medical treatment.

What, then, of capacity? Capacity is a juristic concept whose meaning is arbitrary. A person under the age of 18 has no capacity to vote in elections, simply because the law decrees this to be so. The law could, as easily, establish the cut-off age at 8, 12, or 16. What does the law state is the capacity to consent to treatment?

Capacity to consent to treatment: competency

There are different approaches to defining capacity. The simplest may be referred to as the status approach. Thus a person occupying a certain status is viewed as having capacity. A male or female over the age of 18 has capacity to vote in an election. A person over the age of 12 has capacity to commit a crime. Until recently, this status approach held sway over competency to consent questions. Thus a child, by virtue of being a child, was deemed to be incapable of giving a valid consent to treatment. He or she was incompetent. A person suffering from mental illness, by virtue of that status, was deemed to be incapable of consenting to treatment. Times change, and in more enlightened times, we now eschew the status-based approach to competency.

Competency: a functional approach

The approach now used may be labelled a functional approach. A person's competency to consent to treatment is judged not upon their status, but upon how well they can function and achieve certain tasks. In some ways, this approach is closer to the lay person's understanding of the term competence. A person is a competent driver if, for example, they can perform the motor skills sufficient to propel their car in a desired direction, without the car stalling or hitting another vehicle. A person is a competent teacher if he or she can successfully impart knowledge to students. What tasks, then, are required before a person can be said to be competent to consent to treatment?

Roth, Meisel and Lidz have summarised the different functional approaches that could be used to assess competency. These approaches are:

(a) evidence of choice;
(b) reasonable outcome of choice;
(c) choice based on rational reasons;
(d) the ability to understand; and
(e) actual understanding.

The first test, evidence of choice, requires that a competent patient is one who expresses a choice on whether to undergo treatment or not. No judgment is made on the advisability of such a choice – the test simply focuses upon whether any decision has been made.

The second test, reasonable outcome of choice, states that a patient is competent if he or she makes the decision on treatment which a reasonable person would make.

The third test, choice based on rational reasons, asks whether the patient expressed rational reasons for making his or her choice. If the answer to this question is yes, then the patient is declared to be competent.

The fourth test, ability to understand, focuses upon whether the patient is capable of understanding information which is equally complex as the information on treatment with which he or she is supplied.

The final test, actual understanding, asks whether the patient actually understands the information on the proposed treatment, supplied by the medical practitioner.

Which one of the above, if any, is currently the test used in Australia? It will be appreciated that the first test is too simple to form the basis of a test of competency in Australia. Using this test, there would be very few incompetent patients. The second and third tests seem unduly restrictive of autonomy – who is to say what is reasonable or rational? Why should what is normal be the test in Australian law?

Australian law has adopted the actual understanding test, that is, that the patient must understand the information supplied by the medical practitioner.

Competency as understanding

The term 'understanding' is deceptively simple. Schwartz and Roth note:

> The courts tend to use the words 'inform' and 'understand' interchangeably, reflecting a simplistic assumption that understanding is the natural and expected consequence of adequately informing an individual.

What is meant by 'understanding'? Psychology and philosophy give us precious little guidance. The focus in psychology has been upon how people understand through cognitive and neuropsychological processes. Psychology offers us writings on the structure of memory and understanding, discourse interpretation and the effect of stress on learning abilities. Philosophical works have tended to focus more upon ideas, perceptions and processes of knowing, rather than analysing understanding.

It is possible to isolate three meanings of 'understanding'. The first may be described as 'understanding how'. Thus a person might say, 'I understand how to ride a bicycle'. To understand in this sense means that one is in possession of a certain practical know-how.

A second sense of 'understanding' may be described as 'understanding that'. Thus a person might say, 'I understand that you are a Catholic'. 'Understanding' in this sense is reducible to knowledge of the truth of a matter.

The final sense of 'understanding' is 'understanding what'. This sense differs from the second sense in that a person does not have to believe the truth of what is asserted. Thus a person who is told the sky is falling in, and who is then asked why he is not taking cover, might retort, 'I understand what you are saying, I just don't believe it'.

Which sense of 'understanding' is relevant for competency to consent to treatment? Arguably, 'understanding that'. It is important not only that a patient can make sense of what he or she is told, but that he or she believes the information with which they are supplied and applies that information to their own treatment choices.

A tidier way to express the above type of 'understanding' is the formula suggested by Thorpe J in *Re C (Refusal of Medical Treatment)*. That case concerned a 68 year-old man who was suffering from chronic schizophrenia. The man refused to have a clinically indicated amputation of his leg. Thorpe J noted:

> I consider helpful Dr E's analysis of the decision-making process into

three stages: first, comprehending and retaining treatment information, secondly believing it and thirdly, weighing it in the balance to arrive at a choice. The Law Commission has proposed a similar approach in para 2.20 of its consultation paper 129, *Mentally Handicapped Adults and Decision Making*.

In 1995, The Law Commission of England and Wales recommended that a person should be regarded as lacking capacity if suffering from a mental disability and unable to make a decision because:

(a) he or she is unable to understand or retain the information relevant to the decision, including information about the reasonably foreseeable consequences of deciding one way or another or failing to make the decision; or
(b) he or she is unable to make a decision based on that information.

With respect to both Thorpe J and the Law Commission, it is probably also relevant whether a patient is able to communicate a decision or not.

The next question which arises is, what type of information needs to be understood by a patient?

What is required to be understood to be competent?

Cases have established that the patient need only understand 'in broad terms, the nature of any procedure proposed to be performed upon them'.

What, then, is the nature of the procedure? At the very minimum, the nature of the procedure includes information about the physical contact which is likely to occur if the procedure is carried out. This is because, without consent, any procedure performed would be a battery. Battery is the application of force to another without that other's consent. Is a knowledge of the risks attendant to the procedure also necessary before a patient can be said to have given a valid consent? Courts, both in Australia and in England, have answered this question in the negative. In *Chatterton v Gerson*, a woman suffered pain post-operatively in the region of a scar. Her specialist advised her to undergo an intrathecal block which would block the pain messages from the region. The procedure was competently performed, but the woman's pain became much worse – so much so that she could not bear anything but the lightest of fabrics in contact with the affected area. She sued her specialist in battery and negligence. In relation to the battery allegation, Mrs Chatterton argued that, because her specialist had not informed her of the risks of the procedure, she had not given a valid consent to what otherwise amounted to a battery.

In rejecting Mrs Chatterton's claim for battery, Bristow J said that once a patient was informed in broad terms of the nature of the procedure, and gave her consent then the patient could not complain that a battery had been committed. Any allegation that the patient should have been informed of the risks of a procedure went to a question of negligence, and not battery. This view was followed by the High Court of Australia in *Rogers v Whitaker*. It follows that a patient need not be informed of (nor understand) the risks of a procedure, in order to be competent to consent to treatment.

Factors which impair competency

What sort of factors might impair a person's ability to 'understand' that information with which he or she is provided (ie, believe the information is true, and apply it to his or her own situation)? Some factors might be temporary. In *Re T*, the English Court of Appeal was faced with a situation where it was asked to determine whether a refusal of a caesarean section was a valid wish expressed by a competent patient.

T, who was 34 weeks pregnant, was admitted to hospital following a traffic accident. T was a 20 year-old who had been brought up by her mother (a Jehovah's Witness). Although never a member of that religion, T was sympathetic to its beliefs. T was diagnosed as suffering from pneumonia and had antibiotics, oxygen and pethidine (a narcotic drug) administered to her. T subsequently went into labour. After a period spent alone in the ambulance with her mother, T stated to the doctor and to the nurse that she did not want a blood transfusion. She was told (incorrectly) that other procedures were available and that a blood transfusion was not often necessary with a caesarean section. T then signed a form (which was not read nor explained to her) signifying her refusal of a blood transfusion. T's child was stillborn the following day. T was sedated and placed on a ventilator. A blood transfusion was clinically indicated and so T's boyfriend sought a declaration that it would not be unlawful for the hospital to administer a blood transfusion. The Court of Appeal was persuaded that T had not validly refused consent. She had not been given correct information, and so had not turned her mind to the true situation she was facing. Moreover, there were doubts about her competency. Lord Donaldson, in the course of a decision in which he examined closely the question of a doctor's responsibilities in the face of a refusal of treatment, noted:

> *Prima facie* every adult has the right and capacity to decide whether or not he will accept medical treatment, even if a refusal may risk permanent injury to his health or even lead to premature death. Furthermore, it matters not whether the reasons for the refusal were rational or irrational, unknown or even non-existent. This is so notwithstanding the very strong public interest in preserving the life and health of all citizens. However, the presumption of capacity to decide, which stems from the fact that the patient is an adult, is rebuttable. An adult patient may be deprived of his capacity to decide either by long-term mental incapacity or retarded development or by temporary factors such as unconsciousness or confusion or the effects of fatigue, shock, pain or drugs.

Commenting on the above factors in *Re MB*, Butler-Sloss LJ noted:

> The temporary factors mentioned by Donaldson MR in *Re T* . . . may completely erode capacity but those concerned must be satisfied that such factors are operating to such a degree that the ability to decide is absent. Another such factor may be panic induced by fear. Again, careful scrutiny of the evidence is necessary because fear of an operation may be a rational reason for refusal to undergo it. Fear may also, however, paralyse the will and thus destroy the capacity to make a decision.

Re MB concerned a woman who was needle-phobic. She consented to the performance of a caesarean section on her, but refused consent to the anaesthetist's needle. The Court of Appeal noted that at MB's moment of panic 'her fear dominated all . . . at the actual point she was not capable of making a decision at all. She was at that moment suffering an impairment of her mental functioning which disabled her. She was temporarily incompetent'. A similar case was the case of *Re L*. In that case, the woman concerned was in the middle of an obstructed labour.

An emergency caesarean section was indicated, but L refused the procedure because the caesarean section would involve the use of a needle and she was needle-phobic. Kirkwood J, applying the test outlined by Thorpe J in *Re C*, noted that L's extreme needle phobia amounted to an involuntary compulsion that disabled L from weighing treatment information in the balance to make a choice. Indeed, it was an affliction of a psychological nature that compelled L against medical advice with such force that her own life would be in serious peril.

While there is no principle that just because a patient is suffering from a mental illness then he or she is incompetent, many of the recent cases have focused on patients suffering from mental illnesses. A patient with a mental illness or an intellectual disability which affects one of the capacities outlines in *Re C*, may not be competent. In *Tameside and Glossop Acute Services Trust v CH*, the patient suffered from paranoid schizophrenia and was admitted to hospital under s 3 of the Mental Health Act 1983 (UK). She was found to be pregnant and incapable of consenting or refusing consent for her own treatment, on the basis that she was incapable of meeting the test in *Re C*.

In *Norfolk and Norwich Health Care (NHS) Trust v W*, W arrived at hospital in an advanced state of labour. She denied, however, that she was pregnant. An obstetrician recommended that either a forceps delivery or a caesarean section should be performed. W was examined by a psychiatrist who was undecided whether W was capable of understanding and retaining information about the treatment. He noted that she continued to deny that she was pregnant. The psychiatrist was equally unsure if she believed the information about the proposed treatments. The psychiatrist suggested W was unable to weigh in the balance the information provided to her. The trial judge noted that W:

> . . . lacked the mental competence to make a decision about the treat-

> ment that was proposed because she was incapable of weighing up the considerations that were involved. She was called upon to make the decision at a time of acute emotional stress and physical pain in the ordinary course of labour, made even more difficult for her because of her own particular mental history.

In *Secretary of State for the Home Department v Robb*, the principle that a competent patient could refuse medical treatment was extended to include the refusal of food and water. The respondent in that case was a prisoner who suffered from an anti-social personality disorder. Despite the existence of this psychiatric disorder, the court established that he was competent to make his own decisions about medical treatment (including the provision of food and hydration) and that, therefore, his wish to engage in a hunger strike and starve himself to death had to be respected.

The 1998 decision of the Court of Appeal in *R v Collins; ex parte S* is important because it demonstrates the misuse that can be made of the tag 'mentally ill', in terms of compelling treatment for a patient. The applicant in that case (S) was a 29 year-old woman who was 36 weeks pregnant. She suffered from pre-eclampsia. Medical advice was provided to her that she should be admitted to hospital and undergo a caesarean section. S refused to be admitted to hospital. The local authority had her compulsorily admitted under s 2 of the Mental Health Act 1983 (UK), and a declaration from the court was obtained to carry out 'all necessary treatment' on S.

S's baby was delivered by caesarean section. She sought a review of her admission to hospital and of the declaration made in respect of her treatment.

The Court of Appeal was scathing of the fact that a declaration had been made, and the use of the mental health legislation to detain someone whose views were thought to be bizarre or irrational. They approved the earlier statement of Butler-Sloss LJ in *Re MB* that:

> Every person is presumed to have the capacity to consent to or to refuse medical treatment unless and until the presumption is rebutted. A competent woman who has the capacity to decide may for religious reasons, other reasons, for rational or irrational reasons, or for no reason at all, choose not to have medical intervention, even though the consequence may be the death or serious handicap of the child she bears, or her own death. In that event the courts do not have the jurisdiction to declare medical intervention lawful.

It will be clear from the above that, in England, courts are approached with applications to authorise treatment on mentally ill or intellectually disabled patients of questionable competency. While the test of competency is the same in Australia as it is in England, the approach in most Australian jurisdictions is not to involve the courts. Rather, the services of a Guardianship Board are used.

Children and competency

The law on children's competency is somewhat uncertain. The question of consent to medical treatment for a child has been the subject of a 1996 Law Reform Commission Report. In all States except New South Wales and South Australia, the law regulating competency is common law (ie, judge-made law). In New South Wales and South Australia, there are statutes which govern the question.

The High Court of Australia in *Secretary, Department of Health and Community Services v JWB and SMB* considered the law in Australia relating to children's competency to consent to treatment. In that case, the parents of a 14 year-old girl sought authorisation to perform a sterilisation operation on her. Marion (the pseudonym the court chose for the girl) was severely intellectually and physically disabled. The court was concerned with the question of whether the girl's parents could give consent for a sterilisation procedure, or whether only a court could give such an authorisation. The High Court noted:

> The common law in Australia has been uncertain as to whether minors under sixteen can consent to medical treatment in any circumstances. However, the recent House of Lords decision in *Gillick v West Norfolk AHA* is of persuasive authority. The proposition endorsed by the majority in that case was that parental power to consent to medical treatment on behalf of a child diminishes gradually as the child's capacities and maturities grow and that this rate of development depends on the individual child . . . A minor is, according to this principle, capable of giving informed consent when he or she 'achieves a sufficient understanding and intelligence to enable him or her to understand fully what is proposed'. This approach, though lacking the certainty of a fixed age rule, accord with experience and with psychology. It should be followed in this country as part of the common law.

There are some procedures which the High Court regarded as being so serious that neither child nor parent could give a valid consent to them. These were procedures which involved:

(a) invasive, irreversible and major surgery;
(b) a significant risk of making the wrong decision either as to a young person's present or future capacity to consent or about what are the best interests of a young person who cannot consent; and
(c) where the consequences of making a wrong decision are particularly grave. Such procedures include abortions, sterilisations, the removal of life support, the removal of organs for transplants, gender re-assignment and bone marrow harvest.

It is less clear precisely what amounts to sufficient intelligence and maturity – the threshold a child must reach before he or she can consent to his or her own treatment. Does it, for example, include complex moral and family issues associated with some treatments, as suggested by one of the Law Lords in *Gillick's* case? More troublesome is the question of whether the child's competency to consent includes the competency to refuse treatment. The English Court of Appeal in two cases, *Re R* and *Re W*, thought not. The Court of Appeal in those cases held that no child has the power to refuse health care so as to override a consent given by someone with parental responsibility or a court. Only McHugh J of the High Court addressed the question in *Re Marion*. His Honour suggested that *Re R* should not be followed. The matter awaits further consideration.

The law on child consent to treatment in New South Wales is governed by s 49 of the Minors (Property and Contracts) Act 1970 (NSW). Under that provision, a person who gives medical or dental treatment to a person under the age of 16 is protected from liability if a parent or guardian has consented. A practitioner who performs medical or dental treatment on a person 14 years or older with the consent of that person is similarly protected from liability. In South Australia, the Consent to Medical Treatment and Palliative Care Act 1995 (SA) governs child consent to treatment. Section 6 of that Act provides that a person 16 years of age or older may make decisions about their own medical treatment as validly and effectively as an adult. Section 12 provides that treatment may be provided to a child if the parent or guardian consents or, if the child consents and:

(a) the medical practitioner is of the opinion that the child is capable of understanding the nature, consequences and risks of the treatment and that the treatment is in the best interests of the child's health and well being; and
(b) that opinion is supported by the written opinion of another medical practitioner who has examined the child.

Conclusion

While the law relating to competency has come a long way from the days when the status approach ruled supreme, much still needs to be clarified. The existing tests, while correctly focusing on a patient's abilities, lack the precision needed to provide clear guidance to medical practitioners. Further litigation in this area may be required before authoritative and clear guidelines are produced.

Children

The law relating to children's consent to treatment is complicated by the fact that some States have legislation regulating the area, other States rely upon common law. The law is additionally complicated by the fact that there are both State and Federal statutes which regulate the area.

Until recently, it was thought that, at common law, no person under the age of 18 could consent to (or refuse) treatment. In these circumstances, the child's parents/guardian (or the Family or Supreme Court) could consent or refuse treatment. While it is clear that the Family and Supreme Court retain the jurisdiction to make such orders, it is no longer good law to say that any person under the age of 18 lacks competency to consent to treatment.

Common law

The law in this area has come into focus only in the last 15 years or so. The House of Lords' decision in *Gillick v West Norfolk Area Health Authority* provides central reference point for the discussion.

Gillick v West Norfolk Area Health Authority [1986] 1 AC 112

> **Lord Fraser:**
> . . . the main question in this appeal is whether a doctor can lawfully prescribe contraception for a girl under 16 years of age, without the consent of her parents. The second appellant, the Department of Health and Social Security ('the DHSS') maintains that a doctor can do so. The respondent, Mrs Gillick, maintains that he cannot . . .
>
> In December 1980, the DHSS issued guidance on family planning services for young people, which was a revised version of earlier guidance on the same subject, and which stated, or implied, that, at least in certain cases which were described as 'exceptional', a doctor could lawfully prescribe contraception for a girl under 16 without her parents' consent. Mrs Gillick, who is the mother of five daughters under the age of 16, objected to the guidance and she instituted the proceedings which have led to this appeal, and in which she claims in declarations against both appellants that the advice given in the guidance was unlawful . . .
>
> [The DHSS guidance] expressly states that the doctor will proceed from the assumption that it would be 'most unusual' to provide advice about contraception without parental consent. It also refers to certain cases where difficulties might arise if the doctor refused to promise that his advice would remain confidential and it concludes that the department realises that 'in such exceptional cases' the decision whether or not to prescribe contraception must be for the clinical judgment of a doctor. Mrs Gillick's contention that the guidance adversely affects her rights and duties as a parent must, therefore, involve the assertion of an absolute right to be informed of and to veto such advice or treatment being given to her daughters even in the 'most unusual' cases which might arise (subject, no doubt, to the qualifications applying to the case of a court order or to abandonment of parents' duties).
>
> It was, I think, accepted both by Mrs Gillick and by the DHSS, and in any event I hold, that parental rights to control a child do not exist for the benefit of the parent. They exist for the benefit of the child and they are justified only in so far as they enable the parent to perform his duties towards the child, and towards other children in the family. If necessary, this proposition can be supported by reference to Blackstone,

Commentaries, 17th edn; 1830, Vol 1, p 452, where he wrote: 'The power of parents over their children is derived from . . . their duty.' . . . It would, therefore, appear that, if the inference which Mrs Gillick's advisers seek to draw from the provisions is justified, a minor under the age of 16 has no capacity to authorise any kind of medical advice or treatment or examination of his own body. That seems to me so surprising that I cannot accept it in the absence of clear provisions to that effect. It seems to me verging on the absurd to suggest that a girl or a boy aged 15 could not effectively consent, for example, to have a medical examination of some trivial injury to his body or even to have a broken arm set. Of course, the consent of the parents should normally be asked, but they may not be immediately available. Provided the patient, whether a boy or a girl, is capable of understanding what is proposed, and of expressing his or her own wishes, I see no good reason for holding that he or she lacks the capacity to express them validly and effectively and to authorise the medical man to make the examination or give the treatment which he advises. After all, a minor under the age of 16 can, within certain limits, enter into a contract. He or she can also sue and be sued, and can give evidence on oath. Moreover, a girl under 16 can give sufficiently effective consent to sexual intercourse to lead to the legal result that the man involved does not commit the crime of rape: see *Reg v Howard* [1966] 1 WLR 13, at 15 when Lord Parker CJ said:

> . . . in the case of a girl under 16, the prosecution, in order to prove rape, must prove either that she physically resisted, or if she did not, that her understanding and knowledge were such that she was not in a position to decide whether to consent or resist . . . there are many girls under 16 who know full well what it is all about and can properly consent.

Accordingly, I am not disposed to hold now, for the first time, that a girl aged less than 16 lacks the power to give valid consent to contraceptive advice or treatment, merely on account of her age . . . It is, in my view, contrary to the ordinary experience of mankind, at least in Western Europe in the present century, to say that a child or a young person remains in fact under the complete control of his parents until he attains the definite age of majority, now 18 in the United Kingdom, and that on attaining that age he suddenly acquires independence. In practice, most wise parents relax their control gradually as the child develops and encourage him or her to become increasingly independent. Moreover, the degree of parental control actually exercised over a particular child does in practice vary considerably according to his understanding and intelligence and it would, in my opinion, be unrealistic for the courts not to recognise these facts. Social customs change, and the law ought to, and does in fact, have regard to such changes when they are of major importance. An example of such recognition is to be found in the view recently expressed in your Lordships' House by my noble and learned friend, Lord Brandon of Oakbrook, with which the other noble and learned Lords who were present agreed, in *Reg v D* [1984] AC 778,

Dealing with the question of whether the consent of a child to being taken away by a stranger would be a good defence to a charge of kidnapping, my noble and learned friend said, at p 806:

> In the case of a very young child, it would not have the understanding or the intelligence to give its consent, so that absence of consent would be a necessary inference from its age. In the case of an older child, however, it must, I think, be a question of fact for a jury whether the child concerned has sufficient understanding and intelligence to give its consent; if, but only if, the jury considers that a child has these qualities, it must then go on to consider whether it has been proved that the child did not give its consent. While the matter will always be for the jury alone to decide, I should not expect a jury to find at all frequently that a child under 14 had sufficient understanding and intelligence to give its consent.

That expression of opinion seems to me entirely contradictory of the view expressed by Cockburn CJ in *Reg v Howes* (1860) 3 E & E 332, pp 336–37 in these words:

> We repudiate utterly, as most dangerous, the notion that any intellectual precocity in an individual female child can hasten the period which appears to have been fixed by statute for the arrival of the age of discretion; for that very precocity, if uncontrolled, might very probably lead to her irreparable injury. The legislature has given us a guide, which we may safely follow, in pointing out 16 as the age up to which the father's right to the custody of his female child is to continue; and short of which such a child has no discretion to consent to leaving him.

The question for decision in that case was different from that in the present, but the view that the child's intellectual ability is irrelevant cannot, in my opinion, now be accepted. It is a question of fact for the judge (or jury) to decide whether a particular child can give effective consent to contraceptive treatment.

In times gone by, the father had almost absolute authority over his children until they attained majority. A rather remarkable example of such authority being upheld by the court was *In Re Agar-Ellis* (1883) 24 Ch D 317 which was much relied on by the Court of Appeal. The father in that case restricted the communication which his daughter, aged 17, was allowed to have with her mother, against whose moral character nothing was alleged, to an extent that would be universally condemned today as quite unreasonable. The case has been much criticised in recent years and, in my opinion, with good reason. In *Hewer v Bryant* [1970] 1 QB 357, p 369, Lord Denning MR said:

> I would get rid of the rule in *In Re Agar-Ellis* and of the suggested exceptions to it. That case was decided in the year 1883. It reflects the attitude of a Victorian parent towards his children. He expected unquestioning obedience to his commands. If a son disobeyed, his

> father would cut him off with a shilling. If a daughter had an illegitimate child, he would turn her out of the house. His power only ceased when the child became 21. I decline to accept a view so much out of date. The common law can, and should, keep pace with the times. It should declare, in conformity with the recent *Report of the Committee on the Age of Majority* [Cmnd 3342, 1967], that the legal right of a parent to the custody of a child ends at the 18th birthday, and even up till then, it is a dwindling right which the courts will hesitate to enforce against the wishes of the child, and the more so the older he is. It starts with a right of control and ends with little more than advice.

I respectfully agree with every word of that and especially with the description of the father's authority as a dwindling right . . .

Once the rule of the parents' absolute authority over minor children is abandoned, the solution to the problem in this appeal can no longer be found by referring to rigid parental rights at any particular age. The solution depends upon a judgment of what is best for the welfare of the particular child. Nobody doubts, certainly I do not doubt, that in the overwhelming majority of cases the best judges of a child's welfare are his or her parents. Nor do I doubt that any important medical treatment of a child under 16 would normally only be carried out with the parents' approval. That is why it would and should be 'most unusual' for a doctor to advise a child without the knowledge and consent of the parents on contraceptive matters. But, as I have already pointed out, Mrs Gillick has to go further if she is to obtain the first declaration that she seeks. She has to justify the absolute right of veto in a parent. But there may be circumstances in which a doctor is a better judge of the medical advice and treatment which will conduce to a girl's welfare than her parents. It is notorious that children of both sexes are often reluctant to confide in their parents about sexual matters, and the DHSS guidance under consideration shows that to abandon the principle of confidentiality for contraceptive advice to girls under 16 might cause some of them not to seek professional advice at all, with the consequence of exposing them to the immediate risks of pregnancy and of sexually transmitted diseases. No doubt the risk could be avoided if the patient were to abstain from sexual intercourse, and one of the doctor's responsibilities will be to decide whether a particular patient can reasonably be expected to act upon advice to abstain. We were told that in a significant number of cases such abstinence could not reasonably be expected. An example is *In Re P (A Minor)* (1981) 80 LGR 301 in which Butler-Sloss J ordered that a girl aged 15, who had been pregnant for the second time and who was in the care of a local authority, should be fitted with a contraceptive appliance because, as the learned judge is reported to have said, at p 312:

> I assume that it is impossible for this local authority to monitor her sexual activities, and, therefore, contraception appears to be the only alternative.

There may well be other cases where the doctor feels that because the girl is under the influence of her sexual partner or for some other reason there is no realistic prospect of her abstaining from intercourse. If that is right, it points strongly to the desirability of the doctor being entitled in some cases, in the girl's best interest, to give her contraceptive advice and treatment if necessary without the consent or even the knowledge of her parents. The only practicable course is to entrust the doctor with a discretion to act in accordance with his view of what is best in the interests of the girl who is his patient. He should, of course, always seek to persuade her to tell her parents that she is seeking contraceptive advice, and the nature of the advice that she receives. At least he should seek to persuade her to agree to the doctor's informing the parents. But there may well be cases, and I think there will be some cases, where the girl refuses either to tell the parents herself or to permit the doctor to do so and in such cases, the doctor will, in my opinion, be justified in proceeding without the parents' consent or even knowledge provided he is satisfied on the following matters: (1) that the girl (although under 16 years of age) will understand his advice; (2) that he cannot persuade her to inform her parents or to allow him to inform the parents that she is seeking contraceptive advice; (3) that she is very likely to begin or to continue having sexual intercourse with or without contraceptive treatment; (4) that unless she receives contraceptive advice or treatment her physical or mental health or both are likely to suffer; and (5) that her best interests require him to give her contraceptive advice, treatment or both without the parental consent.

That result ought not to be regarded as a licence for doctors to disregard the wishes of parents on this matter whenever they find it convenient to do so. Any doctor who behaves in such a way would be failing to discharge his professional responsibilities, and I would expect him to be disciplined by his own professional body accordingly. The medical profession have in modern times come to be entrusted with very wide discretionary powers going beyond the strict limits of clinical judgment and there is nothing strange about entrusting them with this further responsibility which they alone are in a position to discharge satisfactorily.

Lord Scarman: . . . The law has, therefore, to be found by a search in the judge-made law for the true principle. The legal difficulty is that in our search we find ourselves in a field of medical practice where parental right and a doctor's duty may point us in different directions. This is not surprising. Three features have emerged in today's society which were not known to our predecessors: (1) contraception as a subject for medical advice and treatment; (2) the increasing independence of young people; and (3) the changed status of woman . . . Family planning services are now available under statutory powers to all without any express limitation as to age or marital status . . .

The law ignores these developments at its peril. The House's task, therefore, as the supreme court in a system largely based on rules of law evolved over the years by the judicial process, is to search the overfull and cluttered shelves of the law reports for a principle, or set of principles recognised by the judges over the years but stripped of the detail which, however appropriate in their day, would, if applied today, lay the judges open to a justified criticism for failing to keep the law abreast of a society in which they live and work . . .

The principle of the law . . . is that parental rights are derived from parental duty and exist only so long as they are needed for the protection of the person and property of the child.

[The Court of Appeal decided, largely for reasons of certainty, that a fixed age of 16 should be the age at which a young person may consent to medical treatment.] Certainty is always an advantage in the law, and in some branches of the law it is a necessity. But it brings with it an inflexibility and a rigidity which in some branches of the law can obstruct justice, impede the law's development, and stamp upon the law the mark of obsolescence where what is needed is the capacity for development. The law relating to parent and child is concerned with the problems of the growth and maturity of the human personality. If the law should impose upon the process of 'growing up' fixed limits where nature knows only a continuous process, the price would be artificiality and a lack of realism in an area where the law must be sensitive to human development and social change. If certainty be thought desirable, it is better that the rigid demarcations necessary to achieve it should be laid down by legislation after a full consideration of all the relevant factors than by the courts confined as they are by the forensic process to the evidence adduced by the parties and to whatever may properly fall within the judicial notice of judges. Unless and until Parliament should think fit to intervene, the courts should establish a principle flexible enough to enable justice to be achieved by its application to the particular circumstances proved by the evidence placed before them . . .

I would hold that as a matter of law the parental right to determine whether or not their minor child below the age of 16 will have medical treatment terminates if and when the child achieves a sufficient understanding and intelligence to enable him or her to understand fully what is proposed. It will be a question of fact whether a child seeking advice has sufficient understanding of what is involved to give a consent valid in law. Until the child achieves the capacity to consent, the parental right to make the decision continues save only in exceptional circumstances. Emergency, parental neglect, abandonment of the child, or inability to find the parent are examples of exceptional situations justifying the doctor proceeding to treat the child without parental knowledge and consent, but there will arise, no doubt, other exceptional situations in which it will be reasonable for the doctor to proceed without the parent's consent . . .

When applying these conclusions to contraceptive advice and treatment, it has to be borne in mind that there is much that has to be understood by a girl under the age of 16 if she is to have legal capacity to consent to such treatment. It is not enough that she should understand the nature of the advice which is being given, she must also have a sufficient maturity to understand what is involved. There are moral and family questions, especially her relationship with her parents; long-term problems associated with the emotional impact of pregnancy and its termination; and there are the risks to health of sexual intercourse at her age, risks which contraception may diminish but cannot eliminate. It follows that a doctor will have to satisfy himself that she is able to appraise these factors before he can safely proceed upon the basis that she has at law capacity to consent to contraceptive treatment. And it further follows that ordinarily the proper course will be for him, as the guidance lays down, first to seek to persuade the girl to bring her parents into consultation and, if she refuses, not to prescribe contraceptive treatment unless he is satisfied that her circumstances are such that he ought to proceed without parental knowledge and consent.

Like Woolf J (in the court at first instance), I find illuminating and helpful the judgment of Addy J of the Ontario High Court in *Johnston v Wellesley Hospital* (1970) 17 DLR (3d) 139, a passage from which he quotes in his judgment. The key passage, at p 143, bears repetition:

But, regardless of modern trend, I can find nothing in any of the old reported cases, except where infants of tender age or young children were involved, where the courts have found that a person under 21 years of age was legally incapable of consenting to medical treatment. If a person under 21 years were unable to consent to medical treatment, he would also be incapable of consenting to other types of bodily interference. A proposition purporting to establish that any bodily interference acquiesced in by a youth of 20 years would nevertheless constitute an assault would be absurd. If such were the case, sexual intercourse with a girl under 21 years would constitute rape. Until the minimum age of consent to sexual acts was fixed at 14 years by a statute, the courts often held that infants were capable of consenting at a considerably earlier age than 14 years.

I feel that the law on this point is well expressed in the volume on *Medical Negligence* (1957) by Lord Nathan, p 176: 'It is suggested that the most satisfactory solution of the problem is to rule that an infant who is capable of appreciating fully the nature and consequences of a particular operation or of particular treatment can give an effective consent thereto, and in such cases the consent of the guardian is unnecessary; but that where the infant is without that capacity, any apparent consent by him or her will be a nullity, the sole right to consent being vested in the guardian.'

I am, therefore, satisfied that the Department's guidance can be followed without involving the doctor in any infringement of parental right . . .

The decision of the House of Lords in *Gillick's* case has been the source of much academic commentary (and criticism).

Some of the more telling points have been neatly summarised in the extract from the Queensland Law Reform Commission's Discussion Paper, outlined below.

Queensland Law Reform Commission: *Consent to Medical Treatment of Young People*, Discussion Paper No 44, May 1995, p 56

A number of criticisms have been levelled at the House of Lords' decision. For example, it has been claimed that:

1. It ignores realities of everyday medical practice. It is doubtful if many adults would satisfy the criteria – let alone young people.
2. Much is likely to depend on the necessarily subjective judgment of individual doctors as to what are the best interests of the young person.
3. Very little indication of precisely what parental interest is infringed by giving a child advice (as distinct from treatment) is given, and more generally, it does little to clarify the scope of parental authority (as distinct from its duration). Woolf J thought parental 'rights' would only be infringed if the conduct in question amounted to a trespass (which advice would not). In the House of Lords, the case was decided on the public law issue that the Department of Health and Social Security advice was not erroneous in law – it sheds no light on the more specific issue of precisely what rights a parent does have in respect of his or her child. In particular, it remains unclear whether a parent could invoke the legal process to prevent a doctor (or other adviser) from merely giving advice to a child.
4. The decision does not indicate whether a legally competent young person is able to refuse treatment which is considered by competent professionals to be in his or her best interests.
5. The decision does not elaborate on whether a legally competent young person's consent to treatment determines the court's power to sanction a treatment.
6. The decision does not elaborate on whether a doctor must independently assess what is in an immature young person's best interests before relying on parental consent to treatment of the young person.

At a more basic level, it is obviously important from the point of clarity to be able to identify whether Lord Scarman or Lord Fraser's view of what amounts to competency is the definitive statement of the law. Note, for example, that the second, third and fourth of Lord Fraser's five 'prerequisites' to a child's competence may point to a conclusion opposite to Lord Scarman's requirements.

Lord Scarman's statement that a child 'understand fully what is proposed' seems at variance with the test for understanding the nature of treatment outlined in *Chatterton v Gerson* (above).

Finally, it has been suggested by some authors (eg, Simon Lee) that Lord Fraser and Lord Scarman may have shifted the focus of decision-making from the parent to the doctor – rather than from the parent to the child.

The House of Lords' decision in *Gillick* was considered, and approved as being part of the common law in Australia in *Secretary Department of Health and Community Services v JWB and SMB* (1992) 175 CLR 218.

Secretary Department of Health and Community Services v JWB and SMB (1992) 175 CLR 218

> Marion, the pseudonym of the teenager who is the subject of this appeal, is now 14 years old. She suffers from mental retardation, severe deafness and epilepsy, has an ataxic gait and 'behavioural problems'. She cannot care for herself. Her parents, who were married in 1976 and who, with their children, are residents of the Northern Territory, applied to the Family Court of Australia for an order authorising performance of a hysterectomy and an ovariectomy (referred to in the application as ovarienectomy) on Marion; alternatively, a declaration that it is lawful for them to consent to the performance of those procedures. A hysterectomy is proposed for the purpose of preventing pregnancy and menstruation with its psychological and behavioural consequences; and ovariectomy is proposed in order to stabilise hormonal fluxes with the aim of helping to eliminate consequential stress and behavioural responses. While the term 'sterilisation' is used throughout this judgment, it must be understood that what the court is concerned with are the two procedures proposed for Marion. The term is used as a shorthand for these procedures in the particular circumstances unless the context indicates that sterilisation in a different sense or in different circumstances is intended.
>
> The appellant, the Secretary of the Northern Territory Department of Health and Community Services, supported by the Attorney General of the Commonwealth as intervener, argued that the guardian of a child has no power to authorise the sterilisation of a child and that application to a court for authorisation of such an operation is mandatory. The Family Court, it was said, has jurisdiction to authorise sterilisation of a child. The respondents, Marion's parents (who are also her joint guardians and custodians), argued that the decision to sterilise a child is not significantly different from other major decisions that parents and guardians have to make for children and that the involvement of the Family Court is optional and of a 'supervisory nature' only. Their argument was that, provided such a procedure is in the best interests of the child, parents as guardians can give lawful consent to a sterilisation on behalf of a mentally incompetent child. In anything but a 'clear case', the respondents said, court involvement is desirable and they agreed with the appellant that the Family Court has jurisdiction to make orders with respect to sterilisation . . .
>
> In a case such as the present one, it is primarily the prospect of surgical intervention which attracts the interest of the law. This is because the law treats as unlawful, both criminally and civilly, conduct which constitutes an assault on or a trespass to the person. Therefore, it is the legality of

the specific medical treatment amounting to a hysterectomy and ovariectomy (or, it may be, tubal ligation or vasectomy) which must be the focus of inquiry. However, to characterise intervention comprising sterilisation as 'medical treatment' is already to make assumptions and to narrow the inquiry, perhaps inappropriately . . .

In the case of medical treatment of those who cannot consent because of incapacity due to minority, the automatic reference point is the minor's parent or other guardian. Parental consent, when effective, is itself an exception to the need for personal consent to medical treatment.

The sources of parental power, including the power to consent to medical treatment of the child, where the parent is also a guardian of a child of a marriage, are the Family Law Act 1975 (Cth), the common law and the [Criminal] Code . . .

The first issue relates to the important threshold question of consent: whether a minor with an intellectual disability is or will ever be capable of giving or refusing informed consent to sterilisation on his or her own behalf. Where the answer to that question is negative, the second question arises. Is sterilisation, in any case, in a special category which falls outside the scope of a parent to consent to treatment? Is such a procedure a kind of intervention which is, as a general rule, excluded from the scope of parental power?

By virtue of legislation, the age of majority in all States and Territories of Australia is 18 years. Every person below that age is, therefore, a minor and under the Family Law Act the powers of a guardian, generally speaking, cease at that age. In some States, a minor's capacity to give informed consent to medical treatment is regulated by statute but in the Northern Territory the common law still applies. The common law in Australia has been uncertain as to whether minors under 16 can consent to medical treatment in any circumstances. However, the recent House of Lords' decision in *Gillick v West Norfolk AHA* is of persuasive authority. The proposition endorsed by the majority in that case was that parental power to consent to medical treatment on behalf of a child diminishes gradually as the child's capacities and maturity grow and that this rate of development depends on the individual child . . .

A minor is, according to this principle, capable of giving informed consent when he or she 'achieves a sufficient understanding and intelligence to enable him or her to understand fully what is proposed'.

This approach, though lacking the certainty of a fixed age rule, accords with experience and with psychology. It should be followed in this country as part of the common law . . .

It is important to stress that it cannot be presumed that an intellectually disabled child is, by virtue of his or her disability, incapable of giving consent to treatment. The capacity of a child to give informed consent to medical treatment depends on the rate of development of each individual. And if *Gillick* is taken to reflect the common law in Australia, as we think it now does, these propositions are true as a matter of law in the Northern Territory.

If it is clear, as it is in the present case, that the particular child is intellectually disabled to such an extent as to be incapable of giving valid informed consent to medical treatment, the second question arises; namely, whether there are kinds of intervention which are, as a general rule, excluded from the scope of parental power to consent to; specifically, whether sterilisation is such a kind of intervention. Thus, the question concerns the limits of parental power other than limits arising from the child's capacity to give personal consent . . .

Australian authority prior to the present case is evenly divided on the question whether court authorisation is a mandatory requirement . . . There are, in our opinion, features of a sterilisation procedure or, more accurately, factors involved in a decision to authorise sterilisation of another person which indicate that, in order to ensure the best protection of the interests of a child, such a decision should not come within the ordinary scope of parental power to consent to medical treatment. Court authorisation is necessary and is, in essence, a procedural safeguard. Our reasons for arriving at this conclusion, however, do not correspond precisely with any of the judgments considered. We shall, therefore, give our reasons. But first, it is necessary to make clear that, in speaking of sterilisation in this context, we are not referring to sterilisation which is a by-product of surgery appropriately carried out to treat some malfunction or disease. We hesitate to use the expressions 'therapeutic' and 'non-therapeutic' because of their uncertainty. But it is necessary to make the distinction, however unclear the dividing line may be.

As a starting point, sterilisation requires invasive, irreversible and major surgery. But so do, for example, an appendectomy and some cosmetic surgery, both of which, in our opinion, come within the ordinary scope of a parent to consent to. However, other factors exist which have the combined effect of marking out the decision to authorise sterilisation as a special case. Court authorisation is required, first, because of the significant risk of making the wrong decision, either as to a child's present or future capacity to consent or about what are the best interests of a child who cannot consent, and second, because the consequences of a wrong decision are particularly grave . . . Our conclusion is that the decision to sterilise a minor in circumstances such as the present falls outside the ordinary scope of parental powers and therefore outside the scope of the powers, rights and duties of a guardian under s 63E(1) of the Family Law Act 1986. This is not a case where sterilisation is an incidental result of surgery performed to cure a disease or correct some malfunction. Court authorisation in the present case is required . . .

It is necessary to consider the precise function of a court when it is asked to authorise the sterilisation of an intellectually disabled child. It is to be remembered that what is sought is not the court's consent as, for example, in the signing of hospital forms, but its authorisation.

> The function of a court when asked to authorise sterilisation is to decide whether, in the circumstances of the case, that is in the best interests of the child. We have already said that it is not possible to formulate a rule which will identify cases where sterilisation is in his or her best interests. But it should be emphasised that the issue is not at large. Sterilisation is a step of last resort. And that, in itself, identifies the issue as one within narrow confines . . .
>
> In the circumstances with which we are concerned, the best interests of the child will ordinarily coincide with the wishes of the parents. In cases of that kind, all that will be necessary is for the court to declare that the procedure in question is or is not in his or her best interests.

A number of issues remain unclear. The Court of Appeal in England has twice held that, although a '*Gillick* competent' child may validly consent to treatment, this does not mean that the same child may validly refuse treatment (see *In Re R* [1992] Fam 11 and *In Re W* [1993] Fam 64). It is suggested that, with respect, this makes a nonsense out of according competent children the right to make their own decisions. There is *dicta* in *JWB and SMB* which suggests that the Court of Appeal's approach is unlikely to be followed here.

Another unresolved question is the situation in which a medical practitioner is faced with a woman under the age of 18 years who presents with her own child, asking for treatment for that child. The normal situation with a non-*Gillick* competent child is that that child's parents consent or refuse treatment for that child. But what if the parent is also a child? The issue is canvassed by the Queensland Law Reform Commission (above), pp 139–45.

Following *Re Marion*, the family Court has, on a number of occasions, been approached to authorise treatment in circumstances where what is proposed is 'invasive, irreversible, or major'. Such applications have included the performance of cardiac surgery on an 11-year-old boy where parental consent was refused – *Re Michael* (1994) FLC 92–471; *Re Michael (No 2)* (1994) FLC 92–486 and the harvest of bone marrow blood cells from a healthy 10-year-old boy for transplant to the child's aunt who was suffering from leukemia – *Re GWW and CMW* (1997) FLC 92–748.

The issue of authorisation to 'sex change' surgery or hormonal treatment for children has been particularly troublesome to Australian courts: *Re Alex* [2004] Fam CA 297 (13 April 2004). This case is extracted below.

Re Alex : Hormonal Treatment for Gender Identity Dysphoria [2004] Fam CA 297 (13 April 2004)

> . . . Anatomically, and in the eyes of the law, Alex is a girl. However Alex has been diagnosed as having what some of the experts define medically as a gender identity disorder and has a profound and longstanding wish to undergo a transition to become male in appearance. I think it questionable whether this condition is properly described as a disorder. I prefer the expression 'dysphoria' which I think is a more accurate description and will use the terminology throughout the remainder of this judgment. A definition appears below in para 100.

No surgical intervention is sought or indeed contemplated by any of the parties or witnesses while Alex is under the age of at least 18 years.

The key issue before me is whether I should authorise medical treatment involving the administration of hormonal therapies that will begin what is colloquially described as a 'sex change' process. In order to reach this decision I must be firmly satisfied upon clear and convincing evidence that the proposed treatment is in Alex's best interests: see *Re Marion (No. 2)* (1994) FLC 92–448 applying the standard established by *Briginshaw v Briginshaw* (1938) 60 CLR 336.

The application was brought by Alex's legal guardian with a view to the commencement of treatment coinciding with Alex beginning secondary school. Alex wants the proposed treatment to start as soon as possible. All of the evidence before me supports such intervention. It indicates that hormonal treatment would be in Alex's best interests and would benefit Alex's mental and emotional health. Some differences emerged, however, among the experts as to the precise course and timing of the hormonal treatment.

. . . I found that the further considerations which go to the question of jurisdiction justified the role of the Court in deciding whether to hear the application. Those considerations are:

- The question of whether Alex can give effective consent to the proposed procedure.
  and
- The nature of the proposed procedure.

The respondents to the application were Alex's mother and the aunt with whom Alex lives. The aunt is an older sister of Alex's mother. The consistent evidence is that the mother is estranged from Alex . . .

The final orders sought in the initiating application

. . . The initiating application sought a declaration that the Secretary of the Department, as the legal guardian of Alex, is authorised to consent to the following medical procedure on his behalf:

(a) that the child be administered a combination of oestrogen and progestogen on a continuous basis until the child turns 16;
(b) on-going psychiatric assessment;
(c) that the further hearing of this matter be adjourned to 6 months before the child's sixteenth birthday to consider authorisation to consent to the child being treated with an LHRH analogue and testosterone administered either in oral form, by monthly injection or by 6 monthly subcutaneous implant;
(d) any other order that this Honourable Court deems met [sic].

Oestrogen and progestogen are female hormones. The effect of continuously administering a combination, which is in effect a contraceptive pill without the usual one-week break, would be to suppress Alex's menses.

LRHR analogue is a drug which would suppress the release of gonadotrophins from the pituitary gland. All ovarian menstruation would be suppressed for as long as Alex continued the treatment. Testosterone is a male sex hormone which would begin the process of masculinisation. It would have certain irreversible effects such as deepening of Alex's voice, the promotion of facial and body hair, muscular development and enlargement of the clitoris.

In final submissions, I was asked to make a declaration which provided authorisation in different terms. In effect, it was submitted that any declaration I make should now authorise all the treatment that is envisaged by the orders sought in the initiating application.

I raised with the parties whether any declaration I make should be prescriptive as to the nature of the hormonal treatment or whether I ought to make a declaration which permits the attending physicians the latitude to adapt the hormonal intervention as the treatment progresses. This would permit some clinical discretion as to whether, for a period of time, the analogue would be administered on its own before testosterone was also administered.

On the final day of the hearing process, the Child Representative submitted the following minute of proposed orders:

1. That until further order the child [birth name] be known as, addressed as and accommodated by the name [male name] and it is requested that all relevant Government departments and/ or agencies give effect to this order and it is further ordered that any requirements for parental consent for any purposes associated with the use of the name of the child be dispensed with and that the consent being the signature of a duly authorised officer of the [Department] be the sole authorisation required including but not limited to the following purposes:–

    (a) Any application to register a change of name pursuant to the [relevant legislation].
    (b) Any application for the issue of [a] passport in respect of [the child].
    (c) Any application and/or request for the issue of a Medicare card in respect of [the child].
    (d) Any application to any authority for identification and/or Learner's Permit including [relevant agencies].
    (e) Without binding the children's court . . . it is requested that in any future applications and/or orders the Court consider referring to the child by the name [male name].

2. That the Child Representative, . . . be duly authorised to communicate with, attend and generally facilitate the issue of the

identifying material referred to [in] the previous paragraph and to explain these orders to appropriate persons.

3. That without the Department admitting the necessity for this order, the Secretary of the said Department ensure that all medical expenses not covered by Medicare including psychiatric and endocrinology expenses, blood tests, ultrasounds and like invoices for [the child] together with all accommodation, education, travel and like expenses including all fees and like payments payable for [the child's] current school are paid by the Department.
4. All extant applications be adjourned to a date to be fixed.
5. Reserve liberty to apply to any party and further reserve liberty to apply on an urgent basis to intervene in these proceedings to:–

   (a) [an educational body associated with the child];
   (b) the Principal of the School from time to time currently attended by the child;
   (c) the [Office which observed the proceedings].

6. I request that the Administrative Judge [of the Court responsible for the child's area of residence] as soon as practicable appoint a Judge Manager of these proceedings.
7. Liberty to the applicant and the Child Representative to provide a copy of this order to all persons and/or organisation[s] relevant to the advancement of [the child's] interests.
8. Certified for Senior Counsel and Solicitor appearing as Counsel.

The Applicant submitted that the responsibilities identified in proposed order 2 were properly those of the Department Secretary as guardian. I suggested that if an order for such matters were made, it could provide for the Secretary to keep the Child Representative informed and this suggestion was acceptable to the Child Representative.

There was discussion in respect of proposed order 3 which I suggested be expressed by way of a notation, a suggestion that did not pose difficulties for either the Applicant or the Child Representative.

I raised with the parties whether proposed order 4, which would have the desirable effect of maintaining the appointment of the Child Representative (albeit in an inactive role unless needed) might be alternatively expressed but there was no disagreement that such continuation of the appointment was desirable. . . .

The applicant

The initiating application was accompanied by a supporting affidavit from Alex's caseworker, Ms R. The annexures to her affidavit included social history and psychiatric reports prepared in 2001 and 2002 for

Children's Court care proceedings. Ms R has been Alex's caseworker since June 2002.

An impressive array of expert medical witnesses with significant publication records and both clinical and teaching experience also gave evidence in the proceedings.

Professor P is an Associate Professor in the Department of Psychiatry at a university faculty of medicine and a consultant child psychiatrist at a hospital for children. Alex was first seen by him in December 2002 for an assessment of mental health issues relating to Alex's gender identity dysphoria and depression. He has seen Alex on roughly a monthly basis since then and has been involved in a number of inter-disciplinary discussions concerning him.

Alex was referred to Professor P by Professor W, who is an Associate Professor in the Department of Paediatrics at the same university as Professor P and a paediatric endocrinologist at the same hospital as Professor P. He has seen Alex three times since November 2002 at approximately six-month intervals.

Both Professor P and Professor W have an on-going treatment role with Alex.

A Dr N also gave evidence. She is a consultant psychiatrist and specialist in child and adolescent psychiatry, particularly gender issues. She has published extensively in the area of sex gender and identity. At the request of the applicant, Dr N assessed Alex and prepared a report focussed on Alex's gender identity issues in anticipation of the present application. She also filed a supplementary report. She is not in a treatment role with Alex.

Dr C is an overseas expert. He is a consultant child and adolescent psychiatrist and an honorary senior lecturer at an English university medical school. He is the director of a specialist clinical service for children and adolescents with gender identity dysphoria. Dr C was requested to comment on current research and treatment options for gender dysphoria. Although he did not see Alex, he was also asked to make comment on a recommended course of treatment based on the facts and opinions outlined in the reports of Ms R, Professor W, Professor P, and Dr N. I treat his evidence as it pertains to Alex in light of this limitation.

Professor P, Professor W and Dr N filed a further affidavit after having the opportunity to peruse the material filed by Dr C and in response to particular matters which I raised during the hearing. In the case of Professor W and Dr N, my questions arose after they together with Dr C gave evidence together by way of telephone link up and made comments on each other's reports.

Dr G is the Head of the Department of Paediatric and Adolescent Gynaecology at the same hospital as Professor P and Professor W. She has not seen Alex. Following some questions I raised at the hearing on

15 January 2004, Dr G swore an affidavit wherein she provided information on the proposed treatment for Alex and:

(a) whether there are any studies regarding the effect on fertility from taking the contraceptive pill (oestrogen and progestogen) for three years;
(b) The impact of taking LHRH analogue with testosterone as compared with administration of the analogue without testosterone for a period of six months first.

The applicant also called Mr H, the principal of the primary school which Alex attended and it also called the principal of his new secondary school, Mr D. Both schools provide a faith-based education setting. Mr H and Mr D gave all of their evidence orally.

The Child Representative

Leave was granted to the Child Representative to issue a subpoena to obtain the mental health file associated with Alex's care proceedings in the Children's Court. It was received into evidence. It contains a report by a child psychiatrist, Dr J, who was not called as a witness.

The Child Representative also arranged for the preparation of a Family Report by a counsellor external to the Court – Mr T who is a probationary psychologist under supervision during his training period. Mr T had been working as a counsellor in the community with Alex between August 2001 and early September 2003. Mr. T was identified as the most appropriate person to make such a report given the relationship he had built up with Alex through counselling him in respect of gender identity and also on matters such as his anger towards his mother and stepfather, his behaviours at home, his peer relationships, and his anxiety about situations where he might have to reveal that he has a female physical appearance.

The hearing process

The evidence in these proceedings was adduced though a hearing process that differed in a number of respects from the traditional form of trial of children's issues in this Court. I think it is fair to say that the Court record indicates that the legal representatives and witnesses shared my view that the procedural modifications to the hearing process enhanced the depth and richness of the evidence, and thereby better served the aim of an outcome which will be in Alex's best interests. I consider that a format such as this is usually to be preferred, at least in relation to special medical procedure cases.

The hearing process was conventional in so far as the evidence in chief was mostly in affidavit form. At the request of the parties, I ordered that all documents including affidavits and exhibits in these proceedings be available to the parties and that the parties be at liberty to provide such material to their expert witnesses.

The hearing process was, however, different in the following major ways:

(a) The hearing was conducted in an inquisitorial rather than adversarial format. In substance, I indicated the type of evidence that I required and what further evidence was needed, after discussions with the parties' legal representatives and some of the witnesses;
(b) The hearing was conducted in a private conference room setting around a table using portable recording equipment. Official transcription services were used to ensure a formal record;
(c) I did not require the aunt and the school principals to give their evidence in chief by affidavit and took such evidence *viva voce*;
(d) It was agreed that the hearing would not necessarily follow the traditional course of each party having a single sequential opportunity to cross-examine witnesses one by one but rather that the questioning of witnesses may alternate between the legal representatives, other witnesses and myself as evidence was proffered. Thus, the hearing often took the form of an orderly discussion between witnesses and legal representatives (including, sometimes, instructing solicitors) and myself;
(e) A distinct benefit of the discussion format from my perspective was hearing witnesses engage in a dialogue in respect of each other's evidence. For example, observations made by Alex's primary school principal were commented upon by his secondary school principal and, on another occasion, there was a very illuminating discussion among medical experts concerning the recommended nature and timing of hormonal treatment in which each commented upon the evidence given by others during the course of a telephone link up;
(f) The nature of the proceedings lent themselves to more than one hearing date rather than a single continuous fixture. This enabled parties to provide further expert material and for witnesses to consider the evidence of other witnesses and to respond in a considered way to material points of difference. The time taken in hearings was considerably less than would have been the case if a traditional format had been employed;
(g) I was informed that Alex wished to meet with me in private and without objection, indeed with the encouragement of the parties, I did so;
(h) So far as the discussion with Alex was concerned, he requested that aspects of it remain confidential. I have honoured that request and insofar as I have acted upon any of the contents of that discussion, I have only done so after referring relevant aspects of it to the witnesses; and
(i) Given the intricacies of the evidence, I arranged for the production of transcripts following each hearing session. A copy was provided to the parties through my chambers as soon as it became available. . . .

Background history

In this section of my reasons, I set out Alex's social history so far as it is relevant to the present application and within the requirements of anonymity which I mentioned earlier. It begins to explain the gender identity issues which have arisen for Alex. I will devote a separate section to a more in-depth discussion later in these reasons.

Family circumstances

Alex was born overseas and was the only child of his married parents. Alex told Professor P that although his parents fought, his father loved his mother. Dr N reported that Alex said that Alex felt rejected from an early age by his mother who he believes 'was affectionless and harsh': affidavit filed 15 December 2003.

Alex and his parents lived with his paternal grandparents when he was very young. The household included an uncle who Alex described as 'crazy, he'd fight with me': (affidavit of Professor P filed 12 December 2003). It is not clear from Professor P's report whether this is the same uncle who Alex told him had tried to 'touch' him in a sexual way, but had not proceeded to do so.

Alex's father died when he was five or six years old, apparently from a cerebrovascular incident. The death was clearly devastating to Alex. He had spent almost all of his waking and sleeping time with his father.

Alex said that they slept in the same bed and he would bathe and shower with his father. None of the evidence suggests any sexual advances by the father towards Alex. Alex told Professor P that apart from the attempted touching mentioned above, he had not been subjected to sexual assault or interference on any other occasion.

Alex said that his father taught him karate and to punch and to kick and to be self-protective. Alex described their relationship as 'like best friends; he told me if he was sad and I told him how I felt' and said his father 'protected [Alex] from [Alex's] own mother who [Alex] said had no love for [Alex]' (affidavit of Professor P, filed 12 December 2003).

Professor P described Alex's account of the death as follows:

> [Alex] related the process of [his] father's death with great distress, saying that [he] still vividly remembers the events around his death. [He] thought something had 'blown up in [the father's] head' and [the father] died on the way to hospital. [Alex] could not see his body for some three days afterwards and still has vivid flashbacks to events around his death. [The father] frequently enters [Alex's] nocturnal dreams.
>
> . . .
>
> [Alex] said [his father] was gentle 'like a girl'. He was 'a good man, he'd speak to people like a man and my mum's family loved him so much.' At times [Alex] felt that [his father] hadn't died and that [his

> father] was just sleeping. At times [he] speaks to [his father] although he knows [his father] is not able to respond. It feels like '[father]'s smiling in my mind.' (affidavit filed 12 December 2003).

Professor P noted in his report that although Alex reported being able to feel at times that his father was alive and able to communicate with him, '[t]here is no evidence of delusions' and '[t]his phenomenon seemed consistent with his own process of bereavement and socially not unacceptable way of managing the loss of [his] father'.

A few years after the death, Alex's mother married a man who sponsored the mother and Alex to Australia. Alex has two younger step-siblings. It would seem that the mother's family was opposed to her remarriage and, according to the evidence of Alex's aunt, the mother ceased all contact with her family. Alex told Dr N that he remains angry at his mother for remarrying, and that he felt that his step-father was 'often rejecting and now he has "*turned*" [his] mother against him'.

Alex and the mother arrived in 2000. Although Alex had little English when he came to Australia, he is now in mainstream education and at the time of the hearing, he was about to make the change from primary to secondary school.

Alex was living with his aunt at the time of the hearing with the support of the applicant as his legal guardian. The aunt's daughter, a university student, also lives at home.

I now turn to summarise the course of the applicant's involvement.

Protective intervention by the applicant

When Alex was 10 years old, approximately nine months after he arrived in Australia, a child protection alert was made and the applicant undertook an investigation. It concluded that Alex had been rejected by his family and that the mother did not wish to work towards Alex returning to her care. The mother had said that she did not want Alex in her life and did not want to see him again.

The applicant's reports to the Children's Court identified circumstances including the following as leading to the initiation of child protection proceedings:

(a) The mother and step-father had taken six months before enrolling Alex in an English language school.
(b) Alex presented as very aggressive to students and had assaulted peers.
(c) The mother had said that Alex had tried to kill his step-brother by running into him with his bicycle and had poked something into the younger child's ear until it bled.
(d) At home, Alex slept in his own bedroom while the mother and the younger two children slept in a locked separate bedroom to prevent Alex from entering.

(e) The mother had said that there is no love between her and Alex and his step-father had said that he has no relationship with Alex and did not see Alex as important.
(f) The mother has said that Alex had threatened to kill his step-siblings and that she wanted Alex out of the home.
(g) The mother had said that in their country of origin, she had asked the authorities to take Alex away but they had refused.

The reports indicated that the child protection alert to the applicant also identified the following as a 'concern':

> '[Alex] presents as very masculine and wears boy's clothes. The mother has said that [Alex] has told her that he wants to be a boy and the school state that [he] has used the boys' toilets at school'. (Affidavit of Ms R filed 12 December 2003, Annexure 'NR3'.)

During the course of the investigation and subsequently, Alex was placed in substitute residential care. Alex's mother refused attempts by the applicant to arrange for her to have contact with Alex and would not become involved with decisions concerning Alex's day-to-day care, safety or well-being. That situation persists.

In his assessment for the 2001 Children's Court proceedings, Dr J considered 'that there is a long-standing conflictual relationship between [Alex and his] mother which appears to be exacerbated by incomplete mourning of the loss of [his] father by [Alex]'. Dr J also said it appeared that Alex's mother demonstrated 'paranoid ideas' regarding Alex, an assessment which seems referable to the mother's fear that Alex is a follower of the devil and would kill family members. Alex told Dr J that if he was to live with his aunt, his mother would accuse him of 'trying to plot to kill [his] family'.

Dr J said that Alex denied experiencing suicidal ideation and reported Alex to have said:

> That's a silly thing. I have a normal life. I want to be male and play with other males. My mother prohibited me from this.

Dr J reported that Alex acknowledged having perceptual disturbances, that he would hear his own voice or the voice of his father, and that Alex had said 'somebody can read my mind and the thoughts in my mind'. Dr J said however that '[t]here was no evidence of delusional disorder or thought disorder' and that Alex's orientation and cognition were intact.

Dr J recommended that the applicant assume responsibility for what may be described as Alex's residence and day-to-day responsibility. He also recommended:

> [Alex's] identification with being a male should be reviewed in the context of [his] incomplete mourning of [his] father's loss in the long-standing conflictual relationship with his mother . . . [His] level of depression should be monitored and treated as necessary both pharmacologically and psychotherapeutically.

Attempts to reconcile Alex with his immediate family were unsuccessful. Alex's mother and step-father excluded Alex from the application they made for permanent resident status. Both wrote to the applicant in October 2001 renouncing their relationship with Alex. (See Affidavit of Ms R filed 12 December 2003, Annexure 'NR4' and 'NR5').

Contact was, however, established with Alex's maternal family and in particular with his aunt, and Alex began residing with the aunt and her daughter in August 2001. Alex was then enrolled in the primary school at which Mr H is the principal.

Ultimately, in its report to the Children's Court, the applicant recommended that it assume guardianship responsibilities for Alex.

Final Orders assigning guardianship responsibilities to the applicant were made in November 2001. The applicant's guardianship responsibility is expected to continue until Alex is 18 years of age.

Alex's placement with his aunt suffered a temporary breakdown in late 2002. His primary school principal, Mr H, was concerned that Alex appeared depressed and was experiencing suicidal thoughts. In evidence before me he said:

> [Alex] was in my office and [he] was definitely quite distraught and wanting to kill [himself] because nobody was taking this whole thing seriously about the gender.

Alex's aunt also reported to Ms R that Alex's behaviour was becoming increasingly difficult to manage around this time. Ms R said in oral testimony that despite an aggressive outburst which brought matters to a head, Alex's aunt continued to want him to live with her. Ms R said:

> We had to put him in a placement though because he was actually threatening to kill himself and saying he would rather be dead and didn't want to live this way, that he wasn't a girl and didn't want to be a girl. I felt very seriously that he actually meant that.
>
> He has detailed to me before I was his worker that there are times when he has tried to kill himself, throwing himself down stairs and things like that. I don't have any evidence that he's done that but knowing how determined he can be I certainly wouldn't play down that or the risk of that in the future.

In the circumstances, the applicant as guardian decided that it would be in Alex's best interests to remove him from the care of his aunt and into a foster care placement. This was to enable Alex to be more closely monitored than his aunt could do given her other commitments and also to allow his aunt a period of respite.

Alex returned three months later to live with his aunt. The temporary placement breakdown drew further attention to issues associated with Alex's gender identity. There was the psychiatric assessment by Dr J to which I have referred, which led to Ms R's facilitation of the involvement of the witnesses Professor P and Professor W.

I now turn to the evidence relating to Alex's sense of his gender.

Alex's gender identity

Professor W's supplementary report of 13 January 2004 confirms that Alex has:

(a) no ambiguity in sexual characteristics;
(b) normal female chromosomes;
(c) hormone levels typical of an adolescent female; and
(d) female reproductive organs.

It is common ground in the material before me that Alex has a long-standing, unwavering and present identification as a male.

In evidence before me, Alex's aunt acknowledged that she had initially tried to dissuade Alex from presenting as male and that she has had difficulty coming to terms with the proposed treatment. Now, however, she accepts him as a boy and introduces him socially as such. She said that she is supportive of the proposed treatment and sees it as 'reasonable' and 'logical'. She said she would be very worried for Alex if the treatment did not proceed because he would react very badly to the disappointment.

Alex's aunt also said that since the commencement of plans to assist Alex become recognised as a boy, he has been happier, with improved behaviour and he 'seems to have some direction and some plan for the future'.

Dr N's supplementary affidavit filed 9 January 2004 states that Alex would be 'intolerant of and resistant to' behavioural treatment aimed at reversing his male gender identification and behaviour. She is also of the view that there is minimal probability of Alex accepting a female role.

Mr H, his primary school principal, recounted that the question of which toilet Alex would use became a major issue. He would wear nappies to school because he was required to use the female toilets but refused to do so. A solution was reached whereby Alex would use the enclosed toilet for people with disabilities within the student toilet block.

In response to a question from me concerning the reactions of other children to Alex, Mr H said:

> [He] was very defensive, wouldn't allow anybody in and so basically [he] would talk to me and the first teacher that [he] had [he] made a reasonable relationship with [him], the second teacher – and that continued. So I would counsel the teacher about the issues that were presenting, things like [Alex] would deliberately stand between the two lines – [he] wouldn't line up with the boys and [he] wouldn't line up with the girls. Always making a statement about all these things. So it was a matter of counselling the staff to say, 'Well, we need to

> accept this,' and staff did. In grade 6 – when [he] went into grade 6 more and more [he] wanted to identify as male and the kids kept saying 'him' and [he] would tell them. [He] also had two little cousins and [he] told the two little cousins to tell all [his] classmates that [he] was really male. We had to deal with that issue as well, and so eventually it was just accepted that [Alex] was different.
>
> When we went on camp, for the grade 6 camp, [he] did Indian arm wrestles with all the boys and, of course, beat everybody. So that actually got [him] some kudos and [he] also in that year, in grade 6, [he] played in the cricket team and [he] was the only supposed girl that played in the cricket team with the boys. So there was a whole acceptance and nothing was – while every now and then things were talked about, it was never a big issue. We sort of tried to keep it as contained as possible, counselling the individual teacher or the other specialist teachers that dealt with [Alex] because [he] can be very defiant and wouldn't do certain things. The first year [he] did go swimming, the second year [he] wouldn't, [he] refused to go swimming. The third year [he] went swimming and enjoyed it.
>
> What we did was we always tried to accommodate the needs of the individual person, in this case [Alex]. When [he] went on camp [he] didn't want to go in with the girls' dorm, [he] wanted to go in the boys' dorm. I said, 'You can't do that,' so in actual fact we had [him] a separate room by [him]self near the staff and [he] had [his] own amenities and the kids accepted that quite readily because there was already a special treatment of [his] case and we treat other people with similar sorts of needs, so that was camp. For swimming what we did was we actually used the disabled change room and [he] actually went there by [him]self and this is in grade 6. So we sort of came to an agreement that we would try and work things through. What I always did was have a meeting with [him] and discussed the issues as I saw them for the school and also what was in [Alex's] bests interests and so usually [he] would sort of comply and say, 'Right, okay, well, we'll go this way'.

Professor P describes Alex as lively, engaging and personable with a tall, striking appearance and 'a fairly masculine face and demeanour'.

Dr N's report states that '[t]here is a well documented history of early-onset and persistent cross gender identification and male behaviour'. (Affidavit filed 15 December 2003).

Ms R reports that Alex's mother had said that Alex 'always acted like a boy since [he] was a small child' and that his cousin (the daughter of his aunt) has told Ms R that Alex had 'always been masculine' and that his mother used to dress him in boy clothes when he was little. The aunt's evidence before me was in similar terms.

Professor P records that Alex had said that his father 'had tried to make [him] like a boy since [he] can remember'. Alex told Professor P:

> . . . he tried to make me a boy; he bought me boy things, he played with me like a boy – lots of action, fighting, punching and karate.

Alex's mother reportedly told Dr. J:

> [He] didn't like dolls. He liked playing with tanks and a sword. [He] had few female friends and was closer to his father than towards his mother.

Ms R commented that '[i]n the past, [Alex] has been noted to respond with anger when it is reinforced to [him] that [he] is a girl'. This corresponds with Professor P's record that '[Alex] said [he] felt very angry and resentful and talked of wanting to punch people who might have confronted [him] about [his] gender'.

During an access visit in June 2001, Alex told his family that he was a boy but that he knew that papers relating to him referred to him as a girl and that the person who had written it 'was stupid'. Ms R's affidavit continues at pars 41–43:

> 41. . . . The family laughed at this statement and did not continue with the discussion.
>
> 42. The department file notes indicate that on 14 June 2001 [Alex] requested that [he] see a doctor to confirm that [he] is a boy. According to the notes [he] told the doctor that [he] 'knows [he] is a girl but would like to be a boy'.
>
> 43. [Alex's] gender identification includes [Alex] telling other people that [he] is a boy and using the boys' toilets at school, particularly when [Alex] was first enrolled at the current school. [Alex] was repeatedly informed of the expectation by [his] school that [he] must use the girls' toilets. [Alex] then started wearing nappies to school and reported to me as recently as 18th November 2003 that [he] would not drink any liquids all day so that [he] did not need to use the toilets during school time.

Professor P's affidavit filed 12 December 2003 states:

> [Alex] has presented a consistent account of the development of [his] own gender identity to myself and to many other professionals involved in [his] care. [He] says [he] has always thought of [himself] as a boy, even though [he] had apparently limited understanding of the human body when first seen in the current context.
>
> . . .
>
> [He] said that [he] grew up in [his] first years of life believing that [he] was a boy.

Professor P reported that Alex had told him that he was distressed about being trapped in a girl's body, that he had been very sad and miserable with his situation for a long time, and that he had wanted to die. Professor P noted that menstruation is extremely distressing because it reminds him that he is not a boy and that Alex is frightened of continued breast development because it will make it impossible to present himself as a boy.

Professor P's report said:

> [Alex] reports that before [his] father died [he] had wanted to be a boy. [He] used to try and urinate standing up and [his] father would take him to the male toilets. [Alex] said 'he taught me to pee like a boy'.
>
> . . .
>
> [Alex] talked of feeling angry with God for having [him] trapped in the wrong body and for [his] father dying and [his] mother not loving [him]. [He] said that [he] had (sic) never seen [his] mother's naked body and [he] said [he] was very distressed when at five years of age [he] did see [his] mother and asked her why her body was different. [Alex] said [he] thought that the whole world was male. [He] said that [he] had never seen [his] parents being 'sexy together'. [Alex] said that some time (sic) [he] dreams at times [he] has a 'dick'. [H]e talks of having some picture in [his] mind of having 'sex with a girl'.

Earlier in the report, Professor P said:

> [Alex] is adamant that [he] is not 'gay or lesbian'. [He] sees this as the worst insult that anyone could make to [him]. [He] says [he] is a boy and would like to have relationships with a girl. Initially, [he] thought he may have children of [his] own but now realizes that if in the long run he proceeds to become a more biological male person he would be unable to have [his] own children.

Under the heading 'Formulation', Professor P concluded:

> [Alex] is a bright, engaging biologically normal 12-year-old girl who has a strong, persistent, longstanding belief and desire to live life as a male. [He] wished to be a boy even though this has its disadvantages within [his] social and family network. [He] has repeatedly stated his desire to be a boy and has behaved as such, going to boys' toilets, dressing in boys' clothes, boys' hairstyles and boys' games and activities. [He] has stopped having relationships with girls as a heterosexual type relationship. [He] feels angry and cheated that [his] body is female and angry that [he] has periods.
>
> [He] has fantasies and persistent thoughts that he would develop a penis. [He] has asked for surgical treatment in order that this might be done. [He] is aware that this is a long, expensive, difficult, process that [he] would not be able to undertake until [he] was at least 18 years of age.
>
> [Alex] has been extremely distressed by [him] feeling trapped in his body. [He] has experiences (sic) of major depression with suicidal ideation.

Professor P's diagnosis was that of: (1) Gender Identity Dysphoria and

(2) History of recurrent depressive episodes (which Professor P said was not 'current' as the time of the report).

Dr N reported in congruent terms:

3. Gender identity assessment

> [Alex] presents as an androgynous appearing young person in male clothes with masculine mannerisms and gestures. [He] gives a clear account of persistent cross-gender identification and insisted that [he] 'is male inside'. [He] is aware that [he] has a normal female body and has been learning about the effect of sex hormones, puberty and hormonal interventions for gender dysphoria.
>
> [Alex] is of the firm belief that [he] 'is male' and requires intervention for bodily change. [He] requests hormones to limit further breast development and prevent 'hip development'. [He] would like facial hair, increased muscle bulk and strength. [He has thoughts of becoming a father in the future and adopting a child.]
>
> [Alex] has feelings of sexual attraction towards girls but is adamant that this is as a male and not as a lesbian. [He] does not want girls to think of [him] as a girl and sees [him]self as in long-term relationships with women as a heterosexual man. [Alex] has not had any sexual experiences and could not describe the sort of sexual behaviour she might engage in as a male. [He] said [he] would tell a female partner [he] 'could not ever have children as a man and has no penis' but had not considered how this might impact on a sexual relationship.
>
> [Alex] has previously considered genital reconstruction surgery but at the time of this assessment is ambivalent about this and was not clear if [he] needed penile construction. [His] main preoccupations are with unwanted breast development and menstruation and [his] desire to maintain a masculine appearance. [He] has some feelings of genital aversion and said, 'I feel my body is disgusting'.
>
> [Alex] has dreams of being in a male body and projects into the future as a male. [He] has thoughts of being a priest or a doctor and helping others. [He] wishes to be accepted by God [his church] as a male and has some feelings of sadness that the church may not be readily accepting of a transgendered person.

4. Formulation

> [Alex]'s cross-gender identification appears to have emerged in the context of an idealised physically close relationship with [his] father, rejection and emotional abandonment by [his] mother, and [his] father's desire for [him] to be a male. This cross-gender formation is stable and there is no evidence that [Alex] has ever developed a psychological identification as female. [His] investment as male sim-

> ultaneously expresses anger towards [his] mother and maintains closeness with [his] dead father.
>
> [Alex]'s feelings of anger, depression and alienation appear to centre around a need to be validated in [his] gender-identity and to rebuild a sense of emotional connection to others. [He] is pre-occupied with feelings of rejection and estrangement from others, which may reflect early emotional abandonment. [Alex] can articulate a desire to be close to others but is wary of rejection:
>
> 'My heart is cold, like ice. I love no one, I don't let anyone in. My mother had a key but chose not to use it. I want a new family.'
>
> [Alex] feels 'sad most of the time' and describes urges to self-harm. [He] has cut [his] arm with a knife and on one occasion hit [his] head on a wall. [He] stated that the hope of being able to be a male has prevented [him] from further acting upon these impulses.
>
> In my opinion [Alex] has a clear Gender Identity Disorder and some additional personality vulnerabilities and unresolved attachment trauma. These issues will need ongoing psychotherapeutic support focussing on consolidation of [his] gender identity and strengthening [his] capacity for reciprocal relationships.

5. Diagnosis

(1) Gender Identity Disorder, transsexual type.
(2) Dysthymic Disorder.

Gender Identity Dysphoria

Dr C's report dated 12 January 2004 provides the following summary of what he described as Gender Identity Dysphoria in children and young people:

> A useful definition of gender identity was given by Stoller who defined it as:
>
> > A complex system of beliefs about oneself: a sense of one's masculinity and femininity. It implies nothing about the origins of that sense (e.g. whether the person is male or female). It has, then, psychological connotations only: one's subjective state (1992). ('Gender identity development and prognosis: a summary'. In *New Approaches to Mental Health from Birth to Adolescence* (eds C. Chiland & J. G. Young), pp. 78–87. New Haven, CT: Yale University Press.)
>
> This refers to the self-perception of being male or female and needs to be differentiated from sexual orientation, which refers to the person's attraction for a member of the same sex, the other sex or both; otherwise known as homosexual, heterosexual or bisexual orientation. Some authors refer to these preferences as sexual identity. Gender Identity Disorder or Gender Dysphoria describes a

> condition characterised by the incongruence between the self-perception of being male and female and the phenotypical body. The diagnostic criteria for gender identity disorders in children and adolescents as defined in the 'Diagnostic and Statistical Manual of Mental Disorders (4th edn) (DSM-IV) by the American Psychiatric Association, 1994', are listed on p 2 of attachment 1 . . .

Attachment 1 is an article published by Dr C. The diagnostic criteria appearing therein are as follows:

> **Criteria for diagnosis of gender identity disorders from the Diagnostic and Statistical Manual of Mental Disorders (4th edn) (DSM-IV; American Psychiatric Association, 1994)**
>
> A A strong and persistent cross-gender identification (not merely a desire for any perceived cultural advantages of being the other sex).
>
> In children the disturbance is manifested by four (or more) of the following:
>
> (a) repeatedly stated desire to be, or insistence that he/she is, the other sex;
> (b) in boys, preference for cross-dressing or simulating female attire; in girls, insistence on only wearing sterotypical masculine clothing;
> (c) strong and persistent preferences for cross-sex roles in make-believe play or persistent fantasies of being the other sex;
> (d) intense desire to participate in the stereotypical games and pastimes of the other sex;
> (e) strong preference for playmates of the other sex.
>
> In adolescents and adults, the disturbance is manifested in symptoms such as:
>
> (a) stated desire to be the other sex;
> (b) frequent passing as the other sex;
> (c) desire to live and be treated as the other sex;
> (d) conviction that he/she has the typical feelings and reactions of the other sex.
>
> **B** Persistent discomfort with his/her sex or sense of inappropriateness in the gender role of the sex.
>
> In children, the disturbance is manifested by any of the following: in boys, the assertion that their penis and testes are disgusting or will disappear, or assertion that it would be better not to have a penis, or aversion towards rough and tumble play and rejection of male stereotypical toys, games and activities; in girls, the rejection of urinating in a sitting position, assertion that they have or will grow a penis, or assertion that they do not want to grow breasts or menstruate, or marked aversion toward normative female clothing.
>
> In adolescents and adults, the disturbance is manifested by symptoms such as preoccupation with getting rid of primary and

> secondary sex characteristics (e.g. request for hormones, surgery or other procedures to alter sexual characteristics physically to simulate the other sex) or belief that they were born the wrong sex.
>
> C The disturbance is not concurrent with a physical intersex condition.
>
> D The disturbance causes clinically significant distress or impairment in social, occupational or other important areas of functioning'.

Dr C's summary then continued:

> Gender identity disorders in children and adolescents can persist into adulthood leading to a condition commonly known as transsexualism, or be a transient experience with the individual developing a self-perception in accordance with his/her biological body. A good proportion of children with Gender Identity Disorder who do not become transsexual adults may develop a homosexual or a bisexual orientation (Green 1987). An important part of the work with children and adolescents with Gender Identity Disorder is to assist them in the development of their gender identity and to monitor the consistency of the experience of their gender identity, which is incongruent with their biological body. After puberty (age 15–16) gender identity disorders tend to persist into adulthood although in a number of cases this can still be a transient experience not leading to adult transsexualism.
>
> As far as causation of gender identity disorders is concerned no single cause has yet been found with certainty. A number of authors would agree that many factors (biological, psychological and social) need to be present simultaneously and work together during a critical period of development to produce a full-blown gender identity disorder.

Alex's sexual identity

The lack of express consideration of the distinction between gender identity and sexual identity in the reasons for judgment of *Re A* (1993) FLC 92–402 has been the subject of comment: see J. Millbank (1995) 'When is A Girl A Boy? Re A (A Child)' 9 *Australian Journal of Family Law*, 173. It is therefore perhaps important to underline that in coming to their diagnosis of gender identity dysphoria, both Professor P and Dr N expressly considered the possibility that Alex's wish for treatment emanates from his attraction to girls. Each reported that Alex responded in a hostile manner to the suggestion that he may be a lesbian.

Such a reaction was also seen by Ms. R. She said in oral evidence:

> . . . early on I actually raised the idea with him that he may simply have a same sex attraction and that this is where his gender issues arise from. He quite vehemently denied that it was anything to do

> with that. I'm still not totally convinced in every single way possible that that isn't part of the issue for him. We could actually be looking at two separate issues rather than just one that's all indicative of the same thing. So I've always advocated that we take the timely sort of approach and not rush into anything and have made sure that he understands that there's a whole range of people in the community and just because he sees a man and a woman and a couple of children and that seems to be the bulk of what he would be exposed to in his own life, that that does not mean that that's all there is in the world.
>
> I take him to places (. . .) where he sees a far greater diversity of people and genders and images and try and get him to see that maybe a far more effeminate looking male might walk past and a very much more masculinised looking woman might be nearby and that this is a whole range of things and it's quite acceptable to be anywhere within that range and that as he gets older he has more power within himself and more options about what he chooses for himself and that what he's dealing with right now doesn't have to continue to be his reality.

Ms R is deeply involved in Alex's well being but of course is not an expert witness of the question of the distinction between gender identity and sexual identity in respect of Alex. I mention though, that notwithstanding that Ms R is not utterly convinced that sexual identity issues are not at play in his wish to have treatment, she and the applicant are in favour of the staged treatment process.

I do not understand the expert witnesses to be ruling out the possibility that with adolescent development Alex may reconsider his gender identity as a male and that if such a change in self-image transpires, he may come to view himself as a lesbian. It is not, however, the current assessment of his state of mind and sense of self.

In light of the adamant nature of Alex's gender identification and the on-going concern as to how traumatised he would be if the proposed treatment were not to otherwise go ahead, I would not delay treatment merely because of the theoretical risk that Alex is constructing his self image as 'really' male when in fact he is 'really' a female lesbian and will come to see himself that way over time.

It is true that if Alex does shift in his self-perceptions after testosterone has begun being administered he will have certain irreversible masculine characteristics. I am satisfied, however, that in the course of the proposed treatment, which includes ongoing psychological and psychiatric assistance, there will be attention to whether there emerges a change in his self-perceptions which impacts upon the treatment plan I am asked to authorise.

The treatment proposed for Alex

Professor P and Dr N identified the question of the form of hormonal intervention to be within the specialist knowledge of Professor W and were supportive of what he proposed. All medical witnesses considered that it is essential that Alex continue to receive on going psychiatric and psychological support.

Professor W's supplementary report of 13 January 2004 was prepared after having had the opportunity to peruse the material provided by Dr C.

Dr C's report made the following diagnostic comments upon the assessments contained in the first affidavits filed by Professor P, Professor W, and Dr. N:

> I have read the very interesting and comprehensive reports by Professor [W], Professor [P] and Dr. [N]. From these reports it seems clear that [Alex] presents with a very well-established gender identity disorder. The self-perception of being a boy dates from a very early age. How much [his] particular family dynamics and traumatic events in [his] life have contributed to the development of her gender identity is difficult to establish with any certainty. Part of a therapeutic exploration with [Alex], if [he] was able to engage in such a process, could be aimed at exploring the foundation of [his] 'atypical gender identity organisation' and relate [his] early experiences to her past and current perception of [his] identity. However even if some understanding could be reached through this work, this may not necessarily lead to a change in [his] convictions as far as [his] gender identity is concerned. One of the aims of this process would be to establish the level of consistency in [his] convictions or whether there is some flexibility in developing alternative self-perceptions. From the report it seems that [his] convictions about being a boy are clear and firm at present. However one should not discount the possibility that [he] might shift during the course of [his] adolescent development . . .

As a first stage intervention, Professor W recommended the continuous administration of Microgynon 30, a combination oral contraceptive pill recommended by Dr G. He said:

> The active pills are taken consecutively and continuously without using the 7 sugar pills that come in every pack. It is almost inevitable that one period would occur 4–6 weeks after the start of treatment but after that, there is a high chance that menses would be completely suppressed. Breakthrough bleeding may occur occasionally, in which case a gynaecological consultation would be obtained.

Professor W commented that the advantages of this 'completely reversible' treatment are that it is routinely used for the suppression of menses as well as for contraceptive purposes. Alex's breasts are unlikely to grow much more as they are already well developed, height growth is not likely to be adversely affected, and bone density will be allowed to increase in the normal way. He said that Alex will need to be warned about the increased risk of thromboembolism associated with the taking of oestrogen and smoking tobacco.

Dr G's affidavit of 18 February 2004 did not express concern that the continuous use of the oestrogen and progestogen pill for three years would have an irreversible effect on Alex's ovarian function and fertility in the unlikely event that he were to decide not to proceed with his transition.

Professor W favoured this option over the administration of a subcutaneous implant of a GnRH analogue which he said would reduce Alex's oestrogen secretion to prepubertal levels. It would render him hormone deficient and at risk of developing osteoporosis and the hormone withdrawal side effects that are similar to women going through menopause.

I pause to mention that it was not suggested to me that any difference in the expert evidence by referring to LHRH or GnRH analogue was of substance to my decision.

Professor W recommended that if Alex at age 16 still holds the desire to be a boy he would recommend the commencement of a GnRH analogue therapy combined with subcutaneous testosterone implants which would induce irreversible masculinisation such as voice change, muscle growth, facial and body hair, growth of the clitoris and behavioural effects 'that would make [Alex] more assertive/aggressive and have a stronger sexual urge.'

Dr C suggested a slightly different approach to the proposed treatment in that there would be a period of GnRH analogue therapy alone before the introduction of testosterone. He explained as follows:

> The Royal College of Psychiatrists' Guidance 1998 (see attachment 3, Gender Identity Disorders in Children and Adolescents – Guidance for Management) recommends that young people have had some experience of themselves in the post-pubertal state of their biological sex before starting any physical intervention. In the case of [Alex], [he] has already had periods and I suppose [he] is very distressed by them and would like them to be stopped. Professor [W] has suggested the use of a combination of oestrogen and a progestogen in tablet form to achieve this. Following this intervention it remains an issue if and when it would be appropriate to use a hypothalamic blocker, such as the GnRH analogue, Leuprorelin, to stop the natural production of oestrogens and give [Alex] an experience of [his] body once more without female sex hormones, as in a pre-pubertal state. Our paediatric and adolescent endocrinologists advise that it is reasonable to initiate this intervention once pubertal growth and development is complete and usually not below the age of 16 years. It is important to monitor bone mineral density

> carefully to avoid the risk of osteoporosis in adult life. For this reason it is also not recommended to use the analogue for longer than one year, at which point it would either need to be stopped or contrary sex hormones introduced, which in the case of [Alex] would be testosterone. This paves the way to stage three. The potential advantage of this intervention is that in our experience a small percentage of teenagers do not want to proceed any further with hormonal treatment after the 'hormonally neutral' period on the analogue. We do not know why this occurs but it does seem that it gives particularly adolescents more time to reflect on their own gender identity while in this neutral biological state.

Dr C also said that use of the analogue alone has the advantage of enabling the introduction of testosterone in a flexible and gradual way. He said that there had been no formal research on the use of the analogue alone for a period of time but that he had not seen any major problems in clinical practice.

The approach suggested by Dr C was commented upon by Dr N in oral testimony. She agreed that a period of the analogue by itself may reduce libido which 'gives these adolescents time to think about the issues, about emotional relationships and delaying sexual intimacy which might be very helpful'.

The desirability or otherwise of administering the analogue without testosterone for a period of time was also considered by Dr G who said in an affidavit filed 18 February 2004:

> LHRH analogues are used fairly regularly in gynaecology – particularly for the treatment of endometriosis, for six-month periods. It is difficult to predict the extent of side effects that will be experienced by any individual. It is fairly common to commence treatment – and then respond if necessary to side effects if they develop. In this case, the appropriate hormonal replacement to avoid symptoms would be androgens – presuming that this remains the wish of this young person. Thus the decision can be delayed and decided upon clinically at the time, with treatment being commenced if and when symptoms develop or at six months if no problems occur during the suppression phase.

Professor W embraced the 'middle course' advised by Dr G. He remarked that he would not wish there to be an order of the Court which prevented him from treating the symptoms of the analogue administered by itself. Professor P made the further recommendation with which I entirely agree, that any orders I make be framed in terms of providing treatment opportunities available to Alex rather than imposing a requirement of taking such treatment.

There is an ongoing commitment by Professor P and Professor W to providing Alex with treatment services. They are, however. professionally affiliated with the same hospital for children and it may be that Alex will begin to receive service from a different medical centre once he turns 16 years of age. There has been consultation in respect of Alex's case with the most likely other medical centre and having heard both Professors, I am satisfied that Alex's mental health and endocrinological treatment would be monitored by a team approach and would, if need be, be the subject of appropriate handover to another medical service centre.

The future arrangements in which the proposed treatment would occur

Residence and guardianship

The evidence discloses the possibility that Alex may wish to change his living arrangements in the period before his 18th birthday. To some extent, it seems that such a wish is associated with a desire to reinvent himself in his male presentation in his home life as well as at school. There is no question about the depth and genuineness of his aunt's care.

As I am not asked in these proceedings to make any orders in respect of residence, it is sufficient for me to say that I am satisfied that the applicant would be able and willing to assist Alex in this regard providing that his reasons for doing so were in his best interests and that his preferences are practicable and realistic.

The aunt, in evidence before me, said she was pleased and appreciative that the applicant's responsibility and involvement would continue and that it is of assistance in her providing Alex with a family home as he can be difficult at times.

Like his aunt, Alex himself is also content for the applicant's continued involvement. As I have commented, he has a good working relationship with his caseworker, Ms R. Professor P noted Alex's confidence in Ms R in his first report.

Ms R has also deposed that she has a close relationship with Alex and appreciates that he would be disappointed if she were to leave her position with the applicant. If that were to occur, she said she would ensure that there was sufficient overlap time to introduce and familiarise a new caseworker. She also said she would be open to maintaining contact with Alex after leaving her current position, if that were permitted by the applicant.

While on the subject of Ms R, I might take the opportunity to say how impressed I have been with the dedication that she has shown in relation to Alex. It is a dedication that goes well beyond what her duties would normally require and I consider that he has been very fortunate to have her support. It is fashionable in some circles to criticise Departmental workers. I consider that Ms R's professionalism is more representative of Departmental workers than that stereotype and is much to be commended.

Alex is appreciative of the action being taken on his behalf by the applicant to arrange the expert assessments he has had and also for the present application to the Court seeking the commencement of hormonal treatment.

There are additional practical benefits to Alex from continued Departmental guardianship. One aspect of such responsibility is to meet Alex's medical and allied health expenses and the applicant will continue to meet them until Alex turns 18 years of age so long as it is his guardian. (See Affidavit of Ms R sworn 20 February 2004.) The applicant also meets Alex's educational expenses until the age of 18 years.

Some further financial assistance may be available in anticipation of needs arising after Alex's 18th birthday. Ms R gave evidence that usually, discussion of such issues would be part of the planning process associated with the discharge of guardianship and transition to independence. It would occur when Alex is 17-and-a-half years old.

Both Mr T and Ms R said that Alex has voiced concern about how he would be able to afford the cost of continuing treatment beyond his 18th birthday, particularly if he decided to seek surgical intervention. In the above-mentioned affidavit, Ms R deposed:

> 'In rare cases where a child is disabled or has special needs which require surgery or financial assistance shortly after he/she turns 18 years old, [the applicant] may provide some assistance if it is apparent that there are not other financial resources available. These decisions are made on a case by case basis. [The applicant] may be in a position to provide financial support shortly after [Alex] turns 18 if he is seeking surgery. However [the applicant] is unlikely to consider providing assistance if [Alex] is undergoing surgery several years after he turns 18 years old.'

Ms R's affidavit then made reference to surgery associated with Alex's desire to live as a male. It indicated that she had been informed that the 'current cost of surgery is approximately $5,000 if one has private health insurance at the top level' and that the expert clinician consulted on this matter had said that the clinician 'will not usually contemplate surgery for a patient prior to 21 years old'.

Ms R's affidavit continued:

> Whilst the cost of surgery is significant, I am aware that [the aunt] has banked all he carer's payments into a joint bank account with [Alex] with the intention of [Alex] having full access to them at the age of 18 years old . . . Carer's payments will continue until [Alex] is 18 years of age unless [Alex] leaves school and obtains employment or is the recipient of other Government benefits. If [Alex] remains at school until 18 years of age and Alex and [his aunt] do not withdraw funds from the account, there will be in excess of $60,000 for [Alex] to access at the age of 18.

Educational

Pursuant to my interim orders, Alex is now enrolled under his newly chosen male name at secondary school. By the time I heard evidence from his principal, Mr D, Alex had been at school for a couple of weeks. He said:

> We're only two or three weeks in but things seem to be going okay. But there will be significant issues.

The very practical question of which toilet Alex uses has been resolved. He uses a male toilet that is not used by the other students except for special reasons. It is in the staff area and used by students who may have celiac disease or irritable bowel syndrome.

Mr D said that it had been determined in conjunction with Alex, that only a limited number of teachers would be informed of his medical issues. He said:

> They may need to know that the student has special needs and there needs to be some sympathetic awareness of that, but they do not need to know the specifics because it is not relevant to designing the learning experience for that student.

Additional support mechanisms have been established for Alex and the school is receiving external assistance and guidance in managing issues as they arise, for example, how Alex may participate in sporting activities. The applicant has committed to being part of this assistance structure and this was an important factor for Mr D in making a judgment as to whether the enrolment should proceed.

Mr D explained that the school has developed 'quite comprehensive anti-harassment, anti-bullying policies and procedures' which involve a range of responses, and Mr D, correctly in my view, saw Alex as not 'being different from the other student who's the subject of unwarranted attention either verbal or physical . . .':

Mr H, Alex's primary school principal said that he had never been approached by parents concerning Alex's gender identity. Mr D said in response that the secondary school has anticipated the possibility of parents' adverse reactions if Alex were to disclose his transition to a fellow student. I found Mr D's answers reassuring:

> I guess the strategies would include meeting such people and assuring them – asking them perhaps, first of all, to indicate in what ways their child is at risk or under some sort of threat, then if there is a perceived risk to deal with that and talk through that. But I would be challenging them to establish their bona fides to make any comment at all in the first instance. I wouldn't be kind of a defensive mode I can assure you. I'd be saying, 'Well, you've got to convince me that there's a case to be answered here before we' – but then if there is a concern about the influence on their child of another child in terms of friendship we would deal with that through counselling

> and discussion and contact. That's not unusual in secondary schools in terms of, for example, same sex – emergent same sex orientation. It's quite common that students can sometimes be the unwanted recipients of attention of other students and families can sometimes express concern about, 'What's the impact of this friendship on my child?' and 'What are you doing about this?' So we've sort of dealt with that over the years routinely . . .
>
> . . .
>
> I see the pastoral issues for the secondary school are similar to disclosure about same sex attraction which is increasingly common. More and more adolescents are feeling more comfortable about coming out at school rather than waiting until they leave school. We've had a number of students at our last place over the last few years who have quite provocatively come out in various ways. A bit like [Alex] sort of saying, 'Well, I want to be' – some of them are a bit naive about the expected kind of response to that . . .

I was also advised by the Child Representative that consideration had been given to what would happen if it transpired that a disclosure led to risks to Alex's safety in the school. In such circumstances, the applicant in conjunction with the associated educationalists involved in Alex's case would be able to find a different school placement for him.

Jurisdiction

In this section of my judgment I explain why I found that I have jurisdiction to hear the present application.

Notwithstanding the agreement or the silence of the parties as to questions of jurisdiction, it is incumbent upon a court to be satisfied that it has jurisdiction to hear an application. Toohey J in *Harris v Caladine* (1991) 172 CLR 84 at 136 defined the term as follows:

> Jurisdiction is the authority which a court has to decide the range of matters that can be litigated before it; . . .

Section 67ZC of the Act is a grant of jurisdiction. It provides:

> (1) In addition to the jurisdiction that a court has under this Part in relation to children, the court also has jurisdiction to make orders relating to the welfare of children.
> (2) In deciding whether to make an order under subsection (1) in relation to a child, a court must regard the best interests of the child as the paramount consideration.

The accompanying Explanatory Memorandum stated that the new provision:

> . . . provides the court with jurisdiction relating to the welfare of children in addition to the jurisdiction that the court has under Part VII in relation to children. This jurisdiction is the parens patriae

> jurisdiction explained by the High Court in SMB and JWB; Secretary, Department of Health and Community Services [sic] Re Marion (1992) 175 CLR 218.

Division 10 of the Act, which contains s 68F, provides for how a court determines the best interests of a child or young person. Section 68F(2) is the well known 'checklist' of factors to which a Court must have regard.

In *Re Marion (No. 2)* (1994) FLC 92–448 I proposed a number of particular matters to be considered when the Court is faced with a special medical procedure application, in that case, a sterilisation procedure. These are:

(i) the particular condition of the child which requires the procedure or treatment;
(ii) the nature of the procedure or treatment proposed;
(iii) the reasons for which it is proposed that the procedure or treatment be carried out;
(iv) the alternative courses of treatment that are available in relation to that condition;
(v) the desirability of and effect of authorising the procedure for treatment proposed rather than available alternatives;
(vi) the physical effects on the child and the psychological and social implications for the child of:

  (a) authorising the proposed procedure or treatment;
  (b) not authorising the proposed procedure or treatment;

(vii) the nature and degree of any risk to the child of:

  (a) authorising the proposed procedure or treatment;
  (b) not authorising the proposed procedure or treatment;

(viii) the views (if any) expressed by:

  (a) the guardian(s) of the child;
  (b) a person who is entitled to the custody of the child;
  (c) a person who is responsible for the daily care and control of the child;
  (d) the child;

to the proposed procedure or treatment and to any alternative procedure or treatment.

Subsequently in *P and P* (1995) FLC 92 615, another sterilisation case, the Full Court said that the matters I suggested 'should prove of practical use to those considering problems of this nature' (at 82 151).

There are three factual issues which determine the Court's capacity to exercise the welfare jurisdiction granted by s 67ZC of the Act.

Whether the child or young person is currently under a care order

. . . two further issues arise from the High Court of Australia's decision in *Secretary, Department of Health and Community Services v JWB and SMB* (1992) 175 CLR 218 (*Marion's* case) which is the relevantly binding Australian authority:

- whether the child or young person is himself competent to consent; and
- whether the subject matter of the application is a 'special medical procedure' to which a parent or guardian cannot consent.

Marion's case involved an application for the sterilisation of a 14-year-old teenager with a severe intellectual disability for the purpose of 'preventing pregnancy and menstruation with its psychological and behavioural consequences'. The gravamen of the decision was that if a child or young person cannot consent her/himself to a medical procedure, parental consent (which for present purposes may be equated with that of a guardian) is ineffective where the proposed intervention is:

- invasive, permanent and irreversible; and
- not for the purpose of curing a malfunction or disease.

Whether the child or young person himself can consent to the procedure

The welfare jurisdiction is a protective jurisdiction. It is paternalistic and, in modern thinking about children and young people, must be understood with regard to their rights.

The circumstances in which a child or young person has the right to make his or her own decisions as to medical treatment are far from precise. There is a significant onus upon the treating professional's assessment of the child or young person. Unless legislation provides otherwise, and it is not applicable in this case, the professional risks liability unless satisfied that the child or young person has 'a sufficient understanding and intelligence to enable him or her to understand fully what is imposed' – *Marion's case* at 237–238. A majority of the High Court were there expressly approving a principle that emerged from House of Lords' decision in *Gillick v West Norfolk and Wisbech Area Health Authority* ('*Gillick's case*') [1986] AC 112. Even though the question of Marion's *Gillick* competency was not, in fact, an issue in that case, given the degree of Marion's disability, the following statement by the High Court majority has been applied by this Court in special medical procedure cases:

'*This* [Gillick] *approach, though lacking the certainty of a fixed age rule, accords with experience and with psychology. It should be followed in this country as part of the common law.*' (at 237–238, footnotes omitted; see for example the Full Court's decision in *P and P* (supra) and, in respect of a procedure other than sterilisation, the first instance decisions of *Re A (A child)* (supra) and *Re GWW and CMW* (supra)).

The majority in *Marion's* case (at 232) described as a 'threshold question of consent; whether a child, intellectually disabled or not, is capable, in law or in fact, of consenting to medical treatment on his or her own behalf'. As submitted by the Commission, I am therefore required to consider whether Alex is competent in the sense that 'competent' is used in *Gillick's* case – whether Alex has achieved 'a sufficient understanding and intelligence to enable him or her to understand fully what is proposed'. The Commission further submitted this was a threshold matter and the first decision I must make.

There is evidence on this matter from Mr T, who prepared the family report and from Professor P, the treating child psychiatrist.

The evidence from Mr T was that Alex was able to describe the stages of treatment he is currently undergoing and those that he will be able to undergo in the next few years. Mr T reported:

> [Alex] was also able to tell me that he is on stage I of the treatment and that the 'pill medication' he is on now, stops his periods, can cause him to feel like he is having a headache or that he wants to vomit. Furthermore, he indicated that he uses 'the medication to go to school as a boy'. In addition, he reported that the medication stops his breasts growing and 'stops hip shape growing like female shape'.
>
> [Alex] reported that stage II would involve him taking 'a male hormone and the injection medication' that is similar to the one he is taking for stage I. With the male hormone, he said, 'it won't affect my bones as I am getting older, while I take the injection. If I take the injection medication by itself, it will affect my bones badly as I am getting older.' At a later session I asked [Alex] how would the bones be affected and he answered, saying 'Make my bones feel weak, won't be strong like now anymore. Feel sick, could break my bones if I do weight lifting'. [Alex] also reported that the male hormone also makes him have a deeper voice, 'it's kinda scarier, stronger and louder than a woman's voice', 'I'll have hair, bones stronger like a boy, man, muscles begin stronger like normal boys'. [Alex] said he hopes that Stage II could be done when he turns 15 'so I look like a young man, like a normal teenager does'.

Mr T's report indicated that Alex appreciated that irreversibility commences with the taking of the testosterone. Mr T also reported:

> In a later session, I asked [Alex] how he got to know the above information, he said from his doctor, from his aunt, from books and from his own thinking. I also asked if anyone had told him how to answer these questions, he said no.

Mr T's conclusion was as follows:

> I am of the professional opinion that while [Alex] appears very knowledgeable about, and would seem to have an intellectual understanding of, the treatment process, including the stages of the

> treatment, some of the intended effects as well as the side-effects of the medications and what the treatment process is for it is not clear whether he understands the full implications of the treatment. I, therefore, concur with [Professor P's] point in his Supplementary Mental Health Report on [Alex] that 'it is not appropriate at age 13 [Alex] should be wholly responsible for the decision to undergo hormone treatment'.

The supplementary reports filed by Professor P and Dr N addressed the question of Alex's present and future capacity to consent to the proposed treatment.

Professor P stated that Alex has an adequate understanding of sex differences and the human reproductive system. He also reported that Alex appreciates the nature of the proposed treatment and its consequences better than he would expect other young people his age to understand it, and that Alex has acquired this information over a fairly short space of time.

Professor P expressed the view and that Alex demonstrates 'good intellectual and cognitive capacity to learn and understand such phenomena'. Professor P is not qualified to undertake formal psychometric assessment but he said he believed that Alex's general intellectual capacities are at least average for his age.

I would refer to two particular statements of Professor P:

> Although [Alex] fully understands at this stage the mechanism of action for the proposed hormone treatment, and side effects and the benefits, I believe that it is not appropriate at age 13 [he] should be wholly responsible for the decision to undergo hormone treatment. This is particularly so since [his] own mother is not currently responsible for his care.
>
> . . .
>
> I believe that [Alex] is able to make an informed judgment about the procedure and its risk in the foreseeable future but that the urgency of treatment is such that it should begin as soon as possible.

These comments would suggest that Alex may in fact have 'Gillick' capacity or may reach that standard soon but that nonetheless it is Professor P's view that the decision should be in the Court's hands in part due to the urgency of the matter. I would also observe that it is unclear to me how Alex being out of his mother's care bears upon the question of Alex's capacity. These matters were not elaborated in oral evidence.

Dr. N's supplementary report was also somewhat non-specific on the question of capacity. Her assessment described Alex as 'a mature, intelligent 12-year-old' who 'concurrently has angry and unresolved feelings towards her mother and a strong identification with her deceased father'. Dr N's opinion of the significance of these matters was as follows:

> The issue here is to what effect these emotional factors impact on

> [his] capacity to understand the proposed treatments. In my opinion, these factors are important underlying determinants, they per se, should not be seen as contraindications to medical intervention or as impairing [Alex's] comprehension.

Dr N's report does not provide a final conclusion on the question of Alex's capacity to give effective consent.

In my view, the evidence does not establish that Alex has the capacity to decide for himself whether to consent to the proposed treatment. It is one thing for a child or young person to have a general understanding of what is proposed and its effect but it is quite another to conclude that he/she has sufficient maturity to fully understand the grave nature and effects of the proposed treatment.

However, in the present case, I have uncontroverted evidence not only that the proposed procedure is entirely consistent with Alex's wishes but also that the expert evidence as to the best interests of Alex accords with those wishes. I therefore take the view that the capacity of Alex to give his own consent would be an academic question unless I were to refuse authorisation. The evidence left me in no doubt that I should make orders authorising at least the continued first stage of the proposed treatment that I had permitted by way of interim orders and, as is discussed subsequently, the second stage of hormonal treatment as well.

Before leaving this topic, I would note the following written submissions of the Commission which responded to a request I made in the course of hearing closing argument:

> 2.5 The general position in Australia in relation to competent minors refusing medical treatment is unclear. While the right of minors to consent to medical treatment has been judicially recognised, their right to refuse treatment has not been the subject of similar discussion. The position in England following the cases of *Re R and Re W* is that a 'Gillick competent' child is unable to refuse treatment, if such refusal has the effect of overriding consent given by the guardian or the court. It is submitted that this view should not be adopted in Australia. It is submitted that the better view – and the view that is most consistent with *Re Marion* and the principles of international law outlined above – is that a court has no power to override either the informed consent or informed refusal of a competent child to medical treatment, or, if it does have such a power, it should not as a matter of discretion exercise that power except, perhaps, in extreme circumstances.

I would interpose here that the Commission had referred to The Convention on the Rights of the Child which specifically concerns under 18 year-olds and provides in Article 12 that they shall be provided the opportunity to be heard in any legal proceedings affecting them, and their views given due weight in accordance with their age and maturity. It was submitted that the Convention therefore 'promotes the right of children to make an informed decision; attempts to ensure that appropriate information is provided to enable this decision to be made; and requires that state parties respect these views and the reasons for their formation'.

The Commission's submission as to competency continued:

> 2.6 Accordingly, it is possible that, on the facts of a particular case, a Court may find that a child is competent to refuse treatment but lacks competency to consent to treatment (or vice versa). This may occur where the treatment issues involved in having the treatment are more complex than the treatment issues involved in refusing it (or vice versa). It is submitted that, on principle, there is no reason why a distinction of this sort cannot be drawn on the facts of a particular case.
>
> 2.7 In short, no presumptions should be drawn as to the issue of whether any individual child of any particular age can give informed consent to receive or refuse medical treatment and in each case the issue will depend on the complexity of the treatment issues involved and 'on the rate of development of each individual'.
>
> 2.8 It is submitted that if this Court finds that the child has achieved 'a sufficient understanding and intelligence' to enable the child 'to understand fully what is proposed', then this Court has no further role in this matter.

I have doubts about the correctness of the proposition set out in the last sentence of para 2.5 of the Commission's submissions and the proposition set out in para 2.8. In the circumstances of the present case it is unnecessary to decide these issues. Much will depend upon what it is that is proposed in each individual case. It seems to me that there is a considerable difference between a child or young person deciding to use contraceptives as in *Gillick* and a child or young person determining upon a course that will 'change' his/her sex. It is highly questionable whether a 13-year-old could ever be regarded as having the capacity for the latter, and this situation may well continue until the young person reaches maturity.

The subject matter of the application

The second issue I must consider is whether the nature of the proposed procedure is one that requires the consent of the Court. Otherwise, it is a procedure to which the applicant may consent as guardian.

While it is the most common type of special medical procedure application, the requirement of court authorisation has not been limited to sterilisation cases. The Family Court of Australia has been called upon to decide applications concerning:

- the surgical gender reassignment of a 14-year-old with a congenital disorder – *Re A* (1993) FLC 92–402;

- the performance of cardiac surgery on an 11-year-old boy where parental consent was refused – *Re Michael* (1994) FLC 92–471; *Re Michael (No 2)* (1994) FLC 92–486; and
- the harvest of bone marrow blood cells from a physically and intellectually healthy 10-year-old boy for transplant to the child's aunt who was suffering from leukemia – *Re GWW and CMW*. (1997) FLC 92–748.

In *Re GWW and CMW* (supra), Hannon J was faced with a challenge to the Court's jurisdiction and made the following comments at 84,108:

> . . . it is necessary to consider whether this is a special case outside the scope of a parent's power to consent to on behalf of his or her child (*Re Marion* FLC at 79,171–79,172; CLR at 232). In *Re Marion* the majority stated that there are features involved in a decision to authorise sterilisation which indicate that in order to ensure the best protection of the interests of a child, such a decision should not come within the ordinary scope of parental power to consent to medical treatment. 'Court authorisation is necessary, and is, in essence a procedural safeguard'. **The court went on to state that court authorisation is required firstly because of the significant risk of making the wrong decision and secondly because the consequences of a wrong decision are particularly grave**. Their Honours constituting the majority of the court, noted in some detail the factors which may contribute to the risk of a wrong decision being made and the gravity of the consequences if that were to occur.
>
> **Although their Honours were there dealing with a case involving sterilisation which they referred to as being 'invasive, irreversible and major surgery', there are passages in the judgment which indicate that it is not only sterilisation which constitutes a special case and therefore is outside the ordinary scope of parental power to consent.** The majority cited with approval a passage from the judgment of Nicholson CJ in *Re Jane* (1989) FLC 92–007 where at page 77,256 his Honour said:
>
> The consequences of a finding that the Court's consent is unnecessary are far reaching both for parents and for children. For example, such a principle might be used to justify parental consent to the surgical removal of a girl's clitoris for religious or quasi-cultural reasons, or the sterilisation of a perfectly healthy girl for misguided, albeit sincere, reasons. Other possibilities might include parental consent to the donation of healthy organs such as a kidney from one sibling to another.
>
> Such procedures involve the invasive, irreversible and major surgery to which the court adverted in *Re Marion* whereas the procedure of harvesting of stem cells sought to be authorised in the present application, although invasive is not irreversible in that the stems regenerate and the blood is reinfused into the donor.' (emphasis added)

I find the passages of his Honour's comments as to principle which I have underlined to be of assistance in the present matter.

Like Hannon J, I do not read their Honours in *Marion's* case to be confining the reasons for authorisation to surgical interventions only. It was a factual element of the case – the sterilisation method proposed for Marion. It is hard to imagine that the principled considerations that I have emphasised in para 176 would be inapplicable if authorisation had been sought for an alternative intervention of similarly irreversible effect for the same purpose, for example the use of radiation or pharmaceuticals.

Returning to *Re GWW and CMW*, Hannon J held that the Court did have jurisdiction, saying at 84,108–9:

> Neither counsel nor I have been able to find any authorities in the United Kingdom or in this country where authorisation from a court has been sought for this procedure although there are a number of cases in the United States of America where this has occurred (Propriety of Surgically Invading Incompetent or Minor for Benefit of Third Party – Gregory). The foundation for the intervention of the Court has been stated to lie in the fact that the state has an interest in protecting the rights of minor children under its *parens patriae* power, the doctrine that all orphans, dependent children and incompetent persons are within the special protection and under the control of the state. Similarly although a guardian may be statutorily authorised to act on behalf of an incompetent in some matters, an intrusion into the body of an incompetent to benefit another requires judicial approval. An important factor emphasised by the courts has been that the operation was not for the child's own benefit but for the benefit of the third party. In my opinion that is an important factor to take into account when the proposed procedure is invasive to the bodily integrity of a child of tender years and involves a surgical procedure although that procedure may be of less gravity than is involved in a sterilisation or an organ transplant.
>
> In summary I accept the submission on behalf of the Attorney-General of the Commonwealth that the circumstances of the present case constitute a 'special case' namely that the purpose is to donate tissue to a third party without any physical benefit to the donor, and it involves general anaesthetic and possibly the injections of a drug. Hence it is a non-therapeutic procedure which at the very least will have an immediate adverse effect upon the child regardless of it not being carried out to promote his physical welfare. The responsibility of the court to protect the welfare of children justifies an intervention.

The application before me would seem a novel one and I was not referred to any Australian or overseas authority with similar fact characteristics.

It is distinguishable from *Re GWW and CMW* (supra) in that the proposed procedures are for the benefit of Alex and not another person and it is not a feature of the proposed treatment that Alex would undergo surgery or a general anaesthetic. The use of injections to administer hormonal treatment is however an option. Alex's case is also distinguishable because the second stage will have irreversible consequences.

Re A (supra) was also a significantly different case. A had been born a genetic female with an extreme degree of masculinisation due to an abnormality in the adrenal gland. A had genital reconstruction in her early years to give her a feminine appearance and was placed on a continuous regime of hormone treatment to prevent the production of any further male hormones by the adrenal gland. During her childhood, however, the recommended level of hormone treatment she received was inadequate as it was not pursued thoroughly by the parents. This led to the further production of male hormones and masculinisation of the external genitalia. At the time of the application to the Court, A was 14 years of age. A felt and the experts agreed, that she would be better as a male and that male gender re-assignment including by way of surgery would be more appropriate.

In the present case, Alex is a physically unambiguous young person who has been diagnosed with a male self image and a clinically recognised psychological urge to become physically male and where the proposed procedure is hormonal treatment, only the second stage of which has irreversible consequences.

Having regard to the original form of the orders sought by the applicant (see para 19 above), I raised with the parties at an early stage of the hearing process whether the Court's authorisation was presently required. I did so because the evidence of the experts indicated that para (a), namely 'that the child be administered a combination of oestrogen and progestogen on a continuous basis until the child turns 16' was uniformly identified as a reversible medical treatment. In contrast, the treatment in para (c), namely, 'the child being treated with an LHRH analogue and testosterone administered either in oral form, by monthly injection or by 6 monthly subcutaneous implant' would have, on the expert evidence, irreversible consequences, but I was not being asked by the application as originally filed, to make orders in the present proceedings for the treatment set out in para (c).

I heard submissions on this topic from Senior Counsel for the applicant and from the Child Representative. I was asked not to view the reversible first stage in isolation from the second stage of hormonal therapy which would have irreversible consequences and may involve injections or an implant.

It seemed to me to be common ground that what may be termed a staged clinical program for Alex should be seen as part of a single package. It was submitted that the evidence showed he was eager for the treatment to commence and that if treatment were to commence, he both perceived and wished it would progress through to the irreversible hormonal treatment contemplated by the application, unless of course Alex elects to cease the treatment or clinical contraindications arise. It was also put on the basis of the expert evidence that to authorise the first stage of treatment but leave the subsequent stages for future application and determination by this Court would be destructive and anxiety-provoking for him.

Submissions by both Senior Counsel for the applicant and the Child Representative as to the form of orders I should finally make proceeded on the basis that my orders would authorise both stages of treatment.

I accept the argument that I should treat the stages of treatment as a single treatment plan. It is respectful of the assessment of Alex that emerges from the expert evidence and my own interview with him. He is adamant in his deep and long-held desire to suppress his biological development as a female and to induce the presence of male characteristics. Compartmentalising the stages of treatment for the purposes of these proceedings would have an air of unreality about it.

In my view, it was proper for the applicant to make the present application and to then alter the form of orders sought to reflect this characterisation. Doing so was sensitive to the limits of the applicant's guardianship authority and the risk of commencing a course of treatment which may have raised false expectations for Alex. I think it would have been detrimental to Alex's best interests for the applicant to have viewed the reversible treatment as within its authority as a guardian and only approached the Court when the second stage was imminent.

It seems to me that there is a further question that I must address as a component of the definition of a special medical procedure that requires court authorisation. That is whether or not the proposed treatment for Alex is, to use the language of the majority decision in *Marion's* case (at 253), 'to cure a disease or correct some malfunction'?

On reviewing the evidence, I am in no way critical that there were no specific submissions before me in this regard. The High Court majority's definition was framed and expressed in a particular context – an application for the sterilisation of a girl for reasons that were not, in a strict sense, medically required.

The aetiology of a compelling desire to make the transition to become the opposite sex has not been definitively established: see *In re Kevin (Validity of marriage of transsexual)* (2001) FLC 93–087 per Chisholm J upheld on appeal to the Full Court in *In Re Kevin (Validity of marriage of transsexual) (No 2)* (2003) FLC 93–127. The Full Court commented at para 56:

> . . . the weight of medical opinion generally agrees that in the instance of a transsexual person, that individual is born with a brain that recognises him or herself as a member of the sex opposite to that whose physiological indicia he or she bears. The expert

> evidence before his Honour, which he accepted, was that this was probably of biological origin within the brain.

I asked the medical experts in this case their views on the research which underpinned the view that there is a physiological basis to transsexualism. Professor W said that he had attended a seminar where a leading proponent of that opinion presented the supporting evidence. He said he did not find there was convincing proof of any biological disorder but went on to say:

> I believe it myself that it is a biological disorder because it can be detected so early in life, you know. It's quite usual now for a transsexual to be diagnosed at the age of five or six. It just makes me believe that it's going to turn out to be biological, but there is no direct evidence, as I understand it.

Dr C commented as follows:

> [The] research which was done in the Netherlands which was for a small group of transsexual people who actually – was on a post-mortem. They found there was one nucleus of (indistinct) which in this male to female transsexual was of the same size in the female population and only in one case of a female to male. It was shown that the size of this nucleus in this female to male transsexual was the same size than it is in the men population. That is what – this study has not been replicated yet. So this is the first point. The second point is that if one looks at gender identity disorder in children and adolescence one is dealing with a wider population because even starting early childhood the children have a gender identity disorder only a minority will progress towards transsexualism later on in life. If one looks at teenagers who present with gender identity disorder of course the proportion of teenagers who have a gender identity disorder who progress towards transsexualism is much higher. But still there is a number of teenagers who present with a gender identity disorder at the age of say 13 or 14 who by the age of 18, 19 no longer wish to pursue gender reassignment. Some of the feature[s] of the gender identity disorder might have disappeared. So this shows that it is much more complex exactly in what might be the causation. The view which I take is that probably it's a combination of biological predisposition or biological factors in association with psychological or social factors. The combination of the three I think is what leads to the disorder which might have from childhood onward various outcome[s].

The current state of knowledge would not, in my view, enable a finding that the treatment would clearly be for a 'malfunction' or 'disease' and thereby not within the jurisdiction of this Court as explained by the majority in *Marion's* case. To my mind, their Honours were seeking in that case to distinguish medical treatment which seeks to address disease in or malfunctioning of organs. In the context of sterilisation for example, they would seem to have had in mind a malignant cancer of the reproductive system which required an intervention that was medically indicated for directly referable health reasons. The present case does not lend itself to such a comparison.

In light of my analysis in this section, I am therefore satisfied that the treatment plan in the present case falls within the category of cases that require court authorisation. There are significant risks attendant to embarking on a process that will alter a child or young person who presents as physically of one sex in the direction of the opposite sex, even where the Court is not asked to authorise surgery. Also, it cannot be said on the evidence that the treatment is to cure a disease or correct some malfunction.

Having reached that view, I would add that I can imagine that Alex and other people who have longed for transition to the opposite sex may find it offensive to find the incompatibility between their sense of self and the sex of their body being categorised as a 'disease' or a 'malfunction'. It is perhaps relevant that the diagnoses of Professor P and Dr N do not use this language.

The categories of cases in which the welfare jurisdiction properly ought to be invoked are not closed. As La Forest J said of the *parens patriae* jurisdiction in *Re Eve* [1986] 2 SCR 407 at 410: 'Its limits (or scope) have not, and cannot, be defined'. This observation is especially apt as the march of science overtakes the perimeters of the settled law. No type of special medical procedure concerning children or young people has been presented for decision by the High Court save for *Marion's* case.

As different fact situations emerge and applications are brought under s 67ZC, each case must be measured against the principled guidance I have set out above.

Speaking more generally, it seems to me that where a reversible treatment in respect of a child or young person is in specific anticipation of an irreversible special medical treatment that requires authorisation by this Court, it would usually be prudent for an application to be made under s 67ZC of the Act at the outset of the clinical intervention. In saying this I am not, however, referring to the assessment and diagnostic procedures that may precede a form of intervention unless such procedures themselves have the qualities of a special medical treatment to them.

Specific additional findings

In addition to the findings I have expressed earlier in this judgment, I will summarise my findings of the specific matters that ought to be considered in special medical procedures cases and then turn to the factors set out in s 68F(2) of the Act.

The Re Marion (No. 2) matters

(i) The particular condition of the child or young person which requires the procedure or treatment

It is common ground that Alex has a gender identity dysphoria which compels him to want to present as a male. That desire is longstanding and most unlikely to change. It has its most likely origins in Alex's biological and psychosocial developmental features.

(ii) The nature of the procedure or treatment proposed

It was submitted, and I accept, that I should view the present application as the question of authorising a single package of reversible and irreversible treatment which Alex can elect to cease at any time.

The two stages of hormonal intervention as contemplated by the initiating application or with a period of the analogue alone will be a matter for clinical advice by the treating physicians for so long as Alex wishes to pursue his transition. The hormonal treatment will be accompanied by on-going psychological and psychiatric support to Alex, in the context of the guardianship and educational supports I have described above.

(iii) The reasons for which it is proposed that the procedure or treatment be carried out

The evidence speaks with one voice as to the distress that Alex is genuinely suffering in a body which feels alien to him and disgusts him, particularly due to menstruation. It is also consistent as to his unwavering and profound wish to present as the male he feels himself to be. The possibility that Alex is an emerging lesbian has been considered but not accepted by the two expert psychiatric witnesses who have assessed him.

(iv) The alternative courses of treatment that are available in relation to that condition

The prognosis for behavioural intervention to change Alex's self-image and behaviour is poor. Hormonal intervention is the agreed expert view and the option of the use of analogue treatment alone at the age of approximately 16 is to be permitted by my order but subject to clinical monitoring and decision-making.

(v) The desirability of and effect of authorising the procedure for treatment proposed rather than available alternatives

The proposed treatment is uniformly recommended by the expert witnesses. It is in keeping with Alex's wishes and will facilitate his socialisation into his chosen identity from the outset of his secondary schooling. In the past, Alex has been depressed and self-harming when he has thought that his deep wish to present as male has not been taken seriously. Those who know him well are supportive of the treatment that is proposed and concerned about self-harming conduct if he is unable to embark on the proposed treatment.

(vi) The physical effects on the child or young person and the psychological and social implications for the child or young person of authorising the proposed procedure or treatment or not authorising the proposed procedure or treatment

I have canvassed above the physical consequences arising from each stage of treatment and I am satisfied that Alex has the capacity and indeed does in fact know the side effects that may arise and further that he wishes the proposed treatment with knowledge of such risks. The social implications of the proposed treatment are that Alex will face challenges in his chosen identity in respect of peer relationships, possible bullying and ostracism, but I am satisfied that impressive steps have been taken to anticipate such risks.

On the other side of the balance, if treatment is not permitted there is consistent concern that Alex will revert to unhappiness, behavioural difficulties at home and self-harming behaviour. Socially, he will be significantly ill at ease with body and self-image during his period of adolescent development until he is competent to make his own treatment decision. Transition into a male public identity will be more difficult than if it occurs at the commencement of secondary school.

(vii) The nature and degree of any risk to the child or young person of authorising the proposed procedure or treatment or not authorising the proposed procedure or treatment

I refer to the risks I explained in the previous paragraph and elsewhere in this judgment. Apart from these immediate and direct consequences, I would also be concerned that his education and residential arrangements and his developmental socialisation would be jeopardised to his long term detriment if authorisation of the proposed treatment were refused.

One important risk that Alex himself understands is that he will need to continue the hormonal treatment and may as an adult wish to have further interventions, all of which will require payment. The evidence persuades me that appropriate arrangements are in place for any transfer of the medical management of his case, and that Alex will have access to the caregiver payments which his aunt has set aside for him to meet the costs of continued treatment after the applicant's guardianship comes to an end.

(viii) The views (if any) expressed by the guardian(s) of the child or young person, a person who is entitled to the custody of the child or young person, a person who is responsible for the daily care and control of the child or young person, and the child or young person himself, to the proposed procedure or treatment and to any alternative procedure or treatment

Alex, his aunt, his cousin and the applicant as guardian all support the proposed treatment and I have referred previously to the evidence that contra-indicates an attempt to change Alex's self-image and behaviour.

The views of his mother are not known but in the circumstances, even if she were opposed to the staged hormonal treatment, I would give such views little weight given the strength of the evidence in favour of authorisation and her withdrawal from a parental role in Alex's life.

Section 68F(2) factors

The Child Representative submitted, and I agree, that I should place considerable weight on the realistic wishes expressed by Alex and the professional concern about the risk to Alex that may occur if the treatment was not authorised. He also submitted, and I agree, that the treating physicians, his schools, his aunt and the applicant as guardian are providing well for Alex's needs, including emotional and intellectual needs and that I should give considerable weight also to the expectation that those relationships are expected to be ongoing. The submissions of the applicant and the Commission were to similar effect.

Paragraph (k) of section 68F(2) of the Act requires me to consider whether to make an order which would be least likely to lead to the institution of further proceedings. Both Senior Counsel for the Applicant and the Child Representative addressed me on the issue of the form of order I should make.

The nub of the applicant's submissions was that it would benefit Alex to have closure of the court proceedings and confidence that there was a treatment plan in place covering both the reversible and irreversible hormonal treatments until he was at least 18 years of age. He said this would have an empowering effect for Alex and provide him with the comfort of an expectation of continued treatment which would be in his best interests. He also advocated the inclusion of liberty to apply provisions in the orders for authorisation he urged me to make.

The Child Representative did not disagree but said the benefit of finality in the proceedings needed to be balanced with an order which would best safeguard Alex's rights through the continued involvement of the Child Representative. To this end, he suggested that the proceedings remain on foot but adjourned for a period so that the appointment of the Child Representative was procedurally maintained so that Alex could call upon him.

I find these suggestions helpful and I note that Counsel for the

Commission indicated that to make orders according with these submissions would not infringe Alex's human rights and she was supportive of the Child Representative's continued involvement as a safeguard.

I would note here too that it was also conceded by Senior Counsel for the applicant that notwithstanding the fact of its guardianship of Alex, if he attains '*Gillick*' competency for the purpose of the proposed treatment, the fact of a guardianship order would put Alex in no different a position than any other child in making his own treatment decisions.

The final matter that I would mention concerning the submissions is one that was raised by the Commission. I think it is appropriately characterised as 'any other fact or circumstances that the court thinks is relevant': section 68F(2)(l) of the Act. In its written submissions, the Commission said:

> 3.8 . . . fundamental human rights are denied when lesbians, gay men and transgender people are not given equal protection without discrimination by the law, or are unable to express their identity through means such as identifying themselves to friends or neighbours, socialising together in public social venues, or openly cohabiting with a partner.
>
> 3.9 Article 8(1) of the [Convention on the Rights of the Child] also provides children with the right to preserve their 'identity'. The concept of 'identity' is not defined in the [Convention], although three elements of identity are listed by way of example – nationality, name and family relations. Sexual identity and gender identity are arguably within the scope of Article 8(1) . . . (footnotes omitted).

The Commission then observed that there is no single definition of 'transgender identity' but, referring to s 38A of the Anti-Discrimination Act 1977 (NSW), noted that the definition of transgender person there included a person 'who identifies as a member of the opposite sex by living, or seeking to live, as a member of the opposite sex'. The Commission described this definition as 'inclusive' in the sense that it is not restricted to persons who have undergone or wish to undergo medical or surgical treatment to reassign their gender. It was submitted that an 'inclusive' definition is to be preferred to a definition that draws a distinction between transgender persons who have undergone medical or surgical treatment and those who have not, and that this definitional approach 'is in keeping with the sentiment' expressed by the Full Court in *Re Kevin (Validity of marriage of transsexual) (No 2)* (supra) at paras 382–384. The Full Court there posed what it termed the 'rhetorical question' of why surgery should be a pre-requisite to establish the fact of a change of sex.

The Commission's submission continued:

> 3.12 On the basis of the above, it is submitted that:
>
> (a) A child has a right to live with a transgender identity, free from discrimination, under international human rights law;

> (b) It is in the child's 'best interests' to have that right respected;
> (c) A child's right to live with a transgender identity should not be limited by a narrow definition of 'transgender identity' that relies on medical or surgical intervention. There is a right to choose how that identity is expressed;
> (d) It follows that respecting a child's right to live with a transgender identity does not, of itself, decide the issue, one way or the other, of whether the authorisation of a medical procedure is in the child's best interests. The latter is a separate yet contextually related question to be decided by the Court, based on its assessment of the child's best interests, and taking into account the right of a child to express their wishes and to be heard . . .

I agree with the submission as a matter of general principle, and in the present case, it weighs in favour of authorisation as being in his best interests.

I would however, add the following caveat to Commission's submission – that it is necessary in each case where the wishes of a child or young person are seen to be significant, and not just medical procedure cases, to give careful consideration to the evidence and opinions concerning the bases for such wishes and the weight they should be accorded: see the discussions by the Full Court in *R and R: Children's Wishes* (2000) FLC 93–000 and *R v R (Children's Wishes)* 2002 FLC 93–108.

Birth certificates – The recorded sex

The orders proposed by the Child Representative in respect of Alex's birth certificate seek that the applicant be authorised to apply to register a change of his recorded name which would reflect the name he is currently using. No change is sought in respect of the record of Alex's sex, however paragraph 3.12 of the Commission's submission invites attention to the laws which govern the issue of a birth certificate which shows a sex that reflects the chosen gender identity of a person.

A helpful collation of Australian law is contained in the September 2003 *Discussion Paper: Changes to Birth Certificates for Transsexual People* by the Victorian Attorney-General's Advisory Committee on Gay, Lesbian, Transgender and Intersex Issues. It provided a consultation mechanism to assist the Attorney to consider 'legislative reforms to enable transsexual people to have the recorded sex on their birth certificate amended to reflect their affirmed sex'. (at 2). The Discussion Paper informs that:

> All Australian States and Territories (except Victoria) enacted legislation between 1988–2002 to provide a legislative mechanism by which an individual who has undergone 'sexual reassignment surgery or procedures', is unmarried and meets the jurisdictional requirements, may apply to have their legal sex (as recorded in the Registry of Births Deaths and Marriages) amended to reflect their

> affirmed sex. New South Wales, the Northern Territory, the Australian Capital Territory, Tasmania and Queensland have included transsexual recognition provisions in their Births Deaths and Marriages Registration legislation. (at 5)

The Discussion Paper then identifies the following statutes: Births Deaths and Marriages Registration Act 1995 (NSW); Births Deaths and Marriages Registration Act 1997 (Northern Territory); Births Deaths and Marriages Registration Act 1997 (Australian Capital Territory); Births Deaths and Marriages Registration Act 1999 (Tasmania) and Registration of Births Deaths and Marriages Act 1962 (Queensland). The Discussion Paper says of these jurisdictions:

> Applications under this model are limited to those who have their birth registered in the jurisdiction. Applications are determined by the Registrar on the basis of whether or not the person complies with the mandatory criteria, namely, that the applicant has undergone sexual reassignment surgery, is unmarried and has birth records registered in that jurisdiction. (at 5)

The Discussion Paper then observes that the Sexual Reassignment Act 1988 (South Australia) and the Gender Reassignment Act 2000 (Western Australia):

> . . . require a Magistrate (SA) or a Gender Reassignment Board (WA) to be satisfied that the person believes that his or her true sex is the sex to which the person has been reassigned and has adopted the lifestyle and has the sexual characteristics of a person of the sex to which the person has been reassigned, and has received proper counselling in relation to his or her sexual identity. In addition, in WA and SA, a copy of the application must be served on the Minister and any other person who should in the Board or Magistrate's opinion be served with notice of the application. If the applicant does satisfy the Magistrate (SA) or Gender Reassignment Board (WA), a 'recognition certificate' is issued. Such a certificate can be taken to other recognising states or to that state's registry of Births Deaths and Marriages for the record to be amended. (at 5)

The Discussion Paper explains that surgery is not required in Western Australia or South Australia. Since in the former, an authorised Magistrate, and in the latter, the Gender Reassignment Board decides:

> . . . whether the person has completed transition based on a range of evidence, the medical treatment criteria does not need to be too prescriptive. These jurisdictions do not require that an applicant for a change of birth certificate has had 'sexual reassignment surgery' as other Australian jurisdictions do. Rather, they require that the applicant 'has the sexual characteristics of a person of the sex to which they have been reassigned'. This factor will then be assessed by the Court or [Gender Reassignment Board of Western Australia] based on the evidence presented. (at 10)

For example, s 3 of the Sexual Reassignment Act 1988 (SA) provides the following definitions and are consistent with the definitions of 'reassignment procedure' and 'gender characteristics' found in s 3 of the Gender Reassignment Act 2000 (WA):

> 'reassignment procedure' means a medical **or** surgical procedure (or a combination of such procedures) to alter the genitals and other sexual characteristics of a person, identified by birth certificate as male or female, so that the person will be identified as a person of the opposite sex and includes, in relation to a child, any such procedure (or combination of procedures) to correct or eliminate ambiguities in the child's sexual characteristics;
>
> 'sexual characteristics' means the physical characteristics by virtue of which a person is identified as male or female (emphasis added)

The Discussion Paper gives consideration to the law concerning people under the age of 18 years and notes that 'most other jurisdictions provide that a parent or the child's guardian may apply for amendment to the recorded sex on their child's birth certificate'. (at 7)

Again, to use the Sexual Reassignment Act 1988 (SA) as an example, in respect of a child under the age of 18 years, s 7(3) provides:

> An application may be made under this section –
>
> (a) by the person to whom it relates; or
> (b) if that person is a child – by the child's guardian.

Section 14(2) Gender Reassignment Act 2000 (WA) is to the same effect.

I consider it is a matter of regret that a number of Australian jurisdictions require surgery as a pre-requisite to the alteration of a transsexual person's birth certificate in order for the record to align a person's sex with his/her chosen gender identity. This is of little help to someone who is unable to undertake such surgery. The reasons may differ but for example in the present case, a young person such as Alex, on the evidence, would not be eligible for surgical intervention until at least the age of 18 years. Thus, for the many purposes for which a birth certificate is required (such as an application for a passport), a person such as Alex in those jurisdictions is required to produce a birth certificate that describes him as a female in circumstances where in all other respects he is living his life as a male.

The Discussion Paper to which I have referred contains illustrations of the hardships that are experienced when the sex recorded on the birth certificate is incongruent with their chosen gender identity. It rightly appreciates that people in these circumstances:

> . . . have to endure the embarrassment of explaining their personal history. Naturally, this will be the source of a great deal of distress and embarrassment for the person as well as increasing the risk of being unfairly discriminated against. (at 3)

Reflecting upon the particular circumstances of this case leaves me anxious about the detrimental consequences that a young person such as Alex would suffer from having to present a birth certificate that is antithetical to his self-image.

A requirement of surgery seems to me to be a cruel and unnecessary restriction upon a person's right to be legally recognised in a sex which reflects the chosen gender identity and would appear to have little justification on grounds of principle.

The requirement of prior surgery in order to establish the fact that a person is a man for the purposes of a valid marriage was questioned in the *Re Kevin* cases (supra): see particularly *In Re Kevin (Validity of marriage of transsexual) (No 2)* (supra) at paras 382–388. The Full Court there also noted (at para 386) the submission of the Commission that the efficacy of surgical intervention is more problematic where the transition is from female to male. Senior Counsel for the Commission in that case said:

> . . . in the circumstances of this case, it is worth accepting that surgical intervention in relation to the removal of gonads may be relatively straightforward, surgical intervention for a male to female transsexual person in relation to the construction of a vagina may be commonplace, surgical intervention which requires the construction of a penis is much more problematic and even where it takes place may or may not give rise to something which would be readily accepted as a penis of a sexual kind which has a particular sexual function.

If one accepts such a submission, a requirement of surgery is not only generally inconsistent with human rights. The requirement is more disadvantageous and burdensome for people seeking legal recognition of their transition from female to male than male to female. Expressed in this way, there is an additional objection to surgery as a pre-requisite; the requirement of surgery is a form of indirect discrimination.

I would urge the various State and Territory Legislatures that make surgery a pre-requisite for a change in birth certificates to reconsider their position.

A scheme for the change of birth certificates which requires a Magistrate or a Board to make a finding of fact but does not make surgery a pre-requisite is, in my view, more consistent with human rights and therefore preferable in comparison with an administrative scheme wherein the applicant must have had surgery to be eligible for the changed birth certificate.

Authorisation and other orders

In the result and for the reasons contained in this judgment, I am satisfied to the *Briginshaw* standard by the evidence and by the submissions that I should make a declaration authorising the administration of hormonal treatment as determined from time to time by the attending physicians without specifying the timing and nature of the treatment. My authorisation will extend to both of the interventions sought in the application and I make it clear that when Alex is older, the question of whether the analogue is administered alone or in combination with testosterone is a matter for the treating clinicians and, of course, Alex. . . .

Alex's case caused much controversy. The issues in this area, and the relevant antecedents are canvassed by Weston-Scheuber and Parlett:

Parlett, K and Weston-Scheuber, KM, Consent to Treatment for Transgender and Intersex Children (2004) 9(2) Deakin Law Review 375–397

More than a decade has passed since the landmark High Court decision in *Marion's Case*, where the Court authorised the sterilisation of a young woman who suffered from a disability. Recently, the principles established in that case were applied by the Family Court in a different context – for the provision of hormonal treatment for a 13-year-old child, some aspects of which are irreversible. Previously, the Family Court had authorised gender reassignment surgery for a child suffering from a physical, congenital condition, but notably in *Re Alex*, the subject child suffered no identified physical condition indicating treatment, but from an identified psychological condition, gender identity dysphoria.

This article considers the issues raised by recent applications of the principles relating to the capacity of children to consent to medical treatment, including the decision in *Re Alex* and the application of those principles to transgender and intersex children. While not all children or adults who identify as transgender or intersex choose the long and difficult path of gender reassignment, some will choose surgical gender reassignment or hormonal treatment at some stage of their lives. In cases where it is proposed that a minor undergo such treatment, the application of the principles of child consent poses particular difficulties.

[Parlett and Weston-Scheuber firstly summarise Gillick and Re Marion, and then continue as follows]

II Overseas authorities

It is relevant before embarking on a discussion of the principles of child consent and their applicability to the transgender or intersex child to consider two cases from the United Kingdom dealing with the capacity of a child to *refuse* consent to medical treatment. To the authors' knowledge, this issue has not arisen for judicial consideration in Australia. In both cases, the English courts limited the *Gillick* principle in two important ways. First, they found that a child who is *Gillick* competent, while able to consent to medical treatment, is not similarly able to *refuse* consent to medical treatment, and in circumstances where a parent authorises treatment against the wishes of a minor, the parental consent will be sufficient to authorise the treatment. The second limitation was a finding that even where a child is *Gillick* competent, the Court in its exercise of the *parens patriae* jurisdiction retains the right to override either a consent or a refusal of the child to medical treatment where that is in the child's best interests.

A *Re R*

Re R involved a 15-year-old ward of the state who was admitted to a treatment centre. She had a disturbed childhood and experienced periods of erratic and violent behaviour interspersed with periods of lucidity and rationality. During an episode of the latter description, she expressed her wishes to a counsellor that she did not wish to take the drugs that the unit personnel wanted to give her and had given her on previous occasions. The local authority commenced wardship proceedings and applied for leave for the unit to administer medication regardless of R's consent or absence thereof.

Although a consideration of the scope of parental authority was not relevant to the decision, Lord Donaldson considered the principle from *Gillick* and found that it did not extend to a right reposed in a minor to refuse consent to medical treatment. With regard to consent, he used the analogy of child and parent as keyholders, each of whom was entitled to 'unlock the door' to medical treatment of the minor. In circumstances where the child refused consent to medical treatment, the parents could still override that consent and authorise medical treatment. To find otherwise would result in doctors being faced with the 'intolerable dilemma' of having to determine who possessed a right of consent at any particular time, with the threat of being sued if a wrong decision was made.

The Court found that R was not *Gillick* competent, on the basis that she was only competent for periods of time before lapsing into phases of irrationality and violence. However, the Court still went on to consider the power of the Court in relation to a child determined to be *Gillick* competent. The Court found that it could, in exercise of its wardship or statutory jurisdiction in relation to minors, override the decision of a *Gillick* competent minor to consent or refuse treatment. In the circumstances it was held to be in the best interests of R that the unit be authorised to administer any treatment to R that it considered necessary.

B *Re W*

Re W concerned a 16-year-old girl suffering from anorexia nervosa. W, who was found by the trial judge to be *Gillick* competent, was being treated at a facility for patients with eating disorders. Her condition was deteriorating steadily, to the extent that doctors feared she might soon suffer damage to her reproductive system and danger to her life if treatment were not administered. W refused consent to her being moved to an alternative treatment centre in London where a more rigorous programme of treatment would be administered.

The Court of Appeal unanimously held that the court, in exercising its unlimited inherent jurisdiction in relation to minors, could override the wishes of a competent child in the best interests of the child, objectively considered. The Court also found that a minor did not have a power of veto in relation to treatment authorised by someone with parental responsibilities for the minor. A power of veto was not provided by s 8 of the Family Law Reform Act 1969 and although the issue of parental power to veto was not at issue in *Re W*, the Court also doubted that the principle in *Gillick* extended to allowing a child an absolute right of refusal in relation to medical treatment. Lord Donaldson, regretting his use of the keyholder analogy in *Re R*, used the analogy of a 'legal flak jacket' which would protect the doctor from litigation in relation to a medical procedure, whether provided by the child or by someone with parental responsibilities. Despite the fact that W was *Gillick* competent, the Court authorised the proposed treatment on the basis that it was in her best interests, given the serious consequences to her health if treatment were not administered.

[The authors then consider Alex's case, outlining relevant facts and findings]

IV Comment: Capacity of the transgender or intersex child to consent (or refuse consent) to treatment

There are a number of issues that arise from a consideration of the principles of child consent in the context of transgender and intersex children. What follows is a discussion of three issues:

1. Despite the Court's endorsement of *Gillick*, are there in fact some types of treatment which are so serious in nature that a minor can *never* consent to them? Would gender reassignment and irreversible hormonal therapy fall into this category?
2. Should a distinction be drawn between the capacity of a minor to consent to medical treatment on the one hand and her or his capacity to *refuse* consent to medical treatment on the other?
3. How should the principles of child consent be applied in the special context of treatment for the transgender or intersex child, given the particular consequences which may result both from administering treatment and withholding treatment?

A Can a minor consent to treatment for the purposes of gender reassignment?

The first issue for consideration is the question of whether there are some types of treatment that are so serious in nature that a minor can never give an effective consent for that treatment. The principle enunciated by the House of Lords in *Gillick* and endorsed by the High Court in *Marion's Case* is that a child is capable of giving consent to medical treatment in circumstances where the child possesses sufficient intelligence and maturity to understand fully the treatment that is being proposed. In *Marion's Case* there was no suggestion that the subject child, who suffered from a severe intellectual disability, had (or ever would have) the capacity to consent to her proposed sterilisation. However, *Re A* and *Re Alex* concerned two children with normal intellectual capacity who wished to undergo medical treatment, some of the consequences of which were irreversible: Alex for the purpose of changing his biological sex and A for the purpose of choosing between the ambiguous sexual characteristics he was born with.

In both cases the Court found that although the children possessed a general understanding of the kinds of treatment that were being proposed, they did not possess the requisite intelligence and maturity to give them the capacity to consent to treatment. However, an examination of the reasons for this finding in *Re Alex* evidences more of a concern about the propriety of a 13-year-old being responsible for such a serious decision than a true inquiry into Alex's capacity to consent to medical treatment.

The Court found that the question of Alex's capacity to consent was an academic question, given that the expert evidence as to the proposed treatment was in accordance with Alex's wishes, nevertheless the Court still gave consideration to the issue. The judgment refers to the evidence of only three people on this point: Mr T (who prepared the family report), Professor P (an Associate Professor in the Department of Psychiatry at a university) and Dr N (Consultant Psychiatrist and specialist in child and adolescent psychiatry). Professor P, in particular, reported that Alex fully understood the mechanism of action for the proposed hormone treatment and its side effects and benefits. Both Mr T and Professor P indicated, however, that they did not consider it appropriate that at age 13 Alex should be wholly responsible for the decision to undergo hormone treatment.

Although holding that a finding of *Gillick* competence did not preclude a court from authorising medical treatment of a minor against her wishes, the judgments in *Re W* evidence a similar reluctance to accept the competence of the minor in question. Despite the trial judge, who heard from W concluding that W was competent, the Court still felt inclined to doubt whether W was truly *Gillick* competent. Lord Donaldson found that 'it is a feature of anorexia nervosa that it is capable of destroying the ability to make an informed choice. It creates a compulsion to refuse treatment or only to accept treatment which is likely to be ineffective'.

One can understand the reluctance of the courts to allow the kinds of treatment being considered (or potentially refused) in these cases to be administered on the basis of the child's consent alone or withheld solely on the basis of the child's refusal. However, if it truly is the case that some treatment is of such a serious nature, or the refusal of treatment would have such serious consequences, that a competent child's right of consent or refusal should not be absolute, then that should be enunciated clearly as a matter of legal principle.

The Court hinted at such a proposition in *Re Alex*. In the course of argument, the Commission made a submission that a court has no power to override either the informed consent or informed refusal of a competent child to medical treatment or, if such a power does exist, the court should not as a matter of discretion exercise that power except perhaps in extreme circumstances. The Court doubted the correctness of that proposition and went on to state, 'It is highly questionable whether a 13-year-old could ever be regarded as having the capacity for the latter, and this situation may well continue until the young person reaches maturity'.

The suggestion here is that there are some types of medical treatment which are so serious that even a child who has a sufficient understanding and maturity to understand fully the nature of the treatment and the consequences of her or his decision, should not be allowed an absolute right to consent to that treatment. Treatment in the nature of gender reassignment surgery and treatment preparatory to that, which is serious in nature and irreversible in consequence, would probably fall into this category.

In the United Kingdom, the power of the courts is unlimited in their exercise of *parens patriae* jurisdiction. Even where a child assessed to be competent has given consent to a medical procedure, a court has the power to override that competent consent where that is considered to be in the child's best interests. The English cases considered above appear to reflect the idea that although competent adults are entitled to consent to or refuse treatment as they see fit, regardless of the consequences, there should be some overarching protection of a *Gillick* competent child to shield her or him from the consequences of an unfettered right to decide whether or not to accept medical treatment. For example, in *Re W*, Balcombe LJ stated that in exercising its ultimate jurisdiction over children the child's wishes would be a material consideration, however:

> there comes a point at which the court, while not disregarding the child's wishes can override them in the child's own best interests, objectively considered. Clearly such a point will have come if the child is seeking to refuse treatment in circumstances which will in all probability lead to the death of the child or to severe permanent injury.

The language of s 67ZC of the Act would appear to support the existence of a similarly unlimited jurisdiction in the Family Court of Australia. Indeed, it has been noted that the United Kingdom position probably applies in Australia. In *Marion's Case*, the majority stated that 'more contemporary descriptions of the *parens patriae* jurisdiction over infants invariably accept that in theory there is no limitation upon the jurisdiction'. They went on to note, however, that the jurisdiction springs from the direct responsibility of the Crown for those who cannot look after themselves. Given that this is the source of the *parens patriae* jurisdiction, it would seem illogical for it to extend to overriding the wishes of a competent minor.

More consideration needs to be given to the issue of whether a child is capable of consenting to serious and irreversible treatment such as treatment for the purposes of gender reassignment, or whether there are certain procedures that only a court can consent to for a minor regardless of whether the minor understands fully the nature and consequences of the treatment. Either through legislation, or through judicial decision, the role of the court needs to be clarified: is its task simply to verify that a child has the requisite capacity to make the decision in question, or is the role of the court to ensure that the best interests of the child are always served, regardless of the competent child's wishes?

B Consent to treatment vs refusal of consent

Another notable feature in the cases and jurisprudence concerning child capacity to consent to medical treatment is the question of whether a distinction should be drawn between capacity to consent to treatment on the one hand and the capacity to refuse consent to treatment on the other (as is suggested in some of the United Kingdom decisions discussed above). The rationale for drawing a distinction between the two is the serious consequences that may result where a child is found competent to refuse consent to life-saving medical treatment, for example by refusing consent to a blood transfusion on religious grounds.

Competent adults, of course, have the ability to consent to, and refuse, a range of medical treatments even where the consequences of that may be serious injury or death. The refusal of life-saving medical treatment on any ground and for any reason is the clearest example. Debates about arbitrary age limits for activities such as voting and driving draw on the argument that although some children are undoubtedly of sufficient intelligence and maturity to vote, some adults do not appear to be. It is generally understood that arbitrary age qualifications such as 18 (for voting and drinking alcohol) are largely a matter of practical convenience, as it would be logistically impossible to assess each individual to determine her or his maturity and intellectual fitness for these activities. Considerations of practical convenience are, of course, irrelevant to the issue of capacity to consent to medical treatment of a serious nature, which is not common and also turns very much on the circumstances of the particular individual seeking treatment, as well as the nature of the treatment itself.

There remains to be considered in the Australian context whether any distinction should be drawn between a child's capacity to consent to medical treatment and a child's capacity to refuse consent. The established position in the United Kingdom is that a *Gillick* competent child may effectively consent to medical treatment, however a refusal of treatment may be overridden by the consent of someone with parental responsibility. This finding is notwithstanding the proposition that 'in logic there can be no difference between an ability to consent to treatment and an ability to refuse treatment'. However there *is* a difference between the two and the distinction lies in the importance of 'medical ethics' and the role it plays in the administration of treatment. When a child, or any person for that matter, 'consents' to medical treatment there is added protection for that person in that the consent does not impose any positive *obligation* on a medical practitioner to administer the treatment or perform the procedure being consented to. A medical practitioner always has a choice as to whether to perform a procedure and is not obligated to treat a patient in circumstances where the practitioner believes that is not in the person's best interests. Lord Donaldson made reference to this when he stated in his summary of principles in *Re W* that '[n]o question of a minor consenting to or refusing medical treatment arises unless and until a medical or dental practitioner advises such treatment and is willing to undertake it'.

Consideration of the role of medical ethics has been a feature of some of the judgments referred to above. For example, in *Re W*, Lord Donaldson considered it 'inconceivable' that a doctor would proceed with a serious procedure (a transplant operation being the example used) unless both child and parents gave their consent to the procedure. Lord Donaldson pointed out that a doctor has a professional duty to act in the best interests of the patient and to advise the patient on that basis. As an additional example, Lord Donaldson and Balcombe LJ indicated that, taking into account medical ethics, there was no real possibility that an abortion would be carried out on a minor against her wishes, unless the procedure was truly in her best interests.

The same inherent safeguard does not apply to a refusal of treatment. In circumstances where treatment is objectively necessary in the patient's best interests, but the person will not consent to that treatment, the harm results from the absence of treatment rather than from the proposed treatment itself. Therefore, it is potentially more significant to allow a child an absolute right to refuse medical treatment than it is to allow the child to consent to medical treatment, as the consent to treatment will only have effect if there is a doctor who is willing to administer the treatment or perform the procedure.

It has been suggested that, where a child is found competent to consent to medical treatment, the child's reasons for refusing medical treatment should be taken into consideration so that, for instance, a decision to refuse treatment which would only prolong a painful and incurable condition should be regarded as a competent one while a decision to refuse treatment on religious grounds would be regarded as invalid as being objectively unreasonable. The authors do not consider that there is much to recommend this proposal. An appraisal of competence is not and should not be concerned with the reasons for decisions but rather with the capacity of the person making the decision to understand the nature of the proposed treatment and the consequences of consenting or withholding consent. If it is to be the case that a competent child is able to refuse consent to medical treatment, then that should be without regard to the motives behind that decision. In the same way that the refusal of treatment by a competent adult is not subject to a requirement that such refusal be reasonable (however that reasonableness could be assessed), a competent child's refusal of treatment should also be unfettered.

Further, we do not consider that there is merit in following the approach taken in the United Kingdom, which enables a child to consent to medical treatment but allows a parent or guardian to override a refusal of treatment by a competent child. Despite the distinction between consent and refusal discussed above, and the added protection that medical ethics provides to the patient in the case of the former, it still should not be presumed that the best interests of the child will always favour administration of treatment rather than the absence of treatment. This is particularly relevant where the treatment is to deal with congenital adrenal hyperplasia, the condition involved in *Re A*.

The consent/refusal dichotomy is particularly relevant in the context of transgender children, where the consequences of administering treatment, sometimes through procedures which have irreversible consequences and may render the patient infertile, can be just as serious as the consequences of failing to administer treatment, which may result in grave psychological problems and result in the minor experiencing emotional problems and even exhibiting suicidal tendencies (as in *Re Alex*). For this reason, it is necessary to discuss the two issues considered above in the particular context of transgender and intersex children.

C The special nature of treatment for transgender and intersex children

Questions about the proper way of 'treating' people with congenital adrenal hyperplasia, gender identity dysphoria and other similar 'conditions' do not have easy answers. Debate currently rages over whether intersex children should have their genitalia surgically altered to make their external appearance match their internal sexual organs. Despite increasing recognition that such procedures performed on small children can have devastating effects in later life, some parents continue to make the decision to subject their children to invasive and irreversible procedures in the interests of helping them to live more 'normal' lives.

Allowing a parent or a court to override the consent of a competent child can, in the context of this kind of treatment, have very serious consequences. It was considered by the English Court of Appeal in *Re W* that it would be unlikely that a doctor would perform an invasive procedure (e.g. an abortion) on a minor against the minor's wishes, however it was indicated that an exception might arise where the procedure was clearly 'in the child's best interests'.

It is not beyond the realms of possibility that anxious parents of a child with ambiguous sexual characteristics might wish their competent child to undergo hormone therapy or even gender reassignment surgery, against the child's wishes, and find a doctor willing to support their decision. Although in Australia, as a result of the decision in *Marion's Case*, it is unlikely that a parent would be able to consent to treatment of the nature of that proposed in *Re A* and *Re Alex*, the distinction between therapeutic and non-therapeutic treatment endorsed by the courts leaves scope for a decision to be made by parents about treatment in circumstances which might be argued to be in the nature of treatment for a disease or illness and therefore therapeutic with the consequence that court consent would not be required.

Even where the consent of the court is required, given the lack of public awareness in relation to transgender and intersex persons, it is possible that a court might consider such treatment to be in a child's best interests even where the child refuses to consent to the procedure. In relation to the treatment of intersex children, concerns have been raised that cosmetic genital surgery is often performed for social and psychological reasons rather than being medically necessary. Although surgery is often performed in the early years of a child's life, when there is no capacity to give consent, the case of *Re A* demonstrates that these issues are also of relevance to intersex young persons who may be developing the capacity to consent to medical treatment for themselves.

One critic of the decision in *Re A* has pointed out the leap in logic that was made by the Court from the fact that A's sexual preference was for females to the conclusion that A was intrinsically male. The same author draws attention to the absence of any discussion of the possibility that A may actually have been a lesbian, or even simply experiencing lesbian tendencies rather than truly identifying as a member of the opposite sex. In *Re A* the treatment that was eventually ordered included bilateral mastectomies, a hysterectomy and oophorectomy, unfolding of the clitoris, closure of the labia to create the appearance of a scrotum and the insertion of prosthetic testes. In A's case, the treatment eventually consented to by the court was in line with the minor's wishes. However, is it possible that a court might sanction treatment where the child is the only person who does not agree?

It is suggested that further consideration should be given to these issues by courts considering cases in the nature of *Re A* and *Re Alex*, and indeed, by the legislature. Is proper weight and consideration being given to the circumstances of the children in these cases and their capacity to consent? Or are the courts simply operating on the unspoken assumption that a child can never independently consent to treatment of this nature and consequently merely paying lip service to the ability of the child to consent to medical treatment? If the latter, it is respectfully suggested that the courts elaborate on the circumstances in which children will *never* be capable of consenting to treatment and the rationale for such a decision. Inevitably, circumstances will one day arise where a child in Alex's or A's position will quite clearly possess the requisite intelligence and maturity to satisfy the *Gillick* test and the court will then, if the concerns we have addressed above are correct, be placed in the position of having to resile from its established endorsement of the *Gillick* principle.

New South Wales legislation regulates the administering of certain 'special medical treatment' on children, defined as persons under 16 years of age. The Children and Young Persons (Care and Protection) Act 1998 prohibits a person from carrying out special medical treatment on a child other than with the consent of the NSW Guardianship Tribunal. Special medical treatment is defined as meaning:

- medical treatment that is intended or is reasonably likely to render a person permanently infertile (not including treatment that is intended to remediate a life-threatening condition and from which permanent infertility or the likelihood of it is an unwanted consequence);
- any medical treatment involving the administration of a long-acting injectable hormonal substance for the purpose of contraception or menstrual regulation;
- any medical treatment in the nature of a vasectomy or tubal occlusion; or
- any other medical treatment declared by the Regulations to be special medical treatment for the purposes of this section.

The Regulations further declare the following treatments to be special medical treatment:

- any medical treatment involving the administration of a drug of addiction over a period of more than 10 days in any 30-day period;
- any medical treatment involving an experimental procedure that does not conform to the *National Statement on Ethical Conduct in Research Involving Humans*; or
- any treatment involving the administration of a psychotropic drug to a child in out-of-home care for the purpose of controlling the child's behaviour.

The first three types of medical treatment referred to above are all kinds of medical treatment that might be involved in a gender reassignment or treatment preparatory to gender reassignment. It is suggested that legislation along these lines at a Commonwealth level should be enacted to clarify the position in relation to child consent if it is considered that minors should not be able to consent to procedures of this nature.

By contrast, the Consent to Medical Treatment and Palliative Care Act 1995 (SA) provides that a person of or over 16 years of age may make decisions about her or his own medical treatment as validly and effectively as if that person were an adult.With respect to children under the age of 16, treatment can be administered either where a parent or guardian consents or where the child consents and the medical practitioner is of the opinion that the child is capable of understanding the nature, consequences and risks and that the treatment is in the best interests of the child's health and well-being and that opinion is supported by the written opinion of at least one other medical practitioner who has personally examined the child. No distinction is drawn between ordinary medical treatment and special medical treatment of the kind discussed above, meaning that hormonal therapy could be administered to a child under the age of 16 against her or his will on the basis of the legislation.

The jurisdiction of the Family Court in relation to the welfare of children derives from the Family Law Act 1975 (Cth) and is based on the powers contained in s 51(xxi) (the marriage power) and s 51(xxii) (divorce and matrimonial causes) of the Constitution. To the extent that there is any inconsistency between the powers vested in the Family Court by federal legislation and restrictions on treatment contained in state legislation, the Family Court's powers will prevail by virtue of s 109 of the Constitution. This has the effect that the Family Court may authorise treatment with respect to a child even where the administration of that treatment would otherwise be unlawful under general state provisions. It is therefore necessary that measures be taken to clarify the position at a federal level, to ensure that a consistent approach applicable to all jurisdictions is developed in relation to these issues.

If it is to be the case that certain procedures for minors require the consent of a court or tribunal, then consideration needs to be given also to what is the most appropriate body to be making these types of decisions. The kinds of issues involved in these cases are complex and extend beyond medical considerations and the wishes and opinions of those immediately involved. Ideally, the process for making decisions should take into account the broader experiences of those who have had the same experiences, and as much as possible take into consideration the range of options available to persons who identify as transgender or intersex. A specialised tribunal might therefore be a more appropriate body for making such decisions than a court.

That is not to suggest, however, that it is appropriate for a court, or any other body, to make the ultimate decision where the child concerned is competent to decide for her or himself. One commentator has suggested that where a child is found to be competent, there should be no distinction drawn between the ability to consent to medical treatment and the ability to refuse consent to treatment. However, an additional safeguard is proposed, namely that there be a requirement that the child provide an *informed* consent, a higher threshold test than that applied to adults. This is consistent with the *Gillick* test which requires of the minor a sufficient intelligence and maturity to *understand fully* the treatment that is proposed. The court's role in such cases would be limited to ensuring that the minor is competent and has made an informed decision.

The authors consider that there is merit in this proposition. Requiring a higher threshold test than that which adults must satisfy is consistent with a recognition of the fact that children generally lack the experience of adults in making difficult decisions and also takes into account the serious consequences that can result where invasive and irreversible procedures are carried out on children. However, it also takes into account that minors, as they approach the age of majority, increase in maturity and that there may be little difference in capacity between a mature 15- or 16-year-old and an 18-year-old.

Ultimately, the procedures of the kinds addressed in *Re A* and *Re Alex* are special in that they are not simply for the purpose of curing an illness or improving health, but are inextricably associated with the patient's self-identity. The consequences of not allowing treatment where that is sought or alternatively, of carrying out treatment where that is not wanted, can be terrible, having consequences lasting throughout a person's lifetime and affecting not only health, fertility and the ability to have a fulfilling sex life, but also psychological well-being and identity. For these reasons, the authors consider that any test ultimately laid down by the courts or the legislature should be one which gives sufficient weight and consideration to the wishes of the minor involved.

V Conclusion

The issues raised by *Re Alex* and *Re A* are of real significance. Recently it was reported that Alan Finch, a 37-year-old man who had his penis and testicles amputated on the recommendation of psychiatrists at a state-funded Melbourne clinic but later reverted to being a male, is claiming damages against the Victorian government and the doctors who work at the clinic. He claims that the doctors followed a rigid ideology of treating gender identity problems by means of surgical intervention without properly considering the possibility of psychotherapy or psychological approaches.

Similarly, a number of congenital adrenal hyperplasia sufferers who underwent surgery as children have recently appeared before the San Francisco Human Rights Commission to testify about the effects that the surgery has had on them, including medical complications, suffering lack of sexual sensation and living lives of secrecy and shame.

These reports highlight the fact that there can be devastating consequences where irreversible procedures of this nature are performed without the consent of the person or where the patient has consented but subsequently changes her or his mind. This is of particular significance when the patient is a child who, even where possessing sufficient intelligence and maturity to satisfy the *Gillick* test, may not have sufficient experience of life or awareness of the various ways of living a transgender or intersex life, to consent to irreversible treatment of this nature. It remains for the courts or the legislature to clarify the limits, if any, on the operation of the *Gillick* principle in Australia, both generally and in the specific context of transgender and intersex children.

Statute

There are two States of Australia in which the common law on child consent to treatment has been modified by statute. They are New South Wales and South Australia.

(a) New South Wales

Minors (Property and Contracts) Act 1970 (New South Wales)

49 (1) Where medical treatment or dental treatment of a minor aged less than 16 years is carried out with the prior consent of a parent or guardian of the person of the minor, the consent has effect in relation to a claim by the minor for assault or battery in respect of anything done in the course of that treatment as if, at the time when the consent is given, the minor were aged 21 years or upwards and had authorised the giving of the consent.

(2) Where medical treatment or dental treatment of a minor aged 14 years or upwards is carried out with the prior consent of the minor, his [or her] consent has effect in relation to a claim by him [or her] for assault or battery in respect of anything done in the course of that treatment as if, at the time when the consent is given, he [or she] were aged 21 years or upwards.

(3) This section does not affect:

(a) such operation as a consent may have otherwise than as provided by this section; or

(b) the circumstances in which medical treatment or dental treatment may be justified in the absence of consent.

(4) In this section:
dental treatment means:

(i) treatment by a dentist registered under the Dentists Act 1934 in the course of the practice of dentistry; or

(ii) treatment by any person pursuant to directions given in the course of the practice of dentistry by a dentist so registered; and

medical treatment means:

(i) treatment by a medical practitioner in the course of the practice of medicine or surgery; or

(ii) treatment by any person pursuant to directions given in the course of the practice of medicine or surgery by a medical practitioner.

The effect of the above section is canvassed by the Queensland Law Reform Commission in their discussion paper.

Queensland Law Reform Commission: *Consent to Medical Treatment of Young People*, Discussion Paper No 44, pp 145–48

New South Wales was the first Australian jurisdiction to address by way of legislation the question of the effect of a young person's consent to medical treatment.

Pursuant to s 49 of the Minors (Property and Contracts) Act 1970 (NSW), people who give medical or dental treatment to a young person under the age of 16 are protected from actions for assault where a parent or guardian has consented. In the case of a young person 14 years of age or upwards, the consent of the young person would similarly be effective. These provisions were adopted from a 1969 Law Reform Commission of New South Wales' Report. The New South Wales' Commission recommended a provision in identical terms to s 49 of the Minors (Property and Contracts) Act 1970 (NSW). The Commission explained the reason for its recommendations as follows:

The law is uncertain at present and we think that this section would effect a useful, though still incomplete, clarification. The section is limited to claims for assault: it has nothing to do with negligence. It would protect persons acting with reasonable care and with consent but that is as far as it goes. In the case of a minor up to 15 years of age, the consent of a parent or guardian of his or her person would be effective; in the case of a minor aged 14 years of age or upwards, the consent of the minor himself [or herself] would be effective. There is an overlap, but we see no harm in that. We think that these special provisions are justified having regard to the fact that the treatment will be by, or under the direction of members of skilled and responsible professions. The consent in question may or may not be contractual in character: the matter is at least an incidental matter within our terms of reference.

The New South Wales' Government in introducing s 49 had no firm views on medical treatment of young people which were ancillary to the object of the legislation but the Government agreed with the Commission's view that there are obvious advantages in laying down standards which will remove the existing uncertainty.

The New South Wales provision, on its face, enables young people aged 14 and upwards to seek medical or dental treatment whether or not they understand the treatment proposed. The effect of such consent would be to relieve the treating doctor or dentist from liability for assault or battery.

An immunity is provided to any practitioner who performs medical or dental treatment upon a child less than 16 years of age, with the prior consent of a parent.

The provision is limited to claims for assault and battery. Any false imprisonment or negligence claim brought on behalf of the young person is not affected. The section provides an immunity and does not affect the common law.

Section 49 does not empower a young person to consent to medical or dental treatment so much as it restricts rights of young people to sue for assault persons who, with their consent, have treated them. The provision does not take away a guardian's powers to withhold or refuse consent to treatment.

Helsham CJ in *K v Minister for Youth and Community Services* (1982) 1 NSWLR 311, p 321 stated in relation to s 49:

> It is a protective section at least in one respect, that is in the case of a 14 to 16 year old, because it takes away a right to sue which he [or she] otherwise would have, notwithstanding his [or her] consent, if the treatment were performed without consent of his [or her] parent or guardian. It does not take away any power of a guardian to withhold consent or to refuse. Whether the section of itself would have the effect of requiring the court to refuse relief to a guardian who sought to restrain an unwarranted operation (take, for example, an unnecessary sterilisation) about to be performed with the consent of a 14 year old, it is unnecessary to decide. I rather think it would not take away the right of a guardian to relief. But in the present case the most that could be said about the operation of the section is that if an abortion were to be performed by a medical practitioner in the course of his or her practice of medicine or surgery then the consent of this girl would free the practitioner from liability under any claim by her for assault or battery because of its performance.

Thus, a parent would probably be entitled to seek a court order prohibiting, in the interests of the child, performance of treatment to which a 14 or 15 year old had consented. The court would then have to decide the dispute according to the principle that the interests of the child are paramount.

Conversely, upon Helsham CJ's view, the New South Wales provision deprives the child of the right to sue a doctor for battery, for treatment to which a parent, but not the child, had consented. Thus, a doctor could lawfully carry out treatment, such as cosmetic surgery, on a patient under 16 in the absence of the patient's consent, if it were otherwise lawful.

For young people of 16 and 17 years of age in New South Wales, it would appear that their wishes must prevail over those of their parents or guardians.

The New South Wales Law Reform Commission is currently reviewing the law governing child consent to medical treatment.

Below is an edited extract from the Issues Paper No. 2 Minor's Consent to Medical Treatment which highlights some of the reform proposals.

Minor's Consent to Medical Treatment, New South Wales Law Reform Commission, June 2004

Introduction

In the past, the question of whether a young person could legally consent to or refuse medical treatment has typically attracted attention in relation to matters involving adolescent health. Adolescents face particular health concerns relevant to the physical, mental and emotional developments of puberty. These concerns include:

- *A heightened preoccupation with body image and the physical changes to their bodies.* Adolescents may seek medical treatment and advice for the changes their bodies undergo in puberty. For some, increased concern for their physical attractiveness may lead to, for example, development of an eating disorder, or even a desire for cosmetic surgery.
- *Increased awareness of sexuality.* Adolescents usually become curious about sex and their own sexuality. Some become sexually active in their teenage years. They may seek medical advice and treatment for contraception, sexually transmitted diseases, or pregnancy.
- *Experimentation with drugs and alcohol.* Some adolescents may begin to experiment with drugs and alcohol. Some may have problems with substance addiction, and may need treatment for the physical and mental effects of addiction.
- *Onset of mental illness, including depression.* The mental health of Australian adolescents has been the subject of much public discussion in recent years, with depression and the threat of suicide posing serious risks to the lives of many young people. Adolescence is also a time when about 75 percent of mental disorders first become apparent. Adolescents may seek counselling, and other forms of treatment, including medication, to address concerns with their mental health.

1.11 Adolescents may be reluctant to share their health concerns with their parents. Adolescence is often characterised by a desire for privacy, greater independence from parents, and a degree of conflict with parents and other authority figures. At the same time, parents will usually be anxious to retain some control and influence over their child's physical and mental well-being. For this group of young people, facing the types of health concerns outlined above, questions of who can consent to or refuse medical treatment raise considerations of ensuring access to medical services, recognising the growing maturity of the adolescent, and promoting the young person's best interests.

Younger children

1.12 It is more difficult to generalise about the typical types of health concerns of younger, pre-adolescent children. Obviously, young children do not yet usually face the health concerns typically associated with puberty. Instead, they are likely to require medical treatment, from time to time, for a wide range of childhood injuries and illnesses, varying from, for example, the common cold, to ear infections, to gastroenteritis, from cuts, to bruises, to broken limbs. They may require regular management of chronic health conditions, such as asthma, juvenile diabetes or eczema. As they develop, they may require treatment for learning or behavioural problems. Parents may seek to immunise their young children against a number of illnesses for which vaccines are now available, such as measles, mumps, chickenpox and hepatitis B. Apart from these more everyday health concerns, there are other health concerns which are more serious and may require decisions about life-saving treatment or invasive and irreversible treatment. Young children may also be found to be medically suited to blood or tissue donation, to benefit, for example, another family member, and the question then arises of who should have the authority to consent to or refuse such a donation.

1.13 Of course, the health concerns outlined above are not limited to young children. They can also affect the general population. The difference for young children is that, because of their immaturity, they are usually voiceless in the way their health concerns are addressed. This vulnerability makes it important to ensure that their welfare is protected and their best interests promoted.

Young people's decision-making capacity

1.14 The capacity of young people to make their own decisions about their medical care has been the subject of psychological theories and empirical research. Piaget developed a model of young people's cognitive development, which asserted that the capacity to make an intelligent choice generally appears in a child between the ages of 11 and 14. At this stage of their cognitive development, children have the ability to deal with abstractions, use deductive and inductive reasoning, apply reason to hypothetical situations and think about the future. They can therefore consider different options and their consequences. In their empirical study, Weithorn and Campbell compared the decision-making capacity of a group of children aged 9 to 14 with a group of adults aged 18 to 21. The 14-year-olds were found to demonstrate a level of competence equivalent to the adults. The 9-year-olds had significantly less developed skills in understanding and reasoning but despite this, did not differ significantly from the adults in the final choices they made about medical treatment. The study concluded that, despite their poorer understanding and failure to consider fully many of the critical elements of disclosed information, the 9-year-olds tended to make clear and sensible treatment preferences, similar to the adults within the sample group.

1.15 While these studies provide some support for the assertion that, at least by the age of 14, young people have attained the same level of cognitive development as adults to make medical treatment choices, other writers have emphasised that young people's decision-making capacity must also be judged according to their 'social development'. Young people may not have developed an internal capability for free, deliberate choice, which results not just from a level of cognitive maturity, but also from emotional development and a sense of distinct 'personhood'. Research suggests that, in early adolescence, young people have a greater tendency than at any other time toward conformity, with the risk of deferential responses to requests for consent being at its greatest until the ages 15–17. Each young person's decision-making capacity should be assessed with reference to the range of his or her experiences, and individual qualities, such as his or her abilities and confidence, relational style with authority and emotional state. A young person's decision-making capacity will also be affected by external factors, such as the nature and circumstances of the particular decision, the nature of the information provided to the young person and the way in which it is communicated, and the expectations of the adults involved in the decision. Cauffman and Steinberg argue that, when determining young people's competence, it is not sufficient simply to consider their cognitive differences and similarities with adults, but also their maturity of judgment. They claim that adolescents are more likely to differ from adults in their sense of responsibility (autonomy, identity and self-reliance), their perspective (sense of morality and context) and their temperance (regulation of emotion, avoidance of extremes and non-impulsivity). However, the way in which these differences affect the young person's maturity of judgment has not been sufficiently subjected to empirical research to make any considered assessment of their decision-making capacity in respect of medical treatment.

Scope of current regulation and State intervention

1.16 At present, there is no single legal framework in New South Wales to regulate the rights and roles of young people, parents, medical practitioners and other interested parties in making decisions about young people's medical treatment. Legislation applies to some aspects of this decision-making process. The relevant pieces of legislation are:

- Minors (Property and Contracts) Act 1970 (NSW);
- Children and Young Persons (Care and Protection) Act 1998 (NSW);
- Guardianship Act 1987 (NSW); and
- Family Law Act 1975 (Cth).

1.17 The scope of current legislative regulation is limited. The legislation says nothing about the rights of young people or their parents to make medical decisions or at least to be involved in such decisions, nor the legal obligations and rights of medical practitioners. It has much more specific aims. For instance, s 49 of the Minors (Property and Contracts) Act 1970 is not concerned with establishing a general framework for the rights of young people to make medical decisions, based on a particular policy position on what such rights should be. Its primary concern is with ensuring that medical practitioners are protected from liability in certain situations. Similarly, the three remaining pieces of legislation, listed above, do not aim to map out a framework for making decisions about young people's medical treatment. Their aim is to place limits on the types of medical treatment to which young people and their parents can consent, and to provide for the intervention of the State for those types of treatment, through several of its courts and tribunals, specifically the NSW Guardianship Tribunal, the Family Court of Australia and the Supreme Court of New South Wales, as well as, though perhaps with less direct involvement, the Children's Court (through the State child protection legislation) and the Mental Health Review Tribunal.

1.18 The common law (judge-made law) reflects greater consideration than current legislation of the rights and responsibilities of young people and parents in the process of making decisions about young people's medical treatment. It has developed a test for determining young people's legal competence to make their own medical decisions, following the courts' consideration of the rights of parents and their children. However, it has not yet developed to the extent of delineating clearly the lines of liability for the medical profession, nor necessarily providing young patients and parents with remedies to enforce their rights in respect of all types of treatment.

1.19 The law assumes that adults are competent to make decisions about their medical treatment, whether it be to consent to, or refuse, such treatment. That assumption is based on the principles of self-determination and autonomy, that is, the notion that individuals, of adult age, have the right to choose how they live and what should be done with their own bodies. That right is absolute, even if the decision made by a particular individual about his or her own medical care is not generally considered to promote his or her best interests. People below the age of 18 neither enjoy that same assumption nor the same recognition of their right to self-determination. Current regulation of the decision-making process for the medical treatment of young people is too limited in its aims to consider, in any meaningful way, whether, and in what circumstances, the continued curtailment of that right can be justified.

Rights and interests at stake

1.20 What should the law be aiming to achieve in regulating the ability of young people and others to make decisions about a young person's medical treatment? In the broadest sense, the State has an interest in ensuring that the medical treatment of young people promotes their best interests. More particularly, it could be argued that the law should aim to achieve, at the least, the following:

- It should ensure that young people have ready access to appropriate medical care;
- It should recognise and protect young people's rights to participate in decisions affecting them and to exercise some control over their own health care relative to their level of maturity;
- It should protect young people from detrimental decisions that may harm them;
- It should recognise the role of parents and the State in participating

in decisions affecting their child's welfare and in determining what is in his or her best interests, and promote the community's interest in encouraging parents to take responsibility for their child's well-being;

- It should provide the medical profession with a workable, clear and consistent framework for treating young people in order to provide them with the best possible care.

1.21 Australia has recognised, both internationally and in its own domestic law, that young people have certain rights that should be protected. These rights include: a right to a good standard of health, a right to have access to health care facilities and the right of young people to participate in decisions affecting them.

1.22 The United Nations Convention on the Rights of the Child acknowledges these rights and represents a promise by its signatories, including Australia, to protect and promote them. Article 24(1) states that:

> States Parties recognize the right of the child to the enjoyment of the highest attainable standard of health and to facilities for the treatment of illness and rehabilitation of health. States Parties shall strive to ensure that no child is deprived of his or her right of access to such health care services.

1.23 Article 12(1) provides that:

> States Parties shall assure to the child who is capable of forming his or her own views the right to express those views freely in all matters affecting the child, the views of the child being given due weight in accordance with the age and maturity of the child.

1.24 At the same time, the Convention also recognises the role of parents, as well as other family and community members, in providing young people with guidance and direction in the exercise of their rights:

> States Parties shall respect the responsibilities, rights and duties of parents or, where applicable, the members of the extended family or community as provided for by local custom, legal guardians or other persons legally responsible for the child, to provide, in a manner consistent with the evolving capacities of the child, appropriate direction and guidance in the exercise by the child of the rights recognized in the present Convention.

1.25 The United Nations Committee on the Rights of the Child has recently given specific consideration to the needs of adolescents and has claimed that signatory States should take additional steps to protect their rights, as enshrined in the Convention on the Rights of the Child. While acknowledging the continuing role of parents in making decisions about adolescents' medical care, the Committee has urged countries to recognise in their domestic law the possibility that the maturing adolescent may be able to give personal consent for medical treatment:

> Before consent is given by parents, adolescents need to be given a chance to express freely their views and they should be given due weight, in accordance with article 12 of the Convention. However, if the adolescent is of sufficient maturity, informed consent shall be obtained from the adolescent her/himself, while informing the parents, if this is in the 'best interest of the child' (article 3).

1.26 Consistent with this emphasis on the increasing autonomy of the maturing adolescent, the Committee has also underlined the importance of maintaining the confidentiality of adolescents' medical information.

1.27 In Australia, federal legislation gives the Human Rights and Equal Opportunity Commission the responsibility of ensuring that federal legislation is not inconsistent with the rights enshrined in the Convention on the Rights of the Child (among other instruments), of promoting an understanding and public discussion of those rights and of reporting on any action that Australia needs to take to comply with the provisions set out in the Convention.

1.28 At a State level, New South Wales has given express recognition in legislation to the importance of protecting and promoting the safety and well-being of young people, while at the same time acknowledging their right to participate in decisions that affect them. The New South Wales Commission for Children and Young People is a government body set up to protect the interests of young people in the provision of government and non-government services and the implementation of legislation and government policies. Its work is governed by three statutory principles, as provided in s 10 of the Commission for Children and Young People Act 1998 (NSW). These are:

(a) the safety, welfare and well-being of children are the paramount consideration;
(b) the views of children are to be given serious consideration and taken into account;
(c) a co-operative relationship between children and their families and community is important for the safety, welfare and well-being of children.

1.29 As is clear from the discussion above, there has been increasing recognition in recent years, both internationally and domestically, of children and young people as people with rights, while at the same time a continuing emphasis on the role, responsibilities and interests of parents and families in caring and making decisions about their children's welfare. A legal framework devised to regulate the area of young people's consent to medical treatment must find a way to recognise and balance these rights and interests.

Medicare: A practical obstacle to medical care?

1.30 It is pointless to consider reform to the decision-making processes concerning young people's medical treatment, without also taking into account practical obstacles that stand in the way of young people gaining ready access to appropriate health care. One of the most obvious, and most significant, obstacles arises from possible problems for young people in making use of the Medicare system. Many young people, with no significant sources of income, are unlikely to be able to seek medical treatment, independently of their parents, unless such treatment is free. There may be some matters for which young people, especially teenagers, do not want to seek medical advice and treatment unless they can do so without involving their parents. Ready access to the Medicare system is important in such situations if these young people are to seek out appropriate medical assistance.

1.31 There are no legislative restrictions on the age at which a person can make use of the bulk-billing health care system. However, the Health Insurance Commission has an internal policy that allows only people aged 15 and above to hold a Medicare card in their own name. Young people below that age must usually use their family's general Medicare card. There is some flexibility in the policy to allow people below 15 to hold their own Medicare cards in some situations, for example, young people who attend boarding schools or otherwise live away from home. However, most young people below the age of 15, who wish to see a medical practitioner and be bulk-billed, must take their family's Medicare card. This may be awkward for them if they do not want their parents to know about the consultation.

1.32 Having said that, there is no legislative or administrative requirement that a patient actually present his or her Medicare card at the medical practitioner's practice in order to be bulk-billed. All that is required is the patient's Medicare number. A young person could, for example, copy out his or her Medicare number from the family Medicare card and present the number to the medical practitioner. There is also a Medicare 'provider hotline' number which medical practices can telephone to obtain or confirm a particular patient's Medicare number. In theory, therefore, a young person below the age of 15 could still make use of the Medicare system without involving his or her parents. However, many young people may not know that they can receive free health care without presenting their Medicare card to the medical practitioner. Moreover, it may be a business decision of the particular medical practice not to bulk-bill patients unless they present their Medicare card at the time of the consultation. Medical practices may also vary in their internal policies concerning the age at which they will allow patients to sign Medicare vouchers for themselves, rather than requiring a parent to sign on the child's behalf.

1.33 Any reforms to the law which are aimed at providing young people with easier access to the health care system will be incomplete unless consideration is also given to possible changes to the Medicare system to allow young people to make greater use of the bulk-billing system independently of their parents. However, any such changes to Medicare can only be made at the federal level, and therefore lie beyond the scope of the NSW Law Reform Commission's role. For this reason, the Commission does not discuss the Medicare system in any detail in this Issues Paper. We have simply raised it in this introductory chapter as a matter that will impinge, in a practical way, on any reforms that we ultimately recommend.

Young people's capacity to make medical decisions – models for reform

The current law is, arguably, unclear and uncertain in a number of respects, lacking a considered and coherent policy direction. Rather than providing a general framework by which to determine young people's competence, the current law has much more specific aims and limited scope.

3.2 In this chapter, the Commission considers various models for legal reform that could be adopted to replace or build upon the existing law. These models would aim to replace what is a fairly piecemeal area of the law with a more cohesive framework that reflects a particular policy stand as regards the rights and interests of young people, their families and the medical profession.

3.3 The models for reform that are discussed below vary in their policy positions, as well as the extent to which they seek to replace and reform the existing law. Ultimately, the decision whether or not to replace the current law, and the particular model that is chosen to replace it, should depend on the policies on which the model is based, and its workability in practice.

Should young people be able to make decisions about their own medical care?

3.4 Should a person below 18 be able to consent to, or refuse, his or her own medical treatment? This question is fundamental to any discussion of possible legal reform and the response that is considered most appropriate will guide the direction that such reform will take.

3.5 There are at least three grounds for arguing that young people should, in some situations at least, be considered legally competent to consent to and refuse medical treatment:

- Some young people may be capable of maturing and developing to a degree that they can, and should, be considered to have the capacity of adults to understand and make decisions about their own health care.
- The law in this area should be in line with the modern view of children as young people with rights, including a right to their own

bodily integrity and a right to control, or at the least to participate in, decisions affecting their bodies. The perception of children as 'chattels' of their parents or their father, over whom parents may exercise complete control, is outmoded and inappropriate.

- It is in young people's best interests to allow them ready access to health care and treatment when needed. In some instances, particularly for matters relevant to adolescent health, young people may not seek medical assistance if they have to involve their parents in the process. It may be necessary to recognise as valid the young person's consent in order to treat him or her.

3.6 One or all of these grounds could provide a basis to justify a legal framework recognising young people's competence to make decisions about their health care. Which of these grounds is given priority, or how they are balanced, will affect the framework that is formulated. For example, if priority is given to the first two arguments, then the law should deny a young person the right to give a personal consent or refusal to medical treatment only to the extent that is necessary to protect them from the consequences of a decision made when they do not have sufficient maturity to give an informed consent or refusal. Once they are sufficiently mature, they should be recognised as autonomous individuals with the same right to make their own decisions as adults. If, on the other hand, priority is given to the third argument, then the law should only recognise as valid a young person's consent or refusal to the extent that this benefits the young person's health and well-being, with less focus on the maturity of the individual.

Issue 3.1 In what situations, if any, should young people be able to make their own decisions about their medical care?

Choosing a model to decide competence

3.7 The Commission puts forward below five possible tests, or models, for deciding when a young person should be considered legally competent to consent to, or refuse, a particular type of medical treatment. We have set out the basic principles of each model and raised issues of concern about each. We are interested in your comments, both generally about each model and about the specific issues raised. A table, summarising the features of each model, as well as its advantages and disadvantages, appears in Appendix A, to help you compare and weigh up the options. As well, there may be other models that we have not considered and that have merit as a means of determining when a young person should be able to give personal consent or refusal to medical treatment. We welcome your suggestions for other such models.

3.8 In considering possible options for reform, it may be helpful to imagine how each model would apply in practice to assess a young patient's legal competence. Here are some situations in which the question of whether young people should be able to consent to treatment may provoke various responses and to which the application of the models suggested below may prove to be more, or less, workable than the existing law:

- A young woman wishes to have cosmetic surgery performed, such as a breast enlargement.
- A young person seeks treatment for depression, including counselling and prescription of anti-depressants.
- A young person suffering from leukaemia wishes to decide for himself or herself the treatment programme, rather than allowing his or her parents to decide.
- A young woman seeks a prescription for the Pill.

A note on the right to refuse treatment

3.9 It is questionable whether a young person's right to refuse medical treatment should be treated separately and differently from the right to consent, and whether a different legal framework should govern any such right to refuse. The Commission considers this question below, at paragraphs 3.35–3.43. For the moment, the five suggested models for reform that follow are formulated in terms of deciding both whether a young person can consent to and refuse treatment. It may be that these models are ultimately considered appropriate only as a means of determining the issue of consent and that different rules are considered desirable to apply to determining if and when a young person can give a valid refusal of medical treatment.

Model One: Assess consent according to each young person's capacity to understand

'Understanding the nature and possible consequences'

3.10 This model encapsulates the common law approach to deciding competence to consent, as reflected in the *Gillick* test. It determines legal competence to consent on an individual, case-by-case basis: a young person may give a valid consent or refusal if he or she is capable of understanding the nature and possible consequences of the treatment. It allows the treating medical practitioner to judge the maturity of each individual and recognises that young people mature at different rates, with varying degrees of understanding about different types of treatment.

3.11 This model has several variations. A young person could give a legal consent or refusal to medical treatment if:

- the treating medical practitioner were satisfied that the young person understood the nature and possible consequences of the treatment; or
- the treating medical practitioner were satisfied that the young person understood the nature and possible consequences of the

treatment and the medical practitioner were satisfied that the treatment was in the young person's best interests; or

- the treating medical practitioner were satisfied that the young person understood the nature and consequences of the treatment, where there was a presumption of maturity over a specified age, such as 13, and the possibility of maturity under that age if it could be proved to the medical practitioner's satisfaction; or
- the treating medical practitioner were satisfied according to one of the above tests, and that opinion was supported by written approval from a second medical practitioner.

What level of understanding should be required?

3.12 What do we mean by 'understanding' the nature and possible consequences of a particular type of treatment? Should this test for competence require simply that a young person reach a certain level of cognitive development to appreciate the procedure that is involved or is there some higher level of understanding that should be required? Is a single test for competence possible in view of the variety of medical procedures that might be the subject of consideration in any particular situation? The Commission has already noted that the current common law is not clear about the level of understanding that a young person must demonstrate under the *Gillick* test in order to be legally competent to consent to medical treatment: should the young person have to demonstrate a high level of understanding, so as to be able to exercise a 'wise choice', understanding not just the nature of the treatment proposed, but also the moral, emotional and family ramifications of the treatment, or should he or she only have to demonstrate a lower level of understanding, one which considers simply the nature of the medical treatment proposed? Should the young person demonstrate not only the cognitive skills to make an intelligent choice about the proposed treatment, but also have the social or emotional maturity to make a 'voluntary' decision, reasonably free from influences such as pressure from peers, the desire to conform or to defer to authority?

3.13 For instance, in the example outlined in paragraph 3.8 of the young woman seeking cosmetic surgery, should she be considered legally competent to consent to the surgery if she has the cognitive skills to understand the procedure and the risks involved? Should the treating medical practitioner also be questioning her level of social and emotional maturity, and her ability to decide independently of a normal adolescent preoccupation with body image and conformity with peers? Is it possible to identify, with any real certainty, a particular point in a young person's development as the threshold past which that young person should be considered legally competent to make decisions about health care?

3.14 It has been suggested that guidelines should be formulated to help medical practitioners assess young people's capacity to understand in a clear, consistent manner, with reference to specified and clearly articulated criteria. The use of guidelines would, firstly, provide the medical profession with an objective standard to enable them to assess young people consistently; and secondly, ensure that medical practitioners provide objective, behaviourally based observations of any incapacitations of a particular patient, which would then be available for subsequent scrutiny by, for example, a court.

Issue 3.2

(a) **Should the law assess a young person's competence to consent to medical treatment in terms of the individual young person's understanding of the nature and possible consequences of the proposed medical treatment, as put forward in Model One of the Commission's Options for Reform?**
(b) **Is there a more appropriate formulation of the test put forward in Model One? For example, should the focus be more on the reasoning process by which the young person reaches a decision about treatment, with an assessment of his or her ability to consider and weigh up various alternatives?**
(c) **Should the law spell out the level of understanding that a young person must demonstrate in order to be competent according to the test put forward in Model One and, if so, how?**
(d) **Would it be helpful to prescribe guidelines by which the treating medical practitioner can assess the individual patient's degree of understanding under this test?**

Finding appropriate safeguards against a medical practitioner's error in judgment

3.15 Model One carries the risk that a medical practitioner will make a mistake about an individual patient's level of maturity. As we noted in the paragraph above, it may not be easy in practice to identify a point at which a young person can be said to pass a specified threshold of maturity to make him or her legally competent to make a decision about a particular medical matter, and it is a question on which medical practitioners might reasonably disagree. There are other factors that might also affect a medical practitioner's ability to make a fair assessment of a young person's competence, such as the medical practitioner's own cultural values and his or her exposure to and experience in treating young patients. The medical practitioner's judgment may go unchallenged or may not be challenged until after the consequences of that judgment have been felt.

Issue 3.3

(a) **Does Model One of the Commission's Options for Reform place too much discretion in the medical practitioner's hands and too much faith in the medical practitioner's ability to assess the young person's level of maturity?**

(b) Does Model One place too much emphasis on the young person's right to autonomy at the risk of exposing him or her to the consequences of a detrimental decision?

3.16 Safeguards could be put in place to check the exercise of the medical practitioner's discretion. For example, the requirement for written support from a second medical practitioner, appearing above as the fourth variation of this model, is one such safeguard.

Issue 3.4

(a) Could a requirement for a second medical opinion in Model One of the Commission's Options for Reform become simply a 'rubber stamp', where approval is granted as a matter of course?
(b) Would such a requirement place too great a burden on medical practitioners, particularly in more isolated, rural areas, to seek a second opinion?
(c) Would such a requirement discourage young people from seeking medical treatment if they knew that the details of their consultation were likely to be disclosed to another medical practitioner?

3.17 Another safeguard that has been previously suggested is provision for a person with 'sufficient interest', including a young person or parent, to apply to a judge to challenge the medical practitioner's decision about the young person's maturity in order either to prohibit the proposed medical treatment or to allow it to take place.

Issue 3.5

(a) Is it practical to include a safeguard in Model One of the Commission's Options for Reform that gives an 'interested person' a right to challenge a medical practitioner's decision about competence in court?
(b) Is there any way in which parents, and other interested people, could be made aware of a medical practitioner's decision before the medical treatment is carried out without compromising the medical practitioner's duty of confidentiality to the young person?
(c) Could a provision, which allowed parents and others to challenge a medical practitioner's assessment of competence, discourage young people from seeking medical assistance?
(d) Are there other safeguards that could be included in Model One, which would be effective in limiting the power vested in the individual medical practitioner in determining a young person's competence to consent or refuse?

A requirement to consider the young person's best interests?

3.18 The second variation of this test includes a welfare provision. That is, the medical practitioner must be satisfied that the treatment in question is in the young person's best interests before relying on the (competent) young person's consent, or refusal.

Issue 3.6

- **(a) If a young person is sufficiently mature to understand the nature and consequences of the medical treatment proposed, should that be enough to validate his or her consent, or refusal, according to Model One of the Commission's Options for Reform?**
- **(b) Is a qualification justifiable that requires young people's decisions about their medical care to be in their own best interests before their consent or refusal becomes legally valid?**
- **(c) If a young person's legal competence to consent, or refuse, is made subject to that consent or refusal being in his or her best interests, how are those best interests to be determined, and by whom?**

Distinguishing between 'consent' and 'informed consent'

3.19 In Chapter 1, the Commission referred to two legal doctrines relating to the notion of consent to medical treatment. The first requires a patient's legally valid consent in order to negate what would otherwise amount to a trespass to the person; the second requires that a patient's consent be based on an informed decision, following a disclosure by the medical practitioner of all the material risks involved in the proposed treatment. In general, at least in the context of treating adult patients, it seems that a consent is legally valid to avoid liability in trespass if it is given by a competent patient who understands the general nature of the procedure that is proposed. Failure to disclose all the material risks to the patient does not invalidate the patient's consent so as to give rise to liability in trespass, but instead exposes the medical practitioner to possible liability in negligence.

3.20 The Commission noted in Chapter 1 that in the current law governing young people's competence to consent to medical treatment, there appears, to some extent at least, a convergence of these two doctrines. Under the *Gillick* test, a young person is competent to consent to treatment, so as to negate what would otherwise be a trespass, if he or she understands the nature *and* the possible consequences of the treatment. Presumably, this would require the treating medical practitioner to disclose not only the general nature of the treatment, but also its possible consequences, including the risks inherent with the procedure. It is not clear how this impacts, if at all, on a medical practitioner's duty to disclose all material risks so as to avoid liability in negligence.

3.21 Model One adopts, to a great extent, the common law test for assessing a young person's competence under the *Gillick* test. If this model is determined to be the preferred option, it may be desirable to consider how it is to interact with the notion of 'informed consent' in the law of medical negligence.

Issue 3.7 How is Model One of the Commission's Options for Reform to be distinguished from the notion of 'informed consent' in the law of medical negligence? Should a medical practitioner be required to

disclose the 'material risks' of a particular type of medical treatment in order to be satisfied of a young person's competence to consent?

Model Two: Assess consent by fixing a general cut-off age

3.22 This model fixes a general age at which a young person is considered legally competent to consent to or refuse medical treatment. All young people of that age are then able to give personal consent or refusal, without the need to obtain parental approval of that decision (unless incapacitated for some reason other than minority, such as an intellectual disability). All young people under that fixed age require their parents' consent, or authorisation from the State, to obtain medical treatment, and their parents generally have sole right to refuse medical treatment for them, subject to the courts' power to intervene. This general rule could be made subject to certain exceptions. For example, different rules could apply to decisions about treating certain types of medical conditions, as discussed at paragraphs 3.27–3.29 below.

3.23 This model has the advantage of certainty for medical practitioners. It removes any discretion from the medical practitioner to make a judgment about the maturity of an individual patient. It avoids the risk that a medical practitioner will sometimes make mistakes in assessing a young person's competence to consent, and that young people with insufficient understanding may consequently consent to health care without their parents' knowledge or guidance. The model does not allow for the possibility that certain individuals may be mature enough to make a decision about their health care at a younger age. It also carries the risk that young people below the cut-off age will be deprived of medical treatment because they do not want to consult with their parents about the medical condition in question. This model gives priority to the need to protect immature young people from making detrimental decisions over the desire to give mature young people the right to autonomy and proper access to health care.

Issue 3.8

(a) Is there any greater likelihood of error in assessing legal competence using a fixed age test, as in Model Two of the Commission's Options for Reform, than in a test that requires the treating medical practitioner to make a judgment about the maturity of an individual patient, as in Model One?

(b) Are concerns about denying young people below the cut-off age proper access to health care adequately met by formulating a list of medical procedures to which a person younger than the cut-off age can consent as exceptions to the general, fixed age rule?

(c) If Model Two were adopted, what would be an appropriate age to fix as the cut-off age? The most common choice in other jurisdictions is 16, although some jurisdictions have fixed the age at 14.

Model Three: Assess consent according to the young person's age *and* capacity to understand

3.24 This model combines an age-based test and a capacity-based test. Young people over a certain age can give a valid consent or refusal to medical treatment if the treating medical practitioner is satisfied that they understand the nature and consequences of the treatment. Young people under that age cannot give a valid consent or refusal, and medical practitioners cannot generally treat them without the parents' consent.

3.25 Here is one formulation of this approach:

- Young people aged 16 and over can legally consent to medical treatment as if they were adults.
- Young people between 12 and 15 can legally consent to medical treatment if they understand the nature and consequences of the treatment. The young person's consent is still valid even if one or both parents object to or refuse the treatment. Parents of a child between 12 and 15 can legally consent to medical treatment for their child. Their consent is still valid even if the child objects to or refuses the treatment, except for certain types of treatment that cannot be performed over the young person's objection, such as termination of pregnancy.
- Young people under 12 cannot legally consent to, or refuse, their own medical treatment. Medical practitioners can generally treat a child under 12 if the child's parents consent to the treatment and the treatment is in the best interests of the child.

3.26 This approach seeks to strike a balance between flexibility and the need to protect immature young people from the consequences of detrimental decisions about their health care. It recognises that some individuals below a certain age may in fact be mature enough to make their own decisions about medical treatment. However, it also recognises the possibility that medical practitioners may make mistakes in assessing competence, and goes some way in protecting young people from those mistakes.

Issue 3.9

(a) Does Model Three of the Commission's Options for Reform find a suitable balance between young people's right to autonomy, parents' interests in protecting and guiding their children and the State's responsibility to protect its young?
(b) Is Model Three too complicated to be workable in practice?

Model Four: Assess consent according to the type of medical treatment

3.27 This model determines a young person's legal competence to give personal consent or refusal, according to the type of medical treatment that is in question. For example, the law could stipulate that a young person, of any age, could give a personal consent to, or refusal of, treatment in respect of one or more of the following:

- contraception;
- termination of pregnancy;
- pregnancy-related health care;
- sexually transmitted diseases;
- drug or alcohol abuse;
- mental health services.

3.28 If desired, legislation giving effect to this model could include an additional provision that the treatment sought (or refused) be in the young person's best interests: that is, a young person could consent to, or refuse, treatment relating to one of the above, if it were in the young person's best interests that the treatment be carried out (or not carried out, as the case may be).

3.29 This model could operate either as a principal test for deciding legal competence, or in addition to a principal test. For example, legal competence to consent could be judged according to a fixed age test (or any other of the models discussed), with the additional provision that a young person of any age could give personal consent to treatment for one of a list of prescribed conditions. The issue here is whether there are certain types of treatment to which a young person of any age should always be able to give a personal consent or refusal, for public policy reasons, regardless of whatever other rules apply generally to decide legal competence to consent. The Commission gives separate consideration to this question at paragraphs 3.44–3.54 below.

Issue 3.10 Should the type of medical treatment in issue determine a young person's ability to consent to, or refuse, medical treatment, either as a principal or a subsidiary test for legal competence? If so, which types of treatment should a young person be automatically considered competent to consent to, or refuse?

Model Five: Assess consent according to specific groups of young people

3.30 According to this model, young people can make their own decisions about their health care if they fall within one of a list of categories, such as:

- young people who are married or living in a de facto relationship;
- young people who are themselves parents;
- young people who live apart from their parents and manage their own financial affairs;
- homeless young people.

3.31 Again, this model can be put forward either as a principal test for determining legal competence, or in addition to a principal test. For example, a young person who is below the fixed age for consent in a fixed age model could still give personal consent if he or she fell into one of the above categories.

Issue 3.11

(a) **Should any or all of the following groups of young people, as listed in Model Five of the Commission's Options for Reform, be considered competent to consent to or refuse medical treatment, regardless of whether they meet the criteria in any general test for assessing legal competence?**

- **Young people who are married or living in a de facto relationship;**
- **Young people who are parents;**
- **Young people who live apart from their parents and manage their own financial affairs;**
- **Young people who are homeless.**

(b) **Are there any other groups of young people who should always be able to give personal consent or refusal to medical treatment?**

(c) **Should these groups of young people be able to consent to or refuse medical treatment as if they were adults, or should there be an additional requirement that the medical practitioner consider the treatment in question, or refusal of that treatment, to be in the patient's best interests?**

Formulating an alternative model: Selecting indicators from each proposed model for reform

3.32 It may be that no single model of the five set out above is considered suitable as the sole means of deciding a young person's legal competence to consent. Instead, each model may contain features that are considered useful as indicators by which to assess competence. Ultimately, the model that is chosen may be a collection of indicators from all, or some, of these models.

Issue 3.12

(a) **Are there any other models for reform that are not included in the five models set out in Chapter 3, which might be effective in determining young people's legal competence to make decisions about their medical care?**

(b) **Which, if any, features, or indicators, of the five models listed in Chapter 3, would you consider useful to retain in any alternative model for reform?**

The role of parents in the proposed model for reform

3.33 Consideration needs to be given to the role that parents should play within any proposed model for reform to the law governing young people's right to consent to and refuse medical treatment. The current law in New South Wales is unclear on the interaction between parents' and young people's rights to consent, and how to resolve possible conflict between a parent and child.

3.34 It may be desirable to clarify the role and rights of parents in participating in decisions about their children's medical care once their children are legally competent to consent to, and refuse, medical treatment themselves. Should parents retain power to make medical decisions on their child's behalf in this situation or should any such power cease as soon as their child becomes legally competent to make those decisions? This question has already been raised in Chapter 2, in Issue 2.4, and the Commission invites your response.

The right to refuse medical treatment: Should different rules apply?

3.35 As the Commission noted in Chapter 2, at paragraphs 2.47–2.53, it is not clear whether, under current law, a mature young person has a right to refuse medical treatment in the same way as he or she has a right to consent to it.

3.36 Should a person under 18 have a right to refuse medical treatment and, if so, when should he or she be able to do so? The following are controversial situations in which these questions may arise:

- A young person with anorexia refuses treatment for the disease.
- A young person with a mental illness or behavioural disorder refuses treatment, in particular refuses prescribed medication.
- A young person suffering from substance addiction refuses treatment, including counselling.
- A young woman refuses to terminate her pregnancy.
- A young person refuses a particular treatment that is preferred by the treating medical practitioner and/or parents, and chooses a different treatment option.

3.37 Some of these examples are complicated by the fact that there are factors additional to the person's age that may have an effect on his or her capacity to understand the consequences of refusing treatment. How should medical practitioners assess the capacity of a young person who suffers from a mental illness or eating disorder: are they to determine first whether the young person has the maturity of an adult, and if so, then judge their capacity to refuse treatment according to the standards used to determine legal capacity of an adult with a mental illness, or is a two-staged determination of this sort completely artificial and impossible to carry out in practice?

3.38 The question of a young person's right to refuse also highlights problems in maintaining patient confidentiality when treating young people. Where a young person refuses treatment that the medical practitioner considers to be in his or her best interest, and the parents are unaware of the young person's health problem or condition, can and should the medical practitioner breach patient confidentiality to inform the parents of the young person's refusal? This is an issue that is discussed in Chapter 9.

Reason for recognising a right to refuse

3.39 The main reason for recognising a young person's right to refuse medical treatment is straightforward. If young people are judged to be sufficiently mature, according to whatever test of maturity is formulated, why should they not be able to refuse medical treatment in the same way that a mature young person is able to consent to medical treatment and in the same way that an adult has a right to refuse treatment? If the law recognises the rights of adults to bodily integrity and control over their own health care, it is discriminatory and unjustifiably paternalistic to deny the same rights to young people who have the mental capacity to make rational decisions for themselves.

Reasons for rejecting a right to refuse

3.40 The following are possible reasons for denying young people a right to refuse medical treatment.

3.41 In most cases, the provision of medical treatment is aimed at benefiting a young person and the refusal of such treatment would be considered, at least in the eyes of the general public, to be to the young person's detriment. If the primary motivation in recognising young people's right to *consent* to medical treatment is to allow them better access to health care, that same concern does not apply to allow them a right to refuse treatment and in fact argues against such a right. At the beginning of this chapter, the Commission referred to three grounds for justifying a young person's right to consent: recognition of young people's ability to mature; recognition of their right to bodily integrity and control over their own health care; and a desire to allow them ready access to medical care. A legal framework that denies young people a right to refuse medical treatment gives priority to the third consideration over the first two considerations.

3.42 It may also be argued that the level of maturity that is needed to appreciate what is involved in refusing medical treatment is different from, and possibly higher than, the level of maturity required in consenting to treatment. Is the reasoning process of the average adolescent, for example, able to appreciate fully the long-term consequences of a decision to refuse treatment?

3.43 Of course, instead of rejecting altogether a young person's right to refuse, a different test, or a more stringent test, could apply to deciding a young person's capacity to refuse treatment than the test to decide his or her capacity to consent to it. Whether it would be practical or workable to have two different tests operating at the same time is open to question. The Commission has already asked, in Issue 2.6, whether young people should ever be considered legally competent to refuse medical treatment. Issue 3.13 seeks your views on the test that should be applied to determine competence to refuse, assuming a right to refuse should be afforded.

Issue 3.13

(a) Assuming that young people should be considered in some situations legally competent to refuse medical treatment, should the same test apply to decide a young person's legal competence to refuse as the test to determine competence to consent to treatment?
(b) If a different test should apply, how should a test to determine competence to refuse be formulated?

Treating certain types of conditions

3.44 In paragraphs 3.27–3.29, the Commission discussed a possible model for deciding consent (and possibly refusal) according to the type of medical condition that was involved. We noted that this model could be used as the primary model for deciding a young person's competence to consent to medical treatment, or as a model additional to another primary model. The fundamental question is whether, regardless of whatever general test is used to decide legal competence to consent and/ or refuse, there are certain types of conditions for which a young person should always have the right to refuse or consent to treatment, without the need to obtain a parent's consent or support.

3.45 We have already suggested a list of conditions and treatment that might fall within this special category of cases. These are:

- contraceptive advice and prescription (excluding permanent or long-lasting forms of contraception);
- sexually transmitted diseases;
- drug and alcohol abuse;
- mental health services;
- termination of pregnancy; and
- pregnancy-related health care.

Contraceptive advice, STDs, substance addiction and mental health services

3.46 In relation to these four conditions and treatment, it could be said that it is in both the interests of the young person and of the general community to allow a young person ready access to treatment, and that a young person of any age should be able to consent to such treatment without first obtaining parental authorisation. Should young people of any age, who are sexually active, have access to contraception, both for their own well-being, in preventing unwanted pregnancies, and for the sake of the community, which may indirectly share the costs of raising an unplanned child? The Commission does not intend to include within this list those forms of contraception that are permanent or long-lasting, such as sterilisation or injectable hormones. These types of medical procedures currently require special authorisation from a court or tribunal and we consider them separately in Chapter 4.

3.47 It is in the interests of the community, as well as the individual, to treat a sexually transmitted disease to prevent further infection. It can also be argued that a young person of any age who suffers from substance addiction should be able to seek treatment for that addiction for his or her own welfare, as well as the interests of the community in reducing the incidence of substance addiction and social problems that follow such addiction.

3.48 Perhaps more controversially would be to allow young people of any age ready access to mental health treatment, without the requirement first to obtain parental consent (and perhaps even without parents' knowledge). Certainly, there is a strong argument for allowing young people ready access to treatment if they suffer from depression, where treatment is likely to prevent a possible suicide. Access to mental health services without parental consent could be limited to these more extreme cases of suicide risk. However, such a limitation may not be practical: it will not necessarily be readily apparent to a medical practitioner, on first meeting with a young person, whether or not that person poses a suicide risk. More fundamentally, it could be argued that young people of any age who are in a state of mental distress should be able to seek help, whether or not they want to tell their parents about the problem first in order to gain their consent for treatment. On the other hand, parents may be concerned that their children are, for instance, receiving counselling and possibly being prescribed drugs without their knowledge or authorisation. Towards the beginning of this Chapter, the Commission cited situations in which the question whether a young person should have a right to consent to treatment might provoke differing responses. One of these situations was of a young person suffering from depression. Should that young person be given the right to consent to counselling, and possibly to medication such as anti-depressants, regardless of whether he or she passes any legal test for competence, or should his or her parents be involved in the decision of whether, and how, to treat the depression?

3.49 There are grounds for arguing that it is in the public interest to allow medical practitioners to treat young people for these four conditions based solely on the young person's consent, without the need to obtain parental consent and, perhaps, despite parental objection. The same justification does not apply to allowing young people of all ages the right to refuse treatment for these four conditions. In fact, the public interest argument provides a ground for arguing that young people of any age should not have a right to refuse treatment for these conditions, regardless of whatever general right to refuse medical treatment is recognised.

Issue 3.14

(a) Should a young person of any age be able to consent to any of the following four types of medical treatment without requiring parental consent:

- **contraceptive advice and prescription (excluding permanent or long-lasting forms of contraception);**
- **treatment for sexually transmitted diseases;**
- **treatment for drug and alcohol abuse;**
- **mental health services?**

(b) Should a young person of any age be able to consent to mental health treatment to prevent a risk of suicide, without requiring parental consent? Should a young person be able to consent to mental health treatment where there is no immediate risk of suicide, without parental consent?

(c) Should a young person be able to refuse any of the forms of treatment listed above in (a)?

(d) If the law recognises a young person's right to give personal consent to any of the forms of treatment listed in (a), should there be an additional requirement that the medical practitioner be satisfied that the treatment is in the young person's best interests?

(e) Should parents be able to consent to, or refuse, any of the four forms of treatment listed in (a), on behalf of their child? Should parents be able to veto a consent given by their child for any of these forms of treatment? Should a young person be able to veto a consent, or refusal, of his or her parents for any of these four forms of treatment?

Termination of pregnancy

3.50 At present, a pregnancy can be lawfully terminated if there is a valid consent and the termination is necessary to protect the woman from serious danger to her physical and mental health. Presumably, under current law, only a young woman who is considered mature according to the *Gillick* test is able to give a valid consent to a termination. A young woman who does not meet this standard would therefore need to obtain her parents' consent before a legal abortion could be performed. It is uncertain in what circumstances a young woman might refuse a termination of her pregnancy if her parents had consented to the termination.

3.51 For a young woman, the decision to terminate a pregnancy is one that, ideally, should be made with the guidance and advice, or at least the knowledge of, a parent. On the other hand, young women who are not considered legally competent to give personal consent may simply resort to 'backyard abortions' rather than inform their parents of the pregnancy, at great risk to their health. It may also seem paradoxical that a young woman can be considered not to be sufficiently mature to have the capacity to consent to an abortion but, failing that termination, is deemed sufficiently mature to give birth and possibly raise a child.

3.52 As for a young woman's right to refuse an abortion, it seems in some way an invidious violation of a woman's right to bodily integrity and right to choose to impose an unwanted termination on her. At the same time, parents and other adults may have grounds for concern that, because of the young woman's immaturity, she does not properly appreciate the demands of giving birth and raising a child.

Issue 3.15

(a) Should all young women below 18 be deemed competent to consent to a termination of pregnancy?
(b) Should all young women below 18 be deemed competent to refuse a termination?
(c) What legal role, if any, should the young woman's parents play in the decision whether or not to terminate her pregnancy?

Pregnancy-related health care

3.53 Should a pregnant woman who is below the age of 18 be able to give personal consent or refusal to pregnancy-related health care, or should the general test for determining competence to consent and refuse apply to this situation? For example, should a pregnant young woman be able to give personal consent to tests and ultrasounds that are routinely carried out to monitor the health of the foetus? Should a pregnant young woman have the right to refuse such tests? Should a young woman be considered competent to give personal consent or refusal to medical assistance in giving birth, such as consenting to or refusing a caesarean birth?

3.54 On the one hand, a woman who is sufficiently mature to have a child could be considered sufficiently mature to make decisions about her antenatal care. On the other hand, parenthood does not necessarily connote maturity and an immature young woman may make decisions about her health care that are detrimental not only to herself but also to the foetus.

Issue 3.16

(a) Should all pregnant women below 18 be considered competent to consent to pregnancy-related health care?
(b) Should all pregnant women below 18 be considered competent to refuse pregnancy-related health care?
(c) What role, if any, should the young woman's parents play in making decisions about her antenatal care?

Treatment requiring court authorisation

3.55 There are currently statutory provisions requiring court authorisation before certain types of treatment can be carried out on a person under 18, whether or not that person is generally considered competent to give personal consent to medical treatment.

(b) South Australia

Consent to Medical Treatment and Palliative Care Act 1995 (SA)

6 A person of or over 16 years of age may make decisions about his or her own medical treatment as validly and effectively as an adult.

12 A medical practitioner may administer medical treatment to a child if:

(a) the parent or guardian consents; or
(b) the child consents and;

 (i) the medical practitioner who is to administer the treatment is of the opinion that the child is capable of understanding the nature, consequences and risks of the treatment and that the treatment is in the best interest of the child's health and well-being; and
 (ii) that opinion is supported by the written opinion of at least one other medical practitioner who personally examines the child before the treatment is commenced.

13(1) – Subject to subsection (3), a medical practitioner may lawfully administer medical treatment to a person (the patient) if:

(a) the patient is incapable of consenting; and
(b) the medical practitioner who administers the treatment is of the opinion that the treatment is necessary to meet an imminent risk to life or health and that opinion is supported by the written opinion of another medical practitioner who has personally examined the patient; and
(c) the patient (if of or over 16 years of age) has not, to the best of the medical practitioner's knowledge, refused to consent to the treatment.

(2) A supporting opinion is not necessary under subsection (1) if in the circumstances of the case it is not practicable to obtain such an opinion.

How does the South Australian statute differ from the New South Wales statute? Which approach is preferable?

Note that all States of Australia make provision for the compulsory examination and treatment of children who are, or who are suspected to be, the subject of abuse.

Procedures not requiring consent (children or adults)

The normal rules governing consent to treatment do not apply in two circumstances:

1 in cases of emergency; and
2 in cases where statutes decree that treatment may be carried out without the consent of the patient.

Emergency

Common law has long recognised that a patient who is in imminent danger of death may have such treatment administered to him as is necessary. It had been thought that the basis of such an imposition was implied consent. Lord Goff in *In Re F* [1990] AC 1 at 77 reiterated the view he had earlier expressed in *Collins v Willcock* [1984] 1 WLR 1172 that implied consent was not the true reason the law allows treatment in an emergency. Rather, the treatment fell within one of the 'actions which are acceptable in ordinary life' as not amounting to battery (cf people being jostled as they walk along the street).

Note that the treatment performed must be necessary and not just 'convenient' – CCH *Australian Health and Medical Law Reporter* 21, p 24, where the Canadian decisions of *Marshall v Curry* (1933) 3 DLR 260 and *Murray v McMurchy* (1949) 2 DLR 442 were contrasted. In the former, while a patient was being operated upon for the purposes of hernia repair, the surgeon noted that the patient had a diseased testicle. In such circumstances, postponing the removal of the testicle may have had the effect of allowing the patient to die of septicemia. The surgeon was found to be justified on the ground of emergency in removing the patient's testicle. In the later case, the tying of a patient's Fallopian tubes at the time that the patient had a caesarean section and removal of fibroid growths was simply convenient and not necessary. The patient could safely have been 'closed up' and asked whether she wished to have her Fallopian tubes tied. In these circumstances, the surgeon was guilty of committing a battery.

The one exception to the legality of what would otherwise be regarded as emergency medical treatment is where the doctor performing the treatment is aware that the patient has indicated that under no circumstances does the patient want the particular type of emergency treatment.

Malette v Shulman (1990) 67 DLR (4th) 321

> A woman was severely injured in a car accident and was rushed to the casualty department of a hospital. The attending doctor decided to administer a blood transfusion. Before he could do so, a nurse discovered a card on the person of the patient. The card stated that the woman was a Jehovah's Witness and that in no circumstances did she wish to receive a blood transfusion. The doctor elected to proceed in spite of the card, on the strength of his conviction that it was his professional responsibility to administer the transfusion. The woman recovered and sued the doctor, the hospital and a number of nurses alleging negligence and battery. She succeeded at first instance. The doctor appealed.
>
> What then is the legal effect, if any, of the Jehovah's Witness card carried by Mrs Malette? Was the doctor bound to honour the instructions of his unconscious patient or, given the emergency and his inability to obtain conscious instructions from his patient, was he entitled to disregard the card and act according to his best medical judgment?
>
> To answer these questions and determine the effect to be given to the

Jehovah's Witness card, it is first necessary to ascertain what rights a competent patient has to accept or reject medical treatment and to appreciate the nature and extent of those rights. The right of a person to control his or her own body is a concept that has long been recognised at common law. The tort of battery has traditionally protected the interest in bodily security from unwanted physical interference. Basically, any intentional nonconsensual touching which is harmful or offensive to a person's sense of dignity is actionable. Of course, a person may choose to waive this protection and consent to the intentional invasion of this interest, in which case an action for battery will not be maintainable. No special exceptions are made for medical care, other than in emergency situations, and the general rules governing actions for battery are applicable to the doctor-patient relationship. Thus, as a matter of common law, a medical intervention in which a doctor touches the body of a patient would constitute a battery if the patient did not consent to the intervention. Patients have the decisive role in the medical decision-making process. Their right of self-determination is recognised and protected by the law. As Justice Cardozo proclaimed in his classic statement: every human being of adult years and sound mind has a right to determine what shall be done with his own body; and a surgeon who performs an operation without his client's consent commits an assault, for which he is liable in damages (*Schloendoff v Society of New York Hospital* (1914) 211 NY 12). See also, *Vitleto v Gennedy* (1981) 33 OR (2d) 497; 125 DLR (3d) 127; 17 CCLT 307 (CA); Linden, *Canadian Tort Law*, 4th edn, 1988, pp 40–43 and p 59 *et seq*; Prosser and Keeton, *The Law of Torts*, 5th edn, 1984, pp 39–42; and Fleming, *The Law of Torts*, 7th edn, 1987, p 234.

The doctrine of informed consent has developed in the law as the primary means of protecting a patient's right to control his or her medical treatment . . . The doctrine presupposes the patient's capacity to make a subjective treatment decision based on her understanding of the necessary medical facts provided by the doctor and on her assessment of her own personal circumstances. A doctor who performs a medical procedure without having first furnished the patient with the information needed to obtain an informed consent will have infringed the patient's right to control the course of her medical care, and will be liable in battery even though the procedure was performed with a high degree of skill and actually benefited the patient.

The right of self-determination which underlies the doctrine of informed consent also obviously encompasses the right to refuse medical treatment. A competent adult is generally entitled to reject a specific treatment or all treatment, or to select an alternate form of treatment, even if the decision may entail risks as serious as death and may appear mistaken in the eyes of the medical profession or of the community. Regardless of the doctor's opinion, it is the patient who has the final say on whether to undergo the treatment. The patient is free to decide, for instance, not to be operated on or not to undergo therapy or, by the same token, not to have a blood transfusion. If a doctor were to proceed in the face of a decision to reject the treatment, he would be civilly liable for his unauthorised conduct notwithstanding his justifiable belief that what he did was necessary to preserve the patient's life or health. The doctrine of informed consent is plainly intended to ensure the freedom of individuals to make choices concerning their medical care. For this freedom to be meaningful, people must have the right to make choices that accord with their own values regardless of how unwise or foolish those choices may appear to others: see generally, Prosser and Keeton, *op cit*, p 112 *et seq*; Harper, James and Gray, *The Law of Torts*, 2nd edn, 1986, Chapter III; Linden, *op cit*, p 64 *et seq*; and *Reibl v Hughes* 114 DLR (3d) 1; [1980] 2 SCR 880; 14 CCLT 1.

The emergency situation is an exception to the general rule requiring a patient's prior consent. When immediate medical treatment is necessary to save the life or preserve the health of a person who, by reason of unconsciousness or extreme illness, is incapable of either giving or withholding consent, the doctor may proceed without the patient's consent. The delivery of medical services is rendered lawful in such circumstances either on the rationale that the doctor has implied consent from the patient to give emergency aid or, more accurately in my view, on the rationale that the doctor is privileged by reason of necessity in giving the aid and is not to be held liable for so doing. On either basis, in an emergency the law sets aside the requirement of consent on the assumption that the patient, as a reasonable person, would want emergency aid to be rendered if she were capable of giving instructions. As Prosser and Keeton, *op cit*, pp 117–18 state:

> The touching of another that would ordinarily be a battery in the absence of the consent of either the person touched or his legal agent can sometimes be justified in an emergency. Thus, it has often been asserted that a physician or other provider of health care has implied consent to deliver medical services, including surgical procedures, to a patient in an emergency. But such lawful action is more satisfactorily explained as privilege. There are several requirements: (a) the patient must be unconscious or without capacity to make a decision, while no one legally authorised to act as agent for the patient is available; (b) time must be of the essence, in the sense that it must reasonably appear that delay until such time as an effective consent could be obtained would subject the patent to a risk of serious bodily injury or death which prompt action would avoid; and (c) under the circumstances, a reasonable person would consent, and the probabilities are that the patient would consent ...

On the facts of the present case, Dr Shulman was clearly faced with an emergency. He had an unconscious, critically ill patient on his hands who, in his opinion, needed blood transfusions to save her life or preserve her health. If there were no Jehovah's Witness card, he undoubtedly would have been entitled to administer blood transfusions as part of the emergency treatment and could not have been held liable for so doing. In those circumstances, he would have had no indication that the transfusions would have been refused had the patient then been able to make her wishes known and, accordingly, no reason to expect that, as a reasonable person, she would not consent to the transfusions.

However, to change the facts, if Mrs Malette, before passing into unconsciousness, had expressly instructed Dr Shulman, in terms comparable to those set forth on the card, that her religious convictions as a Jehovah's Witness were such that she was not to be given a blood transfusion under any circumstances and that she fully realised the implications of this position, the doctor would have been confronted with an obviously different situation. Here, the patient, anticipating an emergency in which she might be unable to make decisions about her health care contemporaneous with the emergency, has given explicit instructions that blood transfusions constitute an unacceptable medical intervention and are not to be administered to her. Once the emergency arises, is the doctor nonetheless entitled to administer transfusions on the basis of his honest belief that they are needed to save his patient's life?

The answer, in my opinion, is clearly no. A doctor is not free to disregard a patient's advance instructions any more than he would be free to disregard instructions given at the time of the emergency. The law does not prohibit a patient from withholding consent to emergency medical treatment, nor does the law prohibit a doctor from following his patient's instructions. While the law may disregard the absence of consent in limited emergency circumstances, it otherwise supports the right of competent adults to make decisions concerning their own health care by imposing civil liability on those who perform medical treatment without consent.

The patient's decision to refuse blood in the situation I have posed was made prior to and in anticipation of the emergency. While the doctor would have had the opportunity to dissuade her on the basis of his medical advice, her refusal to accept his advice or her unwillingness to discuss or consider the subject would not relieve him of his obligation to follow her instructions. The principles of self-determination and individual autonomy compel the conclusion that the patient may reject blood transfusions even if harmful consequences may result and even if the decision is generally regarded as foolhardy. Her decision in this instance would be operative after she lapsed into unconsciousness, and the doctor's conduct would be unauthorised. To transfuse a Jehovah's Witness in the face of her explicit instructions to the contrary would, in my opinion, violate her right to control her own body and show disrespect for the religious values by which she has chosen to live her life: see *In Re Estate of Brooks* (1965, III) 205 NE 2d 435; and *Randolph v City of New York*, an unreported judgment of the Supreme Court of New York released July 12, 1984, Index No 17598/75; reversed (1986) 501 NYS (2d) 837; varied (1987) 514 NYS (2d) 705.

Malette's case must now be considered in light of *Qumsieh's* case. That case suggests that, in some circumstances, a valid refusal of treatment may be overruled using a statutory procedure known as Guardianship. Whether Qumsieh's case is followed is entirely dependent upon the wording of each State's Guardianship law.

Sharin Qumsieh v The Guardianship and Administration Board and Lance Pilgrim [1998] VSCA 45

Supreme Court of Victoria

Winneke P: On 20 February 1998 the appellant was admitted to the Mercy Hospital for delivery of her first child. She is 20 years of age and is married to Nidal Qumsieh. She is a strongly committed Jehovah's Witness and thus holds firmly to the religious belief that she should abstain from blood. Her religious beliefs therefore include the belief that she should abstain from blood transfusions. To her an imposed transfusion of someone else's bodily fluid is the equivalent of rape or abortion.

Although on 20 February 1998 she was successfully delivered of a healthy baby boy, her post-delivery state rapidly declined through haemorrhaging. A radical hysterectomy was performed at the Mercy Hospital and she was later transferred to the intensive care unit of the Western General Hospital, where facilities, so it is said, were more advanced. She remained at that hospital until 24 February 1998 when it would seem she was very anaemic through blood loss and under heavy sedation.

At the Mercy Hospital the applicant had signed a form called a 'consent to operative treatment and administration of anaesthetic' in which she had consented to examination of herself under anaesthetic at the Mercy Hospital by Dr Jansen. In conjunction with such treatment she consented to the 'administration of such anaesthetics as may be considered . . . advisable with the exception of blood transfusion/blood products'. The last four words were in handwriting.

It would seem that when the applicant's post-natal condition began to decline in the Mercy Hospital the applicant's husband, Nidal, produced to the medical staff a document called an 'Advance Medical Directive' signed by the applicant on 15 January 1998 directing that 'no blood transfusions . . . be given to me under any circumstances'.

Early in the morning of 24 February 1998 the applicant's husband, Nidal, went to the offices of Messrs Slater & Gordon, solicitors, and spoke to a Mr Paul Henderson. He told Mr Henderson that he and his wife were both Jehovah's Witnesses, that his wife's condition was at a low ebb and that she had been refusing to have blood transfusions, but that he wished her to be properly treated. Henderson had then rung the Western General Hospital and, having done so, asked the husband whether the appellant had signed what was called an 'enduring power of attorney' pursuant to the provisions of the Medical Treatment Act 1988. The husband told him that the applicant's attorney was a Mr Tawfik Ibrahim. Mr Henderson then tried but was unable to contact Mr Ibrahim.

During the course of 24 February 1998 Mr Henderson told the applicant's husband that a hearing had been arranged before the Guardianship and Administration Board, which was presided over by the second respondent, Mr Lance Pilgrim. At the hearing both Henderson and the applicant's husband were present, as was a Mr John Snowden, who was the hospital's solicitor. It would seem that produced to the Board was the applicant's enduring power of attorney, which clearly was not in compliance with the provisions of the Medical Treatment Act 1988. The proceedings before the Board were conducted as a matter of urgency and, although the Board was told that the applicant had refused a blood transfusion, it is apparent from the material that it was not told 'why'. The Board did not have before it the applicant's 'Advance Medical Directive' to which I have previously referred. The Board asked the applicant's husband whether he wished the applicant to receive a transfusion. The husband replied that he did, and he signed a form which stated:

> I instruct my solicitors . . . to inform the solicitors for the hospital that I wish my wife to have blood and other treatment that is necessary.

The Board was told that the applicant was unconscious and on artificial ventilation. It was told that there was 'a window of opportunity' of only about one hour before irreparable brain damage would occur.

The Board proceeded pursuant to s 32 of the Guardianship and Administration Act which enables a person to apply for a temporary order appointing the Public Advocate as the guardian of a person in respect of whom an application could be made under s 19 of that Act. If the Board considers that the circumstances of the person 'are such that a hearing should be held without unreasonable delay' it must hold a hearing. The Board was satisfied that an urgent hearing should be held and waived notice pursuant to s 20(3) of the Act. Section 33 of the Guardianship and Administration Act stipulates, so far as relevant, that:

> (1) If the Board is satisfied that the person in respect of whom an application has been made under s 32 –
>
> (a) is a person with a disability; and
> (b) is unable to make reasonable judgments in respect of all or any of the matters relating to her person or circumstances; and
> (c) is in need of a guardian –
>
> the Board may make a temporary order appointing the Public Advocate as the limited guardian of that person.

Such a limited order will remain in existence for 21 days.

In exercising its powers the Board reminded itself of its obligations, prescribed by s 4 of the Act, to perform its functions so that, *inter alia*, the best interests of the person with the disability are protected and the wishes of that person are, wherever possible, given effect to.

The Board, on the information before it, was satisfied that Mrs Qumsieh did have a 'disability' within the meaning of s 3 of the Act, a disability which it identified as 'intellectual impairment', and also was satisfied that she was unable to make reasonable judgments with respect to her person or circumstances. The Board stated that it:

> . . . was satisfied on the evidence before it that there was an immediate need for a blood transfusion . . . but whether or not the . . . person received such treatment was a decision for the Public Advocate or a delegated guardian approved by the Board.

The Board noted that there had been put before it the enduring power of attorney dated 11 October 1997 but further noted that the purported agent who was appointed could not act on its authority because it had been executed otherwise than in compliance with s 5A(2) of the Medical Treatment Act. The Board also remarked that:

> . . . it had no evidence before it that the proposed represented person did not want a guardian appointed to make health care decisions, outside her wishes expressed in the . . . informed consent form . . . which was limited to an examination under anaesthetic.

The Board explained the effect of its order to the husband and, although he was in an emotional state, he said he wished to be appointed as the delegated guardian of the Public Advocate. The Board accordingly made its order.

The order having been made, the instructions of the temporary guardian were transmitted to the Western General Hospital. Transfusions were given and Mrs Qumsieh responded to treatment. She was discharged from that hospital about one week later.

She then applied for orders to review the Board's temporary guardianship order, and it was that application which was refused by Beach J in May of this year. The reasons of his Honour were not transcribed but it would seem from the material before this Court that they were brief. By the time the matter came before his Honour, the Board's temporary guardianship order had expired and/or had been revoked.

His Honour, according to the material before us, had said:

> . . . the order was made to save her life and no court would contemplate exercising its discretion to grant a remedy.

The Board was asked to act, as a matter of urgency, upon material which indicated that the appellant was gravely ill, and without any clear indication that the orders sought from it were against the appellant's wishes on religious grounds. Rather they had an application by her husband indicating that he wished to be appointed as his wife's delegated limited medical guardian. The affidavit of the appellant concedes that the Board was not given her Advance Medical Directive 'nor any other evidence which . . . showed that my decision to refuse . . . blood transfusion . . . was made competently and repeatedly . . .'.

Mr Cathcart contends that . . . the evidence of the appellant's competent refusal, shows that the jurisdiction of the Board under s 33 was not attracted. Thus it is said that the Board's expressed satisfaction under s 33 can be challenged notwithstanding the limited evidence before it. I cannot accept that. It would render, in my view, the Board's function almost untenable. Section 33 defines the Board's jurisdiction. It is to act on material which suggests, at the time the application is made to it, that the protected person is under a disability, is unable to make reasonable judgments and is in need of a guardian. The existence of that jurisdiction is not to be denied, in my opinion, because the protected person has previously made a decision that he or she did not want a blood transfusion in different circumstances.

Mr Cathcart puts it that the Board had sufficient before it to make 'alarm bells ring' and that it should have been put on enquiry about the conflict between the husband and the wife. This, I think, puts far too much upon a Board which has embarked, and is empowered to embark, upon an enquiry of urgency. There would be very few enquiries, I think, of this nature in respect of which such potential conflicts would or might not be found. In my view this Act is investing the Board with powers to make urgent decisions in relation to health care matters of persons without having to 'look over its shoulder' to ensure that the material before it is complete and is capable of being acted upon. Such past facts would not, in this case, in my view, have helped to establish the jurisdictional facts which caused the Board to act. Mr Cathcart submits that the 'consent form' was in any event unequivocal evidence of the appellant's informed refusal to accept blood transfusions. However, it seems to me that the Board was entitled to take the view which it did that this was a qualified refusal to have treatment in certain circumstances at the Mercy Hospital some four days before. In any event it must be remembered that the purpose of the Board's order was only to appoint the appellant's husband as the approved delegate of the Public Advocate who could then make whatever decisions were required to be made in respect of the health care of the appellant. The Board was not itself directing those decisions. Mr Cathcart further submitted that the interim order signed by the second respondent manifested the invalidity of the Board's decision because it stated that the husband was himself the appointed person and that this was done contrary to the provisions of s 33. But it is, I think, reasonable in the light of the Board's formal and sealed order to regard the expression in the interim certificate as simply a 'shorthand form' of expressing the order which the Board had in fact made, namely that the husband was the approved delegate of the Public Advocate . . .

All states of Australia have guardianship procedures, which may be accessed through a statutory tribunal, or in some states, by application to the Supreme Court. It is less clear whether the view which commended itself to the Court of Appeal in Victoria in Qumsieh's case about the use which could be made of such procedures, would necessarily hold sway elsewhere.

Statute

Various different statutes prescribe that treatment may be performed on an individual, irrespective of whether that individual consents to the procedure or not. Many of these Acts relate to those suffering from infectious diseases.

All jurisdictions in Australia make provision for the administration of blood transfusions to children in emergency situations in which parents object to such procedures. The details of these provisions are to be found in Queensland, South Australia and the ACT in those jurisdictions' Transplantation and Anatomy Acts; in all other jurisdictions in the Human Tissue (or in NT and WA in the Human Tissue and Transplant) Act.

In the Northern Territory (under the Emergency Operations Act 1973), 'any emergency operation' may be performed without parental consent. In New South Wales, pursuant to the Children (Care and Protection) Act 1987, medical treatment may be performed on a child without parental consent if the treatment is needed to save the child's life or to prevent serious damage.

For a general discussion of the use of battery in medical law, see Seabourne, G, 'The role of the tort of battery in medical law' (1995) Anglo-American Law Review 265.

3

CONSENT TO TREATMENT II – NEGLIGENCE

In Chapter 2, we explored the elements of a battery action as one of the causes of actions which an aggrieved patient might seek to commence against a health care practitioner. The limitation of that action was seen to be the low threshold of information that needs to be provided by the health care practitioner, before he or she can be said to have satisfied his obligations to the patient.

What, though, of the patient who wishes to complain that the health care practitioner did not tell him or her of the risks or side effects of particular treatment? Or, more drastically, the case of a patient who wishes to complain that the health care practitioner has done a 'shoddy' job' in trying to treat the patient?

The cause of action most often invoked, in the above two situations, is the action in negligence. This chapter will explore the elements of such an action, and will examine the actions' limitations in a health care setting.

In *Rogers v Whitaker* (see Chapter 2), the High Court of Australia stated that there were three aspects of a doctor's duty towards his patient: diagnosis, advice and treatment. The law of negligence is relevant to all three aspects. The test for negligence is a court established test.

The law of negligence is not a species of law peculiar to doctor-patient interactions. The law of negligence regulates the interactions of all people. The law requires that a person 'must take reasonable care to avoid acts or omissions which [a person] could reasonably foresee would be likely to injure [his or her] neighbour' (*Donoghue v Stevenson* [1932] AC 562 *per* Lord Atkin). Establishing the exact scope of such acts and omissions has been a painstaking process of judicial decision-making.

Elements of the modern 'duty of care' (as the action in negligence is often called) applying to a health care practitioner may be summarised as:

1 the existence of a duty to take care towards the patient reposing in the health care practitioner;
2 a breach of that duty by the health care practitioner which causes damage to the patient;
3 the type of damage caused was reasonably foreseeable.

I – DIAGNOSIS AND TREATMENT

The High Court has demonstrated a willingness to move away from proximity as one of the limiting factors in determining the existence of a duty of care.

Jones, A. *Personal Injuries Queensland* (looseleaf service, Butterworths) notes 'prior to the decision of the High Court in *Hill v Van Erp* (1997) 188 CLR 159, "the relationship of proximity between plaintiff and defendant was generally regarded as determinative of the existence of a duty of care".' Proximity operated to limit liability to some cases where damage was reasonably foreseeable – where there was some sort of proximate relationship between the parties. Jones comments that the concept of proximity was 'potentially ambiguous'.

Proximity has now been abandoned as 'the conceptual determinant and the unifying theme of the categories of case in which the common law of negligence recognizes the existence of a duty of care to take reasonable care to avoid a reasonably foreseeable risk of injury to another'. *Woolcock Street Investments Pty Ltd v CGD Pty Ltd* (2004) 205 ALR 522. (Jones.)

The abandonment of proximity as a general limiting factor, while important from the point of view of defining the elements of negligence, does not affect the scope of a doctor's liability to his/her patient. The scope of liability remains the same.

Existence and scope of a duty of care

The health care practitioner's duty to take reasonable care has its origins in ancient times in the liability imposed upon members exercising 'a common calling' (a category which included innkeepers and common carriers!) and is independent of any contractual obligation. It is important to note, as Jones, M in his book entitled *Medical Negligence*, 1991, London: Sweet & Maxwell, points out '. . . [the duty] does not depend upon the doctor's status, qualifications or expertise'. The key factor is the undertaking of advice, diagnosis or treatment.

The changing nature of liability in negligence

The law in this field is best understood in its historical perspective.

The law up to 1992

Until **1992**, the law which governed negligence in respect of diagnosis, advice and treatment was that stated in *Bolam's* case. The standard used to assess whether a doctor had been negligent was a practitioner-centred standard. That is, did this doctor act in accordance with a practice accepted as acceptable by a reasonably competent body of medical practice? This test applied to all aspects of a doctor's practice.

The law from 1992–2004

In 1992, the High Court decided the case of *Rogers v Whitaker*. That case distinguished the test which would apply in assessing a breach of duty of care, where what was alleged was a failure to advise of material risks, from other aspects of a doctor's duty of care. In assessing whether a doctor had breached his duty to advise of the material risks of treatment, reference was no longer to be made to what a reasonably competent practitioner would have done. Rather the reference was to whether the doctor had advised of a material risk. That term is explained in the extract from *Rogers v Whitaker* (below).

In *Naxakis*, the High Court determined that, even in those areas of a doctor's professional practice extending beyond advising of risks (i.e diagnosis and treatment); the Court was not necessarily bound by what a reasonably competent body of practitioners would have done. The Court would often be guided by such evidence, but was not bound to follow it.

The Law from 2004–present

The advent of the Civil Liability Acts has, in most jurisdictions of Australia, restored the *Bolam* standard in all areas of medical practice EXCEPT in respect of the duty to advise of risks. The Civil Liability Acts also make important changes to other aspects of medical negligence. These changes are discussed at the end of this chapter.

The classic statement of the medical practitioner's duty of care is that of McNair J in *Bolam v Friern Hospital Management Committee.*

***Bolam v Friern Hospital Management Committee* [1957] 1 WLR 582, pp 586–88**

The plaintiff underwent electro-convulsive therapy at the defendant's hospital. (ECT is commonly known as electric shock therapy and involves the passing of electric current through the brain of a patient). The staff applying the therapy failed to administer a muscle relaxant or to apply manual restraints to the body of the patient. The patient suffered fractured bones. Competing evidence was given as to the normal practice of administering doctors.

> . . . I must tell you what in law we mean by negligence. In the ordinary case which does not involve any special skill, negligence in law means a failure to do some act which a reasonable man in the circumstances would do, or the doing of some act which a reasonable man in the circumstances would not do; and if that failure or the doing of that act results in injury, then there is a cause of action. How do you test whether this act or failure is negligent? In an ordinary case it is generally said you judge it by the conduct of the man on top of a Clapham omnibus. He is the ordinary man. But where you get a situation which involves the use of some special skill or competence, then the test as to whether there has been negligence or not is not the test of the man on the top of a Clapham omnibus, because he has not got this special skill. The test is the standard of the ordinary skilled man exercising or professing to

> have that special skill. A man need not possess the highest expert skill; it is well established law that it is sufficient if he exercises the ordinary skill of an ordinary competent man exercising that particular art . . . in the case of a medical man, negligence means failure to act in accordance with the standards of reasonably competent medical men at the time. That is a perfectly accurate statement, as long as it is remembered that there may be one or more perfectly proper standards; and if he conforms with one of those proper standards, then he is not negligent . . . A man is not negligent if he is acting in accordance with such a practice, merely because there is a body of opinion who would take a contrary view. At the same time, that does not mean that a medical man can obstinately and pigheadedly carry on with some old technique if it has been proved to be contrary to what is really substantially the whole of informed medical opinion. Otherwise you might get men today saying: 'I do not believe in anaesthetics. I do not believe in antiseptics. I am going to continue to do my surgery in the way it was done in the 18th century.' That clearly would be wrong . . .
>
> It is not essential for you to decide which of the two practices is the better practice, as long as you accept that what the defendants did was in accordance with a practice adopted by responsible persons . . . finally, bear this in mind, that you are now considering whether it was negligent for certain action to be taken in August 1954, not in February 1957; and in one of the well-known cases on this topic it has been said that you must not look with 1957 spectacles at what happened in 1954 . . .

Note McNair J's limitation of the scope of the duty, contained in the last sentence of the extract above. This limitation was first explained by Lord Denning in *Roe v Minister of Health*. In that case, Lord Denning also makes some useful comments about risk taking in medical science and its acceptability within a duty of care setting.

Roe v Minister of Health [1954] 2 QB 66

> Two men had undergone operations involving the use of spinal anaesthetic and had subsequently become paralysed. The spinal anaesthetic was stored in glass ampoules, which themselves were stored in carbolic acid. At first instance, evidence was led which suggested that the ampoules must have developed tiny cracks, invisible to the eye, and that this had allowed contamination of the anaesthetic by the carbolic acid.
>
> Leading counsel for the plaintiffs said that staff were negligent in two respects: (i) in not colouring the phenol with a deep dye; (ii) in cracking the ampoules. I will take them in order: (i) The deep tinting. If the anaesthetists had foreseen that the ampoules might get cracked with cracks that could not be detected on inspection they would, no doubt,

have dyed the phenol a deep blue; and this would have exposed the contamination. But I do not think their failure to foresee this was negligence. It is so easy to be wise after the event and to condemn as negligence that which was only a misadventure. We ought always to be on our guard against it, especially in cases against hospitals and doctors. Medical science has conferred great benefits on mankind, but these benefits are attended by considerable risks. Every surgical operation is attended by risks. We cannot take the benefits without taking the risks. Every advance in technique is also attended by risks. Doctors, like the rest of us, have to learn by experience, and experience often teaches in a hard way. Something goes wrong and shows up a weakness, and then it is put right. That is just what happened here. Dr Graham sought to escape the danger of infection by disinfecting the ampoule. In escaping that known danger he, unfortunately, ran into another danger. He did not know that there could be undetectable cracks, but it was not negligent for him not to know it at that time. We must not look at the 1947 accident with 1954 spectacles. The judge acquitted Dr Graham of negligence and we should uphold his decision. (ii) The cracks. In cracking the ampoules, there must, I fear, have been some carelessness by someone in the hospital. The ampoules were quite strong and the sisters said that they should not get cracked if proper care was used in handling them. They must have been jolted in some way by someone. This raises an interesting point of law. This carelessness was, in a sense, one of the causes of the disaster; but the person who jolted the ampoule cannot possibly have foreseen what dire consequences would follow. There were so many intervening opportunities of inspection that she might reasonably think that, if the jolting caused a crack, it would be discovered long before any harm came of it . . . The anaesthetist himself did, in fact, examine it for cracks, and finding none, used it. The trouble was that nobody realised that there might be a crack which you could not detect on ordinary examination. What, then, is the legal position? . . .

In all these cases you will find that the three questions, duty, causation, and remoteness, run continually into one another. It seems to me that they are simply three different ways of looking at one and the same question which is this: is the consequence fairly to be regarded as within the risk created by the negligence? If so, the negligent person is liable for it: but otherwise not . . . Instead of asking three questions, I should have thought in many cases it would be simpler and better to ask the one question: is the consequence within the risk? and to answer it by applying ordinary plain commonsense . . .

Asking myself, therefore, what was the risk involved in careless handling of the ampoules, I answer by saying that there was such a probability of intervening examination as to limit the risk. The only consequence which could reasonably be anticipated was the loss of a quantity of nupercaine, but not the paralysis of a patient. The hospital authorities are, therefore, not liable for it. When you stop to think of what happened in this case, you will realise that it was a most extraordinary chapter of

> accidents ... This has taught the doctors to be on their guard against invisible cracks. Never again, it is to be hoped, will such a thing happen. After this accident a leading textbook, *Professor Macintosh on Lumbar Puncture and Spinal Anaesthesia*, was published in 1951 which contains the significant warning: 'Never place ampoules of local anaesthetic solution in alcohol or spirit. This common practice is probably responsible for some of the cases of permanent paralysis reported after spinal analgesia'.
>
> If the hospitals were to continue the practice after this warning, they could not complain if they were found guilty of negligence. But the warning had not been given at the time of this accident. Indeed, it was the extraordinary accident to these two men which first disclosed the danger. Nowadays it would be negligence not to realise the danger, but it was not then.
>
> One final word. These two men have suffered such terrible consequences that there is a natural feeling that they should be compensated. But we should be doing a disservice to the community at large if we were to impose liability on hospitals and doctors for everything that happens to go wrong. Doctors would be led to think more of their own safety than of the good of their patients. Initiative would be stifled and confidence shaken. A proper sense of proportion requires us to have regard to the conditions in which hospitals and doctors have to work. We must insist on due care for the patient at every point, but we must not condemn as negligence that which is only a misadventure ...

Roe v Minister of Health was applied in the Queensland case of *Dwan v Farquhar* [1988] 1 Qd R 234. In the latter case, it was held that there was no expert opinion, in 1983, that a competent medical practitioner ought to have been aware of the danger of a patient contracting AIDS from a blood transfusion during minor surgery. The existence of that opinion was, however, known at the time the plaintiff commenced his action. The court noted that the relevant time period was when the damage was alleged to have occurred.

(a) When does the duty commence?

Jones, M, *Medical Negligence*, 1991, London: Sweet & Maxwell, p 24

> Although it might be trite to say that a doctor owes a duty of care to his patient, it is not so simple to state precisely when the relationship of doctor and patient begins. This is important because it is equally true to say that a doctor is under no legal obligation (whatever the moral or ethical position) to render assistance by way of examination or treatment to a stranger. This stems from the 'mere omissions' rule: one who chooses to act must do so carefully so as to avoid inflicting harm on others; but, as a general rule, the tort of negligence does not compel a person to take positive steps to confer a benefit on others. There is no legal obligation to rescue someone in danger, even if rescue would

involve little or no effort and no danger to the rescuer. A 'stranger' for these purposes is a person with whom the doctor is not and has never been in a professional doctor-patient relationship. Clearly, if such a relationship does exist a doctor may be liable for failure to attend or treat the patient, just as much as for careless treatment.

The question of whether a doctor who is asked to attend an urgent situation owes a duty of care to anyone who suffers injury as a result of a failure to attend, was considered by the New South Wales Court of Appeal.

***Lowns v Woods, by His Next Friend The Protective Commissioner and Others*, unreported, NSW CA, 5 February 1996**

Cole JA:

The events of 20 January 1987

Mrs Light, as was her custom, rose and went for a walk on the morning of 20 January 1987. She said she left at 8 am, insisting that she had looked at her watch and thus was clear on the time of leaving. Her walk took her 20–25 minutes. She was confident of this and, post incident, had checked that time by repeating her walk in approximately 20 minutes. Thus, she said, she returned at about 8.25 am to find Patrick fitting. She immediately called out to her other children and on their attendance first dispatched her 18-year-old son Harry to get an ambulance, and a few minutes later dispatched her 14-year-old daughter, Joanna, to get a doctor. Mrs Light told her daughter, Joanna, to 'go and get a doctor'. Her daughter immediately changed, took the lift to the ground floor and ran to the doctor's surgery, approximately 300 metres away. Joanna estimated she reached the surgery about five minutes after her mother's initial request.

The account accepted by the trial judge of what then occurred is as follows: 'I knocked on the door, a man came to the door. I told him 'my mother sent me down here, my brother was having a bad fit, and that we needed a doctor, and could he come up?' Q. 'What did he say?' A. 'He asked me to bring my fitting brother down there. He asked me to bring him down.' Q. 'What did you say?' A. 'I said, "He's having a bad fit, we can't bring him down." Q. 'What did he say to that?' A. 'To get an ambulance.' Q. 'What did you say?' A. 'I said, "We need a doctor. We have already got an ambulance." Q. 'What did he say to that?' A. 'He said, 'No, I won't come.'

There was debate regarding whether the conversation set forth occurred at all, and if did, whether it occurred with Dr Lowns. It is important to recognise that, at trial, the issue was not whether Dr Lowns should have gone to Patrick Woods; Dr Lowns accepted that, had the request set out in the conversation quoted been made to him, he would, and should, have gone to the child. His case was that the conversation never occurred. The trial judge found that the conversation had occurred with

Dr Lowns. That is not challenged on appeal. Difficulties were experienced getting the stretcher into the lift from the unit on the sixth floor which delayed the ambulance's departure from outside the unit until approximately 9.20 am; the ambulance arrived at Dr Smeeth's surgery between 9.23 am and 9.26 am; Dr Smeeth gave an injection of Valium 'probably about 9.27 am or 9.28 am'.

The knowledge of Dr Lowns

Dr Lowns denied any knowledge at all of the events because he said there was no conversation between himself and Joanna Woods. However, the appeal has been conducted upon an acceptance of the trial judge's findings that it did occur. On that basis the following was the state of his knowledge.

Patrick Woods was not a patient of Dr Lowns. Dr Lowns did not know Patrick Woods' age or anything about him other than that he was the brother of Joanna Woods who would obviously have been about 14 or 15 years of age. He did not know where Patrick Woods was. He knew nothing of his condition apart from being told he was 'having a bad fit'. He was also told that 'we', presumably meaning Patrick Woods' family, could not 'bring him down' but was informed that 'we have already got an ambulance'. He did not know that Patrick Woods was in a unit on the sixth floor of a building, or that there was any difficulty in the ambulance removing him from the unit. Although he did not know where Patrick Woods was situated, he must have assumed that he was in close proximity because his sister had come on foot to the surgery. He had no reason to believe that the ambulance could not bring Patrick Woods to his surgery immediately on the return of Joanna Woods to the place where Patrick Woods was. The trial judge found it would have taken Dr Lowns 'a minute or so to collect his bag and perhaps leave a message for the receptionist'. Dr Lowns had no reason to think other than that the ambulance could within a time approximate to the time it would take him to go to Patrick Woods, bring Patrick Woods to him.

In those circumstances, whilst denying the conversation occurred, he gave the evidence I have quoted that he would, and should, have gone to Patrick Woods to give him treatment.

Legal principles

The learned trial judge was correct in his holding: 'In general, the common law does not impose a duty to assist a person in peril even where it is foreseeable that the consequence of a failure to assist will be the injury or death of the person imperilled. Something other than the foreseeability of harm is required before the law imposes a duty to intervene. It has been held in other common law jurisdictions that a doctor is under no duty to attend upon a person who is sick, even in an emergency, if that person is one with whom the doctor is not and has never been in a professional relationship of doctor and patient: see Jones, *Medical Negligence*, 1991, at 24, para 2.21, Sweet & Maxwell; Kennedy and Grubb, *Medical Law* (2nd edn), 1994, at 79, Butterworths; *Hurtley v Eddingfield* (1901) 59 NE 1058; *Children v Frye* (1931) 158 SE 744; *Butterworths v Swint* (1938) 188 SE 770; *Findlay v Board of Supervisions of the County of Mohave* (1951) 230 P (2d) 526; *Agnew v Parkes* (1959) 343 P (2d) 118, at 123; *Hister v Randolf* (1986) 17 P (2d) 774. Although there is no Australian authority in which the general proposition has been specifically applied in respect of a medical practitioner, the general principle is clear, and there is certainly no Australian case in which a doctor has been held liable for damages because of a failure to attend upon and treat someone who was not already his patient.'

However, a question arises regarding whether the implicit request to Dr Lowns made by Joanna Woods for him to go with her to treat her brother gives rise to such a relationship of proximity as to give rise to a duty of care, and if so what was the content of that duty. Section 27(2) Medical Practitioners Act 1938, applicable at the time, provided that it was 'misconduct in a professional respect' for a medical practitioner to: '(c) refuse or fail without reasonable cause, to attend, within a reasonable time after being requested to do so, upon a person for the purpose of rendering professional services in his capacity as a registered medical practitioner in any case where he has reasonable cause to believe that such person is in need of urgent attention by a registered medical practitioner but shall not be guilty under this paragraph of such conduct if he causes another registered medical practitioner to attend as aforesaid.'

Dr Lowns, whilst denying the conversation with Joanna, accepted that if it had occurred, as it did, he would have and should have attended upon Patrick at his residence. He did not seek to justify his non-attendance either upon the basis that he had reasonable cause not so to attend because the child was in care of ambulance officers, or upon the basis that the ambulance officers should have brought the child to his surgery. He simply said he was not involved at all.

It was argued that there was no sufficient proximity between Dr Lowns and Patrick Woods to give rise to a duty of care. It was contended there was absent any relevant physical proximity, any circumstantial proximity or any relevant causal proximity in the manner in which those expressions were explained by Deane J in *The Council of the Shire of Sutherland v Hayman* and risk of injury in consequence of the omission to attend not being reasonably foreseeable, no duty of care arose.

In my opinion, this submission fails. Dr Lowns accepted that injury ('damage') to a fitting child was foreseeable if he, once requested, did not attend to treat the child. There was an obvious physical proximity, for Joanna had come on foot. There was also proximity in the sense that Dr Lowns was an adequate medical practitioner to whom a direct request for assistance was made where, on the evidence presented, there was no reasonable impediment or circumstance diminishing his capacity or indicating significant or material inconvenience or difficulty in him responding to the request, in circumstances where he knew, as he must be deemed to have admitted once it is found the conversation occurred, that serious harm could occur to Patrick Woods if he did not respond to the request and provide treatment. Once it is found, as here, that administering Valium at the time determined by the trial judge would have brought an end to the *status epilepticus* before the onset of brain damage causing quadriplegia, causal proximity is also established.

In my opinion, the trial judge was correct to find negligence, in this instance against Dr Lowns.

Kirby P:

Claim for negligent refusal to attend patient

Different considerations arise in respect of negligent omission or failure to act than in the case of positive and careless action. The common law has generally been reluctant to impose upon persons, except in defined circumstances, duties of positive action to prevent injury or damage to others. The reasons for this are explained by Deane J in *Hayman*.

However, in the present case, that problem melts away because Dr Lowns himself acknowledged that within the ordinary standards of a local medical practitioner in his position, had he received the emergency call deposed to by Patrick Woods' sister, he would have been obliged to, and would in fact, have responded. This acknowledgment does not foreclose contrary evidence or prevent a contrary conclusion. But it is powerful testimony (confirming impressionistic understanding of ordinary medical practice in this State) as to what that practice requires.

Section 27(2) of the Medical Practitioners Act 1938, applicable at the time, did not impose a duty for the breach of which, as such, Patrick Woods and his father could sue for civil damages. Yet the subsection reflects the expectations which were accepted as appropriate and proper amongst medical practitioners in responding to a call to the aid of a 'person . . . in need of urgent attention'. This is a high standard. It goes beyond what is expected, and imposed by the law, in the case of other professions. It goes far beyond what may be expected and demanded of an ordinary citizen. But in the noble profession of medicine, it is the rule which Parliament has expressed; which the organised medical profession has accepted; and which Dr Lowns himself acknowledged and did not contest.

I therefore agree with the analysis of the primary judge, and with the reasons of Cole JA for holding that, in the special circumstances, the relationship of proximity between Patrick Woods and Dr Lowns was established, notwithstanding their lack of previous professional association. Having regard to s 27(2) of the Medical Practitioners Act 1938 (then in force) and, indeed, to Dr Lowns' own acknowledgment of his duty in such circumstances, I have no hesitation in concurring in the

> conclusion which Cole JA has reached. Duty and breach are clearly established. The only question upon which I entertain doubt is that of causation.
>
> However, if Dr Lowns had responded to the request for urgent attention to a young boy described as 'having a bad fit', who could not be brought down to him, on the primary judge's conclusions of fact which I would not disturb, Dr Lowns would have administered intravenous diazepam (Valium) once (or possibly twice) to Patrick. This would have been done at 9.15 am or, if two injections were required, by 9.30 am. Had this been done, it was open to the primary judge, in the evidence, to conclude that the risks of brain damage to Patrick would have been 'very low indeed'. The supplementation of the care provided by the ambulance officers would have been critical. The prolonged fitting probably would have been controlled. Profound brain damage would probably have been avoided.
>
> None of these are certain conclusions. This court (like Badgery-Parker J at trial) is being asked to consider what might have been. Obviously the variables include the starting time of Patrick's seizure (not exactly known as his mother was then walking); the probable arrival time of Dr Lowns had he responded to the urgent request; the skill and knowledge of Dr Lowns in appreciating that the correct response to the situation was the administration of Valium; the risk, albeit very small, of an adverse reaction to an injection; the possibility (which Dr Lowns himself rejected) that he might have failed to achieve injection; the risk that he might have been unaware of (or had unavailable to him) intravenous Valium; the possibility that he might have reasonably concluded, that the best course, the ambulance being available, was simply to expedite Patrick's transfer to a hospital, avoiding the delay of any attempted treatment on his own part.
>
> These considerations were carefully weighed by Badgery-Parker J. I see no error of fact-finding or of approach in his Honour's reasons. I therefore agree with his conclusion: 'Duty, breach and causation [are established] and he is entitled to a verdict'.
>
> The consequence is that Patrick Woods is entitled to recover the judgment entered against Dr Lowns. Accordingly, so is his father in the claim for nervous shock. In coming to this conclusion, I agree with the reasons of Cole JA, who dismissed Dr Lowns' appeal.

It remains to be seen whether other Australian jurisdictions follow New South Wales' lead in this regard.

Note that the situation is clearer when a patient attends for treatment at the casualty department of a hospital. Once the patient is 'seen' as a patient by attending staff, a duty of care clearly arises: *Barnett v Chelsea and Kensington Hospital Management Committee* (extracted subsequently).

A related issue is the liabaility of a person who voluntarily comes to the aid of another. Does such a person expose him or herself to liability if he or she acts negligently?

The issue was considered by the Ipp Review (Panel of Eminent Persons to Review the Law of Negligence *Review of the Law of Negligence*, AGPS, Canberra, October 2002). Although the Ipp Report did not recommend legislative protection for those who came to the aid of another (see paras 7.21 and 7.24 of the Ipp Report), legislation has been introduced in NSW, Vic, NT and SA to provide such protection.

Queensland has long had such protection in the Law Reform (Miscellaneous Provisions) Act. Section 26 of the Civil Liability Act 2003 (Qld) supplements these provisions by providing that civil liability will not attach to the provision of first aid to a person in distress if three conditions are met.

Firstly, that the first aid or other assistance is given by the person while performing duties to enhance public safety for an entity prescribed under a regulation that provides services to enhance public safety and secondly, the first aid or other assistance is given in circumstances of emergency and the act is done or omitted in good faith and without reckless disregard for the safety of the person in distress or someone else.

A person in distress is defined in section 25 as including a person who is injured, apparently injured or at risk of injury, and a person who is suffering or apparently suffering an illness.

(b) To whom is the duty owed?

Normally, a duty of care is owed by the health care practitioner only to the patient him or herself. In some circumstances, however, a duty of care will be owed to a third party.

Jones, M, *Medical Negligence*, 1991, London: Sweet & Maxwell, p 27

> There are a number of circumstances in which the medical practitioner may owe duties to persons other than his patient. In some instances, it may be unclear whether a doctor-patient relationship has been created, but nonetheless it is possible to say that the doctor owes a duty of care to the person whom he is examining or advising or reporting upon. For example, when a doctor conducts a medical examination at the request of an employer, prospective employer, or insurance company there can be no doubt that, in addition to the duty owed to the person making the request, the doctor owes a duty of care to the subject of the examination. In *Thomsen v Davison* (1975) Qd R 93, for example, it was held that a doctor who, in a situation in which the relationship of doctor and patient does not exist, undertakes the examination of a person in order to assess his state of health, has a duty of care not merely to his employer but also to that person to conduct the examination competently, and not do or omit anything in the course of performing the examination which is likely to cause the latter damage. This includes a duty to inform himself of the results of pathological tests and advise the person to undergo investigation and treatment if they are adverse. Similarly, in *Stokes v Guest, Keen and Nettlefold (Bolts and Nuts) Ltd* [1968] 1 WLR 1776 Swanwick J held that a factory medical officer was under a

duty to institute six-monthly medical examination of certain employees, given his knowledge of the risk to those employees of contracting cancer from the work in which they were engaged . . .

Where a doctor has negligently permitted a person to come into contact with a contagious disease there would be no difficulty in establishing a duty of care, whether that person was the doctor's patient or not. In *Lindsey County Council v Marshall* [1937] AC 97, the House of Lords held the defendants liable for negligently failing to warn the plaintiff of the risk of infection by puerperal fever when she was admitted to their maternity home, following a recent outbreak of the disease. Similarly, if a doctor negligently discharged an infectious patient from a hospital and, as a result, a third party contracted the disease, the doctor would undoubtedly owe a duty of care to the third party. [*Evans v Liverpool Corporation* [1906] 1 KB 160.]

BT v Oei [1999] NSWSC 1082

Bell J:
The defendant is a medical practitioner in general practice in the inner city of Sydney. AT was his patient. The two claims seek damages for personal injuries arising out of the defendant's alleged negligent failure to diagnose AT's HIV illness and to counsel him (adequately or at all) to undergo an HIV antibody test. It is contended that a general practitioner, in practice in Sydney in 1992, exercising ordinary care and skill would have identified that AT was at risk of having contracted HIV in the light of his history and symptoms. In the event, AT did prove to be HIV positive. BT, who was living with AT as his *de facto* wife (they subsequently married), also contracted HIV.

The plaintiff's personal claim requires consideration of whether the defendant, in addition to the duty to his patient, also owed a duty of care to her as his patient's sexual partner.

The consultations

AT consulted the defendant for the first time on 26 November 1991. He was complaining of a sore throat, fever and a cough. The defendant obtained a history that AT did not suffer from allergies. He was a separated man working as a building contractor who described himself as a non-smoker and social drinker. On examination, the defendant observed lymphadenopathy (swollen glands). He made a provisional diagnosis of viral laryngotrachitis and pharyngitis.

AT next saw the defendant on 28 January 1992. He complained of fever, urinary symptoms, bilateral abdominal pain and lethargy. The defendant observed that AT had a coated tongue, lymphadenopathy, generalised tenderness of the abdomen with a palpable hepatomegaly. He made a provisional diagnosis of appendicitis or hepatitis and arranged for AT to undergo a range of tests including a full blood count, liver function test and hepatitis screen. AT was advised to return the following day.

On 29 January 1992, AT returned for a further consultation as directed. He was still unwell and feverish. By that time the defendant had the results of a test which confirmed a provisional diagnosis of urinary tract infection. The defendant prescribed Augmentin Forte and instructed AT to return when the results of the other tests were available.

AT next saw the defendant on 1 February 1992. He complained of feeling very tired and depressed. The liver function test was suggestive of Hepatitis B. The defendant considered that the combination of Hepatitis B and a urinary tract infection was unusual. It was unusual for a male to develop a urinary tract infection. In evidence the defendant said that urinary tract infections in males may be associated with anal intercourse. During this consultation the defendant questioned AT about his sexual activities; whether he was homosexual or bisexual or had numerous sexual partners. He also asked if AT was an intravenous drug user. AT denied any history in this regard but he referred to 'casual exploits' as a possible source of the Hepatitis B infection.

The defendant says that at the consultation of 1 February he told AT that the Hepatitis B infection could have been acquired as the result of an unprotected sexual encounter and he gave AT three pamphlets, two concerning Hepatitis B and a third relating to safe sex practices, and counselled him in relation to safe sex practices. He recalled AT brushing this off with the comment that he would have 'no energy for it'.

The consultation on 1 February 1992 concluded with the defendant advising AT to rest. He gave him a medical certificate for one week. He ordered further tests and advised AT to return in due course to obtain the result of them.

The defendant next saw AT on 10 February 1992 when AT said that he was feeling a little better. A test result suggested the presence of a phlebolith (kidney stone). AT was concerned about the phlebolith and requested referral for its removal. The defendant was of the view that it was not a matter for concern and so advised AT. He recommended further rest and instructed AT to return for review in two weeks time.

AT returned on 4 March 1992. On this occasion AT reported that he had been feverish and suffering chills, aches and pains. He was given a medical certificate for two weeks and asked to return for further review. He did so on 19 March 1992. On that occasion he indicated that he was feeling much better. The defendant ordered a repeat full blood count, liver function test and other tests.

AT next saw the defendant on 1 December 1992. On this occasion he again presented complaining of fever and aches and pains. He described himself as being very irritable and suffering from a mild headache. The defendant made a provisional diagnosis of viral illness. He ordered a full blood count and further tests.

The defendant next saw AT on 15 January 1993 when he was complaining of bilateral ringing of the ears, feeling unwell with left-sided abdominal pain and constipation. The defendant carried out a physical examination which revealed abdominal tenderness and bilateral ear wax.

On this occasion he arranged for AT to undergo a barium enema.

AT returned to see the defendant on 22 January 1993 and reported that he was feeling a little better. He had undergone a barium enema in the meantime and the results of that procedure revealed spleenomegaly. He was referred for a CAT scan to investigate this more fully.

On 30 January 1993 he again saw the defendant. The CAT scan result revealed heptospleenomegaly suggestive of cirrhosis of the liver. The defendant considered that AT required further investigation and referred him to Dr Bill Bye, Gastroenterologist, for further management. This was the last occasion on which the defendant saw AT.

The relationship between AT and BT

BT met AT around March 1992. It appears that their introduction arose in consequence of one or other of them placing an advertisement in a newspaper. AT collected BT from her home and they went to a nearby coffee shop. They chatted for more than an hour. In the course of this initial discussion AT disclosed that he had contracted Hepatitis B. He told BT that he was better now and that he did not require medication. It was necessary for him to drink a lot of fluid and rest. He also disclosed that, following his separation from his first wife, he had visited a brothel in company with a friend. He said he had had sexual relations with a young Thai girl who was an illegal immigrant.

Following the discussion in the coffee shop the two went to a park and talked further. They spoke about the reasons for the breakdown of AT's marriage.

At the initial meeting AT and BT arranged to meet again. Thereafter there were a number of outings. AT would call to BT's home and escort her out to dinner or a club. He took her home on each occasion. There were no sexual relations between the two. On one occasion AT attended a barbecue at BT's home.

Following the barbecue AT called on BT and told her that he had decided he did not wish to continue seeing her. He explained that he did not believe he could manage a relationship with a woman who had a young child. BT was the mother of a son then aged about six or seven years. However, despite this hesitation, AT subsequently arranged to take BT out again.

At Easter 1992, AT and BT went on a holiday to Young. On the first day of that trip BT asked AT how he was feeling. He told her that he was tired and that he had had a slight fever that day. The following day for the first time the two had sexual intercourse. BT said that they had used a condom on this occasion because AT expressed concerns about her becoming pregnant.

In June 1992, BT started working in the food services department of a hospital. Between Easter and June of 1992, when she commenced employment with the hospital, the two had sexual intercourse on about three or four occasions. On those occasions they did not use a condom. BT had received a prescription for a contraceptive pill in February of 1992. At that time she was suffering menstrual problems and the prescription of the pill was apparently to settle these difficulties and not for contraceptive purposes.

On 9 June 1992, BT consulted her doctor, Dr Subbamma. During that consultation it appears that she told Dr Subbamma that her partner had Hepatitis B. Dr Subbamma noted: 'Wishes to have Hep B test (partner has Hep B).' BT saw Dr Subbamma on a number of occasions in June and July of 1992. Dr Subbamma advised BT to undergo a course of vaccinations to immunise her against Hepatitis B. BT underwent a course of vaccinations between 7 July 1992 and 21 January 1993. BT was advised that she and AT should use condoms until she had completed the full course.

In September 1992, BT and AT commenced living together as *de facto* partners. It appears clear that on occasions, both before and after September 1992, the couple had unprotected sexual intercourse.

On an occasion BT accompanied AT when he saw the defendant at his rooms. BT remained throughout the consultation. AT was complaining of a sensation of ringing in the ears. She was present while the defendant syringed AT's ears. It was BT's recollection that that consultation occurred on an occasion prior to AT's trip to Japan which took place in December 1992 (T170). In cross-examination she agreed that the only complaint so far as she was aware that AT made to the defendant was about ringing in his ears on this occasion but she went on to say 'but got some more problems like stomach pain' (T160).

In February 1993, BT became ill. She had a very severe headache and was not able to move her jaw freely. Her arms and legs were very weak. She had a high temperature and watery eyes and her throat was very sore. She was unable to eat. She attended Dr Salgo on 22 February 1993. She complained of fever and sore throat for a few days. On examination Dr Salgo noted she was very febrile. He queried whether she may have tonsillitis. He prescribed amoxicillin, paracetamol and fluids. For the reasons set out below it is probable that this was BT's seroconversion illness. In the light of that finding, and having regard to the expert evidence as to the interval between infection and the onset of a seroconversion illness I consider that BT contracted HIV on or after 21 January 1993.

In January 1994, AT and BT quarrelled. They separated for a time following this quarrel. On 15 February 1994, BT consulted Dr Subbamma. At that time she was upset and weepy and spoke of her separation from AT. Dr Subbamma arranged for blood tests including an HIV antibody test.

On or about 8 March 1994, BT was advised that her HIV test was antibody positive. She was referred for counselling to the Albion Street Clinic. She followed up on this referral.

BT attributed her HIV positive status to sexual contact with AT. The couple had planned to marry in April 1994. When BT learned that she had contracted the disease she did not inform AT. She was concerned that he might not marry her if he was aware that she had HIV. She was worried about her own financial security and that of her son. She blamed AT for placing her in the predicament in which she found herself.

In October 1994 it appears that Dr Koorey, a specialist who was then treating AT for his liver condition, arranged for him to undergo an HIV test. On 24 November 1994, AT was diagnosed as HIV positive.

On learning of his positive status, AT expressed concern for his wife and suggested that she go to the hospital to undergo a test herself. She said she did not wish to be tested at the hospital because she had worked there. It appears that thereafter AT took her to see Dr Salgo and a further HIV test was conducted. On 9 January 1995, BT was informed by Dr Salgo that she was HIV positive. At no time did she tell either AT or Dr Salgo that she had already been made aware of her HIV positive status.

AT was admitted to Royal Prince Alfred Hospital in February of 1995 for a liver transplant. He died on 26 February 1995 of liver failure. He did not die in consequence of HIV or AIDS.

Evidence was taken from AT before a court-appointed examiner, Mr Tobin QC, on 24 February 1995. In those proceedings he adhered to the contents of an affidavit which he had sworn the previous evening. In the affidavit AT stated that at no time during his treatment by the defendant was he informed that Hepatitis B was something which he might transmit to others through unprotected sexual intercourse. He said that he was given no information regarding any risks that he posed to others in that regard. He said that at no time during his treatment by the defendant was he advised to have an HIV antibody test.

As noted in paragraph 31 above, AT denied that he had received any advice concerning safe sex practices in the course of his treatment with the defendant. It was the defendant's evidence that he had supplied AT with three pamphlets concerning Hepatitis B and safe sex at the consultation on 1 February 1992.

The defendant's notes of his consultation with AT on 1 February 1992 make no reference to any sexual history taking, the provision of pamphlets relating to Hepatitis B or safe sex practices, or general counselling in this regard.

The defendant's notes as to the history taken at the first consultation do not suggest any sexual history was obtained at that time beyond eliciting the information that AT was a separated man. It has not been suggested that there was any need to embark on a detailed sexual history at the initial consultation when it was not known that AT was suffering from any form of sexually transmitted disease.

I find that the defendant questioned AT as to whether he was gay or an intravenous drug user at the consultation on 1 February 1992 when it is common ground he told him that he had probably contracted Hepatitis B through sexual contact. I accept that the defendant had pamphlets concerning safe sex practices and Hepatitis B in his rooms at that time and that he handed AT three such pamphlets in the course of informing him of the likely cause of his infection. I do not consider the fact that the defendant selected copies of pamphlets then on issue (including one which was not available as at February 1992) when he came to make his statement to his solicitors, as being of particular significance.

[The defendant's evidence was:]

> I did not see the patient again until 1 December 1992 when he presented with fever, aches and pains, irritability and headaches. At the time, I recall that the patient seemed unwell and I was concerned that he still appeared to be troubled by the symptoms which he had previously presented with. I once again questioned him about his sexual activity and he denied any homosexual contact or multiple partners. I carried out a full physical examination of the ear, nose and throat which was normal. I also checked his right and left tympanic membrane which were normal. His lymph nodes were normal, however, there was still evidence of hepatomegaly.
>
> I made a provisional diagnosis of a viral illness and once again considered that the patient required further investigation. I therefore ordered a full blood count, ESR and MBA20 (which includes electrolytes, urea, creatinine and liver function test). As I was concerned that the patient had had a lot of viruses, I suggested that an HIV test would be appropriate. The patient, however, did not consider that this was necessary. In view of the patient's reluctance and the fact that his history did not reveal any risk factors, I did not order the test. I asked the patient to return for review as necessary.

I consider it more probable than not that AT was not given any advice to undergo an HIV test at the consultation on 1 December 1992.

The duty of care owed to BT

The plaintiff claims that the defendant owed to her a duty of care. The content of the duty said to have been owed by the defendant to BT was to diagnose AT's HIV infection and/or to give proper counselling and advice to AT as to the need for an HIV test. The duty to BT (and to any other sexual partner of AT) is discharged by the diagnosis and provision of proper advice to the patient.

The defendant submits that no duty was owed by him to BT. The defendant points to the following facts which are not in dispute:

- at no time was BT a patient of the defendant;
- at no time did AT disclose to the defendant the existence of a sexual relationship between himself and BT;
- at no time did AT specifically seek from the defendant any treatment for, or advice about, his HIV status;
- AT's HIV positive status was not caused by any action or inaction on the part of the defendant;
- HIV is a lifelong infection which can be transmitted to other people in a variety of ways both sexually and non-sexually. A person infected can retransmit the infection once acquired.

The plaintiff pleads that she '. . . is within the class of persons who were at risk of foreseeable injury if the defendant failed to properly counsel and advise AT to have an HIV test'. The defendant does not seek to contend that the plaintiff, as a sexual partner of AT, was not a person at risk of foreseeable injury but submits that something more than this consideration alone is required in order to found a duty of care; *Jaensch v Coffey* (1984) 155 CLR 549 *per* Gibbs CJ at 553, *per* Deane J at 581–83; *Bryan v Maloney* (1995) 182 CLR 609 *per* Mason CJ, Deane and Gaurdron JJ at 617–19; *Esanda Finance Corporation Ltd v Peat Marwick Hungerford* (1997) 188 CLR 241 *per* McHugh J at 272.

As the defendant submitted, the identification of the additional element required to give rise to a duty of care is not easy to discern. At the date of making submissions on behalf of the defendant it was noted that proximity is no longer a universal determinant, although it was suggested it may still have some role to play. That was prior to the High Court's judgment in *Perre v Apand Pty Ltd* [1999] HCA 36, (1999) 73 ALJR 1190 which confirms the move away in recent years from seeing proximity as the unifying criterion of the duty of care; see Gleeson CJ at para 9; Gaudron J at para 27, McHugh J at paras 74 and 78; Gummow J at paras 198–201; Hayne J at paras at 330–333.

Perre was a case arising out of a claim for negligently inflicted pure economic loss. However, there are passages in the judgments as to the ingredients of the duty of care which appear of broader application. Gummow J (with whose reasons on this aspect Gleeson CJ agreed) said:

> In determining whether the relationship is so close that the duty of care arises, attention is to be paid to the particular connections between the parties . . . There is no simple formula which can mask the necessity for examination of the particular facts. That this is so is not a problem to be solved; rather, as Priestley JA put it in *Avenhouse v Hornsby Shire Council* (1998) 44 NSWLR 1 at 8: '. . . it is a situation to be recognised.'

Amongst the factors that his Honour identified as justifying a finding that a duty was owed in that case were (i) the defendant's knowledge of the risk; (ii) the appellants had no way of appreciating the existence of the risk to which the respondent's conduct exposed them and, thus, had no avenue to protect themselves (at para 216).

McHugh J placed emphasis on the vulnerability of the plaintiff to incurring loss in consequence of the defendant's conduct. His Honour considered that the defendant's knowledge of the risk and its magnitude would be relevant in all pure economic loss cases and might be relevant in other circumstances (paras 104, 105 and 129).

In *Hill v Van Erp* (1997) 188 CLR 159 the majority found the solicitor owed a duty of care to the third party/beneficiary. That was a case involving a claim for pure economic loss, although the facts did not give rise to concerns as to indeterminacy either in the number or extent of claims. The suggestion that the imposition of a duty in favour of the third party conflicted with the solicitor's duty to her client was rejected, the interests of the solicitor's client and the plaintiff being coincident.

Of the recent decisions of the High Court dealing with constituent elements of the duty of care in the law of negligence to which I was taken, *Pyrenees Shire Council v Day* [1998] HCA 3, (1998) 192 CLR 330 is the only one not concerned with a pure economic loss claim. However, its usefulness for present purposes is limited to some degree by the centrality of the statutory powers of the Council to the way in which their Honours decided the case.

In the course of his reasons in *Pyrenees*, Gummow J observed that the situation occupied by the Shire 'gave it a significant and special measure of control over the safety from fire of persons and property'. His Honour went on:

> [The] statutory enablement of the Shire 'facilitate[d] the existence of a common law duty of care' but the touchstone of what I would hold to be its duty was the Shire's measure of control of the situation including its knowledge, not shared by Mr and Mrs Stamatopoulos or by the Days, that, if the situation were not remedied, the possibility of fire was great and damage to the whole row of shops might ensue. The Shire had a duty of care 'to safeguard others from a grave danger of serious harm', in circumstances where it was 'responsible for its continued existence and [was] aware of the likelihood of others coming into proximity of the danger and [had] the means of preventing it or of averting the danger or of bringing it to their knowledge' (at para 168).

In *Pyrenees*, in determining that a duty of care was owed, Kirby J referred especially to the risk of danger, the latency of the defect and the inability of the claimants to protect themselves (at para 255).

The defendant submitted in a case such as the present in which a duty of care is said to arise in novel circumstances, while a process of reasoning by analogy from decided cases may be appropriate, I would bear in mind the injunction that there is no scope for decision by reference to idiosyncratic notions of justice and morality: *Sutherland Shire Council v Heyman* (1985) 157 CLR 424 *per* Deane J at 498. This is not to say that considerations of public policy do not underlie the determination of the existence of a duty of care in novel cases, as Deane J explained in the above passage. Unsurprisingly both the plaintiff and the defendant have addressed submissions as to what are said to be the competing reasons of policy for and against the existence of a duty.

In the present case the plaintiff submits that the defendant by virtue of his specialist training and knowledge, was in a position to know (or should have known) that in the light of AT's history and symptoms AT was at risk of having contracted HIV. It was reasonably foreseeable that AT, if HIV positive, would transmit the virus to sexual partners. Neither AT nor his sexual partners may be in a position to understand the risk (AT had not progressed to an AIDS-related illness at the material time). In this respect AT's HIV condition was latent. In determining whether a duty is owed it is submitted that the magnitude of the risk is an appropriate matter to take into account.

The plaintiff relied on three North American decisions in which like issues have arisen. In *Pittman Estate v Bain* (1994) 112 DLR (4th) 257, Lang J in the Ontario Court (General Division) dealt with such a case at first instance. A patient undergoing cardiac surgery at the Toronto Hospital in 1984 received a transfusion of blood from a donor who was HIV positive. In 1989 the head of the hospital's blood bank informed the patient's doctor that the transfusion had been contaminated. The doctor was concerned about the effects of this news on his patient's mental and cardiac condition. He took the view, wrongly, that the patient was no longer engaging in sexual intercourse. Having regard to these considerations he determined not to inform his patient of his possible HIV status. The patient died in March 1990 and at that time it was discovered that he was HIV positive. In September 1990 the patient's wife was diagnosed as being HIV positive. She, and the estate of the deceased husband, commenced proceedings against the doctor.

Lang J found that the doctor had a duty to inform his patient of the possibility that he had contracted HIV. He found that the doctor had breached that duty. His Honour went on to observe (at 401) that:

> In this context, it is unnecessary for me to determine whether Dr Bain had an independent duty to Mrs Pittman, because Dr Bain did have an obligation to tell Mr Pittman, and if he had told Mr Pittman, the evidence established that Mr Pittman would have told his wife.

His Honour proceeded to an assessment of damages for the injuries sustained by the plaintiff wife. No alternative basis for compensating her, save that the defendant doctor breached an independent duty owed to her, was advanced. However, as appears from the passage extracted above the decision did not involve an analysis of the basis upon which his Honour arrived at the determination and is thus of little guidance for present purposes.

The plaintiff also relied on the decision of *Reisner v Regents of the University of California* 37 Cal Rptr 2d 518 (1995). In that case a 12-year-old girl received a transfusion of blood contaminated with HIV.

The following day her doctor discovered that the blood was contaminated. He determined not to tell the child or her parents of that fact. Three years later the girl commenced a relationship with the plaintiff. They engaged in sexual intercourse. Two years later the defendant doctor informed the girl of her HIV status. She in turn informed the plaintiff who was tested and found to have contracted HIV. The plaintiff commenced proceedings against the defendant doctor.

The defendant doctor in *Reisner* moved successfully for summary judgment. The plaintiff appealed. The California Court of Appeal noted that the defendant had conceded that:

> When the avoidance of foreseeable harm to a third person requires a defendant to control the conduct of a person with whom the defendant has a special relationship (such as physician and patient) or to warn the person of the risks involved in certain conduct, the defendant's duty extends to a third person with whom the defendant does not have a special relationship (at 520).

In *Reisner* it was the plaintiff's case, as here, that the defendant's duty was discharged by warning his patient (or her parents). The court appears to have accepted the view that the plaintiff was a reasonably foreseeable plaintiff, even though his actual identity was neither known to nor ascertainable by the defendant. It noted (at 521):

> [He] knew or reasonably should have known that, as she matured, Jennifer was likely to enter an intimate relationship.

The court found that the defendant doctor owed a duty to the plaintiff, as a reasonably foreseeable person, to warn his patient of the likelihood that she was infected and of the need, accordingly, for her to take appropriate precautions. It concluded that:

> Once the physician warns the patient of the risk to others and advises the patient how to prevent the spread of the disease, the physician has fulfilled his duty – and no more (but no less) is required (at 523).

It is to be noted that in *Reisner* the defendant doctor's knowledge was of the fact of the transfusion of blood contaminated by HIV antibodies.

The plaintiff also relied on *Di Marco v Lynch Homes-Chester County Inc* 583 A 2d 422 (1990). In that case a health worker suffered a needle stick injury while taking blood from an elderly resident at the defendant's nursing home. She was advised that the resident was a carrier of Hepatitis. She sought medical advice and was informed that if she did not contract Hepatitis within six weeks she would not contract it at all. She was further advised not to engage in sexual intercourse during the six-week period. She refrained from sexual relations for an eight-week period but thereafter resumed a sexual relationship with the plaintiff, with whom she did not live. She and the plaintiff were subsequently diagnosed as suffering from Hepatitis B.

The plaintiff brought proceedings before the Court of Common Pleas of Philadelphia County. The proceedings were dismissed, the court noting that physicians do not have control over the sexual conduct of their patients. The Superior Court of Pennsylvania reversed the finding of the Court of Common Pleas and remanded the matter; *Di Marco v Lynch Homes-Chester County Inc* 559 A 2d 530 (1989).

The decision of the Superior Court was appealed to the Supreme Court of Pennsylvania. The decision of the Superior Court was affirmed by majority (Larsen, McDermott, Papadakos and Cappy JJ; Nix CJ, Flaherty and Zapalla JJ dissenting): *Di Marco v Lynch Homes-Chester County Inc* 583 A 2d 422 (1990). The majority observed that when a physician treats a patient who has been exposed to a communicable disease it is imperative that the physician give the patient proper advice in order to prevent the spread of the disease. Such measures are necessary not for the benefit of the already infected patient, but with a view to the protection of others. They observed:

> . . . the duty of a physician in such circumstances extends to those 'within the foreseeable orbit of risk of harm' . . . If a third person is in that class of persons whose health is likely to be threatened by the patient, and if erroneous advice is given to that patient to the ultimate detriment of the third person, the third person has a cause of action against the physician, because the physician should recognise that the services rendered to the patient are necessary for the protection of the third person (at 424–25).

Their Honours concluded (at 425) that:

> . . . the class of persons whose health is likely to be threatened by the patient includes anyone who is physically intimate with the patient. Those, like the trial court, who insist that we cannot predict, or foresee, that a patient will engage in sexual activity outside of the marital relationship and that thus, we need not protect those who engage in 'casual' sex, are exalting an unheeded morality over reality.

The question of whether a duty is owed by a health service provider to the sexual partner of a patient was considered by the Court of Appeal in *Goodwill v British Pregnancy Advisory Service* [1996] 2 All ER 161. In that case the plaintiff's boyfriend, Mr McKinlay, had undergone a vasectomy before the couple met. When they commenced their sexual relationship he told her of the procedure and of his advice that it had been successful. Subsequently the plaintiff conceived a child and became aware of the pregnancy when it was too late for an abortion. She brought proceedings seeking damages for the expenses associated with her daughter's birth and the costs of raising her. The court found that the defendants were not in a special relationship with the plaintiff such as to give rise to a duty of care. Emphasis was placed on the circumstance that the plaintiff was not Mr McKinlay's sexual partner at the time the defendants advised him. The class to which the plaintiff belonged was any woman who might be a potential sexual partner of Mr McKinlay over the span of his life. This was too uncertain a class to impose any duty of care upon persons advising Mr McKinlay as to his fertility.

It is to be noted that *Goodwill* was a claim for pure economic loss based upon a third party's reliance on negligent advice.

The defendant submitted that before a duty can be held to arise it is essential that the plaintiff is known to or capable of being readily identified by the tortfeasor.

With respect to consequential economic loss the defendant acknowledged that it may sometimes be sufficient if the class is 'capable of being ascertained': *Caltex Oil (Australia) P/L v The Dredge 'Willemstad'* (1976) 136 CLR 529 at 555. In such cases, the defendant submitted, there must nevertheless be a degree of certainty about the identity of the individual. In this sense merely being able to describe a class is not enough. Relying on *Alcock v Chief Constable* [1992] 1 AC 310 at 410E the defendant submitted that the impracticability or unreasonableness of entertaining claims to the ultimate limits of human activity tells against the existence of a duty.

The defendant submitted that the class to which BT belongs must as a matter of logic include not only all sexual partners including future sexual partners but also others at risk of infection by AT. Thus health workers or others who might come into contact with AT's blood products would also fall within it. The members of the class may not be in existence at the time of the tortious conduct. They bear no relation to the defendant and are not capable of being known to him or ascertained by him.

I do not consider that the fact that the members of the class may not be known or be capable of ready identification by the defendant is determinative of there being no duty of care. In *Voli v Inglewood Shire Council* (1963) 110 CLR 74, in finding that the architect owed a duty, Windeyer J observed that the architect:

> . . . knew the purpose for which the hall was being built, and the use to which it would be put. His duty of care extended to persons who would come there to use it in the ordinary way (at 85).

There was no pre-existing relationship between the architect and the plaintiff in that case. The architect at all relevant times was unaware of the plaintiff's existence. The plaintiff could only recover upon the basis that he was a member of a reasonably foreseeable class of persons. The defendant acknowledged as much in his written submissions, observing:

> On some occasions, a known class of people may suffice for a duty to be owed but this is capable of ready identification and has a physical relationship/proximity with the tortfeasor. See *Voli v Inglewood Shire Council* (1963) 110 CLR 74.

The class to whom the architect owed a duty were all those persons who came into the hall lawfully to use it in the ordinary way. Viewed in that way the architect's duty was potentially to a very large and unidentified group.

It does not seem to me that the policy considerations concerning indeterminate liability are raised by the facts of this case more acutely than in *Voli*.

The defendant submitted *Voli* involved the same sort of direct infliction of physical injury as is seen in the motor vehicle collision cases. The stage collapsed because it was constructed in accordance with the defendant's negligently prepared plans. It was in this context that the finding of the duty should be understood. In contrast it was contended that the cause of BT's injury was the sexual contact between her and AT.

The duty alleged by the plaintiff here, so it was submitted, is in effect identical with a duty to rescue; to save BT from a harm which was not caused by the defendant. It is the plaintiff's case that she suffered injury in consequence of the defendant's negligent failure to diagnose and/or adequately advise her sexual partner as to his risk of infection with a fatal sexually transmissible viral illness. On her behalf evidence has been led to establish that the great majority of persons, if made aware of their HIV positive status, will avoid exposing their partners to risk of infection. The rescue analogy requires a restrictive view of the cause of the plaintiff's injury. It does not in my view hold good.

I note the issue of a medical practitioner's duty with respect to rescue was dealt with in *Lowns v Woods* (1996) Aust Torts Reports 81–376. That case has significance for the way in which the Court took into account the obligations imposed on medical practitioners under the Medical Practitioners Act 1938 on the question of whether it was appropriate to impose a duty of care on the doctor in relation to a person (in need of urgent treatment) who was not his patient. The majority held that the primary judge had been right to take into account the statutory obligation (to provide attention) in determining that a relationship of proximity had been made out.

It is to be noted that s 12(1) Public Health Act 1991 requires a medical practitioner who believes on reasonable grounds that his or her patient is suffering from a sexually transmissible medical condition to provide the patient with such information as is required by the Regulations made under that Act. Regulation 4 of the Public Health Regulation 1991 sets out the categories of information which is to be supplied:

(a) means of minimising the risk of infecting other people with the condition;
(b) public health implications of the condition;
(c) responsibilities under s 11 of the Act, including any precautions considered reasonable;
(d) responsibilities under s 13 of the Act;
(e) diagnosis and prognosis;
(f) treatment options.

Section 13 of the Public Health Act makes it an offence for a person who knows that he or she suffers from a sexually transmissible medical condition to have sexual intercourse with another person unless, before the intercourse takes place, the other person has been informed of the risk of contracting a sexually transmissible medical condition and has voluntarily agreed to accept that risk.

The scheme of the Public Health Act thus requires a medical practitioner who reasonably believes his or her patient to have HIV to inform the patient of the public health implications of the condition and of the means of protecting others. The practitioner must inform the patient of the patient's statutory responsibility to warn prospective sexual partners of his or her condition. These provisions seem to me to have some bearing on the submissions with which I next deal concerning conflict of interest, therapeutic privilege and doctor/patient confidentiality as well as the broader question of whether it is appropriate to impose a duty such as that pleaded on a practitioner in relation to the sexual partners of his or her patients.

The defendant submitted that there are policy reasons which tell against a duty being owed by the defendant to BT. First, any such duty, it was submitted, may involve a conflict with the duty owed by the defendant to AT. A doctor's duty to his patient does not permit him to place the interests of any person above those of his patient. A conflict, actual or potential, is a strong policy reason, so it was submitted, to hold against the existence of a secondary duty to a person such as BT. Such a submission would have more force if it were being suggested that the content of the duty required the doctor to warn his patient's sexual partners. That is not the case here. The duty is discharged by the doctor providing his patient with appropriate and adequate advice. In such a circumstance it is difficult to see how as a matter of practical reality a conflict could arise.

The defendant submitted that a potential for conflict arose in the context of the therapeutic privilege which may justify a doctor in withholding information from his or her patient where it is in the patient's best interests so to do. In a case where a medical practitioner believes on reasonable grounds that his or her patient has contracted HIV, therapeutic privilege would not, in the light of the statutory obligation cast on the practitioner, allow of a decision to withhold information either as to the patient's status or obligations with respect to notifying sexual partners.

The defendant also relied upon the confidentiality of the doctor/patient relationship. In written submissions it was put this way:

> The only person who can release the doctor from the obligation of confidence is the patient. But if a duty is owed to a third party by the doctor, then in order to discharge that duty it may be necessary for the doctor to breach the obligation of confidentiality. Which is to prevail? That is an impossible choice. The only course open is to hold that there is no duty.

In the way the plaintiff pleads her case considerations of confidentiality do not strike me as raising issues of real substance. There is no suggestion that the obligation on the doctor extends beyond the provision of adequate advice to the patient.

I consider in the circumstances of this case that the plaintiff has established that the defendant owed to her a duty of care. In arriving at this conclusion I have taken into account the following matters:

- there is no conflict between the duty owed by the defendant to AT and BT as the two are coincident;
- BT was a sexual partner of AT;
- it was reasonably foreseeable that AT, if HIV positive, would transmit the virus to a sexual partner;
- AT was unaware of his HIV status (in this respect the condition was latent);
- the defendant's specialist knowledge and training equipped him to identify the risk that AT had contracted HIV;
- failure to diagnose and adequately counsel AT to undertake an HIV antibody test exposed AT's sexual partner/s to the real risk of contracting a fatal disease.

It is the combination of these factors, together with a consideration of public policy reflected in the statutory obligations placed upon medical practitioners with respect to the treatment of and supply of information to patients with sexually transmissible medical conditions, which to my mind makes the imposition of the duty appropriate in the circumstances of this case.

Breach of duty

The nature and content of the defendant's duty to AT (and by extension to BT) is as set out in *Rogers v Whitaker* (1992) 175 CLR 479, pp 489–90 and 492–93. It is to exercise the reasonable care and skill expected of a general practitioner in 1992. It is alleged that the defendant fell below that standard in his failure both to consider a possible diagnosis of HIV and to advise appropriately. In this case expert evidence as to the practice of general practitioners in 1992 plays an influential role in ascertaining the standard demanded by the law.

The plaintiff submits that reasonably informed general practitioners practising in the inner city suburbs of Sydney in 1992 would have been aware of the association between Hepatitis B (and other sexually transmissible diseases) and HIV.

It is the plaintiff's case that as at 1 February 1992, when AT's Hepatitis B was confirmed and the defendant obtained a history which included reference to AT's 'casual exploits' as a possible source of his infection, the defendant's failure to consider a diagnosis of HIV and to counsel AT to undergo an HIV antibody test fell below the standard of skill and care of an ordinary general practitioner practising in Sydney in 1992.

By the 1 December 1992 consultation when AT returned reporting fever and aches and pains it is submitted that the defendant was even more clearly on notice of HIV as a possible diagnosis such that, even if he suggested an HIV test (which is not accepted), his advice was inadequate and, again, fell below the standard of a general practitioner exercising ordinary care and skill.

The plaintiff relied on the evidence of Drs Law, Furner and Fisher. Dr Fisher is a very experienced general practitioner. His many appointments include a term as President of the Royal Australian College of General Practitioners.

The defendant's evidence is that as at the consultation on 1 December 1992 he had regard to AT's history of viral illnesses and the combination of Hepatitis B with a urinary tract infection and that he considered the possibility of HIV infection. The results of the pyelogram excluded other causes for the urinary tract infection leaving the defendant with the suspicion that AT may have engaged in anal intercourse. The defendant was aware of anal intercourse as a risk factor for HIV. In evidence the defendant said that he advised AT to have an HIV antibody test and that that advice was in strong terms. If that were the case the defendant would have discharged his duty to AT (and BT). For the reasons already given above I do not accept that the defendant advised AT in strong terms to have an HIV test.

If the defendant, mindful of the matters set out in para 118 above, suggested to AT that he consider an HIV test and took the matter no further when AT said that he did not think it was necessary, would his conduct fall below the standard of ordinary care and skill of a general practitioner at that time?

Dr Law stated that patients often cannot accurately assess their level of risk (report para 4, p 3). This seemed to me to be an unexceptional observation and I do not understand any of the expert witnesses to be in disagreement with it. Dr Furner drew a distinction between suggesting that a patient undergo an HIV test and recommending that they do so. In her report of 30 May 1997 Dr Furner said, 'when a patient expresses the sentiment that HIV test is not required, "as they do not feel it is necessary" they should be adequately counselled as to the advantages of having the test performed' (para 3, pp 1–2). Dr Fisher said it was necessary to explore with a patient the reasons for the patient's refusal (T155). It should be observed that the defendant does not assert that AT refused to undergo a test but rather that he said he did not think one was necessary.

It seems to me that if on 1 December 1992 the defendant did turn his mind to the real possibility that, contrary to his assertions, AT had engaged in homosexual relations involving anal intercourse and he knew him to have contracted Hepatitis B and to have a history of recurrent viral illness, it was incumbent on him in the exercise of ordinary skill and care to recommend that he undergo an HIV antibody test. It was necessary to take time to impress the need for this on AT and not to accept an initial expression of disinclination.

As I have indicated I do not accept the defendant's evidence as to the consultation on 1 December 1992. It flows from this that I do not accept the evidence that he was at the time of a mind to suspect that AT had engaged in homosexual relations. I think it more probable than not that the defendant did not give consideration to this (or HIV infection) as a possibility at the time.

Accordingly, I turn now to a consideration of whether in 1992 a general practitioner of ordinary skill and care should have considered a diagnosis of HIV (and advised of the need for a test) in the case of a heterosexual male who presented with Hepatitis B presumed to have been sexually acquired and who had a history of recurrent viral illnesses and a urinary tract infection.

As I have already noted, it is clear that the defendant proceeded upon the basis that AT's Hepatitis B infection was sexually acquired and that the likely cause was a 'casual exploit'.

I accept Dr Fisher's evidence that the presence of Hepatitis B (believed to have been sexually acquired) should have alerted a reasonably competent practitioner in 1992 to the possibility that his/her patient had contracted other sexually transmitted diseases including HIV. However, it does not flow from that that the plaintiff has established that as at the consultation on 1 February 1992 the defendant was negligent in failing to recommend an HIV antibody test. I am mindful of Dr Law's recognition that the demands of general practice are such that on the first occasion a practitioner may not (in 1992) have succeeded in obtaining a detailed sexual history from the patient. Professor Stewart gave evidence that the referral of a patient for an HIV test might itself be traumatic from the patient's perspective. I accept that this consideration may have inclined a competent practitioner to see the need to take a full history before making a decision about referring the patient for an HIV antibody test.

I am satisified that as at 1 December 1992 when AT returned to the defendant's rooms apparently suffering a further viral illness, having regard to the likelihood that the Hepatitis B was contracted as the result of sexual contact and in the light of the earlier history of viral illnesses, a general practitioner exercising ordinary care and skill would have considered a diagnosis of HIV and counselled the need for an HIV antibody test.

I consider that as at 1 December 1992 the defendant was negligent in failing to diagnose the possibility of HIV infection and to counsel AT as to the need to undergo an HIV antibody test.

Causation

Did the defendant's negligent failure to diagnose AT's HIV infection and/or to give adequate counselling and advice to AT as to the need for an HIV test cause or materially contribute to the contraction of that virus by the plaintiff? A number of factual issues need to be determined in order to answer this question.

Had AT undergone an HIV antibody test in the period 1 February 1992 to 30 January 1993 would the test result have shown him to be positive?

When the diagnosis of HIV was made in November 1994 AT's CD4 cell count was 180/ml. It is not possible to deduce from the CD4 cell count the time at which an individual contracted the virus. The rate of decline in CD4 cells varies from one individual to another. One can only in any precise way determine the time of infection by evidence of the change from a negative HIV antibody test to a positive test. Negative tests were not available either with respect to AT or BT. Professor Stewart stated that a reduction in CD4 positive T cells from a normal level of around 1,000/ml to a dangerously low level of below 100/ml occurs over a period of about ten years if the patient is untreated. It is at that point that a high likelihood of the development of life-threatening, opportunistic infections is present.

Dr Adelstein gave evidence that it is difficult to reach a CD4 cell count of 200/ml in less than three years from the date of infection. In Dr Adelstein's view it was likely that AT was infected with the virus some time prior to January 1992.

On the evidence it is entirely possible that AT had been HIV positive for a much longer period than the three years prior to November 1994 referred to by Dr Adelstein in the course of his evidence. That was, having regard to the cell count, the minimum period of probable infection in the doctor's view. I consider that AT had been infected with the virus not later than November 1991. Having regard to the evidence of Dr Furner as to the window period with respect to seroconversion and the detection of infection I consider that HIV antibody testing carried out on AT in the period from 1 February 1992 to 15 January 1993 would have revealed his positive status.

Did BT contract HIV as the result of sexual contact with AT and, if so, when?

BT gave evidence, which I accept, that she had only had sexual intercourse with three persons as at the time she was living in a domestic relationship with AT. She had sexual intercourse with the man who was the father of her first child. Subsequently, she had married an Australian man and lived for some years with him in Australia. Sexual relations between the two of them came to an end in mid-1991. She had not had sexual relations thereafter until forming her relationship with AT. In her home country she had, apart from the relationship with the father of her first child, engaged in intimate contact with two young men falling short of sexual intercourse. The latter explains the reference in one of the histories to her having five sexual partners. It appears that practitioners working in the area of sexual health include in a sexual history risk assessment episodes of intimate contact falling short of intercourse (T56).

BT had no history of risk behaviour in terms of contracting HIV. She commenced a sexual relationship around Easter 1992 with a man who at that time was HIV positive. I accept that BT became infected with HIV in consequence of sexual contact with AT. It was not submitted that I would find otherwise.

For the reasons explained by Professor Stewart in his report it is not possible to say with certainty when BT contracted the virus. Her antibody positive status was determined on 8 March 1994.

On 22 February 1993, BT saw Dr Salgo at a time when she had a high fever and a sore throat. At that time she gave an account of having had the fever for 'a few days'. It was her evidence that she had not previously experienced flu or a flu-like illness. Dr Furner noted that the history given to her of the illness in February 1993, shortly described as a 'severe flu-like illness', was a 'probable seroconversion illness' (T77). In this regard the doctor appears to have considered as significant the circumstance that BT had not experienced other flu-like illnesses to this degree on any other occasion. At the time of expressing the view that the February 1993 history was of a probable seroconversion illness, Dr Furner had access to BT's CD4 cell count from the initial occasion in March 1994 and on subsequent testing. The opinion was expressed in a report of 4 July 1996.

Dr Adelstein said that seroconversion is an illness. When a person is infected with HIV it is the illness associated with their move from the negative antibody status to the positive status. It is itself a positive infection and is associated with the change in status. He was asked if there were any classic or common symptoms to seroconversion illness. He explained that it has symptoms similar to any other viral infection but that it:

> . . . is often described as the worst viral infection anybody has had. It can be associated with swelling glands, but it frequently is more severe than your average flu, although it is often confused with other viral infections (T27).

In evidence Dr Furner made reference to the difficulties in diagnosing seroconversion illness arising out of the fact that it can mimic other illnesses, particularly influenza (T64).

I consider that the illness suffered by BT for which she saw Dr Salgo on 22 February 1993 was a seroconversion illness. Dr Adelstein was asked if there is a commonly understood period between infection and seroconversion. He said that it is usually between seven days and 21 days, somewhere around that range.

Dr Furner gave evidence that a review of the literature indicates the time from exposure to HIV to the onset of acute clinical illness (I took this to be a reference to the seroconversion illness) is typically two to four weeks although the range would be six days to six weeks (T63).

It should be noted that not every person who contracts HIV undergoes a seroconversion illness.

At the time of consulting Dr Salgo, BT had been experiencing flu-type symptoms for 'a few days'. This might take the onset of the illness back to, say, 18 February 1993. That would mean, on Dr Adelstein's evidence, that the probability is that BT contracted the virus some time between 28 January and around 11 February 1993. On Dr Furner's account that the typical interval between infection and seroconversion is two to four weeks, the date of infection might be taken back to around 22 January 1993. It is to be remembered that she put the range as being between six days to six weeks. The date of infection could have been as early as 7 January 1993. The latter view seems unlikely having regard to Dr Furner's review of the literature and Dr Adelstein's evidence. Professor Stewart noted that the interval of six to eight weeks between the date when AT was reported to have visited a prostitute and the date of his febrile illness recorded in the defendant's notes was 'an unusually long incubation period'. The probability in my view is that BT contracted the virus on a date on or after 21 January 1993.

Would AT have undergone an HIV test if counselled to do so?

The defendant could not compel AT to undergo an HIV antibody test. A sample of AT's blood for the purpose of HIV antibody testing could only be taken with AT's consent.

On the evidence as to attendances on both the defendant and Dr Salgo it seems that AT was generally a compliant patient. It happens, on occasions, that patients will refuse an HIV test after receiving competent advice. That, on the expert evidence, appears a relatively unusual occurrence: Dr Furner, report of 30/5/97, para 2, p 1; Dr Fisher at T154. AT was willing to tell Dr Selby that he had had a sexual encounter with a Thai prostitute. As I have noted, he told BT about this episode on the occasion of their first meeting. Although he did not, in terms, refer to relations with a prostitute in his discussion with the defendant he did make reference to 'casual exploits'. These considerations do not lead me to think that AT was likely to be the relatively unusual patient in denial who would steadfastly refuse testing even when the clear desirability of it was pointed out to him.

I do not consider the fact that BT suggested to AT that he have an HIV test (in the course of a conversation relating to his health status as he understood it, namely, that he was suffering from Hepatitis B and cirrhosis of the liver) is a useful guide to what AT might have done had the defendant adequately counselled him to undergo such a test as at December 1992. Any suggestion by BT, who is medically untrained, would not have served to bring home to AT the desirability of undertaking HIV antibody testing.

In November 1994 when Dr Koorey suggested that AT undergo an HIV antibody test he did so.

I consider that AT would have undertaken an HIV antibody test in 1992 had he been advised by the defendant that he should do so.

Would AT have taken appropriate steps to protect BT from contracting HIV from him?

I infer from the circumstances in which AT and BT met (in response to an advertisement placed in a newspaper) that both were interested in meeting a person of the opposite sex with whom they might be compatible with a view to a relationship including a sexual relationship. In this regard AT's hesitancy, after a number of outings, to permit a relationship to develop with a woman who already had a child seems an indicator that he was looking to meet a woman who met his criteria for an ongoing relationship.

At their initial meeting AT disclosed both that he was suffering from Hepatitis B and that he had engaged in sexual relations with a prostitute in a brothel. He also appears to have discussed the break-up of his earlier marriage. It is not clear to me that his reason for disclosing his Hepatitis condition was because of an awareness that it was sexually transmissible and that a prospective sexual partner should be on notice of that fact. BT's evidence in this regard is unclear. She said that she and AT had discussed the risk of sexual transmission of Hepatitis B but that there was '[n]ot much discussion when I first met him, but just when I was living with him' (T126). Elsewhere, in the course of her evidence, she said that the two of them had not discussed the possibility of catching Hepatitis B through sexual intercourse in the period between their first meeting until AT told her he was HIV positive (T132). The cross-examiner came back to this topic (T137) and BT agreed both that Dr Subbamma had told her of the risk of contracting Hepatitis B through unprotected intercourse and that she had discussed that with AT during the six month period that she was undergoing her vaccinations for Hepatitis B. Further, it was BT's evidence that they used condoms when AT was very sick and on occasions when he was complaining of not feeling well. When asked why condoms were used on such occasions she replied, 'Because we said we have to protect each other. He said that' (T171).

When, on one occasion, BT appeared to be denying that there had been any discussion with AT about the possibility of Hepatitis B being sexually transmitted, I considered that she was confused. Having regard to the whole of her evidence it seems to me that she was maintaining that there had been such discussions. Those discussions took place after she and AT commenced living together in September 1992. At the time of those discussions BT had been advised about the risk of sexual transmission of Hepatitis B by her own doctor. As I have already indicated, I accept that when the defendant informed AT that he was suffering from Hepatitis B and noted (as AT confirmed that he did) that the likely source of transmission was sexual intercourse, the defendant gave him pamphlets including one relating to safe sex and that AT brushed the matter off saying something to the effect that he would not have the energy for sex.

AT and BT did not engage in sexual relations for some time following their initial meeting. They went out together on a number of occasions prior to any intimate contact. When they travelled together to Young during the Easter holidays in 1992 they did not have sexual relations on the first day. AT was feeling unwell. They had intercourse on the second day, for the first time, at a time when AT was feeling better. Thereafter they had sexual relations on three or four occasions between Easter and June of 1992. On those occasions no condom was used. BT had not at that time been counselled by Dr Subbamma in relation to the risk of Hepatitis B infection. Such advice as the defendant had given to AT had not resulted in precautions being taken. Even after BT was advised of the risks by Dr Subbamma, and before she had completed her course of Hepatitis B vaccinations, the couple did not always use condoms (T126). Condoms were used on occasions when AT was not feeling well. When AT was feeling well, but during the period prior to January 1993 when BT received her final injection to immunise her against Hepatitis B, they had sexual relations without condoms. BT explained it in this way:

> If I didn't use condoms, because he was very active and energetic on the certain times when we are not using condoms, well what I understand, for the condom is because we do some time, our sexual thing is not in the bedroom' (T171).

I took this to mean that on occasions when AT was feeling well and the couple engaged in sexual relations in spontaneous circumstances they did not take heed of the warning to use condoms to protect BT from the possible contraction of Hepatitis B.

It should be noted that in his affidavit AT stated that it was not until mid-1994 that Dr Salgo advised him and his wife that Hepatitis B could be transmitted by unprotected sexual intercourse and that since that time they had not engaged in sexual intercourse. I do not accept that account. As I have already noted, BT was aware in mid-1993 of the risks of sexual transmission of Hepatitis B and I am satisfied that she discussed that matter with AT. This was a year before the joint consultation with Dr Salgo.

BT states that she and AT stopped having sexual intercourse after he was diagnosed as HIV positive. That was a matter of weeks before his admission to Royal Prince Alfred Hospital on the last occasion. Prior to that in the period between March and late November 1994 the two engaged in sexual relations. At that time BT knew that she was HIV positive. She said that they used condoms on those occasions because of her awareness that she was already sick with HIV. She insisted that they had always used condoms after she found out her status.

On behalf of the defendant, among other things, it was submitted that I would take into account the circumstance that BT had failed to disclose her HIV positive status to her husband and had continued to have sex with him following the discovery of it. Those circumstances do not seem to me to bear relevantly on a consideration of the causation issues raised by BT's claim. I should observe that I accept that BT was sure in her own mind that the source of the infection with HIV in her case was AT. I consider that she blamed AT for infecting her and had, as her primary focus, concern for the future well-being and financial security of her son. She did not disclose her status to AT because she feared he may not marry her. Given her confidence that he was the source of her infection, I do not consider much turns on this aspect.

Given the couple's imperfect understanding of safe sex practices and their apparent willingness to engage in intercourse in circumstances which put BT at risk of infection with Hepatitis B, might it be said that, had AT known of his status, they would have continued, on occasions, to engage in unprotected sexual intercourse? In my view they would not have done so. Hepatitis B, as things turn out, is far more readily transmitted by sexual contact than HIV. It is a debilitating and dangerous condition. However, I do not think it reasonable to assume that the same fear attended the risk of contracting Hepatitis B in 1992 and 1993 as attended the risk of contracting HIV.

AT asserted in his affidavit that, had he been aware of his HIV positive status, he would not have had unprotected sexual intercourse with his wife. Little, if any, weight can be accorded to this assertion for the reasons explained by Kirby P in *Ellis v Wallsend District Hospital* (1989) 17 NSWLR 553 at 560.

AT was aware that his Hepatitis B had likely been contracted as the result of sexual contact. He appears to have had some understanding that the use of condoms can prevent the spread of sexually transmitted disease. Yet the couple did not always use condoms during intercourse. AT's understanding of safe sex practice was limited. It is to be borne in mind that he did not know he was infected with HIV.

Drs Fisher and Law were of the opinion that providing a patient with pamphlets was not a sufficient means of discharging the practitioner's obligation to advise as to safe sex practices. Dr Law emphasised that the giving of pamphlets is not a substitute for the supply of oral information weighted to the patient's situation (report, p 2). In evidence she referred to the need to ensure a patient understands the risks and the means of the practitioner checking that this is so (T51).

Had AT known he was HIV positive and had he received adequate counselling concerning the transmission of HIV and safe sex practices would he have taken measures to protect BT from risk of infection? The expert evidence strongly suggests that he would. Dr Furner, whose expertise in the area of dealing with people who are HIV positive I accept without reservation, stated that it is generally accepted that a very high percentage of persons (of any sexual orientation) if adequately counselled will both notify their sexual partner and change their sexual practices so as not to place their sexual partner at risk.

I consider that BT became infected with HIV in January or February of 1993. By that time the couple were living together in a domestic relationship and, whatever their difficulties, had developed affection for one another. BT's evidence of AT's response when he first became aware of his own HIV status speaks of that. In the light of the expert evidence and having regard to the circumstance that AT and BT were in a stable relationship, I accept that AT would not have engaged in unprotected sexual intercourse with BT had he been aware of his HIV status.

I therefore find that had AT been appropriately counselled as at December 1992 he would have undergone an HIV antibody test. Such a test would have shown he had contracted HIV. Proper advice would have brought home to him the need to protect his partner from risk of infections and the means to do so. The couple would not have engaged in unprotected sexual relations thereafter. In the event, unaware of his HIV condition on an occasion between late January and mid-February 1993, the couple engaged in unprotected sexual intercourse and BT thereby contracted HIV. The defendant's negligent failure to properly advise AT with respect to a possible diagnosis of HIV and the need for an antibody test materially contributed to the plaintiff's infection with the virus.

Accordingly there will be a verdict and judgment for the plaintiff in respect of her personal claim.

Harvey and Ors v PD [2004] NSWCA 97

(Speigelman CJ agreed with the reasons of Santow JA).

SANTOW JA:

Introduction

The appellants, Dr Harvey and Dr Chen appeal against the decision of Cripps AJ. The trial judge concluded that in breach of their professional duty to the respondent 'PD', they failed to take sufficient steps to cause her to be apprised that her future husband ('FH') was HIV-positive when FH had deliberately deceived her into believing that he was not. PD and FH had attended a joint consultation for the purpose, as understood by Dr Harvey who saw the couple together, of having blood tests to ensure that neither carried the Human Immuno-deficiency Virus (HIV) or any other sexually transmitted disease. Dr Harvey knew this was required because they were proposing to get married. He also knew that PD had particular concern about the STD status of her future husband because (as the patient record noted) he came from Ghana. She believed there was a higher risk that a person from Ghana would be HIV positive than one from Australia. FH's deception of PD occurred after PD received her results. She received them not from their doctor at a further joint consultation – none had been advised – but from the clinic's receptionist, who told PD she was not entitled to receive FH's pathology report, which she had requested in view of the earlier joint consultation, but only hers.

14 The focus of the appeal was first on deficiencies in the pre-test counselling and on advice given and omitted to be given by the appellants. The omissions included failing to advise that in the absence of consent,

Dr Harvey was legally prohibited from disclosing any information concerning HIV or AIDS status of one to the other (under s17(2) of the Public Health Act 1991 (NSW)). He also omitted to raise whether the test results were to be conveyed at a further joint consultation or separately.

15 Second, the appeal focussed on the advice and counselling given and omitted to be given to FH **after** the result of the test was known. This was when PD's partner was found to be HIV positive but not PD. I set out below those deficiencies found by the trial judge in the medical advice to FH, and in follow-up after the discordant test results were known:

(a) Dr Harvey did not raise with FH any issue arising out of the joint consultation and in particular asked no questions concerning whether FH was proposing to tell PD the result of his tests;
(b) Not until May 1999 was any check made to determine whether FH kept his appointment with the Royal Prince Alfred Hospital Immunology Clinic (RPAHIC) (Red, 21 at [19]);
(c) PD attended the appellants' clinic on 31 December 1998 for a contraception pill and on 11 February 1999 for vaccines; the results of the joint consultation was not adverted to directly or indirectly on either of these occasions (Red, 21 at [19]);
(d) Dr Chen's counselling of FH (found by the trial judge to fall far short of what was expected of a GP in the circumstances) consisted of the following:

    (i) told he had AIDS not HIV,
    (ii) told 'it kills',
    (iii) told treatment was expensive,
    (iv) did not ask whether he would tell his partner about the illness,
    (v) assumed certain things because of FH's nationality and appearance (Red, 22 at [22]);
    (vi) failing to recognise that people who hear this information often go into denial, often become angry, and not infrequently blame others (Red, 23 at [23]);

(e) Dr Harvey did not contact PD or FH in May 1999 when he received a questionnaire from the Department of Health seeking information about the HIV status of FH; at this time FH and PD were living together (Red, 24 at [26] but she was not to manifest any symptoms till around September 1999 and was found by the trial judge to have contracted the disease in August 1999;
(f) No attempt was made to contact PD or FH after it became known that FH did not attend the RPAHIC; on 15 June 1999 the Alpha Medical Centre received a letter from RPAHIC advising that it had no information that FH had ever attended the clinic;
(g) Sometime in February 2000 PD visited Dr Chen requesting details about FH; during this conversation Dr Chen told PD that FH was HIV positive (Red, 25 at [33–4]).

16 The appellants seek to invoke the statutory obligation to take all reasonable steps to prevent disclosure of test results without consent as placing a fundamental obstacle to attributing any responsibility to the appellants for the respondent's injury. They also contended that the deceit of the husband operated as a superseding event. Moreover, they contend that when the receptionist told PD, correctly, that she was not entitled to see FH's test results, this should have made it clear to her that she was not entitled to rely on the doctors for that information any longer; that is, if indeed (as the appellants deny) she had ever relied on them rather than FH for that information.

17 The respondent challenges that contention frontally. The respondent denies that this is a case about the duty of confidentiality of test results and when it can be breached. Rather, says the respondent, it is a case about the proper management of a couple who attend a doctor together for the known purposes of HIV testing prior to marriage and engaging in unprotected sex. It is also about the proper management of patients after they have been tested for HIV one of whom tests positive. The respondent relies on the finding of the trial judge that each of the doctors were negligent in their management of the situation that was presented to them. That negligence was evinced by their departure from, and ignorance of, established procedures which doctors are supposed to know and follow when dealing with HIV testing (Orange, 52, respondent's written submissions).

18 The respondent has filed a Notice of Contention in which two additional grounds are sought to be put for affirming the decision of Cripps AJ, namely:

(a) His Honour should alternatively have held that there was an implied waiver of confidentiality between the respondent and her former husband (FH), or
(b) His Honour should have found that upon the true construction of the contract between the respondent, FH, and Dr Harvey, there was an implied term of that contract that Dr Harvey would arrange for the blood tests and to advise the respondent of her results as well as the results of FH.

19 The Notice of Contention places particular reliance on the finding (at [48] of the judgment) that the trial judge was '*of the opinion that had the question arisen concerning what the parties* [the respondent and FH] *intended to do with the results when they got them, both would have said that the other could have access to them*'. That is the basis put for there being an implied waiver of any confidentiality between the parties.

20 The respondent brings a cross-appeal on the ground that the trial judge '*erred in failing to award damages based on* ***Griffiths v Kerkemeyer*** *(1977) 139 CLR 161 and* ***Sullivan v Gordon*** *(1998–99) 47 NSWLR 319 in relation to the plaintiff's second child*' and '*in finding that "a link must be established" before damages in the nature of* ***Sullivan v Gordon*** *could be awarded*'.

21 Put briefly, the cross-appeal arises in these circumstances. The respondent after the termination of her marriage to FH, subsequently became engaged to a person also HIV positive, knowing of her condition. After taking such precautions as possible, she gave birth to a second child in 2002, who was not HIV positive. The damages relate to the costs of caring for that second child from the time (2014) when it was found by the trial judge that PD will be incapacitated by her disease, or deceased; that is to say from 2014 when the child would be 12, till the child's maturity at 18. The respondent seeks leave (should it be necessary) to re-argue the decision in *Sullivan v Gordon* (supra). This is to the extent that Beazley JA required a causal relationship between the defendant's negligence and the birth, though contending that, properly understood, Beazley JA's decision did not determine that such a connection was necessary. Beazley JA, it was said, in the face of a submission that the link although necessary was absent, found the causal link established; it was therefore unnecessary for her to determine whether such a causal link was a necessary condition to recovery.

Overview of issues

22 This appeal therefore raises a number of difficult questions, not so far directly dealt with at appellate level in Australia.

Statutory confidentiality and pre-test counselling

23 First, there is the effect of the statutory obligation under s17(2)(b) of the Public Health Act 1991 (NSW) ('the Act'), to take all reasonable steps to prevent disclosure of the test results, unless with consent. What was successfully pressed below as a critical fact was that the tests were undertaken pursuant to a joint consultation and for a purpose whose achievement depended on their truthful joint communication, most reliably achieved through disclosure at a further joint consultation. The question this poses is whether that statutory obligation of confidentiality nonetheless by its constraints precludes any negligence on the part of Dr Harvey from his failing at the initial joint consultation to raise:

(a) the need for consent to disclosure,
(b) the manner of disclosure, or
(c) the possibility of discordant results.

24 The Act also raises questions of what the Act permits in the way consent to disclosure is to be obtained and what constitutes a valid consent.

25 There is a specific finding, potentially relevant to causation bearing upon what would have happened had these matters been raised. The finding was that had the question arisen as to what the parties intended to do with the results when they got them, both would have said the other could have access to them (judgment at [48] Red, 30).

Post-test counselling of FH

26 Then there was the perfunctory and inaccurate post-test counselling of FH. It poses the question, was the failure by either doctor to urge on FH that he disclose his positive test result to PD negligent, or was such a course justified if not mandated by the statutory obligation? The appellants emphasise that the statutory provision is not just an obligation to refrain from disclosure, but a positive obligation to take all reasonable steps to prevent disclosure.

27 It is contended by the appellants that, especially with the test result now known, such urging of FH (to disclose his positive result to PD) would have entailed the doctors breaching their statutory obligation not only to refrain from disclosure, but to take all reasonable steps to prevent disclosure.

28 The appellants put into contention not only the extent of any duty of care, but also whether the injury suffered by PD could truly be said to have causally resulted from any breaches by the doctors. They contend that FH's deception operated as a *novus actus interveniens*, superseding any causative role played by the doctors' negligence, if neglect there were. The appellants contend that had they given the advice and counselling, which the trial judge held should have been given, and whether before or after the test results became available, the injury would still have occurred. This is because FH's conduct showed that he would have ignored such advice and practised the same deceit on PD.

29 Then there is the question whether, in the post-test period, Dr Chen or Dr Harvey should have had a proper system of record-keeping and automatic shared access by all doctors to patient medical records within the medical centre which would have revealed that FH had not disclosed his positive status to PD. This it is said, should have been revealed when PD requested a prescription of an oral contraceptive pill and vaccinations for a trip to Ghana.

30 The appellants contend that in a multi-doctor medical centre it is unreasonable to base legal duties on the theory that every doctor has the knowledge of all of the others about the same patient. They then seek to deal with the matter on the basis that if, contrary to that submission, it would be reasonable so to base the doctors' duties in such a centre, still no liability would ensue.

31 The argument sought to be answered proceeded this way. Let it be assumed that the doctors followed up FH more vigorously than they did and had cross-referenced information. Let it be assumed also that they would from the prescription and vaccinations be on notice of his likely deceit or could verify it by a non-suggestive question of PD ('*were they still together*'). That question would need to be so framed as not to infringe the statutory duty of confidentiality. If PD responded that she was still in a relationship with FH, the doctors under *the Act*, knowing of the probability of unprotected sex from the contraceptive pills, could then notify the Director General.

32 But the appellants argue that the question at the end of that causal chain is whether the Director-General would have taken action having the practical effect of preventing FH continuing in his deceit with PD. The appellant analyses the evidence submitting that it pointed against any such intervention being likely.

PD's Cross-appeal for cost of child care for her second child after PD's anticipated incapacity

33 Finally, there is the difficult question posed by PD's cross-appeal and the further head of damage for care of the second child after PD's anticipated incapacity. It can be considered in causal terms. Did the doctors' negligent failure result in this further head of damage, or was it the result of PD's independent, and it is asserted, unreasonable act in having the further child, knowing that she was now HIV positive? Alternatively, what is the appropriate scope of liability or extent of legal responsibility in relation to each doctor's negligence?

34 Similar questions underlie that issue when framed in terms of an obligation to mitigate damage on the part of PD, or in terms of the proposition that '*recoverability of damages is always bounded by considerations of fairness and reasonableness*' (per Lord Nicholls of Birkenhead in *Rees v Darlington Memorial Hospital NHS Trust* [2003] 3 WLR 1091 at 1098 para 13 citing *Kuwait Airways Corporation v Iraqi Airways Co (Nos. 4 and 5)* [2002] 2 AC 883, 1090–1 paras 69–70).

Salient facts

35 Almost all the salient facts are undisputed. I have set these out below in summary form, indicating any difference between the parties. A more detailed elaboration appears in the judgment of Ipp JA under the heading 'the relevant circumstances', when describing the initial medical interview, its earlier background and its immediate aftermath.

The trial and its result

36 Dr Harvey and Dr Chen were the defendants in proceedings brought against them by PD in the Common Law Division. PD claimed damages for personal injuries said to have been occasioned by breach of professional duty on the part of Dr Harvey and Dr Chen in failing to take sufficient steps to cause her to be apprised that her future husband ('FH') was HIV-positive. The proceedings were heard before Cripps AJ who, on 10 June 2003, gave judgment for the Plaintiff against both Defendants, for $727,437. Dr Harvey and Dr Chen ('the Doctors') have appealed to the Court of Appeal from the judgment of Cripps AJ.

Initial joint consultation for HIV testing

37 PD was a patient of the Alpha Medical Centre at Marrickville ('the Centre') from October 1997 until February 1999. On 16 November 1998, she attended the Centre with her future husband for the purpose, as understood by Dr Harvey who saw them together, of having blood tests to ensure that neither carried the Human Immuno-deficiency Virus (HIV) or any other sexually transmitted disease, because they were proposing to get married. At the time of that consultation, PD and FH were not living together, but had a sexual relationship and practised protected sex. FH came to the Centre for testing at PD's request. Dr Chen was the medical director of the Centre, and he employed Dr Harvey on a regular sessional basis.

38 In the course of the initial joint consultation, Dr Harvey was told that FH came from Ghana. PD was concerned about the STD status of her future husband, because she believed that there was a higher risk that a person from Ghana would be HIV positive than one from Australia. While Dr Harvey did not concede that that accorded with his understanding, he did believe that a person from Ghana was at higher than usual risk of having other sexually transmitted diseases. Following that consultation, he made the following entry on PD's medical record:-

> 16.11.98 Low risk lifestyle
>
> Nil IVDU, no anal sex
>
> Wants STD check
>
> Investigation – HIV
>
> Hep B/RPR See 1/52 Dr Nick Harvey

39 On FH's card, he made the following entry:-

> 16.11.98 Low risk lifestyle
>
> Nil IVDU From Ghana
>
> About to engage in new relationship
>
> Counselled wants blood test for STD
>
> Talk about . . . – Nil. Investigation HIV
>
> Hep B/RPR See 1/52

40 Neither card recorded the circumstance that the consultation was a joint one. PD's card did not record that she was proposing to enter a new relationship of marriage with, it can be taken, unprotected sexual relations replacing the protected sexual relations they had hitherto practised. Dr Harvey did not inform either PD or FH that, in the absence of consent, he was legally prohibited from disclosing any information concerning the HIV or AIDS status of one to the other. How the test results were to be dealt with was not discussed at all. PD believed – the trial judge found, 'reasonably' – that she would have FH's results and he would have hers; but the topic was not raised. The trial judge found, in accordance with evidence apparently given by PD, that she and FH had agreed to exchange pathology results; Red, 20H-M at [13].

41 I interpolate here that the appellants contend that this finding is not unimportant. They submit that, with the finding that how the results were to be dealt with was not addressed by Dr Harvey these findings combine to suggest that PD relied on FH – rather than on the doctors – for the provision of FH's results. That is disputed by the respondent. This is on the basis that the finding is at the least neutral on the matter, submitting that in fact the finding rather supports the inference the respondent seeks to draw to the effect of its Notice of Contention. That inference is that there was an implied waiver of confidentiality between respondent and FH. Also that there was an implied term in a tripartite contract that Dr Harvey would arrange for the blood tests and advise the respondent of her results as well as the results of FH.

42 Both PD and FH gave blood at the joint conference in the presence of each other, and left the surgery. Dr Harvey told them to return to his surgery in about a week's time when the pathology tests would be available.

43 On 23 November 1998, a week later, Dr Harvey received PD's pathology report, which was negative for both Hepatitis B and HIV. The following day, 24 November 1998, he received FH's pathology report, which was positive for Hepatitis B and HIV.

44 PD returned to the Centre sometime between one and two weeks after the initial consultation. The receptionist gave her a copy of the pathology report relating to her. She asked for a copy of FH's pathology report, but was told that it was confidential and could not be given to her. The receptionist did not make any mention that, with consent of FH it could be given to her. It was common ground at the trial that PD should not have received her result from the receptionist but from a medical practitioner (Red, 20D at [14]). She should have been told that the results were not necessarily definitive because of a 'window' of three months prior to the test within which HIV could have been contracted without a positive result.

45 Following his receipt (1 day later) on 24 November 1998 of FH's pathology results, Dr Harvey made the following note in FH's record:-

> 24.11.98 Blood – HIV positive
>
> Unable to contact patient by phone. I have made appointment for immune clinic RPAH 9am Thursday 26.11.98
>
> Letter in notes Dr Nic Harvey

46 According to Dr Harvey, when he received FH's results on 24 November, he telephoned the Centre for FH's phone number. Despite what appears from the medical record, he said that he spoke to FH and made an appointment for him to attend the Royal Prince Alfred Hospital Immunology Clinic ('RPAHIC') at 9am on 26 November 1998. The trial judge accepted that evidence (Red, 21H-L). An appointment was indeed made for FH to attend RPAHIC on Thursday, 26 November

1998, although FH did not keep that appointment. Although there was no copy of the letter in the medical record, the trial judge accepted that the appointment was made, but not kept (Red, 22K-L).

47 In the course of the telephone conversation on 24 or 25 November (Dr Harvey failed to have a face to face meeting with FH and should have done, Judgment Red, 33L-O), Dr Harvey told FH that he had 'very bad news' and that he had tested positive. He thought FH seemed disbelieving of what he was hearing, but Dr Harvey told him that the laboratory was certain of the result. He told him that he had made an appointment for him to attend RPAHIC, and should take a positive attitude towards his condition because of the enormous advances recently made in treatment of people with that illness. FH asked: '*Does this mean I can't have children*?', and Dr Harvey responded: '*At this stage the answer is no*'. Dr Harvey advised him not to have unprotected sex, and that he could not safely father a child. Dr Harvey did not ask whether FH was proposing to tell PD the result of his test nor did Dr Harvey seek consent for the Clinic or himself to make that disclosure to PD.

48 Dr Harvey did not see FH again. FH did not keep the appointment at RPAHIC. Nor did Dr Harvey ever speak to PD again, although she attended the Centre (where she saw a different doctor) on 31 December 1998 for a contraceptive pill, and on 11 February 1999 for vaccines, because she was travelling to Ghana on 31 March 1999, where she proposed to remain for a period of three weeks. Neither the joint consultation nor the test results were adverted to on either of those occasions, and it was not until after mid May 1999 that any check was made to determine whether FH had kept his appointment with RPAHIC.

49 Dr Harvey advised the NSW Health Department in June 1999 (three **months** before PD became infected) that '*more complete and accurate information*' on FH could be obtained from RPAHIC, though he already knew that FH never attended there and that they could not have any information on him at all (Blue, 273X, cross-examination of Dr Harvey, Black, 325V–328P).

50 Dr Harvey accepted that, had he looked at PD's patient history card after he became aware that FH had not attended the appointment at RPAHIC, and had seen that she had attended for oral contraception and vaccination for a trip to Ghana, he '*possibly would have thought*' that they were in a continuing sexual relationship (Black, 328T–329D) and would have made further inquiries of either PD or FH – because it would have been a matter of '*paramount concern*' that PD was in danger of infection.

51 Despite a submission on behalf of PD to the contrary, the trial judge also accepted that Dr Chen spoke to FH at the time of handing him the letter of referral to RPAHIC, and on that occasion urged him to attend RPAHIC (Red, 22V-Y). However, His Honour found that the advice given by Dr Chen 'fell far short of what was expected of a general

practitioner in all the circumstances'. In particular, he told FH that he had AIDS (which he did not); he told him: 'It kills', which the experts agreed was inappropriate; he said FH appeared to understand and shook his head, but thought that he appeared to accept the news. FH raised the question whether treatment was expensive, and was told that it was. Dr Chen said that he formed the view, but without having raised or discussed it with FH, that FH understood his responsibilities and would probably disclose his HIV status to his sexual partner – whose identity Dr Chen did not know. Dr Chen's rationale for this assumption was that FH was a neatly dressed man who appeared to be educated and who – because he was of African origin – would presumably know what HIV was and its basic nature.

52 The trial judge inferred that the reason why Dr Chen did not raise with FH the question of disclosure to his sexual partner was that he did not know who that partner was – let alone that she, PD, was a patient of the Centre. The treatment record card in the case of both PD and FH did not record the fact of the joint consultation, or that PD was about to enter a new relationship (with FH or otherwise) (judgment, Red, 19L-P, 44H-J) Dr Chen's evidence was that he never even knew PD existed, although he did read FH's medical records and would have seen there that FH was in a new relationship about which he asked nothing. The trial judge concluded that Dr Chen's 'counselling' of FH fell far below that expected of a general practitioner, expert evidence on both sides being to the effect that when a GP is conveying grave information concerning life threatening diseases, it is notorious that the recipient although perhaps understanding what has been said, does not fully absorb the consequences, frequently goes into denial, often becomes angry, and not infrequently blames others. Dr Chen, the trial judge thought, apparently recognised none of these matters and thought that having referred him to the RPAHIC he had discharged his duty to FH and did not think that there was any need to check with RPAHIC to see whether FH kept his appointment (judgment Red, 22W–23T).

Deception of PD by FH

53 After PD was refused access to FH's record, she telephoned him and told him she had tested negative. He said that he had tested negative also. He said that he did not wish to see her results, because he accepted her word; she, however, said that she wished to see his results. A few days later, she went to his home and was shown what he represented to be his pathology results, and showed him to have tested HIV negative and Hep B negative. This report was either a forgery, or fraudulently obtained. PD did not keep a copy, and returned it to FH.

54 At the time of the consultation in November 1998 and for some months after, PD and FH continued to live apart, and did not have unprotected sex. They visited Ghana in about March or April 1999, and afterwards commenced living together and engaging in unprotected sex. They married in July 1999, and had a child born on 28 February 2000.

PD visits clinic again

55 On 31 December 1998 PD visited the clinic for oral contraception (Blue, 240) while on 11 February 1999 PD attended the practice for vaccination for a proposed trip to Ghana in March 1999 (Blue, 241). No-one connected these facts or drew any conclusion that she was probably having unprotected sex with her Ghanaian partner, FH. Both dates were before May 1999 when PD and FH commenced cohabitation and September 1999 when PD experienced the first symptoms of a sero-conversion illness, i.e. an HIV infection. With proper record-keeping, the likelihood that she was having unprotected sex with her partner FH should have been identified. But, as the trial judge found (Red, 42R-T) '*From the time PD and FH left the surgery after giving blood on 16 November 1998 they were treated by the practice as two separate and unrelated patients – in circumstances where Dr Harvey knew that was not so and Dr Chen ought to have known it was not so*'.

The Centre receives further information

56 Sometime in May 1999, Dr Harvey received a questionnaire from the Department of Health, seeking information concerning FH's HIV status, which had been notified to the Department by the serum laboratory (which is required by law to provide such information to the Director-General of Health). Neither FH nor PD, who were then living together, were contacted by Dr Harvey; the trial judge did not accept Dr Harvey's evidence that an attempt to contact FH was made at that time.

57 On 15 June 1999, the Centre received from RPAHIC a letter advising that it had no information that FH had ever attended, although its records confirmed that an appointment had been made for him on 26 November 1998. No attempt was made by the Centre to contact PD or FH, the trial judge inferred because the practice considered that it had no further obligation to either. His Honour added that Dr Harvey considered that he had no further obligation to PD after she was given her results by the receptionist and told she was HIV negative, and no further obligation to FH after writing the letter of referral to RPAHIC.

PD contracts HIV

58 In September 1999, PD (already pregnant) was admitted to Canterbury Hospital, with a fever and a rash. This was later recognised as a sero-conversion illness indicating that probably she had become HIV positive. She became aware FH was HIV positive when she found a copy of the genuine pathology report among his papers at the end of 1999 or early 2000. Before she became aware that she was HIV positive, PD attended at the Centre and spoke to Dr Chen, demanding to know why she was not told of her husband's HIV status. A note was made by Dr Chen of that consultation in FH's records, as follows:

(Chen addendum) Patient came (wife) requesting records and info about husband. Explained clearly husband may be unwell – confidentiality issues apply – need to take precautions and advise husband to attend here or any doctor for r/v ASAP, if still has not resolved last 1–2 years issues. Explained records cannot be given to her. Attend with husband to resolve issues best options.

59 Dr Chen said that when he spoke to PD, she told him that she was HIV positive and wanted to see the test results of her husband; he said he would not give them to her because he did not have FH's permission (although he did, to some extent, discuss the results with her); he said that he asked them both to attend together, so that he could get permission to discuss the issue, and that if she believed she was HIV positive, she would need to take precautions. PD said she did not know she was HIV positive when she visited Dr Chen sometime in January or February 2000. She made an almost contemporaneous note of the conversation, and the trial judge accepted her version. Shortly after this meeting, in January 2000, just prior to the expected birth of her child, PD had a further test and found she was HIV positive.

60 The trial judge found that the appellants breached their duty of care to the respondent in nine material respects.

(i) by failing to discuss with PD and FH at the initial consultation the method by which they wanted to receive their results given the distinct possibility of a discordant result (Red, 32T–33K);
(ii) by causing and/or permitting a receptionist in the practice, rather than a medical practitioner, to convey PD's test results to her (Red, 20N);
(iii) by failing to provide pre-test counselling to PD and FH according to the guidelines imposed by the Health Department (Red, 35H–36F);
(iv) by conveying to FH his test results by telephone rather than in a face to face consultation with a medical practitioner (Red, 33L–O);
(v) by failing to provide adequate post-test counselling to FH, especially in relation to his obligation concerning disclosure to sexual partners (Red, 33N–P; 38T–39Q);
(vi) by failing to ask FH whether he intended informing PD of his condition (Red, 38T);
(vii) by failing to follow up the referral of FH to the Royal Prince Alfred Hospital Immune Clinic (Red, 39S);
(viii) by failing to record upon the treatment record card of either D or FH the fact of the joint consultation or that PD was about to enter a new relationship (Red, 19L–P; 44H–J);
(ix) by failing to take fairly obvious steps designed to make PD aware that she was exposed to the danger of infection at a time when the appellants knew or ought to have known such was the case (Red, 42A–E; 44A–J);

61 Cripps AJ found that had one or more of these things been done, it

would have led to PD learning of FH's HIV infection (Red, 41N). But the doctors did nothing at all.

62 Turning to the judgment of the trial judge, a fair summary of that judgment, taken substantially from the appellants' careful summation, is as follows:

(i) Dr Chen (as employer) was vicariously liable for the acts of those whom he employed, including Dr Harvey (judgment Red, 30D–G);
(ii) Although PD was plainly of the opinion that she was entitled to FH's results, and he had consented to her having them before the joint consultation with Dr Harvey, FH did not give his consent to Drs Harvey and Chen to disclose his results to PD (judgment Red, 30J–S);
(iii) The initial joint consultation was inadequate, because no reference was made to what would happen if the results were discordant, bearing in mind the obligations of confidentiality (judgment Red, 32T–33J). The prospect of discordant results, although unlikely, was not wholly remote in the circumstances (judgment Red, 36N–P). Pre-test counselling should have involved at least a brief explanation of the legal issues associated with a positive result, and also explanation of coded notification procedures and confidentiality arrangements (judgment Red, 36D–E). Had the question arisen what PD and FH intended to do with the results when they got them, both would have said the other could have access to them (judgment Red, 30T–V). FH at that time did not know he was HIV positive. If FH had told Dr Harvey at the joint consultation that he was not prepared to make his results available to PD, she would not have married him and in all probability would have discontinued any relationship (judgment, Red, 30W–31N).
(iv) The Doctors' duty of confidentiality did not prevent Dr Harvey placing a note on PD's file that there was a joint consultation with FH, and did not mean that the Centre ceased having any responsibility for the welfare of PD in the circumstances (judgment Red, 32K–M). Implicitly, the trial judge found that such cross-referencing ought to have been made: Dr Chen could not rely by way of exculpation on the circumstance that he did not know of the existence of PD. Still less, that he did not know that she was a patient of the surgery who had attended with FH for a joint consultation, because he should have known of the joint consultation and the connection between PD and FH. The practice had the relevant information and it was not open to Dr Chen to argue that he was justified in paying no attention to any duty the practice might owe to PD because he did not know of her existence. From the time PD and FH left the surgery after giving blood they were treated as two separate and unrelated patients, in circumstances where Dr Harvey knew that was not so, and Dr Chen ought to have known it was not so. PD was never spoken to again

concerning the outcome of the joint consultation, otherwise than by being told that she could not have access to FH's pathology report.

(v) The Centre had an obligation to PD while she remained its patient to ensure as far as could lawfully be done that she had information concerning her proposed husband's HIV status and the risk to which she was exposed (judgment Red, 42V–X).

(vi) The post-test counselling of FH was inadequate; information of the type imparted to him by Dr Harvey should only have been conveyed in a face to face meeting, and Dr Chen's counselling fell short of that expected (judgment Red, 33L–P). Dr Chen did speak to FH when the latter was given his results, although the consultation fell far short of appropriate; Dr Chen did not know of the joint consultation, nor that the person with whom FH was proposing a new relationship was PD, a patient of the practice. That was possibly because of the unsatisfactory system of recording and cross-referencing information, and also because Dr Chen did not refer the matter to Dr Harvey when FH came in for his results (judgment Red, 31X–32D).

(vii) It was not the duty of the Doctors to tell PD (the patient at risk) that her partner or proposed partner was HIV positive (judgment Red, 33R–34R). Nor was it the duty of the Doctors to convey to her by less direct or obvious means of communication the HIV status of FH (judgment Red 34T–35F). However, this did not have the consequence that there was nothing the Doctors could do to protect PD or at least make her aware of the risks to which she was exposed. While the Doctors were not expected to guarantee that PD would not become infected, and were prohibited from giving her direct information, they were not prohibited from undertaking fairly obvious steps designed ultimately to make her aware of the danger she was in (judgment Red, 42D–F). They could have sought advice from experts in the field, they could have sought advice from the Medical Defence Union, and they could have spoken to the Department of Health. In any case the result would have been advice that FH needed to be counselled to ensure he made PD aware of his condition. That duty was not discharged merely by referring him to RPAHIC (judgment Red, 42G–L).

(viii) It was not good enough to send him to RPAHIC without more (judgment Red, 38Y–39B). The Doctors ought to have asked FH whether he was proposing to tell PD of his condition. Had FH been asked whether he proposed to tell his future wife of his condition and reminded that sexual intercourse with her without telling her would be an offence, he would have said he would tell her. It would have been difficult for him to have maintained his deception if those he was proposing to deceive were aware of the joint consultation. A doctor was not entitled to assume PD would become aware of FH's condition (judgment Red, 39E–P). The Doctors ought to have contacted RPAHIC to find out whether

FH kept the appointment and have raised with RPAHIC the circumstance of the joint consultation and (with PD's consent) that PD was HIV negative (judgment Red, 39S–V). The Doctors had an obligation to ensure that a person in FH's position kept an appointment with RPAHIC, there being a public duty to prevent as far as possible the spread of HIV into the community and to protect so far as they were legally able to do so their own patient (PD). Once they became aware FH had not kept his appointment, the Director-General could have been informed (judgment Red, 40A–E).

(ix) Expert evidence established that by a process of counselling and, as a last resort, coercion, HIV positive patients will tell their partners of their condition (judgment Red, 37M–O).

(x) While the doctors could not reasonably have foreseen that FH might present a forged result to PD, they could have foreseen that he may not have told her his result or might have lied to her (judgment Red, 42M–P). There were at least two occasions when it was open to the Doctors to raise with PD her future intentions concerning her marriage to FH: when she attended for a prescription for the oral contraceptive pill and when she attended for vaccinations. Had this matter been mentioned or reference made to the joint consultation on those occasions she would have told them that both were clear and that she was proposing to get married, at which point the Doctors would have been on notice that FH must have lied to her and probably deceived her. Had anyone raised with PD in late December 1998 or early 1999 the test results which followed the joint consultation she would have told that person that she believed FH was HIV negative, and that would have set alarm bells ringing that Dr Harvey did not begin to hear until May 1999 (judgment Red, 46B–G). While they were not at liberty to tell her of the information they had concerning FH's HIV status, the Doctors could and should have taken other steps to ensure that, as far as was legally possible, PD was aware of the danger she was in. Though they could not warn PD in terms of her situation, the Director-General and/or his delegate could. Specialists would have advised the Doctors that FH should be referred for counselling in circumstances where he could be persuaded to disclose his condition to PD. They could have told FH that unless he assured them he was proposing to tell PD of his HIV status, they would assume he was placing her in danger and would remind him of their entitlement to refer the matter to the Director-General. Assuming as was likely that FH would have told the doctors he proposed to tell his wife of his condition, without necessarily intending to do so, it would have justified the Doctors in arranging for another joint consultation when the matter could have been further explored (judgment Red, 38J–M).

(xi) Had the process of counselling been properly commenced before the end of 1998, PD would probably have become aware of the

HIV status of FH well before August 1999 when she became infected (judgment Red, 40L–R). If PD had even a suspicion about FH's honesty concerning his results, she would not have continued the relationship with him (judgment Red, 38Q–S).

(xii) The duty of a medical practitioner to exercise reasonable care and skill in the provision of professional advice and treatment extended to the provision of information in an appropriate case. While the statutory obligations of confidentiality, and the circumstances in which disclosure may take place for the protection of a person, are relevant, the Doctors were not precluded from taking steps to present reasonably foreseeable harm by 'an overriding inconsistent duty'. The obligation to preserve confidentiality is overriding only in the sense that details could not be given to PD without the consent of FH, and the statutory obligation operated as a constraint only. It did not preclude the doctors from taking the steps they should have taken but did not take, which resulted in PD becoming HIV positive. It was significant that there was a joint consultation and although the topic of confidentiality was not raised, the duty of the Centre to PD did not end when the Doctors told her that, contrary to her reasonable expectations, she would not have access to FH's results (judgment Red, 40T–41W).

(xiii) FH's presentation of a forged negative result in late November 1998 was not a *novus actus interveniens*, because though actual forgery may not have been foreseeable, possible deceit or irrational behaviour on his part was (judgment Red, 43H–L). The trial judge observed that '*the medical expert evidence seems to make this clear*' (judgment Red, 43K at [80]).

(xiv) Had the obligation to PD ended when she was given her results by the receptionist and told she could not have those of FH there may then have been an argument that the inadequate pre-test counselling was not causative of the ultimate conduct. However, that obligation did not cease when she was handed her results. Rather it continued while she remained a patient of the practice until at least the end of February. During that period she returned to the practice for further consultations concerning a prescription for the oral contraceptive pill and vaccinations before travel to Ghana. Even if the doctor who saw her on those occasions was unaware of FH's positive result and that FH was the person she was proposing to marry, the Centre had the relevant information and its duty could not be avoided by its inadequate cross-referencing of patient's cards (judgment Red, 44A–I).

(xv) Accordingly, the Defendants were in breach of a duty of care they owed PD and as a result PD became infected with HIV in or about August 1999 (judgment Red, 44K–M).

The appellants' case

63 The appellants' case remains that their statutory obligation of confidentiality to FH under *s17* of *the Act* was such that they could not lawfully have done anything to protect PD. They submit that her only protection was disclosure of FH's HIV positive status and that the only way to have achieved this would have involved breach of that statutory obligation of confidentiality.

64 That statutory obligation is to be found in the mandatory provisions of s17 of the Public Health Act 1991 (NSW) and in particular s17(2)(b), which is in the following terms:

> **17. Protection of identity**
>
> (1) A medical practitioner must not state the name or address of a patient:
>
> (a) in a certificate sent to the Director-General under *section 14* in relation to a Category 5 medical condition, or
> (b) except as may be prescribed, in a written or oral communication made by the medical practitioner for the purpose of arranging a test to find out whether the patient suffers from a Category 5 medical condition.
>
> (2) A person who, in the course of providing a service, acquires information that another person:
>
> (a) has been, or is required to be, or is to be, tested for a Category 5 medical condition, or
> (b) is, or has been, infected with a Category 5 medical condition,
> must take all reasonable steps to prevent disclosure of the information to another person.
>
> (3) Information about a person that is of a kind referred to in subsection (2) may be disclosed:
>
> (a) with the consent of the other person, or
> (b) in connection with the administration of this Act or another Act, or
> (c) by order of a court or a person authorised by law to examine witnesses, or
> (d) to a person who is involved in the provision of care to, or treatment or counselling of, the other person if the information is required in connection with providing such care, treatment or counselling, or
> (e) in such circumstances as may be prescribed.
>
> (4) A medical practitioner or other person who fails to comply with the requirements of this section is guilty of an offence.

Maximum penalty: 50 penalty units.

65 A *'category 5 medical condition' includes 'Acquired Immune Deficiency Syndrome' and 'Human Immunodeficiency Virus infection'.*

66 By s 75 of the Act, mirroring s 17(3), it is an offence to disclose information without lawful excuse. 'Lawful excuse' includes disclosure with the consent of the person to whom the information relates, and prescribed circumstances.

67 The regulations prescribe that disclosure may be made to the Director-General where a healthcare worker has reasonable grounds to believe that a failure to disclose could place the health of the public at risk, in order that the Director-General or his delegate can perform the necessary tracing and take the necessary actions to protect public health. Regulation 10 provides that the Director-General may notify a person whom he or she believes may have been in contact with a person suffering from HIV, of measures to be taken and activities to be avoided in order to minimise the danger of contracting or passing on the condition. Regulation 16 requires a pathology laboratory to notify the Director-General of the confirmed HIV antibody positive result. The notification must not disclose the name or address of the patient. It was in compliance with this obligation that the laboratory passed FH's results to the Director-General in November 1998.

68 Finally, the Act provides for offences. An offence is committed by a person who knows that he or she suffers from a sexually transmissible medical condition and has sexual intercourse with another person without informing the other person of the risk of contracting that condition and the person concerned has '*voluntarily agreed to accept the risk*'; s 13(1) of the Act.

69 Central to the appellants' case is s 17(2)(b) of the Act. Clearly enough s 17(2) was capable of application to and did apply to the appellants. Thus Dr Harvey was '*a person who in the course of providing a service*' namely, procuring the blood test, acquired '*information that another person*' (FH) has been tested for a category 5 medical condition (s 17(2)(a)) and that FH '*is, or has been, infected with a category 5 medical condition*' (s 17(2)(b).

70 I consider that it is clear that the concluding '*another person*' in s 17(2) (to whom disclosure is to be prevented) must mean to another person other than the person (FH) about whom the information had been obtained. In the present context this would certainly include PD unless FH consented to disclosure to her (s17(3)(a)).

71 I agree that the obligation to '*take all reasonable steps to prevent disclosure of the information to another person*', goes further than a simple prohibition on disclosure. It imposes an obligation positively to take steps against disclosure, though no more than the steps which were reasonable.

72 An exception to that prohibition here relevant, is that contained in s 17(3)(a). It permits disclosure where it is '*with the consent of the other person*' meaning in the present case that of FH.

73 The prohibition is one that gives rise to a criminal offence, as s 17(4) makes clear.

74 The appellant's case is fundamentally that liability in negligence on the doctors' part does not comport with the legislative policy exhibited by those statutory requirements. It was submitted by Mr Brereton SC for the appellants in opening that:

> in this State, for public health reasons Parliament has made a policy decision that the responsibility for the decision of someone who suffers from HIV positive status or the acquired immune deficiency syndrome is to notify anyone else of that condition and to take steps to protect the spread of the disease is the responsibility of that person and no one else. The only exception to that is in cases where there is a significant threat to public, as distinct from private, health wherein exceptions prevail. Fundamentally the policy decision has been made in this type of case that uniquely the responsibility is that of the patient alone. [Appeal transcript 1.20–35.]

75 The appellants' capacity to foresee damage for breach of that duty, though an important element, is not sufficient to establish liability if there be a countervailing duty which either denies or cuts down the duty of care upon which the liability is based. The appellants submit that that countervailing duty is here found in the legislation.

76 The appellants contend that in accordance with the well-known passage in the joint judgment of the High Court in *Sullivan v Moody* (2001) *207 CLR 562* at 581 [55], the duty necessary to ground liability in the present case was incompatible with the responsibility imposed by *s17*(2)(b) to prevent disclosure.

77 That passage is as follows:

> [55] More fundamentally, however, these cases present a question about coherence of the law. Considering whether the persons who reported their suspicions about each appellant owed that appellant a duty of care must begin from the recognition that those who made the report had other responsibilities. A duty of the kind alleged should not be found if that duty would not be compatible with other duties which the respondents owed.

78 Further in the joint judgment (at [60]) the possibility of multiple duties is recognised as not of itself ruling out the possibility that a duty of care is capable of being owed to a plaintiff; '*people may be subject to a number of duties, at least provided they are not irreconcilable . . .*' However, '*if a suggested duty of care would give rise to inconsistent obligations, that would ordinarily be reason for denying that the duty exists . . .*'.

79 The trial judge concluded that '*the practice had an obligation to PD while she remained its patient to ensure, **as far as could be lawfully done,** that she had information concerning her proposed husband's HIV status and the risk to which she was exposed*'. [emphasis added]

80 The appellants' case in its essentials comes to this. That compliance

with the statutory obligation to take all reasonable steps to prevent disclosure meant that it could not be lawfully done for the appellants to disclose to PD the result of FH's test, whether directly or by any indirect means. This is said to include means which merely facilitate the information coming to PD. Accordingly, fulfilment by the appellants of their duty to PD, when the content of that duty is thus properly understood, could not have avoided the tragic results for PD following her husband's cruel deception. It was submitted insofar as there were shortcomings in counselling PD or FH, pre or post testing, these were generally not in truth shortcomings when the statutory obligation is taken into account but in any event not such as to have been legally causative of PD's injury.

81 It was accepted by the appellants, for the purposes of this appeal, that in the context of a joint consultation such as occurred here, '*Dr Harvey owed both his patients – PD and FH – a duty to address, in the course of consultation, the question of mutual disclosure of results, and the possibility of discordant results. He did not do so. In that respect breach of duty was established*' (Orange, 28 at para 27).

82 But the appellants contend that this breach of duty was not legally causative of the respondent's loss. This was because the Centre receptionist declined, correctly it is said, to make FH's results available to PD, so the ultimate damage she suffered could not be attributed to that breach of duty. I quote below the appellants' articulation of that argument (Orange, 28):

> '28. However, ultimately, the Centre receptionist told PD that she was not entitled to a copy of FH's pathology report. That advice was correct. By saying that she was not entitled to his results, it was made clear enough that she was not entitled to rely on the Doctors for that information any longer, if she ever had (and the better view is that she relied on FH, not the Doctors, to provide his test results to her). Thus, accepting that there was a breach of duty in respect of the content of the initial joint consultation, nonetheless – as His Honour seems to have found – the eventual damage cannot be attributed to that breach, because in the interim the Centre informed PD that she was not entitled to FH's results, and she ultimately sought and obtained for herself, directly from him, what he represented to be those results.
>
> 29. Accordingly, His Honour, while finding breach of a relevant duty owed to PD in respect of pre-test consultation and counselling, did not find that that breach was causative of damage, and would have erred had he done so. Any shortcomings in pre-test consultation and counselling accordingly cannot form the basis of liability of the Doctors to PD.'

Disposition of the Appeal

83 I consider that the trial judge was correct in concluding that Dr Harvey owed both his patients PD and FH a duty to address, in the

course of that initial joint consultation, the need for consent to disclosure, the manner of disclosure, and the possibility of discordant results. That duty sprang from the obligation the law imposes on a medical practitioner to exercise reasonable care and skill not only in treatment, but also in the provision of professional advice; *Rogers v Whitaker* (1992) 175 CLR 479 at 483. While the existence of that duty was not challenged, the manner of its performance was said to be constrained by the Act.

84 There is however no challenge to the finding that '*the plaintiff believed, and as I find, on reasonable grounds, that she would have FH's results and he would have hers*', though the topic was not raised in the joint consultation; Judgment Red, 19X at [10].

85 At [47], the trial judge concluded, '*PD was plainly of the opinion that she was entitled to FH's results. He had consented to her having them before the joint consultation*'; Red, 30.

86 The trial judge also found that while

> FH did not give his consent to Drs Harvey and Chen to disclose his result to PD, this was because the question had not arisen at the conference by reason of Dr Harvey's negligent failure to inform them of the need for their consents to disclose their results to each other and his negligent failure to raise how they propose to deal with discordant results should that occur; Red, 30 at [47].

87 The critical finding is then made at [48] that 'I am of the opinion that had the question arisen concerning what the parties intended to do with the results when they got them, both would have said the other could have access to them'. Moreover, the trial judge accepted PD's evidence that, 'if FH were not prepared to have results made available to her she would have discontinued her relationship with him'. As to reliance by PD on her doctor, the trial judge records that 'it is common ground that PD should not have received her results from the receptionist but should have received them from a medical practitioner and to have been told, in effect, that the results were not necessarily definitive because of what has been described as the "window" period of three months prior to the test being undertaken within which HIV could have been contracted but without a positive result appearing in the test'; at [14] Red, 20.

88 Those findings need to be coupled with the fact that PD and FH arranged the tests through Dr Harvey by requiring a joint consultation. This was for the clearly stated purpose of ascertaining whether either had any sexually transmitted diseases, before engaging in unprotected sex in contemplation of a new relationship. Those findings and that evidence underpin the conclusion I reach. It is that, had Dr Harvey done what he was in duty bound to do, namely, raised the question of consent to disclosure, mutual disclosure of results, and the possibility of discordant results, the parties would more likely than not have consented to their results being made available to each other by Dr Harvey at a further joint consultation. I also infer that if FH had refused, then their

relationship would have terminated. Had either occurred, I conclude that PD would not have been vulnerable to FH doing what he did, namely hiding his results and substituting forged ones with the tragic result that followed. I elaborate on my reasons below, starting with the statutory impact of s 17(2)(b) of the Act.

89 In my view, s 17(2)(b) of the Act does not preclude a proper process of pre-test counselling encompassing the need for consent, how to receive the test results and dealing with the possibility of discordant results. Care would be needed on the latter, to avoid on the one hand being unduly alarmist while on the other remaining properly candid about the possibilities. The taking of all reasonable steps to prevent disclosure does not extend to require the further unreasonable step of holding back from counselling on those three matters. PD would certainly have wanted to receive the test results for her partner and herself in the most reliable way. Dr Harvey should have been conscious of the possibility of discordant results given PD's expressed concern that FH came from Ghana. This is especially as Dr Harvey accepted there was a greater risk of sexually transmitted diseases from that area (even if he did not concede that his understanding accorded with PD's belief that there was a higher risk that a person from Ghana would be HIV positive than one from Australia). The trial judge moreover had evidence before him that led him to conclude that it was a fact '*that in circumstances where persons may be expected to go into denial, become angry etc responsible behaviour cannot be assumed and certainly not simply because the patient is well dressed and understands English.*' To require the doctor to hold back from raising such a matter because it might encourage a patient's consent in advance to a process of mutual disclosure via the medical practitioner would be to require a step that, in the statutory context, was unreasonable; that is to say, unreasonable in circumstances of an initial joint medical consultation for a couple contemplating marriage who seek that both be tested for sexually transmitted diseases preparatory to engaging in unprotected sex.

90 I conclude that s 17(2)(b) of the Act would not mandate or justify holding back these matters from pre-test counselling in the present circumstances. First, I consider that for a doctor in those circumstances to seek to bring about a situation where it is more likely that both parties' consent would be forthcoming to mutual disclosure at a further joint medical consultation does not involve any failure to take all reasonable steps to prevent disclosure. Moreover, at that time there would be as yet no test results able to be disclosed. There is nothing unreasonable in taking a lead from the couple's own expressed needs in their joint consultation and seek to facilitate a situation of mutual disclosure in the presence of their doctor. Indeed it would call for **unreasonable** steps on the part of the doctor to deny in those circumstances that important element of counselling.

91 What of the fact that at the time of first counselling, the test results are not known; does that vitiate consent to their mutual disclosure at a

further joint conference? It has been said that '*you cannot consent to a thing unless you have knowledge of it*' (per Jessell MR *M R Ex parte Ford; re Caughey* (1876) 1 Ch D 521 at 528). Neither member of the couple can be assumed to know in advance his or her future test result or that of the other. In that sense their knowledge is incomplete. But, analogous to knowing the risks of an operation but not its outcome before the operation is carried out, each of PD and FH must have known that there was a risk of the result testing positive. As the majority judgment in *Rogers v Whitaker* ((supra) at 490) pointed out, the phrase 'informed consent' is amorphous and apt to mislead, depending as it does on contrasting context; for example the consent necessary to negative trespass as against negligence. It would be absurd to construe this legislation, with its evident protective purpose, as precluding the kind of pre-test counselling that should have occurred on the basis that this was to obtain an uninformed consent in advance to such disclosure of test results. Had a further joint consultation occurred by arrangement at which the test results were mutually disclosed through their doctor's facilitation, I consider that there is nothing in this process precluding the necessary prior consent in terms of s 17(3)(a) of the Act. That consent I consider would have been forthcoming by the time of such further joint consultation had such joint consultation occurred for the purpose of mutual disclosure of the test results.

92 Indeed if reliance had to be placed solely on post-test counselling (because no consent given in advance could be an informed one), there would be a much greater constraint on counselling. That is by reason of the concern about breaching s 17(2)(b) when the test results were known. Then the doctor may well feel constrained by knowing the actual test result from giving any hint of it in breach of s 17(2)(b). The doctor would equally be unwilling to risk vitiating any consent under s 17(3)(a), by reason of it being said to result from a breach of s 17(2)(b). However, in view of the conclusion I have reached on the pre-test counselling, and the variety of circumstances that can here arise, I express no conclusion on whether that concern would be well-founded in law.

Causation

93 On causation, I do need to consider whether, if Dr Harvey had provided adequate pre-test counselling of joint disclosure taking into account the possibility of discordant results, FH

(a) would have declined to have his results or their joint results made available at a joint consultation, and
(b) instead insist that they make their results available to each other privately and if so,
(c) whether that would have led to the termination by PD of their relationship.

94 One must hypothesise this occurring in circumstances where Dr Harvey was not in breach of his duty to address in the course of con-

sultation the question of mutual disclosure of results and assume, contrary to what occurred, that he actually raised the matter. It must also be on the hypothesis that Dr Harvey himself (or Dr Chen) would not have breached his duty in having the results made available other than through himself (or Dr Chen) and in particular would not have had the results wrongly made available through the receptionist.

95 The trial judge's findings include the important finding at [49], expressed in the passive voice, that '*if FH were not prepared to have his results* ***made available to her*** *she [PD] would have discontinued her relationship with him*'. One could envisage PD's suspicion from such an insistence by FH that he would not agree to the medical results being given through their jointly consulted doctor but only through him.

96 Indeed the very purpose of the joint consultation was not merely to carry out the relevant tests. That could have been done by a simple referral to a pathologist. Rather it was to obtain advice from their doctor as to sexually transmitted diseases and in particular as to the HIV virus. At a joint consultation with their doctor their results can be shared without risk of concealment and so that their implications, if discordant, can, as they would expect, be properly explained by their doctor. They had clearly signalled, by coming as a couple, that they were seeking joint and not separate advice. I have earlier concluded that the inference properly to be drawn is that had Dr Harvey raised the matter of disclosure and the possibility of discordant results they would either have agreed to joint disclosure or, if FH refused, PD would have discontinued her relationship with him.

97 The expert evidence of Dr Carmella Law supports this. She stated that '*an HIV test should never be performed without pre-test counselling*' (Blue, 8T). While she refers to the possibility of providing one or both parties with the opportunity in a joint consultation for their sexual history to be separately recorded, that in no way detracted from her conclusion that '*the joint session would also provide an opportunity to check the couple's preferences on how they are going to obtain their results i.e. jointly or separately*' and '*how they would manage the situation if one or both of them were to turn out to be positive*'; Blue, 9R–T.

98 Moreover the subject matter of the conference should have included '*making sure the client has an appointment to return to pick up the results in person*'; Blue, 9E.

99 She refers to the need to '*discuss briefly who to tell and how to tell contacts*' again as part of the joint conference. This was to be covered in greater detail if, as here, the individual is assessed to be at higher risk of testing positive so one '*geared the pre-test counselling more towards a likely positive result*'; Blue, 9I–L.

100 Dr Law in cross-examination gave these answers:

> Q: So you cannot assume can you that simply because a couple comes in together, they will authorise the doctor to reveal their result to the other partner, can you?

A: Not usually.
Q: No?
A: But we always check, and in my experience, I don't assume when they come in together that they will have the tests shown to each other, and I say that very clearly, what I do is, I ask them specifically and I document in my notes, 'Are you happy to be in the presence of each other when you get the test results?' and most of the time when they attend together for a test they want the test together, that's the whole idea of about doing this together. T, 118.6–.21.

101 The significance of Dr Harvey's failure to explain the need for consent to access the test results and the understandable misconception on PD's part from that failure is brought out in the following passage of cross-examination of PD:

Q: When you went back to get your tests, what was your understanding as to whether you could have access to your future husband's records or not? Did you have an understanding about that? What did you think?
A: From my understanding, I thought I could just get them because we went together. I didn't know. . . .
Q: That's why you asked for them, I suppose?
A: Yes, but I didn't know the legal, you know, the legal – I'm not a lawyer, but from my understanding I thought I could get them.; T, 137.20–.30.

102 Those answers were given to the trial judge but when counsel for the doctors resumed his cross-examination, the following question and answer indicated the inadequacy of the receptionist's response:

Q: But you were left in no doubt when you went back for your records that you could not have access to his records; correct?
A: I was told that they were confidential. T, 137.32–.35.

103 This passage indicates that instead of the receptionist pointing out that whilst the results were confidential they could be made available with the consent of her partner, PD was simply given the misleading and incomplete information that she could not have access to his records because they were confidential. Had Dr Harvey raised the matter at the initial joint conference, I am satisfied on the findings and evidence that the most likely result is that he would have elicited the response that each consented to the other's results being made available at a further joint conference with Dr Harvey (or another doctor if he were unavailable). Having chosen to get joint medical advice rather than go to a pathologist direct, PD at least would hardly, **if given the choice**, have opted to receive the results from an unqualified receptionist with no knowledge of the circumstances of their original joint consultation. Had the results been conveyed to them together at a joint consultation, I consider that PD's damage would not have occurred. That would satisfy any common sense

notion of causation as well as the 'but for' test; *March v Stramare Pty Ltd* (1991) 171 CLR 506 at 516, 522, 525 and 530.

104 I agree also with the respondent's submission that the appellants cannot rely upon their subsequent breach of duty in permitting the receptionist to consult with PD for the purpose of providing her results. This is in seeking to be relieved of liability for the damage which was caused by Dr Harvey's antecedent breach of duty in failing to discuss with his patients the issue of the provision of results and then failing to have those results made available either through himself or another properly qualified medical practitioner properly informed of the earlier consultation.

105 The trial judge dealt with causation briefly. But in the course of doing so he made this observation:

> Had the obligation to PD with respect to the blood tests ended when she was given her results by the receptionist and told she could not have those of FH there may have been an argument to the effect that although there had been inadequate pre-test counselling the damage she suffered was relevantly 'caused by' the conduct of FH. But, in my opinion, the obligation to the plaintiff did not cease when she was handed her results by the receptionist and told she could not have those of FH. The obligation to look after her interests insofar as that could be lawfully done continued while she was a patient of the practice i.e. until at least the end of February 1999. Red, 43–4 at [82].

106 Beyond raising it as a possible argument, the trial judge did not accept the argument that the damage was relevantly 'caused by' FH. I prefer the reasons I have earlier stated for that conclusion, based on the appellants' failure in **pre-test** counselling and its consequences in rendering PD in trusting FH vulnerable to FH's deceit. Vulnerability is an important factor if not a prerequisite for the protection afforded by the law of negligence, as is made clear by a long line of High Court decisions, such as *Crimmins v Stevedoring Industry Finance Committee* (1999) 200 CLR 1 at 24–6, 39–41, 43 per McHugh J and 85 per Kirby J. In particular I consider that the appellants ought not escape the consequences of their negligence by reason of FH's deceit, when it was itself not unforeseeable. I do so, applying the second limit of the test of causation adopted in *Ruddock v Taylor* [2003] NSWCA 262 at [87]. The normative question to be asked is ought the defendant be held liable for the harm sustained, to which the answer remains yes.

107 It is therefore not necessary, in order for the respondent to succeed, to rely on any failure in post-test counselling. Concededly, the post-test counselling was clearly inadequate. First, each doctor failed to urge upon FH the importance of disclosing his adverse test result to his sexual partners (Red, 33N–P; 38T–39Q). Second, neither doctor ever raised with FH whether he intended informing PD of his condition (Red, 38T). Had Dr Harvey carried out all of the post-test counselling,

he would have been fully aware of PD's and FH's relationship from the earlier joint consultation. Had he properly recorded upon the treatment record card the fact of a joint consultation and that PD was about to enter a new relationship (he did neither) and had there been a system for that record in turn being automatically available to Dr Chen, he would have been aware of the circumstances concerning FH and PD's intention to marry and the purpose of the original tests. His counselling could then have taken that critical circumstance into account. It did not.

108 Making such note of the joint consultation and its purpose could in no way infringe s 17(2)(b) of the Act. Nor, consistent with the trial judge's findings (Red, 32K–M) do I consider it would have infringed any duty of confidentiality to PD or FH. There remains the question whether a multi-doctor medical centre should be excused by that circumstance from the obligation not only to make adequate records but also to ensure their availability by a cross-referencing system to whoever is the treating doctor at the time. Lack of such cross-referencing leaves patients of such a practice at risk that critical information in their files, affecting the safety of on-going treatment, would be unavailable, so creating a serious and from the patient's viewpoint unanticipated hazard. However, as I do not need to reach any concluded view regarding post-test counselling, I consider this related question is best left to be determined in a case requiring its determination.

Conclusion

109 Had Dr Harvey fulfilled his duty to address in the course of the initial joint consultation the question of mutual disclosure of results and the possibility of discordant results the probable result is that Dr Harvey would have secured the consent of FH as well as PD to receiving those results together from Dr Harvey and each would have consented to their respective results being known to the other through Dr Harvey at a further joint consultation. But in the contingency that FH refused, the finding remains that PD would have terminated her relationship with FH. In either case, PD would have escaped the injury she suffered because FH would not have been in a position to deceive her. It is unnecessary for me to consider the matters raised in the respondent's Notice of Contention.

Post-result counselling

110 The appellants deny that they owed any relevant continuing duty to PD, arising from her continuing status as a patient of the Centre, and as a person the doctors ought to have known was at risk from FH's known HIV status. It is however unnecessary to consider that question in light of the conclusion earlier reached. In particular I do not need to reach any final conclusion as to whether the statutory duty imposed by s 17(2)(b) would have precluded the doctors giving post-test counselling urging FH to disclose to PD his positive result or the likely result if they

had. Nor do I need to consider the causal effect of the other inadequacies and omissions in post-test counselling and follow-up in relation to FH, or the likely result if the Director General had been notified. This latter is on the supposition that the doctor concerned worked out from proper cross-referenced medical records that PD and FH were engaging in unprotected sex following her attending for vaccinations to go to Ghana and for a prescription for the contraceptive pill. The appellants contend that to urge or even counsel FH to disclose his HIV status to PD is inconsistent with the statutory obligation imposed by s 17(2)(b) and that in any event it was not reasonable for her to rely on the doctors to procure such disclosure. The appellants contend that the content of the duty is limited to warning the infected patient of the need to take appropriate precautions. Further, that this duty was sufficiently fulfilled by:

(a) Dr Harvey in advising FH not to have unprotected sex, though he did not raise any issue arising out of the joint consultation or ask whether he proposed to tell PD the result (Red, 51 at [18]); and
(b) Dr Chen in telling FH when he attended to collect his results that illness was sexually transmissible and could be transferred to others (Black, T, 191.11–194.17);

citing Bell J in *BT v Oei* [1999] NSWSC 1082 at [60–98].

111 It is unnecessary to consider these issues in light of my earlier conclusion that proper pre-test counselling would have resulted in a joint consultation to obtain the test results from a doctor (or if declined termination of the relationship), and that such disclosure so brought about would not have involved any breach of s 17(2)(b) of the Act or precluded the application of s 17(3)(a). Questions concerning the scope for post-result counselling and the boundary line between on the one hand taking reasonable steps to avoid disclosure and on the other providing proper advice designed to maximise the prospect of lawfully obtained consent to disclosure to a vulnerable partner, is best left to cases that require the resolution of those difficult issues.

Cross-appeal – Recovery of additional costs of child care for PD's second child conceived after PD became aware of her having become HIV positive from a second party

112 The essential facts relevant to this issue are not in dispute and are set out below:

(i) PD had a seroconversion illness in September 1999 (Red, 24U–W);
(ii) PD found out she was HIV-positive in January 2000 (Red, 24W–Z, 27D–F);
(iii) PD's first child – who was the child of FH, and was conceived before she knew she was HIV-positive and probably before she was HIV-positive – was born in February 2000 (Red, 24F);

(iv) PD and FH were divorced in May 2001 (Red, 44T);
(v) Sometime after the divorce in 2001 PD commenced a relationship with a man from Sweden, to whom she became engaged, who was also HIV-positive (Red, 44V–W);
(vi) PD, prior to such engagement, in March 2002, gave a history to Dr Sippe psychiatrist in March 2002 that she was in a relationship with an HIV positive man from Sweden; that she expected he would return to Sweden and that he '*was not ready for commitment*' (Blue, 86I–M). However, they did become engaged. The trial judge concluded that as an HIV positive man, the father would be unlikely to be given permission to reside permanently in Australia (Red, 52);
(vii) PD's treating immunologist Dr Garsie reported in January 2002 that PD was aware that she risked passing on HIV to any future offspring or sexual partner; that she '*displayed a high level capacity to understand and see the implications of the information for her*' (Blue, 60G–K);
(viii) PD's second child was born of that relationship, on 29 November 2002 (Red, 44X);
(ix) That second child was conceived voluntarily by PD in circumstances in which she knew she was HIV-positive;
(x) On the probabilities PD will become afflicted with an AIDS-defining illness in about 2014, and die in about 2016 (Red, 48P–R);
(xi) PD will be able to care for her children until 2014, but not thereafter (Red, 54B–D);
(xii) For the period from 2014, PD was held entitled to damages for loss of future earnings on the footing that she would otherwise have been in full time employment (Red, 45O–46J, 51R–52H). Similarly, she received damages for lost earnings during the 'lost years' on the same basis (Red, 52N–R).

113 There was no evidence before the trial judge that there is an increase in risk of offspring contracting HIV if **both** partners are HIV positive, that is, as distinct from just the mother.

Additional costs of child care

114 The appellants submit that the trial judge correctly declined to award damages under this head, because the cost of future child care for the second child will be the result of the voluntary, informed and unreasonable (in the context of visiting the consequences on the appellants) decision of the respondent. This, importantly, is a category of consequential **economic** loss, though stemming from the injury PD ultimately suffered of HIV-Aids.

115 The appellants further submit:

(i) while, where the compensable injury has reduced a plaintiff's ability to determine whether or not it is appropriate or responsible or reasonable for her to have children, the cost of caring for them may be recoverable; *Sullivan v Gordon* at [67]. That is not so where the plaintiff retains the ability to make that judgment. PD retained that ability, and exercised it. It could not be said that her conduct in having the second child was caused by the appellants' negligence; rather, it was caused by her own informed and deliberate decision. It is not reasonable to impose upon a defendant the cost of care of a child **voluntarily** born by the plaintiff after an injury; *Sullivan v Gordon* at [14]; *Beck v State of New South Wales* [2001] NSWSC 278.

(ii) To allow recovery in this context would be to compensate a plaintiff for the consequences of conduct which is calculated, not to mitigate, but to aggravate, her damages; and to put a defendant at the mercy of a plaintiff's decision to have more children. The implications – given the cost of attendant care, for up to 18 years – are potentially enormous.

(iii) Moreover, any such claim duplicates and overlaps the claim for lost future earnings (including the lost years), which were assessed on the basis of PD being in fulltime employment. Had PD exercised her earning capacity – for the loss of which she is to be compensated – then she would have required child care assistance, at least during the day, in any event.

(iv) Further, the claim ignores the role which the father of the child would play in providing for the care of the children.

116 At the outset one may accept two propositions as not really debatable. First, it was reasonably foreseeable that PD, even knowing of her condition, would decide to have a second child. If one views matters at the time of the original consultation, PD was 24 and had at that time no children. There was nothing to indicate that she intended to hold back from having children at some future date. By the time the second child was born it is true that some four years had elapsed but PD was still under 30. She had already successfully given birth to her first child after undergoing anti-retroviral drug therapy. This, together with having a caesarean delivery, resulted in that child being born HIV free; Red, 45 at [88]. She was able to follow the same course with her second child. There is no evidence to indicate that a father who is HIV positive adds to the risk of a child being born HIV positive from a mother with that condition.

117 So to conclude merely removes an impediment to recovery but is not sufficient of itself to enable PD to succeed.

118 Similarly with the second proposition. As the trial judge recognised, there could be no obstacle to her recovery merely by reason of the special damage being not for the cost of looking after herself but for loss of capacity to care for her second child for the six years till the child turns 18. Such an allowance is properly based on the principles underlying *Griffiths v Kerkemeyer* (1977) 139 CLR 161.

119 *Sullivan v Gordon* thus allowed special damages for the value of the lost capacity to care for the two children born after the accident. As Ipp

JA observes, in the draft judgment that I have had the advantage of reading, that was a claim for loss of **capacity** to care for others and not a financial loss claim as such. This allowance moreover was in *Sullivan v Gordon* in circumstances where it was the accident itself which rendered the plaintiff incapable. The brain damage she suffered made her not only incapable of caring for her two children born after the accident but incapable of deciding responsibly whether or not she wished to have children at all in such circumstances. Here however there is no such direct connection between the defendant's negligence and the birth of a child.

120 The permissibility of recovery for the present claim can be considered in various ways. These the appellants identify. First, whether damage flowed from the original act of negligence such that it should be recoverable. That is a question of causation involving normative issues. But it can be equally framed as a scope of duty question.

121 In that context, the question can be posed, did the scope of the doctors' duty of care comprehend the kind of consequential loss for which claim is made here. Though recovery sought is not for pure economic loss arising out of a relationship, nonetheless as Gleeson CJ expressed it in *Cattanach v Melchior* (2003) 77 ALJR 1312 at [30], liability '*has to be justified by showing that there was a duty of care to protect the claimants from that kind of harm*'.

122 Third, in damage mitigation terms, the issue becomes whether the respondent has been shown to have acted unreasonably in failing to mitigate her damage but rather aggravate it.

123 Professor Jane Stapleton explains in her article 'Cause-in-Fact and the Scope of Liability for Consequences' (2003) 119 LQR 388 that even after one has determined that the negligent conduct in question played a part in bringing about the harm in an historical sense, there is a second aspect concerning '*the "appropriate" scope of liability for the consequences of tortious conduct*' (at 411).

124 Considered as a question of causation the starting point is still the application of common sense (*March v E & M H Stramare Pty Limited* (supra). This is also the test for whether some particular damage resulted from the negligent act or (as here) omission (*Medlin v State Government Insurance Commission* (1995) 182 CLR 1). The appellants as PD's doctors in common sense terms and certainly as a matter of historical involvement, played a significant role in the respondent being faced with the choice of limiting herself to one child or placing herself in likely need of child care once incapacitated. Though it be the case that she chose the latter course, that choice was in a sense forced on her, if she were to have a further child at all. That however still leaves a second question, similar to the scope of duty analysis. That question is whether the doctors '***ought** to be held liable to pay damages for that harm*'. That is the second stage of the two stage enquiry, described by Ipp JA as one which '*may involve normative issues of a general kind . . . and whether the*

damage claimed is too remote.'; *Ruddock & Ors v Taylor* (supra) at [87]. Most recently Hayne J in *Pledge v Roads & Traffic Authority* [2004] HCA 13 speaking in the preferable terms of 'legal responsibility' (at [10]) adopted just such a two stage enquiry:

> The questions that are relevant to legal responsibility are first, whether, as a matter of history, the particular acts or omissions under consideration (here the acts or omissions which led to the presence of the foliage, and the parking bays, and the absence of warning signs) did have a role in the happening of the accident. It is necessary then to examine the role that is identified by reference to the purpose of the inquiry – the attribution of legal responsibility. . . . It is at this second level of inquiry that it may be necessary to ask whether, for some policy reason, the person responsible for that circumstance should nevertheless be held not liable [Stapleton, 'Unpacking "Causation" ', in Cane and Gardner (eds), Relating to Responsibility, (2001) 145 at 166–173].

125 The joint judgment in *Sullivan v Moody* at 415 [49] warns that in determining cases of negligence and causation by reference to what is just and reasonable or fair, principle must have primacy, but that there are also policies at work which can be identified:

> [t]he question as to what is fair, and just and reasonable, is capable of being misunderstood as an invitation to formulate policy rather than to search for principles. The concept of policy, in this context, is often ill-defined. There are policies at work in the law which can be identified and applied to novel problems, but the law of tort develops by reference to principles which must be capable of general application, not discretionary decision making in individual cases.

126 But importantly the High Court did not exclude altogether consideration of what is fair or unfair, for in the next passage (416 at [53]) there is an acknowledgment that:

> [D]evelopments in the law of negligence over the last 30 or more years reveal the difficulty of identifying unifying principles that would allow ready solution of novel problems. Nonetheless, that does not mean that novel cases are to be decided by reference **only** to some intuitive sense of what is 'fair' or 'unfair'. There are cases, and this is one, where to find a duty of care would so cut across other legal principles as to impair their proper application and thus lead to the conclusion that there is no duty of care of the kind asserted. [emphasis added]

127 Here there is no guiding principle which, without recourse as well to legal policy, suffices to answer the scope of duty question. In determining what is here the proper scope of the doctors' duty of care (or the proper scope of their liability for the consequences of its breach) one must begin with the voluntary decision by PD to have a second child, knowing that she was HIV positive. This was when she was in no way

incapacitated from making that decision by reason of the earlier negligence of the doctors, in contrast to the position in *Sullivan v Gordon*. The appellants contend that decision, and the consequences which followed, because it was the product of voluntary and informed conduct, in causation terms must amount to an interruption or termination of the causal force of the original negligence. That conduct, say the appellants, constituted a *novus actus interveniens*, involving independent and unreasonable action on the part of the respondent seeking to recover. That in scope of duty terms, broke the chain of legal responsibility eclipsing any role the doctors' negligence may have played. As I explain, I consider that approach unduly simplistic in its assumption of unreasonableness on the part of PD.

128 Similar issues arose in the well-known case of *McKew v Holland & Hannen & Cubitts (Scotland) Ltd* [1969] 3 All ER 1621. There the defendant, although responsible for initially injuring the plaintiff's leg, was held nevertheless not liable when the plaintiff subsequently fractured an ankle in trying, alone and without even the assistance of a handrail, to descend a steep staircase. Lord Reid at 1623 put the matter in these terms:

> But if the injured man acts unreasonably he cannot hold the defendant liable for injury caused by his own unreasonable conduct. His unreasonable conduct is *novus actus interveniens*. The chain of causation has been broken and what follows must be regarded as caused by his own conduct and not by the defender's fault or the disability caused by it . . . a defender is not liable for a consequence of a kind which is not foreseeable. But it does not follow that he is liable for every consequence which a reasonable man could foresee.

129 Reasonableness in the present case starts with the question whether it was reasonable for PD to have a second child in the circumstances. But that is not the end of the matter. The second question which must be answered is whether, accepting it may have been reasonable for PD to do so, is it reasonable to hold the appellant doctors liable? Was it nonetheless within the proper scope of the doctors' duty of care (or liability for consequences of its breach) for the doctors to be liable to compensate PD for the resultant child care once PD becomes incapacitated to provide it herself. The trial judge simply treats his affirmative answer to the first question as determinative. He concludes that '*conceiving and raising children is a natural incident of the human condition*'; Red, 51 at [114].

130 Beazley JA went further in *Sullivan v Gordon* (at 335): '*In any event, it is probably the case that there is a common law right to procreate*' citing *Re 'Jane'* (1988) 94 FLR 1 and Article 23(a) of the International Covenant on Civil and Political Rights. But as Ipp JA points out in his draft judgment in 1992, the High Court left open the question whether '*there exists in the common law a fundamental right to reproduce which is independent of the right to personal inviolability*'. *Secretary, Department of Health and Community Services v JWB and SMB (Marion's case)*

(1992) 175 CLR 218. More recently Gleeson CJ in *Cattanach v Melchior* (supra), though in the minority, was not contradicted by the majority in observing that '*parents have **the freedom** to choose, and therefore to limit, the size of their family*' (at [23]) [emphasis added]. We are here concerned with the converse of a parental decision to limit the size of a family. It may be expressed as exercising the freedom to choose to have a further child. For the purposes of what follows, I shall assume that such a freedom exists; it is not necessary to go further and characterise it as a right. Here, while the parents face obvious difficulties, it is clearly not a situation that warrants the conclusion that the decision was inherently irresponsible. The trial judge's finding, not challenged, leaves no room for suggesting that PD could not herself care for the child in its early years, until around the age of 12. Nor was there any submission made that the child, given the precautions taken prior to and at the birth, was at high risk of becoming HIV positive in the circumstances.

131 In *March v Stramare* Mason J considered (at 517) that the decision in *McKew* (supra) could be explained as:

> . . . a value judgment that it would be unjust to hold the defendant legally responsible for an injury which, though it could be traced back to the defendant's wrongful conduct, was the immediate result of unreasonable action on the part of the plaintiff. But in truth the decision proceeded from a conclusion that the plaintiff's injury was the consequence of his independent **and unreasonable** action. [emphasis added]

132 Was then the decision of PD to have the second child with her consequent injury (in terms of post-incapacity cost of child care) not just the consequence of her independent action, but itself unreasonable action on her part? For reasons I explain, though indubitably the result of her independent, and indeed fully informed decision, it was not an unreasonable action on her part and from her viewpoint to choose to have a second child. In those terms, there was no *novus actus interveniens* in that decision and subsequent conduct.

133 However, that still leaves the further question in assessing whether the respondent **should** recover, namely the appropriate scope of liability for the consequences of tortious conduct; in short, the scope of the duty. That question is resolved by determining whether in normative terms it would be unjust to hold the appellants legally responsible for that further decision to have a further child, reasonable though it was from PD's viewpoint to do so. That question is not answered simply by invoking the principle that a plaintiff takes a defendant as he find her; compare *Nader v Urban Transport Authority* (1985) 2 NSWLR 501.

134 PD must be taken to have known that before the child reached mature age she, PD, would be incapacitated from looking after her child. This is so whether that age be 12 as the trial judge held or earlier as PD unsuccessfully argued. While the doctor's negligence did not therefore directly lead to the decision to have the second child or remove PD's

capacity to make a reasonable decision in that behalf, nonetheless, but for the doctors' negligence, she could have had a further child without fear of incapacity and consequent need for child care. In causal terms, the link can be said to be more attenuated between the original negligence and the particular head of damage here claimed. That attenuation, while not removing the necessary causal link, is a factor in considering the proper scope of the duty.

135 The following observations of Mason P in *Sullivan v Gordon* remain pertinent:

> The birth of children is also linked to the accident, in a sense, because the appellant's brain damage impacted upon her ability to determine whether it was appropriate or responsible or sensible for her to have children (see at [67] of Beazley JA's reasons). I incline to the view that it would make no difference if this unusual link were absent, but I express no final view on the matter. An injured plaintiff's own need for personal care includes changing needs occurring throughout his or her lifetime. **Nevertheless, it may be necessary to consider whether it is always reasonable to lay at the tortfeasor's door the cost of care for children born after the injury. Pure logic is not the only matter at play in this difficult area of the law**. [emphasis added]

136 One such factor is that there is a **legal** obligation to care for children, as Mason P recognised. That may be compared to the **moral** obligation to care for an aged relative, important though that may be. A similar legal obligation applies here to PD. It cannot be said, contrary to the cross-respondent's submissions, that admitting such a claim ignores the role which the father of the child would play in providing for the care of the children. That role is likely to be a limited one, if PD remains in Australia. The trial judge found the father would be unlikely as an HIV positive person to be permitted to reside permanently in Australia, so his capacity to provide care cannot be counted upon.

137 Nor could it be said that there was a failure to mitigate her damage in the sense that the law requires, namely, that PD not act unreasonably in the circumstances, so as to bring about an increase in the damage she suffered. The burden is of course on the defendant to prove that the plaintiff's refusal to mitigate was unreasonable; Fleming *Law of Torts* (LBC, 1998) 9th ed at 286, approved by the Privy Council in *Geest plc v Lasinquot* [2003] 1 All ER 383. I have already concluded that she did not act unreasonably in exercising her choice to have a second child. It must be kept in mind that she had just turned 24 when she first consulted Dr Harvey with FH and would have had every expectation of having children. PD was a woman of childbearing years who, but for the doctor's negligence would have had every expectation of having a family with no fear of incapacity inhibiting that choice.

138 One way of posing the issue of the appropriate scope of the appellants' legal responsibility, translated into what loss should be recoverable, is to pose this question. What if PD had considered herself forced

by the risks to hold back from having a further child? She might well have done so for fear of the risk of an HIV positive child, a risk apparently not capable of being totally eliminated, though it did not come home here. This could be coupled with a prudential concern about her not being incapacitated by HIV AIDS at a later date while the second child was still dependent. Then one would be considering a claim for loss of what I still assume to be the freedom **safely** to have a further child, in a very approximate sense the converse of a defective sterilisation. (Whether it is also a **right** is not necessary to decide.) An award of damages for pain and suffering from that deprivation might then plausibly be claimed. The argument would then run that the negligent doctor should not be advantaged by PD's willingness to undertake the risks involved in exercising her right to have a further child. Therefore, it would be said, she should recover the extra cost of childcare after her anticipated incapacity. That would be the equivalent to her damage if she had been forced to hold back from having the second child by reason of the risks for the child and her incapacity to look after it once she was incapacitated.

139 One answer is that the head of damage for pain and suffering from being deprived of further children is not the equivalent of the head of damage for cost of childcare after PD's anticipated incapacity by the time the child turns 12, or the equivalent of loss of capacity to care for a child after it turns 12. Moreover there is already an overlap in the claim for lost future earnings (including the lost years) which were assessed on the basis of PD being in full time employment. Finally, while in logic the two situations may appear the converse or reciprocal of each other, this is only in a very approximate sense. It by no means follows that because it may be justified to award damages for being deprived of the capacity safely to have children, damage should also follow when the risk of having further children has been safely circumvented.

140 Ultimately this way of looking at the problem tells against PD's recovery. This is because it opens up the very considerations which in analogous cases pose such difficult issues of recovery. Though the damage is not in the fullest sense to an indeterminate class, it would in its implications open up liability for a potentially indeterminate amount as well as other questions of indeterminacy. It raises the question of just how many children should be potentially within the ambit of damage recovery, given that each later birth would involve an ever longer anticipated period of future incapacity till the child turns 18. Suppose indeed PD's precautions were to fail and she were to have a child that was HIV positive. Could she then recover a further head of damage based upon the additional care obligation for the child that this would entail? What of recovery by the child itself? It is true that this has not occurred and therefore the example is hypothetical. But it illustrates the difficulty of extending liability for the cost of care for the second child or loss of capacity to care for that child, and laying this at the door of the doctors; by what principle, consistently applied, can this be justified?

141 It is true that unlike the sterilisation cases, one can quantify the cost of child care after the age of 12, though a claim for loss of capacity to care for a child is not simply measured in that way as Ipp JA points out in his judgment. Sterilisation cases by contrast present the problem of putting '*a price on the value to the parent of the new life*' (per Hayne J at 200 in *Cattanach v Melchior*). That in the majority view was not ultimately an impediment in this country. In the United Kingdom the opposite result was reached (*McFarlane v Tayside Health Board* [2000] 2 AC 59, followed though not completely, as to the cost of a disabled child in *Rees v Darlington Memorial Hospital NHS Trust* [2003] UKHL 52). That these two ultimate courts of appeal, and by majority, reached such a contrary result, by reasoning inherently plausible, points to those competing legal concerns lying at the heart of this difficult issue as having no pre-ordained resolution; see Cane 'The Doctor, the Stork and the Court; a Modern Morality Play' in (2004) 120 LQR 23. But here the considerations to which I have earlier referred do point to a high degree of indeterminacy of liability which tells strongly against extending liability.

142 Ultimately, whether one puts the matter in neutral terms of 'legal concerns' (Jane Stapleton's preferred terminology in 'The Golden Thread at the Heart of Tort Law' (2003) 24 Australian Bar Review 135 at 136) or in the more influential sense of 'legal policy', albeit still awaiting final recognition as binding principle, I consider that the trial judge was correct in denying this further item of damage. I do so not because I consider that there is no causal link between original negligence of the doctors and later injury suffered in loss of capacity to care for a second child after it turns 12. The doctors were undoubtedly historically involved in that injury. Rather, I do so because I consider that this causal link is too attenuated and its quality altered in a normative sense by PD's independent decision to have the further child, knowing of her condition. Reasonable as it was from her viewpoint to do so, it is unreasonable to hold the doctors legally responsible for its financial consequences.

143 Another most important consideration bearing on that unreasonableness is that recovery would bring about the possibility of far-ranging if not indeterminate liability. As was said by Gleeson CJ in *Perre v Apand Pty Ltd* [1999] 198 CLR 180 at 189 ([5]):

> . . . bearing in mind the expansive application which has been given to the concept of reasonable foreseeability in relation to physical injury to person or property, a duty to avoid any reasonably foreseeable financial harm needs to be constrained by 'some intelligible limits to keep the law of negligence within the bounds of common sense and practicality'. [omitting footnotes]

144 In *Cattanach* the majority gave the greatest weight to '*the increasing judicial aversion to the enjoyment of special privilege or advantage in litigation unless strong reason for its creation or retention can be justified*' (per Callinan J at [295]. Neither *Cattanach* nor this case confer a blanket

immunity upon a category of defendant-like police in the carrying out of their duties. Rather the special advantage lies in denying '*recovery of a particular head of damages for an admitted breach of duty*' (per McHugh and Gummow JJ at [59] in *Cattanach*). But unlike *Cattanach* which was a claim for recovery of pure economic loss, we are here dealing with a claim for financial loss consequential upon personal injury to the plaintiff, a distinction drawn by Gleeson CJ in *Cattanach*.

145 In reaching this conclusion, I frankly acknowledge the part played by a concern which could now fairly be described as one of legal policy if not yet legal principle, namely that of indeterminacy. I should do so explicitly rather than mask what I am doing by mere labelling. The legitimacy of doing so is affirmed by Callinan J in *Cattanach* (at [291]). It is exemplified in the earlier quoted passage from the Chief Justice in *Perre v Apand* (supra).

146 McHugh and Gummow JJ in *Cattanach* at [58] to [82] articulate what is meant by legal policy. They contrast it with what they term a more expedient or ephemeral public policy. At [84], speaking of it, they emphasise that '*The policy of the law should be slow to fix upon something "inherently fluid"*', citing the extra-judicial writings of Lord Radcliffe for that distinction between legal and public policy.

147 Here there is nothing inherently fluid, or expedient, in recourse to longstanding community concern about indeterminate liability, reinforced by burgeoning costs of the Insurance industry. '*If the appellants are said to be subject to an indeterminate liability, that is important to the question of the existence of their duty of care*' (Gleeson CJ in *Cattanach* at [26]). That stricture is especially apposite when read with his earlier warning, applicable here, that '*the modesty of a claim as presented in a particular case might lead a court to overlook the implications, for other cases, of the acceptance of a claim of that character*' (at [20]). There are here strong considerations of legal policy which, with increasing appellate recognition and refinement tested by a sufficiency of cases, may yet acquire the binding character of principle. These, with the factor of PD's informed decision to have a second child emphasised by Speigelman CJ and Ipp JA in their judgments, point strongly against legal recovery. While therefore I believe that they produce a result rather less finely balanced than *Cattanach*, it behoves a judge drawing in part on legal policy in this relatively novel area to avoid undue dogmatism. This is more especially as indeterminacy is itself a matter of degree, though the degree here is considerable.

Overall conclusion

148 I consider that this appeal should fail as also the cross-appeal. Accordingly, I would order that the appeal be disallowed with costs and the cross-appeal likewise disallowed with costs. But I would defer the coming into effect of the latter orders for 14 days to enable the parties if they so choose to make further submissions on costs.

149 **IPP JA:** I have had the benefit of reading the reasons to be published of Santow JA. I set out below my reasons for agreeing with the orders proposed by his Honour. I turn firstly to the appeal.

The alleged breaches of the duty of care

150 The law imposes on a medical practitioner a duty to exercise reasonable care and skill in the provision of professional advice and treatment. The duty extends to the provision of information in an appropriate case: ***Rogers v Whitaker*** (1992) 175 CLR 479 at 483. Dr Harvey undoubtedly owed PD a generalised duty of care that extended to the provision of information. The extent or scope of that duty is in issue.

151 I shall deal only with three of the respects in which PD contended that the appellants breached the duty of care that they owed her, namely:

(a) The appellants failed to inform PD that FH was HIV positive.
(b) They failed to provide adequate pre-test counselling to PD and FH and failed to determine what each intended to do if one or the other was found to be HIV positive.
(c) They failed to counsel PD personally when she attended to receive her test results or arrange for a doctor to counsel her.

The relevant circumstances

152 In 1997 or early 1998 PD met FH. He was a national of Ghana who had entered Australia on a temporary visitor's visa. Their friendship developed into a close relationship and they had sexual intercourse. At that stage, they always took prophylactic measures and only protected sexual intercourse took place between them.

153 In October 1998, FH proposed marriage to PD and she accepted on condition that they first, 'together', underwent tests for sexually transmitted disease ('STD tests'). FH agreed.

154 PD had been a patient of the Alpha Medical Centre ('the Centre') since October 1997. On 16 November 1998 she, together with FH, went to the Centre. They were shown into a room where they met Dr Harvey. PD had not consulted Dr Harvey previously.

155 Dr Harvey was sitting behind a desk. PD and FH sat next to each other on a couch opposite him. They were holding hands. According to Dr Harvey, they appeared to be 'slightly embarrassed'. PD said:

> We are here to perform an HIV test, blood test and also Hepatitis and Hepatitis B, and just general STD checks.

156 Dr Harvey testified that they explained to him that they wanted to have STD tests 'because they were about to begin a new relationship, or about to engage in a new relationship'. In cross-examination, it was put to Dr Harvey that the consultation involved a couple that attended together 'with a view to eliminating the possibility of STDs'. He agreed.

157 Dr Harvey first asked PD some questions. He asked if she had ever used any intravenous drugs. She replied in the negative. He asked if she had ever engaged in anal sex and she again replied in the negative. He asked about her general health and she replied that her general health was good. He asked her whether she thought that she was at a high risk of contracting sexually transmitted diseases and she said that she had never used heavy drugs or 'anything like that'.

158 Dr Harvey then addressed the same questions to FH, including whether he had used any intravenous drugs or had engaged in anal sexual intercourse. FH answered each of these questions in the negative. He said his general health was good. Dr Harvey asked him what country he came from and he replied: 'Ghana'. Dr Harvey then asked FH 'about genital ulceration and groin nodes'. He said he did this because 'there are three STD's which are associated with people from tropical countries'. FH answered these questions in the negative.

159 Blood samples were taken for testing. PD asked Dr Harvey when the results would be available and he said 'in one to two weeks time'. Dr Harvey told them to 'come back' to get the results.

160 Within two weeks PD returned to the Centre and spoke to the receptionist. The receptionist gave her a copy of the pathology report relating to herself. PD asked for FH's pathology report but the receptionist said that that was confidential and could not be given to her. Unbeknown to PD, the Centre had received pathology tests that showed FH to be HIV positive.

161 PD told FH that she had received her test results and they were negative. He said he had received his as well and they were also negative. She was not satisfied with that and asked to see his results. He tried to fob her off but she persisted. He then showed her a false copy of his results that indicated that his tests were negative. This false report deceived PD and stilled her doubts. She married FH, became pregnant by him, and later discovered that she had contracted HIV.

162 The evidence of an expert witness, Dr Carmella Law, who gave evidence on behalf of PD, needs to be mentioned. Dr Law testified that, 'an HIV test should never be performed without pre-test counselling'. She said that the 'joint session' with PD and FH would 'provide an opportunity to check the couple's preferences on how they are going to obtain their results, i.e. jointly or separately' and how 'they would manage the situation if one or both of them were to turn out to be positive'. She said that a medical practitioner in the position of Dr Harvey should '[make] sure the client has an appointment to return to pick up the results in person'. In cross-examination she said that should a couple consult her with a view to obtaining STD tests she would ask them specifically, '[a]re you happy to be in the presence of each other when you get the test results?' She said:

> [M]ost of the time when they attend together for a test they want the test together, that's the whole idea about doing this together.

In context, the reference to 'a couple' wanting the test together meant that they wanted the test *results* together.

Tacit consent by FH to the disclosure of his test results and Dr Harvey's breach of the duty of care

163 I turn now to the question whether the duty of care owed by Dr Harvey to PD extended to telling her that FH's STD test results were positive. The answer to this question would be straightforward, but for ss 17(2) and (3) of the Public Health Act 1991 (NSW) (the 'Act'). This needs some explanation.

164 HIV infection is a 'Category 5 medical condition' under the Act (s 3(1)). Section 17(2) provides that a person who, in the course of providing a service, acquires information that another person has been infected with a Category 5 medical condition, must 'take all reasonable steps to prevent disclosure of the information to another person'. Section 17(3)(a) provides, however, that information of the kind to which s 17(2) applies may be disclosed 'with the consent of the other person'.

165 The effect of these sections is that Dr Harvey could only disclose FH's test results to PD if FH consented.

166 Section 17(3)(a) is to be contrasted with s 42J of the Act. Section 42J concerns the disclosure, in conjunction with the result of a cervical cancer test, of the identifying particulars of any woman who underwent such a test. Section 42J(1)(b) provides that a person may disclose such information only 'with the written consent of the woman'. In contrast with s 17(3)(a), s 42J(1)(b) requires the consent to be in writing.

167 Another section in the Act, of less significance in the present context, but nevertheless relevant, is s 61L(1). This section provides:

> Proceedings for an offence against this Division . . . are not to be commenced without the consent in writing of the Director-General or a person authorised by the Director-General in writing for the purposes of this section.

168 The point to be made is that the Act distinguishes between consents that are required to be in writing and consents that require no formality. The consent required under s 17(3)(a) falls into the category requiring no formality; nothing in the Act precludes a consent in terms of s 17(3)(a) from being given tacitly.

169 Cripps AJ, in dealing with the issue of consent, said:

> An issue has been raised whether I should conclude that in fact FH, by reason of the joint consultation and the way it was conducted, gave his consent for his results to be passed to PD. However, the matter was not discussed at the joint consultation. Neither FH nor PD raised with the doctor, or he with them, whether they consented to information relating to one being available to the other . . .

Accordingly I find that FH did not give his consent to Drs Harvey and Chen to disclose his result to PD.

170 With respect to his Honour, the reasons given do not address the point. The mere fact that the issue of consent did not expressly arise at the consultation says nothing about whether consent was tacitly given.

171 Due significance must be accorded to the fact that PD and FH saw Dr Harvey together, and asked him, together, to be tested for HIV. One must ask: what was the purpose in the two of them going to see Dr Harvey *together* about being tested for HIV? The answer given by Dr Law springs immediately to mind: most of the time, when a couple attend together on a medical practitioner for the purposes of obtaining STD tests, they want to get the results together, 'that's the whole idea [of] doing this together'.

172 This inference was supported by other circumstances. Dr Harvey acknowledged that at November 1998 he knew that there was an elevated risk of HIV in people from Ghana as compared to the Australian population. PD knew that HIV was a serious problem in Africa and that was one of the reasons for her insistence on the STD tests before she would agree to unprotected sex. She had made this clear to FH. The prevalence of HIV in Africa appears to have been well-known. Thus, all three persons at the consultation knew that there were more pressing reasons than the normal in this country for PD to be assured that FH had a clean bill of health before agreeing to their 'new' relationship. This increased the significance of the joint nature of the consultation.

173 The conduct of PD and FH throughout the consultation showed that each regarded the need to discover whether either of them had contracted STDs, generally, and HIV, in particular, as being of the utmost importance to both of them. This was not surprising since they had made it plain to Dr Harvey that they were about to engage in or begin a new relationship, which would involve sexual intercourse, such that each would be vulnerable to infection if the other was already infected.

174 Dr Harvey had no difficulty in asking each, in the presence of the other, a series of questions that concerned potentially life-threatening issues of the utmost sensitivity, intimacy and privacy. The answers to these questions would ordinarily have been confidential to the highest degree. I have mentioned the questions that concerned risks in lifestyle, drug use, anal sex, and groin lesions. Dr Harvey did not feel the need to ask whether either of PD or FH would mind being asked these questions in the presence of each other. He must have understood from the conduct of PD and FH that each consented. This understanding must have been confirmed when each answered these questions readily and candidly.

175 The willingness of PD and FH, despite being embarrassed by the occasion, to disclose information in the presence of each other about these matters was obviously due to a strong desire to learn whether it

would be safe for them to engage in the new relationship contemplated. This knowledge was crucial to the health of each and could become a matter of life or death. The same considerations applied to the STD results. The inference is that PD and FH were equally willing for there to be mutual disclosure of these results.

176 Accordingly, in my view, PD and FH each tacitly consented to the disclosure by Dr Harvey of the results of the STD tests to the other.

177 Further, in my view, all these circumstances lead to the conclusion that Dr Harvey (and Dr Chen who was vicariously liable for Dr Harvey's conduct) breached his duty of care by failing to disclose to PD that FH was HIV positive.

178 I would uphold the Notice of Contention.

179 In any event, if FH did not tacitly consent to Dr Harvey disclosing his test results to PD, then the duty of care owed by Dr Harvey must have extended to requiring him to inform PD and FH, at the consultation of 16 November 1998, of the effect of ss 17(2) and 17(3) of the Act, and to ascertain their wishes as to the disclosure of the test results.

180 Cripps AJ found that:

> If FH were not prepared to have his results made available to her she [PD] would have discontinued her relationship with him.

Santow JA concludes that had Dr Harvey, at the initial consultation, addressed the question of mutual disclosure of results and the possibility of discordant results, Dr Harvey would have secured the consent of FH to his results being disclosed to PD. Were FH to have refused, PD would have terminated her relationship with FH. Santow JA observes:

> In either case, PD would have escaped the injury she suffered because FH would not have been in a position to deceive her.

I agree with his Honour.

The causation issues: the two-limbed test

181 It was argued on behalf of Dr Harvey and Dr Chen that there were two 'supervening causes' that prevented their negligence from being a legal cause of PD's loss.

182 The first was the fact that the Centre's receptionist told PD that she was not entitled to a copy of FH's pathology report. Despite being informed that she could not have access to FH's STD results, PD decided, of her own accord, without any input from the appellants, to have unprotected sex with FH. This 'independent' decision, it was said, broke the chain of causation.

183 The second was FH's deception of PD. It was said that this deception was a matter for which the appellants bore no responsibility and this too broke the chain of causation.

184 Both these arguments raise the issue of the test to be applied when

some independent act of a third party or a decision by the plaintiff materially contributes to the loss sustained.

185 *March v E & M H Stramare Pty Limited* (1991) 171 CLR 506, *Medlin v State Government Insurance Commission* (1995) 182 CLR 1 and *Henville v Walker* (2001) 206 CLR 459 indicate that terminology such as '*novus actus interveniens*' and 'breaking the chain of causation' is no longer appropriate in determining the effect that the act of an independent third party, or the plaintiff herself, might have on whether responsibility for the plaintiff's loss is to be attributed to the defendant.

186 Very often, issues of legal causation may be resolved simply by the application of the 'but for' test. This is usually where the issue of causation is a simple one. But, in some circumstances, the 'but for' test is inappropriate.

187 In more complex cases of causation, a two-limbed test is to be applied. The first limb entails the question whether the defendant's conduct is historically involved in the plaintiff's loss. The second limb requires the question to be asked: *ought* the defendant be held liable for the harm sustained: *Ruddock v Taylor* [2003] NSWCA 262 at [87]. The second question involves a normative weighing of all the relevant circumstances.

188 Thus, there is no single issue that is determinative. Once historical involvement is established, the chain of *factual* causation cannot be broken. Factual causation, however, does not alone establish legal causation. There is no such factor as a *novus actus interveniens* that is determinative of legal causation, although considerable significance will usually be attributed to a single cause that materially contributes to the loss after the defendant's tortious conduct has taken place. The question remains, however, one to be determined by having regard to all the circumstances and then making a value judgment.

189 In *Tambree v Travel Compensation Fund* [2004] NSWCA 24 Sheller JA (with whom Mason P and I agreed) undertook a careful examination of *March v Stramare, Medlin v State Government Insurance Commission* (1995) 182 CLR 1 and *Henville v Walker* and applied the two-limbed test.

190 This approach has most recently been reiterated by Hayne J in *Pledge v Roads and Traffic Authority* [2004] HCA 13, where his Honour said (at [10]):

> The questions that are relevant to legal responsibility are first, whether, as a matter of history, the particular acts or omissions under consideration (here the acts or omissions which led to the presence of the foliage, and the parking bays, and the absence of warning signs) *did* have a role in the happening of the accident. It is necessary then to examine the role that is identified by reference to the purpose of the inquiry – the attribution of legal responsibility. . . . It is at this second level of inquiry that it may be necessary to ask whether, for some policy reason, the person responsible for that

circumstance should nevertheless be held not liable [Stapleton, 'Unpacking 'Causation', in Cane and Gardner (eds), *Relating to Responsibility*, (2001) 145 at 166–173].

191 In my view, the two-limbed test should be applied in this case.

Application of the two-limbed test

192 The negligent conduct of Dr Harvey was undoubtedly an historical cause of PD's loss. In regard to both of the appellants' arguments, it is the second limb that is contentious.

193 Cripps AJ noted that it was common ground that PD should not have received her results from the receptionist but should have received them from a medical practitioner. It is not entirely clear to me whether this means that the appellants conceded that Dr Harvey was negligent in failing to counsel PD personally when she attended to receive her test results or to arrange for a doctor to counsel her. In any event, however, I consider that Dr Harvey was indeed negligent in this respect.

194 I doubt that accepted medical practice has descended to the level where receptionists customarily are allowed to disclose potentially life-threatening information to patients in a mechanical, routine and unfeeling way. Whatever the position may be in this regard, in the particular circumstances of this case, Dr Harvey was duty bound to inform PD, personally, of the STD results. He breached this duty.

195 The receptionist's reply to PD was likely to have caused PD to believe that it was hopeless to try to obtain FH's STD results from Dr Harvey. She was then compelled to rely on the integrity of FH. Thus, the breach of duty on the part of Dr Harvey, in failing to speak to PD personally when she came to find out what her own, and FH's, test results were, or to arrange for another doctor to see her, made her vulnerable to FH's fraud.

196 FH's deception of PD falls into the same category. Dr Harvey's breach of duty in failing to provide the appropriate information to PD enabled FH to deceive PD into believing that his test results were negative. Dr Harvey's conduct was an essential springboard for FH's fraud.

197 In these circumstances, I consider that it would be quite wrong to allow the appellants to rely on Dr Harvey's breaches of duty so as to defeat causation.

198 I would therefore dismiss the appellants' appeal.

The cross-appeal

199 I turn now to the cross appeal. The grounds of the cross appeal are as follows:

(1) His Honour erred in failing to award damages based on *Griffiths v Kerkemeyer* (1977) 139 CLR 161 and *Sullivan v Gordon*

(1999) 47 NSWLR 319 in relation to the plaintiff's second child.

(2) His Honour erred in finding that 'a link must be established' before damages in the nature of *Sullivan v Gordon* could be awarded.

(3) His Honour erred in finding that a link was 'wholly absent' in the birth of the plaintiff's second child.

200 Before addressing the issues raised by these grounds, there are, I think, some comments that need to be made.

Not a claim for cost of child-care

201 Firstly, the head of damage, the subject of the cross appeal, is a claim for the loss of capacity to care for others. This head of damages is related to damages for gratuitous care awarded under the principle in *Griffiths v Kerkemeyer* (1977) 139 CLR 161: see *Sullivan v Gordon* (1999) 47 NSWLR 319; *CSR Limited v Thompson* [2003] NSWCA 329. This means that the loss being compensated for is loss of *capacity* rather than financial loss as such.

202 Therefore, this claim is not a claim for costs of child-care and should not be described as such.

The measure of a *Sullivan v Gordon* loss

203 In claims for *Griffiths v Kerkemeyer* damages, the generally accepted rule is that the damages under this head are measured by the market cost of providing the services: *Van Gervan v Fenton* (1992) 175 CLR 327.

204 In straightforward *Griffiths v Kerkemeyer* claims, the market cost of services is an obvious measure of the plaintiff's need for them. But the same is not necessarily the case in regard to *Sullivan v Gordon* damages for loss of capacity to care for others. This is particularly so when, at the time the loss is incurred (ordinarily, at the date of the tort) the plaintiff was not in fact caring for anyone else and had no need to do so.

205 Take the notional example of a plaintiff who, prior to the tort, has a full-time income-earning occupation and who employs a full-time carer to look after her child. The loss of her capacity to care for her child would not then be measured by the actual cost of caring for the child. In those circumstances that cost would merely be an expense to be met out of the damages awarded for the plaintiff's loss of earning capacity. In the case of a married plaintiff whose spouse is the full-time carer of their children, loss of capacity to care for the children is unlikely to be sustained. Where such a plaintiff spends only part of his or her time caring for the children, the loss of capacity would have to be measured by reference to that part alone. Similar considerations apply to a plaintiff who, prior to the loss of capacity, works part-time and employs a professional carer to look after the children.

206 It would not be correct, therefore, to assume that the measure of damages for loss of capacity to care for others is inevitably the entire cost of caring for the child. For reasons that I later express, this becomes a relevant factor when considering the normative causation question that arises in the cross-appeal.

Not mitigation of damages

207 During the course of argument and, indeed, at trial, there was some suggestion that PD's decision to have a second child constituted a failure to mitigate her damages. That, however, is an erroneous approach to the question.

208 I have observed that Dr Harvey's tortious conduct, as a matter of historical involvement, materially contributed to PD's capacity to care for her second child. Her decision to have a second child can have no bearing on that fact. It is merely a matter to be taken into account in addressing the second limb of the two-limbed test for causation. The question is whether, as a matter of normative judgment, PD's decision precludes a finding that, in law, the appellants' tortious conduct was a cause of her loss of capacity. The issue is one of causation, not mitigation of damage.

The 'right to procreate' and the 'freedom to procreate'

209 In his reasons Santow JA observes that the proposition that a common law right to procreate exists was mentioned, obiter, by Beazley JA (with whom Speigelman CJ, Powell JA and Stein JA agreed) in *Sullivan v Gordon* at 335. Her Honour said:

> [I]t is probably the case that there is a common law right to procreate: see **Re 'Jane'** (1988) 94 FLR 1; see also art 23(a) of the *International Covenant on Civil and Political Rights*.

210 In *Sullivan v Gordon* the Court made no reference to *Secretary, Department of Health and Community Services v JWB and SMB (Marion's Case)* (1992) 175 CLR 218. In that case Mason CJ, Dawson, Toohey and Gaudron JJ referred to *Re 'Jane'* and said (at 254) that they would leave open the question whether 'there exists in the common law a fundamental right to reproduce which is independent of the right to personal inviolability'. Their Honours observed (also at 254):

> It is debatable whether the former [a common law right to reproduce] is a useful concept, when couched in terms of a basic right, and how fundamental such a right can be said to be . . . For example, there cannot be said to be an absolute right in a man to reproduce (except where a woman consents to bear a child), unless it can be contended that the right to bodily integrity yields to the former right, and that cannot be so. That is to say, if there is an absolute right to reproduce, is there a duty to bear children? But if

> the so-called right to reproduce comprises a right not to be prevented from being biologically capable of reproducing, that is a right to bodily integrity. The same applies, though in a different way, to a woman's 'right to reproduce'. Again, if the right is, in fact, a right to do with one's person what one chooses, it is saying no more than that there is a right to bodily and personal integrity. Furthermore, it is quite impossible to spell out all the implications which may flow from saying that there is a right to reproduce, expressed in absolute terms and independent from a right to personal inviolability.

211 Many virtually insoluble questions relate to the recognition of a common law right to procreate or reproduce. One may ask: when does that right accrue? Could it be said to accrue on puberty? In this country the vast majority of parents of a girl of that age would, I think, be appalled at the suggestion that such a right might then accrue. If it arises later, how is the age of accrual to be ascertained? Another difficult question is: what relevance to this notional right has the woman's ability to support the child financially – or even emotionally? Does a woman have that right even if she is not equipped to be an appropriate mother to the child? Does a woman who has abandoned or abused a child in the past forfeit that right for the future? Would the right apply indefinitely, no matter how many children to whom the woman gives birth? The average number of children in two-parent households in Australia is 1.9, and 1.6 for one parent households: *Family Characteristics Australia*, Australian Bureau of Statistics, 1998. Some women have ten children or more, do women have an absolute right to reproduce to this extent and more? For my part, I do not accept such a proposition.

212 *Marion's case* and the difficulties to which I have adverted demonstrate, in my view, that it is quite unhelpful to speak of a common law right to procreate in the present context.

213 In his reasons Santow JA assumes that parents have 'the freedom to choose to have a further child'. I accept that PD was 'free' to have a second child. That 'freedom', in my view, does not determine whether the appellants should be held liable for PD's loss of capacity to care for that child.

The capacity of a plaintiff to decide whether to have children

214 In *Sullivan v Gordon* the tortious conduct of the defendant led to the plaintiff sustaining frontal lobe damage. Beazley JA said in this regard (at 334):

> [T]he appellant's brain damage reduced her ability to determine whether it was appropriate or responsible or reasonable for her to have children, either at all or in the circumstances in which she conceived and bore these children. The appellant's conduct in having children, even if it could be objectively viewed as unreasonable,

was caused by the respondent's negligence and consequently there was no break in the chain of causation.

215 Mason P commented at 324:

> The birth of children is also linked to the accident, in a sense, because the appellant's brain damage impacted upon her ability to determine whether it was appropriate or responsible or sensible for her to have children . . . I incline to the view that it would make no difference if this unusual link were absent, but I express no final view on the matter. An injured plaintiff's own need for personal care includes changing needs occurring throughout his or her lifetime. Nevertheless, it may be necessary to consider whether it is always reasonable to lay at the tortfeasor's door the cost of care for children born after the injury. Pure logic is not the only matter at play in this difficult area of the law.

216 Some point of distinction was sought to be drawn between *Sullivan v Gordon* and the present case on the ground that, unlike the plaintiff in *Sullivan v Gordon*, the negligence of the appellants did not cause any injury to PD's cognitive capacity.

217 In my view, there is a relevant distinction, but it has to be understood in context.

218 It is first necessary to reiterate that we are dealing here, again, with a causation issue that requires the application of the two-limbed test – this time to grounds two and three of the cross-appeal.

219 The second ground of the cross appeal is that the judge erred in finding that 'a link must be established' before damages in the nature of *Sullivan v Gordon* could be awarded. That 'link', in the context of his Honour's reasons, meant a link between the negligence of the appellants and the decision to have a second child.

220 Cripps AJ held that, according to *Sullivan v Gordon*, such a link must be proved before damages for loss of capacity to care for a child can be established. That, however, is not my reading of the judgment of Beazley JA in that case. Her Honour certainly emphasised the importance of the brain damage that the defendant in that case had caused. But this was in the context of determining whether there had been a 'break in the chain of causation'. Thus, in the circumstances of that case, the brain damage was a highly significant consideration. But the inability to make an informed decision whether or not to have children is not an essential condition to the right to recover *Sullivan v Gordon* damages (see in this regard the comments of Mason P referred to above).

221 Again, the two-limbed test for causation illuminates the position.

222 It is a trite proposition that there must be a causal link between the tortious conduct and the damages incurred (whether in the nature of *Sullivan v Gordon* damages or otherwise). To this extent, the judge was plainly correct in finding that 'a link must be established' before *Sullivan v Gordon* damages could be awarded. But the link needed is not a link

between the negligence of the appellants and the decision to have a second child. Instead, it is a link establishing legal causation.

223 The third ground of the cross appeal is that the judge erred in finding that the link between the tortious conduct and the decision to have the child was 'wholly absent'. As a matter of fact, his Honour cannot be faulted in this finding. But, as I have stated, that does not conclude the causation issue. While there is no doubt that there was an historical involvement between the negligence of the appellants and the *Sullivan v Gordon* loss suffered by PD, a live question remains in regard to the second limb of the two-limbed test. That is, the normative question whether, having regard to all the circumstances and, in particular, PD's fully informed decision to have a second child, has causation recognised by the law been established?

224 In answering this normative question, the capacity of PD to make an informed decision plays a considerable, but not necessarily conclusive, part.

The normative question: the second limb of the two-limbed test

225 This question requires several factors to be weighed in the balance.

226 PD's second child was conceived when she already had one child, and when she knew that she was infected with HIV, that her capacity to look after children was reduced, that the father of the second child was also infected with HIV and that he was unlikely to be allowed to stay in Australia permanently.

227 PD's fully informed decision to have a second child has considerable causal potency, but there are other factors, also of a normative kind, that, in my view, must also be taken into account.

228 Cripps AJ said that the circumstances relating to PD's relationship with the father of her second child were 'not really explored during the proceedings'. It is not entirely clear whether the father has made or will make any contribution to the costs of looking after the child, but that seems less than likely. There is no suggestion in the evidence that I have been able to find to the effect that such a contribution has been or might be made. The claim seems to have been put on the basis that the entire expense is recoverable from the appellants. The evidence given by PD on this issue was to the effect that her salary was the only source of income that she could use for the child.

229 It may be said that the reservoir of men from whom PD was able to choose a life partner or a sexual partner has been limited by the appellants' negligence. However, the evidence does not establish that it was so limited as to compel her to acquire, as such a partner, an overseas resident – precluded from gaining permanent entry into Australia – and who does not contribute to the expense of bringing up his own child.

230 I reiterate that the claim is for loss of capacity, and in assessing such loss account is taken of the need of the plaintiff to care for the child. In

the ordinary course, the father will contribute to the cost of bringing up the child (and will be required, by law, to do so). In that event, the father's contribution will reduce the mother's need.

231 Accordingly, in my view, the appellants could not be held liable for loss of capacity measured by reference to the entire cost of bringing up the child. Fairness requires those costs to be excluded which, in the ordinary course, would have been borne by whoever might have been the father of the child (but which in fact will not be so borne – because of PD's deliberate decision to have a child by a man who lacks the ability to contribute to the child's welfare).

232 The question is whether the appellants should be held liable for a lesser amount.

233 I would add that, in this particular case, the child faces a more difficult future by reason of the fact that, as is the case with his mother, his father has a reduced expectation of life and, moreover, is likely – throughout his lifetime – to be absent from the family home for long periods. In my view, the law should not provide an incentive to children being born in such circumstances.

234 The social and moral questions that arise in this case become particularly pointed when one asks: assume that another defendant (in a similar position to the appellants) is faced with a claim for *Sullivan v Gordon* damages where the plaintiff has given birth to two, or three, or four children for whom she cannot properly care because of loss of capacity on her part. How then is the loss of capacity to be measured? The mind baulks at the prospect of the cost of raising all such children being taken into account. As Santow JA asks:

> [J]ust how many children should be potentially within the ambit of damage recovery, given that each later birth would involve an ever longer anticipated period of future incapacity till the child turns 18.

235 In this context, Santow JA asks another telling rhetorical question:

> Suppose indeed PD's precautions were to fail and she were to have a child that was HIV positive. Could she then recover a further head of damage based upon the additional care obligation for the child that this would entail?

In my view, the law should not provide any encouragement to deliberate decisions to have children in circumstances where those children could at birth be infected with HIV.

236 These factors, in my view, collectively compel the normative question to be answered in favour of the appellants. I would dismiss the cross-appeal.

(c) Does the standard of care owed depend on whether the patient is being treated by a city doctor or a country doctor?

In a large country like Australia, where quite a few people live in outback or rural areas, the above question gives pause for thought. The issue was addressed by Simpson J in *Geissman v O'Keefe*.

Geissman v O'Keefe and Another, unreported, Supreme Court of New South Wales, 25 November 1994

Simpson J:
In Professor Nade's report, he refers twice to the standard of care expected of a 'Rural General Practitioner'. It is unclear whether Professor Nade intends to suggest that the standard of care expected of a rural general practitioner is different from, whether greater or lesser than, that demanded of an urban general practitioner, or if this is merely verbiage. I reject any suggestion that there is a different standard of care required to be afforded to residents of rural New South Wales as distinct from those of the city.

II BREACH OF THE DUTY

There are a number of ways in which a health care practitioner could fall below the standard expected of an 'ordinary skilled man exercising or professing to have a special skill'. For the moment, focus will be on those areas which Jones has identified as being specific examples of negligence, supplemented by some categories suggested by recent cases.

(i) Failure to take a medical history

It is obvious that, in order properly to diagnose or treat a patient, a full medical history must be taken of that patient. If a doctor does not take such a history, and injury results to the patient, the doctor will be liable in negligence.

Chin Keow v Government of Malaysia and Another [1967] 1 WLR 813

Viscount Dilhorne, Lord Hodson, Lord Guest, Lord Upjohn, Wooding J:
On the morning of 7 April 1960, Madam Chu Wai Lian, an amah employed in the social hygiene clinic at Sultain Street, Kuala Lumpur, spoke to the staff nurse about an ulcer on her right ankle and swollen glands in her thigh. The nurse ... took her to the respondent, Dr Devadson, who was then medical officer in charge of the clinic. After he had examined her, she was given an injection of procaine penicillin, from which she died within an hour ...

It was not in dispute that before prescribing or authorising the injection to be given Dr Devadson did not enquire into the deceased's medical history. On the contrary, he frankly admitted this himself ...

Dr Tan, a witness for the appellant, stated that when penicillin is

> indicated he would take a careful history. He described what his interrogation would be – an interrogation which he said would not exceed five minutes – and added that all his staff had been trained to ask those questions . . . And Devadson himself admitted that he knew of the possibility of a person developing hypersensitivity to penicillin after having had penicillin before, that he had been told by the nurse that the deceased had had a penicillin injection some years previously, that in such cases there was remote possibility of danger and that, knowing this, he nevertheless carried on because he had had no mishaps before . . . It is plain that Dr Devadson failed in his duty to make appropriate enquiry before causing the penicillin injection to be given which, it was admitted on the pleadings, was the cause of death of the deceased. Had any enquiry been made, he would undoubtedly have been made aware that in 1958, three years after the giving of the injection of which the nurse made mention, the deceased had been given another from which she suffered adverse reactions which led to an endorsement on her outpatient card of the warning 'Allergic to penicillin'. In such circumstances, the fatal injection should never have been given.

It should be noted that the duty to take a medical history is an ongoing duty. That is to say, it is part of a health care practitioner's duty to enquire as to progress of medical treatment. A health care practitioner who fails to listen to a patient complaining of complications may be liable in negligence. This aspect of a health care practitioner's duty was canvassed in the South Australian decision reproduced below.

Giurelli v Girgis (1980) 24 SASR 264

> The plaintiff consulted the defendant (a surgeon) concerning a broken leg. A plate was placed in the leg. The plaintiff was subsequently referred to a physiotherapist. The patient made complaints of severe pain in the leg and commented on its inability to bear any weight. The plaintiff had been a 'difficult' patient, constantly complaining, so the defendant dismissed the patient's view concerning his own leg. When the steel plate was removed, the leg gave way. Another surgeon had to perform an operation on the plaintiff. The plaintiff alleged negligence against the defendant.
>
> **White J:**
>
> > Dr Girgis was either ignoring stronger complaints actually made to him or not understanding them or not allowing sufficient time for the plaintiff to make the comments he was prepared to make about pain or not asking sufficient questions on the topic. In other words, he was not listening to his patient and not prepared to listen to his patient. The lack of probing questions and listening was partly due to the short time allowed for each visit. And the discounting of the significance of any complaints of pain coming to his ears was probably due to Dr Girgis' predisposition to disbelieve the plaintiff in

any event. There was a reason for the latter. On 1 October 1971, Dr Girgis had noted that the plaintiff was a terrible patient. This judgment was based largely upon what he learned from others about the patient's behaviour in hospital. As I said, the plaintiff did not take kindly to hospital. At a time when he may have been delirious, he complained that the windows were dirty. He gave the staff a difficult time with his rowdiness, even getting out of bed; but later he settled down under mild sedatives. He did not like the hospital food and wanted to go home early. Later he apologised to Dr Girgis for his behaviour, some of which he could not remember because it was probably due to genuine pain coupled with some delirium. It was not a sufficient basis for ignoring all of his subsequent complaints of serious pain as attributable almost entirely to a low pain threshold common to people of his nationality or personality. It is probable (and I find) that Dr Girgis learned from Mr Brooks [the physiotherapist], and in a more fragmented way from his own brief consultations with the plaintiff, that the plaintiff was not walking on his injured leg at all in any relevant sense and that he was in fact complaining loudly of pain between mid-October and mid-November 1971, and again between mid-November and early December 1971, whenever required to do so. The explanation, in any relevant sense, was the same – Dr Girgis had made an adverse assessment of the plaintiff as being unreliable in relation to complaints of pain. The plaintiff's description of his symptoms was probably somewhat coloured.

Be that as it may, the task of sifting the grain of truth from the chaff of overstatement should have been undertaken. If he had done so, it is probable that Dr Girgis would have been successful in discovering that the genuine pain suffered by the plaintiff was indicative of far less union than he assumed. After all, the experience of pain on weight bearing was one of the main indicators, indeed the prime indicator, of non-union or slow union of the tibia and of the state of union from time to time. To some extent, the plaintiff has himself to blame for finally (in March 1972) being in the position of the boy who cried 'wolf'. Nevertheless, I do not think it was reasonable for Dr Girgis to discount so much his complaints of pain. The difficulty created by the plaintiff's personality simply called for the exercise of a little greater care and time to sort out real pain from 'imaginary' pain. As it happened, time spent with the plaintiff could be rewarding. The more the plaintiff was pressed during the course of the trial, the more apparent it became that the events which he was describing really happened, even though at times they sounded improbable or exaggerated or even bizarre. Beneath a strangeness of expression arising from his volatility and slight language difficulty, lay a substantial substratum of fact capable of ascertainment with relative ease . . .

Dr Girgis was in the habit of allowing short periods of time – only five to 10 minutes – for consultations. He was heavily pressed by great numbers of patients to be seen. However, pressure of time did not justify the risks of not listening and enquiring. Dr Girgis was also in the habit of relying heavily upon paramedical staff (such as his own sister, the nurses and sisters at the hospital, the bush nursing sister, and the physiotherapist, Mr Brooks). He saw Mr Brooks regularly on ward rounds, at least once a week and more often at times. He must have referred dozens of patients to Mr Brooks during the three months (October, November and December 1971) and they would have had dozens of concurrent patients to discuss at any one time. For example, Dr Girgis would have referred an average of two cases of broken legs each week to Mr Brooks, quite apart from any other patients requiring physiotherapy. If there was a breakdown of communications between them owing to their established procedures or a lack of 'feedback' from Mr Brooks, once again the patient should not suffer as a result. If the patient was thought to be difficult and unreliable, Dr Girgis could have sought out Mr Brooks and made specific inquiry from him about the patient's progress or lack of it. Instead, he relied upon Mr Brooks to come to him and to tell him if there was anything 'unusual'. His evidence was that he could not remember Mr Brooks telling him of the pain and slowness in weight bearing progress. I find it incredible that this 'terrible' patient was not discussed often, even weekly, between Mr Brooks and Dr Girgis. I find on the balance of probabilities that Mr Brooks did pass on to Dr Girgis from time to time the substance of his experience with the plaintiff during the months of October and November 1971 . . .

Dr Girgis was pressed for time with many urgent cases; he saw a hundred or more persons a year with similar leg fractures; and with increasing experience, it took him far less time to examine patients than it did when he was less experienced. Whatever the validity of those factors might be, this was not a routine consultation. An important decision (to remove the plate) was to be made at the end of a difficult case and in the face of complicating factors. The truth of the matter was that something had fairly recently happened causing a dramatic increase in pain and a bowing of the tibia and the breaking and a loosening of the two screws. This consultation was the most significant instance of Dr Girgis not listening sufficiently to his patient. I find that he did not learn from the plaintiff that he had been on light work, that he had been helped by his workmates, that he had sat on a specially made trolley most of the day, or that for most of the time at work, he had been suffering pain on weight bearing . . .

The only doubt that can be raised about the liability of Dr Girgis in negligence in this case is whether his failure to listen to this patient could be said to fall within the category of excusable error, having regard to the patient's tendency to be difficult and to exaggerate his

> complaints of pain by overreacting thereto. Whilst this tendency complicated the task of Dr Girgis to some extent, I find that it was not a gross tendency, and that in the circumstances it was within the competence of a specialist orthopaedic surgeon exercising ordinary competence to discover the truth about the degree of pain experienced by this patient on full weight bearing from time to time. Further, Dr Girgis did have information from Mr Brooks which supported the plaintiff's experience. In addition, Dr Girgis failed to elicit any relevant history before deciding to remove the plate. Taking all of these factors together, and bearing in mind the degree of skill required of a specialist orthopaedic surgeon, I find that Dr Girgis was negligent in the treatment of the plaintiff's fractured tibia, most of the negligence occurring in mid-March 1972.

The standard of care required of Dr Girgis as a specialist is stated by Nathan in *Medical Negligence* thus (p 22):

> A medical man who holds himself out as being a specialist in a particular field, whether it is in the treatment of certain conditions or in the use of certain apparatus or in any other way, will necessarily be judged by higher standards than the ordinary practitioner who does not profess any such specialised skill. But here again the specialist will be required to attain not to the very highest degree of skill and competence but to the ordinary level obtaining amongst those who specialise in the same subject.

Judgment was entered for the plaintiff.

In *Locher and Another v Turner*, unreported, Supreme Court of Queensland, 22 December 1994, Demack J awarded a plaintiff whose life expectancy was then 12 months, damages for medical negligence. The plaintiff had complained to her general practitioner of rectal bleeding. Demack J held that the general practitioner should have listened to the complaint of the patient and ordered further tests, which would have earlier diagnosed the plaintiff's cancer and may have allowed more successful treatment of the cancer.

(ii) Causing an injury to a patient while that patient is undergoing surgery

The most telling example of negligence is that of an anaesthetist who caused an explosion, burning his patient.

***Paton and Another v Parker* [1941] 65 CLR 187**

> The plaintiff was admitted to hospital for an operation. She sustained burns in the operating theatre when a bottle of ether being used as anaesthetic was spilt, and the exposed wires of electric radiator used to heat the room ignited the spirit vapour. She sued on the basis of negligence.

Williams J:

> There is no evidence as to who switched the radiator on or as to how long it had been switched on at the time of the accident . . . There was some evidence from which the jury could infer that the surgeon and anaesthetist had been there for about half an hour. They had both taken part on several occasions in previous operations in the theatre. The radiator was the sole means of heating the theatre . . . Ether is very inflammable and explosive. Approximately speaking, as low a mixture as 1.35% of ether will explode if mixed with 98% of air. There was evidence that it would be hazardous to drop ether on to a mask in the manner already mentioned if there was a heated metal coil six feet away from the operating table, and that if the bottle was broken 'nothing could save a fire'. In a public hospital the surgeon has to accept the services of the anaesthetist on duty and of the staff provided by the hospital. There is a legal duty on the hospital authorities to exercise reasonable care to provide a suitable theatre and equipment, including the warming apparatus, and to select as members of the staff persons who are competent either as surgeons, anaesthetists or nurses. It was the duty of Dr Kirkland to carry out a difficult surgical operation on a woman in a low state of health, and of Dr Paton to administer the necessary quantity of ether to render and keep her in an unconscious state before and during the operation and to safeguard her against the risks inherent in the inhalation of an anaesthetic by a patient in such a condition. These tasks were successfully performed. Both doctors were entitled to assume, in the absence of notice to the contrary, that the theatre was in a suitable condition to enable them to carry out their work, that the anaesthetic in the bottle was ether, that the instruments, gowns, sheets, robes, etc were properly sterilised; and, generally, that the preparations were such that all they would have to do would be to concentrate upon the performance of their respective parts of the operation. It follows, therefore, that they could only be liable for the accident if there was evidence from which the jury could reasonably infer that they knew or ought to have known that the radiator was of the type that contained an open heating element, that it was dangerous to use ether while such a radiator was switched on, and that the theatre sister had failed in her duty to switch it off.
>
> I agree that the evidence that both doctors had been in a small theatre for half an hour before the accident, that they both knew the theatre well, that the operation was being performed in the winter, and that the theatre would have to be heated to protect the patient, would be sufficient, in the absence of any explanation, to enable the jury to draw the inference that they both knew or ought to have known the means for warming the theatre was a radiator of the type already described and that it was switched on. Moreover, there is evidence that it was Dr Kirkland's duty to know that it was hazardous for Dr Paton to drop the ether on to the gauze out of a small

bottle under such conditions. But even if it was his duty to have this knowledge, there is no evidence that the patient's hand was burnt because of his failure to guard against this danger, the effective cause of the accident being the breaking of the bottle when it fell on to the floor. In my opinion, therefore, the learned trial judge was right when he granted the non-suits to Dr Kirkland, so that the appeal should succeed in his case.

It remains to consider the position of Dr Paton. The bottle of ether was in his charge. There is no explanation of how it came to be knocked off his table on to the floor. As there is evidence from which the jury could infer he knew the type of radiator, and that it was switched on, it was his duty to know that there was a danger of explosion if the small percentage of ether already mentioned became mixed with the air. Even if he was entitled to believe that he could drop the ether on to the mask without danger with the radiator on, he ought to have known, if the plaintiffs' evidence is correct, that, if the glass bottle dropped on to the floor and broke, an outbreak of fire was practically certain. If, therefore, he knew the radiator was switched on, he had a duty to take reasonable precautions to see that the patient was safe against explosion and fire, not only in respect of the ether dropped on the gauze but also in the event of the bottle falling on the floor. The action in respect of Dr Paton was remitted for retrial.

[Starke J delivered a judgment which was similar to Williams J. McTiernan J dissented.]

(iii) Errors in treatment

A variation on the theme of causing damage to a patient while that patient is undergoing surgery is the case of the health care practitioner who, faced with one injury and cause of illness, exacerbates the illness of his or her patient by adding a cause of illness. This may occur because of a failure to ensure adequate sterilisation, the choice of the wrong drug treatment, premature discharge of a patient from hospital, or the failure to spot the warning signs of infection. Many of these issues have been addressed in a New South Wales case.

***Geissman v O'Keefe and Another*, unreported, Supreme Court of NSW, 25 November 1994**

Simpson J, No 15758 of 1991:
The plaintiff brings this claim against the defendants, each of whom is a medical practitioner, alleging that each was negligent in the treatment he administered to her in relation to a foot injury in and following August 1986. The first defendant, Dr O'Keefe, practises as an orthopaedic surgeon, the second, Dr Spencer, as a general practitioner.

The plaintiff was born on 7 July 1952 and is now 42 years of age. In August 1986, when the treatment commenced, she was 34 years of age.

She lived in Wellington, NSW, with her husband and three children, on a country property of which her husband was manager, and where she was employed in a part-time capacity as a gardener.

The medical treatment given to the plaintiff by the defendants commenced on 22 August 1986 when she fell in a Wellington street and twisted her left ankle. She attended the surgery of the second defendant, who examined her, and advised her to take some aspirin and bandage her foot. All of this she did. So far as the evidence discloses, there then followed a rather long gap in her treatment. She seems to have next sought treatment during a visit to Mount Tamborine, in November, where she consulted the local doctor, who arranged x-rays, gave her aspirin and diagnosed a torn ligament in the ankle with a 'spur'. His (*sic*) doctor recommended that on her return to Wellington, the plaintiff again consult the second defendant, and in and about December 1986, she did so, taking her Mount Tamborine x-rays with her. The second defendant referred her to an orthopaedic surgeon, a Dr Stratton, whom she saw on 29 December 1986 for assessment of the spur. He applied a plaster cast to the ankle, and this remained on until 11 February 1987 when it was removed by the first defendant to whom the plaintiff was referred by Dr Stratton. This was the plaintiff's first consultation with the first defendant on her own behalf, although she had previously consulted him with and on behalf of her son. The plaintiff described the condition of her foot on the removal of the plaster as 'filthy', and, asked what it smelt like, she replied, graphically, 'It stunk.'

She said:

> It looked dirty and the dirt was there and there was flaky skin and dirt and it felt clammy, sweaty, it was stinking hot, it had been the whole time I had it on, really long hairs, leg was really hairy, it was skinny . . . it was clammy, sweaty, it was dirty.

She said her foot was stiff and when the first defendant injected an anaesthetic into it, it bled. Having injected some local anaesthetic into the foot, the first defendant then injected cortisone.

The plaintiff next saw the first defendant on 25 February 1987 when arrangements were made for her admission to Bathurst Hospital for removal of the spur. During the period between 11 February and her admission to hospital the foot became progressively more painful. It was swollen, and was warmer than the right foot.

On 5 March 1987, a Friday, it was proposed that the plaintiff undergo surgery to be performed by the first defendant and although she was admitted to the Bathurst Hospital on 4 March, and prepared and anaesthetised, for this purpose, she was subsequently told by the first defendant that he had found a strange pus in her foot, and that he had not proceeded to the removal of the spur because removal may have caused infection in the bone. The first defendant then discharged the plaintiff from the hospital, with a prescription for antibiotics, and her foot bandaged. During the weekend the pain in the foot increased, and on the Monday morning she made an appointment to see the second defendant. He told her that the antibiotics she had been given by the first defendant were sufficient, as they were large doses, and 'everything should be fine'. He prescribed painkillers. She returned home, her foot 'still very painful and throbbing and hot'. Its condition deteriorated; by the Wednesday when she saw the second defendant again, it was 'really bad', 'hurting and throbbing' and she had removed the bandage. The second defendant said, 'Yes it's hot, red and angry looking' and admitted her to the local Wellington Hospital. The second defendant accompanied her there, gave her a painkilling injection, a drip and prescribed antibiotics. She remained an in-patient in the Wellington Hospital for nearly three weeks. About a week after her admission another practitioner again opened the foot, and a tube was inserted into the wound, which was flushed out daily with a solution.

She was discharged on 30 March and she said, of the condition of her foot, that:

> It was really no better than what it was when I went in. In fact it was a bit worse.

On 31 March she was feeling 'really sick . . . and in a lot of pain,' and was still taking painkillers. She was having 'terrible muscle spasms' and had to move the foot by lifting it in her hands, because it hurt too much to move it normally.

She consulted the first defendant again on 1 April still feeling 'really sick and in a lot of pain'; he arranged for her admission to the Orange Base Hospital for the purpose of a bone scan. The following day the first defendant told her he feared the foot and ankle were infected, and that he may have to operate, and he identified the infection as osteomyelitis. She remained a patient in the Orange Base Hospital for two weeks, during which time there was some improvement in the foot. For a month or two months after her discharge on 13 April she walked with the assistance of crutches and thereafter a walking stick, which she still uses on occasions. She continues to take painkillers on a regular basis. In July 1987, she returned to Queensland and saw her former general practitioner who referred her to Professor Sikorski on 8 July 1987. Professor Sikorski admitted her to Greenslopes Repatriation Hospital where she was given intensive physiotherapy over a two-week period, resulting in sufficient improvement to permit her to walk without the aid of walking sticks.

The plaintiff suffers considerable restriction in the movement of her foot and her gait has been affected. After prolonged walking she suffers intense pain and throbbing, her foot is painful to lift from the ground and there are occasions when she cannot put weight upon it, and most days, by early afternoon, it is swollen. She is unable now to engage in her chosen occupation in plant nurseries or gardens in the Mount Tamborine area where she has returned to live.

Her present condition has been described by the various medical practitioners in a variety of ways. In August 1987, Dr Sikorski considered that she had three separate problems, all making the situation worse, which he described as:

> The initial problem is almost certainly the injury with a severe mid-foot sprain with or without a sub luxation. Subsequently, the injection and possibly the surgery caused the infection in the hindfoot. Both of these caused weakness and immobility of the foot and she now suffers from the effects of prolonged and excessive immobilisation. She probably has an element of Sudeck's atrophy.

There is, of course, no issue that each defendant was under a duty to the plaintiff to exercise reasonable care and skill in their provision of medical services to her. The only questions are what that duty demanded of each from time to time during the course of the plaintiff s treatment and whether, on the facts as I have recounted them, either defendant failed to discharge that duty. The standard of reasonable care and skill required is that of the ordinary skilled person exercising and professing to have the special skill of the particular defendant, ie a general practitioner and an orthopaedic surgeon: *Rogers v Whitaker* (1992) 175 CLR 479.

This is not one of those cases in which the court is faced with deciding whether or not appropriate information or warnings were given to the plaintiff. It is a case purely about whether the treatment afforded to the plaintiff, at various times over a period of months by the defendants separately at any one of a number of points in that course of treatment, fell short of the standard demanded of the practitioner concerned.

In this respect, the test is no different to cases of negligence generally and is as stated by the High Court in *Wyong Shire Council v Shirt* (1980) 146 CLR 40: see *Darley v Shale*, unreported, 23 October 1992 *per* Wood J and *Crisp v Keng*, unreported, 2 December 1992 *per* Wood J.

It is now clear that the standard is not determined solely or even primarily by reference to the views of medical practitioners (*Rogers v Whitaker*, above) even though those views, and more particularly, the rationale upon which those views are founded, is of enormous assistance in reaching the ultimate conclusion.

The case against the first defendant

The allegations of negligence made against the first defendant can be summarised as follows:

(i) 11 February: At the time of the initial injections, he 'failed to adopt correct procedures to clean and disinfect the foot after the removal of the plaster and before administering the injection'.

(ii) 5 March: At the time of the first operation when the proposed removal of the spur was abandoned the first defendant 'negligently closed the wound without properly draining it, and/or without making any, or any proper provision for draining it'.

(iii) 6 March: The first defendant discharged the plaintiff from hospital:

(a) 'inappropriately early and without adequate care and attention';
(b) 'without making proper provision for the administration of the high doses of antibiotics which were necessary in all the circumstances';
(c) '. . . into the care of the second defendant knowing that (he) was not, or failing to ensure that (he) was adequately qualified to carry out the treatment required with the proper level of skill'.

It is necessary now to consider each allegation of negligence made against the first defendant. Taken chronologically, the first concerns the cleaning procedure he adopted prior to giving the plaintiff the initial injection on 11 February. Some practitioners considered this to be inadequate or inappropriate to the point of constituting a failure to give adequate care . . .

It is generally agreed, and it is the first defendant's own view, that it was at this point that the infection which is the cause of her present problems, entered the plaintiff's skin . . . If it be shown, therefore, that there was some want of care at this point in the first defendant's treatment of the plaintiff, it is a want of care that has had very significant, indeed devastating, consequences for the plaintiff.

Strong diversity of opinion emerges as to whether or not this skin preparation was adequate in the circumstances. [Her Honour then considered the range of views expressed by expert witnesses.]

On this evidence I am not prepared to find that there was any deficiency in the skin preparation such as would constitute a breach of the first defendant's duty to the plaintiff.

Chronologically, the second way in which negligence by the first defendant is alleged relates to the surgery he performed on 5 March 1987 at Bathurst District Hospital. It will be recalled that, at the commencement of this surgery, his intention was to remove the plaintiff's spur. He reported to the second defendant in the following terms:

> I went to remove Mrs Geissman's spur today and found a localised collection of pus. I am not exactly sure why it is there but it is probably the result of one of the . . . steroid injections. I have sent you a copy of culture results and I would be grateful if you would check them and see that she is on an appropriate antibiotic and remove her sutures in one week's time. If the wound becomes very red and angry I would recommend you just remove the sutures and leave it open to granulate and I'd like to review her when I see her son in about a month's time.

The first defendant's operation notes, contained in the hospital file and confirmed by him in evidence, showed that he undertook the operation, applied a tourniquet, found an abscess which he drained, ordered that the fluid or pus so drained be sent for pathology, closed the wound with a nylon suture, and ordered the application of a crepe bandage. He also left some instructions for post-operative care which included the plaintiff's discharge on the following Friday (6 March) with a prescription for a week's supply of antibiotics. These instructions were written on Thursday, 5 March following the operation. The first defendant was in the habit of attending Bathurst Hospital on Mondays and Thursdays each week, but not Fridays but on this occasion, as it happened, he did in fact attend at the hospital on Friday, 6 March and saw the plaintiff. At that time he described to the plaintiff what he had found as 'a strange-looking pus' . . .

The first defendant acknowledged that he realised then that there was potential for the fluid to be infected. But the tissues appeared to be quite normal and healthy, and this fact had a bearing on his doubts about whether the fluid was in fact pus or something else. When the plaintiff was discharged at 6.30 pm on 6 March her temperature was normal. Prior to her discharge the first defendant had been aware of, and unhappy about, the fact that the plaintiff was walking and he requested that crutches be provided to her. He prescribed an antibiotic by the trade name Keflex, which is a broad-spectrum antibiotic. It is, said the first defendant, very useful for potential bone infection.

The criticisms that were made of the first defendant in this respect were twofold. They concern what is said to have been a failure by the first defendant to drain the wound, and the discharge of the plaintiff at too early a stage of care . . .

Associated with negligence with respect to the drainage of the wound and the plaintiff's discharge on 6 March was the claim that the first defendant, in discharging the plaintiff, did so without making proper provision for the administration of necessary high doses of antibiotics, and to the care of the second defendant:

> . . . knowing that the second defendant was not, or failing to ensure that the second defendant was, adequately qualified to carry out the treatment required with the proper level of skill.

The second branch of this allegation, ie with respect to the qualification or capacity of the second defendant, was not really pursued and I put it to one side. The complaint about the antibiotics was not a complaint that the first defendant had failed to prescribe antibiotics for the plaintiff, which, as has been seen, he did . . . The nub of the attack was that the plaintiff was then suffering from some infection which was at that time unidentified. It is now clear, as it was not then, that the infection was pseudomonas aeruginosa – a relatively uncommon infection. The unfortunate aspect of its later learned identity is that it is an infection which is not only not amenable to the effects of Keflex, but is in fact resistant to that drug. In other words, as later acquired information made clear, the plaintiff was being treated with quite the wrong drug. It was therefore the plaintiff's contention that she should have been retained in the hospital until the infection was identified, or, very much as an alternative, she should have been given a more stringent antibiotic regime on her discharge.

The process of analysis of the substance taken from the wound is one which takes, normally, several days – according to the first defendant, he would expect to wait about three days for results. This means, of course, that the plaintiff was discharged from hospital without specific identification of what she was suffering from. What the first defendant had, in effect, done, was to discharge the plaintiff to the care of the second defendant, her general practitioner. In doing so, he dictated a letter to the second defendant, immediately after the operation on the Thursday, but he was unable to say whether that letter had been sent on the Friday or the following Monday. In the letter, the first defendant gave the instructions or advices to the second defendant that have been set out above. Because of uncertainty about when the second defendant would receive the letter, the first defendant spoke to the second defendant by telephone.

The question then is whether the first defendant's decision to discharge the plaintiff in the absence of a complete picture of what was ailing her fell short of the standard demanded.

The first defendant himself said that, notwithstanding his recommendation to the second defendant, he did not expect the wound to become red and angry, and he never believed that *pseudomonas* was the causative organism. I think it is an inference clearly open on the evidence that thought of that organism never entered the first defendant's head until after the receipt of the culture results. That he did not then think of *pseudomonas* at that time is, on the evidence, neither surprising nor negligent.

Despite the apparent segmentation in the statement of claim in the way in which negligence is alleged in respect of the proposed abandoned surgery on 5 March, I think it is most appropriately looked at as a composite course of treatment. Looked at in that way, I am satisfied that the plaintiff has established a failure on the part of the first defendant to exercise reasonable care. By 5 March, it was apparent that the first defendant was dealing with the unknown, so far as the plaintiff's condition was concerned. Her response to what could have been expected to be a routine sprain had been out of the ordinary, and the pus, found by the first defendant at surgery, was of an unfamiliar description, and could not be identified for some days.

Whether it was going to accumulate further in the days following the operation was not known. The first defendant did know that the plaintiff had had a cortisone injection and he was, of course, aware of its potential for infection, although, it must be recognised, it could have been expected that signs of such infection would manifest themselves rather sooner than by 5 March. Nevertheless, discharging the plaintiff on a Friday afternoon in these circumstances, even with fairly explicit advice to the second defendant was, in my opinion, insufficient to satisfy the duty of care which rested on the first defendant.

In the circumstances, therefore, I find that the plaintiff has established her case against the first defendant.

The case against the second defendant

The complaints that are made of the treatment given by the second defendant to the plaintiff concern the consultation on 9 March (the Monday following her discharge from hospital by the first defendant), and the discharge from Bindawalla on 30 March and the alleged cessation of antibiotic treatment at that time. The allegations of negligence are as follows:

(i) 9 March:

- (a) The second defendant failed to obtain or follow consultant's advice as to appropriate treatment on that day;
- (b) He failed to order antibiotics on that day, or to remove the sutures and drain the wound;
- (c) His eventual removal of the sutures, on 12 March, occurred too late.

(ii) 30 March:

- (a) The second defendant ceased antibiotic therapy; and
- (b) Discharged the plaintiff from hospital and at an inappropriately early stage.

In the course of cross-examination, the plaintiff asserted that, on 9 March, when she saw the second defendant, he did not examine her foot. She supported this by saying that the bandage was not removed until she herself removed it on the Wednesday morning. This gave rise to one of the few factual disputes in the case. The second defendant was unable to say with certainty that he had looked at the wound, but he deduced from the fact that, on that day he had written 'abscess' in his notes, that he had done so, his practice being not to make such a notation unless he had conducted an examination. I consider it more likely that the plaintiff is correct in her recollection. The second defendant did not attempt to assert that he had any specific recollection of such an examination, but frankly acknowledged that he was basing his conclusion on reconstruction in the light of his usual practice . . .

The second branch of Dr Mann's (an expert witness) attack on this period of the second defendant's care of the plaintiff arises from the failure to remove the sutures until 12 March. This, in Dr Mann's view, constituted a failure to follow the first defendant's directions to remove the sutures earlier than 12 March should 'the wound become very red and angry'. The sutures were indeed not removed until 12 March, meaning that they remained for the week nominated by the first defendant unless conditions dictated otherwise. Whether the failure to remove the sutures constitutes a disregard of the first defendant's directions depends upon whether the condition adverted to by the first defendant in fact arose, ie whether the wound became very red and angry. It is here that whether or not the second defendant may have examined the plaintiff's foot on Monday, 9 March acquires some significance. If he did not do so, then, of course, he had no way of knowing whether the wound was red and angry, and whether, in accordance with the first defendant's stipulation, he should accelerate the removal of the stitches. The letter from the first defendant clearly signalled the possibility of that event occurring and, in my opinion, put the second defendant on notice of that very possibility. If he failed to make the necessary observations, he deprived himself of the opportunity of complying with the fairly explicit instructions or advice given to him by the first defendant. The second defendant did not do so, I think, because, as he said, on that date he considered the plaintiff s foot was following a fairly normal course and gave him no cause for alarm. Had he done so, and had he found the wound inflamed, he no doubt would have admitted the plaintiff to hospital two days earlier than he did, and removed the stitches then and there.

Can I infer, then, that on the Monday the wound was 'red and angry'? Because the bandage remained on, there is no direct evidence . . .

The second defendant said that warmth is a sign of inflammation whether or not infection were present, and as has already been noted, the plaintiff described the foot as being hot. From all of this I would conclude that on Monday, 9 March the plaintiff's foot fitted the description which, on the first defendant's letter to the second defendant, should have alerted the second defendant to the need for removal of the sutures. Of course, the second defendant did not receive that letter until, at the earliest, 11 March, but for the very reason of the delay which would necessarily occur in its receipt, the first defendant had telephoned the second defendant to convey to him the contents of the letter. Accordingly, I consider it was incumbent upon the second defendant, when the plaintiff complained on Monday, 9 March, to conduct a proper examination to determine the condition of the wound.

I consider his failure to do so constitutes a breach of his duty to her.

Dr Mann's criticism continued, directed to the failure on the part of the second defendant to institute drainage of the wound on the Wednesday (11 March), when he said: 'The signs demonstrated such surgical intervention as a matter of urgency.'

That intervention ultimately occurred on 20 March with the second defendant acting as anaesthetist. It is equally unclear why the second defendant chose not to drain the wound until 20 March . . .

[When Professor Nade, an expert witness, was asked about the course of conduct he said:]

That is understandable after an operation. He is a general

> practitioner, the patient is being treated by a specialist orthopaedic surgeon, I think it is not unreasonable for him to accept what the orthopaedic surgeon has done. When he next saw the plaintiff on the Wednesday he said, 'It appears to me this is worse, I'll admit you to hospital and treat you in a more aggressive way.' I think that is a perfectly reasonable approach to take.
>
> Professor Nade's view, expressed in the second sentence of this paragraph, appears to me to overlook the very contingency alluded to by the first defendant, that is the possibility of a complication the nature of which was spelled out by the first defendant, occurring. I do not think it is legitimate in the light of the first defendant's express warning to the second defendant for the second defendant simply to 'accept what the orthopaedic surgeon has done'.
>
> As with the treatment given to the plaintiff by the first defendant, I consider that that provided by the second defendant must be looked at as a composite. In doing so, I consider that the treatment fell short of what is demanded of a general practitioner. The failure to examine the foot on 9 March prevented the second defendant taking the step of removing the sutures, admitting the plaintiff to hospital and undertaking the necessary treatment. I therefore consider that the second defendant also failed in his duty to the plaintiff.

Other quite stunning examples of negligence through errors in treatment include the administration of an excessive amount of a drug following the misreading of dosage instructions (*Strangeways-Lesmere v Clayton* [1936] 2 KB 11) or administering an excessive amount of anaesthetic, apparently through inexperience (*Jones v Manchester Corporation* [1952] 2 All ER 125).

In *Geissman's* case, Simpson J makes reference to the unreported decision of Wood J in *Darley v Shale*. That case is important not only for the reason identified by Simpson J (that the test of negligence in treatment or diagnosis is the same test as applied to other types of negligent behaviour) but also for the fact that the case demonstrates that not all injury resulting to patients is actionable in negligence.

Darley v Shale involved an action commenced by a patient who suffered a perforated bowel while undergoing a laparoscopy. She alleged that her gynaecologist had been negligent in performing a laparoscopy on her and that he should have, instead, performed a laparotomy on her. Wood J, in *Darley's* case, noted that the complication experienced by Mrs Darley was rare but not unknown and that 'a competent gynaecologist' would have known of the risk. In deciding to take that risk by performing a laparoscopy on his patient, Wood J held that the gynaecologist was not negligent. This was because the gynaecologist had balanced the risks of a laparotomy as opposed to a laparoscopy and was correct in opting to perform the procedure thought to be less risky and of a more minor nature.

In assessing whether there has been an error in treatment sufficient to constitute negligence, Courts have taken into account any underlying conditions of the patient, which might be made worse, should sufficient care not be taken. In this way, the law of medical negligence is broadly reflective of the general law of negligence as expressed in *Paris v Stepney Borough Council* [1951] AC 367.

This principle is seen most clearly in the case of *Markaboui v Western Sydney Area Health Service.*

Fouady Markaboui v Western Sydney Area Health Service t/as Westmead Hospital [2005] NSWSC 649 Hall J

Liability

1 The plaintiff commenced proceedings in the District Court by Ordinary Statement of Claim filed on 4 July 2001 against the defendant with respect to medical treatment administered at Westmead Hospital between 8 October 1999 and 7 November 1999. . . .

Factual background

6 The plaintiff arrived at the Emergency Department of Westmead Hospital at 10.26 am and was assessed by a Dr Brady, a junior medical officer.

7 The emergency department clinical records for 8 October 1999 record that her heart rate was 92 beats per minute but that her blood pressure measurements on the arms could not be taken due to her injuries and pain, she not being able to tolerate placement of a cuff for that purpose. The x-rays revealed the following fractures:

- a minimally displaced spiral fracture of the head and neck of the left humerus;
- a fracture through the olecranon process of the right humerus with some displacement;
- a fracture of the medial condyle of the right femur.

8 The clinical records indicated that the plaintiff was to have a splint applied to the right knee, a slab placed on the right elbow and her left arm placed in a sling before being transferred to the ward.

9 The plaintiff was medicated with oral analgesics (Panadeine Forte) and Endone and was administered, at least from 9 October 1999, with morphine for her pain.

10 The plaintiff alleges that she was negligently treated in the relevant period on the following bases:

- excessive administration of opiate analgesics;
- failure to provide adequate hydration;
- failure to recognise and treat blood loss;
- failure to respond to persistent tachycardia;
- failure to perform necessary investigations;
- failure to diagnose and treat pneumonitis.

11 The analysis in this judgment of the medical evidence has specific

regard to the history of the plaintiff's medical treatment insofar as particular matters are directly or indirectly relevant to each and all of the bases relied upon in support of the claim in negligence.

Chronological analysis

12 The following data have been extracted from Exhibit H, volume one of the medical records of Westmead Hospital relating to the plaintiff's admission:

9 October 1999

0010 IDC inserted. Morphine 10 mg given for pain . . .
0100 . . . unable to attend BP due to deformity of limbs/pain and pts reluctancy . . . IDC attended . . . draining clear urine
0445 . . . Morphine 10 mg given 0200 hours . . . circ obs unchanged, all limbs cool . . . good sensation . . . draining clear urine
1320 . . . Drinking well . . . IDC in situ – draining well. IDC in situ draining well. Panadeine Forte and Endone given for pain as per regular chart. Morphine 10 mg . . . given for pain at @ 0830 hours
1840 Given morphine 10 mg at 1635. Also given regular Panadeine Forte . . . at 1800

10 October 1999

0620 . . . IDC in situ draining small amount overnight . . . lower limbs v cool . . . sensation present. Reg meds given as charted
1315 c/o pain morphine 10 mg given at 1040 – IDC in situ – draining well – tolerating with fluid well . . . regular Panadeine Forte . . . given at 1200
1940 . . . obs satisfactory as charted. Remains tachycardia – 140 bpm . . . refused to eat dinner . . . only had small amount of H20. IDC patent and draining. Given morphine 10 mg at 1930 hours . . . regular Panadeine Forte and Endone given as charted

11 October 1999

0455 Regular analgesia given as charged. Condition stable and unchanged. IDC patent and draining
1110 S/B Dr. Cummine – comfortable . . . will need to stay in for analgesia/nursing care
1420 Pts obs as per chart . . . tolerated fluid well. IDC draining well . . . Pt voiced a lot of pain. R.N. informed medication given as per chart
1445 Morphine 10 mg given @ 1140 hours . . . resting comfortably since analgesia given (also continued on Panadeine Forte 6/24). IDC draining well 600 mls at 1330 hours
2220 Condition satisfactory . . . IDC patent and draining . . . given . . . morphine 10 mg . . . with good effect

12 October 1999

0530 Pt appeared to sleep well. Regular Panadeine Forte . . . IDC draining
Medical registrar present. Pt weak/lethargic . . . speech slurred. Very weak and lethargic. Difficulty breathing.

1150 . . . breathless for 3/7, worse today. Noted by nursing staff to be drowsy today and slurred speech. Meds include Panadeine Forte . . . Endone 10 . . . Morphine 10 mg . . . O/E drowsy xx . . . pupils small, not pinpoint . . . HR 120 reg . . . creps R laterally. Problems – Drowsiness . . . narcotics . . . ECG – sinus tachy. Consider trial Narcan – bloods done – x-ray done – ABC 1 done

1225 Patients observations satisfactory . . . patient complained of being weak and drowsy . . . s/b Dr. Chin . . . pain team consulted re pain control? overnarcotisation – well r/v today

1300 Problems at present – lethargy/drowsiness/weakness up . . . c/o abdominal and back pain . . . urine output 20 mls/hr . . . Clinically . . . pr 140 . . . systolic 110 lethargic but orientated . . . Needs (items 1–11)

1530 Physiotherapy

1600 Nuclear Medicine and Ultrasound. Provisional report only . . . there are bilateral perfusion defects. The patient was unable to ventilate for the scan

1800 CT radiology

1950 Pt returned to ward 1930 hours following . . . scan + CT. Pt orientated but drowsy. Pt given H2O to drink today . . . drowsy Physiotherapy

2245 Drowsy but oriented
Needs: IV access in am? central line – multiple attempt today have failed . . . push oral fluid intake (has been drinking ++). Withhold Endone if not in pain, try paracetamol

13 Dr. Raftos' opinion essentially was that there had been breaches of the hospital's duty of care, including in particular:

(a) a failure to treat for expectant blood loss consequent upon the fractures sustained in the accident giving rise to hypovolaemia;
(b) over-medication with opiate and analgesic medications inducing drowsiness and the development of inhalation pneumonitis.

14 The report of Dr. Raftos dated 30 May 2001 (being part of Exhibit E) provides the analysis in support of those two propositions. I observe here (and will return to them later) that the report omits reference to recorded data in the hospital notes pertaining to:

(a) *urinary output* – data potentially relevant to the issue of the adequacy of the plaintiff's hydration during her hospitalisation. Dr Raftos' opinion on the hydration issue was reached without reference to data consistent with urinary output being 'normal'. He acknowledged in cross-examination that urinary output can, along with factors such as heart rate, blood pressure and peripheral perfusion provide an indication of the level of hydration.

(b) *blood pressure* – Dr Raftos acknowledged that blood pressure readings taken were not hypotensive (ie., low) readings and could be regarded as normal, even if on the low side of normal on some occasions. Dr Raftos, however, relied upon the fact that young people can maintain their blood pressure in the face of a substantial volume loss over an extended period of time, but they will certainly become unwell.

(c) *blood pressure recordings* – these were taken between 9 and 13 October 1999. This is contrary to Dr. Raftos' statement on page six of his report, 'no blood pressure measurements were performed until 13 October 1999'.

15 Mr. Davies, SC, for the hospital, relied upon all of those matters in cross-examination and final submissions. They were said to evidence error in Dr Raftos' opinion and approach in analysing the issues subjacent to the matters relevant to liability. They were also said by the hospital to refute the presence of signs indicative of significant blood loss and of excessive analgesic medication.

16 I note, again at this stage in passing, that normal blood pressure readings are relevant to a further issue raised by Dr Raftos as to 'shock' which he postulated the plaintiff suffered from from the time of her admission on 8 October 1999. (He stated in cross-examination that 'shock' is blood pressure less than 100. He agreed that on the basis of normal blood pressure readings taken on 9, 10, 11 and 12 October, that had a reading been taken on 8 October it probably would also have been normal).

Blood loss

17 Dr. Raftos conceded that the plaintiff's only symptom consistent with the blood loss which he had postulated resulted from the fractures was a high heart rate. He also conceded that both pain and anxiety can cause an elevated heart rate.

18 The hospital relied upon the evidence of Dr Michael Burns, a consultant physician, who has specialised for many years in the field of thoracic medicine. Dr Burns' report dated 27 June 2003 contained a review of the plaintiff's treatment when she was in hospital from 8 October until discharge on 2 November 1999.

19 Both Dr Raftos and Dr Burns agreed that the record did reveal the presence of tachycardia but differed upon its significance. Dr Raftos said tachycardia was a clinical sign of blood loss. Dr Burns was of the view that the record revealed only intermittent, not continuous, tachycardia and therefore discounted it as an indicator of significant blood loss. Dr Raftos observed that on admission the plaintiff's heart beat was recorded as 92 beats per minute, whereas by the early hours of 9 October it had increased to 118 beats per minute which was tachycardia and

indicated he said at that time that the plaintiff was in *hypovolaemia shock*. On the date of her admission to intensive care, her heart beat was 140 to 160 bpm.

20 Whilst the clinical records did indicate an elevated heart rate, it was put to Dr Raftos that this could be explained by other factors such as pain and anxiety. However, he stated that whilst these could cause an elevation in heart rate, it would be unlikely to be beyond a reading of 100. It was put to him in cross-examination:

> *Q: So is it your evidence that the only explanation for the heart rate that she demonstrated from 8 to 12 October was the fact that she had suffered this blood loss?*
>
> *A: Well, given that – combined with the inhalation pneumonitis and the other illnesses, as I said yesterday . . .*

21 Before reviewing Dr. Burns' evidence on specific issues, the essential propositions which he propounded may be summarised as follows:

- The plaintiff did not suffer significant blood loss, a conclusion said to be supported by haemoglobin levels, particularly the reading taken of 121 on 12 October 1999 and the blood pressure readings said to be normal between 9 and 12 October 1999.
- The plaintiff received adequate oral hydration between the time of her admission and 13 October 1999. This conclusion he considered was supported by the urinary output record in that period.
- The plaintiff's admission to the intensive care unit was precipitated by a respiratory failure due to hypoventilation due to sputum retention. The plaintiff may also have had some infection in the chest as well, although this was not proven.

22 Before considering Dr Raftos' evidence, I will first deal with specific aspects of Dr Burns' evidence concerning blood loss:

23 Dr Burns disagreed that the reading taken on 12 October 1999 was a normal reading and was one which was showing *compensation* for blood loss. He accordingly disagreed with Dr Raftos' opinion in this respect. He relied upon readings taken years before showing haemoglobin readings in the 120's.

24 In relation to the blood transfusion that took place on 13 October 1999, Dr Burns stated that it was common for blood to be administered whenever the haemoglobin readings were down:

> *But it's routine when the haemoglobin level is reduced but they give blood because it's usually due to blood loss . . .* (t.473)

25 However, despite this concession, Dr. Burns stated that he did not consider that the blood infused was consequent upon significant blood loss commencing on 8 October, some five days before. He said that by 9 October the fluid would have poured into the blood stream from the system diluting the red cells and the haemoglobin level that was there. By 12 October the blood level should have been lower, but it in fact had

remained within normal range. He accordingly stated 'I don't think there's any good evidence that she sustained major blood loss. She possibly did, but I don't think she did' (t.474).

The hypovolaemia (loss of blood) issue

26 This issue is best approached by:

- placing the question of blood loss in context and identifying its significance to the issue of *'damage'*;
- identifying the way in which it is contended that the plaintiff should have been managed and treated for the blood loss postulated as having been consequent upon the fractures sustained by the plaintiff;
- identifying the competing medical opinions on the question of whether substantial blood loss in fact occurred;
- on the basis that blood loss did occur, identifying whether there was a relevant failure to properly assess and treat the plaintiff for blood loss, given the difficulty of establishing intravenous access.

(i) The issue of hypovolaemia in context

27 Dr Raftos stated essentially that blood loss will always result from significant traumatic injury involving fractures and that, left unaddressed, hypovolaemia will develop which in turn can lead to renal failure or dysfunction. The plaintiff contends that her gravely ill condition for which she was treated in the hospital was, in part, due to renal complications arising from substantial blood loss. Ultimately she required urgent medical treatment by means of a blood transfusion on 12 and 13 October 1999 and treatment otherwise for associated complications in the intensive care unit of the hospital.

28 Dr Raftos explained in evidence that a fracture itself releases blood in that it causes bleeding from the bone itself and from the structures around it. In evidence in chief, he explained that with a fracture of the bone, blood vessels outside the bone and inside it are disrupted and bleeding occurs. He stated that from humerus fractures, probably 500 to 700 mls of blood is lost in general. For fractures of the femora, around the knee, one would assume 500 mls to 1,500 mls of blood loss. He stated that a blood count would provide an idea as to how much blood had been lost. (I note here that Dr Burns stated that he believed a fracture of the humerus would not produce a lot of blood loss but did not quantify how much would result.)

29 The plaintiff's case was that she had suffered significant blood loss (hypovolaemia) and as previously observed it is known that this can lead to renal failure or renal dysfunction. The latter occurred in her case. There is no doubt on the evidence that when she was admitted to the intensive care unit on 13 October 1999, she was gravely ill by reason of a number of conditions or complications. The question was how and why

that came about. She was, in due course, treated successfully in the intensive care unit.

30 Dr Michael Kennedy, consultant physician, gave evidence on behalf of the defendant in the motor vehicle accident proceedings which were heard concurrently with these proceedings. Dr Kennedy considered that the fractures sustained by the plaintiff were *very significant injuries*. He stated that there could be significant blood loss up to 500 mls as acute blood loss, but additionally there exists the possibility of chronic blood loss and that up to two litres of blood could be lost over time. The tachycardia experienced by the plaintiff was consistent with pain and/or blood loss and/or other intercurrent medical condition.

31 Dr Burns, in opining that the plaintiff did not suffer significant blood loss, proceeded upon a fundamental and questionable assumption that her fractures were not sufficient enough to regard her as a severe trauma case. I found Dr Burns' evidence on the issue of blood loss, at times, less than satisfactory. In this regard, and in particular:

(a) His report of 27 June 2003 would lead the reader to understand that he was asserting no blood loss had occurred:
'Close inspection of her hospital file failed to yield any evidence that she had lost blood . . .' (p.4)
'no blood loss was suffered by her.' (p. 6 – under the heading 'overall comment')

(b) In cross-examination, he stated that the latter comment meant there had been no blood loss 'externally', although there had been no indication at all in the report that this is what had been meant.

(c) In cross-examination, Dr Burns then stated that he had *'no doubt that she suffered some blood loss'*. Again, there had been no acknowledgement of this important fact in his report.

(d) In cross-examination he said *'I suspect'* that the plaintiff had neither major or minor fractures but was *'in between'*. However, I note that he considered that a fracture of the humerus generally was not associated with a lot of blood loss. There is cogent medical evidence to the contrary.

(e) He accepted that the purpose of taking haemoglobin readings (the measure of the amount of blood) was to monitor whether there had been significant blood loss and that it was standard practice to do so. However, whilst at first he relied upon the fact that the fractures were not severe enough to warrant taking blood, he, a little later, added that everyone taken to emergency at Westmead would have blood taken but that obtaining blood from the plaintiff was difficult. Given Dr Burns' acceptance that she was an *'at risk'* patient from the day of her admission, I found his evidence on the failure of the hospital staff to consider and then proceed to cannulate the subclavian vein unconvincing (see discussion on that topic later in this judgment).

(ii) The treatment of alleged blood loss as claimed by the plaintiff

32 The plaintiff claims that intravenous access should have been obtained, intravenous fluids then given and blood tests taken and that had this been done she would not have suffered the renal dysfunction, which she claims resulted from the hospital's failure to address significant loss of blood.

33 Dr. Raftos stated in his report of 30 May 2001 that the standard treatment for severely injured persons (of which he considered the plaintiff one) includes the infusion of intravenous fluids and blood products to replace those lost due to injuries. The plaintiff, he said, should have had the infusion of two to three litres of crystalloid fluid initially, by way of replacement of blood lost into the fractures and then routine daily intravenous fluid management of crystalloid fluid. No blood tests were taken in the first five days of hospitalisation.

34 He acknowledged that it may be physically difficult to find a vein from which to take blood for testing, given the plaintiff's condition and pain in her upper limbs. He explained in oral evidence that there was a sequence to be followed:

> *The site of choice is the cephalic vein in the forearm. If that's not readily available, then veins in the cubital fossa at the elbow; if they are not readily available, then consideration needs to be given to accessing the larger veins, either the femoral vein or internal jugular vein.*

35 At the time of placement of the cannula and before infusion of fluid, blood is taken for testing. The blood count provides an idea of how much blood has been lost. The plaintiff weighed about 42 kilograms. A person of 40 kilograms would have a blood volume of 3.5 to four litres. He considered that in this case there was probably a blood loss of about two litres. He rejected that this would mean the plaintiff would have died. Compensatory mechanisms (described below) would, he said, have come into operation.

36 Dr AB Breslin, consultant thoracic surgeon, supported Dr Raftos on the need to insert an intravenous line. He acknowledged the difficulty of inserting a line into somebody in the plaintiff's condition but added:

> *. . . if venous access is required, then you get it. It doesn't matter how you get it, you get it.*

37 Dr Burns spoke of the risk of infection of putting a long line in through the neck, although this in fact eventually had to be done and was done after the plaintiff was placed in intensive care. He acknowledged that had a line been inserted, hospital staff would have been in a better position to have made appropriate observations. In deciding whether the risk of inserting an intravenous line was justified and necessary, Dr Burns assumed that the staff had formed a judgment that severe blood loss was unlikely.

38 The evidence established that in cases such as the present, the issue of intravenous access is one that needs to be considered. The Westmead Hospital's *Guidelines for the Management of Trauma*, 2nd Edition, 1997 (p. 45) (Exhibit N) addresses this question and states, in part:

> *All patients admitted with significant injury,* ***absolutely*** *all who have evidence of blood loss should have two large-bore IV lines inserted as an immediate routine . . .*
>
> *Preferred sites are the large veins in antecubital fossae or cephalic or other large vein in forearm, or cephalic vein in the arm. If there are major injuries to either upper limb, alternative sites are required. These are:*
>
> . . .
>
> *external jugular vein . . .*

39 Dr Kennedy, consultant physician, stated that, with skill, the internal jugular vein can be quite easily cannulated. It gives direct access and has the advantage of permitting measurement of central venous pressures which in turn assists in determining the degree of hydration. He stated that he would not be reluctant to insert a central line because of the dangers of infection (t.448). He identified as a possible complication, the risk of hitting the carotid artery and causing bleeding, injuring the lung and causing pneumothorax. Infection was a long-term complication of a cannula left within the chest. The procedure accordingly is one that requires monitoring once inserted to guard against infection. He stated that the plaintiff's injuries, in his view, were very significant injuries. Whilst noting the reference in the hospital notes to factors which may make an insertion of an intravenous cannula difficult, he went on to state in his report of 11 September 2002 that it was 'normal practice for patients admitted with serious trauma to have an intravenous cannula inserted and intravenous fluids are usually administered until such time as the person is fully assessed in relationship to the need for surgical treatment of the fractures or the possibility of trauma to soft tissue injuries . . .' (report of 11 September 2002, paragraph two). I accept Dr Kennedy in relation to the above evidence.

(iii) Competing opinions on whether substantial blood loss occurred

40 The plaintiff's case on the issue of hypovolaemia essentially raised three issues:

- The first, if intravenous access could not be obtained through one of the peripheral nerves (as in fact was the case), whether intravenous access should have been obtained through the jugular vein.
- The second issue was whether blood loss had occurred as a result of or consequent upon the plaintiff's fractures. It is plain that such loss did in fact occur.
- The third issue was whether the blood loss was a substantial one. If so, whether it could, and should, have reasonably been anticipated

such as to warrant the insertion of an intravenous cannula for the infusion of a crystalloid fluid and the taking of blood counts to assess how much blood had been lost thereby permitting early intervention to have replaced lost blood.

41 Central to Dr Raftos' analysis was the concept of compensatory mechanisms that will often become operative in the event of significant blood loss (hypovolaemia). Dr Kennedy, consultant physician, gave evidence to similar effect. Dr Raftos explained that notwithstanding substantial blood loss, a person may continue to survive by virtue of compensatory mechanisms. He explained that a number of factors operate in this respect but the predominant one involves constriction of the small arteries in the non-essential vascular beds (that is, some of the muscles, the skin, the gastrointestinal tract). Such constriction makes the space into which the blood needs to fit smaller. If normal blood volume was four litres, then it was possible to contract the blood volume down to two litres. In those circumstances, the haemoglobin and certain other readings will be concentrated with the body compensating by fluid moving into the tissues and by the passing of urine.

42 Dr Raftos was challenged in cross-examination as to how such compensating mechanisms could operate without showing symptoms during the first five days apart from a high heart rate. Dr Raftos referred to the altered consciousness that had developed by 12 October, it being noted in the records that the plaintiff was *'weak, lethargic, speech slurred'*.

43 Dr Raftos explained that with contraction of the small arteries the blood flow is maintained to the important organs – the kidneys, heart and brain – in the reduced space. Tachycardia was the predominant symptom. Young people, Dr. Raftos stated, can maintain their blood pressure in face of a substantial volume loss for an extended period of time but they will eventually become unwell.

44 On the basis of his analysis, Dr. Raftos said the haemoglobin reading on 12 October of 121 is not to be seen as a *normal* reading but was an indication of a *concentrated* reading due to blood loss.

45 In resolving the question as to whether blood loss occurred, it soon became apparent in the cross-examination of Dr. Burns that in fact there was no real issue between the medical experts but that the plaintiff had indeed suffered blood loss (issue (ii) above). The principal issues accordingly were, firstly, whether there had been *significant* blood loss and, secondly, whether such blood loss had gone undetected by hospital staff during the period between 8 and 12 October inclusive.

46 There is no clear evidence on this last issue. That is partly because of the fact of an absence of intravenous monitoring being performed and recorded and partly by reason of the conflict of medical opinion which in part turns upon the competing interpretations open on the clinical and recorded data. In this latter respect, the factual information that is available and which was recorded includes the following:

(a) No haemoglobin readings were taken between 8 October and 11

October inclusive. Although Dr Burns assumed that this was because of the risks associated with cannulating the subclavian vein (which, as previously mentioned, was subsequently done on 13 October in intensive care) there is no evidence that this procedure was, in fact, considered by the hospital staff at any stage in that period.

(b) The first haemoglobin reading of 121 was taken on 12 October and although apparently normal, Dr Raftos considered this to be due to haemoconcentration – the process described by him in evidence and referred to above. It will be necessary to refer again to that matter later in this judgment.

(c) After the plaintiff's condition became extremely serious, two haemoglobin readings were taken on the afternoon of 13 October, 60 and 72 respectively, being abnormal and consistent with hypotension. They were shortly followed by blood transfusions of two units and one unit on 13 October which Dr Raftos said was itself consistent with the fact of a significant blood loss which he, in turn, attributed to the fractures.

47 This then was a central point of contention on the issue of blood loss. Dr Burns did not believe that any blood loss for which the transfusion was given was related to the fractures sustained on 8 October. He did, however, concede that it is routine procedure when haemoglobin levels are reduced for blood to be given *'because it's usually due to blood loss'*.

48 Dr Burns pointed to earlier or historical haemoglobin readings taken on 22 June 1995 of 129, on 4 March 1997 of 128 and on 8 April 1999 of 122 and these were consistent, he said, with the reading on 12 October 1999 of 121.

49 Dr Burns postulated that the low readings taken on 13 and 14 October could have been affected by dilution going in through the plastic line that had been established in the right subclavian vein on 13 October. This postulation was, however, not supported by any factual material. The fact of a blood transfusion on the same day (13 October) bespeaks blood loss of a significant amount and cannot be ignored in construing the reading of 121 taken the day before. The real question then became what could have caused such a significant loss?

50 I consider the low haemoglobin readings taken on 13 October were true readings. Indeed, they were seen and acted upon as such by hospital staff who took immediate steps to admit the plaintiff, by then a very ill patient, into intensive care and to undertake on an urgent basis a transfusion of three units of blood in response to an apparent blood loss in a significant quantity of blood. An additional fact pointing to blood loss of significance is the return of haemoglobin readings very shortly after the transfusions took place. I note that Dr Burns conceded that as a matter of medical *possibility* there could have been significant blood loss due to the fractures but he took the view that he did not think that such a possibility had occurred.

51 This then brings back into focus the significance of the haemoglobin reading of 121 on 12 October, Dr Burns saying that it effectively meant there could not have been significant loss on and after 8 October. Dr Raftos' explanation, on the other hand, based on the concept of haemoglobin concentration was shown by the evidence to be an accepted medical theory which could account for what appeared to be a *normal* reading. The basis for disputing concentration in this case was in part based upon blood pressure readings in the period which were within normal range. However Dr Burns conceded in cross-examination that:

- No blood pressure was taken until about 24 hours after admission so that one does not know if, within the initial period which Dr Burns stated was important, hypotension had then existed.
- Twelve hourly blood pressure readings were insufficient to draw conclusions as to whether any variation is taking place because of continuing blood loss – what was required were hourly readings for the first day and four-hourly readings after that, which were not taken.

52 Accordingly, Dr Burns' reliance upon blood pressure readings said to have been within normal range does not in itself constitute a sufficient basis for rejecting Dr Raftos on the issue of blood loss.

53 Returning to the haemocentration theory, Dr Burns conceded in cross-examination such concentration could in fact have been a factor at work but considered that it would not have influenced the haemoglobin reading taken on 12 October:

> *. . . I've never heard of someone having a high haemoglobin four days after blood loss due to body conservation mechanisms. I don't think it's a likely explanation. It's possible, but not likely, in my opinion.* (transcript 489)

54 Causation of a medical condition as a matter of medical *possibility* may be sufficient if there are objective facts that support it in the circumstances of a particular case: *Tubemakers of Australia Limited v Fernandez* (1976) 50 ALJR 720. Here, the haemoglobin readings taken on 13 October, the fact of the blood transfusion in a significant quantity and its apparent effect as discussed earlier, Dr Raftos' analysis of blood loss involving or causing haemocentration, together provide an explanation for the observations taken on 12 and 13 October and are supportive of his conclusion that the fractures at the three sites did produce significant blood loss. Such a condition on the evidence is capable of causing renal dysfunction. I am satisfied on the probabilities that the renal problems of which the plaintiff was diagnosed and to which she was treated in intensive care were causally related to the significant blood loss and not some other unidentified cause as well as to the antecedent failure by hospital staff to identify and treat that blood loss by blood transfusion and close monitoring before 12 October 1999.

Conclusions on the blood loss issue

55 I am satisfied on the evidence of the following matters and make findings accordingly:

(a) The plaintiff's fractures at three sites resulted in a substantial blood loss (hypovolaemia). I accept Dr Raftos' opinion to this effect. This opinion, I observe, has a measure of support from Dr Malka of the hospital who wrote in the hospital notes that her impression was that the plaintiff's decreased level of consciousness was due to 'hypoxia/hypovolaemia' and 'impending renal failure secondary to hypovolaemia'.

(b) Standard procedures of the hospital, in place at the time of the plaintiff's admission, required that intravenous access be obtained for monitoring and maintenance of fluid and blood levels in categories of case which included cases of the severity of the plaintiff's case. The hospital did not follow its prescribed procedure.

(c) Intravenous access in the particular circumstances of the plaintiff by a central venous line was essential and overrode competing risks from such an insertion.

(d) The hospital staff appeared to have acted (wrongly) up until 13 October upon the basis that the fractures involved relatively minor and not severe trauma. I accept Dr Raftos' evidence that the fractures were serious fractures and did result in substantial blood loss at the three fracture sites.

(e) The plaintiff manifested periodic tachycardia. On the basis of Dr Raftos' evidence, which I accept, this was a consistent reaction to substantial blood loss.

(f) The haemoglobin reading of 121 on 12 October was a concentrated or compensated elevated haemoglobin level resulting from substantial blood loss.

(g) The drop in haemoglobin readings on 13 October and the elevation of readings on 14 October, on the probabilities, were indicative respectively of blood loss and replenishment of that loss through the transfusions given on 13 October.

56 It was Dr Raftos' evidence, which I accept, that the blood loss and the pneumonitis (discussed below) contributed to the need for intensive care treatment. It is clear on the evidence that by 12 October both combined to render the plaintiff a very unwell patient to the point that intensive care treatment became an urgent necessity.

57 The hypovolaemia suffered by the plaintiff gave rise to liver dysfunction and coagulation dysfunction. The liver readings, however, did not reach levels indicative of liver failure. The plaintiff was very unwell from 12 October until her discharge from intensive care by reason of haemovolamia and pneumonitis.

The question of the plaintiff's tolerance to opiate medication

58 One issue in the proceedings concerned the plaintiff's tolerance to drugs and of her habituation to opiate medication. The issue was whether she would, by reason of such tolerance/habituation, have required larger doses of opiates in order to obtain appropriate pain relief. Dr Raftos stated that it would not necessarily have had that effect. He added:

> *But . . . it would make you pay more attention to getting the analgesia right.*

59 He also stated habituation to opiates would not generally make any difference to the physiological effect on an excessive prescription of an opiate.

60 Dr Raftos' considered the plaintiff's drowsiness was explicable by the amount of opiate administered in hospital and the fact that her lungs were getting worse and becoming more hypoxic and because she was hypovolaemic.

(a) Excessive use of opiate analgesics

61 The plaintiff was prescribed and given large doses of three opiate analgesics:

- Panadeine forte (paracetamol 500 mg, codeine 30 mg), two tablets, four times per day.
- Endone (Oxychodone 5 mg), two tablets, three times per day.
- Morphine 10 mg intramuscularly, as needed up to three hourly.

62 The following medications were administered in the amounts shown:

Date	Morphine	Panadeine forte	Endone
8.10.99	25 mg IM	4	20 mg PO
9.10.99	40 mg IM	8	30 mg PO
10.10.99	20 mg IM	8	30 mg PO
11.10.99	20 mg IM	8	30 mg PO
12.10.99		2	10 mg PO

63 There were a number of matters of particular relevance to the plaintiff:

- She was a young woman weighing less than 40 kilograms.
- She had had a prior history of heavy analgesic use and of opiate use.
- She had a pre-existing condition of kyphoscoliosis, which potentially restricted her lung function.
- She suffered significant pain whilst in Westmead Hospital arising from her fractures requiring the administration of significant amounts of pain-relieving medication in the form of analgesia and opiates.

64 Dr Burns opined that it was difficult to say from the hospital file that the plaintiff was given excessive doses of opiates but that it could be said that, with her abnormally shaped chest, what she was required to have by way of medication did cause some respiratory depression.

65 In cross-examination by Mr Davies, SC, for the hospital, Dr Raftos accepted that his criticism of drug administration subsequent to the plaintiff's hospital admission was that whilst she should have been put on an opiate drug with a back-up for when the pain broke through the first one's effectiveness, she should not have had a third. He accepted that the doses of morphine and panadeine forte given to the plaintiff were within acceptable limits but said that the Endone was higher than standard dosing.

66 The issue concerning analgesic/opiate drugs is not only related to the allegation of overdose per se but is also related to the question of breathing complications associated with the plaintiff's pre-existing condition. Dr Raftos agreed in cross-examination that the only complication from the administration of the complement of drugs was that of respiratory depression. The three drugs were all capable of causing that condition. Monitoring was required to ensure that the important side effect of respiratory depression did not occur. Drowsiness and constriction would be two relevant signs of that condition.

67 Dr. Burns stated that the combination of the narcotic or analgesic depressing effect and the predisposition to chest trouble from the plaintiff's chest shape meant that 'someone had to be monitoring the thing very closely and according to the notes they did'. I will return to examine this observation by Dr Burns below (see '(c) The need for monitoring').

68 Dr. Burns said that by 12 October it was considered that the plaintiff may have had a problem because the opiate medication was too high:

> *Q: Do I take it that your conclusion ultimately is that that was indeed what caused her problem – that is, the combination of her pre-existing compromised chest and the analgesics.*
>
> A: Yes.

(b) The alleged failure to diagnose and treat inhalation pneumonitis

69 There was no doubt that the plaintiff succumbed to the condition of inhalation pneumonitis whilst she was a patient at Westmead Hospital following her admission on 8 October. The issue was whether or not it was related to the failure to properly manage and treat the plaintiff or whether it arose from some unrelated infection.

70 On 12 October 1999, Dr Chin, orthopaedic intern, noted that the plaintiff was 'weak/lethargic, also speech-slurred. Very weak + lethargic, difficulty breathing'. Dr. Johnston, medical registrar, noted that the plaintiff had been 'breathless for 3 days, worse today. Noted by nursing staff to be drowsy today and slurred speech'.

71 In relation to the latter entry in the clinical notes, the submissions of

the parties focused on whether this latter entry was based upon an account given by the plaintiff herself or whether it had been an observation that had been passed on to Dr. Johnson by a member of the medical or nursing staff. I observe at this point that the notes do indicate from time to time that when statements by the plaintiff were recorded, they were expressly attributed to her. This, however, is not the case with the latter entry.

72 A chest x-ray on 12 October 1999 confirmed that the plaintiff did have pneumonitis. Dr. Malca noted on 13 October 1999 that her impression was that the plaintiff had 'probable respiratory failure/infection'. Upon admission to the intensive care the plaintiff was diagnosed, inter alia, as having sepsis 'probably because of inhalation pneumonitis'. The notes also indicated that she was suffering from 'acute respiratory failure because of a probable combination of inhalation pneumonitis and adult respiratory distress syndrome'.

73 Dr Raftos, in his report of 30 May 2001 (p 5) considered that excessive doses of opiates had made the plaintiff excessively drowsy and suppressed her respiratory drive and her cough reflex. Elsewhere, he stated that both excessive dosages of opiates and untreated blood loss contributed to the plaintiff's state of drowsiness. These, he stated, led directly to her inhaling regurgitated gastric contents causing the inhalation pneumonitis that contributed to her critical illness and admission to the intensive care unit.

74 By 12 October 1999, Dr Raftos considered that the plaintiff clearly was in marked respiratory distress because of the pneumonitis which was the result of the inhalation of gastric contents due to her oversedated state from the time of admission into hospital, but that this had not been suspected or detected until belatedly on 12 October 1999, four days after her admission. Dr Raftos wrote:

> *The failure to prevent, detect, and treat Mrs **Markaboui**'s inhalation pneumonitis until 4 and 5 days after her admission, represents a major departure from accepted standards of hospital medical care and led directly to her developing acute respiratory failure and multiple organ failure.*

75 Dr Raftos also observed in his report that patients, such as the plaintiff, with kyphoscoliosis are at an increased risk of respiratory disease because their chest is physically deformed. Accordingly, he maintained that the plaintiff was, from the outset of her hospitalisation, at increased risk of developing respiratory complications after her accident (and accordingly had to be carefully managed) but, he claimed, hospital staff had paid little attention to that particular risk.

76 In oral evidence, Dr Breslin, consultant thoracic physician, stated that the crepitations of the right base of the lung detected on 12 October were 'new'. Dr Breslin stated that breathlessness over three days could be due to pneumonia.

77 Dr Raftos explained that pneumonitis is an inflammation of the lung

due to inhalation of gastric fluids because of an incompetent gag reflex arising from sedation. He said that was not the same as pneumonia. There is a different cause. He stated that the sort of pneumonia that the plaintiff had was caused by the toxic effects of the gastric acids on the lung, whereas pneumonia is caused by bacteria.

78 In his oral evidence Dr Raftos confirmed the inhalation pneumonitis probably arose because the plaintiff was over-sedated, and this contributed to the need for intensive care treatment. He also stated that there were no other features in the history other than the development of hypovolaemia and inhalation pneumonitis to explain her elevated heart rate.

79 Dr Raftos also made the point that no-one at the hospital seemed to have known or postulated the cause of her emerging and altered consciousness and respiratory distress. He accepted that the plaintiff required substantial quantities of analgesics and opiates to control the pain. But the real issue was the requirement for close monitoring in order to ensure that the important side-effect of respiratory depression did not occur. Such monitoring would include clinical observation by nursing staff.

80 Dr Burns stated that the plaintiff did have respiratory failure which built up on 12 to 13 October 1999 with changes noted in the lungs. He stated in his report of 27 June 2003 (p 5):

> *I believe she had respiratory failure due to hypoventilation due to some sputum retention and could well have had some infection in the chest as well, but it was never proven. Persons, such as Ms* ***Markaboui****, with kyphoscoliosis are subject to impaired breathing if they become ill. I do not think that Ms* ***Markaboui*** *had inhalation pneumonitis.*

81 Dr Burns added, in relation to opiate dose, that he found it difficult from her file to say that she was given excessive doses of opiates but that it could be that, with her abnormally shaped chest, what was necessary by way of analgesia medication did cause some respiratory depression.

(c) The need for monitoring

82 I have referred above to Dr Burns' observation as to the need for monitoring given the depressing effect of medication and the plaintiff's predisposition to chest trouble.

83 Dr Burns assessed or assumed that the plaintiff was provided with a close level of monitoring according to the notes. In this respect he said:

- the physiotherapist paid regular attention to her chest;
- the oxygen levels in the blood were monitored very closely.

84 Dr Burns agreed in evidence that the plaintiff was, at all material times, an 'at-risk' patient, that is, at risk over and above an ordinary person of her age. He considered the 'at-risk' problems were mainly respiratory. (The plaintiff's deformed chest (kyphoscoliosis), meant that

her lungs were restricted from expanding properly but this did not cause a problem when she was up and about.) People with kyphoscoliosis are at risk of hyperventilating, that is, the inadequate ability to expel carbon dioxide and take oxygen in.

85 Dr Burns stated that the combination of the narcotic or the analgesic depression of respiration and the predisposition to chest trouble from the plaintiff's chest shape 'meant that someone had to be monitoring the thing very closely, and according to the notes they did. The physiotherapist paid regular attention to how the chest was. The oxygen level in the blood was monitored very closely and I think she was handled very well in the ward up till the 12th and she went off then fairly quickly'. (t.477).

86 An examination of the hospital's notes, however, reveals that Dr Burns' statement that from the time of her admission the plaintiff received regular attention from the physiotherapist and that the oxygen saturation level in the blood was monitored very closely, is factually incorrect. There was no attendance of the kind he asserted according to the clinical records, until 12 October by which date the plaintiff was very unwell. It was on 12 October and not before that oxygen saturation levels were first investigated.

87 The close monitoring (in the form of physiotherapy review and monitoring of oxygen saturation levels) that was assumed and spoken of by Dr Burns for possible respiration depression resulting from (a) analgesic medication combined with (b) the plaintiff's predisposition simply did not take place. The fact that it did take place impacts significantly upon the opinion Dr Burns expressed as to the adequacy of the monitoring. The clinical notes for 12 October are extensive indeed. They consist of 19 pages of entries for that date alone. They reflect the intensity of urgent attention that, by then, was clearly necessary. It is plain that by that the plaintiff's condition had become grave. Indeed it is of some importance that the third entry for 12 October, at 11.30 hours, records the attendance of Dr. Johnston, medical registrar, who made detailed notes of the plaintiff's condition. (I have referred to the notes earlier.) They include the following note:

> *Breathless for 3/7, worse today. Noted by nursing staff to be drowsy today with slurred speech.*

88 As I have previously stated, it was suggested in submissions that this entry may merely reflect what the plaintiff herself told Dr Johnston. The difficulty in accepting that proposition is that the note does not itself suggest that the plaintiff was giving an account of her own symptoms and of course by the time Dr. Johnston saw her she was drowsy, very unwell and was slurring her speech. Whatever the true position be in this respect, the note does record the fact of breathlessness having developed over the preceding three days. That, of course, is hardly unsurprising, given the level of drug intake and the plaintiff's pre-existing lung function condition. Dr Kennedy stated that the entry would indicate that the

plaintiff had had too much opiate medication administered to her over a period, in all probability, consisting of several days.

89 Dr Burns agreed that the entry as to breathlessness suggested that something 'had been going on' and was presumably worsening. It is true that earlier entries in the clinical notes do not, in fact, note amongst the various recorded observations, symptoms of breathlessness. It is clear, however, that the close level of monitoring of the kind identified by Dr. Burns had from the outset been required as a proactive approach so as to guard against breathing abnormalities developing on and from 8 October. However, that regular monitoring (by the physiotherapist and by taking oxygen saturation levels) did not, in fact occur until 12 October, by which time the plaintiff's clinical condition had become well-established. The failure to monitor in the circumstances (particularly on the evidence of Dr Burns and Dr Raftos) evidences a sub-standard level of care for a patient such as the plaintiff who was in a 'risk' category.

90 Impairment of respiratory function requires medical attention to compensate for a lack of oxygen. This the plaintiff did not receive until 12 October. The respiratory distress leading to impairment of lung function by at least 12 October I find, on the evidence, arose from the hospital's failure to protect or guard against the respiratory risk to which the plaintiff was exposed and its failure to ensure that clinical monitoring and support was maintained to avert the risk by supplementary oxygen supply. In particular, such failure included the failure to undertake appropriate physiotherapy and monitoring of the plaintiff's blood oxygen saturation levels on a frequent or periodic basis. Had such monitoring and support been given, it is likely, either, that the plaintiff would not have developed respiratory complications, or, that early signs of respiratory complications would have been detected soon after admission and effectively managed so as to avoid the condition that did eventually develop and contribute to the need for intensive care.

91 Dr Burns explained the nature of the respiratory complications that were to be avoided in Ms **Markaboul**'s case:

> *That at-risk problems were mainly respiratory, in my opinion, and I believe that the problems she developed were mainly respiratory. She had a deformed chest, kyphoscoliosis – that is, the lungs were restricted from expanding properly – which didn't cause any trouble when she was up and about. But people with kyphoscoliosis are at risk of developing a syndrome (called) hypoventilation, that is, inadequate ability to expel carbon dioxide and take oxygen in. (t.477)*

92 Dr Burns indicated that the cluster of symptoms that became evident on 12 and 13 October in hindsight indicated the need for the plaintiff to have been closely monitored by a specialist physician to have averted respiratory complications. The need for close monitoring of the kind discussed by Dr Burns on the evidence was a foreseeable requirement. The plaintiff's hypoventilation was explained by Dr Burns as 'due to a combination of the shape, the sputum retention, which caused the

pneumonia, and the respiratory suppression from the narcotics'. He went on to explain that '. . . I think they had a physiotherapist in the ward attempting to give her chest physio several times a day'. Sputum retention can arise where the patient is having drugs that suppress coughing and is unable to sit up in order to have physiotherapy. Even if the physiotherapist could not find any sign of sputum retention, material in the airways can be absorbed or aspirated into the lung with secondary infection occurring in the material that has been retained. However, as earlier noted, physiotherapy was only administered later by which time the condition was established.

93 Dr Burns stated that the appropriate care for a patient in the plaintiff's position would have included 'active physiotherapy which would involve a higher level of narcotisation' than she had been having.

94 The evidence of Dr Burns in this respect is much in line with that given by Dr Kennedy. In the context of pain relief administered to the plaintiff, having regard in particular to the issue of tolerance arising from the plaintiff's prior history of drug taking (Panadeine Forte and Endone), Dr Kennedy explained that there is a complex balance between administering drugs for continuing complaint of pain and the risk of respiratory problems. The variables to be considered include:

- The reason for continuing complaints of pain (eg., whether the plaintiff is in the right position, whether they are being nursed appropriately).
- The need to titrate the doses required for pain relief rather than administration by standard dose instruction.
- In a patient with a significant risk (including in particular, those with severe respiratory problems due to muscular disease) there is a need for great caution '. . . because you could be relieving their pain by higher doses, but, in another area, that might be required to relieve their pain, but the ability to drop their respiration is still absolutely sitting there at the very dangerous level. So you have to be very, very careful and watch the patient and you dose the patient. You don't take it out of the text book, you give the dose to the patient and see how they respond.' (t.548–549).
- Increasing pain relief medication is appropriate, provided other factors are under control, including anxiety and oxygen saturation levels are satisfactory and respiratory expansions are appropriate (with low chest expansion, fatigue can set in).

95 Dr Kennedy identified the factors which would have classified the plaintiff as a 'high-risk patient'. These included the fact that the plaintiff had muscular disease, the fact that she had some thoracic problems affecting her lungs and the fractures.

Conclusions in findings in relation to opiate analgesic medication and inhalation pneumonitis

96 The analysis of the evidence supports the following conclusions and findings:

(a) The plaintiff was administered large doses of three opiate analgesic during the period 8 October 1999 to 12 October 1999 inclusive, such medication being administered for significant pain suffered by the plaintiff consequent upon the fractures she sustained in the accident. The plaintiff's prior history of heavy analgesic use and of opiate use, together with the level of pain suffered by her produced a situation whereby large doses of medication were required and appropriate. Accordingly, I do not consider that the allegation of excessive use of opiate analgesics per se is, subject to the question of monitoring below, made out.

(b) The plaintiff's pre-existing condition of kyphoscoliosis meant that the plaintiff was necessarily at risk of developing pneumonitis leading to marked respiratory stress and for that reason required extremely close monitoring of a specialist nature as a preventative measure. The results of such monitoring would provide the basis for appropriate adjustments to medication levels to either prevent the development of pneumonitis or to control any early signs of that condition.

(c) The plaintiff did develop the condition of inhalation pneumonitis and consequent respiratory distress culminating in the need for intensive care treatment.

(d) The close monitoring required for the proper management of the plaintiff upon her admission included physiotherapy review and the taking of oxygen saturation levels at regular intervals. These precautions were not adopted until 12 October, by which time the plaintiff's condition of pneumonitis had become well established.

(e) The development of the condition of pneumonitis in a patient such as the plaintiff, given her predisposition, was clearly a foreseeable complication and had proper or close monitoring measures been adopted from 8 October, the likelihood is that the plaintiff would not have suffered from pneumonitis and consequent respiratory distress syndrome. It was that condition which contributed to the need for the plaintiff to be admitted to the intensive care unit for urgent specialist treatment.

(f) The failure by the hospital to monitor the plaintiff in a proactive way to avoid or control the development of pneumonitis given the level of medication and her predisposition represented a breach of duty on the hospital's part of providing appropriate care and treatment of the plaintiff.

The hydration issue

97 One of the failures of the hospital, according to Dr. Raftos, was the failure to infuse intravenous fluids on a routine daily maintenance basis. This failure (together with the failure to replace blood loss through injury) he considered a major departure from accepted standards of hospital medical care. Dr Raftos claimed that it led directly to the development of cardiovascular collapse, acute renal failure and multiple organ failure.

98 The hospital's clinical records in relation to the plaintiff's admission included a fluid balance chart. The chart did not record oral intake, but did record urinary output. However, the nursing notes do include reference to fluid intake, in particular:

9 October1320 drinking well
10 October1315 tolerated fluids well
11 October1420 tolerated fluids well
11 October1950 given water to drink
12 October2245 oral fluid intake this shift 1.5 litres

99 The urine output was recorded as follows:

9 October1300 mls
10 October1360 mls
11 October1150 mls
12 October1130 mls

100 The hospital relied upon evidence from Dr Burns who maintained that the plaintiff did have adequate oral hydration through until 13 October 1999 when she was transferred to the Intensive Care Unit where the intravenous line was inserted.

101 In his submissions on behalf of the hospital, Mr Davies, SC observed that Dr Raftos had made no mention at all of recorded urinary output in his report. Dr Raftos conceded in cross-examination that urine output, along with other factors such as heart rate and blood pressure and peripheral perfusion, is an indication of the level of hydration. He conceded that he had expressed his view about her hydration levels without reference to recordings of the urine output.

102 I have had regard to Dr Raftos' evidence on this issue, particularly that given in cross-examination. It seems to me that he essentially accepted that the urinary output readings were within normal range even though he sought to adhere to the proposition that urine output had been substantially reduced by reference to the fact that the plaintiff passed 200 mls plus per day whilst in intensive care.

103 Dr Breslin agreed in cross-examination that the urine output figures recorded in the notes were within normal limits, stating:

> They are a bit low, but they are not too bad. (t.281)

104 In particular, he conceded that the reading on 12 October was quite

a good output and that it appeared on the figures that up until and including 12 October urine output was within normal range.

105 Similarly, Dr Kennedy conceded in cross-examination that over the five days upon admission on 8 October, the plaintiff seemed to be maintaining her fluid balance reasonably well on the basis of the figures recorded.

106 The urinary output for 8, 9, 10, 11 and 12 October 1999 was considered by Dr Burns to be a good output and that by 13 October the hospital staff considered it was falling, being the day that the plaintiff went to intensive care.

107 I have had some regard to the entries in the notes which do indicate that the plaintiff was being provided with fluids, even though the quantity of fluids were not recorded. I do not consider that the evidence overall establishes, on the balance of probabilities, that the plaintiff was dehydrated as alleged. I accordingly find that the hospital's care of the patient on the question of hydration, on the evidence, was appropriate and that there was no breach of duty in that respect.

The consequences of the hospital's breach of duty

108 I am satisfied on the balance of the probabilities that the plaintiff suffered pneumonitis and that this condition arose from the administration of opiates and analgesics which acted to depress the plaintiff's breathing, causing a respiratory distress syndrome that was not properly monitored and detected. The lack of proper care by the hospital led to the plaintiff developing inhalation pneumonitis which contributed, along with her hypovolaemia, to the need for intensive care treatment.

109 It is clear on the evidence that the plaintiff's condition that developed in consequence of the hospital's breach of duty had immediate and severe consequences. She, as I have earlier stated, fell into a very grave, potentially life-threatening condition. The immediate effects of the failure to treat in accordance with the standard of care identified in the evidence of Dr Raftos and Dr Burns included:

- hypovolaemia;
- resultant hypertension;
- respiratory compromise/pneumonitis;
- renal dysfunction;
- liver dysfunction.

110 The combination of these conditions rendered the plaintiff in a weakened condition, best described in the hospital notes, in particular, those of 12 and 13 October. These notes refer to the plaintiff's conditions as:

- weak and lethargic;
- difficulty in breathing;
- drowsy and slurred speech;

- anxiety
- decreased level of consciousness.

111 The plaintiff was in intensive care from 13 October to 2 November. She was discharged from Westmead Hospital on 11 November 1999.

112 The plaintiff responded to the treatment in intensive care and substantially recovered from the combination of conditions that led to her admission to the intensive care unit. One important question in these proceedings is, given that the plaintiff, on the evidence, is now in an even more disabled state than she was before 8 October, is her worsened condition due, in any respect, to the hospital's breach of duty of care?

113 The plaintiff relied principally for the answer to that question upon the evidence of Dr Winer, consultant physician in rehabilitation medicine. Dr Winer's report of 29 January 2002 is part of Exhibit E. He also gave evidence on 14 April 2005.

114 I observe at the outset that whilst Dr Winer had the hospital notes for the period of admission between 8 October and 11 November (Exhibit H), he did not have any contemporaneous medical records of treatment after 11 November. To that extent, his opinion on his assessment of the plaintiff's condition and disabilities after 11 November and of his apportionment of any change in her condition arising from medical complications that occurred between 8 October and 2 November is lacking some relevant clinical data.

115 Dr. Winer's report analyses the plaintiff's condition and progress and resultant disabilities under a number of headings. In particular, he discusses the 'before' and 'after' 1999 respective conditions and disabilities. He said, based on the plaintiff's history and his examination of her, 'that there has been a significant increase in her disabilities since October 1999' (p 10). Dr Winer stated that the increased disability was due to a combination of:

- increased weakness in the upper limbs, particularly important in the right arm;
- increased fatigability (tires more easily);
- increased pain (pain more widespread and more severe).

116 Dr Winer also expressed the opinion that the weakness in the right upper limb resulted from a significant period of non-use. I pause here to observe that the inability to move or use the upper limb was, to a large extent, a necessary consequence of the orthopaedic injuries and associated treatment. Dr Winer suggested, however, that some restricted use would also have been consequent upon the time spent in intensive care.

117 Dr Winer explained that weakness in muscles requires more effort and this in turn leads to increased fatigue which Dr Winer stated 'would be experienced by anyone who suffers multiple organ failure . . .'.

118 He went on to express the opinion, 'her increased disability is predominantly attributable to the effects of the multiple organ failure'. I will deal with Dr Winer's evidence in greater detail below.

119 Dr Breslin, in his report of 26 July 2002, analysed the injuries received in the motor vehicle accident as well as the effects of subsequent treatment and management of the plaintiff at Westmead Hospital. He observed that the length of time in hospital, the development of inhalational pneumonitis, which did not receive treatment for several days, caused more severe derangement of the plaintiff's general clinical state and respiratory reserve than the accident purely on its own may have done. Dr Breslin then added:

> I cannot quantify what additional role the treatment or lack of it at Westmead had in the permanent deterioration in her disease that has clearly occurred since the accident, but I believe it made a material contribution . . .

120 In his evidence on 15 April 2005, Dr Breslin stated that the plaintiff's muscles, which were affected by the disease process prior to the accident, had been markedly de-conditioned since the accident and because of her underlying basic condition she has been unable to get back to the way she was prior to the accident in terms of muscle strength and in terms of her general degree of independence.

121 Dr Breslin stated that the long period of inactivity in hospital and the reduced activity since discharge from hospital had de-conditioned all muscles, including the intercostal respiratory muscles. He stated that after a period of five or six weeks spent in hospital, the plaintiff, taking into account her pre-existing condition, did not have the ability to recover the strength in those muscles. Accordingly both the period whilst lying in a hospital bed and the recovery period from the fractures meant that she is less able now to do things that she was able to do beforehand.

122 Dr Breslin also gave evidence as to the following:

- A loss in muscle strength in a patient such as the plaintiff could occur in a matter of days of inactivity.
- The material contribution resulting from the treatment or lack of it at Westmead Hospital referred to in his report (p.6) is a reference merely to a contribution in terms of time spent in hospital.
- In terms of whether the additional period in hospital (including the period spent in the intensive care unit) contributed on an ongoing basis, he was unable to say.

Associate Professor Richard F. Jones, a specialist in the field of rehabilitation medicine, examined the plaintiff on 1 August 2001. In his report of that date (part of Exhibit 5(D1), he said that six weeks of hospitalisation was enough to cause wasting of the muscle. When called to give evidence on 19 April 2005, he was asked to address the question of the respective contribution to the plaintiff's present condition made by the motor vehicle accident and the hospitalisation in terms of whether one or other had added to her existing need arising from her underlying or pre-existing condition or had accelerated the need. He stated that 'the hospitalisation sure didn't help her . . . so in what way did it cause any deterioration? It certainly caused a significant period of increased dysfunction. Did she ever get back to what she was before? Well, she tells me she didn't. Would that be a factor in prescribing for her sleepover? Perhaps.' (t.385). The reference to 'sleepover' was a reference to the need for a carer to live with the plaintiff overnight.

123 Mr Menzies, QC, counsel for the plaintiff, cross-examined Associate Professor Jones on the question as to contribution which the prolonged hospitalisation made to the plaintiff's disabilities as distinct from the accident itself. In the several answers given in cross-examination, he made the following points:

- Apart from the upper limbs, he could see no significant assessable deterioration in the plaintiff's condition because of the accident.
- As between the motor car accident and the prolonged period of hospitalisation (including the 20 odd days in intensive care with multiple organ failure), and the proportion of each of those to her ultimate presentation when he examined her, Associate Professor Jones stated:

  'Initially, and probably for the first year or 18 months, the intensive care problems would have been a higher proportion than they ultimately became. So that issue would diminish with the passage of time . . .' (t.390)

- Following recovery from abnormal liver function, in the longer term, the effects would be small, if any at all.
- Given the disability consequent upon the upper limb injuries, the plaintiff's reduced capacity for personal care came down to the accident itself rather than the intensive care unit hospitalisation period.

124 Medical evidence was led on behalf of the defendant in the motor vehicle accident proceedings (Mr. Gardner). It is unnecessary to detail that evidence and it is sufficient here to note the following:

- Associate Professor Richard F. Jones in his report of 1 August 2001 refers to the accident as having accelerated the plaintiff's condition by some months or perhaps years. He does not suggest that there are ongoing physical effects resulting from the hospital treatment.
- Dr. Alistair Corbett, neurologist, in his report of 8 January 2003 (p 4), states that there had been a marked deterioration in upper limb strength and function as a result of the fractures. He observed that the accident resulted in prolonged period of forced immobility which resulted in loss of strength and contractures. Dr Corbett did not, in particular, identify a contribution to the plaintiff's physical disabilities as a result of medical treatment at Westmead Hospital.

125 Whilst the report of Dr Winer of 29 January 2002 attributes ongoing effects to the hospital treatment specifically to weakness resulting from non-use of the right upper limb and increased fatigue, on analysis, I do not consider that Dr Winer's opinion on these matters

sufficiently takes into account the ongoing effect of the orthopaedic injuries sustained in the accident. I consider that in evaluating what continuing effects, if any, flow from the hospital treatment, it is necessary to bring into account the plaintiff's evidence, the basis identified in Dr Winer's report for his opinion and the concessions made by him in cross-examination.

The plaintiff's pre and post-accident hospitalisation condition

126 The plaintiff relied upon the reports of Dr. Winer to support a claim for ongoing disability arising from her hospital treatment and consequent need for additional personal and domestic care. That claim is complicated as elsewhere observed by reason of her pre-existing disabilities and the effects of the car accident.

The plaintiff's pre-injury condition and need for care

127 Prior to the accident, the plaintiff had two carers attending her home two hours in the morning and two hours in the evening. They assisted with food preparation, dressing, showering and assistance in getting to bed.

128 The plaintiff had limited use of her forearms. She could move both arms from the elbows including her hands. She could move her shoulder a little. She could use her arms to eat and was able to paint and draw.

129 The plaintiff was able to leave her home in the wheelchair being able to utilise its controls. She was also able to operate the remote control for the televison.

The plaintiff's post-hospital condition

130 Ms Markaboui gave evidence as to her post-injury/post-hospitalisation condition. This included evidence as to the following:

- She felt 'nerve pain' when she came out of ICU, described as 'like insects crawling on my skin' that lasted for some months.
- She had pain in her thighs, arms and legs, a pain not previously experienced.
- Her voice was different after the tracheostomy, but it improved over time.
- She had care and assistance when discharged home from her brother Tarek – especially to help with transfers because of her pain, muscle spasms and nerve pain. Accordingly, she had three carers, not two, as before for six months. Other family members also assisted including help to feed her.
- Her condition was worse now than before the accident. She said she could do nothing now with her arms. The carer feeds her now.
- She gets tired with her arms and frustrated.
- She is not able to sit upright in her chair as she falls to the left side.

- The plaintiff said she no longer goes shopping as she has panic attacks.
- She was unable to operate her remote control. Before the accident she could operate it. She cannot operate the mobile phone to make calls. She could do so before the accident.
- The pain in her spine is different from before. She previously had muscular aches. It is now painful on her right side down low.

131 I noted that Dr Winer in his report (pp 4–5) received a history from the plaintiff of increased pain since the accident and increased disability including weakness in the arms and that she fatigues more quickly. The plaintiff agreed that she took pain medication before the accident. She also said that she considered before the accident that she required more personal care than she was in fact then receiving.

132 Dr Winer considered, as earlier noted, that there was generalised weakness in the arms. Importantly, he stated in his report (p 11):

> The weakness in the right upper limb cannot be due to the small fracture at the outer side of the right elbow. The chip fracture was only a minor dislodgment of a small fragment from the long protuberance at the lateral aspect of the elbow . . .
>
> Some of the weakness could be a result of a significant period of non-use and then restricted use during her period of invalidity which would be experienced by anyone during the period of recovery from time in the intensive care unit with multiple organ failure. Muscles weaken and waste comparatively quickly. . . . The effect of such weakness and wasting is all the more significant in a person where the muscles are already at a serious disadvantage as in spinal muscular . . .

133 Dr Winer observed that:

- Whilst some wasting and much weakness can be reversed in an otherwise healthy person, the plaintiff was unable to participate fully in muscle strengthening exercise programmes, partly due to pain, party due to weakness and party due to fatigability.
- The fracture of the left humerus without significant displacement would be followed by recovery from weakness in a normal person. Wasting and weakness from non-use is 'relatively more significant when these occur in muscles which already are partially atrophied and weak' (p 12).
- The loss of residual function of the right upper limb was the most significant loss with gross increased disability in that limb. The inability to exercise vigorously subsequent to October 1999 was partly due to the residual effects of generalised weakness and fatigue.

134 In this way, Dr. Winer linked the medical complications, what he termed multiple organ failure, to the plaintiff's ongoing disabilities. He considered her condition was stationary.

135 In cross-examination, Dr. Winer conceded:

- The plaintiff's scoliosis has probably worsened and this would restrict the lungs and hence breathing and bring on fatigue.
- The scoliosis, however, would not be expected to increase so rapidly as to be a major cause of respiratory compromise.
- Muscle wasting would result from immobility of the arm in plaster, especially in a person who already has muscle atrophy.
- The fact that the plaintiff suffered liver dysfunction as distinct from liver failure did not alter his overall conclusions.
- The factors restricting use of the arm were contractures, pain and fatigue.
- The fatigue is caused by the long term effects of the extreme muscle wasting due to periods of inactivity with further muscle atrophy.

136 In re-examination, Dr Winer restated his view that weakness after 19 days in intensive care and associated immobility in that period produced weakness in the plaintiff. The period of weakness, that is, the combination of fatigue, tiredness and weakness of muscles, in her case would have lasted longer than with the normal patient. She was thereby rendered less able to regain function, particularly in the upper limbs, due to that combination of factors.

137 The hospital's medical witnesses did not deal with the evidence of Dr. Winer on these aspects. Dr. David Bowers, specialist rehabilitation physician, did assess the plaintiff but does not directly or precisely seek to say that the period in intensive care and the dysfunction for which the plaintiff was there treated had made no contribution for her ongoing disabilities. He does state that the motor vehicle accident impacted upon the plaintiff's employment capacity such as it was. He then addressed, in his report of 7 June 2002, her specific needs. He considered that she required, at that time, six hours per day personal care assistance and three and a half hours per week domestic care assistance.

138 The evidence, in fact, supports the conclusion that the plaintiff would have recovered from many of the effects of the conditions due to the hospital's breach of duty and which put her into the intensive care unit and for the treatment given for those conditions following a period of approximately 18 months. The evidence establishes clearly enough that the fractures and the immobilisation consequent upon the treatment for them would themselves have produced muscle wasting within a comparatively short period of time, perhaps days or weeks, and that this contributed to the loss of the flexibility and muscle strength that she formerly had.

139 Accordingly, in assessing damages for breach of duty by the hospital, it is necessary to have regard to:

(a) The nature of the medical conditions produced by the negligent treatment.
(b) The fact that those conditions combined to render the plaintiff gravely ill to the point of being life-threatening.

(c) The need for urgent intensive treatment to address and bring under control the medical conditions resulting from the acts and omissions of the hospital.
(d) The fact that the plaintiff experienced extreme distress, discomfort and dysfunction in terms of her level of consciousness and the other effects which I have earlier set out.
(e) The ongoing effects of (a), (b), (c) and (d) was particularly marked over a period of 18 months.

140 I will return to the assessment of damages in relation to these matters. Before doing so, I turn to the evidence on the plaintiff's psychological condition.

Psychological sequelae

141 Dr Anthony WF Harris, consultant psychiatrist, has treated the plaintiff since her initial referral in 1994. At that time he saw the plaintiff for depressive symptoms, she having had chronic depression which was traced in part to a history of past alleged sexual abuse and the frustrations experienced due to her significantly disabled state.

142 Initial treatment at that time was directed to control of substance abuse and thereafter treatment of the complex mix of depressive and anxiety symptoms.

143 Over the period 1994 to 1998, the plaintiff became more independent, electing to move out of her family home and she took up a TAFE course.

144 At the beginning of 1999, the plaintiff was again referred to Dr Harris, due to an increase in symptoms of depression and anxiety. Over a period of seven months, up to the time of the motor vehicle accident, Dr Harris treated the plaintiff for increased depression, anxiety and anger and this treatment had been ongoing up till the date of the car accident.

145 Dr Harris, who I regard as an impressive witness, stated that subsequent to the car accident, the plaintiff's psychiatric morbidity centred on four areas:

(a) depression as to her loss of independence and increasing levels of disability;
(b) post-traumatic phenomena associated with an increase in anxiety and related panic attacks due to fears surrounding travel;
(c) anger about her treatment in Westmead Hospital;
(d) increase in her pain secondary to the accident.

146 Dr Harris has been treating the plaintiff since 1994 when he worked at the Wentworth Area Health Service and subsequently following his move to the Western Sydney Area Health Service in about 1997 or 1998.

147 In this detailed report of 8 March 2005, Dr Harris sets out the history of the plaintiff's condition and treatment in respect of a

condition of chronic depression, mixed anxiety disorder together with the history of substance abuse, inter-personal difficulties and pain which has troubled the plaintiff for many years.

148 He noted that the number of interacting conditions affecting the plaintiff had led to marked limitation in her daily functioning initially and a difficulty with suicidal ideation on which she had initially acted on at least one occasion. However, over the course of treatment there was substantial improvement in her symptoms and her functioning. He saw her just prior to the motor vehicle accident on 1 October 1999.

149 In February 1999, the plaintiff returned to Dr Harris for treatment following an incident involving sexual abuse. By October 1999, she had improved and Dr Harris, in evidence, stated that his expectation was that she would continue with depression but that she would recover from the exacerbation due to the severe stressor that occurred in February of that year. He expected that she would have been able to get back into life and that the severity of her depression would have reduced and that she would be able to participate in activities such as her interest in art and music.

150 The plaintiff's principal psychiatric symptom since the accident has been the return of her major depression. Associated symptoms included disturbance of sleep pattern, which has also been affected by an increase in symptoms of panic and anxiety and frequent nightmares.

151 Apart from the depressive symptoms, there had been a recurrence of her anxiety-based symptoms subsequent to the accident. Dr Harris said that the plaintiff experienced considerable panic attacks when going outside the house and feels very frightened when she comes to cross over roads, particularly busy roads. Such fears had limited her ability to attend hydrotherapy. These anxiety symptoms, Dr Harris stated, were hallmarks of a post-traumatic stress disorder.

152 Of particular relevance to the proceedings against the hospital, Dr Harris stated that the plaintiff's post-traumatic symptoms were also related to her stay in hospital, particularly the experience of being in the Intensive Care Unit. In 1999, she was required to attend Dr Harris at Westmead Hospital and this had triggered painful memories of her treatment at the hospital and caused increased anxiety. He recorded in his report of 16 May 2002 (p 5) (part of Exhibit E) that she continued to have difficult and frightening dreams, some of which included hospital experiences.

153 In his report of 7 March 2005 (also part of Exhibit E), Dr Harris summarised the history of consultations prior to the motor vehicle accident and then the effect of the motor vehicle accident on her. He observed in the report (p 7) that subsequent to the initial post-accident consultation, her level of depression increased as did her anxiety and agoraphobia. Her symptoms were aggravated by her realisation that she was not regaining her strength and movement and was becoming more restricted than before. Dr Harris, in summary, stated that the plaintiff

> had experienced a significant exacerbation of her mood and anxiety disorders accompanied by an increase in the level of despair that she experiences and recurrent ideas of suicide. She had, in Dr Harris' assessment, become totally dependent upon carers for all her needs.
>
> 154 In cross-examination, Dr Harris confirmed that the anxiety symptoms related to her fear of hospitals arising from her treatment at Westmead remain.
>
> 155 The plaintiff reported being extremely traumatised by the hospitalisation and recounted patchy memories of events during her admission. Subsequent to the initial post-accident consultation, her level of depression increased, as did her anxiety and agoraphobia. The plaintiff's realisation that her strength was not returning and that she was more restricted than before was causing her stress and additionally she experienced panic when outside the house and other anxiety symptoms. Dr Harris said that the hierarchy of fears which the plaintiff experienced subsequent to the accident had many features of a post-traumatic stress disorder.
>
> 156 In cross-examination, Dr Harris gave evidence that in 1988 the plaintiff had a number of attendances upon him in relation to pain, panic attacks and anxiety.
>
> 157 In terms of the plaintiff's past history, he confirmed that the plaintiff had attended Nepean Hospital (June or July 1995) in relation to a suicide attempt and a further admission for a suicide attempt on 5 July 1999, both occasions involving an overdose of therapeutic drugs.
>
> 158 Whilst Dr Harris identified certain fears engendered by her experiences in Westmead Hospital, the severity of her anxiety condition, agoraphobia and mood disturbance appear to be principally related or attributable to the loss of independence consequent upon the injuries received in the motor vehicle accident and the lack of recovery of her physical health. As Dr Harris expressed in his report of 7 March 2005 (p 8), the disturbance in mood has increased as the extent and treatment resistant nature of her physical disability has become evident.
>
> 159 On this basis, it has been the motor vehicle accident and its physical effects that have given rise to an ongoing exacerbation of the plaintiff's pre-accident psychological condition and well-being. The psychological impact or effects of the treatment at Westmead Hospital were of a more limited nature as described in Dr Harris' report.

It should be remembered that it is not every error in treatment which can be said to be negligent.

Only errors which indicate the practitioner has fallen below the standard of a reasonably competent medical practitioner. Thus, a patient who has unsuccessfully undergone a sterilisation procedure may not be successful in pursuing a claim in negligence, if she is only able to prove that the sterilisation procedure failed, and no more. The point is made clear in *Hancock v State of Queensland.*

Hancock v State of Queensland [2002] QSC 27

Atkinson J

[1] Susan Hancock is a woman who has faced much adversity in her life with considerable fortitude. In June 1997, she was in her mid thirties. She had three children: a son aged 16, another son aged 12 and a daughter aged 3. Her second son suffered from a number of disabilities and required constant attention; so much so that she had been reluctant to have another child until almost nine years after his birth. After the birth of her third child, Mrs Hancock and her husband made a definite decision to have no more children.

[2] After consultation with her local general practitioner, Dr Friend, Mrs Hancock decided to undergo a sterilisation procedure at the Gold Coast Hospital.

[3] She attended at the Gold Coast Hospital for a consultation where the nature of a laparoscopic tubal ligation procedure was explained to her. She was told that there was a one to three, or perhaps two, in 1000 failure rate for this procedure. It is common ground that she was given appropriate warnings about the nature of the operation and the possible failure rate. Mrs Hancock was admitted to the Gold Coast Hospital on 3 June 1997 and the tubal ligation by laparoscopy was performed on 4 June 1997. It was apparently a straightforward and uneventful operation with no complications. When she asked a nurse about contraception, she was told she was now sterilised and could cease taking the oral contraceptive pill. However, after two normal menstrual periods she ceased menstruating. She then discovered that she was pregnant with twins. In the event, only one twin developed and Mrs Hancock gave birth to her fourth child, Aaron, on 26 May 1998. The birth of the child so soon after the tubal ligation demonstrates that the operation was not successful in sterilising Mrs Hancock. However, these facts only give rise to some compensable injury if the plaintiffs can establish, on the balance of probabilities, that the loss occurred as a result of the negligence of the defendant.

[4] Particulars of negligence were set out in the second further amended statement of claim filed on 19 July 1999. Most of these were formally or informally abandoned during the trial.

[5] Having had the advantage of seeing Mrs Hancock in the witness box, I agree with the assessment of Dr Byrne, a consultant psychiatrist who examined her for the purpose of these proceedings, when he said that she is an intelligent and fairly resilient individual who has been exposed to substantial adversity. She is an admirable woman who has coped well with the difficulties with which she has been faced and has held her family together, often against considerable odds. In order to succeed in their action in this court, however, the plaintiffs, Mr and Mrs Hancock, must show not only that the operation failed but that the failure of the operation was due to negligence on the part of the servants or agents of the State of Queensland. The negligence in question in this

case would be shown if the defendant had failed to exercise all reasonable skill, care and expertise in performing the medical procedure of tubal ligation by which Filshie clips were applied to Mrs Hancock's fallopian tubes.

[6] A medical practitioner is under a duty to exercise reasonable care and skill in the provision of professional advice and treatment. The standard of care required of a medical practitioner, as a person possessing special skill and competence, 'is that of the ordinary skilled person exercising and professing to have that special skill'.

[7] During the trial, it was agreed between the parties that the damages recoverable by the plaintiffs in the event of success were in the sum of $200,000, inclusive of interest. It was also agreed between the parties that of this sum, $90,000 was the sum attributable to the costs of raising the child, Aaron, born after the sterilisation operation. The only question in issue, therefore, is the question of liability. In order to determine that question, it is necessary to consider the circumstances surrounding and during the sterilisation procedure.

[8] Once Mrs Hancock had made the decision that she wished to be permanently sterilised she saw Dr Friend, her general practitioner. He referred her to the Gold Coast Hospital for a tubal ligation. The referral was dated 27 November 1996. Mrs Hancock then attended at the Gold Coast Hospital where she discussed tubal ligation with Dr Jayasinghe on 27 March 1997. Mrs Hancock asked to have her tubes cut and tied and the doctor told her that this procedure was not usually performed and that the more common current practice was to use Filshie clips to occlude the tubes. The doctor explained to her the nature of Filshie clips, the failure rate of such an operation, the risk of an ectopic pregnancy and that the operation would be performed laparoscopically. Mrs Hancock returned to the hospital on 24 April 1997 when she signed a consent form for the operation to be performed laparoscopically.

[9] A Filshie clip is a titanium hinged clip about 13.9 millimetres in length lined with silicone rubber. It is clipped over the fallopian tubes of a woman in order to block the fallopian tubes to the passage of eggs. Filshie clips must be applied to both fallopian tubes and are applied using an applicator supplied by the manufacturer of the clips.

[10] Mrs Hancock was admitted to the hospital on 3 June 1997. She was seen by an anaesthetist and given pre-operative medication. She also saw Dr Justin Nasser who was to perform the operation. Dr Nasser is now a fellow in obstetrics and gynaecological ultrasound at the Royal Womens' Hospital in Melbourne. He graduated from the University of Queensland with a Bachelor of Medicine and Bachelor of Surgery in 1991. After completing his residency training at the Royal Brisbane and Royal Womens' Hospital, he commenced obstetric and gynaecological training in 1996. In 1997, he obtained a Diploma of the Royal Australian College of Obstetricians and Gynaecologists and in 2000 was admitted to membership of the Royal Australian and New Zealand College of

Obstetricians and Gynaecologists. He was, therefore, a relatively junior doctor or registrar training to be an obstetrician and gynaecologist at the time he performed the operation on Mrs Hancock. At that time, he had assisted in more than 30 operations to attach Filshie clips to the fallopian tubes and had himself performed 10 such operations. He was supervised by a consultant during the procedure. The standard of care expected is not reduced because he was relatively inexperienced. An inexperienced medical practitioner must adhere to the standard of reasonable care expected from a practitioner experienced in that area of practice.

[11] Dr Nasser explained the nature of the laparoscopic procedure and informed Mrs Hancock that if there were any complications such as bleeding he may have to perform a 'bikini line cut' (otherwise known as a mini laparotomy). She agreed to that but told him that unless complications arose during the operation she wanted a laparoscopy.

[12] Because of an unexpected delay in the operating theatre on that day, Mrs Hancock's surgery was postponed to the following day when there was time available for the procedure.

[13] Dr Nasser performed the procedure on Mrs Hancock under the supervision of Dr Joanne Ludlow. Dr Ludlow completed her primary medical degree in the United Kingdom in 1987. In 1988, she commenced working in obstetrics and gynaecology. In 1993, after qualifying as a member of the Royal College of Obstetricians and Gynaecologists in London, she moved to Brisbane. In 1996, she became a Fellow of the Royal Australian College of Obstetricians and Gynaecologists and became a consultant obstetrician and gynaecologist at the Gold Coast Hospital. She presently works as a consultant obstetrician and gynaecologist at the King Edward Memorial Hospital in Perth. At the time she supervised the surgery on Mrs Hancock, she had performed approximately 300 Filshie clip sterilisations and has since performed a further 500.

[14] Neither Dr Ludlow nor Dr Nasser specifically recalls the procedure performed on Mrs Hancock although both recall Mrs Hancock. I accept that neither has specific recollection because the operation was itself uneventful and routine and there was nothing to fix it in their memories. Mrs Hancock was under general anaesthetic at the time so of course has no memory of what occurred during the operation. There are, however, hospital notes prepared immediately after the operation by Dr Nasser which are of some assistance in determining what occurred during the operation. It is also useful to consider the usual practice of both of the medical practitioners concerned before determining whether or not there was any deviation from that usual practice during the procedure under consideration.

[15] Dr Ludlow and Dr Nasser gave evidence that their usual practice is that after the patient is administered an anaesthetic, her abdomen is insufflated with carbon dioxide gas which elevates the anterior abdominal wall from the abdominal contents. Two small incisions are made,

one just under the umbilicus where a 10 millimetre port and a very small camera are inserted; the other is a suprapubic incision where the port for the Filshie clip applicator is inserted.

[16] The camera displays an image of the abdominal contents on a television screen visible throughout the operating room. The patient's pelvic organs are inspected for normality or otherwise. The fallopian tubes are identified and traced to the fimbrial or ampullary end to ensure that the correct structures have been identified. A Filshie clip is placed on the isthmic or narrow portion closest to the uterus of each fallopian tube using the Filshie clip applicator. The applicator is compressed until blanching is seen on either side of the clip ensuring the desired crushing effect of the tube has been achieved. After a clip has been placed on each tube, the tube is then lifted and examined on both sides to ensure that the clip is on the tube, it is on the isthmic portion of the tube and is completely occluding the tubal lumen. The incisions are then closed.

[17] I accept Dr Ludlow's evidence that she was obsessive in following the correct procedure both when she was herself operating and when she was training and supervising and that, in accordance with her usual practice, she carefully checked the fallopian tubes both anteriorly and posteriorly to ensure that the clips had been correctly applied.

[18] That this routine was carried out during the surgery performed on Mrs Hancock on 4 June 1997 is confirmed by notes made by Dr Nasser on that day. It was a routine procedure from which Mrs Hancock made an uneventful recovery.

[19] It was not until Mrs Hancock became aware that she was pregnant that it was revealed that the surgery had not been successful in causing sterilisation. A hysterosalpingogram, which was performed on 23 November 1998, revealed that dye was able to pass along the right fallopian tube and that therefore it had not fully occluded. Four x-ray films were taken during the hysterosalpingogram which show the outline of two closed Filshie clips.

[20] The fact that the procedure has failed to sterilise a woman does not of itself disclose whether the surgeon exercised reasonable skill and care in the performance of the procedure. The known failure rate of this procedure, quoted during the trial as between 1 and 3 in 1000, includes cases where the surgeon has been negligent. In other cases, the failure cannot be explained by any failure to exercise reasonable skill and care.

[21] In order to prove that the failure to sterilise her was due to the negligence of the surgeon, Mrs Hancock relied on expert evidence from Dr Ronald Adam. Dr Adam is a very experienced obstetrician and gynaecologist who is in private practice in Brisbane with an appointment to the Royal Women's Hospital. His first report tendered in evidence was dated 27 October 1999. In that report he speculated that the Filshie clip applicator may not have been properly serviced. He also expressed the view that the failure rate in these procedures using Filshie clips was higher than previously thought. He suggested that further

information about her case could be obtained by doing another laparoscopy to ascertain the circumstances of the failed sterilisation procedure. Such a procedure is invasive and has not been undertaken in this case.

[22] By the time of writing a second report dated 13 September 2000, Dr Adam had examined the x-ray films referred to earlier in these reasons. He concluded that the clip had not been closed correctly as it showed a 'convex curve on the upper limb'. He said that the 'lens of the clip should be parallel to ensure successful occlusion of the tube'. He was of the view that there were three possible reasons for that appearance: the clip was placed on a broad or thick portion of the tube; the clip applicator was defective; the clip was not correctly closed by the operator.

[23] Two matters can be immediately disposed of. Firstly, as to the question of the failure rate raised in his first report, Dr Adam said in his second report that the failure rate was 1 to 3 in 1000. Although in oral evidence he said he believed the failure rate to be much higher, he conceded that in June 1997 a reasonably competent surgeon could properly advise a patient that the failure rate of a Filshie clip sterilisation procedure was 1 to 3 in 1000. This was the failure rate quoted to Mrs Hancock so there was no failure to adequately warn of the failure rate of this particular form of sterilisation procedure.

[24] Secondly, it was common ground between the parties by the end of the trial that the clip applicator which was used had been properly serviced and was not defective. This leaves open only the question of whether the clip was incorrectly applied or placed on the wrong structure or the wrong part of the structure by the surgeon. If either of those occurred, then it would suggest a failure to exercise reasonable skill and care on the part of the surgeon.

[25] In his oral evidence, Dr Adam said that if the clip is correctly closed, the limbs of the clip should be parallel and the top of the clip should be flat. The x ray film shows that the top limb of the clip is convex. He says that in his opinion, if the top limb of the clip is convex, it will not occlude the fallopian tube properly. He then said the top of the clip should be 'flattened and parallel'. He relied for his opinion on two manuals published by Femcare who distribute the Filshie clip. Although the copies of excerpts of those manuals tendered in evidence by the plaintiff do not disclose the edition from which they are excerpted or the publication date, it appears that the first was published in the 1980s and the second was published in the late 1990s. The first edition clearly states that 'the clip must end up with a flat top' and instructs the operator, both in words and by an illustration, to confirm, when finally inspecting the clip, that it has a flat top.

[26] In the later edition of the manual, no such instruction or warning is given although the introduction contains what is described as an illustration of a permanently closed clip and gives the appearance that the top of the clip is flattened. The words accompanying this illustration say that latching has occurred and the clip cannot be opened or removed. On

page 5 of this later edition of the manual, the following instructions appear under the heading 'Applying the Filshie Clip':

> 1. Inspect the tube thoroughly.
> 2. Ensure that the Clip can accommodate the whole diameter of the tube.
> 3. Place the Clip on the isthmic portion of the tube, 1–2 cm from the corner.
> 4. If there is any doubt about the securing of the Clip, a second Clip may be placed immediately adjacent to the first on the uterine side.
> 5. In the unlikely event of the tube being too large for the Clip, use an alternative method of tubal occlusion.
> 6. Having established the best location for the Clip, the applicator should be re-opened and advanced a few millimetres to move the tube gently to the back of the Clip, close to the hinge.
> 7. Lock the Clip into position by applying **firm, but gentle pressure** on the finger bar in a **smooth action** until the stop is reached.
> 8. Do not use an abrupt action or the tube may be transected. Should this happen, a second Clip may be applied on the proximal (uterine) side of the transection. This should be done **very slowly**.
> 9. It is quite noticeable, but quite normal, for the muscle of the tube to 'give' during Clip application.
> 10. When the Clip is locked into position, release the finger bar and the Clip will automatically free itself from the applicator.

[27] Under the heading 'Inspection of Clip' the later manual says:

> Using the empty mouth of the applicator as a probe, inspect the secured Clip, to confirm that the entire tube has been captured, the upper jaw has been compressed and is securely locked under the nose of the lower jaw (Diagram A) and the Clip is in the correct position on the Fallopian tube (not on either the round or ovarian ligament or the fold of the mesosalpinx).

[28] None of this is contrary to the procedure adopted by Dr Nasser under the careful supervision of Dr Ludlow.

[29] Dr Adam also expressed a tentative opinion that the x-ray films might show that the clip on the right side might have been attached to a broader part of the tube than would be preferred but he was unable to be certain from the x-ray. The defence relied on expert evidence from Dr Keeping, who is also a very experienced obstetrician and gynaecologist. In his opinion, the x-ray was too imprecise to show the position of the clip on the tube. The evidence given by Dr Ludlow showed that she carefully supervised and checked the procedure undertaken by Dr Nasser. It is most unlikely that she would not have observed if Dr Nasser had placed the clip on an incorrect structure or on the wrong part of the tube or in some other way had incorrectly placed it. The plaintiff has not

been able to show that this is a probable explanation for the failure of the procedure to sterilise Mrs Hancock.

[30] In Dr Adam's opinion the likely cause of the failure to completely occlude Mrs Hancock's right fallopian tube was that the Filshie clip on that tube had been inadequately closed although he agreed in cross-examination that the x-rays show that the upper limb had been secured under the lip on the lower limb.

[31] Dr Adam was not himself, however, very experienced in the use of Filshie clips. He had only performed 20 or 30 procedures using Filshie clips. He said in evidence that he had never been confident in them since they were first available, that they had gone through a number of different models and so he tended to stay with his previous method of sterilisation, the use of a Fallope ring placed over the tube. He admitted that this procedure gave rise to an increased risk of bleeding or tearing of the tube. It does not appear that it is a more appropriate procedure than the use of Filshie clips. Dr Keeping, who has performed about one thousand sterilisation procedures using Filshie clips, was of the view that laparoscopic sterilisation by clips was the preferred method of permanent contraception.

[32] Dr Adam admitted that his source of information for forming the opinion that the top limb of the clip must be flat before the clip is properly closed was limited to the information contained in the manuals. A number of problems arise from this reliance: firstly, the manuals and the clips have changed from the clips produced 20 years ago and the manual produced in the early 1980s, where the instruction appears that the operator should ensure that the upper limb of the clip is flat. Secondly, Dr Adam was not relying on expertise drawn from his own experience with Filshie clips. Rather, Dr Adam was critical of Filshie clips as a method of sterilisation and it appears this has coloured his views of the causes of the failure of this sterilisation procedure. I cannot accept his opinion that a Filshie clip must have a 'completely flat top limb' before a surgeon could be satisfied that it was completely closed.

[33] My reasons for so concluding are based on the evidence given by Dr Ludlow, Dr Keeping and Dr Clegg. That evidence was supported by the physical appearance of a number of clips which were tendered during the trial. Dr Ludlow carefully described how a surgeon would be able to conclude that a Filshie clip is properly closed. She was not of the view that the flexible upper limb had to be completely flat nor had she received any training or instruction to suggest that was so. Dr Keeping said that the surgeon should try to flatten the clip as it was fastened but its final appearance would depend on a number of variables such as the size, width and fatness of the tube.

[34] Dr Keeping demonstrated the proper method of closing a Filshie clip in the witness box. The upper limb of that clip after closure was slightly flattened once the upper limb was clipped under the lip of the lower limb but it was by no means completely flat and retained some convexity. The extrusion of silicone rubber on either side between the

upper and lower limbs of the clip showed that complete closure had been achieved.

[35] Dr Clegg is a senior lecturer in biomaterials in the School of Mechanical, Manufacturing and Medical Engineering at the Queensland University of Technology. Dr Clegg used an applicator similar to that used in Mrs Hancock's procedure to close a number of clips. He carefully simulated a situation where the applicator was increasingly out of calibration. He also closed clips using the applicator, properly calibrated, as it was when Mrs Hancock's procedure was undertaken. He measured the distance between various parts of the upper and lower limbs of these clips and reproduced the upper profile of the closed clips in the form of a graph or diagram. The more the applicator was out of calibration, the more convex the upper limb of the closed clip became. He also measured the clip on the right fallopian tube as shown in the x-rays. He was obliged to scale back the measurements and average the results from the three x-rays to compensate for distortion and to achieve maximum accuracy. The result was accurate to within 10 percent. Even allowing for this, the profile of the clip in the x-rays was more consistent with the clips correctly closed with a properly calibrated applicator than with the clips which were inadequately closed. The clips used on Mrs Hancock's fallopian tubes were correctly closed; the upper limb was flattened although it retained some convexity which is ordinarily present in a properly closed clip.

[36] I have concluded that the Filshie clip on the right fallopian tube, which did not successfully occlude the tube, was properly closed and placed on the appropriate part of the fallopian tube. While the failure to properly close a clip or the failure to correctly place the clip are common causes of the failure of a sterilisation procedure none of them, individually or in combination, was the cause of the failure in this case. The failure to sterilise Mrs Hancock was an example of the known but inexplicable failure rate of this particular procedure, where the failure was not due to error or negligence on the part of the surgeon. It follows that judgment should be given for the defendant.

Sometimes the allegation is that, while an operation was performed competently, and no negligence is alleged in the performance of the procedure, additional damage is caused to the patient during an operation. By not informing the patient of the addiitonal damage which has occurred, the doctor has behaved negligently in depriving the patient of the opportunity to seek effective treatment for the additional damage. Such was the case in *Wighton v Arnot*.

Wighton v Arnot [2005] NSWSC 637

Studdert J.
The plaintiff, Liza-Lee Wighton, sues the defendant, Richard Arnot, seeking damages for negligence. The defendant has denied liability and, indeed, the contest on this issue has been a strenuous one.

[2] The defendant is a general surgeon who, in 1999, was carrying on his practice in Inverell where the plaintiff lived, and continues to live. The plaintiff developed a lump on the right side of her neck in August of 1999 and the defendant operated on her on three occasions. The plaintiff's case is based upon what happened at the third of the operations and subsequently. Put shortly, it is the plaintiff's case that the defendant severed the right spinal accessory nerve at the third of the surgical procedures undertaken, and that his treatment of the plaintiff thereafter was negligent in that:

(a) he failed to inform the plaintiff of his suspicion that he had severed that nerve;
(b) he failed by appropriate examination to confirm that he had severed the nerve;
(c) he failed to refer the plaintiff to an appropriate specialist for timely remedial surgery.

[3] In response, the defendant's case was that his concerns that he may have severed the nerve were alleviated by submitting the plaintiff to an appropriate test before she was discharged from hospital and that his opportunity to further examine the plaintiff and, if need be, to further treat her or give her appropriate advice as to further treatment was frustrated when the plaintiff failed to attend for a follow-up consultation as requested by the defendant.

[4] Having broadly stated the issues on liability, I propose to record some detail as to the plaintiff's background and the history of her treatment from the time that the lump was detected.

The plaintiff's background

[5] The plaintiff was born on 23 October 1973 and was brought up at Inverell, except between the ages of six and fifteen, when she lived at Quirindi. The plaintiff attended school until year 12 but then worked as a rouseabout for four years and after that worked in a bakery for a short period. Then, in about 1994, the plaintiff obtained employment in a nursing home at Inverell and worked there for two years. In 1996 the plaintiff undertook a traineeship as a kitchen hand in a restaurant at Inverell and was working in that restaurant when the operations were performed upon her in 1999. The plaintiff was also working at that time in a position caring for disabled adults.

[6] Early in 1999 the plaintiff commenced to live with the man who became her husband on 25 March 2000. There are now two sons of that marriage, Bobby, who was born on 9 September 2000, and Riley, who was born on 15 October 2003.

[7] The plaintiff said, and I accept, that she enjoyed good health before the happening of the events which have brought her to this Court. The plaintiff said she enjoyed pre-injury outdoor activities such as waterskiing and fishing and she also played indoor cricket, soccer and hockey. The plaintiff is dominantly right-handed.

The development of the lump and the treatment that followed

[8] The plaintiff said that she felt a lump on the right side of her neck in July 1999 and consulted her general practitioner, Dr Bentel. By the time the plaintiff had consulted Dr Bentel again in August 1999 the lump had grown and the plaintiff was referred to Dr Robilliard in Tamworth. However, he sent her back to Dr Bentel, and Dr Bentel then referred the plaintiff to Dr Arnot. Three surgical procedures followed.

[9] The plaintiff was admitted to Inverell Hospital after Dr Arnot explained he would drain the mass in her neck. For this purpose, the plaintiff was admitted to Inverell Hospital and on 10 August 1999, Dr Arnot operated. His operation report reads (T 440):

> Explore right cervical nodes. Dissection down through the sterno-mastoid muscle to a large lymph node. Blunt dissection leading to a large abscess cavity. Swab sent for culture.

[10] This first procedure was uneventful and the plaintiff was discharged from hospital the same day.

[11] However, the lump recurred and the plaintiff consulted Dr Arnot again on 31 August 1999. According to the plaintiff, Dr Arnot advised that the lump which had recurred was probably a haematoma and he said that this time when he operated he would put a Yates drain in to allow for more drainage. Hence the plaintiff was re-admitted to Inverell Hospital for a second operation on 1 September 1999. The operation notes reveal that following incision steps were taken to drain the recurrent right cervical abscess and a Yates drain was put in position.

[12] On 6 September the drain was removed but, unfortunately, the lump came back, and the plaintiff said she noticed this on her birthday on 23 October 1999. So it was that she saw Dr Arnot again on 25 October 1999. The plaintiff was sent by Dr Arnot for a CT scan and an ultrasound, and, having seen the results, Dr Arnot concluded that the abscess had recurred.

[13] On 28 October 1999 Dr Arnot advised the plaintiff that he would have to operate again to remove the whole mass. The plaintiff was admitted to the Inverell Hospital for the third time on 10 November 1999. Dr Arnot operated on her later that day.

[14] The operation notes are in Dr Arnot's handwriting. He has wrongly stated the date of the operation in those notes to be 9 November 1999. The detail of the notes was read onto the transcript by the defendant in the course of his evidence (T 449–450):

> Q: Can you read very slowly your handwriting in relation to operation?
>
> A: It starts, 'Right radical neck dissection to four node levels and

> removed', I think it says underneath there. Then it says, 'Skin crease incision excising the old scar. Well defined plane identified outside the large lymph node mass. Densely adherent to sternomastoid muscle and the internal jugular vein.' Then there is an annotation underneath it that says, 'Cat gut/black silk/ diathermy haemostasis. Total node clearance (specimen contained a large cavity full of purulent fluid. Good view and preservation of digastric muscle. Internal jugular vein sternomastoid muscle.' *Then in brackets underneath that, '? division of accessory nerve as it enters' – entered or enters – 'entered the sternomastoid muscle, transversed the node mass.'* Then underneath that is 'Repair: Cat gut to platysma', then four slashes, 'zero prolene to skin. Suction drain'. My signature, and then postoperative instructions: '1. Monitor suction drain frequently. 2. Keep neck as still as possible.'
>
> (Emphasis added)

[15] The plaintiff said that the defendant did not inform her that he suspected he had severed the accessory nerve or any other nerve, and the plaintiff's evidence in this regard was not challenged, so I accept it. There is an issue as to what occurred between the plaintiff and the defendant in the time up to her discharge from hospital, but I will return to the detail of the evidence given by the plaintiff and by the defendant over this period when looking at the allegations of negligence. In the present context however, I do no more than record that the plaintiff was kept in hospital after this third procedure until 12 November 1999.

[16] Dr Arnot recorded on the hospital notes for 12 November 1999 that the plaintiff was to see Dr Bentel concerning the stitches and was to see Dr Arnot in three weeks. It is the plaintiff's case that she did attend upon Dr Arnot following her discharge from hospital the third time, but Dr Arnot denies that there was any such consultation.

[17] According to the plaintiff, following discharge from hospital the plaintiff was unable to lift her right arm and could not do the basic things for herself (T 21). Moreover, she said there was constant pain in the shoulder. So it was that the plaintiff consulted a physiotherapist, Ms Kearsey, within a week of her discharge from hospital. The plaintiff saw Dr Bentel in December 1999 and was referred for x-ray and ultrasound. Dr Bentel informed the plaintiff that she had a frozen shoulder.

[18] The plaintiff became aware of her first pregnancy around Christmas 1999.

[19] The plaintiff sought no further treatment for the shoulder during her pregnancy. Her evidence was that she attempted to return to work at the restaurant and found difficulty with that work before eventually ceasing at the end of January 2000. However, the plaintiff obtained work as an access officer working with disabled people. She managed to cope with this work until she was eight months pregnant. Because of the difficulties the plaintiff was experiencing with her shoulder, she said that her colleague was sympathetic and did the more physical tasks required (T 26).

[20] The plaintiff said her arm had not improved by the time of her marriage in March 2000. A photograph of the plaintiff on her wedding day became part of Ex F. That photograph shows wasting, which I am satisfied on the evidence is consistent with the plaintiff's case that the accessory nerve had indeed been severed in the procedure on 10 November 1999.

[21] In November 2000 the plaintiff consulted Dr Harding, a general practitioner, about her shoulder pain and she consulted another general practitioner, Dr Thatcher, in January 2001. Dr Thatcher prescribed Tegretol.

[22] The plaintiff was referred to Dr Lennox in Tamworth and she also saw Dr Diebold, an orthopaedic surgeon, in Inverell. To Dr Diebold the plaintiff said she complained of muscle wasting and of an inability to use the right arm, as well as of her persisting pain. Dr Diebold prescribed physiotherapy which the plaintiff underwent for some months without success.

[23] It was in April 2001 after the plaintiff said she dropped Bobby in the cot that she made an appointment with Dr Lennox. By the time the plaintiff saw Dr Lennox her evidence was that her right shoulder had dropped considerably and that she was experiencing persisting pain.

[24] The plaintiff said that in May 2001 she decided to see Dr Arnot again. By this time Dr Arnot was practising in Lismore, and the plaintiff attended upon him there. The plaintiff told him about her shoulder pain and her reduced ability to use her arm. The plaintiff said that she had suffered chronic pain since the surgery in 1999. Dr Arnot examined her, inter alia performing the 'shrug' test. He asked her to lift her right arm as high as she could. After this examination Dr Arnot said, according to the plaintiff, that he thought the plaintiff had injured her right accessory nerve.

[25] Dr Arnot, in his evidence about the consultation on 31 May 2001, said that there was visible wasting on examination and that there was no sternomastoid muscle movement. By that time Dr Arnot considered a nerve repair would be a waste of time.

[26] Dr Arnot agreed in cross examination (T 468) that when he saw the plaintiff on 31 May 2001 he had little difficulty in coming to a diagnosis that the spinal accessory nerve had been severed, and Dr Arnot went on to acknowledge (T 469) that he had divided the plaintiff's accessory nerve during the surgery that had been undertaken on 10 November 1999. I am satisfied that this is what had occurred.

[27] I am also satisfied on the evidence in this case that it was indeed too late for remedial surgery by May 2001.

[28] The plaintiff's evidence was that Dr Arnot suggested she should see Dr Syme, and the plaintiff did so. However, Dr Syme advised against surgery.

[29] The plaintiff then consulted Dr Lennox for an MRI scan and after that the plaintiff saw Dr Blum in August 2001.

[30] According to the plaintiff, it was Dr Blum who first informed her that her accessory nerve had been damaged in the surgery in November 1999. Dr Blum reported to the plaintiff's general practitioner on 28 August 2001 that when he saw the plaintiff he thought there was activity in the sternomastoid and in the trapezius, and he arranged for electrical studies to be undertaken which suggested that there was reinnervation in the area of the right accessory nerve. Dr Blum acknowledged in evidence in this Court that he was wrong in his examination findings in August 2001 and that the electrical studies he had arranged had provided a wrong result.

[31] In any event, Dr Blum said that he could do nothing for the plaintiff in August 2001. Dr Blum considered that at the time he saw her accessory nerve reconstruction was no longer feasible 'as the motor end plate is not operable after about eighteen months' (see report dated 14 February 2005).

[32] I have the benefit of other opinions in this case which also lead me to conclude that it was too late for repair surgery by the time the plaintiff saw Dr Blum. Dr Lyons, whose speciality includes the area of the neck, wrote in November 2002 that:

> Over a period of time muscle wasting occurs and eventually after one to two years the muscle has wasted so much that nerve grafting can no longer make any difference to the outcome.

[33] No further surgery has been undergone by the plaintiff, and I am satisfied that the opportunity for a successful repair was lost before the plaintiff discovered that her spinal accessory nerve had been severed in November 1999.

Was the defendant negligent in his treatment of the plaintiff and in his failure to advise her what had occurred in the course of surgery?

[34] The mass which the defendant had to remove from the plaintiff's neck measured approximately 3.3 × 2.4 × 2.9 cm in diameter. In evidence (T 453), the defendant said that deep in the surgical wound he encountered 'quite a large structure running from the mass and apparently running between the mass and the muscle, the sternomastoid muscle.' He said he could not be sure whether it was an artery or a vein or a nerve. The structure was divided by him between clips and was tied off with black silk. He went on to say this (T 453):

> A: Having divided it, it looked like a nerve, and I say that because an artery or a vein – there's usually a little spurt of blood when you divide it between clips, or you can often see the actual lumen, the interior of the artery or vein, whereas a nerve has a more solid, cut-end appearance.

> Having divided it, I thought it was probably a nerve – sorry, I thought it was a nerve.

[35] The defendant was then asked these questions and gave these answers:

> *HIS HONOUR*: Q: So, this was quite a deliberate procedure on your part to get to the mass, was it?
>
> A: It was, absolutely so, your Honour, because I did not know what the mass was, and the patient had made it plain that she wanted whatever it was totally removed, and I could not see how I could separate the two without possibly leaving whatever this lump was behind, or part of it behind.
>
> *BURKE*: Q: So, at the time that you were performing the operation, did you form an opinion as to whether or not you could dissect the mass away from the structure that you suspected and, indeed, identified as a nerve at the time?
>
> A: I only identified it as a nerve once it had been divided, and my feeling at the time was that I could not separate the two without possibly leaving some of the lump behind, which could have caused further problems.

[36] The plaintiff does not contend that the defendant was negligent in severing the nerve during the course of the operation. Nor is it contended that the defendant should have repaired the nerve during the surgery on 10 November 1999.

[37] Evidence was introduced through Dr Blum that the nerve ends should have been tagged, and there was evidence that the nerve could have been repaired at the time of the primary procedure. However, Mr Williams made it plain that the plaintiff was not advancing a case that the defendant was negligent either in severing the nerve or in failing to tag the nerve ends or in failing to repair the severed nerve.

[38] I accept that repair of a severed accessory nerve was outside the scope of the defendant's speciality and the exercise of due care on his part did not require of him that he endeavour to repair the severed nerve himself either on the day it was severed or subsequently. What the exercise of due care required of the defendant was that he take reasonable steps to determine whether it was the accessory nerve which had been severed, and that he alert the plaintiff as to what had occurred.

[39] It is clear from the surgical notes which the defendant made immediately after surgery that he at least suspected that the nerve he had divided was the accessory nerve. His note conveys this: '? division of accessory nerve.' When asked (T 454) why he had put a query in the note, the doctor responded:

> I put a query in because it was a large nerve. It was below the area where the accessory nerve normally lies. It was below and more to the front, more anterior than to where one would normally expect the accessory nerve to lie. I was unsure as to – I purely put that in as

> I thought it might be, but it was only a possibility at that stage. I thought it may have been, alternatively, one of the cutaneous nerves that run through the area in that sort of position.

[40] Plainly, it was the defendant's duty to seek to determine whether his suspicion at the time of surgery was well founded. What ought he to have done following the surgery in endeavouring to find out whether he had severed the plaintiff's accessory nerve? This issue was addressed by experts whose evidence was introduced in this case:

(a) Dr Lyons in his report dated 8 November 2004 said there were simple clinical bedside tests that would have established the severance:

> . . . in particular asking the patient to raise her arm over her head and palpating the trapezius muscle whilst attempting active movement would have identified paraesis of the trapezius muscle, this is because active muscle contraction is dependent on an intact neural supply and if the nerve was injured no such active contraction is identifiable. The other clinical test of shrugging the shoulders can sometimes be deceptive as the patient can sometimes simulate shoulder shrugging by utilization of other muscles to assist with the shoulder shrugging, even though these muscles are not the primary muscles involved in this type of movement. Performance of EMG early in recovery period may also have identified the injury.

(b) Professor Sonnabend (T 208) identified the ability to shrug the shoulders strongly as 'the simplest and crudest' test, pointing to its deficiencies in these answers:

> Q: What's the shortfall in that test that leads you to describe it as crude?
>
> A: Well, it is crude in the first instance because pain can limit it. It is crude in the sense that it has to be a full strong shrug because there are other muscles that can produce an apparent shrug of some weakness, so that you would need to shrug – it needs to be tested fairly vigorously, the shrug needs to be tested vigorously.
>
> Q: And that's precluded to a degree by immediate postoperative pain?
>
> A: In the first few days or maybe weeks, yes.

He was then asked (T 209):

> Q: If you have got your accessory nerve sliced, can you put your arm above your head like that?
>
> A: No.

(c) Dr Blum said (T 297) that division of the accessory nerve would affect the ability to shrug and the ability to raise the arm above 90° from the horizontal.

(d) Dr Hodge said (T 500) that if the accessory nerve was divided 'not only was there a problem with being able to shrug the shoulders but also there is a problem with being able to elevate the shoulder', so a clinical test he used was to ask the patient to put the hand behind the head. He went on to say (T 501–502):

> My universal test is that I ask the patient to shrug the shoulders and that is the universal test that people accept as being the test of accessory nerve function.

And then (T 502):

> Q: Is this foolproof, this shrug the shoulders test?
> A: No. The other test that makes it, that you will generally – in the immediate postoperative period you probably would ask the patient only to shrug their shoulders. It would only be if you had a high degree of suspicion that you would do the other clinical test, which is that test like that.
> Q: Indicating raising the arm to the back of the head.
> A: Yes.

(e) Dr McKenzie (T 538–539) gave evidence as follows:

> Q: As at November 1994, what bedside test would you have done in circumstances where you had performed neck surgery and suspected that you had severed the spinal accessory nerve?
> A: In the early stages postoperatively, I would ask the patient to shrug their shoulders, often with my hands on their shoulders to feel the trapezius muscle contracting, and also to offer some resistance that they could push against, and I would also test for weakness of the sternomastoid muscle, which is the other muscle innervated by the spinal accessory nerve, and you do that by placing your hand against the patient's cheek and asking them to press against it from the opposite side. At a later stage, you would also see some evidence of wasting of the muscles, and possibly drooping of the shoulder; possibly.

However, he went on to say he probably would not have done any test in the acute post operative period (T 539):

> Q: Can we go back to that? What would you do in the acute post-operative period?
> A: I probably wouldn't do anything, for the simple reason that the patient is going to have a lot of pain in the neck anyway, and it will be quite difficult to interpret the findings. It is pretty unlikely, after you have had significant surgery to the neck, that you will be able to really raise your shoulders to any great extent, I would think.
> Q: When would you perform, after the initial postoperative period, the test that you have just made reference to?
> A: Well, I guess when I next saw them postoperatively, which would probably be a few weeks postoperatively; two or three weeks.

(f) The plaintiff's evidence (T 34–35), not challenged on this point, was that when she saw Dr Arnot in Lismore in May 2001 he had her shrug her shoulders and raise her right arm:

WILLIAMS: Q: When you went to see Dr Arnot on 31 May 2001, did he conduct any examination or tests upon you?
A: Yes he did.
Q: What happened?
A: You want me to talk about what he did?
Q: Yes?
A: Okay, he did some, like got me to press against his hands.
Q: With your?
A: With my chin to push against his hands on either side and he was looking like he was touching there (indicated).
Q: He was touching in the area where you had had the incision?
A: At the front, well, no. It was, it was in front of the incision.
Q: In front of the actual incision?
A: Yes.
Q: And in that area on the right hand side of your throat?
A: Yes. And he got me to take my shirt off and asked me to shrug my shoulders and then he come over, back over to me, and then he got me to lift my right arm, my right arm out and then asked me to lift it as high as I could and then I got to where I could lift it.
Q: What level was that?
A: It was a little bit higher than where my arm (indicated)–
Q: You are indicating with your left arm a position just a little above parallel to the ground?
A: Yes. Then he raised the arm himself.

[41] That evidence conveys that certainly as at May 2001 Dr Arnot considered the tests he conducted were appropriate to determine whether or not the accessory nerve was functioning.

[42] Notwithstanding what Dr McKenzie said about postponing the performance of the shrug test, the evidence I have reviewed persuades me that the exercise of due care required the defendant to perform at least the shrug test post operatively in the period before the plaintiff was discharged from hospital.

[43] What did the defendant do following the surgery to identify the nerve he had severed? The answer to this question involves consideration of the evidence of the plaintiff and of her husband as well as the evidence of the defendant.

[44] The evidence satisfies me that the defendant saw the plaintiff four times after the surgery and prior to her discharge from hospital two days later. The first of these occasions was on the evening of 10 November 1999; the second and third occasions were during the course of the following day; and the fourth occasion was shortly prior to the discharge of the plaintiff from hospital on 12 November 1999.

[45] The plaintiff gave evidence that after she came out of the anaesthetic following the operation she was experiencing much pain up the back of her arm and across into her neck, and later in the afternoon realised that she was unable to lift her right arm up. She said she mentioned this to her husband and that her husband advised her to be sure to tell Dr Arnot about her shoulder. When Dr Arnot did attend upon her on the evening following the operation, the plaintiff said he wanted to check the nerve in her face and asked her to smile. The plaintiff said that she told Dr Arnot about the difficulty with her shoulder but that he replied he was more concerned about her neck. She said that Dr Arnot did not ask her to shrug her shoulders.

[46] The plaintiff said that she saw the defendant again on the day after the surgery and complained to him of 'really bad pain' in her shoulder. She also told him that she could not lift her arm up. According to the plaintiff, the defendant performed no test on her in response to that complaint, and in particular he did not ask her to attempt to raise her arm. The plaintiff said that her husband was with her on that second visit by Dr Arnot. Whilst the hospital notes record that there was a second visit from Dr Arnot on 11 November, the plaintiff gave no evidence about it.

[47] The plaintiff said that Dr Arnot attended on her again on the morning that she was discharged from hospital. He examined her neck and told her 'everything was going well with it'. Again the plaintiff said she told him she was having trouble dressing because of trouble lifting her arm, but the doctor did not acknowledge this complaint. The plaintiff said that Dr Arnot did not perform any physical test on her.

[48] The plaintiff's account of the defendant's attendances upon her in hospital was supported by the evidence of her husband. Mr Wighton said that when the plaintiff was brought back to the ward after the surgery she complained to him that her shoulder was very sore and that she was unable to lift it, and he urged the plaintiff to tell the defendant about her shoulder. According to Mr Wighton, he was present during the defendant's attendance upon the plaintiff. The defendant said he was not worried about the plaintiff's shoulder, he was concerned about her face and to see whether she could smile. Dr Arnot touched the plaintiff's face and made her smile and, according to Mr Wighton, he lifted the side of her cheek up.

[49] Mr Wighton said that the plaintiff asked him to help her in the shower that night because her shoulder was very sore and she did not feel she could wash herself properly unaided. Mr Wighton complied with his wife's request. Mr Wighton said that he recalled his wife explaining to a nurse why it was that she wanted her husband to help her shower and that she told the nurse that her shoulder was very sore and that she could not lift her arm. The nursing notes do not record this complaint, or, indeed, any complaint about inability to lift the arm following surgery and up to the time of discharge.

[50] Returning to Mr Wighton's evidence, he said he was at the hospital on 11 November and was present when Dr Arnot attended upon his wife on one occasion that day. Mr Wighton said again his wife complained about her shoulder and again Dr Arnot said he was not worried about her shoulder but was more worried about her facial nerves. Mr Wighton's evidence was that on the occasion of neither the visit on 10 November nor the visit on 11 November did the defendant ask the plaintiff to attempt to raise her arm (T 538). According to Mr Wighton, Dr Arnot checked the plaintiff's smile and the side of her face, but performed no other test (T 552).

[51] The defendant gave evidence (T 455) that he recalled visiting the plaintiff in the ward after the surgery on 10 November 1999. He said his practice was to ask visitors and family members to leave the screened off area around the bed whilst he was conducting any examination or discussion with the patient, but he could not recollect whether that practice was followed on this occasion. He said he had a very indistinct recollection of speaking to the plaintiff on 10 November, and went on to say (at T 455): '. . . I have a recollection and I think it was on that occasion, or it may have been one of the subsequent ones, of testing for the function of her trapezius muscle.' When asked how he did that, the defendant said:

> I asked her to shrug her shoulders, but I cannot tell you – not on oath – I cannot be totally certain whether it was on that occasion or one of the other visits.

[52] And then (T 456):

> Q: Are you able to say, after you had asked the plaintiff to shrug her shoulders, be it on that hospital bedside visit or a later one, as to whether the plaintiff did shrug her shoulders?
> A: I was satisfied that she could shrug both her shoulders, apparently equally, and I was reassured, following that examination, that the nerve that I had divided in the neck probably was not the spinal accessory nerve.
> Q: Was that the only test you performed at the bedside, either on that day, or the subsequent bedside visit?
> A: I think that it was. I don't recollect any other test at that stage.
> Q: Do you remember having any conversation with the plaintiff, or she having a conversation with you, when you visited her by the bedside on 10 November 1999?
> A: I'm sure we did have a conversation, but I cannot recollect any detail of it.

[53] When asked, the doctor said that he usually kept notes of examinations in hospital but this was not his invariable practice. He said he often relied on the nursing notes. I observe that the hospital records do not evidence any shrug test being carried out at any time prior to the plaintiff's discharge from hospital.

[54] Dr Arnot had no recollection of the plaintiff complaining of pain other than in the operation area on the side of the neck and he had no recollection of any examination he might have performed on the plaintiff on the day of her discharge. Dr Arnot had no specific recollection concerning any attendances upon the plaintiff on 11 November 1999.

[55] According to Dr Arnot, whenever it was that he asked the plaintiff to perform the shrug test he was satisfied with the response and was reassured that the nerve he had divided probably was not the spinal accessory nerve (T 456).

[56] Was a shrug test performed by the defendant before the plaintiff left hospital? The defendant was relying solely upon his recollection that he had done so, and I found his evidence about this unconvincing. He was unable to be specific about which visit it was on which the test was carried out and there is no hospital note about it. In view of his suspicion that he had severed the accessory nerve, the shrug test result would have been very significant and hence it would have been an important matter to note in the hospital records. Yet there was no note.

[57] The defendant was interrogated in relation to his attendances upon the plaintiff prior to her discharge from hospital. In relation to his visits on 11 and 12 November 1999 he was asked to specify, inter alia, the examinations performed by him and his findings on examination. The defendant's response was that he had no recollection over and above the entries in the hospital records (see interrogatories 24 and 27). I have already observed that the hospital records contain no note of the performance of any shrug test or of relevant examinations.

[58] In his cross examination (T 475), Dr Arnot was unable to say if he examined the plaintiff with regard to the shrug test on 11 November or 12 November. Dr Arnot said as far as he could recollect he only asked the plaintiff to shrug her shoulders on the one occasion (T 486), but that evidence conflicts with the evidence of the plaintiff and her husband which I have reviewed above. I shall consider more closely the submissions made by Ms Burke as to the credibility of the plaintiff and her husband when reviewing the conflicting evidence concerning the issue of the post discharge consultation, but I prefer the evidence of the plaintiff and of her husband to that of the defendant on the issue of whether a shrug test was carried out whilst the plaintiff remained in hospital. I find that no such test was performed.

[59] If, contrary to the finding I have made, the defendant did perform a single shrug test, then I consider that such a test would have been inadequate.

[60] Dr Arnot agreed that if he had conducted a single shrug test on the first post operative visit there was the potential for misdiagnosis (T 631) and there is other evidence to the like effect:

(a) I refer to the evidence of Dr McKenzie (T 544):

> Q: In your report of 5 March you talked about using the shrug test in the acute phase, but I think you have explained to us that

when you say acute, for example, and then immediate post surgical scenario it is not going to be practicable to do it; is that right?

A: Perhaps not fair to the patient, yes.

Q: Would that be the case depending on the degree of discomfort for a period of days?

A: Well, I think the only purpose of doing an investigation in clinical practice or doing a test is if the outcome of that test or investigation is going to influence what you do. Now, in this case the surgeon has a suspicion that he has cut the accessory nerve, he is unable to do anything about it at the time because of the inflammatory response in the neck, so it is not going to be relevant as to just what's going on there in the immediate postoperative period, so I would think that to do any testing of that is not going to alter things at that stage. But when he saw her postoperatively, then would be an appropriate time, I would think, to do that, when the pain had settled, postoperative pain and so on had settled.

Q: I get the impression, doctor, and correct me if I am wrong, that your view is that in this scenario doing the shrug test on the first day or the day of the operation is not indicated and probably useless?

A: I think not indicated and probably inappropriate, yes.

Q: Would that apply, say for a couple of days at least thereafter?

A: I think so, and also to the fact that it is not going to alter, you know, whether the muscle is working or not it is not going to alter at that stage what you do.

Q: Nonetheless, I suppose, doctor, subject to the consideration of how much pain it might occasion the patient, in the acute phase you could, if you were sufficiently concerned about severance of the accessory nerve, test whether the patient could activate the trapezius muscle by seeing if she could raise the arm above shoulder level as I am indicating now, subject to pain levels?

A: You could do that. I don't think it gives you any more information than shrugging the shoulders, especially as there are other muscles which also help you to raise the arm.

Q: If you have got a completely severed accessory nerve you can't activate your trapezius muscle, can you?

A: Exactly.

Q: And if you can't activate your trapezius muscle you can't do that, for example, put your arm straight up in the air, can you?

A: No, but it would be very difficult to interpret if there was pain associated with it because there are other muscles which also tend to rotate the scapula, which is the movement that the trapezius does.

(b) Dr Blum thought the shrug test, if administered on the day of the surgery, could produce a false result (T 296), and then in response to the following questions gave the following answers (T 296):

HIS HONOUR: Q: Do you regard it as reasonable, so I can follow this, that there would have been no bedside test performed on day 2 and day 3 in that scenario?

A: No, your Honour.

BURKE: Q: It is reasonable, is it not, that the bedside tests may not necessarily confirm in the first couple of days or even a week or two postoperatively whether or not the suspicion of severing the spinal accessory nerve is confirmed?

A: I think a week or two is too long. I would have thought that certainly by the third day if she was tested there would be signs that the nerve was unwell.

(c) Dr Hodge said that six hours after surgery (about the time of Dr Arnot's first post operative visit) he would have performed the shrug test (T 515), but he would have repeated it the next day and lifted the plaintiff's arm up (T 516).

[61] The evidence of Dr McKenzie, Dr Blum, and Dr Hodge just referred to, coupled with the defendant's recognition that a single shrug test performed on the first day post operatively could mislead, persuades me that even if, contrary to the finding I have made, the defendant did perform a single shrug test, this would not have sufficed to discharge the duty the defendant owed to the plaintiff to determine whether his suspicion concerning the severance of the nerve was ill founded or not.

[62] I add that I am satisfied on the balance of probabilities that arm abduction examination before the plaintiff left hospital would have established that the nerve had been severed:

(i) Dr Lyons was of the opinion that abduction of the arm would have provided a more definitive answer than the shrug test (T 122);

(ii) Dr Blum was of the opinion that the plaintiff would have been unable to raise her right arm above 90° from the horizontal (T 297);

(iii) Dr Hodge considered that the plaintiff would have been unable to lift the right arm above the shoulder with about three centimetres of nerve severed (T 519).

[63] I find on the balance of probabilities that had the shrug test been performed on two occasions before the plaintiff left hospital the severance of the accessory nerve would have been diagnosed. Moreover, had the defendant been in doubt about the results of that test, the severance would have been confirmed by the arm raise test, a test which should have been carried out in hospital as well. That test the defendant did use when the plaintiff consulted him in May 2001 (para 24 above).

[64] Further, it seems to me that at the time of discharge, even if by that time the defendant did not know it was the accessory nerve he had severed, the plaintiff had a right to know, and the defendant had a duty to inform her, that he had severed a nerve which he suspected was the accessory nerve. Dr Lyons, in his report dated 29 August 2003, expressed the view that the plaintiff should have been advised of the suspected severance 'straight after the surgery', but if not 'certainly . . . at the first signs of any problem with the shoulder' (see also T 116). Accepting as I do the plaintiff's evidence about what occurred in hospital, the need to inform her arose by the time of her discharge.

[65] Dr McKenzie gave evidence concerning informing the patient if the accessory nerve had been divided or was suspected as having been divided. I refer to his evidence at T 550:

> Q: In circumstances where a general surgeon has divided the spinal accessory nerve of 2 to 3 centimetres in length, what is the general surgeon's appropriate standard of care with respect to informing the plaintiff that that has occurred?
>
> A: I think that you would tell the patient. She has already been warned about the possibility of damage to or division to the accessory nerve in the preoperative visit, and you would say, look, this nerve was intimately bound up with the lump we had to remove. It couldn't be separated safely from the lump. It was necessary to remove the lump to cure the condition and so we had to remove a section of the nerve also, and then go on to say that this is unlikely to cause you any great problem, it is part and parcel of the radical operation of neck dissection anyway or has been in the past, and we will see how it's looking when we see you in follow up . . .
>
> Q: . . . My previous question was about actually having knowledge that you have severed a spinal accessory nerve. This question, if a general surgeon suspects that he has severed the accessory nerve and is either consciously or subconsciously aware that if he has in fact done that approximately 2 to 3 centimetres of nerve has been excised, is it your view that the doctor ought to inform the patient postoperatively?
>
> A: I would do that.

[66] Then, at T 551:

> Q: In informing the patient postoperatively where you suspected that you had severed the spinal accessory nerve, would you do that at the bedside time or would you do that in follow up after you had taken steps to ascertain whether or not the plaintiff had symptoms consistent with severance of the spinal accessory nerve?
>
> A: I think that's very difficult to answer because much of the information that you give to patients depends upon how the situation is evolving at the time. If you sense that the patient is wanting to have that information then I would certainly give it at the time. If not, then I think it would be appropriate to do it at the next visit, if there was a problem diagnosed. Some

> patients don't ever seem to want to know anything, many patients want to know lots of things. If the patient wants to know then I think you give them the information.

[67] Dr McKenzie was later asked the following questions and gave the following answers:

> *HIS HONOUR*: Q: Would you consider it appropriate that the doctor informed the patient of his suspicion at a time prior to the follow up consultation stressing the importance of that consultation in the circumstances?
>
> A: I think usually we assume that people will turn up for follow up, I mean particularly patients who have had a significant operation. You would assume they would want to turn up for follow up, so it probably wouldn't have entered his head.
>
> Q: Assuming a suspicion is entertained that he may have severed this nerve, whether he has or whether he hasn't, I take it from what you have said it would be better assessed at some time after discharge from hospital?
>
> A: Yes.
>
> Q: So that the post discharge consultation would be an important one –
>
> A: Important, yes.
>
> Q: – or not? Do you think it would be desirable or not for the doctor to express that to the patient?
>
> A: Well, obviously, in hindsight, it would have been worthwhile.
>
> Q: I am not asking you to look at it in hindsight?
>
> A: Yes.
>
> Q: I am asking you to look at it as a general surgeon, who has this hypothetical problem to consider, prospectively?
>
> A: Well, I think we would stress to the patient they ought to come back and see me at the appointed time.

[68] I conclude then that Dr Arnot failed to exercise due care in the period between the completion of the surgery on 10 November 1999 and the plaintiff's discharge from hospital on 12 November 1999 in failing to carry out appropriate examination of the plaintiff in order to address the suspicion he entertained at surgery that he may have divided the accessory nerve. I also conclude that there was a breach of duty on the doctor's part in failing to inform the plaintiff of the severance of a nerve at surgery and his suspicion that the nerve severed may have been the accessory nerve.

[69] Dr Arnot said that he did not tell the plaintiff in hospital about the severance of the nerve because of her emotional state and because it was only a possibility that he had severed this nerve, and that possibility he considered to be 'probably wrong' because of his examination following surgery (T 476). Acceptance of the doctor's explanation for not alerting the plaintiff to what occurred depends upon acceptance that the shrug test was performed. Since I am not persuaded that it was, I do not find the defendant's explanation for not telling the plaintiff about the division of the nerve to be an acceptable explanation.

[70] I find that the plaintiff should have been informed of the severance no later than the time she was being informed that she should arrange a consultation in three weeks time, thus stressing for her the importance of the follow up consultation.

[71] As it was, the plaintiff was not informed that a nerve which the doctor suspected to have been the accessory nerve was severed and neither was the plaintiff's general practitioner, Dr Bentel. Dr Bentel was eventually sent a copy of the discharge summary from the hospital, which summary was signed by Dr Arnot. The summary is dated 16 November 1999 but a stamp on the copy received by Dr Bentel bears date 10 December 1999. Dr Arnot gave evidence as to the manner in which the discharge summary was prepared. He said that the procedure was that he would dictate the discharge summary on an operating day, probably in the week following the surgery undertaken. A further week would elapse before the summary was typed and ready for his signature. His evidence was that in the present case he probably signed the discharge summary bearing date 16 November the week following. Clearly, Dr Bentel would not have had the summary in time for her examination of the plaintiff on 18 November 1999. Even if Dr Bentel had had that summary available, that doctor would not have been alerted to the possibility that the accessory nerve had been cut because there is no mention of that event in the discharge summary.

[72] Dr Arnot was cross-examined on the issue as to why there was no mention in the discharge summary about the possible severance of the accessory nerve. There was an error in the first draft of the discharge summary because it contained a paragraph which clearly did not relate to the plaintiff at all. That document was not signed and the discharge summary had to be retyped. However, the doctor was unable to explain why he did not insert in the summary a reference to his suspicion concerning the division of the accessory nerve. I do not propose to record in this judgment all the cross-examination that bore upon this question of the lack of any reference to the accessory nerve in the discharge summary, but I must say, to my mind, that Dr Arnot afforded no satisfactory explanation for the omission of this matter. Had Dr Bentel been provided with a discharge summary that referred to the possible division, this may have prompted Dr Bentel to follow the issue up and at least to tell the plaintiff of the suspicion. That did not occur and, as I have already recorded, it was not until the plaintiff saw Dr Blum that she became aware her accessory nerve had been damaged in the surgery in November 1999.

[73] I accept, of course, that the plaintiff was advised by Dr Arnot that she should attend for a follow-up consultation in three weeks time. I accept that the plaintiff was so advised by Dr Arnot prior to her discharge from hospital on 12 November 1999, and in so finding I am mindful of the note which Dr Arnot made in the hospital records on that date to that effect.

[74] Did the plaintiff attend for that follow-up consultation? Whilst Dr Arnot noted the hospital record: 'See me 3 weeks', it was left to the plaintiff to arrange an appointment. There was no system then in place at Dr Arnot's rooms for one of the receptionists there to arrange for the patient's attendance. Dr Arnot has no recollection of any attendance by the plaintiff or of seeing her between the date of her discharge and the appointment made by her in May 2001. Indeed, his evidence went further; the doctor denied that the plaintiff attended as she claimed.

[75] The position at the doctor's rooms at the end of 1999 was that a computer system was in the process of replacing a system of handwritten recording. There was no diary being maintained in which appointments were being recorded. Relevant records consisted of those generated through the computer and also handwritten notes being kept by Dr Arnot. I am satisfied that these records generated by the computer and by Dr Arnot himself contain no record relating to any attendance by the plaintiff upon Dr Arnot in November or December 1999.

[76] Ms Watkins was the practice manager in November 1999 and she gave evidence of the procedure upon the introduction of the computer records. Ms Watkins explained how when a patient made an appointment this was recorded by the computer and once recorded the entry was not supposed to be deleted. If there was a non-attendance, there would be a note that the patient failed to attend. The only way in which the record of an appointment once recorded could be deleted would be by pushing the delete button, and this was not supposed to occur.

[77] The computer record for the plaintiff contained no reference to any appointment with Dr Arnot after 12 November 1999. Moreover, Ex 7 records a list of attendances from August 1999 onwards in respect of which charges were made, and there is no record of any account rendered for a consultation by Dr Arnot after 12 November 1999.

[78] As to this latter matter, the plaintiff said that no charge was made for her attendance at the consultation she claims occurred in Inverell. Neither did the defendant charge the plaintiff for the consultation in May 2001. The plaintiff's evidence to the effect that she was not charged for the attendance in May 2001 is consistent with her medical services claims history, as recorded in Ex P.

[79] The plaintiff said that she did attend Dr Arnot's rooms some two to three weeks after her discharge from hospital. Her evidence was that her grandmother drove her there. The plaintiff described the occasion and described the room in which the consultation occurred. The plaintiff said that the defendant looked closely at her neck. She said there was a patient in another room behind the one in which she was seen and that patient had 'blotchy gauze' on his face. The plaintiff said she told Dr Arnot about her shoulder, the pain she was experiencing and that it was not improving. According to the plaintiff, Dr Arnot did not examine the shoulder. After the consultation the plaintiff said that she approached the receptionist downstairs, a person known to her as 'Jackie', and offered to make payment. However, the receptionist said no payment was required 'because it was a post op'. The plaintiff was strenuously cross-examined on that account but did not resile from her evidence.

[80] Mrs Carter gave evidence which supported the evidence given by her granddaughter. Mrs Carter said that the plaintiff asked her to drive the plaintiff to see Dr Arnot because her neck and her shoulder were too painful for her to drive herself. Mrs Carter said she drove the plaintiff to the doctor's surgery and went upstairs to the waiting room. Mrs Carter said that the plaintiff came out very upset and, upon inquiry as to what was wrong, said that Dr Arnot did not take any notice of her shoulder pain (T 345). Like her granddaughter, Mrs Carter was strenuously cross-examined but denied that she had concocted a story with the plaintiff.

[81] The plaintiff's husband gave evidence that although he did not go to the defendant's surgery with his wife, he rang her to 'see how she got on' at the consultation (T 565). According to Mr Wighton, his wife said she did not want to talk about it over the phone, but that evening the plaintiff complained that Dr Arnot 'blew her off about her shoulder'. The plaintiff conveyed to her husband, according to his version of the conversation, that the defendant was not concerned about her arm or shoulder.

[82] It is difficult to understand why the plaintiff would not have gone back to see Dr Arnot after she had been discharged from hospital. The plaintiff did see Dr Bentel, as she had been requested to do, and, because of the condition of her arm and shoulder, she attended on a physiotherapist, Ms Kearsey, within a week from the time that she left hospital. No reason was suggested in the course of evidence such as might explain why the plaintiff would have ignored Dr Arnot's direction to attend his rooms. For his part, Dr Arnot could advance no reason as to why the plaintiff would have failed to do so (T 488). On the contrary, there was good reason for her to attend upon the defendant because of the problems I am satisfied the plaintiff was experiencing with her arm and shoulder from the time she left hospital. On the other hand of course, why would Dr Arnot not examine the plaintiff's shoulder if indeed the plaintiff attended complaining about pain and loss of movement in the shoulder?

[83] Dr Arnot gave evidence that his practice in Inverell was a busy one and that he saw up to twenty-five patients in his rooms on a non-operating day. Dr Arnot acknowledged that as a general rule, unaided by records, he would not recollect whether he saw a particular patient (T 491), but the defendant said it was 'totally unimaginable' that he would have interrupted his attendance on a patient undergoing a skin cancer procedure in order to see a patient like the plaintiff. He disagreed with the plaintiff's evidence about the post operative consultation at St Elmo's Chambers.

[84] Dr Arnot had not completed his evidence when the Court adjourned on 16 March 2005. On 17 March 2005 I raised with counsel some features of the evidence given by Dr Arnot up to that point in his evidence (T 496). Dr Arnot resumed his evidence on 18 March 2005 and, cross-examination having concluded, counsel for the defendant sought an adjournment to obtain instructions concerning the matters I have raised the previous day. After the adjournment that followed, counsel informed the Court that there would be no re-examination. I certainly do not intend to convey any criticism of counsel for what occurred, but it seems to me that it is appropriate to infer that the defendant was not in a position to give evidence such as would have advanced his case on any of the unanswered matters to which I had drawn attention on the preceding day.

[85] A matter put forward in support of the submission that the plaintiff was not to be believed in her version of events concerning Dr Arnot, was that the plaintiff had earlier lied to Dr Blum when she wrote to him seeking his assistance for her ongoing problems on 9 July 2001 (Ex 1). In that letter the plaintiff wrote:

> . . . I want to let you know that I am not chasing a law suit or damages of any kind . . .

[86] In cross examination (T 254), the plaintiff admitted that when she wrote that letter she had already engaged solicitors and that she lied to Dr Blum in that letter. The plaintiff was then asked these questions and gave these answers:

> *HIS HONOUR*: Q: Why did you lie to Dr Blum when you wrote to him?
> A: I wanted him to see me. I didn't think he would see me if I told him. I wanted an – I don't know whether the words are an unbiased, I wanted him to look after me for medical reasons. I didn't want him to be seeing me like, oh, I just wanted – and I mean I was honest with him at the consultation about that.

[87] In re examination, further evidence in point emerged (T 255):

> *WILLIAMS*: Q: Mrs Wighton, you've made no bones about the fact that you were untruthful in your letter to Dr Blum about litigation. At the time you wrote that had you seen Charlton Shearman?
> A: No, I hadn't.
> Q: Had Abbott Pardy & Jenkins done anything beyond your having first consulted them?
> A: No.
> *HIS HONOUR*: Q: They were still acting for you, were they?
> A: Yes.
> *WILLIAMS*: Q: Why did you put that in the letter?
> A: I didn't think that Dr Blum would have seen me.
> Q: Why did you think that?

A: I had seen another doctor.
Q: Who was that?
A: It was Dr Lennox, and he made quite a few passing comments that doctors would run from this because of the chance of negligence and that if they knew that I had even inquired or was going to see anyone that they probably wouldn't agree to see me.
(Miss Burke sought that the answer be struck out; Allowed to stand.)
Q: As a result of what you had been told by Dr Lennox, what did you perceive might have been Dr Blum's reaction to your request for assistance if he knew you were in the process of suing a fellow surgeon?
A: Well, especially being him, I wouldn't have thought he would have seen me.

[88] It was by no means commendable behaviour on the part of the plaintiff in seeking to deceive Dr Blum but I accept her explanation for having done so as being a truthful explanation.

[89] I had the advantage of observing closely as the various witnesses gave their evidence. Ultimately, I am persuaded on the balance of probabilities that the evidence advanced in the plaintiff's case about the post discharge consultation in the defendant's rooms was truthful evidence. I have come to that conclusion notwithstanding the evidence given by the defendant and the absence of any record of the attendance at the defendant's rooms. The dependability of the computer generated record was, of course, dependent upon human input, and in November 1999 the procedure of record keeping was at a change-over stage. It seems to me that the absence of a record may be explained by human error. I find it more probable than not, having assessed the evidence given by the plaintiff, her husband and her grandmother that the plaintiff did attend as she claimed.

[90] I am satisfied that had due care been taken by the defendant in examining the plaintiff upon a visit two to three weeks after discharge from hospital, that examination would have revealed that the accessory nerve had indeed been severed. The evidence is compelling that there would have been clinical signs of severance of the nerve two weeks after surgery. I am satisfied by the medical evidence in this case that the severance would have been established by due application of the shrug test. I am also satisfied that if the accessory nerve had been severed, it would not have been possible for the plaintiff to raise her arm above her head or to the back of it.

[91] It seems to me that even if the plaintiff had failed to attend upon the defendant as advised, more would have been required of the defendant in discharging his duty of care to the plaintiff than the mere giving of advice to her that she should attend his rooms for follow-up.

[92] There was no system in place in the defendant's practice to follow up a patient who failed to attend for a consultation. Once the defendant severed a nerve during the operation, suspecting that this was the accessory nerve, the exercise of due care required of him that he do more than carry out one shrug test at some time before the plaintiff was discharged from hospital. The performance of that one test in hospital would have been insufficient to base a conclusion that the accessory nerve was intact. I referred earlier to the evidence of Dr Hodge and of Dr McKenzie which supports this conclusion, and which evidence I accept.

[93] Dr Lyons, specialist ear, nose, throat, head and neck surgeon, was of the opinion that if the plaintiff did fail to make an appointment for a follow-up examination, because the defendant thought he had cut the accessory nerve proper standards of practice required him to follow-up the patient. Dr Lyons gave this evidence (T 123):

> Q: If, as alleged, the plaintiff, in fact, just did not turn up following this procedure, where he thought he had cut the accessory nerve, what should the requirements of proper standards of practice have required of this general surgeon?
>
> A: I believe the onus is on the surgeon to, if he suspects that the nerve, a major nerve, has been divided, that he follow up the patient and ensure that the patient attends for follow up.

[94] I accept what Dr Lyons said, and I am satisfied on the evidence that the defendant did not take any step to have the plaintiff attend for examination at any time after he asked her to do so before she left hospital.

[95] Dr Blum was also of the opinion that there was an obligation upon the surgeon who suspected he had sectioned a nerve to inquire why the patient did not attend a follow-up consultation (T 269–270). Dr Blum gave evidence of a procedure in place at the Prince of Wales Hospital under which the registrar was required to find out why a patient failed to attend for follow-up.

[96] In the much cited decision in *Rogers v Whitaker* (1992) 175 CLR 479 at 483 Mason CJ, Brennan, Dawson, Toohey and McHugh JJ said in their joint judgment concerning the duty of care owed by a medical practitioner:

> The law imposes on a medical practitioner a duty to exercise reasonable care and skill in the provision of professional advice and treatment. That duty is a 'single comprehensive duty covering all the ways in which a doctor is called upon to exercise his skill and judgment' (*Sidaway v Governors of Bethlem Royal Hospital* [1985] AC 871); it extends to the examination, diagnosis and treatment of the patient and the provision of information in an appropriate case (*Gover v South Australia* (1985) 39 SASR 543). It is, of course, necessary to give content to the duty in the given case.

[97] It seems to me that, giving content to the duty in the present case, it extended, consistently with the evidence of Dr Lyons and Dr Blum, to the imposition of a requirement upon the defendant that he not only advise the plaintiff to attend for a follow-up consultation, but that he adopt reasonable measures to ensure that the plaintiff did attend.

[98] Here I have found that the plaintiff attended as advised, and in the circumstances I have found that the defendant was in breach of his duty of care owed to the plaintiff in the various respects I have above expressed and which I will now restate in summary form.

The negligence of the defendant

[99] For the reasons above stated, I find the defendant to have been negligent in the following respects:

(i) in the failure to carry out sufficient post operative examinations to determine whether the right spinal accessory nerve had been severed;
(ii) in the failure to advise the plaintiff prior to her discharge from hospital of the suspected severance of that nerve;
(iii) in the failure to carry out appropriate examinations of the plaintiff at the post discharge consultation such as would have established the severance of the accessory nerve;
(iv) in the failure to advise the plaintiff of the need for surgical repair of that nerve by a suitably qualified specialist.

Contributory negligence

[100] In amended Grounds of Defence filed on 11 March 2005 the defendant pleaded contributory negligence, particulars whereof are as follows:

(a) failing to take heed of the defendant's advice to consult him for a post operative review in three weeks time;
(b) failing to inform the defendant of her alleged symptoms after her discharge from hospital; and
(c) failing to contact any medical practitioner with respect to her alleged symptoms from the date of her discharge on 12 November 1999 until her appointment with her general practitioner on 18 November 1999.

[101] The obligation is, of course, upon the defendant to prove this defence, and I am not persuaded that the defendant has established that the plaintiff has failed to exercise due care in any of the respects particularised, in particular:

(a) I have found that the plaintiff did attend upon the defendant at his rooms following her discharge from hospital and as advised by the defendant;
(b) I am satisfied that the plaintiff did complain to the defendant about her problems referable to the severed nerve prior to the time that she

was discharged from hospital and subsequently at the follow-up consultation;

(c) I am not persuaded that the plaintiff failed to exercise due care in seeking medical assistance for her symptoms. I am satisfied on the evidence that the plaintiff sought physiotherapy immediately following her discharge from hospital, that she attended upon Dr Bentel after her discharge from hospital and that she also attended upon the defendant in accordance with the advice he gave her.

[102] In the circumstances, in the absence of any advice given by the defendant that he may have severed the accessory nerve during the operation, I am not satisfied that the plaintiff acted unreasonably in the medical care sought following her discharge from hospital.

[103] The defence of contributory negligence has not been established.

[104] What are the consequences of the negligence established?

[105] The plaintiff must, of course, prove that the negligence established was causative of harm. It is not contended that the defendant was negligent in severing the accessory nerve, and it is necessary to determine what harm, if any, resulted from the negligence I find to have been proved.

[106] Had the plaintiff been alerted to the severance of the nerve promptly after the surgery was performed, and had the plaintiff been advised of the need for surgical repair, I am satisfied on the balance of probabilities that the plaintiff would have undergone repair surgery when advised to do so.

[107] Ms Burke submitted that the plaintiff would not have had surgery until after the birth of the child that the plaintiff discovered she was carrying in January 2000. Delay until after such birth would have reduced the plaintiff's prospects of recovery. The evidence satisfies me that delay in undertaking surgery would, indeed, have reduced its efficacy but I do not find that the plaintiff would have declined to have had it until after the birth.

[108] The plaintiff was cross-examined as to whether she would have undergone surgery in the second trimester if there was an associated risk to the unborn child. The plaintiff's response was that she could not answer that (T 108):

> Q: Let me ask you this. If you were being asked to weigh up and balance the risk between the risk of the nerve repair failing, if it was undertaken in the second trimester of pregnancy, and the risk to an unborn child if the operation was undertaken during the second trimester, that is something you would have to weigh up, is it not?
>
> OBJECTION.
>
> *HIS HONOUR*: Q: Did you understand the question?
> A: I understand the question. I don't know how to answer.

BURKE: Q: Risk versus benefit. Would you forego the benefit that you might receive from having the surgery in a second trimester over and above a risk to your unborn child to –

A: I can't answer that, I don't know how to. I am not in a position now. Back then, is completely different to me sitting here now.

[109] In re examination, the plaintiff gave further evidence in point (T 260):

Q: Have you, during the morning adjournment, been shown, and have you read, the report of Dr Robert Lyneham at page 121? You have been through that and have you seen what Dr Lyneham had to say about surgery in the second trimester?
A: Yes, I have, yes.
Q: If advised along those lines, would you have accepted the surgery in the second trimester for nerve repair to your neck?
A: Yes, I would have.

[110] The report of Dr Lyneham to which the plaintiff was referred was in evidence and Dr Lyneham gave oral evidence to which I now refer.

[111] Dr Lyneham, who is a specialist obstetrician and gynaecologist, responded in his report of 24 February 2003 to three questions:

1. In your opinion, assuming that repair to the accessory nerve was required and the Plaintiff was pregnant, could the accessory nerve be repaired during the second trimester without injury to the developing foetus? Please state your reasons.
   There is no evidence that repair of the accessory nerve during the second trimester would have caused injury to the developing foetus. Surgery in the second trimester is not linked to injury to the infant, and a severed accessory nerve is not an underlying condition which would lead to growth restriction.
2. In your opinion, assuming that the baby was delivered in September 2000, would there be any obstetric and/or gynaecological reasons to prevent surgical repair of the accessory nerve following the birth of the child? Please state your reasons.
   In my view there would have been no obstetric or gynaecological reasons which would have prevented surgical repair after the baby's delivery in September 2000. If Ms Wighton was breastfeeding, formula or expressed breast milk could have been given for a short period.
3. Please comment on any other issues that may be relevant in this matter.
   It is not unusual to plan semi-elective (compared to emergency) surgery during the second trimester. Anaesthetists are well used to administering anaesthetics to pregnant women, and presumably accessory nerve repair is not a procedure carrying a high risk of blood loss or infection.

[112] Dr Lyneham considered the second trimester as the preferred period for any surgery undertaken during pregnancy, in this case from March to May 2000, but he would not have ruled out surgery elsewhere in the pregnancy, even in the third trimester (T 419–420).

[113] Dr Blum, in his speciality as a neurosurgeon, considered it would have been safe for surgery to have been undertaken in the second trimester (T 273), although before undertaking surgery in that period he would have consulted an obstetrician (T 388).

[114] Dr Hodge also considered he would have undertaken surgery in that period, as the following cross examination reveals (T 522):

> Q: Would you assume please that his opinion [that is, the opinion of Dr Lyneham] as to the performance of the procedure in question in this case in 1999 was that of the putative risks that might possibly be involved, namely those of low birth weight and neonatal death, there was no increase in those risks, in a scenario where the cable grafting was to take place in the second trimester. That is to say nil. Would you have been happy to be guided by that opinion?
> A: If the obstetrician was prepared to say there was no risk, then, yes, I would be happy to be guided by that opinion.
> Q: I think you told us that there is a bit of a balancing act, whereby you look at the severity of the symptoms. In this case, if the accessory nerve had been severed in November 1999, it is almost a banality that the longer you leave a cable repair the less sanguine the outcome. Do you agree with that?
> A: Yes.
> Q: From the point of view, inter alia, of retrieving any muscle wasting that would have occurred?
> A: That's right.
> Q: Because somewhere down the track your chance has been obliterated?
> A: Yes.
> Q: It would appear, and I ask you to assume, that the second trimester would have commenced in March of 2000 for this lady. I would like you to have a look please at exhibit F (shown). The first photograph there you may assume was taken on this good lady's wedding day in March of 2000?
> A: Yes.
> Q: Would you direct your attention to her right shoulder area?
> A: (Witness complied).
> Q: There is manifestly evident, is there not, wastage of the trapezius or right shoulder?
> A: There is.
> Q: Given respected obstetric opinion of nil risk to mother or foetus, and given that manifestation, and given ongoing complaints of pain of both types under consideration here, there would not be any question but that she would have been

well-advised to proceed in the second trimester with the graft, would you agree?

A: You realise that she is using her right arm to cut that cake?

Q: Could I very politely I trust ask you to answer my question?

A: Sure. If her symptoms warranted the correction of the nerve, then certainly, from the opinion that you have given me of the obstetrician, then I would be happy to reconstruct the nerve in that period.

[115] There was, however, some disagreement between the experts in this case as to the appropriate timing of repair surgery.

[116] Dr Lyons considered that the ideal time to repair was within a few weeks after the severance, if the repair could not be effected at the time of such severance (T 123). This would allow surgery after the inflammation had settled down and before scar tissue formed (T 132). However, there was, in his view, no absolute time limit for the repair procedure.

[117] Professor Sonnabend considered the accessory nerve should have been repaired as soon as possible and ideally by the fifth day after severance (T 208).

[118] Dr Blum considered that there was some degree of urgency in carrying out the repair. In his report of 14 February 2005 the doctor wrote:

> The semi-urgency of the procedure is because the motor end plate connection with the nerve deteriorates progressively until at 18 months it is not possible for the muscle to contract. The longer the delay, the worse the outcome. A repair in March or April 2000 would have allowed a 60% result of 3+ recovery. Early intervention at Royal Brisbane could have been organized in a matter of days by my ex-registrar in neurosurgery, Dr Rob Campbell.

[119] As to the question of undertaking the surgery during pregnancy, Dr Blum wrote in the same report:

> I need to state that we would be willing to perform the operation in the second trimester of pregnancy between the 13th and 26th weeks, as it is a safe period to perform urgent, or relatively urgent, surgery. The first and third trimester is hazardous for the foetus' development and survival, thus she would have had the repair in early 2000, in March in April.

[120] Dr Hodge was of the view that repair ought not to have been attempted for two months to allow inflammation to settle (T 503).

[121] There is obvious divergence of opinion between the experts, as demonstrated by the above review. It would not have been practicable to carry out the repair within five days of the severance, as Professor Sonnabend would have regarded as desirable, if for no other reason than that the defendant did not have the appropriate expertise to have performed the repair surgery and a referral to some other specialist, which I am satisfied should have been advised and arranged, would inevitably have caused some delay. Indeed, it may well be that it would not have been until December 1999 or January 2000 that the plaintiff would have had the benefit of a consultation with an appropriate specialist surgeon, there being no such specialist available at the time in Inverell.

[122] However, I consider it probable that had it not been for the defendant's negligence, and accepting as I do the evidence in point of Dr Lyneham, Dr Blum and Dr Hodge, the plaintiff would have undergone repair surgery during the second trimester, that is between March and May 2000.

[123] By the time the plaintiff learned of the severance, it was altogether too late to attempt to repair it. Indeed, I do not understand it to be contended otherwise and, certainly for his part, Dr Hodge considered surgery eighteen months after division of the nerve would have been valueless (see his report of 27 April 2004, p 5). However, had the surgery been undertaken within the second trimester, I find that a satisfactory outcome would have been likely.

[124] That does not mean though that the plaintiff would have recovered completely.

[125] Dr Lyons considered that the plaintiff would probably have recovered most of the bulk of the trapezius muscle (T 114) and Dr Lyons considered that the plaintiff would have been likely to have achieved 'normal or near normal shoulder function' (T 118).

[126] I referred above to Dr Blum's report of 14 February 2005. In oral evidence, the doctor explained what he meant by the recovery of sixty percent (T 270–271):

> *HIS HONOUR*: Q: Doctor, can I ask you what the recovery of approximately 60% means. Does that mean there was some improvement following operation in 60% of cases or that on average there was a recovery of 60% of function in each case?
>
> A: The function, your Honour, is graded from 0 to 5, 0 being no recovery and 5 being normal. Most people would say that a recovery of 3 is when you can move the limb or muscle with gravity present and that there was some resistance to you testing it, so 60% would be a 3 or 3 plus result.
>
> Q: But what I am not clear on is whether or not in each of the 66 cases there was a recovery of approximately 60% or whether that was an average?
>
> A: That was an average.

[127] And, later (T 271):

> Q: In general lay terms is grade 3 reasonable function, minimal function?
>
> A: It is reasonable function. It means that the limb can be used but it is not normal.
>
> *HIS HONOUR*: Q: In a work environment?

A: With some degree of difficulty, yes.
Q: What about doing work, for instance, as a nurse's aide, which involves lifting of patients?
A: Lifting, I think she would have difficulty, as she said.
Q: So would I be right in thinking then that assuming repair to a grade 3, the patient would be limited in the work she could do so as to avoid heavy use of the shoulder?
A: Yes.

[128] Dr Hodge, in his report dated 27 April 2004, expressed the opinion that the probability was that surgery after a delay of two months would have been successful, although it would not have alleviated the plaintiff's neuralgic pain, which he considered likely to have been caused by the division of a sensory nerve.

[129] Addressing the issue of causation, I find on the probabilities that as a consequence of the defendant's negligence the plaintiff did not have the repair surgery that she otherwise would have had and that absent appropriate surgery the plaintiff has been left with considerable pain and disability that would have been addressed by such surgery.

[130] I find that such surgery would have been likely to have restored reasonable function in the right upper limb short of normal function and that the plaintiff would have been left with restrictions, being unable to engage in heavy use of the right shoulder. In essence, I accept the detail of the evidence that Dr Blum gave about the practical restrictions which the plaintiff would still have had after successful surgery.

[131] I proceed to assess damages upon the basis of the findings I have expressed. . . . .

(iv) Failure to remove foreign objects inserted into a patient

The very nature of surgery implies the intrusion of foreign materials inside a patient. Commonly, the intrusions would include not only that of a scalpel, but also such implements as forceps, retractors or swabs. Is a surgeon who fails to ensure that such items have been removed from the patient guilty of negligence? The answer would seem to be 'not necessarily' (or 'it depends').

Mahon v Osbourne [1939] KB 14

A patient suffering from a perforated duodenal ulcer was admitted to hospital. The combined effects of his having food in his stomach and poor tolerance of the anaesthetic administered made the emergency operation difficult. At the conclusion of the operation, the surgeon asked the theatre sister (who had been 'flagging' and counting all of the swabs) whether all the swabs had been removed. She replied that they had, but she was in error. The patient died.

At trial, the jury found the theatre sister not to have been negligent, but found the surgeon negligent. He appealed.

Scott LJ:

Before discussing the nature and extent of the surgeon's duty in respect of removing the swabs, it is essential to call attention to certain other medical features characteristic of major abdominal operations and particularly present in the actual operation in question on this appeal . . . (1) It is subjectively of supreme importance that the surgeon's mind should be free throughout the operation to concentrate on his main task, with all its difficulties, problems, surprises and risks, and that it should not be disturbed or diverted. It is objectively of equal importance (2) that a patient should not be kept under operation a moment longer than is necessary; (3) that there should be no pause in the continuity of the operation, even at the time of the count; (4) that his organs should be moved and touched as little as possible; (5) that any extension of the field of operation which involves handling of the organs should be avoided because of the risks (a) of increasing the surgical shock, (b) of causing subsequent 'adhesions' and (c) particularly in abdominal cases of sepsis spreading. The medical evidence below was unanimous in the opinion that for these reasons the actual task of counting the swabs ought not to be put on the surgeon and the learned judge ultimately accepted that view. All three surgeons also stated that it is not in fact the practice for the surgeon to count, and that the whole task of counting is in practice assigned to and performed by the nursing staff present in the theatre whose duty it is to conduct the supply of the swabs. . .

If [a surgeon] professes an art he must be reasonably skilled in it. There is no doubt the defendant surgeon was that. He must also be careful, but the standard of care which the law requires is not insurance against accidental slips. It is such a degree of care as a normally skillful member of the profession may reasonably be expected to exercise in the actual circumstances of the case in question. It is not every slip or mistake which imports negligence and, in applying the duty of care to the case of the surgeon, it is peculiarly necessary to have regard to the different kinds of circumstances that may present themselves for urgent attention. I will mention a few applicable to a major abdominal operation. (1) The multiform difficulties presented by the particular circumstances of the operation; (2) the condition of the patient and the whole set of problems arising out of the risks to which he is being exposed; (3) the difficulty of the surgeon's choice between risks; (4) the paramount need of his discretion being unfettered if he thinks it right to take one to avoid a greater; (5) at the penultimate stage (swab removal) he may, particularly where the patient has been taking the anaesthetic badly and is suffering from shock, be so anxious on surgical grounds to bring the operation to an end as rapidly as possible that, in the exercise of his discretion, perhaps unconsciously exercised, as soon as he has completed the removal of all swabs of which he is at that moment aware he asks the sister for the count and forthwith starts to close the wound. . .

The only other matter on which I desire to say anything is on the relevance to the surgeon's duty with regard to the removal of packing swabs

> of any count by the nurses. His duty is undoubtedly to exercise care in the removal of the swabs, giving proper weight to the rare, but not impossible, risk of a swab having lost its Spencer-Wells clip. This risk, it is worth remembering, is one which depends not on the surgeon but on the nurses. It is their duty to see that each Spencer-Wells clip is in good order and that its safety catch is made well fast when the swab to which it is fastened is placed in the surgeon's hands. So too the check afforded by the count depends on the nurses. Those two risks are wholly external, both to the surgeon and to the patient. If an error has been committed, the surgeon cannot either control it or know it. Nonetheless, I do not doubt that over and above all the many signs of danger to the patient which are forcing themselves on his attention, the surgeon has to keep in mind those two risks of error by the nurses. On the other hand, I do not think the surgeon should be deprived of all support from the count. . .
>
> [MacKinnon J delivered a similar judgment. Goddard LJ dissented. A new trial was ordered.]

In *Chasney v Anderson* (1950) 4 DLR 223, a surgeon was found liable in negligence by the Supreme Court of Canada, when a child died following a tonsillectomy. The child choked on a sponge which was left at the base of his nostrils. The surgeon neither used sponges with tapes attached, nor employed a nurse to count the sponges. He did, however, ask an assistant at the operation whether all sponges had been removed and, receiving a reply in the negative, 'felt around' but could find no sponge. A nurse subsequently removed the sponge.

Jones, M, *Medical Negligence (above), at p 142*

> There is . . . a significant difference between the two cases. In *Mahon v Osbourne,* it was an emergency operation for a duodenal ulcer which the surgeon performed alone. It was a complicated and urgent operation and there was system for counting the swabs. But in *Anderson v Chasney* it was a routine operation in which there was no method for counting. These circumstances may justify a different conclusion on negligence, although *Mahon v Osbourne* probably makes the position in swab cases seem more complicated than it is. In practice such cases are usually settled as indefensible, and most of the cases that are litigated end in a finding of negligence. Even if, on the facts, the conclusion is that the surgeon was not negligent in leaving the swab inside the patient, the result will almost invariably be that the nurse conducting the count was negligent. The position will normally be the same in the case of a surgical instrument left inside the patient's body.

The other 'cases litigated' referred to by Jones include *Hocking v Bell* [1948] WN 21 (when part of a drainage pipe left in a patient, surgeon found negligent), *Gloning v Miller* (1954) 1 DLR 372 (when forceps left in a patient, surgeon found negligent) and *Dryden v Surrey County Council and Stewart* [1936] 2 All ER 535 (when surgical gauze 'plugging' left in patient, surgeon found negligent).

(v) Error in diagnosis

The failure of a health care practitioner to diagnose a condition is not, *per se,* actionable. It will be recalled from the outline of the elements of negligence above that the patient needs also to prove that the failure to properly diagnose caused some loss to the patient. The patient, therefore, needs to demonstrate that, had the health care practitioner successfully diagnosed the condition, the plaintiff would have been able to obtain the necessary treatment and the situation now faced by the plaintiff would not have happened.

This aspect of the action in negligence (referred to as causation) became important in the case below.

***Barnett v Chelsea and Kensington Hospital Management Committee* [1969] 1 QB 427**

Three night watchmen presented at the casualty department complaining of vomiting after consuming tea. The duty casualty officer refused to see them, telling them (via the nurse on duty) to contact their general practitioners. One of the men subsequently died from arsenic poisoning. Evidence was led which indicated that, even if the casualty officer had admitted the man to the wards of the hospital and treated him, he still might have died.

Nield J:
In my judgment, there was here such a close relationship between the hospital and the watchmen that there was imposed upon the hospital a duty of care which they owed to the watchmen. Thus, I have no doubt that Nurse Corbett and the medical casualty officer were under a duty to the deceased to exercise that skill and care which is to be expected of persons in such positions acting reasonably. . .

Let me say at this stage that there is no complaint against Nurse Corbett that she failed in her duty. There are two main questions here: has the plaintiff established, on the balance of probabilities, (1) that the medical casualty officer was negligent, and, if so, (2) that such negligence caused the death of the deceased? The first of those questions can be divided into four questions. (a) Should the doctor have seen the deceased? (b) Should he have examined the deceased? (c) Should he have admitted the deceased to the wards? And (d) should he have treated or caused to be treated the deceased? The first two of those four questions can be answered together. It is not, in my judgment, the case that a casualty officer must always see the caller at his department. Casualty departments are misused from time to time. If the receptionist, for example, discovers that the visitor is already attending his own doctor and merely wants a second opinion, or if the caller has a small cut which the nurse can perfectly well dress herself, then the casualty officer need not be called. . .

Without doubt, the casualty officer should have seen and examined the deceased. His failure to do so cannot be described as an excusable error as has been submitted. It was negligence. It is unfortunate that he was himself at the time a tired and unwell doctor, but there was no one else to do that which it was his duty to do. . .

The third question is, should he have admitted the deceased to the wards? I accept Dr Lockett's opinion that, having regard to all the circumstances, it was the casualty officer's duty to have admitted him.

The fourth question is, should the casualty officer have treated him? . . . In any event, I am satisfied that the deceased's condition of dehydration and malaise was such that intravenous treatment should have been given. Further, I think it would have become plain that it was necessary to test a specimen of the deceased's blood and in the end to send certain other specimens away for analysis to discover what poison it was which was causing the deceased's condition.

Thus, it is that I find that under all four headings the defendants were negligent and in breach of their duty in that they or their servants or agents did not see and did not examine and did not admit and did not treat the deceased.

It remains to consider whether it is shown that the deceased's death was caused by that negligence or whether, as the defendants have said, the deceased must have died in any event . . . I am of the view that the onus of proof remains upon the plaintiff. . .

There has been put before me a timetable which is of much importance. The deceased attended at the casualty department at five or 10 minutes past eight in the morning. If the casualty officer had got up and dressed and come to see the three men and examined them and decided to admit them, the deceased (and Dr Lockett agreed with this) could not have been in bed in a ward before 11 am. I accept Dr Goulding's evidence that an intravenous drip would not have been set up before 12 noon, and if potassium loss was suspected it could not have been discovered until 12.30 pm. Dr Lockett, dealing with this, said: 'If this man had not been treated until after 12 noon the chances of survival were not good.'

Without going in detail into the considerable volume of clinical evidence which has been put before me, it seems to be the case that when death results from arsenical poisoning it is brought about by two conditions; on the one hand dehydration and on the other disturbance of the enzyme processes. If the principal condition is one of enzyme disturbance – as I am of the view it was here – then the only method of treatment which is likely to succeed is the use of the specific antidote which is commonly called BAL. Dr Goulding said in the course of his evidence:

> The only way to deal with this is to use the specific BAL. I see no reasonable prospect of the deceased being given BAL before the time at which he died.

And at a later point in his evidence:

> I feel that even if fluid loss had been discovered death would have

> been caused by the enzyme disturbance. Death might have occurred later.
>
> I regard that evidence as very moderate, and it might be a true assessment of the situation to say that there was no chance of BAL being administered before the death of the deceased. For those reasons, I find that the plaintiff has failed to establish, on the balance of probabilities, that the defendants' negligence caused the death of the deceased.

Modern applications of the causation problem in *Barnett's* case can be seen in the rejection of the action in negligence in *Stacey v Chiddy* (1993) 4 Med LR 345. In that case, a patient alleged that if a general practitioner had made a proper examination of her at an earlier date, her breast cancer could have earlier been detected and cured. The trial judge found the general practitioner was negligent in failing to make proper examination of the plaintiff's breasts and failing to give her proper advice after she had had a 'negative' response to mammograms and ultrasound, but established that the malignancies which formed some 15 months later were unrelated to the presence of earlier cysts which could have been detected by a competent examination.

Similarly is the decision of the Supreme Court of New South Wales in *Smith and Another v Lennard* (unreported decision of Studdert J, 7 September 1994), where a general practitioner failed to request an endoscopy for a patient complaining of dysphagia in 1989. In 1993, an endoscopy of the patient revealed he had a carcinoma of the stomach. Studdert J held that it was unlikely that cancer would have been detected by endoscopy in 1989 even if the gastric reflux the patient then experienced could be attributed to the carcinoma.

In the case below, the plaintiff was successful in establishing that the failure to correctly diagnose an illness deprived him of the chance to obtain medical treatment which could have saved his life.

Wood v Queensland Medical Laboratories, unreported, Supreme Court of Queensland, 16 December 1994

> **Cullinane J:**
>
> The defendant is a firm of pathologists. The plaintiff has instituted proceedings against the defendant claiming damages for negligence in the examination of and report on a lesion which had been excised from the plaintiff's back on 4 October, 1990.
>
> In early October 1990, the plaintiff was in Brisbane visiting his mother and stepfather during school holidays. On or about 4 October 1990, he became concerned about a mole on the left side of his back approximately midway between his armpit and his waist. It was small but he had noticed a change in its colour. He made arrangements to see Dr Whelan, who he describes himself as the family doctor and who practises at Paddington. Dr Whelan examined the mole and excised it and told the plaintiff he would send it away for pathology tests.
>
> The relevant part of the report is in the following terms:

> Specimen: LESION FROM BACK
>
> Macroscopic:
>
> The specimen consists of a skin ellipse measuring 14.0 mm × 5.0 mm × 8.0 mm containing a central 4.0 mm × 2.0 mm mid to dark brown plaque which has a regular margin. Two transverse sections in entirety.
>
> Microscopic:
>
> Sections show a COMPOUND NAEVUS associated with some atypical melanocytic proliferation along the basal layer of the epidermis. No evidence of malignancy can be seen. Excision appears complete.

It is the plaintiff's case that the examination which was carried out by the defendant was carried out negligently and that had an examination been carried out properly it would have revealed a malignant melanoma with an indication of lymphatic permeation.

It was ultimately conceded that there was a malignant melanoma which ought to have been detected. However, the defendant disputed whether there was any evidence suggesting lymphatic permeation or whether it was negligent on the defendant's part to fail to reach such a conclusion and report to this effect.

In mid-1993, the plaintiff moved to Mossman where his grandmother lived. He had for some unspecified time prior to this been feeling unwell and his weight had reduced from about 72.5 kilograms to about 65 kilograms. He suffered from a general tiredness and lack of energy. Not long after he arrived in Mossman he noticed a lump in his left armpit. About a week or so later he saw a general practitioner who prescribed antibiotics. He took these over a period of two weeks but the lump remained.

Shortly after this he spoke to his mother who was at that time employed as a nurse at the Cairns Base Hospital and at her suggestion he saw a doctor at the Mossman Hospital. This occurred on 13 August 1993.

The plaintiff was ultimately admitted to the Cairns Base Hospital on 14 October 1993, when a lymph node biopsy was performed . . . The plaintiff was found to be suffering from metastatic malignant melanoma in some 20 out of 23 lymph nodes in the left axilla . . .

It is, I am satisfied, the case that the malignant melanoma found in the lymph nodes had spread from the primary malignant melanoma which ought to have been detected by the defendant at the time of the examination on 4 October 1990.

Subsequently, the slides produced at the time of the examination in October 1990 were examined by three pathologists. One of these was Dr Cohn, who is either a member of or employee of the defendant. This report is Exhibit 6. It is in the following terms:

> REVIEW OF REPORT – REF NO ZR3570 – SKIN LESION FROM BACK
>
> Sections have been reviewed in the light of metastatic malignant melanoma present in axillary lymph nodes. Upon review the lesion shows atypical junctional activity associated with occasional atypical melanocytes within the overlying epidermis and an occasional mitosis is noted within 'naevoid' cells in the dermis. In some levels these cells show some atypical cytologic features suggesting they do in fact represent invasive malignant melanoma with a maturing naevoid pattern. In one of the levels examined a small space surrounds a tight nest of small 'naeval-like' cells suggesting this could in hindsight represent possible lymphatic vessel permeation. The overall appearance would be consistent with a MALIGNANT MELANOMA OF SUPERFICIAL SPREADING TYPE having a maturing naevoid pattern. No lymphocytic response is seen. The lesion invades to the papillary reticular interface (Level II/III) with a maximum tumour thickness of 0.68 mm.
>
> SUMMARY: UPON REVIEW, THE APPEARANCES WOULD BE CONSISTENT WITH A SUPERFICIAL SPREADING MALIGNANT MELANOMA, LEVEL II/III, TUMOUR THICKNESS 0.68 MM. THE LINE OF EXCISION IS WIDE OF THE MELANOCYTIC CHANGES.

Dr Cohn was not called as a witness . . .

I am satisfied that had the defendant exercised proper care, the malignant melanoma would have been identified and the indications of lymphatic permeation identified and reported on. I find that the defendant was negligent in failing to do so.

The case for the plaintiff was that had the malignant melanoma and the signs which suggested a lymphatic permeation been identified, the plaintiff would have undergone an elective lymphatic node dissection and that given the very small size of the melanoma, his prospects of survival would have been very high, being somewhere in the order of 90% or more. An alternative claim was based upon the proposition that had the melanoma been identified the plaintiff would have been monitored closely and that upon the appearance of the lump in his armpit, he would have then had a significantly increased chance of survival through the performance of a lymph node dissection than is currently the case. This scenario would it seems to me also arise if the indications of lymphatic permeation had been identified and the approach was followed which a witness for the defendant suggested would have been appropriate in the light of such a report.

I turn now to a consideration of the hypothetical course of events had the defendant's examination been carried out with appropriate care and the malignant melanoma and the indications of lymphatic permeation been identified . . .

I think that the plaintiff would have had a dissection recommended to

> him and that it is likely that he would have undergone it. I also accept that it is likely that at the time the examination was carried out by the defendant, the plaintiff had some minor microscopic involvement of the lymph node and that had the dissection been carried out, the plaintiff's prospects of survival would have been very high, approaching 90%. I proceed to assess the plaintiff's damages upon this basis . . .
>
> The assessments which I make under the various heads of damages are arrived at after making an allowance for the risk that the plaintiff may have fallen into the small percentage of persons who would not have survived and also for the possibility that his treatment for the melanoma would not have been by way of elective lymph node dissection in which case he would have had, I am satisfied on the evidence, a greatly reduced chance of survival. The chance of survival in this case would have been measured by the prospects of discovery at an early stage, given the knowledge of the melanoma, of the involvement at an early stage of a lymph node or lymph nodes . . .
>
> [Judgment was entered for the plaintiff.]

Cases in other Australian jurisdictions have reached similar conclusions.

In *O'Shea v Sullivan and Macquarie Pathological Services* (1994) Aust Torts Reports 81–273, a patient was successful in a negligence action against both her general practitioner and the defendant pathology service for failing to diagnose cervical cancer. She had reported post-coital bleeding to her doctor who had ordered a pap smear test. The pap smear test sent to the defendants was falsely represented by them as being negative so the defendants were held liable in negligence. The defendant general practitioner was held to have fallen below the standard of a reasonable general practitioner in that he failed to refer the patient (who showed clear symptoms) to a specialist for treatment.

Stacey v Chiddy (above) should be contrasted with the decision of the Court of Appeal in New South Wales in *Stairmand v Baker* (unreported, 6 February 1992). In that case, damages were awarded on the basis of a 'missed diagnosis' of breast cancer. Priestley, Clarke and Handley JJA found that if the plaintiff had been earlier diagnosed she would have lived an extra seven years and would have experienced less pain and suffering than was otherwise the case. In particular, the judges noted that the plaintiff had to undergo chemotherapy which would have been unnecessary if her doctor had earlier diagnosed cancer.

Medicine, it was noted by Norse LJ in *Thake v Maurice* (supra) is an inexact science. At the same time, an incorrect diagnosis which a reasonable doctor would not have made, which results in a loss of opportunity to undertake efficacious treatment will sound in damages. This 'loss of opportunity' frequently arises where an initial complaint has been misdiagnosed, treatment is provided on the basis of the wrong diagnosis, and progression of the untreated problem precludes effective treatment for that condition. The principle is expounded most tellingly in the case of *Flinders Medical Centre v Waller*.

Flinders Medical Centre and Anor v Waller and Anor [2005] SASC 155

Full Court: Doyle CJ, Perry and Vanstone JJ

61. **PERRY J.** This is an appeal against a judgment given following a trial in the District Court.

62. The respondents, Vivien Kaye Waller 'Mrs Waller' and Kenneth James Waller 'Mr Waller' were the plaintiffs in the proceedings. The appellants, **Flinders Medical Centre** ('FMC') and Richard John Burns ('Professor Burns') were the defendants.

63. At the relevant time FMC, which is a body corporate, managed and conducted a public hospital known by the same name, situated at Bedford Park.

64. For some time before 1975, Professor Burns practised as a medical specialist, more particularly as a neurologist. In 1977, he became Senior Director of Neurology at FMC, and in 1978 an Associate Professor of Medicine at Flinders University.

65. In the proceedings, Mr and Mrs Waller claimed damages for alleged negligent treatment of Mrs Waller by Professor Burns in the course of his practice as a neurologist. The trial judge awarded Mrs Waller damages against both appellants in the sum of $3,202,000 including interest.

66. The trial judge awarded Mr Waller damages of $16,800, including interest.

67. In their notice of appeal, the appellants challenge the trial judge's finding that Professor Burns was negligent, and challenge various aspects of the trial judge's assessment of Mrs Waller's damages.

68. In a notice of cross-appeal, Mrs Waller complains that in various respects the trial judge's assessment of damages was inadequate. She seeks an order that the amount of damages awarded to her be increased.

69. In its defence, FMC admitted liability for the acts and omissions of Professor Burns after 1 July 1997. That admission makes it unnecessary to deal further with the case as against FMC.

70. The trial judge gave a lengthy, carefully reasoned judgment.

71. It was necessary for him to deal with a series of examinations of Mrs Waller by Professor Burns, commencing in 1975 through to 1997.

72. FMC's records relating to Mrs Waller, which included the clinical notes maintained by Professor Burns relating to the period between 1977 and 1988, were destroyed in 1996.

73. There can be no criticism of FMC for destroying the records, as it was not known at that stage that there was a potential legal claim. The destruction was in accordance with its standard procedure.

74. The trial judge found Mrs Waller to be generally an impressive and reliable witness.

75. While accepting Professor Burns' honesty, the trial judge found that he did not have a good recollection of his dealings with Mrs Waller and

he was obliged to rely upon what was recorded in documents then still available.

76. This was no reflection upon Professor Burns, as he had seen many thousands of patients over the intervening period, and there was no particular reason why he should remember the detail of his dealings with Mrs Waller.

77. In the result, as to the course of events over the period in question, the trial judge was obliged to rely, in the main, upon a series of letters written by Professor Burns to Mrs Waller's general practitioner, and Mrs Waller's evidence.

78. I will necessarily have to follow the same course.

79. The narrative account of the background to the matter, which I set out below, will therefore contain a number of references to the terms in which Professor Burns reported to the general practitioners. It is drawn generally from the trial judge's reasons for judgment.

Background

80. Mrs Waller is now aged 51 years. She was born on Kangaroo Island and continued to live there until 2003.

81. She qualified as a hairdresser. Until prevented from doing so by reason of her health, she worked in a hairdressing business on Kangaroo Island, except for periods off when she was caring for her children.

82. Mr and Mrs Waller married in 1972. Mr Waller worked on his father's farm and also as a wool classer.

83. In the early years of their marriage, Mrs Waller was in good health. She played competitive netball and tennis. She led an active social life.

84. On 1 April 1975, while pregnant with her second child, Mrs Waller consulted Dr Alcorn, a general practitioner in Kingscote, complaining of back pain. An x-ray of her thoracic spine was normal.

85. A little later, on 17 April 1975, she consulted Dr Alcorn again, complaining of numbness in her legs and feet, as well as a continuation of the back pain. She exhibited decreased sensation below the level of her breasts and some ankle spasms.

86. Dr Alcorn referred her to Professor Burns. At that stage, Dr Alcorn feared that Mrs Waller had multiple sclerosis ('MS'), but he did not tell her.

87. On 22 April 1975, Professor Burns admitted Mrs Waller to St Andrew's Hospital, where he conducted various examinations and tests.

88. He reported to Dr Alcorn by letter of 24 April 1975. Part of his report reads as follows:

> On examination the cranial nerves were normal as were the upper limbs. In the lower limbs there was weakness of hip flexion and knee flexion, greater on the right and some weakness of dorsiflexion on

> the right foot. Tone was increased in the legs with non-sustained clonus at the ankles and her knee and ankle jerks were hyperactive with bilateral extensor plantar responses. Sensory examination revealed impairment of vibration sense and position sense, mainly in the right foot with some mild but definite pain and temperature impairment on the left side. Hsi level, admittedly subjective to both touch and pain, could be demonstrated at about T6. There was sacral sparing.

89. In the letter, he concluded:

> The signs indicated a probable intramedullary lesion in the thoracic cord. This seemed to be either a post-viral transverse myelitis or a first episode of multiple sclerosis.

90. Professor Burns did not carry out any further investigations at that stage. The trial judge accepted that this was in part attributable to her pregnancy, which he described as 'an inhibiting factor'.

91. Mrs Waller was discharged from St Andrew's on 1 May 1975. On that date, Professor Burns wrote again to Dr Alcorn. In the letter he said:

> The diagnosis I think lies between a first episode of multiple sclerosis versus a transverse myelitis of post-viral origin. . . . I have not mentioned the diagnosis of multiple sclerosis to the patient or her husband. I have told them that it is some type of loss of myelin in the spinal cord of an inflammatory nature and that I am hopeful that in time it will get better. . . . I would very much like to learn of her progress and, if she is coming to Adelaide at some stage in the future, I would be only too pleased to be able to examine her again.

92. By letter of 13 May 1975, Professor Burns wrote again to Dr Alcorn to report the outcome of a further test of the spinal cord which had been made. He reported:

> The results of this patient's I.g.G in the C.5.F indicate that she has .03G per litre compared with the protein which was .10 G per litre. This means that 30% is I.g.G which is a finding greater than normal and consistent with a diagnosis of multiple sclerosis.

93. Mrs Waller's second child was born on 2 November 1975. From about that time, her symptoms began to resolve. They seem to have disappeared by about mid-1976, at which time she started playing competitive netball again and resumed part-time hairdressing.

94. However, in early May 1978, Mrs Waller experienced a recurrence of symptoms in the left leg and intermittent aches in her back and around her waist. Dr Alcorn referred her again to Professor Burns.

95. He reported to Dr Alcorn by letter of 13 June 1978. He explained that on examination he found lowered sensory responses in the left leg which he attributed to:

> . . . an intramedullary thoracic cord lesion on this occasion mainly on the left side involving particularly the posterior columns.

He went on to observe:

> Although the condition is not widely disseminated, the second episode involving the other side of the spinal cord makes a diagnosis of multiple sclerosis much more likely, bearing in mind also the previous elevation of her spinal fluid gamma globulin.

96. Professor Burns told Mrs Waller that he thought her leg would recover by itself in time. He explained to her that she might have a 'benign form of multiple sclerosis'. Importantly, he said in the letter that he had explained to her: '. . . but . . even now I couldn't be certain and in any case it seems to be behaving in a rather benign way'.

97. This was the first time that Mrs Waller was told that she might have MS.

98. Her condition did not improve. She said in evidence that at that stage she was walking with a bad limp, and felt tired and unwell. She stopped playing sport and gave up her part-time hairdressing work. She needed help from her mother-in-law to manage the household chores.

99. When her condition continued to worsen, she was referred again by Dr Alcorn to Professor Burns.

100. He examined her at FMC on 5 December 1979. On the same day, he wrote to Dr Alcorn. In the letter, he reported:

> There is still no evidence of disseminated disease but her thoracic cord lesion is now more obvious. I don't feel inclined to do any further investigations, although visual evoked responses would be of interest. I think she needs lots of reassurance at this stage and I have tried to give her this. It might be worth trying the effects of Baclofen, say 10 mgms b.d. increasing gradually if necessary to 25 mgms b.d. This might alleviate the spasticity and enable her to walk a little better.

101. Mrs Waller was not told by Professor Burns that there was any doubt in the diagnosis of MS, neither did he recommend any further investigation or test.

102. Mrs Waller's condition continued to worsen. She began to have episodes of faecal urgency and incontinence. Her tendency to drag her right leg became more pronounced. She continued to feel very tired.

103. Professor Burns examined her again on 16 September 1980. On the same day, he reported by letter to Dr Jeffries, a partner of Dr Alcorn. The letter reads in part:

> Her neurologic signs remain confined to the thoracic cord. I still believe that demyelination is the most likely pathogenetic mechanism although it is to be noted that she does not have, at the moment, evidence of disseminated neurologic lesions. The natural history so

> far is quite in keeping with this form of Multiple Sclerosis and her recent exacerbation may well have been triggered by increased physical stress and demands placed on her.
>
> As she seems to be improving a little I would not suggest a further course of steroids at the moment although these could be given if her disability does progress. Something like 60 mgms of Prednisolone for ten days could be then tried. In the meantime I think she should continue with her Baclofen. I have advised her to try and rest a little more and I am hopeful that with these measures alone some degree of improvement will occur although it seems likely that some of her neurologic signs are now of a permanent nature.

104. At that stage, Professor Burns did not advise that any further tests or investigations be pursued to confirm or disprove the diagnosis of MS.

105. In 1981, as the plaintiff's ability to walk deteriorated, she took to a wheelchair.

106. In September 1981, she underwent two weeks of physiotherapy and other treatment as a patient in the Multiple Sclerosis Clinic at Memorial Hospital. During that time she was seen by Professor Burns.

107. On 10 September 1981, Professor Burns wrote to Dr Alcorn. Part of the letter is as follows:

> As you know there has been a progressive increase of weakness in her legs in the last six months or so. She required a walking frame at first but now can only walk a few paces with this and uses a wheelchair. . . . Once again there are no symptoms referrable to the upper limbs or cranial nerves.
>
> On examination the signs were as previously confined to the lower half of the body. She had gross weakness of the legs with virtually no hip flexion but the weakness was global being greater on the right side. The distribution was of a pyramidal nature in that knee extension for example, was stronger than knee flexion. She had marked hypertonicity in the lower limbs with bilateral ankle clonus, hyperreflexia of the knee and ankle jerks and extensor plantar responses. Sensory examination revealed a vague level at about T7. Pain and temperature modalities were intact although subjectively impaired in various areas while position sense was grossly impaired in the feet and knees and vibration sense impaired to the iliac crests.
>
> Her neurologic signs remain confined to the thoracic cord involving the cortico-spinal tracts greater on the right and the posterior columns. Despite the fact that she has no neurologic abnormalities rostral to the thoracic cord has always raised slight doubts about the diagnosis but I still think that demyelination is the most likely explanation rather than a spinal cord angioma.
>
> I am afraid that with this type of insidious, progressive paraplegia that occurs in MS, significant recovery is unlikely. . . . She is

> fortunate in that she maintains reasonable sphincteric control and her mental attitude has always been exemplary.
>
> . . . The question of linoleic acid in the diet and also transfer factor remain controversial but I think at the present time it is fair to say that there is no agent that can really offer a significant chance of improvement.

108. Professor Burns did not examine Mrs Waller again until November 1984.

109. Between her spell at the Multiple Sclerosis Clinic at Memorial Hospital until November 1984, Mrs Waller appears more or less to have managed her own treatment. She took multiple vitamins and received massage from a reflexologist, to whom she had been recommended by a friend. The use of her legs appeared to improve.

110. In January 1983, she returned the wheelchair to the Kangaroo Island Hospital, thinking that she had no further need for it. She was able to walk, with occasional support, although she confined herself largely to walking inside the house.

111. On 28 November 1984, Professor Burns examined Mrs Waller again. He reported to Dr Alcorn by letter of that date. He described her has having had a 'remarkable remission and the degree of recovery of function has been most gratifying'. He went on in the letter to say:

> The signs one sees now are presumably the result of her previous spinal cord demyelination. There is nothing to make one think that the disease is active and I just hope that she can remain in remission for an indefinite period.

112. The remission did not last much longer. From about March 1986, her condition again started to deteriorate, and by late 1986, markedly so. By November 1986, she had spasms in her legs and was again using a walking stick. She was advised to resume use of a wheelchair, but resisted it in the hope that she could remain ambulant.

113. However, in May 1988, she twisted her ankle, at which stage she was obliged to use a wheelchair, to which she has been confined ever since.

114. She consulted Professor Burns again in June 1988. Part of his letter of 21 June 1988 to Dr Alcorn is as follows:

> Many thanks for referring Mrs Waller back for review after all these years.
>
> Although it seemed likely that she has gradually deteriorated over a period of some years, things got rapidly worse about a month ago. Until then she was able to walk long distances, usually with the aid of a stick and was capable of doing the housework. . . . She then slipped over and sprained her ankle and since then there has been a rapid deterioration of function. She can no longer walk and in fact

> can barely stand. She is unable to turn in bed and as you indicated she has become incontinent of urine. . . .
>
> Examination revealed signs confined to the lower half of the body with a spastic paraplegia. She was unable to overcome gravity with most muscles; there was increased tone in the legs with knee and ankle clonus and her knee and ankle reflexes were hyperactive, both plantars being extensor. Sensory examination revealed a level at about T10 which involved posterior column modalities, namely vibration sense and position sense. There was some subjective disturbance to pain and temperature but this was less definite.
>
> Her signs then are in keeping with the previously observed deficit of a thoracic cord lesion involving the corticospinal tracts and posterior columns. Multiple sclerosis is the presumed diagnosis despite the absence of disseminated lesions. The pattern of involvement and the exacerbations and remissions would be quite in keeping with this diagnosis but there is always that little doubt in one's mind when the signs are so localised. It is for this reason that I have arranged for her to have a spinal cord MRI just to exclude other much less likely possibilities such as spinal Av malformation.
>
> Hopefully she will improve spontaneously but this cannot be guaranteed. . . . She maintains her brave approach and attitude to her disease although clearly now she is very disabled but gets by because of her strong personality and her very supportive husband.

115. Before writing that letter, Professor Burns had arranged for a magnetic resonance imaging (MRI) scan to be performed at Royal Adelaide Hospital. She underwent the scan on 23 June 1988. As the trial judge indicates in his reasons, the only scanner available at that time in Adelaide was at the Royal Adelaide Hospital, where it had been in operation for a short time only.

116. The scan was performed by Dr Robertson. The latter reported to Professor Burns:

> . . . No evidence of any AVM or tumour was seen from the T6 region down. No definite evidence of any demyelination lesions was seen either.

117. When Professor Burns reported the outcome of the MRI scan to Dr Alcorn by letter of 19 July 1988, he stated that the scan:

> . . . seems to support the diagnosis of multiple sclerosis even though no areas of demyelination were seen on the scan.

What is important to note is that the MRI scan was limited to the T6 region down. The significance of this will appear later.

118. From about that time until July 1997, Mrs Waller did not see Professor Burns again. It appears that her condition, severe though it was, remained relatively static during that period.

119. Professor Burns saw Mrs Waller again in July 1997. By letter of

22 July 1997, he reported to her then general practitioner at Kingscote, Dr LP Jeffries:

> Many thanks for referring Vivien Waller who I remember very well.
>
> She is now aged forty-three and in the last nine years her neurologic disorder has remained more or less unchanged; perhaps her bladder function is a little worse. She has no symptoms referrable to her upper limbs or cranial nerves. She has no power in her legs at all and has no feeling below her breast line. . . .
>
> On examination she was her usual cheerful, alert self. The cranial nerves and upper limbs were normal. She had a complete paraplegia with increased tone in her legs and frequent bouts of clonus. Her deep tendon reflexes were all brisk especially the lower limbs with upgoing plantar responses. She had a complete sensory loss at about T6. This involved posterior column and spinothalamic sensation. She was unable to stand.
>
> She undoubtedly has a lesion in her thoracic cord and as you know a provisional diagnosis of multiple sclerosis has been made although this is not disseminated anatomically. Admittedly her symptoms were intermittent at first but the complete absence of signs above the thoracic cord and the rather dense neurologic deficit with complete spinothalamic involvement is a little unusual in my experience for multiple sclerosis. It was for that reason that an MRI scan was done in 1988 thinking that she might have some other intrinsic cord lesion such as a vascular malformation. I still have some doubts about the diagnosis and after discussing things with Vivien I am arranging for her to have another MRI scan of her cord. The technology is a little better now and although it is unlikely that one will find a treatable lesion, I think it is important to try and establish a diagnosis with more certainty. . . .

120. The MRI scan recommended by Professor Burns was performed on 3 November 1997. The radiologist's report was in part:

> MRI Thoracic Spine: 3/11/97
>
> . . .
>
> FINDINGS: There is a well defined oval expansile intramedullary lesion which extends from the C7-T1 level to the T4/5 level. It measures approximately 8cm in length. . . . It perhaps shows very slight enhancement of its margins on the post contrast images. However there is no discrete solid component.
>
> . . .
>
> CONCLUSION: Large intramedullary lesion likely to be longstanding. The most likely diagnosis is a slow growing cystic cord tumour possibly a haemangioblastoma without a discrete vascular nidus. Presumably there is no history of significant spinal trauma which may have led to development of hydromyelia.

121. Two days later, on 5 November 1997, Professor Burns rang Mrs Waller to say that she did not have MS after all; rather, a tumour on the spine.

122. On 7 November 1997, Professor Burns wrote to Dr Jeffries to report this development. He explained that he would be discussing the matter with a number of other colleagues to decide what course of action should be followed in light of the new diagnosis. In the letter he observed:

> As you know I have always been concerned about the diagnosis of multiple sclerosis for a variety of reasons and while it would be intriguing to find out I don't want to subject her to any procedure if it is going to run the risk of making her worse.

123. The next development was the admission of Mrs Waller to FMC as an in-patient on 16 February 1998. She believed at that time that spinal surgery to remove the tumour would be performed by a neurosurgeon, Mr Brophy. Professor Burns did not examine her on that occasion, but told her that he and Mr Brophy would review the scans, with a view to deciding what was to be done.

124. Mrs Waller did not have any further contact with Professor Burns.

125. The next day, that is, 17 February 1998, a further MRI scan was performed, after which Dr Brophy informed Mrs Waller that he was not intending to do an operation. According to her evidence, which was accepted by the trial judge:

> He thought the nerve damage was too great and I wasn't going to get no better quality of life so that he decided that they weren't going to operate.

126. Dr Brophy suggested that she have another MRI in six months' time to see what the growth rate of the tumour was.

127. While Mrs Waller and her husband were with Dr Brophy, and after he had told them that he was not intending to operate, Mr Waller asked Dr Brophy 'if the tumour had been what caused Mrs Waller her problems for the last 22 years'. He said in answer that the tumour would have caused her problems.

128. Mrs Waller then took a second opinion from another neurologist, Dr Andrew Black, who referred her in turn to Professor Nigel Jones, the Professor of Neurosurgery at the University of Adelaide.

129. After he had seen Mrs Waller, he wrote to Dr Jeffries. In the course of the letter, he said:

> 'Her MRI scan shows an intramedullary tumour which was reported to be most likely a haemangioblastoma. The tumour extends from the T4/5 disc space up to the T1 vertebral level. It appears to be relatively well defined and has some mixed signal intensity within it. There is no nidus of enhancement after gadolinium which I think would be very much against the diagnosis of

haemangioblastoma and the appearances to me are more like an ependymoma.'

130. Mrs Waller decided to go ahead with an operation to remove the tumour. This was performed by Professor Jones on 16 October 1997.

131. Contrary to his expectations, he found that the tumour was an intramedullary epidermoid cyst, which he removed completely.

132. Thereafter, the plaintiff's symptoms remained static. They did not worsen. The paraplegia of the lower part of her body remained unchanged. Mrs Waller continued to live on the farm on Kangaroo Island with her husband. However, their relationship eventually deteriorated, and by the end of 2003, she and her husband agreed that their marriage was finished and that they should separate.

133. Early in January 2004, Mrs Waller moved from Kangaroo Island to Adelaide. Mr Waller remained on Kangaroo Island and continued to run the farm.

Multiple sclerosis

134. It is convenient at this stage to say something about MS.

135. I quote from the trial judge's reasons for judgment:

> [45] MS is a very serious disease which can lead to major disability and death. There is no cure for it. Its causes are unknown. There is no specific diagnostic test for it and diagnosis is only through clinical verification of what are known as the Schumacher criteria. These are:
>
> 1. Neurological examination reveals objective abnormalities of CNS function.
> 2. Examination or history indicates involvement of 2 or more parts of the CNS.
> 3. CNR disease predominantly reflects white matter involvement.
> 4. Involvement of CNS follows 1 or 2 patterns:
>   (i) Two or more episodes, each lasting at least 24h and a month or more apart.
>   (ii) Slow or step-wise progression of signs and symptoms over at least 6 months.
> 5. Patient 10–50 years old at onset.
> 6. Signs and symptoms cannot better be explained by any other disease process. (CNS is Central Nervous System.)
>
> [46] In this case the issue was whether the plaintiff satisfied the criteria Nos 2 and 6. Criterion 2 required disseminated lesions, which is why the disease is called 'Multiple' Sclerosis. The manifestations of MS are such that once a label of MS is placed on a patient any symptoms thereafter displayed by the patient are likely to be attributed to the MS even if they have a different cause. There was

> particular difficulty in the diagnosis of MS from lesions in the spinal cord and rigorous processes were required to ensure that the proper diagnosis was not of some other medical condition which was treatable.
>
> [47] Epidermoid cysts of the type found in 1998 in the plaintiff's thoracic spine are an extremely rare type of tumour. There is no recorded previous instance of such an intramedullary tumour in this State, and there are only about fifty such cases recorded in the world. No doctor who gave evidence or reports in this matter had ever previously seen one. They are benign cysts which are formed before birth and grow slowly. They can become clinically symptomatic at any age, but there was no previous recorded instance of symptoms from them having remitted and returned as occurred with the plaintiff.
>
> [48] Although fairly rare, there were various other types of spinal tumours which could have caused lesions in the plaintiff's spine and have mimicked some of the symptoms of MS. However, generally these tumours were progressive in the onset of their symptoms and did not remit and then recur as was the experience of the plaintiff. Some such tumours were untreatable, but some could be treated.

The basis of the finding of negligence

136. The trial judge correctly identified the duty of care owed by a medical practitioner to a patient as a duty to exercise 'reasonable care and skill in the provision of professional services which extend to the diagnosis and treatment of the patient'.

He correctly identified the applicable standard of care as that of the 'ordinarily skilled neurologist'.

He observed that in a case such as this, the evidence of what other specialists might have done in the same circumstances was 'of considerable significance', but ultimately, it was 'for the court to decide the extent of the duty and whether it had been breached'.

Reaching his findings as to negligence, the trial judge was obliged to consider expert evidence given by a number of neurologists, not all of which was consistent.

Where there were inconsistencies, he preferred the evidence of Dr Hallpike. In his reasons, he said:

> [50] I found Dr Hallpike, a specialist neurologist who had been in practice in Adelaide for many years, to be the most impressive and convincing of the neurologists who gave evidence. I accept his opinions where they are in conflict with those of other neurologists. I accept the expert evidence of the neurosurgeon, Professor Jones. The plaintiffs submitted that I should reject the opinions of Mr North, a neurosurgeon, called by the defendants on neurosurgical practices from 1975 to 1981, which was before Professor Jones had

commenced practice. However, I accept his expertise and integrity, but in my findings below I conclude his opinions are not contrary to the plaintiff's case.

141. Dr Hallpike's evidence was that in light of the findings made in 1975, when Mrs Waller was first seen by Professor Burns, most neurologists would have adopted what he described as a 'conservative (observational) management approach in the short term'. Furthermore, Mrs Waller's pregnancy at that time militated against more invasive investigations, such as a myelogram.

142. As for the attendance by Professor Burns upon Mrs Waller in 1978, neither Dr Hallpike nor another neurologist who gave evidence, Professor McLeod, thought that any question was raised as to the appropriateness of Professor Burns' advice at that time. As of 1978, there had been what appeared to be a complete recovery by Mrs Waller for a substantial period of time which strongly pointed to MS.

143. One of the neurologists who gave evidence, Dr Boyce, was of the opinion that as early as 1975, or soon thereafter, Mrs Waller should have had a full spinal myelogram. But in light of the contrary opinion expressed by Dr Hallpike, the trial judge was not prepared to find Professor Burns negligent in failing to pursue myelography in 1978.

144. However, the trial judge accepted the opinions of Dr Hallpike, Professor McLeod and Dr Boyce, that when Professor Burns saw Mrs Waller in December 1979, he should have pursued further investigations. It is not unimportant to note that Professor McLeod was an expert witness called on behalf of the appellants.

145. The opinion of Dr Hallpike to that effect is set out in his report (undated) addressed to Mrs Waller's solicitors:

> Turning to the situation when Dr Burns saw her again in 1979 (his letter, 5/12/79). There had been progression of the neurological disability. The clinical examination provided clear evidence of a spastic paraparesis with a sensory level at T12. Dr Burns wrote 'there is still no evidence of disseminated disease but her thoracic cord lesion is now more obvious'. It was in this context that the reference was made to the VEP test to look for evidence of another site of CNS involvement. I feel that at this stage there was a need to try and achieve a firm diagnosis. There was a major, persistent – by that time progressive – neurological abnormality. According to Dr Douglas McAlpine in his chapter on 'The Problem of Diagnosis' in *Multiple Sclerosis. A Reappraisal* by Douglas McAlpine, Charles E. Lumsden and E.D. Acheson, Churchill Livingstone, 2nd Edition 1972, the leading clinical textbook on this subject at the relevant time, '*In practice, a provisional diagnosis of multiple sclerosis in a case of paraplegia, especially if progressive, should not be allowed to stand if after a lapse of some months only spinal cord signs are present*' [Dr McAlpine's italics in the text]. What I would understand by '*should not be allowed to stand*' is need for a full re-evaluation of the

problem myelopathy. In this case, I would see such re-evaluation as including plain x-rays of the thoracic spine (if not already done and carefully reviewed), a neuro-ophthalmological examination for any subtle ophthalmic signs of MS, an autoimmune screen (systemic lupus erythematosus can present with a fluctuating/relapse remitting myelopathy and a raised CSF lgG), contact with Mr Paul Weston [senior scientific officer at the time responsible for the clinical neurophysiology at the ACH] about the availability of visually- and auditory-evoked response testing for Mrs Waller. If the total of these investigations gave no support for multifocal neurological disease, there would have been strong indication to proceed with a thoracic myelogram with repeat CSF examination.

146. Dr Hallpike referred to the letter of Professor Burns dated 5 December 1979. I have set out the text of that letter above. It will be seen that part of the letter reads:

> I don't feel inclined to do any further investigations, although visual evoked responses would be of interest.

147. The trial judge found that if a visual evoked response test had been performed in about December 1979, it is likely that the test results would have been normal. If they had been normal, this would have been a strong indication to perform a myelogram, which in turn is likely to have demonstrated the presence of the tumour, which would have displaced the diagnosis of MS, in favour of the tumour being the cause of Mrs Waller's illness.

148. In those circumstances, surgery is likely to have been carried out to remove the tumour at that stage.

149. If that had been the case, the deterioration in Mrs Waller's condition would more than likely have been arrested, and she would have been spared the acute symptoms which developed subsequently.

150. It is that process of reasoning which is at the nub of the finding of negligence against Professor Burns.

151. The way in which the trial judge expressed the matter appears from the following passage in his reasons for judgment:

> [54] I accept the opinion of Dr Hallpike that when the 2nd defendant saw the plaintiff in December 1979 he should as a matter of proper neurological practice in the circumstances which then existed have pursued further investigations to reach a more definite diagnosis. His opinion on this is supported by the opinions of Professor McLeod and Dr Boyce. The plaintiff's condition was then significantly deteriorating and she appeared to be progressing towards paraplegia. There was still no evidence of any second lesion in the central nervous system but outside of the spine which would satisfy the second criterion in the Schumacher Test. There were other possible disease processes which might better explain her symptoms in accordance with criterion 6 in the Schumacher Test.

[55] In his letter of 5 December 1979, quoted above, the 2nd defendant said, 'I don't feel inclined to do any further investigations although visual evoked responses would be of interest.' Visual evoked responses ('VERs') were a new investigation at the time which revealed abnormalities in the visual pathways of 60–75% of persons who definitely had MS. If a VER test had been performed, and had produced abnormal results, that would have been a significant indicator of a para lesion in the optic nerves and confirmatory of MS. If any VER test results of the plaintiff were normal, it would not in itself have refuted a diagnosis of MS, but it would have thrown sufficient doubt on the diagnosis of MS to make tests for other possible causes of the symptoms more imperative. With the benefit of hindsight it is clear that if the plaintiff had undergone VER tests the results would have been normal. Professor McLeod, who practised in Sydney, had VERs performed routinely because facilities for them were readily available to him. Dr Hallpike thought they were not readily available in Adelaide in late 1979 and were only available at the Women and Children's Hospital. However, the 2nd defendant said in his evidence that he was 'pretty sure' that they were available at **Flinders Medical Centre** at the time. Thus there was no inhibition on carrying out such VERs from them being inaccessible.

[56] If VER tests on the plaintiff had been normal, each of Dr Hallpike, Professor McLeod and Dr Boyce said he would then have sought to have the plaintiff undergo myelography to see if that revealed any other possible cause of the symptoms. Myelography is taking plain X-rays of the spinal cord after dye has been injected into it through a lumbar puncture. . . . I find that if myelography had been recommended to her by the 2nd defendant in late 1979 or early 1980 that the plaintiff would have undergone it. . . . In this era myelograms were regularly carried out for many spinal problems, some far less serious than those of the plaintiff. In his many years of practice Dr Hallpike had never known a patient to whom he had recommended a myelogram to refuse to undergo it because of the risks of adverse consequences.

[57] As Dr Hallpike said in his second report:

'. . . the hazards to the plaintiff of overlooking a tumour diagnosis by 1979 *greatly* exceeded any risks associated with the investigation.'

In seeking a definite diagnosis of the cause of a spinal cord lesion myelography was treated in the text books of the time as the gold standard and the highest Court of Appeal. I accept the opinion of Dr Hallpike that if a myelogram had been carried out in about December 1979 on the plaintiff it is highly likely that it would have revealed a swelling in her spinal cord caused by the epidermoid cyst. . . . I accept Dr Hallpike's opinion that if a myelogram of the plaintiff in about December 1979 had revealed swelling of her

> spinal cord it is highly likely that a biopsy would then have been performed at that point in the spinal cord which would have revealed the nature of the epidermoid cyst. If that had been diagnosed in about early 1980, I find that it would have been surgically removed shortly afterwards. . . .
>
> [58] There is no suggestion that the 2nd defendant should have suspected on 5 December 1979 that the plaintiff's symptoms were caused by an epidermoid cyst. From the absence of any second disseminated lesion since the onset of the condition in 1975 the reasonably competent neurologist treating the plaintiff in 1979 should have been looking for any other possible cause of the plaintiff's spinal lesion. There was some, albeit a fairly remote, possibility that the cause could be an intramedullary tumour of some kind such as perhaps an AVM. This possibility could, and should, have been investigated by myelography as there was also some possibility that if some sort of tumour was found it might be treatable. As his subsequent correspondence with the general practitioners on Kangaroo Island showed the 2nd defendant was never sufficiently confident of a firm diagnosis of MS such as to obviate the need to pursue other investigations of alternative, although less likely, causes of the plaintiff's symptoms, and particularly in view of her ongoing descent towards paraplegia. *On the balance of probabilities his failure in December 1979 to pursue VER tests and a myelogram was a breach of his legal duty to the plaintiff* (my emphasis)

152. The trial judge went on to find that even if, contrary to the view which he had expressed, Professor Burns was not negligent in failing to arrange for a myelogram in 1979:

> [60] . . . On similar lines of reasoning he would have been negligent in not recommending one when he saw her in each of September 1980 and September 1981.

153. He did not, however, pursue that aspect of the matter, as he held that her damages would not be any greater, whether the negligence should be dated in either 1979, 1980 or 1981.

The appeal as to the finding of negligence

154. The grounds of appeal advanced in support of the assertion that the trial judge erred in finding a breach of a duty of care by Professor Burns may be summarised as follows:

That the trial judge erred in finding –

- That Professor Burns was negligent in failing to pursue VER tests and the myelogram in December 1979.
- That Professor Burns was negligent in failing to recommend a myelogram in September 1980 or September 1981.
- In finding that Professor Burns was in breach of the standard of

care of the reasonably competent neurologist in failing to perform a myelogram as:

- a myelogram was not indicated;
- there was no evidence of a progressive condition;
- lack of evidence of a second lesion did not detract from a diagnosis of multiple sclerosis.

155. An additional ground of appeal was allowed by way of amendment to the notice of appeal during the course of the hearing (ground 13A). In this ground the appellant contended that the trial judge 'erred in failing to give adequate reasons for his findings on neurological evidence and thereby his findings on breach of duty'.

156. Three neurologists gave expert evidence: Dr Hallpike and Dr Boyce on behalf of Mrs Waller, and Professor McLeod on behalf of Professor Burns and FMC.

157. Professor Burns also gave expert evidence in his own defence.

158. I have set out above, the general findings made by the trial judge as to the expert evidence, and that he preferred the evidence of Dr Hallpike where there was a conflict with others.

159. The trial judge observed in a footnote:

> I received some expert evidence from the 2nd defendant *de bene esse* over an objection that he should not be permitted to give expert evidence because no report from him had been served on the plaintiff pursuant to Rule 38.01. I need not go into the difficult question of whether Rule 38.01 prevents a party giving expert evidence in his own cause as I reject the expert evidence of the 2nd defendant insofar as it conflicts with that of Dr Hallpike.

160. Elsewhere throughout his reasons for judgment, the trial judge specifically referred to the evidence which he preferred, which was more often than not the evidence of Dr Hallpike, on many occasions contrasting it with expert evidence which he was not prepared to accept.

161. During the course of his submissions, Mr Harris QC of counsel for the appellants complained:

> . . . His Honour accepted the opinions of Dr Hallpike where they were in conflict with those of other neurologists (including Professor Burns). However, His Honour, with respect, failed to articulate in the judgment any reasoning process by which the preference of Dr Hallpike could be demonstrated. Relevantly, the learned trial judge dealt with the expert evidence of Professor Burns in a footnote to the judgment and not otherwise.

162. In my view, this complaint is not made out.

163. The fact that the trial judge saw fit to comment on the evidence of Professor Burns in a footnote is of no relevant significance.

164. The trial judge expressly found that Professor Burns was an honest

witness, and he did not suggest that any of the other expert witnesses gave evidence which was other than an honest expression of their views.

165. In cases such as this where there is a substantial body of opinion evidence from a group of highly qualified expert witnesses, it was entirely a matter for the trial judge to evaluate the evidence as best he could, and indicate the evidence which he accepted and that which he rejected, or was otherwise not prepared to rely upon.

166. In some cases, a judge may be able to point to internal inconsistencies in the evidence of an expert witness, or a lack of rationality. In other cases, the trial judge may be able to point to differences in the factual hypothesis upon which an opinion has been expressed, in which case he or she would be entitled to prefer an opinion based upon the factual hypothesis which the judge was prepared to find was accurate.

167. In other cases, such as this case, it may not be possible to point to factors such as that. Where such factors are absent, the preference of one expert over another may come down to the trial judge's impression as to the manner in which the witness gave his or her evidence, and whether the evidence of the witness was convincing.

168. When in this case the trial judge said that he found Dr Hallpike to be '. . . the most impressive and convincing of the neurologists who gave evidence', it was not incumbent upon the trial judge to articulate further why or how he came to that view. Certainly, a finding that one expert was more impressive and convincing than another or others, is not a matter that would admit readily to explanation by reference to a 'reasoning process'.

169. Remarks which I made in *Rowland v Police*, while made in the context of a magistrate's appeal in a criminal matter, are nonetheless apposite:

> [34] . . . it will often be the case that factual issues will be resolved by preferring the evidence of one witness over that of another, particularly where it comes down to a question of 'oath against oath'. In such circumstances, it may be sufficient for a magistrate to say that he or she has preferred the evidence of a witness based on an assessment of demeanour, or because one witness was found to be more convincing than another, or because the evidence given by one witness was inherently implausible or for some other shortly stated reason. See *R v Keyte* per Doyle CJ:
>
> > I do not accept that there is a need to provide a detailed explanation for the decision to prefer the evidence of one witness to another, and for the conclusion of satisfaction of guilt beyond reasonable doubt on the basis of the evidence of that witness, at least when the relevant decision rests substantially upon the impression made by the witness when giving evidence.

170. Once it is accepted that the trial judge did not err in preferring the evidence of Dr Hallpike, or in his explanation as to why he did so, this

goes a long way towards disposing of the grounds of appeal relating to the findings as to breach of duty of care.

171. As the respondents contended, this was a case where Professor Burns consistently indicated a degree of uncertainty in his diagnosis. That uncertainty is reflected in a number of passages in the various letters of report which I have quoted above. I refer again to them.

172. Professor Burns made no firm diagnosis in his letter of 24 April 1975 to Dr Alcorn.

173. In his letter of 1 May 1975, he stated that 'The diagnosis I think lies between a first episode of multiple sclerosis versus a transverse myelitis of post viral origin'.

174. In his letter of 13 June 1978, although he described the diagnosis of multiple sclerosis as 'much more likely', he stated that he could not be certain.

175. In his letter of 5 December 1979, he again referred to the fact that there was 'no evidence of disseminated disease' (an indication of MS), and after indicating that he was not inclined to do any further investigations, he stated that 'visual evoked responses would be of interest'.

176. He noted again in his letter of 16 September 1980 that there was still 'no evidence of disseminated neurological lesions'.

177. In his letter of 10 September 1981, he said:

> 'Despite the fact that she has no neurologic abnormalities rostral to the thoracic cord has always raised slight doubts about the diagnosis . . .'

178. Pausing there, it seems to me that the proper conclusion to be drawn from what Professor Burns was saying in those passages is that the diagnosis of MS was very much a provisional diagnosis, and that the absence of a disseminated distribution of symptoms in particular, made it difficult to reach a firm diagnosis of MS.

179. Against that background, it was open for the trial judge to find, as he did:

> [58] . . . the reasonably competent neurologist treating the plaintiff in 1979 should have been looking for any other possible cause of the plaintiff's spinal lesion.

180. Clearly, from the letter of 5 December 1979, Professor Burns was aware of the availability of a VER test, which he stated 'would be of interest'.

181. A VER test was non-invasive. Professor Burns lacked a definite diagnosis of MS at that stage, or indeed at any stage. There was ample support, not only in the evidence of Dr Hallpike but in other expert evidence, to support the trial judge's finding that Professor Burns owed a duty to conduct further tests, more particularly a VER test in December 1979, which would more than likely have led to a myelogram and the

discovery of the tumour at that stage, and that his failure to do so was a breach of his legal duty to the plaintiff.

I accept the respondent's submission that the weight of the medical evidence, including that given by the medical witnesses and authoritative medical publications, supported the need to pursue further investigations at that stage.

As it was put by Dr Hallpike, in December 1979, the time had come for 'the minimum clinical judgment and the maximum on tests'. Dr Boyce's evidence was:

> Q: As far as you're concerned, presenting with the symptoms that she did in December of 1979, would you have recommended investigations to determine the cause rather than leaving a differential diagnosis.
>
> A: Absolutely.

184. Professor Burns himself accepted in his evidence that visual evoked responses were a most important test when considering a diagnosis of MS.

185. The expert evidence confirmed that myelograms were the 'gold standard'.

186. Notwithstanding the weight of evidence in favour of performing tests as of December 1979, Professor Burns did not recommend or undertake any investigations from about June 1979 and during a period of deterioration of the plaintiff's symptoms up to September 1980 and down to September 1981.

187. The appellants have failed to satisfy me that there is any reason to doubt the soundness of the essential conclusions of the trial judge:

- That at least a VER test should have been carried out in December 1979.
- That knowing what is now known of the plaintiff's condition, a VER test would have been normal.
- A normal VER test would have prompted a reasonably competent neurologist to proceed to a myelogram.
- A myelogram would have identified the swelling in the spinal cord caused by the epidermoid cyst.
- This would have prompted a biopsy, which would have in turn revealed the presence of the cyst.
- A reasonably competent neurologist would then have recommended surgery, very likely in early 1980, to remove the cyst.

188. In my view, that process of reasoning was fully supported by the expert evidence which the trial judge accepted in preference to conflicting evidence.

189. During the course of his argument presented on behalf of the appellants, Mr Harris QC made much of the fact that an epidermoid cyst was a very rare form of tumour, and there was no known precedent

for an intramedullary tumour to give rise to the pattern of symptoms experienced by Mrs Waller.

190. Even accepting those comments, they are, with respect, beside the point. The central question in this case was whether Professor Burns should have pursued further tests in December 1979. No light is thrown on the answer to that question, by reason of the fact that if the tests had been performed, a rare condition would have been found.

191. No ground has been made out by the appellants which would justify interference with that finding.

192. In those circumstances, it is unnecessary to deal with the appellants' complaint that the trial judge erred in finding that even if Professor Burns was not negligent in failing to pursue a myelogram in 1979, he would have been negligent in not recommending such a test when he saw Mrs Waller in September 1980 and September 1981.

193. The finding as to negligence in 1979, which for the reasons I have given should, in my view, be upheld, is sufficient to dispose of the appeal on the issue of negligence.

Causation

194. The contentions of the appellants with respect to causation are summarised in the following grounds of appeal (as amended at the hearing):

> 16. The Learned Trial Judge erred in finding that:
>
> 16.1 After any removal of the cyst in or about early 1980 when the plaintiff's disabilities thereafter would not have been any greater than they were when she was at her best during the period of spontaneous remission between 1982 and 1986, and with the removal of the cyst her disabilities would not have increased from 1986 onwards.
>
> 16.1.A The breaches of duty which His Honour had found in 1979, 1980 and 1981 were the cause of the damage complained of by the first plaintiff in the action.
>
> 16.1.B The epidermoid cyst would have been diagnosed in about early 1980 and that it would have been surgically removed shortly afterwards.
>
> 16.2 That the first plaintiff's claim is not merely for the loss of a chance the detection and removal of the cyst in early 1980 might have improved her subsequent condition.
>
> 16.3 Had the cyst been removed in 1980 then the first plaintiff would have remained reasonably ambulant and fully continent.

195. It is convenient to address ground 16.1B first.

196. The finding by the trial judge to which that ground relates appears in the following passage from his reasons for judgment:

> [57] . . . I accept the opinion of Dr Hallpike that if a myelogram had been carried out in about December 1979 on the plaintiff it is highly likely that it would have revealed a swelling in her spinal cord caused by the epidermoid cyst. Professor Jones gave similar evidence relating to what would have been likely to have been found on a myelogram in 1980, and that supports Dr Hallpike's conclusion. However, a myelogram would have merely revealed the existence and location of swelling of the spinal cord, but it would not have been diagnostic of the cause of swelling. I accept Dr Hallpike's opinion that if a myelogram of the plaintiff in about December 1979 had revealed swelling of her spinal cord it is highly likely that a biopsy would then have been performed at that point in the spinal cord which would have revealed the nature of the epidermoid cyst. If that had been diagnosed in about early 1980, I find that it would have been surgically removed shortly afterwards. I do not accept any view of Mr North to the contrary. He conceded that a progressive worsening of the symptoms, as was the plaintiff's case, would make it more likely that surgery would have been recommended. As to what such surgery in early 1980 would have meant for the plaintiff will be dealt with later in these reasons.

197. Dr Hallpike was asked directly in the course of his evidence in chief whether a biopsy performed in 1979 would have been likely to have identified the tumour. He said that it would.

198. He went on to say in his evidence, that the next step, once the tumour had been identified by biopsy, would be consultation with a neurosurgeon. He said that he was quite sure that a recommendation would have followed that the lesion be 'explored'.

199. In challenging the trial judge's findings based on that evidence, the appellants pointed to the fact that the only neurosurgeon who gave evidence in the case, and who was in practice at the relevant time, was Mr North.

Relevantly, Mr North's evidence was that:

> 'Between 1975 and 1988, the surgical philosophy for managing such a patient with a swelling within the spinal cord would have been conservative, with periodic review.'

201. Insofar as Mr North's view was that surgical intervention would not have been likely, in the passage which I have quoted above from his reasons for judgment, the trial judge clearly was not prepared to accept that evidence, preferring the opinion of Dr Hallpike.

The appellants' contentions on this issue fly in the face of the fact that, as the respondents point out, the point of a myelogram was to diagnose and determine if the condition warranted surgical exploration.

As to ground 16.2, in my view, the trial judge did not err in rejecting the contention which was put to him at the trial, that all that the plaintiff had lost, at best, was a chance that if the tumour had been found and removed in early 1980, this might have improved her subsequent condition.

Whether or not the plaintiffs' case came down to the mere loss of a chance of improvement in her condition, or something more positive than that, was a matter involving an assessment of the evidence as to the likely consequences of removal of the tumour at that stage.

In his reasons for judgment, the trial judge addressed this issue directly. After quoting a passage from the evidence of Dr Hallpike, the trial judge concluded:

> [71] Although it was not directly addressed in the medical evidence, as a matter of commonsense I infer, and find, that after any removal of the cyst in about early 1980 the plaintiff's disabilities thereafter would not have been any greater than they were when she was at her best during the period of spontaneous remission between 1982 and 1986, and with the removal of the cyst her disabilities would not have increased from 1986 onwards. *She has proved this on the balance of probabilities and thus her claim is not merely for the loss of a chance that detection and removal of the cyst in early 1980 might have improved her subsequent condition.* This means that her damages are to be assessed on the basis that in any event she would have had some problems with her legs and have walked with some limp, but she would have remained reasonably ambulant and fully continent. While she would not have been able to run and play sport, and have been restricted in more strenuous activities, she would have been able to perform almost all of her usual household duties and to have engaged in a wide range of social and recreational activities. (my emphasis)

206. Although the trial judge introduces that finding with the expression 'although it was not directly addressed in the medical evidence', the evidence of Dr Hallpike, which he set out before that passage, was to the effect that the more disabled the patient is before the operation, the poorer the outlook for recovery. He went on to say that if Mrs Waller was 'independently ambulant' before the operation (which was the case), 'the outcome . . . would have been very much more favourable on any statistical basis than the outcome when operated on when she was no longer able to stand or walk independently'.

207. The trial judge also referred to the evidence of Dr Hallpike that even intervention as late as 1988 had prospects of considerable improvement. Dr Hallpike's words were that he would have been '. . . quite optimistic of substantial recovery, very significant recovery functionally'.

208. In my view, the trial judge was right to refuse to characterise the case as one where the award should be limited to damages for a lost chance or lost opportunity.

It will always be a question of degree of probability as to whether or not a given result should be so characterised, or whether an affirmative finding that a particular loss is attributable to a negligent act should be made. Given the trial judge's findings, it is unnecessary to deal with the difficult category of cases where the relevant probability is less than 50 per cent.

In this case, once the judge correctly reasoned towards a conclusion that more likely than not, absent the negligence of Professor Burns, the tumour would have been discovered and removed in early 1980 and that this would have had the likely consequence that the later deterioration in Mrs Waller's condition would have been avoided, he was entitled to award damages for the proven consequences of the failure to remove it at that stage.

The findings made with respect to causation were open on the evidence and were not findings which should be disturbed on appeal.

I would dismiss what have been described as the 'causation' arguments, being the matters raised in ground 16 of the notice of appeal.

As for the appeal and cross-appeal with respect to the quantum of damages, I agree with the Chief Justice that the cross-appeal should be allowed, for the purpose of increasing the amount awarded for future economic loss, to $100,000. Save for that adjustment, the appeal and cross-appeal with respect to damages should be dismissed. I agree with the reasons of the Chief Justice as to those matters.

In the result, on all issues, I would dismiss the appeal and cross-appeal, save that the cross-appeal should be allowed for the purpose of increasing the amount awarded in favour of the First Plaintiff to $3,252,000. (Doyle CJ and Vanstone J issued separate judgments agreeing with the reasons of Perry J.)

(vi) Failure to follow-up

Medical practitioners have been found liable in negligence for not chasing up patients to advise them of adverse test results (*Kite v Malycha*), or failing to ensure that a patient is correctly entered onto a surgical list for medical treatment (*Tai v Hatzistavrou*). Extracts from each case are recorded below. Recall also the finding in *Witon v Arnott*.

***Jayne Carlene and Darren John Kite v Peter Malycha; Jayne Carlene and Darren John Kite v Peter Malycha and Peter Malycha Pty Ltd* (1998) 71 SASR 321**

Perry J:
In the principal action Jayne Carlene Kite and her husband Darren John Kite sue Peter Malycha, a general surgeon specialising in breast surgery, for damages arising out of Mr Malycha's examination of Mrs Kite in December 1994.

The gist of the principal action is that Mr Malycha, having taken a needle biopsy of a lump in Mrs Kite's left breast, failed to take proper steps in response to a pathological report indicating that the specimen was highly suspicious of an underlying carcinoma. It is alleged that in the result, Mrs Kite was not offered appropriate treatment at that stage.

Mrs Kite underwent breast surgery in September 1995. There is no doubt that by then Mrs Kite was suffering from ductile carcinoma of the breast which had become metastatic, that is, it had invaded other parts of the body, namely, a number of surrounding lymph nodes. Given the seriousness of her condition, and subsequent developments in it, she has now lived close to, if not beyond, her life expectancy.

The central issue in the case is whether or not the failure properly to diagnose the condition and to offer appropriate treatment in December 1994 robbed her of the chance of successfully curing the cancer, or reduced the life expectancy which she might otherwise have expected to enjoy.

Put shortly, Mr Malycha's case is that while denying negligence, in any event, it would not have made any significant difference if her condition had been diagnosed and treated then.

Mrs Kite saw Mr Malycha at his rooms on South Terrace on 2 December 1994.

During the course of the history which he obtained from her, Mr Malycha elicited that there had been a small lump in her left armpit about a year beforehand, but that it had gone away after it was treated with antibiotics. She explained to him that the lump now present in her left armpit was bigger and tender.

He then examined both breasts, looking for evidence of cancer. He found a lesion in the left axilla. The site of the lesion did not immediately suggest that it was in the axillary tail of the breast as opposed to a position beyond the tail of the breast. It is now clear that the axillary tail of Mrs Kite's breast extended a little beyond the area to which it would commonly extend in other patients.

At all events, Mr Malycha conducted a fine needle aspiration of the lesion.

Aspiration of the lesion with a fine needle was an appropriate procedure. There is no suggestion that it was not performed competently. It involved inserting the needle into the skin and taking several passes, so as to collect in the shaft of the needle a specimen from the area into which the needle was inserted.

In her affidavit Mrs Kite says that Mr Malycha spoke of the possibility of a needle biopsy or needle aspiration, and explained what that involved. She says that she then asked him to perform the needle biopsy. Indeed, according to her, she pressed him to do so as she wanted to be satisfied that there was 'nothing wrong'.

Just why Mr Malycha performed the fine needle aspiration is not entirely clear. In his evidence before me, so far as he could recollect, there was nothing about her condition which prompted him to perform the fine needle aspiration. Indeed, he could not remember having performed it that day on Mrs Kite.

I find, however, that he performed the biopsy, at least in part, as a diagnostic aid. I make that finding in view of the terms of his letter to Dr Sangster of the same day, to which I refer in due course.

She was anxious about her condition. It seems likely that Mr Malycha was prompted to perform the needle biopsy in part as a result of Mrs Kite urging him to do so, and in part, as I have said, as an aid to diagnosis.

After the examination and the needle biopsy, Mr Malycha explained his view as to her condition.

Mrs Kite says that Mr Malycha told her that the condition was no more than infected sweat glands, and that 'they' did not 'turn cancerous'. In technical terms, he had diagnosed hydradenitis. His reference in his note to Clinpath written after the fine needle aspiration had been made, was 'Mass in left axilla? sebaceous material'. On the medical evidence, this is consistent with him having reached a diagnosis of hydradenitis.

Mr Malycha did not make a note of having performed the fine needle aspiration. He said that it was his usual practice to make such a note when he performed that procedure. He was unable to explain why he did not do so on this occasion.

I am satisfied that at the conclusion of the examination and the interview, arrangements were made for Mrs Kite to return in a few weeks time. Despite her evidence to the contrary, I am satisfied that an appointment was made for that purpose for Tuesday 3 January 1995 at 12 noon. I find that she was given a card confirming the details of the appointment before she left Mr Malycha's rooms.

I reject Mrs Kite's evidence that Mr Malycha said that he would have the specimen taken by the needle biopsy tested and if anything 'showed up' he would be in touch with her.

On the contrary, I find that, in accordance with Mr Malycha's usual practice, she was asked to ring his rooms later that day to ascertain the result of the biopsy.

From the specimen which had been aspirated, Mr Malycha prepared two slides. He put them with a printed form provided by Clinpath which he put out for collection by their courier.

I am satisfied that the specimen was collected by them on the same day.

The outcome of Dr Miliauskas's pathological examination is expressed in the following passage in the report dated 2 December 1994 which he sent to Mr Malycha:

> HISTORY
>
> Mass in left axilla. Sebaceous material. Mass 4 × 2 cm.
>
> MACROSCOPY
>
> Received two prepared slides.
>
> MICROSCOPY

> The aspirates are highly cellular and consist of duct epithelial cells, dissociated epithelial cells, background bare nuclei, scant blood cells with many degenerate and distorted epithelial cells. A few scattered small stromal fragments are present. There are some scattered benign duct epithelial cells but many of the epithelial cells show nuclear atypia with nuclear enlargement and focally some nucoleolar prominence. I do not feel that the features are those of a fibroadenoma with associated cellular atypia. The features are those of an atypical epithelial proliferation highly suspicious of an underlying carcinoma.

The evidence adduced by the plaintiff was that a report in those terms was faxed to Mr Malycha's rooms at 5.53 pm. For this purpose, Clinpath utilised an automated facsimile transmitter known as an 'autofax', which is activated at the same time as a hard copy of the report is generated. The autofax process involves a 'handshake', which is an electronic communication from the receiving machine to confirm the receipt of it. If the so-called 'handshake' does not occur, the autofax produces a record indicating that the 'fax failed'.

A print-out of the electronic record does not record any failure in the transmission. It records what it would ordinarily note if the receipt of the fax is confirmed by the machine which receives it.

As well, the hard copy of the report of Dr Miliauskas was said to have been couriered by hand to Mr Malycha's rooms. Clinpath had a number of couriers on their staff. They had various 'runs' or circuits, one of which included Mr Malycha's rooms. The run, which occurred after the autofax was transmitted and after the hard copy report would have been signed, would have reached Mr Malycha's rooms at approximately 8.40 pm.

Mr Malycha's evidence is that he never saw the report in either form, at least until 31 October 1997 when he saw it in circumstances which I refer to below. He was unable to explain why he did not see it at the time.

I have carefully considered his evidence as to that, and all of the other evidence bearing on this aspect of the matter. The other evidence includes the fact that although a copy of the report was, apparently, also sent to Dr Sangster (although it seems likely that it went to the wrong Dr Sangster), and to Dr Krishnan, there is no evidence that either of them saw it. Dr Krishnan denies receipt of it. Neither was the Dr Sangster to whom the report is said to have been delivered called.

I must say that this aspect of the case has given me considerable concern.

At the end of the day, I have reached the view that more likely than not the autofax transmission was received by the fax machine in Mr Malycha's rooms. I am unable to say whether it was printed out, or if it was printed out, what became of it. The practices and procedure as to the handling of the facsimile copy produced by the machine in his rooms left a greater chance for it to be misplaced than would be the case with the hard copy if the hard copy was delivered.

The fax machine was mounted on a bench top. There was no collection tray.

Furthermore, the fax machine was shared by several of the medical practitioners who carried on their practice from the same building, including Mr Malycha. It follows that it is likely that facsimile copies produced by the fax machine were intermingled and distributed by different members of the staff of the various medical practitioners who had access to the machine, which was housed in a shared tea room.

I take a different view as to the probabilities with respect to the hard copy which, as I have said, would ordinarily be delivered later by a courier. As to that, I am satisfied on the balance of probabilities that the hard copy was never delivered.

In reaching that view, I have had particular regard to the absence of evidence that it was received by either of the other two medical practitioners to whom it is said to have been sent. The fact that there is evidence that it was not on Mr Malycha's file when the file was perused by his secretary, Ms Cahill, in October 1997 is also significant.

If the hard copy had been received by his rooms, or if the faxed copy had been received and processed in accordance with the prevailing practice in his rooms, the system was such that it is most unlikely that it would not have been brought to his attention. If it had come to his attention, it is inconceivable that he would have failed to act on it.

In summary, I find on the balance of probabilities that the report was faxed to Mr Malycha's room, but that for some reason or another it was misfiled or mishandled, if in fact the facsimile machine in Mr Malycha's room printed a copy of it, with the result that its contents were never read by Mr Malycha, and it was never placed in his file for Mrs Kite. I find on balance that the hard copy of the report was not delivered to his rooms.

Mr Malycha wrote to Dr Sangster on the same day as his examination of Mrs Kite, that is, on 2 December 1994. The letter is in the following terms:

> Dear John
>
> Re: Mrs Jayne Kite
>
> . . .
>
> Inflamed sebaceous thickening left axilla.
>
> Pigmented birthmark middle upper back.
>
> Thank you for asking me to see Mrs Kite who is twelve weeks into her third pregnancy. She has noticed a tenderness in the left axilla over the last few months. This had been present about twelve months ago but settled with a course of antibiotics. She is understandably anxious about this.

> There is nothing of significance in her past or family history to indicate she would have an increased risk of developing breast cancer.
>
> Examination of her breasts was unremarkable. She is in the early stages of pregnancy so her breasts were quite large and normal other than subdermal thickening in the lateral aspect of left axilla which extended to the upper arm. This was in the area of the apocrine sweat glands and I believe represents an area of hidradenitis (sic) without suppuration. From the history it would appear this had occurred earlier. I performed a fine needle aspiration biopsy as this may show debris or other cells which would further define the diagnosis.
>
> I have given her reassurance. I think she may require a further review and reassurance so I have therefore indicated she can return to see me in the New Year if she wishes.
>
> The pigmented area in the upper middle back results from an old birthmark. It is clinically benign but I think a plain coloured print would be worthwhile. She will obtain this for you to keep in your records.

As to the further appointment for Mrs Kite to see him, it will be seen that in the letter he reported that she was to see him in the New Year 'if she wishes'. In fact, as I have indicated, I am satisfied that a follow-up appointment was made with her before she left his rooms on 2 December 1994.

I am satisfied also that Mrs Kite did not, as had been suggested to her, ring Mr Malycha's rooms later that day.

Events after 2 December 1994

Neither did she keep the appointment arranged for 3 January 1995. She took no other steps to contact Mr Malycha.

When she failed to turn up for the appointment, I am satisfied that, in accordance with his usual practice, Mr Malycha would have reviewed his notes concerning her, although he has no express memory of having done so. I am satisfied that he would have done so with a view to seeing whether there was anything he should follow up, despite the fact that she had not presented for the appointment.

But when he did look at his file, as well as his notes taken at the time of the December examination, he should also have seen the letter to Dr Sangster. If he had read it closely, it would have confirmed that he had taken a fine needle aspiration. I think that he must have given the letter only a cursory look, if he read it at all, as otherwise he would have seen the reference to the fine needle biopsy and would have been prompted to look for the pathology ('cytology') report on it.

In the result, both he and Mrs Kite remained ignorant of the terms of the cytology report until late in 1997.

Mrs Kite's third child was born on 15 June 1995 by caesarean section. By the time of the birth, her impression was that the lump under her armpit had grown marginally larger.

She was not unduly perturbed by this, as Mr Malycha had indicated to her that it was in the nature of swollen sweat glands that the size could vary.

But at some time after the baby was born, not only did she discern that the lump had become larger, but it became uncomfortable and began to annoy her. She decided to make a further appointment to see Mr Malycha. To that end, in August 1995, she telephoned his rooms. She was told that she could not see Mr Malycha for about a month. The earliest was 22 September 1995.

Mrs Kite saw Mr Malycha on that day. At that stage she estimated that the lump had grown from the size of her small fingernail to the size of the last joint on her small finger.

She explained to Mr Malycha that the lump was painful and that she could not easily put her arm down.

Mr Malycha acknowledged that it had grown a little since he last saw it. He expressed the view that the lump was benign. He still attributed it to a swollen sweat gland. But she insisted that he remove it.

For this purpose, she was admitted to St Andrew's Hospital on 25 September 1995.

At the operation, Mr Malycha excised what he described in his operation note as 'the area of concern' in the axilla, which was a 'hard gritty area beneath the skin'. On deeper palpation of the axilla, he located a lymph node which was somewhat hardened. He removed that as well.

After the operation, Mr Malycha informed Mrs Kite that he had removed the lump and also one of her lymph nodes.

On 25 September, the same day as the operation, Clinpath reported that the excised tissue was a cancerous tumour, the maximum diameter being 2.5 centimetres, and that the lymph gland was also malignant, demonstrating metastatic breast carcinoma.

Mr Malycha found it hard to believe that the tumour was in breast tissue. There is much expert evidence to the effect that it was a most unusual position in which to find breast cancer. He rang the pathologist, Dr Miliauskas, to confirm that he was sure that it was breast cancer. Dr Miliauskas confirmed that to be his view.

Mr Malycha arranged to see Mrs Kite two days later, that is, on 27 September 1995.

When he saw her, he told her that the lump was cancerous. He told her that the lymph node which had been removed had also been invaded by the cancer. He suggested further tests at St Andrew's Hospital.

For this purpose, she attended at the hospital the next day. It is unnecessary to go into the detail of the further tests which were performed.

There were several developments thereafter. Mrs Kite ascertained the name of another specialist, Mr Melville Carter. Mr Malycha arranged a reference to Mr Carter, whom Mrs Kite consulted on 11 October 1995. He recommended immediate surgery.

Mr Carter, assisted by Mr Malycha, performed further tests and a partial mastectomy on 19 October 1995 at Ashford Community Hospital. On this occasion, Mr Carter performed an operation known as an axillary clearance of lymph nodes from the left axilla. Ten more lymph nodes were excised.

On histological examination, four of the ten lymph nodes were found to be malignant. This meant that altogether, including the lymph node which had earlier been removed by Mr Malycha, five out of eleven were malignant. This was a bad sign from the point of view of the prognosis.

Thereafter and until the date of trial, the plaintiff has been subjected to intense treatment designed to arrest the spread of the cancer. On 8 November 1995, she began the first of six cycles of chemotherapy treatment. On 17 July 1996, her ovaries were removed in the hope that this would induce hormonal changes which would be conducive to arresting the spread of the cancer. She underwent further surgery involving a breast reduction on 19 December 1996 at Calvary Hospital. By October 1997, tests indicated that the cancer had spread to her liver and bones.

Putting together the various factors to which I have referred, and having regard to the expert opinion which I prefer, I find on the balance of probabilities that if the cancer had been diagnosed in December 1994, and if properly treated then, it would either have been cured, or Mrs Kite would have had a much extended life expectancy compared with the life expectancy which she now enjoys.

Findings and conclusions as to negligence

The law is clear as to the duty of care owed by medical practitioners:

> The law imposes on a medical practitioner a duty to exercise reasonable care and skill in the provision of professional advice and treatment. That duty is a 'single comprehensive duty covering all the ways in which a doctor is called upon to exercise his skill and judgment': [4] it extends to the examination, diagnosis and treatment of the patient and the provision of information in an appropriate case. [5] It is, of course, necessary to give content to the duty in the given case.
>
> The standard of reasonable care and skill required is that of the ordinary skilled person exercising and professing to have that special skill . . . .

In this case, the standard of care and skill owed by Mr Malycha was that of an ordinarily skilled surgeon specialising in oncology, more particularly breast cancer, who also conducted a substantial practice as a clinician in the same area.

Against that background, and having regard to the substantial body of expert evidence given in this case, there is no reason to find fault with Mr Malycha's examination of Mrs Kite on 2 December 1994, or as to the diagnosis which he came to at the conclusion of that examination.

Indeed, many of the eminent experts who gave evidence would have arrived at the same diagnosis (absent the pathological testing) as he came to, having regard to the condition as it was presented at that time.

I have explained the circumstances in which Mr Malycha and Mrs Kite remained ignorant of the terms of the cytology report given by Clinpath following the needle biopsy of 2 December 1994, until much later. The circumstances which gave rise to his failure to become aware of the report are indicative of a failure to answer to the standard of care which was imposed upon him.

Having performed the fine needle aspiration, he owed a duty to record that he had done so in his notes. He did not do so. Furthermore, if perchance the cytology report was not brought to his attention, he should have made some inquiry to find out what had happened to it.

At worst, he should have become aware of it when Mrs Kite did not come in for the appointment on 3 January 1995. His review of his notes at that stage should have alerted him to the fact that he had taken a fine needle aspiration and had not seen the result of it.

Not only did he have no note of the needle biopsy, but he missed the reference to it in the file copy of his letter to Dr Sangster.

Obviously the simplest of systems would have provided a more or less foolproof means of checking whether cytology reports had been forwarded to his rooms. All that would have been needed was a simple running sheet, recording that such a report had been requested, with provision for the particular entry to be ticked off when the report was received.

He had no such system.

Mrs Kite's failures to ring him on 4 December or to attend for the follow-up appointment does not excuse the breach of the duty of care imposed upon him in that respect. Irrespective of any initiative taken by the patient, he owed a duty to find out what the outcome of the pathological examination of the fine needle aspiration was. As Mr Wells QC put it during the course of his address, it is 'unreasonable for a professional medical specialist to base his whole follow-up system, which can mean the difference between death or cure, on the patient taking the next step'.

Mr Malycha owed a duty to inform himself of the outcome of the pathologic test of the specimen, and to offer appropriate treatment in the light of the report.

Contributory negligence

In his defence to the proceedings, Mr Malycha pleads:

13 The first plaintiff (Mrs Kite) was guilty of contributory negligence in that she:

13.1 Failed to contact the defendant's rooms by telephone to obtain the results of her fine needle aspiration biopsy;

13.2 Failed to consult with the defendant at an appointment made for 3 January 1995.

As to the plea in paragraph 13.1, as I have already found, I am satisfied that the witness Ms Tininczky or Mr Malycha made it clear to Mrs Kite that she was to ring to ascertain the results of the fine needle aspiration biopsy. Furthermore, when she left his rooms on 2 December 1994, I am satisfied that an arrangement was made that she would come in again for a further appointment fixed for 3 January 1995.

She did neither.

But if Mr Malycha had ascertained the results of the biopsy in the meantime, as in the ordinary course one would expect would have happened, and if they were adverse, there would then have been a duty on him to contact Mrs Kite, and if it was thought it desirable to do so, to suggest that she might see him sooner. That did not happen, as he did not become aware of the cytology report until much later.

Furthermore, Mrs Kite was entitled to assume that if the cytology report was adverse, she would be told about it. When no communication to that effect was made to her, she not unnaturally assumed that there was no adverse outcome.

But I must say that there is much evidence in the case, which, contrary to the contention put by Mr Wells QC, satisfies me that she was not reliable in keeping appointments.

Be that as it may, it is another matter entirely to characterise her failures to ring or to keep the appointment as evidence from which it would be right to conclude that she was guilty of contributory negligence.

It is true that there are some cases where a medical patient has been held guilty of contributory negligence. Mr Stratford referred in particular to *Locher and Anor v Turner* [7] and *Kalokarinos v Burnett* [8]. I do not pause to go into the circumstances of those cases, as they are simply illustrative of the undoubted fact that general legal principles relating to contributory negligence are applicable in cases such as this.

But each case depends upon its own complex of circumstances. Furthermore, I do not think that the courts should be quick to find contributory negligence on the part of patients who have put themselves in the hands of competent medical practitioners for advice and treatment.

In general terms, Mrs Kite owed a duty to exercise reasonable care for her own safety and well being. But her conduct must be judged in the light of the circumstances as a whole. Mr Malycha concedes that he reassured her as to her condition when she saw him on 2 December 1994. Very likely his reassurance would have led her to believe that a follow-up consultation was not so important as it might otherwise have been. As I have said, irrespective of whether she rang up about it, she was entitled to assume that if the outcome of the testing of the biopsy gave cause for concern, she would be informed. No doubt she would then have sought further advice.

In all the circumstances, I think that it would be going too far to visit her with a finding of contributory negligence based upon her failures to ring up on 2 December 1994 and to keep the appointment made for the following January.

The plea of contributory negligence is not made out.

Tai v Hatzistavrou [1999] NSWCA 306

Priestley JA:

The defendant was a specialist gynaecologist. One of the places where he conducted his practice was in rooms opposite the Auburn District Hospital. He had an operating session at this Hospital on Monday afternoons. The Hospital's booking clerk said he 'usually . . . had one major and probably three minor cases' a session and 'never had a very long waiting list'.

The plaintiff first consulted him in his rooms at Auburn in 1980 when she was 43. A number of women in her family had died of cancer and she was anxious, if she herself were ever to contract it, that it should be found and treated early.

After the first consultation the plaintiff consulted the defendant frequently. For example, she appears to have consulted him seven times in 1991 about her periods and episodes of flushing, and received medication. She had pap smears at least on an annual basis. Also throughout the time she was the defendant's patient, she consulted him about frequent heavy bleeding. In 1983 and 1989 the defendant performed an operation called a D & C on the plaintiff at Auburn District Hospital. In one part of the appeal papers D & C is said to stand for dilatation and curette and in another part diagnostic curette. It is an operation which enables examination of the uterus and the taking of tissue for testing for signs of cancer. On each occasion before recommending the D & C the defendant had examined the plaintiff manually and was of opinion that there were no indications of cancer, but said the operations should be done as a precautionary measure.

The procedure for arranging the operations was that the defendant, who kept a pad of the Auburn District Hospital's admission forms in his rooms, filled one in appropriately, and gave it to the plaintiff who took it over the road and left it with the Hospital's booking clerk. The Hospital would soon afterwards place the plaintiff in the defendant's operating list for one of his Monday afternoon operating sessions and write to the plaintiff telling her the date when she should go to the Hospital for the operation to be carried out. In both 1983 and 1989 this happened, and the operations were done within three weeks of the plaintiff's handing in the form. No sign of cancer was found on either occasion.

Consultation 21 October 1992. By early 1992 the plaintiff had reached menopause. Then, in October 1992, she had bleeding, which she thought of as her period coming back. She went to her general practitioner, Dr Govindan, who wrote a referral for her to the defendant, dated 21 October 1992, 'for routine gynaecological check-up'. She saw the defendant on the same day.

According to the plaintiff, the defendant examined her internally and reassured her that everything was all right. She said he did not on that day suggest a D & C procedure, nor did he give her a form to take to the Hospital. This evidence is different from what is suggested by the defendant's notes entered on the patient's card for that day. These are in abbreviated and hard to read form, translated by the defendant at the trial as saying 'Fluid in the knees. 3 months. Her last period February 92 and 2 weeks now. Her thyroid underactive. Oroxine 200 a day 100 micrograms. Abdomen soft, uterus retroverted, slight bleeding, D & C ADH plus hormone test'.

The defendant said in evidence that the note that the abdomen was soft meant that it felt normal, that the retroversion of the uterus was not a significant observation and that he had seen the slight bleeding through direct visualisation of the cervix using the speculum and a good light. The defendant had no independent memory of what was said at this consultation. His evidence was based on his notes and his regular practice.

He said that the note 'D & C ADH' indicated to him 'that I would have discussed the purpose of the diagnostic curettage with the patient, obtained her consent and handed the patient a form once she's consented and filled in'.

A letter dated 21 October 1992 was in evidence (part of Exhibit E) to Dr Govindan which said:

> Many thanks for referring this patient to my rooms.
>
> She came for a gynaecological check-up.
>
> On examination her abdomen was soft. The uterus was retro-verted and slightly bleeding.
>
> Her name has been placed on the list for Dilatation and Curettage of the Uterus at Auburn District Hospital.
>
> I have arranged for her to have Hormone Blood Tests, and a pap smear was taken.

The trial judge accepted the plaintiff's evidence that she was not given an admission form on this day and said 'although Dr Tai may have noted she was to have a D & C he has somehow overlooked giving her the form'. (The 'may' in this finding is a little hard to understand, but does not matter so far as the appeal is concerned, because there was no challenge to these findings of fact.) The plaintiff did not have a D & C following this consultation.

Consultation 9 December 1992. The plaintiff consulted the defendant again on 9 December 1992. She said this appointment had been made at the 21 October consultation to see if the bleeding problem was going to rectify by itself. The defendant examined her again. Her evidence was that he said:

> . . . Barbara I don't suspect anything but it's a routine you have to have a D & C.
>
> Q: And did he complete a form for you?
> A: Yes.
>
> . . .
>
> Q: Were any of the dates discussed for the timing to have the D & C?
> A: It was nearly Christmas and he says, 'Barbara, no, not at Christmas time, it's safer that you have to wait till they call you from the Hospital'.
> Q: Was anything said to you at that time to alert you as to the possibility that you were a candidate at that time of having cancer?
> A: No, again I told him and he says, 'How many times I'm going to tell you, you know, I'm here for you, there is nothing wrong with you. Don't be afraid'.
> Q: And what did you do with the form that Dr Tai gave you in December of 1992?
> A: The usual, I took it across the road to the Hospital, Auburn Hospital in the admission office.
> Q: When did you do that?
> A: The same day that I went and saw Dr Tai (AB 1/38–39).

It is common ground that the plaintiff did not consult the defendant again until 11 August 1993, following which a D & C was carried out. When asked whether following the consultation in December of 1992 she had continued to have any problems at all in terms of bleeding or difficulties she answered, 'I had the discharge, sometimes from one month to the other. A few times' (AB 1/39, lines 42–46).

An unexpected development at the trial. The first day of the trial was 2 September 1996. It was during cross-examination of the plaintiff on that day (not then completed) that she said she had taken the admission form given to her by the defendant to the Auburn District Hospital on 9 December 1992. The cross-examiner had been careful to pave the way for a prospective later submission that the court should draw the inference that the plaintiff had never lodged the admission form. When the court resumed on 3 September 1996, the defendant's counsel explained that she had been conducting the case on that basis, but in light of what had been so specifically said by the plaintiff, further investigations had been undertaken overnight from which it appeared that the Hospital had a computer record indicating that an admission form for the plaintiff from the defendant had been processed through the computer on 16 December 1992, that date being the date of the processing, not necessarily the date on which the form came into the Hospital. What appeared on the computer screen had not been able to be printed out and at the request of the defendant investigation had been undertaken by the Hospital to trace the actual form.

The defendant's counsel said that her side had been taken by surprise by this new information from the Hospital, as a subpoena had earlier been served which would have caught any document relating to an October or December 1992 admission form, but in response to which no such documents had been produced.

The defendant's counsel added that she was informing the court of these matters first to make it clear that the defendant would no longer advance a case that no form had been lodged by the plaintiff and second to get on record that if in due course the defendant sought to make a claim against the Hospital for contribution, no point could be raised against the defendant on the basis of authorities such as *Port of Melbourne Authority v Anshun* (1981) 147 CLR 589, because through no fault of the defendant, the defendant had not had the necessary knowledge prior to the obtaining of this belated information from the Hospital.

The evidence in the application established that the plaintiff had lodged a recommendation for admission form no later than 16 December 1992. It also established that the usual practice in regard to these forms was that they were filled out by the treating surgeon who nominated the priority with which the patient was to be treated. There was no record of the booking recorded on 16 December 1992 having been cancelled until November in the following year after the plaintiff had had her D & C in August. The container in which the physical form had been kept was last seen by the booking clerk at the beginning of 1996 but could not be found when asked for following the request in September 1996. It was also established that a recommendation for admission form lodged about 9 December 1992 marked with 'routine' priority would, in the case of patients waiting for operation by the defendant, result in notification of a date 'probably early/late February maybe . . . perhaps even March . . .'. The booking clerk was asked what the position would have been, following the lodging of the admission form in December if the fact was that the Hospital did not ring the plaintiff or write to her and the defendant did not cancel the operation.

In the appeal it was agreed that it was common ground that the Hospital had not notified the plaintiff of any time to present herself for the D & C.

The duty issue

For the defendant it was submitted, before coming to the question of duty by reference to the particular facts of the present case, that there was error in the judge's approach to the case indicated by his reference to and apparent reliance on an unreported decision of this court, *Kalokarinos v Burnett* (Mahoney P and Clarke and Powell JJA, 30 January 1996) and by his reference to an analogy to the position of a solicitor who did not advise a client appropriately about the imminence of the expiration of a limitation period. I do not think that the trial judge's references to these two matters either indicated or led to any error in his subsequent reasoning about the extent of the defendant's duty on the facts of the present case.

I agree with the defendant's submission to the extent that I think *Kalokarinos* is not of much help, as an authority, in the present case. There are some differences in the facts, and it was not a considered decision of the court on the question of the duty of a medical practitioner to follow up a recommendation for surgery. An issue at the trial in *Kalokarinos* was whether the plaintiff's account of what happened at a consultation with her doctor should be accepted. The only point raised on the appeal was whether the trial judge was right in accepting the plaintiff's account. This court made it perfectly clear that all it was considering was the attack in the appeal on the trial judge's finding of fact.

That attack failed and the appeal was dismissed.

There were, however, some features in the case relevant to the present. The defendant doctor conceded that if he had behaved as the plaintiff claimed he would have been in breach of duty. The case at least shows there is some medical opinion supporting a wider view of the content of a doctor's duty to a patient than that contended for by the defendant in the present case. I do not think the trial judge in the present case treated *Kalokarinos* as in any way decisive or as binding him to reach the result that he did. He seems to me to have taken it as indicative but not conclusive, either in a factual or a legal sense.

Although it is not strictly relevant in the present case, because in the appeal no question is raised about contributory negligence, it also seems to me to be of some relevance to the general question raised by the defendant that the court in *Kalokarinos* overturned the judge's finding that there had been no contributory negligence by the plaintiff and reduced the damages by 20%. As this finding was the foundation of the court's judgment about contributory negligence, the case is authority for the proposition that, in some factual situations at least, there will be what might be called 'shared responsibility' of doctor and patient in cases of the present kind.

The solicitor analogy which the trial judge mentioned as possibly available, was that if a solicitor advises a client to commence proceedings which might soon exceed a time limitation but then does nothing to ensure that the client is made fully aware of the consequences if the client does nothing within the limitation period, the solicitor would be negligent. I do not think the facts and circumstances are sufficiently similar for the analogy to be of any real help. Nor, however, do I think the trial judge made use of the analogy in his reasoning. He was simply saying, as I understand him, that the analogy he mentioned was closer to the situation he was dealing with than was the competing analogy to which counsel for the defendant had referred before him.

What the trial judge did was to concern himself directly with the duty which, in his view, arose from the facts as he had found them.

In criticising the judge's conclusion about the defendant's duty, the submissions for the defendant emphasised the plaintiff's part in not following up the appointment the defendant had told her to make. This tended to concentrate attention on the plaintiff's fault in the matter. When, however, the question raised by the plaintiff's case is recognised as being whether the defendant was at fault, it seems to me that the way in which the matter was put by the trial judge was persuasive. However, apart from *Kalokarinos*, which was not a case directly deciding the question of a doctor's duty in circumstances analogous to the present, the trial judge referred to no court decisions relating to the duty. In view of the importance which the submissions for the defendant were stressing of the duty and the content of the duty to the practice of medicine generally, it seemed to me prudent to find out whether there had been other judicial decisions relevant to the question. Although counsel had told the court they had been unable to discover any reported decisions of relevance, other than *Kalokarinos*, the court requested further assistance from counsel on the matter of authorities and some were eventually made available to the court by written submission after the close of the oral argument.

Before mentioning the cases and the literature, however, it is convenient to note the two main propositions on which the defendant's submissions relied in regard to the duty issue. The first was based on what was said to be the policy underlying *Rogers v Whitaker* (1992) 175 CLR 479 and the second what was said to be the practical unreasonableness of the duty alleged against the defendant.

The first submission was that the imposition of the duty, or, more accurately, the identification of the content of the duty by the trial judge in the present case, was inconsistent with the autonomy of the adult patient upon which the decision in *Rogers v Whitaker* was based. This court's decision in *O'Brien v Wheeler* (23 May 1997, unreported, Mason P and Powell and Stein JJA) was referred to and the statement there by Mason P, with whom Powell JA had agreed, that the approach in *Rogers v Whitaker*:

> . . . reflects the autonomy of the adult patient, who is regarded as having the right (if properly informed) to decide for himself or herself whether or not to embark on the procedure. An adult

> patient who is in a position to make a choice has the right to elect a surgical procedure which the hypothetical 'reasonable' person in his or her shoes would avoid, and to refuse a procedure which the hypothetical 'reasonable' person in his or her shoes would embrace (at 6).

Although the submission correctly states what Mason P said in *O'Brien*, a little more information about the case is needed to put it in perspective in relation to the present case.

O'Brien was, like *Rogers v Whitaker*, a warning case. The trial judge had held that the doctor's warning to the patient had been deficient. Although that finding was questioned in the appeal, the question was not decided. The appeal was upheld in favour of the doctor on the ground that, even if the doctor's warning had been deficient, the evidence had not established that had an appropriate warning been given the patient would not have undertaken the particular treatment or procedure. The case illustrates what in any event seems quite clear, that there is no inconsistency between requiring that a doctor discharge the various duties to which he or she becomes subject in the course of any doctor/patient relationship and recognising the autonomy of the patient in decision making upon appropriate information. What was submitted on behalf of the plaintiff in the present case, in various forms, was that the defendant here had a duty to remind the patient of the advice that it was necessary for her to have a D & C procedure in order to eliminate the possibility of cancer. Such a reminder would not in any way entrench upon her right to decide whether or not she would undergo the procedure.

In my opinion the trial judge's view that it was the legal duty of the defendant to remind the plaintiff of the need for a timely D & C procedure in no way cut across the patient's autonomy and any rights the law recognises as bound up with that autonomy.

The second main argument on the duty question was that it was too onerous in practical terms to hold that the content of the duty included an obligation on the part of the defendant at the least to inquire why the plaintiff was apparently not taking his advice to have a timely D & C procedure. The trial judge's reasons which have been set out above in my opinion give a quite satisfactory answer to this proposition. In the course of those paragraphs of his reasons the trial judge remarked that there was no reason to think that to have a system by which a patient would be reminded of the doctor's advice and the reasons for following it 'would create enormous practical or administrative difficulties . . . or be prohibitively expensive'. On the materials in this case this seems to me to be a fair observation by the trial judge.

It had been suggested to the defendant in cross-examination that it would be very cheap to have a particular system which would be simple and effective. When asked whether the suggested system would not be a very cheap one, he did not reply (see para 28 above). When asked again, he said he did not know what the cross-examiner meant. There was no re-examination of the defendant on this point.

The court was thus left without any evidence from the defendant's side to support a conclusion that the requirement of a reminder system would be unreasonably onerous upon the defendant. The evidence before the judge was that the defendant had one operating session at the Auburn District Hospital a week at which he usually had one major and probably three minor cases. Even if all his minor cases were D & C procedures, there would not be a great number to keep track of. In the absence of any facts or reasons (other than simple assertion) being advanced why it would be unreasonably onerous for a follow-up system to be put in place and operated by the defendant's receptionist, I do not think the trial judge's view on this point can be reasonably criticised.

In my opinion the two main arguments in the appeal against the trial judge's conclusions on the content of the doctor's duty to the patient fail.

The further researches done by counsel at the request of the court after the oral argument to my mind reinforce the correctness of the decision arrived at by the judge on the materials before him.

First, in a general way, material contained in *International Medical Malpractice Law* by Dieter Giesen (1998), pp 150 to 157 supports the trial judge's position. At p 150 there is reference to *Giurelli v Girgis* (1980) 24 SASR 264 accepting a *dictum* by White J (at 270) that if there is a breakdown of communications between physicians and hospital departments owing to defects in their established procedures or to a lack of 'feed-back' between them, then the patient should not suffer as a result. On the same page two cases are referred to, one from Australia (*Samios v Repatriation Commission* (1960) WAR 219) and the other from Canada), in which hospitals were held liable both for radiologists who failed to forward X-ray results and physicians who consequently misdiagnosed a dislocated shoulder and a dislocated wrist. Then (at 151) a Queensland case, *Thomsen v Davison* (1975) QdR 93, is noted, in which a pathologist to whom samples of blood and other specimens had been sent was held negligent for failing to take reasonable steps to ensure that the results were communicated to the referring physician. Then an English case is mentioned (also at 151) in which it was held negligent to fail to make adequate arrangements for a patient to report to the physician on developments in his condition after treatment.

The following passage then appears (at 152):

> A physician may expect his patient to co-operate in their common effort to restore the patient's health and, thus, may normally also expect a patient to behave reasonably in, for instance, presenting himself for an agreed appointment, heeding an important warning, . . . or returning for treatment or further checks as requested [citations omitted].

The text then proceeds:

> . . . however, a physician may not always be justified in relying on a patient to behave reasonably in following his instructions, and certainly not in cases where difficult instructions have to be heeded and dangerous procedures are to be tried [citations omitted].

The text then refers to various examples where the medical practitioner's duty continues notwithstanding that the patient would be expected to be anxious to co-operate.

These last two passages support the position taken by this court in *Kalokarinos* that responsibility for non-timely presentation may sometimes be shared between doctor and patient, but in doing so, also demonstrate the potential liability of the doctor.

It would seem that all of the cases referred to in the text are, to a greater or lesser degree, distinguishable on their facts from those in the present appeal. They appear, however, generally to support the view that, depending upon the precise facts of the relationship between the doctor and the patient, when a doctor is treating a patient for what may be a serious health problem, and the doctor thinks it necessary, even if only for prudential reasons, that the patient should submit to a particular surgical procedure, then the doctor has a continuing duty to advise the patient to submit to the surgical procedure, so long as the doctor/patient relationship is on foot. This does not mean that the doctor should seek to impose the doctor's view upon the patient against the patient's will, but it does mean that the doctor has a duty to keep the doctor's opinion and advice before the attention of the patient so that the patient can decide upon the patient's course in light of up to date knowledge of the doctor's opinion.

This approach is supported by some observations in vol 1 of *American Law of Medical Malpractice*, by Pegalis and Wachsman (1980), at pp 113 to 115, where it is pointed out that the relationship between doctor and patient, once established, cannot be ended at the mere will of the doctor but lasts until treatment is no longer required or the relationship is dissolved by consent or reasonable notice is given by the doctor to the patient so the patient may have an opportunity to engage the services of another doctor.

A point along these lines had been made on behalf of the plaintiff in the oral submissions in the present appeal although without any great emphasis being put on it as, in effect, a separate point. In the further written submissions the point was put more precisely and the position as stated in the text last referred to, adopted. The submission then continued that in the present case the relationship of patient and doctor continued between the plaintiff and defendant between December 1992 and August 1993, that it was at no stage terminated and that the defendant's duty to ascertain the cause of the plaintiff's post-menopausal bleeding during that period continued, so that his failure to diagnose it until August of 1993 was a breach of his duty.

I am prepared to adopt this submission of the plaintiff. The approach seems to me to be reasonable.

In my opinion the defendant's practice in regard to his sending of patients to the Auburn District Hospital to put into train the fixing of dates for operations he advised them to have, was defective. No doubt, on most occasions, the arrangements made by the patients resulted in their being operated on at an appropriate time, as had happened with the plaintiff's two previous D & Cs. However, the defect in his practice was there and led, in the circumstances now before the court, to a dangerous delay in the diagnosis of the plaintiff's cancer.

Powell JA:

Although, as the decision of the High Court in *Rogers v Whitaker* (1992) 175 CLR 479 (see also *Albrighton v Royal Prince Alfred Hospital* (1980) 2 NSWLR 542; *F v R* (1983) 33 SASR 189, *Battersby v Tottman* (1985) 37 SASR 524; *E v Australian Red Cross* (1991) 27 FCR 310) makes clear, the courts in Australia apply a different standard from that applied in England (see *Bolam v Friern Hospital Management Committee* [1957] 1 WLR 582; [1957] 2 All ER 118; *Whitehouse v Jordan* [1981] 1 WLR 246; [1981] 2 All ER 267; *Maynard v West Midland Regional Health Authority* [1984] 1 WLR 634; *Sidaway v Governors of the Bethlem Royal Hospital* [1985] AC 891) when determining whether, in any particular case, a doctor has discharged his duty of care towards his client, there does not appear to be any difference between the courts in each country as to the nature of that duty. Thus, in *Rogers v Whitaker, supra* at 483, the High Court (Mason CJ, Brennan, Dawson, Toohey and McHugh JJ) said:

> The law imposes on a medical practitioner a duty to exercise reasonable care and skill in the provision of professional advice and treatment. That duty is 'a single comprehensive duty covering all the ways in which a doctor is called upon to exercise his skill and judgment'; it extends to the examination, diagnosis and treatment of the patient and the provision of information in an appropriate case. It is of course necessary to give content to the duty in the given case.

Given the particular problem with which the Court is now concerned to deal, there is some advantage to be gained by setting out, in full, the particular passage in the speech of Lord Diplock to which reference was made in *Rogers v Whitaker, supra*. It was as follows:

> In English jurisprudence the doctor's relationship with his patient which gives rise to the normal duty of care to exercise his skill and judgment to improve the patient's health in any particular respect in which the patient has sought his aid, has hitherto been treated as single comprehensive duty covering all the ways in which a doctor is called upon to exercise his skill and judgment in the improvement of the physical or mental condition of the patient for which his services either as a general practitioner or specialist have been engaged. This general duty is not subject to dissection into a number of

> component parts to which different criteria of what satisfy the duty of care apply, such as diagnosis, treatment, advice (including warning of any risks of something going wrong however skilfully the treatment advised is carried out). The *Bolam* case itself embraced failure to advise the patient of the risk involved in the electric shock treatment as one of the allegations of negligence against the surgeon as well as negligence in the actual carrying out of treatment in which that risk did result in injury to the patient. The same criteria were applied to both these aspects of the surgeon's duty of care. In modern medicine and surgery such dissection of the various things a doctor had to do in the exercise of his whole duty of care owed to his patient is neither legally meaningful nor medically practicable. Diagnosis itself may involve exploratory surgery, the insertion of drugs by injection (or vaccination) involves intrusion upon the body of the patient and oral treatment by drugs, although it involves no physical intrusion by the doctor on the patient's body, may in the case of particular patients involve serious and unforeseen risks.

It seems to me that, in a case such as this was, in which a patient consults a doctor concerning what appears to be a persisting health problem, the doctor is, as a consequence of his being consulted, and with a view to restoring the patient's health, called upon to examine the patient; to carry out, or have carried out, such tests or procedures as might be thought necessary, or desirable, to be carried out to enable or to assist in diagnosis; to diagnose the cause of the patient's problem; to determine what treatment is called for; to prescribe that treatment, or to set in train steps for that treatment to be given; and to advise the patient in relation to the condition diagnosed and the treatment prescribed or proposed.

If this be the scope of a doctor's duty to his patient in such a case, then, as it seems to me, if the doctor, without reasonable cause, fails to carry out, or to have carried out, such of the steps to which I have referred as, in the circumstances, were necessary or desirable, or, although carrying them out, does so without due care and skill, he has failed in the performance of his duty to his patient. When using the phrase 'without reasonable cause', I had in mind the passages – with which I agree – from Gieson: *International Medical Malpractice Law* which Priestley JA has set out in paras 71–72 of his judgment, for while, in some cases – of which *Kalokarinos v Burnett* Court of Appeal 30 January 1996 (unreported) provides an example – a patient's failure to co-operate may rise no higher than contributory negligence, there are in other cases – of which *Forman v Pillsbury* (1990) 753 F Supp 14, to which Priestley JA has referred in para 79 of his judgment, provides an example – when a patient's failure to comply with the doctor's recommendation will dictate a finding of no breach of the doctor's duty of care.

If – as I believe to be the case – what I have written in the preceding paragraph be correct, then it is sufficient to accommodate not only such situations as were considered in *Rogers v Whitaker, supra* and *Kalokarinos v Burnett, supra*, but also such diverse situations as that considered by Jackson SPJ (as he then was) in *Samios v Repatriation Commission* (1960) WAR 219; as that considered by WB Campbell J (as he then was) in *Thomsen v Davison* (1975) Qd R 93; and as that considered by Perry J in *Kite v Malycha* (1998) 71 SASR 321 to which Priestley JA has referred in paragraphs 80–82 of his judgment.

In *Samios v Repatriation Commission supra* at 228–229, Jackson SPJ held that the Commission was negligent, first, in not advising the plaintiff that an immediate operation was necessary, and in letting him leave its hospital on the basis that he could think the matter over and advise his decision on the matter in six weeks' time; and, second, in not following the matter up after the expiry of that period of six weeks.

Thomsen v Davison concerned a trooper in the Citizen Military Forces (as the Army Reserve was then known) who, while on his unit's annual camp, was examined by the defendant who was the unit's Regimental Medical Officer. As tests carried out by the defendant caused him to doubt the plaintiff's state of health he requested the plaintiff to attend a laboratory for the purpose of having further blood and urine tests carried out. However, he failed thereafter to ascertain the result of those tests or to advise the plaintiff as to what they revealed. In the course of his judgment *supra* at 97, WB Campbell J said:

> In my opinion the duty of care owed by the first defendant to the plaintiff extended to the requirement to take all reasonable steps to inform himself of the result of the tests and, if they proved to be adverse, to advise the plaintiff to undergo investigation and treatment. There is ample evidence upon which the jury could find, as it did, that the first defendant failed to ascertain such results and failed to recommend to the plaintiff that his state of health ought to be investigated. Was the jury justified in finding that those failures amounted to negligence? I have already indicated that the evidence is sufficient to establish that Dr Davison should reasonably have foreseen both that his conduct would lead the plaintiff to believe that he was in good health and that causing the plaintiff to have such a belief, and to continue to lead his life accordingly, could result in damage to his health. It is not disputed that it would have been an easy task for the first defendant to have ascertained the test result and he admitted that, had he been aware of them, he would have advised the plaintiff to seek medical treatment because of the likelihood of his suffering from serious kidney disease.
>
> Although the relationship of doctor and patient in the ordinary sense may not have existed between the first defendant and the plaintiff, and assuming for present purposes that it did not, it seems to me that a doctor who undertakes the examination of a person in order to assess his state of health has a duty of care (not merely to the Army, the insurance company or other employer as the case may be), to that person to conduct the examination competently. He is also under a duty to the examinee not to do anything, or to omit to do anything, in the course of performing the examination, which is

> likely to cause the latter damage. Dr Davison set in motion the taking of further tests and there is ample evidence to establish that it was understood by both parties that the doctor would follow up these tests. In effect, the jury have found that the doctor did not complete the examination upon which he had entered and, in the circumstances, this omission was such as to justify a finding that the doctor should reasonably have foreseen that it may cause harm to the plaintiff; the doctor had the task of watching over the health of the soldiers when they were in camp and on army duties, and should have been aware of the confidence and trust they were likely to place in him.

Although the facts differed in their detail from those later considered by Perry J in *Kite v Malycha supra* in their essential features the two cases were the same.

Although, again, the facts in *Thomsen v Davison supra* and *Kite v Malycha supra* differ in their detail from those with which we are concerned to deal in this case, it seems to me that, in substance, they are the same and invite a similar approach to that taken by WB Campbell J and Perry J. In the present case, the Appellant, having considered – rightly – that in order that he might properly diagnose the cause of, and prescribe appropriate treatment for, the Respondent's complaint, he should carry out a dilation and curettage, and having put in train the steps for that to be done, by reason of what appears to have been inadequacies in his own system, failed to ensure that the procedure which he considered necessary in the Respondent's interests was carried out, the results obtained and the Respondent advised accordingly. That being so he, in my view, failed in his duty to the Respondent.

(vii) Failure to counsel patient who might be seriously ill, against leaving hospital

***Wang v Central Sydney Area Health Service & 2 Ors* [2000] NSWSC 515**

Hidden J: This is a very sad case. The plaintiff, Sha Cheng Wang, is seriously and permanently disabled as the result of an assault perpetrated upon him in the Newtown area in the evening of 18 April 1988. His assailant has never been identified. He was then aged 30, and is now 42.

At the time of the assault he was living with friends in the Newtown/St Peters area. Some time after 8 pm on 18 April 1988, he finished work at the newspaper and travelled by train to St Peters. It was while he was walking from that station to his home that he was assaulted. Presumably, the purpose of the assault was robbery but the precise details of the incident are unknown. It does not appear that the plaintiff provided a detailed account to anyone shortly after the event and, as a result of ensuing brain damage, he has not since been capable of doing so. What can be said is that he was struck from behind by a heavy object and fell to the ground. It may be that he was unconscious for a short period.

He managed to walk to his home, and two of his friends there took him by taxi to Royal Prince Alfred Hospital at Camperdown. They waited for some time in the Emergency Department, where they were joined by other associates of his. After some time, and before the plaintiff had been treated, they left and went to the city Superclinic, which was then on Broadway near Railway Square. There, the plaintiff was treated by Dr Andrew Katelaris and returned home.

In the small hours of the following morning his condition deteriorated and he was taken back to Prince Alfred Hospital by ambulance. It seems that his skull was fractured. He was suffering from extradural haemorrhage, and surgical intervention at that stage was unable to prevent irreversible brain damage.

The present proceedings are brought against the Central Sydney Area Health Service, being the statutory body administering the Royal Prince Alfred Hospital (the first defendant), Dr Andrew Katelaris (the second defendant) and Superclinics Australia Proprietary Limited, the company administering the clinic at which Dr Katelaris was working at the relevant time (the third defendant). I shall refer to the first defendant as 'the hospital', and the third defendant as 'Superclinics'. Against each of the defendants the plaintiff seeks damages for negligence. Superclinics is sued on the bases that it is vicariously liable for the negligence of Dr Katelaris and, in any event, was in breach of a non-delegable duty to the plaintiff as a provider of medical services.

All three defendants deny the negligence alleged. By their pleadings, the hospital and Dr Katelaris allege contributory negligence but this was not pursued at the trial. Superclinics also contends that the claim against it, which was made at a late stage of the proceedings, is statute barred.

The hospital cross-claims against Dr Katelaris and Superclinics, seeking contribution or indemnity, as does Dr Katelaris against the hospital.

The plaintiff's companions at the flat where he was living were Li Lang Fu, Li Yun, Li Wei and Barbara Shi. On the night in question Li Lang Fu, Li Yun and Li Wei were at home when the plaintiff arrived. It was Li Lang Fu and Li Yun who took him to the hospital. The people who joined them at the hospital, who knew the plaintiff through their association with the newspaper, were David Siu Ng, Tony Chen and his wife, Christine Chen. Tony Chen was not called. Mrs Chen was, but her recollection of events was so vague that her evidence can be discounted.

What is clear is that the plaintiff arrived at the flat in the mid-evening with a cut to his head, from which blood was oozing. There was blood on his face and clothing. He told his flatmates that he had been assaulted but it appears that he did not elaborate. He said that he was in pain and needed hospital treatment immediately. They put some Chinese medicine, apparently a disinfectant powder, on the wound and Li Yun cleaned his face with a towel. He was then taken to the hospital.

Among those on duty in the Emergency Department at the time were the casualty clerk, Mr Alan Peard, and the triage sister, Sister Sarah

Carruthers. Both gave evidence in the hospital's case. At 10pm, before the plaintiff and his companions had left, Sister Carruthers was relieved by Sister Jennifer Smith. She was not called. Again putting aside expert testimony, the evidence of Sister Carruthers was central to the hospital's case.

The plaintiff's witnesses gave varying estimates of their time of arrival at the hospital. The matter is put to rest by the hospital records. Mr Peard, whose function was effectively that of a receptionist, recorded the time of arrival as 9.25 pm. He had no independent recollection of the plaintiff's attendance. Of the plaintiff's flatmates, it appears that Li Yun had the best English and it was he who did most of the talking. His evidence, which I accept, was that he told Mr Peard that the plaintiff had been hit on the head and that his life was in danger, and he asked that he be seen by a doctor as soon as possible. Mr Peard told him that they would have to wait, as there were a number of people already in the department seeking treatment.

Both Li Lang Fu and Li Yun gave evidence that they remained with the plaintiff and that, prior to their leaving the hospital, he was not examined by a doctor or a nurse. The hospital records suggest otherwise. It is clear that Mr Peard referred the plaintiff immediately to Sister Carruthers, and there is a notation in her hand which reads 'assaulted ?LOC'. At the very least, this is consistent with her evidence that she obtained a history from the plaintiff, using one of his friends as an interpreter. She said that the expression '?LOC' meant that it was possible that there had been a loss of consciousness. She was told that the plaintiff had not lost consciousness but she explained that, as people who have been assaulted may not recall having been unconscious, caution required that that possibility be noted.

Sister Carruthers went on to describe her brief physical examination of the plaintiff. She noted that he walked into her office unaided and appeared to be alert. She had him squeeze her fingers to test his hand grip, which she found to be firm and equal. She checked his pupils by having him close his eyes and open them quickly, and they appeared to be equal and reacting to light.

Triage is the process whereby people attending an emergency department are given priority according to the apparent urgency of their need for treatment, and it was this function which Sister Carruthers was called upon to perform. According to her, because of the possibility of loss of consciousness, she placed him at the top of the list bar one. The patient having priority over him was a woman with a significant abdominal problem. In the meantime, she had the plaintiff sit in the waiting area, where she could observe him in case there was any deterioration in his condition.

Li Yun said that at the hospital the plaintiff looked pale, and appeared to be tired and weak. David Ng, who arrived later, observed that he was still bleeding and appeared to be in pain, although he said that he was 'alright'. Mr Ng noticed that he spoke very slowly. (This may not have been obvious to Sister Carruthers, who did not speak Chinese, and there is no evidence that she was told that there was anything unusual about his speech.) As I have said, Sister Carruthers described him as alert, although she said that he may have been pale and that he was touching his head, looking 'a bit distressed'. She observed blood on his clothing but she said that blood was not oozing from the wound.

The evidence of Li Lang Fu and Li Yun was that, after waiting some time, they approached a woman whom they described as a nurse, saying that the plaintiff's condition was dangerous and that he needed to be seen by a doctor promptly. She replied to the effect that the department was very busy and they would have to wait. It was then that Li Yun telephoned Tony Chen, who lived at Castle Cove, from a public telephone in the waiting area. Apparently, Mr Chen was a business associate of the proprietor of the newspaper where the plaintiff worked. Mr Chen contacted David Ng, who lived in the same area and worked at the newspaper, and Mr and Mrs Chen and Mr Ng travelled to the hospital in Mr Chen's car.

David Ng had quite a good command of English, apparently better than that of Li Yun. He had completed tertiary education at the University of Hong Kong, where the medium of teaching was English. His evidence was that, after waiting some time, he approached a nurse to enquire how long it might be before the plaintiff could be treated. He was told that the department was busy and that a lot of people were waiting. About 15 minutes later he asked her if they could go somewhere else for treatment, perhaps at a private hospital, and she said that they were free to do so. As he put it, she said that 'we can do whatever we want to'. This evidence was not challenged. Most likely, it was Sister Smith to whom Mr Ng spoke on both occasions.

It seems that about ten minutes later the group arrived at a joint decision to seek treatment elsewhere, and they left the hospital. David Ng put this at about 10.45 pm and again, given the sequence of events, I do not believe it could have been any earlier. It may well have been a little after 11 pm, which was Li Yun's recollection. The hospital records contain a handwritten note 'Did not wait to be seen', probably written by Sister Smith, which is not timed. At the end of the day, whether they departed before or after 11 pm is of no moment.

The group travelled to the city Superclinic in Broadway, not far from the hospital, in Mr Chen's car. They arrived there, I infer, at about 11 pm or not very long thereafter. Dr Katelaris made brief but adequate notes of his examination of the plaintiff at the clinic, but he did not note the time of their attendance. There was no-one else at the clinic requiring treatment and Dr Katelaris saw the plaintiff promptly upon their arrival.

Dr Katelaris' evidence about his examination and treatment of the plaintiff, supported to a significant extent by his clinical notes, was not in dispute. He obtained a history of the assault, which alerted him to the possibility of a period of unconsciousness. He observed a deep laceration, about 8 cm in length, towards the back of the plaintiff's head. He debrided the wound and applied a local anaesthetic to it.

He examined the plaintiff's pupils by eye and also using an ophthalmoscope. He tested the grip of both hands, and the extension and flexion of the upper arms. Although he had observed the plaintiff to walk unassisted, he tested the patella reflexes of both legs. Twice he conducted what is known as a Rombergs test, designed to reveal any abnormality in balance. Finally, he sutured the wound and administered a tetanus toxoid injection.

The doctor's evidence was that he then informed the plaintiff's companions that it would be advisable to return to the hospital for an X-ray (a service which he himself was unable to provide at that time). This, he said, was met with 'an instantaneous eruption of displeasure' arising, apparently, from the fact that the plaintiff had not received treatment at that institution earlier. His offer to write a letter to the hospital, so that they would not have to wait, did not change their attitude. His examination of the plaintiff had afforded no evidence of a skull fracture and disclosed no abnormal neurological signs, so he could see no point in trying to persuade them to go back to the hospital. He determined, instead, to advise the plaintiff's companions what action they should take if his condition deteriorated.

To this end, he said, he produced a document which he described as a 'head injury advice form'. He went on to explain what it said, using gestures to ensure that he was understood. He said that an ambulance should be called immediately in the event of vomiting or convulsion, if the plaintiff became drowsy or unrouseable, or if they observed weakness in one or more of his limbs or inequality in the size of his pupils. He told them that the plaintiff should not be left alone. He advised them to take him to a Chinese-speaking doctor the next morning to arrange for an X-ray and for any ongoing care which might be necessary.

At the time the group left the clinic, David Ng observed that the plaintiff's face was pale and that his speech was still very slow. (Again, Dr Katelaris may not have been aware of anything unusual about his speech as the matter was not drawn to his attention.) The doctor gave evidence that 'he certainly looked tired' and that his general demeanour was consistent with someone who had been attacked in the manner described. Tony Chen drove them back to the flat. During the journey, Li Yun asked Mr Chen if he could telephone him if anything untoward happened, as he himself had not been in Australia long and felt that he might need the help of someone with local knowledge. Mr Chen agreed.

The plaintiff, Li Yun and Li Lang Fu were dropped at the flat. Li Yun prepared a light meal for the plaintiff, whereupon all three of them retired. They slept in the same room.

Apparently not much later, the plaintiff woke Li Yun and said that he felt nauseous. Li Yun obtained a bucket, into which he vomited. He said that he felt sick, and he complained of a headache and a pain in his right leg. Nevertheless, he asked Li Yun to turn off the light because he wanted to sleep.

Li Yun left the bedroom, had a meal and took a shower. When he returned to the bedroom, the plaintiff appeared to be asleep but was having some kind of convulsion. His leg was kicking, apparently involuntarily, against the wall. Li Lang Fu awoke and they decided to contact Tony Chen, as they were themselves unsure how to summon an ambulance. They did so from a nearby public phone.

Again, Mr Chen contacted David Ng and drove with him to the flat. Upon their arrival, Mr Ng observed that the plaintiff appeared to be unconscious. He telephoned an ambulance, which arrived promptly. By this time it was after 3 am. The hospital records disclose that the plaintiff arrived there at about 4 am. He then underwent the surgery to which I have earlier referred.

It is likely that the plaintiff would have made a good recovery if he had earlier been treated at the hospital. This was the view of the plaintiff's experts, and Dr Fulde and Dr Raftos gave no evidence to the contrary. It seems that the plaintiff's extra-dural haemotoma was bilateral which, according to Dr Raftos, is relatively rare. Nevertheless, it is clear that intra-cranial bleeding is a well recognised complication of a head injury and, provided it is not detected too late, it can be effectively remedied by surgery.

The plaintiff's case against the hospital is put on two alternative bases. First, it is alleged that Sister Carruthers' examination was inadequate and superficial and that no notice was taken of his friends' insistence that he needed urgent attention, so that he was not afforded the priority which he deserved. Alternatively, accepting that his priority was appropriately assessed, Sister Carruthers should have consulted a doctor about him before she went off duty, and Sister Smith should have done so before the plaintiff left the hospital. In either event, it is said, some attempt should have been made to dissuade the plaintiff from leaving before he had been seen by a doctor. (This last matter was pleaded somewhat differently, but that is the issue which arose on the evidence and to which final submissions were addressed.)

Reliance was placed upon Sister Carruthers' laconic note, 'assaulted? LOC'. The evidence of Ms Fares was that there should have been notes not only of the history provided but also of Sister Carruthers' physical examination, together with her assessment of the urgency of the plaintiff's condition. This, she said, was essential to establish 'a baseline' from which the significance of any change in the plaintiff's condition might be judged, particularly when Sister Carruthers went off duty and was relieved by other staff. The plaintiff's submission was that, quite apart from the need for adequate notes for the benefit of relieving staff, their absence in the present case indicates that no proper examination or assessment was undertaken.

In evidence, Sister Carruthers maintained that the brief note she made accorded with accepted practice at the time and that, when she was relieved by Sister Smith, she gave her an appropriate oral account of the plaintiff's history and condition. As I have observed, Sister Smith was not called. On the other hand, Dr Fulde gave evidence that Sister Carruthers' note would have provided her successor with sufficient information about the plaintiff and that, as the system of triage in 1988 was less formal than it is now, she would not have been expected to record her assessment of his priority. The other experts gave evidence about the practice of keeping notes generally, but none of them was asked to express an opinion about the adequacy of the note in question. It must be borne in mind that Sister Carruthers did not purport to treat the plaintiff, and the only purpose of any note she might make would be in aid of what counsel for the hospital described as 'the sorting process'. Viewed in that light, Dr Fulde's evidence about this should be accepted.

As I have said, it was no part of Sister Carruthers' function to treat the plaintiff. From the whole of the expert evidence, it is clear that her task as triage sister was to make a primary assessment of him with a view to assessing the urgency of his need for treatment. That assessment had to be made in the light of the other demands upon the Department at the time and the available professional resources. Dr O'Sullivan observed that, then as now, patients attending an emergency department who were not in need of immediate resuscitation often had to wait for lengthy periods before being seen by a doctor.

Sister Carruthers' other responsibility was to keep the plaintiff under observation in the waiting area in case his condition worsened. Ms Fares pointed out that the priority afforded to patients in a department at any given time might change, because of deterioration in the condition of any of them or the arrival of a new patient in a critical condition. She agreed with the proposition, put by counsel for the hospital, that 'the underlying principle of triage is to do the greatest good for the greatest number'.

What must be understood, however, is that the observation of the plaintiff required of Sister Carruthers is different from formal neurological observations which might have been maintained if he had progressed to the treatment area. The experts gave evidence about this but it is unnecessary to dwell upon it. It is sufficient to say that a decision to conduct those observations, normally over a period of four hours, would have been made by a doctor, and they would have been carried out by nursing staff in accordance with that doctor's directions.

Allowing for the demands upon the limited resources of hospital emergency departments, this must be so. The effect of Sister Carruthers' evidence is that the plaintiff did not present with symptoms calling for immediate medical intervention, and did not develop any while she was on duty. The fact that he had no such symptoms, and did not deteriorate before he left the hospital, is confirmed by the unchallenged evidence of Dr Katelaris' examination.

Given the significance of resources and the demands upon them, it is necessary to examine such evidence as there is about those matters on the night in question. Sister Carruthers described the Department as very busy. She did not recall how many doctors were on duty, but said that normally there were 'two doctors in the cubicle end and three or four in the ward end'. For the purpose of preparing his report, Dr Fulde was supplied by the hospital with a series of factual assumptions, one of which was that there were four doctors working in the Department at the time (two resident medical officers, a registrar and an intern). I accept that as the fact: cf *Drobek v Braun* [1999] NSWCA 264, *per* Cole AJA at paras 9 and 12.

The pleas of the plaintiff's companions that he be treated urgently, addressed to Mr Peard, Sister Carruthers and Sister Smith, were well motivated and entirely understandable. Nevertheless, they could not influence, let alone dictate, the priority to which he was entitled. That was a matter to be assessed by the hospital staff. As a matter of course, patients who arrived by ambulance were taken immediately to the treatment area. However, there is no evidence that any other patient was called to the treatment area during the period the plaintiff was at the hospital. I could not fairly conclude that, if he had been afforded higher priority, he would have been referred for treatment before the time at which he left.

I turn, then, to the question which has troubled me most. Should hospital staff have attempted to dissuade the plaintiff from leaving? I have referred (at para 21) to the unchallenged evidence of David Ng about his enquiry whether they might seek treatment elsewhere. I am satisfied that that enquiry was directed to Sister Smith and that she did not advise them to wait. It is true that some further time elapsed before they left, and counsel for the hospital submitted that the staff might not have been aware of their departure. However, if appropriate observation of the plaintiff in the waiting area were being maintained, they should have been.

It was common ground that the plaintiff was free to leave and the hospital staff had no power to restrain him. However, varying views were expressed by the experts about how the situation should have been handled. Ms Fares said that normally staff would attempt to persuade a patient from leaving and would find out how soon a doctor might be available, informing the medical staff that the patient was becoming restless.

Dr Mellick also considered that a doctor should have been informed that the plaintiff intended to leave. He said that a number of things might have been done, short of physical restraint, to ensure that he remained at the hospital. For example, he might have been taken to the treatment area and asked to lie on a bed, even though a doctor was not then available to examine him. He added that a patient who had suffered a head injury might be in 'a clouded state of mind' and might not be able to make an informed decision in his own best interests.

It is true that David Ng's enquiry of Sister Smith would have conveyed to her that the plaintiff and his companions intended to seek treatment elsewhere. Equally, it is true that they attended the city Superclinic without delay. Obviously, however, Dr Katelaris did not have available to him the comprehensive resources of the hospital. Sister Smith did not ask Mr Ng where they intended to go, and did not offer any advice about alternative sources of treatment suitable for the plaintiff's condition, should it deteriorate. Indeed, there is no evidence that there was any suitable source at that time of night other than a public hospital. Sister Smith should have counselled the plaintiff to remain at the hospital, explaining why it was in his interests to do so.

The question remains whether the plaintiff would have accepted that advice if it had been tendered. Because of his incapacity, he could not tell us. Nevertheless, it is a matter which he must establish and it would normally be the subject of direct evidence: see, for example, *Ellis v Wallsend District Hospital* (1989) 17 NSWLR 553. However, in the absence of direct evidence, it might properly be inferred: *Qantas Airways Limited v Cameron* (1996) 66 FCR 246 *per* Lindgren J at 293–94.

I have referred (para 22) to evidence that the decision to leave the hospital was made by the plaintiff and his companions jointly. That being so, the attitude of his companions if they had been advised to remain at the hospital is not without importance. Li Lang Fu, Li Yun and David Ng were not asked about this, and that is a significant deficiency in the evidence. Counsel for the hospital also relied upon the fact that Tony Chen did not give evidence, given that he was the man with local knowledge to whom Li Lang Fu and Li Yun had turned for help and who might be seen as the most influential member of the group. There was evidence that Mr Chen had been unwilling to communicate with the plaintiff's solicitor and had evaded service of a subpoena.

It is to be noted, however, that Mr Chen had David Ng accompany him on both occasions when he was called from his home by the plaintiff's flatmates. Although he had not been in this country any longer than the plaintiff, Mr Ng had a good command of English and was the editor of the newspaper where the plaintiff worked. Clearly, he was also in a position of influence. His evidence, and that of Li Lang Fu and Li Yun, impressed me not only for its honesty but also for its demonstration of their genuine concern for the plaintiff's well being. I have no doubt that they joined in a decision to leave the hospital not through any sense of personal inconvenience, but because they believed it was necessary to ensure that the plaintiff received the treatment which he needed.

If the benefits of remaining at the hospital had been explained to Mr Ng, I am satisfied that he would have conveyed that advice to the plaintiff and counselled him to do so. Equally, whatever might have been the attitude of Mr Chen, I am satisfied that the plaintiff would have done so and would have been supported in that decision by his two flatmates. Counsel for the hospital also relied upon the evidence of Dr Katelaris (para 27) that the plaintiff's companions protested when he suggested that they should return to the hospital. That reaction, however, must be understood in the light of the fact that no-one at the hospital had explained to them the benefits of remaining there. They had spent about an hour and a half at that institution and, despite several expressions of concern about the plaintiff's condition, they were told no more than they would have to wait.

It is unnecessary to enter into the debate between counsel about the ambit of the duty of a hospital to a person who attends its emergency department and, in particular, the point at which that duty extends to the provision of 'complete medical services': *Albrighton v Royal Prince Alfred Hospital & Ors* (1980) 2 NSWLR 542 *per* Reynolds JA at 561. Clearly, the primary duty which the hospital owed to the plaintiff was to assign him his appropriate priority through the triage system and to observe him in the waiting area in case his condition deteriorated. I am content to assume that no duty to provide him with medical services arose until he could be accommodated in the treatment area.

The Central Sydney Area Health Service, which administers the hospital, is a statutory authority whose duty was to take reasonable care for the plaintiff's well being in the circumstances, within the limits of its resources: *Crimmins v Stevedoring Industry Finance Committee* (1999) ALJR 1, *per* Gaudron J at para 34. In my view, that duty extended to furnishing the plaintiff with appropriate advice when it was intimated that he might leave the hospital. The hospital failed to discharge that duty, and the plaintiff's present condition is attributable to that failure.

The plaintiff is entitled to a verdict against the hospital. The matter will have to be re-listed for the assessment of damages. I have spent some time considering the various bases upon which the hospital was said to be liable, only to dismiss most of them. The heavy demands upon the limited resources of public hospitals are notorious and, for that reason, I consider that the hospital in the present case should be left in no doubt of the limited ground upon which I have found against it.

Liability of Dr Katelaris and Superclinics

It will be remembered that Dr Katelaris and Superclinics are faced with a claim by the plaintiff and a cross-claim by the hospital. Obviously, neither the plaintiff nor the hospital can succeed against Superclinics, on either of the bases of liability asserted, unless Dr Katelaris himself is found to be liable. To that question I now turn.

All the expert evidence was to the effect that Dr Katelaris' examination and treatment of the plaintiff were competent. Equally, if his evidence about the head injury advice he gave is accepted, that advice was appropriate. In final submissions, counsel for the plaintiff and the hospital did not argue the contrary.

The plaintiff's case involves a challenge to Dr Katelaris' evidence that he told the group they should return to the hospital and that he gave the detailed head injury advice which he described. It is said that, in any event, he should have firmly advised them to go back to the hospital or attend some other public hospital in the general area (eg, St Vincent's Hospital at Darlinghurst), notwithstanding their reluctance to do so. Further, it is said that he allowed the plaintiff to go home without making any enquiry about his domestic arrangements, or about the competence of his companions to maintain the necessary observations and to take prompt action if his condition deteriorated.

The doctor's failure to insist that the plaintiff be taken to a hospital, or to satisfy himself of the capacity of those who would be in his company at home to observe and care for him, are also the allegations upon which the hospital's cross-claim is founded. There is no doubt that advice and inquiries of that kind are embraced within the broad duty of care which a doctor owes to a patient: *Rogers v Whitaker* (1992) 175 CLR 479 at 483.

I accept that Dr Katelaris did provide that advice to the group [to return to the hospital], and that he offered to write a letter in an attempt to ensure that the plaintiff would be seen without delay. I accept also that that recommendation met with firm resistance, such that he saw no point in pursuing it. In evidence, he said that he considered the plaintiff's return home with his companions, armed with head injury advice, to be 'very much a fall-back position'. He acknowledged that it did not occur to him to recommend that the plaintiff be taken to another public hospital. What the reaction of the plaintiff's companions to that suggestion might have been was not explored in their evidence, but I doubt that it would have been any more favourable. As the evidence of Dr Raftos suggests (para 69), it is likely that they would have faced a long wait at any other hospital in the area.

I am satisfied that Dr Katelaris himself saw a return to the hospital as the best course, but I also accept that he could not have persuaded the group to do so. Certainly, the plaintiff has not established the contrary. The question arises, then, whether he might have had the plaintiff remain at the clinic and undertake observations himself over a four hour period. He said that Superclinics did not approve of the use of the clinic as an observation area. He added that a general practitioner would not normally retain a patient at his or her surgery for observations of that kind. In this he was supported by the evidence of Dr Raftos. In any event, he was the only doctor on duty at the clinic that night and may well have had to deal with other patients. There was a receptionist at the clinic but, as counsel for Superclinics pointed out in final submissions, he could not have been entrusted with what is essentially a nursing function. To have kept the plaintiff there for neurological observations was not a practicable option.

As I have said, the plaintiff challenges Dr Katelaris' evidence that he furnished detailed head injury advice. His clinical notes include the notation, 'Home with friends. Head injury advice given'. He was unable to produce a copy of the head injury advice form which he said he gave them, but I consider this to be of little significance. It is clear that advice was furnished at least orally because both Li Yun and David Ng remembered different parts of it (see paras 29 and 30). It is also clear from the expert evidence that the advice which he says he provided was in accordance with the usual practice in head injury cases. For him to have given part only of that advice makes no sense. On this matter also I accept his evidence.

The final matter to be resolved is whether Dr Katelaris ought reasonably to have been satisfied that the plaintiff's companions were competent to maintain the observation of him at home which the situation required. Clearly, as Dr Mellick and Dr Raftos explained, that is a matter which a responsible medical practitioner would wish to determine. Counsel for the plaintiff and for the hospital argued that Dr Katelaris had not done so. It was said that he had not made any adequate inquiry about the association between the plaintiff and his companions, about which of those companions actually lived with him, and whether any of them would be sufficiently alert to attend to the plaintiff's needs over the ensuing hours. Counsel for the plaintiff also submitted that the events of the early hours of the following morning demonstrated his friends' inability to deal with the task which Dr Katelaris had assigned them. (I do not understand that last submission to imply that the plaintiff's flatmates should feel in any way responsible for his present condition. At the hearing it was not suggested by any party that they should.)

The fact remains that Dr Katelaris entrusted the plaintiff to the care of apparently responsible adults, who appeared to be very concerned about him. In evidence, he said of the plaintiff's companions that they 'huddled around him, they were animated about him, they were outraged on his behalf at what had happened'. He added that 'they appeared to be very good friends', and that he had 'a firm impression that they did really care'. This is consistent with my own assessment of those of them who gave evidence. Apart from the advice he furnished about signs of deterioration of the plaintiff's condition, he emphasised that the plaintiff must not be left alone. He was relying as interpreter on a man whose command of English was good and who appeared to be conveying his advice to the others. I consider that his conduct was reasonable in the situation with which he was confronted.

Dr Katelaris and Superclinics are entitled to verdicts in their favour on the plaintiff's claim and the hospital's cross-claim.

(viii) Failure to properly train reception staff to detect and prioritise patients with urgent need

Alexander v Heise & Anor [2001] NSWSC 69

Master Harrison: The plaintiff's claim is brought on her behalf and on behalf of her four children. It is a claim for damages arising from alleged medical negligence.

The plaintiff alleges that Edward Alexander's death would have been prevented had he been examined by a general practitioner, Dr Heise. The first defendant is a registered medical practitioner. He is practising as a general practitioner at a medical surgery in Thornleigh. The second defendant, Keren Heise, acted as a receptionist in the first defendant's surgery. The first and second defendants are husband and wife.

Between 4 and 10 March 1996, the plaintiff's husband was in good health. On 10 March 1996, the plaintiff found her husband unconscious at home on the bed. He was given mouth to mouth resuscitation and transported to Ryde hospital. From Ryde he was transferred to Concord hospital. Edward Alexander died 12 days later on 22 March 1996. The plaintiff's husband had suffered a grade V berry aneurism in the Circle of Willis. At this time the plaintiff was told by the professor managing her husband's case at Concord Hospital that nothing could have been done to save him.

Up until October 1998, the plaintiff viewed her husband's death as inevitable. The plaintiff's knowledge in relation to her husband's chances of survival changed in October 1998, in a moment of serendipity, at a patchwork class. At this class the plaintiff met a neurological intensive care nurse. During a conversation with the nurse the plaintiff was told that grade V aneurisms in the Circle of Willis can be treated. The nurse told the plaintiff that most berry aneurisms are located in the Circle of Willis and if they are observed before they rupture an operation can be performed which prevents the aneurism from rupturing. Once the plaintiff became aware of this she was motivated to obtain legal advice from a friend. She then instructed her current solicitors to take these proceedings.

Background facts

In July 1995 the plaintiff and her family moved from Terrigal to Cheltenham. The plaintiff had selected the first defendant's surgery as the medical practice to which she and her family would attend should the need arise. Up to 4 March 1996 the plaintiff was the only family member who had needed to consult the medical practice. Prior to the events surrounding this cause of action, the plaintiff had consulted Dr Heise on one occasion.

In February 1996 the plaintiff's husband told the plaintiff that he had been suffering a few headaches and attributed their cause as being from the use of a mobile phone. At that time he informed the plaintiff that the headaches he was experiencing were not of a severe nature such that they would require medication. About late February 1996 the plaintiff's husband had suffered from what was thought to be a virus. He had a temperature of 39 degrees. The plaintiff tried to persuade her husband to attend the casualty department of Royal North Shore hospital but he refused to do this because he did not consider that he was sick enough to warrant medical opinion and treatment.

At about 2.00 am on the morning of 4 March 1996, the plaintiff's husband woke her up. He told her that he had a very bad headache which would not go away. He told her that he had already taken two Panadol tablets but that these had had no effect. He requested one of her migraine tablets. She gave him one Mersyndol tablet. He took this tablet and returned to bed. Subsequently, they both fell asleep. It was the plaintiff's view that for her husband to experience a headache of such severity that he was motivated to request one of her migraine tablets was most out of character for him. It concerned her greatly.

When the plaintiff awoke the next morning she told her husband that she would make an appointment for him to see a doctor for a full medical examination. He agreed with this course of action but requested that she make the appointment as late as possible in the evening so as to fit in with his work commitments. He worked as an architect and his office was located in the city whereas the medical practice was located at Thornleigh. That morning the plaintiff's husband indicated that he was feeling well. He went to work as usual.

On the evening of 4 March 1996 the plaintiff, after concluding the prearranged 6 pm appointment with Dr Ginger which lasted 30 minutes, approached the receptionist, the second defendant, firstly to pay her account, and secondly to make an appointment for her husband, Edward Alexander. It is common ground that the plaintiff and second defendant had a conversation at the prior consultation in about September 1995. From this September conversion the plaintiff knew that the second defendant was a trained school teacher but did not have any medical qualifications. The second defendant knew that the plaintiff was also a school teacher, and that they belonged to the same medical benefits fund. It is also common ground that the conversation on 4 March 1996 between the plaintiff and second defendant was conducted in an amicable manner and that the appointment for Edward Alexander was ultimately fixed for 6.45 pm on 11 March 1996. Both the plaintiff and second defendant agreed that at the time of making the appointment the plaintiff mentioned that her husband had been under a lot of stress at work lately. From this point onwards the plaintiff and second defendant's version of the conversation diverge.

The plaintiff, at the time she made the appointment for her husband with the second defendant, had a number of matters she wanted to convey. They were, in order of importance, firstly, that her husband had such a severe headache that he asked her for a migraine tablet; and secondly, she wanted her husband to have a full medical check-up because she thought that the headache may have been related to stress due to his work. Both the plaintiff and second defendant agreed that she mentioned stress due to work. The plaintiff also thought that her husband may have been suffering from high blood pressure but she acknowledged that she did not mention this factor to the second defendant. She also did not mention that he had been suffering from headaches during the previous month. Thirdly, she wanted a blood test to check for prostate cancer. It is more likely than not that Mrs Alexander would have, after requesting an appointment for her husband, said that he had suffered a severe headache during the previous evening and this headache was so out of character that he requested one of her migraine tablets, or words to this effect. Because the headache was out of character it was the catalyst by which she was able to convince her husband (who had been reluctant in the past) to agree to see a doctor. The significance of the headache would have been foremost in her thoughts and so it is most unlikely that she failed to mention it.

I do not accept the second defendant's version that the plaintiff made no mention of a 'severe headache'. It is my view that the plaintiff said words to the effect that Mr Alexander had a severe headache and he had requested one of her migraine tablets which was 'out of character'. It is also more likely than not that the plaintiff would have repeated that she was worried about Mr Alexander's headache as this would have elicited the response by the second defendant in response to being told of the 'severe headache' and asked about Mr Alexander's symptoms that day. The second defendant gave evidence that she was aware that she needed to ascertain the duration and severity of symptoms in order to ascertain how quickly an appointment should be given. This is in accordance with her practice, had she been told of the headache. I accept that Mrs Alexander replied: 'He did not appear sick and was able to go to work this morning.' I do not think that Mrs Alexander stipulated that the appointment had to be by the end of the week but it is more likely, she would have said 'as soon as possible'.

If the plaintiff had just mentioned 'stress at work', the version given by the second defendant, it is unlikely that a long appointment would have been allocated. I prefer the plaintiff's evidence that she said that she required a full medical check-up for her husband. This accords with the diary entry that had recorded 'full medical'. I also accept that Mrs Alexander spoke of a test for prostate cancer being performed at that appointment. As previously stated, the plaintiff had difficulty persuading her husband to consult a doctor. She would have taken the opportunity to get the all matters concerning her husband's health checked.

I do not accept that the second defendant said that she would not make an appointment for Mr Alexander that week because firstly, her husband was working very hard and secondly, she would only make an appointment if several had already been given on that evening, The diary does not bear this out and I accept the second defendant's evidence that she always sought to fit patients into Dr Heise's schedule.

What most likely transpired was that after the conversation referred to earlier took place, the second defendant did not attach any urgency to the headache above the matters mentioned so she allocated a long appointment where there next appeared a number of blank evening spaces, namely 11 March 1996. It is more likely than not that the second defendant did not offer the appointments of Wednesday or Friday evenings.

Nor do I think that the statement to the effect that if there were any cancellations would the second defendant let the plaintiff know, occurred. It is more likely than not that the plaintiff's fears would have been allayed by the making of the appointment on 11 March 1996. The plaintiff was not in a position to realise the significance of a severe headache, other than it was worse than the other headaches her husband had suffered during the previous month.

As previously stated, the plaintiff recounted Mr Alexander's headache and the making of the appointment and her conversation with Dr Heise on a number of occasions to Dr Cook. These statements were made within a few months of her husband's death but by then her focus had been directed to the significance of the headache, namely, it was a warning leak. The importance of Mr Alexander seeing a doctor before the aneurism became life-threatening was also apparent to her. These statements made to Dr Cook convey the same impression as the statement tendered to the court.

Although the plaintiff may have indicated that she was worried about Ted's headache she did not by her manner nor tone of her voice convey a sense of urgency. As previously stated, it is common ground that the conversation was conducted in an amicable manner. Dr Fisher agreed that if a person is requesting an appointment that is absent of any sense of urgency, it makes it much more difficult for the receptionist to pick up a sense of urgency, but according to Dr Fisher, if Mrs Alexander's version is accepted, it does not make any difference to his opinion whether she expressed urgency by tone or not.

It must be acknowledged that the second defendant did not have the benefit of physically observing Mr Alexander's condition, nor was she able to question him so as to gauge urgency of the situation by his responses. The second defendant was aware that Mr Alexander's headache had resolved by the next day and he felt well and went to work in the normal manner. The second defendant had to rely solely upon what the plaintiff told her.

Were the defendants, or either of them, under a duty of care to Mr Alexander?

The statement of claim alleges that the first and second defendants owed a duty of care to the plaintiff and her family to ensure that her concerns were properly managed. The defendants deny that they owed a duty of care to Edward Alexander. The defendants deny that they breached their duty of care and deny that they were negligent. The first defendant does not admit that he was vicariously responsible for any breach of duty of care by the second defendant. According to the defendant there is no duty of care on the part of the administrative staff employed by a doctor, such as receptionist, and nor can a doctor be under any such duty vicariously by means of any information of which his administrative staff became aware during the course of their employment.

In the second defendant's statement of 1 October 1999, she admitted that in 1995 she commenced employment at her husband's surgery for two days per week as a receptionist. Likewise, Dr Ginger gave evidence that the second defendant worked at the practice as a receptionist. It was the doctors of the practice who trained and instructed the receptionist. It is my view that the second defendant was an employee of the first defendant and that the first defendant is vicariously responsible for the acts of the second defendant.

The question to be decided in the case before this court is not whether the first defendant's conduct accords with the practice of his profession or some part of it, but whether it conforms to the standard of reasonable care demanded by the law. That is a question for the courts and the duty of deciding it cannot be delegated to any profession or group in the community. (*Rogers v Whitaker* (1992) Aust Torts Reports 81–189; (1992) 175 CLR 479; (1991) Aust Torts Reports 81–113; (1991) 23 NSWLR 600). The first defendant's duty of care is to exercise the reasonable care and skill expected of a general practitioner in 1996. The expert evidence as to the practice of general practitioners in 1996 plays an influential role in ascertaining the standard demanded by law.

The first issue to be decided is whether the doctor had a duty of care towards Mr Alexander, who had not previously consulted a medical practitioner of the surgery. The defendants submitted that there is no duty of care on the part of a medical practitioner to attend upon a person who is sick, even in an emergency, if that person is one with whom the doctor is not and has never been in a professional relationship of doctor and patient. In *Jones v Manchester Corporation* [1952] 2 All ER 125 (*per* Lord Denning, p 131), it was stated that by accepting a patient for treatment, the hospital authorities came under a duty of care to use reasonable skill and care in their treatment of that patient. The learned author, Michael Jones in the text *Medical Negligence* (Sweet & Maxwell, London, 1996) at p 36, para 2–027 stated that once a person is accepted onto a general practitioner's list they are clearly the doctor's patient, even if the practitioner has never seen that person in a professional capacity. The basis of this assertion was National Health Service (General Medical Services) Regulations 1992 (UK).

In *Lowns & Anor v Woods & Ors* (1996) Aust Torts Reports 81–376, it was held that in special circumstances there was relationship of proximity between the plaintiff and the medical practitioner, a general practitioner, notwithstanding their lack of previous professional association.

The special circumstances arose because it was a medical emergency. Prior to the decision in *Lowns* there was no Australian case in which a doctor had been held liable for damages because of a failure to attend upon and treat someone who was not already his patient. In a recent case, *BT v Oei* [1999] NSWSC 1082, this court held that a general practitioner owed a duty of care to a sexual partner of a patient in certain circumstances.

Policy has a role to pay in deciding whether a duty of care exists. Also the particular connection between the parties, including the second defendant's knowledge of risk compared to the plaintiff's appreciation of risk is a relevant factor in determining whether a duty of care exists (*Perre v Apand Pty Ltd* [1999] HCA 36, para 216). In this regard both Mr and Mrs Alexander had no medical knowledge that would have enabled them to appreciate the risk, whereas Dr Heise, had he been consulted by the receptionist, did have the isolated and specific knowledge that the headache was of a severe nature and would have appreciated the risk. Dr Heise would have firstly recognised the significance of Mr Alexander's headache; secondly, he would have taken steps to investigate this headache, including referral to hospital for a CT scan; and thirdly, he said that he believed that Mr Alexander would have been saved. It is foreseeable to the doctor that if a patient presenting with a severe headache of a significant duration could indicate sinister pathology then urgent medical attention is required to exclude the sinister pathology.

The plaintiff tendered expert reports of Dr Fisher dated 16 November 1999 and 22 November. The defendant tendered a report of Dr McBride of 29 November 1999 (Ex 1). Both doctors gave evidence and were cross-examined. Dr Fisher has been a practising general practitioner for 44 years and retired in 1998. He currently is involved in advisory work for the College of General Practitioners, having been at one time the President of the Royal Australian College of General Practitioners. Dr Fisher has written his report on the basis that the plaintiff's version of the conversation is accepted. Dr Amanda McBride is a practitioner of 20 years' standing. Dr McBride prepared her report on the basis that Mrs Alexander did not indicate urgency or a situation of emergency to the second defendant.

Dr Fisher's view is that when a patient presents by proxy, it is the equivalent of the patient themselves presenting because they are presenting a list of symptoms which they are concerned about. It is common for a doctor to get telephone calls from adults about other adults. Dr McBride said that if a person telephoned the receptionist, who relayed the message back to her, her response would be that she cannot judge the illness of a person over the phone or if a person was seeking to make an appointment for her husband, she would need the husband to contact the practice himself.

Patients presenting to a doctor's surgery with headaches would not be an uncommon occurrence. According to Dr McBride, if a person presented with a problem such as a severe headache, her receptionist would communicate it to her (the doctor). She would request her receptionist to pursue it a little further and find out what it is all about. The reason for this is because while a headache can be a symptom of an utterly benign condition, it can be a condition of an impending catastrophe. Dr Fisher agrees that headache requires a proper history taking and examination to endeavour to establish its course, because it not only can signify haemorrhage but can also signify serious complications such as meningitis, encephalitis or space-occupying lesion.

At the first defendant's practice, if a person presented to the receptionist, requested an appointment for someone else who was not a patient of the practice but was able to describe the symptoms suffered by that other person, the same instructions applied, that is, if the receptionist was unsure, she was to contact the doctor and the doctor would speak to the person involved. No distinction was drawn between whether the person had consulted the practice on previous occasions or whether they were a new patient. This practice is in accordance with Drs Fisher and McBride's views. It is my view that once Mr Alexander's symptoms were described to the receptionist, albeit by his wife, and an appointment was made, Mr Alexander became a patient of the practice and a duty of care was owed to Mr Alexander by at least the first defendant, Dr Heise.

The statement of claim alleges that the defendants breached their duty of care in that firstly, the first defendant failed to instruct or properly instruct the second defendant on the proper management of patients who present with concerns of the kind here; secondly, that the second defendant failed to consult the first defendant about the plaintiff's concerns when she knew or ought to have known that with the history provided by the plaintiff the possibility of sinister pathology could not be excluded and in the circumstances, urgent attention was warranted; and thirdly, the first defendant failed to have in place any adequate protocol or guidelines for a receptionist dealing with a patient presenting with concerns of the kind here.

Both Dr Fisher and Dr McBride agreed a doctor's receptionist should comply with the statements that appear in the Royal Australian College of General Practitioners *Handbook for Medical Receptionists* 1995, 5th Edition (Ex M). The practice recommended in the handbook is one which was adopted in the first defendant's medical practice in any event. There is a section in the handbook headed 'Which Patients require Priority' (p 20). It commences with a warning that unless a receptionist has specific medical training and written instructions, important to the decision on when a patient must been seen are the following:

1 Duration of problem (in minutes, hours, days);
2 Severity of symptoms;
3 Assessment of the patient, eg:

(a) life threatening;
(b) severe pain;
(c) mild discomfort.

Not surprisingly the handbook then states that the receptionist must use his or her judgment. Where there is any doubt a receptionist should ask the doctor, or give the patient the benefit of that doubt.

Under the subheading 'urgent problems to see the doctor today' in relation to the brain, head and neck area the handbook states:

Weakness or paralysis Blurred speech

Fits	Faints
Funny turns	Confusion
Coma	Dizzy spells
Giddy turns	Headache

It should be noted that headache appears on the list of urgent problems to see the doctor today, depending upon the duration and severity of the headache and after an assessment of the patient has been made.

It was Dr Fisher's opinion that a medical receptionist should have specific medical training and written instructions (111.50). It was Dr Fisher's opinion that in a situation where a wife seeks an appointment for her husband, a properly trained receptionist would, when confronted with the statement 'my husband has been under a lot of stress at work lately', explore this further as it may conceal serious problems such as suicide, threat to job, severe depression or, as in this case, headache, all of which would require an urgent consultation. It is common ground that a well trained receptionist would inquire about specific complaints, their severity and duration of the complaint. The receptionist is, in Dr Fisher's opinion, placed in the position of a triage without the specific training of nurses, and where there is a request for any urgency of assessment it should be referred to the doctor. There should not be, in his opinion, intervention or triage by the receptionist.

Dr Fisher considered that if Mrs Heise did receive a history that Mr Alexander had woken up in the early hours of the morning with a severe headache and uncharacteristically requested the plaintiff's migraine tablets, the receptionist should have spoken to the general practitioner concerning the problem. Alternatively, if Dr Heise was not available, then the receptionist should have advised the plaintiff that Mr Alexander should be seen that day either at another practice or hospital.

Likewise, Mrs Heise gave evidence that if there were any concerns presented by a patient regarding the severity of a condition she would go and talk to Dr Heise about it. There was a two-way telephone so she could pick up the phone and ask him for advice. She also said that if a patient was present at the surgery and they were obviously unwell then she felt free to knock on the door, interrupt Dr Heise's consultation and ask him to come out. Her instructions were, if in doubt ask or get him to come out, and this was the practice procedure. The secretaries who Mrs Heise relieved followed this rule of thumb.

Mrs Heise gave evidence that she had been instructed that if a patient presented who was sweaty, grey, with chest pain, migraine, severe headache, asthma, severe pain, problems with visuals and vomiting, children with high temperatures, collapse or trauma or what would be a severe health condition, she was to call the doctor,

> either on the phone or else just go and knock on the door and ask him to come out. This was to happen even if the doctor was with a patient and someone presenting any of these complaints needed immediate attention.

Both Dr Fisher and Dr McBride accepted that a general practitioner has the responsibility for determining whether patients require urgent medical attention. Where there is a doubt as to the urgency, both Dr Fisher and Dr McBride agreed that the receptionist should speak directly to the doctor to obtain the benefit of his or her medical opinion. The second defendant's evidence was that as a matter of practice she consulted the doctor if this situation arose. Both Dr Fisher and Dr McBride gave evidence that a properly trained receptionist acting prudently would be expected to tell the doctor about a patient complaining of a headache which raised their (the receptionist's) index of concern and ensure that an immediate appointment was made. Hence it is my view that a general practitioner has the responsibility to ensure that the patients seeking appointments are properly prioritised. The medical practitioner should have guidelines in place so that, where the receptionist is unsure if the patient's medical condition is of an urgent nature, he or she is to consult the doctor for the doctor's decision as to whether the patient should be seen urgently and, if so, the time period in which he or she needs to been seen. It is also my view that the first defendant is vicariously responsible for the acts of his employees, namely the second defendant. If I am wrong on this issue, it is also my view that a medical receptionist owes a duty of care to the patient to ensure that if he or she presents with a possible urgent medical condition, that patient is seen in a timely manner. If the doctor is unavailable and a patient presents with an urgent medical condition the receptionist should refer the patient elsewhere, such as the nearest hospital accident and emergency section or another medical practice. The answer to the first question is that both defendants owed a duty of care to Mr Alexander.

Did the defendant or either of them breach their duty of care?

Dr Fisher gave evidence that he would expect the receptionist to pick up the concerns and worries of the person who was expressing the worry and if she did so it would be her duty to say to the doctor words like she has a patient who is worried about a person who had a headache this morning and it was an uncharacteristic headache and it has now gone away. She wants him to have a general examination because she says she is worried about it. According to Dr Fisher it was incumbent upon the second defendant to consult the first defendant before giving an appointment one week later. Dr Fisher also adheres to view that where a spouse of a general practitioner is acting as a receptionist, there is a conflict of interest in her concern for the patient and concern for the general practitioner, especially if the receptionist has no medical or receptionist training.

As previously stated, it is important to consider that the second defendant did not have the benefit of observing Mr Alexander to assist her in her assessment as to whether the appointment was of an urgent nature. Clinical assessment is an important tool. Nor did the second defendant have the opportunity to ask Mr Alexander any specific questions and have the benefit of his response. The second defendant was solely reliant on the plaintiff's account to determine whether or not Mr Alexander should see the doctor on an urgent basis. Even though the plaintiff told the second defendant of Mr Alexander's 'severe headache' the night before and that it was so out of character that he asked for a headache tablet, this information was conveyed in the context that she wanted a full medical check-up to take place.

The conversation was amicable and the plaintiff did not articulate that she required an urgent appointment. The second defendant asked about the duration of the headache and knew only that the headache was 'severe'. This, in my view, was not enough to raise the second defendant's index of concern. The second defendant made an assessment of the patient on the information she had available and assessed Mr Alexander's problem as not being life-threatening and, as he was well the next morning and went to work as normal, she was entitled to categorise it as not being urgent. In these circumstances no obligation arose to consult the doctor, the first defendant, for his opinion. Mr Alexander made a choice not to see a doctor on an urgent basis but chose to delegate the making of a medical appointment to his wife. He chose to go to work rather than see a doctor that day. Mr Alexander was only willing to attend an appointment for a full medical check-up if it could be conducted after 6.00 pm; that placed limitation on the range of appointments that could be given. In these circumstances, I agree with Dr McBride where she gave the following evidence.

Dr McBride stated (138.5–10):

> The words 'severe headache' would alert someone that there is something untoward going on. However, it was followed by the fact that the interpretation of his wife as a non-medical practitioner was that it was stress related and her husband had agreed to have a medical examination, which indicates to me that he did not really want a medical examination, that his wife was worried and that a certain group of people in this community are very stoic and do not want to have medical examinations no matter what was happening.
>
> And, therefore, quite properly she was trying to get him in for a full check-up. She really wanted him checked out thoroughly because this does not happen very often. Having a migraine tablet to settle down a severe headache at that point in time, a migraine tablet can be, with due respect – what is recommended in accident and emergency is three aspirins and that is often there recommended.

It was her view that it would be an uncommon occurrence if a Mersyndol would settle down a headache of severe intensity. The taking of a migraine tablet would not have alerted her that there was anything wrong that would warrant an appointment that day.

It is my view that the first defendant, the general practitioner, had a duty of care to properly instruct the second defendant, the medical receptionist, on the proper management of patients who presented with complaints which may warrant urgent attention. It is my view that the first defendant had properly instructed the second defendant on the proper management of patients who present with complaints that may warranted urgent treatment. In the circumstances where Mrs Alexander expressed a number of concerns about her husband's medical condition in an amiable manner and wanted these checked out in the context of a full medical check-up where there was no patient to assess, it is my view that the medical receptionist acted reasonably and prudently in allocating an appointment the following Monday. The second defendant was aware that the severe headache had subsided the next morning and Mr Alexander was well and had gone to work. In these circumstances the second defendant's index of concern would not have been heightened. A medical receptionist acting reasonably and prudently would not have appreciated that Mr Alexander could have a life-threatening condition on the information provided. The risk of him suffering a grade V aneurism or some other life-threatening illness on what she was told by the plaintiff was not foreseeable. The first and second defendants did not breach their duty of care that they owed to Mr Alexander.

Further, in relation to the alternate allegation that the first defendant failed to have adequate protocol or guidelines for the reception, the only external training course the second defendant attended was in July 1993 when she attended a week long seminar conducted by the Ku-ring-gai District Medical Association. This covered bookings, handling of complaints, and determining the priority of patients. There were no regular training sessions given by the practice but the medical practitioners in the practice would try to have either second or third monthly meetings with the staff to go through issues and problems.

The second defendant stated that the first defendant instructed her on how to perform duties at the surgery. Training of receptionists at the first defendant's medical practice was that after every session they had in general practice they used to talk to the receptionists. They would give the doctors a list of phone calls or messages that were required. The doctors would go through – sometimes, if there was an issue the doctors would discuss those issues after the session as well. Nevertheless, the first defendant was aware of matters requiring urgent attention and where there was a doubt she was to consult the doctor. She was also aware of how to assess a patient and explore the duration of the problems and the severity of the symptom. It is my view that the first defendant had in place adequate guidelines for a patient presenting with a severe headache. The answer in respect of whether the defendants breached their duty of care is no.

An appeal against the above decision was dismissed by the Court of Appeal: *Alexander v Heise & Anor* [2001] NSWCA 422.

PART III: FAILING TO ADVISE OF 'MATERIAL RISKS'

In Chapter 2, we saw that a health care practitioner must disclose information as to the nature of the treatment, to allow a patient the decision of whether or not to consent to treatment (*Chatterton v Gerson* (1981)). If he fails to do so, a patient will have an action in battery.

In addition, a health care practitioner must disclose to a patient certain information about risks or side effects. If the health care practitioner fails to do so, the risk materialises causing damage to the patient and the patient gives evidence that if he or she had known of the risk he or she would not have consented to the treatment, then the health care practitioner will be liable in negligence.

Until the High Court's decision in *Rogers v Whitaker* (1992), this latter duty to warn of risks was judged according to the *Bolam* standard, viz would a competent body of medical practitioners disclose such a risk?

Dissatisfaction with the *Bolam* test can be seen in *F v R* (1983) 33 SASR 189 and *Battersby v Tottman and State of South Australia* (1985) 37 SASR 524. In those cases, a patient-centred test of disclosure was applied. A good outline of the state of Anglo-Australian law pre-*Rogers v Whitaker* is Cassidy, DI, 'Malpractice – medical negligence in Australia' (1992) 66 ALJ 67. For comparisons of the *Bolam* standard with the broader-based American law, see Crooke, GW, 'Consumerism, accountability and recent trends in medical litigation' (1991) QLSJ 373 and Robertson, G, 'Informed consent to medical treatment' (1981) 97 LQR 102.

Rogers v Whitaker marked an important point of departure for Australian law. Its effects have survived the passing of the Civil Liability Acts.

Rogers v Whitaker (1992) 175 CLR 479

Mason CJ, Brennan, Dawson, Toohey JJ:

The appellant, Christopher Rogers, is an ophthalmic surgeon. The respondent, Maree Lynette Whitaker, was a patient of the appellant who became almost totally blind after he had conducted surgery upon her right eye. The respondent commenced proceedings against the appellant for negligence in the Supreme Court of New South Wales and obtained judgment in the amount of $808,564.38. After an unsuccessful appeal to the Court of Appeal of New South Wales, the appellant now appeals to this court.

There is no question that the appellant conducted the operation with the required skill and care. The basis upon which the trial judge, Campbell J, found the appellant liable was that he had failed to warn the respondent that, as a result of surgery on her right eye, she might develop a condition known as sympathetic ophthalmia in her left eye. The development of this condition after the operation and the consequent loss of sight in her left eye were particularly devastating for the respondent as she had been almost totally blind in her right eye since a penetrating injury to it at the age of nine. Despite this early misfortune, she had continued to lead a substantially normal life: completing her schooling, entering the workforce, marrying and raising a family. In 1983, nearly 40 years after the initial injury to her right eye and in preparation for a return to the paid workforce after a three-year period during which she had looked after her injured son, the respondent decided to have an eye examination. Her general practitioner referred her to Dr Cohen, an ophthalmic surgeon, who prescribed reading glasses and referred her to the appellant for possible surgery on her right eye.

The respondent did not follow up the referral until 22 May 1984 when she was examined by the appellant for the first time. The appellant advised her that an operation on the right eye would not only improve its appearance, by removing scar tissue, but would probably restore significant sight to that eye. At a second consultation approximately three weeks later, the respondent agreed to submit to surgery. The surgical procedure was carried out on 1 August 1984. After the operation, it appeared that there had been no improvement in the right eye but, more importantly, the respondent developed inflammation in the left eye as an element of sympathetic ophthalmia. Evidence at the trial was that this condition occurred once in approximately 14,000 such procedures, although there was also evidence that the chance of occurrence was slightly greater when, as here, there had been an earlier penetrating injury to the eye operated upon. The condition does not always lead to loss of vision but, in this case, the respondent ultimately lost all sight in the left eye. As the sight in her right eye had not been restored in any degree by the surgery, the respondent was thus almost totally blind.

In the proceedings commenced by the respondent, numerous heads of negligence were alleged. Campbell J rejected all save the allegation that the appellant's failure to warn of the risk of sympathetic ophthalmia was negligent and resulted in the respondent's condition. While his Honour was not satisfied that proper medical practice required that the appellant warn the respondent of the risk of sympathetic ophthalmia if she expressed no desire for information, he concluded that a warning was necessary in the light of her desire for such relevant information. The Court of Appeal (Mahoney, Priestley and Handley JJA) dismissed all grounds of the appellant's appeal from the judgment of $803,564.38 on both liability and damages; the court also dismissed a cross-appeal by the respondent on the question of general damages. The respondent does not pursue the latter issue in this court but the appellant has appealed on the questions of breach of duty and causation.

Breach of duty

Neither before the Court of Appeal nor this court was there any dispute as to the existence of a duty of care on the part of the respondent. The law imposes on a medical practitioner a duty to exercise reasonable care and skill in the provision of professional advice and treatment That duty is a 'single comprehensive duty covering all the ways in which a doctor is called upon to exercise his skill and judgment'; it extends to the examination, diagnosis and treatment and the provision of information in an appropriate case. It is of course necessary to give content to the duty in the given case.

The standard of reasonable care and skill required is that of the ordinary skilled person exercising and professing to have that special skill, in this case the skill of an ophthalmic surgeon specialising in corneal and anterior segment surgery. As we have stated, the failure of the appellant to observe this standard, which the respondent successfully alleged before the primary judge, consisted of the appellant's failure to acquaint the respondent with the danger of sympathetic ophthalmia as a possible result of the surgical procedure to be carried out. The appellant's evidence was that 'sympathetic ophthalmia was not something that came to my mind to mention to her'.

The principal issue in this case relates to the scope and content of the appellant's duty of care: did the appellant's failure to advise and warn the respondent of the risks inherent in the operation constitute a breach of this duty? The appellant argues that this issue should be resolved by application of the so-called *Bolam* test. In *Sidaway v Governors of Bethlem Royal Hospital*, Lord Scarman stated the *Bolam* principle in these terms:

The *Bolam* principle may be formulated as a rule that a doctor is not negligent if he acts in accordance with a practice accepted at the time as proper by a responsible body of medical opinion even though other doctors adopt a different practice. In short, the law imposes the duty of care: but the standard of care is a matter of medical judgment.

Before the primary judge there was evidence from a body of reputable medical practitioners that, in the circumstances of the present case, they would not have warned the respondent of the danger of sympathetic ophthalmia; there was also, however, evidence from similarly reputable medical practitioners that they would have given such a warning. The respondent, for her part, argues that the *Bolam* principle should not be applied if it entails courts deferring to the medical experts in medical negligence cases and that, in any event, the primary judge was correct in the circumstances of this case in not deferring to the views of those medical practitioners who gave evidence that they would not have warned the respondent . . .

One consequence of the application of the *Bolam* principle to cases involving the provision of advice or information is that, even if a patient asks a direct question about the possible risks or complications, the making of that inquiry would logically be of little or no significance; medical opinion determines whether the risk should or should not be disclosed and the express desire of a particular patient for information or advice does not alter that opinion or the legal significance of that opinion. The fact that the various majority opinions in *Sidaway*, for example, suggest that, over and above the opinion of a respectable body of medical practitioners, the questions of a patient should truthfully be answered (subject to the therapeutic privilege) indicates a shortcoming in the *Bolam* approach. The existence of the shortcoming suggests that an acceptable approach in point of principle should recognise and attach significance to the relevance of a patient's questions. Even if a court were satisfied that a reasonable person in the patient's position would be unlikely to attach significance to a particular risk, the fact that the patient asked questions revealing concern about the risk would make the doctor aware that this patient did in fact attach significance to the risk. Subject to the therapeutic privilege, the question would therefore require a truthful answer.

In Australia, it has been accepted that the standard of care to be observed by a person with some special skill or competence is that of the ordinary skilled person exercising or professing to have that special skill. But, that standard is not determined solely or even primarily by reference to the practice followed or supported by a responsible body of opinion in the relevant profession or trade. Even in the sphere of diagnosis and treatment, the heartland of the skilled medical practitioner, the *Bolam* principle has not always been applied. Further, and more importantly, particularly in the field of non-disclosure of risk and the provision of advice and information, the *Bolam* principle has been discarded and instead, the courts have adopted the principle that, while evidence of acceptable medical practice is a useful guide for the courts, it is for the courts to adjudicate on what is the appropriate standard of care after giving weight to 'the paramount consideration that a person is entitled to make his own decisions about his life' . . .

Acceptance of this approach does not entail an artificial division or itemisation of specific, individual duties, carved out of the overall duty of care. The duty of a medical practitioner to exercise reasonable care and skill in the provision of professional advice and treatment is a single comprehensive duty. However, the factors according to which a court determines whether a medical practitioner is in breach of the requisite standard of care will vary according to whether it is a case involving diagnosis, treatment or the provision of information or advice; the different cases raise varying difficulties which require consideration of different factors. Examination of the nature of a doctor-patient relationship compels this conclusion. There is a fundamental difference between, on the one hand, diagnosis and treatment and, on the other hand, the provision of advice or information to a patient. In diagnosis and treatment, the patient's contribution is limited to the narration of symptoms and relevant history; the medical practitioner provides diagnosis and treatment according to his or her level of skill. However, except in cases of emergency or necessity, all medical treatment is preceded by the patient's choice to undergo it. In legal terms, the patient's consent to the treatment may be valid once he or she is informed in broad terms of the nature of the procedure which is intended. But the choice is, in reality, meaningless unless it is made on the basis of relevant information and advice. Because the choice to be made calls for a decision by the patient on information known to the medical practitioner but not to the patient, it would be illogical to hold that the amount of information to be provided by the medical practitioner can be determined from the perspective of the practitioner alone or, for that matter, of the medical profession. Whether a medical practitioner carries out a particular form of treatment in accordance with the appropriate standard of care is a question in the resolution of which responsible professional opinion will have an influential, often decisive role to play.

Whether the patient has been given the relevant information to choose between undergoing and not undergoing the treatment is a question of a different order. Generally speaking, it is not a question the answer to which depends upon medical standards or practice. Except in those cases where there is a particular danger that the provision of a relevant information will harm an unusually nervous, disturbed or volatile patient no special medical skill is involved in disclosing the information, including the risk attending the proposed treatment. Rather, the skill is in communicating the relevant information to the patient in terms which are reasonably adequate for that purpose having regard to the patient's apprehended capacity to understand that information.

In this context, nothing is to be gained by reiterating the expressions used in American authorities, such as 'the patient's right of self-determination' or even the oft-used and somewhat amorphous phrase 'informed consent'. The right of self-determination is an expression which is, perhaps, suitable to cases where the issue is whether a person has agreed to the general surgical procedure or treatment, but is of little assistance in the balancing process that is involved in the determination of whether there has been a breach of the duty of disclosure. Likewise, the phrase 'informed consent' is apt to mislead as it suggests a test of the validity of a patient's consent. Moreover, consent is relevant to actions framed in trespass, not in negligence. Anglo-Australian law has rightly taken the view that an allegation that the risks inherent in a medical procedure had not been disclosed to the patient can only found an action in negligence and not in trespass; the consent necessary to negative the offence of battery is satisfied by the patient being advised in broad terms of the nature of the procedure to be performed. In *Reibl v Hughes*, the Supreme Court of Canada was cautious in its use of the term 'informed consent' . . .

The law should recognise that a doctor has a duty to warn a patient of a material risk inherent in the proposed treatment; a risk is material if, in the circumstances of the particular case, a reasonable person in the patient's position, if warned of the risk, would be likely to attach significance to it or if the medical practitioner is or should reasonably be aware that the particular patient, if warned of the risk, would be likely to attach significance to it. This duty is subject to the therapeutic privilege.

The appellant in this case was treating and advising a woman who was almost totally blind in one eye. As with all surgical procedures, the operation recommended by the appellant to the respondent involved various

> risks, such as retinal detachment and haemorrhage infection, both of which are more common than sympathetic ophthalmia, but sympathetic ophthalmia was the only danger whereby both eyes might be rendered sightless. Experts for both parties described it as a devastating disability, the appellant acknowledging that, except for death under anaesthetic, it was the worst possible outcome for the respondent. According to the findings of the trial judge, the respondent 'incessantly' questioned the appellant as to, amongst other things, possible complications. She was, to the appellant's knowledge, keenly interested in the outcome of the suggested procedure, including the danger of unintended or accidental interference with her 'good', left eye. On the day before the operation, the respondent asked the appellant whether something could be put over her good eye to ensure that nothing happened to it; and entry was made in the hospital notes to the effect that she was apprehensive that the wrong eye would be operated on. She did not, however, ask a specific question as to whether the operation on her right eye could affect her left eye.
>
> The evidence established that there was a body of opinion in the medical profession at the time which considered that an inquiry should only have elicited a reply dealing with sympathetic ophthalmia if specifically directed to the possibility of the left eye being affected by the operation on the right eye. While the opinion that the respondent should have been told of the dangers of sympathetic ophthalmia only if she had been sufficiently learned to ask the precise question seems curious, it is unnecessary for us to examine it further, save to say that it demonstrates vividly the dangers of applying the *Bolam* principle in the area of advice and information. The respondent may not have asked the right question, yet she made clear her great concern that no injury should befall her one good eye. The trial judge was not satisfied that, if the respondent had expressed no desire for information, proper practice required that the respondent be warned of the relevant risk. But it could be argued, within the terms of the relevant principle as we have stated it, that the risk was material, in the sense that a reasonable person in the patient's position would be likely to attach significance to the risk, and thus required a warning. It would be reasonable for a person with one good eye to be concerned about the possibility of injury to it from a procedure which was elective. However, the respondent did not challenge on appeal that particular finding.
>
> For these reasons, we would reject the appellant's argument on the issue of breach of duty.
>
> For the foregoing reasons, we would dismiss the appeal.

Do you agree that 'no special medical skill' is involved in communication of risk of a treatment to a patient?

Note that the High Court acknowledges an exception to the requirement that a medical practitioner divulge information on material risks viz where doing so would cause great harm to the patient. This is known as 'the therapeutic privilege'.

The High Court clarified the position expressed in *Rogers v Whitaker* in the later case of *Rosenberg v Percival.* That case concerned an experienced nurse who consulted an oral and maxillofacial surgeon about a worsening malocclusion. The surgeon performed an operation called a sagittal split osteotomy, but did not inform the patient of the risk of temporomandibular joint problems, a risk which eventuated.

The nurse sued the surgeon for failing to disclose a material risk.

Rosenberg v Percival [2001] HCA 18

Gleeson CJ:

Two main issues were argued in this Court. The first is whether the appellant was in breach of his duty of care to his patient, the respondent, when he failed to bring to her notice the risk of a certain kind of harm she might suffer in consequence of surgery he undertook to perform. The second is whether, if there had been such a breach of duty, it was causally related to the respondent's injuries. That in turn involved the question whether, if she had been made aware of the risk, the respondent would have decided not to undergo the surgery. The trial judge found against the respondent on both issues. [The Court of Appeal allowed an appeal against the trial judge] . . .

The case was conducted at trial, in the Full Court, and in this Court, upon the basis that the decision of this Court in *Rogers v Whitaker* established the nature of the appellant's duty of care, as distinct from its practical content in the circumstances of the particular case. It is important to note what *Rogers v Whitaker* decided, and what it did not decide. Rejection of the doctor's argument [in that case] involved deciding not to follow the English decisions of *Bolam v Friern Hospital Management Committee* [4], and *Sidaway v Governors of Bethlem Royal Hospital* [5]. This Court preferred the approach of Lord Scarman, who dissented in *Sidaway*, and who said:

> In my view the question whether or not the omission to warn constitutes a breach of the doctor's duty of care towards his patient is to be determined not exclusively by reference to the current state of responsible and competent professional opinion and practice at the time, though both are, of course, relevant considerations, but by the court's view as to whether the doctor in advising his patient gave the consideration which the law requires him to give to the right of the patient to make up her own mind in the light of the relevant information whether or not she will accept the treatment which he proposes.

As the above passage, which was quoted with approval in *Rogers v Whitaker*, makes clear, the relevance of professional practice and opinion was not denied; what was denied was its conclusiveness. In many cases, professional practice and opinion will be the primary, and in some cases it may be the only, basis upon which a court may reasonably act. But, in an action brought by a patient, the responsibility for deciding the content of the doctor's duty of care rests with the court, not with his or her professional colleagues.

In *Rogers v Whitaker*, once the issues of duty, and breach of duty, had been resolved, there was no serious question of causation. The trial judge had accepted that, if the patient had been warned of the risk of what ultimately occurred, she would not have undergone the surgery.

The patient had shown anxious concern about the possible risks. The trial judge's finding on that factual issue was affirmed in the Court of Appeal [7]. Causation was not in dispute by the time the matter reached this Court.

Although this Court came to the same conclusion about the duty of care as had been reached in North American cases, the Court warned against uncritical use of certain concepts, which ought to be valuable currency, but which are susceptible to rhetorical inflation. Mason CJ, Brennan, Dawson, Toohey and McHugh JJ said:

> In this context, nothing is to be gained by reiterating the expressions used in American authorities, such as 'the patient's right of self-determination' or even the oft-used and somewhat amorphous phrase 'informed consent'. The right of self-determination is an expression which is, perhaps, suitable to cases where the issue is whether a person has agreed to the general surgical procedure or treatment, but is of little assistance in the balancing process that is involved in the determination of whether there has been a breach of the duty of disclosure. Likewise, the phrase 'informed consent' is apt to mislead as it suggests a test of the validity of a patient's consent. Moreover, consent is relevant to actions framed in trespass, not in negligence. Anglo-Australian law has rightly taken the view that an allegation that the risks inherent in a medical procedure have not been disclosed to the patient can only found an action in negligence and not in trespass; the consent necessary to negative the offence of battery is satisfied by the patient being advised in broad terms of the nature of the procedure to be performed. In *Reibl v Hughes* the Supreme Court of Canada was cautious in its use of the term 'informed consent'.

Having rejected the *Bolam* principle, the Court went on to formulate the test to be applied in determining whether there was a breach of duty. However, in the light of the way the case had been argued, and in the light of the facts of the case, it was sufficient to do so in general terms.

The joint judgment continued:

> The law should recognise that a doctor has a duty to warn a patient of a material risk inherent in the proposed treatment; a risk is material if, in the circumstances of the particular case, a reasonable person in the patient's position, if warned of the risk, would be likely to attach significance to it or if the medical practitioner is or

> should reasonably be aware that the particular patient, if warned of the risk, would be likely to attach significance to it.

The trial judge had found that the case fell within the second of the two alternative tests of materiality, but not the first. Having regard to the patient's conduct before surgery, there was no challenge in this Court to that finding.

In the circumstances of that case, it was unnecessary for the Court to explore some of the potential factual difficulties in the concept of a duty to warn about a material risk inherent in the proposed treatment. What was meant by materiality was explained; but the practical application, in a given case, of the concepts of warning, and risk, may raise difficult issues for judgment.

Ordinary people live their lives surrounded by adverse contingencies that are foreseeable, in the sense that they are not far-fetched or fanciful. Transportation to a doctor's surgery may be accompanied by a foreseeable risk of serious injury in a motor vehicle accident, but such a risk is usually regarded as inconsequential. Even when surgical procedures are classified as elective, most people who undergo such procedures believe they have a serious reason for doing so; and doctors who recommend such procedures normally have the same belief. Thus, information about risk is being considered in the context of a communication between two people who have a common view that there is a serious reason in favour of the contemplated surgery. The more remote a contingency which a doctor is required to bring to the notice of a patient, the more difficult it may be for the patient to convince a court that the existence of the contingency would have caused the patient to decide against surgery.

That is the difficulty which confronted the respondent in the present case. The adverse contingency which resulted in her post-operative problems was remote. The respondent failed to prove that her problems resulted from incompetence in the manner in which the surgery was performed. In the alternative, she sought to make out a case based on a failure to warn of the contingency. Expert medical opinion at the trial was divided on the degree of remoteness of the contingency, and the need to warn about it. However, as the evidence emerged, it became clear that there was a serious question whether, even if the contingency had been brought to the attention of the respondent, it might have been expected to make any difference to her decision. This question was then addressed by the respondent in evidence, belatedly, and, in the opinion of the trial judge, unconvincingly.

There is an aspect of such a question which may form an important part of the context in which a trial judge considers the issue of causation. In the way in which litigation proceeds, the conduct of the parties is seen through the prism of hindsight. A foreseeable risk has eventuated, and harm has resulted. The particular risk becomes the focus of attention. But at the time of the allegedly tortious conduct, there may have been no reason to single it out from a number of adverse contingencies, or to attach to it the significance it later assumed. Recent judgments in this Court have drawn attention to the danger of a failure, after the event, to take account of the context, before or at the time of the event, in which a contingency was to be evaluated [10]. This danger may be of particular significance where the alleged breach of duty of care is a failure to warn about the possible risks associated with a course of action, where there were, at the time, strong reasons in favour of pursuing the course of action.

The trial judge's findings on the issue of causation did not depend solely upon the adverse opinion he formed as to the respondent's credibility, although that was important. He also took into account the seriousness of her need for corrective surgery, her evident willingness to undergo the risks of a general anaesthetic, with which she was familiar by reason of her professional background, her failure to ask specific questions about risk, and the fact that the possibility of which, on her case, she should have been warned, was 'very slight'. The conclusion that the respondent had not established that, if her attention had been drawn to the risk in question, she would not have gone ahead with the surgery, was justified by the evidence and supported by cogent reasons. It should not have been overturned by the Full Court.

I would allow the appeal with costs, set aside the orders made by the Full Court, and order that the appeal to the Full Court be dismissed with costs.

McHugh J:
The test for causation where there has been a failure to warn a patient of risks.

Under the Australian common law, in determining whether a patient would have undertaken surgery, if warned of a risk of harm involved in that surgery, a court asks whether this patient would have undertaken the surgery. The test is a subjective test [11]. It is not decisive that a reasonable person would or would not have undertaken the surgery. What a reasonable person would or would not have done in the patient's circumstances will almost always be the most important factor in determining whether the court will accept or reject the patient's evidence as to the course that the patient would have taken. But what a reasonable person would have done is not conclusive. If the tribunal of fact, be it judge or jury, accepts the evidence of the patient as to what he or she would have done, then, subject to appellate review as to the correctness of that finding, that is the end of the matter. Unlike other common law jurisdictions [12], in this field Australia has rejected the objective test of causation in favour of a subjective test.

It follows from the test being subjective that the tribunal of fact must always make a finding as to what this patient would have done if warned of the risk. In some cases where there is no direct evidence as to what the patient would have done, the judge may infer from the objective facts that the patient would not have undergone the procedure. In exceptional cases, the judge may even reject the patient's testimony as not credible and then infer from the objective facts that the patient would not have proceeded. The judge might find, for example, that the patient was a person whose general credibility was so poor that no reliance could be placed on that person's oral evidence. Yet, notwithstanding the rejection of the patient's oral testimony, the judge might infer that nevertheless this patient would not have undergone the procedure. That inference would ordinarily be based not only on the objective facts but also on the tribunal's assessment of the general character and personality of the patient.

Appellate review of the causation issue where there has been a failure to warn

When the tribunal of fact has accepted the patient's evidence that he or she would not have undertaken the surgery, an appellate court will often be in a stronger position to reverse that finding than when the tribunal of fact has rejected the patient's evidence. That is because, human nature being what it is, most persons who suffer harm as the result of a medical procedure and sue for damages genuinely believe that they would not have undertaken the procedure if they had been warned of the risk of that harm. Thus, the demeanour of the patient in the witness box will often not restrain appellate review of this finding of fact to the extent that it does in respect of fact finding in many other appeals [13]. Nevertheless, where the tribunal of fact has accepted the evidence of the patient, an appellate court cannot entirely disregard the 'subtle influence of demeanour' on the tribunal of fact.

When the tribunal of fact has rejected the patient's evidence that he or she would not have proceeded with the surgery, however, the ordinary restrictions on appellate review of fact finding apply. If the tribunal of fact is a judge, as in the present case, an appellate court must respect the advantage that the judge has had over the appellate court in seeing and hearing the patient give evidence. Ordinarily, the appellate court cannot reverse the finding of the judge unless it is satisfied 'that any advantage enjoyed by the trial judge by reason of having seen and heard the witnesses, could not be sufficient to explain or justify the trial judge's conclusion' [15]. Unless that condition is satisfied or the judge has misdirected himself or herself or has misapprehended the evidence or has indicated that the demeanour of the patient played no part in the finding, the appellate court cannot reverse it. These restrictions on appellate review also apply when the trial judge makes a positive finding that the patient would have undertaken the procedure if warned of the relevant risks.

Moreover, in the circumstances of this case, the patient could not succeed on the causation issue unless her evidence concerning that issue was credible. The objective facts in her favour were not so strong that a court could infer from them that, if warned, she would not have proceeded with the surgery even though the court found that no reliance whatsoever could be placed on her oral testimony. All members of the Full Court implicitly recognised that this was so by sending the causation issue for a re-trial instead of making their own findings on that issue.

No doubt it was for this reason that Wallwork J did not suggest that, even if the patient's evidence on the causation issue was rejected, it was still open to the trial judge to find that she would not have had the surgery. His Honour merely said that the judge had 'rejected the proposition that the [patient] would have not had the surgery had she been warned of the possible risks'. That is true. But the trial judge did more than reject this proposition. He also made a positive finding that 'even if the [patient] had been warned of the slight possibility . . . she would have proceeded with the surgery in any event'. Given the evidence and the advantage that he had of seeing and hearing the patient give evidence, this finding was also open to him.

The finding was the product of a number of matters. They included:

- the rejection of the patient's testimony on the causation issue;
- the assessment of the patient's character and personality;
- the 20 years experience that the patient had had as a qualified nurse with a doctorate of philosophy in nursing and a senior lectureship in nursing at a university;
- the patient knowing that surgical operations carry inherent risks of harm;
- the patient suffering from a worsening condition of malocclusion for a number of years;
- the consulting of several specialists for the purpose of remedying the condition and getting the best result;
- the osteotomy procedure being the operation most likely to produce the best result in her case;
- the osteotomy being a common operation;
- the risk of suffering the harm that the patient suffered being very small; and
- the patient subsequently undergoing another operation to correct the consequences of the temporomandibular joint disorder.

Conclusion

Australian law is committed to a subjective test in determining whether a patient would have refused to undergo a medical procedure if that person had been warned of the risk of relevant injury. If the patient is believed, he or she succeeds even though the objective facts point the other way. If the evidence of the patient is rejected, he or she carries the heavy evidentiary burden of persuading the court to make a favourable finding on the causation issue solely by reference to the objective facts and probabilities. Courts frequently make findings as to states of mind based on nothing more than the objective facts and probabilities of the case. But usually such findings refer to the mental state that simultaneously accompanied some act or omission of a person. Thus, courts often have to determine whether an act causing harm was done with intent to kill or inflict grievous bodily harm, whether a representation was made with knowledge of its falsity, whether an omission to account for trust moneys was done with intent to defraud or whether a publication was made maliciously. The very doing of the act or the omitting to do the act, when considered in its context, generally throws much light on the mental state of the person concerned. But these cases are different from the 'What if?' situation that arises when the court has to determine what a patient would have done if warned of a risk. In the 'What if?' situation, the relevant mental state has not accompanied any act or omission of the patient.

In terms of causation theory, the critical fact is whether the patient would have taken action – refusing to have the operation – that would have avoided the harm suffered. But that fact can only be determined by making an anterior finding as to what the patient would have decided to do, if given the relevant warning. It is not possible to find what the patient would have done without deciding, expressly or by necessary implication, what decision the patient would have made if the proper warning had been given. If the court finds that the patient would have decided not to have the operation, it concludes that he or she would not have had the operation. What the patient would have decided and what the patient would have done are hypothetical questions. But one relates to a hypothetical mental state and the other to a hypothetical course of action. The answer concerning the hypothetical mental state provides the answer to the hypothetical course of action. The onus is on the patient to prove that he or she would have decided not to have the operation if given a warning of the risk of harm. That means that the patient must prove what he or she would have decided to do. When the direct testimony of that person on the causation issue has been rejected, it is unlikely, as a matter of fact, that the patient will succeed on that issue unless the objective evidence in favour of the patient is very strong.

In the present case, as the judgment of Kennedy J shows, a number of matters supported the patient's case. But neither individually nor collectively were they strong enough for the patient to succeed without the trial judge accepting her evidence that she would have decided not to have the operation. Gunning DCJ rejected her evidence and, given the limits of appellate review in respect of findings of fact based, wholly or partly, on the assessment of a witness's credibility, character or personality, it was not open to the Full Court to set aside his finding on the causation issue.

Gummow J:
There are two major issues arising out of this appeal. The first is whether the Full Court was correct in holding that the appellant had breached his duty of care ('the materiality issue'); and, secondly, whether the Full Court erred in principle in overturning the trial judge's findings on credibility and in ordering a re-trial of the causation issue.

At first blush, it may appear that, if the second issue were to be decided in the affirmative, the appeal to this Court could be allowed without the need to investigate the materiality issue. However, in this case, the issues of materiality and causation are so interrelated that this is not the proper approach. Observations by Gaudron J in *Bennett v Minister of Community Welfare* [21] indicate the point. Her Honour said 'questions of the sufficiency of the precaution to avert the harm are inevitably subsumed in the finding that there was a duty.' It should be emphasised that a determination of whether the failure to warn of a risk was causative depends to a large extent on the definition or identification of the risk in question. Central to the identification of the risk are considerations of degree and severity. Those same considerations are also central to the question of whether the risk was material. If the Court comes to one view of those considerations when dealing with the materiality issue, the same view will direct the resolution of the causation issue.

Of course, notwithstanding the logical difficulties involved, cases may be conducted on the basis, or may reach this Court on the footing, that materiality or causation but not both are in issue. *Rogers v Whitaker* was fought on the issue of materiality not causation, whereas in *Chappel v Hart* the issue was the other way around. Here, as indicated, both issues are involved. The appellant submits to this Court that the Full Court failed properly to identify the risk in question and had erred in determining its materiality. He further submits that the Full Court erred in principle in overturning the findings of the trial judge concerning the credibility of the respondent's evidence. These submissions should be accepted and the appeal allowed.

The path to be followed in these reasons to reach that conclusion involves consideration of the identification of the risk to the patient, the materiality of that risk, and the causation of the injury she suffered.

The identification of the risk

It is established by *Rogers* that a medical practitioner owes a duty 'to warn a patient of a material risk inherent in the proposed treatment'. However, that proposition in turn poses further questions.

The first question is 'what "risk" is being spoken of here?' Put another way, it is 'what are the facts and circumstances, the possibility of the occurrence of which constitutes that "risk"?' Once that question is answered one may turn to consider whether the risk is 'material'. Where the action is brought in negligence and the plaintiff is seeking compensation for an injury suffered, the relevant risk is the possibility that the proposed treatment will result in the injury that in fact occurred [25]. It is not, for example, the risk that the patient will make an uninformed decision or choose the wrong option, although that may well underpin the rationale behind the duty.

It is important to understand the decision in *Rogers* in the context in which it was decided. Before *Rogers* dealt with the law in Australia, the law in England was that evidence of medical practice was the sole determinant of the appropriate standard. Thus, if evidence that it was the practice of a respected body of medical practitioners not to give a warning in the circumstances of the case were accepted by the tribunal of fact, any such failure to warn would not be negligent. This approach was described as the *Bolam* test. The decision of this Court in *Rogers* rejected the *Bolam* test. The Court held that the standard to be observed by medical practitioners was not to be determined solely or even primarily by medical practice. Rather, it was for the courts to judge what standard should be expected from the medical profession. In the joint judgment that standard was identified and fixed. Hence the statement by Gaudron and McHugh JJ in *Breen v Williams* that:

> *Rogers* took away from the medical profession in this country the right to determine, in proceedings for negligence, what amounts to acceptable medical standards.

The structure and sequence of their Honours' reasoning can be understood from the following six passages:

(i) 'In Australia, it has been accepted that the standard of care to be observed by a person with some special skill or competence is that of the ordinary skilled person exercising and professing to have that special skill. But, that standard is not determined solely or even primarily by reference to the practice followed or supported by a responsible body of opinion in the relevant profession or trade.'

(ii) '[I]t is for the courts to adjudicate on what is the appropriate standard of care after giving weight to "the paramount consideration that a person is entitled to make his own decisions about his life".'

(iii) 'The duty of a medical practitioner to exercise reasonable care and skill in the provision of professional advice and treatment is a single comprehensive duty. However, the factors according to which a court determines whether a medical practitioner is in breach of the requisite standard of care will vary according to whether it is a case involving diagnosis, treatment or the provision of information or advice; the different cases raise varying difficulties which require consideration of different factors.'

(iv) 'There is a fundamental difference between, on the one hand, diagnosis and treatment and, on the other hand, the provision of advice or information to a patient. In diagnosis and treatment, the patient's contribution is limited to the narration of symptoms and relevant history; the medical practitioner provides diagnosis and treatment according to his or her level of skill. However, except in cases of emergency or necessity, all medical treatment is preceded by the patient's choice to undergo it. In legal terms, the patient's consent to the treatment may be valid once he or she is informed in broad terms of the nature of the procedure which is intended. But the choice is, in reality, meaningless unless it is made on the basis of relevant information and advice.'

(v) 'Whether a medical practitioner carries out a particular form of treatment in accordance with the appropriate standard of care is a question in the resolution of which responsible professional opinion will have an influential, often a decisive, role to play; whether the patient has been given all the relevant information to choose between undergoing and not undergoing the treatment is a question of a different order. Generally speaking, it is not a question the answer to which depends upon medical standards or practices.'

(vi) 'We agree that the factors referred to in *F v R* by King CJ must all be considered by a medical practitioner in deciding whether to disclose or advise of some risk in a proposed procedure. The law should recognise that a doctor has a duty to warn a patient of a material risk inherent in the proposed treatment; a risk is material if, in the circumstances of the particular case, a reasonable person in the patient's position, if warned of the risk, would be likely to attach significance to it or if the medical practitioner is or should reasonably be aware that the particular patient, if warned of the risk, would be likely to attach significance to it. This duty is subject to the therapeutic privilege.'

Thus, the Court, in (vi), sets the standard that the law demands of medical practitioners in relation to the provision of information. This standard does not deal with the foreseeability of the risk in question, save to the extent that the risk must be 'inherent' in the procedure. In this respect the general law of negligence still applies. Support for this view can be found in the concurring judgment of Gaudron J. Her Honour stated that a real and foreseeable risk was required to found a duty to warn and, further, saw 'no basis for treating the doctor's duty to warn of risks . . . as different in nature or degree from any other duty to warn of real and foreseeable risks'. A risk is real and foreseeable if it is not far-fetched or fanciful, even if it is extremely unlikely to occur. The precise and particular character of the injury or the precise sequence of events leading to the injury need not be foreseeable. It is sufficient if the kind or type of injury was foreseeable [38], even if the extent of the injury was greater than expected. Thus, in *Hughes v Lord Advocate*, there was liability because injury by fire was foreseeable, even though the explosion that actually occurred was not.

A misunderstanding as to what is involved in the notion of risk in cases such as this case may lead to an exaggerated view as to the nature of the burden imposed upon defendants. That appears to have infected some of the reasoning of the Full Court in this case. Wallwork J said:

> The question of the risk in this case was not dependent on it being known to the operating surgeon or the other experts concerned that there were pre-operative signs of a [TMJ] disorder. On the overwhelming evidence it was a risk which existed because of the

> likelihood of some patients having complications after the operative procedure. Once there is a risk which is generally known to the profession, there is a duty to warn.

What is lacking here is an identification of the 'risk' with which the court should be concerned. For example, there is no reference to the severity of the potential injury or the likelihood of its occurrence. Indeed, in the present case it appears that the risk which the Full Court had in mind was a general risk of the occurrence of 'TMJ complications'. However, such a broad definition is of little use in determining either materiality or causation. Nor did the Full Court identify or give content to the notion of materiality, a matter dealt with later in these reasons.

One of the factors relevant to, but not decisive of, the question of what a reasonable medical practitioner ought to have foreseen is the state of medical knowledge at the time when the duty should have been performed [40]. A reasonable medical practitioner cannot be expected to have foreseen an event wholly uncomprehended by medical knowledge at the time.

This reflects the fundamental proposition that the law demands no more than what was reasonable in all the circumstances of the case.

In the words of Barwick CJ in *Maloney v Commissioner for Railways* (NSW) [41]:

> [T]he respondent's duty was to take reasonable care . . . It is easy to overlook the all important emphasis upon the word 'reasonable' in the statement of the duty. Perfection or the use of increased knowledge or experience embraced in hindsight after the event should form no part of the components of what is reasonable in all the circumstances.

More recently, it was said in *Perre v Apand Pty Ltd* that:

> . . . it needs to be kept in mind . . . that the criterion is 'reasonable foreseeability'. Liability is to be imposed for consequences which [the respondent], judged by the standard of the reasonable man, ought to have foreseen.

With this in mind, the first step must be to define the relevant risk. It is appropriate in this context to define the risk by reference to the circumstances in which the injury can occur, the likelihood of the injury occurring, and the extent or severity of the potential injury if it does occur. These factors are to be considered from the point of view of what a reasonable medical practitioner in the position of the defendant ought to have foreseen at the time. This approach directs attention to the content of any warning that could have been given at the time.

Material risk

The next question is whether the risk, in the above sense, was 'material'. Under the *Rogers* test set out in para (vi) above, a risk is material if:

1 in the circumstances of the case, a reasonable person in the patient's position would be likely to attach significance to it ('the objective limb'); or
2 the medical practitioner was, or should have been, aware that the particular patient would be likely to attach significance to it ('the subjective limb').

Both *Rogers* and *Chappel v Hart* were concerned with the subjective limb; in this case, it is the objective limb. However, what is of immediate importance is that the key to the formulation in both limbs is the phrase 'likely to attach significance to'. Some of the difficulty which appears to be encountered in the application of the passage in para (vi) may stem from a failure to read what is said there with the judgment of King CJ in *F v R*, with which the joint judgment in *Rogers* expressly agreed in that very passage. In *F v R*, the Chief Justice of South Australia discussed five factors that are useful in determining whether a reasonable patient or the particular patient respectively, would be 'likely to attach significance to' the risk. This discussion merits careful attention. However, by way of summary, it can be seen that these factors are in effect an adaptation of the criteria set out by Mason J in *Wyong Shire Council v Shirt* for determining breach of duty. Those criteria were 'the magnitude of the risk and the degree of the probability of its occurrence', balanced against 'the expense, difficulty and inconvenience of taking alleviating action and any other conflicting responsibilities which the defendant may have'.

Clearly, in cases of a medical practitioner's failure to warn, the extent or severity of the potential injury is of great importance in applying the test in *Rogers* of 'likely to attach significance to', as is the likelihood of the injury actually occurring. These two matters, the extent or severity of the potential injury and the likelihood of it coming to pass, are to be considered together. A slight risk of a serious harm might satisfy the test, while a greater risk of a small harm might not. It is also important to note that, in considering the severity of the potential injury, that severity is judged with reference to the plaintiff's position. Thus, the risk of blindness in one eye would ordinarily be considered serious; if however, as in *Rogers*, the patient is already blind in one eye and stands to lose sight entirely, that risk becomes one of an altogether greater magnitude.

These considerations need to be weighed against the circumstances of the patient. The patient's need for the operation is important, as is the existence of reasonably available and satisfactory alternative treatments. A patient may be more likely to attach significance to a risk if the procedure is elective rather than life saving. As will be seen, these factors merge with the issue of causation.

The second, or subjective, limb of the test in *Rogers* for material risk requires further discussion. The second limb recognises that the particular patient may not be a 'reasonable' one; he or she may have a number of 'unreasonable' fears or concerns. These will be given full weight under the second limb if the medical practitioner was or should have been aware of them. One way of satisfying that condition is if the patient asked questions revealing the fear or concern. However, that is not the only means of satisfying the second limb. There are a multitude of potential circumstances in which a court might find that the medical practitioner should have known of a particular fear or concern held by the patient. Courts should not be too quick to discard the second limb merely because it emerges that the patient did not ask certain kinds of questions.

The phrase 'likely to attach significance to' as it appears in both limbs does not present a threshold issue of the same nature as that presented by the issue of causation. In the authorities, reference has been made to 'information that is relevant to a decision or course of action' [45] and 'matters which might influence the [decision]'. It is not necessary when determining materiality of risk to establish that the patient, reasonable or otherwise, would not have had the treatment had he or she been warned of the risk in question. The test is somewhat lower than that. However, it is necessary that the reasonable patient or particular patient respectively would have been likely seriously to consider and weigh up the risk before reaching a decision on whether to proceed with the treatment. The authorities referred to above should be read in that way. This case does not fall within the second, or subjective, limb of the *Rogers* test. The respondent did not ask questions identifying a particular area of concern and there is no indication of any relevant physical or mental characteristics peculiar to the respondent of which the appellant should have been aware. Therefore, the test of whether the risk was material falls to be determined by reference to the first, or objective, limb and thus to the reasonable person in the patient's position. From the findings of fact made at trial, the relevant factors to consider include: the temporary nature of any potential harm; the possibility of some pain, but not severe pain; the 10% chance of such complications arising; the fact that the respondent was concerned about her malocclusion, she wanted the 'best result' and the osteotomy was the most effective way to remedy the problem; the respondent was an experienced and knowledgeable nurse who was certainly aware that all surgery carried some risk and the fact that the respondent had received advice from a number of sources indicating that she should proceed with the treatment.

In light of these factors, it was open to the trial judge to conclude that a reasonable person in the respondent's position would not, in the sense of *Rogers*, be 'likely to attach significance to' the risk. Therefore the risk was not a material risk.

Causation

The question of whether a failure to warn of a material risk was causative of the plaintiff's injury involves two distinct levels of inquiry. At the first level, the risk must be related in a physical sense to the injury that was suffered. Thus, a medical practitioner will not be held liable for the failure to warn a patient of a material risk of damage to 'her laryngeal nerve', if the injury that eventuated resulted from a misapplication of anaesthetic. This is so despite the fact that the patient would not have had the treatment and therefore would not have suffered the injury from the misapplication of anaesthetic if the patient had been warned of the risk to 'her laryngeal nerve'. This can be seen as an example of a situation where the application of the 'but for' test would lead to an unacceptable result.

At the second level, there must be a causal connection, in the legal sense, between the failure to warn of the material risk and the occurrence of the injury. Cases involving a failure to warn of a risk encounter difficulties of causation that do not arise in cases of, for example, a negligent physical act 'causing' injury. The failure to warn the patient of the risk can never amount in the same sense to the cause of the injury.

Moreover, the issue of failure to warn usually arises when the performance of the physical cause of the injury was not negligent. Indeed, the present is such a case, given the finding that the appellant conducted both operations upon the respondent with the required skill and care.

It is well understood that the legal concept of causation differs from notions of causation which appear in the speculations of philosophers and the perceptions by scientists of the operation of natural laws. This is because the legal concept of causation is primarily concerned with attributing responsibility. It has been said that the test of causation is one of common sense, but, as Lord Hoffmann has observed:

> [C]ommon sense answers to questions of causation will differ according to the purpose for which the question is asked. Questions of causation often arise for the purpose of attributing responsibility to someone, for example, so as to blame him for something which has happened or to make him guilty of an offence or liable in damages. In such cases, the answer will depend upon the rule by which responsibility is being attributed.

Again, in *Chappel v Hart*, Gaudron J said [51]:

> Questions of causation are not answered in a legal vacuum. Rather, they are answered in the legal framework in which they arise. For present purposes, that framework is the law of negligence. And in that framework, it is important to bear in mind that that body of law operates, if it operates at all, to assign a duty to take reasonable steps to prevent a foreseeable risk of harm of the kind in issue.

In this case the purpose of the relevant rule is that stated in para (vi) of the extracts from the joint judgment in *Rogers* which have been set out above. This imposes an obligation upon medical practitioners adequately to warn their patients of the consequences of the treatment they are contemplating. If the medical practitioner should fail to warn the patient of a particular consequence and that consequence in fact eventuates then, subject to the question of materiality, the rule seeks to hold the medical practitioner liable for that consequence. In *Bennett v Minister of Community Welfare*, Gaudron J put the matter this way:

> [T]he issue is approached on the basis that 'when there is a duty to take a precaution against damage occurring to others through the default of third parties or through accident, breach of the duty may be regarded as materially causing or materially contributing to that damage, should it occur, subject of course to the question whether performance of the duty would have averted the harm'.

From this consideration, it can be seen that causation, in the present kind of case, requires satisfaction of two criteria. The first criterion is a breach of the duty to warn of a material risk, that risk having eventuated and caused, in the physical sense, injury to the plaintiff. The second criterion is that, had the warning been given, the injury would have been averted, in the sense that the relevant 'patient' would not have had the treatment in question.

In Australia the relevant 'patient' for the purposes of the second criterion is the particular patient and, in that sense, the criterion is a subjective one [53]. The question is whether the particular patient would not have had the treatment had a warning been given. This subjective criterion, it has been recognised, involves practical questions of proof. The court must deal with hypothetical considerations as to what the patient in question would have done had a warning been given. In *Gover v State of South Australia and Perriam*, Cox J said [54]:

> The court has to reach a decision about a topic to which the patient, in most cases, will not have addressed his mind at the time that matters most. His evidence as to what he would have done is therefore hypothetical and is very likely to be affected, no matter how honest he is, by his own particular experience.

His Honour added [55]:

> It will often be very difficult to prove affirmatively that a plaintiff would not have taken a risk, say, that the evidence shows that many other people freely take. I am not sure that the application of the subjective test will always be disadvantageous to a plaintiff, rather than the other way round.

The way in which the law deals with some of these difficulties was explained by McHugh J in *Chappel v Hart*. His Honour said:

> [T]he onus of proving that the failure to warn was causally connected with the plaintiff's harm lies on the plaintiff. However, once the plaintiff proves that the defendant breached a duty to warn of a risk and that the risk eventuated and caused harm to the plaintiff, the plaintiff has made out a *prima facie* case of causal connection. An evidentiary onus then rests on the defendant to point to other evidence suggesting that no causal connection exists. Examples of

> such evidence are: evidence which indicates that the plaintiff would not have acted on the warning because of lack of choice or personal inclination . . . Once the defendant points to such evidence, the onus lies on the plaintiff to prove that in all the circumstances a causal connection existed between the failure to warn and the injury suffered by the plaintiff.

These matters also have been discussed in recent English authority. In *Smith v Barking, Havering and Brentwood Health Authority*, Hutchison J said:

> [T]here is a peculiar difficulty involved in this sort of case – not least for the plaintiff herself – in giving, after the adverse outcome of the operation is known, reliable answers as to what she would have decided before the operation had she been given proper advice as to the risks inherent in it. Accordingly, it would, in my judgment, be right in the ordinary case to give particular weight to the objective assessment. If everything points to the fact that a reasonable plaintiff, properly informed, would have assented to the operation, the assertion from the witness box, made after the adverse outcome is known, in a wholly artificial situation and in the knowledge that the outcome of the case depends upon that assertion being maintained, does not carry great weight unless there are extraneous or additional factors to substantiate it. By extraneous or additional factors I mean, and I am not doing more than giving examples, religious or some other firmly-held convictions; particular social or domestic considerations justifying a decision not in accordance with what, objectively, seems the right one; assertions in the immediate aftermath of the operation made in a context other than that of a possible claim for damages; in other words, some particular factor which suggests that the plaintiff had grounds for not doing what a reasonable person in her situation might be expected to have done.

His Lordship's reference to the giving of particular weight by the tribunal of fact to what he called 'the objective assessment' should not be taken too far. At a jury trial, as the litigation in *Hocking v Bell* strikingly demonstrated, and as the decision in *Puntoriero v Water Administration Ministerial Corporation* recently emphasised, the ultimate question on any appeal will be whether it was open to the jury to return a verdict for the plaintiff; the jury, for example, may prefer the evidence of a lay plaintiff to that of experts. Where the tribunal of fact is a judge sitting without jury, the reasoning process will be disclosed, or should be apparent, from the reasons for judgment.

In this case, the trial judge rejected the respondent's evidence. His Honour, as has already been noted, based this decision primarily on his assessment of her credibility. However, his Honour found support for this assessment from a number of objective considerations. These included the low probability of the risk occurring, the fact that the likely consequences were not very severe, the desirability of the treatment and the respondent's awareness, as an experienced nurse, of the risks inherent in any surgery. There was no evidence of substantial fears or concerns that could counter these objective considerations. Consequently, the trial judge held that, even if the risk was material, the failure to warn was not causative. Subject to the observations made above as to the dangers involved in considering causation divorced from materiality, his Honour's reasoning did not disclose appealable error.

Rosenberg v Percival represented the last in a line of similar cases, where courts viewed sceptically a patient's statement that, had he/she known of the risks, he/she would not have consented to the procedure. The earlier cases are discussed by Campbell, and by Robinson and Yeldham in the articles extracted below.

Campbell, F, 'Causation and the failure to advise of risks associated with medical procedures' (1995) 3 No 6 *Australian Health Law Bulletin* 1

In two recent decisions involving allegations of failure to advise of risks, the court found that the plaintiffs were in fact warned by their medical practitioners of the material risks associated with the procedures. Furthermore, in both cases, the court found that the plaintiffs would have undergone the procedures in any event regardless of the risks involved.

***Berger v Mutton* (unreported), Twigg DCJ Dist Ct**

(NSW, 22 November 1994, 3584 of 1990)

Berger is an illustration of the extent to which a court will impute to the patient plaintiff knowledge of the attendant risks of a procedure, despite the plaintiff's evidence that she had no idea at the time of giving her consent, of the risks which were associated with the procedure.

Facts

The plaintiff was a 48-year-old woman who was trained and worked as a nurse. She had extensive experience in surgery, trauma and oncology wards over a period of 15 years. At the time her claim arose she was a director of a nursing home. She was familiar with the importance of consent to surgical procedure forms and of the significance of ensuring that a patient understands the contents of such forms before signing.

Following recurring abdominal pain of about two years' duration, accompanied by vaginal and rectal bleeding, the plaintiff consulted the defendant with a real fear that she might have cancer. She had had particularly heavy bleeding, loose bowels and chronic pain in the abdomen over the preceding two weeks. She also experienced inter-menstrual bleeding. The defendant recommended an examination under anaesthetic with dilatation and curettage, and a diagnostic laparoscopy.

In the course of the operation, the defendant found no abnormalities present. However, during the procedure the plaintiff's bowel was perforated requiring immediate suturing. The plaintiff remained in hospital for six days. Her recovery was uneventful save that she complained that insufficient analgesia was administered to her post-operatively.

The plaintiff claimed she was not warned of the risk of perforation of the bowel as a result of which she suffered initial shock, an extended hospital stay, pain, anxiety, insomnia and nightmares. She also claimed damages for an alleged unsightly scar.

A psychiatrist diagnosed a severe anxiety disorder which was characterised as a post-traumatic stress disorder, said to have developed as a consequence of the operation and the subsequent events, causing a dependency on sleeping pills and alcohol. He concluded that the plaintiff had fully recovered, functioning satisfactorily in both an occupational and social capacity.

The defendant gave evidence that he followed his usual practice of advising the plaintiff of the risks involved in an operation including the risk of bowel trauma and perforation, and of the risks associated with anaesthesia.

Findings

Rogers v Whitaker was followed in determining the material risks about which the plaintiff should have been warned. Applying the *Rogers v Whitaker* test, Twigg DCJ found that the defendant was not in breach of his duty of care. He found that, not only did the defendant make the plaintiff fully aware of the risks involved in the procedure, the plaintiff had ample knowledge of the procedure and was aware of the risks involved.

His Honour rejected the plaintiff's claim that she had no idea of what was involved in a laparoscopy at the time of giving her consent to the procedure. Her previous personal experience of a similar operative procedure (cholecystectomy in 1965) and her professional experiences of surgery made it impossible to accept that she was unaware that this surgical procedure might involve misadventure, specifically a risk of perforating the bowel. He found the plaintiff s evidence was coloured by her anger towards the defendant because she blamed him for all the events which occurred during and after the operation.

Further, Twigg DCJ rejected the plaintiff's evidence that if the defendant had given a more detailed explanation of the risks involved, she would not have had the operation but would have sought a second opinion. In his Honour's opinion, the plaintiff was anxious and concerned about the possibility that she might have cancer. She had observed in her professional and personal life the devastation caused by the disease. She was determined to have the operation so as to determine whether she had cancer somewhere in her body.

Bustos v Hair Transplant Pty Ltd and Peter Wearne

(unreported, Cooper DCJ, Dist Ct NSW 20 December 1994, 30978 of 1986)

In *Bustos*, the court found that the plaintiff was keen to the point of desperation to undergo the procedure.

Facts

In this action, the plaintiff sued Hair Transplant Clinic Pty Ltd and Dr NV, claiming damages for the consequences of an alleged negligently performed hair transplant in 1982. The plaintiff also alleged that Dr W failed to warn of material risks associated with the procedure, including the failure of the transplanted section to cover the recipient area; a 'droop' caused by an excess of skin at the recipient site, a lump or 'dog ear' where the hair and skin to be transplanted is rotated 180 degrees and placed at the donor site; altered sensation; and neuroma (a non-cancerous tumour made up of nerve cells and fibres) causing headaches.

At the time of the procedure, the plaintiff was 33 years old and was concerned about his thinning hair. He was born in Argentina and returned there in 1981 where he met an uncle who had similarly receding hair. The uncle had undergone a hair transplant by a Dr J who pioneered the 'Juri flap' procedure. The plaintiff thought his uncle looked 15 years younger and, the court found, decided at that point that he wanted to have the same operation.

The plaintiff claimed that as a result of the procedure he suffered extensive scarring, a droop and excess skin on the left (donor) side, a cosmetic defect as the flap reaches only two centimetres past the mid-line of his forehead, severe pain during the operation, headaches ever since (commencing immediately after the procedure), resulting in a psychiatric disorder, the breakdown of his marriage, the collapse of his restaurant and a subsequent inability to work.

Findings

His Honour, Cooper DCJ, found that while the Juri flap procedure was reasonably new in Australia, it was common ground that inherent in such a procedure were a number of possible complications. These are primarily of a cosmetic nature but also include pain, swelling and painful neuroma formation.

His Honour stated that to the knowledge of each of the defendants the plaintiff was undertaking elective surgery for the express purpose of improving his appearance. Further, it was known to them that he managed a restaurant. Therefore, his Honour found, each risk was a 'material risk' within the meaning of that phrase as it was formulated in *Rogers v Whitaker*. A risk is a material risk if, in the circumstances of the particular case, a reasonable person in the patient's position, if warned of the risk, would be likely to attach significance to it or if the medical practitioner is or should be reasonably aware that the particular patient, if warned of the risk would be likely to attach significance to it.

The plaintiff stated that if he had known of any of the consequences he would not have had the operation. He said that at the consultation with the doctor he was not warned of any of the risks.

Before being seen by Dr W, the plaintiff received counselling from the managing director of the clinic. At the counselling session, a consent booklet containing detailed information about the alternative procedures was given to, and signed by, the plaintiff. It did not, however, outline the risks of the procedure(s).

Dr W gave evidence of a consultation with the plaintiff after the plaintiff had had counselling with the clinic. Dr W stated he did not in any way rely on the counselling the plaintiff received from the clinic to discharge his own duty to the plaintiff. Further, he did not rely on the plaintiff reading the booklet but rather he would have given a detailed explanation of the operation and possible complications to the plaintiff himself. Dr W stated that, with one exception (the plaintiff's mention of his uncle undergoing the procedure), he had no memory of the conversation with the plaintiff but was relying on his normal practice.

His Honour accepted the evidence of Dr W in preference to that of the plaintiff and found that an appropriate warning was given by Dr W. He found this despite also finding that the plaintiff's evidence was given with conviction and sincerity stating that the plaintiff's many subsequent misfortunes coloured his recollection of events.

Cooper DCJ said the plaintiff's evidence that he would not have undergone the operation had he been warned is not conclusive of the issue, following Kirby J in *Ellis v Wallsend District Hospital* (1989) 17 NSWLR 553, at 560. He said that, however honest the patient may be, self interest and, again, the knowledge of the misfortunes that have followed the treatment will colour the patient's response to that question.

His Honour said that in this case the answer was to be found in the circumstances which led the plaintiff to the clinic in the first place. He was a young man who had noticed a receding hairline for five or six years previously. He was in the public eye, owning a restaurant which was doing well. He believed an improved appearance was helpful to his business. Having seen the vast improvement in the appearance of his uncle, he wanted to achieve the same transformation. He wanted the 'Juri flap' procedure which his uncle had undergone.

Accordingly, he nominated that form of treatment to the clinic when he contacted it in 1981. Neither the clinic nor the doctor recommended it to him. At the initial 'interview' with the clinic the various techniques were traversed. However, the plaintiff wanted the Juri flap procedure his uncle had. By his own evidence he was keen, if not desperate, to have the operation.

His Honour said the only thing that would have stopped him was if it were effectively brought home to him that his appearance would be worse after the operation, a prognosis which was not reasonable in light of the medical experience in 1982.

Importantly, his Honour found:

> . . . the plaintiff had in his mind's eye the picture of his uncle and it was this picture which motivated him to undergo the operation regardless of what warnings Dr W or anyone else gave him.

His Honour also said:

> I would further add that if the plaintiff had so satisfied me that the defendant was in breach of his duty to adequately advise the plaintiff of the risks, then he has failed to satisfy me that he would not have undergone the operation if so advised by the second defendant.

Comment

The *Rogers* decision has gone a long way towards clarifying the extent of the duty the court will impose on the medical profession in relation to the provision of advice to patients. The issue of causation, as revealed by these two decisions, remains a significant determining factor in litigation involving medical advice.

In both cases, the court accepted the evidence of the doctor over the patient with respect to what information was given. The difficulty became one of determining the accuracy of the plaintiff's recollections and the degree to which disappointment and mistrust had affected their recollection. In these circumstances, both judges found that the evidence, while given with conviction, was not factually accurate.

When applying the *Ellis* test of what a patient would have done if properly advised, knowledge of the events as they occurred must be excluded. The question is whether if they had been warned (assuming the court has found a warning was not given) of material risks, they would have nonetheless proceeded at the time their consent was given.

In both cases, the plaintiff had decided to undergo surgery if not prior to the consultation, then independently of the information given at the consultation. In *Berger*, the plaintiff was an experienced oncology nurse and was anxious to exclude cancer by diagnostic surgery. The plaintiff in *Bustos*, the court found, would have been dissuaded from surgery only if it were brought home to him that his appearance would be worse after the operation than before, an unreasonable prognosis in 1982.

In both decisions, the court seems to deviate from what is a perceived deference to the patients' stated view. In *Bustos*, his Honour considered the subjective evidence of the plaintiff that he would have declined to have the procedure, with the totality of the objective evidence and found that, at the time of consent and without the benefit of hindsight, the

> facts suggest that he would have proceeded in any event – short of demonstrating that he would have looked worse after the transplant.
>
> Similarly in *Berger*, the court rejected the plaintiff's evidence that she would not have undergone the procedure if she had known of the risk of a perforated bowel, on the basis that the objective facts painted a picture of an anxious and concerned woman, well aware of the signs and devastation of cancer, who wanted to exclude it from her diagnosis. The balance of the evidence, leaving aside the plaintiffs' stated view, provided a basis in both cases for the court to hold that the procedure would have been undertaken regardless of the risks involved.
>
> The weight to be given to a patient's desire to undergo a procedure, regardless of the associated risks has not, historically, been well argued. As a matter of causation, in elective and plastic surgery cases especially, there may be greater scope to submit that the patient elected to undergo treatment and had a desire to attain the desired result such that they would have consented to the procedure regardless of the risks associated with it.

Bustos' case has also been discussed by Robinson and Yeldham in a note in the Journal of Law and Medicine. Extracted below are the authors' summaries of some other unreported decisions which apply.

Robinson, WA and Yeldham, BA, 'The application of *Rogers v Whitaker* in the courts' (1996) 3 *Journal of Law and Medicine*, pp 222–24

> ... *Karpati v Spira* (NSW, Spender AJ, 6 June 1995) is another recent decision where *Rogers v Whitaker* was applied. This case goes some way towards offering the medical profession a guide as to the factors that will assist the court in determining negligence on the part of a medical practitioner, and how best to prevent a finding of negligence.
>
> In this case, the patient sued Dr Paul Spira, neurologist, Dr Peter Blum, neurosurgeon, and the Eastern Area Health Service for damages after undergoing an operative procedure known as stereotactic thalamotomy to eliminate a tremor caused by the onset of Parkinson's Disease. The operation was performed in 1987 and as a result of the operation the patient suffered a stroke which left him with a significant right-sided hemiparesis. The evidence at the hearing was that the extent of the risk of hemiparesis or stroke at the end of 1987 ranged from 0.5–1% up to 5% and that this information had been conveyed to the patient prior to his consent being obtained.
>
> Although the doctors were found to have adequately warned their patient of the risks of an operative procedure, Spender A J stated that the use of subjective terminology, such as 'small risk', 'slight risk' and 'rare', do not adequately or relevantly convey the true nature of the risk and should not be used in advising patients about the risks of treatment. His Honour concluded that, where possible, the patient should be

advised of the risk in percentage terms if there is a known figure, or a band or range of figures.

The need for clear and detailed notating has also become increasingly important in light of the decision in *Rogers v Whitaker*. In *Vale v Ho* (unreported, District Court, NSW, Sinclair DCJ, 11 May 1995), the patient alleged that Dr Ho failed to warn the patient of the risks involved before a second procedure to correct an apparent deviation of the patient's nose following plastic and reconstructive surgery. Dr Ho based his evidence on his extensive and detailed contemporaneous notes which contradicted much of the patient's evidence in relation to when, and if, warnings were given and their substance. His Honour Judge Sinclair found that he preferred the evidence of the doctor as the doctor's notes were made contemporaneously and before any complaint was made by the patient.

The dangers of not keeping adequate notes are also discussed in the Queensland decision of *Locher v Turner* (unreported, Court of Appeal, Qld, 21 April 1995). Here, the facts concerned a failure adequately to investigate a condition of the colon until more than 12 months after initial complaint.

The Court of Appeal held that neither the evidence of the patient nor that of the doctor as to matters not recorded in the notes could necessarily be taken to be correct. The doctor's notes of the consultations were in evidence but were not very full and it was necessary for the doctor to attempt to add to them matters from her recollection when giving evidence.

In the circumstances, the court stated that it could not decide the appeal on the basis that the doctor's evidence, 'filling in' gaps in and omissions from her written notes, should be treated as reliable, as to do so would go well beyond the proper function of an appellant court dealing with factual findings. Obviously, more detailed notes would have assisted the court, and perhaps led to a more satisfactory conclusion from the medical practitioner's point of view.

In *Sturch v Willmott* (unreported, Supreme Court, Qld, Thomas J, 13 April 1995), the judge discussed the distinction drawn in *Rogers v Whitaker* between diagnosis and treatment on the one hand, and the provision of advice or information to a patient on the other. His Honour held:

> In the former area, the prevailing professional opinion and practice at the time may have an influential and often decisive role to play. In the latter, the question does not depend so much upon medical standards or practice.

As his Honour found that the case before him was concerned with acts or omissions in relation to diagnosis and treatment, he held that the doctor fell within the standard of skill as expounded in *Rogers v Whitaker*:

> the standard of . . . skill required is that of the ordinary skilled person exercising and professing to have that special skill.

In South Australia, the case of *Hribar v Wells* (unreported, Supreme Court, SA, King CJ, Boland and Duggan JJ, 8 June 1995) provides a useful discussion of the court's attitude to the awarding of damages for the detriment resulting from a patient having undergone an operation which the patient would not have undergone if properly warned. The case involved an action for negligence in the failure to give adequate prior warning of the risks involved in dental surgery by a dental surgeon specialising in oral and maxillofacial surgery.

The doctor performed an operation on the patient to break and realign the jaws to correct a malocclusion on 15 April 1989. The operation left the patient with pain and disability and the patient had claimed damages for breach of duty and in negligence, alleging, among other things, that the doctor had failed to adequately advise her of the possible adverse effects of the operation.

The doctor was unsuccessful on appeal because, although it was held that it was the doctor's normal practice to give a warning to his patients regarding the probability of pain and swelling following the operative procedure, the doctor was held not to have given adequate warning to the patient about other 'possible untoward consequences of the operation', in particular, permanent and painful nerve damage.

One issue left unresolved was whether all complications flowing from the procedure should attract compensation, or only those relating to the particular complication about which the doctor failed to warn. One appeal judge thought that, logically, the former should be the case whereas the other two judges expressed reservation. Most recently, in *O'Sullivan v Little* (unreported, Supreme Court, ACT, Miles CJ, 10 August 1995), the judge found that a doctor's evidence as to his usual practice about warning patients expressing an interest in undergoing laparoscopic sterilisation was sufficiently compelling for him to find that the patient had not proved her allegation that the doctor had failed to warn her that the operation might fail by reason of the inaccurate application of Filshie clips or from any other reason. Importantly, it was also found in this case that consent forms signed by the patient which stated:

> The effect and nature of the operation has been explained to me and I understand that:
>
> (a) the effect is permanent;
> (b) there is small chance of the tubes rejoining naturally;
> (c) operation to rejoin the tubes may not be successful;
> (d) there is no effect on hormone activity,

supported the hypothesis that the doctor had followed his usual practice of informing the patient as the doctor made a habit of pointing out that the form for sterilisation is poorly worded and that there is a chance of becoming pregnant after the operation.

In conclusion, it can be seen that the standard of care to be applied in failure-to-warn cases in accordance with the decision in *Rogers v Whitaker* is no longer determined solely or even primarily by reference to the views of medical practitioners, even though those views, and more particularly the rationale on which those views are founded, are still of enormous assistance to the courts in reaching their ultimate conclusion: *Geissman v O'Keefe* (unreported, Supreme Court, NSW, Simpson J, 25 November 1994, p 11). It is now clear that, when applying the two tests formulated in *Rogers v Whitaker* to a factual situation, courts will have regard to such things as the contemporaneous notes made by doctors of consultations, consent forms and information pamphlets (when explained to patients), and in particular the invariable practice of the doctor.

It would now seem that *Rogers v Whitaker* is not as monstrous a decision as first imagined. The recent cases demonstrate that the courts do not expect doctors to be infallible; that not all possible risks of a surgical outcome need to be explained to the patient: and that the courts will not always accept that a patient would have avoided the procedure even if fully informed.

It is clear that, in order to prove causation, the patient needs to prove that if he or she had been informed of the risk, he or she would have avoided the risk. This, however, is not to say that the patient needs to prove that he or she would not have had the medical procedure performed. The High Court has held that, if the patient had been informed of the risk and would have elected to have the procedure performed by a more experienced (and thus more competent) practitioner, then causation is satisfied. This would seem to be on the basis that the chances of the risk actually occurring lessen if a more competent practitioner performs the procedure.

Note below the strong dissenting judgment of McHugh J.

Clive A Chappel v Beryl Jean Hart [1998] HCA 55

Gaudron J:

The facts may be simply stated. Mrs Hart underwent surgery at the hands of Dr Chappel without warning as to the possible consequences should her oesophagus be perforated and infection set in. That is what happened and, in consequence, Mrs Hart suffered damage to her laryngeal nerves, paralysis of her right vocal cord and voice loss.

The condition for which Dr Chappel operated on Mrs Hart is one which is relentlessly progressive. Thus, Mrs Hart would inevitably have required surgery of the kind performed. And the surgery would have been subject to the risk which eventuated – although not necessarily in the same degree – no matter when or by whom it was undertaken. Had Mrs Hart been aware of that risk, she would not have had surgery when she did. And she would have taken steps to have it performed by 'the most experienced [surgeon] with a record and a reputation in the field'.

Mrs Hart commenced proceedings against Dr Chappel in the Supreme Court of New South Wales, claiming damages for the injuries which she sustained. She recovered a verdict in the sum of $172,500.61. Included in the verdict was an amount of $30,000 for general damages. Dr Chappel appealed to the Court of Appeal of the Supreme Court of New South Wales and Mrs Hart cross-appealed, complaining that the amount awarded for general damages was inadequate. Both the appeal and cross-appeal were dismissed. Dr Chappel now appeals to this Court.

The primary contention made on behalf of Dr Chappel is that there was no causal connection between his failure to give adequate warning of the risks involved in the surgery and the damage suffered by Mrs Hart. The contention was made in a context in which it is clear that the surgery was performed with skill and care and the infection which set in and led to the injuries which Mrs Hart sustained was a random event which might occur no matter when or by whom the surgery was performed. It was put that, as surgery was inevitable and carried the risk which, in fact, eventuated, '[t]here was no loss of any "real and valuable chance", nor . . . any substantial prospects of the risk being diminished or avoided'. Alternatively, it was put that the damage sustained by Mrs Hart resulted from the random risk which, in fact, eventuated and her 'voluntary willingness to undertake that risk'.

The primary argument for Dr Chappel proceeds on the basis that the damage sustained by Mrs Hart was not physical injury but the loss of a chance to have surgery performed by somebody else at some other time. And as the risk which eventuated was ever present, no matter when or by whom the surgery might be performed, Mrs Hart did not, according to the argument, lose a chance of any value. Although the nature of the risk was the same, the evidence does not bear out the proposition that the degree of that risk was the same regardless of the experience of the surgeon involved. That issue can, for the moment, be put to one side, because, clearly, the damage sustained by Mrs Hart was not the loss of a chance – valuable or otherwise – but the physical injury which she, in fact, sustained.

The argument that the damage sustained by Mrs Hart was simply the loss of a chance must be considered in a context concerned with the assignment of legal responsibility. In that context, philosophical and scientific notions are put aside and causation is approached as a question of fact to be answered 'by applying common sense to the facts of [the] particular case'. That is so both for the question whether a particular act or omission caused any damage at all and for the question whether some particular damage resulted from the act or omission in question.

Questions of causation are not answered in a legal vacuum. Rather, they are answered in the legal framework in which they arise. For present purposes, that framework is the law of negligence. And in that framework, it is important to bear in mind that that body of law operates, if it operates at all, to assign a duty to take reasonable steps to prevent a foreseeable risk of harm of the kind in issue.

It was not disputed in this Court that Dr Chappel was under a duty to inform Mrs Hart of the possible consequences in the event of the perforation of her oesophagus and subsequent infection, including the possibility of damage to her voice. The duty was called into existence because of the foreseeability of that very risk. The duty was not performed and the risk eventuated. Subject to a further question in the case of a duty to provide information, that is often the beginning and the end of the inquiry whether breach of duty materially caused or contributed to the harm suffered. As Dixon J pointed out in *Betts v Whittingslowe*, albeit in relation to a statutory duty, 'breach of duty coupled with an accident of the kind that might thereby be caused is enough to justify an inference, in the absence of any sufficient reason to the contrary, that in fact the accident did occur owing to the act or omission amounting to the breach'.

Where there is a duty to inform it is, of course, necessary for a plaintiff to give evidence as to what would or would not have happened if the information in question had been provided [9]. If that evidence is to the effect that the injured person would have acted to avoid or minimise the risk of injury, it is to apply sophistry rather than common sense to say that, although the risk of physical injury which came about called the duty of care into existence, breach of that duty did not cause or contribute to that injury, but simply resulted in the loss of an opportunity to pursue a different course of action.

The matter can be put another way. If the foreseeable risk to Mrs Hart was the loss of an opportunity to undergo surgery at the hands of a more experienced surgeon, the duty would have been a duty to inform her that there were more experienced surgeons practising in the field.

Because the risk was a risk of physical injury, the duty was to inform her of that risk. And that particular duty was imposed because, in point of legal principle, it was sufficient, in the ordinary course of events, to avert the risk of physical injury which called it into existence. And the physical injury having occurred, breach of the duty is treated as materially causing or contributing to that injury unless there is 'sufficient reason to the contrary'.

The second argument with respect to causation is that there is 'sufficient reason to the contrary' to preclude a finding that Dr Chappel's failure to inform Mrs Hart of the risks involved was causally related to the injuries which she sustained. More precisely, it was argued that, even if he had adequately informed her of those risks, it would not have averted the harm suffered. There are two aspects to that argument. The first is that, as surgery was inevitable and the risk which eventuated was inherent in that surgery, Mrs Hart did not, in fact, suffer any damage. The second aspect asserts that the harm resulted from the 'random risk' of infection, which, in fact, eventuated, and Mrs Hart's 'voluntary willingness to undertake that risk'.

The first aspect of the argument must be rejected. It assumes that the degree of risk – as distinct from the nature of the risk – was the same regardless of the experience of the surgeon concerned. That is a matter to which it will be necessary to return. For the moment, however, it can be put to one side. There is a more fundamental flaw. The argument proceeds on the erroneous footing that the damage sustained by Mrs Hart was simply exposure to risk, not the harm which eventuated. And to say that Mrs Hart would inevitably have been exposed to risk of the harm which she suffered is not to say that she would inevitably have suffered that harm.

The second aspect of the argument, which asserts that the harm suffered by Mrs Hart resulted from the 'random risk' of infection which eventuated and her 'voluntary willingness to undertake that risk', must also be rejected. It may be that, at some stage, Mrs Hart would have voluntarily undertaken whatever risk was involved in the surgery then necessary for her condition. However, it cannot be said that that or any other risk was voluntarily undertaken when Dr Chappel operated but nothing presently turns on that point. The second aspect of the argument must be rejected because it treats the infection which occurred as a supervening event breaking the chain of causation which would otherwise begin with Dr Chappel's failure to inform Mrs Hart of the possible consequences in the event of perforation and subsequent infection. It is contrary to common sense to treat part of the very risk which called the duty into existence as a supervening event breaking the chain of causation beginning with the breach of that duty.

The question whether the infection which set in following perforation of Mrs Hart's oesophagus broke the chain of causation can also be answered by asking what would or would not have happened if Dr Chappel had provided her with adequate information as to the risk involved. If he had, Mrs Hart would not then have undergone surgery and would not then have suffered the injuries which she did or their consequences. Thus, Dr Chappel's 'breach was "still operating", or, continued to be causally significant when [those injuries were sustained]'.

The arguments advanced on behalf of Dr Chappel with respect to causation cannot succeed. Accordingly, it is necessary to turn to the question of damages. As already indicated, damages fell to be assessed, as the courts below recognised, on the basis that Mrs Hart suffered physical injury, not merely the loss of a chance to undergo surgery at the hands of some other surgeon at some other time. However, it was argued for Dr Chappel that, even on that basis, Mrs Hart suffered no damage at all, or, at most, only nominal damage.

It is well settled that an award of damages must take account of the probability that some or all of the damage suffered by the plaintiff would have occurred in any event [14]. In this context, it was put on behalf of Dr Chappel that, '[e]ven with the benefit of a more experienced surgeon, the increased chance of avoiding the injury by reason of the surgeon's greater experience and skill . . . would be minimal with the result that there was no damage; or alternatively the damages are nominal'. That argument would also seem to be infected with the notion that the damage suffered by Mrs Hart was the loss of a chance rather than the physical injury which she sustained. Whether or not that is so, the argument is premised on an assumption which is made possible only by an ambiguity inherent in the proposition that surgery would involve the very risk which, in fact, eventuated, no matter when or by whom it was performed.

It is not in doubt that a risk of perforation and infection was and is inherent in surgery of the kind performed on Mrs Hart. In that sense, the risk of injury was the same, no matter when or by whom the surgery was performed. However, that is not to say that the likelihood of that risk eventuating was the same. This was recognised by Donovan AJ, at first instance, his Honour stating that '[t]here [was] no evidence that the risk in the sense of its being likely to occur as it did would be the same'. Moreover, Professor Benjamin gave evidence from which it might be inferred that the risk of perforation, without which the injury sustained by Mrs Hart could not have occurred, diminished with the skill and experience of the surgeon concerned. And that inference was drawn by the Court of Appeal.

In the Court of Appeal, Handley JA (with whom Mahoney P and Cohen AJA agreed on this point) found that '[w]hile perforations could occur . . . without negligence, superior skill and experience could reduce [that] risk'. His Honour added that, on the evidence, Mrs Hart was likely to 'have retained the best and most experienced surgeon available' had she been fully informed of the risks involved and concluded that 'the risk . . . in the actual and hypothetical situations was not the same'. That conclusion was clearly open.

Once it is accepted, as in my view it must be, that the risk of injury would have been less if, as Mrs Hart deposed, she had retained the services of the most experienced surgeon in the field, the argument that, at best, Mrs Hart was entitled to nominal damages must be rejected. Rather, Mrs Hart is entitled to damages for the injuries suffered. In the calculation of those damages, however, the question arises whether there was a probability that Mrs Hart would have suffered harm of the kind that eventuated no matter when or by whom surgery was performed. If that was a probability, allowance should have been made for it [15]. However, neither the trial judge nor the Court of Appeal adverted to the question.

The evidence was that the harm suffered by Mrs Hart is extremely rare and cannot occur unless the oesophagus is perforated and infection sets in. The risk was described in evidence as 'random'. Apparently, no surgery of the kind performed on Mrs Hart can be described as completely free of the risk of harm of the kind that, in fact, eventuated. However, the uncontroverted evidence that it is both rare and random precludes the risk being described as other than speculative. That being so, there is no basis for a finding that it was, in any degree, probable that Mrs Hart would, in any event, have suffered harm of the kind she in fact suffered.

There is, thus, no basis for any reduction of the damages awarded at first instance.

The appeal should be dismissed with costs.

McHugh J (dissenting): The question in this appeal is whether a doctor who performed an operation with reasonable care is nevertheless liable for an accidental injury occurring in the course of the operation. The question has to be determined in the context that the doctor, in breach of his duty, failed to warn his patient that such an injury could occur and that the patient, if warned, would have had the operation carried out by 'the most experienced person with a record and a reputation in the field'.

Proof of a cause of action in negligence or contract requires the plaintiff to prove that the breach of duty by the defendant caused the particular damage that the plaintiff suffered. In civil cases, causation theory operates on the hypothesis that the defendant has breached a duty owed to the plaintiff and that the plaintiff has suffered injury; but causation theory insists that the plaintiff prove that the injury is relevantly connected to the breach of duty. The existence of the relevant causal connection is determined according to common sense ideas and not according to philosophical or scientific theories of causation. The reason for this distinction was pointed out by Mason CJ in *March v Stramare (E & MH) Pty Ltd* [17]:

> In philosophy and science, the concept of causation has been developed in the context of explaining phenomena by reference to the relationship between conditions and occurrences. In law, on the other hand, problems of causation arise in the context of ascertaining or apportioning legal responsibility for a given occurrence.

In *March* this Court specifically rejected the 'but for' test as the exclusive test of factual causation. Instead the Court preferred the same common sense view of causation which it had expressed in its decision in *Fitzgerald v Penn*. There, the Court said that the question is to be determined by asking 'whether a particular act or omission . . . can fairly and properly be considered a cause of the accident'. As a natural consequence of the rejection of the 'but for' test as the sole determinant of causation, the Court has refused to regard the concept of remoteness of damage as the appropriate mechanism for determining the extent to which policy considerations should limit the consequences of causation-in-fact. Consequently, value judgments and policy as well as our 'experience of the "constant conjunction" or "regular sequence" of pairs of events in nature' are regarded as central to the common law's conception of causation.

The rejection of the 'but for' test as the sole determinant of causation means that the plaintiff in this case cannot succeed merely because she would not have suffered injury but for the defendant's failure to warn her of the risk of injury. However, his failure to warn her of the risk was one of the events that in combination with others led to the perforation of her oesophagus and damage to the right recurrent laryngeal nerve.

Without that failure, the injury would not have occurred when it did and, statistically, the chance of it occurring during an operation on another occasion was very small. Moreover, that failure was the very breach of duty which the plaintiff alleges caused her injury. The defendant's failure to warn, therefore, must be regarded as a cause of the plaintiff's injury unless either common sense or legal policy requires the conclusion that, for the purposes of this action, the failure is not to be regarded as a cause of the plaintiff's injury.

Underlying the rejection of the 'but for' test as the determinant of legal causation is the instinctive belief that a person should not be liable for every wrongful act or omission which is a necessary condition of the occurrence of the injury that befell the plaintiff. As Mason CJ emphasised in *March*, causation for legal purposes is concerned with allocating responsibility for harm or damage that has occurred. So the mere fact that injury would not have occurred but for the defendant's act or omission is often not enough to establish a causal connection for legal purposes. Thus, in *Leask Timber and Hardware Pty Ltd v Thorne*, members of this Court accepted that the driving of a crane by an uncertificated driver was not causally related to the death of the plaintiff's husband, notwithstanding that driving a crane without a certificate was a breach of the law and that the death would not have occurred but for that breach. Windeyer J said:

> Possession of a certificate means that the driver has satisfied an inspector that he can drive a crane competently, and is a trustworthy person. If, however, he fails to exercise the competence he has and drives a crane improperly, unskilfully and negligently, it will not avail him or his employer that an inspector had certified that he was capable of doing so properly and skilfully; nor is it material that an inspector thought he was trustworthy if trust in him should prove misplaced. On the other hand, a person might have skill and competence but no certificate. If he drives a crane carefully, skilfully and competently then he is not liable in negligence for the consequences of an accident that occurs without fault on his part. That is how the matter would stand in an action for negligence.

Similarly, in *The Empire* Jamaica Willmer J held that the act of the owners of a ship in sending it to sea with a master who had no certificate, contrary to a local Ordinance, was not a legal cause of a collision occurring on the voyage, notwithstanding that the master was guilty of negligent navigating.

Before the defendant will be held responsible for the plaintiff's injury, the plaintiff must prove that the defendant's conduct materially contributed to the plaintiff suffering that injury. In the absence of a statute or undertaking to the contrary, therefore, it would seem logical to hold a person causally liable for a wrongful act or omission only when it increases [28] the risk of injury to another person. If a wrongful act or omission results in an increased risk of injury to the plaintiff and that risk eventuates, the defendant's conduct has materially contributed to the injury that the plaintiff suffers whether or not other factors also contributed to that injury occurring. If, however, the defendant's conduct does not increase the risk of injury to the plaintiff, the defendant cannot be said to have materially contributed to the injury suffered by the plaintiff. That being so, whether the claim is in contract or tort, the fact that the risk eventuated at a particular time or place by reason of the conduct of the defendant does not itself materially contribute to the plaintiff's injury unless the fact of that particular time or place increased the risk of the injury occurring.

In principle, therefore, if the act or omission of the defendant has done no more than expose the plaintiff to a class of risk to which the plaintiff would have been exposed irrespective of the defendant's act or omission, the law of torts should not require the defendant to pay damages. Similarly, if the defendant has done no more than expose the plaintiff to a risk for which the defendant has not undertaken responsibility and to which the plaintiff was always exposed, the law of contract should not require the defendant to pay damages for injury arising from that risk even if it follows upon a breach of contract. No principle of the law of contract or tort or of risk allocation requires the defendant to be liable for those risks of an activity or course of conduct that cannot be avoided or reduced by the exercise of reasonable care unless statute, contract or a duty otherwise imposed by law has made the defendant responsible for those risks.

For these reasons, in *Carslogie Steamship Co Ltd v Royal Norwegian Government*, where a vessel was delayed so that damage caused by the defendant's negligence could be repaired, the House of Lords had no difficulty in concluding that further damage to the vessel as the result of a severe storm after it resumed its voyage was not causally connected with that negligence. The House so concluded, notwithstanding that the further damage probably would not have occurred but for the delay. No doubt the House would have reached a different conclusion if the delay had increased the risk that the vessel might suffer damage from severe storms. Increased risk as the result of breach of duty was the reason that, in *Monarch Steamship Co Ltd v Karlshamns Oljefabriker (A/B)*, the House of Lords held the defendant liable for the cost of transhipment arising from the outbreak of war. The House held that the defendant's breach of duty had resulted in delay which had increased the chance that the cargo would have to be delivered after the outbreak of war.

Cases such as *Carslogie* and *Monarch* were concerned with damage following negligent acts. But logically the same principles must apply to the wrongful omissions as well as the wrongful acts of the defendant. Thus, if the defendant negligently fails to warn the plaintiff that a particular route is subject to landslides, no causal connection will exist between the failure to warn and subsequent injury from a landslide if every other available route carried the same degree of risk of injury from a landslide. In such a case, the injury suffered is simply an inherent risk in the course of action pursued by the plaintiff. Although the negligence of the defendant has resulted in the plaintiff being in the place where and at the time when the landslide occurred, that negligence is to be regarded as merely one of the set of conditions that combined to produce the injury. Because the negligent failure of the defendant to give a warning did not increase the risk of injury to the plaintiff, the defendant should not incur liability for the plaintiff's injury.

On the other hand, if there were alternative routes involving a lesser risk of landslide and the plaintiff would probably have taken one of them, if given a warning, the defendant's failure to warn would be causally connected with the plaintiff's injury. That is because the failure to warn deflected the plaintiff from taking a safer course and increased the chance that he or she would suffer injury. By doing so, the defendant has materially contributed to the occurrence of that injury. The case is *a fortiori* if the plaintiff, on being warned, would have abandoned the journey.

Furthermore, a defendant is not causally liable, and therefore legally responsible, for wrongful acts or omissions if those acts or omissions would not have caused the plaintiff to alter his or her course of action. Australian law has adopted a subjective theory of causation in determining whether the failure to warn would have avoided the injury suffered. The inquiry as to what the plaintiff would have done if warned is necessarily hypothetical. But if the evidence suggests that the acts or omissions of the defendant would have made no difference to the plaintiff's course of action, the defendant has not caused the harm which the plaintiff has suffered.

Moreover, even when the defendant's wrongful act or omission has exposed the plaintiff to a risk to which the plaintiff would not have been exposed but for that act or omission, the correct conclusion may nevertheless be that no causal connection exists between the negligence and the injury suffered. Thus, in *Central of Georgia Railway Co v Price*, a railway company was held not liable for injury sustained as the result of a lamp exploding in a hotel where the plaintiff had to stay as the result of the company negligently taking her beyond her destination. The risk of such an event occurring in that hotel on that particular night was so insignificant and therefore so abnormal as to be fairly described as a coincidence, rather than an event causally connected to the defendant's negligence.

The foregoing observations lead me to the following conclusions concerning whether a causal connection exists between a defendant's failure to warn of a risk of injury and the subsequent suffering of injury by the plaintiff as a result of the risk eventuating:

(1) a causal connection will exist between the failure and the injury if it is probable that the plaintiff would have acted on the warning and desisted from pursuing the type of activity or course of conduct involved;

(2) no causal connection will exist if the plaintiff would have persisted with the same course of action in comparable circumstances even if a warning had been given;

(3) no causal connection will exist if every alternative means of achieving the plaintiff's goal gave rise to an equal or greater probability of the same risk of injury and the plaintiff would probably have attempted to achieve that goal notwithstanding the warning;

(4) no causal connection will exist where the plaintiff suffered injury at some other place or some other time unless the change of place or time increased the risk of injury;

(5) no causal connection will exist if the eventuation of the risk is so statistically improbable as not to be fairly attributable to the defendant's omission;

(6) the onus of proving that the failure to warn was causally connected with the plaintiff's harm lies on the plaintiff. However, once the plaintiff proves that the defendant breached a duty to warn of a risk and that the risk eventuated and caused harm to the plaintiff, the plaintiff has made out a *prima facie* case of causal connection. An evidentiary onus then rests on the defendant to point to other evidence suggesting that no causal connection exists. Examples of such evidence are: evidence which indicates that the plaintiff would not have acted on the warning because of lack of choice or personal inclination; evidence that no alternative course of action would have eliminated or reduced the risk of injury. Once the defendant points to such evidence, the onus lies on the plaintiff to prove that in all the circumstances a causal connection existed between the failure to warn and the injury suffered by the plaintiff.

Upon the unusual facts of the present case – they are set out in detail in other judgments – the defendant in my opinion can escape liability only if the proper conclusion is that the plaintiff did not prove that the defendant's failure to warn resulted in her consenting to a procedure that involved a higher risk of injury than would have been the case if the procedure had been carried out by another surgeon.

It is clear from the evidence that mediastinitis is not an inevitable result of the perforation of the oesophagus. For practical purposes, the occurrence of mediastinitis is the result of the random chance of bacteria being present in the oesophagus when the perforation occurs. Given the principles of causation to which I have referred, the existence of a causal connection between the occurrence of mediastinitis and the defendant's failure to warn depends upon whether the plaintiff has proved that the failure to warn required her to assume a risk of mediastinitis occurring that was greater than the risk of it occurring if she had been warned. That depends in the first place on whether the effect of Professor Benjamin's evidence is that there are other surgeons who could perform the procedure with less risk of a perforation than the defendant.

I do not think that it is possible to read Professor Benjamin's evidence as asserting that either he or other unidentified surgeons could perform the procedure with greater care or more skill than the defendant ordinarily performed it. In the Court of Appeal, Handley JA read one of Professor Benjamin's answers as meaning that he had performed between 100 and 150 operations without a perforation of the oesophagus. If that interpretation had been correct, it would have provided an evidentiary foundation for the argument, if not the conclusion, that the defendant's failure to warn had denied her the alternative of having the procedure performed with a reduced risk of perforation of her oesophagus. However, the plaintiff did not really dispute that his Honour misunderstood Professor Benjamin's answer and that the effect of the Professor's evidence was merely that he had carried out that number of operations without the onset of mediastinitis.

Indeed, it is possible to read one of Professor's Benjamin's answers as indicating that perforations have occurred on a number of occasions when he or a team of surgeons of which he was a member has carried out the procedure [40].

Nothing in the evidence suggested that there was available to the plaintiff the services of a surgeon of such skill that he or she would never perforate the oesophagus while performing this procedure. Nor did the evidence suggest that either Professor Benjamin or any other surgeon was so superior in skill to the defendant that an operation by that person carried with it a statistically significant lesser risk of perforation than an operation by the defendant. Professor Benjamin was no doubt a pre-eminent surgeon in this field and had performed the operation on many more occasions than the defendant. It is also true that risk of perforation will vary depending upon the degree of care taken on a particular occasion. But the evidence did not suggest, let alone prove, that an operation by the defendant carried with it a statistically significant greater risk of perforation than that of any other qualified surgeon. There is not even a suggestion that the defendant had perforated the oesophagus in any previous operation. The evidence was all one way that perforation of the oesophagus was an inherent risk of the procedure. That is to say, it was an injury that could occur even when reasonable skill and care were exercised. The fact that it happened on this occasion says nothing about whether an operation by the defendant carried with it a statistically significant greater risk of injury.

The plaintiff's claim must fail. This follows from her failure to prove that there was open to her an alternative course of action which would have reduced the inherent chance of a perforation and consequent onset of mediastinitis and damage to the recurrent laryngeal nerve. The highest that her case can be put is that the defendant's failure to warn her resulted in her having the procedure at an earlier date and no doubt at a different place with a different surgeon than would have been the case if the defendant had carried out his duty and warned her. On the evidence, the carrying out of the procedure by the defendant on the day and at the place did not increase the risk of injury involved in the procedure. That being so, the defendant's failure to warn did not materially contribute to the plaintiff's injury. Her claim that a causal connection existed between that failure and her injury must be rejected.

On the view that I take of the case, it is of no relevance that, if she had been warned, another surgeon would have performed the procedure and that the chance of her suffering damage to the laryngeal nerve in that procedure was very remote. Perforation of the oesophagus with consequential mediastinitis and inflammation resulting in damage to the laryngeal nerve is such a rare event that it is close to a certainty that the plaintiff would have avoided mediastinitis and consequential damage to the laryngeal nerve if another surgeon had performed the procedure.

Perforation of the oesophagus can and does occur in carrying out the procedure even though the surgeon exercises reasonable skill and care. When it does occur, it will lead to mediastinitis only if bacteria are present in the oesophagus. According to the evidence of Professor Benjamin, it is 'very rare' for a perforation to be complicated by mediastinitis. Even then, as the learned trial judge found 'the likelihood is that the problems would clear up'. It seems almost certain, therefore, that if the plaintiff had been warned and had had the operation performed by another surgeon she would have avoided damage to her laryngeal nerve.

However, it is also close to a certainty that neither mediastinitis nor damage to the laryngeal nerve would have occurred if the defendant had performed the operation on some other day or even at some different hour on that day. He was not as experienced a surgeon as Professor Benjamin but he had performed the operation successfully on previous occasions. If reasonable care is exercised, there is only a remote possibility that damage to a laryngeal nerve resulting from mediastinitis will lead to paralysis of the vocal cords, as happened with the plaintiff, irrespective of which surgeon performs the procedure. Moreover, given the plaintiff's abandonment of any claim that the defendant had performed the operation negligently, he must be taken to have exercised reasonable skill and care on this occasion. His performance on this occasion was differentiated from that of others only by the eventuation of a risk that is inherent in the procedure whoever performs it.

To hold the defendant liable on the basis that if the plaintiff had been given a warning of the risk of mediastinitis occurring she would have avoided that condition is simply to apply the 'but for' test, a course which *March* [41] rejects. If, as the result of the defendant warning the plaintiff about the risk of perforation, the plaintiff had sought out another surgeon who had operated and accidentally perforated the plaintiff's oesophagus with consequent mediastinitis, only the most faithful adherents to the 'but for' test would argue that the defendant's warning had caused the perforation and mediastinitis. To so argue would seem an affront to common sense. Similarly, with great respect to the learned judges in the courts below, it seems contrary to common sense to conclude that the defendant's failure to warn caused or materially contributed to him perforating the plaintiff's oesophagus on this occasion. From a common sense point of view, the cause of the perforation and the consequent mediastinitis was the examination of the oesophagus with a rigid endoscope, an examination which carried with it an inherent risk of perforation.

The attractiveness of the proposition that the defendant's failure to warn caused or materially contributed to the plaintiff's perforation and mediastinitis derives, I think, from the language in which the proposition is expressed. Authorities on writing recognise that using a noun instead of a verb to express action (nominalisation) and omitting an actor from a sentence are fertile sources of imprecise communication [42]. The use of a nominalisation and the omission of an actor can also conceal reasoning errors. The question: 'Did the defendant's failure to warn cause or materially contribute to the perforation of the oesophagus?' is more readily answered in the affirmative than the question: 'Did the defendant's failure to warn cause or materially contribute to him perforating the defendant's oesophagus?'

The first question uses a noun (perforation) instead of the verb (perforate) and expresses no action. Because the perforation follows the failure to warn and the question identifies no action or actor, that question implicitly suggests a connection between the failure to warn and the perforation. But it is merely a temporal or sequential connection between the omission and the injury. When analysed, therefore, the posing of the first question can be of little, if any, assistance in determining whether the defendant by failing to warn of the risk of injury materially contributed to him perforating the oesophagus of the plaintiff.

The second question focuses on the defendant and makes his actions central to the inquiry. Its very statement suggests a negative answer. His omission to warn had nothing to do with him perforating the oesophagus on that particular day, except as one of many events that combined to place him in the theatre that day operating on the plaintiff. For the purpose of legal causation theory, his omission to warn was no more causative of the perforation than were his medical qualifications, no more causative of the plaintiff's injury than the lack of a crane driving certificate was causative of the deceased's injury in *Leask Timber*.

It follows that the learned judges of the Supreme Court and the Court of Appeal erred in finding that there was a causal connection between the defendant's failure to warn and the plaintiff's injury.

The plaintiff also sought to rely on an alternative case that she lost the chance of having the procedure performed without a perforation occurring. However, this is not a case concerned with 'loss of a chance' as that phrase is understood in the many cases that have come before the courts since *Chaplin v Hicks* [44] authoritatively decided that a loss of a chance or opportunity was compensable in damages. No part of the relationship between the plaintiff and the defendant involved her being given the opportunity to seek a higher standard of care or better treatment from another surgeon or an opportunity to have the procedure carried out without perforation of the oesophagus [45]. Her relationship with the defendant gave her a legal right to have her condition examined, diagnosed and treated with reasonable care and skill by the defendant and to be informed and advised by him of any material risk inherent in the proposed procedure. But nothing in that relationship required the defendant to provide opportunities of the kind to which I have just referred. The damage that the plaintiff suffered was physical injury, not loss of a chance or opportunity. That being so, her claim stands or falls according to whether the physical injury that she suffered was causally connected for legal purposes with the defendant's failure to warn.

The appeal must be allowed.

Gummow J:

The facts

The appellant, Dr Chappel, is an ear, nose and throat specialist. On 10 June 1983, the respondent, Mrs Hart, underwent surgery at the hands of Dr Chappel for the removal of a pharyngeal pouch in her oesophagus. During that procedure, her oesophagus was perforated and there ensued an infection known as mediastinitis. This was caused by bacteria present in the oesophagus escaping through the perforation into the mediastinum which is part of the chest cavity. While Mrs Hart appears by November 1984 to have recovered from the perforated oesophagus and mediastinitis, the infection damaged the laryngeal nerve and led to a paralysis of the right vocal cord. This affected the performance by Mrs Hart of her duties in a senior position in the New South Wales Department of School Education. In 1985 she was retired from that position on medical grounds.

The surgical procedure was 'elective' for the respondent in June 1983, although at a later stage the position would have been reached where it could no longer sensibly be deferred. The evidence did not indicate with any precision when Mrs Hart's condition would have reached that stage.

Mrs Hart sued Dr Chappel in the Supreme Court of New South Wales. She pleaded her action in contract and in the tort of negligence. She did not allege that the operation had been performed negligently. Rather, Mrs Hart alleged that on 20 April 1983 she had consulted Dr Chappel for advice concerning medical problems relating to her throat and that, after the receipt of his advice to undergo a surgical procedure, she engaged Dr Chappel to carry out that procedure. The trial judge made findings to that effect.

Mrs Hart pleaded that her agreement with Dr Chappel contained an implied term that he would warn her of all risks associated with the procedure, that he had failed to warn her of those risks and that he caused or allowed to be caused her injuries. Mrs Hart also pleaded that Dr Chappel had been negligent in advising her in relation to the procedure by failing to warn her of any risks associated with its performance. In particular, she alleged that Dr Chappel, before obtaining her consent to the carrying out of the procedure, had failed to warn her of the risks of sustaining the injuries which she in fact sustained. Mrs Hart further alleged that, in consequence of this negligence and breach of contract, she had sustained a perforated oesophagus and consequent paralysis of the right vocal cord. Finally, she contended that she had incurred out-of-pocket expenses and sustained economic loss by reason of her compulsory retirement in 1985.

This Court decided in *Rogers v Whitaker* [46] that a medical practitioner has a duty to warn a patient of a material risk inherent in a proposed procedure or treatment and that:

> . . . a risk is material if, in the circumstances of the particular case, a reasonable person in the patient's position, if warned of the risk, would be likely to attach significance to it or if the medical practitioner is or should reasonably be aware that the particular patient, if warned of the risk, would be likely to attach significance to it.

Mrs Whitaker sued successfully in tort, for negligence. In this Court, there was no challenge to the holding that Mrs Whitaker would not have undergone the surgery had she been advised of the risk of sympathetic ophthalmia. That finding was treated as one going to the establishment of causation.

In the present case, the primary judge held that Dr Chappel had breached the duty to warn of a material risk, which is formulated in the above passage in *Rogers v Whitaker* and which, in the circumstances of the case, Dr Chappel had owed to his patient. Further, the injury resulting from the sequence of the perforation, the infection (mediastinitis), the damage to the laryngeal nerve and the paralysis of the right vocal cord had been, on the evidence, reasonably foreseeable. In this case, unlike *Rogers v Whitaker* itself, the outcome of the appeal turns upon questions of causation and the measure of damages. Damage was the gist of her action in negligence. Breach of the contract entitled Mrs Hart to a verdict and at least nominal damages, but recovery beyond that would have required her to establish an element of causation analogous to that in tort.

The trial judge found that Dr Chappel had reassured Mrs Hart that what was proposed was 'a common operation' and that, whilst he mentioned the risk of perforation as a recognised complication, he did not warn her of the risk of injury to the laryngeal nerve and the consequent risk of partial or total loss of her voice. His Honour accepted Mrs Hart's evidence that if she had been warned of this risk she would not have undergone surgery when she did. It followed that 'but for' the failure of Dr Chappel to warn Mrs Hart she would not have undergone surgery on 10 June 1983 and she would not have sustained the injuries which then ensued from the surgery undergone at that particular time.

However, Dr Chappel challenges the finding against him with respect to causation. In particular, he bases this challenge on the finding by the trial judge that, even if Mrs Hart had elected to defer surgery after receipt of an adequate warning of the risk, sooner or later she would have had the operation. This would have carried the risk of the complication which in fact had come to pass after the surgery performed on 10 June 1983. Mrs Hart's injuries were a random event which could have resulted whenever the surgery was performed. In ground 3A of the Amended Notice of Appeal [50], Dr Chappel contends that damages should have been assessed 'as a loss of a chance rather than as the physical injuries which, in fact, the [r]espondent suffered'.

The analysis of the issues in this Court was confused by a failure properly to distinguish those factors which are relevant to the issue of causation and those that are to be considered in the assessment of damages.

Causation

In Australia, it is settled by the decision of this Court in *March v Stramare (E & MH) Pty Ltd* that the legal concept of causation differs from philosophical and scientific notions of causation. Mason CJ said:

> In philosophy and science, the concept of causation has been developed in the context of explaining phenomena by reference to the relationship between conditions and occurrences. In law, on the other hand, problems of causation arise in the context of ascertaining or apportioning legal responsibility for a given occurrence.

Mason CJ (with whom Toohey J and Gaudron J agreed) also held that, generally speaking, a sufficient causal connection is established if it appears that the plaintiff would not have sustained the injuries complained of had the defendant not been negligent. However, the 'but for' test is not a comprehensive and exclusive criterion, and the results which are yielded by its application properly may be tempered by the making of value judgments and the infusion of policy considerations. So, it may be 'unjust' to hold a defendant legally responsible for an injury which, though it may be traced back to the wrongful conduct of the defendant, was the immediate result of unreasonable action on the part of the plaintiff.

In *Environment Agency (formerly National Rivers Authority) v Empress Car Co (Abertillery) Ltd*, the leading judgment in the House of Lords was given by Lord Hoffmann. His Lordship stressed that whilst 'the notion of causation should not be overcomplicated', it should not 'be oversimplified'. He went on to emphasise that (a) the legal issue is not what caused the result complained of, but did the defendant cause it, and (b) 'common sense' answers to questions of causation will differ according to the purpose for which the question is asked and the rule by which responsibility is being attributed. In particular, 'one cannot give a common sense answer to a question of causation for the purpose of attributing responsibility under some rule without knowing the purpose and scope of the rule'.

Lord Hoffmann illustrated these points [61] by the following discussion of *Stansbie v Troman*:

> A decorator working alone in a house went out to buy wallpaper and left the front door unlocked. He was held liable for the loss caused by a thief who entered while he was away. For the purpose of attributing liability to the thief (eg in a prosecution for theft) the loss was caused by his deliberate act and no one would have said that it was caused by the door being left open. But for the purpose of attributing liability to the decorator, the loss was caused by his negligence because his duty was to take reasonable care to guard against thieves entering.

His Lordship concluded:

> Before answering questions about causation, it is therefore first necessary to identify the scope of the relevant rule. This is not a question of common sense fact; it is a question of law. In *Stansbie v Troman* the law imposed a duty which included having to take precautions against burglars. Therefore breach of that duty caused the loss of the property stolen.

The nature and purpose of a duty with the content established in *Rogers v Whitaker* [64] concern the right of the patient to know of material risks which are involved in undergoing or forgoing certain treatment. This, in turn, arises from the patient's right to decide for himself or herself whether or not to submit to the treatment in question. That choice 'is, in reality, meaningless unless it is made on the basis of relevant information and advice'.

In the present appeal, not only was the damage which Mrs Hart suffered reasonably foreseeable, but the fact that the relevant conjunction of circumstances could occur should have been the subject of any adequate warning and the reason for giving it. It is true that in some cases of a failure to warn by a medical practitioner an application of the 'but for' test without qualification could lead to absurd or unjust results. Such would have been the situation if, for example, instead of suffering damage to her laryngeal nerve, Mrs Hart had been injured through the misapplication of anaesthetic. Whilst it would still be open to conclude that, but for Dr Chappel's failure to warn her of the possibility of damage to her voice, she would not have opted for the operation at that time and would not have been injured by the anaesthetic, the law would not conclude that the failure to warn of the risk of injury to the laryngeal nerve caused the injury resulting from the anaesthetic.

The present appeal is significantly different from the situation described. In Mrs Hart's case, the very risk of which she should have been warned materialised. In his written submissions filed by leave after the hearing of the appeal, Dr Chappel conceded that, if the surgery had been performed at a different time, then '[i]n all likelihood' Mrs Hart 'would not have suffered the random chance of injury'. In addition, the particular risk involved had been the subject of a specific inquiry by Mrs Hart of the medical practitioner who then was engaged by her to perform the surgery. She was a person for whom the potential consequences of damage to her voice were more significant than the 'statistical' risk. Those additional factors combined with the satisfaction of the 'but for' test were sufficient to establish causation in this case.

Here, the injury to Mrs Hart occurred within an area of foreseeable risk. In the absence of evidence that the breach had no effect or that the injury would have occurred even if Dr Chappel had warned her of the risk of injury to the laryngeal nerve and of the consequent risk of partial or total voice loss, the breach of duty will be taken to have caused the injury.

In those circumstances the task of Dr Chappel was to demonstrate some good reason for denying to Mrs Hart recovery in respect of injuries which she would not have sustained at his hands but for his failure adequately to advise her. Dr Chappel founds his case upon the circumstance that injuries of the nature which were sustained by his patient may be caused without negligent performance of the procedure. He joins to that consideration three matters. The first is the circumstance that sooner or later (though it does not appear whether this would have been before Mrs Hart's retirement in August 1985 or, indeed, at any particular time) Mrs Hart would have been obliged to submit to the procedure. The second is the finding by the trial judge that at some future time Mrs Hart would in fact have done so, even after being made adequately aware of the risk. The third is that this later operation would have carried the same risk of injury. Thus, it was said to follow that Mrs Hart had lost no 'real and valuable chance . . . of the risk [of injury] being diminished or avoided'. In support of that conclusion, reliance was placed upon passages in *Sellars v Adelaide Petroleum NL* [68] which deal with lost opportunities or chances to acquire benefits. However, as is emphasised later in these reasons, Mrs Hart did not sue to recover the value of an opportunity or chance lost to her by the act or omission of Dr Chappel.

In this way the submissions for Dr Chappel tended to divert attention from the central issue, namely whether there was adequate reason in logic or policy for refusing to regard the 'but for' test as the cause of the injuries sustained by Mrs Hart, by the allurement of further cogitation upon the subject of 'loss of a chance'.

Once the criterion for assessment of the adequacy of causation has been determined as a matter of law, the question whether the plaintiff has suffered some damage and therefore has a complete cause of action in tort is normally established by evidence which satisfies the civil standard of proof [69]. If causation is not established in this way, then the plaintiff will fail and recover nothing [70].

The difficulties which this standard of proof may present to plaintiffs in certain types of litigation have attracted attention in recent times. In

Snell v Farrell, Sopinka J, who gave the judgment of the Supreme Court of Canada, referred with approval to the treatment of the subject by Professor Fleming. That scholar had written:

> This traditional approach has come increasingly under challenge in dealing with non-traumatic injuries such as man-made diseases linked to dust, deafness, dermatitis, asbestosis, or linked to chemical products like Thalidomide, DES, and Agent Orange. Another group of cases involves medical procedures depriving patients of a chance of survival or cure. It is often difficult to prove medical causation by 'particularistic' evidence, that is direct, anecdotal, non-statistical evidence from the mouth of witnesses.

The result of the application of the traditional criterion of proof may be to deny plaintiffs any recovery in tort. There has been discussion of alternatives to denial of recovery in obedience to the 'more probable than not' civil standard of proof. Writing in 1989, Professor Fleming said of these alternatives:

> One is to lower the conventional standard and accept exposure to the risk of injury instead of actual injury as a compensable event. Another is to limit liability in an amount proportionate to the risk created by each individual agent. Both of these modifications have gained reluctant and by no means universal acceptance by Anglo-American courts.

In *Snell v Farrell*, Sopinka J referred to material suggesting that in the United States the loosening of the criteria for recovery in medical malpractice suits had been followed by the withdrawal of some major insurers from the market [76]. Subsequently, in *Laferrière v Lawson*, the Supreme Court of Canada held that it had not been proved on the balance of probabilities that the failure in 1971 of the defendant to inform his patient that the growth removed by him was cancerous had caused her death in 1978. The evidence was that the patient's chances of survival would not have been greater had she been informed in 1971 of the diagnosis. The Court also held that the theory of liability for loss of a chance was not to be adopted in such a case.

The present appeal does not involve any consideration of whether such means should be adopted to assist recovery by plaintiffs in certain cases. Mrs Hart did not plead that she contracted for the benefit of a chance of avoiding physical harm or damage. She alleged an obligation to warn her of all risks associated with the procedure, and the failure to discharge that obligation. Nor does Mrs Hart submit in tort that the deprivation of the chance of a full recovery should be accepted as the equivalent of or substitute for her physical injury and damage.

To the contrary, it is Dr Chappel who seeks (in ground 3A of the Amended Notice of Appeal) to intrude considerations of risk and chance with the objective of denying recovery to Mrs Hart. I have set out earlier in these reasons the steps by which Dr Chappel seeks to achieve that result. However, this is not a case in which Mrs Hart seeks damages for the loss of an opportunity or chance to acquire or receive a benefit with a value to be ascertained by reference to the degree of probabilities or possibilities. As is explained in *Sellars v Adelaide Petroleum NL*, in Australia this generally is what is involved in the 'loss of a chance' cases. Similarly, in *Athey v Leonati* the Supreme Court of Canada observed:

> The [loss of chance] doctrine suggests that plaintiffs may be compensated where their only loss is the loss of a chance at a favourable opportunity or of a chance of avoiding a detrimental event.

Rather, Mrs Hart claimed damages for the injuries she sustained. To make good her case and to obtain the award of damages she recovered, Mrs Hart was not required to negative the proposition that any later treatment would have been attended with the same or a greater degree of risk.

This is not a case such as *Hotson v East Berkshire Area Health Authority*. There, the facts precluded the adoption of the plaintiff's hypothesis that he would have escaped disability to his hip joint but for the negligence of the defendant in failing to diagnose a fracture and to treat it promptly.

In the present case, the chain of causation appears from the historical facts found to have intervened between the negligent omission of Dr Chappel and the injuries sustained by Mrs Hart. There was no difficulty in demonstrating what would have happened if Dr Chappel had given Mrs Hart the warning required by *Rogers v Whitaker* before the surgical procedure on 10 June 1983 in which her oesophagus was perforated, leading to the development of mediastinitis and the paralysis of her right vocal cord. Mrs Hart would not have undergone that procedure at the hands of Dr Chappel. She would have wanted 'the most experienced person with a record and reputation in the field', such as Professor Benjamin.

Professor Benjamin, a pre-eminent specialist in throat surgery, was called by Mrs Hart. He was asked questions concerned with the incidence of perforation of the oesophagus, followed by the mediastinum infection and then by injury to the laryngeal nerve. It indicates that, had Mrs Hart undergone the same surgical procedure in other circumstances, the cumulative risks which produced her injuries were so unlikely to recur as to border upon the speculative. In chief, the matter was dealt with as follows:

> Q: To your knowledge what was the incidence of perforation of the oesophagus in this type of procedure?
>
> A: Well, I think it is higher than most surgeons would recognise. We have done studies simply by taking an X-ray of every patient who has this operation within an hour of the operation and I would think that, depending upon the experience and care with which the surgery is done, it could occur as often as one in 20 or 30 or 40 operations, but it is usually just an escape of a few

bubbles of air and the patient is asymptomatic. It is very rare indeed for that to then be complicated by what we call mediastinitis. That is a very severe infection.

Q: If there is a full perforation, does mediastinitis always follow?

A: That depends on what a full perforation is. If there is any perforation mediastinitis can follow.

Q: What would be the process, if it be the case, [whereby] the mediastinitis would compromise the laryngeal nerve?

A: There you have me guessing again. It is an abscess, pus formation in a smaller or larger quantity. If there is a delicate nerve in the area one must presume it could undergo some form of damage.

In cross-examination there was the following exchange:

Q: Just, finally, you have given evidence as to this complication of perforation being one in twenty or forty; that is, the complication of perforation at all. Of course, that statistic applies to any perforation whatsoever, most of which, as I understand it, don't lead to any complication of any significance at all. Is that right?

A: That's correct.

Q: Can you give us, likewise, a statistic of this complication arising that does lead to mediastinitis? You say it is very rare. Are you able to translate that in similar terms to the way you have expressed yourself *apropos* the statistic of one in twenty to forty, or not?

A: Could I give my own experience?

Q: Yes?

A: I believe, not having counted it, that I have performed between 100 and 150 operations and have not had a patient with that complication. Nevertheless, I think every practising ear nose and throat surgeon, whether he does this operation or not, is aware of the possibility of perforation and mediastinitis that may follow the operation.

The reference by Professor Benjamin to experience and care in the particular case underlines the significance of several observations by Gonthier J in delivering the majority judgment in the Supreme Court of Canada in *Laferrière v Lawson*. His Lordship said [84] that he was not prepared to conclude that 'particular medical conditions should be treated for purposes of causation as the equivalent of diffuse elements of pure chance, analogous to the non-specific factors of fate or fortune which influence the outcome of a lottery'. He had earlier identified [85] loss of chance cases where the damage can only be understood in probabilistic terms as those where there was no factual context in which to evaluate the likely result other than the realm of 'pure statistical chance', so that 'the pool of factual evidence regarding the various eventualities in the particular case is dry'. Gonthier J concluded:

> I can certainly see no reason to extend such an artificial form of analysis to the medical context where faults of omission or commission must be considered alongside other identifiable causal factors in determining that which has produced the particular result in the form of sickness or death. As far as possible, the court must consider the question of responsibility with the particular facts of the case in mind, as they relate concretely to the fault, causation and actual damage alleged in the case.

In the present case, the obtaining of adequate advice as to the risks involved was a central concern of Mrs Hart in seeking and agreeing to undergo the surgical procedure in question. It would, in the circumstances of the case, be unjust to absolve the medical practitioner from legal responsibility for her injuries by allowing decisive weight to hypothetical and problematic considerations of what could have happened to Mrs Hart at the hands of some other practitioner at some unspecified later date and in conditions of great variability.

Assessment of damages

Once the liability of Dr Chappel was established in contract and in tort, as was properly done, there may have been a question when assessing Mrs Hart's loss of what, if any, reductions arising from the uncertainty of future events properly were to be taken into account.

The principles applicable were laid down in *Malec v JC Hutton Pty Ltd*. In that case, the plaintiff was entitled to be compensated for the near certainty that, as a result of the defendant's negligence between 1975 and 1977, he would suffer from a psychiatric condition and be unemployable for the rest of his life. However, the majority in the Queensland Full Court had found that it was 'likely' that, independently of the defendant's negligence, as a result of the plaintiff's unemployability, he would have developed a similar neurotic condition. This Court held that the Full Court had erred in refusing to award damages for economic loss suffered after May 1982. The case was returned to the Supreme Court to determine if the damages otherwise recoverable should be reduced to provide for the chance that, independently of the negligence of the defendant, the plaintiff would have been placed in a similar position by May 1982. A chance expressed in terms of probability as 'say less than 1 per cent' would properly be disregarded as speculative.

In the present case, it would have been for Dr Chappel to show that Mrs Hart's damages were to be reduced to reflect the possibility, being more than a speculation, that independently of his negligence Mrs Hart would have sustained at some later date the injuries of which she complained. That was not the way in which the case for the appellant was presented. Rather, the attempt was to show a lack of causation and to deny any liability. The submissions by Dr Chappel in a large measure attempt to turn speculative matters, which are relevant, if at all, upon the assessment of damages, to account by disrupting the principles governing causation. In this Court, as in the Court of Appeal, Dr Chappel seeks an order setting aside the verdict for Mrs Hart and its replacement by a judgment in his favour.

In any event, by her Notice of Contention Mrs Hart submits that Dr Chappel would have failed in any attempt at trial to obtain a Malec discount and I agree. The evidence of Professor Benjamin, which is set out earlier in these reasons, and the observations in the Supreme Court of Canada to which I have referred, indicate the serious difficulty that would have arisen in this case in passing from the speculative to the ascertainment of a degree of probability. That consideration serves also to emphasise the strength of Mrs Hart's case on causation.

Conclusion

The appeal should be dismissed with costs.

Kirby J: This is yet another appeal concerned with the difficult topic of causation.

Causation: a complex and controversial problem

Establishing a causal connection between an alleged wrongdoer's conduct or default and the harm complained of is a pre-condition to the legal liability to pay damages. But, as Professor Dieter Giesen has observed, establishing a causal connection between medical negligence and the damage alleged is often the most difficult task for a plaintiff in medical malpractice litigation (as, indeed, in other negligence actions). Judges in common law countries can take only the smallest comfort from the fact that determining what caused an injury, for the purposes of legal liability, is also regarded as a most difficult task by the courts of civil law countries. Like courts of the common law, those courts have searched for principles to provide a 'filter to eliminate those consequences of the defendant's conduct for which he [or she] should not be held liable'. The search sets one on a path of reasoning which is inescapably 'complex, difficult and controversial'. The outcome is a branch of the law which is 'highly discretionary and unpredictable' [96]. Needless to say, this causes dissatisfaction to litigants, anguish for their advisers, uncertainty for judges, agitation amongst commentators and friction between healthcare professionals and their legal counterparts.

There are no easy solutions to these problems. This is apparent from the many cases concerned with causation in the context of medical negligence coming before final and other courts of appeal in England, Canada, the United States of America and Australia.

It is further illustrated by the division of opinions in this case: Gaudron J and Gummow J favouring the dismissal of the appeal; McHugh J and Hayne J being in favour of allowing it. I agree with the remarks of my colleagues that the case is a difficult one involving an unusual chain of events. But, it is not unique. Other cases exist which bear certain similarities [103]. Whilst avoiding the dangers of endless theoretical argument and acknowledging the disputability of a result depending upon the drawing of lines which fix the outer perimeter of legal liability, this Court must endeavour to give guidance in this case as to the approach to be taken when problems of this kind arise in the future, as surely they will.

A patient is not warned and suffers damage

The issues in the appeal were even further refined before this Court.

Mrs Hart's claim against Dr Chappel was limited to a complaint that he had failed to warn her adequately, or at all, of the dangers involved in the operation: specifically, that there was a danger that her voice could be compromised by the complications which, in fact, occurred. A claim that Dr Chappel had conducted the operation negligently, although initially pleaded, was not supported by evidence and was abandoned at the trial.

Although originally strongly contested, Dr Chappel (for the purpose of the appeal) accepted (as the primary judge had found), that when asking about the risks prior to the operation, Mrs Hart had said to him words to the effect: 'I don't want to wind up like Neville Wran'. This remark was taken to be an allusion to a contemporaneous problem which, following operation, the then Premier of New South Wales (Mr NK Wran) had experienced with his voice which had only been partly restored by a teflon injection to his vocal cords. After the subject operation, Mrs Hart came under the care of Professor BN Benjamin. In treating the damaged laryngeal nerve to allow her improved use of the vocal cords he actually injected teflon. However, this procedure left Mrs Hart's voice weak and affected, much as Mr Wran's voice had been. Dr Chappel fought this appeal on the footing that he had failed properly to respond to his patient's inquiry. To that extent he was in breach of his duty to provide information to his patient which this Court's decision in *Rogers v Whitaker* required him to give.

The aetiology of the damage to Mrs Hart's laryngeal nerve was not in doubt. It required the coincidence of three events: (1) the operative tear to the oesophagus; (2) an escape of bacteria from the oesophagus; and (3) consequential impingement of the resulting infection upon the nearby right vocal cord causing paralysis and damage. Each of these preconditions was accepted to be very rare. A tear could occur (according to Professor Benjamin's evidence) once in every 20, 30 or 40 operations. Usually, it resulted in nothing more than the 'escape of a few bubbles of air'. The complication of mediastinitis that occurred in this case was 'very rare indeed'. It had not occurred in the 100 to 150 operations performed by Professor Benjamin. However, it was a recognised possibility. Once a patient asked a question about that possibility, he or she was entitled to have an accurate and candid answer so that the patient could make an informed decision about the surgery. For Mrs Hart, the consequences were important and they were large.

The condition which originally took Mrs Hart to Dr Chappel was 'relentlessly progressive'. Surgery was the 'only relief' for it. Without surgery there would not only be soreness and difficulty in swallowing but the danger that food might become caught in the throat needing emergency attention. It was therefore accepted that, even if Mrs Hart had been warned of the danger of damage to her voice, she would eventually have undergone an operation on her throat. In any such operation the slight risk would exist of the kind that followed Dr Chappel's procedure. Mrs Hart did not dispute this. Dr Chappel conceded that, if the surgery had in fact been postponed and carried out at a different time, '[i]n all likelihood [Mrs Hart] would not have suffered the random chance of injury' to her vocal cord. This represented nothing more than acceptance that such injury was an extremely rare occurrence. It was not even mentioned in some clinical textbooks.

Mrs Hart swore that if she had been told by Dr Chappel of the risks to her voice she would not have gone ahead with the operation by him. She would have sought further advice. She would have wanted the operation performed by the most experienced person available. Professor Benjamin was posited as such a person. The evidence showed that he had performed many more operations of this kind than Dr Chappel had. The primary judge accepted that Mrs Hart was a witness of truth. Her claim must therefore be assessed on the footing that, with the warning that the law required Dr Chappel to give her, she would not have gone ahead with the operation when she did. She would thus not in fact have suffered the damage which ensued.

Dr Chappel contended that, in the foregoing facts, Mrs Hart was not entitled to recovery. The random chance of complications could just as easily have struck during an operation at a later time and place and conducted by a different surgeon. In the absence of proof of negligence in the performance of the operation, his accepted failure to warn Mrs Hart had not caused her damage. Mrs Hart, armed with the decisions below, contended that she had established sufficient facts to demonstrate a causal connection and to retain her damages.

Causation: general legal propositions

To answer the problem presented by the appeal, it is useful to collect a number of propositions, established by authority, relevant to a case such as the present:

1 A practical question: the starting point is to remember the purpose for which causation is being explored. It is a legal purpose for the assignment of liability to one person to pay damages to another. It

is not to engage in philosophical or scientific debate, still less casuistry.

As Windeyer J explained in *The National Insurance Co of New Zealand Ltd v Espagne*:

> Philosophy and science seek the explanation of phenomena and look to relationships and concurrences. Law is not concerned *rerum cognoscere causas*, but with attributing responsibility to persons.

The law allocates responsibility by a process which at once determines the entitlement of the particular plaintiff and sets the standards of conduct that may be expected of other persons in positions analogous to the defendant. The law's concern is entirely practical. 'In the varied web of affairs, the law', said Lord Wright, 'must abstract some consequences as relevant, not perhaps on the grounds of pure logic but simply for practical reasons'. Where a breach of duty and loss are proved, it is natural enough for a court to feel reluctant to send the person harmed (in this case a patient) away empty handed. However, such reluctance must be overcome where legal principle requires it.

It must be so not only out of fairness to the defendant but also because, otherwise, a false standard of liability will be fixed which may have undesirable professional and social consequences.

2 A commonsense approach: causation is essentially a question of fact. It is to be resolved as a matter of commonsense. This means that there is usually a large element of intuition in deciding such questions which may be insusceptible to detailed and analytical justification. As Dixon CJ, Fullagar and Kitto JJ remarked in *Fitzgerald v Penn* 'it is all ultimately a matter of common sense' and '[i]n truth the conception in question [ie, causation] is not susceptible of reduction to a satisfactory formula'. Similarly, in *Alphacell Ltd v Woodward*, Lord Salmon observed that causation is 'essentially a practical question of fact which can best be answered by ordinary common sense rather than by abstract metaphysical theory'. Yet, a losing party has a right to know why it has lost and should not have its objections brushed aside with a reference to 'commonsense', at best an uncertain guide involving 'subjective, unexpressed and undefined extra-legal values varying from one decision-maker to another. Nevertheless, despite its obvious defects, the commonsense test has been embraced by this Court as a reminder that a 'robust and pragmatic approach' to such questions is the one most congenial to the common law.

3 The 'but for' consideration: If, but for the negligent act or omission, the actual damage suffered by a plaintiff would not have occurred, it will often be possible, as a practical matter, to conclude the issue of causation in the plaintiff's favour. Similarly, where the damage would probably have happened anyway, it will often be possible to conclude that the act or omission was not the cause for legal

purposes [120]. In this sense, the 'but for' test, so qualified, remains a relevant criterion for determining whether the breach of duty demonstrated is a cause of the plaintiff's damage. However, it is not the exclusive test. Nor is it sufficient on its own to demonstrate the causal link for legal purposes. It is a mistake to read this Court's cautionary words about the 'but for' test as an expulsion of that notion from consideration where the question of causation is in contest. On the contrary, a sufficient causal connection will, generally speaking, be established if it appears that the plaintiff would not have suffered the damage complained of but for the defendant's breach of duty. The Court has simply added the warning that it is necessary to temper the results thereby produced with 'value judgments' and 'policy considerations'. This qualification has been expressed lest a party, shown to have been in breach of duty, is forever thereafter to be liable for every misfortune that follows in time whatever the breach demonstrated and however irrelevant it may appear to the damage which ensued. As Windeyer J observed in *Faulkner v Keffalinos*:

> But for the first accident, the [plaintiff] might still have been employed by the [defendants], and therefore not where he was when the second accident happened: but lawyers must eschew this kind of 'but for' or *sine qua non* reasoning about cause and consequence.

In an attempt to assist decision-makers in the task of drawing lines and in the assignment of legal responsibility, various phrases have been proffered by generations of judges to mark out a legally relevant cause (such as 'proximate cause', 'legal cause', 'true cause', 'effective cause', 'substantial cause', 'direct cause', 'foreseeable cause' or 'cause in fact'). These phrases, whilst well-intentioned, beg the question that is to be answered. They also carry dangers of their own. So does the attempt to convert the inquiry, as McHugh J has suggested, from the passive to the active voice as if this will solve the quandary of causation. That quandary remains, however it is expressed in verbal formulation.

4 The plaintiff's legal onus: it is elementary to say that it is a precondition to recovery of damages for an established breach of a legal duty that the onus is upon the plaintiff to prove that the breach alleged was the cause of the damage shown. It is important to keep separate the questions of liability and the calculation of damages. Where, as in this case, a plaintiff relies on a claim in contract, proof of breach of that contract will entitle the plaintiff to nominal damages at least. For recovery of compensation beyond nominal damages in contract, the plaintiff must prove that the breach was the cause of the damage. This is as true of a claim based on the tort of negligence as of one framed in contract. In this sense, the legal burden of proving causation is, and remains throughout the proceedings, upon the plaintiff. It is not an insubstantial burden. In

some medical contexts it has even been described as Herculean. In cases similar to the present, it has been characterised as 'the most formidable obstacle confronting health care consumers'. The reasons include the imprecision of, and uncertainty about, some medical conditions; the progressive nature of others; the complexity of modern medical practice and technology; and the fact that some mistakes, serious enough in themselves, have no untoward results which can properly be attributed to them. In the present case, Dr Chappel argued that he fell into the last stated class of exemption. The recognised difficulties of causation for plaintiffs in medical negligence cases have occasionally given rise to legal devices designed to lighten their burdens. Some of these will be mentioned below.

5 Displacing apparent causation: in certain circumstances, the appearance that there is a causal connection between the breach and the damage, arising from the application of the 'but for' test and the proximity of the happening of the damage, has been displaced by a demonstration that:

(a) the happening of the damage was purely coincidental and had no more than a time connection with the breach;
(b) the damage was inevitable and would probably have occurred even without the breach, for example by the natural progression of an undetected, undiagnosed or unrevealed condition, or because the condition presented a life threatening emergency which demanded instant responses without time for the usual warnings and consents;
(c) the event was logically irrelevant to the actual damage which occurred;
(d) the event was the immediate result of unreasonable action on the part of the plaintiff; or
(e) the event was ineffective as a cause of the damage, given that the event which occurred would probably have occurred in the same way even had the breach not happened.

6 Reinforcing the duty to warn: in judging the performance of a health care or other professional, the law does not require perfection. It recognises the variability of professional skills. Even an expert, acting at the highest standards of the profession, may turn in a less than perfect performance on a particular day. However, the requirement to warn patients about the risks of medical procedures is an important one conducive to respect for the integrity of the patient and better health care. In Australia, it is rigorous legal obligation. Its rigour was not challenged in this appeal. It must be accepted that, by establishing the requirement to warn patients of a risk to which they would be likely to attach significance, or of which they should reasonably be aware, the law intends that its obligations be carefully observed. Breaches must be treated seriously. Because in some cases the failure to warn would have no, or no relevant, consequences, proof of a breach will not of itself be sufficient to

establish an entitlement to damages for every harm that thereafter occurs to the patient. To reason in such a way would involve the logical fallacy of *post hoc ergo propter hoc*. The plaintiff's legal obligation to show the causal connection remains throughout the proceedings.

7 Accepting subjective intentions: In considering the suggested consequences of a failure on the part of a medical practitioner to advise a patient about the risks of a particular procedure, courts in Australia have adopted a 'subjective' approach which has regard to what the particular patient's response would have been had proper information been given. A contrary ('objective') approach, having regard to the response of a reasonable person in the patient's situation, was not urged in this case, although it has found favour in Canada and the United States of America. The subjective criterion involves the danger of the 'malleability of the recollection' even of an upright witness. Once a disaster has occurred, it would be rare, at least where litigation has commenced, that a patient would not be persuaded, in his or her own mind, that a failure to warn had significant consequences for undertaking the medical procedure at all (where it was elective) or for postponing it and getting a more experienced surgeon (as in this case). Yet, these dangers should not be over-stated. Tribunals of fact can be trusted to reject absurd, self-interested assertions. Where such a conclusion is reached the case will rarely come before an appellate court. The present appeal must be approached on the footing accepted by the primary judge. This was that, if she had been warned, Mrs Hart would not have had the operation, not have suffered the physical injuries which then ensued and would have sought a more experienced surgeon when the time for operation eventually came.

8 Shifting the evidentiary onus: one means of alleviating the burden cast by law on a plaintiff to establish a causal relationship between the breach and the damage concerns the evidentiary onus. Australian law has not embraced the theory that the legal onus of proof shifts during a trial. Nevertheless, the realistic appreciation of the imprecision and uncertainty of causation in many cases – including those involving alleged medical negligence – has driven courts in this country, as in England, to accept that the evidentiary onus may shift during the hearing.

Once a plaintiff demonstrates that a breach of duty has occurred which is closely followed by damage, a *prima facie* causal connection will have been established. It is then for the defendant to show, by evidence and argument, that the patient should not recover damages. In *McGhee v National Coal Board*, a Scottish appeal, Lord Wilberforce explained why this was so. Although Lord Wilberforce's statement in McGhee has proved controversial in England, it has received support in this Court. Its principle has also been accepted by international experts such as Professor Giesen. I find Lord Wilberforce's exposition compelling:

> [T]he question remains whether a pursuer must necessarily fail if, after he has shown a breach of duty, involving an increase of risk of disease, he cannot positively prove that this increase of risk caused or materially contributed to the disease while his employers cannot positively prove the contrary. In this intermediate case there is an appearance of logic in the view that the pursuer, on whom the onus lies, should fail – a logic which dictated the judgments below. The question is whether we should be satisfied, in factual situations like the present, with this logical approach. In my opinion, there are further considerations of importance. First, it is a sound principle that where a person has, by breach of a duty of care, created a risk, and injury occurs within the area of that risk, the loss should be borne by him unless he shows that it had some other cause. Secondly, from the evidential point of view, one may ask, why should a man who is able to show that his employer should have taken certain precautions, because without them there is a risk, or an added risk, of injury or disease, and who in fact sustains exactly that injury or disease, have to assume the burden of proving more: namely, that it was the addition to the risk, caused by the breach of duty, which caused or materially contributed to the injury? In many cases . . . this is impossible to prove, just because honest medical opinion cannot segregate the causes of an illness between compound causes. And if one asks which of the parties, the workman or the employers, should suffer from this inherent evidential difficulty, the answer as a matter of policy or justice should be that it is the creator of the risk who, *ex hypothesi* must be taken to have foreseen the possibility of damage, who should bear its consequences.

9 Valuing a lost chance: A further way in which, in some circumstances, the difficulties of causation for a plaintiff are alleviated is by treating the plaintiff's loss as a 'loss of a chance'. In cases in which this approach is permissible, it may allow evaluation of the plaintiff's loss in terms of comparing the chances of suffering harm (given the breach which has occurred) against those that would have existed (if the breach is hypothesised away). In *CES v Superclinics (Aust) Pty Ltd* I indicated my attraction to this approach as a more rational and just way of calculating damages caused by established medical negligence. It is clearly laid down by the authority of this Court that, in some circumstances, a plaintiff may recover the value of a loss of a chance caused by a wrongdoer's act or omission. The approach also has some judicial support in the context of medical negligence in England, Canada and the United States. A number of commentators favour this approach because of the failure of orthodox reasoning to do justice to some patients' losses and because it invites a more empirical calculation of loss, with the use of statistics which might offer outcomes that are more accurate and

fair to all concerned. On the other hand, the weight of judicial opinion in England and Canada and some academic writing appears to be critical of the application of the loss of a chance theory to cases of medical negligence. In part this is because, where medical negligence is alleged, 'destiny [has] taken its course', arguably making an analysis by reference to chance inappropriate or unnecessary in the view of the critics of this approach.

Alternatively, the loss of a chance calculation has been criticised on the ground that it would discard commonsense, undermine the plaintiff's onus of proving the case and submit the law to the 'paralysis' of statistical abstractions.

10 Discounting damages: if it is established that damage was caused by the breach alleged, it remains to calculate the amount of compensation recoverable. It is then proper to reduce any damages which a defendant should pay for the harm it has caused to a proper proportion actually attributable to its breach. If, independently of the breach on the part of a defendant, the evidence shows that the plaintiff would have suffered loss, the damages may be reduced by reference to the estimate of the chances that this would have occurred. If those chances are less than 1%, this Court has held that they may properly be disregarded as speculative. Dr Chappel argued that, even if he had given the requisite warning to Mrs Hart, and she had postponed the procedure and later undergone an operation by a more experienced surgeon, there was still the same random chance that she would have suffered the complications that occurred; neither more nor less. Mrs Hart argued that the true comparison was between the loss that had in fact occurred to her and the concededly small risk that such loss would have happened at the postulated postponed operation. She resisted any reduction in her damages, submitting that a chance of injury in a postponed operation was minuscule, ie, 'speculative' in the sense described by this Court.

Conclusion: causation was established

The application of the foregoing principles to the facts of this case, as now established, presents difficult puzzles upon which reasonable minds may differ; as indeed they have. The strongest arguments for Dr Chappel, as it seems to me, are those which lay emphasis upon a logical examination of the consequences which would have flowed had he not breached his duty to warn his patient. Dissecting the facts in that way affords a powerful argument which would banish from consideration the events which in fact occurred in the operation which he carried out. All that would have happened, had he given the requisite warning, would have been a change in the timing of the operation and of the identity of the surgeon. For Dr Chappel, these were irrelevant changes as the evidence showed that, whenever the operation was performed and whoever did it, the tripartite chances which had to combine to produce the misfortune which Mrs Hart suffered were extremely rare. There was thus an equivalence of unlikelihood. They were risks inherent in the procedure, not wholly avoidable even by the most skilful and experienced of surgeons. In the view which Dr Chappel urged of the case, Mrs Hart was left with nothing more than the time sequence. To burden a surgeon, in whose actual performance no fault could be found, with civil liability for randomised chance events that followed the surgery would not be reasonable. It would penalise him for chance alone. It would do nothing to establish a superior standard in the performance of the work of surgeons generally.

For a time I was attracted to Dr Chappel's arguments. Ultimately, I have concluded against them. The 'commonsense' which guides courts in this area of discourse supports Mrs Hart's recovery. So does the setting of standards which uphold the importance of the legal duty that was breached here. This is the duty which all health care professionals in the position of Dr Chappel must observe: the duty of informing patients about risks, answering their questions candidly and respecting their rights, including (where they so choose) to postpone medical procedures and to go elsewhere for treatment.

In *Environment Agency (formerly National Rivers Authority) v Empress Car Co (Abertillery) Ltd*, Lord Hoffmann emphasised that commonsense answers to questions of causation will differ according to the purpose for which the question is asked. The answer depends upon the purpose and scope of the rule by which responsibility is being attributed. In *Rogers v Whitaker*, this Court decided that 'a doctor has a duty to warn a patient of a material risk inherent in the proposed treatment' and that:

> . . . a risk is material if, in the circumstances of the particular case, a reasonable person in the patient's position, if warned of the risk, would be likely to attach significance to it or if the medical practitioner is or should reasonably be aware that the particular patient, if warned of the risk, would be likely to attach significance to it.

These standards have fairly been described as onerous. They are. But they are the law. They are established for good reason. When not complied with (as was held to be so in this case) it should occasion no surprise that legal consequences follow. This was an unusual case where the patient was found to have made very clear her concerns. The practicalities are that, had those concerns been met as the law required, the overwhelming likelihood is that the patient would not, in fact, have been injured. So much was eventually conceded. In such circumstances, commonsense reinforces the attribution of legal liability. It is true to say that the inherent risks of injury from rare and random causes arise in every surgical procedure. A patient, duly warned about such risks, must accept them and their consequences. Mrs Hart was ready to accept any general risks of the operation of which she was warned. However, she declined to bear the risks about which she questioned the surgeon and received no adequate response. When those risks so quickly eventuated, commonsense suggests that something more than a mere coincidence or irrelevant cause has intervened. This impression is reinforced once it is accepted that Mrs Hart, if warned, would not have undergone the operation when she did.

Although no statistical or other evidence was called to demonstrate that recourse to a more experienced surgeon would necessarily have reduced the risk of the kind of injury that occurred (and while some risk was unavoidable), intuition and commonsense suggest that the higher the skill of the surgeon, the less is the risk of any perforation of the oesophagus into the mediastinum. In 100 to 150 operations of this kind, Professor Benjamin had never experienced mediastinitis. Whilst that may indeed be the result of chance and amount to good luck on his part (and on the part of his patients) intuition and commonsense suggest that the greater the skill and more frequent the performance, the less the risk of perforation. And without perforation (already a rare occurrence) the second and third events necessary to produce paralysis of the vocal cords in a patient like Mrs Hart (occurrences even more rare) would not occur. As Gaudron J points out, the nature of the risk would be the same. But the degree of risk would be diminished. This was the view taken by the Court of Appeal. It is a view which involved no error.

Once Mrs Hart showed the breach and the damage which had immediately eventuated, an evidentiary onus lay upon Dr Chappel to displace the inference of causation which thereupon arose. He failed to do so. Nor, in my view, causation being established, did he prove that Mrs Hart would have been exposed to the same, or substantially the same, possibilities of like injury if she had postponed the procedure and had it done by someone more experienced, as was her right. On the contrary, the evidence demonstrated that the chances of her receiving such injury in any other operation were minuscule. For the reasons stated those chances would probably be even smaller in the hands of a surgeon with the experience and skill of Professor Benjamin.

To the complaint that Professor Benjamin (or his equivalent) could not possibly undertake every Dohlman's operation (any more than the most skilful barrister can appear for every client) the answer comes back. This was not an ordinary patient. It was an inquisitive, persistent and anxious one who was found to have asked a particular question to which she received no proper answer. Had a proper answer been given, as the law required, it was found that she would not have undergone the operation at the hands of Dr Chappel when she did. It is virtually certain, then, that she would not have suffered mediastinitis at all. She would not have been injured. She would not have been obliged to bring her case before the courts. She therefore adequately proved causation. Dr Chappel did not displace the inferences to which her evidence gave rise. Nor was it shown that the damages to which she was entitled should be reduced on the footing that they would have occurred in any event.

As to the question of loss of a chance, Dr Chappel, by leave, added a ground of appeal to assert that Mrs Hart's damages should have been assessed in those terms. Mrs Hart resisted the amendment but, in any case, said that it mattered not. At trial, the only claim for damages, which she had asserted, was in respect of the physical injury done to her vocal cords and its sequelae. She neither pleaded, nor sought to prove, a case expressed in terms of a loss of a chance. Accordingly, no evidence was tendered as to the value of that chance. The case is therefore not one in which an entirely new perspective should be adopted at such a late stage. One day loss of a chance in this area of discourse will return to this Court. However, this case must be approached on the footing that the loss suffered by Mrs Hart was that claimed: physical injury and its consequence – nothing more.

Order

The appeal should be dismissed with costs.

Hayne J (dissenting): At trial, the respondent's claim that the appellant conducted the original procedure negligently was not pressed and no evidence was led in support of that claim. The respondent limited her claim to an allegation that the appellant had failed to warn her of the risks of the operation. The primary judge found (and it is not now disputed) that in the course of the consultation with the appellant in May 1983 the respondent told him that 'I don't want to wind up like Neville Wran' – a comment which the respondent described in her evidence as being a 'throw-away line' but which was taken by the primary judge to be a clear indication by the respondent to the appellant of concern for the safety of her voice. It was found that the appellant did warn the respondent that there was a risk of perforating the oesophagus in the course of the procedure but he did not warn her that the operation posed a risk to her voice. The primary judge found (and again this is not now disputed) that in the light of her reference to Neville Wran the risk to the respondent's voice was a material risk of which she should have been warned [170]. The risk was slight but if it was realised, the consequences for the respondent were large.

The central question debated on the hearing of the appeal to this Court was the question of causation. Did the appellant's failure to warn of the risk to the respondent's voice cause all or any part of the loss she claimed?

There are several features of the case which it will be necessary to bear steadily in mind:

1 The appellant's breach of duty was his failure to warn the respondent of the risk to her voice; he performed the procedure concerned without negligence. In particular, to perforate the oesophagus in the course of the procedure, while not intended, was not negligent.

2 The respondent's condition was one which could be treated only by surgery and her condition was one the symptoms of which, it was accepted, were correctly described by Professor Benjamin as being 'relentlessly progressive'.

3 Although perforation of the oesophagus in the course of a procedure like that performed by the appellant on the respondent was not uncommon (according to Professor Benjamin a perforation might occur once in every 20 or 30 or 40 operations) it is very rare for that then to be complicated by infection of the mediastinum (mediastinitis). According to the Professor, the compromise of the recurrent laryngeal nerve, which the respondent suffered, may have been caused by operative trauma, intubation trauma during anaesthesia or spread of infection from the mediastinitis. In his report prepared in May 1994 and tendered in evidence at trial, Professor Benjamin said:

> With respect to the paralysis of the right vocal cord and the cause, it is very difficult to say which is the most likely idiological factor. Vocal cord paralysis during or after an uncomplicated or a complicated endoscopic operation for pharyngeal pouch is very uncommon. However in view of the mediastinitis and the long term nature of the paralysis perhaps it is likely the paralysis was associated with perforation of the oesophagus and mediastinal infection.

4 Because the pharyngeal pouch could be treated only by surgery and because the respondent's symptoms would have grown worse over time, it was accepted that she would have had an operation of the kind she did have at some time.

5 The respondent swore that, if the appellant had told her of the risks to her voice, she would not have had the operation when she did but would have sought further advice because she would have wanted the operation performed by the most experienced person with a record and reputation in the field. (The primary judge accepted the respondent as a witness of truth.) There was some evidence to suggest that the better the surgeon, the less likely was there to be a perforation of the oesophagus.

The elementary proposition that a defendant is liable in negligence only if the damage suffered by the plaintiff was caused by the defendant's negligent act or omission identifies the connection between the defendant's act or omission and the plaintiff's damage as that of causation. As is said in *Bennett v Minister of Community Welfare*:

> In the realm of negligence, causation is essentially a question of fact, to be resolved as a matter of common sense. In resolving that question, the 'but for' test, applied as a negative criterion of causation, has an important role to play but it is not a comprehensive and exclusive test of causation; value judgments and policy considerations necessarily intrude.

The resolution of that question will often find expression in an assertion of its result without any lengthy articulation of reasons. Especially would that be so in a case where policy considerations do not assume prominence in the process.

In this case, however, it is as well to try to identify the process of reasoning that is adopted.

The search for causal connection between damage and negligent act or omission requires consideration of the events that have happened and what would have happened if there had been no negligent act or omission. It is only by comparing these two sets of facts (one actual and one hypothetical) that the influence or effect of the negligent act or omission can be judged.

If the damage of which the plaintiff complains would have happened without the intervention of the negligent behaviour, it will often be possible to conclude that the negligent behaviour was not a cause of that damage. Thus, to take examples cited in Prosser and Keeton on the *Law of Torts*:

- a failure to fence a hole in the ice plays no part in causing the death of runaway horses which could not have been halted if the fence had been there;
- a failure to have a lifeboat ready is not a cause of the death of a person who sinks without trace immediately upon falling into the ocean;
- the omission of crossing signals by an approaching train is of no significance when a car driver runs into the sixty-eighth car in the line.

If, however, the damage of which the plaintiff complains would not have happened without the intervention of the negligent behaviour, it will often be possible to conclude that the negligent behaviour was a cause of that damage. Thus, the plaintiff in *Rogers v Whitaker* would not have had surgery on her blind eye if she had been warned of the risk that the operation posed to her good eye. The negligent failure to warn her of that risk was held to be a cause of her damage.

The 'but for' test is, however, neither a comprehensive nor exclusive test of causation. To take but one example where its application is not conclusive, it does not readily resolve the case where two causes are at work and either of them, alone, would have been sufficient to bring about the result. If two separate fires, negligently lit by separate persons, merge to destroy the plaintiff's home, and each fire would have been sufficient in itself to cause the damage, is each of the fire lighters liable? If the 'but for' test were to be applied to each defendant's conduct separately then neither would be liable. And what if neither fire, by itself, would have destroyed the plaintiff's house?

The 'but for' test is of most use as a negative test. If it is not satisfied, it is unlikely that there is the necessary causal connection. But showing that 'but for' the defendant's conduct, the plaintiff would not have suffered damage does not demonstrate the required degree of connection between the defendant's act or omission and the plaintiff's damage. The application of a 'but for' test does not identify what might be called the 'quality' of the causal connection. No doubt it is with this in mind, that the cases and literature use many different epithets to describe the kind of causation that is necessary – 'proximate cause', 'legal cause' and so on – as opposed to 'causation in fact'. (No doubt also, those epithets will sometimes reflect the value judgments or policy considerations mentioned in cases like *March v Stramare (E & MH) Pty Ltd.*)

The importance of examining the nature of the connection between the negligent conduct and the damage can be demonstrated in this way. If the respondent had not been operated on when she was, but had had her operation on another day, the chances are that she would not have suffered the damage to her laryngeal nerve that she did. There may have been no perforation of the oesophagus, there may have been no infection, there may have been no damage to the nerve. The whole tenor of the evidence given at the trial was that if it was the infection that led to paralysis of the laryngeal nerve (and this was the explanation favoured by Professor Benjamin in his written report) infection was such a rare event that it was unlikely (indeed very unlikely) that it would have happened if the operation had been performed on another day. Of course, the respondent did suffer a perforated oesophagus, she did suffer an infection, she did suffer paralysis of the laryngeal nerve. But if she had not attended the hospital on that day, the probabilities are that none of this would have happened. And if the appellant had told her of the risk to her voice, she would not have had the operation when she did. But precisely the same argument would be open if, instead of suffering damage to her voice, as she has, the operating theatre in which her procedure was performed had been struck by lightning, or a runaway truck, and she had been injured. But for the negligent failure to warn she would not have been in harm's way.

No doubt the case of the lightning strike or the runaway truck invite consideration of *novus actus interveniens* and whether, although 'the earlier wrongful act or omission may have amounted to an essential condition of the occurrence of the ultimate harm, it was not the true cause or a true cause of that harm'. But that is no more than a particular example of the general proposition that the tort of negligence requires a particular kind of causal relationship between the negligent act or omission of the defendant and the damage suffered by the plaintiff.

Being able to say that the damage would not have happened but for the negligent act or omission is not enough. As Windeyer J said in *Faulkner v Keffalinos* (where the plaintiff had been injured in a car accident, and then injured in a separate car accident before the trial):

> The consequences that flow from the second accident cannot I think be regarded as caused, in any relevant sense, by the defendant's tort

> I realise that philosophers and casuists may see these as indirect consequences. But for the first accident, the respondent might still have been employed by the appellants, and therefore not where he was when the second accident happened: but lawyers must eschew this kind of 'but for' or *sine qua non* reasoning about cause and consequence.

In my view, the only connection between the failure to warn and the harm the respondent has suffered is that but for the failure to warn she would not have been in harm's way. The appellant's conduct did not affect whether there would be pathogens present in the respondent's oesophagus when the procedure was carried out; his conduct did not affect whether the pathogens that were present would, in all the circumstances, produce the infection which they did; his conduct did not affect whether that infection would damage the laryngeal nerve as it did. Of course, he manipulated the instrument which perforated the oesophagus but he did so without negligence.

I should mention the recent decision of the House of Lords in *Environment Agency (formerly National Rivers Authority) v Empress Car Co (Abertillery) Ltd.* Lord Hoffmann, who gave the leading speech, said that:

> . . . common sense answers to questions of causation will differ according to the purpose for which the question is asked,

and that:

> . . . one cannot give a commonsense answer to a question of causation for the purpose of attributing responsibility under some rule without knowing the purpose and scope of that rule.

So much may be accepted. But consideration of the purposes of asking about causation in a case like the present should not be permitted to obscure the fact that the search is for a relationship between the negligent act or omission of one party and the damage which the other party alleges has been sustained.

The law of negligence may be seen as directed to several purposes but purposes of compensating the injured and promoting reasonable conduct are prominent among them. In this particular area of negligent advice by a medical practitioner it is important to bear in mind 'the paramount consideration that a person is entitled to make his own decisions about his life'.

With these purposes in mind, it may be suggested that a sufficient causal relationship is established by showing that the subject-matter of the negligent conduct – a failure to warn of risk to the voice – is the very subject-matter of the damage. But that connection is not enough. If it were enough, it would follow that if the operating theatre had been struck by lightning and the respondent had suffered damage to the laryngeal nerve (because of the resulting power surge affecting the diathermy equipment being used in the operation) the appellant would be liable but that he would not if the power surge caused burns to her body. Similarly, it would mean that the appellant would be liable if the respondent's voice were damaged as a result of an infection stemming from some failure of the hospital to sterilise, properly, instruments or other items used in the procedure.

No doubt the fact that what I have called the subject-matter of the negligent conduct and the subject-matter of the damage are the same is important to that intuitive process of analysis that is referred to when it is said that questions of causation are questions of fact to be resolved as a matter of commonsense. But important as this consideration is, it is not determinative.

Nor is it enough to say that a purpose of this area of the law is to promote reasonable conduct by medical practitioners and, particularly, the giving of advice necessary to enable people to make their own decisions about their lives. Enlarging the circumstances in which damages will be awarded if there has been a negligent failure by a medical practitioner to advise a patient of risks may well tend to promote the giving of fuller advice. So too may the imposition of a penalty for failing to give proper advice. But the ambit of the liability is not to be decided only according to whether enlarging that ambit will promote careful conduct. The question of causation must still be answered. What is the connection between the negligent act or omission and the damage sustained?

The difficulty in the analysis that looks only to whether the subject-matter of the negligent conduct (failure to warn of risk to voice) and the damage suffered (damage to the voice) are the same is that it does not pay sufficient heed to the comparison that the law requires between the facts of what happened and the hypothetical facts of what would have happened if there had been no negligent act or omission.

It was accepted in this case that, if the respondent had been given proper advice of the risks of the operation, she would, nevertheless, have had the operation which she did. She would have had it at a different time and may have had it performed by a different doctor but she would have had it done. Until she had the operation, she would have continued to suffer the discomforts and dangers that she was suffering when she consulted the appellant – persistent sore throat, difficulty in swallowing, a constant danger of food being caught in her throat. But the hypothetical situation that was to be considered was one in which the respondent had the operation in any event.

If she had had the operation at some later time and if she had engaged the appellant to perform it, the risk of her suffering the consequences to her voice that in fact befell her would, for all practical purposes, have been the same. If she had been given proper advice, even if she would have then deferred the operation, that would not have altered the risk that her voice would be affected (any more than it would have affected the risk that the operating theatre would be struck by lightning).

If, on being given proper advice, she would have deferred the operation, I would conclude that the respondent did suffer damage and would suffer damage because she did not defer the operation. But the damage she would suffer in those circumstances would not be the damage to her voice – it would be the loss of the period for which she would have deferred the operation and have had her voice and her job, subject nevertheless to the continuing disabilities of her untreated condition. Thus, if, because of the failure to warn, she had the operation (say) two years earlier than she otherwise would have had it and if the damage to her voice thus occurred two years earlier than it might have occurred in a later operation, she would have lost two years of employment and attendant enjoyment of life, discounted to take account of the disabilities she would have suffered during that period of two years. But the damage to her voice would not be caused by the failure to warn.

The respondent's claim focused upon the damage to her voice. The evidence that was led, and the arguments that were advanced on her behalf, were all directed to showing that the appellant's failure to warn caused the respondent the physical damage which she had suffered (the damage to the laryngeal nerve with consequent effects on her voice) and the economic consequences that were said to follow from that damage. No evidence was led to suggest that the respondent, if advised of the risks to her voice, would have deferred the operation for any significant period. She said that she would have sought 'a second opinion . . . perhaps several opinions' and no doubt this would have taken time but it was not suggested that she would then have put off the operation for some months let alone years. Thus no factual foundation was laid for a claim based upon delaying the operation.

It will be seen that the comparison I have drawn is between the times at which she would have confronted the risk about which she should have been warned. It is not a comparison that involves any prediction of whether that risk would have occurred if the operation had been deferred. That is because the operation has risks even if reasonable care is exercised; those risks cannot be eliminated by the exercise of reasonable care. It was not alleged in this case that the appellant performed the procedure negligently. That is, it was not alleged that the risk which the respondent faced in undergoing this operation could be eliminated if the surgeon was careful. This is not to deny that professional performance varies: that some surgeons are better than others. But the law is not concerned to do more than enforce standards of reasonable care. The respondent could ask no more than that the doctor she engaged to perform this procedure should exercise reasonable care in doing so, and the appellant did just that.

There was evidence that if she had been properly advised of the risks to her voice, the respondent would not have had the procedure performed by the appellant, but by another doctor. There was, as I have said, some evidence which suggested that the better the doctor, the less the chance of perforation of the oesophagus. That evidence was, at best, exiguous and stopped far short of identifying any sound basis for assessing what effect the surgeon's skills may have had on the unusual chain of events which happened in this case. Nevertheless, it was submitted that the evidence permitted the conclusion that the appellant's failure to give a proper warning of the risks deprived the respondent of a chance to seek better treatment, or exposed the respondent to a greater risk of injury than she faced in undergoing the procedure at the hands of the appellant.

I deal first with the contention that the failure to warn deprived the respondent of a chance to seek better treatment.

I do not think it necessary or appropriate to analyse this case as one of loss of a chance. There are several reasons why that is so.

First, the case was not put in this way at trial. The damage which the respondent alleged that she had suffered was the physical damage to her voice and the economic consequences of that damage. She did not seek to make any loss of chance case at trial.

Secondly, the chance which it is now said that the respondent lost is the chance to engage a better doctor. She said in evidence that she 'would have wanted the most experienced person, with a record and reputation in the field'. But it was never part of the respondent's case that the appellant should have told her to seek a better doctor; it was never suggested that there had been some negligent failure by the appellant to refer the respondent to another doctor. Moreover, it is important to bear steadily in mind that it was not said that the appellant had performed the procedure negligently. Thus it was never suggested that she was deprived of the opportunity to have the procedure performed properly – only that had she been advised of the risks to her voice she (of her own volition) would have sought out the 'most experienced' practitioner in the field.

I do not consider that the appellant should be held responsible for the loss of that chance. No doubt it may be said that the failure to warn led to this result – in the sense that 'but for' the negligent failure to advise, the respondent would have pursued the course that she described in her evidence – but why should the law provide for compensation for loss of that chance and what is it that she lost?

The law of negligence is intended to compensate those who are injured as a result of departures from standards of reasonable care. It is not intended to compensate those who have received reasonable care but who may not have had the best available care. To hold that the appellant's failure to warn the respondent of the risks of the operation caused her to lose the chance of the best available care would depart from that fundamental premise of the law of negligence.

Further, what is it that is lost when it is said that the respondent lost a chance of better treatment? It is said that by going to the best doctor in the field she could have reduced the chance of an adverse outcome of the operation. She could not, however, have eliminated those risks. How then is this alteration in the size of the risks to be measured and how is the loss of it to be compensated?

Leaving aside whatever may have been the difficulty of assembling evidence that bore upon the point (and those difficulties may have been very large) what kind of enquiry would have to be undertaken? Presumably the comparison to be made would be a comparison between the risks if the procedure was carried out by the appellant and the risks if the best available doctor carried it out. But how would that be measured? Any observer of skilled professionals at work knows that some are better than others but it is equally obvious that the performance of even the best is subject to variation. Is the comparison to be made a comparison with the best performer doing his or her best work? But how is that to be demonstrated? It is often enough difficult to identify what reasonable care requires; proof of what would be the best available care would be harder. And why should the law of negligence concern itself with more than what reasonable conduct would require?

Further, the risks of which we are speaking are risks that are very small. If the risk of disaster is assessed as being (say) 1 in 100 if the procedure is performed by the appellant but 1 in 200 if performed by another, what use is to be made of that data? If we are to speak in the language of loss of chance, has the respondent lost the chance of a 99.5% chance of successful operation in return for a 99% chance? Has she, that is, lost a 0.5% chance of success? What is that worth? (The point is all the sharper if the comparison is between a 1 in 10,000 and a 1 in 20,000 chance.) Or is the relevant conclusion that the chances of disaster could have been halved?

Whichever description of the change in the risks is adopted, how does one assess the value of the chance that has been lost? It was suggested in the course of argument that it is reflected in the assessment of damages by discounting the damages otherwise allowed. But that invites attention to what are those damages that are to be discounted – is it, as the argument appeared to assume, the damages attributable to the physical consequences which the respondent suffered? That could be so only if the physical consequences which the respondent suffered were caused by the appellant's negligence.

All of these considerations point to the conclusion that the loss of chance analysis is flawed and should not be adopted. I therefore need not (and do not) express any view on the difficult questions that arise where a plaintiff claims damages for negligence, as opposed to contract, and contends that the damage suffered is the loss of a chance.

Much, if not all, of what I have said about the contention that the respondent lost a chance of better treatment applies equally to the mirror contention that she was exposed to greater risk.

I agree with McHugh J that there is insufficient evidence in this case to say, on the balance of probabilities, that the appellant's failure to warn exposed the respondent to greater risk of injury. The respondent would have had the operation at some time. The operation has risks even if performed by the most skilled surgeon available. There was very little evidence on the difference between the risk of injury actually faced by the respondent and the risk that she would have faced had the operation been performed by, say, Professor Benjamin.

I do not need to deal separately with the respondent's claim in contract. If the appellant's failure to warn the respondent of the risks of the operation was a breach of contract, for the reasons I have given earlier, I do not consider that that breach caused damage to her voice or caused her to lose a chance of better treatment or exposed her to greater risk.

I have said that the resolution of the question of causation will often be asserted without lengthy articulation of reasons. Since it is a question of fact resolved as a matter of commonsense and experience, the conclusion is often reached intuitively. The description of the steps involved in that kind of process is difficult and is apt to mislead. Articulating the reasoning will sometimes appear to give undue emphasis to particular considerations. No doubt if policy and value judgments are made, they should be identified. But the lengthy analysis which I have made should not be taken as intending to state any qualification upon the generality of the propositions recognised in cases like *March v Stramare (E & MH) Pty Ltd*. Causation is a question of fact to be resolved as a matter of commonsense. I have made the extended analysis which I have in order to draw out the various considerations which I consider bear upon the resolution of a difficult and unusual case, not because I consider that a trial judge should be expected (except, perhaps, in the most unusual case) to do more than record the conclusion that he or she reaches about whether the plaintiff's damage was caused by the defendant's negligence.

The respondent did not establish that she had suffered damage as a result of the appellant's negligence. The claim having been framed in breach of contract and breach having been established, she is, of course, entitled to nominal damages but, in my view, to no more. I would allow the appeal.

The Law on causation has been significantly changed by the Civil Liability Act (see below).

PART IV THE CIVIL LIABILITY ACTS – EVERYTHING OLD IS NEW AGAIN

Enactment of Civil Liability Acts in most States of Australia has altered the law. The major parts of those Acts as they affect medical practice are outlined below. For ease of reference, Queensland law is chosen as the paradigm example, though reference to other States' Acts is also made. Prior to a discussion of the wording of the various sections of the Civil Liability Acts, sections from the Ipp Report which informed the process of change, are extracted.

(a) Duty of care – general principles

For a good overview of the effect of the Civil Liability Acts on the concept of 'duty of care' see Dietrich, J. 'Duty of Care Under the Civil Liability Acts' (2005) **Tort Law Journal** 17. Dietrich's commentary is broad ranging and not limited to doctor-patient interactions.

(b) Causation

The Civil Liability Act deals has altered the troubled issue of causation. The background to the issue is canvassed by the Ipp report:

Panel of Eminent Persons to Review the Law of Negligence Review of the Law of Negligence, AGPS, Canberra, October 2002, paragraphs 3.19–3.43

Causation and remoteness of damage

3.1 A person cannot be liable for damages for failure to take care to prevent personal injury or death unless negligent conduct on his or her part (whether act or omission) caused the harm, and unless that harm was not too 'remote' from the negligent conduct. The current law in Australia (as laid down by the High Court) appears to be that whether negligent conduct caused the harm in question is to be answered by the application of 'commonsense'. A problem with this approach is that it gives courts and parties to negligence claims very little guidance about when negligent conduct will be considered to have caused harm.

The two-pronged test of causation: factual causation

The basic rule

3.2 Despite this appeal to commonsense, it is accepted that causation has two aspects. The first – the factual aspect – is concerned with whether the negligent conduct in question played a part in bringing about the harm that is the subject of the claim. The long-accepted basic test for answering this question is whether the conduct was a necessary condition of the harm, in the sense that the harm would not have occurred but for the conduct. In one case, for example, it was held that a hospital that had turned away a patient who had been poisoned was not liable for negligent failure to treat him because even if he had been treated, he would have died anyway. Although there are some cases with which the 'but for' test does not deal satisfactorily (involving 'causal over-determination' of harm – that is, harm that is attributable to more than one sufficient condition), the law has devised rules for resolving such cases in ways that are generally considered to be satisfactory and fair. We therefore make no recommendations on this aspect of the law.

Evidentiary gaps

3.3 However, there are several issues that have arisen in this context that are currently the cause of considerable controversy. One is the problem of what have been called 'evidentiary gaps'.[1] The cases identify two types of situation in which an evidentiary gap may exist.

3.4 One involves harm which is brought about by the cumulative operation of two or more factors, but which is indivisible in the sense that it is not possible to determine the relative contribution of the various factors to the total harm suffered. This was the situation in the English case of *Bonnington Castings v Wardlaw*,[2] which lays down the principle that any of the contributory factors can be treated as a cause of the total harm suffered, provided it made a 'material contribution' to the harm. The effect of this rule is that a defendant may be liable for the total harm suffered by a plaintiff even though it cannot be said that, but for the conduct of the defendant, the plaintiff would not have suffered the total harm; and that it can only be said that but for the conduct of the defendant the plaintiff would not have suffered some of that harm.

3.5 It should be noted that the term 'material contribution to harm' is often used not in the sense in which it was used in *Bonnington Castings v Wardlaw*, but merely to express the idea that a person whose negligent conduct was a necessary condition of harm may be held liable for that harm even though some other person's conduct was also a necessary condition of that harm. In this sense, both joint and concurrent tortfeasors materially contribute to the harm resulting from their respective conduct.

3.6 A recent illustration of the second type of case in which an evidentiary gap may exist is provided by the decision of the English House of Lords in *Fairchild v Glenhaven Funeral Services Ltd* [2002] 3 WLR 89. The plaintiffs contracted mesothelioma as a result of successive periods of exposure to asbestos while working for different employers. The scientific evidence about the aetiology of mesothelioma did not justify a conclusion, in relation to any of the plaintiffs' employers, that but for the negligence of that employer, the plaintiffs would not have contracted the disease. The court held that in such a case, proof (on the balance of probabilities) that the defendant's negligent conduct 'materially increased the risk' that the plaintiffs would contract mesothelioma, would suffice to establish a causal connection between the conduct and the harm. The status of this principle in Australian law is unclear.[3] The High Court has not yet had a chance to consider it.

1 The Panel's consideration of and recommendations about causation have been greatly assisted by the work of Jane Stapleton, especially 'Causation and the Scope of Liability for Consequences' (2003) 119 *LQR* (forthcoming).

2 [1956] AC 613.

3 In *Bendix Mintex Pty Ltd v Barnes* (1997) 42 NSWLR 307, Mason P seems to have rejected it, but Stein J apparently accepted it.

3.7 The 'material contribution to harm' and 'material contribution to risk' principles both allow negligent conduct to be treated as a factual cause of harm even though it cannot be proved on the balance of probabilities that there was in fact a causal link between the conduct and the harm. In other words, in certain circumstances, it may be appropriate to 'bridge the evidentiary gap' by allowing proof that negligent conduct materially contributed to harm or the risk of harm to satisfy the requirement of proof of factual causation.

3.8 The Panel's opinion is that, in certain types of cases, bridging the evidentiary gap in this way would be widely considered to be fair and reasonable. The decisions in *Bonnington Castings and Fairchild* support this conclusion, as does the practice of the New South Wales Dust Diseases Tribunal which, apparently, has felt itself able to deal with such cases by taking a 'robust and pragmatic' approach to factual causation in cases where the scientific evidence about causation has not provided a solid basis for finding that the 'but for' test has been satisfied.[4]

3.9 The major difficulty with the 'material contribution to harm' and 'material contribution to risk' approaches is to define those cases in which the normal requirements of proof of causation should be relaxed. It is extremely important to note that this is a normative issue[5] that depends ultimately on a value judgment about how the costs of injuries and death should be allocated. The Panel believes that detailed criteria for determining this issue should be left for common law development. Nevertheless, we consider that it would be useful to make explicit the normative character of the issue by including in the Proposed Act a provision that, in deciding whether proof that conduct that materially contributed to, or materially increased the risk of, harm should suffice as proof of causal connection, it is relevant to consider whether (and why) responsibility for the harm should be imposed on the negligent party, and whether (and why) the harm should be left to lie where it fell (that is, on the plaintiff) (see paragraph (f) of Recommendation 29).

3.10 Another way in which it has sometimes been suggested that the problem of evidentiary gaps might be dealt with is by shifting the onus of proof on the issue of factual causation from the plaintiff to the defendant once the plaintiff has established that the defendant was under a duty to take reasonable care to avoid the risk in question and failed to take the required care. In the Panel's opinion, this approach is undesirable because it does not squarely address the issue of the evidentiary gap but rather hides it. This is because in practice, the onus of proof that is shifted to the defendant will be impossible to discharge precisely because there is an evidentiary gap. For this reason, the Panel

4 See, e.g. the judgment of O'Meally J in *McDonald v State Rail Authority* (1998) 16 NSWCCR 695, esp 714–717.

5 It should be noted that this is a different normative issue from that discussed in paragraph 7.41. It should also be noted the normative issue being discussed here arises in the context of factual causation.

believes that it would be valuable to state legislatively that the onus of proof of any fact relevant to causation always rests on the plaintiff.

3.11 The Panel believes that this recommendation has a wider significance. In *Bennett v Minister for Community Welfare* (1992) 176 CLR 408, 420–421 Gaudron J said:

> . . . generally speaking, if an injury occurs within an area of foreseeable risk, then, in the absence of evidence that the breach had no effect or that the injury would have occurred even if the duty had been performed, it will be taken that the breach of the common law duty of care caused or materially contributed to the injury.[6]

3.12 The effect of this approach is to cast the onus of proof on the issue of causation onto the defendant, once it has been established that the defendant owed the plaintiff a duty of care and breached that duty, and that the plaintiff has suffered a foreseeable injury. This principle, which has been referred to with approval by various courts in recent cases, represents a fundamental change in the traditional law about causation and proof of causation, and has the potential significantly to expand liability for negligence. The objection to the principle is that it applies regardless of whether there is an evidentiary gap, and without requiring consideration of whether there is any good reason (over and above the existence of duty, breach and damage) to relieve the plaintiff of the requirement to prove factual causation. A legislative restatement of the basic rule that the onus of proof of any fact relevant to causation always rests on the plaintiff may discourage courts from adopting this approach. This will promote the objectives of the Terms of Reference.

Cases in which causal link depends on the plaintiff's hypothetical reaction

3.13 A second issue[7] that needs to be considered in this context concerns situations in which the question, of whether the harm would have occurred but for the negligent conduct, cannot be answered without

6 Cited with approval in *Rosenberg v Percival* (2001) 205 CLR 434, 461 per Gummow J; *Chappel v Hart* (1998) 195 CLR 232, 240 per Gaudron J, 257, per Gummow J, 273, per Kirby J; *Naxakis v Western General Hospital* (1999) 197 CLR 269, 279 per Gaudron J.

7 This was one of the three issues raised in paragraph 3.85. Another issue raised there was 'the proper basis of assessment of damages in cases of breach of a duty to inform' by a medical practitioner. Suppose that a surgeon negligently fails to warn a patient of a risk of harm inherent in an operation, that the patient would not have had the operation if the warning had been given, and that the risk materialises despite the exercise of all reasonable care by the surgeon in performing the operation. The possibility we had in mind was that damages in such a case might be assessed, not by reference to the physical harm suffered by the plaintiff, but rather by reference to the impairment of the plaintiff's decision-making autonomy as a result of the negligent failure to warn. Having given this matter further consideration (concerning the Panel's timetable of work see paragraphs 1.44–1.46), our view is that the proper basis for assessment of damages in such cases is the harm suffered. As this is the position under the current law, we make no recommendation on this topic.

asking a further question about what the plaintiff would have done if the defendant had not been negligent.[8] Suppose, for example, that an employer unreasonably fails to provide its employee with a particular safety device that would have prevented the harm suffered by the plaintiff if it had been used. Suppose further, however, that the employer alleges that even if it had been provided, the employee would not have used it. Or take as another example the leading Australian case of *Chappel v Hart* (1998) 195 CLR 232, in which it was held that a doctor had failed to fulfil the reactive duty to inform a patient of an inherent risk of a surgical operation which materialised, thus harming the patient. The plaintiff alleged that she would not have had the operation, at the hands of the defendant or at the time it was performed, and hence would almost certainly not have suffered harm, if she had been warned of the risk.

3.14 In both of these cases, the question of what the plaintiff would have done if the defendant had not behaved negligently could be decided either 'subjectively' or 'objectively'. The subjective approach depends on asking what the plaintiff would actually have done if the defendant had not been negligent, whereas the objective approach depends on asking what the reasonable person in the plaintiff's position would have done if the defendant had not been negligent. A serious problem that affects the subjective approach is that, once the harm has been suffered, it is unrealistic to expect the plaintiff to testify that he or she would have had the operation (or not used the safety device) even if he or she had been given the relevant information. The objective test overcomes this problem. But in the medical context, at least, it is open to several serious objections. First, it might be thought to put too little weight on the patient's interest in making decisions about his or her own health. Secondly, it threatens to undermine the reactive duty to inform. That duty requires the doctor to give the patient information that the doctor knows or ought to know the patient wants, regardless of whether the reasonable patient would want the information. If the doctor fails to give such information, it would seem inconsistent to answer the question, of how the patient would have acted if the information had been given, on the basis that the patient was a reasonable person. Rather, the question to be asked is what that patient would have done if the information had been given. Thirdly, the objective test provides an answer to the non-causal question, 'what should have happened', not the causal question, 'what would have happened', if the defendant had not been negligent.

3.15 Australian law currently adopts the subjective approach, whereas in medical negligence cases (but not in other cases), Canadian law adopts a version of the objective approach under which the question to be answered is not simply what a reasonable person would have done, but rather, what the reasonable person in the plaintiff's position and

8 The same issue arises where the question is what a third party would have done if the defendant had not been negligent.

with the plaintiff's beliefs and fears would have done. A problem with this approach is that it may require an answer to the nonsensical question of what a reasonable person with unreasonable views would have done.

3.16 Our view is that the arguments against the objective test are much stronger than those in its favour, and that Australian law is right to adopt the subjective test. On the other hand, the Panel is also of the view that the question of what the plaintiff would have done if the defendant had not been negligent should be decided on the basis of the circumstances of the case and without regard to the plaintiff's own testimony about what they would have done. The enormous difficulty of counteracting hindsight bias in this context undermines the value of such testimony. In practice, the judge's view of the plaintiff's credibility is likely to be determinative, regardless of relevant circumstantial evidence. As a result, such decisions tend to be very difficult to challenge successfully on appeal. We therefore recommend that in determining causation, any statement by the plaintiff about what they would have done if the negligence had not occurred should be inadmissible.[9]

The two-pronged test of causation: liability for consequences

3.17 As we have noted, the first aspect of the causation issue concerns the factual question of whether the allegedly negligent conduct played a part in bringing about the harm in question, in the sense that it was a necessary condition of the occurrence of the harm. Answering this question positively is not enough to justify the imposition of liability for negligence because every event has an infinite number of necessary conditions, and there is an important sense in which all necessary conditions are of equal salience in explaining how the harm came about. But the ultimate question to be answered in relation to a negligence claim is not the factual one of whether the allegedly negligent conduct played a part in bringing about the harm, but rather a normative one[10] about whether the defendant ought to be held liable to pay damages for that harm. In other words, the question is: should the defendant be held liable for any of the harmful consequences of the negligence and if so, for which? These questions can be said to concern the appropriate 'scope of liability' for the consequences of negligence.

3.18 It is the Panel's considered opinion that at least some of the confusion and uncertainty in this area of the law is a result of failure to distinguish clearly between the factual question, of whether the negligence was a necessary condition of the harm, and the normative

9 This recommendation could be extended to cover any case in which the issue of causation depends on what a person – whether the plaintiff or a third party – would have done if the defendant had not been negligent.

10 It should be noted that this is a different normative issue from that discussed in paragraph 7.33.

question about which consequences of the negligence the defendant should be held liable for. A danger here is that a finding that the negligent conduct was a necessary condition of the harm may, by itself, be thought to justify a conclusion that the defendant ought to be held liable for the consequences of the negligence. The point is not that imposition of liability may not be justified, but only that a finding that the negligence was a necessary condition of the harm is not, by itself, sufficient to support that conclusion, because there is an infinite number of necessary conditions of every event. For this reason, the Panel recommends a legislative statement to the effect that the issue of causation has two elements – factual causation and scope of liability – both of which need to be addressed.

3.19 It is in the context of the second element – namely scope of liability for consequences – that the statement that causation is a matter of commonsense is most often made. However, courts use various other terms and phrases to describe the sort of connection between negligent conduct and harm that can justify the imposition of legal liability to pay damages. These include ‘real cause’ and ‘effective cause’. It is also said that if another necessary condition ‘intervenes’ between the defendant’s conduct and the harm and ‘breaks the chain of causation’, the defendant will not be liable for the harm.

3.20 The concept of foreseeability is used in this context as well. A basic rule of negligence law is that a negligent person will not be held liable for unforeseeable consequences of their negligence (although there are important qualifications to this rule – such as the principle that the victim of negligently-caused harm must be ‘taken as found’ – that need not be discussed in detail here). A point that should be noted is that the rule laid down in the Shirt case (discussed in paragraph 7.12 above), that a person cannot be liable for failing to take precautions against a far-fetched or fanciful (albeit foreseeable) risk of harm, does not apply in this context. Once a person is held to have behaved negligently, they can, in theory at least, be held liable for foreseeable consequences of that negligence, even if they were of a very low probability.

3.21 None of these terms and phrases provides very much guidance as to the likely outcome of individual cases, and the question of ‘the scope of liability for consequences’ tends to be seen as one that has to be answered case-by-case rather than by the application of detailed rules or principles. This is not to say that there are no relevant guidelines in the law. For instance, it is said that a person is not liable for ‘coincidental’ consequences of their negligence. Suppose that a driver negligently injures a pedestrian, who is further injured when the ambulance in which she is being taken to hospital is involved in a collision as a result of negligence on the part of the ambulance driver. The first driver would not be held liable for the injury resulting from the second accident, because the sequence of events would be considered a ‘coincidence’, even though the first driver’s negligence was a necessary condition of the harm suffered in the second accident. On the basis of this example, it is easy to see the appeal of the 'coincidence principle' as an outworking of ideas about personal responsibility.

3.22 However, this principle of 'no liability for coincidences' is not of universal application. For instance, in *Chappel v Hart*, the failure of the defendant to warn the plaintiff was accepted to have been a necessary condition of the materialisation of the risk because the plaintiff would not have had the operation, at the defendant's hands or when it was performed, if she had been warned; and in that case she would almost certainly not have suffered the harm. But the fact that the risk materialised despite the exercise of reasonable care by the defendant could be called a coincidence. The best explanation of the difference between this case and the example discussed in paragraph 7.45 is not that the doctor caused the patient's harm whereas the first negligent driver did not cause the harm suffered in the second accident. Rather, the explanation would seem to lie in differing ideas about the responsibilities of doctors to their patients on the one hand, and the responsibilities of drivers to pedestrians on the other. In *Chappel v Hart*, several of the judges made this point by saying that the doctor should be liable because the risk that materialised was precisely the risk about which (in discharge of the reactive duty) he should have warned the patient.

3.23 For present purposes, the important point is that there appears to be a perception amongst various groups that courts are too willing to impose liability for consequences that are only 'remotely' connected with the defendant's conduct. In other words, there is a feeling that the net of responsibility for the consequences of negligence is being cast too widely. The question that confronts the Panel is whether there is anything that we can usefully propose by way of legislative statement that might reduce the element of uncertainty in the law and indicate to courts that issues of responsibility are directly relevant in this context.

3.24 A major difficulty here is to strike a balance between making legislative statements that are so abstract and general as to be more or less useless, and making detailed provision that denies courts the flexibility they need to deal with the infinitely various facts of individual cases. What is needed is a provision that will suggest to courts a suitable framework in which to resolve individual cases. Terms and phrases such as 'effective cause', 'foreseeability' and 'commonsense causation' do not provide such a framework because they express a conclusion without explaining how that conclusion was reached. They discourage explicit consideration and articulation of reasons, for imposing or not imposing liability for the consequences of negligence, that are securely grounded in the circumstances of individual cases and address issues of personal responsibility.

3.25 The Panel believes that it is possible to give some helpful legislative guidance that holds out a reasonable prospect of furthering the objectives of the Terms of Reference. Such a provision would be to the effect that in determining liability for the harmful consequences of negligence (whether in such terms or in terms of 'legal cause', 'effective cause', 'commonsense causation', 'foreseeability', 'remoteness of damage' and so on), it is relevant to consider, (a) whether (and why) responsibility for the harm should be imposed on the negligent party, and (b) whether (and why) the harm should be left to lie where it fell.

Section 11 of the Queensland Act states that a decision that a breach of duty caused harm comprises two elements:

- that the breach of duty is a necessary condition of the occurrence of the harm; and
- that it is appropriate that the scope of liability extends to the harm caused.

The former is factual causation, the latter is the scope of liability. The explanatory notes suggest that an objective test is to be used when determining the scope of liability.

Factual causation restates the operation of the 'but for' test. Section 11 states that a breach of duty must be a 'necessary condition' of the occurrence of harm. While the meaning of this is not clear, Jones suggests that presumably it does not require anything beyond the common law test of a contributing cause which is more than negligible (*Chapman v Hearse* (1961) 106 CLR 112).

Section 11(3) of the Act deals with the circumstance of what the defendant would have done, for example if he or she had been warned. In such circumstances, deciding what would have occurred is to be determined 'subjectively in light of relevant circumstances'. That is, the question may not be determined by reference to what a reasonable person in the position of the plaintiff would have done. Statements made by people as to what they might have done are inadmissible unless the statements are against that person's interest.

This represents a major change to the existing law. In *Chappel v Hart* (supra) the plaintiff was permitted to give evidence as to what she would have done had she been warned of the risk of mediastinitus happening, damaging her voice. As noted in the text page 218ff, although plaintiffs were permitted to give evidence as to what they would have done, the Court took into account other, objective evidence to determine the veracity of the evidence.

Section 12 of the Act confirms that the plaintiff bears the onus of proving any fact in relation to causation. This puts to rest the suggestion made in *Chappel v Hart* that a reversal of onus may sometimes occur.

Section 11(2) of the Act acknowledges the existence of exceptional cases where, although factual causation cannot be made out, a breach of duty which was a 'material contribution to the harm' exists. In these circumstances, a court can determine that causation has been established, provided that they consider, amongst other things whether or not and why responsibility for the harm should be imposed on the party breaching the duty of care. Once this has been done, the Court next has to apply the scope of liability test in section 11(1)(b) of the Act.

The scope of exception cases is not clear. Jones notes that in the Ipp Report two categories were suggested. Firstly, where it is proved a harm is caused by the cumulative operation of two or more factors, without sufficient proof of the relative contribution of those factors to the total harm suffered. Paragraph 7.28 of the Ipp Report notes 'but for the conduct of each defendant the plaintiff would have suffered some of the harm and not all of it'.

The second instance mentioned by the Ipp Report is where the conduct of the defendant 'materially increases the risk' that plaintiff will suffer harm. The third category is a recognition of the decision of the House of Lords in *Fairchild v Glenhaven Funeral Services Ltd* [2002] 3 WLR 89.

Jones notes that the Civil Liability Act does not provide an alternative test for establishing causation in exceptional cases – the content of the test is left to the Courts to determine.

The operation of the tests of causation under the Civil Liability Acts has been considered by Tracey Carver in 'Causation – Queensland Civil Liability Act' (2004) 24 (4) *Queensland Lawyer* 189 and by Tracey Carver and Tina Cockburn in 'Determining Liability Under the Civil Liability Act Queensland' (2004) 24(6) Proctor 15.

Carver and Cockburn suggest that the operation of the Civil Liability Act advocates 'an approach to causation founded upon a more transparent analysis of policy considerations'. In their article they consider some relevant cases from New South Wales as to the interpretation of the Civil Liability Act. Their analysis of the cases is reproduced below.

Carver, T and Cockburn, T; Determining Liability Under the Civil Liability Act Queensland (2004) 24(6) Proctor 15.

Ruddock v Taylor

In *Ruddock*, the Court of Appeal found in favour of the plaintiff, who claimed false imprisonment consequent upon the wrongful cancellation of a visa.

Noting that at common law there are fundamental questions involved in the determination of causation in tort the court stated:

> The first relates to the factual aspect of causation, namely, the aspect that is concerned with whether negligent conduct in question played a part in bringing about the harm the subject of the claim.
>
> The second aspect concerns 'the appropriate' scope of liability for the consequences of tortious conduct.

In other words, the ultimate question to be answered when addressing the second aspect is a normative one, namely, whether the defendant ought to be held liable to pay damages for that harm . . .

Applying this test to the facts, as 'but for' the Minister's wrongful decision to cancel the visa detention would not have occurred, 'factual causation' was established. Secondly, in relation to 'scope of liability', as it is a 'fundamental purpose of the common law to protect the personal liberty of individuals', Justice Ipp concluded that the appellants ought to be held liable to pay damages because 'it would be unjust to hold otherwise'.

He noted this approach to causation formed the basis of s 5D of the Civil Liability Act 2002 (NSW).

Finch v Rogers

In *Finch*, the plaintiff was successful in a medical negligence claim arising from a medical practitioner's failure to adequately monitor the plaintiff's condition and thus avoid unnecessary chemotherapy resulting in permanent tinnitus. In determining causation, Justice Kirby applied section 5D of the Civil Liability Act 2002 (NSW). He noted that this provision 'fundamentally reflects the common law' and concluded

> in short, I consider that the defendant's negligence was a necessary condition of the harm that ensued.(s 5D(1)(a)) I further believe that it is appropriate that the scope of the defendant's liability extend to the harm so caused (s 5D(1)(b)).

Tambree v Travel Compensation Fund

In *Tambree*, the respondent (having met claims arising upon the collapse of a travel agency) claimed damages from accountants and auditors for professional negligence, and pursuant to s 42 of the Fair Trading Act 1987 (NSW), for failing to take reasonable care in the preparation of accounts and the giving of audit certificates (which were lodged to obtain the renewal of the agency's licence).

Justice Sheller (with whom President Mason and Justice Ipp agreed) applied Ruddock's two limbed test to determine causation as follows:

> On the evidence . . . I am satisfied that a proper discharge of Mr Roseby of his auditing duties or by Mr Tambree of his duties as an accountant would have led to a chain of regulatory events that would have prevented the losses being suffered by the claimaints or, alternatively, would have provided a means for meeting them without recourse to TCF.
>
> The next question is whether, bearing in mind the particular circumstances in which they negligently made misleading representations, Mr Tambree and Mr Roseby should be held responsible for all of TCF's loss.
>
> It is a matter of public importance that accountants should not, when asked to prepare financial reports of business entities, to be used by an agency such as TCF, act so negligently as to produce a misleading report. Even more so can this be said of an auditor. . . .

However the respondent's claim failed to the extent that it related to amounts paid pertaining to a period during which the agent unlawfully carried on a business, as here there was insufficient causal connection between the accountant's and auditor's acts and the payments made.

Harvey v PD

In *Harvey*, a medical practitioner was held liable in negligence for failing to disclose to the plaintiff that her future husband was HIV-positive. The couple had attended a joint consultation, for the purpose, known to the doctor, of determining prior to marriage whether either party had HIV or any other sexually transmitted disease. The couple subsequently had unprotected sex, the plaintiff contracted HIV, and twice fell pregnant.

As to causation, Justice Ipp said:

> In more complex cases of causation, a two-limbed test is to be applied. The first limb entails the question whether the defendant's conduct is historically involved in the plaintiff's loss. The second limb requires the question to be asked: ought the defendant be held liable for the harm sustained: *Ruddock v Taylor* . . . The second question involves a normative weighing of all the relevant circumstances.

The test was applied, as follows, to determine whether *Sullivan v Gordon* damages (for the value of the lost capacity to care for children ought after an accident) were available.

> It is a trite proposition that there must be a causal link between the tortious conduct the damages incurred . . . To this extent the judge was plainly correct in finding that 'a link must be established' before *Sullivan v Gordon* damages could be awarded. But the link needed is not a link between the negligence of the appellants and the decision to have a second child. Instead, it is a link establishing legal causation.
>
> The third ground of the cross appeal is that the judge erred in finding that the link between the tortious conduct and the decision to have the child was 'wholly absent'. As a matter of fact, his Honour cannot be faulted in this finding. But . . . this does not conclude the causation issue. While there is no doubt that there was an historical involvement between the negligence of the appellants and the *Sullivan v Gordon* loss suffered by PD, a live question remains in regard to the second limb of the two-limbed test. That is, the normative question whether, having regard to all the circumstances and, in particular, PDs fully informed decision to have a second child, has causation recognized by the law been established?

As to the normative question, Justice Ipp considered that several factors balanced to deny causation including:

- Whilst 'PD's fully informed decision to have a second child had considerable causal potency' there were other normative factors that also must be taken into account.

- 'Fairness requires these costs to be excluded which, in the ordinary course, would have been borne by whoever might have been the father of the child (but which in fact will not be so borne – because of PD's deliberate decision to have a child by a man who lacks the ability to contribute to the child's welfare'.
- That the child faced a more difficult future 'by reason of the fact that, as is the case with his mother, his father has a reduced expectation of life and, moreover, is likely – throughout his lifetime – to be absent from the family home for long periods. In my view, the law should not provide an incentive to children being born in such circumstances'.
- Socially and morally 'the law should not provide any encouragement to deliberate decisions to have children in circumstances where those children could at birth be infected with HIV'.

Justice Speigelman agreed with Justice Ipp, subject to the following observations:

> First, the two-limbed test for causation, which His Honour applies, is apt in the circumstances of the case. I wish to preserve my position on its more general application.
>
> Secondly, on the normative issue I am content to rest the conclusion on PD's informed decision to have a second child. I do not find it necessary or appropriate to give weight to the other factors to which IPP JA refers.

Harriton v Stephens

(*Harriton v Stephens* involved 'wrongful life' claims. The court held no duty of care was owed, but nonetheless made comments on causation).

(Having considered the first, 'historical' limb of causation, Justice Ipp turned to the normative considerations in the second limb)

- 'Idiosyncratic attempts to extend liability in tort law by fundamentally changing established principles and rules, motivated as they are by sympathy for plaintiffs, come at an immeasurable cost to the community, and involve judicial legislation that will ultimately result in loss of respect for the law'.
- No corrective or distributive justice considerations justify altering the established compensatory principle.
- Whilst legislatures throughout the country are legislating to restrict liability for negligence 'it would be quite wrong to expand, by judicial fiat, the law of negligence into new areas'.
- 'Discoveries and potential discoveries in the field of genetics should make courts cautious in altering established principle so as to accommodate claims for wrongful life. At this stage of genetic science it is simply not possible to know what consequences would follow from the making of such changes'.

- Sanctity of life 'militates against the recognition of a duty of care owed to a child to take steps that might lead to the child not being born'.
- 'The law already affords a remedy for damage brought about by medical negligence resulting in the birth of disabled children. That remedy is the action available to the parents of such children by which they can claim the financial expenses if raising and maintaining the children.'

Concluding comments

Concern has been expressed as to the fragmentation of the law which would arise if the statutory tests of causation were applied in some actions and the common law in all other actions . . . [the cases suggest] that the Civil Liability Act's test [of causation] may be held to have a wider application than originally intended, in determining causation in other areas of tort law. However, to what extent remains to be seen.

. . . The recent New South Wales decisions provide guidance as to the interpretation and application of the causation provisions in Queensland's Civil Liability Act. In any even, as noted by Justice Kirby in *Finch v Rogers*, the Act appears to essentially re-instate the common law, although advocating an approach to causation founded upon a more transparent analysis of policy considerations. For as stated by Lord Hoffman (in relation to the English position);

> . . . there is sometime a tendency to appeal to commonsense in order to avoid having to explain one's reasons.

More recently in Ruddock, Justice Ipp said:

> Terminology such as 'commonsense causation' and 'proximate' or 'dominant' or 'effective' or even 'legal cause' conceal judicial reasoning rather than explain it.

It is therefore to be hoped that the application of the Civil Liability Act's causation provisions, though involving a two-limbed test encompassing an open consideration of policy issues, will prove not to be 'overly analytical and complicated'. As with all things, transparency in the legal process is to be favoured wherever possible.

Douglas, RJ; Mullins, GR; Grant, SR; The Annotated Civil Liability Act 2003 (Qld) Butterworths, Sydney, 2004 at 25.

Corresponding legislation

Section 5D of the Civil Liability Act 2002 (NSW), s 51 of the Wrongs Act 1958 (Vic) and s 13 of the Civil Liability Act 2002 (Tas) are in substantially the same terms as s 11. Section 5C of the Civil Liability

Act 2002 (WA) as amended by the Civil Liability Amendment Act 2003 (WA) is similar except in subs (2) it refers the court to both the circumstances of the plaintiff and the defendant. Section 45 of the Civil Law (Wrongs) Act 2002 is also in terms that replicate s 11 except for subs (3). Section 45(3) refers instead to the application of the common law in circumstances where a number of defendants are responsible for exposing a plaintiff to loss. The Personal Injuries (Liabilities and Damages) Act 2003 (NT) does not deal with these issues. Similar to the ACT legislation, s 34 of the Wrongs Act 1936 (SA), as amended by the Law Reform (Ipp Recommendations) Bill 2003 will be in substantially the same terms as s 11 except that it does not apply the 'exceptional circumstances' test in subs (2) and prefers the multiple defendant application used by the ACT.

(c) Restoration of a modified Bolam *principle for all BUT duty to warn cases*

The background to this change is discussed in the Ipp Report at paragraphs 3.1–3.18:

Panel of Eminent Persons to Review the Law of Negligence Review of the Law of Negligence, AGPS, Canberra, October 2002, paragraphs 3.1–3.18

Treatment

The principal issue

3.26 The issue that principally causes controversy in regard to the standard of care applicable to the treatment of patients is whether the court should be the ultimate arbiter of the standard of care or whether it should defer to some designated body of opinion within the medical profession. Until *Rogers v Whitaker* (1992) 175 CLR 479, it was thought by many that the law on this question in Australia was embodied in the so-called '*Bolam* rule', although courts had expressed reservations about its application in Australia. The rule derives from a famous statement by McNair J in the English case of *Bolam v Friern Hospital Management Committee* [1957] 1 WLR 582:

> a doctor is not guilty of negligence if he has acted in accordance with a practice accepted as proper by a responsible body of medical men skilled in that particular art . . . merely because there is a body of opinion that would take a contrary view.

3.27 There are several points that need to be made about this statement:

3.28 Although it refers specifically to medical practitioners, there are reasons to think that it may apply to other occupational groups.

1. The *Bolam* case involved treatment rather than the giving of information about treatment.

2. Under the rule the defendant will be held to have exercised reasonable care if what was done was in accordance with 'a responsible body of medical opinion'.

3.29 Our consultations suggest that there is a significant body of opinion, especially among the medical profession, in favour of reinstating the *Bolam* rule in its original form. However, the Panel has formed the view, for the reasons which follow, that it should not recommend the reintroduction of the *Bolam* rule in its original form but rather a modified version of that rule.

Should the court defer to expert medical opinion?

3.30 Under the current law, courts are never required to defer to expert opinion as such. What the law says is that the court is entitled to accept a responsible body of expert opinion, unless there is a strong reason to reject it. The principle underlying this approach is that it is always for the court to decide what the test of reasonable care requires in particular cases, and it is always for the court to decide whether to defer to any particular body of expert opinion in the case before it. By contrast, the traditional *Bolam* rule requires courts to defer to responsible medical opinion, so that if the defendant acted in accordance with a responsible body of expert opinion, the court cannot decide that the defendant acted without reasonable care.

3.31 The choice between these two options may depend, in part at least, on how the body of professional opinion to which deference is accorded is defined. There are various options in this regard.

The Bolam *rule*

3.32 As already noted, under the *Bolam* rule, deference is accorded to a 'responsible body' of medical opinion. A common objection to the *Bolam* rule is that it gives too much weight to opinions that may be extreme and held by only a very few experts, or by practitioners who (for instance) work in the same institution and so are unrepresentative of the views of the larger body of practitioners. The *Bolam* rule also gives added importance to the influence of so-called 'rogue experts'. The problems with the *Bolam* rule in its original form are well-illustrated by two instances.

3.33 The first is discussed in *Bolitho v City and Hackney Health Authority* [1998] AC 232 by Lord Browne-Wilkinson, referring to *Hucks v Cole* [1993] 4 Med. L.R. 393, 397 (a 1968 case), in which 'a doctor failed to treat with penicillin a patient who had septic spots on her skin even though he knew them to contain organisms capable of leading to puerperal fever. A number of distinguished doctors gave evidence that they would not, in the circumstances, have treated [the patient] with penicillin'. Despite this body of supportive opinion, the Court of Appeal held the doctor to have been negligent because he had knowingly taken a risk of causing grave danger even though it could have been easily and inexpensively avoided.

3.34 The second instance concerns the events described in the *Report of the Committee of Inquiry into Allegations Concerning the Treatment of Cervical Cancer at National Women's Hospital and into Other Related Matters* (1988). The report arose out of a research programme, conducted over the course of almost 20 years, at the National Women's Hospital (Auckland, New Zealand), to determine the natural history of carcinoma-in-situ of the female genital tract. The programme involved leaving untreated women who returned positive Pap smears. A positive Pap smear may be indicative of carcinoma-in-situ, which may develop into invasive cancer. This procedure involved deliberately omitting to treat women in accordance with standards accepted elsewhere, in order to determine whether they would later develop invasive cancer. The approach followed in the programme was accepted by many other practitioners, within and outside the hospital, and formed the basis for under-graduate and post-graduate teaching. According to the Report, several women died as a result of the failure to offer conventionally-accepted treatment. Under a strict application of the *Bolam* rule as originally formulated, the practitioners involved arguably were not negligent.

3.35 These examples demonstrate that the *Bolam* rule, when strictly applied, can give rise to results that would be unacceptable to the community. They show the main weakness of the *Bolam* rule to be that it allows small pockets of medical opinion to be arbiters of the requisite standard of medical treatment, even in instances where a substantial majority of medical opinion would take a different view. It is well-established that in many aspects of medical practice, different views will be held by bodies of practitioners of varying size and in different locations. This can result in the development of localised practices that are not regarded with approval widely throughout the profession. Thus, the *Bolam* rule is not a reliable guide to acceptable medical practice. The Panel therefore recommends that *Bolam* rule, in its original form, not be reinstated.

3.36 The question then is whether deference to a body of expert medical opinion would be acceptable if the relevant body of opinion were differently defined.

3.37 Term of Reference 3(d) suggests that deference should be paid to 'the generally accepted practice' of the medical profession. A problem with this formulation is that it does not allow for cases in which there is a genuine difference of opinion about whether generally accepted practice represents best practice, and it gives no scope for the properly regulated development of new techniques with a view to their future general adoption as best practice.

3.38 A third possibility, which would overcome the problems both of the *Bolam* test as originally formulated, and of the test suggested by Term of Reference 3(d), is a rule that a defendant could not be held liable where the court is satisfied that the conduct in question was in accordance with an opinion widely held by a significant number of respected practitioners in the relevant field.

3.39 In this formulation, the requirement that the opinion be 'widely held' is designed to prevent reliance being placed on localised practices that develop in isolation from the mainstream of professional activity. The requirement of 'a significant number' is designed to filter out idiosyncratic opinions. The requirement of 'respected practitioners' is designed to ensure that the opinion deserves to be treated as soundly based.

3.40 The Panel considers that the test set out in paragraph 3.13 is preferable both to the *Bolam* rule as originally formulated, and to the test suggested by Term of Reference 3(d). If it were thought right to require courts to defer to expert medical opinion relating to the standard of care applicable to medical treatment, the Panel's view is that the rule for determining the standard of care in all cases in which a medical practitioner is alleged to have been negligent in providing treatment to a patient should be as follows: 'A medical practitioner is not negligent if the court is satisfied that the treatment provided was in accordance with an opinion widely held by a significant number of respected practitioners in the relevant field'.

3.41 As we have noted, however, under current law a court is never required to defer to medical opinion, although in the normal run of cases, it will. A serious problem with this approach is that it gives no guidance as to circumstances in which a court would be justified in not deferring to medical opinion.

3.42 This problem could be addressed by adding to the rule suggested in paragraph 3.15 the following proviso: 'unless the court considers that the opinion was 'irrational'. This proviso follows the law as laid down by the English House of Lords in *Bolitho v City and Hackney Health Authority* [1998] AC 232. In the opinion of the Panel, this formula gives doctors as much protection as is desirable in the public interest, because the chance that an opinion which was widely held by a significant number of respected practitioners in the relevant field would be held irrational is very small indeed. But, if the expert opinion in the defendant's favour were held to be irrational, it seems right (in the opinion of the Panel) that the defendant should not be allowed to rely on it. The Panel therefore recommends that this formula be adopted as the test of standard of care in relation to medical treatment administered by medical practitioners.

3.43 The proviso relating to 'irrational treatment' needs further elaboration. Under the recommended rule, it is for the court to decide whether treatment is irrational. It would be rare indeed to identify instances of treatment that is both irrational and in accordance with an opinion widely held by a significant number of respected practitioners in the field. Such a rare instance is the finding of the court in *Hucks v Cole* [1993] 4 Med. L.R. 393, referred to in paragraph 3.8.

The Civil Liability Act has restored the *Bolam* principle in respect of all areas of medical practice EXCEPT where the allegation made is that there was a failure to advise of material risk.

Section 22(1) of the Civil Liability Act (Qld) states that a professional does not breach a duty if it is established that the professional acted in a way that, at the time that the service was provided, was widely accepted by peer opinion or by a significant number of respected practitioners in the field as competent professional practice.

Section 22(5) notes that the above exclusion does not apply to a failure to advise of a material risk.

The section is NOT limited to medical practitioners – it applies to all professionals. The fact that there are many differing opinions does not prevent one of them being accepted as proper (section 22(3)).

The limitation that it be accepted as competent *at the time that the service was provided* provides a statutory recognition of the rule in *Roe v Ministry of Health.*

The common practice will not relieve from liability where it is irrational, or contrary to a written law (section 22(2)).

The term 'irrational' is not defined. The Explanatory Memorandum to the Civil Liability Act explains that the impugned opinion must be 'clearly outside the scope of community expectation.' (p 10, explanatory memorandum).

Jones speculates that peer opinion which is manifestly wrong must also be irrational following *Ainsworth v Levi CA* (NSW) unreported, 30 August 1995.

Douglas *et al* suggest the term 'irrational' should be interpreted consistent with the view that 'the accepted procedure is not capable of withstanding logical analysis' (citing *Bolitho v City and Hackney Health Authority* [1988] AC 232 at 243).

Douglas, RJ; Mullins, GR; Grant, SR; The Annotated Civil Liability Act 2003 (Qld) Butterworths, Sydney, 2004 at 41 (Note the following concerning section 22)

Under subs (1) a professional needs to introduce evidence in support of his or her conduct that satisfies four criteria:

1. The conduct was widely accepted, meaning that the conduct was not only accepted by one particular regional group, but by various groups. This may mean that the practice may need to be accepted nationally, or internationally, dependent upon the professional concerned.
2. The conduct was accepted by a significant number of practitioners, meaning that, having regard to the number of practitioners in practice, a large proportion accepted the behaviour. It does not mean that over half of practitioners need to accept the conduct; subs (3)

and (4) support that it is possible for a number of 'schools of thought' to exist in relation to the practices within a profession.

3. The practitioners providing evidence in support must be 'in the field' of practice under review, and 'respected' in that field. Accordingly, in areas of speciality medicine and research, there will exist a limited number of professionals who will be able to provide the evidence necessary.
4. The evidence must support that the conduct in question was 'competent'. This implies a different consideration to whether the conduct is in fact reasonable. This slight change may allow a greater scope for argument based upon subs (2) that, whilst competent, the conduct is irrational.

Douglas, RJ; Mullins, GR; Grant, SR; The Annotated Civil Liability Act 2003 (Qld) Butterworths, Sydney, 2004 at 63.

Corresponding legislation

Sections 5O and 5P of the Civil Liability Act 2002 (NSW) basically replicate s 22, but provides the only relevant opinion is an Australian opinion. Similarly, ss 59 and 60 of the Wrongs Act 1958 (Vic) basically replicate s 22. The Civil Liability Act 2002 (WA) as amended by the Civil Liability Amendment Act 2003 (WA) will remain silent on the issue. Section 22 of the Civil Liability Act 2002 (Tas) and the Personal Injuries (Liabilities and Damages) Act 2003 (NT) do not deal with the issue. Section 41 of the Wrongs Act 1936 (SA) as amended by the Law Reform (Ipp Recommendations) Bill 2003, will replicate the New South Wales Provision.

Content of the duty to warn of material risks

The Ipp Report considered this area of the law in some detail. In the extract from the report, below, note which parts of the law it recommends should be subject to legislative enactment, and which parts should be left to the common law.

Panel of Eminent Persons to Review the Law of Negligence Review of the Law of Negligence, AGPS, Canberra, October 2002, paragraphs 3.44–3.79

The provision of information

Basis for treating provision of information differently: the patient's right to decide

3.44 People have the right to decide for themselves whether or not they will undergo medical treatment. Originally, consent to medical treatment was seen as relevant only to the question of whether a medical practitioner administering the treatment could be sued for trespass to the person (battery), for interfering with the patient's bodily integrity. In this context, the law only required the medical practitioner to tell the patient, in general terms, about the nature of the proposed treatment.

3.45 Under current law, however, the giving of information by the medical practitioner, and the giving of consent by the patient, are seen as relevant to the issue of whether the medical practitioner has exercised reasonable care in relation to the patient. More importantly, it is now thought that medical practitioners must provide the patient with sufficient information to enable the patient to give 'informed consent'. This obligation is commonly (although inaccurately) referred to as the 'duty to warn'.

3.46 An important implication of the patient's right to give or withhold consent is that the opinions of medical practitioners about what information ought to be given to patients should not set the standard of care in this regard. The giving of information on which to base consent is not a matter that is appropriately treated as being one of medical expertise. Rather, it involves wider issues about the relationship between medical practitioners and patients and the right of individuals to decide their own fate. The court is the ultimate arbiter of the standard of care in regard to the giving of information by medical practitioners.

To whom the duty should apply: the relevant occupations

3.47 As stated, the obligation of medical practitioners to provide information derives originally from the law relating to trespass to the person.

3.48 In regard to professions and occupations other than the medical profession, the law does recognise duties on the part of service providers to give particular categories of information in particular circumstances. The historical source of these duties, and their nature and scope, differ from the duty of medical practitioners to inform their patients. Moreover, while duties to inform have from time to time been imposed, they have yet to be analysed and categorised into a principled set of rules. This is very much a developing area and in the view of the Panel it is desirable to make a legislative statement of certain aspects of duties to inform in the medical context only.

3.49 Accordingly, the Panel recommends that any legislative statement of duties to provide information should relate only to medical practitioners. When dealing with the duty to provide information, the Panel will confine the discussion accordingly.

When the duty arises and who owes it

3.50 In all of the cases to which the Panel has been referred and which the Panel has considered in its own research, it has been assumed by the parties that it is the treating medical practitioner who owed the relevant duty to inform. While in most instances this will be the case, it is not necessarily so.

3.51 In many instances of modern medical practice, the treatment of a patient, while under the direction of what (in common practice) is known as the 'attending medical officer', is shared by several health care providers. For example, in the course of pre-operative treatment, the operation itself and post-operative treatment, the patient might be attended by the general practitioner, a physician, a radiologist, a principal surgeon and an assisting surgeon, a registrar, an intern, an anaesthetist, theatre nurses and ward nurses. Each one of these persons may administer treatment to the patient. It is unlikely that each will incur an obligation to inform the patient about the treatment administered, but is quite possible that more than one of these persons will incur such an obligation.

3.52 The law is undeveloped in regard to determining precisely when a duty to inform will arise and on whom it will be imposed. The Panel considers it inadvisable to attempt to lay down any rules or principles in this connection. Often, the answer will lie in responsibilities assumed by the various practitioners, and orders given and accepted. The Panel considers that this aspect should be left for the development of the common law.

The nature of the duty: a duty to take reasonable care

3.53 Some of the statements made concerning the duty to provide information make no reference, either expressly or impliedly, to the duty to inform being a duty of reasonable care. In these statements, the content and scope of the duty to inform are looked at solely from the point of view of the patient. In the Panel's view, however, this should not be the case. It should always be borne in mind that the duty to inform is part of the law of negligence, and accordingly is a duty to take reasonable care to inform. This means that consideration must be given to the situation of the practitioner.

3.54 It is by no means unknown, for example, for general practitioners in country areas to conduct surgery of a kind that elsewhere would be conducted by specialist surgeons. We are not here talking of instances where general practitioners profess skill that they do not have. The example we are giving is of general practitioners who hold themselves out as having only the skill of a general practitioner, but who are requested by their patients to carry out surgery that would elsewhere be carried out by specialist surgeons. Such general practitioners may not have the same knowledge as specialist surgeons would have of (for instance) risks of surgery. The law must accommodate this fairly, and will do so if it is recognised that the practitioner only has a duty to exercise reasonable care in giving information, and does not have a duty to give whatever information can be obtained.

3.55 An express statement that obligations to give information are obligations only to take reasonable care may help to reassure doctors that the law does not require of them unrealistic standards of behaviour, even though the law does not defer to medical opinion in this area to the extent that it does in relation to treatment. For instance, a doctor is not required to ensure that the patient fully comprehends the information given, but only to take reasonable care in this and other respects.

3.56 On the other hand, it is important to note that the information that the doctor must take reasonable care to provide is the information necessary to enable the patient to give informed consent, not the information that the reasonable doctor would consider necessary for this purpose.

Analysis of the categories of information to be provided

3.57 It is necessary to distinguish between two different kinds of obligation to provide information.

3.58 An obligation to give information about treatment might be imposed on the practitioner regardless of whether the practitioner knows or ought to know that the patient wants to be given the information. The Panel will call this the 'proactive duty to inform'. On the other hand, an obligation to give certain information might be imposed only when the practitioner knows or ought to know that the patient wants or expects to be given the information. The Panel will call this the 'reactive duty to inform'.

3.59 The proactive duty to inform relates to information that the practitioner must give a patient even when the particular patient does not ask for it or otherwise communicate a desire to be given it. The reactive duty to inform relates to information the practitioner must give when the particular patient asks for information, or otherwise communicates a desire to be given it.

The proactive duty to inform

3.60 Under current Australian law, the proactive duty to inform requires the medical practitioner to put the patient in a position to make an informed decision about whether or not to undergo the treatment by telling the patient about material risks inherent in the provision of the treatment, and by providing other relevant information. A risk is material if, in the circumstances of the particular case, a reasonable person in the patient's position would attach significance to it in deciding whether or not to undergo the treatment.

3.61 It seems clear that the proactive duty to inform is not confined to information about risks but extends to other types of information that may be needed to enable patients to make an informed decision about their health. What types of information are required to be given will depend on the circumstances of each case, and it is not possible or desirable to make general provision about this matter.

3.62 The test for determining what information the proactive duty to inform requires to be given should be objective, but should take account of the personal characteristics of the patient. In determining what information the reasonable person would want, relevant factors might include the nature and effects of the treatment, the nature and probability of inherent risks of the treatment, and alternatives to the treatment.

3.63 Accordingly, we recommend that the proactive duty to inform should be formulated to the effect that the practitioner must exercise reasonable care to give the patient such information as the reasonable person in the patient's position would, in the circumstances, want to be given before making a decision whether or not to undergo treatment.

3.64 It is important that this formula be applied by reference to the time at which the decision whether or not to undergo the treatment was made and not with the benefit of hindsight. This is the current law. Research by psychologists suggests that it is very difficult to eliminate the effects of 'hindsight bias'. This problem may be thought particularly great where the question is what a person would have done if they had been given certain information that they were not given. So, in this context (at least), the Panel recommends providing explicitly that the question of what information the reasonable person in the patient's position would have wanted to be given is to be answered by reference to the time at which the relevant decision was made and not at a later time. This provision will, at least, require the issue of hindsight to be explicitly addressed.

Giving the proactive duty to inform greater specificity

3.65 On the basis of its consultations and investigations, the Panel has formed the view that the medical profession finds the current legal specification of the proactive duty to inform unsatisfactory because it gives insufficient guidance as to what information the medical practitioner has to give to the patient in order to avoid legal liability for negligence. There is anecdotal evidence that this may be having an adverse and distorting effect on medical practice. For example, it is sometimes said that medical practitioners may spend more time giving patients information than examining them. The Panel wishes to avoid further distortion of medical practice.

3.66 One way of addressing this concern might be to attempt to frame detailed, prescriptive legislative provisions specifying the matters about which information must be given to satisfy the proactive duty to inform. The Panel's considered view, however, is that this course of action would be impractical and undesirable. The precise content of the obligation has to depend on the facts and circumstances of individual cases, which are likely to be extremely diverse and incapable of being dealt with in such a way.

3.67 Another proposal that has been made in this regard is that the medical colleges (or the National Health and Medical Research

Council) should develop guidelines, protocols or codes of practice concerning provision of information. We have not been able to investigate the feasibility of such developments. However, our view is that while compliance (or non-compliance) with such advisory regimes would (in accordance with current law) be relevant to the legal issue of reasonable care, it could never be treated as conclusive of the issue. For this reason, such proposals are not directly relevant to the Panel's Terms of Reference.

3.68 A specific issue raised in the course of the Panel's consultations is whether the proactive duty to inform requires the practitioner to tell the prospective patient that the treatment is also available from other more skilled or experienced practitioners. This question cannot be answered in the abstract. Although, generally, such an obligation would not arise, there might be exceptional circumstances in which it would. It would be neither desirable nor practicable to attempt to spell these out in legislative form.

Persons to whom the proactive duty to inform is owed, and the circumstances in which it does not arise

3.69 There are cases in which the proactive duty to inform would be appropriately owed to someone other than the patient (who might be called 'the substitute decision-maker'): for instance, where the patient is an infant, or unconscious, or otherwise lacking in decision-making capacity. The identity of the appropriate substitute decision-maker would be determined in accordance with the law of the relevant jurisdiction dealing, for instance, with the rights and obligations of parents and guardians of minors. In such cases, the content of the proactive duty to inform would be to give the substitute decision-maker such information as, in the circumstances, a reasonable person in the substitute decision-maker's position would want to be given to enable him or her to make a decision in the best interests of the patient.

3.70 There are three main situations in which the proactive duty to inform would not arise:

3. Where its performance has been waived by the person to whom it is owed. This would be the case where the person to whom the duty to inform is owed has explicitly or impliedly told the person who owes the obligation that he or she does not want to be given information, or information of a particular kind, about proposed treatment.
4. Where the treatment is provided on an emergency basis. To constitute an emergency, three conditions must exist: first, a threat of death or serious physical or mental harm to the person to whom the duty to inform is owed; second, the person to whom the obligation is owed temporarily lacks decision-making capacity; third, there is no appropriate substitute decision-maker for that person. In such cases, the proactive duty to inform is suspended, but not cancelled. When the person to whom the treatment is provided regains

decision-making capacity, the practitioner is under a proactive duty to give that person such information as a reasonable person in the patient's position would, in the circumstances, want to be given about the treatment that was provided.

5. Where a medical practitioner reasonably believes that the very act of giving particular information to a patient would cause the patient serious physical or mental harm. This is the so-called therapeutic privilege. In this context, the phrase 'serious physical or mental harm' does not include harm likely to be suffered by reason only of a decision not to undergo the treatment in question. If it did, the patient's freedom to choose whether or not to undergo the treatment could be seriously compromised by a decision of the practitioner that the patient did not know what was in his or her own best interests.

3.71 The Panel considers that the development of these principles is best left to the common law.

Obvious risks

3.72 In the course of the Panel's consultations, the suggestion was repeatedly made that an obligation to give information should not entail an obligation to warn of obvious risks. Such a provision is consistent with the principle underlying the Terms of Reference that people should take more responsibility for their own safety. The Panel therefore recommends enactment of a legislative provision to the effect that a medical practitioner cannot be held to have breached the proactive duty to inform merely by reason of a failure to give the patient information about a risk or other matter that would, in the circumstances, have been obvious to the reasonable person in the patient's position, unless giving the information was required by statute.

3.73 The term 'obvious risk' is intended to include risks that are patent or matters of common knowledge. In the Panel's view, the mere fact that a risk is of low probability does not prevent it being an obvious risk. Beyond this, however, the Panel considers that it would be undesirable and impractical to attempt to define obviousness of risk. Whether or not a risk is obvious must ultimately depend on the facts of individual cases and, in the end, will be a matter for the court to decide.

The reactive duty to inform

3.74 Under current law, the reactive duty to inform is an obligation to take reasonable care to give to the particular patient information about risks inherent in the treatment (and other matters) to which the practitioner knows or ought to know the patient would attach significance in deciding whether or not to undergo the treatment. In other words, the reactive obligation relates to information that the patient has asked for or otherwise communicated a desire to be given.

3.75 As in the case of the proactive duty to inform, the reactive obligation is not limited to information about risks but may extend to other types of information about the treatment that the practitioner knows or ought to know the patient wants to be given before making the decision about whether or not to undergo the treatment.

3.76 So far as concerns the issue of to whom the reactive duty is owed (see paragraph 3.59), it is the view of the Panel that, in cases where the proactive duty to inform would be owed to a substitute decision-maker, the reactive duty to inform would also be owed to that person.

3.77 Concerning the issue of the circumstances in which the reactive duty might not arise, waiver (described in paragraph 3.60(a)) is obviously not relevant in this context. In emergency situations, described in paragraph 3.60(b), the Panel's view is that the reactive duty to inform would be suspended in the same way and to the same extent as the proactive duty to inform. The application of the therapeutic privilege, described in paragraph 3.60(c), to the reactive duty to inform raises difficult questions of policy that the Panel has not had time to consider.

3.78 The application of these issues to the reactive duty to inform has yet to be settled. The Panel considers that this should be left to the common law to develop.

3.79 So far as obvious risks are concerned, if a medical practitioner knows or ought to know that the patient wants to receive particular information before making the decision whether or not to undergo treatment, then the practitioner should be under an obligation to give that information, even if it concerns a risk or other matter that would, in the circumstances, have been obvious to the reasonable person in the patient's position.

Section 21 of the Civil Liability Act restates the obligation established by the High Court, that a doctor has duty to warn of material risks of treatment. It does not alter the content of the duty or the operation of the test of material risks. (Douglas, RJ; Mullins, GR; Grant, SR *The Annotated Civil Liability Act 2003* (Qld) at 39). Note that this section is not replicated in other jurisdictions.

See also sections 15 and 16 of the Civil Liability Act 2003 (Qld).

Expressions of Regret

The Civil Liability Act introduces recognition of an expression of regret. Section 72 of the Queensland Act states that any oral or written statement expressing regret for an incident, provided it does not contain an admission of liability, is not admissible. This provision only applies to statements made by individuals.

Douglas, RJ; Mullins, GR; Grant, SR; The Annotated Civil Liability Act 2003 (Qld) Butterworths, Sydney, 2004 at 123

Corresponding legislation

Section 69 of the Civil Liability Act 2002 (NSW), s 14J of the Wrongs Act 1958 (Vic), s 5AH of the Civil Liability Act 2002 (WA) as amended by the Civil Liability Amendment Act 2003 (WA), s 7 of the Civil Liability Act 2002 (Tas), s 14 of the Civil Law (Wrongs) Act 2002 (ACT) and s 13 of the Personal Injuries (Liability and Damages) Act 2003 (NT) provide for the evidential effect of 'apologies' or 'expressions of regret' under the comparative provisions in the relevant jurisdiction. Section 75 of the Wrongs Act 1936 (SA) amended by the Law Reform (Ipp Recommendations) Bill 2003 [is to the same effect].

Recoverability of damages for negligent sterilisation

It has been established for some time in Australian law that a negligently performed sterilisation may sound in damages.

In *Cattanach v Melchior*, the High Court considered the extent of recoverable damages. The High Court's judgment is summarised below.

Devereux, JA Actions for wrongful birth (2004) XXXIII No 3 INSAF (2001) Aust Torts Reports 81–597

English common law traditionally resisted a claim for damages in circumstances where what was complained of was the birth of a healthy child following a failed sterilization. Such claims had been dismissed as being contrary to public policy.

Recent cases in England and Australia have allowed such claims (commonly referred to as 'wrongful birth' cases). The latest in the line of Australian decisions considering legal issues in reproduction is *Cattanach v Melchior*.[12] A decision as remarkable for its conclusions as it is for the misconceptions it has raised in the popular press. *Cattanach v Melchior* is important for two reasons. Firstly, it emphasises the growing unease and contradictions inherent in an application of the rules governing pure economic loss post-*Perre v Apand Ltd.*[13] Secondly, it places Australian law on remoteness 'out of kilter' with the majority of the common law world.

This article presents a detailed analysis of *Cattanach v Melchior,* together with a comparison of relevant English cases which have reached contrary conclusions to the Australian decision. It is hoped that

12 *Cattanach v Melchior* (2003) 199 ALR 131.

13 (1999) 198 CLR 180.

this article may be of assistance to Malaysian lawyers confronting the issue of 'wrongful birth'.

Facts

Mrs Melchior was referred by her general practitioner to the defendant, a specialist gynaecologist and obstetrician. In the course of her consultations with the defendant, the plaintiff explained that she wished to have a sterilization procedure performed. She also told him that, when she was fifteen, she had had an appendectomy. The plaintiff's mother had informed her that the surgeon had removed not only her appendix, but also her right fallopian tube.

In March 1992 the defendant performed a laparoscopic tubal ligation procedure on the plaintiff. The procedure involving the application of a Filshie clip to the plaintiff's left fallopian tube.

Four years after the procedure Mrs Melchior fell pregnant and subsequently gave birth to a healthy child.

Originally the plaintiff and her husband commenced proceedings on the basis that the defendant must have incorrectly applied the Filshie clip. At the birth of Mrs Melchior's child, the Filshie clip was noted to be intact. It transpired that Mrs Melchior had become pregnant because her right fallopian tube was also intact, though obscured by scar tissue and convoluted. An ovum had transmigrated from her left ovary to her right fallopian tube, rendering her fertile.

Mrs Melchior and her husband sued alleging both breach of contract and negligence. The former cause of action could not be maintained as the defendant had carried out the sterilization procedure in the course of his duties in a public hospital. The particulars of negligence pleaded were a failure to warn of the risk of pregnancy, a failure to seek the hospital records of the appendectomy performed on Mrs Melchior in 1967 and a failure to perform a hystereosalpingogram on Mrs Melchior. A hystereosalpingogram may have indicated the presence of two functioning fallopian tubes.

Decision at First Instance

At first instance[14] Justice Holmes dismissed the last two particulars of negligence. She described as 'impracticable' the notion that a doctor be required to 'cross-check' fully the medical history of every patient. The hystereosalpingogram was described as painful and not always entirely accurate.

Given, however, that the defendant could not be entirely sure that the plaintiff's right fallopian tube had been removed, the trial Judge determined that the defendant ought to have warned the plaintiff, that, in the

14 (2001) Aust Torts Reports 81–597

absence of proof of the removal of the fallopian tube, the risk of her falling pregnant was of the order of magnitude of 10 times more than that which existed in a 'normal' sterilization procedure. He should then have advised her to undergo a hystereosalpingogram.

As has been noted elsewhere,[15] the mere failure to advise of a risk is insufficient to sound in damages. The plaintiff needs to prove causation in that, had she been advised of the risk, she would have taken steps to avoid the risk. In the present case, Justice Holmes was satisfied that, had Mrs Melchior been advised of the increased risk of pregnancy, she would have elected to have the hystereosalpingogram, the presence of the intact right fallopian tube would have been detected and appropriate precautions against conception would have been taken. The trial judge awarded damages for birth and confinement and costs of raising the child until the child turned 18.

Decision of the Court of Appeal

The Queensland Court of Appeal[16] dismissed unanimously the appeal as to liability. The court was, however, divided as to the recoverability of the claim for maintenance of the child. While the Court unanimously agreed with the trial Judge's characterization of the loss suffered by the Melchiors as pure economic loss, only President McMurdo and Justice Davies opined that the costs of maintaining the child, until the child turned 18, were recoverable.

The defendants submitted there was a distinction to be made between economic loss occasioned by the pregnancy and birth, and economic loss occasioned by the child's existence in the family. If damages were recoverable at all for economic loss, the defendants submitted they were limited to the former.

The defendants were granted leave to appeal to the High Court, but only as to the question of whether the costs of maintaining the child until 18 were recoverable.

Relevant antecedents

There were few prior Australian cases on point. Of the three directly relevant, two were from Queensland. In *Dahl v Purnelh*,[17] the District Court of Queensland allowed a claim for the birth of a child following a failed vasectomy. Although damages were awarded for the costs of maintaining the child until it reached majority, the amount awarded was

15 See generally Devereux, JA 'Throwing The Baby Out With The Bathwater: An Antipodean Perspective On Claims For Failed Sterilisation' (2002) 2 No. 1 *Commonwealth Law Journal* 141. The article in the *Commonwealth Law Journal* was written prior to the hearing of the High Court action *in Cattanach v Melchior*.

16 [2001] QCA 246.

17 (1993) 15 QLR 33.

discounted to account for the benefits to the parents of having a child. In *Veivers v Connolly*,[18] the Queensland Supreme Court awarded damages following the birth of child who was severely disabled. The particulars of negligence were that the medical practitioner had failed to diagnose the mother's rubella.

Then, in *CES v Superclinics (Australia) Pty Ltd*,[19] damages were awarded to a woman who gave birth to a healthy child in circumstances where she had been deprived of the opportunity to seek an abortion. The first pregnancy test conducted by the defendants wrongly indicated she was not pregnant. The second test, which indicated she was pregnant, was wrongly communicated to the plaintiff as indicating she was not pregnant.

The New South Wales Court of Appeal, by majority, permitted damages to be awarded – but not for the costs of maintaining the child until it turned 18. Justice Meagher, dissenting, refused the award of damages at all because the woman, by failing to adopt out the child, had failed to mitigate her loss. President Kirby would have been happy to award the plaintiff damages until the child turned 18, pointing out that the widespread use of contraception put paid to the myth that the birth of a child was universally regarded as a blessing. In an effort to produce a workable outcome for the plaintiff, however, he reluctantly agreed with Priestley JA that the award of damages be confined to the costs of birth and confinement.

An important antecedent was the House of Lords decision in *MacFarlane v Tayside Health Board*.[20] The case is authority for the view that, in England and Scotland, damages are recoverable for the birth of a child following a failed sterilization, but not for the upkeep of the child until majority.

Applying the principles applicable to negligence claims in England, the House of Lords found that it would not be 'fair, just and reasonable' to allow recovery for costs of maintaining the child. Lords Slynn, Steyn and Clyde were not persuaded that there were compelling public policy arguments against allowing the recovery of damages for birth. Lord Hope rejected recourse to public policy arguments, saying public policy was more properly the province of the legislature.

In dissent, Lord Millett suggested that allowing parents the benefits of parenthood while avoiding the costs would be 'subversive of the mores of society' – accordingly he rejected all elements of the parents' claim including damages for birth and upbringing of the child.

18 [1995] 2 QdR 326.
19 (1995) 38 NSWLR 47.
20 [2000] 2 AC 59.

The High Court Decision in *Cattanach v Melchior*

The High Court in *Cattanch v Melchior,* by a majority of 4–3, dismissed the defendant's appeal. Young provides a good overview of the High Court's decision.[21] The summary of the various judgments in *Cattanach* below is modelled on Young's approach, modified and expanded for present purposes.

Justices McHugh and Gummow

Justices McHugh and Gummow considered whether, consistent with the approach of the High Court in *Brodie v Singleton Shire Council*[22] an immunity could be found for doctors against damages for maintaining the child. Their Honours could find no compelling reason to grant such an advantage in litigation to doctors.[23]

As a matter of policy, the law recognized underlying values respecting the importance of life and nurturing of infant children. Their Honours could find no values or 'general recognition'[24] which would deny the plaintiffs their normal common law remedies flowing from a proven breach of duty. In particular, viewing the birth of a child as always a blessing denied the reality of widespread community use of contraception,[25] and their Honours did not think that damages should be precluded simply due to speculation as to the psychological damage which might be occasioned to publicly labelling a child as unwanted.[26] Their Honours could find no distinction in terms of recovery between the birth of a healthy child or a disabled child.[27]

The defendants had argued that, were recovery for costs of upbringing permitted, set-off should be made for the benefits of having children. Their Honours held that no such set-off should be allowed – since the benefits of having children were of a different class of damages than the cost of raising the children. The analogy provided was that of a coal miner 'forced to retire because of injury, [who] does not get less damages for loss of earning capacity because he is now free to sit in the sun each day reading his favourite newspaper'.[28]

21 Young, R '*Cattanach v Melchior*' (2004) 11 *Journal of Law and Medicine* 153.
22 (2001) 206 CLR 512.
23 Note 12 at 153.
24 Note 12 at 153.
25 Note 12 at 154.
26 Note 12 at 154.
27 Note 12 at 154.
28 Note 12 at 156–157.

Justice Kirby

Justice Kirby was not convinced that the loss could properly be characterized as pure economic loss – rather it was loss consequent upon direct injury to the parents.[29]

He considered that, in the present circumstances, there were five possible answers to the question of recoverability of damages:[30]

1. No recovery permitted if a healthy child was born
2. Recovery limited to birth and immediate circumstances
3. Recovery of additional costs if the child is disabled or if the parents are disabled
4. Recovery permitted but offset by the benefits of the birth of a child
5. Full recovery

His Honour dismissed the first approach since the notion that the birth of child was a blessing, he stated, was unconvincing and based on a legal fiction.[31] The second approach his Honour thought involved severing the causal link between various outcomes of pregnancy which was 'incontestably arbitrary.'[32] Both kinds of damage (birth and upbringing) he thought were equally foreseeable as a consequence of negligence. Each is directly caused. Neither is too remote.[33]

Adopting the third approach, his Honour noted, would not 'stick in the gullet of Lord Steyn's hypothetical underground traveller'[34] [the updated 'man on the Clapham omnibus'] – but was arbitrary and therefore unacceptable.[35] It also reinforced views about disability that are 'contrary to contemporary Australian values reinforced by the law'.[36]

The fourth approach involved a comparison of different types of costs and benefits and was inconsistent with Australian law, except as it acknowledged 'any proved economic benefits' derived by the parents from the birth of the child.[37]

His Honour chose the last outcome as being that most consistent with the ordinary principles of negligence.[38]

Justice Callinan

Justice Callinan, after reviewing relevant overseas authorities which limited recovery so as to not include damages for upbringing of a child,

29 Note 12 at 180.
30 Note 12 at 168.
31 Note 12 at 169–174.
32 Note 12 at 175.
33 Note 12 at 175.
34 Note 12 at 176.
35 Note 12 at 176.
36 Note 12 at 177.
37 Note 12 at 179.
38 Note 12 at 180.

noted that such authorities were based on 'emotional and moral values' rather than the law.[39] Although finding the assessment of damages in the present case to be distasteful, His Honour noted the normal principles of the law required that it be done.[40] The matter was one which involved pure economic loss and recovery of damages should be permitted.[41]

Chief Justice Gleeson

The Chief Justice, dissenting, noted that the immediate cause of the damage was the normal process of human reproduction resulting in a parent-child relationship.[42] The Chief Justice noted that the law imposed obligations on parents to support the child – which was inconsistent with viewing such obligations as damage.[43]

The Chief Justice stated the law should not assign a value to the creation of such a relationship. Assessing the plaintiffs' claim involved indeterminacy both as to quantum and potential claimants.[44] The Chief Justice also questioned why the cut-off for damages should be the child's majority. In the present circumstances, why could the defendant not also be liable for the costs of tertiary education, or the child's wedding?[45]

The Chief Justice concluded that the defendant's claim 'displays all the features that have contributed to the law's reluctance to impose a duty of care to avoid causing loss. The liability sought to be imposed is indeterminate. It is difficult to relate coherently to other rules of common law and statute. It is based upon a concept of financial harm that is imprecise. . .it is incapable of rational or fair assessment. Furthermore, it involves treating, as actionable damage, and as a matter to be regarded in exclusively financial terms, the creation of a human relationship that is socially fundamental.'[46]

Justice Hayne

Justice Hayne, also in dissent, stated that the focus in the present case ought to always be on the actionable wrong – the failure by the doctor to give the correct advice.[47] Labelling the claim as involving questions of reproductive autonomy, he noted, distracted from, and clouded, the real issue.[48]

39 Note 12 at 209.
40 Note 12 at 211.
41 Note 12 at 213.
42 Note 12 at 133.
43 Note 12 at 143.
44 Note 12 at 144.
45 Note 12 at 141.
46 Note 12 at 144.
47 Note 12 at 182.
48 Note 12 at 183.

His Honour started from the view that all damages which were directly caused by the breach of duty were prima facie recoverable.[49] The emphasis was then on arguments which suggested that a particular class of damages was not recoverable.[50] His Honour considered a number of such arguments[51] – 'the child as blessing argument', 'the set-off for benefits of the child', 'the impossible prediction as to the future of the child', 'the award of damages could damage the child', 'the relevance of the motive for seeking sterilization'. Taking into account all these arguments, and the decision of the House of Lords in *MacFarlane v Tayside*, His Honour expressed himself satisfied that public policy dictated limiting the award of damages. This was because the birth of a child involved both benefits and burdens to a parent. Allowing a parent to claim for the economic consequences of bringing up a child involved requiring the parent to prove all the costs involved, inevitably ending up in a conclusion that bringing up the child 'was more trouble than it was worth'.[52] Such a commodification of the child was contrary to public policy. The one exception his Honour permitted was extra costs associated with a child with special needs.[53]

Damages for birth and confinement did not offend public policy because those costs were costs 'which affected the parent alone'.[54] In utilising public policy arguments to reach his conclusions, His Honour cited with approval Oliver Wendell Holmes' idea that public policy is 'the secret root from which the law draws all the juices of life'.[55]

Justice Heydon

Justice Heydon, dissenting, suggested that there were three reasons why the Court of Appeal had erred.[56] The reasoning of the Court of Appeal presupposed a loss in circumstances where what has occurred was not really a loss. This was because 'since the law assumes that human life has unique value and brings into existence corresponding duties of a unique kind, the impact of new life in a family is incapable of estimation in money terms'.[57] 'Secondly, that an award of damages encouraged parents to exaggerate the abilities of their children or the troubles of their children, which was "entirely alien to the assumptions and goals of the legal system" '.[58] Finally, that an award of damages generated litigation which

49 Note 12 at 183.
50 Note 12 at 183.
51 Note 12 at 184–188.
52 Note 12 at 200.
53 Note 12 at 201.
54 Note 12 at 201.
55 Note 12 at 191.
56 Note 12 at 227.
57 Note 12 at 227.
58 Note 12 at 227.

causes distress to children if they hear about the litigation.[59] The latter Justice Heydon found most repellent, especially given the general thrust of the law to safeguard the best interests of the child as a paramount concern.

Justice Heydon described the policy of the law to treat the birth of a child as valuable *per se*, not because it conferred blessings or economic advantages, but because it was life. A child was not a commodity capable of recompense.[60]

Like the Chief Justice, Justice Heydon expressed concerns about determining the exact length of time for which a child could expect to be maintained.[61] He also pointed out that, since the common law recognizes no caps on damages awards, the possibility existed for a very large damages claim in respect of a child born into a rich family.[62]

Further thoughts

It is hard not to agree with Seymour's comment that 'reading *Cattanach v Melchior* is a dispiriting experience. . . . Too often the analysis is cumbersome and discursive, with the result that it is frequently difficult to discover the precise basis for the conclusions reached.'[63]

Part of the problem would seem to be that the majority and minority judgments approach the same issue using a different analysis. On the one hand, there is reliance upon what Seymour describes as the 'personal views and the perceptions of desirable public policy.' This arises from the analysis of the issue as determining the monetary value of Jordan Melchior. On the other, again, Seymour's description, is 'a search for firm legal principle' arising from the question of the foreseeability (or remoteness) of damages for the upkeep of a child.

The minority judges, while strongly rejecting the commodification of children, seem perfectly prepared to do so when what is involved is not a healthy child, but a disabled child. There is less logic here than sympathy for the plight of those who must shoulder the burden of a sick child.[64] Understandable perhaps, but hardly consistent with the logical development of principle.

59 Note 12 at 227.

60 Note 12 at 228–231.

61 Note 12 at 215.

62 Note 12 at 214–215.

63 Seymour, J. '*Cattanach v Melchior*. Legal Principles and Public Policy' (2003) *Torts Law Journal* 14. Similar frustration is expressed by Vranken. M. 'Damages for Wrongful Birth – The Australian Perspective' (2003) *International Journal of Family Law* 210 '. . . unfortunately, an apparent inability, whether deliberate or not, among the current members of the High Court of Australia to act as team players makes for rather user-unfriendly case law. Six separate judgments, totaling some 165 pages and 605 footnotes, are testing even for the most dedicated of law students or practitioners'.

64 Seymour above, note 55.

This is not to assert that the position in other common law countries is any better. Kirby J describes the unfolding of the law in England as exhibiting a mixture of 'exhausted principle and obscure pragmatism'.[65]

English courts, having denied recovery for the upkeep of a healthy child (again rejecting commodification of the child) now permit damages for the birth of a disabled child[66] and, somewhat curiously, for the birth of a healthy child to a disabled mother.[67] Drawing the line between someone who has a healthy child (for which no recovery is possible) and someone with an unhealthy child, or who herself is suffering a disability (for whom recovery is possible) is deceptively easy. Waller LJ in Rees asks:

> Assume the mother with four children [who had] no support from husband, mother or siblings, and then compare her with the person who is disabled but who has a husband, siblings and a mother all willing to help. I think ordinary people would feel uncomfortable . . . that it was simply disability which has made a difference.

The analysis is further advanced by Priaulx. She notes:

> Parallels can be drawn. The diminished ability to care for a child need not derive from disability alone. Lone parenthood, coupled with a lack of social and familial support, typifies an analogous situation where individuals may honestly believe themselves to be diminished in their capacity to care for a child. . . . Courts may well find themselves unable to identify an appropriate demarcation between 'suffering a disability' and 'suffering hardship' in one's ability to care for a child.[68]

An alternative danger has been highlighted by Weir. He argues that inferior courts in England may well 'illustrate their antipathy' to the strictures of the *McFarlane* decision by finding disabilities, where there are, in fact, none.[69]

In Australia, at least one court has been able to find lawful grounds for an abortion in circumstances where continuance of the pregnancy did not pose a threat to the physical mental health of the mother – but where mental health problems following the birth of the child did do.[70] What then, of the situation in England where a healthy woman seeks sterilization, the sterilization is negligently performed, and the healthy mother gives birth to a healthy child – but the woman subsequently develops

65 Quoting with approval the view expressed in Hoyano, LCH 'Misconceptions about Wrongful Conception' (2002) *Modern Law Review* 883 at 905.

66 *Parkinson v St James and Seacroft University Hospital NTiS Trust* [2001] 2 FLR 401; *Groom v Selby* [2002] Lloyds Med Rep 1.

67 *Rees v Darlington Memorial Hospital NHS Trust* [2002] 1 FLR 799.

68 Priaulx, N. 'Parental Disability and Wrongful Conception' (2003) *Family Law Journal* 117.

69 Weir, T. *Rees v Darlington Memorial Hospital* [2002] 6 *Edinburgh Law Review* 248.

70 *CES v Superclinics.*

health problems as a result of childbirth? Are damages recoverable for wrongful birth? Douglas[71] and Prialux[72] think so.

The stage has now been reached where, unlike the majority of jurisdictions in the US,[73] and in England and Scotland, Australian courts have determined that damages are recoverable for the maintenance of an unwanted child, until that child turns 18. In choosing to depart from the common law world, it might have been thought that the High Court would clearly delineate the public policy considerations which make Australian parents (and their children) different from the rest of the common law world. Yet there is precious little in the decision which points to such differences. The High Court identifies no peculiarities of Australian society, its values or aspirations, which make it a 'distinct society' and deserving of different rules.

It is, of course, true that Australian law, adopting as it does the tests of liability for pure economic loss in *Perre v Apand*, has already departed from the 'fair, just and reasonable' test of the English Courts. But have we really gained anything useful? There would seem to be such a plurality of approaches to economic loss in *Perre v Apand* that it is hard to surmise any more than that the test is ultimately so flexible so as to allow the law on economic loss to be the modern day equivalent of 'the length of the Chancellor's foot'.

All bar one of the High Court Judges found that *Melchior*'s claim *was* one of pure economic loss (and thus was subject to the tests in *Perre v Apand*) – yet each of them came to such a different conclusion as to how the claim should be determined.

It has been stated elsewhere[74] that it is impossible not to be struck by McMurdo P's comments that there are obvious differences between the *Melchior's case* and *Perre v Apand.* The doctor and patient relationship is quite different to the commercial relationship between the parties in the *Perre* case. Moreover, in *Melchior,* unlike *Perre,* there was no question that the defendants owed the plaintiffs a duty of care; by the time the dispute reached the High Court, the question in *Melchior* was whether the damages concerned were too remote.

There remains a live question whether the loss suffered in *Melchior* was

71 Douglas, G [2002] *Family Law* 348. Priaulx, note 56.

72 Priaulx above, note 60.

73 The cases are reviewed by McMurdo P in the Court of Appeal's decision in *Melchior v Cattanach* note 7. *Rieek v Medical Protective Co of Fort Wayne Ind* 219 NW 2d 242 (1974); *Terrell v Garcia* 496 SW 2d'124 (1974); *Wilbur v Kerr* 628 SW 2d 568 (1982); *Cockrum v Baumgartner* 447 NE 2d 385 (1983); *McKernan v Aasheirn* 687 P 2d 850 (1984); *Girdley v Coates* 825 SW 2d 295 (1992). Opposing cases are *Custudio v Baker* 27 ALR 3d 884 (1967); *Sherlock v Stillwater Clinic* 260 NW 2d 190 (1977); *Ochs v Borrelli* 187 Conn 253 (1982); *Burke v Rivo* 551 NE 2d 1 (1990); *Lovelace Medical Centre v Mendez* 805 P 2d 603 (1991).

74 Note 8 at 150.

truly pure economic loss.[75] The loss to Mr. Melchior may well be described in this way. But surely the loss to Mrs Melchior was consequential upon a direct injury to her? If this is right, then the determination of her claim should proceed along normal remoteness lines, and Mr. Melchior's claim should have proceeded along the *Perre v Apand* lines. It is untidy, perhaps, that this should be so. The situation becomes further complicated by the possibility of sequential claims being made, in circumstances where the parents of the unwanted child are divorced. As Thomas JA pointed out, in these circumstances the father's claim might be the cost of maintenance he might otherwise be obliged to pay, and the mother's claim might be for the balance of the child's needs.[76]

The question of set-off for the benefits of having a child is likely to prove troublesome. While it is true that some of the benefits of having a child are difficult to quantify (such as companionship), others are more readily identifiable. Social security benefits routinely accrue to parents – why is it not possible to account for these? Justices McHugh and Gummow's coal miner analogy bears further thought. It might be true that a parent who gives birth to an unwanted child might enjoy some collateral benefits (similar to the coal miner's sitting in the sun reading his favourite newspaper) – but social security benefits, for one, would seem to be directly correlative and not collateral. The same could presumably be said of those families where children maintain their parents in their dotage – a matter referred to by the Chief Justice.

The issue of set-off for the benefits of having a child has been considered in US cases where, somewhat unsurprisingly perhaps, similar problems have been encountered in trying to decide whether such set-offs should be permitted.[77] The issue there arises out of section 920 of the Restatement (Second) of Torts – 'the benefit rule':

> When the defendant's tortious conduct has caused harm to the plaintiff or his property and in so doing has conferred a special benefit to the interest of the plaintiff that was harmed, the value of the benefit conferred is considered in mitigation of the damages, to the extent that this is equitable.

In the restatement, it is important to note that the interest of the plaintiff which has been harmed must be carefully identified – for it is only benefits relating to that interest for which 'set-off' is allowed. This 'same interest' limitation prevents damages resulting from the injury to one

75 The point has been made elsewhere see Devereux, JA *Melchior v Cattanch* (2001) 8 *Journal of Legal Medicine* 248. See also Lavery, J 'Rearing Expenses after Unwanted Pregnancy: Australia versus the United Kingdom' (2000) 9(2) *Australian Health Law Bulletin* 19 and McGivern, B 'Tortious Liability for (Selected) Genetic Harm: Exploring the Arguments' (2002) 10 *Torts Law Journal* 3 at note 68.

76 Note 8 at 149.

77 The American cases on set-off and mitigation of loss summarized in this note are discussed by Milsteen, below, note 78.

particular interest from being diminished by showing that some other interest has been benefited. Within the Australian context, a strict application of the benefit rule would suggest, for example, that social security benefits, or maintenance in old age, are pecuniary benefits which are the same interest as that which has been damaged by the failed sterilization. Companionship, on this analysis, would not be able to be offset.

Some US Courts have been willing to construe widely the interest affected by the birth of an unwanted child. So, in *Troppi v Scarf*,[78] where pregnancy followed a pharmacist supplying tranquillizers instead of contraceptive pills, the Court permitted offset of all aspects of childbirth, by non-pecuniary benefits that might accumulate to the parents from the birth of a child. A similar approach to *Troppi's* case is *Sherlock v Stillwater*.[79]

To the extent to which the benefit rule has been allowed to offset pecuniary benefits with non-pecuniary ones the Illinois Appellate Court opined that this had been a misapplication of the rule *(Cockrum v Baumgartner)*.[80] The rewards of parenthood were described as emotional in nature and thus different from the plaintiff's financial interests. Similarly, this is the approach of the Court in *Custodio v Bauer.*[81]

Focussing on the interest affected, in order to assess whether set-off should be permitted for benefits is interesting, conceptually, for another reason. Being precise about exactly what interests are affected may provide the solution for navigating the maze of damages or not in the failed sterilization debate.

Reading the English, American and Australian cases leads to the conclusion that the focus is very much on the 'child as damage'. Thus expressed, views as to the extent of recoverability of damage will always be sharply divided; dependent upon the factors identified above by Seymour.

If the focus is changed slightly, the outcome becomes less contentious.[82] So in *Coleman v Garrison*[83] as well as *Bushman v Burns Clinic*;[84] the cause of action was expressed to be wrongful pregnancy or wrongful conception. Viewed in this way, the focus is squarely upon pregnancy, rather than birth, as the wrong for which redress is sought. Damages for the costs of confinement, loss of income etc. are readily recoverable – but not so the costs of maintaining the child which may be considered too remote.

An alternative, and perhaps more realistic way to view the matter, is to start by acknowledging that unwillingly falling pregnant may be viewed

78 31 Mich App 240 (1971).
79 260 NW (2d) 169 (1977).
80 99 Ill App (3d) 271 (1981).
81 251 Cal. App (2d) 303 (1967).
82 See generally on this point Milsteen below, note 78.
83 327 A. (2d) 757 (1974).
84 83 Mich App 453 (1978).

as disastrous by different people, for different reasons. That is to say, for different people, different interests will be affected. For some, the reason not to have another child may be based on a well grounded fear of harm to self; for example, for a woman who has been warned that falling pregnant again could be disastrous to her health. For others, the reason may be economic – the inability to properly provide for 'another mouth to feed'. For still others there may be social or work related reasons why it may be inappropriate to fall pregnant. A dancer in a ballet company may not, for example, be permitted to continue dancing while pregnant.

Since the law of torts is directed toward the compensation of individuals ... for losses which they have suffered in respect of all their legally recognised interests, a determination of the specific interests the parents sought to protect through sterilization would necessarily relate to the appropriateness of damages to be awarded.... Only after the motivation, 'the why', has been discovered may the courts properly determine 'how much'.[85]

Milsteen[86] suggests there are three primary motivations for avoiding pregnancy. These he describes as The Therapeutic Motivation, The Eugenic Motivation and The Socio-Economic Motivation. Milsteen suggests that the courts, when assessing claims for wrongful birth, should focus on 'the motivation' for avoiding pregnancy in the first place.

In the therapeutic motivation, avoidance of pregnancy is sought to protect the physical or mental health of the parents. Milsteen's example is the case of *Custodio v Bauer*,[87] where the female concerned was advised to undergo a sterilization procedure to avoid aggravating an existing bladder and kidney condition. Viewed in this way the Court was able to note:

> The purpose of the operation was to save the wife from the hazards to her life which were incident to childbirth. It was not the alleged purpose to save the expense incidental to the pregnancy and delivery.... The expenses alleged are incidental to the bearing of a child, and their avoidance is remote from the avowed purpose of the operation.[88]

Identifying the damage caused as limited to the health to the mother has the effect of limiting the offset which might be thought to accrue from the benefit of having a child. Since having the child is unlikely to have any benefit to the health of the mother, no offset would be permitted.

The Eugenic Motivation focuses on a couple deciding not to have children to avoid the known possibility of having a disabled child. If this is the motivation for having a sterilization, and that sterilization fails, then damages should be awarded for the costs of birth and confinement plus

85 Prosser, W *Handbook on the Law of Torts* West Publishing, 4th ed, 1971 at para 1. Quoted in Milsteen below, note 65.

86 Milsteen, JL 'Recovery of Childrearing Expenses in Wrongful Birth Cases: A Motivational Analysis' (1983) 32 *Emory Law Journal* 1167.

87 251 Cal App (2d) 303 (1967).

88 251 Cal App (2d) at 318.

the extraordinary costs of raising a disabled child – medication, prostheses, care etc. Again, set-off would not be available as companionship is different from economic costs.

The Economic Motivation focuses on one of two motivations. A 'pure' economic motivation – where the parents simply cannot afford to have more children; or a 'socio-economic' motivation – where parents choose not to have any more children, for fear that it would impact upon their desired lifestyle and activities. In either case, the interest damaged is having the child and damages should be awarded accordingly.

Milsteen's argument is appealing, but leaves unanswered some questions. What, for example, of the parents for whom the eugenic motivation is the key motivation in having a sterilization – which fails. The mother then gives birth to a child – who is perfectly healthy. Would such a woman be denied damages on the basis that her interests were limited to avoiding the birth of an *unhealthy* child, which was not infringed by the birth of a *healthy* child?

Despite the possible shortcomings of Milsteen's analysis, it is clear that at least some judges are keen to analyse the loss occasioned following a failed sterilisation in terms of the particular interests of the plaintiff which have been affected. Thus, McMurdo P in *Melchior* notes that the loss for which the Melchiors claimed was precisely the type of harm which, by undergoing the sterilization, they were keen to avoid. Similarly, Priaulx, commenting on the decision of the court in Rees notes:

> An interesting aspect of the judgment in Rees is the critical emphasis placed upon the claimant's communication of her purpose in undergoing the operation as being relevant to the issue of the surgeon's assumption of responsibility . . .[89]

American courts have carefully considered the argument that, by failing to adopt out her child, or to seek a lawful abortion, the plaintiff in a wrongful birth action has failed to mitigate her loss – and that damages should be reduced accordingly. In America, this issue is referred to as 'the unavoidable consequences doctrine', the clearest statement of which appears in section 918 of the Restatement (Second) of Torts 'one injured by the tort of another is not entitled to recover damages for any harm that he could have avoided by the use of reasonable effort or expenditure after the commission of the tort'.

American courts have been scathing in their commentary on the suggestion that a woman should be forced to have an abortion, in order to mitigate her loss. In *Troppi v Scarf*,[90] the Court noted three reasons against forcing a woman to have an abortion or adopt out her child. Firstly, the Court noted there was an interest in permitting a child to be

89 Priaulx above, note 60.
90 31 Mich App 240 (1971).

raised by his natural parents. Secondly there was the mother's right to keep the child unless she was proven unfit. Finally there was the possibility of psychological harm that might result to a child from being adopted out.

In *Rivera v New York*,[91] the Court held that requiring a woman to have an abortion would 'constitute an invasion of privacy of the grossest and most pernicious kind.' In *Mason v Western Pennsylvania Hospital*[92] Justice Brosky suggests that requiring a woman to undergo an abortion 'carries a pungent odour of moral depravity'. Echoes of the American courts' findings can be seen in *CES v Superclinics*.[93] It is a pity the High Court did not make more of the opportunity presented to it in *Cattanch's* case to either affirm the view expressed in CES – or to distance itself from such a view.

In permitting recovery of damages for maintenance of a child, the arbitrariness of the age of majority as the cut-off point for maintenance requires further thought. As the Chief Justice points out, there are foreseeable obligations on a parent which may survive the child's majority – university education or marriage, for example. Why should these damages be regarded as too remote?

That the decision in *Melchior* was settled by the narrowest of majorities suggests the matter is one which may subsequently be reconsidered. Already the Queensland legislature has acted to prevent a repeat of such a damages award.[94] Developments in other common law jurisdictions are eagerly awaited.

Fordham M, 'Blessing or burden? Recent developments in actions for wrongful conception and wrongful birth in the UK and Australia [2004] Sing JLS 462

Introduction

In a case which came before the Singapore courts recently, a child suffering from Down's syndrome was named as co-plaintiff in an action brought by his mother against the obstetrician who allegedly failed to diagnose the child's condition in time for him to be aborted. The child's action, based on the financial hardship and pain which he had endured as a result of being born, appeared to fly in the face of established law. For it is accepted in just about every jurisdiction that no action is available in tort to a person who seeks to argue that he should have been spared a life which is so compromised that it lacks any value. On the occasions when an action of this nature has been attempted, the courts

91 94 Misc. (2d) 157 (1978).

92 268 Pa Super 354 (1981).

93 Above note 7.

94 Justice and Other Legislation Amendment Act 2003 (Qld).

have balked at the notion that a legal remedy should be available to the claimant, and for reasons of public policy they have thus far refused to recognize a duty to prevent life in such circumstances. On the other hand, the mother's claim seeking compensation for, *inter alia*, the costs of raising her disabled child, was based on somewhat firmer foundations. For actions brought against medical authorities by the parents of children born with disabilities and, indeed, the parents of healthy but unplanned children born following unsuccessful sterilisation procedures – have succeeded in a number of situations and jurisdictions since the decision of the English Court of Appeal in *Emeh v. Kensington & Chelsea & Westminster Area Health Authority*.' The distinction drawn between the two types of claim is that while one (the child's claim for 'wrongful life') would require a court to determine the worth – or lack thereof – of a human existence, the other (the parents' claim for 'wrongful conception' or 'wrongful birth' merely requires it to make a financial assessment of the costs associated with child-rearing. The distinction has, however, always had its detractors!) and decisions involving claims for the cost of raising children in wrongful conception and wrongful birth situations have gone both ways. The willingness of the English courts to allow claims for the cost of raising children – at least where those children are born without disabilities to able-bodied parents – ceased just before the millennium with the House of Lords' decision in *McFarlane and Another v. Tayside Health Board*. In the wake of *McFarlane*, there was uncertainty about the direction which the law might take in other jurisdictions, and questions were raised about the position in England should the courts in future be faced with claims involving parents or children suffering from disabilities. Those questions were answered to an extent when, in 2002, following a number of first instance decisions involving children born with disabilities, the English Court of Appeal decided in *Parkinson v. St James and Seacroft University Hospital NHS Trusts* that a mother could recover damages for the proportion of the costs which she would incur in raising her child which was attributable purely to the child's disabilities. Then in 2003 two more cases came before the highest courts – the first in Australia and the second in England. In the first case, *Cattanach v. Melchior* the Australian High Court narrowly decided to allow a claim for damages by the parents of a healthy child. However, in the second, *Rees v. Darlington Memorial Hospital NHS Trust*, the House of Lords, after considering *McFarlane, Parkinson* and *Melchior*, reaffirmed the views expressed in *McFarlane* and arguably went even further in holding that the disabled parent of a healthy child should receive no compensation for the cost of rearing that child. This article will examine the judicial approaches taken in these cases, *and* will seek to determine whether any consistency can be discerned in this morally cloudy area of the law.

II. THE CASES

McFarlane

McFarlane (an appeal from the Scottish Inner House of the Court of Session) offered the House of Lords its first opportunity to consider the question of whether damages should be awarded for the cost of raising a child who had been born as a result of an act of medical negligence. The case involved a claim for damages for wrongful conception brought by the parents of a healthy baby girl. The child was conceived and born after the husband had wrongly and negligently been informed, following a vasectomy, that he was now sterile and that he and his wife need no longer use contraceptives. The question before the House was therefore whether the doctor responsible for giving the negligent advice – and, more significantly, his employers, the local health authority – should be held liable for the costs associated with the child's upbringing. When *McFarlane* was decided, the prevailing English law – as represented by *Emeh* and the cases which had followed it – recognized liability by a medical authority for the cost of raising a child, whether healthy or disabled, in circumstances where the authority was responsible for wrongly preventing the conception and/or birth of the child in question. This position was, moreover, generally regarded as being consistent with the category of claims for pure economic loss arising from professional negligence which had come to be recognized following the House of Lords' application of the principle established in *Hedley Byrne & Co. Ltd. v Heller & Partners* in *Henderson v. Merrell Syndicates Limited.* Yet in *McFarlane* all five members of the court – for reasons which, it must be said, were neither fully canvassed nor entirely consistent – held that claims for the cost of raising a healthy child should cease to be allowed. In spite of the obvious moral and ethical connotations of the case, their Lordships sought to distance themselves from issues of public policy – although their judgments indicate the impossibility in practice of separating the law from social considerations in a case of this kind. Lord Millett based his judgment on the premise that a healthy child, whether planned or not, should always be treated as a blessing, and that it would be 'subversive of the mores of society for parents to enjoy the advantages of parenthood while transferring to others the responsibilities which it entails'. Lord Hope considered that, since the benefits of having a healthy child were incalculable, it could not be said that the financial obligations involved in raising such a child outweighed the benefits of parenthood, and so it would not be fair, just or reasonable to relieve the parents of these obligations. Lord Clyde (who preferred an analysis based on extent of loss rather than duty of care) referred to 'the expense of child rearing [being] wholly disproportionate to the doctor's culpability', and Lord Slynn, taking a similar view albeit from a duty angle, stated that '[t]he doctor undertakes a duty of care in regard to the prevention of pregnancy: it does not follow that the duty includes also avoiding the costs of rearing the child if born and accepted into the family'. Lord Steyn was the only judge openly to recognize the moral aspect of the case. He drew on the perceived views of the general public (in the form of commuters on the London Underground) in concluding that, if such ordinary men and women were to be asked 'Should the parents of an unwanted but healthy child be able to sue the doctor or hospital for compensation equivalent to the cost of bringing up the child for the years of his or her minority?':

> I am firmly of the view that an overwhelming number . . . would answer the question with an emphatic 'No'. And the reason for such a response would be an inarticulate premise as to what is morally acceptable and what is not . . . The realisation that compensation for financial loss in respect of the upbringing of a child would necessarily have to discriminate between rich and poor would, surely, appear unseemly to them. It would also worry them that parents may be put in a position of arguing in court that the unwanted child, which they accepted and care for, is more trouble than it is worth. Instinctively, the traveller on the Underground would consider that the law of tort has no business to provide legal remedies consequent on the birth of a healthy child, which all of us regard as a good thing. Even Lord Steyn, though, asserted that his judgment was based ultimately on considerations of distributive justice rather than on pure considerations of morality. The unanimous finding that there could be no liability for the child's upbringing did not lead their Lordships to conclude that the health authority should be entirely immune from liability. All five judges agreed that some claim should be available with respect to the unplanned pregnancy, although there was limited agreement as to exactly what this claim should cover. All except Lord Millett were willing to treat the mother's condition as physical injury, and thus to award damages for the pain, suffering and inconvenience of pregnancy and childbirth. Lord Millett was not willing to award anything to the mother for the pain and suffering associated with the pregnancy and birth, although he would have been prepared to make a conventional award of £5,000 to recognise the parents' loss of autonomy in choosing to limit the size of their family. The majority – again with the exception of Lord Millett, and apparently Lord Clyde – considered that the mother should also recover for loss of earnings during pregnancy, and Lord Hope (and possibly Lord Slynn) would even have been prepared to extend this to her loss of earnings for an undetermined period following the baby's birth. But these were comparatively minor concessions in a decision which effectively eradicated the possibility of suing in negligence for the cost of raising a healthy child.

Parkinson and its precursors

In the immediate aftermath of *McFarlane*, three wrongful birth claims came before the lower courts. In the first case, *Rand*, antenatal screening had failed to detect that a foetus had Down's Syndrome. Had the parents been aware of this, they would have had the opportunity to terminate the pregnancy, and having been denied this opportunity, they claimed compensation for expenses associated with the child's disabilities. The judge, Newman J, concluded that wrongful birth cases (where the pregnancy was initially desired, but would have ceased to have been so had the parents been made aware of the disabled condition of the foetus) were different from wrongful conception cases like *McFarlane* (where the pregnancy itself – although resulting in the birth of a healthy child – was undesired) and should thus be treated differently. One difference was that since the parents in a wrongful birth case intended to have a child, they could not claim that the birth itself was damage, and so their only claim was for economic loss. However, the arguments which had prevailed for refusing to allow a claim for economic loss in *McFarlane* were not applicable in a wrongful birth case, where the incalculable benefits of bearing a healthy child were not relevant, and where the hypothetical commuter on the London Underground would be unlikely to consider it morally repugnant to focus on compensation for the consequences of disability. It was foreseeable that if the relevant health authority failed properly to screen mothers, thus depriving parents of their rights under the Abortion Act 1967, those parents would suffer damage, and that damage should be recoverable under the extended *Hedley Byrne* principle. Newman J awarded compensation to cover the economic consequences flowing from the child's disability. The case was settled before appeal, but a similar issue then arose in *Hardman*. In this case, Henriques J, faced with a claim brought by a mother who gave birth to a child with severe disabilities after doctors failed to diagnose that she had contracted rubella while she was pregnant, held that *McFarlane* did not affect the law concerning children born with disabilities and awarded damages for the costs associated with the child's condition. *Hardman* was followed by *Lee*, in which antenatal screening had failed to diagnose that a foetus was suffering from spina bifida, and the child in question had therefore been born with severe congenital abnormalities. The parents had specifically sought the screening since they feared foetal disability as a result of medication which they were both taking. Toulson J, deciding the case, was of the view that the two main lines of reasoning to be drawn from *McFarlane* were that either the birth of a child was a blessing, for which no compensation should be given, or that doctors should not be made to compensate parents for the disproportionately large expense of raising a child whose very existence would be enriching (the first approach being attributed to Lords Millett, Steyn and Hope and the second to Lords Slynn and Clyde). Neither line of reasoning could apply in the case of a child born with disabilities. Toulson J therefore awarded damages for the cost of raising the child.

It was against this background that the Court of Appeal reached its decision in *Parkinson*. The case was an unusual one since it concerned a child born with behavioural problems attributable to an unidentifiable condition following a failed sterilisation procedure. The mother had been informed during her pregnancy that the child might be disabled, but she had chosen not to have an abortion. *Parkinson* therefore straddled the divide between actions for wrongful conception and actions for wrongful birth, involving as it did a claim for the cost of raising a disabled child who had been conceived following a failed medical procedure. The Court of Appeal decided that the mother could recover damages for the costs associated with her child's condition, even though her sterilisation had *not* been carried out specifically for the purpose of preventing the birth of a disabled child, thus effectively sidelining *McFarlane* in claims for the cost of raising a child born with disabilities.

In her judgment, Hale LJ embarked on an extensive examination of the wide-reaching implications of pregnancy, childbirth and motherhood, and traced the limitations which all three conditions placed on a woman's autonomy. Had she not been constrained by the binding decision in *McFarlane*, she would have treated the cost of raising a child not as purely economic loss but rather as a consequential loss flowing from invasion of that autonomy by a doctor who failed to control a woman's fertility. She discerned little consensus in their Lordships' reasoning in *McFarlane*, and observed that the unintended effect of the decision might well be to encourage abortions among women who had sought to be sterilized for economic reasons and who would now have no means of obtaining financial assistance in raising their unplanned children. She also questioned Lord Steyn's arguments about distributive justice and commuters on the Underground on the basis that:

> The traveller is not here being invoked as a hypothetical reasonable man but as a moral arbiter. We all know that London commuters are not a representative sample of public opinion. We also know that the answer will crucially depend upon the question asked and the amount of relevant information and argument given to help answer it. The fact that so many eminent judges all over the world have wrestled with this problem and reached different conclusions might suggest that the considered response might be less emphatic and less unanimous.

However, Hale LJ considered that even if one *were* to assume that the Underground commuters would object to allowing a claim for the cost of raising a healthy child, this objection would not be likely to extend to a disabled one. Drawing on some of the judgments in *McFarlane* to frame the notion of 'deemed equilibrium' (under which the benefits associated with raising a healthy child would be deemed to balance out the costs, thus negativing the claim), her Ladyship concluded that although this concept carried the danger of commodifying children – an objection subsequently relied on heavily by the minority in *Melchior* – it crucially allowed a disabled child to be regarded as having the same worth and as offering the same benefits as a healthy child, but to be classified differently when it came to compensation because he cost more. This she felt would be regarded as unobjectionable by Lord

Steyn's 'Underground commuters'. Brooke LJ also discerned few common features in the judgments *in McFarlane* (concluding that their Lordships 'spoke with five different voices') and was of the view that, whatever its findings with respect to healthy children, the decision gave no clear indication of the position to be adopted in cases concerning those born with disabilities. He therefore considered himself free to reason from first principles. Most of these principles (such as the fact that it was foreseeable that a child might be conceived if a surgeon were to carry out a sterilisation procedure negligently, and that the category of claimants in such cases would be limited to the parents of the unwanted child in question) would have been equally applicable to healthy children and were clearly based on what his Lordship saw as the quite reasonable position under which such claims had been allowed prior to *McFarlane*. However, the key finding – and the one which was confined to situations involving disabled children – was that it was fair, just and reasonable to award damages to cover the special ('often staggering and quite debilitating') costs involved in bringing up a child with serious disabilities. In terms of distributive justice, he considered that most people would find such an award acceptable as long as that award were to be confined to the additional expenses associated with the child's condition. Sir Martin Nourse agreed that damages should be awarded. The Court of Appeal refused leave to appeal to the House of Lords and the defendant, the National Health Service (N.H.S.), did not pursue the matter.

Melchior

Into this picture came the decision of the Australian High Court *in Melchior*. The case concerned a couple who conceived their third child after the mother, Mrs Melchior, had undergone a tubal ligation. While carrying out the procedure, the defendant doctor, Dr Cattanach, had failed to clip her right fallopian tube, since he wrongly believed it had been removed. He did not, therefore, warn her after the procedure that she might still be fertile. She subsequently became pregnant and gave birth to a healthy child. Following the birth of this child, the parents sued the defendant in contract and tort for the cost of raising the child. The contract claim was not pursued, but at trial the defendant was found liable in negligence for failing to inform the mother of the possibility that the procedure might not succeed due to the presence of her functioning right tube. An appeal by the defendant to the Queensland Court of Appeal failed, and the defendant then appealed to the High Court. The only question before the High Court was whether the Court of Appeal had been wrong to hold that the parents were entitled to damages for the reasonable costs of maintaining their child, since the issues of duty, breach, causation and remoteness, together with liability for the mother's pecuniary and non-pecuniary losses arising from her pregnancy, were all agreed in the claimants' favour. By a majority of four to three the court held that the Court of Appeal had been correct in upholding the trial judge's decision to award damages for the costs of raising the child. The three very detailed majority judgments (only McHugh and Gummow JJ produced a joint judgment) contained a number of common threads, as did the three similarly full minority ones. The majority, having accepted the existence of the elements of a negligence claim, found it comparatively straightforward to conclude that compensation was thus required under normal tort principles. The minority, on the other hand, based their decision primarily on policy objections to the claim. Of the majority judges, Kirby J, normally a willing advocate of the open consideration of policy issues, regretted the demise in Australia of the *Caparo* test, the absence of which he feared would lead to a less transparent approach to such matters. Without *Caparo* to assist him, he based his judgment on what he described as 'ordinary principles of tort liability'. In his opinion, the case was not confined by the parameters of pure economic loss, since it involved damages for the economic consequences of a physical event. Moreover, to deny a claim of this nature would 'provide a zone of legal immunity to medical practitioners engaged in sterilisation procedures that is unprincipled and inconsistent with established legal doctrine'. Kirby J recognised that five alternative outcomes were possible. The first (conforming with the views of Lord Millett in *McFarlane)* would be to hold that every child should be regarded as a 'blessing,' and thus to refuse to recognise any claim in negligence in these circumstances, whether the child in question was healthy or disabled. This alternative Kirby J rejected both on the basis that it was a fiction to assume that every child indeed constituted a blessing, and on the basis that the claim was, anyway, not a claim with respect to the child's very existence but rather a claim for the costs involved in raising it. The second alternative (in line with the decision in *McFarlane)* would be to accept the validity of a claim in negligence in these circumstances, but to confine it to the immediate physical and economic consequences of pregnancy and delivery. The third would be to extend damages to the cost of maintaining a child, but only if the child (as in *Parkinson)* and/or its parent or parents' suffered from a disability. Both outcomes Kirby J regarded as 'arbitrary' and 'unjust' or 'unacceptable'. The fourth alternative – and one which Kirby J admitted to having initially found attractive – would be to extend damages to cover the costs of maintaining any child, whether healthy or disabled, but with a reduction to reflect the joys and benefits of parenthood. On consideration, however, his Honour was of the opinion that, as a matter of legal principle, there was no justification for taking account of such benefits, which had 'nothing to do with the legal wrong for whose foreseeable consequences the tortfeasor must restore the parents'. He therefore concluded that the fifth alternative – that of extending damages to the cost of raising any child with no reduction to take account of the benefits of child-rearing – was the correct one. In the case at hand, this alternative would 'entitle the victims of the appellants' wrong to recover from the appellants all aspects of their harm that are reasonably foreseeable and not too remote'. Like Kirby J, McHugh and Gummow considered that not every birth could be regarded as a blessing and that, anyway, a claim for the cost of raising a child must be separated from the emotional issues involved:

The unplanned child is not the harm for which recompense is sought in this action; it is the burden of the legal and moral responsibilities which arise by reason of the birth that is in contention. The expression 'wrongful birth' . . . is misleading and directs attention away from the appropriate frame of legal discourse. What is wrongful in this case was not the birth of a third child to Mr. and Mrs. Melchior but the negligence of Dr. Cattanach. Neither were their Honours impressed by the possibility (which they considered to be 'speculative' at best) that an award of damages now might later harm the child when he learned that his conception had been undesired and that his birth had given rise to a claim for compensation. Moreover, there was no argument to justify reduction of damages to take account of the pleasures of child-rearing, since '[t]he benefits received from the birth of a child are not legally relevant to the head of damage that compensates for the cost of maintaining the child.' Callinan J while acknowledging that he found it 'personally distasteful to be required to assess damages of the kind claimed' nevertheless considered the decision to be a relatively simple one to reach.

The appellants were negligent. The respondents as a result have incurred and will continue to incur considerable expense. That expense would not have been incurred had the first appellant not given negligent professional advice. All of the various touchstones for, and none of the relevant disqualifying conditions against, an award of damages for economic loss are present here. The minority judges were (not surprisingly) more impressed by the reasoning in *McFarlane*, and in particular by the views of the most cautious of the judges in that case, Lord Millets. Approving Lord Millett's analysis, Hayne J held that public policy militated against an inquiry into the monetary worth of the child, an inquiry which would encourage parents to argue that the burdens of child-rearing outweighed the benefits, and which would lead them to treat 'the child as a commodity to be given a market value'. He would therefore have restricted any claim in circumstances such as these to 'those matters which affect the parent alone'. Heydon J, too, relied heavily on public policy in his judgment, and shared the view that it would be wrong to allow the 'commodification' of the child:

A child is not an object for the gratification of parents, like a pet or an antique car or a new dress. Nor is it a proprietary advantage which has accompanying burdens needing to be met if the advantage is to be fully secured . . . His judgment was, however, also concerned with the practical consequences of allowing claims of this kind. He asked how the appropriate level of compensation could be assessed and wondered what would (or should) happen in claims by families with high expectations about private schooling up to the age of 18 – and possibly beyond, or in situations where an additional child might make the family wish to move to a bigger house or to extend their existing one. Moreover, in comparison with personal injury litigation, where there were a number of moral and legal safeguards against exaggerating the damage for which a claim was being made, his Honour worried that claimants would be more likely to overstate the expenses associated with bringing up a child:

> . . . [A] new order of litigation would arise if the law permitted plaintiffs to sue in respect of the apprehended cost of future events relating to the ordinary needs and weaknesses of their children. The restraints on plaintiffs exaggerating the needs and weaknesses of their children are likely to be much more attenuated than the restraints against plaintiffs exaggerating their own needs and weaknesses.

Gleeson CJ expressed similar concerns about the means of assessing such claims ('If the cost of birthday and Christmas presents is to be included, why not . . . the expense associated with a wedding? If the cost of schooling is included, why not . . . the cost of tertiary education?'). His concerns in this respect were influenced – much as the judgments of Lords Clyde and Slynn had been in *McFarlane* – by the view that it would not be reasonable to hold a doctor liable for such expenses, since this would go beyond the 'reasonable restitution' required by tort law. His Honour concluded that the claim involved:

> . . . treating, as actionable damage, and as a matter to be regarded in exclusively financial terms, the creation of a human relationship that is socially fundamental. The accepted approach in this country is that 'the law should develop novel categories of negligence incrementally and by analogy with established categories.' The recognition of the present claim goes beyond that, and is unwarranted.

Rees

Some of their Honours in *Melchior* referred to the recent decision of the English Court of Appeal in *Rees*, and to the fact that the case had been appealed to the House of Lords, but that their Lordships' decision was still awaited. Some three months later that decision was delivered. *Rees* involved a healthy baby born, following a negligently performed sterilisation procedure, to a mother who was severely visually handicapped. She had sought to be sterilised primarily, although not exclusively, because of her disability. Her action against the relevant medical authorities was for the additional costs which she would incur in raising her child due to her condition. The trial judge, Stuart Brown QC, held (somewhat reluctantly) that the decision in *McFarlane* precluded the claim, since the mother's losses – in employing extra help or calling on friends and family to assist – would be the same as those of many other mothers and were not of the same nature as those in the case of a handicapped child. On appeal to the Court of Appeal, two of the three judges – Hale and Robert Walker LJJ – reversed this finding, although their reasons for doing so were rather different. Hale LJ, adopting her own analysis in *Parkinson*, drew on the concept of 'deemed equilibrium' which she had favoured in that case. In her opinion, *McFarlane* was distinguishable from the present case because, unlike a healthy parent, a disabled parent could not raise a child unaided and must necessarily draw on the assistance of others. Robert Walker LJ, on the other hand, did not find any grounds for the 'deemed equilibrium' view in the judgments in *McFarlane*, and preferred to draw on what he saw as the 'moral intuition' of the courts in both that case and *Parkinson*. The claimant's disability (which had been known to the surgeon and had been accepted by him as the main reason for her requiring sterilisation) meant that it was fair, just and reasonable to hold that he had assumed a responsibility to her. Given the increasing recognition of the need to treat disabled persons with special consideration, there was nothing morally repugnant about awarding damages for expenses which she would incur due to her visual impairment. Waller LJ dissented. In a powerfully worded judgment, he expressed his discomfort with the notion that the mother's disability alone should enable her to claim when healthy parents (however desperate their circumstances) were not able to do so. He also considered that, once the claimant adjusted to life with the child, she might actually find her son's presence to be beneficial. In the House of Lords, a bench of seven Law Lords was asked to consider two issues. The first was whether *McFarlane* should be overruled, and the second was whether, if *McFarlane* remained good law, it would preclude recovery for the costs incurred by a disabled parent in raising a healthy child. All seven judges agreed that *McFarlane* had been correctly decided and should not be overruled. By a bare majority the court reversed the decision of the Court of Appeal and held that the costs of raising the child were irrecoverable. The majority – Lord Bingham of Cornhill, Lord Nicholls of Birkenhead, Lord Millets and Lord Scott of Foscoe – held that no damages should be awarded to cover the costs of bringing up the child which flowed from the mother's disability (although, as established by *McFarlane*, the mother could recover for the pain and suffering associated with pregnancy and birth). They did, however, hold – in a decision which drew on the views of Lord Millets in McFarlane – that she should receive a conventional award, set at £15,000, to reflect the wrong which she had suffered in being denied the opportunity to live as she had planned. Lord Bingham, who discussed at length both *McFarlane* and *Melchior* (and in particular Kirby J's formulation of the possible outcomes in a case of this kind), acknowledged that an orthodox application of tort principles would have allowed recovery in *McFarlane* under the rules governing liability for negligent misstatements. Their Lordships in *McFarlane* had adopted different approaches when refusing to apply the orthodox principles, but all had refused to do so 'for reasons of policy (legal, not, public policy),' which Lord Bingham considered to be completely justified, and which he now applied in *Rees*. However, his Lordship felt that some payment should be made to recognise the fact that the mother had lost the right to choose to remain childless, and he concluded:

I would . . . support the suggestion favoured by Lord Millett in *McFarlane* . . . that in all cases such as these there would be a conventional award to mark the injury and loss . . . (I have in mind a conventional figure of £15,000) and I would add this to the award for pregnancy and birth. This solution is in my opinion consistent with the ruling and rationale in *McFarlane*. The conventional award would not be, and would not be intended to be, compensatory. It would not be the product of calculation. But it would not be a nominal, let alone a derisory, award. It would afford some measure of recognition of the wrong done. And it would afford a more ample measure of justice than the pure *McFarlane* rule. I would for my part apply this rule also, without differentiation, to cases in which either the child or the parent is (or claims to be) disabled. Lord Nicholls took the view that while 'on ordinary principles the foreseeable adverse financial consequences of a legal wrong may expect to be borne by him who committed the wrong', it was nevertheless crucial to bear in mind that '[r]ecoverability of damages is always bounded by considerations of fairness and reasonableness.' Based on such considerations, and in particular on the idea that it would be 'a disproportionate response to the doctor's wrong' to hold the National Health Service liable for the costs of bringing up the child, he agreed that the decision in *McFarlane* should stand. He further agreed with the award of £15,000 to recognise the wrong which the mother had suffered. While recognising the essentially arbitrary nature of the sum decided upon, he preferred this to the alternative of means-testing. Lord Millett, who in *McFarlane* had firmly opposed the notion of compensating parents for the costs of raising healthy children, unsurprisingly saw no reason to make an exception where the parents of such children were themselves disabled. He believed that although the individual judgments in *McFarlane* had involved differences of approach, they had been based on the underlying idea expressed in his own judgment that '[i]t is morally offensive to regard a normal, healthy baby as more trouble and expense than it is worth.' In this respect, he was openly critical of Hale LJ's analysis both in *Parkinson* and in the Court of Appeal in this case that the decision in *McFarlane* had rested on a theory of 'deemed equilibrium' 'such a theory cannot be extracted from the speeches; on the contrary, it is entirely inconsistent with them.' His Lordship considered that the question of whether *Parkinson* had been correctly decided was not relevant to this case and should be left open, although he did recognise that the costs associated with raising a disabled child could be treated differently from those associated with raising a healthy one, and expressed the view that he would not 'find it morally offensive to reflect this difference in an award of compensation.' However, he saw no justification for extending this principle to disabled parents, and drew heavily on the dissenting judgment of Waller LJ in the Court of Appeal to stress the arbitrariness of awarding damages to a disabled parent when no able-bodied parent, however dire the circumstances, would be able to recover, and to make the point that the birth of a healthy child to a disabled parent might in fact prove to be an advantage as the child grew up and became able to assist the parent. With respect to the conventional award which he alone had favoured in *McFarlane*, but which was now being approved by the majority in this case, Lord Millett observed that such an award 'would not, of course go far towards the costs of bringing up a child ... but it would not be meant to ... a modest award would, however, adequately compensate for the very different injury to the parents' autonomy.' The last of the majority judges, Lord Scott, agreed that general principles would require the claimant 'to be placed in the same position he or she would have been in if the professional advice or services had been competently provided' but concluded that simply applying such general principles was difficult in cases of this kind 'because the consequence of the negligence is the birth of a human being and because assessments about the value or burden of a particular human life are impossible.' *McFarlane*, rightly in his Lordship's view, had established an exception to general principles which recognised the uniqueness of such claims. This case differed from *McFarlane* only because the mother was blind, which his Lordship did not consider sufficient to take it outside the ambit of that decision ('a balance sheet of detriment and benefit ... cannot be drawn up'). Although not critical to this case, Lord Scott questioned the decision to award damages in the case of a disabled child in *Parkinson*, since the parents in that case had asked for the relevant sterilisation to be performed simply to avoid conception in general, rather than to avoid the conception of a disabled child. Only in the latter category would his Lordship have been willing to make an exception to *McFarlane*. He agreed that in this case a conventional sum of £15,000 should be awarded. The three dissenting judges – two of whom (Lord Steyn and Lord Hope) had decided *McFarlane* – considered that this case fell outside the *McFarlane* principle. Lord Steyn and Lord Hope were, moreover, extremely critical of the legal basis for the conventional award favoured by their majority colleagues. Lord Steyn was of the view that their Lordships in *McFarlane* had not addressed their minds to the issue of a disabled mother giving birth to a healthy child, which meant that the matter now had to be considered for the first time. Although impressed by the dissenting opinion of Waller LJ in the Court of Appeal, in which his Lordship had stressed the arbitrariness of making awards to disabled parents when even the most needy healthy ones had no claim, Lord Steyn was more persuaded by the views of Robert Walker LJ who, while recognising the danger of arbitrary lines being drawn, had nevertheless held that recovery should not be denied to a deserving category of claimants. Lord Steyn concluded:

> It is unrealistic to say that there is only one right answer. But a decision must be made, and that decision must represent the best available choice and hopefully a decision defensible as delivering justice . . . it is logically not straightforward to treat the present case simply as an extension of *Parkinson*. On the other hand, I consider (like Hale and Robert Walker LJJ) that the law should give special consideration to the serious disability of a mother who had wanted to avoid having a child by undergoing a sterilisation operation. I am persuaded that the

> injustice of denying to such a seriously disabled mother the limited remedy of the extra costs caused by her disability outweighs the considerations emphasised by Waller LJ.

In his judgment, Lord Hope took issue with Lord Millett's view that the judges in *McFarlane* had basically shared his view that it was morally offensive to treat a healthy child as more trouble than it was worth ('I did not base my decision on a belief that it was morally repugnant to award damages for the birth of a healthy child . . . the fundamental value which is attached to human life is an ethical, not an economic, concept, and the problem . . . [is] legal, not theological'). Lord Hope regarded the real problem in cases of this kind to be the calculating the additional costs which a disabled parent would incur. Like Lord Steyn, he was impressed by the views of Waller LJ in the Court of Appeal, and he accepted that there might be considerable difficulties in determining the extent to which a mother's disability increased the cost of raising her child. However, also like Lord Steyn, Lord Hope ultimately preferred the reasoning of Robert Walker LJ, and held that these difficulties should not deter a court from considering the possibility of recovery. While accepting Lord Millett's point that a parent's reason for not wanting any (or more) children is normally irrelevant, his Lordship concluded:

> On balance . . . I have come to the view that the fact that the child's parent is seriously disabled does provide a ground for distinguishing *McFarlane* and that it would be fair, just and reasonable to hold that such extra costs as can be attributed to the disability are within the scope of the tortfeasor's duty of care and are recoverable . . . I have referred to the parent in whose favour the exception exists as 'seriously disabled'. The word 'serious' is important. The normal incidents of an otherwise healthy life must be held to be covered by the *McFarlane* principle . . .

Lord Hutton shared the view that difficulties of determination and assessment of damages should not lead to denial of a rule allowing recovery. He considered that, as an exception to the normal rules, *McFarlane* should not apply to either a disabled child or a disabled mother. The reservations of Lord Hope and Lord Steyn about the conventional award of £15,000 were very strongly worded. Lord Hope pointed out that although conventional awards are common in the field of personal injury, where it is impossible to place an accurate financial value on the loss of a limb or an eye, no such problem of assessment exists in cases involving financial loss. To make a conventional award in such circumstances would not only be novel, it would effectively mean the division of damages into two parts – general and special – with the intention of allowing the first while rejecting the second. This would be contrary to the compensatory function of tort law. Although Lord Bingham had appeared to acknowledge that the award would not be compensatory, the other majority judges had not done so, which left considerable doubt as to the basis for the award. Lord Steyn was similarly concerned. He observed that, if applied in the way suggested by Lord Bingham (the only judge specifically to state that the award would apply to all cases without differentiation), it would require a departure from *McFarlane* and a reversal of the position in *Parkinson*, and, like Lord Hope, he objected to the fact that, having been rejected by the majority in *McFarlane*, the concept of a conventional award was now being mooted at a late stage in this appeal without having had the benefit of being considered in either of the courts below. Lord Steyn (expressing views shared by Lord Hope) observed:

> It is a great disadvantage for the House to consider such a point without the benefit of the views of the Court of Appeal. And the disadvantage cannot be removed by calling the new rule a 'gloss'. It is a radical and most important development which should only be embarked on after rigorous examination of competing arguments . . . No United Kingdom authority is cited for the proposition that judges have the power to create a remedy of awarding a conventional sum in cases such as the present. There is none . . . Like Lord Hope I regard the idea of a conventional award in the present ease as contrary to principle . . . In my view the majority have strayed into forbidden territory . . . If such a rule is to be created it must be done by Parliament.

The fact is, however, that it would be a hugely controversial legislative measure.

III. DISCUSSION

The law in this area has never been jurisdictionally consistent, but the present position is less settled – and more confused – than at any time since *Emeh* was decided almost twenty years ago. Although the lack of judicial consensus is perhaps not particularly surprising, given the fact that, as Lord Steyn observed *in Rees*, there is no 'right answer' *to* the questions which the courts face in cases of this kind, it is unfortunate that decisions in recent years have done little to focus or clarify the position. One noteworthy feature of wrongful conception *and* wrongful birth cases in both England and Australia is the acceptance by the courts that the claims satisfy the requirements for recovery under the general principles of tort law, and that only if an exception to these general principles is recognised will the claims fail. This is noteworthy because, in spite of the fact – at least in wrongful conception cases – that the mother's claim for damages for pregnancy and childbirth stems *from* her physical condition and its economic consequences, most judges treat the claim for the costs of maintaining the child whom she bears as an action for pure economic loss. Pure economic loss is, of course, an area of damage which normally poses considerable problems for claimants in negligence actions; and although several of the cases (like *McFarlane* and *Melchior*) have involved the more readily compensable category of economic loss caused by negligent misstatements, others (like *Rees*) have involved claims for economic loss caused by negligent acts, an area in which the English courts, in particular, operate an almost blanket prohibition against recovery. Yet even the English courts have generally eschewed this line of reasoning, largely because of the notion of 'professional responsibility', under which a claimant may succeed against a professional who has negligently caused him harm, regardless of whether the negligence takes the form of an act or a statement and of whether it causes physical damage or economic loss. As a result, the class of damage in wrongful conception and wrongful birth claims is treated as fundamentally allowable, with the legitimacy of the claims being questioned (by those who do question their legitimacy) not because – or at least not primarily because – the claims relate to economic loss, but because they involve difficult questions of moral, ethical and distributive justice. And it is these difficult questions which are responsible for the uncertainties and inconsistencies to be found in the law as it presently stands. For while most judges (with some refreshing exceptions, particularly in the Australian High Court) seek to distance themselves from the idea that their judgments are based on matters of public or social policy, in practice these are the concerns which are at the very heart of their decisions. To describe – as Lord Bingham did in *Rees* – the decision in *McFarlane* as being based on 'legal, not public policy', is to create a distinction so fine that it is almost meaningless. That is not to say that had there been more openness about public policy considerations in *McFarlane* the case would have been decided any differently. Whether a judge acknowledges that a decision is being reached for reasons of policy, or whether he rationalises it in terms of 'justice and reasonableness', or according to principles of causation or extent of loss, the outcome is likely to be the same, because his instinctive view of what is right will be the same whatever label he uses to communicate that view. However, if their Lordships in *McFarlane* had been willing to reach a consensus on the underlying reasons for their decision (even if this consensus had been nothing more than the open acknowledgment of a desire to protect the already under-funded and over-stretched National Health Service from further calls on its resources) there would have been a far greater chance of that decision offering a concise and clearly-stated precedent, which in turn might have led to its concise and clearly-stated application in subsequent cases. Instead, we have witnessed a number of disparate views being expressed at length in a number of cases, culminating in the decisions in *Parkinson* and *Rees*. Indeed, it is largely because of the difficulty in drawing a single ratio from the five judgments in *McFarlane* (beyond the fact that the costs of raising a healthy child are not recoverable), that judges in cases like *Parkinson* and now *Rees* have become embroiled in such a complicated process of reasoning and distinguishing. This writer considers the decision in *McFarlane* to have been unjustifiably rigid in its refusal to award damages for the costs of raising children born as a result of medical negligence, and is therefore to some extent grateful that the decision did not close the door to recovery in all such cases. But it must be said that the law in this area has not been well-served by the lack of a clear and coherently articulated principle in *McFarlane*. Nor can the Australian High Court really be said to have contributed to the search for clarity in this area. The decision in *Melchior* is extremely long, and the six separate judgments make few concessions to the need for a clear statement of law. Moreover, although the decision allows for recovery even in the case of a healthy child, the narrow margin by which it was decided suggests that the future for this area of law might not be as secure as the outcome would otherwise indicate. At least one state has already reversed the decision by legislation, and even if it survives in other states, the endorsement of *McFarlane* in *Rees* and the decision not to follow the path set by *Melchior* suggest that we are unlikely to see the English courts liberalising their stance during the next few years. *Rees* is an important precedent. Not only is it the most recent case in this area, it is also a case decided by seven Law Lords. It is, however, open to criticism on several grounds. One is the acceptance by all seven judges that the decision in *McFarlane* was correct. Although not entirely surprising given *McFarlane's* relative newness, added to the fact that three of their Lordships (Lords Millett, Slynn and Hope) were common to both cases, the refusal to reconsider the blanket prohibition of claims for the costs of raising healthy children was still regrettable. Another ground for criticism is the reasoning which led the majority to leap from endorsement of *McFarlane* to the conclusion that, since no able-bodied parents could claim expenses associated with raising a healthy child, it would be wrong to allow any disabled parent to claim. As the minority in *Rees* demonstrated, this was by no means the obvious or automatic conclusion to be drawn from an application of *McFarlane*. Claims by disabled parents for the costs of raising healthy children will never be so numerous as to pose a danger of floodgates, and to take the view that it is effectively better to be unfair to all parents of healthy children rather than to make a concession for those who face special problems in raising such children involves a questionable application of logic. Moreover, underlying sympathy for the defendant and for its precarious financial position ought not to form the basis for a refusal to allow actions by persons whom the defendant has harmed. Another doubtful aspect of *Rees* is the majority's decision to make a conventional award in circumstances where the damage claimed was capable of being assessed in financial terms. Not only was the decision to make a conventional award in such circumstances unprecedented, but the taking of this radical step was also, as Lords Hope and Steyn observed, made without full debate or detailed consideration of the consequences. Their dissent was couched in such critical terms that it seems unlikely that this will be the end of the story where this aspect of the decision is concerned. However, if the conventional award *does* find acceptance it might well, as Lord Steyn warned, effectively spell a reversal of *Parkinson,* under which the additional costs associated with raising a disabled child are recoverable. For although Lord Scott was the only one of their Lordships in *Rees* directly to suggest that he opposed the decision in *Parkinson*, Lord Bingham, who gave the leading judgment with respect to the conventional award, indicated that the award should in future apply to all cases of wrongful conception or wrongful birth, whether the child or the parent be healthy or disabled.

IV. CONCLUSION

When their Lordships decided *McFarlane in* 1999, they sought to draw a line under the law in this area. Instead, their decision spawned a number of conflicting and incompatible decisions and led to strong disagreement among the judiciary in terms of both legal principle and damage assessment. In England, the decision in *McFarlane* has been confirmed and extended in *Rees*, with the result that no damages – apart from a conventional award – are available to the parents (whether able-bodied or not) of any healthy but unwanted child. While the decision of the Court of Appeal in *Parkinson* still appears to allow claims for the extra costs involved in raising a disabled child, it is unclear how this will be affected by the conventional award introduced in *Rees*. In Australia, the High Court in *Melchior* has allowed a claim for the cost of raising a healthy child, but by the barest of majorities and in the face of fierce opposition which now seems to be leading to legislative reversal. This is not an area of law which brims with certainty or inspires confidence. Unlikely as it is that the English courts will have either the opportunity or the inclination to reconsider the current position in the near future, that is nevertheless what this writer would wish to see. All judges when faced with wrongful conception or wrongful birth cases agree that basic principles of tort law favour the claimants. Only by a process of convoluted and subjective reasoning do some of them then manage to take the cases outside these basic principles. The law would be better served by a more straightforward approach. If a state-financed defendant is insufficiently funded to compensate a claimant, then that is something which the state should address. Sympathy for the fact that the defendant is economically stretched does not justify a situation in which victims of negligence are left without any meaningful remedy. Nor is there any basis for refusing claims simply because conventional wisdom considers a child to be a blessing. A blessing can also be a financial burden – and if that burden has been created by the negligence of a defendant, then it is one which tort law should require him to shoulder.

Abolition of effect of *Cattanach v Melchior*

In *Cattanach v Melchior* [2003] HCA 38, the High Court determined that damages were recoverable for the costs of maintaining a child born as a result of a negligently performed failed sterilisation. Section 49A of the Civil Liability Act reverses the effect of this decision for any future cases in Queensland.

Douglas, RJ; Mullins, GR; Grant, SR; The Annotated Civil Liability Act 2003 (Qld) Butterworths, Sydney, 2004 at 123

Corresponding legislation

Section 71 of the Civil Liability Act 2002 (NSW) . . . amended by the Civil Liability Amendment Act 2003 (NSW) limits damages for the costs of raising a child substantially similar to [the Queensland provision]. [All other relevant State Acts] are silent on this point with the exception of section 67 of the Wrongs Act 1936 (SA) amended by the Law Reform (Ipp Recommendations) Bill 2003 which limits damages for the costs of raising a child substantially similar to [the Queensland provision].

Empirical studies on consent

There has been surprisingly little by way of Australian empirical work on what patients expect from their health care practitioners, to what level they understand information provided on a consent form, etc. For some interesting studies which have been carried out, see DeLuca, RJ, 'Patient information and informed consent: a linguist's perspectives on ethical dilemmas' (1995) 13 No 4 *Monash Bioethics Review* 10; Dawes, PJD and Davison, P, 'Informed consent: what do patients want to know?' (1995) 13 No 4 *Monash Bioethics Review* 20; Harth, S and Thong, Y, 'Parental perceptions and attitudes about informed consent in clinical research involving children' (1993) *Journal of Medical Ethics*; Dharmanda, V, 'Informed consent to medical treatment: practices, processes and beliefs' (1992) *Western Australian Law Reform Commission*; The Victorian Law Reform Commission Informed Decisions About Medical Procedures: Doctor and Patient Studies 1989. A joint project of the Victorian Law Reform Commission, the Australian Law Reform Commission and the New South Wales Law Reform Commission also produced a collection of papers on Informed Consent entitled 'Symposia 1986' as well as a discussion paper dated October 1987 entitled 'Informed Consent to Medical Treatment'.

Review of the use of negligence actions in health care settings

In 1991, the Federal Government established a Review of Professional Indemnity Arrangements for Health Care Professionals. The Final Report of this body's review of Compensation and Professional Indemnity in Health Care was issued in November 1995. Among the recommendations of this Review (referred to as 'the Tito Review' after the name of its Chair, Fiona Tito) is that access to the court system be improved to ensure that victims of 'adverse patient outcomes' be allowed to seek compensation. The Review found no evidence of a 'litigation explosion' in this field (as was noticeable in, for example, the United States). The Review was, however, critical of the fact that almost 60% of cases of medical negligence were not settled within seven years of the negligent act. The Review rejected, however, the idea of abandoning the principles of negligence law in favour of a 'no fault' compensation scheme.

The Tito Review also suggested that there had been a change in the role of health care consumers from passive recipients to 'active partners with health care professionals'. One of the dominant reasons health care consumers gave for resorting to law to obtain redress was that they were unable to ascertain what had happened to them in the provision of health care and they were suspicious that information was being withheld from them. The Review recommended that legislation be enacted to ensure that patients gain access to their own medical records.

See generally Review of Professional Indemnity Arrangements for Health Care Professionals, *Compensation and Professional Indemnity in Health Care*, AGPS, Canberra, 1995.

Trade Practices Act and the Fair Trading Act – sleepers?

The impact of the above two Acts has yet to be determined. Both Acts require providers of services (including medical services) to refrain from certain practices when providing services. The prohibited conduct includes 'misleading or deceptive conduct'. The ambit of the Acts' possible impact on a doctor-patient relationship has been considered by Laufer, S in her article, 'Aggrieved patients who claim they were not told: a new avenue of redress?' (1990) 20 *UWALR* 489.

4

CRIMINAL LAW ASPECTS OF TREATMENT

Although medical treatment is generally perceived as being beneficial, in some circumstances the administration of treatment can make a health care practitioner liable to criminal sanctions. This chapter explores three types of treatment which have given rise to such penalties. In the first part of this chapter, we will explore the application of the law of criminal battery (often called assault) or wounding to medical treatment. In the second part, we examine the law regulating abortion. In the final part we examine the law relating to euthanasia.

PART I: CRIMINAL BATTERY (ASSAULT)

In Chapter 2, we saw that treatment for which no consent was obtained would give rise to an action in battery. The action examined was an action for tortious battery. It is also the case that nonconsensual treatment may give rise to an action for criminal battery, or for wounding (the latter in the case of a treatment which breaks the skin of a patient). If the type of treatment administered inflicts a serious injury on the patient, it might also amount to the offence of doing bodily harm or grievous bodily harm. Note the provisions of the Criminal Codes reproduced below.

Queensland Criminal Code 1899

245 A person who strikes, touches, or moves, or otherwise applies force of any kind to the person of another, either directly or indirectly, without his consent, or with his consent if the consent is obtained by fraud, or who by any bodily act or gesture attempts or threatens to apply force of any kind to the person of another without his consent, under such circumstances that the person making the attempt or threat has actually or apparently a present ability to effect his purpose, is said to assault that other person, and the act is called an assault.

The term 'applies force' includes the case of applying heat, light, electrical force, gas, odour, or any other substance or thing whatever if applied in such a manner as to cause injury or personal discomfort.

246 An assault is unlawful and constitutes an offence unless it is authorised or justified or excused by law . . .

343 Any person who unlawfully assaults another is liable on summary

conviction to a fine of five hundred dollars, inclusive of costs, and in default of payment to imprisonment for six months . . . or to imprisonment for six months in the first instance . . .

343A Any person who unlawfully assaults another and thereby does him bodily harm is liable on summary conviction to a fine of 1,000 dollars inclusive of costs and in default thereof to imprisonment for two years, or to imprisonment for two years in the first instance . . .

320 Any person who unlawfully does grievous bodily harm to another is guilty of a crime, and is liable to imprisonment for 14 years.

323 Any person who:

(1) Unlawfully wounds another; or
(2) Unlawfully, and with intent to injure or annoy any person, causes any poison or other noxious thing to be administered to, or taken by, any person, is guilty of a misdemeanour, and shall be liable to imprisonment for seven years . . .

288 It is the duty of every person who, except in a case of necessity, undertakes to administer surgical or medical treatment to any other person or to do any other lawful act which is or may be dangerous to human life or health, to have reasonable skill and to use reasonable care in doing such act; and he is held to have caused any consequences which result to the life or health of any person by reason of any omission to observe or perform that duty.

Northern Territory Criminal Code

187 In this Code 'assault' means:

(a) the direct or indirect application of force to a person without his consent or with his consent if the consent is obtained by force or by means of menaces of any kind or by fear of bodily harm or by means of false and fraudulent representations as to the nature of the act or by personation; or
(b) the attempted or threatened application of such force where the person attempting or threatening it has an actual or apparent present ability to effect his purpose and the purpose is evidenced by bodily movement or threatening words other than the application of force:
(c) when rescuing or resuscitating a person or when giving any medical treatment or first aid reasonably needed by the person to whom it is given or when restraining a person who needs to be restrained for his own protection or benefit or when attempting to do any such act;
(d) in the course of a sporting activity where the force used is not in contravention of the rules of the game; or
(e) that is used for and is reasonably needed for the common intercourse of life.

Tasmanian Criminal Code Act

182 (1) An assault is the act of intentionally applying force to the person of another, directly or indirectly, or attempting or threatening by any gesture to apply such force to the person of another if the person making the attempt or threat has, or causes the other to believe on reasonable grounds that he has, the ability to effect his purpose; or the act of depriving another of his liberty.

(2) Words alone cannot constitute an assault.

(3) An act which is reasonably necessary for the common intercourse of life done only for the purpose of such intercourse, and which is disproportionate to the occasion, does not constitute an assault.

(4) Except in cases in which it is specially provided that consent cannot be given, or shall not be a defence, an assault is not unlawful if committed with consent of the person assaulted unless the act is otherwise unlawful, and injury is of such a nature, or is done under such circumstances, as to be injurious to the public, as well as to the person assaulted, and to involve a breach of the peace.

184 Any person who unlawfully assaults another is guilty of a crime.

149 (1) Subject to the provisions of Subsection 2 it is the duty of a person who undertakes to administer surgical or medical treatment to another, or to do any other lawful act of a dangerous character which requires special knowledge, skill, attention, or caution, to employ in so doing a reasonable amount of such knowledge, skill, attention, and caution.

(2) In a case of necessity, and where no person having such knowledge or skill as aforesaid can be procured by reasonable means to do such act, it is lawful for a person not having such knowledge or skill to do such act, but it is his duty to employ in so doing such amount of attention and caution as is reasonable in the circumstances.

152 A person who without lawful excuse omits to perform any of the duties mentioned in this chapter shall be criminally responsible for such omission if the same causes the death of or grievous bodily harm to any person to whom such duty is owed, or endangers his life, or permanently injures his health.

Note that Western Australia also has a Criminal Code whose provisions on the above matters are substantially the same as in Queensland. The position in those States which do not have a criminal code (ie, Victoria, New South Wales and South Australia) is broadly the same as that under the Codes except that, of course, reference is made to the common law as modified by the various Crimes Acts rather than to sections of a Criminal Code. (See generally, Fisse, B, *Howard's Criminal Law*, 5th edn, 1990, Sydney: Lawbook Co, pp 138–39.)

Note that the Queensland and Western Australian Codes have a section which provides a defence to those carrying out 'surgical operations'.

Section 282 Qld (s 259 WA): A person is not criminally responsible for performing in good faith and with reasonable care and skill a surgical operation upon any person for his benefit, or upon an unborn child for the preservation of the mother's life, if the performance of the operation is reasonable, having regard to the patient's state at the time and to all the circumstances of the case.

The section's relevance with respect to abortions will be canvassed in Part III of this chapter. For the moment, some comments as to the general ambit of the section will be made.

O'Regan, RS, 'Surgery and criminal responsibility under the Queensland Criminal Code' (1990) 14 Criminal Law Journal 73

Section 282 applies to anyone who performs a surgical operation, whether qualified as a medical practitioner or not. Thus, it might avail a nurse, a dentist, a physiotherapist, an ambulance officer rendering first aid or anyone engaging in the wide range of activity comprehended by the term 'surgery'. This, according to the *Oxford English Dictionary*, is 'the art or practice of treating injuries, deformities and other disorders by manual operation or instrumental appliances'. It is obvious, therefore, that the potential scope of the section is very wide. Any treatment involving the use of force by manual or mechanical means may be a 'surgical operation'.

Reasonable care and skill

Compliance with the requirement of 'reasonable care and skill' depends upon the circumstances in which the surgical operation is performed and upon the status of the person performing it. What is reasonable in a situation of emergency may be unreasonable in other situations. Moreover, what is reasonable for a lay person may not be so for a surgeon. The standard of care and skill is a relative one, as it is in the civil law of negligence. Thus, in the civil case of *Philips v William Whiteley Ltd* [1938] 1 All ER 566, Goddard J held that a jeweller piercing a woman's ears for earrings was required to observe the standard of care and skill expected of a jeweller performing such an operation, not that of a surgeon. It is submitted that the same flexible approach should be taken in determining whether s 282 is applicable.

Apart from precluding reliance on s 282 as a defence, the absence of reasonable care and skill in performing a surgical procedure may also have a direct inculpatory effect. It may attract the operation of s 288 of the Code . . .

It is settled that the negligence here referred to [in s 288] is of a higher order than that which suffices for civil liability. It must be shown that, in the oft quoted words of Hewart LCJ in *Bateman* (1925) 19 Cr App R 8, at 13 there was negligence which 'went beyond a mere matter of compensation between subjects and showed such disregard for the life and safety of others as to amount to a crime against the State and conduct deserving punishment'.

For the benefit of the person

The test under s 282 is couched in terms of the purpose for which the operation was performed. It must be for the 'benefit' of the patient. The benefit may assume various forms. It may, for instance, be social, economic or therapeutic. Moreover, some operations, such as the removal of organs for transplant or the removal of blood for transfusion into others, benefit persons other than the patient. Experimental operations may advance science and benefit the wider community, but not those who submit to them. The section is incapable of application in many of these situations.

It is doubtful whether the word 'benefit' in this context would be given any wider meaning than 'therapeutic' benefit. That, of course, suffices to protect many kinds of operations from the mundane and the exotic. Voluntary castration to overcome uncontrollable sexual urges could be excused on therapeutic grounds. The section could also protect a surgeon performing a prefrontal leucotomy to effect a change of personality in a mentally ill patient. Some routine procedures pose more problems. Male circumcision for religious reasons seems to be outside the protection of the section. So too would tattooing and ear piercing were the legality of such operations not assumed in the Health Act 1937 [s 100A]. Cosmetic surgery, although not medically necessary, may enhance the self-esteem of the patient, and the notion of therapeutic benefit might be just stretched to cover it. However, sterilisation for contraceptive purposes without any medical indication is not so readily accommodated. In England, the legality of such procedures was put beyond doubt by legislation, the National Health Service (Family Planning) Amendment Act 1972, but in Queensland the matter is governed solely by s 282 of the Code, and that seems to be inapplicable. Even a sterilisation performed to prevent the transmission of genetic disease or to prevent a pregnancy likely to threaten the physical or mental wellbeing of another – a spouse or other sexual partner – would not be within the narrow protective ambit of the section, confined as it is to consideration of the benefit of the patient only. In the result, there is now no correspondence between the criminal law as enacted and the criminal law as enforced. Sterilisations of the kind referred to are now commonly performed without prospect of prosecution.

Perhaps it was for this reason that in 1977 the legislature in New Zealand, which also has a Code based on the English Draft Code, including s 61 in terms similar to s 282, supplemented that section by s 61A as follows:

(1) Everyone is protected from criminal responsibility for performing with reasonable care and skill any surgical operation upon any

person if the operation is performed with the consent of that person, or of any other person lawfully entitled to consent on his behalf to the operation, and for a lawful purpose.

(2) Without limiting the term 'lawful purpose' in subsection (1) of this section, a surgical operation that is performed for the purpose of rendering the patient sterile is performed for a lawful purpose.

The amendment directs attention to two additional criteria – consent and lawful purpose. As will be seen later, the former, although not referred to explicitly, is relevant to s 282 because it bears upon the reasonableness of the operation. The latter is an entirely different criterion, and a much more extensive one than the notion of benefit to the patient.

Obviously, s 282, confined as it is to operations for the benefit of the patient, provides no exoneration from criminal liability in respect of operations for the removal of blood or regenerative tissue from one person for the benefit of another. Such an exoneration has now been provided by the Transplantation and Anatomy Act 1979, which excuses a person who in good faith and without negligence and with the consent of the patient removes blood for transfusion or for other therapeutic purposes or for other medical or scientific purposes. Parental consent in the case of a donor who is a child is also necessary. A medical practitioner who administers a transfusion to a child without parental consent incurs no criminal liability if in his opinion this was necessary 'to preserve the life of the child'.

The Act also provides a defence for a medical practitioner who removes regenerative tissue for transplantation or for other therapeutic purposes or for other medical or scientific purposes. Again, the operation must be performed in good faith and without negligence, and the consent of the donor, if an adult, or of a parent, if the donor is a child, must be obtained. There are stringent safeguards to ensure that informed consent has been freely given . . .

Section 282 makes no reference to the consent or dissent of the patient. It does not follow that the matter is irrelevant to criminal responsibility for offences which might be charged in relation to a surgical operation. The performance of the operation must be reasonable, having regard to the patient's state at the time and to all the circumstances of the case. Obviously, one material circumstance would be whether the patient consented. It would be unreasonable to operate on an adult patient capable of an informed and rational choice without consent or on a person too young or ill to give consent without the approval of a parent or other person *in loco parentis*. It would be different where the parent or other person from whom consent was sought unreasonably refused to give it. If in those circumstances the operation were considered reasonably necessary to save life, prevent serious injury to health or relieve suffering, its performance would be reasonable, and protected by s 282. Again, where emergency surgery is indicated it could be undertaken without the consent of others.

There are no Code decisions to support these propositions, but it is submitted that they are sustainable on a fair reading of the section and that they are consistent with the public interest. The autonomy of the patient should not lightly be disregarded, but it is also important that a doctor not be deterred by the risk of criminal prosecution from performing with reasonable care and skill an operation which he honestly and reasonably considers should be done for therapeutic reasons. However, the relevance of consent should be made explicit. That was done in s 61A of the New Zealand Crimes Act 1961, which has been set out above, and also in s 51 of the Tasmanian Criminal Code – a section which, like Queensland's s 282, derives from s 68 of the English Draft Code. The Tasmanian section provides:

(1) It is lawful for a person to perform in good faith and with reasonable care and skill a surgical operation upon another person, with his consent and for his benefit, if the performance of such operation is reasonable, having regard to all the circumstances.
(2) In the case of a child too young to exercise a reasonable discretion in such a matter, such consent as aforesaid may be given by his parent or by any person having the care of such child.
(3) In the case of a person in such a condition as to be incapable of giving such consent as aforesaid, such operation may be performed without such consent.

Conclusion

Section 282 in its present form gives inadequate protection to those who provide modern medical treatment. Its scope is uncertain in many respects. The relevance of consent should be made explicit and the extent of the section's application to abortion should be clarified. Furthermore, if the legislature is of the view that other procedures such as sterilisation, although arguably not for the benefit of the patient, should not, either generally or in specific circumstances, attract the sanctions of the criminal law, then specific legislative provision should be made for them.

The common law position with respect to consent to a medical intervention which would otherwise amount to a battery is similarly unclear. Although the law is clear in stating that a person cannot consent to the doing of bodily harm to him or herself (as to which see *R v Brown* [1994] 1 AC 212), it is equally clear that there are exceptions to this rule which encompass properly conducted games and sports, dangerous exhibitions and lawful surgical intervention. The failure to give consent to treatment could give rise to an action in criminal battery. The High Court has endorsed this position in *Secretary of State for Health v JWB and SMB* (above).

Prosecutions against doctors for criminal battery are rare.

PART II: ABORTION

Unlike the United States, in Australia there is no constitutionally protected right of a woman to seek an abortion. The law on abortion in Australia is governed by State criminal statutes which regulate the circumstances in which women may undergo an abortion (and in which a doctor may lawfully perform such an operation). For a good history of the law relating to abortion in Anglo-Australian society, see Waller, L, 'Any reasonable creature in being' (1987) 13 Monash University Law Review 37. The current law on abortion is succinctly summarised by Petersen and Fisse.

Petersen, K, 'Criminal abortion laws: an impediment to reproductive health?', in Freckelton, I and Petersen, K, *Controversies in Health*, Law Federation Press, Sydney, 2000

Introduction

In contemporary Australia, abortion is a common medical procedure which affects at least a third of all women and the majority of families. Nevertheless, throughout Australia, abortion is still regulated by criminal statutes. The incongruence between abortion laws on the 'statute books' and practice, plus concerns about the health interests of women, led to the former Women's Health Committee of the National Health and Medical Research Council (NHMRC) commissioning an Expert Panel (the Panel) to prepare a report on abortion services throughout Australia in 1992. In keeping with the NHMRC's mandate, the terms of reference specifically focused on the health care aspects of abortion. However, in November 1996, the NHMRC considered the draft report prepared by the Panel and refused to endorse the report or its recommendations because of the controversy surrounding abortion and pressure from various quarters to suppress publication. It directed that the findings of the expert panel were to be published merely as an Information Paper rather than an NHMRC report. Hence, 'An Information Paper on Termination of Pregnancy in Australia' quietly appeared in government bookshops in June 1997. The Preface contains a disclaimer statement by the NHMRC and the Introduction refers to the 'great silence on the part of millions of Australian women who have experienced abortion', expressing the hope that 'this Report will break that silence, and will assist all concerned to improve the care available to women'.

The Panel recommends the decriminalisation of abortion and claims that adequate regulation could be achieved through professional self-regulation. It is noted that:

> Existing provisions in the Medical Practitioners Act (s 1) or equivalent in each State are adequate to ensure that only qualified medical practitioners can legally perform abortions, and that their skill and competence are subject to normal community and peer scrutiny.

In this chapter I shall discuss the major findings of the Information Paper concerning abortion practice and consider these findings in the context of unclear and inconsistent laws throughout Australia. I also examine the effects that unclear abortion laws have on the ethical and legal components of the therapeutic relationship between women and medical practitioners.

Abortion practice in Australia

There is a range of public and private abortion services throughout Australia. Abortion is listed on the Medical Benefits Schedule as a medical service. In a financial sense it has been 'normalised' as a health service in Australia, but evidence in the Information Paper demonstrates that there is one abortion law for the private patient and another law for the public patient.

The incidence of abortion

We have statistical information on the incidence of abortion from the following sources: South Australia, where the law imposes recording requirements, and from Medicare and Casemix data. This information constitutes the official record. However, it may not be totally accurate as abortions can be paid for privately or recorded for public funding purposes under another item of the Medicare remuneration schedule. Reliable statistics are a recent development but historically the high incidence of criminal abortion was regarded as a major health problem and subject to a number of inquiries before World War Two. As the Information Paper points out, abortion was 'the largest single cause (20–30%) of maternal mortality during most of this century, until abortion-related deaths were virtually eliminated following legal liberalisation in the early 1970s and the resultant availability of safer medical services'. The Panel received evidence claiming the incidence of abortion is now lower than earlier in this century but found no evidence of 'backyard' abortions being performed in Australia today. Table 4.1 in the Information Paper (following page) shows on the basis of Medicare and State Health Department statistics that 80,000 terminations are performed in Australia each year and the abortion rate per 1,000 women aged 15–44 years is 19.6. Using the South Australian figures as a baseline, the Panel calculated that the overwhelming majority of abortions, that is, 95%, are performed in the first trimester of pregnancy. Comparisons with other countries show that Australian figures are on the lower end of the scale, keeping company with those in Norway, Denmark and Sweden. It is worth observing that there is a very low rate of abortion in the Netherlands, suggesting that their sexual education and fertility control programmes have a very positive influence on the incidence of unwanted pregnancies.

Table 4.1 Terminations of Pre Bane Australian States and Territories 1990

Australian State or Territory	*Estimated resident population, females aged 15–44 years 30 June 1990*	*Medicare claims for terminations annual average for Jul 1989–June 1997*[1]	*State Health Dept statistics 1990*[1]	*Total terminations 1990*	*Abortion rate per 1,000 women aged 15–44 years*
NSW	1,344,129	28,068	2,912	30,980	23.0
Vic	7,043,943	78,793	2,810	21,603	20.7
Qld	687,873	10,435	28	10,463	15.2
SA	335,011	1,867	2,920	4,781	14.3
WA	394,983	7,504	973	8,477	21.3
Tas	704,794	784	410	1,194	17,4
NT	41,901	234	383	617	74.7
ACT	76,577	7,274	n/a	1,274	16.6
Unknown	–		–	9	
TOTAL AUSTRALIA	4,029,205	68,962	70,376	79,338	79.6

Australian Demographic Statistics, March
Quarter 1991. Canberra: Australian Bureau of Statistics, September 1991. Source of Medicare statistics: Health Insurance Commission.

1 Services provided by hospital doctors to public patients in public hospitals.

(Source: Chan, A, from data supplied by Health Insurance Commission and State Departments of Health.) This Table is found in 'An information Paper on termination of pregnancy in Australia', 1996, AGPS, p 4.

Access and equity

Information

Laws and practices throughout Australia result in information about abortion services being suppressed. Consequently, women are denied access to information regarding sexual and reproductive health which is essential to reproductive decision making. The lack of information and even deliberate suppression of information about abortion services in Australia has an adverse effect on the reproductive rights and health of many Australian women. The Panel suggests that the history of criminal abortion laws and the lack of consensus about abortion laws has contributed to this problem.

Availability

A striking feature of the Australian delivery system is the overwhelming predominance of private services. Approximately 87% of abortions are performed privately and the higher rates occur in jurisdictions where women have access to private clinics. The Panel found that 'private specialised clinics provide prompt services of generally good quality on a day-case basis'. Provision for public patients throughout Australia is far less satisfactory and there is an acute undersupply of services in the public sector. Services for public patients in Queensland's public hospitals are the lowest in the nation and many women seek the services of private clinics in Queensland and the border town, Tweed Heads. There is a similar situation in Tasmania where approximately 40% of women seeking abortions travel interstate, incurring extra cost, extended absences, stress and problems with follow-up care and counselling.

One of the most damning criticisms made in the Information Paper concerns the implications of these delays on women's health. Family Planning South Australia has been monitoring the waiting lists in public hospitals since 1988 and according to their records waiting times for the first appointment are generally between one and four weeks. And the total time from first contact to procedure can extend to between five and six weeks. Obviously, these delays contribute to the incidence of late-term abortions. As the Information Paper notes, the ban on free-standing clinics in South Australia does not promote the health interests of women. However, the establishment of a special clinic by the Queen Adelaide Hospital in Adelaide in 1992 has substantially reduced the waiting time for women seeking abortions.

The experience of service providers in South Australia indicates that the undersupply of services is a problem for those who are dependent on the public hospital system, resulting in delays and, for some patients, the incurring of hardship in order to pay for private care, either locally or by travelling interstate to use a private clinic. The resort to private interstate services occurs to some extent in South Australia, Tasmania and the Northern Territory.

Variation in abortion practices

The variation in abortion rates throughout Australia is considerable. Geographic and socio-economic disparities raise a number of equity and health issues. Women living in an *urban environment are more likely to be able to exercise reproductive* choice than rural women. As the Information Paper notes:

The quality, accessibility, and affordability of abortion is generally better for women living in cities than for those in rural and remote areas where abortion is virtually unobtainable. Accessibility is markedly better for those able to use private health services, and provision of services in public hospitals is generally inadequate.

Abortion facilities are available throughout all jurisdictions but when access is restricted to public hospitals, availability will be influenced by the way the law is interpreted by medical practitioners and hospital managers. Limited resources can also affect the availability of services in the public sector. Hospital practices are described in the Information Paper as follows:

> Every State and Territory has some level of service for public patients who present with grounds for abortion which fit within the particular hospitals and/or practitioner definition as acceptable. In some cases this interpretation is limited to instances where the life of the woman is threatened by the pregnancy or where fetal abnormality has been detected. In other cases a woman's assessment of her personal circumstances, well-being and wishes in relation to pregnancy are accepted as relevant considerations.

The incidence of abortion is higher in jurisdictions where private clinics are permitted than in jurisdictions where abortions are only available in 'prescribed' hospitals. The abortion rate per 1,000 women aged between 18 and 44 years reflects this. New South Wales (23.0), Victoria (20.7) and Western Australia (21.3) have the highest rates; Tasmania (11.4), South Australia (14.3) and the Northern Territory (14.7) have the lowest rates; and Queensland (15.2) and the Australian Capital Territory (16.6) are in the middle. Queensland figures are deceptive. This State is in the middle range even though it has a number of 'owner operated' clinics and this is most likely attributable to Queensland women attending abortion clinics in the border town, Tweeds Heads, where the figures will appear in the New South Wales statistics. Access to private clinics is clearly the most significant determinant of abortion rates.

Australian abortion laws

Throughout the Australian federation, abortion comes under State law. There are two main legal models: a 'judicial' model and a 'statutory' model. In this section of the chapter I shall make a few introductory points about the medical framework in which the laws operate and then I shall discuss the content of the abortion laws.

Medical practitioners: legal gatekeepers

At the outset, I wish to emphasise that abortion laws in all Australian jurisdictions appoint medical practitioners as the legal gatekeepers to abortion services. Doctors, rather than the unwillingly pregnant woman, decide if an abortion is indicated even when – as in the majority of cases – the reasons are non-medical. Nevertheless, the Panel found that there is 'no standard or protocol of practice for medical practitioners in the assessment of legality of a woman's grounds for wanting an abortion'. This raises two questions. First, how do doctors satisfy themselves that a woman has legal grounds for a termination? Secondly, on what basis are judgments made about the personal, social or moral reasons for an abortion? The answers to these questions will depend partly on a doctor's knowledge of unclear and complicated laws but mostly on the personal attitudes of the medical practitioners to abortion. As the Information Paper notes:

> The current system often means that women have to present within

> the terms that the doctor considers valid, terms shaped not only by legal requirements and the doctor's personal views about abortion itself, but also by the training of doctors, the medical and popular discourse on the dangers of abortion, and the doctor's personal values . . . some practitioners consulted for referral and/or abortion ask questions (designed to establish the legal or moral justification for an abortion) which can be readily interpreted by women as an assessment of whether they 'deserve' an abortion. Assessment of grounds often requires the revelation of the woman's personal, sexual, familial, relational, financial and career circumstances, as well as her medical and emotional well-being.

This finding hardly complies with principles expressed in the NHMRC Guidelines which refer to the importance of an open exchange between patients and doctors.

The diversity of medical attitudes to abortion has a profound influence on the provision of abortion. For example, some doctors hold conscientious objections to abortions and will not perform them or even provide a woman with a referral; whilst others believe that women have enough moral maturity to make their own reproductive decisions. In addition 'some doctors express resentment of this gatekeeping role, which they feel is not a proper part of their professional practice'. Presumably, there are also many doctors who do not have particularly strong attitudes to abortion either way, but who believe it is safer to avoid any dealings with an unclear legal situation which still attracts some professional stigma. Obviously, women who can afford to attend private clinics are more likely to have their reproductive autonomy respected than those attending public hospitals.

Minors

Competency is fundamental to the law of consent and is particularly relevant when a minor seeks an abortion. New South Wales and South Australia have statutes addressing the health care of minors. Western Australia has specific statutory provisions for involving parents in the decision making process when a dependent minor under the age of 16 years seeks an abortion. In the other Australian jurisdictions, consent to medical treatment is covered by the 'mature minor' principle which is far from clear. According to this principle, a minor who is capable of fully understanding the nature and consequences of a particular medical procedure is capable of giving consent. This approach has been endorsed in the English case *Gillick v West Norfolk and Wisbech Area Health Authority* and accepted into Australian common law by the High Court in *Secretary, Department of Health and Community Services v JWB and SMB* (*Marion's* case). This ruling permits a doctor to decide if a minor is 'Gillick competent' and has the capacity to give a valid consent. Teenage pregnancies are often a symptom of dysfunctional families, abuse and a breakdown of family communication. In an ideal world parents would be involved in making a decision which would encompass all the options and promote the best interests of the pregnant girl. However, it is recognised that it is sometimes against the best interests of a minor to involve her parents. If a minor is not regarded as mature enough to give consent to an abortion, does this mean that she is mature enough to decide to relinquish a child for adoption? Or to be a parent for a child?

In *Marion's* case the High Court held that the right to consent to the sterilisation of a child is not within the ordinary scope of parental powers because of the grave consequences flowing from the procedure and the significant risk of a wrong decision being made. The court also recognised that levels of competence vary and found the *Gillick* principle applies to all minors. The question of whether an abortion falls within the same category as a sterilisation procedure has not been tested. However, it could be argued that when a minor is assessed as being incompetent for reasons of disability or immaturity the Family Court rather than the parents may have to give authorisation for an abortion.

The 'judicial' model

In Victoria, New South Wales and Queensland, the courts, rather than the legislatures, have liberalised the original criminal statutes. There has not been a test case in Tasmania. The pivotal case, *R v Davidson*, was decided in Victoria in 1969. Dr Davidson was charged during a period when the Homicide Division of the Victorian Police Force was purging the activities of 'medical abortionists' and the government was wrestling with allegations of police corruption and abortion practices. Under s 65 of the Crimes Act 1958 (Vic), which is similar to abortion provisions in other States, any person who 'unlawfully uses any instrument . . . with intent to procure the miscarriage of any woman' shall be guilty of an indictable offence. The word 'unlawfully' has been interpreted by the courts to exclude a doctor who honestly believes on reasonable grounds that an abortion is necessary to preserve the life and good health of a pregnant woman. In *Davidson's* case Menhennitt J ruled that the defence of necessity (also known as 'the choice of two evils doctrine') was permitted in an abortion prosecution. He also ruled that the Crown must prove *beyond reasonable doubt*:

- that the accused performed an unlawful abortion;
- that the accused did not honestly believe on reasonable grounds that the abortion was necessary to preserve the woman from serious danger to her life, or her physical or mental health; and
- that the abortion was not proportionate to the danger presented by the pregnancy.

Shortly after *Davidson's* case, Levine J extended the ruling to include socio/economic reasons in the New South Wales decision, *R v Wald*.

Subsequently, *Davidson's* case was accepted into Queensland law by McGuire J in *R v Bayliss and Cullen*. The criminal standard of proof coupled with the problem of proving that a doctor did not hold an honest belief makes it extremely difficult for the Crown to secure a conviction.

Child destruction

In Victoria, no specific reference to gestation limits is made in s 65 of the Crimes Act 1958 (Vic) but s 10(1) of the Act makes it an offence if a person 'with intent to destroy the life of a child capable of being born alive, by any wilful act unlawfully causes such child to die before it has an existence independent from its mother'. The words 'capable of being born alive' are not defined in the Act and under s 10(2) of the Crimes Act 1958 (Vic) a foetus is presumed to be capable of being born alive at 28 weeks gestation and earlier. There is no Australian legal precedent on the relationship between Menhennitt J's ruling and Victorian child destruction law. However, as s 10 is similar to the Infant Life (Preservation) Act 1929 (Eng), an Australian court may seek guidance from English cases. In the event of a prosecution for child destruction, a court would have to decide if it would follow English authorities when interpreting the words 'capable of being born alive'. In *C v S*, the English Court of Appeal held that a foetus at 18 to 21 weeks is not 'capable of being born alive' under the 1929 English statute because it could not breathe naturally or unnaturally. More recently, it was held in *Rance v Mid-Downs Health Authority* that a foetus of 26 to 27 weeks gestation was 'capable of being born alive'. The court also found that if a foetus is born alive and is able to breathe on its own it is 'capable of being born alive' within the meaning of the Infant Life (Preservation) Act 1929 (Eng). Technological advances in this area may lead to further legal developments.

The word 'unlawfully' is not defined in s 10 of the Crimes Act 1958 (Vic) and has not been defined judicially. If a court determined that it was bound by *R v Davidson*, it would have to decide whether the accused honestly believed on reasonable grounds that the abortion was 'necessary to preserve the woman from serious danger to her life or her physical or mental health'. Even though foetal screening during pregnancy is common, it is not always understood by women and doctors that foetal abnormality *per se* is not a ground for an abortion because the law is framed to protect the health of the pregnant woman. However, it can be argued that the circumstances could present a serious danger to the pregnant woman's health – particularly her mental heath. Proportionality of risk is easier for the Crown to establish in late-term pregnancies because the risks of the abortion for the mother begin to outweigh the risks of continuing with the pregnancy after 16 weeks gestation. This is an area of considerable legal uncertainty and a cause for concern amongst medical practitioners. Nevertheless, medical lawyer, Loane Skene, considers it unlikely that a doctor performing a late termination because of serious foetal abnormality would necessarily be prosecuted for child destruction:

> Even if a case of alleged abortion or child destruction by therapeutic termination of pregnancy were to reach the court, it is not likely that a doctor would be convicted. Surely a judge or jury would take a compassionate view of the doctor's actions, as the courts did in earlier cases concerning abortions to preserve the mother's life or health. It is therefore difficult to imagine that a doctor would be convicted of a criminal offence when acting in what he or she honestly believed to be the mother's best interests, even if her 'interests' related solely to not bearing a seriously disabled child.

The 'judicial' model fails to distinguish clearly between criminal and non-criminal abortions and doctors and women remain vulnerable to prosecution. Two doctors were unsuccessfully prosecuted in these jurisdictions in the 1980s. Moreover, because abortion law in the 'judicial' models is unclear it is subject to idiosyncratic judicial interpretation. In the wrongful birth case, *CES v Superclinics (SC)*, Newman J in the NSW Supreme Court found the defendant doctors and the clinic had breached their duty of care by failing to diagnose her pregnancy until she was 19.5 weeks pregnant but denied the woman plaintiff's claim for damages on the ground she had merely lost the opportunity to perform a hypothetically illegal abortion. He drew an analogy between this woman and an unsuccessful bank robber claiming damages against another party who intentionally obstructed the robbery. Newman J was overruled by the Court of Appeal in *CES v Superclinics (CA)* and Kirby ACJ found that Newman J had incorrectly applied the tests in *Davidson and Wald* by failing to recognise the true nature of the evidentiary burden. However, the Court of Appeal decision was not unanimous and the High Court appeal, which could have led to an authoritative ruling either way, was settled out of court. Consequently, abortion laws remain unclear and unpredictable in these jurisdictions.

The 'statutory' model

Since 1998 there have been two versions of the 'statutory' model of abortion law in Australia. The first and earlier version was adopted in South Australia and the Northern Territory. The second and more recent version has been adopted in Western Australia and the Australian Capital Territory. At the time of writing, the Health Regulation (Maternal Health Information) Act 1998 (ACT) has not been fully gazetted and has therefore not yet been proclaimed.

South Australia and the Northern Territory have followed the United Kingdom's approach to abortion regulation. Instead of repealing original criminal 19th century abortion statutes, these jurisdictions have enacted 'reform' statutes which provide defences to criminal laws for medical practitioners who perform abortions in good faith and comply with various procedural and reporting/recording requirements. If two doctors examine a woman and both form the *bona fide* opinion that the risk of continuing a pregnancy is more dangerous to the physical and mental health of the woman than a termination, lawful grounds for an abortion will exist in these jurisdictions. The law also requires abortions to be performed in 'prescribed' hospitals. No time limits are included in the South Australian legislation but child destruction laws make it an offence to destroy a foetus 'capable of being born alive'. Legislation in the Northern Territory is similar to South Australia but between 14 and 23 weeks gestation, lawful abortions can only be performed if necessary to prevent grave injury to the woman's physical or mental health. An abortion may be performed at any stage of a pregnancy to preserve the woman's life.

South Australian medical practitioners are required to nominate a specific medical reason for the procedure on the required form. Even though therapeutic abortions are legal, 95% of the grounds are officially recorded as 'anxiety and/or depression as a result of the pregnancy'. Moreover, between 1990 and 1994, the label 'Current Psychiatric' was used to describe the grounds for the overwhelming majority of abortions performed in South Australia. It is not clear why a psychiatric label is used by doctors to classify the main reason for women seeking abortions. It is suggested in the Information Paper that it may be due to administrative factors or a myriad of other reasons, including concerns about protecting confidentiality and privacy. However, I would add two further points: first this practice reinforces perceptions that women seeking abortions are deviant, and second, it has the ring of a former era when women had to threaten to commit suicide in order to obtain abortions.

The South Australian and Northern Territory statutes clearly distinguish *between criminal and non-criminal abortions*. Nevertheless, the grounds for abortion are based on a comparative risks assessment and can be perceived as confusing. The law requires two doctors to decide if it is safer for the woman to have an abortion or carry the foetus to term. Statistically, an abortion performed up to approximately the 16th week of pregnancy is safer than carrying a foetus to term. According to this view of the law, all first trimester abortions should be available upon request. However, not everyone agrees with this interpretation. Commenting on a similar provision in British law, the Lane Committee decided that statistical risks must be taken into account but every case must also be assessed individually.

The Acts Amendment (Abortion) Act 1998 (WA) and the Health Regulation (Maternal Health Information) Act 1998 (ACT) can be described as a 'hybrid statutory' model. The Western Australian legislation repeals and amends parts of the Criminal Code Act 1913 (WA), which deals with procuring an abortion, and amends the Health Act 1911 (WA) and the Children's Court of Western Australia Act 1988 (WA). The most significant change is the repeal of the former s 200 of the Criminal Code Act 1913 (WA) which penalised women who had unlawful abortions. In every other Australian jurisdiction a woman can be still be charged with having an unlawful abortion.

Under s 199(1) of the Criminal Code Act 1913 (WA) there is a presumption that an abortion is unlawful unless certain conditions are satisfied. Specifically, an attempt to perform an abortion, whether or not the woman is pregnant, is a criminal offence unless:

- the abortion is performed by a medical practitioner;
- the abortion is performed in good faith with reasonable care and skill; and
- the abortion is justified under s 334 of the Health Act 1911 (WA).

Section 334(3)(a) of the Health Act 1911 (WA) provides that an abortion is 'justified' if the woman gives her informed consent and is no more than 20 weeks pregnant. Essentially this constitutes abortion 'on request'. An abortion will also be justified if the woman has serious social/personal problems, or medical or mental health reasons for requiring an abortion and has given her informed consent unless it is impracticable in the circumstances. Under this Act the 'informed consent' must be given freely by a woman to a medical practitioner who neither performs nor assists with the procedure. Furthermore, a woman is deemed to have given her 'informed consent' if she has received information about the medical risks of termination or carrying the foetus to term, and if she has been offered the opportunity of referral for appropriate and adequate pre-abortion or post-abortion counselling. Presumably, a guardian will have to be appointed under s 43(4) of the Guardianship and Administration Act 1990 (WA) to provide an 'informed consent' on behalf of a disabled woman who has reached 18 years and is not legally competent.

Two major qualifications are imposed on the provision of legal abortion in Western Australia. The first one concerns gestation limits and the second one concerns dependent minors. Under s 334(7) of the Health Act 1911 (WA) an abortion is not justified after a woman has been pregnant for 20 weeks unless two medical practitioners who are members of a government-appointed panel agree that the pregnant woman or the foetus have a 'severe medical condition' justifying an abortion. There is no further guidance in the statute on the meaning of a 'severe medical condition' and presumably this is regarded as a matter for clinical discretion. Many foetal abnormalities can now be diagnosed before 20 weeks gestation. Medical practitioners usually calculate the length of the pregnancy from the last menstrual period (LMP). Today the calculation would usually be made with the assistance of an ultrasound diagnosis. The Act is not specific about the way in which gestation is to be calculated.

Under s 334(8) of the Health Act 1911 (WA) the definition of 'informed consent' has been expanded and requires that the custodial parent or guardian of a dependent minor under 16 years must be informed that an abortion is being considered and given the opportunity to participate in the counselling and medical consultations. However, under s 334(9) the Children's Court may grant an order exempting the minor from involving the parents or guardian in the decision-making process. An order made by the Children's Court in these terms is final. The consent in these circumstances must be given by the minor if she is regarded as legally competent. However, if she is not legally competent and it is not in her interests for the parents or guardian to be involved, it is possible that an application would have to be made to the Family Court in Western Australia.

The Health Regulation (Maternal Health Information) Act 1998 (ACT) (as yet not proclaimed) complements existing criminal abortion provisions in the Crimes Act 1900 (ACT) and the legality of an abortion is not affected by either the compliance or the failure of any person to comply with the 1998 legislation. Sections 5 and 12 of the Act require abortions to be performed by medical practitioners in facilities that have been approved by the Minister for Health and Community Care.

The major features of this legislation concern the provision of information and the introduction of a 'cooling-off' period. Sections 6 and 7 of the Act stipulate that the medical practitioner must provide a woman seeking an abortion with information which includes the medical risks of termination and of carrying a pregnancy to term as well as particular risks to the woman. The practitioner must also tell the woman of any particular risks associated with the type of abortion procedure proposed and the gestational age of the foetus. The practitioner must also offer the woman the opportunity of referral to counselling and provide her with a pamphlet which includes information about medical risks and pictures of a foetus. This information is to be approved by an Advisory Panel to consist of seven members from various branches of the health professions. Section 8 requires both the doctor and woman to make a joint declaration in writing that all these conditions have been met.

Under s 9 of the Act the abortion cannot be performed unless her consent is obtained in writing not less than 72 hours after the s 8 declaration has been made. Arguably, s 9 of the Act encroaches on the right to personal inviolability by imposing a serious qualification on the capacity of a legally competent woman to give a valid consent.

Privacy and notification requirements are included in both the Western Australian and the Australian Capital Territory statutes. Both Acts stipulate that the privacy of the woman must be protected and that all abortions must be officially reported. In Western Australia the report has to be made by the medical practitioner who performs the abortion within 14 days of the procedure. The notification form has been drafted in a way which protects the identity of the woman and consequently limits the amount of demographic information available. In the Australian Capital Territory, on the other hand, more information is available because of a different system of reporting. Instead of requiring a doctor to make a report after each procedure, s 16 requires the manager of an approved facility to provide the Minister of Health and Community Care with a report every three months. Specific information is required which includes: the incidence of abortion, reasons for women having abortions, ages of the women, gestational ages of the foetuses and the number of women who had previously had an abortion at the facility.

The therapeutic relationship

Little attention has been paid to the effect of the criminal law on the therapeutic relationship between the doctor and the woman seeking an abortion. This relationship is grounded in the doctor's ethical duty to act in the best interests of the patient and the legal duty to obtain a valid consent. Moreover, in the NHMRC *Guidelines on Information* one of the principles states that 'Patients should be encouraged to make their own decisions'. Criminal abortion laws place a wedge between the doctor and the patient by creating ethical and legal conflicts for the medical practitioner. The unwillingly pregnant woman is the patient and the person to whom the doctor owes a duty of care. The ethical values of respect for autonomy and beneficence are undermined when criminal laws require a doctor to make a medical assessment based on legal grounds rather than the needs and best interests of the woman. If, for example, the doctor does not honestly believe the legal grounds exist but believes it would be in the woman's best interests to have an abortion, he or she is confronted with a difficult legal and ethical dilemma. The Information Paper puts it this way: 'Health care providers are constrained by legal requirements which limit the woman's autonomy. This conflict between best practice and the legal framework is one of the major difficulties arising in the delivery of TOP services in Australia.' The ethical ideal of consent being a process of shared and informed decision-making does not fit easily with a patient/doctor relationship clouded by the shadow of criminal laws which appoint the doctor as the legal gatekeeper – a concept which explicitly diminishes the woman's role in the decision-making process.

Consent laws are designed to secure the right of an individual to act in an autonomous and self-determining way, to impose an obligation on physicians to disclose relevant information (so that the exercise of autonomy is meaningful), and to protect doctors from legal suits. The legal standing of a woman's consent to an abortion is an issue which is rarely addressed. At the outset, it is worth emphasising that a person cannot give a valid consent to an illegal act. As the legal status of the majority of abortions performed in the 'judicial model' jurisdictions is unclear and unpredictable, it is very difficult for a doctor to be certain when an abortion is lawful. Nevertheless, Kirby ACJ in *CES v Superclinics Australia Pty Ltd* made it clear that an abortion is *prima facie* lawful in jurisdictions which follow the *Davidson* ruling until a jury decides that the doctor did not honestly believe that abortion was lawful beyond reasonable doubt. Any treatment performed without a valid consent may lead to an action in trespass, that is, battery or assault. It is unlikely that a competent adult woman would sue a medical practitioner in these circumstances. However, parents could possibly sue in trespass where a doctor has been convicted of performing an abortion on a minor without parental consent.

The common law requires doctors to give patients sufficient information about a proposed procedure to equip them to make an informed medical decision. In *Rogers v Whitaker* the High Court held: 'In legal terms, the patient's consent to treatment may be valid once he or she is informed in broad terms of the nature of the procedure which is intended. But the choice is, in reality, meaningless unless it is made on the basis of relevant information and advice.' The exact nature of the information a woman seeking an abortion should be given will depend on the main purpose of the consultation and the stage of gestation. In some cases the woman will be requesting advice from the doctor as part of her decision-making process. In other cases, the woman will be proposing the particular course of treatment to the doctor. The nature of the relevant information may differ, but in all cases the woman has the right to be informed about options, risks and consequences. If a woman suffered some emotional or medical 'harm' as result of the abortion and she decided to sue her doctor, she would have to demonstrate on the balance of probabilities that if the doctor had warned her of the risk she would not have proceeded with the abortion; or would not have proceeded with the abortion at that time with that doctor. The Information Paper suggests:

> Adequate information about abortions (when, what, where, how long, cost, etc) should be routinely provided for all women seeking abortion. The basic principle of client self determination or personal autonomy assumes the presence of adequate information and support to enable people to make a decision, after consideration of all the options. If abortion is the chosen option, information about the procedure and the associated risks is essential for informed consent.

Many of these issues have not been seriously addressed because of the stigma associated with abortion and the unclear laws. The repeal or clarification of abortion laws would enable more attention to be focused on these important aspects of the therapeutic relationship.

Conclusions

The Information Paper contains a wealth of material about the Australian abortion delivery system. It demonstrates that, although abortion is a common practice which is supported by the public purse, the law is confusing and unclear. Access to abortion services is a lottery for women who are obliged to depend on public services but virtually an entitlement for women who can afford to attend private clinics. On the basis of these findings, the Information Paper recommends that abortion should be decriminalised, defined as a health issue and monitored through professional regulatory bodies. The Panel takes the view that decriminalising abortion would promote women's health and permit health professionals to act in the best interests of their patients.

Since the Information Paper was published, the Western Australian Parliament has paved the way towards decriminalising abortion laws. The transfer of some abortion regulation from criminal to health law is symbolic. Furthermore, abortion is *prima facie* unlawful but it is no longer a criminal offence for a woman to have an abortion and the ground of 'informed consent' up to 20 weeks gestation is relatively permissive. This model of abortion law attempts to balance the competing interests of the pregnant woman by restricting late-term abortions to a serious medical condition for the foetus or the pregnant woman. Mrs Gillick would no doubt approve of the new restrictions placed on dependent minors seeking an abortion. In some respects, therefore, the Western Australian abortion law addresses many of the concerns raised in the Information Paper and the *modus operandi* of the government-appointed panel and the procedures adopted by the Children's Court will be under national scrutiny. Doctors remain the legal gatekeepers in Western Australia. However, the therapeutic relationship is enhanced by the new 'informed consent' ground for abortion in the first 20 weeks of gestation.

Throughout the rest of Australia, abortion laws remain unclear, unjust and discriminatory. Formal criminal laws are prohibitive and antithetical to the health interests of women. They also diminish the political and social status of women by denying women control over reproduction and by treating women as inferior citizens who are not capable of exercising mature moral judgment. This sentiment is captured in the classic statutory phrase 'married women, infants and lunatics' which was on our statute books for a greater part of this century. The 'Alice In Wonderland' characteristic of our approach to these questions may have spared this country the volatility and violence experienced in the United States but the dignity and health interests of many Australian women have not been spared. A scant perusal of the abortion statistics will show that the Western Australian model of abortion law is more in line with practice than other legal models in Australia, where law and practice have little in common. This has led to a state of confusion which masks the reality of abortion practice and, amongst other things, denies the community the opportunity to make an informed appraisal of appropriate legal frameworks concerning this important aspect of women's health.

Fisse, B, *Howard's Criminal Law*, 5th edn, 1990, Sydney: Lawbook Co, pp 166–68

There are three indictable offences connected with abortion: the attempted abortion of V [victim] by D [defendant], the attempted abortion of V by herself and the supply of means for abortion with knowledge that those means are intended to be used for that purpose . . . The various definitions of attempted abortion are substantially the same. Section 65 of the Crimes Act 1958 (Vic): '[W]hosoever with intent to procure the miscarriage of any woman whether she is or is not with child unlawfully administers to her or causes to be taken by her any poison or other noxious thing, or unlawfully uses any instrument or other means with the like intent . . .'

As the reservation that it is immaterial whether V is pregnant or not implies, the overriding element in attempted abortion is D's intentions. This rule receives its most important application in connection with the word 'unlawfully', which excludes surgical operations performed in good faith from the scope of the offence. The Queensland and Western Australian Codes have the following rule [282 Queensland Criminal Code]: 'A person is not criminally responsible for performing in good faith and with reasonable care and skill a surgical operation upon any person for his benefit, or upon an unborn child for the preservation of the mother's life, if the performance of the operation is reasonable, having regard to the patient's state at the time and to all the circumstances of the case.' The equivalent section in the Tasmanian Code is not limited to the case where D believes the abortion necessary to preserve V's life, but merely lays down the general element of reasonableness in all the circumstances. At common law for many years, the only case directly in point was the well-known prosecution in Bourne, where an obstetric surgeon of the highest qualifications deliberately drew the attention of the English authorities to his performance of an abortion on a young girl, who had been badly raped, in order to provoke proceedings which would clarify the law. He was acquitted after the trial judge had directed the jury substantially to the same effect as the Queensland and Western Australia rule quoted above.

In 1969, there were two important developments in Australia. In Victoria in *Davidson*, Menhennitt J directed a jury that at common law 'to establish that the use of an instrument with intent to procure a miscarriage was unlawful, the Crown must establish either (a) that the accused did not honestly believe on reasonable grounds that the act done by him was necessary to preserve the woman from a serious danger to her life or her physical or mental health (not being merely the normal dangers of pregnancy and childbirth) which the continuance of the pregnancy would entail; or (b) that the accused did not honestly believe on reasonable grounds that the act done by him was in the circumstances proportionate to the need to preserve the woman from a serious danger to her life or her physical or mental health (not being merely the normal dangers of pregnancy and childbirth) which the continuance of the pregnancy would entail. In short, D must believe that the abortion is both necessary and proportionate when measured against the danger to the mother if his act is to be lawful. It has been suggested that the requirement of proportionality in this direction is intended to emphasise that the later in pregnancy an abortion takes place, the greater the danger to the mother from its performance, and that the introduction of the idea of necessity provides a means for further judicial amelioration of the law.

The other development was a statutory amendment in South Australia. In that State an abortion is lawful, in addition to the common law, if it is either performed in a hospital and in the opinion of two doctors 'the continuance of the pregnancy would involve greater risk to the life of the pregnant woman or greater risk of injury to the physical or mental health of the pregnant woman than if the pregnancy were terminated', or alternatively in their opinion 'there is a substantial risk that if the pregnancy were not terminated and the child were born to the pregnant woman, the child would suffer from such physical or mental abnormalities as to be seriously handicapped', or, if it is not performed in a hospital, the pregnancy is terminated by a doctor in whose opinion termination is immediately necessary to save the life, or to prevent injury to the physical or mental health, of the pregnant woman. The operation of the Act is limited to women who have resided in South Australia for at least two months before the abortion.

Other limitations on attempted abortion arise from the statutory statements of the means which are prohibited by law. The words 'poison and instrument' are reasonably clear, and it has been held that a 'noxious thing' in this context is limited to something likely to harm a pregnant woman. All the statutes, however, include an apparently general reference to 'other means', which might be understood as bringing within the offence any attempt to induce abortion, however ridiculous the method used. As to this, the South Australian Court of Criminal Appeal in *Lindner* declined to accept the view that the legislature intended to catch people who might believe in the efficacy of prayer or witchcraft and limited 'means' to 'something that is, in the common experience of mankind and in some reasonable degree, capable of producing the result'.

O'Regan, in his discussion of s 282 of the Queensland Criminal Code, analyses some cases on abortion post those discussed in the extract by Fisse. It may be noted that O'Regan is sceptical whether the common law as outlined by Fisse and apparently applied in the Code States should apply in the Code States.

O'Regan, 'Surgery and criminal responsibility under the Queensland Criminal Code' (above)

As already indicated, Sir Samuel Griffith included the reference in s 282 to 'a surgical operation . . . upon an unborn child for the preservation of the mother's life' in order to provide a defence to a charge of child destruction under s 313 . . . That offence relates to action taken by the accused 'when a woman is about to be delivered of a child' and proscribes what if the child were born alive and then killed would be unlawful homicide. However, the words have been taken as providing a defence to the very different charge of attempting to procure an abortion contrary to s 224, an offence which relates to the termination of pregnancy before childbirth has begun. The legality of abortion depends, according to the Queensland courts, upon whether the operation was performed 'for the preservation of the mother's life' . . .

[after discussing *Bourne's* case]

In the Queensland case of *Ross and McCarthy* in 1955, the accused relied unsuccessfully on the 'preservation of the mother's life' component of s 282 to found a defence under that section on a charge of unlawful abortion. The trial judge had left the defence to the jury but on appeal the accused complained that the direction concerning it had been defective. The trial judge had merely read s 282 to the jury without explanation. However, the Court of Criminal Appeal held that this was sufficient. Mansfield SPJ disposed of the point summarily in these terms:

> The words 'preservation' and 'life' do not bear any technical meaning, and although in *Bourne* the meaning of similar words was explained to the jury, it is my opinion that no such explanation is necessary in this case.

He did not go on to say why. It is suggested that a direction confined to a reading of the section without more would be much less favourable to the accused than that given in *Bourne*. According to Macnaghten J, the onus of establishing that the operation was performed to preserve the mother's life would be satisfied by showing that a probable consequence of continuance of the pregnancy would be 'to make the woman a physical or mental wreck'. As Lord Diplock has remarked, this phrase, although vivid, is 'unfortunately lacking in precision'. It is clear enough, however, that the consequence referred to is not the death of the mother: it is to quality of life, not to its termination. Unless a trial judge placed this gloss upon the word 'life' as Macnaghten J did, it is likely that a jury would take the section as referring only to an operation performed to prevent the mother from dying as a result of continuance of the pregnancy or of the ultimate birth.

The test formulated in *Bourne* was applied in a somewhat different statutory context by Menhennitt J in 1969 in the Victorian case of *Davidson*. The relevant provision of the Victorian Crimes Act 1958 proscribing unlawful abortion provided no guidance as to what constituted unlawfulness. Nor was there any local counterpart to s 1(1) of the Infants Life (Preservation) Act (Imp). Menhennitt J therefore looked elsewhere and found that the common law doctrine of necessity supplied the answer. He concluded:

> For the use of an instrument with intent to procure a miscarriage to be lawful, the accused must have honestly believed on reasonable grounds that the act done by him was (a) necessary to preserve the woman from a serious danger to her life or her physical or mental health (not being merely the normal dangers of pregnancy and childbirth) which the continuance of the pregnancy would entail; and (b) in the circumstances not out of proportion to the danger to be averted.

In *K v T*, GN Williams J expressed the view that the same test would apply in Queensland under s 282. This observation, however, was *obiter*. The issue to be decided was whether an interlocutory injunction should be granted on the application of a man to prevent a woman pregnant to him from having an abortion. The application was refused on the ground that, as the applicant was not suing on the relation of the Attorney

General, he had no standing, and on the further ground that in the absence of evidence it could not be assumed that the abortion would be outside the protection of s 282.

McPherson J in *Re Bayliss* agreed with the opinion of GN Williams J, but again what he said was *obiter*. McPherson J was there reviewing a decision of a magistrate refusing to impose as a condition of bail a requirement that the doctor charged with procuring an abortion and conspiring to procure an abortion not commit an offence. It had been submitted that, after being admitted to bail, he might in the conduct of his practice perform unlawful abortions. McPherson J rejected the submission in the following passage: 'It does not from that follow that every, or even any, of such miscarriages will constitute an offence under s 224. Section 224 refers to the "unlawful" procurement of a miscarriage and it will therefore be necessary for the Crown to establish that requirement as well as to exclude the provisions of s 282 of the Criminal Code. Section 282 excludes in the circumstances there specified a surgical operation for the preservation of the mother's life. The meaning of that expression was considered in the well-known case of *Bourne*. That and other cases were in turn considered in Queensland by G N Williams J in *K v T* in a passage which I respectfully accept as representing the law in Queensland. Moreover, in addition to excluding s 282 the Crown may also, depending on the circumstances, be bound to prove that the miscarriage or the conspiracy to procure the same was not procured under an honest but reasonable and mistaken belief in the existence of a state of things envisaged by s 282.'

Most recently, in 1986, Maguire DCJ, in an elaborate ruling in *Bayliss and Cullen* (1986) 9 QL 8, while accepting that Sir Samuel Griffith had included the words 'upon an unborn child for the preservation of the mother's life' to provide a defence to a charge under s 313, concluded that they provided a defence to unlawful abortion also and that, as suggested by G N Williams and McPherson JJ, the jury should be directed in terms of *Bourne* and *Davidson*.

It by no means follows from these cases that the law on the point is now settled. Certainly, *Ross and McCarthy* provides no support for the conclusion that the word 'life' in that part of the section should be construed expansively as in *Bourne*. The Full Court in *AG (ex rel) Kerr v T*, an unsuccessful appeal against the refusal of GN Williams J in *K v T* to grant an interlocutory injunction, left the point open. Furthermore, resort to common law principles to supplement and explain statute law, as in *Davidson*, while readily permissible in Victoria, must be regarded as very unusual in Queensland, which has a comprehensive Criminal Code, and one which does not have common law defences. The provision in the Code which is closest to the common law defence of necessity is s 25, which provides a defence for 'an act . . . done . . . under such circumstances of sudden or extraordinary emergency that an ordinary person possessing ordinary powers of self-control could not reasonably be expected to act otherwise'. Reference to powers of self-control seems inappropriate in relation to the performance of a surgical operation. It is submitted that s 282 alone, or, as McPherson J suggested in *Re Bayliss*, in combination with s 24 (honest and reasonable mistake of fact), renders abortion lawful.

The question remains whether the first or the second limb of the section provides the relevant defence, that is, whether the purpose of the operation must be preservation of the mother's 'life' (however that word is construed) or whether it is enough if the purpose of the operation is therapeutic and its performance is reasonable. The Court of Criminal Appeal in *Ross and McCarthy* assumed it was the first. It is, however, a curious use of language to describe attempting to procure the miscarriage of a woman by surgical means as 'a surgical operation . . . upon an unborn child', where such words are apt to provide a defence to a charge of child destruction under s 313.

This, as already noted, is what Sir Samuel Griffith intended by including them. If as a matter of drafting technique he had chosen to specify this defence in s 313 instead, there could be no argument about the matter. Experience elsewhere confirms this. The Codes of Tasmania, New Zealand and Canada, like the Queensland Code, were strongly influenced by the English Draft Code and all have sections corresponding to ss 282 and 313, but with one important difference. In these Codes, the defence for a surgical operation provided in s 282 by the expression, 'upon an unborn child for the preservation of the mother's life', appears not in the sections equivalent to s 282 but in the sections equivalent to s 313. It has never been held there that this defence applies to abortion as well as to child destruction. In Canada and New Zealand, other specific provisions indicate when abortion is lawful. These involve prior approval of the abortion by a medical committee which has satisfied itself that prescribed criteria have been satisfied. In Canada, the criterion is danger to life or health. In New Zealand, there are a number of alternatives, including serious danger to life or health, pregnancy of a subnormal woman and pregnancy as a result of incest. Even before these provisions were enacted in New Zealand in 1977, the Court of Appeal held in *Woolnough* that the lawfulness of abortion was not to be tested by reference to the child destruction defence.

In Tasmania, it would appear that s 51 of the Code which corresponds to s 282 but without the incorporation of the 'preservation of the mother's life' formula provides the relevant defence; that is, a therapeutic abortion attracts no criminal responsibility if it is one performed with reasonable care and skill and is reasonable, having regard to all the circumstances. It is arguable that the law in Queensland is the same and that the second and not the first limb of s 282 is applicable. However, the Court of Criminal Appeal would probably now be reluctant to reverse the clear trend of the authorities.

A recent case on abortion is reproduced below.

Bayliss and Cullen (1986) 9 QL 8

[Doctors Bayliss and Cullen were accused of conducting an abortion, contrary to s 24 of the Queensland Criminal Code.]

The process of inducing the miscarriage of a pregnant woman is commonly called an abortion. Abortion is not strictly a legal term and in the relevant statute 'miscarriage' is preferred. 'Abortion or miscarriage, as a legal term, means expulsion of the contents of the womb of a pregnant woman at any period of gestation short of full term.' (*Encyclopedia of the Laws of England*, 3rd edn, Vol 1, p 22.)

In the common, though not legal, use of the term, 'miscarriage' has reference to accidental termination of pregnancy, whilst 'abortion' has the more sinister meaning of a deliberate and improper procuring by artificial means of the expulsion of the contents of the pregnant uterus.

The purposes of the proscription of abortion in s 224 seem to be twofold. Clearly, one purpose is to protect the life, or the potential for life, of an unborn child, but I think the second purpose must also have been to protect the mother, having regard to the grave dangers, which until comparatively recent times, were attendant upon induced abortions.

As well as s 224 of the Criminal Code, of particular relevance for present purposes is s 282 of the Code. Section 282 provides as follows:

[Macguire DCJ then outlined s 282]

In *R v Wald* (1971) 3 NSWDCR 25, medical practitioners were charged under s 83 of the Crimes Act 1900 (NSW) with unlawfully using an instrument with intent to procure the miscarriage of women. Section 83 of the New South Wales Act is in similar terms to s 224 of the Queensland Criminal Code. Levine J applied the *Davidson* test. His Honour said:

> The criteria for unlawfulness must relate to the acts of the accused in relation to the operations performed upon the women. In my view the general principle laid down in *Davidson's* case (above) does provide adequate criteria where the operation to terminate the pregnancy is skillfully performed, with the woman's consent, by a duly qualified medical practitioner. If any meaning is to be given to the word 'unlawful' in the section at all, in my view in relation to this case *Davidson's* case provides the answer . . .

In my view, it would be for the jury to decide whether there existed in the case of each woman any economic, social or medical ground or reason which in their view could constitute reasonable grounds upon which an accused could honestly and reasonably believe there would result a serious danger to her physical or mental health. It may be that an honest belief be held that the woman's mental health was in serious danger as at the very time when she was interviewed by a doctor, or that her mental health, although not then in serious danger, could reasonably be expected to be seriously endangered at some time during the currency of the pregnancy, if uninterrupted. In either case, such a conscientious belief on reasonable grounds would have to be negatived before an offence under s 83 of the Act could be proved . . .

In *K v Minister for Youth and Community Services* (1982) 1 NSWLR 311, a 15 year old ward of the State of New South Wales got pregnant. She desired an abortion. Under the relevant legislation, consent to that course of the Minister of Youth and Community Services was necessary. The Minister refused consent. Proceedings were instituted by the girl's mother to enlist the court's aid as *parens patriae* to enable the abortion to be performed.

Helsham CJ in Equity in his judgment said (at 318–19):

> If the law be, as it was stated to be by Levine, Chairman of Quarter Sessions, in *R v Wald* (1971) 3 NSWDCR 25, at 29, then there is no legal wrongdoing if a miscarriage is procured by a person who has an honest belief on reasonable grounds that the termination of pregnancy was necessary to preserve the woman involved from serious danger to her life or physical or mental health and that in the circumstances the danger of the operation was not out of proportion to the danger intended to be averted. Reasonable grounds can stem from social, economic or medical bases. As it was not submitted on behalf of the Minister that this was not a correct statement of the law, I am content to accept it as such. Of course, the lawfulness of the procedure in this case postulates consent and proper performance. Applying this to the present facts, I have not the slightest doubt that there would be no legal impediment to the carrying out of an abortion on the plaintiff. There is ample material upon which a conclusion could be reached that the social and medical situation of this girl constitutes reasonable grounds upon which an honest belief could be formed that an abortion is necessary to prevent serious danger to her physical or mental health. Indeed, I would go so far as to say that in my view there is virtually no evidence before me to the contrary. The only real evidence against the necessity for termination of this girl's pregnancy is that it may now be too late, that the risk to her of terminating the pregnancy may be a greater one than continuing with it; this must mean physical risk. A specialist gynaecologist has expressed the view that it is not too late and that she would be very happy to recommend termination of the pregnancy; that was five days ago. Bearing in mind the danger to this girl's health, and in the light of the opinion of this specialist, it would be open for a qualified person to reach the conclusion that the danger of the operation was not out of proportion to the danger intended to be averted, provided the person upon whom the procedure is to be performed is aware of this and consents. In the light of the preponderance and weight of the material pointing to the necessity for the abortion in order to avoid putting this girl's whole future in danger, one wonders how it could be refused her on any legal grounds. If there were to be found a competent person willing to perform the necessary procedures, then

> there exist ample grounds for reaching an honest belief that their performance is necessary to preserve this girl from serious danger to her health and that any danger in carrying them out ought to be run.

At 326 the Chief Justice in Equity said:

> I have reached the conclusion that if an abortion can now be lawfully performed, that is to say, within the parameters of the legal requirements laid down in *R v Wald* then it is essential in this child's best interests that it be done. There is a serious danger to her health, but I think the adverse effects on her of being forced to bear her child are likely to be so grave that they make it essential. She is fifteen and a half and has been up against it all her life . . .

For myself, I think the courts must act on principle and not on hunch or intuition. For this reason, I lean on the side of necessity as the guiding principle . . . It is argued for the Crown that the common law defence of necessity has no application under the Queensland Criminal Code unless the defence is specially reserved by the Code. I agree with that as a general proposition. However, Glanville Williams did express the opinion that the *Bourne* direction 'is a striking vindication of the legal view that the defence of necessity applies not only to the common law but even to statutory crimes'. With respect, I think there is merit in the learned author's view. The history of the development of certain branches of the law shows that there are times when logic has been sacrificed on the altar of expediency. In the words of the great Mr Justice Oliver Wendell Holmes' oft quoted aphorism: 'The life of the law has not been logic; it has been experience.' And as Lord Macmillan said in *Read v J Lyons & Co Ltd* [1947] AC 156, at 175: 'Arguments based on legal consistency are apt to mislead for the common law is a practical code adapted to deal with the manifold diversities of human life' . . .

Section 282 and the unborn child

It would appear clear that s 321 of the draft is the section to which Griffith intended to refer in his footnote to s 289 [the latter represents the current s 282].

Section 321 of Griffith's draft Code reads as follows:

> **Killing unborn child**
>
> 321 Any person who, when a woman is about to be delivered of a child, prevents a child from being born alive by any act or omission of such a nature that, if the child had been born alive and had then died, he would be deemed to have unlawfully killed the child, is guilty of a crime, and is liable to imprisonment with hard labour for life.

It seems to me, therefore, that reference to the unborn child in s 282 of the Queensland Criminal Code has to be related to s 313 [Griffith's draft

> s 321] of the Code. I am therefore of opinion that the reference to 'unborn child' in s 282 of the Code means a viable child, that is, one capable of being born alive.
>
> However, if I am wrong, or if there is doubt about the construction I have placed on the words 'or for the preservation of the mother's life' contained in s 282 of the Queensland Criminal Code, it seems to me that the phrase 'for the preservation of the mother's life' in the abortion law contexts has a more or less judicially settled meaning. I have traced the authorities at some length. Without exception, the phrase has been interpreted to include preservation of health in one form or another.
>
> For these reasons, the exact scope of s 282 is indeed difficult to define. The matter is further complicated by s 288 of the Queensland Criminal Code which defines the duty of persons undertaking surgical or medical treatment. However, for the reasons previously stated, I am of opinion that s 282 as it affects the unborn child should be read in conjunction with s 313 dealing with the killing of an unborn child, and that the mischief which it was designed to remedy was an apparent gap between the law on abortion, on the one hand, and the law of homicide, on the other. As I have said, Griffith himself said as much in his notes to the relevant provisions of his draft Code to which I have earlier made detailed reference.
>
> The law in this State has not abdicated its responsibility as guardian of the silent innocence of the unborn. It should rightly use its authority to see that abortion on whim or caprice does not insidiously filter into our society. There no legal justification for abortion on demand.

It would appear that Australian law is beginning to take a broader view of when the continuation of a pregnancy could be said to pose a threat to a mother's health. In *Veivers v Connolly* [1995] 2 Qd R 326, de Jersey J considered an action brought by a 25 year old woman who had given birth to a severely disabled child following the contraction of rubella during pregnancy. One of the questions facing the court was whether, if the plaintiff had been correctly informed of the likelihood of her child being born handicapped, the plaintiff could have sought an abortion. Justice de Jersey held that a relevant serious risk to the mother could arise not only during the term of the pregnancy but even after the birth of the child. This view was approved of and applied by Kirby P in *CES v Superclinics* ((1995) Aust Torts Reports 81–360) who noted that, in light of the growing recognition of postnatal depression and other 'serious economic and social pressures', the dangers of pregnancy have to be evaluated as they apply to each woman. An appeal from the decision of the Court of Appeal in the *CES* case was lodged with the High Court, but the appeal has now been withdrawn as the parties to the matter settled their dispute.

For further reading on abortion, see: Crowley-Smith, L, 'Therapeutic abortions and the emergence of wrongful birth actions in Australia' (1996) 4 No 3 Journal of Law and Medicine 359; Finlay, HA, 'Abortion – right or crime?' (1990) 10 University of Tasmania Law Review 1; Cica, N, 'The inadequacies of Australian law on abortion' (1991) 5 AJFL 37.

PART III: ASSISTED SUICIDE, EUTHANASIA AND ADVANCE DIRECTIVES

Although suicide is no longer a crime in any Australian jurisdiction, assisting someone else to end his or her own life is in most jurisdictions. The term of art for such a procedure is euthanasia. It should be noted at the outset that an enormous variety of material has been published about the legal, philosophical, theological and moral issues involved in euthanasia. For reasons of space, it is not possible to cover all such issues here. Readers interested in the area of euthanasia from an Anglo-Australian perspective are referred to: Alschuler, A, 'The right to die' (1991) 141 NLJ 1637; Browne, A, 'Assisted suicide and active voluntary euthanasia' (1989) 11 No 2 Canadian Journal of Law and Jurisprudence 35; Bunney, L, 'A right to die: has patient autonomy gone too far?' (1993) 2 Australian Health Law Bulletin 29; Johnson, E, 'Euthanasia: is it murder?' (1988) 21 No 1 The Australian Journal of Forensic Science 26; Kelly, P, 'Euthanasia: law and morality' (1988) 6 No 1 Auckland University Law Review 224; Lanham, D, *Taming Death by Law*, 1993, Melbourne: Longman Cheshire; Lanham, D, 'Euthanasia, painkilling, murder and manslaughter' (1994) 4 Journal of Law and Medicine 146; Law Reform Commission of Western Australia, *Medical Treatment for the Dying*, Project No 84, 1988; Mackinnon, P, 'Euthanasia and homicide' (1984) 26 Criminal Law Quarterly 483; Otlowski, M, 'Mercy killing cases in the Australian criminal justice system' (1993) 17 Criminal Law Journal 10; Shinn, M, 'Physician-assisted suicide' (1994) 2 No 8 Australian Health Law Bulletin 96; Smith, GP, 'Re-thinking euthanasia and death with dignity: a transnational challenge' (1990) 12 Adelaide Law Review 480; Victorian Parliamentary Social Development Committee, *Final Report on Dying with Dignity*, 1986.

It should be noted that the law in some jurisdictions permits a health care practitioner to ameliorate suffering by using drugs, even if one of the possible side effects is the death of that patient *provided that causing the death of the patient was not the intention of the health care practitioner*. This is known as the principle of double effect.

Note also that *Bland's* case (below) confirmed that Anglo-Australian law draws a distinction between causing the death of a patient (which is unlawful, see *R v Cox* referred to in *Bland*) and permitting a terminally ill patient to die by withdrawal of treatment (which *in some circumstances* is permissible).

A competent patient is able to choose when he or she does not want to undergo further treatment. Moreover, in three States of Australia, legislation specifically allows patients to make 'living wills', which direct which treatment they do or do not want, in the event that they are incompetent when the time comes to make such decisions. Relevant extracts from the legislation are reproduced below.

A competent patient may refuse any treatment – including life-sustaining treatment

In Chapter 2, we saw that it is a competent patient's right to decide what treatment is performed on him or her. This right clearly extends to the refusal of life-sustaining treatment. The courts will, however, carefully scrutinise any such decision, to ensure that the patient had capacity to make the decision and freely made the decision.

In Re T (Adult: Refusal of Treatment) [1993] Fam 95

T, who was 34 weeks pregnant, was admitted to hospital following a traffic accident. T was a 20 year old who had been brought up by her mother (a member of the Jehovah's Witnesses). Although never a member of that religion, T was sympathetic to their beliefs. T was diagnosed as suffering from pneumonia and had antibiotics, oxygen and pethidine (a narcotic drug) administered to her. T subsequently went into labour. It was decided to deliver the baby by Caesarean section. After a period spent alone in the ambulance with her mother, T stated to the doctor and nurse that she did not want a blood transfusion. She was told by the doctor that a transfusion was not usually necessary and (incorrectly) that other procedures were available. She then signed a form which was neither read to her or explained to her signifying her refusal of blood transfusions. The following day, her child was delivered stillborn and a blood transfusion was medically indicated. She was sedated and placed on a ventilator.

T's boyfriend and father applied for a declaration that it would not be unlawful for the hospital to administer a blood transfusion to her. At first instance, the declaration was granted. The Official Solicitor (as guardian *ad litem* for T) appealed.

Staughton LJ:

An adult whose mental capacity is unimpaired has the right to decide for herself whether she will or will not receive medical or surgical treatment, even in circumstances where she is likely or even certain to die in the absence of treatment. Thus far the law is clear. The difficulty arises when it is uncertain whether or not the competent adult (as I call her for brevity) does or does not consent to the proposed treatment . . .

One such occasion will be when the adult is brought to hospital unconscious after an accident, and has had no opportunity to signify whether she consents to treatment or not. In those circumstances treatment can only be justified by the principle of necessity . . .

In any individual case there are three possibilities: (a) the patient consents, (b) the patient has expressed no decision and (c) the patient refuses consent. A further complication arises because an apparent consent, or apparent refusal to consent, may not be a true consent or a true refusal. I use the word 'true' to express the notion that consent, or refusal of consent, may be inoperative in law for one of three reasons; there may perhaps be others, but only these three are relevant to the present case.

The first reason is that the apparent consent or refusal was given as a result of undue influence. It is, I think, misleading to ask whether it was made of the patient's own free will, or even whether it was voluntary. Every decision is made of a person's free will, and is voluntary, unless it is effected by compulsion. Likewise, every decision is made as a result of some influence: a patient's decision to consent to an operation will normally be influenced by the surgeon's advice as to what will happen if the operation does not take place. In order for an apparent consent or refusal of consent to be less than a true consent or refusal, there must be such a degree of external influence as to persuade the patient to depart from her own wishes, to an extent that the law regards it as undue. I can suggest no more precise test than that. The cases on undue influence in the law of property and contract are not, in my opinion, applicable to the different context of consent to medical or surgical treatment. The wife who guarantees her husband's debts, or the widower who leaves all his property to his housekeeper, are not in the same situation as a patient faced with the need for medical treatment. There are many different ways of expressing the concept that what a person says may not be binding upon him; a Greek poet wrote 'My tongue has sworn, but no oath binds my mind'.

The second reason why an apparent consent or refusal of consent may not be a true consent or refusal is that it may not have been made with reference to the particular circumstances in which it turns out to be relevant. A patient who consents, even in the widest terms, to a dental operation under anaesthetic does not give a true consent to the amputation of a leg. Nor does a patient who refuses consent in some circumstances necessarily give a true refusal of consent to treatment in any quite different circumstances which may arise: an example is to be found in *Werth v Taylor* (1991) 475 NW (2d) 426.

The third reason is that at the time of apparent consent or refusal the patient may not, for the time being, be a competent adult. Her understanding and reasoning powers may be seriously reduced by drugs or other circumstances, although she is not actually unconscious.

The notion that consent or refusal of consent may not be a true consent or refusal presents a serious problem for doctors. It does not arise so much when the doubt lies between (a) consent and (b) no decision. In such a case, the surgeon may lawfully operate, in the knowledge that he can be justified either by consent or by the principle of necessity, whichever is in fact applicable. But what if the choice is, as in this case, between (b) no decision and (c) refusal of consent? The surgeon will be liable in damages if he operates when there is a valid refusal of consent, and liable in damages if he fails to operate in accordance with the principle of necessity when there was no valid decision by the patient. That is the intolerable dilemma described by Lord Bridge of Harwich in *In re F (Mental Patient: Sterilisation)* [1990] 2 AC 1, 52. In *Malette v Shulman*, 67 DLR (4th) 321, a Canadian court upheld an award of $20,000 to a patient who had been given a blood transfusion in order to save her life but against her known wishes. I doubt if an English court would have awarded such a sum; but the liability would exist.

Some will say that, when there is doubt whether an apparent refusal of consent is valid in circumstances of urgent necessity, the decision of a doctor acting in good faith ought to be conclusive. In this case, there was an application at the judge's lodgings at 11 o'clock at night, a procedure which may not always be available. However, I cannot find authority that the decision of a doctor as to the existence or refusal of consent is sufficient protection, if the law subsequently decides otherwise. So the medical profession, in the future as in the past, must bear the responsibility unless it is possible to obtain a decision from the courts.

In the present case, I agree with Lord Donaldson of Lymington MR and Butler-Sloss LJ that there was no valid refusal of consent, and that the doctors were justified in their treatment of Miss T by the principle of necessity. I would dismiss this appeal.

Lord Donaldson MR:

Summary

1 *Prima facie* every adult has the right and capacity to decide whether or not he will accept medical treatment, even if a refusal may risk permanent injury to his health or even lead to premature death. Furthermore, it matters not whether the reasons for the refusal were rational or irrational, unknown or even non-existent. This is so notwithstanding the very strong public interest in preserving the life and health of all citizens. However, the presumption of capacity to decide, which stems from the fact that the patient is an adult, is rebuttable.

2 An adult patient may be deprived of his capacity to decide either by long-term mental incapacity or retarded development or by temporary factors such as unconsciousness or confusion or the effects of fatigue, shock, pain or drugs.

3 If an adult patient did not have the capacity to decide at the time of the purported refusal and still does not have that capacity, it is the duty of the doctors to treat him in whatever way they consider, in the exercise of their clinical judgment, to be in his best interests.

4 Doctors faced with a refusal of consent have to give very careful and detailed consideration to what was the patient's capacity to decide at the time when the decision was made. It may not be a case of capacity or no capacity. It may be a case of reduced capacity. What matters is whether at that time the patient's capacity was reduced below the level needed in the case of a refusal of that importance, for refusals can vary in importance. Some may involve a risk to life or of irreparable damage to health. Others may not.

5 In some cases, doctors will not only have to consider the capacity of the patient to refuse treatment, but also whether the refusal has been vitiated because it resulted not from the patient's will, but from the will of others. It matters not that those others sought, however strongly, to persuade the patient to refuse, so long as in the end the refusal represented the patient's independent decision. If, however, his will was overborne, the refusal will not have represented a true

decision. In this context the relationship of the persuader to the patient – for example, spouse, parents or religious adviser – will be important, because some relationships more readily lend themselves to overbearing the patient's independent will than do others.

6 In all cases, doctors will need to consider what is the true scope and basis of the refusal. Was it intended to apply in the circumstances which have arisen? Was it based upon assumptions which in the event have not been realised? A refusal is only effective within its true scope and is vitiated if it is based upon false assumptions.

7 Forms of refusal should be redesigned to bring the consequences of a refusal forcibly to the attention of patients.

8 In cases of doubt as to the effect of a purported refusal of treatment, where failure to treat threatens the patient's life or threatens irreparable damage to his health, doctors and health authorities should not hesitate to apply to the courts for assistance.

[Butler-Sloss LJ delivered a judgment which agreed with Lord Donaldson and Staughton LJ.]

Note that the principle of refusing treatment also extends to the situation of refusing food and water: *Secretary of State for the Home Department v Robb* [1995] Fam 127. In that case, it was held that a prisoner, though suffering from a personality disorder, was competent to make the decision to engage in a hunger strike and starve himself to death. This wish had to be respected by prison authorities.

The distinction between causing death and letting die

Although a competent patient may decide to refuse treatment even though this results in death, what is the position of an unconscious and incompetent patient with no prospects of recovery? Must doctors keep such a patient alive? Put another way, would a doctor who decided to cease feeding or hydrating such a patient (or a doctor who discontinued life support for such a patient) be guilty of causing the patient's death, or being a party to causing the patient's death?

The law relating to the difference between causing death and letting die came into sharp focus in the case of *Airedale NHS Trust v Bland*. In that case, Tony Bland (the subject of the appeal) was in a persistent vegetative state with no prospect of recovery. The very nature of his condition meant that he was unable to express any preference as to treatment or non-treatment and he was insensate.

Airedale NHS Trust v Bland [1993] AC 789, pp 860–73

Lord Goff:

The central issue in the present case has been aptly stated by Sir Thomas Bingham MR to be whether artificial feeding and antibiotic drugs may be lawfully withheld from an insensate patient with no hope of recovery when it is known that if that is done the patient will shortly thereafter die . . . [there is] no absolute obligation upon the doctor who has the patient in his care to prolong his life, regardless of the circumstances ... It is scarcely consistent with the primacy given to the right of self-determination in those cases in which the patient of sound mind has declined to give his consent that the law should provide no means of enabling treatment to be withheld in circumstances where the patient is in no condition to indicate if that was his wish, that he did not consent to it ... It has to be stressed that the law draws a crucial distinction between cases in which a doctor decides not to prolong or to continue to provide for his patient treatment which could or might prolong his life, and those in which he decides, for example, by administering a lethal drug, actively to bring his patient's life to an end. It is not lawful for a doctor to administer a drug to his patient to bring about his death, even though that course is prompted by a humanitarian desire to end his suffering, however great that suffering may be: see *R v Cox* (1992) 12 BMLR 38 *per* Ognall J in the Crown Court at Winchester. So to act is to cross the Rubicon which runs between on the one hand the care of the living patient and on the other hand euthanasia – actively causing his death or to avoid his suffering. Euthanasia is not lawful at common law. I return to the patient who, because, for example, he is of unsound mind or has been rendered unconscious by accident or illness, is incapable of stating whether or not he consents to treatment or care. In such circumstances, it is now established that a doctor may lawfully treat such a patient if he acts in his best interests, and indeed that, if the patient is already in his care, he is under a duty so to treat him: see *F v West Berkshire Health Authority* [1989] 2 All ER 545, [1990] 2 AC 1, in which the legal principles governing treatment in such circumstances were stated by this House. For my part, I can see no reason why, as a matter of principle, a decision by a doctor whether or not to initiate, or to continue to provide, treatment or care which could or might have the effect of prolonging such a patient's life should not be governed by the same fundamental principle. Of course, in the great majority of cases, the best interests of the patient are likely to require that treatment of this kind, if available, should be given to a patient. But this may not always be so. To take a simple example given by Thomas J in the High Court of New Zealand in *Auckland Area Health Board v AG* [1993] 1 NZLR 235, at 253, to whose judgment in that case I wish to pay tribute, it cannot be right that a doctor, who has under his care a patient suffering painfully from terminal cancer, should be under an absolute obligation to perform upon him major surgery to abate another condition which, if unabated, would or might shorten his life still further. The doctor who is caring for such a patient cannot, in my opinion, be under an absolute obligation to prolong his life by any means available to him, regardless of the quality of the patient's life. Common humanity requires otherwise, as do medical ethics and good medical practice accepted in this country and overseas. As I see it, the doctor's decision whether or not to take any such step must subject to his patient's ability to give or (withhold his consent) be made in the best interests of the patient ...

It is of course the development of modern medical technology, and in particular the development of life support systems, which has rendered cases such as the present so much more relevant than in the past. Even so, where, for example, a patient is brought into hospital in such a condition that, without the benefit of a life support system, he will not continue to live, the decision has to be made whether or not to give him that benefit, if available. That decision can only be made in the best interests of the patient. No doubt, his best interests will ordinarily require that he should be placed on a life support system as soon as necessary, if only to make an accurate assessment of his condition and a prognosis for the future. But, if he neither recovers sufficiently to be taken off it nor dies, the question will ultimately arise whether he should be kept on it indefinitely. As I see it, that question (assuming the continued availability of the system) can only be answered by reference to the best interests of the patient himself, having regard to established medical practice. Indeed, if the justification for treating a patient who lacks the capacity to consent lies in the fact that the treatment is provided in his best interests, it must follow that the treatment may, and indeed ultimately should, be discontinued where it is no longer in his best interests to provide it. The question which lies at the heart of the present case is, as I see it, whether on that principle the doctors responsible for the treatment and care of Anthony Bland can justifiably discontinue the process of artificial feeding upon which the prolongation of his life depends.

It is crucial for the understanding of this question that the question itself should be correctly formulated. The question is not whether the doctor should take a course which will kill his patient, or even take a course which has the effect of accelerating his death. The question is whether the doctor should or should not continue to provide his patient with medical treatment or care which, if continued, will prolong his patient's life. The question is sometimes put in striking or emotional terms, which can be misleading. For example, in the case of a life support system, it is sometimes asked: should a doctor be entitled to switch it off, or to pull the plug? And then it is asked: can it be in the best interests of the patient that a doctor should be able to switch the life support system off, when this will inevitably result in the patient's death? Such an approach has rightly been criticised as misleading, for example, by Professor Ian Kennedy (in his paper in *Treat Me Right, Essays in Medical Law and Ethics* (1988)), and by Thomas J in *Auckland Area Health Board v AG* [1993] 1 NZLR 235, at 247. This is because the question is not whether it is in the best interests of the patient that he should die. The question is whether it is in the best interests of the patient that his life should be prolonged by the continuance of this form of medical treatment or care.

The correct formulation of the question is of particular importance in a case such as the present, where the patient is totally unconscious and where there is no hope whatsoever of any amelioration of his condition. In circumstances such as these, it may be difficult to say that it is in his best interests that the treatment should be ended. But, if the question is asked, as in my opinion it should be, whether it is in his best interests that treatment which has the effect of artificially prolonging his life should be continued, that question can sensibly be answered to the effect that it is not in his best interests to do so . . .

[In PVS cases] there is in reality no weighing operation to be performed. Here the condition of the patient, who is totally unconscious and in whose condition there is no prospect of any improvement, is such that life-prolonging treatment is properly regarded as being, in medical terms, useless. As Sir Thomas Bingham MR pointed out in the present case, medical treatment or care may be provided for a number of different purposes. It may be provided, for example, as an aid to diagnosis, for the treatment of physical or mental injury or illness, to alleviate pain or distress, or to make the patient's condition more tolerable. Such purposes may include prolonging the patient's life, for example, to enable him to survive during diagnosis and treatment. But for my part, I cannot see that medical treatment is appropriate or requisite simply to prolong a patient's life when such treatment has no therapeutic purposes of any kind, as where it is futile because the patient is unconscious and there is no prospect of any improvement in his condition. It is reasonable also that account should be taken of the invasiveness of the treatment and of the indignity to which, as the present case shows, a person has to be subjected if his life is prolonged by artificial means, which must cause considerable distress to his family – a distress which reflects not only their own feelings but their perception of the situation of their relative who is being kept alive. But in the end, in a case such as the present, it is the futility of the treatment which justifies its termination. I do not consider that, in circumstances such as these, a doctor is required to initiate or to continue life-prolonging treatment or care in the best interests of his patient. It follows that no such duty rests upon the respondents, or upon Dr Howe, in the case of Anthony Bland, whose condition is in reality no more than a living death, and for whom such treatment or care would, in medical terms, be futile.

In the present case, it is proposed that the doctors should be entitled to discontinue both the artificial feeding of Anthony and the use of antibiotics. It is plain from the evidence that Anthony, in his present condition, is very prone to infection and that, over some necessarily uncertain but not very long period of time, he will succumb to infection which, if unchecked, will spread and cause his death. But the effect of discontinuing the artificial feeding will be that he will inevitably die within one or two weeks.

Objection can be made to the latter course of action on the ground that Anthony will thereby be starved to death, and that this would constitute a breach of the duty to feed him which must form an essential part of the duty which every person owes to another in his care. But here again it is necessary to analyse precisely what this means in the case of Anthony. Anthony is not merely incapable of feeding himself. He is incapable of swallowing, and therefore of eating or drinking in the normal sense of those words. There is overwhelming evidence that, in the medical profession, artificial feeding is regarded as a form of medical treatment and, even if it is not strictly medical treatment, it must form part of the medical care of the patient. Indeed, the function of artificial feeding in the case of Anthony, by means of a nasogastric tube, is to provide a form of life support analogous to that provided by a ventilator which artificially breathes air in and out of the lung of a patient incapable of breathing normally, thereby enabling oxygen to reach the bloodstream. The same principles must apply in either case when the question is asked whether the doctor in charge may lawfully discontinue the life-sustaining treatment or care; and, if in either case the treatment is futile in the sense I have described, it can properly be concluded that it is no longer in the best interests of the patient to continue it. It is true that, in the case of discontinuance of artificial feeding, it can be said that the patient will as a result starve to death; and this may bring before our eyes the vision of an ordinary person slowly dying of hunger and suffering all the pain and distress associated with such a death. But here it is clear from the evidence that no such pain or distress will be suffered by Anthony, who can feel nothing at all. Furthermore, we are told that the outward symptoms of dying in such a way, which might otherwise cause distress to the nurses who care for him or to members of his family who visit him, can be suppressed by means of sedatives. In these circumstances, I can see no ground in the present case for refusing the declarations applied for simply because the course of action proposed involved the discontinuance of artificial feeding.

In *F v West Berkshire Health Authority* [1989] 2 All ER 545, [1990] 2 AC 1, it was stated that, where a doctor provides treatment for a person who is incapacitated from saying whether or not he consents to it, the doctor must, when deciding on the form of treatment, act in accordance with a responsible and competent body of relevant professional opinion, on the principles set down in *Bolam v Friern Hospital Management Committee* [1957] 2 All ER 118, [1957] 1 WLR 582. In my opinion, this principle must equally be applicable to decisions to initiate, or to discontinue, life support, as it is to other forms of treatment. However, in a matter of such importance and sensitivity as discontinuance of life support, it is to be expected that guidance will be provided for the profession; and, on the evidence in the present case, such guidance is for a case such as the present to be found in a discussion paper on *Treatment of Patients in Persistent Vegetative State*, issued in September 1992 by the medical ethics committee of the British Medical Association. Anybody reading this substantial paper will discover for himself the great care with which this topic is being considered by the profession. Mr Francis for the respondents drew to the attention of the Appellate Committee four safeguards in particular which, in the committee's opinion, should be observed before discontinuing life support for such patients. They are: (1) every effort should be made at rehabilitation for at least six months after the injury; (2) the diagnosis of irreversible PVS should not be considered confirmed until at least 12 months after the injury, with the effect that any decision to withhold life-prolonging treatment will be delayed for that period; (3) the diagnosis should be agreed by two other independent doctors; and (4) generally, the wishes of the patient's immediate family will be given great weight.

In fact, the views expressed by the committee on the subject of consultation with the relatives of PVS patients are consistent with the opinion expressed by your Lordships' House in *F v West Berkshire Health Authority* that it is good practice for the doctor to consult relatives. Indeed, the committee recognises that, in the case of PVS patients, the relatives themselves will require a high degree of support and attention. But the committee is firmly of the opinion that the relatives' views cannot be determinative of the treatment. Indeed, if that were not so, the relatives would be able to dictate to the doctors what is in the best interests of the patient, which cannot be right. Even so, a decision to withhold life-prolonging treatment, such as artificial feeding, must require close co-operation with those close to the patient; and it is recognised that, in practice, their views and the opinions of doctors will coincide in many cases.

Study of this document left me in no doubt that if a doctor treating a PVS patient acts in accordance with the medical practice now being evolved by the medical ethics committee of the British Medical Association he will be acting with the benefit of guidance from a responsible and competent body of relevant professional opinion, as required by the *Bolam* test. I also feel that those who are concerned that a matter of life and death, such as is involved in a decision to withhold life support in a case of this kind, should be left to the doctors who do well to study this paper. The truth is that, in the course of their work, doctors frequently have to make decisions which may affect the continued survival of their patients, and are in reality far more experienced in matters of this kind than are the judges. It is nevertheless the function of the judges to state the legal principles upon which the lawfulness of the actions of doctors depend; but in the end the decisions to be made in individual cases must rest with the doctors themselves. In these circumstances, what is required is a sensitive understanding of both the judges and the doctors of each other's respective function, and in particular a determination by the judges not merely to understand the problems facing the medical profession in cases of this kind, but also to regard their professional standards with respect. Mutual understanding between the doctors and the judges is the best way to ensure the evolution of a sensitive and sensible legal framework for the treatment and care of patients, with a sound ethical base, in the interests of the patients themselves. This is a topic to which I will return at the end of this opinion, when I come to consider the extent to which the view of the court should be sought, as a matter of practice, in cases such as the present . . .

Certainly, in *F v West Berkshire Health Authority*, your Lordships' House adopted a straightforward test based on the best interests of the patient; and I myself do not see why the same test should not be applied in the case of PVS patients, where the question is whether life-prolonging treatment should be withheld. This was also the opinion of Thomas J in *Auckland Area Health Board v AG* [1933] 1 NZLR 235, a case concerned with the discontinuance of life support provided by ventilator to a patient suffering from the last stages of incurable Guillain-Barre syndrome. Of course, consistent with the best interests test, anything relevant to the application of the test may be taken into account; and, if the personality of the patient is relevant to the application of the test (as it may be in cases where the various relevant factors have to be weighed), it may be taken into account, as was done in *Re J (A Minor) (Wardship: Medical Treatment)* [1990] 3 All ER 930, [1991] Fam 33. But, where the question is whether life support should be withheld from a PVS patient, it is difficult to see how the personality of the patient can be relevant, though it may be of comfort to his relatives if they believe, as in the present case, and indeed may well be so in many other cases, that the patient would not have wished his life to be artificially prolonged if he was totally unconscious and there was no hope of improvement in his condition.

I wish to add, however, that, like the court below, I have derived assistance and support from decisions in a number of American jurisdictions to the effect that it is lawful to discontinue life-prolonging treatment in the case of PVS patients where there is no prospect of improvement in their condition. Furthermore, I wish to refer to the section in Working Paper No 28 (1982) on *Euthanasia, Aiding Suicide and Cessation of Treatment* published by the Law Reform Commission of Canada concerned with cessation of treatment, to which I also wish to express my indebtedness. I believe the legal principles as I have stated them to be broadly consistent with the conclusions summarised in the Working Paper (pp 65–66), which was substantially accepted in the Report of the Commission (1083), pp 32–35. Indeed, I entertain a strong sense that a community view on the legal principles applicable in cases of discontinuing life support is in the course of development and acceptance throughout the common law world.

In setting out my understanding of the relevant principles, I have had very much in mind the submissions advanced by Mr Munby on behalf of the Official Solicitor, and I believe that I have answered, directly or indirectly, all his objections to the course now proposed. I do not, therefore, intend any disrespect to his argument if I do not answer each of his submissions *seriatim*. In summary, his two principal arguments were as follows. First, he submitted that the discontinuance of artificial feeding would constitute an act which would inevitably cause, and be intended to cause, Anthony's death; and as such, it would be unlawful, and indeed criminal. As will be plain from what I have already said, I cannot accept this proposition. In my opinion, for the reasons I have already given, there is no longer any duty upon the doctors to continue with this form of medical treatment or care in his case, and it follows that it cannot be unlawful to discontinue it. Second, he submitted that discontinuance of the artificial feeding of Anthony would be a breach of the doctor's duty to care for and feed him; and since it will (as it is intended to do) cause his death, it will necessarily be unlawful. I have considered this point earlier in this opinion, when I expressed my view that artificial feeding is, in a case such as the present, no different from life support by a ventilator, and as such can lawfully be discontinued when it no longer fulfils any therapeutic purpose. To me, the crucial point in which I found myself differing from Mr Munby was that I was unable to accept his treating the discontinuance of artificial feeding in the present case as equivalent to cutting a mountaineer's rope, or severing the air pipe of a deep sea diver. Once it is recognised, as I believe it must be, that the true question is not whether the doctor should take a course in which he will actively kill his patient, but rather whether he should continue to provide his patient with medical treatment or care which, if continued, will prolong his life, then, as I see it, the essential basis of Mr Munby's submission disappears. I wish to add that I was unable to accept his suggestion that recent decisions show that the law is proceeding down a 'slippery slope', in the sense that the courts are becoming more and more ready to allow doctors to take steps which will result in the ending of life. On the contrary, as I have attempted to demonstrate, the courts are acting within a structure of legal principle, under which in particular they continue to draw a clear distinction between the bounds of lawful treatment of a living patient and unlawful euthanasia.

I turn finally to the extent to which doctors should, as a matter of practice, seek the guidance of the court, by way of an application for declaratory relief, before withholding life-prolonging treatment from a PVS patient. Sir Stephen Brown P considered that the opinion of the court should be sought in all cases similar to the present. In the Court of Appeal, Sir Thomas Bingham MR expressed his agreement with Sir Stephen Brown P in the following words (see p 842, above):

> This was in my respectful view a wise ruling, directed to the protection of patients, the protection of doctors, the reassurance of patients' families and the reassurance of the public. The practice proposed seems to me desirable. It may well be that with the passage of time a body of experience and practice will build up which will obviate the need for application in every case but for the time being I am satisfied that the practice which Sir Stephen Brown P described should be followed.

Before the Appellate Committee this view was supported both by Mr Munby for the Official Solicitor and by Mr Lester as *amicus curiae*. For the respondents, Mr Francis suggested that an adequate safeguard would be provided if reference to the court was required in certain specific cases, ie, (1) where there was known to be a medical disagreement as to the diagnosis or prognosis, and (2) problems had arisen with the patient's relatives – disagreement by the next of kin with the medical recommendation; actual or apparent conflict of interest between the

> next of kin and the patient; dispute between members of the patient's family; or absence of any next of kin to give their consent. There is, I consider, much to be said for the view that an application to the court will not be needed in every case, but only in particular circumstances, such as those suggested by Mr Francis. In this connection, I was impressed not only by the care being taken by the medical ethics committee to provide guidance to the profession, but also by information given to the Appellate Committee about the substantial number of PVS patients in the country, and the very considerable cost of obtaining guidance from the court in cases such as the present. However, in my opinion, this is a matter which would be better kept under review by the President of the Family Division than resolved now by your Lordships' House. I understand that a similar review is being undertaken in cases concerned with the sterilisation of adult women of unsound mind, with a consequent relaxation of the practice relating to application to the court in such cases. For my part, I would therefore leave the matter as proposed by Sir Thomas Bingham MR; but I wish to express the hope that the President of the Family Division, who will no doubt be kept well informed about developments in this field, will soon feel able to relax the present requirement so as to limit applications for declarations to those cases in which there is a special need for the procedure to be invoked . . .
>
> For these reasons, I would dismiss the appeal.

Bland's case has been followed in *Frenchay Healthcare NHS Trust v S* [1994] 2 All ER 403. Note that the Official Solicitor in England has issued a Practice Note (see [1994] 2 All ER 413) which states that, in cases of patients in a PVS, leave of a judge must be sought before discontinuing feeding.

The applicability of *Bland* in Australia is somewhat unclear. There are indications the case would likely be followed – see the discussion of *Bland*'s case by Morris J in *Gardner*, re BWV (below).

Although actively causing the death of another remains a crime in Australia, there is some indication that courts have not always applied the full rigour of the law in so called 'mercy killing' cases. Margaret Otlowski has studied a number of largely unreported decisions in euthanasia. Note that not all of the cases referred to by Otlowski involve health care practitioners assisting in the death of others.

Otlowski, M, 'Mercy killing cases in the Australian criminal justice system' (1993) 17 Crim LJ 10, pp 13–28

> . . . cases of mercy killing coming to the attention of the Justice system in Australia have been few, those which have arisen have, almost invariably, been treated with exceptional leniency. A review of the Australian mercy killing cases sampled in this study confirms a number of mechanisms within the criminal justice system have been invoked to temper the rigours of the criminal law in true instances of mercy killing or assisted suicide. These include the exercise of prosecutorial discretion, acquittals (either by the judge or the jury) or findings of guilt on a lesser charge,

lenient sentencing by the courts, the parole determinations, and the exercise of executive clemency . . .

Prosecution discontinued

There have been cases of mercy killing where, in the exercise of prosecutorial discretion, a decision has been taken not to proceed with a prosecution. One such case arose in the Australian Capital Territory in 1983, when the Attorney General decided not to proceed with a charge of murder against a woman who had allegedly killed her sister who had been suffering from a terminal illness and had expressed a wish to die. The murder charge followed a coronial inquiry into the death in which a *prima facie* case of murder was found to have been established against the defendant. In explaining the reasons for the decision not to proceed with the prosecution, it was stated that the evidence against the defendant was largely circumstantial and such that a jury would be unlikely to convict. However, it was emphasised by the Attorney General that the decision not to proceed with the prosecution was based wholly on the exceptional circumstances of the case and should not be taken as signalling any particular approach to cases of this kind. In furtherance of this decision not to proceed with the prosecution, the Crown entered a bill of *nolle prosequi* in the Australian Capital Territory Supreme Court.

Another example of a discontinued prosecution can be found in the Tasmanian case of *Baker* (Unreported, *Mercury* 5, 6 December 1972). The defendant, Reginald Baker, was charged with murder as a result of shooting his sick wife in the forehead with a .22 calibre rifle. The deceased's health had been failing for some time as a result of a number of strokes and in the months preceding the shooting, it had significantly deteriorated rendering the deceased incapable of caring for herself. In a statement made to the police, the defendant stated that his wife had a dread of being placed in a nursing home. He told police that in light of her worsening condition he had summoned the courage to prevent any more unhappiness and pain by taking her life. The defendant pleaded not guilty to the charge. Following committal proceedings the defendant was committed for trial. Medical evidence presented at committal proceedings raised some doubt as to whether the deceased had, in fact, died from the bullet wound or was already dead at the time the shot was fired. In view of this evidence, the Crown decided not to file an indictment and the defendant was discharged.

As noted above, the sufficiency of evidence is an important consideration in the exercise of prosecutorial discretion and, having regard to the equivocal medical evidence, it is possible that a reasonable jury, properly instructed, would have had a reasonable doubt as to the cause of death in this case. However, having regard to the tragic circumstances of the case, the conclusion appears inescapable that considerations of sympathy for the defendant also played some role in the interpretation of the medical evidence.

Prosecution for lesser charge

Another way in which prosecutorial discretion may be manifest in genuine mercy killing cases is for the Crown to proceed with a lesser charge. This is illustrated in the case of *Austen* (unreported, Supreme Court (NSW), 5 March 1990) in which the defendant, an elderly man of outstanding character, was indicted for manslaughter rather than murder for the killing of his wife, who was suffering from Alzheimer's disease. From discussions with Crown prosecutors, it would appear, however, that this course would normally only be taken in circumstances where there is sound justification for reducing the charge.

Acceptance by the prosecution of plea of guilty for lesser offence

In cases where prosecution for the more serious offence is set to proceed, the Crown may be prepared to accept a plea of guilty from the defendant to a lesser offence in full satisfaction of the charge. Whilst the decision to accept a plea for a lesser offence lies within the discretion of the Crown, there are general principles, and in some jurisdictions, specific guidelines, which guide the exercise of this discretion. It appears to be widely accepted amongst prosecutors that there must be good justification before a decision is taken to accept a lesser plea. A plea should not be accepted unless it reasonably reflects the nature of the criminal conduct of the defendant and provides an adequate basis upon which a court can impose an appropriate sentence. Where there is a plea of guilty to a lesser offence, the Crown may, for the purposes of sentencing, agree to proceed on an accepted factual basis favourable to the defendant.

The Victorian case of *Larkin* (unreported, Supreme Court (Vic), 14 April 1983) illustrates the Crown's role in accepting a plea to a lesser offence in full satisfaction of the charge. In that case, the defendant, a nurse, was initially charged with the murder of her lover, a manic depressive, who had, on a number of occasions, threatened to commit suicide. The deceased had taken an overdose of tablets whilst the defendant was at work. When the defendant returned from work the deceased once again expressed his wish to die and attempted to inject himself with a fatal dose of insulin. The defendant responded to her lover's plea and administered the fatal injection. The defendant subsequently pleaded guilty to a charge of aiding and abetting suicide under the Crimes Act 1958 (Vic) and the Crown accepted this plea.

Another case in point is that of *Thompson* (unreported, Supreme Court (NSW), 25 November 1981). The charges against the defendant in this case arose as a result of a confession that he had made to the police concerning the murder of his father in 1969, some 12 years earlier. The defendant's father had been suffering from Parkinson's disease for several years. He had been in poor physical and mental condition, but had declined to go into a nursing home. The defendant had employed a nurse to look after him, but he often did the nursing of his father himself. On Christmas Day 1969, the defendant killed his father by placing a plastic bag over his head. There was evidence that the defendant was under considerable pressure and strain at this time because of his family circumstances, which could have affected the defendant's reasoning. The defendant, 52 years of age, pleaded not guilty to a charge of murdering his father, but guilty to the lesser charge of manslaughter and this plea was accepted by the Crown in full satisfaction of the charge.

A final example of the role of the Crown in accepting a plea of guilty for a lesser offence can be found in the case of *Thiel* (unreported, Supreme Court (NSW), 27 September 1990). The defendant in this case, a 74 year old man, had suffocated his ailing wife and then attempted to commit suicide. The evidence indicated that he was depressed and wanted to take his own life but felt he could not leave his wife on her own and therefore felt compelled to take her life as well. The Crown accepted a plea of guilty of manslaughter on the grounds of diminished responsibility.

The Crown's role in accepting a plea of guilty from the defendant to a lesser offence in full satisfaction of the charge is in practice likely to be particularly relevant in those jurisdictions where there is still a mandatory sentence of life imprisonment for murder. For the purpose of the jurisdictions, if the Crown accepts a plea of guilty to a charge of manslaughter or assisted suicide rather than murder, the possibility is there opened up for discretion in the sentencing of the defendant.

Jury acquittals

Of those cases which have proceeded to trial, a significant proportion have resulted in the acquittal of the defendant by the jury often against the weight of the evidence. Juries have considerable discretion in verdicts they bring in, since they are general verdicts only and juries do not have to give reasons for their decisions. Here too, in practice, jury acquittals may be particularly relevant with regard to murder prosecutions in jurisdictions where there is still a sentence of mandatory life imprisonment.

One example of a jury acquittal is the case of *Meares and Wanless* (unreported, Supreme Court (NSW), July 1989) in which charges arose out of the fatal shooting of a 54 year old cancer victim. The deceased, Mervyn Meares, had been in severe pain from terminal cancer and had apparently wanted to end his life. Mr Wanless, a 45 year old invalid pensioner and a close friend of the deceased, was charged with the murder. The deceased's wife, Mrs Meares, a 58 year old pensioner, was charged with having solicited Wanless to murder her husband. Both had pleaded not guilty to the charges. Notwithstanding the admission into evidence of a very incriminating police record of interview given by the defendant Meares, her defence counsel succeeded with a 'no case to answer' application on the grounds that there was insufficient evidence of communication with the co-defendant with the object of soliciting the murder. Maxwell J accordingly directed the jury to find the defendant Meares not guilty of the charge of having solicited the co-defendant Wanless to murder her husband. The case did, however, proceed against the co-defendant, Wanless. The Crown case relied on both motive and opportunity in that Wanless felt compassion for his sick friend and had visited him the day the shooting had occurred. Further, the Crown alleged that the deceased had continually begged for assistance to put an end to his suffering. There was also evidence connecting Wanless with the weapon which had been used in the killing. Wanless gave evidence that he had visited the deceased that day but that he had not killed his friend. Notwithstanding the strength of the Crown case, the jury found the defendant Wanless not guilty of the charge and he was acquitted.

Another case where the jury acquitted the defendant against the evidence was *Austen*. As noted above, the manslaughter charges in this case arose out of the killing of the deceased, a sufferer of Alzheimer's disease, by her husband. The defendant had been caring for his wife for a number of years but her condition had deteriorated and he was finding it increasingly difficult to cope with the situation. Evidence for the Crown was that he had suffocated his wife by putting his hand over her nose and a handkerchief in her mouth. The defendant had pleaded not guilty to the charge but did not dispute the evidence that he had suffocated his wife. In his evidence, he simply said that he could not really believe that he had done it or explain why or how. There was evidence before the court that the defendant had been suffering from depression and was emotionally disturbed at the time of the killing. In his address to the jury, counsel for the defendant made a plea for a merciful verdict (without really putting any legal basis for such a verdict), and the jury returned a verdict of not guilty.

Yet another instance of a sympathetic jury verdict can be found in the case of *Barnes* (unreported, Supreme Court (NSW), 16 November 1981). The defendant, a nurse's assistant, was charged with attempted murder after allegedly administering an unauthorised dose of pethidine to an elderly patient. He then proceeded to administer an overdose of pethidine to himself, in an apparent attempt to take his own life. The patient survived the overdose but died some weeks later from natural causes. In the police record of interview, the defendant admitted administering a large dose of pethidine to the patient in order to kill her but claimed that she had been in severe pain and that he acted out of merciful motives. The defendant pleaded not guilty to a charge of attempted murder. At his trial, he denied having administered the dose and said that he could not recall what had happened on the day in question. Evidence was also put before the court that the defendant had been receiving psychiatric treatment and was under great emotional stress prior to this incident. The jury returned a verdict of not guilty.

There have also been mercy killing cases in Australia where the jury has found the defendant guilty but has made strong recommendations for leniency in the treatment of the defendant.

Leniency in sentencing

In cases involving conviction of the offender (mostly arising from pleas of guilty), the courts have generally shown great leniency with respect to the sentencing, at least in those jurisdictions where the court has a discretion to do so.

For example, in the case of *Thompson*, noted above, in which the Crown had accepted the defendant's plea of guilty to the lesser offence of manslaughter in respect of a deliberate killing, Hunt J deferred passing sentence and placed the defendant on a $5,000 bond to be of good behaviour for five years. His Honour then went to some lengths to justify this decision. Whilst recognising that some people in the community would object to the decision, and regard it as 'weakly merciful', he felt that in the circumstances of the evidence disclosed, a term of imprisonment would serve no benefit to the prisoner or to the community. Hunt J accepted that the defendant's dominant motive in acting as he did was to put his father out of his misery. He also accepted that the matter was only brought to light by the defendant's own confession, which was a strong indication of his contrition. His Honour said that he had taken into consideration that the defendant had no relevant prior record as well as his position and acceptance in the community. Furthermore, he said that he could not imagine that the defendant would offend again. Weight was also attached to the defendant's impaired mental state at the time the crime was committed, arising from the stress of his father's situation. Hunt J was of the view that, in these circumstances, where the defence of diminished responsibility has been raised on the facts, the subjective considerations with regard to sentencing were paramount and the issue of public deterrence was of limited relevance.

Another striking example of judicial leniency in sentencing can be found in the case of *Johnstone* (unreported, Supreme Court (SA), 21 January 1987) in which the defendant, a 62 year old electrical engineer, had pleaded guilty to the murder of his mentally ill wife. The deceased had been suffering from a severe mental illness for many years. She had attempted suicide on numerous occasions but these attempts were unsuccessful, largely due to the defendant's efforts in obtaining appropriate medical treatment. Her mental condition had deteriorated significantly in the years preceding the commission of the crime and the defendant had assumed responsibility for her care and for the running of the household. Prior to her death, the deceased had often requested that the defendant help her to die. As her condition worsened, she became increasingly concerned about the prospect of being institutionalised. The defendant shared these concerns and refused to have his wife committed despite her deteriorating condition. He eventually acceded to her wish to die and, with her help, electrocuted her by placing wet face washers and foil on her arms and wiring her body to a radiator.

The defendant appeared before Bollen J in the South Australian Supreme Court for sentence. Bollen J explained that he was required by statute to pass the mandatory sentence of life imprisonment for the crime of murder. However, the court was also required to fix a period during which the prisoner may not be released on parole and his Honour said that there was no doubt that the defendant was entitled to leniency in fixing of this non-parole period. In sentencing Johnstone, Bollen J said he accepted that the defendant's act of killing was not done out of desire for personal benefit but out of a deep compassion and love for his wife. His Honour was of the view that in the special circumstances neither the punitive nor the preventative elements in sentencing demanded an actual stay in prison. With regard to the issue of general deterrence, his Honour stated that the actual period of imprisonment served by the defendant would make no difference to the deterrent effect of the sentence. His Honour felt that, in the circumstances of the case, the community would not profit in any way by the defendant actually serving any real term of imprisonment. In fact, he indicated that if he had the power to say that it was inappropriate to order punishment and immediately release the defendant, he would have done so. Bollen J proceeded to fix what he described as a 'token non-parole period' of 10 days, to be calculated from the date when the defendant first came before the court.

This sentence of a 10-day non-parole period following the imposition of the mandatory life sentence for the crime of murder (apparently the shortest in South Australian history) was welcomed by the press as a victory for the law, justice and commonsense. However, the Crown appealed against the sentence on the grounds that the non-parole period was manifestly inadequate. The Crown argued *inter alia* that Bollen J had given insufficient weight to the question of general deterrence and that the non-parole period did not reflect the importance of society's maintenance of the sanctity of life. King CJ, giving judgment for the Court of Criminal Appeal, described the Johnstone case as both important and distressing. He accepted that it was natural to be moved by the sad predicament in which the defendant had found himself but said that it would be wrong to allow one's pity to blind one to the stark reality of what the defendant had done. His Honour said:

> Cases such as this present great difficulty to the sentencing judge and to an appellate court. People cannot be permitted to take life in defiance of the law, however altruistic their personal motives may be. It is the responsibility of the court to impose punishments which maintain respect for the law and deter others from defying it.

Whilst acknowledging that in circumstances where murder is committed by a loved one who is moved by the plight and entreaties of the victim, there is considerable scope for compassion and leniency in fixing non-parole period.

King CJ said that even in this type of case, the gravity of the crime and the need for deterrence must not be overlooked. His Honour went on to say that:

> When those factors are given proper weight, it is difficult to visualise a case, even the most compassionate of cases, in which the end punishment could be served adequately other than by a substantial non-parole period probably of some years. The nominal non-parole period which the learned sentencing judge imposed and the remarks which accompanied it, lead me to the conclusion that his Honour allowed his understandable pity for this unfortunate man to cloud his appreciation of the necessity for the non-parole period to affirm the values which the law enshrines and to deter people from disregarding them. I think that the failure to give proper weight to those factors had caused the sentencing process to miscarry.

Although the court was of the view that there had been an error in the sentencing process and that the non-parole period set by Bollen J was inadequate, it was not prepared to interfere with the sentence. King CJ referred to the well-established principle that in a Crown appeal, an error in the sentencing process does not lead inevitably to intervention by the court and acknowledged that there are cases in which the ends of justice are best served by establishing the correct principles and standards without interfering with the result in the particular case.

His Honour expressed the view that despite the gravity of the crime which the defendant had committed, to return him to prison after he had been at liberty for about six months, would smack of cruelty. The appeal was accordingly dismissed, but the court emphasised that the case should not be regarded as a precedent and that the proper application of the appropriate standards and principles would have resulted in a much longer non-parole period.

The decision of the Court of Criminal Appeal in this case is significant. Through its strong disapproval of the token non-parole period fixed in the case, it seeks to preserve intact established principles with regard to sentencing, particularly in relation to the general deterrent aspect of sentencing. At the same time, by refusing to interfere with the actual outcome in this case (although not uncommon in appeals by the Crown) the court demonstrated some leniency towards the defendant in the exceptional circumstances of the case.

A further instance of judicial leniency towards mercy killers with respect to sentence can be found in the cases of *Kelly* (unreported, Supreme Court (Qld), 12 May 1989) and *Hollinrake* (unreported, Supreme Court (Vic), 29 June 1992) which involved very similar circumstances. In the case of *Kelly*, which came before the Queensland Supreme Court, the defendant, an 81 year old man, pleaded guilty to the attempted murder of his wife who had suffered several strokes. There was evidence before the court that the deceased had been an invalid for some years and the defendant had conscientiously taken care of her. Following a further stroke which resulted in a marked deterioration of her condition, the defendant had shot his wife in an attempt to put her out of her misery. She survived the shooting but died some months later from coronary artery disease. Ryan J sentenced the defendant to three years of probation. In passing sentence, he referred to the advanced age of the prisoner, his good background, his close relationship with his wife, his perception of her condition as one of misery, and his depressed state at the time of the offence. His Honour concluded that, in those circumstances, a custodial sentence was not demanded and would not serve any useful purpose.

In the Victorian case of *Hollinrake*, the defendant, 80 years of age, was charged with the attempted murder of his 79 year old wife who had been his partner for 51 years. Mrs Hollinrake had had a stroke which affected her vision and speech and left the right side of her body paralysed. The defendant had slit the wrist of his wife's paralysed right arm while she was in hospital. He then went home and tried to kill himself by cutting his wrists and forearm in the shower. A note written by the defendant, informing staff of a euthanasia and suicide pact between the couple, was found beside Mrs Hollinrake. His wife was revived by medical staff and his own suicide attempt was foiled when a visitor unexpectedly arrived at his home. The defendant pleaded guilty in the Victorian Supreme Court to the charge of attempted murder. He was placed on a three-year good behaviour bond. In sentencing the defendant, Coldrey J said that the circumstances of the case were truly tragic. His Honour accepted that the defendant's motivation in attempting to kill his wife stemmed from his love and compassion for her. There was also evidence before the court that the couple had previously discussed the issue of mercy killing. Both had considered the prospect of being dependent in a nursing home totally unacceptable and each had pledged to act to end the life of the other in such circumstances. The judge said that mercy killing could not be accepted or condoned by the court and that it was the court's duty to uphold the sanctity of life. However, he did not believe that the community would want retribution against the defendant in this exceptional case. Nor did he think that special deterrence needed to be given weight in the circumstances of this case. Although acknowledging the court's duty in sentencing offenders in an attempt to deter others from embarking on similar behaviour, his Honour was of the view that, given the rarity of this type of offence, the principal of general deterrence did not need to be accorded prominence. Coldrey J said that the courts must dispense justice, but in the circumstances of the case, that justice may be tempered with mercy. The defendant had no prior convictions in an otherwise unblemished life. The judge also said that the defendant's plea of guilty to the charge had been taken in account in his favour. In all the circumstances, his Honour came to the conclusion that a sentence of imprisonment was not warranted.

The case of *Thiel*, in which the 74 year old defendant pleaded guilty to the manslaughter of his ailing wife (discussed above), further illustrates the significance of judicial leniency in sentencing mercy killers. Finlay J of the New South Wales Supreme Court described this as a case of infinite sadness. After reviewing the evidence, he said that in the very exceptional circumstances of the case a custodial sentence was not called for.

His Honour deferred passing sentence and ordered the defendant's release upon his entering into a recognisance.

There have also been a number of cases of assisted suicide before the courts in which the defendant was dealt with rather leniently. For example, in the Victorian case of *Larkin* discussed above, following a plea of guilty to a charge of aiding and abetting suicide under the Crimes Act 1958 (Vic) (carrying a maximum penalty of 14 years), the defendant was placed on a three-year good behaviour bond with the condition that she attend psychiatric counselling. Nicholson J of the Victorian Supreme Court (as he then was) observed that in the circumstances of the case, there was no requirement that the sentence be retributive, nor were considerations of general or special deterrence of relevance, the offence being so unusual and the defendant having acted with the highest of motives, 'if misguided'. His Honour found that the community interest would best be served by not imposing a custodial sentence upon the defendant.

The New South Wales case of *Den Heyer* (unreported, Parramatta District Court (NSW), 28 September 1990) also serves to illustrate the leniency shown by the courts in cases of this kind. There was evidence before the court that the deceased was suffering from terminal cancer and was experiencing severe pain. He had on a number of previous occasions attempted to commit suicide. The defendant, 28 years of age, was charged with aiding and abetting the suicide of his father by supplying the gun with which the father had shot himself. The defendant pleaded guilty to the charge. Judge Court was firmly of the view that none of the principal objectives of sentencing, namely individual deterrence, general deterrence, retribution and rehabilitation, in any way called for the imposition of a custodial sentence in this case. A conviction was recorded and the defendant was sentenced to the rising of the court.

Judicial leniency in sentencing was also evident in the case of *Savage* (unreported, Newcastle District Court (NSW), 27 March 1992). The defendant in this case, a well-known Australian artist 62 years of age was charged with aiding his wife's suicide. The defendant had been diagnosed some years earlier as having chronic lymphatic leukaemia and his wife had advanced bowel cancer. The couple had decided to die together in a suicide pact rather than be institutionalised because of their illnesses. They drank a lethal cocktail of drugs and alcohol with fatal consequences for Mrs Savage. The defendant, however, survived the suicide attempt. He pleaded guilty to the charge of aiding his wife's suicide and delivered an hour-long statement from the witness stand, describing his love for his wife and their decision to die together. Judge Freeman, sitting in the Newcastle District Court, acknowledged that in some people's eyes, the defendant's intentions were understandable, honourable, even laudable. In sentencing the defendant, his Honour said it would be easy in the emotion-charged atmosphere of the court to say that the defendant had been punished already by his survival of the suicide pact. He went on to say that the court must be careful to avoid that sort of reaction because the decision of the court must not be taken to be a warrant or support for any like action. Judge Freeman noted that s 31(c) of the Crimes Act 1900 (NSW) provides for a maximum penalty of 10 years' imprisonment for the offence of aiding suicide, indicating that the legislature clearly regards this as a crime of some significance. Whilst accepting that the case before him did not have a sinister nature, he noted that the role played by the defendant had been long and thought out and was no mere fleeting assistance. His Honour was, however, of the view that in all the circumstances, a custodial sentence was not appropriate and he ordered that the defendant perform 200 hours of community service.

The foregoing cases usefully illustrate judicial leniency in sentencing in genuine cases of mercy killing. In reviewing the special characteristics of these cases, it is readily apparent that they involve quite exceptional circumstances. Certain observations can be made about these cases which also apply more generally to the cases under review in this study. In all of these cases, the defendants had apparently acted out of compassionate motives. This was usually evident from the circumstances; the victim's condition, the victim's requests to be helped to die in most of these cases, and the close and loving relationship between the defendant and the victim. In all of these cases, the defendants had no relevant prior record and, in fact, in many of these cases, there was character evidence before the court testifying to the defendant's unblemished background and the high esteem in which the defendant was held in the community. In all cases, the defendants had been exceptionally co-operative with police, even to the extent of confessing their crime and in all of the cases reviewed here, defendants had pleaded guilty to the offence charged. In quite a number of these cases the defendants were elderly, including two cases where the defendants were in their eighties. Another significant feature in a number of these cases was the depressed or imbalanced state of mind of the offender, although not of such magnitude as to have affected the legal liability for the crime.

In sentencing these offenders, the courts have been responsive to special circumstances of mercy killing. In many of these cases, sentencing remarks of the judges reflect the careful consideration which has been given to sentencing principles and contain justification why a more severe sentence (usually in the nature of a custodial sentence) was not appropriate in the circumstances. In view of the special circumstances of mercy killing cases, the courts have been able to say with some confidence that the defendant is most unlikely to reoffend and therefore does not present a threat to the community. As a result, individual deterrence and rehabilitation of the offender has not been an issue in these cases. Furthermore, courts presented with the tragic circumstances of a mercy killing case have on occasion expressed the view that there is no need to include a retributive element in the sentence, partly in the light of the suffering that the defendant has clearly already undergone. The most troublesome aspect for the courts in sentencing mercy killers has been the issue of general deterrence, that is, the need to deter others who are minded to commit similar crimes. Although this is often said to be one of the paramount considerations in sentencing, in these mercy killing cases, the courts have frequently held that this factor is outweighed by other considerations. In a number of the cases, judges have, in justifying their decision to give less than usual attention to the issue of general deterrence in sentencing, referred to the rarity of mercy killing cases and the exceptional circumstances that they involve. It has also been pointed out that the issue of general deterrence may have less relevance in circumstances where the criminal act is prompted by strong emotion such as compassion, as is the case in a mercy killing.

Whilst leniency in sentencing is clearly a significant factor in the treatment of mercy killing cases in the Australian criminal justice system, it should be noted that in some Australian jurisdictions, a mandatory sentence of life imprisonment still applies in respect of the crime of murder. Consequently, if a defendant is convicted of murder, the court has no discretion with regard to the sentence it imposes.

Necessity as a defence to criminal conduct

In the case of *Dudley and Stephens* (1884) 14 QBD 273, it had been clearly established that necessity was not a defence to causing the death of another. That case concerned a group of people, survivors of a ship disaster who, convinced they would not otherwise survive, drew lots to see who would be eaten. The cabin boy drew the short straw and was consumed by the others.

Given this principle, the separation of conjoined twins (so called 'Siamese twins') in circumstances where separating the twins was likely to cause the death of one of the twins, was always going to be fraught with legal difficulty.

The resolution of this problem is found in an English case, *Re A*, and a Queensland case *Re Nolan*.

Re A [2001] 2 WLR 480

Lord Justice Ward:

I Introduction to the case of the Siamese twins

In the past decade an increasing number of cases have come before the courts where the decision whether or not to permit or to refuse medical treatment can be a matter of life and death for the patient. I have been involved in a number of them. They are always anxious decisions to make but they are invariably eventually made with the conviction that there is only one right answer and that the court has given it.

In this case the right answer is not at all as easy to find. I freely confess to having found it exceptionally difficult to decide – difficult because of the scale of the tragedy for the parents and the twins, difficult for the seemingly irreconcilable conflicts of moral and ethical values and difficult because the search for settled legal principle has been especially arduous and conducted under real pressure of time.

The problems we have faced have gripped the public interest and the case has received intense coverage in the media. Everyone seems to have a view of the proper outcome. I am very well aware of the inevitability that our answer will be applauded by some but that as many will be offended by it. Many will vociferously assert their own moral, ethical or religious values. Some will agree with Justice Scalia who said in the Supreme Court of the United States of America in *Cruzan v Director, Missouri Department of Health* (1990) 110 S. Ct. 2841, 2859:

> The point at which life becomes 'worthless', and the point at which the means necessary to preserve it become 'extraordinary' or 'inappropriate', are neither set forth in the constitution nor known to the nine Justices of this Court any better than they are known to nine people picked at random from the Kansas City telephone directory.

It is, however, important to stress the obvious. This court is a court of law, not of morals, and our task has been to find, and our duty is then to apply the relevant principles of law to the situation before us – a situation which is quite unique.

It truly is a unique case. In a nutshell the problem is this. Jodie and Mary are conjoined twins. They each have their own brain, heart and lungs and other vital organs and they each have arms and legs. They are joined at the lower abdomen. Whilst not underplaying the surgical complexities, they can be successfully separated. But the operation will kill the weaker twin, Mary. That is because her lungs and heart are too deficient to oxygenate and pump blood through her body. Had she been born a singleton, she would not have been viable and resuscitation would have been abandoned. She would have died shortly after her birth. She is alive only because a common artery enables her sister, who is stronger, to circulate life sustaining oxygenated blood for both of them. Separation would require the clamping and then the severing of that common artery. Within minutes of doing so Mary will die. Yet if the operation does not take place, both will die within three to six months, or perhaps a little longer, because Jodie's heart will eventually fail. The parents cannot bring themselves to consent to the operation. The twins are equal in their eyes and they cannot agree to kill one even to save the other. As devout Roman Catholics they sincerely believe that it is God's will that their children are afflicted as they are and they must be left in God's hands. The doctors are convinced they can carry out the operation so as to give Jodie a life which will be worthwhile. So the hospital sought a declaration that the operation may be lawfully carried out. Johnson J. granted it on 25th August 2000. The parents applied to us for permission to appeal against his order. We have given that permission and this is my judgment on their appeal.

Exceptionally we allowed the Archbishop of Westminster and the Pro-Life Alliance to make written submissions to us. We are grateful for them. We are also very grateful for the very considerable research undertaken by the Bar and by the solicitors and for the powerful submissions counsel have advanced which have swayed me one way and another and left me at the conclusion of the argument in need of time, unfortunately not enough time, to read, to reflect, to decide and then to write.

II The facts in more detail

A cautionary word – the injunction

Enough is known about this case for everyone to understand what a hideous nightmare it must be for these parents. If anyone is entitled to peace and privacy it is this mother and father and their babies. To protect them, Johnson J made an order preventing the publication of anything calculated to lead to the identification of the parties or even their addresses – and that includes for the avoidance of doubt the country in which they live. The identities of the medical witnesses are likewise protected to keep them free from intrusion as they go about their private and professional lives. In order, however, to put into the legitimate public domain all that the public needs to know, I shall set out the facts as fully as possible (indeed more fully than I would ordinarily do for law-reporting purposes).

The parents

The father is forty-four years old; his wife is ten years younger. They have been married for two years and have no other children. Life is hard for them. There is simply no work for the husband. He has been unwillingly unemployed for eight years. The mother was more fortunate but her work terminated during her pregnancy. They have, somehow, managed to accumulate very modest savings and were in the process of building a home for their expected family.

When about four months pregnant, an ultrasound scan revealed that the mother was carrying twins and that they were conjoined. A doctor at the hospital had trained at St. Mary's Hospital, Manchester, and knew of its expertise and excellence. He advised that they should seek treatment there.

Through long established links between their government and ours their country is allowed to send a number of patients to be treated here on our National Health Service. We explain this because we read of what may be a concern to some that the parents are Kosovan refugees unjustifiably draining our resources. They are not, nor anything of the kind. That said, we remind the curious that the injunction covers any publication of any matter 'calculated to lead to the identification' of the parents' address.

The assessment panel in their homeland not surprisingly judged that theirs was a case which local resources could not manage and in that way their government paid for the mother to travel to Manchester in mid-May for treatment during her pregnancy. The father has managed somehow to join her there.

Further scans were taken and an MR scan was undertaken at Sheffield. To quote from the parents' statement:

> As a result of these scans it became clearer during the latter stages of the pregnancy that the difficulties with the twins were more than had originally been suspected and for a number of weeks towards the latter end of the pregnancy the clear indication was given to us by the treating doctors that sadly the smaller of the two twins would probably not survive. Indeed it was not thought that the smaller of the twins would survive birth. This was something we had to consider carefully and for a long time during the pregnancy we have always been aware that both of our babies were in great danger. In (our homeland), the termination of any pregnancy is illegal. When we came to England . . . there was talk . . . of (the mother) being able to undergo a termination because of the difficulties with the unborn children. This was not something (we) could give any serious consideration to because we are Roman Catholics and our beliefs are very important to us and we believe very strongly that everyone has a right to life. It was God's will for (the mother) to carry twins and it is God's will that those twins have been born alive and are continuing to make progress and indeed have made progress in the first seven days of their lives.

The consultant obstetrician said this:

> I have had many discussions with them (the parents) about their wishes with regard to their children. I have at all times tried to accommodate their wishes within what I believe to be ethically and acceptable guidelines. As a result of their desire for non-intervention I took the unusual step of allowing the twin pregnancy to continue until she went into spontaneous labour at 42 weeks. Normally one considers delivery before that time because of a concern as to whether the placenta can adequately nourish both fetuses. Also, as agreed with them, I delivered them by Caesarean section at the last possible moment in labour. This was to meet their desire that the pregnancy was as non-interventionist as possible.

The birth

The twins were born on 8th August 2000. Their combined birth weight was 6 kg. They were immediately taken to a resuscitation venue. The notes on Jodie record:

> Baby crying and active ... making respiratory effort ... Easily intubated ... Baby making spontaneous breathing effort ... Kept intubated in view of condition of other twin.

As expected it was very different for Mary. Her notes read:

> Making spontaneous respiratory effort on arrival from theatre. Face mask oxygen given ... Intubated ... Very stiff to ventilate. No audible air entry. Position rechecked and tube replaced to confirm tracheal placement. Still unable to ventilate. No chest movement or breath sounds.

An hour later it was noted that:

> No assistance to breathing being given. No active intervention at the moment. Outlook for Twin 2 still bleak despite surprisingly stable condition at the moment.

In his evidence the consultant neonatologist said:

> The fetal scans – in other words, those done before the delivery took place – suggested that there was a large quantity of fluid within the chest where the lungs should be, and that there was a large heart, and probably lung tissue. The real test came when the baby was born and we expected her – she had sufficient lung tissue to support herself breathing – that she would with our initial help be able to do so. My consultant anaesthetist colleague, who was intubating and resuscitating Mary, found that although he could pass the end of the clear tube into her main airway he was not able to make her chest move and he was not able to detect any gasway at all, nor when he put a monitor into the ventilator to track for excretion of carbon dioxide did he detect that any carbon dioxide, which should be being exhaled, was coming out. So we never had any evidence that she has breathed for herself at all.

The conjoined twins

They are ischiopagus (ie joined at the ischium) tetrapus (ie having four lower limbs) conjoined twins. The ischium is the lower bone which forms the lower and hinder part of the pelvis – the part which bears the weight of the body in sitting. The lower ends of the spines are fused and the spinal cords joined. There is a continuation of the coverings of the spinal cord between one twin and another. The bodies are fused from the umbilicus to the sacrum. Each perineum is rotated through ninety degrees and points laterally.

The reports and medical literature did not prepare me fully for the almost numbing surprise at first seeing the twins in the photographs which were produced to us, though not to Johnson J. After the initial shock one is filled with desperate sadness and sympathy for these helpless babies and their devastated parents. These photographs are taken from the side and show the twins lying end to end on their backs. Jodie's head seems normal but Mary's is obviously enlarged, for she has a swelling at the back of the head and neck, she is facially dysmorphic and blue because she is centrally cyanosed. Between these two heads is a single torso about forty centimetres long with a shared umbilicus in the middle. Two legs, Mary's right and Jodie's left, protrude at an acute angle to the spine at the centre of the torso, lying flat on the cot but bending to form a diamond shape. The external genitalia appear on the side of the body. The consultant's report reads:

> The nature of the conjoin produces a grossly abnormal laterally placed vulval configuration on each side and a markedly splayed perineum. The vulva for each twin is composed of two halves, each coming from the other twin. There is a single orifice in each vulva, which drains urine and meconium, and each twin has an imperforate anus. Each twin has two hemi-vaginae and two hemi-uteri. Such ano-urogenital disposition is consistent with a cloacal abnormality. The gonads and fallopian tubes could not be assessed.

Internally each twin has her own brain, heart, lungs, liver and kidneys and the only shared organ is a large bladder which lies predominately in Jodie's abdomen but which empties spontaneously and freely through two separate urethras.

For our purposes the absolutely crucial anatomical fact is that:

> Jodie's aorta feeds into Mary's aorta and the arterial circulation runs from Jodie to Mary. The venous return passes from Mary to Jodie through a united inferior vena cava and other venous channels in the united soft tissues.

The twins' present condition

The information concerning the twins' condition was originally given in a number of statements by the treating doctors, and by the evidence they gave Johnson J. It is worthy of noting, and we commend Johnson J for his typically sensible approach, that the evidence of the doctors was taken by a video link facility outside the confines of the Royal Courts of Justice. Sooner, rather than later, fully efficient facilities ought to be established here. Since there was a degree of urgency about the hearing, no second opinion was available. This left us with a slight sense of unease that there may have been a rush to judgment and so we encouraged, and all parties agreed to, the Great Ormond Street Hospital for Children reporting to us and we are grateful for the speed with which they did so. During the course of the hearing, we have had up-dating reports on the twins' progress.

Jodie's present condition

The consultant gave this description of Jodie nine days into her life:

> She has an anatomically normal brain, heart, lungs and liver. Her

> bowel is also normal and appears to be totally separate from that of twin Mary. There is an abnormal vertebra in the lower thoracic area of the spine. She has two kidneys and a full spinal cord. She has two normal lower limbs, which move normally but are widely spaced because of the pelvic diastasis. The hip joints are both normal but the sacroiliac joints are dislocated and externally rotated causing the lower limbs to lie at right angles to the spine.

Neurologically the position is this:

> She has various neonatal responses which appear to be normal including a Moro response, plantar grasp and palmar grasp responses, a withdrawal response and an asymmetrical tonic neck response. There is normal routing response and a glabellar tap. In the cranial nerves, the optic fundi are normal and she has normal external ocular movement. Facial movements are normal and she is capable of sucking and swallowing. In the limbs, appearance, tone, movements and muscle development seem satisfactory. The tendon reflexes are present and equal and the plantar responses are equivocal. Touch, pain and temperature are well perceived. In the trunk there appears to be normal development of the chest wall and the diaphragmatic movements are satisfactory. No obvious abnormality was seen in the cervical, dorsal and lumbar spine. The bladder is shared with her co-twin Mary. The pictures of the ultrasound brain scan showed no obvious abnormality. My finding suggests that Jodie may have normal brain development.

So far as her intelligence is concerned:

> The feeling from the team is that Jodie's behaviour and anatomical studies, ultrasound scans and such like suggest that she has a normal brain, which is expected to function normally and of normal intelligence insofar as one can tell that at this point in time.

We are told that at three weeks of age she showed: 'normal reactions and normal development as expected for a child of her age and gestation'.

Of particular concern is the capacity of her heart to sustain life for herself and her sister. At three weeks:

> Jodie's heart remains stable and appears to be coping well with the circumstances. . . . these results (of blood gas analysis) are below normal indicating a degree of oxygen deprivation for both twins. Despite this presently Jodie does not show any clinical signs of concern.

There are some complications in that there is only one external opening which communicates with the urinary bladder and vagina and there is no opening of the anus.

The neonatologist who gave evidence to Johnson J on 22nd August 2000 said:

> I last saw her yesterday evening and she was, as I described just now, very sparkling really, wriggling, very alert, sucking on a dummy and using her upper limbs in an appropriate manner, very much a with it sort of baby.

After that hearing Jodie suffered a severe blood infection with Staphylococcus aureus and needed urgent intravenous resuscitation with plasma and antibiotics for which treatment the parents gave consent. It was effective and she soon returned to normal. The antibiotics have been discontinued and she is not receiving and indeed she does not require any medical support, though she has retained the intravenous catheter which was surgically placed at the time of her collapse.

A report from the hospital dated 31st August states that:

> Her heart remains stable and shows no signs of strain from supporting, virtually completely, her sister Mary as well as herself. She feeds normally by mouth and appears to be a bright little girl achieving the expected developmental milestones. Her blood gas analysis has been consistently below normal for blood oxygen, probably as a result of admixture with the severely de-oxygenated blood of her sister Mary. This has not as yet presented any detectable clinical problem.

The Great Ormond Street paediatric surgeon told us that:

> Jodie appeared alert, responsive and was seen to feed well. She is quite thin but is undistressed. Cardiac and pulmonary function appeared normal. There was nothing abnormal to feel in her abdomen either.
>
> During the time I observed them, the twins appeared entirely contented. There was nothing to suggest pain or distress in either twin.

Their cardiologist reported:

> Jodie was comfortable breathing air, alert and hungry. She was observed to feed from a bottle without distress. She is on demand oral feeds . . . Oxygen saturation was 100% . . . Arterial pulses were palpable in all limbs. There was good peripheral perfusion. Leg blood pressure was recorded as 80/50 mmHg. The precordial impulse was not overactive. Heart sounds were normal. I could not hear a heart murmur.

It is interesting that Great Ormond Street made the following comment:

> At the present time, the twins' calorie intake is insufficient to allow growth. It is a feature of Siamese twins, even when both are neurologically normal, that one is more active and feeds less than the other. Conversely, the active, feeding, twin is thinner than the fatter one. A similar situation is developing here where Mary does very little and her twin does all the work. Although Jodie is feeding on demand, she is not at present receiving enough calories to grow

> normally and this is not a favourable situation for her in the long term. Presumably her feeding can be supplemented when this is deemed necessary.

On 13th September Mr Adrian Whitfield QC, counsel for St. Mary's Hospital, reported that:

> The cardiac assessment this morning shows that Jodie's heart remains steady and there is no sign of failure. The surgeons are therefore not in any great hurry, as from the cardiac point of view things remain steady. However, the surgeon, from his usual observations, has noticed that Jodie is not growing as he would expect, and he has noticed this since last week, as has the nurse. Mary is growing normally. From the physical point of view, Jodie is not growing – although she is eating well – and the surgeon thinks that it may be that Mary is drawing nutrition from Jodie, and growing at her expense. This could have implications for the timing of the operation but there is no immediate rush. The surgeon is thinking of monitoring over the next week or so, and unless he continues to observe failure to grow in Jodie, he would still put the point of separation at three plus months. If, however, there was a continued failure to thrive, the operation would be advanced by about four weeks.

Mary's present position

Mary is severely abnormal in three key respects.

Firstly she has a very poorly developed 'primitive' brain. The brain scan showed various abnormalities including reduced cortical development, ventricular enlargement, partial agenesis of the corpus callosum and a Dandy Walker type malfunction of the hindbrain. A neuronal migration defect may have occurred. These are the result of a major malformation which was probably present early in fetal life. Similar brain malformations are not compatible with normal development in post-natal life. The neurologist gave evidence and these passages are pertinent:

> Q: How would you describe the degree of abnormality of Mary's brain?
>
> A: Very severe indeed . . . It is possible that this child is progressively developing hydrocephalus which might be to its detriment. Corpus callosum in later childhood is associated with seizure disorders/epileptic fits. It is also associated with developmental delay and learning difficulties.

The second problem is with her heart. Hers is very enlarged, almost filling the chest with a complex cardiac abnormality and abnormalities of the great vessels. In his evidence the cardiologist said:

> It (her heart) is very dilated and very poorly functioning. In terms of actually pumping blood out round the body it is doing very little

> work of its own accord. In terms of structure, the actual way the heart is formed is probably normal and, as I say, the problem is much more the functioning aspects, it is just not squeezing well at all . . .
>
> Q: So far as Mary's heart is concerned, is there any further deterioration that can occur in her heart that will cause any problems?
>
> A: I think, as has already been said, if Jodie wasn't covering Mary's circulation she wouldn't be alive now if they were separate twins. There is no flow at all into her heart. I don't think things could get any worse than they are at present.

Thirdly there is a virtual absence of functional lung tissue (severe pulmonary hypoplasia).

The neonatologist said of her:

> It has become apparent that she has no functioning lung tissue and does not shift air at all in and out of the chest, and has very poor heart function . . . together with the fact that she has several very significant brain spectral problems . . .
>
> . . . the combination of the abnormal lung tissue development, which is virtually non-existent, and the very abnormal cardiac function which, for a single twin, would have meant that we would not have been able to resuscitate her from the word go, had she been just a single baby, plus a combination of the inter-cranial abnormalities makes me feel that her outlook is really extremely poor.

Great Ormond Street confirmed that Mary:

> . . . is not capable of separate survival because of grossly impaired cardiac performance and no useful lung function, with no prospect of recovery.

That is the sad fact for Mary. She would not have lived but for her connection to Jodie. She lives on borrowed time, all of which is borrowed from Jodie. It is a debt she can never repay.

The available options and the doctors' views

There are three ways of treating this appalling situation.

(a) Permanent union: at the moment the twins survive virtually unaided, though Mary has to be fed by tube. The summary of the hospital view is that:

> This (permanent union) condemns a potentially normal Jodie to carry her very abnormal sister, Mary, throughout the life of both. In view of the anatomical disposition Jodie will be unable to walk or even sit up appropriately. She is liable to progressive high output heart failure, which may lead to her earlier death within weeks or months.

This was examined in the evidence led before the judge. The cardiologist said:

> At the moment the function of Jodie's heart is very good. We are happy with its functioning now. The difficulty we envisage for her is that at the moment she is pumping blood round both babies' circulations, and the analogy I give staff in the unit, so that it is easy to understand, is that it is like asking anybody's heart to pump up to a ten foot person. So if we suddenly grew about four feet overnight we are asking our heart to suddenly adapt and manage to deal with that for the foreseeable future. So the difficulty these hearts get into is that in time it places such an extra strain on the heart that they begin to show signs of failure.
>
> Q: And what would the effect of that failure be?
> A: At the time the heart failed to pump blood round both babies both Jodie and Mary would have less blood going to the vital organs and the kidneys would potentially fail . . . the brain would be again further starved of blood and oxygen and that would lead to the death of both infants.
> Q: Are you able to express an opinion upon when, if at all, it is likely that Jodie will suffer this condition of high cardiac output failure?
> A: In terms of conjoined twins it is very difficult to be precise . . . but I think three to six months is a reasonable guide of the kind of time we could be looking at.

In cross examination he was asked:

> Are there circumstances in which Mary could die but Jodie's heart continues to function?
>
> A: I think at the moment . . . because Jodie is essentially pumping for the vital organs of both twins as they breathe, I think that is unlikely . . . I think that while Jodie is performing o.k., Mary will survive. I think if she was to deteriorate to the point where Mary was to die because of Jodie's heart being compromised I think probably both twins would die simultaneously.

Great Ormond Street were not quite as pessimistic. The paediatric surgeon says:

> Although my impression is they can live together for many months, or perhaps even a few years, it does not seem likely that they can survive in this fashion long term.

The cardiologist said:

> Jodie's heart provides sub-total perfusion of Mary's tissues. Cardiac work in Jodie will be substantially increased as a result, and consequently she is at risk of heart failure. This can be defined as the inability of her heart to pump sufficient blood for the needs of the body, which in this case, also includes Mary's body.

> The estimated life expectancy of three to six months . . . was reasonable, in my opinion. Any estimate of anticipated survival in this case will have wide confidence limits, and may need revision according to observed progress. Since the suggested 80–90% chance of death by age six months was made, more than two weeks has elapsed without evidence of haemodynamic deterioration. Jodie's heart continues to provide adequate tissue perfusion to both her own body and that of Mary without the need for pharmacological support. I do not know how long the twins will survive without surgical intervention. However, with the benefit of the longer follow up to date, I would estimate the chance of survival to beyond six months to be greater than the 10–20% likelihood previously suggested . . .
>
> Life expectancy with non-surgical supportive care is difficult to estimate. However progress to date suggests that the chance of survival of both twins to beyond the age of six months is probably greater than the previously suggested 10–20%.
>
> I cannot provide an accurate estimate for an 'upper limit' for life expectancy but this estimate would gradually increase with time if the present satisfactory progress from the point of view of Jodie's cardiac performance is maintained.

Elective separation: the summary of the hospital's view on this is that:

> (It) will lead to Mary's death, but will give Jodie the opportunity of a separate good quality life. There are concerns regarding the possibility of acute heart failure for Jodie at the time of separation. Jodie may have bladder and anorectal control problems and is likely to require additional operative intervention over time. She may have musculoskeletal anomalies, which may also require surgical correction. It is expected, however, that separation will give Jodie the option of a long-term good quality life. She should be able to walk unaided and relatively normally. Separation should allow Jodie to participate in normal life activities as appropriate to her age and development.

I will need to explore the prognosis for Jodie in more detail.

Semi-urgent/urgent separation

> [This] may need to be considered in the event of an acute catastrophe such as Mary's death, the development of progressive heart failure for Jodie, or the development of a life threatening condition . . . The prognosis for Jodie would be markedly reduced and mortality highly likely, particularly following the death of Mary. For Jodie the prospects of urgent separation are less good (60% mortality) when compared with those of a planned elective separation (6% mortality). Clearly, for Mary, separation will always mean death. If it is possible it would be preferable to plan for an elective separation than to avoid 'urgent' procedures.

No-one in the case advances this option. The probability seems to be that Jodie would die first and Mary's death would follow immediately. So long as Mary is alive the real problems in the case remain whether it is elective surgery or surgery undertaken in response to the intervening event.

The hospital and all concerned with the treatment and care of the twins are in favour of elective separation. The leader of the team gave this evidence:

> I think every one of us involved in the team considering these issues, as indeed with many other issues we face in daily life, has to form their own judgment and form their own approach as to what in conscience, for instance, they are able to accept. We have taken the attitude that we would consult very widely with all members of the team giving opportunity to everyone to discuss and to bring up points for discussion. No-one has been forced into anything. I took the occasion after your comments yesterday to ask the members of the nursing staff on the neonatal unit, where the twins are presently being looked after, whether they or anyone they knew had any feelings or views which precluded them from being part of the team, or whether they had any conscientious objections and I was told that no-one could think of any individual who wished to opt out on a conscience basis knowing the full implications of what was proposed. So it has been discussed. People have had their views very definitely, but the feeling from everyone is that everyone is on board.

The nature of the proposed operation to separate the twins

The surgeon gave the judge this explanation of the operation:

> The operation will be in separate parts. The first bit will be to explore the anatomy to confirm that which we have been seeing on various investigations, so in other words can we confirm which bits are definitely whose and such like. We need also to determine – much of this can only be done at the time of surgery – from which parts each bit of each organ is being supplied so that we know which bit to give to whom. So that will be the first part of the operation. We would then be looking to proceeding with the separation of the bladders, giving whichever bit to each patient and also looking at the anatomy of the anal rectum. Once it is established which bits are going to whom, the actual separation then starts by separating the bones, the pelvic bones, one from another anteriorly and then proceeding fashioning skin and such like as you go along towards the spine, where the two spinal bones are joined together at their tip. That will need to be separated, the bones would need to be separated, within that we expect to find the common channel between the linings of the spinal cord which will need to be separated and similarly the terminal ends of the spinal cord.

> Once we reach that stage, we should be left with possibly some muscle union at the pelvic floors, that will need to be divided so that each has its own two halves. Finally and eventually we have a major blood vessel, which is the continuation of Jodie's aorta, which is bringing blood across to Mary, and similarly the vena cava, which is returning blood from Mary to Jodie. Those would need separating, dividing. It is at that point that we would expect that Mary would then die.
>
> The rest of the operation for Jodie would then be essentially a reconstructive operation, attempting to bring the pelvic bones together. One needs to break them and divide them at the back in order to allow rotation and apposition in front and then forming the buttocks and forming the anus and the vagina and urethra and essentially closing the abdominal wall anteriorly.
>
> It is a major procedure and it will take many hours and it will involve various teams of surgeons: ourselves, the orthopaedic surgeons and one of the neurosurgeons in particular, as well as an anaesthetist for each baby and his team.

Further important points about the operation need to be noted.

Firstly, as the surgeon reported to us in answer to a question, 'Would the separation operation impinge on the bodily integrity of Mary?', the response was:

> Separation of the twins would necessarily involve exploration of the internal abdominal and pelvic organs of both twins and particularly the united bladder. It is expected however that each twin would have all its own body structures and organs. It is not anticipated or expected to take any structure or organ from either twin to donate to the other.

Secondly, there was a suggestion in the oral evidence to the judge that as a matter of prudence, given the utterly hopeless outcome for Mary, it would be better to favour Jodie 'in relation to the skin element to ensure that we could close the surgical wound with Jodie'. In evidence to us the surgeon explained that although that was the prudent course, it was not a necessary course and, if required not to do so, that precaution would not be taken, so that, putting it crudely, no part of Mary would be given to Jodie. It is important to recognise that this is not a case involving any organ transplant nor indeed the donation of any bodily parts from one child to the other.

Thirdly as to where the clamping of the aorta would occur, he explained in a report to us that:

> Interruption of the blood supply from Jodie supporting Mary would occur at the level of the united sacrococcygeal vertebrae. The site could be biased towards Jodie.

A report from the spinal surgeon was also placed before us and he is of the opinion that:

> As far as one can see her spinal deformity is a single hemi-vertebra at the thoracolumbar level, together with the contiguous sacra. Her hemi-vertebra is unlikely to require treatment, but will require follow-up by a spinal surgeon. It is unlikely to cause anything other than a minor deformity and should not be the source of any functional decifit.
>
> With respect to her contiguous sacra, given that she has normal bladder function it is likely that the nerve supply to the lower limbs will be sufficient to enable her to walk reasonably normally. She will of course require surgery to stabilise her pelvis.
>
> Overall, the outlook from the point of view of her musculoskeletal problems is good.

The prognosis for Jodie

If the twins remain united, then, as already set out, Jodie's heart may fail in three to six months or perhaps a little longer. But it will eventually fail. That is common ground in this case. Her prospect of a happy life is measurably and significantly shortened. As to the manner of her death the surgeon told us that:

> (Jodie) has, so far as we can make out, a perfectly normal brain and therefore we could expect that in the event of heart failure, with increasing breathlessness, increasing difficulty with oxygenation, with swelling of the liver, swelling of the legs, that she would become uncomfortable and would eventually find it an unpleasant experience to say the least.

Those effects could be palliated with drugs and the use of a ventilator. A similar breathlessness would occur if she suffered hypoxia, a drop in the oxygen concentration in the blood, usually as a result of infection. Such an infection might be septicaemia, some forms of which are not always successfully treated by antibiotics. Very young babies often suffer necrotising enterocolitis but the risk is decreasing as time goes by. If they suffered respiratory infection, she may again need to be placed on a ventilator. If she were to survive without the onset of illness, she would, ordinarily, attempt to roll over so that she is lying on her abdomen, ultimately to get into a crawling position. This would happen between five to eight months of age. She would instinctively want to try these movements but it will not be possible due to the attachment of Mary who, by reason of her brain anomalies, would not be developmentally at the stage where she would be wishing to undertake the same manoeuvre. For Jodie there will be the frustration of not being able to move.

> Her attachment to Mary means that she is not going to be able to walk or to stand, she is going to need to lie or to be carried wherever, and that will therefore limit her ability to develop as a normal child whereas if she survives this operation and walks, as she is

> expected to, she can have a relatively normal or as close to normal free existence.

If the operation to separate is carried out, there is a 5–6% chance the children might die. Great Ormond Street were more confident. They reported:

> Surgery would probably be a low risk procedure for Jodie. The operation itself and the possibility of later complications would probably carry an overall risk of death of perhaps 1–2%.

As to her life expectancy St. Mary's surgeon said:

> From what we know at this time of Mary, there is nothing which suggests that the life expectancy should be any shorter than normal . . . Jodie's problems are functional, if you like, rather than life-threatening. Against those risks must be balanced the opinion that there is a 64% chance of death if an emergency operation had to be undertaken and the 80–90% prospect of death within three to six months, or perhaps a little longer, if no surgery is undertaken at all.

Evidence was given that the literature suggested:

> . . . that the separation is usually well accepted without any serious or other psychological effects on the survivor. . . . it is unlikely that she will have any major psychological consequences from that separation.

So far as her mobility is concerned, the surgeon said:

> All the indicators and also the experience from the literature suggest that she should be able to stand and she should be able to walk on her own without support, so, yes, we would expect her to have reasonably normal mobility. I hesitate to say normal because obviously there are serious concerns here. That will be the expectation: that she will be able to get around sensibly, as close to normal as possible on her own and unsupported.

He was asked for the worst possible scenario and said:

> In the worst scenario, yes, it is possible that she will never walk, she may need a wheelchair, she may need an appliance in the form of a crutch or a brace or something like that but it is not what is expected.

He explained:

> In the first instance she is going to need her pelvis sorting out at the time of first operation in order to allow closure and such like. Any further operative procedures will depend on whether the pelvis and the spine were stable, whether there was any progression of any adverse circumstance, so she may need no operations at all. If as she was growing it became obvious that the spine was beginning to bend, for instance, as a scoliosis, then the spinal surgeon may

> consider it relevant to institute therapy for that, be it conservative with plaster and/or surgery. . . . The most common situations which arise when they do arise relate to the pelvis re-spreading so that the limbs go into a lateral position, so we have a sort of wobbling gait, rather than feet facing forwards they face laterally. So a further operation at some stage to re-adjust the configuration of the pelvis and to bring the feet into a more normal alignment for walking would be one area. Another would be the question of a bend in the spine, as I have mentioned, scoliosis, developing and progressing and that would be a scenario where surgery would be relevant to correct the bend and join the bones, tying the bones together such that the bend is stabilised. But it may be that she would never come to any surgery. The literature says that in looking towards the long-term future one should have regard to potential musculoskeletal concerns and we have taken that on board along with every other system.

He was a little more cautious about the anorectal situation saying:

> It is not normally formed, it is an imperforate anus and therefore we are going to have to reconstruct in a manner of an imperforate anus and if you add to that the split of the floor, which is where the muscles are, then it does make it rather more difficult. So there are good points and there are bad points. The nerves going to the muscles seem to be normal but the muscles themselves are split and the whole area is not normally formed. Therefore when you come to reconstruct all that there are very many factors at which one has to look in terms of continence so I am little bit cautious at saying to you that it is going to be all right. I hope it will be.

He explained the difficulty. The prospect is that the anus will learn to open and close normally. If that has not been achieved by about school age, it may need wash-outs and enemas and such like and the possibility of a colostomy. The family would need some form of medical nursing support initially to help them in learning how to care for the attachment of the colostomy bag and there may be practical difficulties in finding a ready availability of those bags in their homeland. As the surgeon observed:

> A colostomy would perhaps be regarded as a much greater handicap than it would be in this country for instance.

The surgeon is hopeful, though he cannot be certain, that they would be able to preserve what seems like a relatively normal bladder function. Again the worst case scenario would be that Jodie would have to have a urinary diversion with a bag. The surgeon commented in evidence:

> Of themselves, they reduce your quality of life but they do not destroy your life. There are several children and people who live with such diversions. It may be it is not an entirely normal life. I think perhaps the most relevant ones would be serious musculo-

> skeletal problems, which would directly interfere with her life and in the longer term she may require further attention to her vagina which may to a certain extent affect how she functions sexually, but it certainly is reconstructable. . . . Jodie at the moment has normal vaginal structures and uterus, they are unfused, they are in two parts instead of one, they are in the form of two tubes as they develop embryologically instead of one tube, so she needs some attention to that vagina in order to make it one channel. . . . (She) has two half uteri and two half wombs both of which normally grow sufficiently to make a full pregnancy without concern, so the uteri do not need surgery. We do not know as yet what is the status with her gonads, with her ovaries. The normal expectation is that she should have two normal ones. . . . So one would expect that as long as she is able to perform normally sexually there is no reason why she should not conceive in the course of time and have her own children.

The long term prognosis following surgery offered by Great Ormond Street is much more optimistic and I bear in mind the greater experience they bring to bear. Their surgeon says: –

> Jodie . . . will require further surgery. It seems likely to me that her large bowel is normal and, therefore, I would expect her to have normal bowel control. However, given that the attachments of the muscle in the pelvis will be absent or at least tenuous on one side, one could not be absolutely certain that bowel control will be normal. I would, however, be hopeful in regard to this aspect.
>
> At present, it seems that the twins void normally. One would hope, therefore, that this would continue after surgery.
>
> Further operations will be required to provide a functioning vagina. This is a procedure which is commonly performed and the results are variable. Nonetheless, the great majority of children achieve a functioning vagina after reconstruction.
>
> From the available literature, it seems that gait is normal, or near normal. Jodie does have a hemi-vertebra at the lower end of her thoracic spine. It is possible that she would need scoliosis surgery should a curvature of the spine develop. At present the need for surgery cannot be predicted and one would need to await further spinal growth.

The consultant surgeon said:

> As far as one can see her spinal deformity is a single hemi-vertebra at the thorocolumbar level, together with the contiguous sacra. Her hemi-vertebra is unlikely to require treatment, but will require follow-up by a spinal surgeon. It is unlikely to cause anything other than a minor deformity and should not be the source of any functional deficit.

The prognosis for Mary

If the operation to separate the twins is carried out, Mary will be anaesthetised against all pain and death will be mercifully quick. The surgeon was frank in acknowledging there was really no benefit for Mary in the operation. This was put to him:

> Q: The phrase you used, which is a harsh one, but the reality nonetheless has to be faced, is that effectively during this operation you would be, to use your own words, killing off Mary.
> A: Yes and that is a very serious worry for all of us involved in such an act and we would only look to taking it on if we felt that there was really and truly in the best interest, taking the whole situation as it is, of Jodie and if Mary's long-term survival was so poor that it was not really a sensible proposition, also leaving them united together detracts markedly and severely from the quality of life for both really.
> Q: Just focusing on Mary for a moment, there cannot really be any doubt, can there, that, as His Lordship said, it is in Mary's best interests to maintain the status quo?
> A: Can I question 'best interests'? It is only in Mary's best interests insofar as it is her only means of survival to continue to use Jodie as her oxygen supply and her circulatory pump . . .
> Q: Is there any therapeutic benefit for Mary in the operation being performed?
> A: If you look at it in terms of Mary dying, no, there is not a therapeutic benefit. If you look at it in terms of what Mary's life would be like attached forever to her sister, then it is not a benefit for her to remain attached to her sister: she will be much happier if she is separate.

The neonatologist expressed himself slightly differently. In his report he said:

> It is sadly therefore in Mary's best interests that the ultimate aim should be planned separation of these twins accepting the fact that this would terminate the life of Mary.

Asked about that he said in evidence: –

> I think my perception of the quality of her life is that it would be so poor that I do not feel that it is a life that she will enjoy. I think her limitations would be so severe that inter-reactions with and development and progress would be so severely interrupted, prevented really, that in my view it is acceptable to acknowledge that Mary should be allowed to die . . .
>
> Q: . . . I do not think you have quite answered my question. Is it really your view that the best option for Mary is to terminate her life?
> A: I think I come back to the fact that the quality of any life that

> she will have will be so poor that, yes, I feel that it is appropriate to terminate her life.

If the twins are to remain fused, the evidence is that Mary will have a 75% or more chance of developing hydrocephalus which would be 'extremely difficult' to treat because usually the end of the shunt system would either go into the abdominal cavity which is abnormal in her case or into the heart which is also not possible in her case. The effect of untreated hydrocephalus will be to increase brain damage. She is at risk of suffering epilepsy. Lack of sufficient oxygen will progressively cause cellular damage and brain damage. In the view of the neonatologist, her condition is not terminal but severe.

There is great uncertainty as to the extent to which she suffers pain. The paediatric surgeon in the evidence he gave us said:

> What we see at present is a child whose responses are extremely primitive. They are more like mass movements to a stimulus, be it what is regarded as a pleasurable stimulus or a painful stimulus. They are withdrawal type and grimacing and such like. So we are not really able to differentiate at this time, and even at four weeks of age now, whether this twin actually appreciates pleasure or pain. Certainly there is a response to stroking and there is a response to pinprick, but they are the same.

The neonatologist explained that:

> . . . she just screws her face up in what appears a painful sort of way, and that is the only facial expression I see her make, and that is not an irritant stimulation, it's really gentle, it's patting her or stroking her head.

Sadly the same reaction is produced to a pinprick. He explained to the judge:

> That might be a reflex response to sensation.

The judge commented:

> But this baby cannot cry because this baby has no lungs. So how would you know, in the situation that I am putting to you, whether Mary is suffering pain or not?
>
> A: It is extremely difficult, sir, I do not have a straightforward answer for you . . . My Lord, the responses that Mary shows are certain stereotype responses that we can observe as doctors, but it is how you interpret those responses which matters. If that response occurs to being tugged or pulled, her being pricked to obtain a blood sample, the interpretation that one might place on that stereotype response is possibly pain. On the other hand, if you get a similar response to gentle stroking it might not imply pain.

The paediatric neurosurgeon, observing that her brain is not functioning normally and that she would not achieve the development one would expect in the next three to six months in a child with a normal brain, then said, in answer to the question whether she had any ability to feel pain or suffering:

> I was impressed by the observation of being dragged around, which was going to be if not painful certainly very uncomfortable, and I would further subscribe to that by saying that having your skin dragged over any sort of surface is likely to be very uncomfortable, if not constantly painful, and I agree – I think that is an horrendous scenario, to think of being dragged round and being able to do nothing about it. I think with the increasing activity of Jodie, Mary's situation becomes worse.

Miss Parker QC on Jodie's behalf asked the surgeon a 'very theoretical question' whether Mary could be kept alive if she were attached to a heart lung machine immediately after the common aorta was severed. He agreed that it was possible but he went on to say:

> It is not something that we would have planned as part of the procedure because this is the sort of situation that one would set up if one was looking towards a survivor. It is a holding situation, pending whatever is your final operation that is going to lead to a separate viable entity. Here for the weaker of the twins, unless there was a heart and lungs available for transplant instantly there would not really be all that much point, and then one has to take into context the rest of the problems which the child has . . . which really do not suggest that there is any point in taking on a heart/lung transplant for this child.

Great Ormond Street agreed. In their opinion:

> This would not be appropriate as the only accepted indication for this very intensive form of treatment is in the context of potentially recoverable abnormality, or possibly as a short term bridge to transplantation. Heart and lung transplantation in Mary is not an option. Heart and lung transplantation has not been performed in early infancy to my knowledge; even if it was considered to be technically feasible, donor organs of appropriate size are not available.

Miss Parker wisely and properly did not pursue this line. It would make a mockery of law and medicine to escape some of the difficulties in this case by hooking this child into a heart/lung support machine and then seeking permission to discontinue that treatment given the futility of prolonging her life. *Bland* has already left the law, as Lord Mustill commented, in a 'morally and intellectually misshapen' state. It would be quite wrong, as the doctors recognise, to contemplate this an acceptable outcome to the case. But it remains a poignant irony in the case. At one end of life, the pregnancy could have been lawfully terminated, Mary would have died but no offence would have been committed because she is not viable. Now at the other end, were it ethically permissible to do so, life could have been preserved artificially and then ended on *Bland* principles.

The medical literature

A considerable body of medical literature has been placed before us, as well as a number of helpful articles referring to the legal and ethical problems in dealing with conjoined twins. It has been fully discussed in the judgment of Brooke LJ, a copy of which I have read in draft, and, rather than repeat any of it in this judgment, I gratefully adopt his exposition.

The parents' views

It is a laudable feature of this case that despite holding such different views about the twins' future, the parents and the hospital have throughout maintained a relationship of mutual respect. The highly commendable attitude of the parents is shown in this passage in their statement:

> We have been spoken to on many occasions by all the treating doctors at St. Mary's Hospital and we were fully aware of the difficulties . . . We have been treated with the utmost care and respect at St. Mary's Hospital and we have no difficulties or problems with any of the medical staff that are treating (us).

As parents of the children, their views are a very important part of this case. It is right, therefore, that I set them out as fully as possible:

> We have of course had to give serious consideration to the various options as given to us by our daughters' treating doctors. We cannot begin to accept or contemplate that one of our children should die to enable the other to survive. That is not God's will. Everyone has the right to life so why should we kill one of our daughters to enable the other to survive. That is not what we want and that is what we have told the doctors treating Jodie and Mary. In addition we are also told that if Jodie survives and that is not known at all, then she is going to be left with a serious disability. The life we have . . . is remote . . . with very few, if any facilities which would make it extremely difficult not only for us to cope with a disabled child but for that disabled child to have any sort of life at all.
>
> . . . there is a small hospital where you can receive emergency treatment but certainly they do not have the staff or facilities to cope with someone with serious ongoing difficulties. Any treatment would have to be undertaken (some distance away) where there is a hospital and a further hospital is being built which should be completed in about three years' time. However if specific treatment is required it may be necessary for us to go further afield and indeed

come back to St. Mary's Hospital in Manchester for further treatment. That is how we came to St. Mary's Hospital in the first place to ensure that our babies had the best possible treatment.

These are things we have to think about all the time. We know our babies are in a very poor condition, we know the hospital doctors are trying to do their very best for each of them. We have very strong feelings that neither of our children should receive any medical treatment. We certainly do not want separation surgery to go ahead as we know and have been told very clearly that it will result in the death of our daughter, Mary. We cannot possibly agree to any surgery being undertaken that will kill one of our daughters. We have faith in God and are quite happy for God's will to decide what happens to our two young daughters.

In addition we cannot see how we can possibly cope either financially or personally with a child where we live, who will have the serious disabilities that Jodie will have if she should survive any operation. We know there is no guarantee of survival but she is the stronger of the two twins and if she should survive any surgery then we have to be realistic and look at what we as parents can offer to our daughter and what care and facilities are available to her in our homeland. They are virtually nil. If Jodie were to survive she would definitely need specialist medical treatment and we know that cannot be provided. Jodie would have to travel, on many occasions, possibly to England to receive treatment. It concerns us that we would not have any money for this treatment and we do not know if this is something (our) government would pay for.

This has meant that we have also had to give very careful consideration to leaving Jodie in England, should she survive, to be looked after by other people. We do not know if other people would be willing to look after such a seriously disabled child, but we do know that this is something that if we had any other choice we would not even give it consideration. It would be an extremely difficult, if not impossible decision for us to reach, but again we have to be strong and realistic about matters and understand that certainly Jodie would receive far better care and importantly the required medical treatment should she continue to reside in England as opposed to her being taken home. We do not know whether it is possible or feasible for Jodie to remain in England. We do not know if it is possible or feasible for her to be fostered by another family so that we can have an involvement in her upkeeping or whether she would have to be adopted and we could have no contact with her at all. That would break our hearts. We do not want to leave our daughters behind, we want to take them home with us but we know in our heart of hearts that if Jodie survives and is seriously disabled she will have very little prospects on our island because of its remoteness and lack of facilities and she will fare better if she remains in this country. . . . So we came to England to give our babies the very

> best chance in life in the very best place and now things have gone badly wrong and we find ourselves in this very difficult situation. We did not want to be in this situation, we did not ask to be in it but it is God's will. We have to deal with it and we have to take into account what is in the very best interests of our two very young daughters.
>
> We do not understand why we as parents are not able to make decisions about our children although we respect what the doctors say to us and *understand that we have to be governed by the law of England.* We do know that everyone has the best interests of our daughters at heart and this is a very difficult situation not only for us as their parents but also for all of the medical and nursing staff involved in Mary's and Jodie's treatment. [I have added the emphasis to make it clear that the parents accept the jurisdiction of the English courts to decide the awesome question laid before us.]

I said when this appeal opened that we wished at the very beginning to emphasise to the parents, strangers in our midst, how we sympathise with their predicament, with the agony of their decision – for now it has become ours – and how we admire the fortitude and dignity they have displayed throughout these difficult days. Whether or not we agree with their view does not diminish the respect in which we hold them.

The nature of these proceedings

I am satisfied there has been the closest consultation between the medical team, the parents, their friends, their priest and their advisers. Just as the parents hold firm views worthy of respect, so every instinct of the medical team has been to save life where it can be saved. Despite such a professional judgment it would, nevertheless, have been a perfectly acceptable response for the hospital to bow to the weight of the parental wish however fundamentally the medical team disagreed with it. Other medical teams may well have accepted the parents' decision. Had St. Mary's done so, there could not have been the slightest criticism of them for letting nature take its course in accordance with the parents' wishes. Nor should there be any criticism of the hospital for not bowing to the parents' choice. The hospital have care of the children and whilst I would not go so far as to endorse a faint suggestion made in the course of the hearing that in fulfilment of that duty of care, the hospital were under a further *duty* to refer this impasse to the court, there can be no doubt whatever that the hospital is entitled in its discretion to seek the court's ruling. In this case I entertain no doubt whatever that they were justified in doing so.

Thus they issued an originating summons on 18th August entitled 'In the exercise of the inherent jurisdiction of the High Court and in the matter of the Children Act 1989'. The relief which was sought was:

> A declaration that in the circumstances where (the children) cannot give valid consent and where (the parents) withhold their consent, it shall be lawful and in (the children's) best interests to

(a) carry out such operative procedures not amounting to separation upon (Jodie and/or Mary);
(b) perform an emergency separation procedure upon (Jodie and/or Mary); and/or
(c) perform an elective separation procedure upon (Jodie and Mary).

There has been some public concern as to why the court is involved at all. We do not ask for work but we have a duty to decide what parties with a proper interest ask us to decide. Here sincere professionals could not allay a collective medical conscience and see children in their care die when they know one was capable of being saved. They could not proceed in the absence of parental consent. The only arbiter of that sincerely held difference of opinion is the court. Deciding disputed matters of life and death is surely and pre-eminently a matter for a court of law to judge. That is what courts are here for.

The judgment of Johnson J

His judgment was given, as so frequently happens in this kind of case, under even greater pressure of time than we have felt. He did not have the benefit of the searching arguments we demanded and received of counsel.

The case as it was presented to him and the case in the shape into which we knocked it are as different as chalk and cheese. I would like to record my sympathy for the judge, sitting alone, having to take such a decision as this in such difficult circumstances. He found that Jodie would be able to lead 'a relatively normal life':

> All in all, the evidence, which has not been, and in my judgment could not be, the subject of serious dispute is that in medical terms Jodie's life would be virtually as long as and would have the quality of that of any ordinary child. . . . For Jodie separation means the expectation of a normal life; for Mary it means death.

He directed himself that the children's welfare was paramount. He attached 'great weight to the wishes of the parents'. He asked:

> If in a situation such as this, parents' rights are to be regarded as anything less than of the most vital importance, then what rights, I ask, are there in a free society?

He said:

> If, which I do not, I were to balance the interests of Jodie against those of Mary, then Jodie's chance of a virtually normal life would be lost in order to prolong the life of Mary for those few months. . . .
>
> Mary's state is pitiable. . . .
>
> However pitiable her state now, it will never improve during the few

> months she would have to live if not separated. During the course of the hearing I raised with counsel and with one of the paediatricians the question of pain. Mary cannot cry. She has not the lungs to cry with. There is no way that can be remotely described as reliable by which those tending Mary can know even now whether she is hurting or in pain. When lightly touched or stroked her face contorts. When pinched there is the same reflex. But she cannot cry. So I ask, what would happen as the weeks went by and Jodie moved, tried to crawl, to turn over in her sleep, to sit up. Would she not, I ask, be pulling Mary with her. Linked together as they are, not simply by bone but by tissue, flesh and muscle, would not Mary hurt and be in pain? In pain but not able to cry. One very experienced doctor said she thought that was an horrendous scenario, as she put it being dragged around and not being able to do anything about it. Accordingly, weighing up those considerations I conclude that the few months of Mary's life if not separated from her twin would not simply be worth nothing to her, they would be hurtful. . . . To prolong Mary's life for these few months would in my judgment be very seriously to her disadvantage.

He dealt with the parents' wishes, quoting at length from their statement:

> . . . as one way of my emphasising to the parents that I have truly taken into account their feelings as loving parents. I recognise, as they do that what is proposed has not only an inevitability for Mary but also creates at best the chance for Jodie of a life that will have social and emotional problems over and above those problems which can be medically cured. But as I have sought to emphasise throughout this judgment my focus has been upon Mary and what is best for her. And about that I am in no doubt.

He dealt with the lawfulness of the proposed act observing that:

> If the operation is properly to be regarded as a positive act then it cannot be lawful and cannot be made lawful. I have found this to be the most difficult element in my decision.

He held:

> I was at first attracted by the thought prompted by one of the doctors, that Jodie was to be regarded as a life support machine and that the operation proposed was equivalent to switching off a mechanical aid. Viewed in that way previous authority would categorise the proposed operation as one of omission rather than as a positive act. However on reflection I am not persuaded that that is a proper view of what is proposed in the circumstances of this particular case. I have preferred to base my decision upon the view that what is proposed and what will cause Mary's death will be the interruption or withdrawal of the supply of blood which she receives from Jodie. Here the analogy is with the situation in which the court

authorises the withholding of food and hydration. That, the case is made clear, is not a positive act and is lawful. Jodie's blood supply circulates from and returns to her own heart by her own circulation system, independent of the supply and return from Mary. So it was suggested that one could theoretically envisage a clamp being placed within Jodie's body to block the circulation to Mary, so that there would be the immediate consequence for Mary without any invasion of her own body. I emphasise that this was simply part of the arguments to see how the operation should be categorised in order to judge its lawfulness. It was simply one of a number of arguments, analogies and illustrations that were canvassed in final submissions which I have not found it possible to record more extensively in what is effectively an *ex tempore* judgment. Nevertheless I have concluded that the operation which is proposed will be lawful because it represents the withdrawal of Mary's blood supply. It is of course plain that the consequence for Mary is one that most certainly does not represent the primary objective of the operation.

So he made the declaration asked.

The grounds of appeal

The parents have appealed on the grounds that the learned judge erred in holding that the operation was (i) in Mary's best interest, (ii) that it was in Jodie's best interest, and (iii) that in any event it would be legal. The appeal has accordingly ranged quite widely over many aspects of the interaction between the relevant principles of medical law, family law, criminal law and fundamental human rights. I propose to address them in that order.

III Medical law

1. The fundamental principle

The fundamental principle, now long established, is that every person's body is inviolate: see Lord Goff of Chieveley in *In Re F (Mental Patient: Sterilisation)* [1990] 2 AC 1, 72 E. The importance of this principle was emphasised by Lord Reid in *S v McC, W v W* [1972] AC 24, 43 where he said:

> There is no doubt that a person of full age and capacity cannot be ordered to undergo a blood test against his will. . . . the real reason is that English law goes to great lengths to protect a person of full age and capacity from interference with his personal liberty. We have too often seen freedom disappear in other countries not only by coups d'etat but by gradual erosion: and often it is the first step that counts. So it would be unwise to make even minor concessions.

It follows that:

> It is well established that, as a general rule, the performance of a medical operation upon a person without his or her consent is unlawful, as constituting both the crime of battery and the tort of trespass to the person . . . per Lord Goff in *Re F* at p. 71 D.

2. The principle of autonomy and the consequence of an adult patient's refusal to consent to treatment

In *Re F* Lord Goff at p. 73C endorsed the libertarian principle of self-determination which, to adopt the words of Cardozo J (in *Schloendorff v Society of New York Hospital* (1914) 105 NE 92, 93) recognised that:

> Every person being of adult years and sound mind has a right to determine what shall be done with his own body . . .

The patient's right of veto is absolute:

'This right of choice is not limited to decisions which others might regard as sensible. It exists notwithstanding that the reasons for making the choice are rational, irrational, unknown or even non-existent . . .' per Lord Donaldson of Lymington MR in *In Re T (Adult: Refusal of Treatment)* [1993] Fam. 95, 102, following *Sidaway v Guardians of Bethlem Royal Hospital and Maudsley Hospital* [1985] AC 871, 904–905.

The principle was also recognised in *Airedale NHS Trust v Bland* [1993] AC 789, and it might be useful to cite two passages:

> It is established that the principle of self-determination requires that respect must be given to the wishes of the patient, so that if an adult patient of sound mind refuses, however unreasonably, to consent to treatment or care by which his life would or might be prolonged, the doctors responsible for his care must give effect to his wishes, even though they do not consider it to be in his best interests to do so . . . To this extent, the principle of the sanctity of human life must yield to the principle of self-determination . . . and for present purposes perhaps more important, the doctor's duty to act in the best interests of his patient must likewise be qualified: per Lord Goff at p. 864C.
>
> Any invasion of the body of one person by another is potentially both a crime and a tort . . . How is it that, consistently with the proposition just stated, a doctor can with immunity perform on a consenting patient an act which would be a very serious crime if done by someone else? The answer must be that bodily invasions in the course of proper medical treatment stand completely outside the criminal law. The reason why the consent of the patient is so important is not that it furnishes a defence in itself, but because it is usually essential to the propriety of medical treatment. *Thus, if the consent is absent, and is not dispensed with in special circumstances by operation of law, the acts of the doctor lose their immunity* . . . If the

> patient is capable of making a decision whether to permit treatment and decides not to permit it his choice must be obeyed, even if on any objective view it is contrary to his best interests. A doctor has no right to proceed in the face of objection, even if it is plain to all, including the patient, that adverse consequences and even death will or may ensue . . .: per Lord Mustill at p. 891F. (I have added the emphasis).

3. *Treatment of the incompetent adult*

Where no one is capable of giving consent for an adult patient who does not have the capacity to give consent himself for whatever reason, Lord Goff in *Re F.* seized upon the fact that:

> There exists in the common law a principle of necessity which may justify action which would otherwise be unlawful . . . p. 74A.

The basic requirements, applicable to such a case of necessity, are that to fall within the principle:

> . . . not only (1) must there be a necessity to act when it is not practicable to communicate with the assisted person, but also (2) the action taken must be such as a reasonable person would in all the circumstances take, acting in the best interests of the assisted person, p. 75H.

4. *The power to give proxy consent for a young child to undergo treatment*

The parents if they are married have this power: if they are not, it is the mother's.

> It is abundantly plain that the law recognises that there is a right *and duty* of parents to determine whether or not to seek medical advice in respect of their child, and, having received advice, to give or withhold consent to medical treatment . . . per Lord Scarman in *Gillick v West Norfolk AHA* [1986] 1 AC 112, 184G.

I have added the emphasis to show the close link between parental right and duty. Failure to perform the duty may be a culpable omission. Lord Scarman went on to note that the parental right derives from parental duty and that is recognised in the common law. He referred at p. 185 A to *Blackstone's Commentaries*, 17th Ed. (1830) Volume 1, Chs. 16 and 17 where Blackstone:

> analyses the duty of parents as the 'maintenance . . . protection, and . . . education' of the child: p. 446. He declares that the power of parents over their children is derived from their duty and exists to enable the parent more effectively to perform his duty, and partly as a recompense for his care and trouble in the faithful discharge of it: op. cit., p. 452.

The current law is contained in the Children Act 1989. Each of the parents, or the mother if she is unmarried, has parental responsibility over the child. That is defined, perhaps rather unsatisfactorily, in Section 3 of the Act in these terms:

> (1) In this Act 'parental responsibility' means all the rights, duties, powers, responsibilities and authority which by law a parent of a child has in relation to the child and his property.

So in the current law the right and the duty to give consent to medical treatment is an incident of parental responsibility vested in the parent.

5. *The effect of the parents' refusal*

Since the parents are empowered at law, it seems to me that their decision must be respected and in my judgment the hospital would be no more entitled to disregard their refusal than they are to disregard an adult patient's refusal. To operate in the teeth of the parents' refusal would, therefore, be an unlawful assault upon the child. I derive this from *In Re R (A Minor) (Wardship: Consent to Treatment)* [1992] Fam. 11 where Lord Donaldson of Lymington MR said at p. 22:

> It is trite that in general a doctor is not entitled to treat a patient without the consent of someone who is authorised to give that consent. If he does so, he will be liable in damages for trespass to the person and may be guilty of a criminal assault.

There is, however, this important safeguard to ensure that a child receives proper treatment. Because the parental rights and powers exist for the performance of their duties and responsibilities to the child and must be exercised in the best interests of the child,

> . . . the common law has never treated such rights as sovereign or beyond review and control, per Lord Scarman in *Gillick* at p. 184A.

Overriding control is vested in the court. This proposition is well established and has not been the subject of any challenge in this appeal. Because of the comment in the media questioning why the court should be involved, I add this short explanation. Long, long ago the sovereign's prerogative to protect infants passed to the Lord Chancellor and through him to the judges and it forms a part of the inherent jurisdiction of the High Court. The Children Act 1989 now contains a statutory scheme for the resolution of disputes affecting the upbringing of children. If a person having a recognisable interest brings such a dispute to the court, the court must decide it.

There are abundant examples of this happening. One such case is *In Re B (A Minor) (Wardship: Medical Treatment)* [1981] 1 WLR 1424. There a child who was born suffering from Down's Syndrome and an intestinal blockage, required an operation to relieve the obstruction if she was to live more than a few days. If the operation were performed, the child might die within a few months but it was probable that her life expectancy would be 20–30 years. Her parents, having decided that it would be kinder to allow her to die rather than live as a physically and mentally disabled person, refused to consent to the operation. The local authority made the child a ward of court and, when a surgeon decided that the wishes of the parents should be respected, they sought an order authorising the operation to be performed by other named surgeons. Templeman LJ said at p. 1423/4:

> On behalf of the parents Mr Gray has submitted very movingly . . . that this is a case where nature has made its own arrangements to terminate a life which would not be fruitful and nature should not be interfered with. He has also submitted that in this kind of decision the views of responsible and caring parents, as these are, should be respected, and that their decision that it is better for the child to be allowed to die should be respected. Fortunately or unfortunately, in this particular case the decision no longer lies with the parents or with the doctors, but lies with the court. It is a decision which of course must be taken in the light of the evidence and views expressed by the parents and the doctors, but at the end of the day it devolves on this court in this particular instance to decide . . .

Dunn LJ said at p. 1424:

> I have great sympathy for the parents in the agonising decision to which they came. As they put it themselves, 'God or nature has given the child a way out'. But the child now being a ward of court, although due weight must be given to the decision of the parents which everybody accepts was an entirely responsible one, doing what they considered was best, the fact of the matter is that this court now has to make the decision. It cannot hide behind the decision of the parents or the decision of the doctors; and in making the decision this court's first and paramount consideration is the welfare of this unhappy little baby.

So it is that at this point we move into the realm of family law.

IV Family law

1. The test for overriding the parents' refusal

This is trite law. In *In Re B (A Minor) (Wardship: Sterilisation)* [1988] AC 199, 202 Lord Hailsham of St. Marylebone LC said:

> There is no doubt that, in the exercise of its wardship jurisdiction the first and paramount consideration is the well being, welfare, or interest (each expression occasionally used, but each, for this purpose, synonymous) of the human being concerned . . .

Insofar as these proceedings are brought under the inherent jurisdiction of the court, that is the test that governs. In any event the position is regulated by section 1(1) of the Children Act 1989 under which these proceedings are also brought. That provides:

> When a court determines any question with respect to:
>
> (a) The upbringing of a child; . . .
>
> the child's welfare *shall* be the court's paramount consideration. (Emphasis added)
>
> The peremptory terms of this section should be noted. It places the court under a duty to do what is dictated by the child's welfare.

2. The meaning of welfare

In *J. v C.* [1970] AC 668, 710 Lord MacDermott addressed the question of construction as to the scope and meaning of the words in the Guardianship of Infants Act, 1925, '. . . shall regard the welfare of the infant as the first and paramount consideration', and he said:

> I think they connote a process whereby, when all the relevant facts, relationships, claims and wishes of parents, risks, choices and other circumstances are taken into account and weighed, the course to be followed will be that which is most in the interests of the child's welfare as that term has now to be understood.

In *Re M.B. (Medical Treatment)* [1997] 2 FLR 426, 439 Butler-Sloss LJ said:

> Best interests are not limited to best medical interests.

In *Re A (Male Sterilisation)* [2000] 1 FLR 549, 555 Dame Elizabeth Butler-Sloss, as President, said that:

> In my judgment best interest encompasses medical, emotional and all other welfare issues.

3. The interface with the criminal law

It should not need stating that the court cannot approve of a course of action which may be unlawful. The stark fact has to be faced in this case that to operate to separate the twins *may* be to murder Mary. It seems to me, however, that the question of what is in the best interests of the child is a discrete question from whether what is proposed to be done is unlawful. A patient in terminal decline, racked with pain which treatment may not be able fully to alleviate, may beg to die and it may be said – at least by some – that it is in his best interests that he should be allowed to do so, but that would not justify unlawfully killing him. In my judgment, although the nature of what is proposed to be done has a bearing on how one ascertains where the patient's best interests lie, the ascertainment of those interests is the first but a separate stage of the court's task. If the operation is in the best interests of a child patient, then the court can, as Stage 1 of the task which it has to undertake, override the parents' refusal and approve the operation but conditionally, always subject to and dependent upon the outcome of the second stage of the court's enquiry which is whether or not the carrying out of that operation would be lawful.

4. The main issues in this appeal

On the basis of foregoing analysis, the crucial questions which arise in this appeal are:

(1) Is it in Jodie's best interests that she be separated from Mary?
(2) Is it in Mary's best interests that she be separated from Jodie?
(3) If those interests are in conflict is the court to balance the interests of one against the other and allow one to prevail against the other and how is that to be done?
(4) If the prevailing interest is in favour of the operation being performed, can it be lawfully performed?

5. But first, a preliminary issue: is this a fused body of two separate persons, each having a life in being?

All parties took for granted in the court below that Mary is a live person and a separate person from Jodie. In the literature which was placed before us, some commentators had questioned whether this was the right approach to adopt. Consequently we invited counsel to address the question. Before dealing with the law, I should set out the facts, including further material placed before us by the hospital on this particular point.

There is no unanimity of view in answer to the hypothetical question: if Mary had not been joined to Jodie, would she have been born alive? The neonatologist said:

> Had Mary been born with very tiny lungs she could well have been born alive but would then have been unresuscitatable.

The consultant radiologist said:

> There would have been a significant risk of her dying of heart failure during the pregnancy . . . Mary may well have deteriorated further and died in pregnancy, though I am unable to quantify the risk of this.

The obstetrician felt that:

> With the degree of abnormalities of the circulatory system I feel that probably Mary would have been born dead.

The cardiologist expressed the firmest view:

> If Mary and Jodie had been separate and Mary's cardio-respiratory system in utero was as weak as it is now, I think it is 100% likely she would have died at birth had she survived the pregnancy.

Nevertheless he was equally emphatic about her present position:

> I first reviewed Mary at 72 hours of age, (not at birth) and at that stage although her heart was very large and weak, it was pumping, but contributing probably less than 10% of the circulatory requirements of Mary.

The neonatologist was also clear:

> When Mary was born the clinicians' judgment was that she did have functions indicative of life. Her heart was beating regularly, she did make some spontaneous respiratory efforts and there were movements of all her limbs.

There was total unanimity about their individuality. The neonatologist said:

> The twins are considered to be separate individuals. There are two heads, two brains and at different times of the day and night they exhibit different states of wakefulness/alertness and clearly their feeding abilities and patterns are very different.

The cardiologist said:

> Although the twins share some common tissue, they each have separate hearts, brains, etc., and thus medically I feel are separate individuals.

In the face of that evidence it would be contrary to common-sense and to everyone's sensibilities to say that Mary is not alive or that there are not two separate persons. It is, therefore, unnecessary to examine the law in any depth at all. In one of the early cases, *R v Poulton* (1832) 5 C & P 329 Littledale J in his summing-up to the jury in a murder trial stated:

> With respect to the birth, being born must mean that the whole body is brought into the world . . . Whether the child was born alive or not depends mainly on the evidence of the medical men.

In *R v Handley* (1874) 13 Cox 79, 81 Brett J told the jury they would have to consider whether the child was born alive:

> . . . ie whether it existed as a live child, breathing and living by reason of breathing through its own lungs alone, without deriving any of its living or power of living by or through any connection with its mother.

Brooke J, as he then was, in *Rance v Mid-Downs HA* [1991] 1 QB 587, 621 adopted a similar definition, saying that a child is born alive:

> . . . if, after birth, it exists as a live child, that is to say, breathing and living by reason of its breathing through its own lungs alone, without deriving any of its living or power of living by or through any connection with its mother.

I think I can guarantee that when My Lord said that, he did not relate his observations to Siamese twins.

Here Mary has been born in the sense that she has an existence quite independent from her mother. The fact that Mary is dependent upon Jodie, or the fact that twins may be interdependent if they share heart and lungs, should not lead the law to fly in the face of the clinical judgment that each child is alive and that each child is separate both for the purposes of the civil law and the criminal law.

I would not wish to leave this topic without saying firmly that the notions expressed in earlier times that Siamese twins were 'monsters' is totally unacceptable, indeed repugnant and offensive to the dignity of these children in the light of current medical knowledge and social sensibility. I deprecate any idea of 'monstrous birth'.

6. Jodie's welfare: where do her best interests lie?

Mr Taylor, on the parents' behalf, faces an uphill struggle to persuade this court that Johnson J was wrong to find that the operation would be in Jodie's best interests, and to be fair to him, he recognises the difficulty. There was abundant evidence before the judge to justify his conclusion which could not be attacked on appeal unless it was plainly wrong, that is to say unless it fell outside the generous ambit within which reasonable disagreement is possible. Far from being plainly wrong, Johnson J was in my judgment plainly right to conclude that the operation would be in Jodie's best interest.

The salient facts are these. The operation itself carries a negligible risk of death or brain damage. On the contrary the operation is overwhelmingly likely to have the consequence that Jodie's life will be extended from the period of 3–6 months or a little more to one where she may enjoy a normal expectancy of life. Prolonging her life is an obvious benefit to her. In general terms, she will live a normal or fairly normal life. Her present intellectual functioning is good and there is no reason to think that she will not have the mental capacity fully to enjoy her life. There is every chance that she will walk reasonably normally though future operations cannot be ruled out. She will have her own bladder and should be capable of controlling it. There is no certainly about bowel control though it is interesting to note that the opinion of Great Ormond Street is hopeful in this respect. At worst she will have to wear a colostomy bag. She is expected to be capable of satisfactory sexual functioning. The judge's findings are amply confirmed by (1) the report from the Great Ormond Street Hospital which must carry great weight with the court because it is independent and because they are world-recognised experts and (2) the spinal surgeon's report both of which are set out in the discussion on Jodie's prognosis.

I will deal separately with the problems that will or may arise in the parents or others giving care to Jodie but in the context of the argument which has dominated this case, namely the sanctity of life and the worthwhileness of life, it seems to me impossible to say that this operation does not offer infinitely greater benefit to Jodie than is offered to her by letting her die if the operation is not performed.

7. A more difficult question – Mary's welfare: where do her best interests lie?

7.1 The difficulties in the judge's approach

The steps in the analysis of Mary's best interests as carried out by Johnson J are:

(i) her 'pitiable' state will never improve;
(ii) there is no reliable way to test whether she is hurting or in pain; but,
(iii) linked as they are, Jodie's wish to move 'pulling Mary with her' would hurt Mary: this was an 'horrendous scenario';
(iv) accordingly 'the remaining few months of her life if not separated would not simply be worth nothing – they would be hurtful';
(v) 'to prolong Mary's life for those few months would be very seriously to her disadvantage'.

The careful criticisms of counsel have revealed some flaws in these propositions and lead me to the preliminary conclusions that:

(i) I agree with the judge's assessment: one pities Mary because her position is utterly dire for she exists pathetically on borrowed time.
(ii) Although there may be no reliable way of telling whether she can differentiate between pleasure and pain, the Great Ormond Street observations would suggest that she tends ordinarily to be quite comfortable.
(iii) The evidence seized on by the judge (given, one has observed, in answer to his promptings) may sit a little uneasily with his main finding of the uncertainty of the extent to which her primitive brain can register pain. The horror of the scenario is more likely, therefore, to impinge upon Jodie who, being sentient, may find it more difficult to cope with this hindrance to her instincts and development.
(iv) The conclusion that the ensuing months of Mary's life are worth nothing brings the dichotomy between quality of life and sanctity of life into critical focus.
(v) Whether the operation to separate the twins is properly to be viewed in terms of a prolongation of her life, as opposed to its termination, is again a critical element of the analysis.

7.2 The welfare assessment

The question of Mary's best interest is one of the key and one of the difficult issues in the case and it calls for thorough exposition.

That Mary's welfare is paramount is a trite observation for family lawyers. Welfare dictates the outcome of the question relating to her upbringing which is before the court. It means no more and no less than that the court must decide what is best for her, taking all her interests and needs into account, weighing and then bringing into balance the advantages against disadvantages, the risks of harm against the hopes of benefit which flow from the course of action under consideration.

The first step must be to characterise that course of action. Here it is proposed to operate to separate Mary from Jodie. So the first question is what are the gains and losses from that intervention? I would judge the answer by application of the test expressed by Lord Brandon of Oakbrook in *In Re F* at p55 F:

> The operation or other treatment will be in their best interests if, but only if, it is carried out in order either to save their lives, or to ensure improvement or prevent deterioration in their physical or mental health.

The only gain I can see is that the operation would, if successful, give Mary the bodily integrity and dignity which is the natural order for all of us. But this is a wholly illusory goal because she will be dead before she can enjoy her independence and she will die because, when she is independent, she has no capacity for life. The operation is not capable of ensuring any other improvement to her condition or prevent any deterioration in her present state of health. In terms of her best health interests, there are none. To be fair to the hospital, they do not pretend that there are.

If one looks to the operation as a means of meeting any other needs, social, emotional, psychological or whatever, one again searches in vain. One cannot blind oneself to the fact that death for Mary is the certain consequence of the carrying out of this operation.

7.3 Introducing Bland

If the search is to find how, if at all, there can be any benefit from an operation which it is known will terminate her life, then one must look to *Airedale NHS Trust v Bland* [1993] AC 789 for guidance because there, as here, it was known that the proposed course of action would terminate life. Tony Bland's awful predicament is well known. He was a young supporter of Liverpool FC who was caught in the Hillsborough crush which reduced him to a persistent vegetative state. The hospital applied for a declaration that it might lawfully discontinue all life-sustaining treatment and medical support measures designed to keep him alive in that state, including the termination of ventilation, nutrition and hydration by artificial means. That declaration was granted. As I pointed out in argument, the speeches in the House of Lords have been the subject of much academic scrutiny: see for example Kennedy and Grubb, *Withdrawal of Artificial Hydration and Nutrition: Incompetent*

Adult (1993) 2 Med. L. Rev. 359; Kennedy and Grubb, *Medical Law*, 2nd Edn., Ch. 16; J. Finnis, *Bland, Crossing the Rubicon*, (1993) 109 LQR 329 and J. Keown, *Restoring Moral and Intellectual Shape to the Law after Bland* (1997) 113 LQR 481. Looking at the matter very broadly, the drift of their Lordships' thinking was along these lines.

(i) There was some recognition that the intention was to cause death.
(ii) Actively to bring a patient's life to an end is:

> to cross the Rubicon which runs between on the one hand the care of the living patient and on the other hand euthanasia – actively causing his death to avoid or to end his suffering. Euthanasia is not lawful at common law: per Lord Goff at p865F.

(iii) Withdrawal of treatment was, however, properly to be characterised as an omission.
(iv) An omission to act would nonetheless be culpable if there was a duty to act.
(v) There was no duty to treat if treatment was not in the best interests of the patient.
(vi) Since there was no prospect of the treatment improving his condition the treatment was futile and there was no interest for Tony Bland in continuing the process of artificially feeding him upon which the prolongation of his life depends.

We see shades of *Bland* in the way Johnson J framed his vital fourth and fifth proposition, and the way in which he wrestled with the problems of acts and omissions. I must, therefore, examine his propositions (iv) and (v) in the light of the speeches in the House of Lords and the academic commentary thereon.

7.4. Would Mary's life if not separated from her twin 'be worth nothing to her'?

The judge must have reached that conclusion by forming an assessment of the quality of her life. How did the quality of life argument enter the jurisprudence? As far as I can trace, it seems to have been introduced by *In Re B* in 1981, the case of the Down's Syndrome baby with the intestinal blockage. It should be noted that that case came before the High Court judge in the morning and was decided by the Court of Appeal in the afternoon. The test adopted by Templeman LJ at p1424 B was:

> . . . whether the life of this child is demonstrably going to be so awful that in effect the child must be condemned to die.

Dunn LJ observed at p1424H that:

> There is no evidence at all as to the quality of life which the child may expect. As Mr Turcan on behalf of the Official Solicitor said, the child should be put into the same position as any other Mongol

> child and must be given the chance to live an existence. I accept that way of putting it.

That was practically all I had to go on when deciding Baby C's future: *In Re C (A Minor) (Wardship: Medical Treatment)* [1990] Fam. 26. That cruelly disadvantaged baby was dying. Although I (not for the first time nor for the last) failed to express myself with 'felicity', the Court of Appeal did not appear to disapprove of the twin strands of my approach: firstly that no treatment would alter the hopelessness of the child's position and, secondly, that insofar as I was able to assess the quality of life 'which as a test in itself raises as many questions as it can answer' I judged the quality of her life to be demonstrably awful and intolerable following *In Re B.*

In Re J (A Minor) (Wardship: Medical Treatment) [1991] Fam. 33 which followed shortly thereafter, was another damaged young baby case, though here she was not terminally ill. The court rejected the Official Solicitor's first submission, which was (see p42B):

> His first, or absolutist, submission is that a court is *never* justified in withholding consent to treatment which could enable a child to survive a life-threatening condition whatever the pain or other side effects inherent in the treatment and whatever the quality of life which it would experience thereafter. I add the emphasis.

Having rejected it, the court was left only with the quality of life argument and whether life would be intolerable to the child as judged from the perspective of the child. [Since a 'substituted judgment' approach has been rejected by *Bland*, I doubt whether that view is still good law. That, however, is not the main point]. John Keown in his penetrating analysis of *Bland* seems to me correctly to identify that counsel in *In Re J* was confusing the doctrine of vitalism on the one hand and the true principle of sanctity of life on the other. Vitalism holds that human life is an absolute moral value and that it is wrong either to shorten it or to fail to lengthen it. This is too extreme a position to hold.

The sanctity of life doctrine holds that human life is created in the image of God and is therefore possessed of an intrinsic dignity which entitled it to protection from unjust attack. The 'right to life' is essentially a right not to be intentionally killed, according to John Keown. Taylor LJ began his judgment in *In Re J* by setting out three preliminary principles not in dispute. The first was that welfare is the court's paramount consideration.

> Secondly, the court's high respect for the sanctity of human life imposes a strong presumption in favour of taking all steps capable of preserving it, save in exceptional circumstances. The problem is to define those circumstances.
>
> Thirdly, and as a corollary to the second principle, it cannot be too strongly emphasised that the court never sanctions steps to terminate life. That would be unlawful. There is no question of approving,

> even in a case of the most horrendous disability, a course aimed at terminating life or accelerating death. The court is concerned only with the circumstances in which steps should not be taken to prolong life.

The Archbishop puts as his first 'overarching moral consideration':

> Human life is sacred, that is inviolable, so that one should never aim to cause an innocent person's death by act or omission.

The report of the Select Committee of the House of Lords on Medical Ethics (HL Paper 21-I, Para. 237) similarly provides:

> The (prohibition of intentional killing) is the cornerstone of law and social relationships. It protects each one of us impartially, embodying the belief that all are equal. We do not wish that protection to be diminished . . .

A joint statement by the Anglican and Roman Catholic Archbishops in the aftermath of the House of Lords' judgment in *Bland* included the following passage to which the Archbishop of Westminster has helpfully drawn our attention:

> Those who become vulnerable through illness or disease deserve special care and protection. Adherence to this principle provides a fundamental test as to what constitutes a civilised society . . . Because human life is a gift from God to be preserved and cherished, the deliberate taking of life is prohibited except in self-defence or the legitimate defence of others . . . a pattern of care should never be adopted with the intention, purpose or aim of terminating life or bringing about the death of a patient.

What the sanctity of life doctrine compels me to accept is that each life has inherent value in itself and the right to life, being universal, is equal for all of us.

The sanctity of life doctrine does, however, acknowledge that it may be proper to withhold or withdraw treatment. The Archbishop points out that in Roman Catholic moral theology one is justified in declining 'extraordinary' treatment where the prospective benefits of treatment do not clearly warrant the burdensome consequences it is likely to impose such as physical pain, psychological stress, social dislocation, and financial expenditure.

John Keown argues, to my mind very persuasively, that:

> The question is always whether the *treatment* would be worthwhile, not whether the patient's *life* would be worthwhile. Were one to engage in judgments of the latter sort, and to conclude that certain lives were not worth living, one would forfeit any principled basis for objecting to intentional killing. He has added the emphasis.

In my judgment, that is essentially what the court was doing in *In*

Re J and what I was trying to do in *In Re C.* Lord Goff makes the point in *Bland* at p. 868 E–H:

> But if the question is asked, as in my opinion it should be, whether it is in his best interests that treatment which has the effect of artificially prolonging his life should be continued, that question can sensibly be answered to the effect that his best interests no longer require that it should be.

Even so, a distinction may be drawn between (i) cases in which, having regard to all the circumstances (including, for example, the intrusive nature of the treatment, the hazards involved in it, and the very poor quality of life which may be prolonged for the patient if the treatment is successful), it may be judged not to be in the best interests of the patient to initiate or continue life-prolonging treatment, and (ii) cases such as the present in which, so far as the living patient is concerned, the treatment is of no benefit to him because he is totally unconscious and there is no prospect of any improvement in his condition. In both classes of case, the decision whether or not to withhold treatment must be made in the best interests of the patient. In the first class, however, the decision has to be made by weighing the relevant considerations. For example, in *In Re J (A Minor) (Wardship: Medical Treatment)* [1991] Fam. 33, the approach to be adopted in that case was stated by Taylor LJ as follows, at p 55:

> I consider the correct approach is for the court to judge the quality of life the child would have to endure if given the treatment and decide whether in all the circumstances such a life would be so afflicted as to be intolerable to that child.

In Keown's analysis:

> From the standpoint of the sanctity doctrine, a central objection to the Quality of life philosophy is that it denies the ineliminable value of each patient and engages in discriminatory judgments, posited on fundamentally arbitrary criteria such as physical or mental disability, about whose lives are 'worthwhile' and whose are not. The arbitrariness is highlighted when it is asked *which* disabilities, and to which *degree*, are supposed to make life not worth living? Again it is his emphasis.

7.5 Conclusions as to the worth of Mary's life

Given the international Conventions protecting 'the right to life', to which I will return later, I conclude that it is impermissible to deny that every life has an equal inherent value. Life is worthwhile in itself whatever the diminution in one's capacity to enjoy it and however gravely impaired some of one's vital functions of speech, deliberation and choice may be. I agree with the Archbishop that:

> The indispensable foundation of justice is the basic equality in worth of every human being.

This accords with the observation of Lord Mustill in *Bland* at p894D:

> . . . whilst the fact that a patient is in great pain may give him or her a powerful motive for wanting to end his or her life, to which in certain circumstances it is proper to accede, is not at all the same as the proposition that because of incapacity or infirmity one life is intrinsically worth less than another. That is the first step on a very dangerous road indeed, and one which I am not willing to take.

Neither am I. In my judgment Johnson J was wrong to find that Mary's life would be worth nothing to her. I am satisfied that Mary's life, desperate as it is, still has its own eneliminable value and dignity.

7.6 Johnson J's fifth proposition: 'To prolong Mary's life . . . would be very seriously to her disadvantage'.

My difficulty with that proposition lies in the characterisation that the treatment under consideration is a course of action which will prolong Mary's life. This again derives from *Bland.* It is best seen in Lord Goff's speech. At p865D he points out that the law draws a crucial distinction between cases in which a doctor decides not to provide life-prolonging treatment, and those in which he decides, for example by administering a lethal drug, actively to bring his patient's life to an end. The latter course crosses the Rubicon (p865F). At the heart of the distinction is the difference between acts and omissions. He says at p866F:

> The distinction appears, therefore, to be useful in the present context in that it can be invoked to explain how discontinuance of life support can be differentiated from ending a patient's life by a lethal injection. But in the end the reason for that difference is that, whereas the law considers that discontinuance of life support may be consistent with the doctor's duty to care for his patient, it does not, for reasons of policy, consider that it forms any part of his duty to give his patient a lethal injection to put him out of his agony.

The decision to discontinue treatment which prolongs life is governed by the patient's best interests (p867C). The question at the heart of the case is on what principle the doctor can justifiably discontinue the process (p867H). He continues on p868A:

> It is crucial for the understanding of this question that the question itself should be correctly formulated. The question is not whether the doctor should take a course which will kill his patient, or even take a course which has the effect of accelerating his death. The question is whether the doctor should or should not continue to provide his patient with medical treatment or care which, if continued, will prolong his patient's life. The question is sometimes put in striking or emotional terms, which can be misleading. For

> example, in the case of a life-support system, it is sometimes asked: should a doctor be entitled to switch it off, or pull the plug? And then it is asked: can it be in the best interests of the patient that a doctor should be able to switch the life support system off, when this will inevitably result in the patient's death? Such an approach has rightly been criticised as misleading, for example by Professor Ian Kennedy in his paper *Treat Me Right, Essays in Medical Law and Ethics* and by Thomas J in *Auckland Area Health Board v Attorney-General* [1993] 1 NZLR 235, 247. This is because the question is not whether it is in the best interests of the patient that he should die. The question is whether in the best interests of the patient that his life should be prolonged by the continuance of this form of medical treatment or care.

He concludes at p869D:

> But for my part I cannot see that medical treatment is appropriate or requisite simply to prolong a patient's life, when such treatment has no therapeutic purpose of any kind, as where it is futile because the patient is unconscious and there is no prospect of any improvement in his condition . . . But in the end, in a case such as the present, it is the futility of the treatment which justifies its termination.

Finally, at p837C he says:

> To me, the crucial point at which I find myself differing from Mr. Munby was that I was unable to accept his treating the discontinuance of artificial feeding in the present case as equivalent to cutting a mountaineer's rope or severing the airpipe of a deep sea diver. Once it is recognised, as I believe it must be, that the true question is not whether the doctor should take a course in which he will actively kill his patient, but rather whether he should continue to provide his patient with medical treatment or care which, if continued, will prolong his life, then as I see it, the essential basis of Mr Munby's submission disappears.

7.7 Act or omission in this case?

I set out earlier (I realise with embarrassment a lot earlier) how this operation would be performed. The first step is to take the scalpel and cut the skin. If it is theoretically possible to cut precisely down the midline separating two individual bodies, that is not surgically feasible. Then the doctors have to ascertain which of the organs belong to each child. That is impossible to do without invading Mary's body in the course of that exploration. There follow further acts of separation culminating in the clamping and then severing of the artery. Whether or not the final step is taken within Jodie's body so that Jodie's aorta and not Mary's aorta is assaulted, it seems to me to be utterly fanciful to classify this invasive treatment as an omission in contra-distinction to an act. Johnson J's valiant and wholly understandable attempt to do so cannot be supported and although Mr Whitfield QC did his best, he recognised his difficulty. The operation has, therefore, to be seen as an act of invasion of Mary's bodily integrity and unless consent or approval is given for it, it constitutes an unlawful assault upon her.

7.8 Is the course of action one which can be characterised as not continuing to provide the patient with treatment which will prolong the patient's life?

The answer to that has to be no. Mary is not receiving treatment (or any substantial treatment) at the present time. Such care as she receives in hospital will of course prolong her life but there is no question of withdrawing that care or that treatment. What is under consideration is the active invasion of her body. That will not prolong her life. It will terminate it. With respect to the judge he asked the wrong question. The question is not: is it in Mary's best interests that the hospital should continue to provide her with treatment which will prolong her life? This case is not about providing that kind of treatment. What is proposed should be done and what the court is being asked to sanction demands that the question be framed in this way: is it in Mary's best interests that an operation be performed to separate her from Jodie when the certain consequence of that operation is that she will die? There is only one answer to that question. It is: no, that is not in her best interests. In my judgment the judge's approach is fatally flawed and his assessment of Mary's best interests falls with it.

7.9 Conclusion as to Mary's best interests

The question is whether this proposed operation is in Mary's best interests. It cannot be. It will bring her life to an end before it has run its natural span. It denies her inherent right to life. There is no countervailing advantage for her at all. It is contrary to her best interests. Looking at her position in isolation and ignoring, therefore, the benefit to Jodie, the court should not sanction the operation on her.

8. On the sharpest horns of dilemma: what does the court do now?

I have found this a very difficult question to answer. Subject to having regard to the parents' wish, which I will consider shortly, the operation will be in Jodie's interests but not in Mary's. Can that conflict be resolved and if so how?

In the course of argument I speculated that Mary's interests may not be overborne and that consequently approval for the operation can not be given. Miss Parker QC on Jodie's behalf submits very strongly that it can. She submits that judges in the Family courts are frequently presented with a clash of interests between children whose upbringing they have to regulate and that when that arises the judges balance the interests of one against the other and choose the least detrimental alternative. So they do, but is it right that they do so and can one's right to life be traded against another's?

There is no clear authority on the point. In *Birmingham City Council v H (A Minor)* [1994] 2 AC 212, the House of Lords was invited to express its opinion of this question but was able to avoid doing so. In that case the local authority applied for a care order in respect of a young baby. The mother was only 15 and was a 'child' herself. Application was made pursuant to Section 34(4) of the Children Act 1989 for an order authorising the local authority to refuse contact between the baby and the mother. No conflict arose because the question to be determined by the court related to the baby's upbringing and it was the baby's welfare that was to be the court's paramount consideration, even where the mother herself was a child in care. Section 34(3) enabled the court to 'make such order as it considers appropriate with respect to the contact which is to be allowed between the child and that person'. Lord Slynn of Hadley said at p222:

> For this purpose, 'the child' is the child in care in respect of whom an order is sought by one of the four categories of person. That child is the subject matter of the application. The question to be determined relates to that child's upbringing and it is that child's welfare which must be the court's paramount consideration. The fact that the parent is also a child does not mean that both parent's and child's welfare is paramount and that each has to be balanced against the other.

The case was decided on that narrow basis.

The Court of Appeal had proceeded differently: see the report in [1993] 1 FLR 883. The Court of Appeal considered that the upbringing of both mother and daughter was involved and that section 1(1) of the Act governed the position. Balcombe LJ said at p. 890–2:

> So the question of contact between R (the baby) and M (the mother) relates to the upbringing of each of them and in each case the Act requires that their welfare shall be the court's paramount consideration. But this is an impossibility. 'Paramount' means 'above all others in rank, order or jurisdiction; supreme' – see the *Shorter Oxford Dictionary* (3rd Edn.) On one and the same issue, contact between them, M's welfare cannot rank above R's welfare and his above hers. This potential difficulty which may occur when cases of two or more siblings come before the court, was foreseen by the Law Commission in their studies leading up to the 1989 Act – see Working Paper No. 96, para. 6.16 and Report No. 172, paras. 3.13 and 3.14 and s 1(2) of the Draft Bill appended to the Report.
>
> However, for whatever reason, the draughtsman of the 1989 Act did not adopt the Law Commission's recommendations on this point, and we have to resolve the dilemma ourselves.

> Where the court is faced with what appears to be an impossibility, it must try and give the statutory provision such meaning as it can sensibly bear, having regard to any other provisions of the Act which may throw light on the intention of the legislature.
>
> . . .
>
> In my judgment, therefore, we are thrown back upon the words of s 1(1) of the 1989 Act. I can think of no reason why Parliament should have intended, when a question with respect to the upbringing of two children is before the court, that the court should regard one child's interests as paramount to that of the other. Accordingly, in my judgment, while the welfare of M and R, taken together is to be considered as paramount to the interests of any adults concerned in their lives, as between themselves the court must approach the question of their welfare without giving one priority over the other. You start with an evenly balanced pair of scales. Of course, when you start to put into the scales the matters relevant to each child – and in particular those listed in s 1(3) – the result may come down in favour of one rather than the other, but that is a balancing exercise which the court is well used to conducting in cases concerning children.

Kennedy LJ and Evans LJ agreed but Evans LJ added this at p896:

> The question in issue in this case is whether contact should be allowed between M, the child's mother, and R, her son, who is now aged 15 months. This question concerns the upbringing of R and is therefore subject to s 1(1) of the Act, which provides that the child's welfare shall be the court's paramount consideration. The problem arises because M herself is a child, 16 years, and is herself in care of the same local authority as R. If the same question is also one 'with respect to her upbringing', then s1(1) makes her welfare the court's paramount consideration and on the judge's findings, her welfare and R's are in conflict . . . The Act does not provide expressly for the case where the parent is herself a child nor for the situation where the question of welfare may arise between two children in other circumstances, for example, between siblings. The Law Commission drew attention to the latter problem . . . but the Act is silent. We therefore have to attempt to apply the general provisions of the Act to the exceptional, though unhappily not unique, circumstances of this case.
>
> It seems that there is no reported authority, whether before or after 1989, where this or any similar question has arisen between a child and a parent who is herself a child
>
> . . .
>
> The starting point must be the correct interpretation of ss 1 and 34 of the Act . . .

He concluded at p899:

> But the welfare of the two individuals cannot both be 'paramount' in the ordinary and natural meaning of that word. If that is the requirement of s 1(1) in the circumstances, then the Act presents the court with an impossible task. For this reason, I agree with Balcombe LJ that the requirement must be regarded as qualified, in the cases where the welfare of more than one child is involved, by the need to have regard to potential detriment for one in the light of potential benefit for the other. Only in this way, it seems to me, can the section be applied and the manifest objects of the Act achieved.

The House of Lords expressed no view as to the correctness or otherwise of that approach. It seems to me, therefore, that it must stand as at least persuasive, if not binding, authority. Moreover the question arises directly in this case and because it is the right to life of each child that is in issue, the conflict between the children could not be more acute. If the duty of the court is to make a decision which puts Jodie's interests paramount and that decision would be contrary to the paramount interests of Mary, then, for my part, I do not see how the court can reconcile the impossibility of properly fulfilling each duty by simply declining to decide the very matter before it. That would be a total abdication of the duty which is imposed upon us. Given the conflict of duty, I can see no other way of dealing with it than by choosing the lesser of the two evils and so finding the least detrimental alternative. A balance has to be struck somehow and I cannot flinch from undertaking that evaluation, horrendously difficult though it is. Before doing so, I must decide what weight to give to the parents' wishes.

9. *Giving due weight to the parents' wishes*

9.1 The parents and the courts

As I have shown, the parents in their statement accept that they are governed by the law of England: there is no challenge to the court's jurisdiction. Furthermore Mr Taylor on their behalf does not challenge the judge's approach, only his conclusion.

Since the parents have the right in the exercise of their parental responsibility to make the decision, it should not be a surprise that their wishes should command very great respect. Parental right is, however, subordinate to welfare. That was the view of the House of Lords in *In Re KD (A Minor) (Ward: Termination of Access)* [1988] 1 AC 806, 824–5 where Lord Oliver of Aylmerton said:

> My Lords I do not, for my part, discern any conflict between the propositions laid down by your Lordships' House in *J v C* and the pronouncements of the European Court of Human Rights in relation to the natural parent's right of access to her child. Such conflict as exists, is, I think, semantic only and lies only in differing ways of giving expression to the single concept that the natural bond in the

> relationship between parent and child gives rise to universally recognised norms which ought not to be gratuitously interfered with and which, if interfered with at all, ought to be so only if the welfare of the child dictates it. The word 'right' is used in a variety of different senses, both popular and jurisprudential . . . Parenthood, in most civilised societies, is generally conceived of as conferring upon parents the exclusive privilege of ordering, within the family, the upbringing of children of tender age, with all that that entails. That is a privilege which, interfered with without authority, would be protected by the courts, but it is a privilege circumscribed by many limitations imposed both by the general law and, where circumstances demand, by the courts or by the authorities upon whom the legislature has imposed the duty of supervising the welfare of children and young persons. When the jurisdiction of the court is invoked for the protection of the child the parental privileges do not terminate. They do, however, become immediately subservient to the paramount consideration which the court has always in mind, that is to say, the welfare of the child. That is the basis of the decision of your Lordships' House in *J v C* [1970] AC 668 and I see nothing in *R v United Kingdom* (Case 6/1986/104/152) which contradicts or casts any doubt upon that decision or which calls now for any re-appraisal of it by your Lordships. In particular the description of those familial rights and privileges enjoyed by parents in relation to their children as 'fundamental' or 'basic' does nothing, in my judgment, to clarify either the nature or the extent of the concept which it is sought to describe.

In *J v C* at p175 Lord MacDermott set out the rule which has served the test of time:

> While there is now no rule of law that the rights and wishes of unimpeachable parents must prevail over other considerations, such rights and wishes, recognised as they are by nature and society, can be capable of ministering to the total welfare of the child in a special way, and must therefore preponderate in many cases. The parental rights, however, remain qualified and not absolute for the purposes of the investigation the broad nature of which is still as described in the fourth of the principles enunciated by FitzGibbon LJ in *In Re O'Hara* [1900] 2 IR 232, 240.

That fourth principle which itself was derived from *Reg v Gyngall* [1893] 2 QB 232, is stated thus:

> 4. In exercising the jurisdiction to control or to ignore the parental right the court must act cautiously, not as if it were a private person acting with regard to his own child, and acting in opposition to the parent only when judicially satisfied that the welfare of the child requires that the parental right should be suspended or superseded.

Finally, it is perhaps useful to repeat the passage in the judgment of Sir

Thomas Bingham MR in *In Re Z (A Minor) (Identification: Restrictions on Publication)* [1997] Fam. 1, 32, in accordance with which Johnson J approached this part of the case. The Master of the Rolls said:

I would for my part accept without reservation that the decision of a devoted and responsible parent should be treated with respect. It should certainly not be disregarded or lightly set aside. But the role of the court is to exercise an independent and objective judgment. If that judgment is in accord with that of the devoted and responsible parent, well and good. If it is not, then it is the duty of the court, after giving due weight to the view of the devoted and responsible parent, to give effect to its own judgment. That is what it is there for. Its judgment may of course be wrong. So may that of the parent. But once the jurisdiction of the court is invoked its clear duty is to reach and give the best judgment that it can.

That is the law. That is what governs my decision. That is what I am desperately trying to do. I do not discern any very significant difference between the law, as set out above, and the Archbishop's fifth overarching moral consideration which he expresses in these terms:

> Respect for the natural authority of parents requires that the courts override the rights of parents only when there is clear evidence that they are acting contrary to what is strictly owing to their children.

9.2 The role of the court: reviewer or decision-maker?

Is the court reviewing the parental decision as it reviews an administrative decision or does the court look at the matter afresh, in the round, with due weight given to the parental wish? If there was doubt about that, it has been resolved in favour of the latter approach by the decision of this court in *In Re T (Wardship: Medical Treatment)* [1997] 1 WLR 242. That was an agonising decision for the court to take. The baby, a year old, had a life threatening liver defect. An operation when he was 3½ weeks old was unsuccessful. The unanimous medical opinion was that without a liver transplant he would not live beyond the age of 2½ years. His parents refused to consent to that operation. Their wish eventually prevailed. On this particular point Butler-Sloss LJ said at p250 F:

> . . . The first argument of Mr Francis that the court should not interfere with the reasonable decision of a parent is not one that we are able to entertain even if we wish to do so. His suggestion that the decision of this mother came within that band of reasonable decisions within which a court would not interfere would import into this jurisdiction the test applied in adoption to the refusal of a parent to consent to adoption. It is wholly inapposite to the welfare test and is incompatible with the decision in *In Re Z*.

Waite LJ said at 254C:

> An appraisal of parental reasonableness may be appropriate in

> other areas of family law (in adoption, for example where it is enjoined by statute) but when it comes to an assessment of the demands of the child patient's welfare, the starting point – and the finishing point too – must always be the judge's own independent assessment of the balance of advantage or disadvantage of the particular medical step under consideration. In striking that balance, the court will of course take into account as a relevant, often highly relevant, factor the attitude taken by the natural parent, and that may require examination of his or her motives. But the result of such an enquiry must never be allowed to prove determinative. It is a mistake to view the issue as one in which the clinical advice of doctors is placed in one scale and the reasonableness of the parent's view in the other.
>
> . . .
>
> It can only be said safely that there is a scale, at one end of which lies the clear case where parental opposition to medical intervention is prompted by scruple or dogma of a kind which is patently irreconcilable with principles of child health and welfare widely accepted by the generality of mankind; and that at the other end lie highly problematic cases where there is genuine scope for a difference of view between the parent and the judge. In both situations it is the duty of the judge to allow the court's own opinion to prevail in the perceived paramount interest of the child concerned, but in cases at the latter end of the scale, there must be a likelihood (though never of course a certainty) that the greater the scope for genuine debate between one view and another the stronger will be that inclination of the court to be influenced by a reflection that in the last analysis the best interests of every child include an expectation that difficult decisions affecting the length and quality of its life will be taken for it by the parent to whom its care has been entrusted by nature.

Roch LJ expressed a similar view.

9.3 The weight to be given to these parents' wishes

I would wish to say emphatically that this is not a case where opposition is 'prompted by scruple or dogma'. The views of the parents will strike a chord of agreement with many who reflect upon their dilemma. I cannot emphasise enough how much I sympathise with them in the cruelty of the agonising choice they had to make. I know because I agonise over the dilemma too. I fear, however, that the parents' wish does not convince me that it is in the children's best interest:

(i) From Jodie's point of view they have taken the worst possible scenario that she would be wheelchair bound, destined for a life of difficulty. They fail to recognise her capacity sufficiently to enjoy the benefits of life that would be available to her were she free and independent.

(ii) She may indeed need special care and attention and that may be very difficult fully to provide in their home country.
This is a real and practical problem for the family, the burden of which in ordinary family life should not be underestimated. It may seem unduly harsh on these desperate parents to point out that it is the *child's* best interests which are paramount, not the *parents'*. Coping with a disabled child sadly inevitably casts a great burden on parents who have to struggle through those difficulties. There is, I sense, a lack of consistency in their approach to their daughters' welfare. In Mary's case, they are overwhelmed by the legitimate, as I have found it to be, need to respect and protect her right to life. They surely cannot so minimise Jodie's rights on the basis that the burden of possible disadvantage for her and the burdens of caring for such a child for them can morally be said to outweigh her claim to the human dignity of independence which only cruel fate has denied her.

(iii) They are fully entitled to recoil at the idea, as they see it, of killing Mary. That is wholly understandable. This lies at the core of their objection. Yet they came to this country for treatment. They were aware of the possibility that Mary might be stillborn and they seemed reconciled to an operation which would separate Jodie from her. They seemed to have been prepared, and presented their case to Johnson J on the basis that they would agree to the operation if Mary predeceased Jodie. The physical problems for Jodie would be the same, perhaps even worse in such an event. The parents appear to have been willing to cope in that event, and the burdens for parents and child cannot have changed. Mary is lost to them anyway.

(iv) In their natural repugnance at the idea of killing Mary they fail to recognise their conflicting duty to save Jodie and they seem to exculpate themselves from, or at least fail fully to face up to the consequence of the failure to separate the twins, namely death for Jodie. In my judgment, parents who are placed on the horns of such a terrible dilemma simply have to choose the lesser of their inevitable loss. If a family at the gates of a concentration camp were told they might free one of their children but if no choice were made both would die, compassionate parents with equal love for their twins would elect to save the stronger and see the weak one destined for death pass through the gates.

This is a terribly cruel decision to force upon the parents. It is a choice no loving parent would ever want to make. It gives me no satisfaction to have disagreed with their views of what is right for their family and to have expressed myself in terms they will feel are harshly and unfairly critical of them. I am sorry about that. It may be no great comfort to them to know that in fact my heart bleeds for them. But if, as the law says I must, it is I who must now make the decision, then whatever the parents' grief, I must strike a balance between the twins and do what is best for them.

10. How is the balance to be struck?

The analytical problem is to determine what may, and what may not, be placed in each scale and what weight is then to be given to each of the factors in the scales.

(i) The universality of the right to life demands that *the right* to life be treated as equal. The intrinsic value of their human life is equal. So the right of each goes into the scales and the scales remain in balance.

(ii) The question which the court has to answer is whether or not the proposed treatment, the operation to separate, is in the best interests of the twins. That enables me to consider and place in the scales of each twin the worthwhileness of the treatment. That is a quite different exercise from the proscribed (because it offends the sanctity of life principle) consideration of the worth of one life compared with the other. When considering the worthwhileness of the treatment, it is legitimate to have regard to the actual condition of each twin and hence the actual balance sheet of advantage and disadvantage which flows from the performance or the non-performance of the proposed treatment. Here it is legitimate, as John Keown demonstrates, and as the cases show, to bear in mind the actual quality of life each child enjoys and may be able to enjoy. In summary, the operation will give Jodie the prospects of a normal expectation of relatively normal life. The operation will shorten Mary's life but she remains doomed for death. Mary has a full claim to the dignity of independence which is her human entitlement. In the words of the Rabbinical scholars involved in the 1977 case in Philadelphia, Mary is 'designated for death' because her capacity to live her life is fatally compromised. The prospect of a full life for Jodie is counterbalanced by an acceleration of certain death for Mary. That balance is heavily in Jodie's favour.

(iii) I repeat that the balancing exercise I have just conducted is *not* a balancing of the Quality of life in the sense that I value the potential of one human life above another. I have already indicated that the value of each life in the eyes of God and in the eyes of law is equal. Remember Lord Mustill's observation in *Bland*.

(iv) In this unique case it is, in my judgment, impossible not to put in the scales of each child the manner in which they are individually able to exercise their right to life. Mary may have a right to life, but she has little right to be alive. She is alive because and only because, to put it bluntly, but nonetheless accurately, she sucks the lifeblood of Jodie and she sucks the lifeblood out of Jodie. She will survive only so long as Jodie survives. Jodie will not survive long

> because constitutionally she will not be able to cope. Mary's parasitic living will be the cause of Jodie's ceasing to live. If Jodie could speak, she would surely protest, 'Stop it, Mary, you're killing me'. Mary would have no answer to that. Into my scales of fairness and justice between the children goes the fact that nobody but the doctors can help Jodie. Mary is beyond help.

Hence I am in no doubt at all that the scales come down heavily in Jodie's favour. The best interests of the twins is to give the chance of life to the child whose actual bodily condition is capable of accepting the chance to her advantage even if that has to be at the cost of the sacrifice of the life which is so unnaturally supported. I am wholly satisfied that the least detrimental choice, balancing the interests of Mary against Jodie and Jodie against Mary, is to permit the operation to be performed.

11. Conclusion on the Family Law aspect of this case

I would grant permission for the operation to take place provided, however, what is proposed to be done can be lawfully done. That requires a consideration of the criminal law to which I now turn.

IV The criminal law

1. Introduction

It is obvious that the question whether or not this operation can be lawfully performed is crucial to the outcome of the appeal. What I confess I had not fully appreciated was how rooted in obscurity the answer to those difficulties was. Brooke LJ was fully aware of all the intricacies and he set counsel a rigorous reading list to meet our concerns. I am, therefore, grateful to him for leading the way. In his judgment which I have read in draft, he so fully sets out the relevant material that I am happy to adopt it and I will not add to this lengthy judgment by needless repetition. In the light of his full exposition of the law, I can state the gist of my reasons for agreeing with him quite shortly.

2. Is there some immunity for doctors?

Archbold 2000: Criminal Pleading Evidence & Practice, para. 19–38, states that:

> Bona fide medical or surgical treatment is not 'unlawful' and therefore death resulting therefrom does not amount to murder, even though death or serious injury is foreseen as a probable consequence. Nor does it amount to manslaughter, unless the person giving the treatment has been guilty of 'gross negligence'.

No authority is given for this sweeping statement. It is true that in *Gillick* Lord Scarman said at p190:

> The bona fide exercise by a doctor of his clinical judgment must be a complete negation of the guilty mind which is an essential ingredient of the criminal offence of aiding and abetting the commission of unlawful sexual intercourse.

Lord Mustill speaks of it in *Bland.* Yet hanging over *Bland* is the spectre of murder. To have crossed the Rubicon would have been to murder. I, therefore, approach the question of lawfulness of the proposed separation on the basis that, whatever immunity doctors do enjoy, they have no complete immunity. I have to be satisfied that in this case they will not be guilty of unlawfully killing Mary by active intervention – and perhaps of unlawfully killing Jodie by omitting to act in her interests if there is a duty upon them to do so.

3. Murder

Stripping away the inessential elements, for present purposes I have to examine whether there would be (1) an unlawful (2) killing of a person (3) with intent to kill or cause grievous bodily harm. Each of those elements calls for consideration.

4. Intention

4.1 The proper test

It is sufficient for present purposes simply to note that, despite several earlier attempts by the House of Lords to clarify the mens rea required to establish murder, 'the law of murder was in a state of disarray': per Lord Steyn in *Reg v Woollin* [1999] 1 AC 82, 91 A. *Woollin* is binding upon us and, despite Mr Owen QC's submission that Article 2 of the European Human Rights Convention will require us to recast the definition, I do not propose to do so. Law which has long needed to be settled should be left to settle. The test I have to set myself is that established by that case. I have to ask myself whether I am satisfied that the doctors recognise that death or serious harm will be virtually certain (barring some unforeseen intervention) to result from carrying out this operation. If so, the doctors intend to kill or to do that serious harm even though they may not have any desire to achieve that result. It is common ground that they appreciate that death to Mary would result from the severance of the common aorta. Unpalatable though it may be – and Mr Whitfield contends it is – to stigmatise the doctors with 'murderous intent', that is what in law they will have if they perform the operation and Mary dies as a result.

4.2 The doctrine of double effect

This teaches us that an act which produces a bad effect is nevertheless morally permissible if the action is good in itself, the intention is solely to produce the good effect, the good effect is not produced through the bad effect and there is sufficient reason to permit the bad effect. It may be difficult to reconcile with *Woollin*. Nevertheless it seems to enjoy some approval from Lord Donaldson MR – see *In re J* at p46C – and Lord Goff – see *Bland* p867C. I can readily see how the doctrine works when doctors are treating one patient administering pain-killing drugs for the sole good purpose of relieving pain, yet appreciating the bad side-effect that it will hasten the patient's death. I simply fail to see how it can apply here where the side-effect to the good cure for Jodie is another patient's, Mary's, death, and when the treatment cannot have been undertaken to effect any benefit for Mary.

5. Causation

I appreciate, of course, that in one sense Mary will die because she is simply incapable of living. She is not a viable child. But as she is alive at the time of the operation is undertaken, the operation serves to hasten her inevitable death just as the lethal injection accelerates the death of a patient at a terminal stage. So I do not see how, in law, the severance of the artery will not be treated as a cause of her death.

6. Killing

I have already explained why the operation will be an active invasion of Mary's body and by that act the doctors will kill her.

I seem to be the lone voice raising the unpalatable possibility that the doctors and even – though given the horror of their predicament it is anathema to contemplate it – the parents might kill Jodie if they fail to save her life by carrying out the operation to separate her from Mary. Although I recoil at the very notion that these good people could ever be guilty of murder, I am bound to ask why the law will not hold that the doctors and the parents have come under a duty to Jodie. If the operation is in her interests the parents must consent for their duty is to act consistent with her best interests: see Lord Scarman in *Gillick* in the passages I have already set out. I know there is a huge chasm in turpitude between these stricken parents and the wretched parents in *R v Gibbins and Proctor* (1918) 13 Cr. App. R. 134 who starved their child to death. Nevertheless I am bound to wonder whether there is strictly any difference in the application of the principle. They know they can save her. They appreciate she will die if not separated from her twin. Is there any defence to a charge of cruelty under section 1 of the Children and Young Persons Act 1933 in the light of the clarification of the law given by *Reg v Sheppard* [1981] AC 395 which in turn throws doubt on the correctness of *Oakey v Jackson* [1914] 1 KB 216? Would it not be manslaughter if Jodie died though that neglect? I ask these insensitive questions not to heap blame on the parents. No prosecutor would dream of prosecuting. The sole purpose of the enquiry is to establish whether either or both parents and doctors have come under a legal duty to

Jodie, as I conclude they each have, to procure and to carry out the operation which will save her life. If so then performance of their duty to Jodie is irreconcilable with the performance of their duty to Mary. Certainly it seems to me that if this court were to give permission for the operation to take place, then a legal duty would be imposed on the doctors to treat their patient in her best interests, ie to operate upon her. Failure to do so is a breach of their duty. To omit to act when under a duty to do so may be a culpable omission. Death to Jodie is virtually certain to follow (barring some unforeseen intervention). Why is this not killing Jodie?

7. *Unlawfully*

7.1 The search for settled principle

The search for settled principle is difficult where the law is as uncertain in this area as Brooke LJ's masterly analysis has shown it to be. Doing the best I can, I have come to these conclusions.

7.2 Necessity

Necessity in the *Dudley and Stephens* sense arises where A kills B to save his own life. The threat to A's life is posed by the circumstances, rather than an act of threat by B on A in conventional self-defence terms.

7.3 Duress

Similar considerations apply to duress. There is, of course, a difference between them but as Lord Hailsham of St. Marylebone LC said in *Reg v Howe* [1987] 1 AC 417, 427:

> This, however, is, in my view a distinction without a relevant difference, since on this view duress is only that species of the genus of necessity which is caused by wrongful threat. I cannot see that there is any way in which a person of ordinary fortitude can be excused from one type of pressure on his will rather than the other.

7.4 The policy of the law

The policy of the law is to prevent A being judge in his own cause of the value of his life over B's life or his loved one C's life, and then being executioner as well. The policy of the law was expressed in similar terms in *Hale's Pleas of the Crown* (1736), Vol. 1, p51, and *Blackstone, Commentaries on the Laws of England* (1857 Ed.) Vol. 4, p28. Blackstone wrote that a man under duress 'ought rather to die himself than escape by the murder of an innocent'. The sanctity of life and the inherent equality of all life prevails. Several passages in *Howe* show this. Lord Hailsham said:

> This brings me back to the question of principle. I begin by affirming that, while there can never be a direct correspondence between law and morality, an attempt to divorce the two entirely is and has always proved to be, doomed to failure, and in the present case, the overriding objects of the criminal law must be to protect innocent lives and to set a standard of conduct which ordinary men and women are expected to observe if they are to avoid criminal responsibility: p428E.
>
> Other considerations necessarily arise where the choice is between the threat of death or *a fortiori* of serious injury and deliberately taking an innocent life. In such a case a reasonable man might reflect that one innocent human life is at least as valuable as his own or that of his loved one. In such a case a man cannot claim he is choosing the lesser of two evils. Instead he is embracing the cognate but morally disreputable principle that the end justifies the means: p433C.
>
> It may well be thought that the loss of a clear right to a defence justifying or excusing the deliberate taking of an innocent life in order to emphasise to all the sanctity of a human life is not an excessive price to pay in the light of these mechanisms: p433F.

Lord MacKay of Clashfern was equally emphatic:

> It seems to me plain that the reason that it was for so long stated by writers of authority that the defence of duress was not available in a charge of murder was because of the supreme importance that the law afforded to the protection of human life and that it seemed repugnant that the law should recognise in any individual in any circumstances, however extreme, the right to choose that one innocent person should be killed rather than another. In my opinion, that is the question which we still must face. Is it right that the law should confer this right in any circumstances, however extreme? p456E.

The question posed by Lord MacKay is the crucial question to resolve in this case. To arrive at the right answer, it is in my view necessary to state two important features of this case.

7.5 A legal duty?

The first important feature is that the doctors cannot be denied a right of choice if they are under a duty to choose. They are under a duty to Mary not to operate because it will kill Mary, but they are under a duty to Jodie to operate because not to do so will kill her. It is important to stress that it makes no difference whether the killing is by act or by omission. That is a distinction without a difference: see Lord Lowry in *Bland* at p877. There are similar opinions in the other speeches. Lord Browne-Wilkinson said at p885G:

> Finally, the conclusion I have reached will appear to some to be

> almost irrational. How can it be lawful to allow a patient to die slowly, though painlessly, over a period of weeks from lack of food but unlawful to produce his immediate death by lethal injection, thereby saving his family from yet another ordeal to add to the tragedy that has already struck them? I find it difficult to find a moral answer to that question. But it is undoubtedly the law . . .

Lord Mustill said at p887C:

> The acute unease which I feel by adopting this way (drawing a crucial distinction between acts and omissions) through the legal and ethical maze is I believe due in an important part to the sensation that however much the terminologies may differ the ethical status of the two courses of action is for all relevant purposes indistinguishable.

The Archbishop would agree. He tells us that:

> To aim at ending an innocent person's life is just as wrong when one does it by omission as when one does it by a positive act.

7.6 The effect of a conflict of duty

What then is the position where there is a conflict of duty? In *Pleas of the Crown* (1803) Vol. 1, Chap. 5, para 7, East explained that 'justification is founded upon some positive duty: excuse is due to human infirmity'. Much later, Wilson J, speaking only for herself, gave a similar explanation in *Perka v The Queen* 13 DLR (4th) 1, 36:

> . . . The ethical considerations of the 'charitable and the good' must be kept analytically distinct from duties imposed by law. Accordingly, where necessity is invoked as a justification for violation of the law, the justification must, in my view, be restricted to situations where the accused's act constitutes the discharge of a duty recognised by law. The justification is not, however, established simply by showing a conflict of legal duties. The rule of proportionality is central to the evaluation of a justification premised on two conflicting duties since the defence rests on the rightfulness of the accused's choice of one over the other.

So far I agree. But she goes on to say:

> As the facts before the court in the present case do not involve a conflict of legal duties it is unnecessary to discuss in detail how a court should go about assessing the relative extent of two evils. Suffice it to say that any such assessment must respect the notion of right upon which justification is based. The assessment cannot entail a mere utilitarian calculation of, for example, lives saved and deaths avoided in the aggregate but must somehow attempt to come to grips with the nature of the rights and duties being assessed. This would seem to be consistent with Lord Coleridge's conclusion that

> necessity can provide no justification for the taking of a life, such act representing the most extreme form of rights violation. As discussed above, if any defence for such a homicidal act is to succeed, it would have to be framed as an excuse grounded on self-preservation. It could not possibly be declared by the court to be rightful.

She is adhering to the sanctity of life principle. What are the doctors to do if the law imposes upon them a duty which they cannot perform without being in breach of Mary's right to life if at the same time the respecting of her right puts them in breach of the equally serious duty of respecting Jodie's right to life? A resort to a sanctity of life argument does not enable both rights to receive the equal protection the doctrine is supposed to provide each of them equally. In those circumstances it seems to me that the law must allow an escape through choosing the lesser of the two evils. The law cannot say, 'heads I win, tails you lose'. Faced as they are with an apparently irreconcilable conflict, the doctors should be in no different position from that in which the court itself was placed in the performance of its duty to give paramount consideration to the welfare of each child. The doctors must be given the same freedom of choice as the court has given itself and the doctors must make that choice along the same lines as the court has done, giving the sanctity of life principle its place in the balancing exercise that has to be undertaken. The respect the law must have for the right to life of each must go in the scales and weigh equally but other factors have to go in the scales as well. For the same reasons that led to my concluding that consent should be given to operate so the conclusion has to be that the carrying out of the operation will be justified as the lesser evil and no unlawful act would be committed.

I should emphasise that the doctors do not cease to owe Mary a duty of care, they must continue to furnish such treatment and nursing care as may be appropriate to ensure that she suffers the least pain and distress and retains the greatest dignity until her life comes to an end.

7.7 Offending the sanctity of life principle

The second reason why the right of choice should be given to the doctors is that the proposed operation would not in any event offend the sanctity of life principle. That principle may be expressed in different ways but they all amount to the same thing. Some might say that it demands that each life is to be protected from *unjust attack*. Some might say as the joint statement by the Anglican and Roman Catholic bishops did in the aftermath of the *Bland* judgment that because human life is a gift from God to be preserved and cherished, the deliberate taking of human life is prohibited *except in self-defence or the legitimate defence of others*. The Archbishop defines it in terms that human life is sacred, that is inviolable, so that one should never aim to cause an *innocent* person's death by act or omission. I have added the emphases. The reality here – harsh as it is to state it, and unnatural as it is that it should be happening – is that Mary is killing Jodie. That is the effect of the incontrovertible medical evidence and it is common ground in the case. Mary uses Jodie's heart and lungs to receive and use Jodie's oxygenated blood. This will cause Jodie's heart to fail and cause Jodie's death as surely as a slow drip of poison. How can it be just that Jodie should be required to tolerate that state of affairs? One does not need to label Mary with the American terminology which would paint her to be 'an unjust aggressor', which I feel is wholly inappropriate language for the sad and helpless position in which Mary finds herself. I have no difficulty in agreeing that this unique happening cannot be said to be unlawful. But it does not have to be unlawful. The six year boy indiscriminately shooting all and sundry in the school playground is not acting unlawfully for he is too young for his acts to be so classified. But is he 'innocent' within the moral meaning of that word as used by the Archbishop? I am not qualified to answer that moral question because, despite an assertion – or was it an aspersion? – by a member of the Bar in a letter to *The Times* that we, the judges, are proclaiming some moral superiority in this case, I for my part would defer any opinion as to a child's innocence to the Archbishop for that is his territory. If I had to hazard a guess, I would venture the tentative view that the child is not morally innocent. What I am, however, competent to say is that *in law* killing that six year old boy in self-defence of others would be fully justified and the killing would not be unlawful. I can see no difference in essence between that resort to legitimate self-defence and the doctors coming to Jodie's defence and removing the threat of fatal harm to her presented by Mary's draining her life-blood. The availability of such a plea of quasi self-defence, modified to meet the quite exceptional circumstances nature has inflicted on the twins, makes intervention by the doctors lawful.

8. Conclusion

For these reasons, very shortly expressed, I conclude that the operation which I would permit can be lawfully carried out.

V Enter the Human Rights Act 1998

The Act will be in force in ten days' time. It is idle to pretend it should not apply. If the doctors are to operate they are in any event likely to operate after 2nd October. It will then be unlawful for the hospital as a public authority, as it will be unlawful for the court, to act in a way which is incompatible with a Convention right. Article 2(1) provides in the first sentence that everyone's right to life shall be protected by law. As applied to the State, this essentially requires there to be adequate laws against murder and so forth. If so construed there are adequate laws binding on the hospital to afford protection to patients. On that basis the hospital's resort to the court is an adequate and equal safeguard for Mary and Jodie. If, on the other hand, the right to life is more literally construed, the protection has to be offered equally to both children and where there is a conflict there is the same impossibility of performance which has dominated the whole of this judgment. I cannot believe that the court in Strasbourg would reach any other conclusion for solving that dilemma than we have done. Mr Anderson QC in his powerful written submissions argues that the negative obligation to refrain from the intentional deprivation of life in effect trumps the positive obligation to take steps to protect the enjoyment of the right to life. In my judgment Mr Owen QC was right to point out that that is not the view the Commission took when deciding the abortion case, *Paton v United Kingdom* (1980) 3 EHRR 408 where, in para. 23, the Commission construed Article 2 to be subject to an implied limitation which would justify the balancing act we have undertaken.

For reasons more fully expressed by my Lords, with which I agree, I find nothing in the forthcoming Human Rights Act which calls for a different answer to the problem to the one I have already given.

VI Conclusion

In my judgment the appeal must be dismissed. Lest it be thought that this decision could become authority for wider propositions, such as that a doctor, once he has determined that a patient cannot survive, can kill the patient, it is important to restate the unique circumstances for which this case is authority. They are that it must be impossible to preserve the life of X without bringing about the death of Y, that Y by his or her very continued existence will inevitably bring about the death of X within a short period of time, and that X is capable of living an independent life but Y is incapable under any circumstances (including all forms of medical intervention) of viable independent existence. As I said at the beginning of this judgment, this is a very unique case.

LORD JUSTICE BROOKE:

Introduction

If this appeal had been concerned only with difficult issues of family law, I would have been content if the judgment of Ward LJ, with which I agree, had been issued as a single judgment of the court. Although my heart goes out to the parents of Jodie and Mary in the cruel dilemma in which they find themselves, Parliament has directed us to consider the interests of the children to be paramount. The devout wishes of the children's parents must form an important factor in the balancing equation, but I am completely satisfied, for the reasons given by Ward LJ, that if what is now proposed is a lawful operation, the best interests of Jodie compel us to authorise that operation. It would give her a very good prospect of living a happy, fulfilled life, and provided that the operation is lawful we should not allow Jodie's interests to be overridden by Mary's interests where those interests are in conflict. I also entirely agree, for the reasons he gives, with Ward LJ's analysis of the situation from Mary's standpoint, and with the criticisms he makes of the judge's conclusions in this respect.

We have been told by an independent paediatric surgeon from the Great Ormond Street Hospital that surgery would probably be a low risk procedure for Jodie. He would expect her to have normal bowel control, although he cannot be absolutely certain about this. She voids normally, and he hopes that this will continue. She will need further operations to provide a functioning vagina, but in his experience the great majority of children achieve a functioning vagina after reconstruction. It seems that her gait will be normal, or near normal, although he cannot exclude the possibility of surgery should a curvature of the spine develop. Some of the media comment about this case has focussed on the extreme possibilities of untoward outcomes in relation to all these matters, in contrast to what we have been told is the likely outcome, not only by the Manchester team but also by the independent expert from Great Ormond Street, for whose assistance we are very grateful.

There is one aspect of the facts which I would mention in addition to the very full summary provided by Ward LJ. He has mentioned the pressures on Jodie's heart if the present situation continues for any significant length of time. The consultant paediatrician from Manchester mentioned two other threats which Mary posed to Jodie. The first was that persistent hypoxia in Mary might lead to the release of cytokines which would be capable of crossing over to Jodie's circulation. Such cytokines are known to be damaging to the brain and might lead to white matter damage, which in turn might lead to the development of irreversible cerebral palsy. Persistent hypoxia in Mary might also lead to the generation of thromboplastins which would enter Jodie's circulation and cause an abnormality in coagulation, causing a prolongation in clotting time and a tendency to bleed. In evidence, this witness added that chronic hypoxia over many days and weeks would promote cell destruction in Mary, and there was a possibility that it would have a similar effect on Jodie. The dangers posed to Jodie by Mary's continued attachment to her cannot simply be limited to the serious dangers posed to Jodie's heart.

Although I am in full agreement with Ward LJ on the family law issues in this appeal, I have been constrained to prepare a judgment of my own because of the exceptionally difficult issues of criminal law which this appeal has raised. In this judgment I am happy to adopt the description of the facts of this case which Ward LJ has set out. In order to understand more fully the issues we have to decide, I have also found it valuable to consider in some detail the effect of the medical and other literature which has been put before the court.

The medical literature

The birth of conjoined twins is a comparatively rare event. In 1975 one expert suggested that they constituted 1 in 50,000 live births. There has been a more recent estimate of 1 in 100,000. In 1986 another expert estimated that on the continent of Africa 1 in 14,000 births were of conjoined twins. 40–60% of these twins were stillborn, and a further 35% survived for only one day after birth.

Conjoined twins are always the product of a single fertilised egg, and they always have the same chromosomal composition and sex. It is believed that they result from an incomplete division of the inner cell mass about 15–16 days after the egg is fertilised, and about seven days after what is called monozygotic twinning is said to occur. The exact reason for the complex fusion which may result from such late cleavage is still unknown, and it takes a wide range of different forms. The incomplete division of the embryo appears to be associated with a process which inhibits the complete differentiation of the various organ systems. Conjoined twins with fused organs therefore usually enjoy incomplete development. This may be manifested for instance, in conjoined hearts or livers, or conjoined gastro-intestinal and genito-urinary tracts.

There are a few centres of medical and surgical excellence in different parts of the world which specialise in the care and, on very rare occasions, the separation of conjoined twins. The Great Ormond Street Children's Hospital in London has now established itself as one such centre. The Children's Hospital of Philadelphia is another, and we have been greatly assisted by being afforded the opportunity to read two papers written by Professor James O'Neill, formerly of the Department of Surgery at that hospital. The first, entitled '*Surgical Experience with Thirteen Conjoined Twins*', was a paper he presented to a specialist gathering in San Francisco in 1988. The other is his chapter on Conjoined Twins in the second volume of his textbook '*Pediatric Surgery*' (5th Edition), which was published much more recently. We also obtained much assistance from a 1989 article entitled '*Twenty Three Year Follow-up of Separated Ischiopagus Tetrapus Conjoined Twins*', by Dr Hoyle and Dr Thomas of the School of Medicine in the University of North Carolina. This article summarises the outcome of the 33 reported attempts at surgical separation of the type of conjoined twins with which we are concerned in this case. While the authors were engaged in preparing this summary, they conducted a survey of more than 600 publications in the medical literature concerned with the topic of conjoined twins.

Doctors give the name 'ischiopagus conjoined twins' to twins of this type. The Greek derivation of the first part of this word means 'pelvis', and the second part of the word means 'fixed'. In 1988 Professor O'Neill believed that ischiopagus twins constituted about 6% of the total number of conjoined twins. They are joined, as their name suggests, at the pelvis, and they often possess shared genito-urinary structures, recta and livers. They may possess a ruptured omphalocele – a hernia of abdominal organs through the umbilicus (navel) – and they usually have either three or four lower extremities. They can therefore be categorised as ischiopagus tetrapus (four legs), like the twins in this case, or ischiopagus tripus (three legs). Bipus (two legs) twins also feature in the literature. There may be substantial differences in the way in which the bones and organs of the bodies of ischiopagus conjoined twins develop in the womb.

Ward LJ has described the anatomical structures of these two children, and I need not repeat what he has said. One feature of these structures is that this is not one of those cases in which there would have to be any organ transplantation from Mary to Jodie as a part of any surgical separation. Apart from the organs they share (which would have to be divided) and their divided organs (which would have to be united) they each have a complete set of separate organs, although in Mary's case some of them (and in particular her heart, lungs and brain) are severely underdeveloped.

Because they may develop differently, there can be no single solution to the legal issues that arise from any proposal to separate twins joined at the pelvis, let alone all conjoined twins. About 75% of all conjoined twins are joined at the thorax or the navel. These very often have conjoined hearts, and surgical separation is regarded as likely to be hopeless in the vast majority of such cases. The next main category (pygopagus: 18%) are joined at the rear, at sacrum level, and a tiny minority (craniopagus: 1.5%) are joined at the head. There are also (heteropagus) children born with parasitic attachments that are attached as duplicates to any part of their bodies, or even within their bodies. We are not of course concerned in this case with any of these other types of conjointure, which form 94% of the total.

The general scene has been well described by Sally Sheldon and Stephen Wilkinson, of the law and philosophy departments of Keele University, in their recent article '*Conjoined Twins: the Legality and Ethics of Sacrifice*' (1997) 2 Med LR 149 at p 150:

> At one end of the spectrum is the case of two fully grown, fully equipped bodies with a minor connection which is easy to remove, leaving two complete individuals who could survive into old age. At the other end is one complete body with a small number of extra parts which could be removed to leave just one complete individual. Between these two extremes are a range of gradations including two fairly complete bodies which are so heavily fused that they cannot be separated; two bodies which can be separated but at a substantial risk; and two which can be separated with the inevitable consequence that one of them will die.

We are concerned with the last of these three situations. The authors of the article are correct to add, and we cannot stress this point too strongly, that each situation will raise its own unique problems.

Although the Roman writer Pliny referred to a pair of conjoined twins nearly 2,000 years ago, and although the Maids of Biddenden, who were born in England in 1100 and survived into adult life, joined laterally from hips to shoulders, gained a reputation which has lasted to the present day, conjoined twins were not mentioned in a significant medical treatise until 1678, and the earliest recorded successful surgical separation was performed in 1689. It is a measure of the extreme rarity of the operation (at any rate until very recent times) that Professor O'Neill has said that only about 100 successful separations (featuring the survival of one or both twins) were reported in medical literature between 1689 and 1988. In the latest edition of his text book on paediatric surgery he raised that figure to 150, and in 1997 another review (conducted by N C Freeman and others) updated Dr Hoyle's figures and concluded that there were now 210 reports of surgical separation operations for conjoined twins reported in world medical literature.

Conjoined twins obtained international notoriety (and a name now universally used) in the nineteenth century when Eng and Chang Bunker, born in Siam in 1811, toured the world with P T Barnum's circus, living fertile and successful lives until their deaths, within three hours of each other, at the age of 63. Notwithstanding the obvious happiness of these two men, conjoined twins were described as 'double-headed monsters' in medical literature well into the twentieth century. Very few of them, if born alive, survived for more than a few days, and a tiny handful grew up into adulthood. Separation was hardly ever attempted before about 1955.

As I have said, we are concerned in this case only with the surgical separation of twins joined at the pelvis. Hoyle and Thomas reported 33 such operations in the medical literature up till 1989 and listed them conveniently in a table. The later operations in this series, from about 1979 onwards, on the whole display more or less consistently successful outcomes, although the survivors were inevitably still very young when their article was written. On the other hand, of the 26 children involved in the 13 operations undertaken between 1955 and 1974 only 15 survived, and one of these died when only two years old.

More significantly for the purposes of the present case, in two of these early cases one of the twins is said to have been sacrificed. In one of these cases the sacrificed twin suffered from anencephaly (ie it lacked all or most of the cerebral hemispheres, but was capable of using its lungs). In the other case, the first in the series, the sacrificed twin was said to have been deformed and moribund. In that case the surviving twin was lost to follow-up at the age of ten, but at that time she was said to be doing quite well except for her short stature and abnormal gait due to the absence of a symphysis pubis.

We have also been shown a 1998 article, '*Urological problems in conjoined twins*', written by a senior registrar at Great Ormond Street Hospital in conjunction with others at that hospital. Between 1985 and 1995 seven sets of conjoined twins were surgically separated at Great Ormond

Street. Urological problems were encountered in three of these sets of twins, all of whom were joined at the pelvis. They were also all joined at the navel, and two of them were joined at the breast bone as well. Their separation operations took place at the ages of 8 months, 10 months and three years respectively. One of these children died three days after her operation, probably secondary to cardiac insufficiency, and another died a year after separation from aspiration of a foreign body.

The pre-operative and post-operative conditions of all these children were different, and because they were either bipus or tripus twins, all the survivors now possess an artificial limb. One of them, at 8 years old, was said to have urinary control, with normal renal function. Of the second set, one twin was having problems with his renal function and bladder at the time of his death. The other was having very considerable problems with renal function, had no urinary control, and at the age of 4 was awaiting stone removal and further genital reconstruction. Pre-operatively those twins had possessed medial kidneys fused on the midline and displayed very complex problems in the genital region. Both twins in the pair who both survived (until the age of ten at least) were experiencing continuing difficulties of a urological nature. One of them was still incontinent of urine despite an injection into the neck of his bladder, while the other was fitted with suprapubic catheterization to control his bladder emptying functions. Other centres were said to have reported greater success in achieving urinary continence in such children following their separation.

Another article, '*Experience with Uro-Genital Reconstruction of Ischiopagus Conjoined Twins*', discussed the comparable experience of the Philadelphia Children's Hospital between 1957 and 1993. Their 20 surgical separations included six pairs of twins joined at the pelvis. Ten of them survived – one of the two deaths resulted from a cause unconnected with the surgery – but many of them experienced continuing urinary problems, or were awaiting further surgical intervention. The authors concluded that with careful observation and judicious intervention it was possible to maintain normal kidney function, provide bladder continence, and make normal sexual activity and fertility achievable goals, so that the individuals concerned might have satisfying well-adjusted lives.

Although more than 200 surgical separations have now been carried out, neither counsel nor the members of the court were able to discover any reported judgment of any court in any jurisdiction that has addressed the issues that are at the centre of the present appeal. It appears that in the United States of America proposals to separate conjoined twins may now be referred to hospitals' ethics committees, and not to a court, no doubt because of features of United States law that are different from English law.

We were shown, however, one article that contained a vivid description of a case in Philadelphia in 1977 in which a three-judge panel of a local Family Court retired for only three minutes before deciding that a surgical separation might go ahead. This was a case similar to ours, where the survival of both twins following separation was out of the question. It therefore raised the same ethical (and legal) question: could one twin be sacrificed so that the other might have a chance to live?

In that case the parents, who were deeply religious Jews, would not consent to the separation without rabbinical support. Many of the nurses at the hospital were Catholic, and they would not allow themselves to become involved in the proposed operation unless a priest assured them that it was morally acceptable to proceed. In the event, both the rabbinical scholars and the archdiocesan authorities gave favourable answers, for reasons to which I will refer later in this judgment. The court authorised the surgery, although sadly the surviving twin died three months later.

It is possible to draw two fairly clear conclusions from the medical literature before the court:

Although surgical separation of conjoined twins is still a very rare event, it is now being performed more frequently, and there is a substantial volume of writing available to assist medical and surgical teams, like the teams at Manchester, who are undertaking the operation for the first time;

The separation of twins joined at the pelvis is complicated by the incidence of shared (or divided) organs in the genito-urinary and gastro-intestinal regions. Such separations, however, are now being undertaken more frequently, with reasonably good results although there is always a need for careful post-operative monitoring and for further surgical intervention, if and when it is required.

The law of murder and the sanctity of human life

I turn from this general introduction to the issues of criminal law that have been raised by this appeal. As is apparent from the judgment of Ward LJ, issues of life and death are presented in the starkest terms. The operation to save Jodie would kill Mary. If the operation is not performed, both will probably live for a few more months and they will both then die. The question is: would such an operation be lawful?

To answer this question we must go first to the law of murder and the defences that are available to a charge of murder. An important part of this examination must be devoted to the defences that may be available to surgeons performing life-saving operations in accordance with good surgical practice. And because this operation, if permitted, is likely to take place after 2nd October 2000, when the Human Rights Act 1998 comes into force, we must also consider the effect of relevant provisions of the European Convention on Human Rights.

First, then, the law of murder. Murder is a common law offence. The classic definition of murder is contained in *Coke's Institutes* (*Co Inst* Pt III, Ch.7, p 47). It is in these terms:

> Murder is when a man of sound memory and of the age of discretion, unlawfully killeth within any county of the realm any reasonable creature *in rerum natura* under the king's peace, with malice aforethought, either expressed by the party or implied by law . . .

I omit the requirement, recently repealed by statute, that the death had to occur within a year and a day after the causative act or omission. The editors of the 2000 edition of *Archbold* have suitably modified this definition so that it conforms with the present state of the law:

> Subject to three exceptions, the crime of murder is committed where a person of sound mind and discretion unlawfully kills any reasonable creature in being and under the Queen's peace with intent to kill or cause grievous bodily harm . . .

None of the three exceptions are relevant in this case. They relate to the defences of provocation, diminished responsibility and action in pursuance of a suicide pact. These serve, if available, to reduce to manslaughter what would otherwise be an offence of murder.

The words or phrases in the *Archbold* definition which need to be explored in the present case are the words 'unlawfully', 'kills', 'any reasonable creature' and 'with intent to kill'. It is first, however, necessary to say a little about the value protected by the law of murder, namely the sanctity of human life.

The right to life is one of the most important values protected by our law. The penalty for murder is a mandatory sentence of life imprisonment. Before 1957 the mandatory penalty for murder was death. When I consider, in due course, the circumstances in which the law is willing to recognise that an act which would otherwise constitute a crime was not unlawful, it will be evident that our common law judges, right up to the present day, have shown very great reluctance to extend those defences when an innocent life has been taken deliberately. As the law now stands, for example, duress is available as a defence to a charge of aircraft hijacking but not to a charge of murder or attempted murder. In recent years Parliament has greatly increased the penalties for certain driving offences that result in death. In exercising their sentencing discretion in cases of involuntary manslaughter, where death arises by accident from a quite trivial act of unlawful violence, the judges have always laid stress on the fact that a life has been needlessly lost. Successive Governments, and Parliaments, have set their face against euthanasia. I cannot better what Sir Thomas Bingham MR said about the sanctity of human life in his judgment in *Airedale NHS Trust v Bland* [1993] AC 789, 808, in the passage quoted by Robert Walker LJ in his judgment.

We received a written submission from the Archbishop of Westminster which began along these lines:

> The arguments presented in this submission stem from the belief that God has given to humankind the gift of life, and as such it is to be revered and cherished. Christian belief about the special nature

> and value of human life lie at the root of the western humanist tradition which continues to influence the values held by many in our society and historically underpins our legal system.

The first of the five 'overarching moral considerations' which governed the Archbishop's submission was in these terms:

> Human life is sacred, that is inviolable, so that one should never aim to cause an innocent person's death by act or omission.

As the Archbishop observed, the same sentiment is expressed (in secular terms) in Article 2 of the European Convention on Human Rights:

> Everyone's right to life shall be protected by law. No one shall be deprived of his life intentionally save in the execution of a sentence of a court following his conviction of a crime for which this penalty is provided by law.

The Archbishop told us that he was articulating principles of morality which the Catholic Church held in common with countless others who value the Judaeo-Christian tradition.

There can, of course, be no doubt that our common law judges were steeped in the Judaeo-Christian tradition and in the moral principles identified by the Archbishop when they were developing our criminal law over the centuries up to the time when Parliament took over the task. There can also be no doubt that it was these principles, shared as they were by the other founder members of the Council of Europe 50 years ago, which underlay the formulation of Article 2 of the European Convention on Human Rights. Although parts of our criminal law, as enacted by Parliament, reflect a shift away from some of the tenets of Judaeo-Christian philosophy (in particular, for example, a shift away from the Catholic Church's teaching on abortion) in favour of the views of the majority of the elected representatives of an increasingly secular (and increasingly multi-cultural) modern state, there is no evidence that this process is at work in that part of our law concerned with the protection of human life between the moment of birth and the moment of death.

The emphasis that English law places on the importance of the protection of human life is also reflected in the caselaw of the European Court of Human Rights in Strasbourg. In *McCann v United Kingdom* A324 (1995), 21 EHRR 97, the case concerned with the shooting of suspected IRA terrorists in Gibraltar, the court said at para 147:

> It must also be borne in mind that, as a provision which not only safeguards the right to life but sets out the circumstances when the deprivation of life may be justified, Article 2 ranks as one of the most fundamental provisions in the Convention. . . . Together with Article 3 ['No one shall be subjected to torture or to inhuman or degrading treatment or punishment'], it also enshrines one of the basic values of the democratic societies making up the Council of Europe . . .

It is against this background that I turn to the four words or phrases whose meaning has to be explored in this case: 'unlawfully', 'kills', 'any reasonable creature', 'with intent to kill'. I will consider first the words 'any reasonable creature'.

Is Mary a reasonable creature?

For the reasons given by Ward LJ and Robert Walker LJ, with which I agree, I am satisfied that Mary's life is a human life that falls to be protected by the law of murder. Although she has for all practical purposes a useless brain, a useless heart and useless lungs, she is alive, and it would in my judgment be an act of murder if someone deliberately acted so as to extinguish that life unless a justification or excuse could be shown which English law is willing to recognise.

In recent editions of *Archbold*, including the 2000 Edition, the editors have suggested that the word 'reasonable' in Coke's definition (which they wrongly ascribe to Lord Hale in para 19.1) related to the appearance rather than the mental capacity of the victim and was apt to exclude 'monstrous births'. Spurred on by this suggestion, and because the present case broke so much novel ground, we explored with counsel some of the thinking of seventeenth century English philosophers in an effort to ascertain what Coke may have meant when he used the expression 'any reasonable creature' as part of his definition. We had in mind their absorbing interest in the nature of 'strange and deformed births' and 'monstrous births' (see Thomas Hobbes, *Elements of Law*, II.10.8, and John Locke, *An Essay Concerning Human Understanding*, III.III.17, III.VI.15 and 26 and III.XI.20).

In *Attorney-General's Reference (No.3 of 1994)* [1998] AC 245, Lord Mustill referred at p 254F to another statement in *Coke's Institutes*, not mentioned in that passage in *Archbold*, where after referring to prenatal injuries which lead to the delivery of a dead child, Coke writes (*Co Inst* Pt III, Ch.7, p 50):

> if the childe be born alive, and dieth of the potion, battery, or other cause, this is murder; for in law it is accounted a reasonable creature, *in rerum natura*, when it is born alive.

In these circumstances I have no hesitation in accepting the submission by Miss Davies QC (whose assistance, as the friend of the court, was of the greatest value), which was in these terms:

> In '*The Sanctity of Life and the Criminal Law*' (1958), Professor Glanville Williams stated at p 31:
>
> There is, indeed some kind of legal argument that a 'monster' is not protected even under the existing law. This argument depends upon the very old legal writers, because the matter has not been considered in any modern work or in any court judgment.
>
> After discussing the meaning of the word 'monster' (which might originally have connoted animal paternity) he states at pp 33–34:

> Locked (Siamese) twins present a special case, though they are treated in *medical* works as a species of monster. Here the recent medical practice is to attempt a severance, notwithstanding the risks involved. Either the twins are successfully unlocked, or they die (emphasis added).

It is implicit in this analysis that the author is of the view that 'Siamese' twins are capable of being murdered and the amicus curiae supports this view.

> Advances in medical treatment of deformed neonates suggest that the criminal law's protection should be as wide as possible and a conclusion that a creature in being was not reasonable would be confined only to the most extreme cases, of which this is not an example. Whatever might have been thought of as 'monstrous' by Bracton, Coke, Blackstone, Locke and Hobbes, different considerations would clearly apply today. This proposition might be tested in this way: suppose an intruder broke into the hospital and stabbed twin M causing her death. Clearly it could not be said that his actions would be outside the ambit of the law of homicide.

Modern English statute law has mitigated the prospective burden that might otherwise fall on the parents of severely handicapped children and their families if they are willing to avail themselves of its protection at any time up to the time the child (or children) is born. Section 1(1)(d) of the Abortion Act 1967, as substituted by Section 37(1) of the Human Fertilisation and Embryology Act 1990, provides:

> Subject to the provisions of this section, a person shall not be guilty of an offence under the law relating to abortion when a pregnancy is terminated by a registered medical practitioner if two registered medical practitioners are of the opinion, formed in good faith—
>
> . . .
>
> that there is a substantial risk that if the child were born it would suffer from such physical or mental abnormalities as to be severely handicapped.

Once a seriously handicapped child is born alive, the position changes, and it is as much entitled to the protection of the criminal law as any other human being. The governing principle is sometimes described as the universality of rights. In the Canadian case of *Perka v The Queen* 13 DLR (4th) 1 Wilson J said at p 31 that the principle of the universality of rights demands that all individuals whose actions are subjected to legal evaluation must be considered equal in standing.

It follows that unless there is some special exception to which we can have recourse, in the eyes of the law Mary's right to life must be accorded equal status with her sister Jodie's right to life. In this context it is wholly illegitimate to introduce considerations that relate to the quality, or the potential quality of, each sister's life.

The meaning of the word 'kills'

I turn now to the word 'kills' in the definition of murder. In the Tony Bland case (*Airedale NHS Trust v Bland* [1993] AC 789) the House of Lords was much exercised with the question whether the cessation of medical treatment and care to a patient who had been in a persistent vegetative state for three years constituted an intentional killing of that patient for the purposes of the law of murder. Lord Goff identified what he described as a crucial distinction in these terms at p 865:

> I must however stress, at this point, that the law draws a crucial distinction between cases in which a doctor decides not to provide, or to continue to provide, for his patient treatment or care which could or might prolong his life, and those in which he decides, for example by administering a lethal drug, actively to bring his patient's life to an end. As I have already indicated, the former may be lawful, either because the doctor is giving effect to his patient's wishes by withholding the treatment or care or even in certain circumstances in which (on principles which I shall describe) the patient is incapacitated from stating whether or not he gives his consent. But it is not lawful for a doctor to administer a drug to his patient to bring about his death, even though that course is prompted by a humanitarian desire to end his suffering, however great that suffering may be: see *Reg v Cox* (unreported), 18 September 1992. So to act is to cross the Rubicon which runs between on the one hand the care of the living patient and on the other hand euthanasia – actively causing his death to avoid or to end his suffering. Euthanasia is not lawful at common law.

In the Tony Bland case the House of Lords was satisfied that the cessation of life-prolonging treatment or care could not be categorised as a positive act for the purposes of the law of murder, and since on the facts of that case the doctors owed no duty to the patient to prolong his life (since that course, the House of Lords held, would not be in their patient's best interests), they could not be found guilty of a culpable omission to act, either.

It was this distinction between acts and omissions which the judge had in mind when he held that it would be lawful to perform the proposed operation. He explained his thinking in the long passage which Ward LJ has recited fully in his judgment. He believed, in short, that the proposed operation was not unlawful because it did not represented a positive act but merely the withdrawal of Mary's blood supply.

On the hearing of the appeal only Mr Whitfield QC sought to persuade us to uphold the judge's approach. I am satisfied that the judge's approach was wrong. The proposed operation would involve a number of invasions of Mary's body, in the process of identifying which organ belonged to which child, before the positive step was taken of clamping the aorta and bringing about Mary's death. These acts would bear no resemblance to the discontinuance of artificial feeding sanctioned by the

House of Lords in the Tony Bland case. They would be positive acts, and they would directly cause Mary's death.

The intention to kill

Next, the words 'intent to kill'. There is a technical difficulty about one aspect of the meaning of 'intention' in this context. It seems to me that the best way to describe it is to start with an extract from the Law Commission's 1993 report on *Offences Against the Person and General Principles*, Law Com. No 218 at pp 8–10:

> 7.1 Clause 1(a) of the Criminal Law Bill [at p 90 of the report] provides for the purposes of the offences in Part I of the Bill that
>
> a person acts . . . 'intentionally' with respect to a result when –
>
> it is his purpose to cause it; or
>
> although it is not his purpose to cause that result, he knows that it would occur in the ordinary course of events if he were to succeed in his purpose of causing some other result.
>
> . . .
>
> 7.4 In all but the most unusual cases, courts and juries will only be concerned with the basic rule in clause 1(a)(i) of the Criminal Law Bill: that a person acts intentionally with respect to a result when it is his purpose to cause that result.
>
> 7.5 The concept of purpose is ideally suited to express the idea of intention in the criminal law, because that law is concerned with results that the defendant causes by his own actions. These results are intentional, or intentionally caused, on his part, when he has sought to bring them about, by making it the purpose of his acts that they should occur . . .
>
> 7.6 . . . [I]n almost all cases when they are dealing with a case of intention, courts will not need to look further than paragraph (i) of clause 1(a). Paragraph (ii) is however aimed at one particular type of case that, it is generally agreed, needs to be treated as a case of 'intention' in law, but which is not covered by paragraph (i) because the actor does not act in order to cause, or with the purpose of causing, the result in question. . . .
>
> 7.7 The point was formulated by Lord Hailsham of St Marylebone in *R v Hyam* [1975] AC 55, 74. A person must be treated as intending 'the means as well as the end and the inseparable consequences of the end as well as the means'. If he acts in order to achieve a particular purpose, knowing that that cannot be done without causing another result, he must be held to intend to cause that other result. The other result may be a *pre-condition*; as where D, in order to injure P, throws a brick through a window behind which he knows P to be standing; or it may be a necessary *concomitant* of the first result; as where . . . D blows up an aeroplane in flight in order

> to recover on the insurance covering the cargo, knowing that the crew will inevitably be killed. D intends to break the window and he intends the crew to be killed.
>
> 7.8 There is, of course, no absolute certainty in human affairs. D's purpose *might* be achieved without causing the further result; P might fling up the window while the brick is in flight; the crew *might* make a miraculous escape by parachute. These, however, are only remote possibilities, as D (if he contemplates them at all) must know. The further result will occur, and D knows that it will occur, 'in the ordinary course of events'. This expression was used in Clause 18 of the [Law Commission's 1989 *Draft Criminal Code Bill*] to express the near-inevitability, as appreciated by the actor, of the further result.

In paragraph 7.2 of its report the Law Commission touched on some of the problems that existed in 1993 in this corner of the law. These problems were vividly described by Lord Steyn in his speech in the recent case of *R v Woollin* [1999] 1 AC 82 at pp 90E–93F, with which the other members of the House of Lords agreed. Apart from mentioning at p 91A the 'state of disarray' into which the House of Lords had plunged the law of murder in the case of *R v Hyam* [1975] AC 55, it is not necessary to go into any further detail about these problems. Suffice it to say that Lord Steyn restated the law along the lines suggested by the Law Commission six years earlier. The effect of his speech at p 96B–H is that in this rare type of case a judge should direct the jury in accordance with the following principles:

> Where the charge is murder and in the rare cases where the simple direction is not enough, the jury should be directed that they are not entitled to find the necessary intention, unless they feel sure that death or serious bodily harm was a virtual certainty (barring some unforeseen intervention) as a result of the defendant's actions and that the defendant appreciated that such was the case.
>
> Where a man realises that it is for all practical purposes inevitable that his actions will result in death or serious harm, the inference may be irresistible that he intended that result, however little he may have desired or wished it to happen.

Now that the House of Lords has set out the law authoritatively in these terms, an English court would inevitably find that the surgeons intended to kill Mary, however little they desired that end, because her death would be the virtually certain consequence of their acts, and they would realise that for all practical purposes her death would invariably follow the clamping of the common aorta.

The doctrine of double effect

We received interesting submissions from Mr Owen QC and Mr Whitfield in which they suggested that the doctrine of double effect would relieve the surgeons of criminal responsibility in these circumstances. This doctrine permits a doctor, in the best interests of his or her patient, to administer painkilling drugs in appropriate quantities for the purpose of relieving that patient's pain, even though the doctor knows that an incidental effect of the administration of these drugs will be to hasten the moment of death. In his speech in *Airedale NHS Trust v Bland*, Lord Goff, while describing the doctor's duty to act in the best interests of his patient, said at p 867C–E:

> It is this principle too which, in my opinion, underlies the established rule that a doctor may, when caring for a patient who is, for example, dying of cancer, lawfully administer painkilling drugs despite the fact that he knows that an incidental effect of that application will be to abbreviate the patient's life. Such a decision may properly be made as part of the care of the living patient, in his best interests; and, on this basis, the treatment will be lawful. Moreover, where the doctor's treatment of his patient is lawful, the patient's death will be regarded in law as exclusively caused by the injury or disease to which his condition is attributable.

In *Re J* [1991] Fam 33 Lord Donaldson MR identified the relevant principles in these terms at p 46C–D:

> What doctors and the court have to decide is whether, in the best interests of the child patient, a particular decision as to medical treatment should be taken which as a side effect will render death more or less likely. This is not a matter of semantics. It is fundamental. At the other end of the age spectrum, the use of drugs to reduce pain will often be fully justified, notwithstanding that this will hasten the moment of death. What can never be justified is the use of drugs or surgical procedures with the primary purpose of doing so.

Mr Whitfield relied on these dicta in support of his argument that what matters in this context is the surgeon's 'primary purpose' (a phrase used by Ognall J in summing up to the jury in *R v Cox* 12 BMLR 38), and that the fact that Mary's accelerated death would be a secondary effect of the surgeon's actions would not justify his conviction for murder. He also referred us to the passage at pp 179–180 in an essay by Professor Ashworth, *Criminal Liability in a Medical Context: the Treatment of Good Intentions*, which is published in *Harm and Culpability* (edited by AP Simester and ATH Smith, Oxford, 1996). Mr Whitfield summarised Professor Ashworth's argument as follows:

(i) the true meaning of intention is purpose;
(ii) one may purpose ends or means;
(iii) one does not purpose a side-effect;
(iv) therefore a consequence, even if prohibited, is not intended if it is a side effect.

Mr Owen QC, for his part, referred us to a passage in the 2nd Edition of

Medical Law, in which Professors Ian Kennedy and Grubb criticise the doctrine of double effect in so far as it is advanced as negating the necessary elements of intention or causation for the crime of murder, saying at p 1207:

> The more appropriate analysis is as follows: the doctor by his act intends (on any proper understanding of the term) the death of his patient and by his act causes (on any proper understanding of the term) the death of his patient, but the intention is not culpable and the cause is not blameworthy because the law permits the doctor to do the act in question.

It is not necessary for the purpose of this case to decide authoritatively whether this is the correct analysis, answering as it does the anxieties about the manipulation of the law of causation expressed by Lord Mustill in *Airedale NHS Trust v Bland* [1993] AC 789 at pp 895D–896B. There are certainly some powerful dicta in support of a proposition that if a surgeon administers proper surgical treatment in the best interests of his or her patient and with the consent (except in an emergency) of the patient or his or her surrogate, there can be no question of a finding that the surgeon has a guilty mind in the eyes of the criminal law: see in particular *Gillick v West Norfolk and Wisbech Area Health Authority* [1986] 1 AC 112, per Lord Fraser of Tullybelton at pp 174G–175A and Lord Scarman at p 190F–G. The reason why it is not necessary to decide these matters now is that the doctrine of double effect can have no possible application in this case, as the judge rightly observed, because by no stretch of the imagination could it be said that the surgeons would be acting in good faith in Mary's best interests when they prepared an operation which would benefit Jodie but kill Mary.

In this context it is relevant to quote the second and third overarching moral considerations identified by the Archbishop of Westminster in his written submission:

> (b) A person's bodily integrity should not be involved when the consequences of so doing are of no benefit to that person; this is most particularly the case if the consequences are foreseeably lethal.
>
> (c) Though the duty to preserve life is a serious duty, no such duty exists when the only available means of preserving life involves a grave injustice. In this case, if what is envisaged is the killing of, or a deliberate lethal assault on, one of the twins, Mary, in order to save the other, Jodie, there is a grave injustice involved. The good end would not justify the means. It would set a very dangerous precedent to enshrine in English case law that it was ever lawful to kill, or to commit a deliberate lethal assault on, an innocent person that good may come of it, even to preserve the life of another.

It is of interest to note in this context that when the Catholic nurses at the Children's Hospital in Philadelphia consulted their archdiocesan authorities in a similar case in 1977 (with the sole distinguishing factor that the parents of the 'sacrificed' child were willing to consent to the operation once they had received favourable rabbinical advice) the comfort they received was based on the double effect doctrine. It was argued that the tying of the carotid artery was done not to terminate the life of the sacrificed twin but to preserve the life of the other twin by protecting it from the poisons that would built up in the sacrificed twin's blood after its death: see *Siamese Twins: Killing One to Save the Other*, by George J Annas (Hastings Center Report, April 1987, 27 at p 28) and *The Ethics of Caring for Conjoined Twins*, by David C Thomasma and others (Hastings Center Report, July–August 1996, 4 at p 9). I do not consider that this method of applying the doctrine of double effect would have any prospect of acceptance in an English court.

It follows from this analysis that the proposed operation would involve the murder of Mary unless some way can be found of determining that what was being proposed would not be unlawful. This, the fourth and final part of the investigation, is far the most difficult. It is worth noting at the outset that Miss Davies supported the contentions of Mr Whitfield and Mr Owen to the effect that what was proposed would not be unlawful. They were opposed by Mr Taylor (for the parents) and Mr Harris QC (instructed by the Official Solicitor on behalf of Mary). At the close of his final submissions on behalf of Mary, however, Mr Harris, acting on the Official Solicitor's express instructions, took us back to the final page of his original written argument to this court, which had ended in these terms:

> It is difficult to accommodate the proposed treatment which, notwithstanding the above comments, it is recognised the Court may well consider to be desirable, within the framework of established legal principle. It might be argued that the basic principles of medical law cannot be applied to these facts. Existing case law is based upon the presumption of bodily integrity. John Locke's assertion that 'every Man has a Property in his own Person. This no Body has any Right to but himself' (*Two Treatises of Government*, 1690) which underpins much of the moral dialogue in this area is difficult to apply in the case of conjoined twins. Both twins' physical autonomy was compromised at birth with the result that they now have fundamentally inconsistent interests and needs. In these circumstances, the Court may wish to explore the possibility of a development of the law to enable a doctor lawfully to undertake surgery to preserve the life and achieve the independence of one twin even though that may result in the death of the other provided that:
>
> (i) The actions of the doctor viewed objectively constitute a proportionate and necessary response to the competing interests viewed as a whole; and
> (ii) Such actions are approved in advance by the Court.
>
> How any development of the law in this area might be reconciled

> with M's best interests and right to life is a question which it is easier to ask than answer.

This explicit encouragement by the Official Solicitor that we should explore the possibility of developing the law so as to enable such surgery to be undertaken lawfully was not at all unwelcome. We pointed out repeatedly to Mr Taylor and Mr Harris during the course of argument that if their contentions were correct, no separation surgery which would inevitably involve the sacrifice of one conjoined twin could ever lawfully take place, however ardently their parents wished one of their children to survive, and however severely compromised the condition of the other twin. It would also follow, if their arguments based on the effect of Article 2 of the European Convention on Human Rights (bolstered on this occasion by the written arguments of Mr David Anderson QC on behalf of the Pro-Life Alliance) are well-founded, that no separation surgery involving the sacrifice of a conjoined twin could take place in any of the member states of the Council of Europe. Mr Taylor and Mr Harris accepted, realistically, that this was indeed the effect of their submissions.

The doctrine of necessity

We received some interesting and powerful submissions about the doctrine of necessity, and the ways in which it might be called in aid to justify the operation proposed by the doctors. Although for many years cases involving pleas of necessity were notable for their absence from our caselaw, the doctrine has recently been given a new lease of life by Lord Goff of Chieveley, first in *In re F (Mental Patient: Sterilisation)* [1990] 2 AC 1, and more recently, in a speech with which the other members of the House of Lords agreed, in *R v Bournewood Community and Mental Health NHS Trust ex parte L* [1999] 1 AC 458.

This doctrine is so obscure, and it has featured so seldom in our caselaw in the criminal courts, that I must describe it in considerable detail, and identify the problems it throws up, before I go on to decide whether it is permissible to apply it to the facts of the present case.

In *In re F* Lord Goff said at p 74A–C in the context of the law of tort:

> That there exists in the common law a principle of necessity which may justify action which would otherwise be unlawful is not in doubt. But historically the principle has been seen to be restricted to two groups of cases, which have been called cases of public necessity and cases of private necessity. The former occurred when a man interfered with another man's property in the public interest – for example (in the days before we would dial 999 for the fire brigade) the destruction of another man's house to prevent the spread of catastrophic fire, as indeed occurred in the Great Fire of London in 1666. The latter cases occurred when a man interfered with another's property to save his own person or property from

> imminent danger – for example, when he entered upon his neighbour's land without his consent, in order to prevent the spread of fire onto his own land.

Lord Goff then went on to consider a third group of cases, also founded upon the principle of necessity, which were concerned with actions taken by someone as a matter of necessity to assist another person without his consent. We are not, however, concerned in the present case with this application of the doctrine, because the law confers on the parents of an infant child the authority to consent on her behalf, and because there is also the residual right of consent vested in the court.

In the *Bournewood* case, Lord Goff had recourse to this doctrine again when holding that doctors were entitled to rely on it as the basis for their authority to care for compliant incapacitated patients of adult years and treat them without their consent. At the end of his speech in that case, he mentioned some old cases which authorised (in so far as this was shown to be necessary) the detention of those who were a danger, or potential danger, to themselves or others. He added (at p 490C–D):

> I must confess that I was unaware of these authorities though, now that they have been drawn to my attention, I am not surprised that they should exist. The concept of necessity has its role to play in all branches of our law of obligations – in contract (see the cases on agency of necessity), in tort (see *In re F (Mental Patient: Sterilisation)* [1990] 2 AC 1), and in restitution (see the sections on necessity in the standard books on the subject) and in our criminal law. It is therefore a concept of great importance. It is perhaps surprising, however, that the significant role it has to play in the law of torts has come to be recognised at so late a stage in the development of our law.

Public and private necessity in the criminal law

In the present case we are concerned with what is said by some of those who appeared before us to be a case of private necessity in the eyes of the criminal law. Bracton, writing in the thirteenth century *On the Laws and Customs of England* (Selden Society Edition 1968, at Vol 2, 340–341) identified this type of necessity, in the context of the law of homicide, in these terms:

> Of necessity, and here we must distinguish whether the necessity was avoidable or not; if avoidable and he could escape without slaying, he will then be guilty of homicide; if unavoidable, since he kills without premeditated hatred but with sorrow of heart, in order to save himself and his family, since he could not otherwise escape [danger], he is not liable to the penalty for murder.

Five hundred years later the same concept of necessity, which still forms part of our law today, was expressed as follows by Lord Hale in his *Pleas of the Crown* Vol I, 51:

> . . . but if he cannot otherwise save his own life, the law permits him in his own defence to kill the assailant; for by the violence of the assault, and the offence committed upon him by the assailant himself, the law of nature and necessity hath made him his own protector *cum debito moderamine inculpatae tutelae* as shall be further shewed, when we come to the chapter of homicide *se defendendo*.

Later in the same volume Hale identifies two kinds of necessity which justify homicide: necessity which is of a private nature, and the necessity which relates to the public justice and safety (with which we are not here concerned). He added (at p 478):

> The former is that necessity which obligeth a man to his own defence and safeguard, and this takes in these enquiries:
>
> (1) What may be done for the safeguard of a man's life . . .
>
> As touching the first of these, viz. homicide in defence of a man's own life, which is usually called *se defendendo*
>
> . . .
>
> Homicide *se defendendo* is the killing of another person in the necessary defence of himself against him that assaults him.

Blackstone, in Volume IV of his *Commentaries on the Laws of England*, had recourse to the law of nature as the source of a person's authority to use proportionate force in self-defence, saying at p 30:

> In such a case [viz. a violent assault] he is permitted to kill the assailant, for there the law of nature, and self-defence its primary canon, have made him his own protector.

During the seventeenth century there were suggestions that the right of self-preservation extended beyond the right to use appropriate force in self-defence. Thus in his *Elements of the Common Laws of England* (1630) Lord Bacon wrote:

> Necessity is of three sorts – necessity of conservation of life, necessity of obedience, and necessity of the act of God or of a stranger. First, of causation of life; if a man steal viands to satisfy his present hunger this is no felony nor larceny. So if divers be in danger of drowning by the casting away of some boat or barge, and one of them get to some plank, or on the boat's side to keep himself above water, and another to save his life thrust him from it, whereby he is drowned, this is neither *se defendendo* nor by misadventure, but justifiable.

Similar sentiments appear in Thomas Hobbes's *Leviathan* at p 157:

> If a man by the terror of present death, be compelled to doe a fact against the Law, he is totally Excused, because no Law can oblige a man to abandon his own preservation. And supposing such a Law were obligatory; yet a man would reason thus, if I doe it not, I die

> presently; if I doe it, I die afterwards; therefore by doing it, there is time of life gained; Nature therefore compels him to the fact.
>
> When a man is destitute of food, or other thing necessary for his life, and cannot preserve himselfe any other way, but by some fact against the law; as if in a great famine he take the food by force, or stealth, which he cannot obtaine for mony nor charity; or in defence of his life, snatch away another mans Sword, he is totally Excused, for the reason next before alledged.

Both these extensions of the doctrine of necessity have been authoritatively disapproved as propositions of English law. For the disapproval of the idea that in order to save himself a man is entitled to deprive another of the place of safety he has already secured for himself, see *R v Dudley and Stephens* (1884) 14 QBD 273 per Lord Coleridge CJ at pp 285–6 ('if Lord Bacon meant to lay down the broad proposition that a man may save his life by killing, if necessary, an innocent and unoffending neighbour, it certainly is not law at the present day') and *R v Howe* [1987] 1 AC 417 per Lord Hailsham of St Marylebone LC at p 431E, to similar effect. For the equally strong disapproval of the idea that if a starving beggar takes the law into his own hands and steals food he is not guilty of theft, see *Southwark LBC v Williams* [1971] 1 Ch 734 per Lord Denning MR at pp 743H–D and Edmund-Davies LJ at pp 745E–746C. See also on these topics Hale's *Pleas of the Crown* Volume I, 51 and 54 and Blackstone's *Commentaries*, Volume IV, pp 30 and 31–32.

Nineteenth century attempts at codifying the doctrine of necessity

Nineteenth century Governments appointed commissions from time to time with the laudable purpose of consolidating or codifying our criminal law. Inevitably, these commissions addressed issues related to the existence and scope of the doctrine of necessity. It is not at all surprising that they found them difficult to handle.

For example in 1839 the Commissioners on Criminal Law wrote (see *Fourth Report of HM Commissioners on Criminal Law*, Parliamentary Papers XIX) at p xxi:

> There are necessarily some occasions, which, upon general principles of criminal jurisprudence, and independently of the motive or state of mind of the party who causes the death control the generality of the abstract rules founded on mere intention, and which tend to justify or excuse, or to extenuate the act of homicide. Of the former class, that is, of those which serve to justify or excuse the act, the most present are those founded on a principle of necessity where the act is essential to the defence of a man's person or property. The rule as to the latter class, ie where the occasion saves to extenuate criminality is also founded on a mixed principle of necessity and policy.

In 1846, in the *Second Report of HM Commissioners for Revising and*

Consolidating the Criminal Law ((1846) Parliamentary Papers), the Commissioners dealt with self-defence as a potential justification for homicide in Article 16 of their Draft Code, but they decided on policy grounds not to provide a more general defence of necessity. In a footnote to Article 19 they wrote:

> The treatises generally contain a provision justificatory of the homicide of an unoffending party committed in order to save the life of the accused, or rather because the accused reasonably thought that the homicide was indispensable for preserving his own life. We propose to omit any justification rule for these occasions. Independently of the question which has been much discussed by ancient and modern jurists of the right *in foro conscientiae* of a person depriving another of life under such circumstances, we conceive that there would be less inconvenience in leaving persons to the mercy of the Crown who have thus acted under circumstances of sudden and extreme peril, than in holding out protection to the general disposition of all persons to overrate the danger to which they are exposed, and to place too low an estimate on the life of another when placed in the balance against prospect of additional safety to themselves. The Indian Law Commissioners . . . express themselves on this subject in the following terms: 'There are, as we have said, cases in which it would be useless cruelty to punish acts done under fear of death, or even of evils less than death. But it appears to us impossible to precisely define these cases; we have, therefore, left them to the Government, which, in the exercise of its clemency, will doubtless be guided in a great measure by the advice of the Court'.

When the Criminal Code Bill Commissioners took up the challenge in 1879 they were equally baffled by definitional difficulties, although they were readier to leave open the possibility of establishing a lawful justification based on necessity. They said:

> Ingenious men may suggest cases which though possible have not come under practical decision in courts of justice. . . . We are certainly not prepared to suggest that necessity should in every case be a justification. We are equally unprepared to suggest that necessity should in no case be a defence; we judge it better to leave such questions to be dealt with when, if ever, they arise in practice by applying the principles of law to the circumstances of the particular case.

Sir James Stephen was one of these Commissioners, and his initial views on this elusive topic are to be seen in the second volume of his *History of the Criminal Law of England*, at pp 108–110. He began his discussion of the subject at p 108:

> Compulsion by necessity is one of the curiosities of law, and so far as I am aware is a subject on which the law of England is so vague that, if cases raising the question should ever occur the judges

> would practically be able to lay down any rule which they considered expedient. The old instance of the two drowning men on a plank large enough to support one only, and that of shipwrecked persons in a boat unable to carry them all, are the standing illustrations of this principle. It is enough to say that should such a case arise, it is impossible to suppose that the survivors would be subjected to legal punishment.

After referring to the dilemmas created by cases where a boat will sink unless it is relieved of one or more of its passengers, he found some comfort in the judgment of Lord Mansfield in *R v Stratton* (21 St Tr 1224), from which he derived the proposition that it was just possible to imagine cases in which the expediency of breaking the law was so overwhelming that people might be justified in breaking it. He went on to say (at pp 109–110):

> . . . [B]ut these cases cannot be defined beforehand, and must be adjudicated upon by a jury afterwards, the jury not being themselves under the pressure of the motives which influenced the alleged offenders. I see no good in trying to make the law more definite than this, and there would I think be danger in attempting to do so. There is no fear that people will be too ready to obey the ordinary law. There is great fear that they would be too ready to avail themselves of exceptions which they might suppose to apply to their circumstances.

He ended by saying that these considerations applied also to the case of a choice of evils. One of the two examples he gave in this context was of a ship so situated that the only possible way of avoiding a collision with another ship (which would probably sink one of both of them) involved running down a small boat.

The Queen against Dudley and Stephens

This was the legal background against which the case of *R v Dudley and Stephens* (1884) 14 QBD 273 was set. In AWB Simpson's *Cannibalism and the Common Law* (1984) the author described how the three survivors of the yacht Mignonette were landed from a German sailing barge at Falmouth in September 1884, a year after Stephen's *History of the Criminal Law of England* was published. On the day they landed all three of them described the circumstances in which the fourth member of the crew, the ship's boy had been killed and eaten on their twentieth day of survival on the open sea without water or food (apart from two tins of turnips). As part of the historical background of the case Mr Simpson describes in Chapter 5 of his book (gruesomely entitled 'The Customs of the Sea') a large number of similar instances in the nineteenth century of shipwrecks leading to cannibalism, some of which were described by Samuel Plimsoll in 1875 in a parliamentary debate.

The law report shows how a jury at the Devon and Cornwall Assizes had found the facts of the case in a special verdict. The case was then ordered to be argued in London before a court of five judges. In giving the judgment of the court Lord Coleridge CJ considered earlier writings (including the judgment of a circuit court in Pennsylvania in *United States v Holmes* 26 Fed Cas 360 (1842)) about necessity being a possible justification for homicide before he concluded that the facts stated in the jury's verdict provided no legal justification for the homicide in the present case. His reasoning can be seen in two passages towards the end of his judgment (at pp 286–288):

> Now it is admitted that the deliberate killing of this unoffending and unresisting boy was clearly murder, unless the killing can be justified by some well-recognised excuse admitted by the law. It is further admitted that there was in this case no such excuse, unless the killing was justified by what has been called 'necessity'. But the temptation to the act which existed here was not what the law has ever called necessity. Nor is this to be regretted. Though law and morality are not the same, and many things may be immoral which are not necessarily illegal, yet the absolute divorce of law from morality would be of fatal consequence; and such divorce would follow if the temptation to murder in this case were to be held by law an absolute defence of it . . .
>
> It is not needful to point out the awful danger of admitting the principle which has been contended for. Who is to be the judge of this sort of necessity? By what measure is the comparative value of lives to be measured? Is it to be strength, or intellect or what? It is plain that the principle leaves to him who is to profit by it to determine the necessity which will justify him in deliberately taking another's life to save his own. In this case the weakest, the youngest, the most unresisting, was chosen. Was it more necessary to kill him than one of the grown men? The answer must be 'No' –
>
> 'So spake the Fiend, and with necessity,
> The tyrant's plea, excused his devilish deeds.'
>
> It is not suggested that in this particular case the deeds were 'devilish', but it is quite plain that such a principle once admitted might be made the legal cloak for unbridled passion and atrocious crime. There is no safe path for judges to tread but to ascertain the law to the best of their ability and to declare it according to their judgment: and if in any case the law appears to be too severe on individuals, to leave it to the Sovereign to exercise that prerogative of mercy which the Constitution has entrusted to the hands fittest to dispense it.

Sir James Stephen was not a member of the court, although he authorised Lord Coleridge to say that the language he had used about necessity in his *History of the Criminal Law of England* was not meant to cover a case like this. Three years later, in his *Digest of the Criminal Law* (1887),

Stephen attempted a description of the doctrine of necessity in these terms at pp 9–11:

> An act which would otherwise be a crime may in some cases be excused if the person accused can show that it was done only in order to avoid consequences which could not otherwise be avoided, and which, if they had followed, would have inflicted upon him or upon others whom he was bound to protect inevitable and irreparable evil, that no more was done than was reasonably necessary for that purpose, and that the evil inflicted by it was not disproportionate to the evil avoided.
>
> The extent of this principle is unascertained. It does not extend to the case of shipwrecked sailors who kill a boy, one of their number, in order to eat his body.

It is not necessary for present purposes to refer to the detail of the long footnote in which he commented, not always favourably, on the judgment of the court in *R. v Dudley and Stephens.*

That case has sometimes been taken as authority for the proposition that necessity can never under any circumstances provide a legal justification for murder. While it is true that a passage in the speech of Lord Hailsham in *R v Howe* [1987] 1 AC 417 at p 429C–D might be interpreted to this effect, in my judgment neither that passage nor a similar passage in Lord Mackay of Clashfern's speech at p 453 C–D displays any evidence that they had in mind a situation in which a court was invited to sanction a defence (or justification) of necessity on facts comparable to those with which we are confronted in the present case. I accept Miss Davies's submission that *R v Dudley and Stephens*, endorsed though it was by the House of Lords in *R v Howe*, is not conclusive of the matter.

Necessity: the recent studies by the Law Commission

We have also been shown how the Law Commission tackled this troublesome doctrine in the criminal law between 1974 and 1993. In 1974 a very experienced Working Party was brave enough to recommend codified proposals for a general defence of necessity (Law Commission Working Paper No 55 pp 38–9). Three years later the Commission itself retreated so far from this proposition that it recommended that there should be no general defence of necessity in any new Code, and that if any such general defence existed at common law it should be abolished (Law Com No 83 (1977), p 54). It felt that it would be much better if Parliament continued to create special defences of necessity, when appropriate. Because euthanasia was so controversial, and because the Criminal Law Revision Committee was engaged in work on offences against the person, the Commission thought it better to leave to that committee any questions relating to the provision of a defence in that area of the law.

This retreat, influenced by the responses it had received on consultation, particularly from practitioners (see pp 24–25), evoked a storm of protest from academic commentators (see, for instance, the articles entitled '*Necessity*' by Glanville Williams [1978] Crim LR 12 and '*Proposals and Counter Proposals on the Defence of Necessity*' by PHJ Huxley [1978] Crim LR 141, and the powerful criticism (to the effect that the proposals represented 'the apotheosis of absurdity') by Sir Rupert Cross in a Canadian university law journal cited by Professor Glanville Williams in a footnote on page 202 of the Second Edition of his *Textbook on Criminal Law* (1983).

Professor Williams returned to the topic of necessity in Chapter 26 of that book. He observed at p 602 that the main difficulty felt by the Law Commission appeared to have been in respect of certain 'human rights', whereas the doctrine of necessity was an expression of the philosophy of utilitarianism. He referred, however, to a suggestion by an American writer, Paul Robinson, to the effect that the recognition of important values did not entirely exclude a defence of necessity. In the determination of cases where those values did not appear, their existence could not affect the outcome, and even where they did appear, they could be given special weight in estimating the balance of interests.

In his powerful Section 26.3 ('Necessity as a reason for killing') Professor Williams addressed the issues with which we are confronted in this case. He began his treatment of the subject by saying that many people believed in the sanctity of life, and consequently believed that killing was absolutely wrong. It was for this reason, he said, that the defence of necessity, if allowed at all, was given very narrow scope in this area. He distinguished private defence from necessity (although the two overlapped) on the grounds that (unlike necessity) private defence involved no balancing of values, while on the other hand private defence operated only against aggressors (who, with rare exceptions, were wrongdoers) whereas the persons against whom action was taken by necessity might not be aggressors or wrongdoers. In this context, he mentioned *R v Bourne* [1939] 1 KB 687 (where Macnaghten J had suggested in his summing up that there might be a duty in certain circumstances to abort an unborn child to save the life of the mother), as an example of the defence of necessity, even though it was a case not of homicide but of feticide.

Professor Williams came to the heart of the matter at p 604:

> *Might this defence apply where a parent has killed his grossly malformed infant?*
>
> Doubtless not. It may of course be argued that the value of such an infant's life, even to himself, is minimal or negative, and that if parents are obliged to rear him they may be disabled from having another and normal child. But it is not a case for applying the doctrine of necessity as usually understood. The child when born, unlike the fetus, is regarded as having absolute rights. Besides, there is no emergency.
>
> The usual view is that necessity is no defence to a charge of murder.

> This, if accepted, is a non-utilitarian doctrine; but in the case of a serious emergency is it wholly acceptable? If you are roped to a climber who has fallen, and neither of you can rectify the situation, it may not be very glorious on your part to cut the rope, but is it wrong? Is it not socially desirable that one life, at least, should be saved? Again, if you are flying an aircraft and the engine dies on you, it would not be wrong, but would be praiseworthy, to choose to come down in a street (where you can see you will kill or injure a few pedestrians), rather than in a crowded sports stadium.
>
> *But in the case of cutting the rope you are only freeing yourself from someone who is, however involuntarily, dragging you to your death. And in the case of the aircraft you do not want to kill anyone; you simply minimise the slaughter that you are bound to do one way or the other. The question is whether you could deliberately kill someone for calculating reasons.*
>
> We do regard the right to life as almost a supreme value, and it is very unlikely that anyone would be held to be justified in killing for any purpose except the saving of other life, or perhaps the saving of great pain or distress. Our revulsion against a deliberate killing is so strong that we are loth to consider utilitarian reasons for it.
>
> But a compelling case of justification of this kind is the action of a ship's captain in a wreck. He can determine who are to enter the first lifeboat; he can forbid overcrowding; and it makes no difference that those who are not allowed to enter the lifeboat will inevitably perish with the ship. The captain, in choosing who are to live, is not guilty of killing those who remain. He would not be guilty even though he kept some of the passengers back from the boat at revolver-point, and he would not be guilty even though he had to fire the revolver.

Between 1985 and 1993 the Law Commission returned to the topic of necessity on three separate occasions. In 1985 it published a report prepared by three professors of criminal law, who included Professor John Smith, on *The Codification of the Criminal Law* (1985 Law Com No. 143). Their recommendation (at para 13.26) was in these terms:

> Necessity is not a topic to which we can apply our normal procedure of restatement, for which the present law does not provide suitable material. We cannot ourselves conduct a law reform exercise and propose a general defence of necessity of our own devising. And, as indicated above, we cannot support the Law Commission's totally negative proposals. In these circumstances our main proposal is that necessity should remain a matter of common law. That is, to the extent that the defence is now recognised, it should be unaffected by the Criminal Code Act; and (probably more important, because the present status of the defence is so limited and uncertain) the courts should retain the power that they now have to develop or clarify the defence. Necessity, that is to say, would fall

> within the general saving for common law defences declared by clause 49. Our only specific necessity provision is clause 46, which admits a defence in circumstances so closely analogous to those of the duress defence that it might indeed be 'the apotheosis of absurdity' to admit the one and to deny the other. The kind of situation catered for by clause 46 has, indeed, sometimes been called 'duress of circumstances'.

In 1989 the Law Commission itself accepted this recommendation without taking the matter any further (see *A Criminal Code for England and Wales* (1989 Law Com. No 177, Volume I, Draft Criminal Code Bill clauses 4(4) and 45(c), and the commentary in Volume II, para 12.41(ii)). Following further consultation the Law Commission maintained this approach in its report on *Offences Against the Person and General Principles* (1993 Law Com No 218). After discussing the defence of duress by threats, the Commission said at para 35.5 of this report:

> By contrast with the defences of duress just discussed, there appear to be some cases, more properly called cases of 'necessity', where the actor does not rely on any allegation that circumstances placed an irresistible pressure on him. Rather, he claims that his conduct, although falling within the definition of an offence, was not harmful because it was, in the circumstances, justified. Such claims, unlike those recognised by the duress defences, do seem to require a comparison between the harm that otherwise unlawful conduct has caused and the harm that that conduct has avoided; because if the latter harm was not regarded as the greater the law could not even consider accepting that the conduct was justified. Nor, fairly clearly, does the defence depend on any claim that the actor's will was 'overborne': on the contrary, the decision to do what, but for the exceptional circumstances, would be a criminal act may be the result of careful judgment, as in the case of the kind of professional decision referred to in the next paragraph.

The Commission went on to mention Lord Goff's speech in *In re F (Mental Patient: Sterilisation* [1990] 2 AC 1) where he had relied on the doctrine of agency of necessity as providing a legal justification for the sterilisation of a mentally incapable adult without her consent. It added (para 35.6):

> A perhaps more straightforward example is that given by Lord Goff in his judgment in the same case: 'a man who seizes another and forcibly drags him from the path of an incoming vehicle, thereby saving him from injury or even death, commits no wrong'. In such cases there is no question of the defence depending on the actor's resistance being overcome, in the sense discussed in paragraph 29.11 above; rather, the courts decide that in all the circumstances the actor's, freely adopted, conduct was justified.

It will be seen that the Law Commission envisaged that in exceptional circumstances a comparison might have to be made, perhaps as a matter of careful professional judgment and not in the throes of a life or death emergency, between the harm that otherwise unlawful conduct has caused (or would cause, if performed) and the harm that that conduct has avoided (or would avoid).

Necessity: modern academic writers

Those who prepared that report would have been familiar with a modern update of the 'two men on a plank' dilemma (which dates back to Cicero, *de Officiis*) and the 'two mountaineers on a rope' dilemma which was mentioned by Professor John Smith in his 1989 Hamlyn Lectures (published under the title '*Justification and Excuse on the Criminal Law*'). At the coroner's inquest conducted in October 1987 into the Zeebrugge disaster, an army corporal gave evidence that he and dozens of other people were near the foot of a rope ladder. They were all in the water and in danger of drowning. Their route to safety, however, was blocked for at least ten minutes by a young man who was petrified by cold or fear (or both) and was unable to move up or down. Eventually the corporal gave instructions that the man should be pushed off the ladder, and he was never seen again. The corporal and many others were then able to climb up the ladder to safety.

In his third lecture, '*Necessity and Duress*', Professor Smith evinced the belief at pp 77–78 that if such a case ever did come to court it would not be too difficult for a judge to distinguish *R v Dudley and Stephens*. He gave two reasons for this belief. The first was that there was no question of choosing who had to die (the problem which Lord Coleridge had found unanswerable in *R v Dudley and Stephens* at p 287) because the unfortunate young man on the ladder had chosen himself by his immobility there. The second was that unlike the ship's boy on the Mignonette, the young man, although in no way at fault, was preventing others from going where they had a right, and a most urgent need, to go, and was thereby unwittingly imperilling their lives.

I would add that the same considerations would apply if a pilotless aircraft, out of control and running out of fuel, was heading for a densely populated town. Those inside the aircraft were in any event 'destined to die'. There would be no question of human choice in selecting the candidates for death, and if their inevitable deaths were accelerated by the plane being brought down on waste ground, the lives of countless other innocent people in the town they were approaching would be saved.

It was an argument along these lines that led the rabbinical scholars involved in the 1977 case of conjoined twins to advise the worried parents that the sacrifice of one of their children in order to save the other could be morally justified. George J Annas, '*Siamese Twins: Killing One to Save the Other*' (Hastings Center Report, April 1987 at p 27, described how they:

> . . . reportedly relied primarily on two analogies. In the first, two men jump from a burning aeroplane. The parachute of the second man does not open, and as he falls past the first man, he grabs his legs. If the parachute cannot support them both, is the first man morally justified in kicking the second man away to save himself? Yes, said the rabbis, since the man whose parachute didn't open was 'designated for death'.
>
> The second analogy involves a caravan surrounded by bandits. The bandits demand a particular member of the caravan be turned over for execution; the rest will go free. Assuming that the named individual has been 'designated for death', the rabbis concluded it was acceptable to surrender him to save everyone else. Accordingly, they concluded that if a twin A was 'designated for death' and could not survive in any event, but twin B could, surgery that would kill twin A to help improve the chance of twin B was acceptable.

There is, however, no indication in the submission we received from the Archbishop of Westminster that such a solution was acceptable as part of the philosophy he espoused. The judge's dilemma in a case where he or she is confronted by a choice between conflicting philosophies was thoughtfully discussed by Simon Gardner in his article '*Necessity's Newest Inventions*' (*Oxford Journal of Legal Studies* Vol II, 125–135). He explored the possibility of rights-based justifications based on a principle that otherwise unlawful actions might be justified where the infraction was calculated to vindicate a right superior to the interest protected by the rule, but he was perplexed by the idea that judges in a democracy could make their own decisions as to what was right and what was wrong in the face of established law prohibiting the conduct in question. The whole article requires careful study, but its author concluded that in jurisdictions where rights were guaranteed, the judicial vindication of a guaranteed right would be seen as protecting democracy rather than contravening it. This consideration does not, however, assist us in a case where there are conflicting rights of apparently equal status and conflicting philosophies as to the priority, if any, to be given to either.

Before I leave the treatment afforded to the topic of necessity by modern academic writers of great distinction (there is a valuable contemporary summary of the issues in the Ninth Edition of Smith and Hogan's *Criminal Law* (1999) at pp 245–252), I must mention the section entitled '*Justifications, Necessity and the Choice of Evils*' in the Third Edition (1999) of '*Principles of Criminal Law*' by Professor Andrew Ashworth. After referring to the facts of the Zeebrugge incident he said at pp 153–4:

> No English court has had to consider this situation, and it is clear that only the strongest prohibition on the taking of an innocent life would prevent a finding of justification here: in an urgent situation involving a decision between n lives and n + 1 lives, is there not a strong social interest in preserving the greater number of lives?

> Any residual principle of this kind must be carefully circumscribed; it involves the sanctity of life, and therefore the highest value with which the criminal law is concerned. Although there is a provision in the Model Penal Code allowing for a defence of 'lesser evil', it fails to restrict the application of the defence to cases of imminent threat, opening up the danger of citizens trying to justify all manner of conduct by reference to overall good effects. The moral issues are acute: 'not just anything is permissible on the ground that it would yield a net saving of lives'. Closely connected with this is the moral problem of 'choosing one's victim', a problem which arises when, for example, a lifeboat is in danger of sinking, necessitating the throwing overboard of some passengers, or when two people have to kill and eat another if any of the three is to survive. To countenance a legal justification in such cases would be to regard the victim's rights as morally and politically less worthy than the rights of those protected by the action taken, which represents a clear violation of the principle of individual autonomy. Yet it is surely necessary to make some sacrifice, since the autonomy of everyone simply cannot be protected. A dire choice has to be made, and it must be made on a principle of welfare or community that requires the minimisation of overall harm. A fair procedure for resolving the problem – perhaps the drawing of lots – must be found. But here, as with self-defence and the 'uplifted knife' cases, one should not obscure the clearer cases where there is no need to choose a victim: in the case of the young man on the rope-ladder, blocking the escape of several others, there was no doubt about the person who must be subjected to force, probably with fatal consequences.

Necessity: the work of Parliament

I turn now from twentieth century academic writing and the work of the Law Commission and its specialist working parties to consider the way in which Parliament and the courts have addressed these issues.

So far as I am aware, Parliament has never even debated these issues in a general sense, in spite of the recommendations of the Law Commission and the increasingly insistent pleas for Parliamentary assistance which have been made by senior judges in the context of the rapidly developing new defence of 'duress of circumstances'. Parliament has, however, to an increasing extent included 'necessity' defences or justifications in modern offence-creating statutes, and where such provisions are present the Parliamentary intention is clear. In 1974 the Law Commission's Working Party identified such provisions in the Infant Life Preservation Act 1929 s 1(1), the Education Act 1944 s 39(2)(a), the Fire Services Act 1947 s 30(1), the Road Traffic (Regulation) Act 1967 s 79, the Abortion Act 1967 s 1(1) and the Road Traffic Act 1972 s 36(3). The Criminal Damage Act 1971 s 5(2)(b) provides another example from that period, and this statutory process has continued up to the present day, although, as is common with piecemeal law reform, the defences are not always framed along the same lines.

The Abortion Act provides a particularly good example of this process at work, expanding and clarifying the law for the benefit of the courts and for everyone else who, for whatever reason, needs to have recourse to the law in this controversial area. Before its enactment Macnaghten J in the case of *R v Bourne* derived a 'necessity' defence out of the word 'unlawfully' in Section 58 of the Offences against the Person Act 1861 ('Any person who unlawfully uses an instrument with intent to procure a miscarriage shall be guilty of felony'). Macnaghten J said at p 691 that he thought that the word 'unlawfully' imported the meaning expressed by the proviso in Section 1(1) of the Infant Life Preservation Act 1929 ('Provided that no person shall be guilty of an offence under this section unless it is proved that the act which caused the death of the child was not done in good faith for the purpose only of preserving the life of the mother'). He went on to direct the jury at p 693:

> In such a case where a doctor anticipates, basing his opinion upon the experience of the profession, that the child cannot be delivered without the death of the mother, it is obvious that the sooner the operation is performed the better. The law does not require the doctor to wait until the unfortunate woman is in peril of immediate death. In such a case he is not only entitled, but it is his duty to perform the operation with a view to saving her life.

That, as I have observed earlier, was the common law defence of necessity at work when a judge was interpreting what he believed Parliament must have meant when it used the word 'unlawfully' in a codifying statute. Parliament's current intentions in this field are now clearly set out in the substituted Section 1(1) of the Abortion Act 1967. It would of course be very helpful, once Parliament has had the opportunity of considering the implications of the judgments in the present case, if it would provide similar assistance to the courts and to all other interested parties (and in particular parents and medical practitioners) as to what is legally permissible and what is not legally permissible in the context of separation surgery on conjoined twins. Parliament would of course now have to take account of the relevant provisions of the European Convention of Human Rights when formulating any new legislation.

Necessity: the courts and the defence of duress of circumstances

In addition to the major work that has been undertaken by Parliament in creating statutory excuses or justifications for what would otherwise be unlawful, the courts have also been busy in this field, at all events in those cases where a defendant maintains that he/she was irresistibly constrained by threats or external circumstances to do what he/she did.

So far as duress by threats is concerned, it was common ground between counsel that the solution to the present case is not to be found in the caselaw on that topic which Lord Hailsham has described as 'that species of the genus of necessity which is caused by wrongful threats' (see *R v Howe* [1987] 1 AC 417, 429C). After no fewer than three split 3–2 decisions the House of Lords and the Privy Council have now both ruled that 'duress by threats' is not available as a defence to murder (*Howe*) or attempted murder (*R v Gotts* [1992] 2 AC 412): see also, in this series *DPP for Northern Ireland v Lynch* [1975] AC 653 and *Abbott v The Queen* [1977] AC 755.

The work of academic writers and of the Law Commission has, however, led to one significant development in the common law. This lies in the newly identified defence of 'duress of circumstances'. The modern development of this defence began in the field of driving offences.

In *R v Kitson* [1955] 39 Cr App R 66, the defendant, who had had a lot to drink, went to sleep in the passenger seat of a car driven by his brother-in-law. When later charged with driving the car under the influence of drink, he said in his defence that when he woke up, he found that the driving seat was empty, and the car was moving down a hill with the hand brake off. He managed to steer the car into a grass verge at the bottom of the hill. He was convicted of driving a car under the influence of drink, and when the Court of Criminal Appeal dismissed his appeal on the basis that the ingredients of the offence were made out, and he had undoubtedly been driving the car within the meaning of the Act, nobody suggested that he was entitled to rely on a defence of necessity or duress of circumstances.

Thirty years later, this potential line of defence first saw the light of day in *R v Willer* (1986) 83 Cr App R 225. The defendant had been convicted of reckless driving (for which he was given an absolute discharge, although his licence was endorsed with ten penalty points) because he had been seen driving his car quite slowly on the pavement in front of a shopping precinct. He wished to defend the case on the basis that this had seemed to him to be the only way in which he could escape from a gang of 20–30 youths who had already banged on his car and threatened to kill him, and were now bent on doing him further violence. The assistant recorder, however, ruled that a defence of necessity was not available to him on those facts. On his appeal Watkins LJ said that the court doubted whether the defence of necessity was in point, but the court held that the jury ought to have been left to decide whether 'the appellant was wholly driven by force of circumstances into doing what he did, and did not drive the car otherwise than under that form of compulsion, ie under duress'.

A similar issue arose in *R v Conway* [1989] QB 290, another case of reckless driving. The defendant said that the reason why he had driven recklessly was that he was in fear for his life and that of his passenger. Woolf LJ said at pp 296–7 that the court found itself bound by the decision in *Willer* to rule that a defence of duress was available. He added that it was convenient to refer to this type of duress as 'duress of circumstances' (being the expression adopted by the Law Commission's

Criminal Code Working Party four years earlier: see 1985 Law Com No 143, para 13.26). He said that the defence would be available where the defendant was constrained by circumstances to drive as he did in order to avoid death or serious bodily harm to himself or some other person. He added that whether 'duress of circumstances' was called 'duress' or 'necessity' did not matter. What was important was that whatever it was called, it was subject to the same limitations as the 'do this or else' species of duress.

In *R v Martin* [1989] 1 All ER 652, Simon Brown J gave the judgment of the Court of Appeal (which included Lord Lane CJ) in a case where the defendant had wished to advance a defence to the effect that the only reason why he had driven while disqualified was that he had felt constrained to drive his stepson to work because his stepson had overslept. His case was that his wife (who had suicidal tendencies) had been threatening suicide unless he drove the boy to work, since she was so worried that her son might lose his job. Simon Brown J, relying on the earlier decisions in *Willer* and *Conway*, said that a defence was available to the defendant (however sceptically one might regard its prospects of success) and that he ought to have been allowed to place it before a jury. He added at pp 653g–654a:

> The principles may be summarised thus: first, English law does, in extreme circumstances, recognise a defence of necessity. Most commonly this defence arises as duress, that is pressure on the accused's will from the wrongful threats or violence of another. Equally however it can arise from other objective dangers threatening the accused or others. Arising thus it is conveniently called 'duress of circumstances'.
>
> Second, the defence is available only if, from an objective standpoint, the accused can be said to be acting reasonably and proportionately in order to avoid a threat of death or serious injury.
>
> Third, assuming the defence to be open to the accused on his account of the facts, the issue should be left to the jury, who should be directed to determine these two questions: first, was the accused, or may he have been, impelled to act as he did because as a result of what he reasonably believed to be the situation, he had good cause to fear that otherwise death or serious physical injury would result; second, if so, would a sober person of reasonable firmness, sharing the characteristics of the accused, have responded to that situation by acting as the accused acted? If the answer to both those questions was Yes, then the jury would acquit; the defence of necessity would have been established.

In the course of the last eleven years, the scope of this defence has been broadened. In *R v Pommell* [1995] 2 Cr App R 607 the Court of Appeal ruled that it was available to a defendant convicted of possessing a loaded sub-machine gun who had wished to advance a defence to the effect that on the previous evening he had taken it 'off a geezer who was going to do some damage with it'. Kennedy LJ, giving the judgment of the court, said at pp 613E–614D:

> The strength of the argument that a person ought to be permitted to breach the letter of the criminal law in order to prevent a greater evil befalling himself or others has long been recognised (see, for example, Stephen's *Digest of Criminal Law*), but it has, in English law, not given rise to a recognised general defence of necessity, and in relation to the charge of murder, the defence has been specifically held not to exist (see *Dudley and Stephens* (1884) 14 QBD 273). Even in relation to other offences, there are powerful arguments against recognising the general defence. As Dickson J said in the Supreme Court of Canada in *Perka v R* (1985) 13 DLR (4th) 1, at p 14:
>
>> '. . . no system of positive law can recognise any principle which would entitle a person to violate the law because on his view the law was conflicted with some higher social value'. The Criminal Code has specified a number of identifiable situations in which an actor is justified in committing what would otherwise be a criminal offence. To go beyond that and hold that ostensibly illegal acts can be validated on the basis of their expediency, would import an undue subjectivity into the criminal law. It would invite the courts to second-guess the Legislature and to assess the relative merits of social policies underlying criminal prohibitions.
>
> However, that does not really deal with the situation where someone commendably infringes a regulation in order to prevent another person from committing what everyone would accept as being a greater evil with a gun. In that situation it cannot be satisfactory to leave it to the prosecuting authority not to prosecute, or to individual courts to grant an absolute discharge. The authority may, as in the present case, prosecute because it is not satisfied that the defendant is telling the truth, and even if he is vindicated and given an absolute discharge, he is left with a criminal conviction which, for some purposes, would be recognised as such.

This reasoning is strikingly different from the reasoning in the context of a murder charge which led Lord Simon of Glaisdale (then in a minority) in *DPP for Northern Ireland v Lynch* [1975] AC 653 at p 687C–G and Lord Hailsham of St Marylebone in *R v Howe* [1987] 1 AC 417 at p 433C–G to hold that the availability of administrative as distinct from purely judicial remedies (the discretion not to prosecute, the Royal prerogative, the role of the Parole Board, etc) were strong enough techniques to 'mitigate the hardships which might otherwise occur in the most agonising cases' (see Lord Hailsham in *R v Howe* at p 433D) if duress was not available as a defence to murder.

In *R v Abdul-Hussain* (CAT 17th December 1998: see [1999] Crim LR 570) the Court of Appeal held that the defence of duress (whether by threats or from circumstances) was generally available in relation to all substantive crimes, except murder, attempted murder and some forms of treason. Rose LJ, speaking with the authority of the Vice-President of the Criminal Division of the Court of Appeal, said that this was now the fourth occasion in five years on which the court wished to emphasise the urgent need for legislation to define duress with precision.

In that case all the appellants except one (whose appeal was dismissed) had wished to put forward a defence to the effect that the reason why they had hijacked a Sudanese airbus on a flight from Khartoum to Amman and had forced it to fly to Stanstead Airport in England was that they were terrified that the Sudanese authorities might deport them to Iraq where they faced the prospects of imprisonment in conditions of extreme hardship, torture and summary execution.

Rose LJ said that the judgment of Simon Brown J in *Martin* afforded the clearest and most authoritative guide to the relevant principles in relation to both forms of duress. He also gave further guidance on the law as it now stands. In particular, he said that the imminent peril of death or serious injury to the defendant (or those for whom the defendant has responsibility) was an essential feature of both forms of duress, and that this peril must operate in the mind of the defendant at the time when he commits the otherwise criminal act (so as to overbear his will). The execution of the threat need not, however, be immediately in prospect. He added (see [1999] Crim LR 570) that:

> the period of time which elapsed between the inception of the peril and the defendant's act was a relevant but not determinative factor; [and] that all the circumstances of the peril, including the number, identity and status of those creating it, and the opportunities (if any) to avoid it were relevant . . . when assessing whether the defendant's mind was affected so as to overbear his will.

In his judgment Rose LJ described how in the course of that hijacking an air hostess was seized and threatened with a plastic knife, an imitation grenade was produced (accompanied by a threat to blow up the plane), a knife was held for a very long time to the captain's back, passengers believed to be security officials were tied up, and one of the defendants pretended to instruct the others to blow up the plane if there was any movement on board. The defendants had declined to release the women and children at Larnaca, in Cyprus, where the plane stopped to refuel. The atmosphere on board was said to have been very tense.

I mention these facts to show that the Court of Appeal is now willing to entertain the possibility of a defence of duress even in a case as extreme as this if it is arguable that 'the will of the accused has been overborne by threats of death or serious personal injury so that the commission of the alleged defence was no longer [his] voluntary act' (see *R v Hudson* [1971] 2 QB 202 per Lord Parker CJ at p 206E). The defence is available on the basis that if it is established, the relevant actors have in effect been compelled to act as they did by the pressure of the threats or other circumstances of imminent peril to which they were subject, and it was the impact of that pressure on their freedom to choose their course of action that suffices to excuse them from criminal liability.

I have described how in modern times Parliament has sometimes provided 'necessity' defences in statutes and how the courts in developing the defence of duress of circumstances have sometimes equated it with the defence of necessity. They do not, however, cover exactly the same ground. In cases of pure necessity the actor's mind is not irresistibly overborne by external pressures. The claim is that his or her conduct was not harmful because on a choice of two evils the choice of avoiding the greater harm was justified.

Necessity: a Canadian perspective

In his judgment in *R v Pommell* Kennedy LJ cited an extract from the judgment of Dickson J, with which three other members of the Canadian Supreme Court agreed, in *Perka v The Queen* 13 DLR (4th) 1. In that case a ship bound on a voyage between Columbia and Alaska was driven by mechanical breakdowns and deteriorating weather to seek refuge on the west coast of Vancouver Island. Canadian police officers boarded the ship and seized over 33 tons of cannabis *marijuana*, which would not have come within the jurisdiction of the Canadian courts but for the emergencies which forced the ship to seek shelter in Canadian waters.

It was not in issue in that case that necessity was a common law defence, since it was expressly preserved by section 7(3) of the Canadian Criminal Code. What was in issue was whether it was available to the defendants on the facts. Dickson J held that although the residual defence of necessity could not be conceptualised as a justification for wrong-doing, it might properly be identified as an excuse where someone does a wrongful act under pressure which, in the words of Aristotle's *Nichomachean Ethics*, 'overstrains human nature and which no one could withstand'. He was therefore concerned with that type of necessity which in modern English law would be characterised as 'duress of circumstances'.

In her judgment Wilson J cavilled at Dickson J's conclusion that the appropriate jurisdictional basis on which to premise the defence of necessity was exclusively that of excuse. She was firmly of the view that a door should be left open, in an appropriate case, for justification to be adopted as the jurisdictional basis of the defence. She said that an act might be said to be justified where an essential element of the offence was absent, whereas an act might be excused if all the elements of the offence were present but the jury was requested to exercise compassion for the accused's predicament in its evaluation of his claim that 'I could not help myself'. In making this distinction Wilson J drew on the recent writings of Professor GR Fletcher ('*The Individualisation of Excusing Conditions*' 47 SO Cal.L.R. 1264 at p 1269 (1974)). She referred to some

American cases as illustrations of situations where someone's criminally wrongful act was treated as 'normatively involuntary', and therefore blameless, in the particular circumstances in which he or she was situated.

She could see no reason why a court should not regard an act as justified on the grounds of necessity if it could say that the act was not only a necessary one but that it was also rightful rather than wrongful. She did not think that the fact that one act was done out of a sense of immediacy or urgency and another after some contemplation could serve to distinguish its quality in terms or right or wrong. Instead, she considered that any justification of a wrongful act must be premised on the need to fulfil a legal duty which was in conflict with the duty which the accused was charged with having breached. She gave two Canadian cases as examples. In *R v Walker* (1973) 48 CCC (2d) 126, it was held to be legitimate to break the law where it had been necessary to rescue someone to whom one owed a positive duty of rescue (because failure to act in such a situation might itself constitute a culpable act or omission: see *R v Instan* [1893] 1 QB 450). In *Morgentaler v The Queen* [1976] 1 SCR 616 Laskin CJC (taking forward the thinking of Macnaghten J in *R v Bourne*) perceived a doctor's defence to an abortion charge as his legal duty to treat the mother rather than his alleged ethical duty to perform as unauthorised abortion.

At p 36 Wilson J said:

> . . . [W]here necessity is involved as a justification for violation of the law, the justification must, in my view, be restricted to situations where the accused's act constitutes the discharge of a duty recognised by law. The justification is not, however, established simply by showing a conflict of legal duties. The rule of proportionality is central to the evaluation of a justification premised on two conflicting duties since the defence rests on the rightfulness of the accused's choice of one over the other.

She made it reasonably clear, however, that she could not conceive of any circumstances in which this application of the doctrine of necessity could be extended to provide justification of an act of homicide. Her recourse to the principle of the universality of rights showed that she envisaged that everyone was of equal standing in relation to their right to life. For this reason she went on to say at p 36:

> The assessment cannot entail a mere utilitarian calculation of, for example, lives saved and deaths avoided in the aggregate, but must somehow attempt to come to grips with the nature of the rights and duties being assessed. This would seem to be consistent with Lord Coleridge's conclusion that necessity can provide no justification for the taking of a life, such an act representing the most extreme form of rights violation. As discussed above, if any defence for such a homicidal act is to succeed, it would have to be framed as an

> excuse grounded on self-preservation. It could not possibly be declared by the court to be rightful.

I found this a valuable way of forcing us to think more clearly about the reasons why it is ever permissible to admit a defence drawn from what Lord Hailsham would describe as the genus of necessity as a means of establishing that a defendant is not in law guilty of a crime even though the requirements of *mens rea* (a guilty mind) and *actus reus* (a guilty act) appear to be satisfied. In the last resort, however, it does not provide the solutions we are seeking in the present case for three reasons. The first reason is that English criminal law does not make any clear-cut distinction between a justification and an excuse. As Professor John Smith said at p 12 of his first Hamlyn lecture in 1989,

> Whether the act is one which society wants to be done, or merely tolerates, is a question which is not easy to answer if society has not expressed its wishes in the form of legislation or judicial decision. Not unnaturally there is a disagreement between the theorists. So far as the successful defendant is concerned, it matters not in the least whether the court, or anyone else, says that he is justified or merely excused; he is simply found not guilty in either event.

Secondly, as he points out at p 18 of that lecture, the distinction between those who save others out of a legal duty and those who do the same act for reasons which cannot be so characterised is not always very easy to sustain. Thirdly, Wilson J made it clear that she did not regard the analysis as available when someone's right to life was in question.

The European Convention on Human Rights

I have already observed how in 1983 Professor Glanville Williams discussed the way in which the increasing emphasis on the importance of human rights might be difficult to reconcile with the doctrine of necessity, being as it is an expression of the philosophy of utilitarianism. The fundamental importance of the right to protection of life is so ingrained in the English common law that I do not consider that any different solution to the dilemma we face can be found in the language of the European Convention of Human Rights ('ECHR') on which we received helpful oral submissions from Mr Owen and Mr Taylor in addition to Mr Anderson's written submissions.

I can take the ECHR points quite shortly because I have read in draft the judgment of Robert Walker LJ on these matters, with which I agree. I do not consider that the *Woollin* extension of the meaning of the word 'intention' is appropriate when determining whether a doctor who performed a separation operation on conjoined twins in circumstances like these was intentionally killing the twin whose life was to be sacrificed. The doctor's purpose in performing the operation was to save life, even if the extinction of another life was a virtual certainty. Like Robert Walker LJ I do not consider that the adoption of an autonomous meaning of the word 'intentionally' in Article 2(1) of the Convention need have any effect on the interpretation of the concept of 'intention' in our national law, which has at long last been settled by the House of Lords in *Woollin*.

I should add that I was unattracted by Mr Owen's fall-back argument, to the effect that Article 2 contained an implied implication that the right it proclaims may be violated if it is in conflict with another person's Article 2 right. He based his argument on some words used by the European Commission on Human Rights in its decision in *Paton v United Kingdom* (App No 8416/78), 3 EHRR 408, 416, at para 23. The doctrine of inherent (or implied) limitation still appears to be in its infancy as a matter of Convention law (see *Theory and Practice of the European Convention on Human Rights*, Third Edition, by P van Dijk and GJH van Hoof at pp 763–5), and on the present state of Convention law I would be reluctant to hold, unless and until compelled to do so, that a right as fundamental as the right identified in Article 2 can be subject to an implied limitation which destroys its value.

Mr Anderson also relied, much less convincingly, on Articles 3 and 8 of the Convention. The medical evidence, which was not available to him, was to the effect that it is most unlikely that Mary can suffer pain, and I do not consider that her treatment during the course of the proposed operation (in which she will be under a general anaesthetic) could properly be described as inhuman or degrading within the meaning of Article 3. The facts of *Ireland v United Kingdom* A25 (1978), 2 EHRR 25, paras 96 and 167 and *D v United Kingdom* RSD 1997 – III 778, 24 EHRR 423, paras 51–53, are a very long way away from the present case. So far as Article 8 is concerned, once it is established on the welfare principle that Jodie's interests are to be preferred, then the reference to the protection of the rights and freedoms of others in Article 8(2) provides a justification for what would otherwise be a wrongful inference with Mary's Article 8(1) rights (which include a right not to be subjected to compulsory medical interference: see *Peters v Netherlands* 77A DR 75 (1994) at 79).

After this long analysis of the doctrine of necessity in our criminal law, I turn finally to the question whether it is, uniquely, available in the present case to provide a lawful justification for what would otherwise be an offence of murder.

Conclusion

I have considered very carefully the policy reasons for the decision in *R v Dudley and Stephens,* supported as it was by the House of Lords in *R v Howe*. These are, in short, that there were two insuperable objections to the proposition that necessity might be available as a defence for the Mignonette sailors. The first objection was evident in the court's questions: Who is to be the judge of this sort of necessity? By what measure is the comparative value of lives to be measured? The second objection was that to permit such a defence would mark an absolute divorce of law from morality.

In my judgment, neither of these objections are dispositive of the present case. Mary is, sadly, self-designated for a very early death. Nobody can extend her life beyond a very short span. Because her heart, brain and lungs are for all practical purposes useless, nobody would have even tried to extend her life artificially if she had not, fortuitously, been deriving oxygenated blood from her sister's bloodstream.

It is true that there are those who believe most sincerely – and the Archbishop of Westminster is among them – that it would be an immoral act to save Jodie, if by saving Jodie one must end Mary's life before its brief allotted span is complete. For those who share this philosophy, the law, recently approved by Parliament, which permits abortion at any time up to the time of birth if the conditions set out in Section 1(1)(d) of the Abortion Act 1967 (as substituted) are satisfied, is equally repugnant. But there are also those who believe with equal sincerity that it would be immoral not to assist Jodie if there is a good prospect that she might live a happy and fulfilled life if this operation is performed. The court is not equipped to choose between these competing philosophies. All that a court can say is that it is not at all obvious that this is the sort of clear-cut case, marking an absolute divorce from law and morality, which was of such concern to Lord Coleridge and his fellow judges.

There are sound reasons for holding that the existence of an emergency in the normal sense of the word is not an essential prerequisite for the application of the doctrine of necessity. The principle is one of necessity, not emergency: see Lord Goff (in *In re F* at p 75D), the Law Commission in its recent report (Law Com No 218, paras 35.5 to 35.6), and Wilson J in *Perka* (at p 33).

There are also sound reasons for holding that the threat which constitutes the harm to be avoided does not have to be equated with 'unjust aggression', as Professor Glanville Williams has made clear in Section 26.3 of the 1983 edition of his book. None of the formulations of the doctrine of necessity which I have noted in this judgment make any such requirement: in this respect it is different from the doctrine of private defence.

If a sacrificial separation operation on conjoined twins were to be permitted in circumstances like these, there need be no room for the concern felt by Sir James Stephen that people would be too ready to avail themselves of exceptions to the law which they might suppose to apply to their cases (at the risk of other people's lives). Such an operation is, and is always likely to be, an exceptionally rare event, and because the medical literature shows that it is an operation to be avoided at all costs in the neonatal stage, there will be in practically every case the opportunity for the doctors to place the relevant facts before a court for approval (or otherwise) before the operation is attempted.

According to Sir James Stephen, there are three necessary requirements for the application of the doctrine of necessity:

(i) the act is needed to avoid inevitable and irreparable evil;
(ii) no more should be done than is reasonably necessary for the purpose to be achieved;
(iii) the evil inflicted must not be disproportionate to the evil avoided.

Given that the principles of modern family law point irresistibly to the conclusion that the interests of Jodie must be preferred to the conflicting interests of Mary, I consider that all three of these requirements are satisfied in this case.

Finally, the doctrine of the sanctity of life respects the integrity of the human body. The proposed operation would give these children's bodies the integrity which nature denied them.

For these reasons I, too, would dismiss this appeal.

Lord Justice Robert Walker:

Conjoined twins

The tragic situation of Jodie and Mary is very rare indeed in medical terms, and it appears to be unprecedented anywhere in the world in terms of full consideration of the legal position by a court. The basic statistics are that about one in ninety live births produces twins. About one in 250 live births produces monozygotic twins (identical twins from the division of a single fertilised ovum). Very rarely (a suggested figure is once in 100,000 births, although this figure is far from precise and seems to vary in different parts of the world) monozygotic twins fail to separate completely (as normally occurs about a fortnight after conception), resulting in conjoined twins. Rather over half of all conjoined twins are still-born, and a further third both die within 24 hours. Only about 6 per cent of conjoined twins are classified as ischiopagus (joined at the pelvic level) and only about two per cent as ischiopagus tetrapus (joined at the pelvic level and having four legs).

Jodie's and Mary's medical condition is therefore very rare indeed. Their condition is even more exceptional in that – quite apart from abnormalities of their bodily organs in the region where they are joined – Mary has very grave defects in her brain, her heart, and her lungs. For practical purposes her lungs are non-existent. She is wholly dependent for life on oxygenated blood circulated through Jodie's lungs and Jodie's heart. The consultant paediatric and neonatal surgeon, Mr B, has described her as 'totally supported' by Jodie. It is the strain on Jodie of supporting her sister as well as herself which is very likely to lead to the deaths of both twins within a matter of months, if they remain joined, because Jodie is likely to suffer what is called high output heart failure. There is no practical possibility of Mary being put on a heart-lung machine or receiving a heart-lung transplant. In an article (Hoyle and Thomas, 1989) reviewing 33 separations of ischiopagus tetrapus twins reported throughout the world between 1955 and 1986, only two seem to have been cases in which, for reasons other than a shared vital organ, one identified twin had no prospect of surviving the surgery (one was already dying when the surgery was undertaken, and the other was anencephalic).

The legal position has been considered in some published articles, including an article by Sally Sheldon and Stephen Wilkinson ('Conjoined twins: the legality and ethics of sacrifice' [1997] *Medical Law Review* 149) which contains a helpful discussion. But the only decision of a court referred to in any of the medical and legal literature is the decision in 1977 of a three-judge panel of the Family Court in Philadelphia which authorised an operation to separate thoracopagus twins with a conjoined heart (see George J Annas, 'Siamese twins: Killing one to save the other, Hastings Center Report April 1987). The article also mentions a similar operation in Philadelphia in 1987 in which the hospital obtained prior clearance from the District Attorney and approval from its own ethics committee, but did not go to court. It appears that in the 1977 case the parents (who were deeply religious Jews) had consented to the operation after taking rabbinical advice; and the hospital nurses (most of whom were Roman Catholics) had also been reassured by a priest. The application to the Family Court was made by the surgeon for his own protection. It does not appear whether the Family Court gave a reasoned judgment (the court is said to have deliberated for only a few minutes, so probably it did not).

In these circumstances this court has to start with some very basic questions. Are these conjoined twins two persons or one in the eyes of the law? If they are two persons, was Mary born alive? (If she was not born alive, there can be no possible question of criminal liability for her unlawful killing.)

Mr Adrian Whitfield QC (appearing with Mr Huw Lloyd for the Healthcare Trust) conceded that Jodie and Mary must be regarded as two separate persons, and he was clearly right to do so. They have two brains and two nearly complete bodies, despite the grave defects in Mary's brain and her heart and lungs. There are cases of incomplete (or heteropagus) twinning in which a child is born with abnormalities which can be regarded as no more than a parasitic attachment. But it has not been and could not be suggested that this case comes anywhere near that category.

The evidence also indicates that Mary, although incapable of separate existence, was born alive. A 'stillborn' child is defined (by the Births and Deaths Registration Act 1953 s. 41, as amended) as:

> 'a child which has issued forth from its mother after the twenty-fourth week of pregnancy and which did not at any time after being completely expelled from its mother breathe or show any signs of life.'

The medical notes from the hospital show that Mary was struggling to breathe, although sadly in vain, when she and Jodie were brought from the operating theatre into the recovery ward. Mr B (who would lead the operating team) was clear in his oral evidence to this court that Mary was not stillborn, but that she could not be resuscitated and was not viable. Since her umbilical cord was cut she has been dependent for life on her sister. The fact that she is alive as a distinct personality, but is not viable as a separate human being, is the awful paradox at the centre of this case.

The definition in the 1953 Act applies only for the purposes of that statute, but it appears to correspond closely (except in the precision of the minimum 24-week term, which is not relevant here) to the position at common law: see generally the full historical review by my lord, Brooke J in *Rance v Mid-Downs Health Authority* [1991] 1 QB 587, 617–23. Mr David Harris QC (appearing with Mr Andrew Hockton, instructed by the Official Solicitor, for Mary) drew the court's attention to some passages in the speeches in *Airedale NHS Trust v Bland* [1993] AC 789 (most notably in the speech of Lord Browne-Wilkinson at pp 878–9) pointing out that as medical science has developed new techniques and equipment for the prolongation of human life, the law has had to redefine death (in terms of brain-stem death rather than cessation of unaided cardiovascular functioning). Mr Harris submitted that just as the law has had to redefine death, so it may have to redefine the concept of being born alive. There are a number of difficulties in the way of that argument but they need not be considered further since Mr Whitfield (and all other counsel who might have been concerned to argue the contrary) have rightly conceded that Mary is a human being and was born alive.

It hardly needs to be said that there is no longer any place in legal textbooks, any more than there is in medical textbooks, for expressions (such as 'monster') which are redolent of superstitious horror. Such disparagingly emotive language should never be used to describe a human being, however disabled and dysmorphic. But having studied the medical evidence and the photographs, the court must recognise that if the twins remain as they are, solidly joined at their trunks, with their genitals and legs at right angles to their bodies, and if the specialists from Great Ormond Street Hospital prove right in their prediction that a longer life-span is possible, there would be grave physical and (for Jodie) psychological problems to be faced. The appellant parents' counsel, Mr Simon Taylor, himself used emotive language to describe that prospect when he drew attention to the new medical evidence.

The welfare principle

The twins are not wards of court, nor have they been taken into care under the Children Act 1989. The Healthcare Trust's application to the court was made under the inherent jurisdiction of the court. But the proceedings are proceedings with respect to the twins' upbringing (which is defined in s 105 of the Children Act so as to include care). Therefore the court is bound by the overriding welfare principle in s 1(1) of that Act:

> the child's welfare shall be the court's paramount consideration.

In this case the court has to consider the welfare (or best interests – the expressions are synonymous) of each of the twins. The court has on several occasions had to consider a situation in which the interests of two minors appeared to be in conflict. In *Birmingham City Council v H (a minor)* [1994] 2 AC 212 the House of Lords had to consider a conflict between the interests of a mother (aged 14 when her child was born) and her son (who was aged 2 when the appeal was heard). The issue was resolved on the narrow ground that the only question to be determined by the court was in respect of the baby's upbringing. But in cases where questions as to the upbringing of two siblings are before the court, it appears that the court must normally undertake a balancing exercise to achieve the situation of least detriment, as the Court of Appeal had held in the case of the child mother and her baby: see *Re H* [1993] 1 FLR 883; also *Re T and E (proceedings: conflicting interests)* [1995] 1 FLR 581, 584–7.

However the decisions in which those conflicts of interests arose were decisions as to matters such as residence and contact which, however anxious and difficult, are routinely made by family judges. They were not decisions on a matter of life or death. The notion that the court should ever undertake the evaluation of the lives of two innocent human beings, with a view to deciding which should live and which should die, could not be reconciled with the law's respect for the sanctity (or inviolability) of human life, either before or after the incorporation of the European Convention on Human Rights. In his enumeration of the salient principles in *Airedale NHS Trust v Bland* [1993] AC 789, 808, Sir Thomas Bingham MR put this first:

> A profound respect for the sanctity of human life is embedded in our law and our moral philosophy, as it is in that of most civilised societies in the East and in the West. That is why murder (next only to treason) has always been treated here as the most grave and heinous of crimes.

This court has been shown many similar statements, both in law reports and in academic work, but it is unnecessary to multiply citations.

The court was referred to a number of reported decisions in which judges of the Family Division, or this court, have authorised the withdrawal of treatment (or the withholding of treatment on a future emergency) in the case of severely disabled children. It is not necessary to refer to all the cases which were cited. All are concerned primarily with the question of the best interests of a single child, and the weight to be given to the wishes of devoted parents. None goes far into the issue of lawfulness, since it did not arise.

In *Re B (a minor) (wardship: medical treatment)* [1981] 1 WLR 1421 this court (reversing the trial judge) authorised surgery, against the parents' wishes, for an intestinal blockage of a Down's syndrome baby who was only a few days old. The baby was not very severely disabled. In *Re J (a minor) (wardship: medical treatment)* [1991] Fam 33 this court (upholding the trial judge) authorised non-resuscitation (on a future emergency) of a six-month-old child who had been born very prematurely and had suffered very severe brain damage. Lord Donaldson MR said (at p46):

> What doctors and the court have to decide is whether, in the best interests of the child patient, a particular decision as to medical treatment should be taken which *as a side effect* will render death more or less likely. This is not a matter of semantics. It is fundamental. At the other end of the age spectrum, the use of drugs to reduce pain will often be fully justified, notwithstanding that this will hasten the moment of death. What can never be justified is the use of drugs or surgical procedures with the primary purpose of doing so.

In the same case Taylor LJ set out three principles which were not in dispute. The first related to the welfare principle and the weight to be given to parents' wishes. Taylor LJ went on (at p 53):

> Secondly, the court's high respect for the sanctity of human life imposes a strong presumption in favour of taking all steps capable of preserving it, save in exceptional circumstances. The problem is to define those circumstances.
>
> Thirdly, and as a corollary to the second principle, it cannot be too strongly emphasised that the court never sanctions steps to terminate life. That would be unlawful. There is no question of approving, even in a case of the most horrendous disability, a course aimed at terminating life or accelerating death. The court is concerned only with the circumstances in which steps should not be taken to prolong life.

In *Re T (wardship: medical treatment)* [1997] 1 FLR 502 this court (reversing the trial judge) upheld the objections of devoted parents to an 18-month-old child undergoing an operation for a liver transplant after previous surgery had been unsuccessful, and had caused the child pain and distress. Butler-Sloss LJ (who was a member of the court) has since described the case as exceptional and as lying near one end of the spectrum of cases. One of its special features was that if the child were to have a successful liver transplant, it would require total commitment by the caring parent to the proposed treatment.

Re T (wardship: medical treatment) confirms, following *Re Z (identification: restrictions on publication)* [1997] Fam 1, that where parents withhold consent to a particular course of action the court's function is not limited to reviewing the parents' decision and reversing it only if it is unreasonable (as with an appellate court asked to reverse a lower court's exercise of discretion). The court exercises its own judgment. In *Re Z* Sir Thomas Bingham MR put it as follows (at pp 32–3):

> I would for my part accept without reservation that the decision of

> a devoted and responsible parent should be treated with respect. It should not be disregarded or lightly set aside. But the role of the court is to exercise an independent and objective judgment. If that judgment is in accord with that of the devoted and responsible parent, well and good. If it is not, then it is the duty of the court, after giving due weight to the view of the devoted and responsible parent, to give effect to its own judgment. That is what it is there for. Its judgment may of course be wrong. So may that of the parent. But once the jurisdiction of the court is invoked its clear duty is to reach and express the best judgment it can.

There are to my mind particularly strong reasons for having regard to the parents' views in this case, even if they have been (as the judge put it) 'overwhelmed by the circumstances that confront them'. They have sincerely-held religious views (formed after discussion with a priest near the hospital, and now backed by the Archbishop of Westminster). Their views might be described as controversial but (unlike the objections to blood transfusion held by Jehovah's witnesses) they are not obviously contrary to any view generally accepted by our society. Still less are their views contrary to those generally accepted in the remote community from which they have come to this country. Healthcare services (and, it may be, social security) are less readily available in that community and the parents are naturally concerned about what the future would hold. No one suggested that it was selfish or unreasonable that they should have concerns about their ability, either financially or personally, to care for Jodie at home, if there is a separation operation which Jodie alone survives (they assume that there is no possibility of their taking both twins home without separation). That is so, I think, even if they have taken what is on the medical evidence a rather pessimistic view of the likely outcome for Jodie after elective surgery.

I would add, to avoid any possible misunderstanding, that the doctors and officers of the Healthcare Trust have themselves shown every consideration to the parents. This court has had the benefit of hearing oral evidence from Mr B, and has read transcripts of all the oral evidence given to the judge. It is impressive both for its sensitivity to the feelings and wishes of the twins' parents, and for its intellectual honesty. The medical specialists have faced up to the consequences for Mary of elective separation, but remain of the view that that separation is the best course.

The judge (who did not have the benefit of the very full and carefully-prepared arguments which this court has heard, and for which we are greatly indebted to all counsel and solicitors in the case) dealt with the matter by considering first the best interests of Jodie, then the best interests of Mary, and then (as a separate matter) the issue of lawfulness. Those issues are (in all too real a sense) not easily separated, and Mary's best interests cannot be fully considered except in the context of the decision of the House of Lords in *Airedale NHS Trust v Bland* [1993] AC 789, and the (perhaps even more difficult) questions of possible unlawfulness and criminal liability which arise on the facts of this case.

So far as it was appropriate to consider Jodie's best interests on their own the judge had ample material on which to conclude, as he did, that elective separation of the twins would be in the best interests of Jodie, despite the risk (which is put at about 6 per cent) of her not surviving the operation, and despite the risks of her quality of life being affected by incontinence, difficulty in walking, and the need for protracted reconstructive surgery. Those are risks – not probabilities, still less near-certainties – and they were fully addressed in the medical evidence. The judge mentioned them at the beginning of his judgment. Nevertheless he rightly said that for Jodie, separation means the expectation of a normal life.

The judge came to the conclusion that separation would also be in Mary's best interests, even though it would result in her immediate death. As I have said, this raises very difficult issues. At present I deal primarily with the judge's findings of fact about Mary's condition. It is uncertain how far she can feel pain, but the evidence did not positively establish that she cannot feel pain. It did establish that she cannot cry, as she has no effective lungs. The judge was obviously very concerned about that, and about the prospect of Mary being caused pain and discomfort as Jodie becomes more mobile. He referred to the oral evidence of the paediatric neurosurgeon:

> I think that is an horrendous scenario, to think of being dragged around and being able to do nothing about it. I think with the increasing activity of [Jodie], [Mary's] situation becomes worse.

Mr Taylor and Mr Harris have respectfully but firmly criticised the judge for fastening on this evidence, to the exclusion of other evidence that Mary probably cannot feel pain. There may be some force in that criticism, although this court would be slow to differ from the findings of this very experienced family judge who had seen and heard all the witnesses. But even if it were assumed that Mary is no more capable of feeling pain or discomfort than she is of any pleasant sensation or emotion, it is hard to see any benefit to her from continued life. In *Bland*, Lord Goff (at p868) drew a distinction between cases in which the patient has (or may come to have) some awareness of his or her quality of life, and cases of total unconsciousness. Whichever category Mary should be put in I do not differ from the judge's conclusion that to prolong Mary's life for a few months would confer no benefit on her but would be to her disadvantage. If Mary had been born separated from Jodie but with the defective brain and heart and lungs which she has, and if her life were being supported, not by Jodie but by mechanical means, it would be right to withdraw that artificial life-support system and allow Mary to die.

Airedale NHS Trust v Bland

The facts of *Airedale NHS Trust v Bland* [1993] AC 789 are well known. A young man (aged 17 at the time of his injury, but of full age at the time of the application to the court) was so severely injured in the Hillsborough disaster that he was in a persistent vegetative state. His cerebral cortex had been destroyed and he had no awareness of his condition and no sensation of pain. But his brain stem was alive and (although he could not swallow and required feeding through a nasal tube) he could breathe spontaneously. (His condition was therefore the converse of a patient with Guillain-Barré syndrome as in the Canadian case of *Nancy B v Hôtel-Dieu de Québec* (1992) 86 DLR (4th) 385; she had all her mental faculties but could not breathe and depended for continued life on a ventilator. The patient in the New Zealand case of *Auckland Area Health Board v Attorney-General* [1993] 1 NZLR 235 was in a more advanced state of that syndrome, in which the brain is alive but incapable of controlling the body because the conductivity of the nervous system has been destroyed.)

In the *Bland* case the House of Lords (upholding this court and the President of the Family Division) authorised the withdrawal of treatment (that is, artificial nutrition and hydration) but made clear that positive action to bring about the patient's death would be unlawful. Lord Goff said [1993] AC 789, 865:

> . . . the law draws a crucial distinction between cases in which a doctor decides not to provide, or to continue to provide, for his patient treatment or care which could or might prolong his life, and those in which he decides, for example by administering a lethal drug, actively to bring his patient's life to an end. As I have already indicated, the former may be lawful, either because the doctor is giving effect to his patient's wishes by withholding the treatment or care, or even in certain circumstances in which (on principles which I shall describe) the patient is incapacitated from stating whether or not he gives his consent. But it is not lawful for a doctor to administer a drug to his patient to bring about his death, even though that course is prompted by a humanitarian desire to end his suffering, however great that suffering may be: see *Reg v Cox* (unreported), 18 September 1992. So to act is to cross the Rubicon which runs between on the one hand the care of the living patient and on the other hand euthanasia – actively causing his death to avoid or to end his suffering. Euthanasia is not lawful at common law.

The practical result was that the patient died slowly from lack of nutrition and hydration, a process which caused him no pain, but which seems likely to have caused distress to the nurses who were caring for him. Switching off a ventilator is also regarded as a withdrawal of treatment (that is, as an omission rather than a positive act) even though it results (and is expected to result) in immediate death.

Many of the judges who considered the *Bland* case were understandably anxious about the intellectual robustness of the distinction between death brought about by an omission, on one hand, and death caused by a positive act, on the other hand. That appears very clearly in the speech of Lord Mustill. He said (at p 887):

> The conclusion that the declarations can be upheld depends crucially on a distinction drawn by the criminal law between acts and omissions, and carries with it inescapably a distinction between, on the one hand what is often called 'mercy killing', where active steps are taken in a medical context to terminate the life of a suffering patient, and a situation such as the present where the proposed conduct has the aim for equally humane reasons of terminating the life of Anthony Bland by withholding from him the basic necessities of life. The acute unease which I feel about adopting this way through the legal and ethical maze is I believe due in an important part to the sensation that however much the terminologies may differ the ethical status of the two courses of action is for all relevant purposes indistinguishable. By dismissing this appeal I fear that your Lordships' House may only emphasise the distortions of a legal structure which is already both morally and intellectually misshapen.

At pp 897–8 he set out an argument which he regarded as 'logically defensible and consistent with the existing law', but added (at p898):

> I must recognise at once that this chain of reasoning makes an unpromising start by transferring the morally and intellectually dubious distinction between acts and omissions into a context where the ethical foundations of the law are already open to question. The opportunity for anomaly and excessively fine distinctions, often depending more on the way in which the problem happens to be stated than on any real distinguishing features, has been exposed by many commentators, including in England the authors abovementioned, together with *Smith & Hogan on Criminal Law*, 6th ed (1988), p 51, H Beynon at [1982] Crim LR 17 and M J Gunn and J C Smith at [1985] Crim LR 705. All this being granted we are still forced to take the law as we find it and try to make it work.

(The academic writers to whom Lord Mustill had already referred were Professor Skegg, Professor Glanville Williams and Professor Kennedy. This court has been referred to much of this material and has also considered more recent work, including some valuable articles by Professor Ashworth, Professor Finnis and Dr Keown.)

Lord Browne-Wilkinson was equally candid. He described his conclusion as reached on narrow, legalistic grounds. He said at the end of his speech (at p 885)

> . . . the conclusion I have reached will appear to some to be almost irrational. How can it be lawful to allow a patient to die slowly, though painlessly, over a period of weeks from lack of food but unlawful to produce his immediate death by a lethal injection, thereby saving his family from yet another ordeal to add to the tragedy that has already struck them? I find it difficult to find a moral answer to that question. But it is undoubtedly the law and nothing I have said casts doubt on the proposition that the doing of

> a positive act with the intention of ending life is and remains murder.

To the same effect Lord Lowry referred (at p 877) to a possible 'distinction without a difference'. Several of their lordships referred to the need for these questions of life and death to be determined by the democratic processes of Parliament, rather than by the court.

The switching-off or disconnection of a ventilator has also been regarded by the New Zealand court as a withdrawal of treatment: see the judgment of Thomas J in *Auckland Area Health Board v Attorney-General* [1993] 1 NZLR 235, to which Lord Goff (at p 867) paid tribute in *Bland.* The Canadian case of *Nancy B* was different in that the court's function was to recognise the rights of self-determination of a mentally competent but physically disabled patient.

The decision of the House of Lords in *Bland* has (unsurprisingly, in view of its very controversial subject-matter) attracted criticism. So far as legal academic literature is concerned this court has been referred in particular to two well-argued articles in the Law Quarterly Review, (1993) 109 LQR 329 (Professor Finnis) and (1997) 113 LQR 481 (Dr Keown). But as Parliament has not since 1993 intervened to make any change in the law the decision in *Bland* is binding on this court, and it is important to identify the principle of the decision as precisely as possible.

The following points seem to be stated or approved in all five of their lordships' speeches and led to the result that the appeal in *Bland* should be dismissed. (1) The artificial feeding of the patient through a nasogastric tube constituted (at any rate in conjunction with other nursing care) medical treatment. (2) The discontinuance of artificial feeding should be regarded as an omission, since although the removal of the tube was a positive act the substance of the matter was the discontinuance of a treatment; and an omission to give treatment could not be unlawful or contrary to the patient's best interests unless there was a duty to treat him. (3) There was no duty on the doctors to administer to the patient treatment which was futile and contrary to his best interests. (4) None of this authorises or legalises a positive act intended to cause the patient's death, since (as Lord Goff put it at p 866) the law 'does not, for reasons of policy, consider that it forms any part of [a doctor's] duty to give his patient a lethal injection to put him out of his misery'. It is that reasoning which led Lord Goff to say (at p 868),

> . . . the question is not whether it is in the best interests of the patient that he should die. The question is whether it is in the best interests of the patient that his life should be prolonged by the continuance of this form of medical treatment or care.

The judge's decision and the issues in the appeal

The judge considered whether elective separation would be in the best interests of Jodie and whether it would be in the best interests of Mary.

In each case he concluded that it would be. He then considered the question of lawfulness, which he regarded as the most difficult element in his decision. If the operation is carried out Mary's death would be the inevitable result of positive action by the surgeons, who would at some stage place a clamp within Jodie's body and cut off the supply to Mary's body of oxygenated blood from Jodie's heart and lungs. She would die immediately. The judge said that he had not been presented with any argument based on the doctrine of double effect. He referred to the difficulty in this area of distinguishing between an act and an omission, and to the 'Rubicon' which might be crossed. This was an indirect reference to a passage (already cited) in the speech of Lord Goff in *Bland*, [1993] AC 789, 865. Having referred to these difficulties the judge said:

> I was at first attracted by the thought prompted by one of the doctors, that Jodie was to be regarded as a life support machine and that the operation proposed was equivalent to switching off a mechanical aid. Viewed in that way previous authority would categorise the proposed operation as one of omission rather than as a positive act. However on reflection I am not persuaded that that is a proper view of what is proposed in the circumstances of this particular case. I have preferred to base my decision upon the view that what is proposed and what will cause Mary's death will be the interruption or withdrawal of the supply of blood which she receives from Jodie. Here the analogy with the situation in which the court authorises the withholding of food and hydration. That, the cases make clear, is not a positive act and is lawful.

There are some serious difficulties about this way of looking at the case, as Mr Taylor and Mr Harris have pointed out. It is impossible, they submitted, to describe the proposed surgery as being a withdrawal of treatment. It is active surgical intervention which will be invasive of the bodies of both Jodie and Mary, and will result in the latter's death. Nevertheless Mr Harris recognised that the principle of bodily integrity, which is fundamental to the court's approach to these problems, is difficult to apply in the case of conjoined twins. Where twins are born alive but conjoined their physical integrity and autonomy has already been gravely prejudiced by the rare accident of incomplete separation at an early stage of gestation. But Mr Harris urged this court to take a principled approach, and not to decide this case in a way which might distort the development of the law. In this context he and other counsel drew attention to some cautionary observations in recent cases in the House of Lords (*R v Kingston* [1995] 2 AC 355, 375, 377; *Hunter v Canary Wharf* [1997] AC 655, 707; *Kleinwort Benson v Lincoln City Council* [1999] 2 AC 349, 378–9).

The case put forward by Mr Taylor and Mr Harris is straightforward, and is supported by two important decisions of the House of Lords. A surgical operation to separate the twins would be a deliberate, positive act. It would be invasive of Mary's body and it would cause her death.

Necessity, counsel said, is not a defence to murder: *R v Howe* [1987] AC 417. Nor is it a defence to say that the defendant did not wish to cause death, if it is for all practical purposes inevitable that that will be the result of his actions: *R v Woollin* [1999] 1 AC 82. Nothing in the cases on medical treatment, including *Bland*, is in any way inconsistent with those principles.

Against that apparently simple and compelling case various lines of argument have been put forward by those counsel who argued for elective separation (that is Mr Whitfield and Mr Tim Owen QC, who appeared for Jodie to argue the issues of criminal law; they received some degree of support from Miss Nicola Davies QC, Mr David Perry and Mr Gareth Patterson, who were appointed by the Attorney-General to assist the court, but made clear that they were not arguing for any particular outcome). These arguments overlap to some extent, as became apparent as soon as counsel's written submissions were delivered. It is convenient to note at the outset certain lines of argument which were not pursued (at any rate with any enthusiasm) in this court. No one argued that Mary could not be a victim of unlawful killing. No one other than Mr Whitfield argued that the operation could be equated with a withdrawal of treatment such as was regarded (in *Bland*) as an omission. That seems to have been the ground on which the judge based his decision as to lawfulness. Mr Whitfield sought to uphold this ground of decision, while candidly recognising the difficulties in his way. He pointed out that in the proposed operation no bodily organ or skin of Mary's would be transferred to Jodie (their shared bladder would be divided into two). Nevertheless it would be invasive of Mary's body. On the clear and undisputed evidence as to what the proposed operation would involve, it cannot be described as a withdrawal of treatment, or as an omission rather than a positive act.

The main submissions in favour of upholding the judge's order were based on intention and necessity (including the species of necessity sometimes referred to as private defence); and some counsel (although not Miss Davies) also relied on the doctrine of double effect, which no one had relied on below, but which can be seen as a sort of bridge between the issue of intention and the issue of necessity. The arguments run into each other. What follows is a summary treatment of difficult issues which are more fully and profoundly considered in the judgment of Brooke LJ.

Criminal law issues

There are various ways in which English criminal law gives effect to the general intuitive feeling that a defendant should not be convicted of a serious crime unless he did the prohibited act intentionally and in circumstances in which he should be held responsible for the consequences. Many of these are concerned with cases (which can all be loosely called cases of necessity) where the defendant's freedom of choice has in one way or another been constrained by circumstances.

But if a defendant's action is of its nature certain, or virtually certain, to produce a harmful result, he cannot normally be heard to say that he did not intend that result. In *R v Woollin* [1999] 1 AC 82 an angry father threw his three-month-old son on to a hard surface. The child suffered a fractured skull and died. The father was convicted of murder but because of a misdirection the House of Lords allowed his appeal (substituting a verdict of guilty of manslaughter). That was the context in which their lordships approved (as part of a model direction to the jury) the passage at p 96:

> Where a man realises that it is for all practical purposes inevitable that his actions will result in death or serious harm, the inference may be irresistible that he intended that result, however little he may have desired or wished it to happen.

The decision of the House of Lords in *Woollin* has (it is to be hoped) finally resolved a debate as to the mental element requisite for murder ('malice aforethought' is the traditional but archaic phrase) which has been continuing intermittently since *DPP v Smith* [1961] AC 290, with legislative intervention in the form of s 8 of the Criminal Justice Act 1967. Mr Owen submitted that *Woollin* may have to be reconsidered in the light of the Human Rights Act 1998 and Article 2 of the European Convention on Human Rights. I would not accept that submission, if it were relevant, for reasons set out later in this judgment.

However the stark facts of *Woollin* and the speeches in the House of Lords in that case say nothing at all about the situation in which an individual acts for a good purpose which cannot be achieved without also having bad consequences (which may be merely possible, or very probable, or virtually certain). This is the doctrine (or dilemma) of double effect which has been debated by moral philosophers (as well as lawyers) for millennia rather than centuries. In one class of case the good purpose and the foreseen but undesired consequence (what Bentham called 'oblique intention') are both directed at the same individual. That can be illustrated by a doctor's duty to his patient. The doctor may in the course of proper treatment have to cause pain to the patient in order to heal him. Conversely he may in order to palliate severe pain, administer large doses of analgesics even though he knows that the likely consequence will be to shorten the patient's life. That was recognised by Lord Donaldson MR in the passage of his judgment in *Re J* which I have already cited (note its references to primary purpose and side effects; similar language was used by Ognall J in his summing-up to the jury in *R v Cox* (1992), the case of the doctor who administered potassium chloride to a dying patient). Similarly Lord Goff referred in *Bland* (at p 867) to:

> . . . the established rule that a doctor may, when caring for a patient who is, for example, dying of cancer, lawfully administer painkilling drugs despite the fact that he knows that an incidental effect of that application will be to abbreviate the patient's life. Such a decision

> may properly be made as part of the care of the living patient, in his best interests; and, on this basis, the treatment will be lawful.

In these cases the doctrine of double effect prevents the doctor's foresight of accelerated death from counting as a guilty intention. This type of double effect cannot be relevant to conduct directed towards Mary unless the mere fact of restoring her separate bodily integrity, even at the moment of death, can be seen as a good end in itself and as something which ought to be achieved in the best interests of Mary as well as Jodie.

There is another class of case in which a person may be faced with the dilemma of whether to save himself or others at the cost of harm or even death to a third person. The dilemma generally rises as the result of an emergency, and the examples (real or imagined) are typically concerned with disasters at sea, or emergencies during mountaineering or other hazardous activities. If a person, faced with such a dilemma, acts with the intention of saving his own life (or the lives of others) it may be said that that leaves no room for a guilty intention to harm or even kill the third person. Equally it may be said that although he must (on *Woollin* principles) be taken to have intended the death which he foresaw as virtually certain, he has a defence of necessity. That is the way the submission was put by Miss Davies.

Of the many real and imagined examples put before the court it is worth mentioning two incidents which really did happen, although neither was the subject of a court decision. One is the awful dilemma which faced the commander of an Australian warship, in peacetime, when a very serious fire occurred in the engineroom. He ordered the engine room to be sealed off and flooded with inert gas, in order to save the ship and the rest of the crew, although the order meant certain death for anyone who was still alive in the engineroom. The other is the equally awful dilemma of a mountaineer, Simon Yates, who held his fellow-climber, Joe Simpson, after he had slipped and was dangling on a rope over a precipice at 19,000 feet in the Andes. Yates held Simpson for an hour, unable to recover him and becoming increasingly exhausted. Yates then cut the rope. Almost miraculously Simpson landed on a snowy ice bridge 100 feet below, and survived. When they met again Simpson said to Yates, 'You did right'. This incident is mentioned in Professor Smith's 1989 Hamlyn Lectures, Justification and Excuse in the Criminal Law, p 79.

The House of Lords has made clear that a doctrine of necessity does form part of the common law: see *Re F (mental patient: sterilisation)* [1990] 2 AC 1 (especially in the speech of Lord Goff at pp 74–8) and *R v Bournewood Community and Mental Health Trust ex parte L* [1999] 1 AC 458. In the latter case Lord Goff said (at p 490):

> The concept of necessity has its role to play in all branches of our law of obligations – in contract (see the cases on agency of necessity), in tort (see In *re F (Mental Patient: Sterilisation)* [1990] 2 AC 1), and in restitution (see the sections on necessity in the standard books on the subject) and in our criminal law. It is therefore a

> concept of great importance. It is perhaps surprising, however, that the significant role it has to play in the law of torts has come to be recognised at so late a stage in the development of our law.

In *R v Howe* [1987] AC 417 the House of Lords held that duress by threats is no defence to a charge of murder (and in *R v Gotts* [1992] 2 AC 412 that has, by a bare majority, been extended to attempted murder; the dissenting speech of Lord Lowry merits careful study). In *Howe* Lord Hailsham (at p 429) referred to what he called the famous and important case of *R v Dudley and Stephens* (1884) 14 QBD 273, in which two shipwrecked mariners, adrift in a boat, killed the ailing cabin-boy and survived by eating his flesh. They were convicted of murder but the death sentence was commuted. Lord Hailsham said that that case was generally regarded as an authority on the 'supposed defence of necessity' but he went on:

> There is, of course, an obvious distinction between duress and necessity as potential defences; duress arises from the wrongful threats or violence of another human being and necessity arises from any other objective dangers threatening the accused. This, however, is, in my view a distinction without a relevant difference, since on this view duress is only that species of the genus of necessity which is caused by wrongful threats.

Similarly the defence of private defence (action in defence of one's own life, person or property, or in defence of the life, person or property of another) can be seen as a species of a more general defence based on necessity. The law lays great stress on action in self-defence being no more than is necessary: see *Palmer v R* [1971] AC 814, especially at pp 828–9. But it is clear that deliberate killing in self-defence can sometimes be justified.

Duress of circumstances can therefore be seen as a third or residual category of necessity, along with self-defence and duress by threats. I do not think it matters whether these defences are regarded as justifications or excuses. Whatever label is used, the moral merits of the defence will vary with the circumstances. The important issue is whether duress of circumstances can ever be a defence to a charge of murder. There is authority that it can be a defence to the very serious crime of aircraft hijacking contrary to s 1 of the Aviation Security Act 1982 (for which the maximum punishment is life imprisonment): see *R v Abdul Hussain and others* (Court of Appeal Criminal Division, 17 December 1998). The judgment of the court in that case, delivered by Rose LJ, examined the development of the defence. Rose LJ stated the principles which he derived from the authorities, the first three principles being as follows:

> 1. Unless and until Parliament provides otherwise, the defence of duress, whether by threats or from circumstances, is generally available in relation to all substantive crimes, except murder, attempted murder and some forms of treason (*R v Pommell* [1995] 2 Cr App R 607 at 615C). Accordingly, if raised by appropriate evidence, it is

> available in relation to hijacking aircraft; although, in such cases, the terror induced in innocent passengers will generally raise issues of proportionality for determination, initially as a matter of law by the judge and, in appropriate cases, by the jury.
>
> The courts have developed the defence on a case-by-case basis, notably during the last 30 years. Its scope remains imprecise (*Howe*, 453G–454C; *Hurst* [1995] 1 Cr App R 82 at 93D).
>
> Imminent peril of death or serious injury to the defendant, or those to whom he has responsibility, is an essential element of both types of duress (see *Southwark LBC v Williams* [1971] 1 Ch 734, per Lord Justice Edmund-Davies at 746A; *Loughnan*, by the majority at 448 and the dissentient at 460; and *Cole* at page 10).

The hijacking case concerned Shiite Muslims from southern Iraq. Many members of their families had been tortured and killed and they faced similar threats. Duress of circumstances was therefore a much more suitable description of their plight than the dilemma facing the doctors in this case. The doctors are not faced with any threat to themselves, but they are faced with the awful dilemma of trying to perform the professional duties which they owe to their two infant patients.

The special features of this case are that the doctors do have duties to their two patients, that it is impossible for them to undertake any relevant surgery affecting one twin without also affecting the other, and that the evidence indicates that both twins will die in a matter of months if nothing is done. Whether or not that is aptly described as duress of circumstances, it is a situation in which surgical intervention is a necessity if either life is to be saved.

I do not find any clear principle in *R v Howe, R v Gotts* or *R v Abdul-Hussain* which applies to the clinical dilemma which faces the doctors in this case. Like the other members of the court I have derived assistance from the minority judgment of Wilson J given in the Supreme Court of Canada in the case of *Perka and other v The Queen* (1984) 13 DLR (4th) 1. The facts of that case were totally different (a ship used by drug smugglers had been driven ashore by a storm) but the judgment of Wilson J discusses the underlying principles and the importance of a conflict between legal (as opposed to moral) duties.

Wilson J said at pp 34–5:

> Accordingly, not only can the system of positive law not tolerate an individual opting to act in accordance with the dictates of his conscience in the event of a conflict with legal duties, but it cannot permit acts in violation of legal obligations to be justified on the grounds that social utility is thereby increased. In both situations the conflicting 'duty' to which the defence arguments point is one which the court cannot take into account as it invokes considerations external to a judicial analysis of the rightness or wrongness of the impugned act. As Lord Coleridge CJ succinctly put it in

> *Dudley and Stephens, supra*, at p 287: 'Who is to be the judge of this sort of necessity?'
>
> On the other hand, in some circumstances defence counsel may be able to point to a conflicting duty which courts can and do recognize. For example, one may break the law in circumstances where it is necessary to rescue someone to whom one owes a positive duty of rescue (see *R v Walker*) (1979), 48 CCC (2d) 126, 5 MVR 114 (Ont. Co. Ct.), since failure to act in such a situation may itself constitute a culpable act or omission: see *R v Instan*, [1893] 1 QB 450. Similarly, if one subscribes to the viewpoint articulated by Laskin CJC in *Morgentaler, supra*, and perceives a doctor's defence to an abortion charge as his legal obligation to treat the mother rather than his alleged ethical duty to perform an unauthorized abortion, then the defence may be invoked without violating the prohibition enunciated by Dickson J in *Morgentaler* against choosing a non-legal duty over a legal one.

She said at p 36:

> The justification is not, however, established simply by showing a conflict of legal duties. The rule of proportionality is central to the evaluation of a justification premised on two conflicting duties since the defence rests on the rightfulness of the accused's choice of one over the other.
>
> As the facts before the court in the present case do not involve a conflict of legal duties it is unnecessary to discuss in detail how a court should go about assessing the relative extent of two evils. Suffice it to say that any such assessment must respect the notion of right upon which justification is based. The assessment cannot entail a mere utilitarian calculation of, for example, lives saved and deaths avoided in the aggregate but must somehow attempt to come to grips with the nature of the rights and duties being assessed. This would seem to be consistent with Lord Coleridge's conclusion that necessity can provide no justification for the taking of a life, such an act representing the most extreme form of rights violation. As discussed above, if any defence for such a homicidal act is to succeed, it would have to be framed as an excuse grounded on self-preservation.

Wilson J's reference to a conflict of duties in relation to abortion must be treated with caution because of the well-established rule that English law (like Canadian law, but here differing markedly from the teaching of the Roman Catholic church) does not regard even a viable full-term foetus as a human being until fully delivered: see the account in *Rance v Mid-Downs HA* [1991] 1 QB 587, 617–23 to which I have already referred, and also *St George's Healthcare NHS Trust v S* [1999] Fam 26, 45–50. There is in law no real analogy between Mary's dependence on Jodie's body for her continued life, and the dependence of an unborn foetus on its mother.

In truth there is no helpful analogy or parallel to the situation which the court has to consider in this case. It is unprecedented and paradoxical in that in law each twin has the right to life, but Mary's dependence on Jodie is severely detrimental to Jodie, and is expected to lead to the death of both twins within a few months. Each twin's right to life includes the right to physical integrity, that is the right to a whole body over which the individual will, on reaching an age of understanding, have autonomy and the right to self-determination: see the citations from *Bland* collected in the *St George's Healthcare* case at pp 43–5.

In the absence of Parliamentary intervention the law as to the defence of necessity is going to have to develop on a case by case basis, as Rose LJ said in *R v Abdul-Hussain*. I would extend it, if it needs to be extended, to cover this case. It is a case of doctors owing conflicting legal (and not merely social or moral) duties. It is a case where the test of proportionality is met, since it is a matter of life and death, and on the evidence Mary is bound to die soon in any event. It is not a case of evaluating the relative worth of two human lives, but of undertaking surgery without which neither life will have the bodily integrity (or wholeness) which is its due. It should not be regarded as a further step down a slippery slope because the case of conjoined twins presents an unique problem.

There is on the facts of this case some element of protecting Jodie against the unnatural invasion of her body through the physical burden imposed by her conjoined twin. That element must not be overstated. It would be absurd to suggest that Mary, a pitiful and innocent baby, is an unjust aggressor. Such language would be even less acceptable than dismissing Mary's death as a 'side-effect'. Nevertheless, the doctors' duty to protect and save Jodie's life if they can is of fundamental importance to the resolution of this appeal.

The European Convention on Human Rights

Article 2 of the European Convention on Human Rights provides for the right to life. It is in the following terms:

1. Everyone's right to life shall be protected by law. No one shall be deprived of life intentionally save in the execution of a sentence of a court following his conviction of a crime for which this penalty is provided by law.
2. Deprivation of life shall not be regarded as inflicted in contravention of this article where it results from the use of force which is no more than absolutely necessary:

   (a) in defence of any person from unlawful violence;
   (b) in order to effect a lawful arrest or to prevent the escape of a person lawfully detained;
   (c) in action lawfully taken for the purpose of quelling a riot or insurrection.

The right has, naturally enough, been described as one of the most fundamental provisions of the Convention (*McCann v United Kingdom* A 324 (1995), para 146).

Article 2 was in the forefront of the written submissions of Mr David Anderson QC on behalf of the Pro-Life Alliance. Mr Anderson also made submissions based on Articles 3 and 8 of the Convention and on Article 2 of the Fourth Protocol to the Convention. The last-mentioned submissions would be relevant only if there were a dispute, which at present there is not, about the twins being moved to another country. Mr Anderson's submissions on Article 2 of the Convention were on the same lines as those of Mr Taylor and Mr Harris, but were more fully developed. Mr Anderson submitted that the word 'intentionally' in Article 2(1) should be given its natural and ordinary meaning, and that the Strasbourg jurisprudence has no hint of the doctrine of double effect. It does not admit of necessity. The positive obligation in the first sentence of Article 2(1) (which is the only provision on which Jodie could rely) is a very much weaker obligation (see *Osman v United Kingdom* 1998 – V111 3124, para 116).

Mr Owen did not seek to rely on any part of Article 2(2). He rightly accepted that Mary's dependence on Jodie's cardiovascular system, however life-threatening to Jodie, could not be described as unlawful violence. But Mr Owen and Mr Whitfield both relied strongly on the word 'intentionally' (in French 'intentionnellement') in Article 2(1). Mr Owen seized on Mr Anderson's submission that the word should be given its natural and ordinary meaning. That meaning, he said, was limited to the purpose of an action. The *Woollin* principle, extending intention to foreseen but undesired consequences, did not apply. That was why the draftsmen of Article 2 did not think it was necessary to include further qualifications relating to double effect. (Mr Owen went so far as to submit that the *Woollin* principle will have to be modified as a result of the coming into force of the Human Rights Act 1998. I do not follow that submission. The Convention does not in any way restrict a contracting state as to how the most serious form of homicide is defined in its domestic law.)

Mr Anderson's submissions were clearly and skilfully developed but I do not accept them. The Convention is to be construed as an autonomous text, without regard to any special rules of English law, and the word 'intentionally' in Article 2(1) must be given its natural and ordinary meaning. In my judgment the word, construed in that way, applies only to cases where the purpose of the prohibited action is to cause death. It does not import any prohibition of the proposed operation other than those which are to be found in the common law of England. The coming into force of the Human Rights Act 1998 on 2 October next does not therefore alter my view of the case. The incorporation of the Convention into domestic law is a very important event but in this case its effect is to confirm, and not to alter, pre-existing law.

The Archbishop's submissions

This court has also accepted written submissions made by the Roman Catholic Archbishop of Westminster, the Most Reverend Cormac Murphy-O'Connor. Those submissions make five salient points based on Roman Catholic faith and morality. These are, first, that human life is sacred and inviolable. Secondly, a person's bodily integrity should not be invaded when that can confer no benefit. Thirdly, the duty to preserve one person's life cannot without grave injustice be effected by a lethal assault on another. Fourthly, there is no duty on doctors to resort to extraordinary means in order to preserve life. Fifthly, the rights of parents should be overridden only where they are clearly 'contrary to what is strictly owing to their children'. The rest of the submissions are very largely submissions as to English law and cover points already considered in this judgment.

The five salient points made by the Archbishop are entitled to profound respect. In general they underpin some important foundations of English law (although the fifth point does not form part of English law) and they have no doubt been reflected in the advice which the twins' parents have received from their local priest. But they do not explain or even touch on what Roman Catholic moral theology teaches about the doctrine of double effect, despite its importance in the Thomist tradition (there is some evidence that the doctrine was considered by the Roman Catholic Archdiocese of Philadelphia in the case in 1977 which I have already mentioned: see Thomasma and other, The Ethics of Caring for Conjoined Twins, Hastings Center Report July–August 1996, p 9). The term 'casuistry' has come to have bad connotations but the truth is that in law as in ethics it is often necessary to consider the facts of the particular case, including relevant intentions, in order to form a sound judgment.

I do not by that imply any criticism of the Archbishop's moderate and thoughtful submissions, which the court has anxiously considered. But ultimately the court has to decide this appeal by reference to legal principle, so far as it can be discerned, and not by reference to religious teaching or individual conscience.

Conclusions

In this case highly skilled and conscientious doctors believe that the best course, in the interests of both twins, is to undertake elective surgery in order to separate them and save Jodie. The surgery would not be intended to harm Mary but it would have the effect of ending her life, since her body cannot survive on its own (and there is no question of her life being prolonged by artificial means or by a heart-lung transplant). The doctors' opinion cannot be determinative of the legality of what is proposed – that responsibility has fallen on the court – but it is entitled to serious respect. In *Gillick v West Norfolk and Wisbech AHA* [1986] AC 112, 190 Lord Scarman (with whom Lord Fraser and Lord Bridge agreed) said (in relation to the supply of contraceptives to a girl under 16):

> The bona fide exercise by a doctor of his clinical judgment must be a complete negation of the guilty mind which is an essential ingredient of the criminal offence of aiding and abetting the commission of unlawful sexual intercourse.

Here the court is concerned with the possibility of the commission of a much more serious criminal offence, that is murder. But in the wholly exceptional case of these conjoined twins I consider that the same principles apply. In *Bland*, Sir Thomas Bingham MR (whose judgment was approved in the House of Lords by Lord Goff and a majority of their lordships) was prepared to put the matter very broadly ([1993] AC 789 at p 815):

> For present purposes I do not think it greatly matters whether one simply says that that is not an unlawful act, or that the doctor lacks criminal intent, or that he breaches no duty or that his act did not cause death.

In this case the doctors would perform a positive act of invasive surgery, but they would do so for the well-intentioned purposes which I have mentioned. The surgery would plainly be in Jodie's best interests, and in my judgment it would be in the best interests of Mary also, since for the twins to remain alive and conjoined in the way they are would be to deprive them of the bodily integrity and human dignity which is the right of each of them. As Thomas J said in the *Auckland* case [1993] 1 NZLR 235, 245:

> Human dignity and personal privacy belong to every person, whether living or dying.

Much of this judgment has necessarily been rather technical, and I am conscious that some of it may seem rather remote from the deeply troubling dilemma which Jodie's and Mary's condition presents. Every member of the court has been deeply troubled by this case, but we have to decide it in accordance with the principles of existing law as we perceive them to apply to this unprecedented situation. I will summarize my conclusions as to the applicable principles as simply as I can.

(i) The feelings of the twins' parents are entitled to great respect, especially so far as they are based on religious convictions. But as the matter has been referred to the court the court cannot escape the responsibility of deciding the matter to the best of its judgment as to the twins' best interests.

(ii) The judge erred in law in equating the proposed surgical operation with the discontinuance of medical treatment (as by disconnecting a heart-lung machine). Therefore the Court of Appeal must form its own view.

(iii) Mary has a right to life, under the common law of England (based as it is on Judeo-Christian foundations) and under the European Convention on Human Rights. It would be unlawful to kill Mary intentionally, that is to undertake an operation with the primary purpose of killing her.

(iv) But Jodie also has a right to life.

(v) Every human being's right to life carries with it, as an intrinsic part of it, rights of bodily integrity and autonomy – the right to have one's own body whole and intact and (on reaching an age of understanding) to take decisions about one's own body.

(vi) By a rare and tragic mischance, Mary and Jodie have both been deprived of the bodily integrity and autonomy which is their natural right. There is a strong presumption that an operation to separate them would be in the best interests of each of them.

(vii) In this case the purpose of the operation would be to separate the twins and so give Jodie a reasonably good prospect of a long and reasonably normal life. Mary's death would not be the purpose of the operation, although it would be its inevitable consequence. The operation would give her, even in death, bodily integrity as a human being. She would die, not because she was intentionally killed, but because her own body cannot sustain her life.

(viii) Continued life, whether long or short, would hold nothing for Mary except possible pain and discomfort, if indeed she can feel anything at all.

(ix) The proposed operation would therefore be in the best interests of each of the twins. The decision does not require the court to value one life above another.

(x) The proposed operation would not be unlawful. It would involve the positive act of invasive surgery and Mary's death would be foreseen as an inevitable consequence of an operation which is intended, and is necessary, to save Jodie's life. But Mary's death would not be the purpose or intention of the surgery, and she would die because tragically her body, on its own, is not and never has been viable.

The approach is Queensland is somewhat different, due to the use of section 282 of the Criminal Code (1899) as discussed by O'Regan (above).

State of Queensland v Nolan & Anor [2001] QSC 174

[1] **Chesterman J:** Alyssa Grace Nolan and Bethany Rose Nolan were born on 3 May 2001 by caesarean section at the Royal Womens' Hospital. They are conjoined craniopagus twin girls. The condition is extremely rare. Of all conjoined twins those joined at the head account for only 2–6%. Surgery to separate such twins is extremely complicated and the survival rate for even one of the twins is not high. The first occasion on which the operation was successfully performed was 1953 when one of a set of twins was saved.

[2] Alyssa has only one kidney. Bethany has no kidneys and no bladder.

As well she has a condition commonly referred to as club foot which is sometimes an indication of underlying brain damage. Though joined at the head the girls have separate brains though they share the cranial draining veins ('venous draining sinuses'). They thus share blood flow. This has enabled Bethany to survive, Alyssa's one kidney removing waste from the bloodstream of both girls.

[3] In the days prior to 25 May 2001 Bethany developed increasing hypertension from a cause which could not be ascertained. Her high blood pressure proved resistant to drug therapy and she developed hypertrophy in the left ventricle of the heart. A difficulty in treating Bethany's hypertension is that Alyssa's blood pressure is not elevated. The drugs which lower Bethany's blood pressure also reduce Alyssa's with the potential to diminish the flow of blood to her brain or compromise the function of the one shared kidney.

[4] During the evening of 25 May Bethany's condition deteriorated rapidly. Her hypertension caused cardiac failure. As well she developed severe pulmonary oedema (fluid in the tissues and air spaces of the lungs). These clinical signs indicated that Bethany's death was an immediate prospect. Should she have died while still joined to her sister, Alyssa too would have died within hours. The skill of the staff at the Royal Childrens' Hospital kept Bethany alive but the prognosis was that even with all possible assistance she could not survive more than about 24 hours, or a little longer.

[5] Late on 25 May the State of Queensland applied to the Supreme Court for an order permitting an operation to separate the twins. Its purpose was to save the life of Alyssa but in circumstances where there was no prospect that Bethany could live beyond it. Apart from her compromised heart the operation would leave her without an essential cerebral vein and, of course, no kidney. She is too young for dialysis.

[6] The court's sanction to the procedure was sought because although necessary for the preservation of Alyssa's life it would prove immediately fatal to Bethany.

[7] The jurisdiction appealed to is that which was formally vested in the Sovereign but was transferred in centuries past to the Lord Chancellor and from him personally to the Courts of Chancery and then to those courts which, like the Supreme Court, exercise the jurisdiction of that court. It is exercised to protect the person and property of subjects, particularly children who are unable to look to their own interests. The court has a wide power in relation to the welfare of infants. The dominant factor in the exercise of the jurisdiction is always what is in the best interests of the child in question. In a passage approved by Brennan J in *Marion's case* (1991–1992) 175 CLR 218 at 280 it was described by Lord Esher MR in *R v Gyngall* [1893] 2 QB 232 at 241:

> The court is placed in a position by reason of the prerogative of the Crown to act as supreme parent of children, and must exercise that

> jurisdiction in the manner in which a wise, affectionate, and careful parent would act for the welfare of the child.

The power is to be exercised for the protection of those whose plight enlivens it. See also *Fountain v Alexander* (1982) 150 CLR 615 at 633.

[8] Although the court may make orders contrary to the wishes of a child's parents if satisfied that it is in the child's best interest to do so this is not such a case. Mr and Mrs Nolan have given their consent to the operation notwithstanding the inescapable consequence it must have for Bethany. Dr Isles, who attended the hearing, informed me that he had explained their daughters' plight to them, the surgical options available, and the risk to Alyssa involved in the procedure. A note made of the conversation signed by Dr Isles, Dr Theile and Dr Campbell as well as by Mr and Mrs Nolan contains the summary:

> Bethany has had a rapid demise over the last 12 hours . . . her death is felt to be immanent. Surgical separation has been recommended and confirmed with several second opinions.
>
> Result of surgery: chance of Alyssa dying = 60–80%
> chance of Bethany dying = 100%.
>
> . . . The operation will be performed to attempt to save Alyssa's life . . .
>
> It was Dr Isles' opinion that Mr and Mrs Nolan understood the explanation and agreed that the operation should be performed.

[9] The court was approached for two reasons: (a) to confirm, in the exercise of its protective jurisdiction, that it is in the best interests of Alyssa and Bethany that the operation should proceed; and (b) to obtain the opinion of the court as to whether performing the operation which will lead to Bethany's death will be to do an unlawful act. Distressing as the thought may be in the present circumstances it is the case that a strict application of the *Criminal Code* ('the Code') might result in those taking part in the operation having committed an offence. It is, obviously, a crime for any person unlawfully to kill another unless the killing is justified excused or authorised by law. Any person who causes the death of another, directly or indirectly, by any means whatever, is deemed to have killed that other person.

[10] The provisions of the Code have another relevance to the application. It would not be in a child's best interests that it be subjected to an unlawful, especially a criminal, act.

[11] There were thus two considerations that had to be addressed before the application could be decided. They were:

(a) is it in the best interests of the children, and in particular of Bethany, that the operation be performed?
(b) will the operation amount to the unlawful killing of Bethany?

[12] The stark, indeed the brutal, facts which underlie the application are that Bethany's life will come to an end within a few hours. Her death

will lead to her sister's loss of life. An operation performed almost immediately will hasten Bethany's end but provide the best chance for Alyssa to survive and grow into normal childhood, adolescence and maturity.

[13] The application throws up the harsh reality that there is no commonality of interest between the sisters in undergoing the operation. It will benefit Alyssa by giving her a chance of a normal life but it will lead to Bethany's death. It confers no advantage on her. What, then, is in the best interests of the children?

[14] The same problem confronted the (English) Court of Appeal in September last year and I gratefully accept the analysis and conclusions of the judges who decided *Re A (Children) (Conjoined Twins: Surgical Separation)* [2001] 2 WLR 480. In this case, as in that, the operation cannot bring about any improvement in Bethany's condition or prevent any deterioration to her health.

Notwithstanding the handicaps with which she was born and the ineluctable consequence they have for her life expectancy, it cannot be said that her life is worthless or is intrinsically worth less than her sister's. The application is not to be decided by a comparison between the respective worth or value of the two lives. That was the approach of the Court of Appeal and I agree with it.

The court approached the dilemma posed by the conflicting interests by accepting that the right to life of both twins is equal. It then turned to consider whether the proposed treatment was in the best interests of both. The answer was that the operation was of decided advantage to one but there would not be a *corresponding* detriment to the other. Although her life would be shortened she was 'doomed for death . . . because her capacity to live . . . (was) fatally compromised'. According to Ward LJ:

> The prospect of a full life for J is counterbalanced by an acceleration of certain death for M. That balance is heavily in J's favour. (p 529).

[15] Robert Walker LJ summarised his opinion on this point in much the same terms. He said (592):

> . . . an operation to separate them would be in the best interests of each . . .
>
> In this case the purpose of the operation would be to separate the twins and so give J a reasonably good prospect of a long and reasonably normal life. M's death would not be the purpose of the operation, although it would be its inevitable consequence . . . She would die, not because she was intentionally killed, but because her own body cannot sustain her life.
>
> Continued life, whether long or short, would hold nothing for M . . .

> The proposed operation would therefore be in the best interests of each of the twins. The decision does not require the court to value one life above another.

[16] The reasoning is entirely apposite to the present application and is, with respect, an inexorable product of the circumstances. The condition of the twins and their future without surgery indicate what is to be done in their bests interests.

[17] In *Re A* it does not provide the same assistance with respect to the second point: whether the operation will be lawful. This is for the reason that two of the Lords Justices answered the question in the affirmative by reference to the little invoked doctrine of necessity which justifies conduct otherwise criminal. The doctrine is, however, a creature of the common law and finds only a very limited role in the Code.

[18] The defence of necessity was explained by Brooke LJ (in *Re A* 567):

> . . . the argument that a person ought to be permitted to breach the letter of the criminal law in order to prevent a greater evil befalling himself or others has long been recognised . . . but it has, in English law, not given rise to a recognised general defence of necessity, and in relation to the charge of murder, the defence has been specifically held not to exist . . . no system of positive law can recognise any principle which would entitle a person to violate the law because on his view the law conflicted with some higher social value . . . To . . . hold that ostensibly illegal acts can be validated on the basis of their expediency would import an undue subjectivity into the criminal law . . . However that does not . . . deal with the situation where someone commendably infringes a regulation in order to prevent another person from committing what everyone would accept as being a greater evil . . . In that situation it cannot be satisfactory to leave it to the prosecuting authority not to prosecute . . .

[19] The English courts have also recognised a similar but not identical defence of 'duress of circumstances' which is available where it is established that the person in question has been compelled to act as he did by the pressure of threats or other circumstances of imminent peril to which he was subjected. The impact of that pressure on his freedom to choose his course of action excuses him from criminal liability. This part of the concept is recognised by s 25 of the Code. It differs from the defence of necessity in which the person's mind is not irresistibly overcome by external pressures. The basis for the defence of necessity is that the conduct in question is not regarded as harmful because on a comparison of two evils the choice of avoiding the greater harm was justified (See In *Re A* at 568–9).

Applying that principle to the English twins Brooke LJ thought that the operation was needed to avoid inevitable and irreparable evil (ie the death of J); no more was to be done than was reasonably necessary for the purpose of saving J's life; and that the evil inflicted (ie the death of M) was not disproportionate to the evil avoided (ie the death of J).

Therefore by the doctrine the death of M by the operation was necessary to avoid a greater evil in the death of both girls.

[20] The judgment of Robert Walker LJ (588) recognises that the difficulty presented to the law by these cases is unique. There is no precedent nor even truly helpful analogy 'to the situation which the court has to consider'. His Lordship went on:

> . . . the law as to the defence of necessity is going to have to develop on a case by case basis . . . I would extend it, if it needs to be extended, to cover this case. It is a case of doctors owing conflicting legal and not merely social or moral duties. It is a case where the test of proportionality is met, since it is a matter of life and death, and on the evidence M is bound to die soon in any event. It is not a case of evaluating the relative worth of two human lives, but of undertaking surgery without which neither life will have the . . . wholeness which is its due.

[21] The approach to this part of problem taken by Ward LJ was slightly different. It is an approach which does have a counterpart in the Code. He said (534–536):

> (The doctors) are under a duty to M not to operate because it will kill (her), but they are under a duty to J to operate because not to do so would kill her.
>
> . . .
>
> What then is the position where there is a conflict of duty? . . . Justification is founded upon some positive duty . . . What are the doctors to do if the law imposes upon them a duty which they cannot perform without being in breach of M's right to life if at the same time the respecting of her right puts them in breach of the equally serious duty of respecting J's right to life? . . . In those circumstances . . . the law must allow an escape through choosing the lesser of the two evils. . . . Faced as they are with an apparently irreconcilable conflict, the doctors should be in no different position from that in which the court itself was placed in the performance of its duty to give paramount consideration to the welfare of each child. The doctors must be given the same freedom of choice as the court has given itself and the doctors must make that choice along the same lines as the court has done . . . so the conclusion has to be that the carrying out of the operation will be justified as the lesser evil and no unlawful act would be committed.

[22] It is, I think, right that the conflict referred to by Ward LJ arises under the Code. Section 286 provides that:

> (1) It is the duty of every person who has care of a child under 16 years to –
>
> (a) provide the necessaries of life for the child; and
> (b) take the precautions that are reasonable in all the

> circumstances to avoid danger to the child's life, health or safety; and
>
> (c) take the action that is reasonable in all the circumstances to remove the child from any such danger;
>
> and he or she is held to have caused any consequences that result to the life and health of the child because of any omission to perform that duty . . .

The person who has 'care of a child' is extensively defined by subsection (2). The definition is capable of extending to the hospital and doctors who undertook, or were given the responsibility of, caring for the babies. They have an obligation imposed by the section to supply such medical and surgical care and skill as is reasonable in the circumstances to prevent them coming to harm. It may not be stretching things to say that the obligation would, in some circumstances, extend to performing an operation to save Alyssa's life. That obligation, if discharged by the performance of the operation, will result in the death of Bethany. The operation which is compelled by law is a justification for the act which has that result. The killing is therefore not unlawful.

[23] There is another reason why the operation would not constitute a criminal offence. Section 282 of the Code provides that:

> A person is not criminally responsible for performing in good faith and with reasonable care and skill a surgical operation upon any person for the patient's benefit, or upon any unborn child for the preservation of the mother's life, if the performance of the operation is reasonable, having regard to the patient's state at the time and to all the circumstances of the case.

[24] It may be taken as certain that Sir Samuel Griffith did not have the present sort of case in mind when drafting that section but his terms are wide enough to encompass it. The section expressly recognises that there may be some medical exigencies in which an operation to save one life will result in the loss of a potential (ie unborn) human life but the act which causes the loss will not give rise to criminal liability. That situation is not identical to the present case. The law does not regard human existence as beginning until birth though, of course, there are provisions protecting the unborn. Here two actual lives are in existence. Nevertheless s 282 abnegates criminal responsibility for a surgeon who performs an operation in good faith and with reasonable skill upon any person if it is for the patient's benefit and if the operation is reasonable having regard to all the circumstances of the case. The language is wide enough to encompass the relevant facts here.

[25] The operation is one to save the life of Alyssa. The circumstances, including the loss of Bethany, would, in my opinion, make the operation reasonable for the purposes of the section. Alyssa is to be regarded as the patient.

[26] The court cannot authorise the commission of an unlawful act,

particularly a criminal act. The purpose of the application was not to obtain the court's sanction for conduct that would otherwise be criminal. What was sought was a declaration, in the exercise of the court's protective jurisdiction, that the operation was in the girls' best interests (though conventional legal terminology is pathetically inadequate in the case of Bethany) and the court's opinion that the surgery would not offend against the Code.

[27] The application was brought on as a matter of urgency at 11.00 p.m. on Friday 25 May and did not conclude until close to midnight. The operation was scheduled for 6.30 the next morning. There was no time for the preparation or delivery of reasons. I indicated that I would prepare reasons which would be published in the normal way in order that there should be a public record of the application, the circumstances that led to it and the reasons which led me to sanction the proposed cause of action.

[28] The orders formally made were:

1. I declare that an operation to separate the conjoined twins Alyssa Grace Nolan and Bethany Rose Nolan may be lawfully carried out in an attempt to save the life of Alyssa Grace Nolan.

2. I order that Alyssa Grace Nolan and Bethany Rose Nolan be permitted to undergo, and the applicant's servants and agents be permitted to perform surgery to effect the physical separation of the children.

3. No orders to costs.

4. Time for bringing the application be abridged.

Several States in Australia have passed legislation allowing a patient to specify, in advance, if he or she does not wish to have certain treatments even if, without the specified treatments, the patient would die.

Medical Treatment Act 1988 (Vic)

3 In this Act:

'Medical practitioner' means a legally qualified medical practitioner.

'Medical treatment' means the carrying out of:

(a) an operation;
(b) the administration of a drug or other like substance; or
(c) any other medical procedure but does not include palliative care.

'Palliative care' includes:

(a) the provision of reasonable medical procedures for the relief of pain, suffering and discomfort; or
(b) the reasonable provision of food and water.

'Refusal of treatment certificate' means a certificate in the form of Schedule 1 and, if that certificate is modified, includes that certificate as modified and in force for the time being.

4 (1) This Act does not affect any right of a person under any other law to refuse medical treatment.

(2) This Act does not apply to palliative care and does not affect any right, power or duty which a medical practitioner or any other person has in relation to palliative care.

5 (1) If a registered medical practitioner and another person are each satisfied:

(a) that a patient has clearly expressed or indicated a decision

(i) to refuse medical treatment generally; or
(ii) to refuse medical treatment of a particular kind for a current condition; and

(b) that the patient's decision is made voluntarily and without inducement or compulsion; and
(c) that the patient has been informed about the nature of his or her condition to an extent which is reasonably sufficient to enable the patient to make a decision about whether or not to refuse medical treatment generally or of particular kind (as the case requires) for that condition and that the patient appeared to understand that information; and
(d) that the patient is of sound mind and has attained the age of 18 years the registered medical practitioner and the other person may together witness a refusal of treatment certificate.

(2) A refusal of treatment certificate must be in the form of Schedule 1.
(3) For the purposes of subsection (1)(a), the patient may clearly express or indicate a decision in writing, orally or in any other way in which the person can communicate.

6 A registered medical practitioner must not, knowing that a refusal treatment certificate applies to a person, undertake or continue to undertake any medical treatment which the person has refused, being treatment for the condition in relation to which the certificate was given.

7 (1) A refusal of treatment may be cancelled or modified by the patient to whom the certificate applies clearly expressing or indicating to a registered medical practitioner or another person a decision to cancel or modify the certificate.

(2) For the purposes of subsection (1), a person may clearly express or indicate decision in writing, orally or in any other way in which the person can communicate.
(3) A refusal of treatment certificate ceases to apply to a person if the

medical condition of the person has changed to such an extent that the condition in relation to which the certificate was given is no longer current.

8 (1) This section applies to a refusal of treatment certificate and to a written notice of a cancellation or modification of a refusal of treatment certificate.

(2) In any civil or criminal proceeding, production of either of the instruments mentioned in subsection (1) is:

(a) evidence; and
(b) in the absence of evidence to the contrary, proof that the patient has refused medical treatment or has cancelled or modified a refusal of treatment certificate.

(3) This section does not affect other methods of proving a decision to refuse medical treatment.

9 (1) A registered medical practitioner or a person acting under the direction of a registered medical practitioner who, in good faith and in reliance on a refusal of treatment certificate, refuses to perform or continue the medical treatment which the person has refused is not:

(a) guilty of misconduct or infamous misconduct in a professional respect;
(b) guilty of an offence; or
(c) liable in any civil proceedings;

because of the failure to perform or continue that treatment.

(2) For the purposes of this s and s 6 a person who acts in good faith in reliance on a refusal of treatment certificate but who is not aware that the certificate has been cancelled or modified, is to be treated as having acted in good faith in reliance on a refusal of treatment certificate.

Natural Death Act 1988 (NT)

3 Definitions. In this Act, unless the contrary intention appears:

'extraordinary measures' means medical or surgical measures that prolong life, or are intended to prolong life, by supplanting or maintaining the operation of bodily functions that are temporarily or permanently incapable of independent operation;

'recovery', in relation to a terminal illness, includes a remission of symptoms or effects of the illness;

'terminal illness' means such an illness, injury or degeneration of mental or physical faculties:

(a) that death would, if extraordinary measures were not undertaken, be imminent; and

(b) from which there is no reasonable prospect of a temporary or permanent recovery, even if extraordinary measures were undertaken.

4 Power to Make Direction.

(1) A person of sound mind who has attained the age of 18 years and who desires not to be subjected to extraordinary measures in the event of his or her suffering from a terminal illness, may make a direction in the prescribed form.
(2) A direction under subsection (1) is of no effect unless witnessed by two witnesses who have attained the age of 18 years, neither of whom is the medical practitioner responsible for the treatment of the person.
(3) Subject to subsection (2), where a person who is suffering from a terminal illness has made a direction under this s and the medical practitioner responsible for the treatment of the person has notice of that direction, it shall be the duty of that medical practitioner to act in accordance with the direction unless there is reasonable ground to believe that the person:

 (a) has revoked, or intended to revoke, the direction; or
 (b) was not, at the time of making the direction, capable of understanding the nature and consequences of the direction.

(4) This s does not derogate from any duty of a medical practitioner to inform a patient who is conscious and capable of exercising a rational judgment of all the various forms of treatment that may be available to the patient's particular case so that the patient may make an informed judgment as to whether a particular form of treatment should, or should not, be undertaken.

5 Act Not to Affect Other Rights.

(1) This Act does not affect the right of a person to refuse medical or surgical treatment.
(2) This Act (other than s 6) does not affect the legal consequences (if any) of taking, or refraining from taking:

 (a) therapeutic measures (not being extraordinary measures) in the case of a patient who is suffering from a terminal illness, whether or not the patient made a direction under this Act; or
 (b) taking or refraining from taking, extraordinary measures in the case of a patient who has not made a direction under this Act.

6 Certain Aspects of Causation of Death.

(1) For the purposes of the law of the Territory, the non-application of extraordinary measures to, or the withdrawal of extraordinary

measures from a person suffering from a terminal illness does not constitute a cause of death where the non-application or withdrawal was as a result of and in accordance with a direction made under s 4(1) by the person.

(2) This s does not relieve a medical practitioner from the consequences of a negligent decision as to whether or not a patient is suffering from a terminal illness.

7 Savings.

(1) Nothing in this Act prevents the artificial maintenance of the circulation or respiration of a dead person:

(a) for the purpose of maintaining bodily organs in a condition suitable for transplantation; or
(b) where the dead person was a pregnant woman – for the purpose of preserving the life of the foetus.

(2) Nothing in this Act authorises an act that causes or accelerates death as distinct from an act that permits the dying process to take its natural course.

Medical Treatment Act 1994 (ACT)

4 The objectives of this Act are:

(a) to protect the right of patients to refuse unwanted medical treatment; and
(b) to ensure the right of patients to receive relief from pain and suffering to the maximum extent that is reasonable in the circumstances.

5 (1) This Act does not affect any right of a person under any other law of the Territory to refuse medical treatment.

(2) This Act does not apply to palliative care and does not affect any right, power or duty that a health professional or any other person has in relation to palliative care.
(3) The refusal or withdrawal of medical treatment under this Act does not limit any duty of a health professional or other person:

(a) to advise and inform the patient or the patient's agent or guardian; or
(b) to provide medical treatment other than the medical treatment that has been refused or withdrawn.

10 A direction ceases to apply to a person if the medical condition has changed to such an extent that the condition in relation to which the direction was given is no longer current.

11 (1) Before complying with a direction in respect of a person who is still competent to make a rational judgment, the health professional

shall take all reasonable steps to ensure that the person has been informed about:

(a) the nature of his or her illness;
(b) any alternative forms of treatment that may be available;
(c) the consequences of those forms of treatment; and
(d) the consequences of remaining untreated.

(2) A health professional shall not give effect to the direction unless the health professional believes on reasonable grounds that the person has:

(a) understood the information provided under the subsection (I); and
(b) weighed the various options and, as a result of this consideration, affirms the decision:

(i) to refuse medical treatment; or
(ii) to have medical treatment withdrawn.

12 A health professional shall not withhold or withdraw medical treatment from a person in accordance with a direction unless the health professional believes on reasonable grounds that:

(a) the direction complies with this Act; and
(b) the person has not revoked the direction or in any way changed his or her decision since making the direction.

20 (1) A health professional or other person who becomes aware that a patient in a hospital, hospice or nursing home:

(a) has made a direction or granted a power of attorney; or
(b) having made the direction or granted the power of attorney, has revoked it; shall notify the superintendent of that fact and the circumstances in which the direction or power of attorney was made, granted or revoked.

(2) A superintendent who is notified under subsection (1) shall take reasonable steps to ensure that:

(a) a copy of the direction, power of attorney or revocation; or
(b) if it is not possible to obtain a copy of the direction, power of attorney or revocation – a notation of the direction, power of attorney or revocation;

is placed with the patient's file.

21 A health professional incurs no liability for a decision made by him or her in good faith and without negligence as to whether a person:

(a) revoked, or intended to revoke, a direction or power of attorney; or
(b) was, or was not, at the time of making a direction or granting a power of attorney, capable of understanding the nature and consequences of the direction or power of attorney.

22 A health professional or a person acting under the direction of a health professional who, in good faith and in reliance on a decision that he or she believes on reasonable grounds complies with this Act, withholds or withdraws medical treatment from a person is not:

(a) guilty of unsatisfactory professional conduct under any law of the Territory;
(b) guilty of an offence against any law of the Territory; or
(c) liable in any civil proceedings;

in connection with the withholding or withdrawal of medical treatment.

23 (1) Notwithstanding the provisions of any other law of the Territory, a patient under the care of a health professional has a right to receive relief from pain and suffering to the maximum extent that is reasonable in the circumstances.

(2) In providing relief from pain and suffering to a patient, a health professional shall pay due regard to the patient's account of his or her level of pain and suffering.

Consent to Medical Treatment and Palliative Care Act 1995 (SA)

Anticipatory grant or refusal of consent to medical treatment

7 (1) A person of or over 18 years of age may, while of sound mind, give a direction under this s about the medical treatment that the person wants, or does not want, if he or she is at some future time:

(a) in the terminal phase of a terminal illness, or in a persistent vegetative state; and
(b) incapable of making decisions about medical treatment when the question of administering the treatment arises.

(2) A direction under this section:

(a) must be in the form prescribed by Schedule 2 or in a form prescribed by regulation; and
(b) must be witnessed by an authorised witness who completes a certificate in the form prescribed by Schedule 2 or in a form prescribed by regulation.

(3) If:

(a) a person by whom a direction has been given under this section:

(i) is in the terminal phase of a terminal illness or in a persistent vegetative state;
(ii) and is incapable of making decisions about his or her medical treatment; and

(b) there is no reason to suppose that the person has revoked, or intended to revoke, the direction, the person is to be taken to have consented to medical treatment that is in accordance with the wishes of the person as expressed in the direction and to have refused medical treatment that is contrary to those expressed wishes.

Appointment of agent to consent to medical treatment

8 (1) A person of or over the age of 18 years of age may, while of sound mind, by medical power of attorney, appoint an agent with power to make decisions on his or her behalf about medical treatment.

(2) A medical power of attorney:

- (a) must be in the form prescribed by Schedule 1 or in a form to similar effect; and
- (b) must be witnessed by an authorised witness who completes a certificate in the form or to the effect of the certificate in Schedule 1.

(3) A person is not eligible to be appointed under a medical power of attorney unless over 18 years of age.

(4) The fact that a person has an interest under the will, or in the estate, of the grantor of a medical power of attorney does not invalidate the appointment of that person as a medical agent, or the exercise of any power by that person under a medical power of attorney.

(5) A person is not eligible to be appointed an agent under a medical power of attorney if that person is, in a professional or administrative capacity, directly or indirectly responsible for or involved in the medical care or treatment of the person by whom the medical power of attorney is to be given and, if a person who is validly appointed as a medical agent becomes so responsible or involved, the person is disqualified from acting as a medical agent under the medical power of attorney.

(6) If a medical power of attorney appoints two or more agents, it must indicate the order of appointment and, in that case, if the person designated first in order of appointment is unavailable, the power is to be exercised by the person designated second in the order of appointment, if the first and second are not available, by the person designated third in order of appointment, and so on, but a medical power of attorney may not provide for the joint exercise of the power.

(7) A medical power of attorney:

- (a) authorises the agent, subject to any conditions and directions contained in the power of attorney, to make decisions about the medical treatment of the person who granted the power if that person is incapable of making decisions on his or her own behalf; but
- (b) does not authorise the agent to refuse:

(i) the natural provisions or administration of food and water; or
(ii) the administration of drugs to relieve pain or distress; or
(iii) medical treatment that would result in the grantor regaining the capacity to make decisions about his or her own medical treatment unless the grantor is in the terminal phase of,

a terminal illness.

(8) The powers conferred by a medical power of attorney must be exercised:

(a) in accordance with any lawful conditions and directions contained in the medical power of attorney; and
(b) if the grantor of the power has also given an anticipatory direction – consistently with the direction,

and subject to those requirements, in what the agent genuinely believes to be the best interests of the grantor.

(9) The grantor of a medical power of attorney may, by any form of representation that indicates an intention to withdraw or terminate the power, revoke the power of attorney.

(10) The grantor of a medical power of attorney may, on regaining capacity to make decisions about his or her medical treatment, vary or revoke any decision taken by the medical agent during the period of incapacity.

Exercise of powers under medical power of attorney

9 (1) A medical agent is only entitled to act under a medical power of attorney if:

(a) the agent produces a copy of the medical power of attorney for inspection by the medical practitioner responsible for the treatment of the grantor of the power; and
(b) the medical agent is not disqualified from acting under the medical power of attorney; and
(c) the medical agent is of full legal capacity.

(2) A medical agent will only be regarded as available to act under a medical power of attorney if:

(a) the medical practitioner responsible for the treatment of the grantor of the medical power of attorney is aware of the appointment; and
(b) the medical agent is entitled to act under the medical power of attorney; and
(c) it is reasonably practicable in the circumstances for the medical practitioner responsible for the grantor's treatment to obtain a decision from the medical agent.

Review of medical agent's decision

10 (1) Supreme court may, on the application of:

(a) the medical practitioner responsible for the treatment of the grantor of a medical power of attorney; or
(b) any person who has in the opinion of the Court a proper interest in the exercise of powers conferred by a medical power of attorney,

review the decision of a medical agent.

(2) The court may not review a decision by a medical agent to discontinue treatment if:

(a) the grantor is in the terminal phase of a terminal illness; and
(b) the effect of the treatment would be merely to prolong life in a moribund state without any real prospect of recovery.

(3) The purpose of the review is:

(a) to ensure that the medical agent's decision is in accordance with lawful conditions and directions contained in the medical power of attorney and, if the grantor of the power has also given an anticipatory direction, is consistent with that direction; and
(b) to ensure as far as possible that the medical agent's decision is in accordance with what the grantor would have wished if the grantor had been able to express his or her wishes.

(4) A decision of a medical agent that is not contrary to lawful conditions and directions given by the grantor will, in the absence of proof to the contrary, be presumed to be in accordance with what the grantor would have wished if the grantor had been able to express his or her wishes but this presumption does not apply if:

(a) the grantor is not in the terminal phase of a terminal illness; and
(b) the effect of the medical agent's decision would be to expose the grantor to the risk of death or exacerbate the risk of death.

(5) The court may:

(a) confirm, cancel, vary or reverse the decision of the medical agent; and
(b) give advice and directions that may be necessary or desirable in the circumstances of the case.

(6) The court must conduct a review under this s as expeditiously as possible.

(7) A person must not publish by newspaper, radio or television a statement or representation:

(a) by which the identity of a person who is, or has been, the subject of proceedings under this s ('the patient') is revealed; or

(b) from which the identity of a person who is, or has been, the subject of proceedings under this s ('the patient') might be inferred.

Penalty: $10,000

(8) Subsection (7):

(a) ceases to apply if or when the patient recovers and then gives his or her consent to the publication of the information; or
(b) ceases to apply after the death of the patient.

(9) In subsection (7):

'newspaper' means any journal, magazine or other publication that is published daily or at periodic intervals.

Penalty for fraud, undue influence, etc

11 (1) A person who, by dishonesty or undue influence, induces another to execute a medical power of attorney is guilty of an offence.

Penalty: Imprisonment for 10 years

The relevant legislation in Queensland is the Powers of Attorney Act 1998 (Qld). The law in New South Wales is governed by a set of guidelines entitled Guidelines for End of Life Care and Decision-Making. They were published on 22 March 2005.

(2) A person who purports to act as a medical agent under a medical power of attorney knowing that the power has been revoked is guilty of an offence.
Penalty: Imprisonment for 10 years.
(3) A person convicted or found guilty of an offence against this s forfeits any interest that the person might otherwise have had in the estate of the grantor of the power of attorney.

Note that, in 1995, a Bill entitled the Medical Care for the Dying Bill 1995 was introduced into the Western Australian Parliament. The Bill is closely modelled on the Victorian Medical Treatment Act. For a brief discussion of the Bill, see Mendelson, D, 'Medical care for the dying' (1995) 3 No 4 Journal of Law and Medicine 315. The Bill was not enacted.

For a first-class discussion of the issues raised by the above Acts, see Mendelson, D, 'Medico-legal aspects of the right to die legislation in Australia' (1993) 19 MULR 112 and, by the same author on broader-based 'letting die' issues, see 'Jurisprudential aspects of withdrawal of life support systems from incompetent patients in Australia' (1995) 69 ALJ 259.

Guidelines for end-of-life care and decision-making

Purpose

NSW Health places a high priority on health professionals working collaboratively with each other, and with patients and their families throughout all phases of end-of-life care. Such care is dependent on open and early communication in an environment of trust. These guidelines set out a process for reaching end-of-life decisions. This process promotes such communication, compassionate and appropriate treatment decisions, fairness, and seeks to safeguard both patients and health professionals.

Ideally, patients are able to determine their own decisions for end-of-life care. Some aspects of the guidelines apply to these patients. Often, however, patients lose decision-making capacity before their wishes for the use of life sustaining treatment have been determined. In those situations, the treating team and family together need to plan care that considers the patient's best interests: reflecting the patient's wishes and values as much as possible and avoiding both inappropriate over- and under-treatment. These guidelines are particularly relevant to such situations where a consensus building approach is recommended.

Dying patients are cared for in many settings including intensive care units, hospital wards, hospice facilities, aged care facilities and the home. These guidelines provide useful advice for health professionals about a process for negotiating end of life decisions wherever that care is delivered.

These guidelines replace the *Dying with Dignity: interim guidelines on management (1993)*.

1 . . .

Guidelines for end-of life care and decision-making NSW Health 2

2 Principles

A large part of this document focuses on building consensus, in particular where patients do not have the capacity to decide on life-sustaining treatment for themselves. Consensus building is the most inclusive process for determining what is the best treatment for that individual, at that time, and in that place. A consensus view about best treatment is ethically based when it is in accordance with the following guiding principles.

Respect for life and care in dying

A primary goal of medical care is preservation of life, however when life cannot be preserved, the task is to provide comfort and dignity to the dying person, and to support others in doing so.

The right to know and to choose

All persons receiving healthcare have a right to be informed about their condition and their treatment options. They have a right to receive or refuse life-prolonging treatment. Caregivers have an ethical and legal obligation to acknowledge and honour these stated choices and preferences in accordance with these guidelines.

Appropriate withholding and withdrawal of life-sustaining treatment

Appropriate end-of-life care should intend to provide the best possible treatment for an individual at that time. It recognises that if the goals of care shift to primarily accommodate comfort and dignity, then withholding or withdrawal of life-sustaining medical interventions may be permissible in the best interests of the dying patient.

A collaborative approach to care

Families and healthcare professionals have an obligation to work together to make compassionate decisions for patients who lack decision-making capacity, taking account of previously expressed patient wishes where known. Many health professionals in the treating team play a role in end-of-life care and a collaborative approach should be fostered.

Transparency and accountability

In order to preserve the trust of those receiving health care, and to ensure that decisions are fairly made, the decision-making process and its outcomes should be clear to the participants and accurately recorded.

Non-discriminatory care

Treatment decisions at the end of life should be non-discriminatory and should be dependent only on factors that are relevant to the patient's medical condition, values and wishes.

Rights and obligations of healthcare professionals

Health professionals are under no obligation to provide treatments that, in the circumstances, are unreasonable, in particular, those that offer negligible prospect of benefit to the patient. Patients have a right to receive care, and health professionals have a responsibility to practise, in accordance with community and professional norms and legal standards.

Continuous improvement

Health professionals have an obligation to strive for ongoing improvement in standards of end-of-life care. This situation requires education and support for those health professionals managing dying patients and their families.

Planning in advance

Decision-making capacity is often lost as serious illness or death approaches. Therefore timely and appropriate decision-making about end-of-life care is more likely where those close to the patient understand the patient's wishes in advance.

With discussion and planning, the patient's preferences and values can inform decision-making as priorities change during the time leading to the patient's death. Currently in NSW, people can plan in advance for end-of-life care by:

developing an advance care plan in conjunction with their health-care professionals while being treated in a care setting;

discussing their preferences for life-sustaining treatment with their family before they are acutely ill;

formally appointing and informing an enduring guardian;

writing an advance care directive.

The critical element for effective advance care planning by any of the above approaches is discussion between the patient and those close to him or her while the patient still has decision-making capacity.

NSW Health has developed best practice guidelines for health professionals on advance care planning for end-of-life care titled *Using Advance Care Directives (NSW)*. Those guidelines should be read in conjunction with this document in order to assist advance care planning where possible and at the earliest appropriate stage. The guidelines are available at www.health.nsw.gov.au (see also paragraph 7.6 of these guidelines).

3 . . .

4 Foundations of sound decision-making

The following section discusses a number of factors that support a sound process for end-of-life decision-making. The process itself is discussed in more detail in section 5. These factors include:

the changing context of treatment limitation decisions at the end of life;

the relationship between the treating team and the patient with decision-making capacity;

the collaborative nature of the treating team;

the consensus building model where the patient has no decision-making capacity;

accountability;

the importance of palliative care.

4.1 The changing context of treatment limitation decisions at the end of life

Because planning for end-of-life care usually takes place in the context of ever-changing circumstances, it is useful to follow the cyclic feedback process for end-of-life decision-making set out in section 5 (see 5.1). One reason for this constant change is the difficulty in predicting, with certainty, an individual's response to particular treatment. Often life-sustaining treatment will be commenced while further investigations are carried out or information sought in order to make a more accurate prognosis. When all available information has been collected, the appropriateness of continuing the treatment is reviewed with the treating team, patient and/or their family. Furthermore, patients' wishes may change as they develop an appreciation of their clinical condition. This process of review, decision-making and treatment trial may be repeated a number of times as the patient's condition improves or deteriorates. These decisions are often based on probabilities, rather than certainties.

4.2 The relationship between the treating team and the patient with decision-making capacity

People are said to have decision-making capacity if they are able to comprehend, retain and weigh up relevant information and then make a choice. A person's decision-making capacity may be adversely affected by a number of chronic or acute illnesses. As a result, decision-making capacity may vary over time and therefore necessitate re-assessment periodically. An adult patient with decision-making capacity may accept or refuse life-sustaining treatment, even where that decision may lead to serious deterioration in health or death. It is crucial that the patient is properly informed of the consequences of refusing such treatment. A patient may make choices about treatment consistent with his or her own values, even where these values differ from those of the treating team. A patient with decision-making capacity does not share decision-making authority with treating health professionals. Rather the treating team acts in an advisory capacity to the patient enabling him or her to make choices regarding reasonable treatment options. Such patients may choose to make decisions without reference to family or others close to them. It is essential that health professionals continue to keep patients informed about their medical condition as they improve or deteriorate, and as the patient's decision-making capacity fluctuates. Patients should be given the opportunity to participate in treatment decisions consistent with their level of decision-making capacity. The general principles regarding consent for medical treatment apply in relation to the treatment of dying patients as they do for other patients. Healthcare professionals must be familiar with the Department's policy on consent PD2005_406 (Circular 2004/84).

4.3 The collaborative nature of the treating team

The treating team involved in end-of-life care, either through direct decision-making or in supportive roles, may variously include medical specialists, surgeons, general practitioners, nurses and allied health workers such as social workers, patient advocates, chaplains or pastoral care workers. Individual members of the treating team may have closer or prolonged involvement with the patient and may be aware of the patient's values and wishes. Other team members may be more involved in how the patient is psychologically or spiritually coping with illness. Each member may bring valuable perspectives and information to the process of planning care and their collaborative involvement should be actively pursued. Junior nurses and doctors should not be excluded where end-of-life decisions are considered, although they should be supervised in any discussions about end-of-life decisions with patients or their families. Reaching agreement within the treating team about appropriate care is an important initial step in a collaborative approach, particularly where the patient no longer has decision-making capacity. It can help reduce subjectivity or bias, particularly in cases of uncertainty.

Nurses and doctors have independent ethical duties towards patients, and the particular burdens that treatment limitation decisions place on nurses should be recognised. Nurses play a significant role in providing clinical and social information about or to the patient and family; in the potential initiation of treatment limitation discussions; and as managers of the dying process. Nurses must be part of the collaborative process whereby the treating team develops a management plan with patients and/or their families.

4.4 A consensus-building model when the patient lacks decision-making capacity

A consensus building approach to end-of-life decision-making that considers the patient's best interests as paramount is recommended where the patient lacks the capacity to determine his or her own care. This collaborative process aims to draw on the family and treating team's knowledge and understanding of the patient's personal values and medical condition. A consensus is sought within the treating team, and between the treating team and family about a plan of care that is as consistent with the patient's wishes and values as possible, and which also supports the family in the degree of involvement it wishes to have. The approach of shared decision-making is recommended as sole decision-making by any one party, either the senior treating clinician or the family, may fail to achieve the best possible treatment decision. A consensus approach with appropriate involvement from both treating team and family:

> avoids placing a senior treating clinician in a position of guessing at a patient's wishes concerning end-of-life treatment without the participation of others, or precipitously withholding or withdrawing treatment

is consistent with a desire by many patients for their family to be involved in end-of-life decisions when they are not able;

avoids imposing possibly additional stress on a family who may perceive that they carry the burden of decision-making and which may later contribute to feelings of guilt;

minimises inappropriate input to decisions where concerns arise about conflict of interest within a family or a family's inability to understand medical aspects of care.

The treating team, and senior treating clinician in particular, should therefore not merely outline treatment options then delegate decision-making responsibility to families, but rather they should make recommendations for management based on their understanding of the patient's medical condition and prognosis, allow time for discussion and reflection, while continuing to work with, and support, a family and reach a consensus decision. Families should be provided with a contact point for appropriate members of the treating team, hospital or community-based staff after the patient's death to discuss unanswered questions, as this may be beneficial in allaying guilt or uncertainties.

Elements that are critical to the success of this approach and options for resolving disagreements are discussed in section 5.

4.5 Accountability

The senior treating clinician is accountable, as leader of the treating team, to the patient, the family, the employing health authority, and ultimately the courts for the process whereby a consensus about end-of-life decisions is sought, and the reasonableness of the planned course of action. Following the process set out in these guidelines and adequate documentation of that process will ensure that the senior treating clinician and the treating team meet the obligations required for accountability in end-of-life treatment decisions.

4.6 Importance of palliative care

The provision of palliative care for patients should continue throughout all phases of terminal illness, and especially during the dying phase. This care should encompass controlling pain, relieving other systems of disease and providing emotional and psychological support in preparation for death. Other issues such as relief of psychological suffering, spiritual care and addressing any unresolved issues for the patient may be raised during discussions about end-of-life care. The specific details of palliative care should be documented. See 7.3

5 Developing a management plan

Planning end-of-life care is an iterative or cyclic process based on **assessment, disclosure, discussion** and **consensus building** with the patient and/or their family and the treatment team. This process can take place over a short period, such as hours, where the patient suddenly or unexpectedly deteriorates, but it can also extend over weeks or months. The key points in each step of this process (section 5.1) are discussed in the following sections.

5.1 Process of end-of-life decision-making

5.2 Assessment

A sudden or unexpected deterioration, or uncertainty about prognosis, usually requires efforts to stabilise the patient so that a complete assessment can be undertaken and potential reversibility of the condition be established. The treating team should undertake this assessment at the earliest appropriate time. Life-sustaining treatment already commenced may be subsequently withdrawn if deemed appropriate upon assessment of the patient's wishes or clinical condition.

Where there is reasonable doubt about the medical assessment in the treating team, advice should be sought from other senior clinicians with experience in the condition if possible. Second opinions should be documented.

Assessment should also include evidence of the patient's preferences and values where available from the patient, or his or her family if the patient has no capacity to express those wishes. Patients' preferences for life sustaining treatment are not static over time and should be regularly reviewed by the treating team.

A patient's desire regarding direct communication and information must be respected. The patient also has a choice to nominate someone to receive information on his or her behalf, or to exclude family members from discussions and decision-making processes. The desire for autonomous-style decision-making or the preference for a collective or delegated approach to end-of-life decisions may vary among patients from different cultural or religious backgrounds. This aspect should be explored on an individual basis to avoid inappropriate clinical decisions and poor interaction with patients and families. The informal use of untrained interpreters such as other family members should be avoided where possible to prevent role confusion and misinterpretation of clinical information.

Failure to demonstrate any improvement in clinical condition over an extended period appropriately generates questions about further initiation or continuation of treatment. The patient, the treating team or the family may initiate such discussions.

Clinical deterioration/non-response to treatment or patient's desire to limit treatment

Assessment

Discussion

Conflict

Disclosure Consensus

Management plan

Options

- Time and repeat discussion
- Second medical opinion
- Facilitation
- Guardianship Tribunal
- Transfer of care
  - physician or institution
- Legal intervention.

5.3 Disclosure

Honest information in non-technical language should be provided to patients and their families for them to participate meaningfully in decisions about end-of-life care. Uncertainty about prognosis or likely response to treatment should be communicated to patients and their families. Prognostic information is ideally given by a health professional who is respected as an expert. Patients and families may be caught off guard when conversations about the goals of care and possible treatment cessation occur suddenly, very late, without preparation, or when they have not received a balanced picture of the patient's prognosis. Patients and their families should be engaged in open communication about possible outcomes early in treatment, especially where the patient is seriously or critically ill, in order to prevent unrealistic expectations about what can be achieved with treatment. Early, honest and regular communication can also help create the trust needed for shared decision-making and to defuse tension.

5.4 Discussion

Discussions with patients and their families about treatment limitation should ideally occur in stages over a period of time, preferably while the patient can determine the appropriateness of treatment or its cessation. The presence of nursing staff, or other key members of the treating team, at these discussions is recommended to support and facilitate communication between the treating team and the family.

Strategic opportunities for the treating team to initiate or revisit discussion about end-of-life care may include recent hospitalisation with severe, progressive illness or repeated recent admissions, inquiries from the patient or family about palliative or hospice care or an expression by the patient of a wish to die.

Having the same person/s communicate with the patient or family on behalf of the treating team throughout this process can be useful, as minor differences in explanation of the patient's condition or progress can seem to patients and families like major disagreements or discord in the team. Ideally, this health professional should be experienced in conducting such discussions, have earned trust before treatment limitation is discussed, and be able to discuss prognostic information.

The phrases 'do everything' or 'do nothing' are unproductive and should be avoided: neither term is ever strictly enacted and such terminology is a barrier to informed discussion regarding the benefits and burdens of certain courses of action. The ongoing care with the goal of providing comfort to the dying patient should be emphasised with the patient and his or her family where limitation of life-sustaining treatment is planned.

5.5 Documenting a consensus decision

The agreed management plan for end-of-life care, and decisions about the use of life-sustaining treatment within that plan, should be documented and conveyed to all members of the treating team. Such communication may be difficult where many staff care for the patient but adequate documentation may assist in this regard. The senior treating clinician is responsible for summarising discussions held with the patient, family and treating team in the patient notes. These notes must clearly state:

medical facts leading to the decision, including prognosis;

persons involved in the discussion;

statement of the patient's wishes, where known;

goals of treatment;

details about medical treatments to be provided, timeframe before review, or details about treatments to be withdrawn/withheld.

Management plans may cover a shorter or longer period of time, depending on the clinical situation of the patient. Decisions that involve withholding treatment such as CPR should be regularly reviewed in accordance with fluctuations in the patient's condition. A change in the appropriateness of withholding treatment such as CPR needs to be re-documented. (See also 7.5.) Other appropriate treating team members should continue to document other aspects of care that will be maintained or enhanced, such as comfort measures. Thorough documentation of decision-making processes and subsequent care enables greater transparency and accountability in the care provided and ensures that all health professionals fulfil their professional and legal obligations.

6 Resolving disagreements

In most situations where a patient is dying, the patient, family and treating team readily come to an agreement on appropriate medical management. However, disagreements can arise regarding treatment limitation decisions, or about other aspects of end-of-life care. Most disagreements between the treating team, the patient or the family can be prevented by early, sensitive and proactive communication that clarifies goals of treatment, possible outcomes and the patient's values and wishes.

6.1 Disagreement in the healthcare team

In circumstances where one team member is in disagreement with the others, the team as a whole should consider the basis for disagreement and seek the opinions of professionals from the same discipline as the disagreeing member. In the event that support for this position cannot be found, it may be appropriate for the dissenting member not to continue being involved in the treating team. As in other areas of clinical practice, a health professional may exercise conscientious objection and not participate in a particular practice which is contrary to his or her moral beliefs.

Counselling or other psychological support may be appropriate where disagreement occurs about the appropriateness of treatment limitation, particularly for nurses who, in some settings and by their more intimate involvement in the care of dying patients, may be more acutely aware of the patient's distress.

6.2 When a patient's family disagrees with a patient's decision

The wishes of the adult patient with decision-making capacity are paramount. If the patient's expressed wishes regarding active treatment or refusal of treatment prior to loss of decision-making capacity are known, then these wishes prevail over the wishes of the family. Disagreements between the patient and his or her family may arise if the family is not properly informed by the treating team about the directions given by the patient, and every effort should be made to communicate this information to the family.

6.3 Inappropriate requests for continuing treatment

At times a family or a patient requests a test or intervention that appears unreasonable or inappropriate to the treating team. Such a request may appear inappropriate in the following scenarios:

> where the patient's condition continues to deteriorate even with optimal therapeutic interventions;
>
> where the treatment would not be successful in producing the clinical effect for which it is ordinarily used;
>
> where the treatment might successfully produce a clinical effect, but still fail to serve important patient goals such as independence from life-support devices, survival in order to leave hospital, or improvement from permanent unconsciousness.

A focus should be kept on the patient. All requests for continuing treatment should be given due consideration before decisions about the appropriateness of treatments are made. Any request should lead to a review of the diagnosis and prognosis and the margins of certainty in each aspect. Health professionals should initially endeavour to explain to the patient or family why they think the desired test or treatment is inappropriate.

Families of patients without decision-making capacity who demand continued treatment in such situations might have unrealistic expectations about what can be achieved. More often though, a family will ask for 'everything to be done' if they are not ready to accept the patient's inevitable death. This situation may be exacerbated when the family are not engaged early in treatment planning prior to the onset of the dying process (see 5.2) or where guilt may be associated with fractured or distant relationships within the family.

Resolving disagreements

The efforts of nursing and medical staff, pastoral care workers, social workers or other counsellors should be directed to supporting family members and assisting them to resolve their difficulties in accepting the reality of the patient's impending death. In such circumstances, it is preferable to continue treatment until conflict with relatives is resolved; however time critical situations pose extremely difficult choices and challenges (see 6.5).

6.4 Potentially inappropriate requests for cessation of treatment by the patient

Unrelieved pain, suffering or depression may influence a patient's request for treatment cessation. Under such circumstances, it is appropriate to explore the patient's feelings, possibly with the assistance of a qualified professional, and to address any issues that may be resolvable.

It may be appropriate to negotiate with the patient an agreed plan of continuing treatment and further discussion in the near future, while acknowledging that sustained wishes for treatment refusal in the competent patient are ultimately paramount.

6.5 Options for resolving disagreement

The following approaches are possible avenues for resolving disagreements in the end-of-life care setting. Not all options will be available in all clinical contexts. However, the simple approaches should be taken first.

Time and repeat discussion

Unless decisions about life-sustaining treatment need to be made urgently, giving families time to come to terms with the impending death of the patient, and to seek further discussion with family or others providing support may be sufficient to resolve outstanding issues.

Second medical opinion

A request for a second medical opinion may be raised with, or directed to, any member of the treating team. Offering a second opinion may also be appropriate if the family are displaying anxieties or uncertainties regarding diagnosis or prognosis. It is the responsibility of the senior treating clinician to facilitate any second medical opinion. This opinion should be from a health professional with relevant expertise in the patient's condition and who is demonstrably independent from the treating team.

Time-limited treatment trial

Such a course of action may be undertaken to clarify prognostic uncertainty or resolve disagreement about prognosis, provided the trial is in the best interests of the patient. It may be advisable to clarify with the treating team and family what treatments are being commenced or continued, the criteria for assessment and the timeframe for review before possible continuation or withdrawal.

Facilitation

Involvement of a third party may assist in clarifying and addressing the concerns of the patient and/or family members, or in finding agreement where an impasse has occurred between the family and the treating team. The third party may be a senior member of the hospital administration, a senior health professional, or another person agreed upon by those involved. The person should have sufficient seniority, be respected by all parties, and be demonstrably independent of the treating team.

Patient transfer

When the above steps have not resolved the situation, the practicality of transferring the care of the patient to another institution or another suitable treating clinician within the same institution should be investigated with those involved.

Guardianship Tribunal

The Guardianship Tribunal may provide advice in relation to end-of-life care for patients lacking decision-making capacity. Advice may include whether it is appropriate for the Tribunal to deal with an application for consent to a proposed treatment on behalf of such a patient. As palliative care is medical treatment under Part 5 of the Guardianship Act, consent may be sought for it to be provided to replace more active treatment. The application must set out the proposed treatment, and any alternative treatments, and the nature and degree of any significant risks associated with either the proposed treatment or the alternatives to it.

Legal intervention

The NSW Supreme Court, or the Family Court of Australia in respect of children and young people under 18 years old, has jurisdiction to hear matters relating to treatment limitation decisions. Senior treating clinicians or their delegates may consider initiating a Court action when they are unsure of whether the proposed treatment or treatment limitation is in accordance with their duties as medical practitioners, and when all of the above steps have failed to resolve their concerns.

Before initiating a Court action, the senior treating clinician should usually have:

obtained a second specialist medical opinion in writing;

received senior institutional advice;

discussed this course of action with the family;

sought advice from the Guardianship Tribunal if the patient does not have decision-making capacity;

informed the hospital executive of the proposed approach.

Where this option is taken, continued consultation should take place with family members to assist in clarifying the issues and to determine whether a legally acceptable solution that is in the best interests of the patient can be reached. Family members or 'persons responsible' may decide to independently initiate a Court action if they have concerns regarding end-of-life decisions where the patient lacks decision-making capacity. Family members or person responsible should be specifically informed that they have this option, where appropriate.

7 Specific issues

7.1 Distinction between euthanasia, assisted suicide and lawful treatment limitation decisions

Euthanasia and assisted suicide both involve deliberate acts or omissions that are undertaken with the intention of ending a person's life and are inconsistent with the duties of a medical practitioner.

Euthanasia and assisted suicide are different from withholding or withdrawing life-sustaining treatment in accordance with good medical practice by a medical practitioner. When treatment is withheld or withdrawn in these circumstances, and a patient subsequently dies, the law classifies the cause of death as the patient's underlying condition and not the actions of others (see 7.3). Care of terminally ill patients that is lawful never involves an intention to end a patient's life. Both euthanasia and assisted suicide are crimes under the Crimes Act 1900 (NSW) and are not endorsed in this document, or by the NSW Department of Health.

7.2 Children and young people

End-of-life decisions in children pose particular difficulties. This difficulty is in part because, unlike adults, children are often unable to understand or fully understand choices concerning life-sustaining treatments or functional states, and the implications for decision-making. Children are also less likely to have expressed values that would, in adults, be known by the family and inform treatment decisions. Parents and the treating team may nevertheless consider that continued treatment is not appropriate where the child's condition is intolerable to the child or where the child is dying.

Older or mature minors (that is, between 14 and 18 years) may not make treatment limitation decisions solely by themselves, even where their capacity to make other medical decisions is not in doubt. However, older minors should be involved in discussions with their parents and the treating team regarding their prognosis and treatment, as appropriate to their level of understanding, emotional maturity and in accordance with their best interests. Multidisciplinary support, as described below, may be necessary where a child's expressed wishes about end-of-life treatment are contrary to those of his or her parents.

Where the treating clinician and parents differ in their assessment of what is in the best interests of the child, or where the parents disagree with each other, the following strategies (additional to those discussed in 6.5) may be useful.

The understandable anxieties of parents in relation to treatment limitation decisions may be complicated by potential feelings of guilt and responsibility for the child's subsequent death. Appropriate multidisciplinary support for parents should be provided at this time. This assistance may ultimately involve working with parents to refocus their hopes and goals.

Assessment of the family dynamics and possible genesis of disagreement within that family by an appropriately qualified mental health or social work professional and family counsellor.

Appointment of an appropriately qualified professional, such as a counsellor, in the treating team to advocate independently for the interests of the child.

The consensus-building approach to treatment limitation decisions outlined elsewhere in these guidelines is also applicable in this setting. Where the process fails to bring a consensus about the appropriateness of treatment limitation, resolution will require application to the Court. In situations where the child is subject to a care order conferring parental responsibility on the Minister for Community Services generally or specifically for medical decisions, the law treats the Minister as the child's parent. The treating clinician should consult with the Minister about the appropriateness of life-sustaining medical treatment by contacting the Department of Community Services. Treatment should continue to be provided, time permitting, while consultation takes place. Disagreements between the treatment team and the Minister or Minister's delegate about the appropriate course of action should be resolved by the same processes as apply to other parents as outlined in these Guidelines.

7.3 Appropriate use of analgesia and sedation

Analgesia and sedation should be provided by whatever route is necessary for relief, in proportion with clinical need, and with the primary goal of relieving pain or other unwanted symptoms. Such administration will not be unlawful provided the intention of the medical practitioner is the relief of symptoms, even if the medical practitioner is aware that the administration of the drug might also hasten death.

7.4 Artificial hydration and nutrition

Use of artificial hydration and nutrition is an intervention with its own possible burdens and discomforts, for example, those related to having tubes in situ or regularly replaced. Withdrawal of artificial hydration and nutrition, like the withdrawal of other medical interventions, can be seen as a treatment limitation decision that may be made in accordance with these guidelines. It is recognised that the provision of artificial hydration and nutrition may be a particularly sensitive matter for some in the community who believe that it must be continued, unless specifically refused by the patient. The offering of food and fluids by ordinary, non-medical means should be part of the care of dying patients as appropriate to their clinical condition or wishes.

7.5 No CPR orders

The term No Cardiopulmonary Resuscitation (No CPR) order is preferred as less ambiguous than Do Not Resuscitate (DNR) or Not For Resuscitation (NFR) orders and the interventions to which they apply.

The principles for withholding CPR are consistent with those for withdrawing life-sustaining treatment as outlined in these guidelines. Decisions relating to withholding CPR should be made on an individual basis, not involving blanket decisions or policies, for example, related to age or disability. (See also section 3 Planning end-of-life care in advance.) A No CPR order may be compatible with providing the patient with maximum therapeutic care, short of CPR. The treating clinician and treating team should reassure the patient, or his or her family, that all comfort and other appropriate care will be provided.

No CPR orders should be clearly written in the patient's medical notes as with other treatment decisions. Use of covert symbols on charts, medical notes or wristbands is not appropriate. Where the decision to apply a No CPR order has not been discussed with the patient because he or she lacks decision-making capacity, that fact should be documented.

Where no explicit decision has been made about the appropriateness, or otherwise, of attempting resuscitation of the hospitalised patient, then resuscitation should be commenced until a senior doctor is available who should determine, based on likely prognosis, whether CPR should continue and then direct the team accordingly.

Where paramedics have been called to a patient whose condition has deteriorated and cardiac arrest occurs, there is a presumption that emergency medical care is appropriate.

7.6 Advance care directives

A number of conditions, outlined below, should be met before the treatment decisions in an advance care directive (see Glossary) are followed:

> the directive is intended to apply to the clinical circumstances that have arisen;
>
> the directive must be sufficiently clear and specific to guide clinical care;
>
> there must not be any evidence to suggest that the directive does not reflect the current intentions of the patient, or was made as a result of undue influence;
>
> the directive should be made by the patient him or herself and should reflect his or her wishes, rather than the wishes of another person.

In addition, it is best practice, but not legally necessary, that:

> the patient should periodically review the directive, for example, once a year, after an illness, or with a change in health status;
>
> the directive should be available at the time decisions need to be made, for example, by ensuring the likely person responsible and primary healthcare provider have a copy of the directive and any of its revisions;
>
> the directive should be signed and witnessed;
>
> a medical practitioner should be involved in discussions with the patient to assist with the development of the directive.

See also section 3 of these guidelines. For more detailed information about advance care directives and advance care planning, see *Using Advance Care Directives (NSW)*, NSW Health, 2004.

7.7 Persistent vegetative state (post-coma unresponsiveness)

Treatment limitation for a severely brain-injured patient is a decision that should be made in accordance with these guidelines. Diagnosis of persistent vegetative state is difficult and usually protracted, often taking months to confirm. The National Health and Medical Research Council has released advice on this matter titled *Post-coma unresponsiveness (vegetative state): a clinical framework for diagnosis*. It is available on www.nhmrc.gov.au.

7.8 Emergency treatment

In some circumstances, for example where a patient's condition suddenly deteriorates and his or her wishes or likelihood of recovery are unknown, a treating clinician or health professional may provide medical treatment without consent (from either the patient or the person responsible) if the treatment is necessary as a matter of urgency. Such situations might be to:

save the patient's life;

prevent serious damage to the patient's health; or, except in cases of special medical treatment, alleviate significant pain or distress.

This treatment should be no more than is reasonably required in the best interests of the patient.

This does not apply, however, if the patient, when competent, has unequivocally refused the provision of such treatment in the applicable circumstances and the clinician is satisfied on the available evidence that such a direction has been made.

Developing local policy

These guidelines should form the basis of local policy on end-of-life decision-making, considering local conditions and resources. Local policy development is recommended for the following situations:

no CPR orders;

minimum standards for documentation of decisions about withholding, or withdrawal of, treatment;

dispute resolution for patients, families and staff.

Local policy may expand on these guidelines by, for example, identifying relevant persons or contacts within the hospital/Area Health Service who may serve certain roles.

Quality improvement activities for end-of-life care that incorporate self-audit, with other sources of performance feedback, such as complaints and commendations, should be developed to guide future practice. Area Health Services or individual hospitals should identify an appropriate implementation group to undertake local policy development using these guidelines.

8 Advance care directives

An advance care directive contains instructions that consent to, or refuse, the future use of specified medical treatments. It becomes effective in situations where the patient no longer has the capacity to make treatment decisions.

Family

For the purposes of this document and recognising the collaborative nature of end-of-life care, the term 'family' is used to refer to a person or persons who have a close, ongoing, personal relationship with the patient, whom the patient may have expressed a desire to be involved in treatment decisions, and who have themselves indicated a preparedness to be involved in such decisions. This person or persons may or may not include the immediate biological family. However, it may include other relatives, partner (including same sex and de facto partners), friend, or 'person responsible' according to any expressed wishes of the patient.

Life-sustaining treatment

Life-sustaining treatment is any medical intervention, technology, procedure or medication that is administered to forestall the moment of death, whether or not the treatment is intended to affect life-threatening diseases or biological processes. These treatments may include, but are not limited to, mechanical ventilation, artificial hydration and nutrition, cardiopulmonary resuscitation or certain medications (including antibiotics).

Palliative care

Palliative care is competent and compassionate care which provides coordinated medical, nursing and allied health services for people who are terminally ill, delivered where possible in the environment of the patient's choice. It provides relief from pain and other distressing symptoms, integrates psychological and spiritual aspects of care, focuses on supporting patients to live as actively as possible until death, and includes grief and bereavement support for the patient, family and other carers during the life of the patient, and continues after the death of the patient.

Patient

For the purposes of this document, the patient describes the person receiving end-of-life care in an institution such as an intensive care unit, hospital ward, hospice facility, aged-care facility and the home.

Person responsible

The Guardianship Act 1987 (NSW) establishes who can give valid consent for medical treatment to an incompetent patient aged 16 years and over. Consent of the person responsible is required in relation to provision of minor and major medical treatment. The Act establishes a hierarchy for determining who is the person responsible as follows:

> The patient's lawfully appointed guardian (including an enduring guardian) but only if the order or instrument appointing the guardian extends to medical treatment.
>
> If there is no guardian, a spouse including a de facto spouse and same sex partner with whom the person has a close continuing relationship.
>
> If there is no such person, a person who has the care of the patient (otherwise than for fee and reward).
>
> If there is no such person, a close friend or relative.

See the Department's consent policy (circular 2004/84) for further information on substitute consent and persons responsible.

Treatment limitation decisions

Decisions that involve the reduction, withdrawal or withholding of life-sustaining treatment.

Treating team

The multidisciplinary team of health professionals involved in the patient's management and care, including medical, nursing, allied health, social workers and counsellors, carers and spiritual advisors.

Gardner; re BWV [2003] VSC 173 (29 May 2003)

Morris J:

1. The plaintiff is the Public Advocate of Victoria. This position is a statutory position created by s 14 of the Guardianship and Administration Act 1986.

2. By reason of s 16(1)(a) of that Act the Public Advocate may be appointed by the Victorian Civil and Administrative Tribunal ('the Tribunal') to be a guardian, whether plenary or limited, of a person who needs representation.

3. On 28 February 2003 the Tribunal appointed the Public Advocate to be a limited guardian of BWV, a woman aged 68 years who suffers from dementia. The appointment constituted the Public Advocate as a limited guardian of BWV with powers and duties to make decisions concerning her medical treatment.

4. BWV suffers from a progressive and fatal form of dementia, probably

Pick's Disease. She has not appeared conscious, or to have any cortical activity, for approximately three years. She appears to have no cognitive capacity at all and has no bodily functions, other than those which are reflexive. Further, she appears to have no conscious perception of input from any of her sensory pathways.

5. BWV receives fluid and nutrition, via a percutaneous endoscopic gastrostomy ('PEG'), which process keeps her alive.

6. BWV requires full nursing care: she is doubly incontinent; she receives regular pressure care; she is moved into a shower by a hoist; and she receives medications, as well as nutrition and hydration, through the PEG.

7. Although the brain stem of BWV continues to function normally, the medical evidence is that the damage to the cortex is irreparable. There is no prospect of any recovery, or improvement of any kind in BWV's condition.

8. The evidence of the three medical witnesses who examined BWV is that the provision of nutrition and hydration, via the PEG, is futile, in the sense that it has no prospect whatever of improving her condition.

9. It is in these circumstances that the plaintiff seeks declarations from the Court that:

(a) provision of nutrition and hydration via a percutaneous endoscopic gastrostomy ('PEG') to BWV constitutes 'medical treatment' within the meaning of the term in the Medical Treatment Act 1988; and
(b) refusal of further nutrition and hydration administered via a PEG to BWV constitutes refusal of 'medical treatment', rather than refusal of 'palliative care', within the meaning of the Medical Treatment Act 1988.

10. The significance of the distinction between 'medical treatment' and 'palliative care', in the context of the Medical Treatment Act 1988, revolves around the provisions of ss 3, 4 and 5B of that Act, which effectively allows a guardian, on behalf of a patient, to refuse medical treatment, but not to refuse palliative care.

11. If the declarations sought are made, the Public Advocate, on behalf of BWV, intends to refuse further medical treatment in the form of the provision of nutrition and hydration via the PEG (subject to satisfying certain other conditions required by the Act). If this occurs BWV will die within one to four weeks of the withdrawal of such nutrition and hydration.

Parties and amicus curiae

12. The application was made by way of an originating motion, without naming any defendant.

13. On 13 May 2003 Master Kings ordered that the Attorney-General for the State of Victoria be given leave to intervene. Counsel for

the Attorney-General subsequently explained to the Court that the application to intervene had been made to ensure that there was a proper contradictor; and, also, to ensure that certain matters concerning the public interest were considered by the Court.

14. On 14 May 2003 I considered an application by Right to Life Australia Incorporated to be joined as a party to the proceeding and be given leave to intervene in the proceeding. I refused this application. I considered that Right to Life Australia Incorporated could not demonstrate any legal interest which would entitle it to be made a party or be given leave to intervene. Further, I indicated, that I would have refused to give leave for Right to Life Australia Incorporated to be joined as a party as a matter of discretion.

15. Nonetheless I did decide that Right to Life Australia Incorporated should be given leave to appear before the Court as *amicus curiae*; subject to the condition that, subject to any further order, its participation in the hearing be confined to making written submissions and oral submissions (confined to one hour) concerning the interpretation of the Medical Treatment Act 1988 in the context of the application for declarations in the case.

16. The Most Reverend D J Hart, Catholic Archbishop of Melbourne, and Catholic Health Australia Incorporated also appeared before me on 14 May 2003. These persons did not seek to be joined as parties, or be given leave to intervene in the proceeding; but they did apply to be given leave to appear *amicus curiae*. I granted such leave, on the same basis as that set out above in relation to Right to Life Australia Incorporated.

17. In refusing the application of Right to Life Australia Incorporated to be joined as a party, and in granting the applications for leave to appear *amicus curiae*, I had regard to the comments of Brennan CJ and Kirby J in *Levy v Victoria*. It is unusual for the status of *amicus curiae* to be given to a person in a hearing before the Trial Division of this Court. However, it struck me that the nature of the proceeding, the novelty of the issues raised, the possible implications of any decision and the uncertainty about the precise role that the Attorney-General might play in the proceeding all justified this course. (As matters transpired, the Attorney-General played a substantial role in the hearing and made submissions contrary to those of the Public Advocate.)

Evidence

18. The Public Advocate has given evidence to the Court that he has obtained information in relation to BWV's current condition from four medical practitioners, being:

- Dr Michael Woodward, MBBS, FRACP, consultant physician in geriatric medicine and general medicine and rehabilitation;
- Dr Noel G Whitty, BWV's treating general practitioner;
- Professor Michael Ashby, MD, MRCP, FRCR, FRACP, FAChPM, Head of Palliative Care Unit at the Monash Medical Centre; and

- Professor Malcolm Horne, MBBS, PhD, FRACP, Director of Neurological Sciences at the Monash Medical Centre.

19. The Public Advocate has also given evidence to the Court that he has consulted with the family of BWV, which consists of the husband of BWV and six adult sons and daughters of BWV. By reference to these matters, the Public Advocate has formed the view that it would be contrary to the wishes of BWV to continue to receive nutrition and hydration through the PEG and that the continuation of these measures constitutes a continuing denial of her wishes. Further, the Public Advocate has formed the view, after consultation with the medical practitioners and the members of BWV's family, that BWV would, after giving serious consideration to her health and wellbeing, consider that the medical treatment she is receiving is unwarranted and unreasonable.

20. The affidavit of the Public Advocate also set out statements of the family of BWV as to what they knew of BWV's wishes if she was ever to be in her current condition. It was argued that this part of the Public Advocate's evidence was inadmissible as hearsay; and I expressly reserved ruling on this question until the giving of judgment. As matters transpired it has become unnecessary for me to make any ruling as my decision can be made without relying on this evidence.

21. Dr Ashby, who is highly qualified in the field of palliative medicine, visited BWV on 14 April 2003 and subsequently provided a report to the Public Advocate. He expressed the opinion that BWV is slowly dying of advanced dementia. In his view it is in accordance with good medical practice, and in particular good palliative care, for the PEG to be removed and for the provision of fluids and nutrition to cease. He believes the present nutrition and hydration regime does not accord with the 'reasonable provision of food and water' because it is only having the effect of prolonging the natural dying process.

22. Professor Horne is a highly qualified expert in neuroscience. He saw BWV on 13 April 2003, made investigations and subsequently provided a report to the Public Advocate. His report, which provides a basis for the findings set out earlier in this judgment, concludes by stating that BWV has no prospect of any recovery, or any improvement of any kind.

23. Dr Michael Woodward, a consultant physician in geriatric medicine, also provided a report to the Public Advocate. This report offers further support to the findings set out earlier in this judgment. However Dr Woodward's report did differ in that he stated that, in his opinion, the maintenance of hydration and nutrition is not generally regarded as medical treatment. By this he meant that the actual administration of the nutrition and hydration, through the PEG, is not regarded as medical treatment. In his oral evidence Dr Woodward shifted from this view and he told the Court that he would certainly regard the provision of food and fluid, via a PEG, as an example of a medical procedure, if not medical treatment.

24. However, in my opinion, medical opinion as to whether or not the

administration of nutrition and hydration through a PEG is, or is not, medical treatment is not directly relevant in the context of the Medical Treatment Act 1988, because the expression 'medical treatment', when used in the Act, carries a special, statutory meaning.

25. Evidence was also given to the Court by Dr Peter John McCullagh. Dr McCullagh is now retired, but has previously worked in medical research and has been the President of the National Brain Injury Foundation. The circumstances in which Dr McCullagh gave evidence were somewhat unusual. In December 2002, prior to the VCAT hearing, an officer of the Public Advocate had contacted Dr McCullagh seeking information about the circumstances in which artificial nutrition and hydration, via a PEG, might be refused. Dr McCullagh had apparently written a book, which had not then been published, on questions relating to brain injuries. Dr McCullagh provided a short series of comments on 15 December 2002 in relation to the withdrawal of PEG feeding. The matter was left there and would have remained there, but for the fact that Dr McCullagh decided to attend the first day of the hearing. On that day counsel for Right to Life Australia Incorporated raised a concern that the Public Advocate was not being candid with the Court because he was not calling Dr McCullagh to give evidence. Subsequently the Public Advocate explained that he did not have any personal knowledge that Dr McCullagh had been contacted by a junior officer in his employ. I accept that evidence. Nonetheless, in order to remove any possible concern, Mr Burnside QC, who appeared with Dr Freckelton for the Public Advocate, called Dr McCullagh to give evidence.

26. Although I have found reading the transcript of Dr McCullagh's evidence informative and helpful in relation to some of the issues I am called upon to decide, his evidence cannot be regarded as being in the same category as the evidence of Dr Ashby, Professor Horne or Dr Woodward. Dr McCullagh has not examined BWV and, really, he is in no position to give evidence about her condition.

27. Having regard to what was put to me, I do wish to record that I am satisfied that the Public Advocate has displayed candour with the Court. It was suggested at one stage that I was having the wool pulled over my eyes. If that is the case, I certainly have not detected it.

Submissions

28. Essentially the Public Advocate submitted that the matter before the Court was governed by the Medical Treatment Act. It was submitted that the administration of nutrition and hydration via a PEG was (what I will call) *prima facie medical treatment* because it was either the administration of a substance like a drug or some other medical procedure. Further it was submitted that such administration, or procedure, did not constitute palliative care, whether by reference to the natural meaning of the words 'palliative care', or any of the included words. In relation to paragraph (b) of the definition of palliative care, it was sub-

mitted that the proper meaning of the expression 'the reasonable provision of food and water' was the ordinary provision of food or water, being food or water provided for oral consumption. Alternatively it was submitted that, if the provision of food and water by artificial means, through a PEG, was embraced by the words in paragraph (b) of the definition of palliative care, then this was not 'reasonable' in all the circumstances.

29. Counsel for the Attorney-General took issue with a number of elements of this argument. Ms Tate, SC who appeared with Ms Brophy for the Attorney-General, questioned whether the administration of artificial nutrition and hydration to BWV could be regarded, *prima facie*, as within the definition of medical treatment. Further, it was submitted that such a process could constitute palliative care, as being the reasonable provision of food and water, which would result in it failing to be regarded as medical treatment under the Act. The Attorney-General submitted that the Court should consider whether to exercise its power within the *parens patriae* jurisdiction of the Court and make an order, or give a consent, which would provide a remedy in the circumstances of this case, without impacting upon the operation of the Medical Treatment Act.

30. The Public Advocate responded to this argument by contending that the parliament had put in place the Guardianship and Administration Act 1986 and the Medical Treatment Act 1988 to deal with guardianship issues and issues relating to the refusal of medical treatment, including by agents and guardians on behalf of other persons. He contended that it was the intention of parliament that these statutes largely govern the circumstances which arise in this case. Counsel for the Public Advocate did not deny the continued existence of the *parens patriae* jurisdiction, but submitted that it should be reserved for extraordinary circumstances. Nonetheless, it was submitted that, should the application in relation to the Medical Treatment Act fail, it would be appropriate in those circumstances for the Court to ultimately make an order in its *parens patriae* jurisdiction.

31. Written and oral submissions were made on behalf of the Most Reverend Hart, Catholic Archbishop of Melbourne, Catholic Health Australia Incorporated and Right to Life Australia Incorporated, all as *amicus curiae*, in relation to the interpretation of the Medical Treatment Act in the context of the application for declarations. These submissions were comprehensive and thought provoking and have assisted the Court in its task.

Key issues

32. The key issues in this case which the Court must address are:

- what is the meaning of the words used in the definitions of medical treatment and palliative care in the Act;

- whether, having regard to the meaning of the defined terms and the facts, it is appropriate to make the declaration sought by the Public Advocate or decline to make such declarations, either absolutely or because it would be better for the Court to exercise its powers within the *parens patriae* jurisdiction of the Court.

Legal context

33. In 1988 the Victorian Parliament passed the Medical Treatment Act 1988, with the intention of clarifying the law relating to the right of patients to refuse medical treatment. Subsequently, in 1990, the Act was amended to enable an agent or guardian to make decisions about medical treatment on behalf of an incompetent patient.

34. The present application arises in the context of the Medical Treatment Act; it is not an application which relies upon the common law right of a person to refuse medical treatment; nor, for that matter, is it an application in which the plaintiff calls in aid the Court's *parens patriae* jurisdiction. At least three things follow from this.

35. First, decisions in other jurisdictions which were made by reference to common law principles, whilst of general assistance, are not directly relevant.

36. Second, the Court is in a position where the parliament has turned its mind to the circumstances where an agent or guardian may refuse treatment on behalf of a patient. This issue is of public interest and will inevitably involve different views, having regard to the nature of the philosophical, legal, moral and social issues involved. But I must emphasise: the Medical Treatment Act is part of the law of Victoria; it is the role of a judge of this Court to discharge his or her office according to law; and in giving its judgment the Court should be taken as giving effect to the will of parliament, not making new law.

37. Third, in the interpretation of provisions of the Medical Treatment Act, a construction that would promote the purpose or object underlying the Act should be preferred to a construction that would not promote that purpose or object. This will require consideration of the whole of the Act, so that particular provisions can be interpreted in their context. Further, in seeking to interpret particular provisions of the Act, consideration may be given to relevant documents that form part of the legislative history, including reports of proceedings before the Legislative Assembly and Legislative Council and reports of parliamentary committees.

Medical Treatment Act 1988

38. In order that this decision can be understood in its full legal context, it is necessary to set out substantial extracts from the Medical Treatment Act 1988. It is convenient to set out the relevant extracts in the same order as they are contained in the Act.

Preamble

The Parliament recognises that it is desirable –

(a) to give protection to the patient's right to refuse unwanted medical treatment;
(b) to give protection to medical practitioners who act in good faith in accordance with a patient's express wishes;
(c) to recognise the difficult circumstances that face medical practitioners in advising patients and providing guidance in relation to treatment options;
(d) to state clearly the way in which a patient can signify his or her wishes in regard to medical care;
(e) to encourage community and professional understanding of the changing focus of treatment from cure to pain relief for terminally-ill patients;
(f) to ensure that dying patients receive maximum relief from pain and suffering.

1. Purpose

The purposes of this Act are –

(a) to clarify the law relating to the right of patients to refuse medical treatment;
(b) to establish a procedure for clearly indicating a decision to refuse medical treatment;
(c) to enable an agent to make decisions about medical treatment on behalf of an incompetent person.

. . .

3. Definitions

In this Act –

. . .

'medical treatment' means the carrying out of –

(a) an operation; or
(b) the administration of a drug or other like substance; or
(c) any other medical procedure–
but does not include palliative care;

'palliative care' includes –

(a) the provision of reasonable medical procedures for the relief of pain, suffering and discomfort; or
(b) the reasonable provision of food and water;

. . .

4. Other legal rights not affected

(1) This Act does not affect any right of a person under any other law to refuse medical treatment.

(2) This Act does not apply to palliative care and does not affect any right, power or duty which a registered medical practitioner or any other person has in relation to palliative care.

(3) This Act does not –

(a) affect the operation of section 6B(2) or 463B of the Crimes Act 1958; or
(b) limit the operation of any other law.

(4) A refusal of medical treatment under this Act does not limit any duty of a registered medical practitioner or other person –

(a) to advise and inform the patient or the patient's agent or guardian; or
(b) to provide medical treatment, other than medical treatment that has been refused.

5. Refusal of treatment of certificate

(1) If a registered medical practitioner and another person are each satisfied –

(a) that a patient has clearly expressed or indicated a decision –
    (i) to refuse medical treatment generally; or
    (ii) to refuse medical treatment of a particular kind – for a current condition; and
(b) that the patient's decision is made voluntarily and without inducement or compulsion; and
(c) that the patient has been informed about the nature of his or her condition to an extent which is reasonably sufficient to enable the patient to make a decision about whether or not to refuse medical treatment generally or of a particular kind (as the case requires) for that condition and that the patient has appeared to understand that information; and
(d) that the patient is of sound mind and has attained the age of 18 years – the registered medical practitioner and the other person may together witness a refusal of treatment certificate.

. . .

(3) For the purposes of sub-section (1)(a), the patient may clearly express or indicate a decision in writing, orally or in any other way in which the person can communicate.

5A. Agents and guardians

(1) A decision about medical treatment of a person may be made in accordance with this Act –

(a) if the person has appointed an agent in accordance with this section, by that agent;
or
...
(b) if the person is a represented person and an appropriate order has been made under the Guardianship and Administration Act 1986 providing for decisions about medical treatment, by the person's guardian.

5B. Refusal of treatment certificate by agent or guardian

(1) If a registered medical practitioner and another person are each satisfied –

(a) that the patient's agent or guardian has been informed about the nature of the patient's current condition to an extent that would be reasonably sufficient to enable the patient, if he or she were competent, to make a decision about whether or not to refuse medical treatment generally or of a particular kind for that condition; and
(b) that the agent or guardian understands that information –
the agent or guardian, on behalf of the patient –
(c) may refuse medical treatment generally; or
(d) may refuse medical treatment of a particular kind –
for that condition.

(2) An agent or guardian may only refuse medical treatment on behalf of a patient if –

(a) the medical treatment would cause unreasonable distress to the patient; or
(b) there are reasonable grounds for believing that the patient, if competent, and after giving serious consideration to his or her health and well-being, would consider that the medical treatment is unwarranted.

(3) Where a refusal is made by an agent or a guardian, a refusal of treatment certificate must be completed in the form of Schedule 3.

...

6. Offence of medical trespass

A registered medical practitioner must not, knowing that a refusal of treatment certificate applies to a person, undertake or continue to undertake any medical treatment to which the certificate applies, being treatment for the condition in relation to which the certificate was given.

Penalty: 5 penalty units.

7. Cancellation or cessation of certificate

. . .

(3) A refusal of treatment certificate ceases to apply to a person if the medical condition of the person has changed to such an extent that the condition in relation to which the certificate was given is no longer current.

. . .

9. Protection of registered medical practitioners

(1) A registered medical practitioner or a person acting under the direction of a registered medical practitioner who, in good faith and in reliance on a refusal of treatment certificate, refuses to perform or continue medical treatment which he or she believes on reasonable grounds has been refused in accordance with this Act is not –

(a) guilty of misconduct or infamous misconduct in a professional respect; or
(b) guilty of an offence; or
(c) liable in any civil proceedings –
because of the failure to perform or continue that treatment.

39. The effect of these provisions in this case is that the Public Advocate, as guardian of BWV with the power to make decisions concerning her medical treatment, may refuse 'medical treatment' of a particular kind for the current condition of BWV, if:

- the medical treatment would cause unreasonable distress to BWV; or
- there are reasonable grounds for believing that BWV, if competent, and after giving serious consideration to her health and wellbeing, would consider that the medical treatment is unwarranted.

40. However the Public Advocate cannot refuse treatment pursuant to the Act, on behalf of BWV, if that treatment is not 'medical treatment'. Further, if a procedure or practice constitutes palliative care, it cannot be refused pursuant to the Act, because it would then be excluded from the definition of medical treatment.

Purposes of Medical Treatment Act

41. The inclusion of a preamble to the Act and the matters set out in s 1 of the Act make it relatively easy to discern the purposes of the Act. In the context of the present case, two purposes stand out:

- to both clarify and give legal effect to the right of a patient to refuse unwanted medical treatment; and
- to enable an agent (including a guardian) to make a decision about medical treatment on behalf of an incompetent patient.

42. Much was said during the hearing about the sanctity of life. There is no doubt that this is a fundamental principle of every civilised society, although I believe that the principle is better referred to as the inviolability of life. But as Hoffmann LJ observed in *Bland*:

> But the sanctity of life is only one of a cluster of ethical principles which we apply to decisions about how we should live. Another is respect for the individual human being and in particular for his right to choose how he should live his own life. We call this individual autonomy or the right of self determination. And another principle, closely connected, is respect for the dignity of the individual human being: our belief that quite irrespective of what the person concerned may think about it, it is wrong for someone to be humiliated or treated without respect for his value as a person.

43. In *Bland* the English courts adopted an approach which sought to balance these competing values and which established a common law position, in that country, which revolves around what is said to be in the 'best interests' of the patient. It is unnecessary to decide whether that same principle applies as part of the common law in Victoria. Nonetheless it is important to note that, both legally and ethically, it will always be necessary to achieve some accommodation between different moral principles. In this respect, I agree with Hoffmann LJ, in *Bland* when he said:

> I do not suggest that the position which English law has taken is the only morally correct solution. Some might think that in cases of life and death, the law should be more paternalist even to adults. The point to be emphasised is that there is no morally correct solution which can be deduced from a single ethical principle like the sanctity of life or the right of self determination. There must be an accommodation between principles, both of which seem rational and good, but which have come into conflict with each other.

44. The Medical Treatment Act 1988, combined with the Guardianship and Administration Act, seeks to achieve an appropriate accommodation between these principles in Victoria. This does not mean that the Act articulates the only morally correct solution. But it is the solution which forms part of the law in this State.

Legislative history

45. This is a case where it is appropriate to have regard to the legislative history in carrying out the task of interpreting the provisions of the Medical Treatment Act, particularly the definitions of medical treatment and palliative care.

46. The legislative history of the Act is unusual, and requires some background.

47. Victoria has two houses of parliament, the Legislative Assembly

and the Legislative Council. The Legislative Assembly is the lower house and, in 1988, consisted of 88 members. The majority party in the lower house forms the government. During the relevant period the Australian Labor Party formed the majority in the Legislative Assembly and constituted the government. In 1988 the Legislative Council consisted of 44 members. Twenty two members were drawn from the Australian Labor Party; and 22 members were drawn from conservative political parties (the Liberal Party of Australia and the National Party). Of course, for legislation to be approved, it needed to be carried by both houses of parliament.

48. In 1988 the President of the Legislative Council was a member of the Australian Labor Party. As president, this member did not have a deliberative vote, but could only cast a vote if the number of votes for and against were the same. This effectively meant that the government of the day could only get its legislation through both houses of parliament if at least one member of the conservative parties in the Legislative Council voted for a proposed Act or abstained from voting.

49. On 17 December 1985 the Social Development Committee of the parliament was asked to conduct an inquiry and make recommendations to the parliament in relation to a number of matters which were subsequently described as options for dying with dignity. The members of the Committee were drawn from all political parties and from both the Legislative Council and the Legislative Assembly. The chair person of the Committee was the Honourable J L Dixon, a member of the Australian Labor Party and of the Legislative Council. The Committee conducted an extensive inquiry and subsequently produced at least two reports.

50. In April 1987 the second and final report of the Committee was published and was titled 'Inquiry into Options for Dying with Dignity'. Amongst other things, the Committee concluded that:

> . . . the primary mechanism for clarification of the common law right to refuse medical treatment is by means of legislation. Such legislation should verify the right of a competent adult to refuse medical treatment or *life support systems*, thereby protecting the individual concerned, their relatives or care-givers, and the medical team caring for the individual. [My emphasis.]

51. In the course of its discussions the Committee also discussed the concepts of a 'right to die' and a 'right to die with dignity'. The Committee reported:

> The Committee found that, while opinions were divided on definitions of a 'right to die', there appeared to be considerable common ground as to what a 'right to die peacefully with human dignity' means, in a practical, everyday sense among the major religious and philosophical traditions in our community. In essence, there appears to be common ground among these traditions that a

dying person has a basic right to die with dignity. From a moral perspective such a basic right comprises two elements:

(a) that it is morally acceptable to forego medical treatment which is 'disproportionate' or 'extraordinary' or 'burdensome'; and
(b) that it is morally acceptable to administer pain-killing medication with the intention of relieving pain and suffering, even though the medication may shorten life.

52. The drafting of a Bill to give effect to the Committee's recommendations proved to be no easy task. According to Hansard debates the final version was in fact the ninth draft. However, for present purposes, it is sufficient to refer to the last three drafts.

53. On 27 October 1987 a Bill was introduced into the Legislative Council, known as a Bill for the Medical Treatment Act 1987. This Bill did not contain any definition of 'palliative care'. However the definition of medical treatment was as follows:

> 'Medical Treatment' means the carrying out of –
>
> (a) an operation; or
> (b) the administration of a drug or other substance; or
> (c) any other medical procedure
>
> except for the purposes of relief of pain, suffering or discomfort.'

This Bill was not proceeded with.

54. On 23 March 1988 the Honourable E H Walker, on behalf of the Honourable J H Kennan, (both members of the government) moved that the Medical Treatment Bill (No 2) be read for a second time. This Bill contained a different definition of 'medical treatment' and a new definition of 'palliative care', as follows:

> 'Medical Treatment' means the carrying out of –
>
> (a) an operation; or
> (b) the administration of a drug or other like substance; or
> (c) any other medical procedure
>
> but does not include palliative care. 'Palliative Care' means a medical procedure for the purposes of relief of pain, suffering or discomfort, including the provision of food or water (or other medical care) which is not burdensome to the patient.

55. It is to be observed that the Bill introduced in 1988 differed from that introduced in 1987, not only by introducing the definition of palliative care, but also by specifically referring to the provision of food or water as part of palliative care (and, hence, not part of medical treatment). This is of potential significance as part of the task facing the Court is to give effect to parliament's will in relation to the meaning of the words

> the 'provision of food and water'.

56. In the course of his second reading speech, Mr Walker referred to the fact that a definition of palliative care had been included in the Bill. He then said:

> 'The definition of "palliative care" covers treatment for the relief of pain, suffering or discomfort and specifically includes the provision of food or water or other medical care which is not burdensome to the patient. The inclusion of non-burdensome treatment within the definition is intended to meet concerns that the Bill as originally drafted addressed only the medical, pain relieving aspect of treatment and did not recognise necessary *non-medical care, especially in the area of physical sustenance.*' [My emphasis.]

57. The conservative parties strongly opposed the Medical Treatment Bill (No 2). This opposition was lead by the Honourable B A Chamberlain, a senior and respected member of the Council. He was supported in the debate by other members of the conservative parties, though, interestingly, not by the Honourable R I Knowles or the Honourable R M Hallam who, with Mrs Dixon, had been members of the inquiry into options for dying with dignity.

58. Mr Chamberlain was strongly critical of some of the concepts employed in the Bill, stating that it was possible 'to drive a truck through the concepts'. In describing the Bill Mr Chamberlain commenced by saying:

> The scheme of the Bill is as follows: firstly, the Act does not apply to pain relieving care and the ordinary provision of food; those are items which cannot be refused under a refusal of treatment certificate.

59. The Honourable Judy Dixon made a lengthy speech in support of the Bill. During the course of this speech she distributed a list of amendments that the government proposed to make when the Bill was considered in its committee stage. One of these amendments was to alter the definition of 'palliative care' so it would read:

> 'Palliative care' includes –
>
> (a) the provision of reasonable medical procedures for the relief of pain, suffering and discomfort; or
> (b) the reasonable provision of food and water.

60. In the course of her speech Mrs Dixon said:

> I shall foreshadow important amendments that the government will move during the Committee stage. The amendments concern palliative care, which was an issue raised by Mr Chamberlain. The subject is difficult and all honourable members acknowledge that the consultative process has been long and trying. We were very concerned to make sure that no one was ever in the situation where he or she would be refused, or where anyone could refuse on his or her behalf, food and water. Working out that particular definition was difficult.

> Honourable members have before them the definition of 'palliative care'. That definition will resolve the problem. It means that palliative care is now divided into two separate elements; the first is the provision of reasonable medical procedures for the relief of pain and suffering and discomfort; and the second is the reasonable provision of food and water. *This definition will overcome confusion that has arisen because of the use of the term 'medical procedures' as one which embraced the provision of food and water.* I shall not go into further detail because the subject will be explained during the committee stage. [My emphasis.]

Unfortunately the matter was not further explained during the committee stage.

61. Another speaker during the second reading debate was the Honourable JVC Guest, a member of the Liberal Party and a former barrister. In the course of his contribution he said:

> I turn now briefly to what will be the ninth version of the Bill. Mrs Dixon referred to the care taken, and the amendments made or proposed, to ensure that a patient cannot refuse food and drink. At least two further questions arise from that: one is whether that means that the food will be forced into the mouth of a patient. Is it yet another case of the government not having thought the matter through? Does this really mean that the patient cannot refuse any food and drink? A number of cases that were not commented on adversely which were related in the Committee's report were of old people who simply refused to eat. Will those people suffering from the terminal illness of old age have their mouths levered open and food shoved into them? Possibly this is not just a failure of the government to think clearly but also a failure to bite the bullet. If the patients are not fed orally, will they have tubes inserted into their veins so that they obtain the nutrients compulsorily? The government has failed to spell out the detail of the proposed legislation that would help members of the medical profession in this respect as well as other drafting problems referred to by Mr Chamberlain.

62. The speaker who followed Mr Guest was the Honourable M A Lyster, who later became Minister for Health in the Kirner government. In the course of her speech she referred to the rider to the definition of medical treatment, namely that it did not include palliative care. In relation to patients choosing palliative care rather than medical treatment Mrs Lyster said:

> 'They may not use those words, quite obviously, but what they want is to be able to die with dignity. That is where the palliative care issue becomes so important. Clause 3 of the Bill defines palliative care as 'a medical procedure for the purposes of relief of pain, suffering or discomfort, including the provision' – for those who imagine for some reason that we are in some cruel, barbaric, uncivilised State – 'of food or water'. I have heard people say that this Bill

> will preclude the provision of food and water to people with terminal illness. I do not know where that view could possibly come from.'

After an interjection, she continued:

> I cannot imagine what sort of barbaric thinking would lead anybody to imagine that this government would even contemplate including that in legislation; and, worse still, I do not know how anybody who had known of the effort, the compassion, concern and sensitivity that have gone into the Social Development Committee's Inquiry could contemplate in any way that members of that committee would support proposed legislation that talked about not providing food and water to a person who was dying. There are some very sick minds around.

63. The comments of Mr Walker, Mr Chamberlain and Mrs Lyster appeared to have been made in relation to the original version of the Bill debated on 19 April 1988. By contrast, the comments made by Mrs Dixon and Mr Guest appeared to have been directed to the definitions foreshadowed by Mrs Dixon (which ultimately became part of the Act). However all of these contributions would seem to be relevant in ascertaining what the parliament ultimately meant when it enacted a definition of palliative care that included the reasonable provision of food and water.

64. The second reading in the Legislative Council was adjourned and resumed on 3 May 1988. During the course of this debate the Honourable A J Hunt, a former leader of the Liberal Party in the Legislative Council, indicated that he intended to abstain from voting so that the Bill would be read a second time and proceed to the committee stage. Subsequently, when a division was called, the vote was 21 in favour and 21 against; which enabled the President of the Legislative Council to exercise a casting vote in favour of the motion to read the Bill a second time.

65. When the Legislative Council came to debate the clauses of the Bill in committee the Minister for Health moved the amendment to the definition of palliative care previously foreshadowed by Mrs Dixon. Mr Chamberlain spoke against the amended form of clause 3 and criticised the lack of precision in the concepts being employed. The Honourable D R White, Minister for Health, replied by stating:

> The common law is vague and attempts no definition of medical treatment. The Bill gives structure where none exists in common law.

Interestingly, notwithstanding that Mr Chamberlain announced that the Opposition would oppose the clause, the Legislative Council agreed to the clause without dividing.

66. Subsequently, during the committee stage, the Legislative Council defeated those parts of the Bill which would have allowed an agent or

guardian to refuse medical treatment on behalf of a patient. This was an important change. Following this change the Legislative Council carried a motion to read the Bill for a third time, at which stage it was sent to the Legislative Assembly.

67. In presenting the second reading speech in the Legislative Assembly on 5 May 1988 the Attorney-General, Mr McCutcheon, read a similar speech to that which had been read by Mr Walker (on behalf of Mr Kennan) in the Legislative Council. There was one significant change. By contrast to what has been set out previously, Mr McCutcheon said:

> A definition of 'palliative care' is included in the Bill. The definition of 'palliative care' covers treatment for the relief of pain, suffering or discomfort and specifically the reasonable provision of food or water.

68. The debate in the Legislative Assembly, where the government had the numbers, provides fewer clues as to the meaning of the legislation than the debate which was held in the Legislative Council. Nonetheless it can be noted that the lead speaker for the Liberal Party, Mr John, adopted a similar approach to Mr Chamberlain in describing the main provisions in the Bill, stating:

> Firstly, it does not apply to pain-relieving care and the ordinary provision of food.

69. The Legislative Assembly approved the Bill, reinstating provisions which would have allowed an agent or guardian to refuse medical treatment on behalf of a patient. However, when this was sent back to the Legislative Council, the Council stood its ground and refused to approve legislation that would permit such a course. The Legislative Assembly then reluctantly accepted the position which the Council had taken.

70. Thus the key definitions with which the Court is concerned were originally contained in an Act which did not permit an agent or guardian to refuse medical treatment on behalf of a patient; although they were inserted in the context of a Bill whereby the government hoped to invest agents or guardians with the power to refuse medical treatment on behalf of a patient.

71. On 3 May 1989 the Medical Treatment (Enduring Power of Attorney) Bill was first debated in the Legislative Council. Essentially, this Bill sought to re-introduce, in a much revised form, the provisions which the Legislative Council had rejected in 1988. The revisions that had been made were designed to ensure that satisfactory safeguards were in place to prevent the abuse, by agents or guardians, of the power to refuse medical treatment on behalf of some other person. The lead speaker on behalf of the Opposition in the Legislative Council was Mrs Tehan, who announced that the Liberal Party would not oppose the Bill, subject to certain amendments. She said:

> The Bill will have the full support of the three parties in this chamber, will eventually be passed and become law in Victoria.

Mrs Tehan proved correct. The Legislative Council subsequently passed numerous amendments, and then the whole Bill, without division. When the matter was then considered by the Legislative Assembly it was overwhelmingly supported with 65 members in favour and 16 against.

Medical Treatment Act – method of approach

72. Having regard to the framework of the Medical Treatment Act, it is convenient to first consider whether the provision of nutrition and hydration to BWV, via a PEG, falls within paragraphs (a), (b) or (c) of the definition of medical treatment; and, second, if it does fall within any of these paragraphs, to then consider whether it falls within the definition of palliative care. It is convenient to describe an action which falls within paragraphs (a) (b) or (c) of the definition of 'medical treatment' as being 'prima facie medical treatment'.

73. This approach acknowledges that there is some overlap between prima facie medical treatment and palliative care. So much is clear, not only from para (a) of the definition of palliative care, but also from the final words in the definition of medical treatment. The extent to which the concepts overlap and, in particular, whether there is any overlap between prima facie medical treatment and para (b) of the definition of palliative care are important matters which I will come to later in this judgment.

Prima facie medical treatment

74. It is clear that the administration of artificial nutrition and hydration in this case is not an operation. It is thus necessary to consider whether it is a medical procedure or the administration of a drug or other like substance.

75. In my opinion, a medical procedure can generally be described as a procedure that is based upon the science of the diagnosis, treatment or prevention of disease or injury, or of the relief of pain, suffering and discomfort. It is not a simple matter to say what is and what is not a medical procedure. Some procedures, such as blood letting, might once have been regarded as medical procedures but may no longer be regarded as such. Other procedures, such as applying dressings to wounds, might be medical procedures in some contexts, but not in other contexts (such as applying a band-aid to a grazed knee). I think there is some force in Mr Burnside's submission that whether or not a procedure is a medical procedure depends upon whether the medical knowledge upon which it is based has become so widespread within the community that it might now be regarded as common knowledge, not medical knowledge.

76. It is not necessary to explore all the circumstances which might be said to constitute a medical procedure: because, unquestionably in my judgment, the use of a PEG for artificial nutrition and hydration, or for

that matter any form of artificial feeding, is a 'medical' procedure. Artificial nutrition and hydration involves protocols, skills and care which draw from, and depend upon, medical knowledge. Artificial nutrition and hydration will inevitably require careful choice of and preparation of materials to be introduced into the body, close consideration to dosage rates, measures to prevent infection and regular cleaning of conduits. These are not matters of common knowledge. In this regard, I particularly rely upon the evidence given to the Court by Dr Woodward, Professor Ashby and Professor Horne.

77. In my opinion, the claim that artificial nutrition and hydration, via a PEG, can be performed in the home by an informed lay person does not mean that this procedure is not a medical procedure. Quite apart from the fact that the evidence is that such artificial nutrition and hydration must necessarily be performed under regular medical and nursing supervision, such a procedure involves skills and protocols which the lay person would need to specifically obtain by drawing upon medical knowledge.

78. I also find that the administration of artificial nutrition, via a PEG, to BWV is the administration of a substance like a drug: and, hence, is also within the meaning of the words in paragraph (b) of the definition of medical treatment. The nutrition administered to BWV consists of Osmolite, which is said to be a high nitrogen isotonic liquid nutrition. Mr Burnside emphasised that Osmolite consists of a number of specified minerals, vitamins and other constituents. However, as I observed in argument, the same could be said of a banana. Nonetheless Osmolite is quite different to most foods in that it is intended to provide complete, balanced nutrition, without the need for any other food whatsoever. Osmolite is included in the 1998 edition of the Australian Prescription Products Guide and in the 2002 MIMS Annual (which claims to be the byword for accurate, reliable, comprehensive and independent drug information). Both publications emphasise that Osmolite provides complete, balanced nutrition and that it is suitable for both oral feeding and tube feeding. The label on the can of Osmolite specifies that it should be used under the supervision of a physician. Indeed, when Professor Horne was asked whether Osmolite fitted more closely into the category of a drug or a food, he answered that it fitted more closely into the category of a drug because it was formulated in concentrations that one would not normally expect in a food and would have consequences if it was administered in an inappropriately high or inappropriately low dosage. Having regard to these characteristics of Osmolite I find that it is within the meaning of the words 'other like substance' in paragraph (b) of the definition of 'medical treatment'.

79. Of course, that is not the end of the exercise: it is now necessary to consider whether the artificial nutrition and hydration in this case would also fall within the definition of 'palliative care'. This not only involves consideration of the words used in that definition, but also consideration

of the extent of overlap between prima facie medical treatment and palliative care.

Palliative care – natural meaning

80. The definition of 'palliative care' must first be considered by reference to its natural meaning, in the context of the Act. This context includes the right of a person, or a person's agent or guardian, to refuse medical treatment. Such a right would be worthless if the parliament meant the expression 'palliative care', standing alone, to encompass most medical procedures. Further, the context includes the preamble to the Act. Having regard to this context, in my opinion the expression 'palliative care', standing alone, means care, not to treat or cure a patient, but to alleviate pain or suffering when a patient is dying. Indeed, palliative care extends to care for the relatives of the dying patient. In its second and final report 'Inquiry Into Options For Dying With Dignity', the Social Development Committee of the parliament discussed the meaning of the expression 'palliative care' in its natural sense. Various explanations are given of the nature of palliative care. And the report quotes various submissions, including a submission from Right to Life Victoria, which emphasises that when death has become inevitable, treatment should be adjusted, since the patient's best interest would then be served by treatment that emphasised relief, rather than futile attempts to cure.

81. I find that the administration of artificial nutrition and hydration, via a PEG, cannot be regarded as palliative care, where that expression is used in its natural sense. Such a procedure is, in essence, a procedure to sustain life; it is not a procedure to manage the dying process, so that it results in as little pain and suffering as possible.

The . . . provision of food and water

82. The Medical Treatment Act makes it clear that the reasonable provision of food and water is not to be regarded as medical treatment. But what did the parliament mean when it referred to the provision of food and water? Did it mean making food and water available, to be consumed naturally, that is orally? Or should it be taken to have meant any nourishment, or water, which is put into the body? Dictionary definitions are of limited assistance. And cases, in other contexts, provide little guidance.

83. There may be some significance in the use of the words 'food' and 'water', rather than 'nutrition' and 'hydration'. However I do not think that this choice of words is decisive. It is necessary to also consider the language used in para (b) of the definition of palliative care compared with the language used in para (a) of that definition and the language used in the definition of medical treatment. It is also necessary to consider what would appear to be the purpose of para (b) in the definition

of palliative care. And, in seeking to discern the intent of parliament, the legislative history and parliamentary debates ought be considered.

84. After carefully studying the definitions in the Medical Treatment Act, I have concluded that para (b) of the definition of palliative care is not intended to be understood so as to overlap with what I have called prima facie medical treatment. In this respect I draw attention to the different language used in para (a) to that used in (b) of the definition of palliative care; the legislative history leading to the separation of para (b) from para (a); and the comments of Mr Walker and Mrs Dixon in this regard. Indeed, I am persuaded by the argument put by Mr Santamaria QC that there is no overlap between prima facie medical treatment and para (b) of the definition of palliative care. Of course, when he put this argument he was seeking to persuade the Court that the consequence of such a conclusion was that the expression 'medical procedure' in para (c) of the definition of medical treatment should be confined. But his contention also means that if the provision of artificial nutrition and hydration is a medical procedure (as I have found) it should not be regarded as being within the concept of the provision of food and water.

85. In my opinion, the intent of parliament in excluding the provision of food and water from the concept of medical treatment was to ensure that a dying person would have food and water available for oral consumption, if the person wished to consume such food or water. It can hardly have been the parliament's intention that dying patients would be forced to consume food and water. Further, in my opinion, the extension of the concept to artificial nutrition and hydration would produce odd results, contrary to the purpose of the legislation to allow patients, or agents or guardians on their behalf, to choose to refuse medical treatment and to die with dignity. In this respect, I agree with the analysis of the Canadian author Dr Margaret Somerville, the founding director of the McGill Centre for Medicine, Ethics and Law, in her recent book 'The Ethical Canary, Science, Society And The Human Spirit':

> One such request by patients that healthcare professionals and families often find difficult to respect – and which some people vehemently oppose implementing – is that to withdraw artificial hydration and nutrition when a person's life is dependent on them. Images of a person dying of dehydration and starvation come to mind. This situation can be viewed differently, however, if we think of the terminally ill person as suffering from a failed alimentary system and the withdrawal of artificial hydration and nutrition as withdrawal of artificial alimentary system support. In short, respecting a refusal of this type of treatment is no different from accepting a person's refusal of respiratory support for a failed respiratory system. We have tended to see these situations differently because of the values and symbolism attached to the provision of food and drink for those in our care, especially babies and young children. We have wrongly equated artificial hydration and nutrition

> (a medical life-support treatment) with natural food and drink and, thereby, have mistakenly equated the withholding of them. I hasten to add that I am not suggesting we are always justified in withholding or withdrawing artificial hydration and nutrition. Rather, the basis on which this decision should be made is the ethics of the withholding or withdrawal of artificial life-support treatment, not that of food and water.

86. The parliamentary debates set out above assist the Court in ascertaining the intent of parliament when it referred to the provision of food and water. These debates make it clear that the parliament was intending to refer to the ordinary, non-medical provision of food and water. This is especially evident in the speeches of Mr Walker, Mr Chamberlain, Mrs Dixon, Mr Guest, Mrs Lyster and Mr John.

87. It is also useful to consider the position immediately after the Medical Treatment Act came into operation on 1 September 1988. At that time only a patient, not an agent or guardian, could refuse medical treatment. One might imagine a lucid patient suffering from throat cancer who had lost the ability to swallow. The prognosis might be that the patient had one week to live; but, if a PEG was installed to provide artificial nutrition and hydration, the prognosis might be three months. In my opinion, it cannot have been the case that the parliament was enacting a law whereby the patient could not have refused to have a PEG installed. But, if the provision of food and water included artificial nutrition and hydration, it would not have been open for the patient to have refused such an operation pursuant to the Act unless it could be shown that such provision of nutrition and hydration was not reasonable.

88. Of course, it is said that different considerations arise when the decision to refuse medical treatment is being made by an agent or guardian, rather than a patient. But it is most unlikely that the meaning of the words 'the . . . provision of food and water' changed when the Medical Treatment Act 1988 was amended by the Medical Treatment (Enduring Power of Attorney) Act 1990 on 6 August 1990. On the contrary, there is every indication that the parliament intended to put the patient's agent or guardian in exactly the same position as the patient, when it came to refusing medical treatment, provided that the safeguards added into the Act by the Medical Treatment (Enduring Power of Attorney) Act were complied with. These safeguards include a formal process for the appointment of an agent (s 5A(2)), the provision of information to the agent or guardian about the nature of the patient's current condition (s 5B(1)), a right to refuse treatment only in limited circumstances (s 5B(2)), the requirement that a formal refusal of treatment certificate be completed (s 5B(3)), the ability for the Victorian Civil and Administrative Tribunal to suspend or revoke the appointment of an agent (s 5C(1)), which might be done on the application of either the Public Advocate or a person who has a special interest in the affairs of the donor of the power (for example, the treating medical practitioner)

(s 5C(2)), penalties for procuring or obtaining the execution of a certificate by deception, fraud, misstatement or undue influence (s 5F), and the inapplicability of a refusal of treatment certificate if the medical condition of the patient changes to the extent that the condition in relation to which the certificate was given is no longer current (s 7(3)). These safeguards have the effect of substantially reducing the risk of an agent or guardian acting unlawfully, or even criminally, in refusing medical treatment on behalf of another person.

89. Mrs Morrish, on behalf of Right to Life Association Inc, emphasised the possibility that the Medical Treatment Act may be abused by an agent or guardian. In this respect, she relied upon a number of cases decided in contexts other than the Medical Treatment Act, such as the criminal law. For my part, I believe the safeguards that have been put in place will prove to be appropriate in the overwhelming number of situations that will arise. It must be remembered that most agents of dying patients will be loving relatives who have been trusted by the patient to make life and death decisions on the patient's behalf. In any event, what is more important, is that the parliament has decided upon the appropriate safeguards and, indeed, that an agent or guardian can make the decision to refuse medical treatment on behalf of some other person.

90. I note that my conclusion that artificial nutrition and hydration is medical treatment, not palliative care, pursuant to the Medical Treatment Act is consistent with the approach of other courts where artificial nutrition and hydration has been considered in the context of the natural meaning of the expression 'medical treatment'. Thus in *Bland* Lord Goff noted that the effect of discontinuing the artificial feeding of Anthony Bland would be that he would inevitably die within one or two weeks. Lord Goff then said:

> Objection can be made to the latter course of action on the ground that Anthony will thereby be starved to death, and that this would constitute a breach of the duty to feed him which must form an essential part of the duty which every person owes to another in his care. But here again it is necessary to analyse precisely what this means in this case of Anthony. Anthony is not merely incapable of feeding himself. He is incapable of swallowing, and therefore of eating or drinking in the normal sense of those words. There is overwhelming evidence that, in the medical profession, artificial feeding is regarded as a form of medical treatment; and even if it is not strictly medical treatment, it must form part of the medical care of the patient. Indeed, the function of artificial feeding in the case of Anthony, by means of a nasogastric tube, is to provide a form of life support analogous to that provided by a ventilator which artificially breathes air in and out of the lungs of a patient incapable of breathing normally, thereby enabling oxygen to reach the bloodstream.

91. In the Irish case of *In the Matter of a Ward of Court* the Supreme Court of Ireland found that artificial nutrition and hydration through a nasogastric tube constituted 'medical treatment' and not merely 'medical care'. Dame Elizabeth Butler-Sloss reached a similar conclusion in *NHS Trust A v M.* The issue was also addressed by Schreiber J of the Supreme Court of New Jersey, United States of America, in the matter of *Conroy* where he considered a possible distinction between the termination of artificial feedings and the termination of other forms of life-sustaining medical treatment. He offered the view:

> Certainly, feeding has an emotional significance. As infants we could breathe without assistance, but we were dependent on others for our lifeline of nourishment. Even more, feeding is an expression of nurturing and caring, certainly for infants and children, and in many cases for adults as well. Once one enters the realm of complex, high technology medical care, it is hard to shed the 'emotional symbolism' of food. However, artificial feedings such as nasogastric tubes, gastrostomies, and intravenous infusions are significantly different from bottle feeding or spoon feeding – they are medical procedures with inherent risks and possible side effects, instituted by skilled health care providers to compensate for impaired physical functioning. Analytically, artificial feeding by means of a nastogastric tube or intravenous infusion can be seen as equivalent to artificial breathing by means of a respirator. Both prolong life through mechanical means when the body is no longer able to perform a vital bodily function on its own. Furthermore, while nastogastric feeding and other medical procedures to ensure nutrition and hydration are usually well tolerated, they are not free from risks or burdens; they have complications that are sometimes serious and distressing to the patient.

The 'reasonable' provision of food and water

92. Having regard to my conclusion that the parliament did not intend the words 'the . . . provision of food and water' to include artificial feeding or artificial hydration (for example, by way of a PEG), it is unnecessary to resolve what is meant by the word 'reasonable' in order to make the declarations sought by the Public Advocate. But as the matter was argued before me, it may be desirable if I make a few observations.

93. In *Mounsey v Lafayette* Nettle J considered the meaning of the expression 'reasonable' in the context of the steps which must be taken for purchase of a ticket to travel on public transport. After referring to a number of cases, he observed that the essential idea is what a reasonable person would regard as being reasonable in the circumstances. In one sense this does not take us very far. However it does indicate that the concept of what is 'reasonable' is a practical concept which depends

upon the circumstances and which calls in aid the everyday judgment of a fair-minded person. In my opinion, this is the manner in which the word 'reasonable' is employed in paras (a) and (b) of the definition of palliative care in the Medical Treatment Act. It must also be kept in mind that the reasonableness of the provision of, for example, food and water must be determined in the context that such provision is for the purpose of palliative care.

94. An example of the application of this concept, in the context of the provision of food and water, might be where food or water is not provided to a dying patient in circumstances where it is not being requested and, when provided on previous occasions, has not been consumed. This could be a case of the carer paying heed to what Professor Ashby told the Court was a Latvian proverb that 'he or she has put down the spoon', meaning that the patient no longer wished to eat or drink but wished to die peacefully.

95. If my conclusion as to the meaning of the expression 'the . . . provision of food and water' is wrong, and instead this expression includes the provision of artificial nutrition or hydration, the question would then arise whether, in the circumstances of BWV, the continued provision of artificial nutrition and hydration was 'reasonable'. If I was required to answer this question, I would find that the further provision of artificial nutrition or hydration was not reasonable in all the circumstances. In forming this view I would rely upon the evidence of the medical witnesses who observed BWV, the view of her guardian that it would be contrary to her wishes to continue to receive nutrition and hydration through the PEG, her existing condition, the period for which she has been in her existing condition, her prognosis and the fact that continued feeding is doing no more than merely postponing the natural dying process.

The *parens patriae* alternative

96. I now turn to the submission made on behalf of the Attorney-General that, if the Court considers that there is uncertainty as to whether the administration of artificial nutrition and hydration via a PEG is medical treatment under the *Medical Treatment Act*, the most appropriate course would be for the Court to proceed, on a case by case basis, to consider whether it should grant authority for the cessation of such a procedure using its *parens patriae* jurisdiction. It was common ground, and I accept, that the Court does possess a *parens patriae* jurisdiction.

97. In a comprehensive submission, Ms Tate SC explained the history and nature of the *parens patriae* jurisdiction. She referred the Court to the statement by Lord Brandon made in *In Re F (Mental Patient: Sterilisation)* where he said the *parens patriae* jurisdiction:

> . . . is an ancient prerogative jurisdiction of the Crown going back as far perhaps as the 13th Century. Under it the Crown as *parens*

> *patriae* had both the power and the duty to protect the persons and property of those unable to do so for themselves, a category which included both minors (formerly described as infants) and persons of unsound mind (formerly described as lunatics or idiots).

The nature of the jurisdiction has been further discussed by the High Court of Australia in *Marion's Case*.

98. Ms Tate submitted that the Court could exercise the *parens patriae* jurisdiction of its own motion, provided that there was a matter before the Court. She argued that this followed from the fact that the jurisdiction was based upon a duty and was to be exercised in the public interest. I do not doubt this submission, but it is unnecessary to determine it. The Public Advocate agreed that if the Court was to proceed in its *parens patriae* jurisdiction (instead of making the declarations sought) the case would need to be adjourned and a further application could be made, supported by further evidence.

99. Although the *parens patriae* jurisdiction of the Court is of considerable historical interest, I doubt if it should play any current role in the day to day administration of guardianship matters. Victoria has comprehensive laws in relation to guardianship and administration matters. These laws have established the statutory office of Public Advocate, with roles and responsibilities somewhat akin to those which might once have been adopted by the Court. A wide jurisdiction is also vested in the Victorian Civil and Administrative Tribunal to resolve disputes concerning guardianship matters and to consider applications where there is some perceived threat to the integrity of the guardianship system. The Medical Treatment Act sets out parliament's intent in relation to the procedure whereby a person may refuse medical treatment; and, further, the procedure whereby an agent may make a decision about medical treatment on behalf of an incompetent person.

100. In my opinion, the Court would be failing to give effect to the will of parliament if it refused to make the declarations sought by the Public Advocate in this case by reference to some discretionary consideration. The fact that a type of reserve power exists provides no logical justification for bypassing the Guardianship and Administration Act and the Medical Treatment Act.

101. It is clearly *not* the intention of parliament that the usual method whereby an agent might refuse medical treatment on behalf of a patient who is dying be one where the agent seeks to invoke either the common law jurisdiction or the *parens patriae* jurisdiction of the Supreme Court. The parliament has set in place a careful statutory scheme whereby such decisions can be made by agents or guardians, subject to safeguards to prevent abuse. Further, the parliamentary debates demonstrate that recourse to the Supreme Court was seen as problematic: for reasons of cost, delay and emotional trauma to the families concerned.

102. It is apparent from my judgment that I do not regard there to be any uncertainty as to whether the administration of artificial nutrition

and hydration via a PEG is medical treatment under the Medical Treatment Act 1988. Hence the basis for the submission made on behalf of the Attorney-General falls away. In any event, for the reasons set out above, I do not believe it to be desirable for the Court to make an order in its *parens patriae* jurisdiction in lieu of making the declarations sought by the Public Advocate.

Declarations

This is an appropriate case for the making of the declarations sought by the Public Advocate. The circumstances of BWV are real, not hypothetical. The issues have been fully and competently argued. The Court has formed the firm conclusion that artificial nutrition and hydration is medical treatment within the meaning of the Medical Treatment Act. The making of the declarations will remove any doubts that the Public Advocate may have had in relation to the decisions open to him, in relation to BWV, under the Act; and will enable the Public Advocate to decide, on behalf of BWV, whether it is now time to allow her to die with dignity.

Are advance directive statutes useful?

The question arises as to whether 'advance directives' as permitted by the above statutes are useful.

Sommerville, A, 'Are advance directives really the answer? And what was the question?', in McLean, SAM, *Death, Dying and the Law*, Dartmouth, Aldershot, 1996, pp 40–46

Do advance directives offer genuine advantages?

The House of Lords' report [on Medical Ethics] lists advantages and disadvantages which witnesses raised in regard to advance directives. The perceived advantages include giving patients control of their destiny and therefore peace of mind, providing opportunity for dialogue, guiding health professionals in difficult cases and removing responsibility for difficult decisions from relatives.

The primary perceived advantage of advance directives lies in protecting patient autonomy beyond the onset of incapacity but this may arguably be a 'symbolic' rather than a practical expression of autonomy. Many forms of advance directives offer the drafter a choice of specifying personal instructions and/or nominating a proxy to decide. US surveys indicate that people are most likely to select proxy decision-making by their family or their doctor. A US study published in 1992 indicated that, of 104 patients with a life-threatening illness who were offered advance directives, 69 took up the offer and most asked for non-aggressive treatment if 'the burdens of treatment outweigh the expected benefits', although none gave any other personal instructions and all of them designated a proxy. However, other evidence suggests that proxies are more likely than patients themselves to opt for life-prolonging treatment. While choosing to transfer the decision is just as much an expression of autonomy as deciding oneself, it does not require an advance directive to do so.

In any case, people are not entirely autonomous in their decision-making, but are influenced to some degree by the advice and information they receive and how the options are portrayed to them. It is increasingly recognised that the concept of non-directive counselling on complex issues is often no more than a sham. Dialogue with health professionals is an important facet of making an informed advance directive, but health professionals, although exhorted to make their advice non-directive, find this hard to achieve. Nor is it easy to find specialised counselling about the likely future options for patients with specific diseases. Autonomy is only protected if the instructions are available at the right moment and the directive is clear. An ambiguous statement will complicate, rather than simplify, the situation.

Discussions of 'autonomy' sometimes appear to juggle theories but offer little by way of practical guidance. In Dworkin's view, when an individual is conscious but mentally incapacitated, two autonomies are in play: the autonomy of the demented patient and the autonomy of the person who became demented. These two autonomies can conflict, and the resulting problems are complex and difficult. Of course, some philosophers resolve this dilemma by attributing no autonomy to the demented person and recognising the 'residual interests' of the previously competent individual as paramount. A cluster of fascinating psychological and philosophical questions arise here about an individual's ability to make decisions, in advance, on matters of life and death on behalf of the person he or she will be in the future when some part of the individual 'self' – mental faculties, memories and awareness of continuity – has been lost. As Dworkin implies, the competent person who makes the anticipatory decision can be seen as fundamentally different and 'other' to the incapacitated individual who lives out (or does not) the consequences of the decision. While individuals can only make advance directives for 'themselves', a person who becomes severely mentally disordered or brain-damaged is, in some sense, no longer 'herself'.

Much of Western philosophy has been preoccupied with the importance of 'personhood', personal identity and the relationship between mind and body. Harris, for example, sees the individual's capacity to assess and value his life as fundamental to personhood. There is a tradition of trying to resolve problems of identity by citing continuity of mind and mental state as the important criterion. Yet, continuity of the body is irrelevant. If the mind ceases to function as a mind, then that 'person' ceases to exist although the bodily shell may continue. A competent individual, therefore, is arguably not making advance decisions for him or herself but for the relics of that individual which he or she once was.

Although it is philosophically complex, on a practical level this issue is not necessarily intractable. If we allow 'persons' to make testamentary disposition for their material possessions, why not permit the same for their bodily shell after the cessation of the rational faculties? 'Ownership' of the body was the notion that sparked off the original idea of a living will: Luis Kutner's proposal was that a competent adult should be able to execute a document 'analogous to a revocable or conditional trust, with the patient's body as the res (the property or asset), the patient as the beneficiary and grantor, and the doctor and the hospital as trustees'. The concept of property is based on the idea that there is a system of rules governing access to, and control of, some resources, whether material or incorporeal. In this case, the property would be very much corporeal, and the owner, when competent, might be assigned legal rights about how it is treated in future. The owner of the body would retain an enduring interest in the body until it decays and would continue to inhabit it or be allowed to vacate it in accordance with his prior direction.

Some modern philosophers, such as Parfit, argue that survival of identity need not be viewed as an 'all or nothing' issue but as a matter of degree, and this has some intuitive plausibility . . . It is trite to observe that people's views change with their circumstances. Parfit imagines the possibility of the diffusion of 'self' along several different potential branches of development. He talks, for example, of 'my most recent self', 'one of my earlier selves' and 'one of my distant selves' – each of these showing a different degree of psychological connectedness with the past self. From a practical perspective, would this mean that a greater weight should be attached to an advance directive made comparatively recently by an individual who is still more or less the same self? If we recognise varying degrees of psychological continuity with former and future selves, it leaves unresolved the same question of whether it is morally correct for subsequent selves to be locked in by the provisions of an advance directive which fails to reflect their current interests. In life, of course, we do recognise that individuals make bad or risky choices in the development of their 'successive selves' but that these should generally be respected.

Theorising aside, concern for the welfare of people with severe and permanent incapacity or dementia is often used as an argument for imposing limits on the scope of advance directives. The incapacitated individual may show all signs of wanting to be nourished, to receive treatment and to live, oblivious to the views of the former self. Despite such difficulties, it is not my intention to diminish the importance of respect for autonomy, imperfect though the exercise of it may be in practice.

Some disadvantages of advance directives were noted by the House of Lords. They include the difficulties patients experience in making their views known unambiguously, the risks of pressure or other forms of abuse being brought to bear upon the drafter and the danger of misdiagnosis. Unfortunately, however, none of these are restricted to anticipatory decision-making, but may apply to any treatment situation. Admittedly, the matter of ensuring unambiguous expression may be more complex in the case of anticipatory refusals. An example from the *Lancet* drew attention to a dilemma facing doctors treating an elderly woman with advanced cancer of the colon and intestinal obstruction. Her acute pain was unamenable to narcotics but could have been relieved by a colostomy under local anaesthetic. Her advance directive refused any 'heroic' intervention in the case of incurable illness and did not distinguish between life-prolonging and pain-relieving measures. On the brief evidence given, however, such a directive might have been justifiably challenged under the criteria specified by Lord Donaldson in the 'T' case, as arguably, the patient had insufficient information when she drafted the directive. It might also be argued that the circumstances which arose were not precisely those envisaged in advance.

A potentially more damaging disadvantage would arise if advance directives were seen as a covert measure for reducing treatment costs or limiting the amount of care given to the elderly and terminally ill. Any encouragement by health professionals for the drafting of directives would then create suspicion and mistrust. A comparison of costs and benefits was offered in the Schneiderman study which, although it admittedly involved relatively small patient numbers, showed that while most patients with advance directives wanted to limit expensive high-technology treatments, in the actual implementation of their directive there was no significant difference in overall provision of terminal care or costs between these patients and others who made no anticipatory choice. This conclusion obviously leads to the question of whether advance directives are likely to work or have any genuine value outside the realm of theoretical debate.

The study mentioned above indicated that, in 1992, advance directives made little or no difference to treatment of the seriously ill in the State of California. No significant differences were found between those with and without advance directives in terms of patient satisfaction, general wellbeing, length of survival and amount of narcotics given. Patients with directives spent more days in hospital than those in the control group without directives, and similar treatment costs were incurred by all patients in the last month of life. The authors identify several reasons for this lack of divergence. They suggest, for example, that doctors may simply have ignored the directive or limited 'heroic' treatment in equal measure to those with and without directives or that the document was not applicable to the circumstances. One of the most significant findings is that, contrary to expectation, most of the patients in the study retained decision-making capacity in the terminal stages. For those facing mental incapacity through diseases such as AIDS, 'discussion before death was so extensive it precluded dependence on the advance directive'.

Clearly, it is inadvisable to generalise from such limited data, but one inevitable conclusion is that even where advance directives are potentially most useful, they are superfluous in practical terms if good opportunities for dialogue already exist . . .

Another factor influencing the usefulness of directives concerns the venue where treatment is provided. Community-based services, short-stay hospital or hospice care, community nursing and better liaison between [the health service], social services and voluntary sector can promote patient choice. Even when complicated technical interventions are required, people who die in their own homes supported by carers, specialised nurses or hospice outreach programmes are likely to have greater control over the final stages of life. There are persistent fears, however, that hard-pressed health authority budgets will increasingly be used to purchase acute services rather than provide palliative care for people at home. Funding for hospice and palliative care is no longer ring-fenced as it was in the past . . .

Fears undoubtedly abound that life-prolonging measures are likely to be increasingly unavailable for patients with poor long-term prognoses, even if they want them. In its position paper to the House of Lords' Select Committee, the Alzheimer's Disease Society implies that a concentration on autonomy may distract from broader needs. It suggests that people might be willing to sacrifice the right to consent to treatment if they could use a living will to will themselves appropriate medical care when they need it. The Society goes on to say that good terminal care for people with dementia is decreasing and 'it is likely that many people in the last stages of Alzheimer's disease will have very little prospect of high-quality and appropriate health care in the early part of the next century'. This is not to say that advance directives will become superfluous but rather that they may need to change to allow those who want treatment to register a claim.

In real life, the practicalities of combining directives with proxy decision-makers may also raise difficulties. The pattern of population trends is such that the proportion of older people in the UK who may want to appoint proxies will exceed the number of those they know and can be confident will survive them. Women, in particular, live longer than men, are more likely to experience widowhood and are less likely to remarry. At present, half of the women of 65 years and over and a fifth of older men live alone. Dementia occurs in about 5% of the population over 65 and in up to 20% of those over 80. The very old (85 years and over) often live in institutional settings and carry the highest risk of dementia. Will there be trusted proxies available for them in future?

Conclusion

All the signs are that advance directives – at least in their present form – may not be the best or only answer for people with deteriorating mental faculties. Despite the rhetoric, only a small minority of people presently have sufficient confidence to commit themselves about future choices, and they may be aiming wrongly to ward off treatments which are increasingly never even on offer. In a climate of genuine patient choice, advance statements could usefully broaden in scope and offer a way forward to better communication and negotiation. In practice, this can only be achieved if opportunities for unhurried or repeated discussion are built into the provision of health care. These are rarely available at present. The attitudes of health professionals are also vital . . .

Developments in the Northern Territory

The Northern Territory passed legislation making legal a doctor ending the life of his or her patient in accordance with that patient's request. This legislation was the first of its kind in the world, although it should be noted that similar legislation was enacted in the American State of Oregon and recently in the Netherlands. The American legislation has been beset by constitutional challenges. The Northern Territory legislation is also not without its problems. A challenge to the constitutional validity of the legislation was launched in June 1996 by a conglomerate of churches and the local branch of the Australian Medical Association. The Northern Territory Supreme Court dismissed the challenge. A Private Members' Bill was introduced in the Federal Parliament which had the effect of making invalid the NT's legislation. (The Northern Territory is not a sovereign State, but enacts laws based on a grant of power from the Commonwealth.) The effect of Kevin Andrew's Private Members' Bill was to deny the Northern Territory Parliament the legislative competence to pass laws allowing for euthanasia.

Note that the former NT legislation addresses not only the criminal law issue of liability for causing the death of another, but also associated questions such as the ethical liability of health care practitioners, the insurance law consequences of taking one's own life and the effect on the law of wills.

Rights of the Terminally Ill Act 1995 (NT)

3 Interpretation

In this Act, unless the contrary intention appears:

'assist', in relation to the death or proposed death of a patient, includes the prescribing of a substance, the preparation of a substance and the giving of a substance to the patient for self-administration, and the administration of a substance to the patient;

'certificate of request' means a certificate in or to the effect of the form in the Schedule that has been completed, signed and witnessed in accordance with this Act;

'health care provider', in relation to a patient, includes a hospital, nursing home or other institution (including those responsible for its management) in which the patient is located for care or attention and any nurse or other person whose duties include or directly or indirectly relate to the care or medical treatment of the patient;

'illness' includes injury or degeneration of mental or physical faculties;

'medical practitioner' means a medical practitioner who has been entitled to practise as a medical practitioner (however described) in a State or a Territory of the Commonwealth for a continuous period of not less than five years and who is resident in, and entitled under the Medical Act to practise medicine in, the Territory;

'qualified psychiatrist' means:

(a) a person entitled under a law of a State or Territory of the Commonwealth to practise as a specialist in the medical specialty of psychiatry;
(b) a specialist whose qualifications are recognised by the Royal Australian and New Zealand College of Psychiatrists as entitled the Person to fellowship of that College;
(c) a person employed by the Commonwealth or a State or Territory of the Commonwealth, or an Agency or authority of the Commonwealth or a State or Territory, as a specialist or consultant in the medical specialty of psychiatry;

'terminal illness', in relation to a patient, means an illness which, in reasonable medical judgment will, in the normal course, without the application of extraordinary measures or of treatment unacceptable to the patient, result in the death of the patient.

PART 2 – Request For and Giving of Assistance

4 Request for assistance to voluntarily terminate life

A patient who, in the course of a terminal illness, is experiencing pain, suffering and/or distress to an extent unacceptable to the patient, may request the patient's medical practitioner to assist the patient to terminate the patient's life.

5 Response of medical practitioner

A medical practitioner who receives a request referred to in s 4, if satisfied that the conditions of s 7 have been met, but subject to s 8, may assist the patient to terminate the patient's life in accordance with this Act or, for any reason and at any time, refuse to give that assistance.

6 Response of medical practitioner, etc not to be influenced by extraneous considerations

(1) A person shall not give or promise any reward or advantage (other than a reasonable payment for medical services), or by any means cause or threaten to cause any disadvantage, to a medical practitioner or other person for refusing to assist, or for the purpose of compelling or persuading the medical practitioner or other person

to assist or refuse to assist, in the termination of a patient's life under this Act. Penalty: $10,000.

(2) A person to whom a reward or advantage is promised or given, as referred to in subsection (1), does not have the legal right or capacity to receive or retain the reward or accept or exercise the advantage, whether or not, at the relevant time, he or she was aware of the promise or the intention to give the reward or advantage.

7 Conditions under which medical practitioner may assist

(1) A medical practitioner may assist a patient to end his or her life only if all of the following conditions are met:

(a) the patient has attained the age of 18 years;
(b) the medical practitioner is satisfied, on reasonable grounds, that

(i) the patient is suffering from an illness that will, in the normal course and without the application of extraordinary measures, result in the death of the patient;
(ii) in reasonable medical judgment, there is no medical measure acceptable to the patient that can reasonably be undertaken in the hope of effecting a cure; and
(iii) any medical treatment reasonably available to the patient is confined to the relief of pain, suffering and/or distress with the object of allowing the patient to die a comfortable death;

(c) two other persons, neither of whom is a relative or employee of, or a member of the same medical practice as, the first medical practitioner or each other:

(i) one of whom is a medical practitioner who holds prescribed qualifications, or has prescribed experience, in the treatment of the terminal illness from which the patient is suffering; and
(ii) the other who is a qualified psychiatrist, have examined the patient and have confirmed,
(iii) in the case of the medical practitioner referred to in subparagraph (i):
(A) the first medical practitioner's opinion as to the existence and seriousness of the illness;
(B) that the patient is likely to die as a result of the illness; and
(C) the first medical practitioner's prognosis; and

(iv) in the case of the qualified psychiatrist referred to in subparagraph (ii) – that the patient is not suffering from a treatable clinical depression in respect of the illness;

(d) the illness is causing the patient severe pain or suffering;

(e) the medical practitioner has informed the patient of the nature of the illness and its likely course, and the medical treatment, including palliative care, counselling and psychiatric support and extraordinary measures for keeping the patient alive, that might be available to the patient;

(f) after being informed as referred to in paragraph (e), the patient indicates to the medical practitioner that the patient has decided to end his or her life;

(g) the medical practitioner is satisfied that the patient has considered the possible implications of the patient's decision to his or her family;

(h) the medical practitioner is satisfied, on reasonable grounds, that the patient is of sound mind and that the patient's decision to end his or her life has been made freely, voluntarily and after due consideration;

(i) the patient, or a person acting on the patient's behalf in accordance with s 9, has, not earlier than seven days after the patient has indicated to his or her medical practitioner as referred to in paragraph (f), signed that part of the certificate of request required to be completed by or on behalf of the patient;

(j) the medical practitioner has witnessed the patient's signature on the certificate of request or that of the person who signed on behalf of the patient, and has completed and signed the relevant declaration on the certificate;

(k) the certificate of request has been signed in the presence of the patient and the first medical practitioner by another medical practitioner (who may be the medical practitioner referred to in paragraph (c)(i) or any other medical practitioner) after that medical practitioner has discussed the case with the first medical practitioner and the patient and is satisfied, on reasonable grounds, that the certificate is in order, that the patient is of sound mind and the patient's decision to end his or her life has been made freely, voluntarily and after due consideration, and that the above conditions have been complied with;

(l) where, in accordance with subsection (4), an interpreter is required to be present at the signing of the certificate of request, the certificate of request has been signed by the interpreter confirming the patient's understanding of the request for assistance;

(m) the medical practitioner has no reason to believe that he or she, the countersigning medical practitioner or a close relative or associate of either of them, will gain a financial or other advantage (other than a reasonable payment for medical services) directly or indirectly as a result of the death of the patient;

(n) not less than 48 hours has elapsed since the signing of the completed certificate of request;

(o) at no time before assisting the patient to end his or her life had

the patient given to the medical practitioner an indication that it was no longer the patient's wish to end his or her life;
- (p) the medical practitioner himself or herself provides the assistance and/or is and remains present while the assistance is given and until the death of the patient.

(2) In assisting a patient under this Act, a medical practitioner shall be guided by appropriate medical standards and such guidelines, if any, as are prescribed, and shall consider the appropriate pharmaceutical information about any substance reasonably available for use in the circumstances.

(3) Where a patient's medical practitioner has no special qualifications in the field of palliative care, the information to be provided to the patient on the availability of palliative care shall be given by a medical practitioner (who may be the medical practitioner referred to in subsection (1)(c)(i) or any other medical practitioner) who has such special qualifications in the field of palliative care as are prescribed.

(4) A medical practitioner shall not assist a patient under this Act where the medical practitioner or any other medical practitioner or qualified psychiatrist who is required under subsection (1) or (3) to communicate with the patient does not share the same first language as the patient, unless there is present at the time of that communication and at the time the certificate of request is signed by or on behalf of the patient, an interpreter who holds a prescribed professional qualification for interpreters in the first language of the patient.

8 Palliative care

(1) A medical practitioner shall not assist a patient under this Act if, in his or her opinion and after considering the advice of the medical practitioner referred to in s 7(1)(c)(i), there are palliative care options reasonably available to the patient to alleviate the patient's pain and suffering to levels acceptable to the patient.

(2) Where a patient has requested assistance under this Act and has subsequently been provided with palliative care that brings about the remission of the patient's pain or suffering, the medical practitioner shall not, in pursuance of the patient's original request for assistance, assist the patient under this Act. If subsequently the palliative care ceases to alleviate the patient's pain and suffering to levels acceptable to the patient, the medical practitioner may continue to assist the patient under this Act only if the patient indicates to the medical practitioner the patient's wish to proceed in pursuance of the request.

9 Patient who is unable to sign certificate of request

(1) If a patient who has requested his or her medical practitioner to assist the patient to end the patient's life is physically unable to sign

the certificate of request, any person who has attained the age of 18 years, other than the medical practitioner or a medical practitioner or qualified psychiatrist referred to in s 7(1)(c), or a person who is likely to receive a financial benefit directly or indirectly as a result of the death of the patient, may, at the patient's request and in the presence of the patient and both the medical practitioner witnesses (and where, in accordance with s 7(4) an interpreter has been used, also in the presence of the interpreter), sign the certificate on behalf of the patient.

(2) A person who signs a certificate of request on behalf of a patient forfeits any financial or other benefit the person would otherwise obtain, directly or indirectly, as a result of the death of the patient.

10 Right to rescind request

(1) Notwithstanding anything in this Act, a patient may rescind a request for assistance under this Act at any time and in any manner.

(2) Where a patient rescinds a request, the patient's medical practitioner shall, as soon as practicable, destroy the certificate of request and note that fact on the patient's medical record.

11 Improper conduct

(1) A person shall not, by deception or improper influence, procure the signing or witnessing of a certificate of request.
Penalty: $20,000 or imprisonment for four years.

(2) A person found guilty of an offence against subsection (l) forfeits any financial or other benefit the person would otherwise obtain, directly or indirectly, as a result of the death of the patient, whether or not the death results from assistance given under this Act.

PART 3 – Records and Reporting of Death

12 Medical records to be kept

A medical practitioner who, under this Act, assists a patient to terminate the patient's life shall file and, subject to this Act, keep the following as part of the medical record of the patient:

(a) a note of any oral request of the patient for such assistance;
(b) the certificate of request;
(c) a record of the opinion of the patient's medical practitioner as to the patient's state of mind at the time of signing the certificate of request and certification of the medical practitioner's opinion that the patient's decision to end his or her life was made freely, voluntarily and after due consideration;
(d) the reports of the medical practitioner and qualified psychiatrist referred to in s 7(1)(c);
(e) a note by the patient's medical practitioner:

(i) certifying as to the independence of the medical practitioner and qualified psychiatrist referred to in s 7(1)(c) and the residential and period of practice qualifications of the patient's medical practitioner;
(ii) indicating that all requirements under this Act have been met;
(iii) indicating the steps taken to carry out the request for assistance; and
(iv) including a notation of the substance prescribed,

and such other information, if any, as is prescribed.
Penalty: $10,000 or imprisonment for two years.

13 Certification as to death

(1) A medical practitioner who, under this Act, assists a patient to end the patient's life shall be taken to have attended the patient during the patient's last illness for the purposes of Part IV of the Registration of Births, Deaths and Marriages Act or any provision in substitution for that Part.
(2) A death as the result of assistance given under this Act shall not, for that reason only, be taken to be unexpected, unnatural or violent for the purposes of the definition of 'reportable death' in the application of Part 4 of the Coroner's Act, or be a reportable death by reason only of having occurred during an anaesthetic.

14 Medical record to be sent to Coroner

(1) As soon as practicable after the death of a patient as the result of assistance given under this Act, the medical practitioner who gave the assistance shall report the death to a Coroner by sending to the Coroner a copy of the death certificate under the Registration of Births, Deaths and Marriages Act and so much of the medical record of the patient (including that required by s 12 to be kept) as relates to the terminal illness and death of the patient.
(2) As soon as practicable after the end of each financial year the Coroner shall advise the Attorney General of the number of patients who died as a result of assistance given under this Act and the Attorney General, in such manner or report as he or she thinks appropriate, shall report the number to the Legislative Assembly.

15 Coroner may report on operation of Act

The Coroner may, at any time and in his or her absolute discretion, report to the Attorney General on the operation, or any matter affecting the operation, of this Act and the Attorney General shall, within three sitting days of the Legislative Assembly after receiving the report, table a copy of the report in the Assembly.

PART 4 – Miscellaneous

16 Construction of Act

(1) Notwithstanding s 26(3) of the Criminal Code, an action taken in accordance with this Act by a medical practitioner or by a health care provider on the instructions of a medical practitioner does not constitute an offence against Part VI of the Criminal Code or an attempt to commit such an offence, a conspiracy to commit such an offence, or an offence of aiding, abetting, counselling or procuring the commission of such an offence.
(2) Assistance given in accordance with this Act by a medical practitioner or by a health care provider on the instructions of a medical practitioner is taken to be medical treatment for the purposes of the law.

17 Certificate of request is evidence

A document purporting to be a certificate of request is, in any proceedings before a court, admissible in evidence and is prima facie evidence of the request by the person who purported to sign it or on whose behalf it is purported to have been signed, for assistance under this Act.

18 Effect on construction of wills, contracts and statutes

(1) Any will, contract or other agreement, whether or not in writing or executed or made before or after the commencement of this Act, to the extent that it affects whether a person may make or rescind a request for assistance under this Act, or the giving of such assistance, is not valid.
(2) An obligation owing under a contract, whether made before or after the commencement of this Act, shall not be conditioned or affected by the making or rescinding of a request for assistance under this Act or the giving of that assistance.

19 Insurance or annuity policies

The sale, procurement or issuing of any life, health or accident insurance or annuity policy or the rate charged for such a policy shall not be conditioned on or affected by the making or rescinding of a request for assistance under this Act or the giving of that assistance.

20 Immunities

(1) A person shall not be subject to civil or criminal action or professional disciplinary action for anything done in good faith and without negligence in compliance with this Act, including being present when a patient takes a substance prescribed for or supplied to the patient as the result of assistance under this Act to end the patient's life.
(2) A professional organisation or association or health care provider shall not subject a person to censure, discipline, suspension, loss of licence, certificate or other authority to practise, loss of privilege, loss of membership or other penalty for anything that, in good faith

and without negligence, was done or refused to be done by the person and which may under this Act lawfully be done or refused to be done.

(3) A request by a patient for assistance under this Act, or giving of such assistance in good faith by a medical practitioner in compliance with this Act, shall not constitute neglect for any purpose of law or alone constitute or indicate a disability for the purposes of an application under s 8 of the Adult Guardianship Act.

(4) A health care provider is not under any duty, whether by contract, statute or other legal requirement, to participate in the provision to a patient of assistance under this Act, and if a health care provider is unable or unwilling to carry out a direction of a medical practitioner for the purpose of the medical practitioner assisting a patient under this Act and the patient transfers his or her care to another health care provider, the former health care provider shall, on request, transfer a copy of the patient's relevant medical records to the new health care provider.

For a summary of some early uncertainties relating to the Rights of the Terminally Ill Act 1995, see the special issue of the Journal of Law and Medicine (1995) 3 No 2 Journal of Law and Medicine.

5

INFORMATION AND MEDICAL PRACTICE

This chapter explores the dual issues of access to records and confidentiality. It will become apparent that the issues represent two sides of the same coin.

PART I: CONFIDENTIALITY

Patients in their interactions with health care practitioners have the right to have their privacy respected. This right emerges from three sources:

(i) a health care practitioner's ethical obligations;
(ii) the contract between the patient and the health care practitioner;
(iii) implications from a branch of law called equity.

Ethical obligations

It will be recalled from Chapter 1 that the AMA's code of ethics directs doctors to preserve their patients' confidences.

Contract

In Chapter 2, we noted that a contract exists between a health care provider and his or her patient. Although it would be rare for there to exist an explicit term of such a contract guaranteeing the patient's confidences, such a term is likely to be implied by operation of law. This would be consistent with the decisions of *Thake v Maurice* and *Eyre v Measday* referred to in Chapter 2.

Equity

The operation of the principles of Equity in this field have been aptly summarised by Chalmers and Dalpont.

Dalpont, G and Chalmers, D, *An Introduction to Equity in Australia and New Zealand*, 1996, Sydney: Lawbook Co, pp 80–82

> A confidence is formed whenever one party ('the confider') imparts to another ('the confidant') private or secret matters on the express or implied understanding that the communication is for a restricted

purpose. In these circumstances, equity will restrain the confidant from making unauthorised use of the information and if need be, will hold her or him accountable for any profits acquired by its improper use. This is because the law recognises that 'it is the privilege of all persons who possess information to keep that information confidential'.

The information, the subject of equitable protection, may be in written or verbal form. This serves to distinguish the action for breach of confidence from the action for breach of copyright, where information itself is not protected, but only its mode of expression, whether in the form of words, diagrams, drawings, photographs, etc. The law of confidential information can also be distinguished from the law of patents in that the information in question need not be novel, merely private or not in the public domain.

Jurisdictional basis and elements

Courts in Australia, New Zealand and the United Kingdom have recognised that independently of any question as to a right at law, a court of equity has an original, inherent and independent jurisdiction to prevent the violation of a confidence. Therefore, equity will grant relief against an actual or threatened abuse of confidential information, though not involving any tort, breach of express or implied contractual provision, wider fiduciary duty or copyright or trademark right.

There is a common law aspect to protection of confidential information which the courts have characterised as the enforcement of a common law property right . . .

The jurisdiction is based on the principles of good faith and fair dealing with the work of another. It is such that a person who has received information in confidence shall not take unfair advantage of it or fraudulently abuse the trust reposed in her or him. In fact, the jurisdictional basis of protection of confidences may in the future be subsumed into the general equitable notion of unconscionability.

The importance of the purely equitable jurisdiction is twofold. First, it affords a ground for relief in circumstances where there exist no or limited contractual or property rights. Secondly, it opens the door to equitable remedies. However, there is overlap between the equitable and legal protections for confidential information and it is inaccurate to categorise them as mutually exclusive. For example, the court may find that the information in question is protected by both an implied contractual term and the equitable doctrine of confidence. In these circumstances, the full spectrum of legal and equitable remedies may be available to the plaintiff . . .

Courts in Australia and New Zealand have accepted the approach propounded by Megarry J in *Coco v AN Clark (Engineers) Ltd* [1969] RPC 41, at 47 as representing the correct formulation of the elements upon which the equitable duty of confidence is based, namely:

> . . . three elements are required if, apart from contract, a case of breach of confidence is to succeed. First, the information itself. . . must 'have a necessary quality of confidence about it'. Secondly, that information must have been imparted in circumstances importing an obligation of confidence. Thirdly, there must be an unauthorised use of that information.

> Whether a court will enforce personal confidences depends upon the nature of the communication, the relationship between confider and confidant, and prevailing notions of public policy . . . The prevailing view is that an objective test must be applied to determine whether the circumstances of communication are confidential. The approach was clearly expressed by McInerney J in *Mense v Milenkovic* [1973] VR 784, at 801:

> > If the circumstances are such that any reasonable man standing in the shoes of the recipient of the information would have realised that upon reasonable grounds the information was being given to him in confidence, then this should suffice to impose on him the equitable obligation of confidence.

> Therefore, equity may impose an obligation of confidence upon a defendant having regard to not only what the defendant knew, but to what he ought to have known in all the relevant circumstances.

In *Hunter v Mann* [1974] QB 767, Boreham J at P 772 noted that a doctor 'is under a duty not to [voluntarily] disclose, without the consent of the patient, information which he, the doctor, has gained in his professional capacity'. His Lordship's statement suggests two qualifications to the rule respecting confidences. Firstly, where the doctor is compelled by law to make disclosure of information. Secondly, where the patient gives his or her consent to the publication of information. These exceptions will be explored subsequently. For the moment, it may be instructive to consider some applications of the confidence rule, as it applies in medical practice.

Firstly, Gurry, F, in *Breach of Confidence*, 1984, Oxford: Clarendon, suggests that the health care practitioner's duty of confidence extends not only to information acquired directly from the patient, but also to information acquired from other persons in the practitioner's capacity as a health care provider.

Secondly, enforcement of the duty may lead to not only damages for the breach of confidence *per se*, but also liability for any consequential losses which might flow.

The case of *Furness v Fitchett* is instructive in this regard.

Furness v Fitchett [1958] NZLR 396

> **Barraclough CJ:**
> The duty which, in Mr Gazley's submission, the doctor owed to his patient was, if I may express it very loosely, a duty not to disclose to a third party in the circumstances of this case his opinion of his patient's

mental condition. The relationship between the plaintiff and the defendant was that of doctor and patient. The doctor knew – he admitted that he knew – that the disclosure to his patient of his opinion as to her mental condition would be harmful to her. He was careful not to tell her directly what that opinion was. Nevertheless, he wrote out and gave to Mrs Furniss' husband a certificate, expressing that opinion. If he ought reasonably to have had in contemplation that Mrs Furniss might be injured physically, though not financially, as the result of his giving that certificate – and that on the evidence is beyond dispute – then it seems clear that he should have regarded her as 'his neighbour' in Lord Atkin's phrase. If she was his neighbour in that sense, he was under a duty to take care to avoid an act which he could reasonably foresee would be likely to injure her physically though not financially. Whether Mrs Furniss was to be regarded as his neighbour for that purpose, and whether he ought reasonably to have foreseen that the giving of a certificate, though true and correct, might nevertheless injure her, are questions of fact which would ultimately be for decision by the jury . . .

On the facts, it is clear that if Mrs Furniss were to be confronted by this certificate, it was likely to do her harm. The certificate was handed to Mr Furniss, who was then living with his wife. Their relations were extremely strained. She regarded him as mentally unsound and as intent on doping or poisoning her. She had not hesitated to make these accusations against him, and it was because of her accusations that he had been brought to the distraught condition in which he found himself when he begged the doctor to give him a certificate. In these circumstances, it seems to me not only likely, but extremely likely, that when the husband was charged by his wife with mental instability, he would be goaded into a '*tu quoque*' retort, and that he would disclose to her either the certificate or at all events its contents. That he apparently did not disclose it, and that the certificate remained hidden from Mrs Furniss for a whole year, speaks volumes for the husband's restraint. It is also to be noted that, in giving the certificate to Mr Furniss, the doctor placed no restrictions on its use. It was not even marked 'confidential'. On that evidence, I can only conclude that Dr Fitchett ought reasonably to have foreseen that the contents of his certificate were likely to come to his patient's knowledge, and he knew that if they did, they would be likely to injure her in her health. I do not hold that the doctor ought to have foreseen the precise manner in which the contents of his certificate did in fact come to Mrs Furniss' knowledge, though, I think, that, in the circumstances disclosed by the evidence, he ought to have foreseen that the certificate could be expected to be used in some legal proceedings, in which his patient would be concerned and thus come to her knowledge. It is sufficient to say that, in my view of the evidence in the special circumstances of this case, Dr Fitchett should have foreseen that his patient would be likely to be injured as the result of his action in giving to her husband such a certificate as he did give, and in giving it to him without placing any restriction on its use. In these circumstances, I am of opinion that, on the principle of *Donoghue v Stevenson* [1932] AC 562, there arose a duty of care on his part. I have not forgotten that the certificate was true and accurate, but I see no reason for limiting the duty to one of care in seeing that it is accurate. The duty must extend also to the exercise of care in deciding whether it should be put in circulation in such a way that it is likely to cause harm to another. I conclude, therefore, that, in the circumstances to which I have referred the doctor owed to his patient at common law a duty to take reasonable care to ensure that no expression of his opinion as to her mental condition should come to her knowledge. The doctor did not take any precautions in that respect, and, in my opinion, a cause of action was thus disclosed in the statement of claim . . . I have already held in dealing with the first part of the motion that the doctor's duty of care to his patient includes a duty not to give to a third party a certificate as to his patient's condition, if he can reasonably foresee that the certificate might come to the patient's knowledge, and if he can reasonably foresee that that would be likely to cause his patient physical harm. But I cannot think that the duty is so absolute as to permit, in law, not the slightest departure from it. Take the case of a doctor who discovers that his patient entertains delusions in respect of another, and in his disordered state of mind is liable at any moment to cause death or grievous bodily harm to that other. Can it be doubted that the public interest requires him to report that finding to someone? Take the case of a patient of very tender years or of unsound mind. Commonsense and reason demand that some report on such a patient should be made to the patient's parent or other person having control of him. But public interest requires that care should be exercised in deciding what shall be reported by this and to whom. Publication or communication of the report to other than to appropriate persons could still be a breach of the duty owed by the doctor if the patient thereby suffers unnecessary physical harm. That which will justify a departure from the general rule must depend on what is reasonable professional conduct in the circumstances under consideration in the particular case, and as such is a question for the jury. In the present case, I think, the doctor was under a general duty to take care that the certificate which he issued would not cause physical harm to his patient. Nevertheless, I think that in certain circumstances, the issue of a certificate might have resulted in benefit to the patient. Indeed, that was Dr Fitchett's own contention. He thought that as a result of it, Mrs Furniss would not be committed to a mental institution without previous examination by a specialist in psychiatry. Dr Fitchett thought that committal would not be in his patient's interest. Accordingly, I do not think that in this respect there was any misdirection of the jury. It were told, in effect, that it could find for the plaintiff if it came to the conclusion that, by reason of the particular manner of the disclosure in this case, the doctor's action did not conform with reasonable and accepted standards of professional conduct . . .

This case suggests that the health care practitioner's duty of care to his patient extends to an obligation to avoid doing his patient harm by releasing confidential information.

It is important to note that, additionally to the duties implied by the three sources above, in most States, legislation requires confidentiality on the part of health care practitioners employed by the State.

CCH *Australian Health and Medical Law Reporter*, paras 31,430–31,433

New South Wales

The Health Administration Act 1982 makes it unlawful for any person to disclose any information in connection with the administration of that or any other Act conferring responsibilities on (amongst others) departmental or hospital staff except with the patient's consent or in special specified circumstances – this provision is applicable to medical records, and considerable emphasis is placed on it in the administration of hospitals, particularly public hospitals. It is also unlawful to disclose information that has been obtained in connection with the administration or execution of the Medical Practice Act 1992 without the patient's consent.

Queensland

The Health Act 1937 makes it an offence for the Director General of Health or officers administering the Act to directly or indirectly disclose or make use of information gained by them in the course of carrying out their work. The penalty is a monetary fine of 10 penalty units.

South Australia

The South Australian Health Commission Act 1976 makes it an offence for staff of the Commission at the hospitals or health centres to divulge personal information relating to patients. The Act permits the disclosure of confidential information to researchers and employees providing technical, administrative or secretarial support without any breach of any law or any principle of professional ethics. Confidential information is defined as 'information relating to a health service in which the identity of the patient or person providing the service is revealed'. Confidential information disclosed pursuant to s 64d of the Act must not be divulged even to a board, tribunal or court. If a person is appearing as a witness and is asked a question which would require divulging of confidential information, the person is not required to answer.

The Supported Residential Facilities Act 1992 prohibits people from performing functions under the Act to use confidential information gained by virtue of their official positions for the purpose of securing a private benefit for themselves. The intentional disclosure of confidential information is not permitted unless the person to whom the information relates consented to the disclosure, disclosure is necessary to enable officers to perform their official duties or the disclosure is authorised by a court or tribunal.

The Public and Environmental Health Act 1987 also provides that a person cannot intentionally disclose medical information or information as to the personal affairs of another obtained in the course of official duties. There are exceptions, however, where the disclosure is made in the course of official duties or with the consent of the other person or is required by a court or tribunal.

Victoria

The Health Services Act 1988 prohibits staff from communicating or divulging information concerning patients. The Mental Health Act 1986 requires those employed in connection with mental health services not to give information to another that would identify patients or former patients of psychiatric hospitals. Information may only be given about patient care with the person's consent or if a court or other official body requires it. Information may only be given to an agency concerned with medical or social research with the approval of an ethics committee.

Tasmania

Part IX (Discipline and Conduct) of the Tasmanian State Service Act 1984, imposes penalties for disclosure of 'confidential information' in patients' medical records.

Administrative instructions and guidelines

Western Australia

The Health Department of Western Australia issued guidelines in 1986 dealing with the release of or access to health records. That document, among other things, deals with requests for information by relatives, the police, the media and for research purposes.

In addition to the statutory measures mentioned above, s 5(1) of the Health Services Act 1991 (Qld) requires employees of a Regional Health Authority or public sector health service to maintain patient confidentiality.

The Northern Territory has, in its Criminal Code, a unique provision designed to restrain breaches of confidence. Its meaning and import was considered by Angel J in the case extracted below.

Snell v Pryce (unreported), Supreme Court of the Northern Territory SC No 458 of 1989, 15/2/96

Angel J:

Section 222 of the Criminal Code provides:

> Any person who unlawfully abstracts any confidential information from any register, document, computer or other repository of information with intent to cause loss to a person or with intent to publish the same to a person who is not lawfully entitled to have it or receive it, or with intent to use it to obtain a benefit or advantage for himself or another, is guilty of a crime and is liable to imprisonment for three years . . .

At the time of the alleged offence, the appellant was employed as a public servant in the communications section of the Police Department. Located deep within the police headquarters at Berrimah is the communications room which is not fenestrated. To gain access to that part of the police building, a person must first pass through a security door in the reception area of police headquarters by use of a magnetic card, thence to a communication area which is designated 'restricted area', from where one enters the communications section through a door opened with a key. Within the communications section is a computer. Access to the computer is restricted. In order to use the computer a person must insert, first, his or her (I lapse into computer jargon) 'user identification', and secondly, a password known only to that person. It is physically impossible for a member of the public to enter the communications room; only authorised personnel have access to that room and only persons with appropriate facilities can use the computer once there.

The evidence discloses, and the learned Special Magistrate found, that the police department maintains strict security arrangements concerning the use of the computer and the availability of the information in it . . . In what can only be described as a flagrant breach of the terms of her employment and a deplorable breach of faith, the appellant, contrary to the express instructions of her superiors and contrary to the dictates of the computer manual, the contents of which were well known to her, extracted certain names and addresses and some dates of birth from the computer, which information she passed on to her *de facto* husband. He was a licensed enquiry agent seeking certain persons' whereabouts, apparently to assist him to serve process.

Within the communications centre of the police department there are certain computer terminals, one of which was used by the appellant for her purposes. There is within Darwin a computer known as a mainframe. Certain government departments, including the Police Department, Motor Vehicle Registry and the Department of Lands and Housing, store information on the mainframe computer. The respective departments have certain access to that information. The appellant, from within the communications room at police headquarters, could procure information from the mainframe that had been stored from either the Motor Vehicle Registry or the Department of Lands and Housing or the Police Department. The names and addresses and information abstracted by the appellant in the present case did not comprise a list of people with anything in common, eg convictions of a particular type. They were names and addresses selected by the choice of the appellant. The evidence does not particularise which information came from which department's contribution to the store of information on the mainframe computer.

It was submitted before the learned Special Magistrate and before this court, that the information abstracted was not confidential, comprising as it did names, addresses and dates of birth. In particular, it was argued before the learned Special Magistrate that because the information was 'in the public domain' and accessible from other sources, it was therefore not confidential. The learned Special Magistrate rejected that submission . . . the learned Special Magistrate reached his conclusion from the way the police treated the information, including their instructions to the appellant, and without regard to the intrinsic nature or quality of the information itself . . . the expression 'confidential information' appearing in ss 76 and 222 of the Criminal Code is not defined. Section 222, I was informed by counsel for the respondent, is unique to the Northern Territory and this is the first instance of a prosecution under it. The learned Special Magistrate resorted to certain dictionary definitions of the words 'confidential' and 'secret' in reaching his conclusions.

Sections 76 and 222 of the Code speak of 'confidential information'. They do not speak of 'information communicated in confidence', cf *Corrs Pavey Whiting and Byrne v Collector of Customs (Vic) and Anor* (1987) 74 ALR 428, at 430, 443, 444, or 'breach of confidence'. The sections concern conduct in relation to information of a certain intrinsic quality or nature rather than any relationship or arrangement or intangible notion of a confidence between persons; cf Gurry, 'Breach of Confidence' in *Essays in Equity*, edn Finn, 1985, Law Book Co, Chapter 6, p 116 and Finn, 'Confidentiality and the public interest' (1984) 58 ALJ 497, at 508. It is true Section 222 speaks, *inter alia*, of information on a 'register'. It draws no distinction between a private and a public register. Of course, public registers are in places to which the public have access, usually on payment of a fee; one thinks of births, deaths and marriages, lands titles and the like. However, I do not think one can seize on the word 'register' and say that it follows that confidential information means information imparted in confidence whatever its nature and whether available to the public or not. One may surmise there are registers containing information of the highest confidentiality. One can imagine medical registers listing the carriers of AIDS and other communicable diseases. But I do not pursue these speculations about registers any further. Whatever be the limits of the expression 'confidential information', it cannot, in my opinion, without more, include matters of common knowledge or readily accessible information such as names and addresses published in the telephone directory. In order to be confidential, information has to have, in the oft cited words of Lord Greene MR, 'the necessary quality of confidence about it': *Saltman Engineering Co Ltd v Campbell Engineering Co Ltd* (1947) 65 RPC 203, at 215; *Moorgate Tobacco Co Ltd v Philip Morris Ltd and Anor (No 2)* (1983/84) 156 CLR 414, at 438. As Deane J said in the latter case: 'Relief under the jurisdiction is not available . . . unless it appears that the information in question . . . is significant, not necessarily in the sense of commercially valuable . . . but in the sense that the preservation of its confidentiality or secrecy is of substantial concern to the plaintiff.'

It must not be trivial (*Coco v AN Clark (Engineers) Ltd* (1969) RPC 41, at 48) or 'pernicious nonsense' (*Church of Scientology v Kaufman* (1973) RPC 635, at 658) and, as Megarry J said in *Coco*, above, at 47:

> However confidential the circumstances of communication, there can be no breach of confidence in revealing to others something which is already common knowledge.

If information is 'public property and public knowledge' (*Saltman*, above, at 215), 'common knowledge' (*Coco*, above, at 47), 'information available to the public', 'generally available for the public' (*Ackroyds (London) Ltd v Islington Plastics Ltd* (1962) RPC 97, at 104), it cannot be confidential regardless of the circumstances in which it is conveyed. One cannot confide the notorious. That is not to say confidentiality is lost by partial or limited communication, not made with a view to general communication; information can be confidential even though secrecy may be imperfect: *Interfirm Comparison (Australia) Pty Ltd v Law Society of New South Wales* (1975) 2 NSWLR 104, at 118, 119. As Cross J said in *Franchi v Franchi* (1967) RCC 149, at 152–53; in a passage approved in *Attorney General's Department and Anor v Cockcroft* (1986) 64 ALR 97, at 108: 'Clearly a claim that the disclosure of some information would be a breach of confidence is not to be defeated simply by proving that there are other people in the world who know the facts in question besides the man as to whom it is said that his disclosure would be a breach of confidence and those to whom he has disclosed. It must be a question of degree depending on the particular case, but if relative secrecy remains, the plaintiff can still succeed.'

The position at general law is summed up by Gummow J in *Corrs Pavey v Collector of Customs*, above, at 437: 'It is now settled that in order to make out a case for protection in equity of allegedly confidential information, a plaintiff must satisfy certain criteria. The plaintiff (i) must be able to identify with specificity, and not merely in global terms, that which is said to be the information in question, and must also be able to show that (ii) the information has the necessary quality of confidentiality (and is not, for example, common or public knowledge), (iii) the information was received by the defendant in such circumstances as to import an obligation of confidence, and (iv) there is actual or threatened misuse of that information: *Saltman Engineering Co Ltd v Campbell*

Engineering Co Ltd (1948) 65 RPC 203, at 215; *Commonwealth v John Fairfax and Sons Ltd* (1980) 147 CLR 39 at 50–51; 32 ALR 485, at 491–92; *O'Brien v Komesaroff* (1982) 150 CLR 310, at 326–28; 41 ALR 255, at 266–68. It may also be necessary, as Megarry J thought probably was the case (*Coco v Clark (AN) (Engineers) Ltd* [1969] RPC 41, at 48), and as Mason J (as he then was) accepted in the Fairfax decision was the case (at least for confidences reposed within government), that unauthorised use would be to the detriment of the Plaintiff.'

The matters enumerated (i) and (ii) by Gummow J are important in the present case. It was for the prosecution to define the precise information filched by the appellant and to demonstrate that it was secret or inaccessible or relatively so, ie confidential within the accepted tests: *Pioneer Concrete Services Ltd and Anor v Galli and Anor* (1985) VR 675 at 714. And see generally: *Attorney General v Guardian Newspapers Ltd and Ors (No 2)* [1988] 3 All ER 545, at 648, 649 *per* Lord Griffiths, at 658, 659, 661, 662 *per* Lord Goff of Chieveley.

Unquestionably, the Police Department treats information stored in its computer or accessible through its terminals as confidential and so instructed its staff, including the appellant. However, in my view, that is not enough. If the name and address of the Prime Minister were to be deposited in the bowels of a police department computer with grave restrictions on access and strict instructions as to its use, that could not render the name and address confidential. The fact that such information was on the computer could be confidential, but that is another matter.

Counsel for the respondent pressed upon me the importance of the learned Special Magistrate's findings as to the policy of the Police Department and the steps taken by it to protect and control access to the information. He relied upon the observations of Megarry VC in *Thomas Marshall (Exports) Ltd v Guinle* [1979] Ch 227, at 248. But I respectfully agree with Professor Finn ('Confidentiality and the Public Interest', above at 499, fn 18) that the learned Vice Chancellor's views in that case must be treated 'with circumspection' and that the matters referred to by the learned Special Magistrate are not decisive of the question of confidentiality.

The prosecution case here falls short of proof. I have already noted that the precise details of the filched names and addresses and birth dates are not in evidence. The evidence does not disclose when, by whom or in what circumstances the information was first entered on the mainframe computer. Apparently much of the information was available to the public via the telephone directory and readily accessible electoral rolls and, upon payment of a fee, from the Lands Department terminals. Of course, publicly available information may be rendered confidential through its association with other facts: Gurry, *Breach of Confidence*, Clarendon Press, 1984, pp 78–80, but as I have said, all we have here are mere names and addresses. They have no context. They have no proven common denominator independent of their utility to the appellant's *de facto* husband. Their reason for being in the police records is not known. Whilst the names and addresses of themselves may not be confidential, had they been shown to comprise some sort of list linked by a common denominator, for example, a list of police suspects, the list might then have been confidential, cf Gurry, *Breach of Confidence*, above, p 71.

Mere names and addresses of themselves do not suggest confidentiality. The current address of Salman Rushdie is no doubt confidential. There is nothing to suggest any of the persons here were in hiding. Even though the appellant's *de facto* husband was an enquiry agent seeking to serve process, one cannot infer from this that the names and addresses in question were secret or relatively secret. The prosecution led no evidence that the addresses were otherwise inaccessible. No evidence was led to demonstrate confidentiality on grounds of the information being topical, the basis of the English sports results and news cases: *Exchange Telegraph Company Ltd v Gregory and Co* [1896] 1 QB 147; *Exchange Telegraph Company Ltd v Central News Ltd* [1897] 2 Ch 48; or, perhaps, if once known, largely forgotten: *Schering Chemicals v Falkman Ltd and Ors* [1982] QB 1 at 28 D E *per* Shaw LJ, 37 F at 38A *per* Templeman LJ; and see too *Attorney General for the United Kingdom v Heinemann Publishers Australia Pty Ltd and Anor* (1987) 10 NSWLR 86, at 168–69; (1987) 75 ALR 353, at 432, 433; Meagher Gummow and Lehane, *Equity Doctrines and Remedies* 2nd edn, 1984, Butterworths, at para 4113; *Attorney General v Guardian Newspapers Ltd and Ors* [1987] 1 WLR 1248, at 1319 B E *per* Lord Oliver of Aylmerton; *Attorney General v Guardian Newspapers Ltd and Ors (No 2)*, above, at 625g, 626g *per* Bingham LJ, at 661g, 663b *per* Lord Goff of Chieveley.

In the present case, it is sufficient to say that the prosecution has failed to identify precisely the abstracted information and prove its confidential quality. It follows the appellant must succeed . . .

Exceptions to confidentiality

Mason, JK and McCall-Smith, RA, *Law and Medical Ethics*, 1994, London: Butterworths, pp 169–71

Consent to publish

The first, and most easily recognised exception is when the patient or his legal adviser consents to a relaxation of secrecy. The situation is simple when viewed from the positive angle: a positive consent to release of information elides any obligation to secrecy owed by the person receiving that consent. Equally, an explicit request that information should not be disclosed is binding on the doctor save in the most exceptional circumstances . . .

Looked at from the negative aspect, however, the position is not so clear and may be frankly unsatisfactory. How many patients know whether the person standing with the consultant beside the hospital bedside is another doctor, social worker or just an interested spectator? Would they have consented to their presence if they had been informed? The consultant may be responsible if, as a result, there is a breach of confidence – but this is small consolation to the patient who feels his rights have been infringed. What patient at a teaching hospital outpatient department is likely to refuse when the consultant asks, 'You don't mind these young doctors being present do you?' The pressures are virtually irresistible and truly autonomous consent is impossible, yet the confidential doctor-patient relationship which began with his general practitioner has, effectively, been broken.

In practice, it is obvious that such technical breaches must be, and generally are, accepted – a modern hospital cannot function except as a team effort and new doctors have to be trained, the return for a technical loss of patient autonomy being access to the best diagnostic and therapeutic aids available . . .

The doctor in society

The doctor's overriding duty to society represents what is arguably the most controversial permissible exception to the rule of confidentiality in so far as it rests on subjective definitions. Society is not homogeneous but consists of groups amenable to almost infinite classification – regional, political, economic, by age and so on. It follows that what one man regards as a duty to society may be anathema to another. Individual doctors are bound to weigh the scales differently in any particular instance while, in general, all relative weighting must change from case to case. There is, for example, a great deal of difference in respect of confidentiality between a bee sting and venereal disease. While it is clear that no rules can be laid down, some aspects of this societal conflict are of sufficiently wide importance to merit individual consultation.

The most dramatic dilemma is posed by the possibility of violent crime. What is the doctor to do if he knows his patient has just committed rape – particularly if there is evidence that this is but one of a series of attacks on women? Perhaps even more disconcertingly, what if it becomes apparent that his patient is about to commit such an offence? Statute law is helpful here only in a negative sense – misprison of felony, other than as related to treason is no longer an offence. There is case law to the effect that the doctor need not even assist the police by answering their questions concerning his patients although he must not give false or misleading information (*Rice v Connolly* [1966] 2 QB 414). The obligation on the prosecution to disclose to the defence all unused material which might have some bearing on the offences charged has caused some difficulty for police surgeons. Generally speaking, an accused gives consent to disclosure of specific information only. Other information may, however, come to light during the course of the examination and once this is in the police notes, the police may feel it is their duty to include it in their 'disclosure' notes despite the fact that there is no consent to their so doing. The police surgeon may, therefore, feel it his ethical imperative to conceal his knowledge – but the decision must, at times, be difficult to make.

In the early part of this century, both medical and legal opinion was divided on the issue of disclosure of serious crime. Discussion was, however, based largely on the subject of illegal abortion which has emotional overtones of its own. Nevertheless, it was in that context that Avery J made his well-known observation:

> There are cases where the desire to preserve [the confidential relation which exists between the medical man and his patient] must be subordinated to the duty which is cast on every good citizen to assist in the investigation of serious crime . . .

This conflict between the private interest of a patient in having his confidentiality respected and the public interest in preventing crime was considered in the English case of *W v Egdell.*

W v Egdell [1990] 1 Ch 359

The plaintiff was detained in a secure hospital following the killing of five people. The plaintiff attempted to have himself transferred to a regional secure unit (which might eventually mean his release into the community). In support of his application, he commissioned the defendant (a psychiatrist) to compile a report on his mental state. The report was unfavourable to the plaintiff, so the plaintiff withdrew his application to be transferred and refused his consent for the defendant to release the report to the medical officer at the hospital. The defendant released the report. The plaintiff attempted to obtain an injunction preventing the release of the report.

Bingham LJ:

> It has never been doubted that the circumstances here were such as to impose on Dr Egdell a duty of confidence owed to W. He could not lawfully sell the contents of his report to a newspaper, as the judge held. Nor could he, without a breach of the law as well as professional etiquette, discuss the case in a learned article or in his memoirs or in gossiping with friends, unless he took appropriate steps to conceal the identity of W . . .
>
> The breadth of such a duty in any case is, however, dependent on circumstances. Where a prison doctor examines a remand prisoner to determine his fitness to plead or a proposer for life insurance is examined by a doctor nominated by the insurance company or a personal injury plaintiff attends on the defendant's medical adviser . . . the professional man's duty of confidence towards the subject of his examination plainly does not bar disclosure of his findings to the party at whose instance he was appointed to make his examination. Here, however, Dr Egdell was engaged by W, not by the tribunal or the hospital authorities.

He assumed at first that his report would be communicated to the tribunal and thus become known to the authorities but he must, I think, have appreciated that W and his legal advisers could decide not to adduce his report in evidence before the tribunal.

The decided cases very clearly establish: (1) that the law recognises an important public interest in maintaining professional duties of confidence but (2) that the law treats such duties not as absolute but as liable to be overridden where there is held to be a stronger public interest in disclosure. Thus, the public interest in the administration of justice may require a clergyman, a banker, a medical man, a journalist or an accountant to breach his professional duty of confidence (*Attorney General v Mulholland* [1963] 1 All ER 767 at 771; [1963] 2 QB 477, at 489–90, *Chantrey Martin & Co v Martin* [1953] 2 All ER 691; [1953] 2 QB 286). In *Parry-Jones v Law Society* [1968] 1 All ER 177; [1969] 1 Ch 1, a solicitor's duty of confidence towards his clients was held to be overridden by his duty to comply with the law of the land, which required him to produce documents for inspection under the Solicitors' Accounts Rules. A doctor's duty of confidence to his patient may be overridden by clear statutory language (as in *Hunter v Mann* [1974] 2 All ER 414; [1974] QB 767). A banker owes his customer an undoubted duty of confidence, but he may become subject to a duty to the public to disclose, as where danger to the State or public duty supersede the duty of agent to principal (*Tournier v National Provincial and Union Bank of England* [1924] 1 KB 461, at 473, 486, [1923] All ER Rep 550 at 554, 561). An employee may justify breach of a duty of confidence towards his employer otherwise binding on him when there is a public interest in the subject matter of his disclosure (*Initial Services Ltd v Putterill* [1967] 3 All ER 145; [1968] 1 QB 396, *Lion Laboratories v Evans* [1984] 2 All ER 417; [1985] QB 526). The qualifications of the duty of confidence arise not because that duty is not accorded legal recognition but for the reason clearly given by Lord Goff in his speech in *Attorney General v Guardian Newspapers Ltd (No 2)* [1988] 3 All ER 545, at 659; [1988] 3 WLR 776, at 807 (the *Spycatcher* case), quoted by Scott J ([1989] 1 All ER 1089, at 1102; [1989] 2 WLR 689, at 710):

> The third limiting principle is of far greater importance. It is that, although the basis of the law's protection of confidence is that there is a public interest that confidences should be preserved and protected by the law, nevertheless that public interest may be outweighed by some other countervailing public interest which favour disclosure. This limitation may apply, as the judge pointed out, to all types of confidential information. It is this limiting principle which may require a court to carry out a balancing operation, weighing the public interest in maintaining confidence against a countervailing public interest favouring disclosure.

These principles were not in issue between the parties to this appeal. Counsel for W accepted that W's right to confidence was qualified and not absolute. But it is important to insist on the public interest in preserving W's right to confidence because the judge in his judgment concluded that while W had a strong private interest in barring disclosure of Dr Egdell's report he could not rest his case on any broader public interest. Here, as I think, the judge fell into error. W of course had a strong personal interest in regaining his freedom and no doubt regarded Dr Egdell's report as an obstacle to that end. So he had a personal interest in restricting the report's circulation. But these private considerations should not be allowed to obscure the public interest in maintaining professional confidences.

The fact that Dr Egdell as an independent psychiatrist examined and reported on W as a restricted mental patient under s 76 of the Mental Health Act 1983 does not deprive W of his ordinary right to confidence, underpinned, as such rights are, by the public interest. But it does mean that the balancing operation of which Lord Goff spoke falls to be carried out in circumstances of unusual difficulty and importance. We were referred, as the judge was, to the current advice given by the General Medical Council to the medical profession pursuant to s 35 of the Medical Act 1983. Rule 80 provides: It is a doctor's duty, except in the cases mentioned below strictly to observe the rule of professional secrecy by refraining from disclosing voluntarily to any third party information about a patient which he has learnt directly or indirectly in his professional capacity as a registered medical practitioner . . . Where, as here, the relationship between doctor and patient is contractual, the question is whether the doctor's disclosure is or is not a breach of contract. The answer to that question must turn not on what the doctor thinks but on what the court rules. But it does not follow that the doctor's conclusion is irrelevant. In making its ruling, the court will give such weight to the considered judgment of a professional man as seems in all the circumstances to be appropriate.

The parties were agreed, as I think rightly, that the crucial question in the present case was how, on the special facts of the case, the balance should be struck between the public interest in maintaining professional confidences and the public interest in protecting the public against possible violence. Counsel for W submitted that on the facts here the public interest in maintaining confidences was shown to be clearly preponderant . . . Where a man has committed multiple killings under the disability of serious mental illness, decisions which may lead directly or indirectly to his release from hospital should not be made unless a responsible authority is properly able to make an informed judgment that the risk of repetition is so small as to be acceptable. A consultant psychiatrist who becomes aware, even in the course of a confidential relationship, of information which leads him, in the exercise of what the court considers a sound professional judgment, to fear that such decisions may be made on the basis of inadequate information and with a real risk of consequent danger to the public is entitled to take such steps as are reasonable in all the circumstances to communicate the grounds of his concern to the responsible authorities. I have no doubt

> that the judge's decision in favour of Dr Egdell was right on the facts of this case . . . [May LJ and Brown P delivered judgments agreeing with Bingham LJ.]

If the Medical Board of a particular State wrote, with the Police Department, a letter to all medical practitioners requesting them to divulge details of any patients they suspected may have committed a series of attacks on young girls, how should medical practitioners respond? See Mendelson, D, 'Mr Cruel and the medical duty of confidentiality' (1994) 1 Journal of Law and Medicine 120.

On whether the 'public interest exception' to the ethical duty of confidentiality incorporated in the AMA ethical guidelines (referred to in Chapter 1) is too broad, see Harris, L, 'Patient confidentiality: is the public interest exception a cause for concern?' (1996) 16 No 4 Proctor 25.

Is there a duty of disclosure?

A question arises following *Egdell's* case: although a doctor has permission to divulge confidential information, does he have a duty to do so?

Abadee, A, 'The medical duty of confidentiality and the duty to disclose: can they co-exist?' (1995) 3 Journal of Law and Medicine 75, pp 80–86

> Whether an affirmative duty to disclose exists is a question which courts have been prone to evade, if not deny. This tendency is not surprising: if an affirmative duty to disclose is admitted, then at some point the duty of confidentiality must be overridden. If recognition is given to a new duty, doctors are taken out of the realm of balancing public interests and towards resolving conflicting duties.
>
> **Potential existence of a duty of disclosure**
>
> *(a) The Tarasoff decision*
>
> In *Tarasoff v Regents of University of California*, the Supreme Court of California ruled that a psychiatrist was under a duty of care to warn a potential victim of a patient's dangerous condition if the psychiatrist should reasonably have known that the patient presented a serious danger of violence to the individual.
>
> Under the prevailing 'public interest' exception to the duty of confidentiality, it might be expected that a voluntary disclosure to an endangered third party would be considered justifiable: while there was a public interest in safeguarding the confidentiality of treatment of mental illness, there was a corresponding and overriding public interest in protecting members of the public by warning endangered citizens. But *Tarasoff* went one step further: Tobringer J recognised the general rule that people are under no obligation to control others' conduct, but then fashioned an exception: where a doctor stands in a 'special relationship'

– either to a person whose conduct needs to be controlled or to a foreseeable victim of that conduct – a doctor has an affirmative duty for the benefit of a third party. The impact of this ruling on the duty of confidentiality is potentially revolutionary. This ruling suggests that the protection of injury to confidentiality 'ends where public peril begins'. The judge eschewed the 'balancing of interests' test in declaring:

> If the exercise of reasonable care to protect the threatened victim requires the therapist to warn . . . we see no sufficient societal interest that would protect and justify concealment.

Before I examine the scope of such a duty, its potential legal and ethical bases are considered.

(b) The legal basis for a duty

In his survey of the duties of affirmative action, Fleming detects an increasing trend away from the '*laissez-faire* approach of the common law', which 'shrank from converting the law into an agency for forcing them to help each other', towards a sense of 'heightened social obligation and other communitarian tendencies'. But still, the distinction between non-feasance and misfeasance endures, and there is no general duty of care in the former case.

The immediate question is upon what legal basis a duty to warn might rest. If one takes the typical *Tarasoff* situation – where one individual's dangerous propensities are known by a person who has some degree of control over that individual – the notion that the person exercising control has a duty to someone who might be affected by the other individual's dangerous propensities, potentially comes within the realm of tort law's duty to control others. This duty is actuated by the duty of care to the endangered third party. There is no reason to doubt that a doctor may owe a duty of care to a third party outside of the doctor's relationship with the patient. This duty of control fundamentally rests upon the idea that 'certain relations call for special assurances of safety in accordance with prevailing assumptions of social responsibility'. Of course, the crucial prerequisite is the right to control – in the absence of which there can be no duty to exercise it for others' protection.

The question as to where a doctor's degree of control resides must be considered. There is a qualitative difference between the degree of control exercised in, say, the relationship between gaoler and prisoner and the control exerted between therapist and patient. In the latter case, the doctor ultimately 'has no right or power . . . to use compulsion in order to assert his will over that of the patient'.

Fashioning a duty of care confronts the additional problem that courts are reluctant to impose a special duty of care where the victim belongs to an unascertained class and is not at particular risk. Although this analysis rejects the notion of control as the touchstone for imposing a duty, a similar source – short of control – may justify the duty: the doctor's 'unique capacity' to modify a patient's behaviour, either in the treatment provided or the advice given. It is possible that a special social responsibility owed by a doctor to an endangered third party might produce the requisite degree of proximity for imposing a legal duty.

(c) *The ethical basis for a duty*

The *Tarasoff* decision sat uncomfortably with Norrie's view that the injection of a 'Good Samaritan' principle into English law, with its imposition of an affirmative duty to take preventative action when a special relationship exists, should be resisted. It has been noted that the law's reluctance to embrace affirmative duties reflects *laissez-faire* individualism, but other commentators are sceptical of imposing an affirmative duty upon doctors for other professional and ethical reasons. As Mendelson rhetorically asks, is society seeking to designate doctors as protectors and guardians of public safety, or is it their primary duty to adopt a non-judgmental approach which focuses on the best interests of the individual patient, without prejudice? Plueckhahn and Cordner emphasise that the right to professional secrecy is the patient's right, not the doctor's. Paragraph 6.2.2 of the Australian Medical Association's Code of Ethics states that the 'overriding consideration' for doctors, in considering whether to disclose information without the patient's consent, is 'the adoption of a line of conduct that will benefit the patient or protect his interests'. This code of conduct reflects a view of the professional role of doctors and that profession's relationship to the community. Some commentators, like Prins, believe there is no dilemma: the interests of the public are paramount. Other critics, sensing a potential conflict of duties, point out that if disclosure is found to be unjustified, doctors are liable to disciplinary proceedings for breach of the duty of confidentiality. At this point, it is important to recollect that the duty of confidentiality may be conceptualised in relative terms. Thomson cites another policy underlying the duty of confidentiality not always considered: the maintenance of public confidence and trust in the medical profession. Just as the protection of public health is served by the observance of and occasional departure from the duty of confidentiality, so public confidence in the profession, which entails the expectation that confidences are respected, might also entail the expectation that a doctor would breach the duty of confidentiality so as to prevent harm to members of the community. This focus upon public expectations and the public good reflects a shift away from justifying breaches of confidence in the name of 'interpersonal impropriety' towards a justification framed in terms of 'anti-public behaviour'. It is contended that there are strong legal and ethical grounds that would justify a medical practitioner breaching, in the strict sense, the duty of confidentiality when confronted by a situation such as *Tarasoff*. But the legal and ethical grounds for imposing an affirmative duty of disclosure are not so clearly established. Prior to dismissing its existence, it is proposed to consider the potential scope of a duty of disclosure, in the light of comparative analysis and its conceivable practical application.

(i) The American experience

Quite uniquely, the *Tarasoff* principle was subjected to almost immediate review. Edgley details that whereas the '*Tarasoff* One' principle created a duty to warn a victim of a potentially violent client, '*Tarasoff* Two' yielded a degree of latitude for professional judgment: When a therapist determines, or pursuant to the standards of the profession should determine, that his patient presents a serious danger of violence to another, he incurs an obligation to use reasonable care to protect the intended victim against such danger.

The immediate question arises as to how such professional standards are to be assessed. One issue is the time when the danger of violence towards a third party becomes apparent. The dissentient in *Tarasoff*, Mosk J, believed that the burden on a psychotherapist in predicting potential violence was intolerable. The history of American case law post-*Tarasoff* has featured mixed attempts in formulating the proper scope of the duty. This history has involved the variable application of the duty in various States.

In *Brady v Hopper*, a District Court in Colorado limited the psychiatrist's duty to warn only when there was a specific, identifiable victim. By contrast, a Federal District Court in *Lipari v Sears, Roebuck & Co* gave an expansive interpretation to the *Tarasoff* principle, holding that a psychotherapist has a duty to warn when he or she could 'reasonably foresee that the risk engendered by the patient's condition would endanger others'. Thus, the identity of the victim was irrelevant for the purposes of the duty.

Similar inconsistency has bedevilled development of the duty in California. While the Supreme Court favoured the limited interpretation, resting the duty on a 'readily identifiable' victim in *Thompson v County of Alameda*, the same court, in *Hedlund v Superior Court of Orange County*, extended the definition of 'readily identifiable' victims to include family members of a victim. Indeed, it was possible that the duty extended to warning all bystanders who might be injured. In extending the range of victims, American courts are effectively, if not in a conceptually convincing way, moving towards a situation whereby 'foreseeability' is the touchstone for the imposition of a duty to disclose. Ironically, in view of the value that a duty to disclose places upon protection of the public at large from dangerous individuals, as the range of identifiable victims grows, a warning to every 'victim' may produce a 'cacophony of warnings that by reason of their sheer volume would add little to the effective protection of the public'. This is why the court, in *Thompson*, offered the clearest standard reached by American courts: the duty does not arise in cases of 'non-specific threats. . . directed at non-specific victims'.

(ii) English experience

There are conceptual and practical reasons which suggest that an affirmative duty to disclose confidential information to endangered third parties will be rejected in English law. It has been clearly accepted that there is no obligation in law to take positive steps to confer benefits on others by preventing harm, and no obligation to rescue someone in danger, unless a special relationship can be established between the doctor and a third party. As Lord Reid observed in *Home Office v Dorset Yacht Co Ltd*, mere 'accidental propinquity' may attract a moral duty to act, but a legal duty is impracticable.

The Court of Appeal recently held that foreseeability of harm to a victim is insufficient in the absence of a proximate relationship between plaintiff and defendant. If a doctor cannot be said to 'have control' over a dangerous patient, there is nothing – short of foreseeability of harm – upon which to base the duty.

Notwithstanding the theoretical accommodation, in principle, between the duty of confidentiality and the duty of disclosure, the practical problem of determining the content of the latter duty remains. In this respect, there are two concerns:

(1) The assumption underlying a duty to give a warning to an endangered third party is that it is possible for a therapist to do so. It may be wondered how a therapist may warn an unascertained class of individuals not specifically threatened. The situation is, of course, different when danger is focused on a single individual.
(2) There is the difficulty in determining what steps were reasonable for the therapist to take in all the circumstances to prevent injury to the third party.

It is submitted that as English law presently stands, a doctor who believes that a patient poses a potential risk to a third party may disclose otherwise confidential information in exercise of the 'public interest' exception to confidentiality. But it is argued that a doctor is under no duty to do so. To extend the public interest exception to mandate affirmative conduct would radically overstep the requirements of reasonable foreseeability and proximity which lie at the core of the duty of care.

(iii) Australian law

Mendelson notes that Australian law follows the English practice that in the custodial setting whereby a doctor exercises control over a 'dangerous' patient, a 'special relationship' exists between a doctor and a third party such that the doctor must take positive action to ensure that the patient does not injure the third party. But Mendelson doubts, even in the same custodial setting, whether a doctor would have a positive duty to issue warnings to protect third parties, since this action would run counter to certain statutory provisions imposing penal sanctions for breach of professional secrecy. Certain statutory exceptions to the duty of confidentiality have been referred to above, but a common element in each of them is that disclosure is directed only to proper authorities. If the distinction between 'positive' misconduct and non-feasance is accepted, a decision not to warn an endangered third party would be considered an instance of the latter. Confirmation of this distinction was made by the High Court in *Sutherland Shire Council v Heyman*, where Deane J reiterated:

> The common law imposes no *prima facie* general duty to rescue, safeguard or warn another from or of reasonably foreseeable loss or injury or to take reasonable care to ensure that another does not sustain such loss or injury.

Thus a mere failure to do an act will not ordinarily attract an action unless the defendant had a prior duty. Foreshadowing later acceptance in English law, Deane J emphasised the dual requirements in grounding a duty of care:

> . . . reasonable foreseeability of a likelihood that such loss or injury will be sustained in the absence of any positive action to avoid it does not of itself suffice to establish such proximity of relationship as will give rise to a *prima facie* duty on one party to take reasonable care to secure avoidance of a reasonably foreseeable but independently created risk of injury to the other.

Therefore, an injured third party, in purporting to establish a *Tarasoff* duty of care, would need to establish a relationship of proximity. In *Heyman*, Mason J noted that the concept of proximity 'involves in most cases a degree of reliance'. But as McHugh J points out, reliance is not sufficient to create a duty without a further element such as the defendant's assumption of responsibility. Mason J determined in *Heyman* that such a 'further element' existed because of the specific reliance of the plaintiff upon a public authority. But Mason J also considered the possibility of the more general reliance which individuals place upon public authorities. The source for that reliance is the product of the grant . . . of powers designed to prevent or minimise a risk of personal injury . . . recognised by the legislature as being of such magnitude or complexity that individuals cannot . . . take adequate steps for their own protection.

It is difficult in the abstract to determine the source of any powers that doctors might have to prevent or minimise the risk of injury to third parties. Thus third parties would not have a general reliance upon doctors. Short of circumstances indicating specific reliance, it is unclear on which basis a general duty will lie.

A recent case where sufficient proximity led to the imposition of a duty of care owing to a third party was the decision of the Supreme Court of South Australia in *Swan v South Australia*. That case ruled that a duty of care was owed by State agencies to those who might be foreseen to be likely to suffer harm from a paedophile released in breach of a parole condition. Crucially, the court held that if the relationship of proximity could be established, public policy would not deny a duty of care.

This decision resembles the more restricted interpretation of *Tarasoff*: that any duty will only be owed to a specifically identified class of victim. By implication, it is possible, on this reasoning, that notwithstanding the public policy of preserving medical confidentiality, and provided proximity is established between a doctor and a third party, a duty of care to a third party might entail the breach of medical confidentiality. But viewed in terms of Mason J's specific/general reliance analysis in *Heyman, Swan* merely involved a consideration of a State agency's obligations under statute. Unless a third party could point to specific reliance, there is no source of statutory power practitioners to protect third parties, and therefore no general reliance which might denote proximity.

Mendelson notes that it is theoretically possible, in a *Tarasoff*-like situation for a doctor to owe a duty of care to a third party where the third party reasonably relied upon care being taken and where the doctor induced the reliance. But Mendelson doubts whether this situation could be realised since the presence of a medical code of ethics, which discourages the disclosure of information, makes it unlikely that the court could infer a reasonable reliance. Conceivably, it is only where the third party was also a patient of the doctor that he or she would specifically rely on a doctor.

In view of the absence of general reliance by a third party and the competing interests for and against disclosure already outlined, the present state of Australian law suggests an alignment with English law: at most, a doctor will have a discretion to breach the duty of confidentiality. As has been argued, although disclosure would not be mandatory, it may be justified in the public interest.

Compulsion due to statutory requirement

Although a medical practitioner is generally bound, both ethically and legally, to respect his or her patient's confidences, a statutory duty to divulge information *must* be heeded by a medical practitioner – even if this means betraying his or her patient's confidential information.

Hunter v Mann [1974] QB 767

Section 168 of the Road Traffic Act 1972 (UK):

> (2) Where the driver of a vehicle is alleged to be guilty of an offence . . .
>
> (a) the person keeping the vehicle shall give such information as the identity of the driver as he may be required to give by or on behalf of the chief officer of police, and
> (b) any other person shall if required as aforesaid give any information which it is in his power to give and may lead to the identification of the driver . . .

> (c) . . . a person who fails to comply with the requirement of Subsection (2)(b) above shall be guilty of an offence.

The defendant doctor knew information which might lead to the identification of the driver of a stolen car. He was asked by a police officer to provide that information and refused on the basis of the duty of confidence he owed to his patient. The doctor was convicted of an offence under s 168. The doctor appealed.

> I accept that the doctor . . . has no right to refuse to disclose confidential information in the course of judicial or quasi-judicial proceedings; but I also accept that the judge in certain circumstances, and in the exercise of his judicial discretion, may refuse to compel the doctor to do so. Further than this, in my judgment, the authorities which have been cited to us do not go. Moreover each one of those authorities was concerned with legal proceedings. In the present case it is important to bear in mind the distinction between privilege which is to be claimed in legal proceedings and a contractual duty not to disclose; which distinction is marked by a passage in the judgment of Diplock LJ in *Parry-Jones v Law Society* [1969] 1 Ch 1, at 9:
>
>> So far as Mr Parry-Jones' point as to privilege is concerned, privilege . . . is irrelevant when one is not concerned with judicial or quasi-judicial proceedings because, strictly speaking, privilege refers to a right to withhold from a court, or a tribunal exercising judicial functions, material which would otherwise be admissible in evidence. What we are concerned with here is the contractual duty of confidence, generally implied though sometimes expressed, between a solicitor and client. Such a duty exists not only between solicitor and client, but, for example, between banker and customer, doctor and patient and accountant and client. Such a duty of confidence is subject to, and overridden by, the duty of any party to that contract to comply with the law of the land. If it is the duty of such a party to a contract, whether at common law or under statute, to disclose in defined circumstances confidential information, then he must do so, and any express contract to the contrary would be illegal and void.
>
> With those words in mind, I proceed to the conclusion drawn by Mr Bingham from his contentions. He says that when one comes to construe the statute one should approach it thus; that Parliament must not be taken to have overridden or to have attempted to override the duty of confidence to which reference has been made, except by clear language or necessary implication. He says, and this is the burden of his whole contention, that 'any other person' in s 168(2)(b) must be read in a restricted way so that that duty is not breached . . .
>
> It seems to me that my first duty is to look at the section and give the words their ordinary natural meaning, and in the absence of

equivocation or ambiguity to give effect to such meaning unless of course there is something in the context of the section or of the Act itself which suggests that a special or restricted meaning should be given.

I find the words clear and unequivocal. I accept as Mr Bingham has suggested, that one should assume that Parliament has passed this Act, and this section in particular, with the existing law in mind. Accepting that, then it seems to me that Parliament must have been conscious of the use of very wide words here and if it had been intended to create exceptions, why then it would then have been easy enough to do so. It has not been done. Moreover I ask myself the question: if there is to be a restriction how far is it to go? Where is it to stop? I find it impossible to provide an answer to that question.

In these circumstances, I am driven to the conclusion that a doctor acting within his professional capacity, and carrying out his professional duties and responsibilities, is within the words 'any other person' in s 168(2)(b).

The next limb of Mr Bingham's argument was directed at the words 'in his power' in the expression 'information which it is in his power to give'. He contends that power must include a legal right, that there is no legal right or power to disclose so far as a doctor is concerned and, therefore, that he is not caught by those words.

I am not going to attempt to define 'power'. It seems to me a word of fairly common understanding and reading it in its ordinary way I have no difficulty in coming to the conclusion that a doctor in the circumstances in which the defendant found himself had the power. It may be that but for the section in the Act he would not have exercised that power, because of his duty to his patient, but that seems to me to beg the question for that would have been in accordance with his duty not to make voluntary disclosure. Once it is decided that the defendant is a person to whom the statutory duty imposed by s 168(2)(b) applies, then I have no doubt that he had the power . . .

In my view, it is important when one is considering this section to have in mind that on many occasions serious accidents are caused by people who take away, without consent, other people's motor cars and who have no hesitation in leaving the scene as quickly as they possibly can so as to avoid detection. I, therefore, find it a comfort to think that the section gives the police a wide power for the purpose of detecting people who may cause damage to others.

May I say, before leaving this case, that I appreciate the concern of a responsible medical practitioner who feels that he is faced with a conflict of duty. That the defendant was conscious of a conflict and realised a duty both to society and to his patient is clear from the finding of the justices . . . although the judgment goes against him . . .

[May J concurred. Lord Widgery CJ delivered a judgment in which he agreed with Boreham J.]

Similar provisions to the UK Road Traffic Act exist in most Australian jurisdictions.

Court ordered access

All documents (with some exceptions relating to 'privileged communications') are subject to court orders which compel their disclosure during litigation. There currently exists no privilege against disclosure which applies to medical documents.

PART II: ACCESS TO RECORDS

Do patients own their medical records?

Although a patient may require a doctor to keep private, information concerning him or her, does that mean that the patient 'owns' that information? Put another way, in the absence of a relevant statutory provision, can a patient force a doctor to divulge that patient's medical records? Until recently, the High Court's decision in *Breen v Williams* determined the question.

Breen v Williams (1996) 186 CLR 71, High Court of Australia

> In a democratic society, changes in the law that cannot logically or analogically be related to existing common law rules and principles are the province of the legislature. From time to time, it is necessary for the common law courts to re-formulate existing legal rules and principles to take account of changing social conditions. Less frequently, the courts may even reject the continuing operation of an established rule or principle. But such steps can be taken only when it can be seen that the 'new' rule or principle that has been created has been derived logically or analogically from other legal principles, rules and institutions.
>
> In the present case, it is not possible, without distorting the basis of accepted legal principles, for this court to create either an unrestricted right of access to medical records or a right of access, subject to exceptions. If change is to be made, it must be made by the legislature.
>
> **Gaudron J, McHugh J:**
>
> **The right of access**
>
> A claim that a patient has a right of access to his or her medical records is a question of great social importance. But absent a contractual term, such a claim has no foundation in the law of Australia. Nevertheless, every possible argument that could be made in support of the claim by Ms Breen was put. Dr Cashman who appeared for Ms Breen, contended that one or more of five legal principles or doctrines supported or gave to Ms Breen a right of access to records in the possession of Dr Williams that relate to his treatment of her, subject to lawful exceptions.

First, the common law gave her a 'proprietary right and interest' in the actual information contained in Dr Williams' records. Second, the common law implied a term in the contract between her and Dr Williams to the effect that she had a right of access to the documents in Dr Williams' file. Third, there was an innominate common law right of access to medical records. Fourth, the common law recognised a patient's 'right to know' all necessary information concerning his or her medical treatment including, where requested, access to records containing that information. Fifth, the law imposed on Dr Williams a fiduciary duty, enforceable in a court of equity, to give her access to her medical records.

Did Ms Breen have a proprietary right or interest in the medical records?

Dr Cashman did not submit that Ms Breen owned the actual documents which comprised the medical file. She did not, he said, 'seek to divest the doctor of the pieces of paper' comprising the records. The concession that Ms Breen did not own the documents was plainly correct. Professional persons are not ordinarily agents of their clients even though they often have express, implied or ostensible authority to enter into contracts on their clients' behalf. Documents prepared by an agent are ordinarily the property of the principal. But documents prepared by a professional person to assist him or her to do work for a client are the property of the professional, not the client.

The doctor-patient relationship, like that of valuer and client, is not one of agent and principal. Dr Williams' notes were prepared to assist him to fulfil his professional duties. The property in the medical records relating to Ms Breen which he prepared belongs to him; Ms Breen has no proprietary right in respect of those records. The right of ownership of Dr Williams is, statute or contract apart, good against the world and entitles Dr Williams to prevent any person from having access to those records.

Although Dr Cashman conceded that Ms Breen did not own the records, he contended that she had a proprietary right or interest in the documents that entitled her to access to them. The premise of this argument was that the records were not owned by anybody. However, the idea that an item of personal property that has not been abandoned has no owner is ill-founded. Ownership may be divisible in the sense that one or more of the collection of rights constituting ownership may be detached and vested in a number of persons. Ownership may also be divorced from possession in numerous circumstances. But the notion that personal property that has not been abandoned may have no owner is one that is foreign to the common law. Statute or contract apart, medical records prepared by a doctor, are the property of the doctor. That property right entitles the doctor to refuse other persons access to the records.

Was a right of access an implied contractual term?

The doctor-patient relationship is contractual in origin. In general terms, '[a] doctor offers a patient diagnosis, advice and treatment, the objectives of which are 'the prolongation of life, the restoration of the patient to full physical and mental health and the alleviation of pain'. Given the informal nature of the relationship, however, a contract between a doctor and a patient rarely contains many express terms. Because that is so, the courts are obliged to formulate the rights and obligations of the parties to the contract. As Lord Wilberforce has put it, in cases where the parties to a contract have not attempted to spell out all the terms of their contract, the function of the court is 'simply . . . to establish what the contract is, the parties not having themselves fully stated the terms'. The court does so by implying terms in the contract in accordance with established legal principles.

The common law draws a distinction between terms which are implied in fact and terms which are implied by law. Leaving aside terms that are presumed to apply because of the custom of a trade or business, the courts will only imply a term in fact when it is necessary to give efficacy to the contract. A term implied in fact purports to give effect to the presumed intention of the parties to the contract in respect of a matter that they have not mentioned but on which presumably they would have agreed should be part of the contract. A term implied by law on the other hand arises from the nature, type or class of contract in question. Some terms are implied by statutes in contracts of a particular class, for example, money lending and home building contracts. Such terms give effect to social and economic policies which the legislature thinks are necessary to protect or promote the rights of one party to that class of contract. Other terms are implied by the common law because, although originally based on the intentions of parties to specific contracts of particular descriptions, they 'became so much a part of the common understanding as to be imported into all transactions of the particular description'. Many of these terms are implied to prevent 'the enjoyment of the rights conferred by the contract [being] rendered nugatory, worthless, or, perhaps . . . seriously undermined', the notion of necessity being central to the rationale for such an implication. The distinction between terms implied by law and terms implied in fact can tend in practice to 'merge imperceptibly into each other'.

The argument for Ms Breen started with the premise that, by implication of law, a doctor always contracts with a patient to act in the patient's 'best interests'. To support this premise, Dr Cashman relied on the following statement of Lord Templeman in *Sidaway v Governors of Bethlem Royal Hospital:*

> The doctor, obedient to the high standards set by the medical profession impliedly contracts to act at all times in the best interests of the patient.

From this premise, Dr Cashman argued that, as an incident of the 'best interests' term, the doctor must make available medical records concerning a patient when the patient seeks access to them. The leap from the premise to the conclusion is a long one. But we can pass that by.

While the notion of 'best interests' is a relevant consideration in some areas of the law, such as the law relating to child welfare, a doctor does not impliedly promise that he or she will always act in the 'best interests' of the patient. The primary duty that a doctor owes a patient is the duty 'to exercise reasonable care and skill in the provision of professional advice and treatment'. The doctor does not warrant that he or she will act in the patient's best interests or that the treatment will be successful. If a doctor owed such a duty, he or she would be liable for any act that objectively was not in the best interests of the patient. The doctor would be liable for treatment that went wrong although he or she had acted without negligence. That is not the law of Australia.

There are good reasons why Australian courts do not imply a 'best interests' term, as a matter of law, into all doctor-patient contractual relationships. First, [w]here a term is implied into a contract it will usually embody a contractual promise and therefore create a legal duty. Such a duty would be inconsistent with the existing contractual and tortious duty to exercise reasonable care and skill in the provision of professional advice and treatment. The existence of a tortious duty of care militates against 'the implication of . . . a general contractual duty of care', particularly where 'the incidents of an independent general contractual duty of care would differ from those of an independent tortious duty. Second, the meaning and application of an implied term must be reasonably certain. The notion of 'best interests' has been criticised as uncertain in the context of child welfare. That criticism is just as pertinent, if not more so, in the context of contract law which places a premium on certainty.

Even if Australian law implied a term in the contract between doctor and patient that the doctor would act in the patient's best interests in the sense that Lord Templeman propounded in *Sidaway*, it would not assist Ms Breen's claim to a right of access to medical records concerning her. Lord Templeman was not asserting that a doctor owed a general duty to act in the best interests of the patient. He used the term in the context of medical advice and treatment. In the paragraph preceding the statement upon which Dr Cashman relies, Lord Templeman had said that '[a] doctor offers a patient diagnosis, advice and treatment'. It was in that context that his Lordship went on to say that the doctor 'impliedly contracts to act at all times in the best interests of the patient'. The duty was not one applying in respect of all matters arising out of the doctor-patient relationship and subsisting for an indefinite period. Only within the context of 'diagnosis, advice and treatment' was the duty to act in the 'best interests' of the patient active. Moreover, '[i]t is difficult to see how a duty to act in the patient's 'best interests' can differ in any substantive way from a doctor's duty to exercise reasonable care in practising the skills of medicine. In addition, Lord Templeman was not formulating an objective test of 'best interests'. The whole point of his speech in *Sidaway* was that it was primarily a matter for the doctor to determine what was in the patient's best interests. He said that 'the doctor, bearing in mind the best interests of the patient and bearing in mind the patient's right of information which will enable the patient to make a balanced judgment must decide what information should be given to the patient and in what terms that information should be couched.'

For these reasons, the common law did not imply a term in the contract between Dr Williams and Ms Breen that he would always act in her best interests or that she had a right of access to his record of her treatment. So far as advice and treatment were concerned, the only relevant contractual term implied by law was to exercise reasonable care and skill.

Finally, no ground exists for implying a 'best interests' term as a matter of fact. The term was not 'so obvious that "it goes without saying" ', nor was it 'necessary to give business efficacy to the contract'.

Accordingly, no implied term of the contract between Ms Breen and Dr Williams entitles her to access to the medical records in his possession.

Is there an innominate common law right of access to medical records?

Dr Cashman relied on the decision of the English Court of Appeal (Nourse Evans LJJ and Sir Roger Parker) in *R v Mid-Glamorgan Family Health Services* to assert that there is an 'innominate' common law right of access to medical records. The Court of Appeal held in that case that a public health authority had a 'duty to administer its property in accordance with its public purposes' and that, as the owner of a patient's medical records, the authority may deny a patient access to his or her records if it is in the best interests of the patient to do so. The Court of Appeal upheld the primary judge's conclusion that an offer to make the records of the plaintiff available to his medical advisers satisfied this duty.

Contrary to the view that we have expressed, Nourse LJ thought that Lord Templeman's speech in *Sidaway* had decided that a doctor had a duty to act at all times in the best interests of the patient and that it was a 'general duty'. Nourse LJ went on to say that '[t]hose interests would usually require that a patient's medical records . . . should usually, for example, be handed on by one doctor to the next or made available to the patient's legal advisers if they are reasonably required for the purposes of legal proceedings in which he is involved.' But, as we have said, we do not think that Lord Templeman intended to lay down so sweeping a duty. In any event, for the reasons that we have given, in Australia no such duty is implied in the contractual relationship between a doctor and patient.

It follows that *Mid-Glamorgan Family Health Services* is not an authority that has any persuasive effect in this country.

Does a doctor have a fiduciary duty to a patient to give the patient access to that person's medical records?

Dr Cashman contends that the doctor-patient relationship is fiduciary in nature and that a doctor who denies a patient reasonable access to medical files concerning that patient is in breach of this fiduciary duty. In our opinion, this submission must be rejected.

Australian courts have consciously refrained from attempting to provide a general test for determining when persons or classes of persons stand in a fiduciary relationship with one another. This is because, as counsel for Dr Williams pointed out, the term 'fiduciary relationship' defies definition. In *Hospital Products Ltd v United States Surgical Corporation*, Gibbs CJ said:

> I doubt if it is fruitful to attempt to make a general statement of the circumstances in which a fiduciary relationship will be found to exist. Fiduciary relations are of different types, carrying different obligations . . . and a test which might seem appropriate to determine whether a fiduciary relationship existed for one purpose might be quite inappropriate for another purpose. For example, the relation of physician and patient, and priest and penitent, may be described as fiduciary when the question is whether there is a presumption of undue influence, but may be less likely to be relevant when an alleged conflict between duty and interest is in question.

As the law stands, the doctor-patient relationship is not an accepted fiduciary relationship in the sense that the relationships of trustee and beneficiary, agent and principal, solicitor and client, employee and employer, director and company and partners are recognised as fiduciary relationships. In *Hospital Products*, Mason J pointed out that in all those relationships 'the fiduciary acts in a "representative" character in the exercise of his responsibility'. But a doctor is not generally or even primarily a representative of his patient.

Circumstances which have indicated the presence of a fiduciary relationship have included: the existence of a relation of confidence; inequality of bargaining power, an undertaking by one party to perform a task or fulfil a duty in the interests of another party, the scope for one party to unilaterally exercise a discretion or power which may affect the rights or interests of another; and a dependency or vulnerability on the part of one party that causes that party to rely on another.

Some aspects of the doctor-patient relationship exhibit characteristics that courts have used to find a fiduciary relationship. For example, from the most mundane consultation with a general practitioner through to the most complicated surgical procedure by a specialist surgeon, a patient is invariably dependent upon the advice and treatment of his or her doctor. Patients also invariably confide intimate personal details about themselves to their doctors. In some circumstances, the dependency of the patient or the provision of confidential information may make the relationship between a doctor and patient fiduciary in nature. But that does not mean that their relationship would be fiduciary for all purposes. As Mason J pointed out in *Hospital Products*, a person may stand in a fiduciary relationship to another for one purpose but not for others.

In *Birtchnell v Equity Trustees, Executors and Agency Co Ltd*, Dixon J said that in 'considering the operation of [fiduciary principles], it is necessary to [ascertain] the subject matter over which the fiduciary obligations extend'. In the present case, if Dr Williams owed a fiduciary duty to Ms Breen, the duties and obligations which arose from their fiduciary relationship could only come from those aspects of the relationship which exhibited the characteristics of trust, confidence and vulnerability that typify the fiduciary relationship. They could only attach in respect of matters that relate to diagnosis, advice and treatment.

A consideration of the fundamental obligations of a fiduciary shows that Dr Williams owed no fiduciary duty to Ms Breen to give her access to the records that he had created. The law of fiduciary duty rests not so much on morality or conscience as on the acceptance of the implications of the biblical injunction that '[n]o man can serve two masters'. Duty and self-interest, like God and Mammon, make inconsistent calls on the faithful. Equity solves the problem in a practical way by insisting that fiduciaries give undivided loyalty to the persons whom they serve. In *Bray v Fora*, Lord Herschell said:

> It is an inflexible rule of a Court of Equity that a person in a fiduciary position, such as the respondent's, is not, unless otherwise expressly provided, entitled to make a profit; he is not allowed to put himself in a position where his interest and duty conflict. It does not appear to me that this rule is, as has been said, founded upon principles of morality. I regard it rather as based on the consideration that, human nature being what it is, there is danger, in such circumstances, of the person holding a fiduciary position being swayed by interest rather than by duty, and thus prejudicing those whom he was bound to protect. It has, therefore, been deemed expedient to lay down this positive rule.

In the present case, it is impossible to identify any conflict of interest, unauthorised profit or any loss resulting from any breach of duty.

In the present case, there was no breach of fiduciary duty in the conditional denial of access because there was no pre-existing duty on the part of Dr Williams to give access to the records.

It is also impossible to identify any profit that Dr Williams may have derived from the relationship beyond the payment of his authorised professional fees. Nor is the case one where Dr Williams seeks to make or has made a profit from confidential information that he obtained in the course of his relationship with Ms Breen.

The problem of reconciling the alleged fiduciary duty to act in the best interests of Ms Breen with other rights and obligations of Dr Williams and Ms Breen also makes it difficult to see how there could be a fiduciary duty to give access to records relating to her medical treatment. In *Hospital Products*, Mason J explained the relationship of fiduciary obligations and contractual rights and obligations as follows:

> That contractual and fiduciary relationships may co-exist between the same parties has never been doubted. Indeed, the existence of a basic contractual relationship has in many situations provided a foundation for the erection of a fiduciary relationship. In these situations, it is the contractual foundation which is all important because it is the contract that regulates the basic rights and liabilities of the parties. The fiduciary relationship, if it is to exist at all, must accommodate itself to the terms of the contract so that it is consistent with, and conforms to, them. The fiduciary relationship cannot be superimposed upon the contract in such a way as to alter the operation which the contract was intended to have according to its true construction.

The right of access claimed by Ms Breen is not one given by the contract between her and Dr Williams. Nor can it arise from any undertaking, express or implied, by Dr Williams to act as the representative of Ms Breen because no such undertaking was given. Moreover, the contract between the parties gives her no right to or interest in the medical records. They remain the property of Dr Williams. Furthermore, a fiduciary duty that Dr Williams would always act in Ms Breen's best interests, which is the foundation of the claim of a fiduciary obligation to provide access to the records, would conflict with the narrower contractual and tortious duty to exercise reasonable care and skill in the provision of professional advice and treatment that Dr Williams undertook.

In addition, Dr Williams is the owner of the copyright in the records. By federal law, ownership of the copyright gives Dr Williams a number of exclusive proprietary rights including the right to reproduce the records in any material form. He is the beneficial owner of those rights. He does not hold them on trust for Ms Breen. In the absence of an undertaking, express or implied, on the part of Dr Williams to allow her to copy the records, it is difficult to see how Ms Breen could be allowed to copy the records even if she had a right of access to the records.

In our view, there is no basis upon which this court can hold that Dr Williams owed Ms Breen a fiduciary duty to give her access to the medical records. She seeks to impose fiduciary obligations on a class of relationship which has not traditionally been recognised as fiduciary in nature and which would significantly alter the already existing complex of legal doctrines governing the doctor-patient relationship, particularly in the areas of contract and tort. As Sopinka J remarked in *Norberg v Wynrib*:

> Fiduciary duties should not be superimposed on these common law duties simply to improve the nature or extent of the remedy.

The 'right to know'

Dr Cashman contended that the law in Australia governing the doctor-patient relationship has moved to or is moving towards a recognition of the patient's 'right to know' and that this was a reason why the court should hold that a patient has a right of access to medical records concerning that person. He argued, relying particularly on the decision of this court in *Rogers v Whitaker*, that this movement is recognisable in the law in five ways: an acceptance of the principle of personal inviolability; a rejection of a paternalistic approach which had been previously accepted; the rejection of the notion that the patient's interests are to be determined by standards exclusively fixed by the medical profession; the imposition of judicially imposed standards; and the acceptance of patient autonomy. Dr Cashman did not contend, however, that this 'movement' in the law of itself gave Ms Breen the right of access for which he argued. Rather, he suggested that it advanced the validity of his other arguments.

While recent decisions of Australian courts have rejected the attempt to treat the doctor-patient relationship as basically paternalistic, it would require a quantum leap in legal doctrine to justify the relief for which Dr Cashman contends. *Rogers* took away from the medical profession in this country the right to determine, in proceedings for negligence, what amounts to acceptable medical standards. But the decision also rejected the notion of 'the patient's right of self-determination' as providing any real assistance in the 'balancing process that is involved in the determination of whether there has been a breach of the duty of disclosure'.

Any change in the law must be for Parliament

No doubt there are people in this country who think that a patient should have an unrestricted right of access to medical records that concern that patient. Many others, Ms Breen among them, no doubt think that a patient should have access to such records, subject to limited exceptions. Perhaps only a very small minority of persons in Australia would think that in no circumstances should patients have access to information contained in their medical records. But absent a contractual right, the common law of Australia does not give a patient a right to have access to records, compiled by a medical practitioner, which relate to that patient. Nor, for the reasons that we have given, is it possible for this court to develop existing principles to create such a right.

Advances in the common law must begin from a baseline of accepted principle and proceed by conventional methods of legal reasoning. Judges have no authority to invent legal doctrine that distorts or does not extend or modify accepted legal rules and principles. Any changes in legal doctrine, brought about by judicial creativity, must 'fit' within the body of accepted rules and principles. The judges of Australia cannot, so to speak, 'make it up' as they go along. It is a serious constitutional

> mistake to think that the common law courts have authority to 'provide a solvent' for every social, political or economic problem. The role of the common law courts is a far more modest one.
>
> [Brennan CJ and Gummow J delivered separate judgments; Dawson and Toohey JJ delivered a joint judgment. All judges dismissed Ms Breen's appeal.]

The effect of the Privacy Amendment (Private Sector) Act 2000 has been to amend the Commonwealth's Privacy Act. An important development is the statutory reversal of the rule in *Breen v Williams*. Patients are now (subject to exceptions outlined in the National Privacy Principles) permitted to access their own health information. The Privacy Act requires individuals and organisations to comply with the National Privacy principles, which are set out in schedule III of the Privacy Act. Principle 6 requires that access be granted to people about whom the information is written (subject to some exceptions). Principle 7 requires that people in possession of the private information must alter that information if it is inaccurate.

An Information Privacy Commissioner has been established to enforce the new requirements. Some aspects of the new legislation are outlined in the extract below.

Devereux, JA, 'Privacy and medical confidentiality' (2000) 21 Law and Technology 4

> The Privacy Amendment (Private Sector) Bill 2000 has been described by the Attorney-General, the Hon Daryl Williams AM, QC, as 'the most significant development in the area of privacy law in Australia since . . . 1988':
>
> > Its impact upon health practice should not be underestimated. The advent of federal legislation applying to private health practices is best understood against a background of increasing storage and access of personal health information in electronic form, greater linkage of that information which is said to support clinical decision making, and the increased gathering of information on health care matters by non-health care practitioners (for example, gyms, counsellors, superannuation providers and workers' compensation providers). [Crompton, M, 'Application of national principles for fair handling of personal information to personal information', Office of the Federal Privacy Commissioner, 25 May 1999 at p 7.]
>
> There have been significant developments at a State level which have attempted to address concerns relating to privacy. Such attempts have included the ACT's Health Records/Privacy and Access Act 1987, the Privacy and Personal Information Act 1998 INS and the Victorian Department of Human Services Information Privacy Principles. Such attempts, combined with industry Codes of Practice (such as the Royal

College of General Practitioners Code of Practice for the Management of Health Information in General Practice) have led to there being a patchwork of voluntary and mandatory standards in this area.

The amendments to the Federal Privacy Act seek to provide some clarity and broad coverage. The amendments draw upon the 1980 OECD Guidelines for the Protection of Privacy and Transborder Flows of Personal Data. Rather than consisting of detailed legislative provisions, the Act establishes principles which should apply across the board.

Private organisations are encouraged to develop Codes of Practice in respect of the handling of personal information. Where the industry has not developed such a Code, the principles in the Act will apply. Before an industry Code can operate, it must be approved by the Privacy Commissioner. He may only approve Codes if they provide at least the same amount of consumer protection as the National Principles.

If an individual is not happy with the way his or her personal information is being handled by an organisation, he or she may make a complaint with the organisation. Organisations are permitted to set up complaint-handling mechanisms.

Such complaints procedures are required, by virtue of the Privacy Act 1988 amendments, to meet specific standards as to independence and transparency. In the absence of a specific industry code as to complaints handling, the Privacy Commissioner takes on the role of resolving a dispute through mediation.

The decision-making process employed by an industry mediator or the Privacy Commissioner may be judicially reviewed under the Administrative Decisions (Judicial Review) Act 1977. Any order made by an industry mediator or the Privacy Commissioner may be enforced through the Federal Court or the Federal Magistrates Court.

Carter points out that a major problem with the proposed regime as far as health information is concerned is that the regime is complaints based. Carter argues 'in the health sector the most vulnerable consumers are unlikely to make complaints because of the potential to prejudice their ongoing treatment. In addition, in an electronic environment individual consumers may not even know that their privacy has been abused'. (Carter, M, 'Protecting consumers' interest in their health records' (1999) 8 No 2 Australian Health Law Bulletin 15.)

A key part of the new regime is that individuals should be able to access and correct information about themselves. Access to health information is guaranteed, except where there are legitimate reasons for denying access (such as 'therapeutic privilege' where a grant of access would pose a serious threat to the person). Unfettered access to records represents a change to the common law as expounded by the High Court in *Breen v Williams* (1996) 186 CLR 71. There the High Court held there was no right of patient access to records, since such records belonged to the doctor.

The Australian Medical Association, in their Legal Issues web page (see http://www.amo.com.au), have attacked the new regime for its failure to accord with *Breen v Williams*. They argue also that the new regime needs to be accompanied by an 'adequately funded education programme to alert the profession to the requirements of the new law'. They claim that the Privacy Act amendments will cause concern to the medical practitioners who 'are concerned about bureaucratic interference in medical practice and the doctor-patient relationship'. It might be legitimately pointed out, though, that the Privacy Act amendments apply to all organisations which handle personal information, and not just the medical profession.

The thorny issue of the use of information for research purposes has been the subject of a recent English High Court decision, *R v Department of Health ex parte Source Informatics Ltd* [1999] 4 All ER 185. In that case the Court held that it was an actionable breach of confidence for doctors or pharmacists to supply, without patient consent, information gleaned from prescriptions – even where such information was provided in a de-identified form. The Privacy Act amendments provide that, where information is provided for the purpose of research, it must be done so with patient consent or, where this is not practicable, in accordance with safeguards relating to the public interest and approved guidelines.

The Health Records Act 2001 (Vic) and the Health Records and Information Privacy Act 2002 (NSW) allow patients in those states to gain access to their medical records from a private or public health services provider.

Patient records and FOI legislation

Although *Breen v Williams* established that a patient cannot force a medical practitioner to divulge medical records, statute has intervened to give patients a right of access to the medical records held by government authorities (including hospitals).

The relevant pieces of Freedom of Information Legislation are extracted by MacFarlane, P in his book *Health Law*, 1995, pp 140–42, Sydney: Federation. Broadly, most states have legislation allowing a patient to access his or her own records. In the event that the records contain information of a 'medical or psychiatric nature' and that it is felt that the disclosure of the records might have an adverse effect on the health of the patient, then the records may be disclosed to a registered medical practitioner of the patient's choice, rather than to the patient him- or herself.

Privacy guidelines

Reference has already been made to the Western Australia guidelines on privacy and confidentiality (for details of these guidelines, see CCH *Australian Health and Medical Law Reporter*). Another, very thorough set of guidelines was produced by the Queensland Department of Health Departmental Standing Committee on Privacy in Health and Medical Records in April 1986. These guidelines are reproduced below. Note that these guidelines have been replaced by Information Standard 42A which is extracted at the end of this chapter.

Queensland Department of Health Privacy Guidelines for Hospitals

PREFACE

There is a growing concern in society about invasions of personal privacy, whether actual or potential. Health records (that is, all medical records, whether used for treatment or for other legitimate purposes such as public health surveillance) may contain large amounts of personal information of a nature which many people would regard as sensitive. Therefore, it is necessary to ensure that all personal information is handled wisely. This Department's policy on privacy in health and medical records is embodied in the general principles listed below.

General principles of privacy for health and medical records

The social justification principle

The collection of personal data (eg medical records) should be for a general purpose (eg provision of effective health care and specific uses (eg treatment of a particular individual or planning bed numbers) which are socially acceptable. That is, both the intent and the actions must be socially acceptable.

This principle aims to ensure that personal data are not collected for any purpose which, even if strictly legal, would not be generally socially acceptable.

The collection limitation principle

The collection of personal data should be restricted to the minimum necessary for the achievement of a socially acceptable purpose and such data should not be obtained by unlawful or unfair means.

The object of this principle is to reduce the likelihood that personal information be transmitted unnecessarily by ensuring that data collected are kept to a minimum; for example, irrelevant personal details should not, as sometimes happens, be recorded as a matter of routine.

The purpose specification principle

The purposes for which personal data are collected should be specified to the individual concerned no later than at the time of data collection or should, at the least, be implicit in publicly accepted common ethical practice. Subsequent use of the data should be limited to the fulfilment of those purposes specified and/or implied or to such others as are not incompatible with those purposes.

The aim of this principle is to ensure that the individual concerned is aware, when personal information is collected, of the ways in which it might be used.

The information quality principle

Personal data should, for the purpose for which they are to be used, be accurate, complete and kept up-to-date.

The object of this principle is to ensure that an individual is not misrepresented or inappropriately treated as a result of personal data being at any time inaccurate.

The security safeguards principle

Personal data should be protected by security safeguards which are reasonable and appropriate for the purpose of preventing loss or destruction of data or the unauthorised access to, use of, modification of or disclosure of data.

This principle recognises the need for security measures for the protection of stored data, although it should be noted that absolute protection cannot be expected, owing to cost factors.

The policy of openness principle

There should be a general policy of openness about developments, practices and policies with respect to personal data.

The object of this principle is to maintain a high level of awareness in the community generally about the type of personal information which is commonly collected and the way in which it is used.

The accountability principle

There should be in respect of personal data, an accountable officer who should be responsible for making every reasonable effort to give effect to these principles.

This principle is considered sufficiently important to be included because it emphasises the fact that there is a need for individuals to accept responsibility in this area if policy is to be implemented effectively.

The individual participation principle

In relation to health and medical records, the individual concerned should have communicated to him or to his nominated medical practitioner such information as is deemed to be desirable or necessary for his continued wellbeing.

It is in this way that the right of the individual to have access to such personal data is given recognition.

The disclosure limitation principle

Personal data should not be disclosed or made available except with the consent of the individual concerned, the authority of law or pursuant to a publicly known usage or common and routine ethical practice.

This principle is designed to permit the individual concerned to control the disclosure of personal information which has been given to an agent (eg health service provider, health service planner), except under certain well-recognised circumstances.

The time limitation principle

Personal data in a form which permits identification of the individual concerned should, where the purposes of the data have expired be destroyed, archived or de-identified.

This principle simply ensures that sensitive personal information is not stored in an identifiable form for longer than is necessary. The risk of undesirable disclosure is thus reduced.

CONFIDENTIALITY

Hospitals have a responsibility to maintain the privacy of patient information. This includes medical records and those documents and registers not normally regarded as being part of the medical record, such as admission, casualty and operating theatre registers, radiographs, financial records and other similar material. Documents should not be viewed by unauthorised persons, whether staff members or the general public.

Conversations regarding confidential information should not be conducted in the presence of, or overheard by, unauthorised persons.

Note: Special problems for country hospitals.

All hospitals have problems in maintaining patient privacy.

These include controlling access to medical records, responding to third party requests for information and ensuring privacy during medical examinations. However, this is particularly a problem in country hospitals which serve small communities.

The community

In general, a country hospital serves a relatively small population. Therefore, knowledge may spread quickly through informal networks and cause patients embarrassment or distress.

Sensitivity in matters of confidentiality affecting patients is especially important when the hospital is the only available source of medical care. A person on a high income can easily go out of the area to see a doctor or be admitted to another hospital outside the area. However, people on lower incomes cannot afford this. If they are afraid to come to the hospital for treatment, they may not seek treatment at all.

The staff

Community residents employed by the hospital who care for patients or process patient information may find it difficult to maintain confidentiality with respect to medical information about their friends, relatives or neighbours. Moreover, most community residents employed in the hospital will not have received training in medical ethics and consequently the idea of confidentiality may be foreign to them at first. In addition, doctors and other staff members who are not from the community and who are accustomed to working in large medical institutions may be insensitive to some of the special problems of confidentiality which arise in a country hospital.

Imagined problems

Even if a hospital protects patient privacy adequately, some community members may be afraid to use it. They may fear that their friends or neighbours working in the hospital will gossip or that the hospital will report something about them to outside agencies, such as the police, the immigration authorities or welfare department. Many people may distrust the hospital from the start because they have had bad experiences with public institutions in the past. It is a special challenge to the country hospital to overcome such fears as these and to achieve the respect and trust of the community it serves.

BREACHES OF CONFIDENCE

(a) BREACHES AND POTENTIAL BREACHES

It is important to determine what constitutes a breach of confidence. Certain kinds of breaches are easy to define: staff members gossiping about patients; patients overhearing private medical consultation; staff members releasing information without patient consent; or people seeing medical records when they have no business seeing them.

However, there are some occurrences which may or may not constitute a breach of patient confidence. The following illustrations are included to show that the problem of defining a breach of confidentiality is very complex.

A doctor tells a woman that her husband has cancer before he tells the man; he wants the wife to be prepared to give her husband emotional support when he learns the diagnosis.

A ward sister arranges to get a domiciliary nurse to help care for an elderly patient at the patient's request. The ward sister tells the nurse all relevant health information about the patient without obtaining the patient's express consent.

In the cases just cited, it is hard to determine whether invasions of privacy have occurred. How does one determine what is in the patient's best interest? If a patient tells a health worker in confidence that she has saved 50 sleeping tablets because she is planning to commit suicide, the health worker may decide to notify someone in the hospital in order to prevent the suicide. If a patient tells a staff member in confidence that he is an alcoholic, but that he does not want anyone in the hospital to know, what if anything should the staff member do with this information?

These examples serve to illustrate that not all problems of confidentiality have clear-cut answers.

(i) Patient-staff interactions

Many kinds of patient-staff encounters occur both inside and outside the hospital. These may include home visits by a domiciliary care team, reception at the hospital, referrals, medical examinations and treatment. During any of these confidential encounters, it is possible that people who have no legitimate reason for knowing what is said will overhear the conversation between the patient and staff member.

(ii) Staff handling of patient information

Following an interview with a patient, a staff member might violate the confidence of the patient in a number of ways: he might tell his spouse about the interview, as a way of getting an emotional burden off his chest; he might tell a friend or relative of the patient about the interview, as an expression of sincere concern; he might legitimately discuss the interview with another staff member and be overheard; or he might release information that he received during the interview to a third party, such as an insurance agent, without the patient's consent.

(iii) Entries in medical records

Good medical records facilitate high-quality, comprehensive care by making detailed and relevant patient information (both current and historical) readily available to care givers. Therefore, all pertinent patient information should be entered in the record. However, entries can threaten patient privacy if they contain particularly sensitive or personal information that is irrelevant to patient care.

(b) THE EFFECTS OF BREACHES

(i) Potential harm to the patient

One cannot predict how a patient will be affected when a medical institution commits a breach of confidence. The effects may range from mild embarrassment to mental anguish, from loss of job to defamation, from deterioration of health to suicide. A breach of confidence may permanently disrupt a person's life.

For example, if a woman goes to hospital for a pregnancy termination and word later leaks out of the hospital that she has had an abortion, she might be ostracised by her friends and neighbours. If a man goes to a hospital for psychiatric help and the hospital reveals his psychiatric problems to his employer, the man might lose his job.

It is easy to imagine the consequence for a patient if sensitive medical information (eg information about venereal disease, psychiatric problems or drug addiction) is not kept confidential. However, it must be stressed that all patient information should remain confidential. Information that does not appear sensitive to anyone in the hospital may harm the patient if it is divulged.

For example, a staff member might casually mention to a patient that she had seen the patient's husband at the hospital outpatient department the previous week. If the man had not told his wife, it could cause some domestic problems: the woman might be hurt that her husband had not confided in her.

Indeed, if information that appears to be non-sensitive is freely revealed, patients might reasonably believe that other information is treated similarly and thus they might be reluctant to use the hospital services.

(ii) Potential harm to the hospital

If a hospital fails to maintain strict confidentiality of patient information, the people it is supposed to serve will eventually realise that they cannot trust the hospital to keep their personal health information private.

The hospital may be legally liable for breaking confidences. A patient might sue for retrieval of damages if he is able to prove that the hospital wrongfully disclosed information about him.

(c) MEASURES TO PREVENT BREACHES

The likelihood of the occurrence of breaches of confidence and subsequent loss of the patient's trust will be reduced if five general principles are observed.

The collection limitation principle

The collection of personal data should be restricted to the minimum necessary for the achievement of a socially acceptable purpose and such data should not be obtained by unlawful or unfair means.

The purpose specification principle

The purposes for which personal data are collected should be specified to the individual concerned no later than at the time of data collection or should, at the least, be implicit in publicly accepted common ethical practice. Subsequent use of the data should be limited to the fulfilment of those purposes specified and/or implied or to such others as are not incompatible with those purposes.

The security safeguards principle

Personal data should be protected by security safeguards which are reasonable and appropriate for the purpose of preventing loss or destruction of data or the unauthorised access to, use of, modification of or disclosure of data.

The time limitation principle

Personal data in a form which permits identification of the individual concerned should, where the purposes of the data have expired, be destroyed, archived or de-identified.

The accountability principle

There should be, in respect of personal data, an accountable officer who should be responsible for making every reasonable effort to give effect to these principles. Patient information is necessarily shared among many people in medical institutions; health care providers, medical record personnel, data collectors, accounts personnel and students all have access to it. The administration should determine which staff members must have access to what patient information in order to provide good patient care. In many cases, individual staff members will have to use their own judgment in determining what information they should acquire and share with others.

STAFF MEMBERS DO NOT HAVE AN AUTOMATIC RIGHT TO HAVE ACCESS TO PATIENT INFORMATION PURELY BECAUSE THEY ARE DOCTORS, NURSES, ALLIED HEALTH PROFESSIONALS OR ACCOUNTS PERSONNEL.

Administrative efficiency should not supersede issues of confidentiality. Each hospital should try to limit, wherever possible, the numbers and categories of staff who have access to patient information. At the same time, the policies should not interfere with delivery of good medical care.

In order for all staff to be acquainted with their responsibilities in respect of patient information, each new member should (a) be required to sign a declaration that he or she will respect the confidentiality of patient information and (b) be reminded that breaching confidentiality can lead to being charged with an offence under s 44 of the Hospitals Act. All students and regular volunteer workers should also be required to give a similar written declaration. Volunteers who provide assistance in emergency situations should be reminded of the need for confidentiality.

(i) Patient-staff interactions

Sensitivity of staff members to the needs and feelings of patients is central in guaranteeing privacy for patients. The nature of the patient-staff encounter and the place in which it is held determines those who may legitimately be present.

During medical examinations and treatment, the presence of several medical and allied health staff members may be necessary and should pose no threat to patient privacy. However, staff members should be sensitive to the patient's feelings about who should or should not be present.

Orientation and training of employees is crucial in maintaining confidentiality. Employees such as receptionists and volunteers such as drivers, who frequently interact with patients but who do not give direct patient care, may need special in-service training so as to learn how to avoid causing embarrassment to patients. Privacy may be particularly difficult to achieve in busy hospitals. Certain kinds of patient-staff interactions demand greater privacy than others. All medical examinations and treatment should be carried out in privacy. Examining rooms should be walled off and doors closed. Interviews with psychiatrists, psychiatric social workers and venereal disease investigators and others require the greatest possible privacy. The hospital administration should ascertain what patient-staff encounters require privacy, and whether the rooms in which these interviews take place afford privacy. Each department or team might be requested to identify additional places where leaks occur and to heighten the sensitivity of staff members to the issues. Privacy requirements should be accorded due consideration when plans for new buildings are being drawn up.

(ii) Staff handling of patient information

Such intangible conditions as the psychological atmosphere prevalent in the hospital and the attitudes of professional staff toward one another can affect the extent to which employees will be inclined to talk irresponsibly about patients.

When a member of staff is deeply troubled about the condition of a patient, he should be able to discuss his concern with his supervisor, thereby relieving himself of the temptation to discuss it with a close friend inside or outside the hospital. Any health professional troubled by the problems of a patient often has a need to share the concerns with another person. When the supervisory or team structure does not meet this need, the hospital administration should consider designating a sympathetic staff member, such as a medical director or social worker, with whom other employees can talk things out in an informal way that does not threaten patient privacy.

Legitimate discussion among staff members

Even during a necessary and legitimate discussion about patients which occurs among staff members (eg a team conference whether formal or informal, a supervisory session, a medical consultation), patient privacy can be violated if the discussion is overheard by people who are not involved in the patient's care. Doctors, dentists, nurses and others must be careful not to talk about their patients in hallways, lifts, waiting rooms or coffee rooms.

Team conferences

Confidential patient information is discussed in detail at team conferences. The team should decide for itself what information about a patient should and should not be shared openly at these meetings. Team members may at times misunderstand the informal atmosphere among colleagues and they may feel that they can similarly share patient information with others outside the team conference. All staff members must clearly understand that such information must not be discussed outside team conferences, except when it is necessary to do so in order to give the patient proper treatment. Real conflict can arise for a staff member who has promised a patient not to reveal certain information that the patient has given in secrecy. The staff member should not share the information without the patient's consent unless (1) the situation is urgent and the health of the patient or his family depends upon immediate disclosure, or (2) the information is such that statute requires the staff member to report it. If, for legal reasons the staff member must report it, or for medical reasons he must immediately share it, he should inform the patient he will have to break a confidence. In many cases, it will be possible to convince the patient that it is in the interest of his medical care for the staff member to reveal the information to the doctor or other staff members.

Case conferences for the purpose of training

As a part of in-service training or continuing education, health care workers often have conferences with one another and their supervisors during which cases are discussed. Although these conferences are designed to educate staff members, they also contribute to patient care by encouraging the exchange of ideas and suggestions about individual patients and families. It is of prime importance that staff members keep the rights and interests of the patient at heart during training conferences. They should preserve the anonymity of the patient or family as far as possible.

Other necessary discussions of patients

In addition to team and training conferences, other discussions of patients among staff members are essential to patient care. Medical consultation among physicians, for example, is an effective means of bringing more knowledge and better judgment to a case than one doctor can provide alone. These consultations most often occur informally, between appointments or after hours. The staff members involved should make sure that such consultations occur in privacy. Facilities should be organised in such a way that such discussions can take place during rest pauses and meal breaks.

(iii) Entries in medical records

Each staff member who makes entries in medical records should conscientiously apply his judgment in determining what kinds of information should go into the record. However, this is not a matter that can be decided by individual judgment alone. Senior staff should formulate guidelines stating what kinds of information are extraneous, 'gossipy' or just too sensitive to be written into a permanent record.

(iv) Personnel and training

Every hospital employee should be familiar with rules and written policies designed to protect patient information, because almost everyone who works in a hospital may eventually come into contact with patient information. Policies should dictate the expected code of behaviour for employees. They should also tell staff members what to do if they are asked to divulge patient information to outside persons or agencies.

Although policies dealing with confidentiality are necessary, hospitals should guard against becoming 'rule dominated'. Most studies on administrative competence, leadership and production indicate that rule-bound agencies tend to be low in morale and output. Respect for the dignity of the patient and of the staff member should be the starting point for hospital policies on confidentiality.

Prevention of all the kinds of breaches of confidence discussed above depends largely on the ways in which the hospital hires, trains and supervises staff members. These depend, in turn, on the ability of policy-making bodies, advisory boards, and administrators to develop policies and practices that demonstrate active concern for patient privacy.

The following suggested policies might help to prevent breaches of confidence.

In selecting employees for positions in a hospital, administrators should take special care to hire people who are mature, who can think independently but can take direction, who have commonsense, who are not known to be gossips, and who are not malicious. Hospital staff members should be able to deal with intimate personal information, both medical and social, without becoming shocked, depressed, or unduly inquisitive. This is particularly important in hospitals whose employees are likely to know patients personally.

Administrators should try to determine how selection procedures can be designed to ensure that persons who are hired will respect the patients. In particular, they should screen out people who tend to gossip, who are emotionally immature or who feel obliged to notify public authorities about patients' private concerns.

Before he begins to work, a new employee should become thoroughly acquainted with the importance of confidentiality during his overall orientation to the hospital. Orientation should include an explanation of the goals of the hospital, with special emphasis on the objective of giving health care with dignity. A new employee should understand that people who have access to personal patient information hold a position of special trust.

The entire staff should receive in-service orientation and training in confidentiality. Such training should encourage a deep exploration of the issues of confidentiality which all staff members face, rather than restrict itself to problems which a particular segment of the staff is likely to encounter. This broader approach will create a better understanding of the complicated issues and stimulate the entire staff to work together to solve confidentiality problems. It should also help the individual see where his role in protecting patient confidentiality fits into the overall operation of the hospital.

In-service education by departments or by teams is also important. Staff members who are likely to encounter particular problems should participate in departmental or team orientation sessions which deal with those specific problems.

Good supervision of employees is crucial in the protection of patient privacy. Supervision should support staff members: an employee should feel free to discuss with his supervisor any breaches of confidence that he is responsible for, in order that he may avoid similar mistakes in the future. Supervision that is highly authoritarian can create a repressive atmosphere in which employees might chatter among themselves about patients, as a way of escaping or a way of expressing dissatisfaction, rather than discuss the matter with the appropriate supervisor. Supervision that is devoid of genuine and active concern for the employee and the problems he faces in his job may also lead to dissatisfaction and a sense of uselessness that engenders gossip about patients.

(v) Controlling access to records

Administrators should consider the following suggestions for preserving the confidentiality of records:

- Carefully screen medical record personnel for maturity and sound judgment before hiring. Educate them regarding ethics and confidentiality. Supervise them closely and instruct them carefully about policies related to confidentiality.
- Allow only medical record personnel and certain designated staff to have direct access to records on the shelves or in cabinets in the record department.
- If records are kept in cabinets, lock the cabinets at night. In record departments which use open shelving, lock the record department at night. Keys should be held by certain designated members of the night staff.
- Establish rules and policies about the reproduction of medical records on copying machines or other reproducing equipment in the hospital.
- Pay particular attention to the privacy of medical records of hospital employees.
- Always have a supervisor present when the medical record department is being cleaned, or when equipment is being installed.

The Medical Superintendent has overall responsibility for hospital medical records (ss 12 and 13 of the Hospitals Act Regulation). Once records leave the Medical Record Department, they should be the responsibility of the staff member to whom they are signed out. The Medical Record Administrator or the clerk in charge of medical records should know as far as possible where each record is at all times within the hospital. Therefore, sign-out procedures should be defined, and they should be understood and followed by all staff members who handle records. The following are suggested as a general guide, although local conditions will require their own particular solutions:

- Assign certain staff members from the Medical Record Department the responsibility of transporting medical records from one part of the hospital to another, or have professionals collect their records; alternatively, develop another secure transport system to suit your hospital.
- Do not allow staff members to leave records lying around on table tops or desks where passers by might have access to them. Assign to a person within each department the responsibility of checking to see that records are returned to the record department.
- When records are sent by carrier to satellite centres (eg day hospitals not on site), place them in sealed envelopes. Instruct the carrier never to leave them unattended.
- Devise a system for determining location of records (eg ward, satellite centre, pathology and so on).
- Devise a system that ensures that the medical records of discharged

and deceased patients are returned to the Medical Record Department.

There are times when certain files or records have to be destroyed. Whenever there is a legitimate reason for destroying confidential patient records, the administration should see that the records are completely destroyed (eg shredded and then burned).

RELEASE OF PATIENT INFORMATION

There are two general principles which should be observed in relation to disclosure of any information about patients.

The disclosure limitation principle

Personal data should not be disclosed or made available except with the consent of the individual concerned, the authority of law or pursuant to a publicly known usage or common and routine ethical practice.

The individual participation principle

In relation to health and medical records, the individual concerned should have communicated to him or to his nominated medical practitioner such information as is deemed to be desirable or necessary for his continued wellbeing.

Health institutions constantly face the problems of when, in what form, and to whom patient information should be released. They must solve these problems systematically and justly in order to protect patients from probing agencies and individuals. Information contained in medical records is equivalent to confidential communication between patients and medical personnel. When unwarranted release of information from medical records occurs, the relationship of privacy and trust between the patient and the health professional becomes meaningless.

The patient, or person legally responsible for the patient, has the right to authorise release of information pertaining to him. Unwarranted divulgence intrudes on his privacy and violates his right of individual freedom by making this decision for him.

It is suggested that all patient information, whether personal, social, psychological or medical, be considered confidential. This includes basic information (such as name, address, age, sex and physician's name) which is frequently not treated as such.

Requests for patient information occur frequently and come from many sources: outside health care institutions, insurance companies, researchers, police, social service agencies, investigation agencies, the armed forces, and private individuals. Requests are made in person, by telephone and in writing. Hospital personnel should be prepared to respond appropriately to every request. A sound rule is to refer all requests to the Medical Superintendent, his appointee, or to the patient's attending physician. (However, see below for advice on releasing information to relatives and friends.) Information must not be released or made available to any person, including staff, unless it is established that he has a legitimate right to it.

Hospital administrators should note the following:

- The responsibility of offices other than the Medical Record Department (such as accounts office, pathology department or public relations) to release medical information should be defined, preferably in a policy manual.
- Channels should exist for prompt rulings by the Medical Superintendent on novel or difficult questions.

In situations where a copy of all or part of a record is supplied to a person or organisation legitimately requiring the information, it is strongly recommended that this be noted on the original record, together with all relevant details (information supplied, to whom, for what purpose). All copies should be clearly marked 'confidential'. In general, the practice of photocopying whole or part of a file in substitution for a well-compiled medical report or case summary is to be discouraged.

(a) TO THE PATIENT

As a general principle, it is the policy of this Department that the individual should have communicated to him, or to his nominated medical practitioner, such information as is deemed to be desirable or necessary for his continued wellbeing.

In any record-keeping system, the need for the individual concerned to have access to his own record relates to his right to ensure the accuracy, timeliness, relevance and objectivity of its contents, particularly when the record is to provide the basis for important decisions, including non-medical ones (such as an employer's decision to make an offer of appointment or a life insurance company's decision to issue a policy).

Therefore, a patient should be given by his medical attendant all the information about his illness that he can understand and accept. It is believed that direct access to his medical record might in some cases, prove detrimental to the patient's medical care, especially in highly sensitive areas such as psychiatric illness, alcohol and drug dependence, cancer, venereal disease and all kinds of terminal illness. The treating doctor should not release such information which, in his professional judgment, might prove damaging to the patient's health or prognosis.

In summary, therefore, a medical practitioner should communicate to his patient, in intelligible form, all information relevant to his condition, while withholding items for which there might be a good and specific reason for doing so, as, for example, in the case of an unconfirmed diagnosis of cancer.

(b) TO RELATIVES AND FRIENDS

Friends and relatives frequently request information, ranging from current address of a patient to the exact nature of his diagnosis and treatment. This information should not be released by anyone (except the patient's physician in certain cases) without patient consent. As a service to the patient, the Medical Record Department may agree to inform the patient of any request from an individual, in case the patient himself wishes to get in touch with the inquirer.

Where a patient requests that no information be released at all, his wishes must be respected. In hospitals, doctors frequently discuss the condition of a patient with the patient's spouse, relatives or close friends without the explicit consent of the patient. When a physician does not have the explicit or implied consent to discuss a case with a patient's relative but feels it is in the best interest of the patient to do so, he must weigh the situation very carefully before making his decision.

Where the patient is a minor, disclosure of confidential medical information to parents, although contrary to the wishes of the patient, may appear to be desirable or even unavoidable in some cases. However, it is important that children not be thus discouraged from seeking medical advice or treatment. In such circumstances, therefore, it is better to explain to the patient the reasons for parents needing to be informed and to encourage him or her to initiate the disclosure than to override the individual's right to privacy. Note carefully the provisions of the Mental Health Services Act 1974–84, s 17(2), which permits a person who has attained the age of 16 years to seek and obtain psychiatric treatment without parental consent.

(c) TO HOSPITAL STAFF

Staff members do not have an automatic right to have access to patient information purely because they are doctors, nurses, allied health professionals or accounts personnel, nor do former employees of the hospital have any right to examine patient records. Information should only be released to staff when it is established that there is a legitimate right to it. This is particularly important in hospitals whose employees are likely to know patients personally.

(d) FOR MEDICO-LEGAL REASONS

(i) To the courts

The courts, Royal Commissions and Commissions of Inquiry have the power to subpoena persons or documents for the purpose of obtaining evidence relevant to the proceedings. For example, the Coroners Act 1958–84 permits the coroner to:

> . . . summon any person whose evidence he may deem it necessary to obtain to attend the inquest at a time and place mentioned in the

> summons and then and there to give evidence and be examined and may further require him to produce then and there at the inquest any books, documents, or other writings or any other thing whatever in his custody or control which he is required by the summons to produce (s 29(4)(a)).

In addition, the coroner may, if he thinks necessary:

> . . . direct or request any medical practitioner who attended professionally the deceased person at or immediately prior to his death or during his last illness to submit to the coroner a report for the assistance of the person making the postmortem examination (s 18(6)(ii)).

Other courts have similar powers in relation to information concerning persons either deceased or living. This has implications for the handling of medical records. When a subpoena is received, certified copies of the records which have been requested should be forwarded in a sealed envelope to the Clerk of the Court. A receipt detailing the name of the court, date of receipt and the name of the person accepting the envelope at the court should be obtained. The attention of the Medical Superintendent should be drawn to any case that might involve the hospital. Where the person whose health record has been subpoenaed is not a party to the proceedings before the court, he should be notified by the hospital that the subpoena has been received and advised of the place, date and time of the court hearing.

Access to records may also be required as a consequence of the legal process of 'discovery'. This is the process whereby either party to a civil dispute is able to obtain from the other party information as to the existence of documents relevant to the case; the court may subsequently order that any relevant documents, including those held by a third party (for example, medical records held by a hospital) be produced. If should be emphasised that only material relevant to the case is required to be released in these circumstances.

(ii) To the police

In general, a police officer has no more right to confidential patient information than has any private citizen. Police requests to view patient records should be directed to the Medical Superintendent. However, the common law right to silence can be overridden by legislation, as is the case with the Traffic Act 1949–84. Under this Act:

> . . . any member of the police force may make all inquiries that he deems necessary or desirable in order to investigate any road accident resulting in death, injury or damage to property and, furthermore, a person may not, without lawful excuse, refuse to provide the required information (s 33);

> . . . every person, if requested by a police officer, is required to give any information which he may have which may lead to the

identification of a driver alleged or suspected to have committed an offence (s 41);

any member of the police force has the power of entry to any premises for the purpose of carrying out any investigation which he is required or authorised to do under the Traffic Act (s 43).

It can be seen, therefore, that police powers under the Traffic Act are very broad. In order to protect patient confidentiality, it would be prudent for a medical officer to supply all information requested in relation to road accidents and offences, so that there would be no necessity for any member of the police force to examine medical records.

In relation to other requests, information about patients should not generally be released unless there appears to be extreme and immediate danger to the person or to another person (for example, when the patient has informed his doctor that he is about to kill someone). It is generally said that a physician may release information in these circumstances without violating confidentiality.

Although it may have been customary to do so, there is no legal requirement to hand over to the police the medical record of a deceased person who has become the subject of a coronial inquiry. Indeed, it is possible that disclosure of the contents of the record to unauthorised persons could embarrass or prejudice the interests of the family of the deceased. In such a case, the family would have legitimate grounds for a complaint against the hospital.

In the event of a dispute over disclosure of information to the police, the local police superintendent should be required to make a detailed statement explaining the reasons for the request.

(iii) Statutory right of access

Some individuals or bodies have statutory right of access to certain types of information. Before medical records are released in response to a statutory demand, the authority of the person requesting access and the nature of the access requested should be checked to ensure that only material relevant to the statutory demand is released.

(iv) Compulsory notification

In certain circumstances, disclosure of patient information is compulsory. That is, notification of certain facts to the relevant authority is a statutory responsibility. For example, a medical practitioner must notify the coroner of any death which occurs in suspicious circumstances (s 13 Coroners Act) and will be considered to be guilty of misconduct under s 35 of the Medical Act 1939–84 if he does not notify the police of any information which indicates that non-accidental injury has been caused to a person or that an attempted or completed crime has been committed (Refer MOP 18–30–65). In addition, some diseases are the subject of statutory notification. Cancer cases must be notified to the Cancer Registry. The Director General must be informed of any case of the following disease: amoebiasis, ancylostomiasis, anthrax, brucellosis, cholera, dengue, diphtheria, diarrhoea in a closed institution, encephalitis, epidemic polyarthritis, filariasis, food poisoning in two or more associated cases, genital herpes, hepatitis (type A (infective) and type B (serum)), hydatid disease, leprosy, leptospirosis, malaria, melioidosis, meningitis, psittacosis (ornithosis), plague, poliomyelitis, Q fever, rubella, salmonella infections, shigella infections, smallpox, taeniasis, tetanus, trachoma, tuberculosis (all forms), typhoid, typhus (all forms), venereal disease including acquired immune deficiency syndrome and yellow fever (Health Act 1937–84, ss 30 and 54(5)). Also under the Health Act, Division IXB, a medical practitioner who suspects maltreatment or neglect of a child is obliged to notify this within 24 hours to a person authorised by the Director General to receive and act upon such information. This Act specifically states that notification so given in good faith shall not be held to constitute a breach of professional ethics.

In all situations where notification is mandatory or access to information is given under statute (for example, under the provisions of the Mental Health Services Act 1974–84, medical psychiatric reports must be provided, in certain circumstances, to the Director of Psychiatric Services and/or the Patient Review Tribunal), the patient should be informed of this, although his permission is not required.

(v) Other medico-legal requests

Where requests for information are received from solicitors, insurance companies, compensation authorities and others, such information should only be released on receipt of the patient's written consent to the release of the information. However, in cases where the patient's own solicitor requests information, this can be released on receipt of the solicitor's unequivocal statement in writing that he is acting on behalf of the patient.

A health professional should always be involved in the handling of these requests to ensure that only information relevant to the request is released. Where the information sought is thought to be particularly sensitive, the information should be forwarded directly to the patient and the solicitor or other person advised accordingly. The patient can then decide whether the information should be released.

In general, requests for complete photocopies, 'all notes and records' and similar broad, non-specific requests should be refused pending details of the specific information required.

(e) TO OTHER INSTITUTIONS OR AGENCIES

(i) Emergency situations

In emergency situations, the Medical Record Administrator or clerk should respond to requests for patient information immediately. If, for example, another health care institution calls about a patient whom it is treating on an emergency basis, and asks for information about the patient's blood type, drug sensitivities, current diagnosis, or medications, etc the information should be given, even though patient consent has not been obtained. In responding to emergency requests for patient information, medical record personnel should find out what information is needed, take down the name and number of the physician treating the patient, look up the required information (eg concerning drug allergies) and ask a professional to call the physician back. Calling back the institution will verify that the request actually came from that institution. The professional should make a note in the patient's record of what information was released, to whom it was released, and the nature of the emergency.

(ii) Non-emergency situations

A doctor or health care institution often requests a summary of a patient's medical record from the physician or institution that previously cared for him. However, a request for patient information should not be honoured simply because it comes from a doctor. If the patient's new physician requests a copy of the record, this should not be supplied without the patient's knowledge and should not be supplied at all if the patient objects to the information being released. The Disclosure Limitation Principle states that information may be released 'pursuant to a publicly known usage or common and routine ethical practice'. It is important that this be borne in mind when issuing discharge summaries. If there is any doubt as to whether the patient is aware of the practice, steps should be taken to inform him that a detailed discharge summary will be sent to the referring practitioner. Similar practices should be followed when patient information is supplied to other 'care-giving individuals or organisations, such as a Community Health Service or a domiciliary nursing service.

Health institutions often release patient information to a social welfare agency either because agency staff feel that they have a legitimate 'need to know' or because of an unwritten rule of 'agency co-operation'. Nevertheless, it is necessary to obtain the proper patient authorisation before releasing patient information to such an agency. There is a danger that the requesting agency will either subordinate the patient's interest to its own interest or misinterpret medical information. The hospital should avoid exchanging confidential patient or client information with other agencies solely in the interest of 'inter-agency co-operation'. The patient or client must be allowed to decide whether an agency has a legitimate need to have confidential information about him.

(f) TO EMPLOYERS

Special care should be exercised in the release of information to an employer, even with the consent of the patient. It is desirable to give only information related to the accident, disease or condition for which the employer (or his insurance company) has assumed financial responsibility and to withhold information which is not relevant.

Where the hospital itself is potentially the employer of a person who has been one of its own patients, no attempt should be made during the selection process to peruse the applicant's medical record. If there are any doubts about the applicant's health, a routine medical examination and report should be requested.

(g) TO RESEARCHERS

Disclosure of information to researchers is the responsibility of the Medical Superintendent, who acts in such matters for the Hospital Board. The Medical Superintendent should, however, have access to an ethics committee to provide advice on research applications. Membership of the committee should include medical, legal and other non-medical persons.

'Research' is understood here to mean any study or investigation which involves contact with patients or their records or both, excepting only those studies required as part of peer review or clinical audit, which are essential elements in the process of maintaining quality of care within the hospital. (See s 2(c)(ii).)

The Medical Superintendent, without referral to the ethics committee, may authorise retrospective reviews of medical records or prospective studies involving detailed documentation of clinical practice by the staff involved in the care of the patient. However, any study in which contact is to be made with a patient by a research worker not involved with the patient's treatment should be referred to the ethics committee. Where patients are to be contacted directly by the researcher, the informed consent of each patient should be obtained prior to access being granted.

Intending researchers, whether or not they are members of the hospital staff, should be given the following instructions:

- All research proposals submitted for approval should be accompanied by a comprehensive protocol detailing the aims, methods and reasons for study. Where access to records is requested, the nature of the access should be clearly specified and the safeguards for privacy outlined.
- Any researcher who has contact with patient information is expected to treat that information as absolutely confidential. With knowledge comes the risk of inadvertent or accidental disclosure, so that maintenance of confidentiality requires constant vigilance on the part of the researcher.

- Information collection (eg data from files, patient interviews) should be restricted to a minimum, recording only that which is essential for the study. This precludes the accumulation of data which might have a future, as yet unspecified, use.
- Records should not, under any circumstances, be removed from the hospital precincts.
- In publishing, reporting on or presenting (eg seminar) research results, the researcher must preserve the anonymity of patients. Nothing should be presented in such a way that an individual patient might be identified; this includes the use of initials or pseudonyms in case studies, which can lead to identification or, possibly even worse, misidentification. If, despite the absence of a patient's name, it may be possible to identify a patient because of special circumstances such as the rarity of the condition, the patient's consent should be obtained prior to publication.

(h) TO THE MEDIA

The greatest invasion of patient privacy, and possibly the greatest risk of legal action against a health care institution, may occur when information is released to the press, radio or television because of the broad publicity resulting from such disclosures. These situations usually arise when an accident victim, a person involved in a police case, or a well-known public figure is receiving treatment in a health care facility. In general, hospitals should always require consent of the patient before releasing any information to the media. Since these situations are complex, and are likely to come up with little advance warning, hospitals should develop specific policies and procedures to deal with them. For example, the condition of the patient may be released in some circumstances. Requests for information should be referred to the Medical Superintendent. Wherever possible, the wishes of the patient should be ascertained in such circumstances, since some types of information may indirectly identify the patient. Media photographers or camera operators should obtain the consent of the Medical Superintendent before filming any area of a hospital or clinic, so that patients' rights to privacy and confidentiality are not infringed.

SUMMARY GUIDELINES

1. Health and medical records should be viewed as confidential always.
2. Members of staff do not have an automatic right to have access to patient information purely because they are doctors, nurses, allied health professionals or accounts personnel.
3. Staff must be selected and trained so that breaches of confidence do not occur. This means that staff should:

   (a) acknowledge that patients have a right to information privacy;
   (b) be aware of the potential for breaches of confidence;

(c) be aware of the possible harmful effects of breaches;
(d) receive accurate information about persons and organisations having legal right to have access to the information contained in records;
(e) be aware that other persons and organisations have no right to such information.

The Queensland Department of Health's principles would seem to be derived from the OECD 1981 Guidelines on the Protection of Privacy and Transborder Flows of Personal Data.

How do the 1986 Guidelines differ from Information Standard 42A reproduced below?

Information Standard No. 42A
Information Privacy for the Queensland Department of Health

1. Overview/Purpose

The purpose of this information standard is to establish a framework for the responsible collection and handling of personal information in the Queensland Department of Health.[1] In September 2001 Cabinet decided that, in implementing an information privacy scheme for the Queensland public sector, the Queensland Department of Health would comply with the National Privacy Principles (NPPs) (rather than the Information Privacy Principles (IPPs)) contained in the Commonwealth Privacy Act 1988. The IPPs, which govern other Queensland public sector agencies are contained in Information Standard No. 42. Information Standard No. 42A applies the NPPs to the Queensland Department of Health, but otherwise reflects the content and mandatory requirements contained in Information Standard No. 42.

1.1 Scope

Information standards are issued under the authority of ss 22(2) and 56(1) of the Financial Management Standard 1997. This information standard applies only to the Queensland Department of Health. Information Standard No. 42A requires personal information to be managed in accordance with a set of NPPs adapted from the Commonwealth NPPs contained in the Privacy Act 1988 (Cth). It should be noted that the requirement for the Queensland Department of Health to comply with this Information Standard is administratively based. This means that:

where conflicting requirements exist any legislative requirements

1 The Queensland Department of Health is bound by Information Standard No. 42A. Statutory bodies (within the meaning of the Financial Administration and Audit Act 1977) administered by the Minister for Health are bound by Information Standard No. 42.

will supersede compliance with the Information Standard; for example, section 63 of the Health Services Act 1991; and

compliance is subject to any existing outsourcing arrangements, contracts and licences. Any future outsourcing arrangement, contracts and licences will be expected to comply with Information Standard No. 42A.

1.2 Exempt personal information[2]

The following personal information is exempt from Information Standard No. 42A:

Personal information about an individual arising out of or in connection with a controlled operation or controlled activity within the meaning of the Police Powers and Responsibilities Act 2000;

Personal information about an individual arising out of or in connection with a covert undertaking of an operation, investigation or function of a law enforcement agency;

Personal information about an individual arising out of a warrant issued under the Telecommunications (Interception) Act 1979 of the Commonwealth.

Witness protection

Personal information about a witness who is included in a witness protection program under the Witness Protection Act 2000 or who is subject to other witness protection arrangements made under an Act.

Disciplinary actions and misconduct

Personal information about an individual arising out of a complaint made under Part 7 of the Police Service Administration 1990.

Personal information about an individual arising out of an investigation of misconduct or official misconduct under the Criminal Justice Act 1989.

Whistleblowers

Personal information about an individual that is contained in a public interest disclosure within the meaning of the Whistleblowers Protection Act 1994, or that has been collected in the course of an investigation arising out of a public interest disclosure.

2 The provisions pertaining to exempt personal information do not relieve anyone from existing requirements to obtain that personal information through either a legislative authority or under subpoena or warrant.

Cabinet and Executive Council documents

Personal information about an individual that is contained in a document of a kind referred to in sections 36 and 37 of the Freedom of Information Act 1992 (ie Cabinet and Executive Council documents).

Commissions of inquiry

Personal information about an individual arising out of a Royal Commission or commission or inquiry.

1.3 Codes of Practice

Information Standard No. 42A permits a code of practice to be developed and approved for the Queensland Department of Health. A code of practice may modify the application of any one or more of the NPPs, but may not modify the NPPs themselves. A code can apply to any one or more of the following:

any specified class of personal information;

any specified activity or specified class of activity;

any class of designated person.

Codes of Practice may be developed by the Department of Health, approved by the Department of Justice and Attorney-General (after consultation with the Department of Innovation and Information Economy, Sport and Recreation Queensland, if appropriate) and then issued by the Department of Health.

2. Policy Statement

Personal information held by the Queensland Department of Health must be responsibly and transparently collected and managed (including any transfer or sale of personal information held to other agencies, other levels of Government or the private sector) in accordance with the requirements of the National Privacy Principles.

3. Policy Principles

The Queensland Department of Health must comply with ten NPPs, which govern how personal information is collected, stored, used and disclosed. The NPPs deal with the following:

Principle 1: Collection of personal information;

Principle 2: Use and disclosure;

Principle 3: Data quality;

Principle 4: Data security;

Principle 5: Openness;

Principle 6: Access and correction;

Principle 7: Identifiers;

Principle 8: Anonymity;

Principle 9: Transborder flows; and

Principle 10: Sensitive information.

3.1 Mandatory requirements

It is mandatory that the Queensland Department of Health:

> nominate a privacy contact officer who will be the first point of contact for privacy issues. The privacy contact officer may also, at the discretion of the chief executive, be the first point of contact for any privacy complaints made to the Queensland Department of Health;
>
> develop a privacy plan to give effect to the NPPs;
>
> publish their privacy plan on their website;
>
> implement the privacy plan according to a schedule developed in the privacy plan, subject to any existing contractual obligations, licences or other outsourcing arrangements;
>
> review and update the privacy plan annually;
>
> develop and place on their website a privacy and security statement;
>
> be responsible for accessing and correcting records; and
>
> be responsible for ensuring mechanisms are in place for complaint resolution.

3.1.1 National Privacy Principle 1

1.1 An organisation must not collect personal information unless the information is necessary for one or more of its functions or activities.

1.2 An organisation must collect personal information only by lawful and fair means and not in an unreasonably intrusive way.

1.3 At or before the time (or, if that is not practicable, as soon as practicable after) an organisation collects personal information about an individual from the individual, the organisation must take reasonable steps to ensure that the individual is aware of:

(a) the identity of the organisation and how to contact it;
(b) the fact that he or she is able to gain access to the information;
(c) the purposes for which the information is collected;
(d) the organisations (or the types of organisations) to which the organisation usually discloses information of that kind;
(e) any law that requires the particular information to be collected; and
(f) the main consequences (if any) for the individual if all or part of the information is not provided.

1.4 If it is reasonable and practicable to do so, an organisation must collect personal information about an individual only from that individual.

1.5 If an organisation collects personal information about an individual from someone else, it must take reasonable steps to ensure that the individual is or has been made aware of the matters listed in sub-clause 1.3 except to the extent that making the individual aware of the matters would pose a serious threat to the life or health of any individual.

1.6 If the information is required under a statutory collection the organisation which collects the information is not required to ensure that the individual is or has been made aware of the matters listed in subclause 1.3.

3.1.2 National Privacy Principle 2

2.1 An organisation must not use or disclose personal information about an individual for a purpose (the *secondary purpose*) other than the primary purpose of collection unless:

(a) both of the following apply:

- (i) the secondary purpose is related to the primary purpose of collection and, if the personal information is sensitive information, directly related to the primary purpose of collection;
- (ii) the individual would reasonably expect the organisation to use or disclose the information for the secondary purpose; or

(b) the individual has consented to the use or disclosure; or

(c) if the information is not sensitive information and the use of the information is for the secondary purpose of direct marketing:

- (i) it is impracticable for the organisation to seek the individual's consent before that particular use; and
- (ii) the organisation will not charge the individual for giving effect to a request by the individual to the organisation not to receive direct marketing communications; and
- (iii) the individual has not made a request to the organisation not to receive direct marketing communications; and
- (iv) in each direct marketing communication with the individual, the organisation draws to the individual's attention, or prominently displays a notice, that he or she may express a wish not to receive any further direct marketing communications; and
- (v) each written direct marketing communication by the organisation with the individual (up to and including the communication that involves the use) sets out the organisation's business address and telephone number and, if the communication with the individual is made by fax, telex or other electronic means, a number or address at which the organisation can be directly contacted electronically; or

(d) if the information is health information and the use or disclosure is necessary for research, or the compilation or analysis of statistics, relevant to public health or public safety:

   (i) it is impracticable for the organisation to seek the individual's consent before the use or disclosure; and
   (ii) the use or disclosure is conducted in accordance with guidelines approved for the purposes of this subparagraph; and
   (iii) in the case of disclosure – the organisation reasonably believes that the recipient of the health information will not disclose the health information or personal information derived from the health information; or

(e) the organisation reasonably believes that the use or disclosure is necessary to lessen or prevent:

   (i) a serious and imminent threat to an individual's life, health or safety; or
   (ii) a serious threat to public health or public safety; or

(f) the organisation has reason to suspect that unlawful activity has been, is being or may be engaged in, and uses or discloses the personal information as a necessary part of its investigation of the matter or in reporting its concerns to relevant persons or authorities; or
(g) the use or disclosure is required or authorised by or under law; or
(h) the organisation reasonably believes that the use or disclosure is reasonably necessary for one or more of the following by or on behalf of an enforcement body:

   (i) the prevention, detection, investigation, prosecution or punishment of criminal offences, breaches of a law imposing a penalty or sanction or breaches of a prescribed law;
   (ii) the enforcement of laws relating to the confiscation of the proceeds of crime;
   (iii) the protection of the public revenue;
   (iv) the prevention, detection, investigation or remedying of seriously improper conduct or prescribed conduct;
   (v) the preparation for, or conduct of, proceedings before any court or tribunal, or implementation of the orders of a court or tribunal.

(Note 1: It is not intended to deter organisations from lawfully co-operating with agencies performing law enforcement functions in the performance of their functions.
Note 2: Sub-clause 2.1 does not override any existing legal obligations not to disclose personal information (for example, section 63 of the Health Services Act 1991). Nothing in sub-clause 2.1 requires an organisation to disclose personal information; an organisation is always entitled not to disclose personal information in the absence of a legal obligation to disclose it.
Note 3: An organisation is also subject to the requirements of National Privacy Principle 9 if it transfers personal information to a person in a foreign country.)

2.2 If an organisation uses or discloses personal information under paragraph 2.1(h), it must make a written note of the use or disclosure.

2.3 *(Sub-clause 2.3 deleted – not relevant in the case of the Queensland Department of Health).*

2.4 Despite sub-clause 2.1, an organisation that provides a health service to an individual may disclose health information about the individual to a person who is responsible for the individual if:

(a) the individual:

  (i) is physically or legally incapable of giving consent to the disclosure; or
  (ii) physically cannot communicate consent to the disclosure; and

(b) a natural person (the *carer*) providing the health service for the organisation is satisfied that either:

  (i) the disclosure is necessary to provide appropriate care or treatment of the individual; or
  (ii) the disclosure is made for compassionate reasons; and

(c) the disclosure is not contrary to any wish:

  (i) expressed by the individual before the individual became unable to give or communicate consent; and
  (ii) of which the carer is aware, or of which the carer could reasonably be expected to be aware; and

(d) the disclosure is limited to the extent reasonable and necessary for a purpose mentioned in paragraph (b).

2.5 For the purposes of sub-clause 2.4, a person is *responsible* for an individual if the person is:

(a) a parent of the individual; or
(b) a child or sibling of the individual and at least 18 years old; or
(c) a spouse or de facto spouse of the individual; or
(d) a relative of the individual, at least 18 years old and a member of the individual's household; or
(e) a guardian of the individual; or
(f) exercising an enduring power of attorney granted by the individual that is exercisable in relation to decisions about the individual's health; or
(g) a person who has an intimate personal relationship with the individual; or
(h) a person nominated by the individual to be contacted in case of emergency.

2.6 In sub-clause 2.5:

child of an individual includes an adopted child, a step-child and a foster-child, of the individual;

parent of an individual includes a step-parent, adoptive parent and a foster-parent, of the individual;

relative of an individual means a grandparent, grandchild, uncle, aunt, nephew or niece, of the individual;

sibling of an individual includes a half-brother, half-sister, adoptive brother, adoptive sister, step-brother, step-sister, foster-brother and foster-sister, of the individual.

(Note: Sub-clauses 2.4–2.6 do not override any law with respect to assisted and substitute decision making; for example, the Guardianship and Administration Act 2000 and the Powers of Attorney Act 1998).

3.1.3 National Privacy Principle 3

An organisation must take reasonable steps to make sure that the personal information it collects, uses or discloses is accurate, complete and up-to-date.

3.1.4 National Privacy Principle 4

4.1 An organisation must take reasonable steps to protect the personal information it holds from misuse, loss and unauthorised access, modification or disclosure.

4.2 An organisation must take reasonable steps to destroy or permanently de-identify personal information if it is no longer needed for any purpose for which the information may be used or disclosed under National Privacy Principle 2.

3.1.5 National Privacy Principle 5

5.1 An organisation must set out in a document clearly expressed policies on its management of personal information. The organisation must make the document available to anyone who asks for it.

5.2 On request by a person, an organisation must take reasonable steps to let the person know, generally, what sort of personal information it holds, for what purposes, and how it collects, holds, uses and discloses that information.

(Note: Sub-clauses 5.1–5.2 do not affect the Department's obligation to develop and make publicly available a privacy plan setting out:

the nature of the records of personal information kept by or on behalf of the Department (including public registers managed within the Department);

the purpose for which each type of record is kept;

the classes or types of individuals about whom records are kept;

the period for which each type of record is kept;

the persons who are entitled to have access to personal information contained in the records and the conditions under which they are entitled to have that access; and

the steps that should be taken by persons wishing to obtain access to that information.

3.1.6 National Privacy Principle 6

(The text of this principle has been deleted – right of access and correction is limited to the Freedom of Information Act 1992 *and/or the Department of Health's Administrative Access to Health Records policy.)*

3.1.7 National Privacy Principle 7

7.1 An organisation must not adopt as its own identifier of an individual an identifier of the individual that has been assigned by:

(a) an agency; or
(b) an agent of an agency acting in its capacity as agent; or
(c) a contracted service provider for a Commonwealth contract acting in its capacity as contracted service provider for that contract.

7.1A *(Sub-clause 7.1A deleted – not relevant in the case of the Queensland Department of Health.)*

7.2 An organisation must not use or disclose an identifier assigned to an individual by an agency, or by an agent or contracted service provider mentioned in sub-clause 7.1, unless:

(a) the use or disclosure is necessary for the organisation to fulfill its obligations to the agency; or
(b) one or more of paragraphs 2.1(e) to 2.1(h) (inclusive) apply to the use or disclosure.
(c) *(Sub-clause 7.2(c) deleted – not relevant in the case of the Queensland Department of Health.)*

7.3 In this clause:

identifier includes a number assigned by an organisation to an individual to identify uniquely the individual for the purposes of the organisation's operations. However, an individual's name or ABN (as defined in the A New Tax System (Australian Business Number) Act 1999) is not an ***identifier***.

3.1.8 National Privacy Principle 8

Wherever it is lawful and practicable, individuals must have the option of not identifying themselves when entering transactions with an organisation.

3.1.9 National Privacy Principle 9

An organisation in Australia or an external Territory may transfer personal information about an individual to someone (other than the organisation or the individual) who is in a foreign country only if:

(a) the organisation reasonably believes that the recipient of the information is subject to a law, binding scheme or contract which effectively upholds principles for fair handling of the information that are substantially similar to the National Privacy Principles; or
(b) the individual consents to the transfer; or
(c) the transfer is necessary for the performance of a contract between the individual and the organisation, or for the implementation of pre-contractual measures taken in response to the individual's request; or
(d) the transfer is necessary for the conclusion or performance of a contract concluded in the interest of the individual between the organisation and a third party; or
(e) all of the following apply:
    (i) the transfer is for the benefit of the individual;
    (ii) it is impracticable to obtain the consent of the individual to that transfer;
    (iii) if it were practicable to obtain such consent, the individual would be likely to give it; or
(f) the organisation has taken reasonable steps to ensure that the information which it has transferred will not be held, used or disclosed by the recipient of the information inconsistently with the National Privacy Principles.

3.1.10 National Privacy Principle 10

10.1 An organisation must not collect sensitive information about an individual unless:

(a) the individual has consented; or
(b) the collection is required by law; or
(c) the collection is necessary to prevent or lessen a serious and imminent threat to the life or health of any individual, where the individual whom the information concerns:
    (i) is physically or legally incapable of giving consent to the collection; or
    (ii) physically cannot communicate consent to the collection; or
(d) *(Sub-clause 10.1(d) deleted – not relevant in the case of the Queensland Department of Health.)*
(e) the collection is necessary for the establishment, exercise or defence of a legal or equitable claim.

10.2 Despite sub-clause 10.1, an organisation may collect health information about an individual if:

(a) the information is necessary to provide a health service to the individual; and
(b) the information is collected:

 (i) as required or authorised by law; or
 (ia) by a designated person with the approval of the chief executive; or
 (ii) in accordance with rules established by competent health or medical bodies that deal with obligations of professional confidentiality which bind the organisation.

10.3 Despite sub-clause 10.1, an organisation may collect health information about an individual if:

(a) the collection is necessary for any of the following purposes:

 (i) research relevant to public health or public safety;
 (ii) the compilation or analysis of statistics relevant to public health or public safety;
 (iii) the management, funding or monitoring of a health service; and

(b) that purpose cannot be served by the collection of information that does not identify the individual or from which the individual's identity cannot reasonably be ascertained; and
(c) it is impracticable for the organisation to seek the individual's consent to the collection; and
(d) the information is collected:

 (i) as required or authorised by law; or
 (ia) by a designated person with the approval of the chief executive;
 (ii) in accordance with rules established by competent health or medical bodies that deal with obligations of professional confidentiality which bind the organisation; or
 (iii) in accordance with guidelines approved for the purposes of this subparagraph.

10.4 If an organisation collects health information about an individual in accordance with sub-clause 10.3, the organisation must take reasonable steps to permanently de-identify the information before the organisation discloses it.

10.5 *(Subclause 10.5 deleted – not relevant in the case of the Queensland Department of Health.)*

(Note: For the purpose of sub-clause 10.3, the chief executive may delegate the power to approve the collection of information by a designated person).

4. Authority

In September 2001 Cabinet decided that in implementing an information privacy scheme for the Queensland public sector the Queensland Department of Health would comply with the National Privacy

Principles (NPPs) rather than the Information Privacy Principles (IPPs) contained in the Commonwealth Privacy Act 1988.

5. Guidelines

(Guidelines to be developed.)

6. References/Supporting Documentation

Commonwealth Attorney-General's Department (http://www.law.gov.au/privacy) [2001, February 7] Office of the Federal Privacy Commissioner http://www.privacy.gov.au) [2001, February 7]

7. Definition of Terms

Agency means:

(a) a Minister of the Commonwealth; or
(b) a Department of the Commonwealth; or
(c) a body (whether incorporated or not), or a tribunal, established or appointed for a public purpose by or under a Commonwealth enactment, not being:

  (i) an incorporated company, society or association; or
  (ii) an organisation within the meaning of the Conciliation and Arbitration Act 1904 or a branch of such an organisation; or

(d) a body established or appointed by the Governor-General, or by a Minister of the Commonwealth, otherwise than by or under a Commonwealth enactment; or
(e) a person holding or performing the duties of an office established by or under, or an appointment made under, a Commonwealth enactment, other than a person who, by virtue of holding that office, is the Secretary of a Department of the Commonwealth; or
(f) a person holding or performing the duties of an appointment, being an appointment made by the Governor-General, or by a Minister of the Commonwealth, otherwise than under a Commonwealth enactment; or
(g) a Federal Court; or
(h) the Australian Federal Police; or
(i) an eligible case manager; or
(j) the nominated AGHS company; or
(k) an eligible hearing service provider.

Chief executive means the Director-General of the Queensland Department of Health.

Commonwealth contract means a contract, to which the Commonwealth or an agency is or was a party, under which services are to be, or were to be, provided to an agency.

Consent means express consent or implied consent.

Contracted service provider, for a government contract, means:

(a) an organisation that is or was a party to the government contract and that is or was responsible for the provision of services to an agency or a State or Territory Authority under the government contract; or
(b) a subcontractor for the government contract.

Department means the Queensland Department of Health.

Designated person means:

(a) a health service employee appointed under the Health Services Act 1991(Qld); or
(b) a public service employee, within the meaning of the Public Service Act 1996 (Qld), employed in the Queensland Department of Health under the Public Service Act 1996 (Qld); or
(c) the chief health officer appointed under the Health Act 1937 (Qld); or
(d) a health practitioner who works for a public sector health service, within the meaning of the Health Services Act 1991 (Qld), but is not an employee (for example, an agency nurse or a contracted visiting medical officer); or
(e) a person being educated or trained at a public sector health service within the meaning of the Health Services Act 1991 (Qld); who is subject to a statutory duty of confidentiality.

Eligible hearing service provider means an entity (within the meaning of the Hearing Services Administration Act 1997):

(a) that is, or has at any time been, engaged under Part 3 of the Hearing Services Administration Act 1997 to provide hearing services; and
(b) that is not covered by paragraph (a), (b), (c), (d), (e), (f), (g), (h) or (j) of the definition of **agency**.

Enforcement body means:

(a) the Australian Federal Police; or
(b) the National Crime Authority; or
(c) the Australian Customs Service; or
(d) the Australian Prudential Regulation Authority; or
(e) the Australian Securities and Investments Commission; or
(f) another agency, to the extent that it is responsible for administering, or performing a function under, a law that imposes a penalty or sanction or a prescribed law; or
(g) another agency, to the extent that it is responsible for administering a law relating to the protection of the public revenue; or
(h) a police force or service of a State or a Territory; or
(i) the New South Wales Crime Commission; or
(j) the Independent Commission Against Corruption of New South Wales; or

(k) the Police Integrity Commission of New South Wales; or
(l) the Criminal Justice Commission of Queensland; or
(m) the Queensland Crime Commission; or
(n) another prescribed authority or body that is established under a law of a State or Territory to conduct criminal investigations or inquiries; or
(o) a State or Territory authority, to the extent that it is responsible for administering, or performing a function under, a law that imposes a penalty or sanction or a prescribed law; or
(p) a State or Territory Authority, to the extent that it is responsible for administering a law relating to the protection of the public revenue.

Generally available publication means a magazine, book, newspaper or other publication (however published) that is or will be generally available to members of the public.

Government contract means a Commonwealth contract or a State contract.

Health information means:

(a) information or an opinion about:

 (i) the health or a disability (at any time) of an individual; or
 (ii) an individual's expressed wishes about the future provision of health services to him or her; or
 (iii) a health service provided, or to be provided, to an individual; that is also personal information; or

(b) other personal information collected to provide, or in providing, a health service; or
(c) other personal information about an individual collected in connection with the donation, or intended donation, by the individual of his or her body parts, organs or body substances.

Health service means:

(a) an activity performed in relation to an individual that is intended or claimed (expressly or otherwise) by the individual or the person performing it:

 (i) to assess, record, maintain or improve the individual's health; or
 (ii) to diagnose the individual's illness or disability; or
 (iii) to treat the individual's illness or disability or suspected illness or disability; or

(b) the dispensing on prescription of a drug or medicinal preparation by a pharmacist. **Individual** means a natural person.

Individual concerned in relation to personal information or a record of personal information, means the individual to whom the information relates.

Lead agency for the purposes of this Information Standard means the Department of Justice and Attorney-General.

National Privacy Principle means any of the National Privacy Principles set out in Section 3 of this Information Standard.

NPP means a National Privacy Principle

Organisation means the Queensland Department of Health or a designated person.

Personal Information means information or an opinion (including information or an opinion forming part of a database), whether true or not, and whether recorded in a material form or not, about an individual whose identity is apparent, or can reasonably be ascertained, from the information or opinion.

Privacy Plan means a plan setting out –

the implementation schedule for giving effect to the NPPs;

the legislation administered by the Department of Health and the legislative requirements, if any, related to personal information that will supersede the NPPs;

the nature of the records of personal information kept by or on behalf of the Department (including public registers managed within the Department);

the purpose for which each type of record is kept;

the classes or types of individuals about whom records are kept;

the period for which each type of record is kept;

the persons who are entitled to have access to personal information contained in the records and the conditions under which they are entitled to have that access;

the steps that should be taken by persons wishing to obtain access to that information; and

the contact details for the Department's privacy contact officer.

Record means:

a document; or

a database (however kept); or

a photograph or other pictorial representation of a person; but does not include:

a generally available publication; or

anything kept in a library, art gallery or museum for the purposes of reference, study or exhibition; or

public records as defined by sub-section 2(2) of the Libraries and Archives Act 1988 that are in the open access period as defined in the regulation to that Act; or

letters or other articles in the course of transmission by post.

Sensitive information means:

(a) Information or an opinion about an individual's:

- (i) racial or ethnic origin; or
- (ii) political opinions; or
- (iii) membership of a political association; or
- (iv) religious beliefs or affiliations; or
- (v) philosophical beliefs; or
- (vi) membership of a professional or trade association; or
- (vii) membership of a trade union; or
- (viii) sexual preferences or practices; or
- (ix) criminal record; that is also personal information; or

(b) health information about an individual.

State contract means a contract, to which a State or Territory or State or Territory Authority is or was a party, under which services are to be, or were to be, provided to a State or Territory Authority.

Statutory collection means:

(a) a register or collection of personal information that an organisation is required or authorised to maintain under an Act for the purposes of monitoring public health issues, including morbidity and mortality trends, planning and evaluating health services or facilitating and evaluating treatment; or
(b) personal information collected by an organisation pursuant to a provision of an Act which requires a person to give it to the organisation.

Use, in relation to personal information, does not include mere disclosure of the information, but does include the inclusion of the information in a publication.

Attachment A – Implementation Schedule

Department of Health privacy plan with implementation schedule completed and approved by CEO (Date to be 6 months from date of Cabinet endorsement of Information Standard).

Copy of privacy plan published on website.

Privacy and security statement placed on website. (Date to be 15 days after date privacy plan completed and approved).

Update privacy plan as appropriate annually.

6

AIDS AND MEDICAL LAW

It is perhaps a misnomer to hive off a branch of this book and call it 'AIDS and Medical Law'. All of the principles thus far explored in this book have application to those patients suffering from AIDS. In this chapter, we will explore some laws which have specific application to AIDS patients. One theme will be identified: that much of the law is premised on the fact that AIDS is contagious and should therefore be treated in the same way as other more contagious diseases (such as tuberculosis). The wisdom of this approach is questioned. In considering the extract from the statutes reproduced subsequently, ask yourself the following question: if HIV can only be transmitted by exchange of bodily fluids (blood, semen or vaginal secretions), why should the law require such stringency normally associated with airborne infections?

PART I: WHAT IS AIDS?

In order to evaluate the usefulness or efficacy of present laws relating to AIDS, we need firstly to understand what AIDS is.

Macher, AM, 'HIV Disease/AIDS: medical background', in Webber, D (ed), *AIDS and the Law*, 1992, New York: John Wiley and Sons, pp 3–5

> Acquired Immune Deficiency Syndrome (AIDS) is a specific group of diseases or conditions that indicate severe immunosuppression related to infection with the human immunodeficiency virus (HIV) . . .
>
> The immunodeficiency that occurred in AIDS patients was measurably different from immunological disorders previously recognised in adults. Severe and apparently irreversible, the immunodeficiency predisposed these individuals to frequent and devastating infections. The immunological deficiency appeared to be qualitatively different in that previously uncommon entities, such as aggressive multifocal Kaposi's sarcoma, disseminated Mycobacterium avium infections, chronic enteric cryptosporidiosis, and disseminated toxoplasmosis, all were unusually common compared to other immunosuppressed populations.

Immune system

The human immune system is a complex network of specialised cells that has evolved to defend the body. When functioning properly, the immune system fights off infections by agents such as bacteria, viruses, fungi, protozoa, and other parasites.

The organs of the immune system are stationed throughout the body. They are generally referred to as lymphoid organs because they are concerned with the growth, development, and deployment of lymphocytes, the white blood cells that are the key operatives of the immune system. Lymphoid organs include the bone marrow and the thymus, as well as the lymph nodes, spleen, tonsils and adenoids, appendix, and clumps of lymphoid tissue in the small intestine known as Peyer's patches. The blood and lymphatic vessels that carry lymphocytes to and from the other structures can also be considered lymphoid organs.

Cells destined to become immune cells, like all other blood cells, are produced in the bone marrow, the soft tissue in the hollow shafts of long bones. The descendants of some so-called stem cells become lymphocytes, while others develop into a second group of immune cells typified by the cell- and particle-devouring white cells known as phagocytes (including granulocytes, monocytes, and macrophages).

The two major classes of lymphocytes are B cells and T cells. The B cells complete their maturation in the bone marrow. Each B cell is programmed to make one specific antibody. For example, one B cell will make an antibody that blocks a virus causing the common cold, while another produces an antibody against a bacterium causing pneumonia. When a B cell encounters its triggering antigen (the common cold virus, or the bacterium that causes pneumonia) it (along with collaborating T cells and accessory cells) gives rise to many large plasma cells. Every plasma cell is essentially a factory for producing antibodies. Each of the plasma cells descended from a given B cell (which are all members of the same family or clone) manufactures millions of identical antibody molecules and pours them into the bloodstream. A given antibody matches an antigen much as a key matches a lock. Thus, the antibody interlocks with the antigen and thereby marks it for destruction.

The T cells, on the other hand, migrate to the thymus, a multi-lobed organ that lies high behind the breastbone. There they multiply and mature into cells capable of producing an immune response; that is, they become immunocompetent. The T cells contribute to the immune defences in two major ways. Regulatory T cells are vital to orchestrating the elaborate immune system. The B cells, for instance, cannot make antibody against most substances without T cell help. Cytotoxic T cells, on the other hand, directly attack body cells that are infected or malignant.

Chief among the regulatory T cells are helper/inducer cells. Identifiable by the T4 (CD4+) cell marker (CD4 is a protein embedded in the cell surface of helper T-lymphocytes), helper T cells are essential for activating B cells and other T cells as well as natural killer cells and macrophages. Another subset of T cells, carrying the T8 marker (a protein embedded in the cell surface of suppressor T-lymphocytes), acts to turn off or suppress these cells.

Cytotoxic T cells, which carry the T8 marker, are killer cells. In addition to ridding the body of cells that have been infected by viruses or transformed by cancer, they are responsible for rejecting tissue and organ grafts.

T cells work primarily by secreting substances known as cytokines or, more specifically, lymphokines. Lymphokines (which are also secreted by B cells) are potent chemical messengers. Binding to specific receptors on target cells, lymphokines call into play many other cells and substances, including the elements of the inflammatory response. They encourage cell growth, promote cell activation, direct cellular traffic, destroy target cells, and incite macrophages. One of the first cytokines to be discovered was interferon. Produced by T cells and macrophages, interferons are a family of proteins with antiviral properties.

HIV infection and the immune system

In 1983, Luc Montagnier and his research team at the Pasteur Institute in France identified the virus that causes AIDS. Discovery of this virus, now designated human immunodeficiency virus (HIV), opened new avenues of research into every aspect of the disease. By 1985, a blood test (serology) for detecting infection with HIV had been developed. The test detects antibodies that have been produced in response to the host's invasion by HIV. An HIV infection is confirmed by the use of a series of tests that include two ELISAs (enzyme-linked immunosorbent assay is a testing method to detect antibodies to HIV) and a Western blot (a test for the presence of specific antibodies, more accurate than the ELISA test).

HIV-infected individuals develop a wide spectrum of disease states ranging from the asymptomatic carrier state to full-blown AIDS. The clinical features of HIV infection range from: (1) an acute mononucleosis-like illness to (2) chronic fever, weight loss, malaise, diarrhoea, lymphadenopathy (abnormal enlargement of the lymph nodes), and finally to (3) AIDS in individuals whose cellular immune systems are unable to defend the hosts against opportunistic infections. It is believed that the majority of those who are infected with HIV will eventually develop AIDS.

HIV has been found in only a small fraction of cells in infected individuals. However, the cell population most profoundly affected by HIV is the helper subset of T lymphocytes. *In vitro* studies (an artificial environment created outside a living organism, such as a test tube) allowing the detection of HIV genes in infected cells have shown that HIV genes are present in one in 10,000 to one in 1,000,000 lymphocytes in tissues from patients with AIDS. These infected lymphocytes are

> primarily T lymphocytes. This same *in vitro* analysis technique has also detected HIV genes in the brain tissues of patients with AIDS.
>
> The human immune system demonstrates both acute and chronic effects after HIV infection. HIV invades cells by first attaching to CD4 molecule (CD4 receptor). The most devastating effect on an HIV-infected individual is the gradual but progressive depletion of helper T lymphocytes, leading to an as yet irreversible immunodeficiency state. Although HIV interacts with the same cell population as human T lymphotropic viruses Type I and II (HTLV-I and HTLV-II), rather than cause T helper cell malignant transformation, HIV causes T helper cell death. *In vitro* (outside the living body), a major mechanism of T cell death is through cell-cell fusion and the formation of multinucleated giant cells, which die within 24–48 hours.
>
> *In vivo* (inside the living body), a series of white blood cell abnormalities contribute to the profound immunodeficiency that develops in individuals infected with HIV, allowing other viruses, parasites, and tumour cells to proliferate.

It should be noted that not all patients who 'catch' HIV develop 'full-blown' AIDS. There is presently no cure for AIDS.

The best source of information on legal aspects of AIDS is a book entitled *Australian HIV/AIDS Legal Guide* by Godwin, Hamblin, Patterson and Buchanan. Published by the Federation Press, the book is now in its second edition. Readers wanting more information on this area of the law are referred to this book. The book contains first-class chapters on insurance, anti-discrimination, confidentiality and public health. Extracts from the book on testing and transmission offences will be considered subsequently.

Note firstly that HIV is a notifiable disease in all jurisdictions of Australia (Schedule 1, Public Health Act 1991 (NSW), s 32A(1) of the Health Act 1937 (Qld), Regulation 198 of 1991, Public and Environmental Health Act 1987 (SA), Public Health (Notifiable Diseases) Regulations 1967–89 (Tas), Health (Infectious Diseases) Regulations 1990 (Vic), Infectious Diseases Order 1983 and Dangerous Infectious Diseases Order 1983 (WA), Public Health (Infectious and Notifiable Diseases) Regulations 1983 (ACT), Notifiable Diseases Act 1981 (NT)).

PART II: TESTING FOR HIV

In what circumstances does a patient have a right to be consulted before being tested for AIDS? There are some aspects of some general law which regulate the issue, as modified by relevant Australian statutes.

In the extract below, the law of battery is discussed.

Grubb, A and Pearl, D, 'Blood testing, AIDS and DNA profiling' [1990] Family Law (Jordan and Sons), pp 3–21

> Although the legality of HIV testing must be considered within the framework of both the civil and criminal law, it is principally the torts of

battery and negligence which concern us here because the prospect of a criminal prosecution being brought against a doctor is unlikely. A battery may be defined as the deliberate (ie intentional) touching of (or application of force to) another which is offensive or harmful and which is done without the consent of that other. A negligence action may arise when harm results from a doctor's breach of duty to inform his patient of the reasons for taking blood . . .

It can be seen from the above definitions that valid consent in law is relevant to both battery and negligence. In principle, HIV testing should not take place without the patient's consent. The ability to consent and the reality of a patient's consent would seem to be essential to lawful HIV testing.

Let us assume that the patient who is to be tested for HIV infection is a competent adult that is capable of understanding what is involved in the suggested procedure. Once ability to consent is established, the most important legal issue will be the reality of the patient's consent to the HIV test and precisely what, as a matter of law, is meant by a real consent.

Our analysis requires us to look at . . . different situations:

(a) where there is explicit consent to test for HIV infection;
(b) where there is no consent to test at all;
(c) where there is consent to test generally;
(d) where there is consent to perform particular tests not including HIV infection;
(e) where the doctor only decides to test the patient's blood for infection after it is extracted . . .

(a) Explicit consent to test

Where a doctor extracts blood to be tested indicating to the patient that sample will be tested for HIV infection and the patient consents to this, there can be no question but that the doctor has acted lawfully. While the law will not give effect to an individual's consent in exceptional circumstances, no public policy considerations would prevent the patient's real and informed consent from being valid whatever the motivation for the test whether consented to for himself, out of a concern for the doctor's wellbeing or as a public-spirited citizen as part of a prevalence investigation.

(b) No consent at all to test

At the other extreme is the situation where a doctor extracts the patient's blood to test for HIV infection without seeking his consent to the extract at all. This is rather an unlikely event in reality but it highlights the underlying principle that the patient must consent. Here, he does not. Therefore, the doctor would act unlawfully because he would commit a battery.

(c) Consent to test generally

It is in situations which fall factually between these two extremes, ie between telling the patient everything and telling him nothing, that legal difficulties arise. We must therefore examine what the law regards as relevant information of which a patient must be aware before his assent to the extraction of blood for testing can be a legally valid consent.

Let us first examine the situation where a doctor takes blood from a patient intending to test the blood for HIV infection without explicitly informing the patient of his intention. The doctor may take the blood informing the patient that he intends to test it generally without specifying precisely for what. Is the doctor's conduct lawful? This, along with the next situation, could arise most often in the everyday practice of medicine. It is necessary in these circumstances to discuss first the law of battery and then the law of negligence.

(i) The law of battery

Express consent

A patient may, of course, expressly consent to a medical procedure. The first question which must be addressed is whether a patient who has not been informed that his blood will be tested for HIV infection has sufficient information about the procedure to be performed so that his consent is valid in law.

(a) The content of a valid consent. As regards the law of battery, the patient's consent will be valid if he understands the nature and purpose and thus the quality of the touching. As Bristow J stated in *Chatterton v Gerson* [see Chapter 2], once the patient is informed in broad terms of the nature of the procedure which is intended and gives . . . consent, that consent is real and hence no battery will be committed. The difficulty here is to determine what information is relevant to the nature (and purpose) of a touching and what information is merely collateral to it. Ignorance of the latter will not affect the validity of the patient's consent, although non-disclosure might give rise to an action in negligence. It is difficult to know exactly what information goes to the nature of a particular touching . . .

    Does the lack of knowledge that blood is being extracted in order to test it for HIV infection affect the quality of the touching by the doctor? Is it knowledge of the insertion of a needle in the patient's vein (and its implications) or is it this knowledge plus the knowledge of the underlying purpose of the procedure (ie, HIV testing) which is vital in order for a patient to have the necessary understanding of the quality of the touching for his consent to be valid?

(b) Public policy. The answer to this question must lie in an assessment of the needs of public policy. It is this issue which is at the heart of the many cases concerned with the difficult legal task of distinguishing between essential (nature) information and irrelevant (collateral) information. Public policy requires that such information should be considered essential to the patient's decision and goes to the quality of the touching assented to by the patient. HIV infection is not simply another medical condition and a number of factors mark out its singular nature. First, the medical prospects for infected individuals are horrendous when the virus attacks the immune system so as to produce drastic immune deficiency. The subsequent stages of infection, namely AIDS-Related Complex and full-blown AIDS, will have catastrophic effects on not just the individual's physical health but also his mental health. Indeed, merely to discover that you are seropositive may, in itself, have a serious effect on a person's mental health. The importance of pretesting counselling (impossible in the case of secret testing) emphasises the need for full disclosure to the patient.

Secondly, individuals who are seropositive may also be subjected to discrimination in the workplace and in society generally. Even though the nature of the information is confidential, as a matter of practice, this cannot always be ensured. The irrational fear engendered in society towards AIDS sufferers is not something that public policy (and hence the law) should ignore . . . HIV status may also affect an individual's ability to obtain life insurance coverage. Existing policies may be affected and future coverage may be refused if the patient has to disclose (as good faith requires) his HIV status. He may even be prejudiced by required disclosure that he tested negative.

These grave and adverse personal and social consequences make the knowledge that a doctor is going to test an individual's HIV status so important and basic to an individual's consent to be tested that the courts should require the doctor to inform the patient of his intention. Only then may the patient decide whether, and how, he wishes to discover his HIV status. One legal commentator on AIDS in the US expresses his position as follows:

> HIV testing without knowledge or consent goes against the very purpose of the test: facilitating education and counselling. The prevailing view is that patients should be informed of the potential consequences of positive HIV test results; the possibility that the test may be falsely positive; the behaviour that is desirable to help prevent further spread of HIV; the potential psychological impact; and the locations where the patient can get personal, social, and financial support in coping with the burden of the disease. By neglecting to inform the patient that the test will be performed, [doctors] fail to provide the patient with the dignity and help that is now uniformly acceptable in the practice of medicine. [Gostin, L, 'Hospitals, health care professionals, and AIDS' (1989) 48 Maryland Law Review 12, p 41.]

Perhaps only through the law of battery can this public policy be effectively achieved. It is, after all, the tort of battery which has traditionally protected the inviolability of the individual's person.

(c) Some contrary arguments. Two arguments can be made against this position. First, a general one. A series of recent decisions has been hostile to the application of battery to medical procedures. In these cases, the plaintiffs alleged that the doctor's failure to disclose a risk inherent in a medical procedure vitiated the patient's consent. However, the courts confined the plaintiffs to the tort of negligence in pursuing their claims of non-disclosure of information. In *Hills v Potter* [1984] 1 WLR 641, at 653, Hirst J said: 'I should add that I respectfully agree with Bristow J [in the earlier case of *Chatterton v Gerson*] in deploring reliance on these torts in medical negligence cases of this kind . . .'.

However, these cases should be seen in their proper context. It is suggested that the judges were emphasising that normally the tort of negligence more appropriately fits allegations of non-disclosure in medical cases. Battery still has a role, albeit a limited one, in this area. Each of the cases concerned the non-disclosure of a risk incidental to a medical procedure. It is surely the case that the risk of an unpleasant (perhaps even dangerous) side effect is collateral to the information essential to the nature and purpose of the medical procedure. The nature and purpose of the procedure does not necessarily require any reference to undesirable side effects. Informing a patient of these side effects does not help describe, let alone define, what is being done by the doctor. The patient's consent may not be fully informed, and so may give rise to an action in negligence, but it is nevertheless a valid consent for the purposes of battery. Where secret HIV testing is the issue, however, this is not so. The nature and purpose of the procedure cannot intelligibly be expressed without reference to the fact that the patient's blood will be tested for HIV infection. Without knowledge of this, the patient thinks he is consenting to a materially different procedure. The patient's consent is not just uninformed, it relates to something quite different in kind.

Secondly, a more specific argument needs to be addressed. The view that the doctor need not disclose that the blood extracted will be tested for HIV is usually based upon an application of the criminal case of *R v Clarence* (1888) 22 QB 23 . . . Clarence transmitted a venereal disease, gonorrhoea, to his wife through sexual intercourse. He was charged with assault occasioning actual bodily harm and with maliciously inflicting grievous bodily harm upon his wife. He was acquitted. A majority of the court held that both offences required proof of an assault or battery and hence it was necessary to prove that his wife had not given a valid consent to sexual intercourse with him. A majority of the court held that her consent was valid even though Clarence had failed to disclose his medical condition. It was not essential that Clarence's wife assent to sexual intercourse with knowledge of her husband's infectious condition.

Is there an analogy between a consent to sexual intercourse obtained without informing a person that you are infected with a sexually transmissible disease and a consent to test a blood sample generally if the doctor secretly intends to test for HIV infection? Some would argue that there is. If, however, *Clarence* is examined carefully, and in its social and historical context, it does not provide any support for the legality of secret testing. It is important to remember that the case was decided over one hundred years ago. It concerned serious criminal charges brought against a husband for harm caused to his wife during otherwise lawful sexual intercourse. It is clear from reading the judgments that the court was greatly influenced by these features of the case. It is a decision of Victorian judges who were predisposed to support the social climate of the times that husbands were the dominant partner in a marriage and that it was no place for the court to create a criminal offence arising out of the exercise of a husband's conjugal rights. The judges referred in support of their view to the rule that a husband cannot rape his wife. Her consent is presumed once the marriage is contracted. Further, the novelty of the suggestion that transmission of contagious disease should be a criminal offence was noted by the judges. Finally, the judges were clearly influenced by the fact that they considered a contrary view would lead to the creation of a new criminal offence and this was something which should be better left to the wisdom of the legislature. Added to which, as Stephen J pointed out, legislation relating to the transmission of disease had been repealed in 1886, but even this legislation had not criminalised sexual transmission of disease.

(d) Explaining the decision in *Clarence*. Seen in context, *Clarence* may be understandable in 1888 but it does not, in our view, resolve the issue we are concerned with here. We are not concerned with the criminalisation of interspousal sexual conduct. Nor are we concerned with criminalising the sexual transmission of disease. As Professor Glanville Williams has said:

> . . . people have infected each other with disease since the beginning of mankind, and whether this should be made a criminal offence, in the absence of intention, is a delicate social question which should be left to Parliament [Williams, G, 'Alternative elements and included offences' [1984] Criminal Law Journal 290, at 293].

Criminal law, interspousal conduct, the doctrine of unity between man and wife, and the sexual transmission of disease defined the context of *Clarence*.

Bearing in mind the judges' clear preference in *Clarence* not to introduce the criminal law into interspousal sexual relations, a further reason can be seen why the court chose not to consider knowledge of infection as a matter going to the quality of the touching permitted. Suppose the court in *Clarence* had held that his wife lacked sufficient knowledge. Could Mrs Clarence have given a valid consent to sexual intercourse even if she had known that her husband was infected? If the answer is no, then a court with the motivations apparent in *Clarence* to keep the criminal law out would be reluctant to require knowledge. Arguably, as cases such as *R v Donovan* [1934] 2 KB 498 and *Attorney General's Reference (No 6 of 1980)* [1981] QB 715 illustrate, she could not have knowingly consented because as Lord Lane CJ said in the latter case '. . . it is not in the public interest that people should try to cause, or should cause, each other actual bodily harm for no good reasons.' So, even if the court in *Clarence* had required that Mrs Clarence be aware of her husband's physical condition, and even if she had had that knowledge, her consent would, at least as far as the criminal law is concerned, have been invalid. This would have gone against the judges' underlying desire to keep the criminal law out. It was simpler for the judges to ensure that knowledge was irrelevant. Mrs Clarence was consenting to something she knew about and no harm resulted from that, and so there could be no countervailing public policy to justify the law ignoring her consent.

In the context we are concerned with, perhaps it is equally undesirable to invoke the criminal law when a doctor is acting in what he perceives to be his patient's best interests, albeit secretly. There is obviously some merit in this argument. But ultimately, the criminal law does have its part to play in determining the outer legal boundaries of the doctor-patient relationship. It is a rare case of criminal law that arises out of the practice of medicine when a doctor is (or alleges that he is) acting in his patient's best interests. In any event, it is the civil law of battery which will be of greater practical importance.

Is there any other reason to believe that *Clarence* may be relevant today in determining the legality of secret HIV testing? In the case of *Sidaway v Bethlem Royal Hospital Governors* [1984] QB 494, when the case was before the Court of Appeal, both Lord Donaldson MR and Dunn LJ approved *Clarence*. The judges accepted that *Clarence* decided that lack of knowledge of something which went to the nature of an act vitiates consent. We, of course, agree with this, but have argued above that a patient's knowledge that blood is being taken to test for HIV infection is essential for him to understand the nature of the procedure. Public policy, which will help determine the legality of secret HIV testing, would respond differently to the case where a doctor extracts blood without explicit consent.

Let us now turn to consider a different set of arguments that are sometimes thought to be relevant here.

Implied consent

A patient may not only explicitly consent to a medical procedure but he may also do so impliedly as a result of his conduct or in the light of the prevailing circumstances. An old example from the US will illustrate the point. In the Massachusetts case of *O'Brien v Cunard*, the plaintiff was attempting to immigrate into the US. Whilst on a boat approaching Boston, the plaintiff stood in a line of persons who were being vaccinated as an entry requirement to the US. The plaintiff held out her arm and was vaccinated. Her subsequent action for battery was dismissed because she had impliedly consented to the doctor's actions by holding out her arm. Could it be said that a patient who consents to his blood being tested generally impliedly consents to HIV testing also?

Some have argued that a patient does impliedly consent in these circumstances. Those who argue this rely upon the fact that doctors frequently take blood for testing and carry out a whole range of routine tests without specifying them in advance. We do not subscribe to this view. In our view, there is a significant difference. First, it is not at all clear that testing blood for HIV infection is routine within the medical profession in the sense that it is (or may be) done as a matter of course in every case. Indeed, the evidence contradicts such an assertion. Secondly, in any event this mode of analysis misses the point. We should not be concerned with procedures accepted as routine within the medical profession. Instead, we must look to a patient's expectations of what will (or may) be done with his blood once it has been taken for testing. This is the important matter for the law. Patient's expectations may be conditioned to an extent by professional practice but this is not necessarily so. The law is, after all, seeking to determine what can be implied by the patient's conduct in agreeing to his blood being tested.

Thirdly, a much more important line of reasoning exists which denies the argument that testing for HIV may be implied from a general consent to test. A general consent will not in law be taken to extend so as to include consent to touchings which are *prima facie* contrary to public policy. Such touchings, if they can be consented to at all, require explicit consent. Thus, if a professional footballer D causes injury to another player P during the course of the game, can it be said that P, by agreeing generally to play, has thereby consented to the injury caused by the touching? If the injury is caused by conduct within the rules of the game, the law implies that P consented to the touching. But what if D's action, which causes injury, is outside the rules? Would the law imply that P has consented to this unlawful conduct also? If D's conduct is part of the generally recognised and tolerated behaviour within the particular sport, then even though it is unlawful under the rules of the game, P would be taken to have consented to this touching and it would not be unlawful under the law of the land. If, however, the injury is caused by an 'off-the-ball' kick or punch then, as a matter of public policy, P would not be taken to have impliedly consented to it.

The analogy here is particularly important. A doctor in our situation is acting in furtherance of the enterprise which P has agreed to take part in, namely the testing of blood. However, just as the sportsman would not be taken in law by his general consent to have consented to a touching which public policy condemns, so a patient would not be taken to have consented impliedly to testing for the specific purposes of determining his HIV status.

The consequences for a patient that flow from a positive HIV test (or in some instances even a negative test) are so serious for him that a court would consider it to be contrary to public policy to regard consent to testing as including (by implication) a procedure with such far-reaching consequences for the patient.

(a) Therapeutic and non-therapeutic testing

The assumption in the discussion of battery and consent has so far been that the patient's blood is to be tested for HIV infection for reasons concerned with the patient's health. In other words, the touching of the patient, albeit without full disclosure of the doctor's underlying reasons, is for a therapeutic purpose. Any other tests which might be carried out on the patient's blood will also be for therapeutic reasons. Therefore, the touching is always intended (and understood to be) for therapeutic purposes. However, if the doctor's reason for testing for HIV infection is not out of a concern for the health interests of his patient, or is only partly so, a further argument arises which supports the view that the patient has not given a valid consent to be touched. The doctor might, for example, wish to test the patient's blood out of a concern for the health interests of himself and other health care providers who might come in contact with the patient's blood. Alternatively, the doctor might be concerned about the health of his patient's spouse or partner who may also be his patient. In this situation, the primary purpose for the doctor's touching is different from that which the patient understands to be the case. The touching has a non-therapeutic purpose. The law does not assume that a patient who consents to treatment also consents to research. Here, the patient cannot be said to understand the 'nature and purpose' of the touching and hence his consent is not valid. Alternatively, it cannot be said that a patient impliedly consents to a touching which is not intended exclusively to be for his benefit. Only this result will demonstrate the law's concern for the rights of the patient.

(d) Consent to perform particular tests

(i) The law of battery

The arguments we made above, establishing that a general consent to take a blood sample and test it does not amount to either an express or an implied consent to test for HIV, apply with as much, if not greater force when the patient and doctor have agreed that particular tests will be performed on the blood taken from the patient but no mention is made of HIV testing.

Here, however, there is a further argument to support the view that a doctor must inform his patient explicitly of his purpose if his action is to be lawful. The doctor's failure to inform may be considered in law as fraud or misrepresentation which would vitiate any consent even if it would otherwise be valid. Two distinct situations should be considered: first, where the doctor informs his patient that he intends to perform certain tests but actually he intends only to test for HIV infection; and secondly, where he does intend to perform the specified tests but, in addition, he intends to test for HIV infection.

(a) He intends to test only for HIV infection

When the doctor expresses a false intention to his patient, he thereby acts fraudulently and misrepresents the intended purpose of the touching. In some circumstances, fraud by a doctor will vitiate what would otherwise be a valid consent. If a doctor must explicitly obtain the patient's permission to test for HIV infection because this information goes to the nature and purpose of the touching, then a doctor who lies, necessarily commits a battery. The fact that the doctor is acting fraudulently is irrelevant because whether the patient's ignorance of the underlying purpose arises through mistake on his part or through the fraud of the doctor, he does not have sufficient information to give a valid consent.

The important point for our purposes is to determine whether fraudulent representation of information not going to the nature and purpose of the procedure may vitiate consent. There is not much English authority to help us. In *Chatterton v Gerson*, Bristow J provided some support for a wide fraud exception '. . . if information is withheld in bad faith, the consent will be vitiated by fraud.' His comments are consistent with the view that had the doctor fraudulently represented the possible side effects the plaintiff might have been able to succeed in a battery action. Bristow J's view finds strong support in the leading decision of the Supreme Court of Canada in *Reibl v Hughes* (1980) 114 DLR (3d) 1. Like the judge in *Chatterton*, the Canadian court limited the availability of battery when a doctor has failed to disclose risks inherent in a medical procedure but recognised that battery might be the appropriate cause of action in cases of fraud or misrepresentation. Laskin CJ stated that 'unless there has been misrepresentation or fraud to secure consent to the treatment, a failure to disclose the attendant risks, however serious, should go to negligence rather than to battery'.

However, when the *Sidaway* case was before the Court of Appeal, Sir John Donaldson MR expressed a view which conflicts . . . This, of course, is a much narrower view of the fraud exception and, as we stated above, it is really no exception at all since there cannot be a valid consent, whether or not there is fraud, if the patient does not understand the nature and purpose of the doctor's touching.

We have already examined *Clarence* and doubted its relevance in a modern setting concerned with medical touchings. However, in *Hegarty v Shine* (1878) 4 LR Ir 288 a similar result was reached in a civil case where a mistress unsuccessfully sued her lover for infecting her with venereal disease. Many of the arguments directed against the *Clarence* decision cannot be made against *Hegarty*; the case was a civil one and not criminal; the parties were not married and so the issues arising out of the doctrine of unity between husband and wife did not arise. Nevertheless, *Hegarty* has been the subject of considerable criticism itself . . .

The picture is confused by a statement of Sir John Donaldson MR in the case of *Freeman v Home Office* decided shortly after *Sidaway*. In this case, he seems to accept a wider view of the fraud exception. First, he identifies that for the purposes of battery 'real consent' is necessary. By this, he undoubtedly means that the patient understands the nature and purpose of the medical procedure. 'Real consent,' he concludes, 'provides a complete defence to a claim based on a tort of trespass to the person.' It is at this point that he appears to have changed his view on the scope of the fraud exception he expressed in *Sidaway* because he adds '[c]onsent would not be real if procured by fraud or misrepresentation but, subject to this and subject to the patient having been informed in broad terms of the nature of the treatment, consent in fact amounts to consent in law.' So, even a patient who has been informed in broad terms of the nature of the touching will be able to sue in battery if the doctor has acted fraudulently as to matters not going to the broad terms of the nature of the treatment.

It is our view, therefore, that a doctor who informs his patient that he is taking blood to test for specific purposes and intends to test only for HIV infection will be liable in an action for battery because his fraud will vitiate any apparent consent the patient may have given.

(b) He intends to test for the specific purposes and for HIV infection

Here it could not be said that the doctor is lying. Instead, it could be said that he is just not telling the whole truth. In many areas of the law, a half truth is no better than an outright lie. Even if silence could not be described as a fraudulent representation, the same cannot be said of the 'half truth'. The latter is much closer, and in our view is indistinguishable from, an outright lie. Secondly, a doctor who expressly states his purposes for taking the blood, omitting to disclose his intention to test for HIV, makes an implied representation of his present intention. This implied representation, which is false, is itself sufficient for his conduct to be considered fraudulent.

(e) The doctor who decides to test later

> Up to this point, we have been concerned with the legality of the conduct of a doctor who secretly intends to test for HIV infection when he seeks the patient's consent to extract the blood sample. But what happens when the doctor only forms the intent to test for HIV infection sometime after he has extracted the blood? An analysis based upon battery is now inappropriate. The legality of the touching must be determined at the time of touching and since there was no concealment or lie at that time, the patient's consent would be valid. However, the doctor's conduct may still be unlawful . . .
>
> In addition to his duty, at the time he seeks the patient's consent to take the blood sample, a doctor will have a continuing duty to advise and counsel his patient after the blood has been extracted. The consequences of HIV testing remain the same regardless of what precise point in time a doctor decides to test the patient's blood. Consequently, a failure to inform a patient of his intention to carry out an HIV test on blood he has already extracted would be a breach of his duty of care and could result in a negligence action.

Three jurisdictions in Australia have passed legislation regulating the conduct of 'AIDS tests'. These States provide that patients must be given certain information about AIDS.

Godwin, J, Hamblin, J, Patterson, D, Buchanan, D, *Australian HIV/AIDS Legal Guide*, 2nd edn, 1993, Sydney: Federation, pp 182–183

[Notations in square brackets indicate changes to the legislation.]

New South Wales

The Public Health Act 1991 provides:

> A medical practitioner who believes on reasonable grounds that a person receiving medical attention from the medical practitioner suffers from a sexually transmissible medical condition must, as soon as practicable, provide the person with such information concerning the condition as is required by the regulations (s 12(1)).
>
> A medical practitioner who fails to comply with this section is guilty of offence unless the Court is satisfied that the medical practitioner knew that the information to which the offence relates had been supplied to the patient by another medical practitioner. Penalty: 50 penalty units (s 12(2)).

The Public Health Regulations 1991 provide:

> A medical practitioner is required in relation to a sexually transmissible scheduled medical condition to provide information on such of the following matters as are relevant in the particular case:

(a) means of minimising the risk of infecting other people with the condition;
(b) public health implications of the condition;
(c) responsibilities under s 11 of the Act (which imposes a duty to take reasonable precautions in public) including any precautions considered reasonable;
(d) responsibilities under s 13 of the Act (which relates to the duty to disclose the condition prior to sexual intercourse);
(e) diagnosis and prognosis;
(f) treatment options (Reg 4).

Victoria

Where a person requests an HIV test, the medical practitioner must, before carrying out the test, give the person 'information about the medical and social consequences of being tested and the possible results of the test', and must, if the result of the requested test is positive, advise the person of 'information about the medical and social consequences of being infected and guidelines on ways to prevent the transmission of the virus to others' (s 127 Health Act 1958).

Northern Territory

Under the Notifiable Diseases Act 1981, a medical practitioner who diagnoses that a person is a 'carrier' of HIV or who suspects a person of being a 'carrier' or suspects that a person may have 'been exposed to' an infected person must advise the person of the nature of the disease, the measures needed to be taken to prevent the spread of the disease and the treatment required (ss 5 and 10). [Note: there has been a change in the terminology of this Act, and the word 'carrier' is no longer used. Instead, the term 'infected person' includes a person who is a carrier of a notifiable disease, see s 5.] Where the person is under 16 years, the parents or guardians of the person must be informed. If the person is a child who has attained the age of 16 years, the medical practitioner has a discretion whether to advise the parents or guardians (s 10(c)).

Public health statutes in all jurisdictions allow for the testing of people thought to be suffering from AIDS. Their scope, as well as the scope of provisions allowing for compulsory detention, is explored in the extract below.

Godwin, J, Hamblin, J, Patterson, D, Buchanan, D, *Australian HIV/ AIDS Legal Guide*, 2nd edn, 1993, Sydney: Federation, pp 2–34

New South Wales

Public Health Act 1991

Public Health Regulation 1991

Public Health (Scheduled Medical Condition) Regulation 1991

Infectious diseases appear in Schedule 1 of the Public Health Act 1991. The Public Health (Scheduled Medical Conditions) Regulation 1991 provides that AIDS is a Category 2 condition (to be notified by medical practitioners) and human immunodeficiency virus (HIV) infection is a Category 3 condition (to be notified by laboratories). AIDS is also listed in Schedule 3 as a notifiable disease. Both AIDS and HIV infection appear in Category 5 of Schedule 1.

1.2.1 Notification

A medical practitioner who believes on reasonable grounds that a person receiving medical attention from the medical practitioner suffers from a Category 2 medical condition, or as a result of any kind of postmortem examination, believes on reasonable grounds that a person has died as a result of such a medical condition must:

(a) as soon as practical, record in accordance with the regulations particulars concerning the person; and
(b) keep the record for the prescribed period; and
(c) immediately after having recorded the particulars, send to the Director General a certificate that relates to the particulars and is in an approved form that does not provide for the provision of information that the medical practitioner is prohibited by s 17 from disclosing (s 14(1), (2)).

This does not apply to a medical practitioner dealing with a person in a hospital where the hospital's chief executive officer has notified the Director General that that person has a notifiable disease (ss 14(2A), 69).

This provision also binds other persons in prescribed occupations (s 14(3)). The particulars required are set out in the 'Doctor/Hospital Notification Form' and the 'AIDS Notification Form' published by the Department of Health.

If a medical practitioner requests a serological or other prescribed test for the purposes of detecting whether a person is suffering from a Category 3 medical condition and the test has a positive result, the person who, in response to the request certifies the result of the test to the medical practitioner must, as soon as practicable, send to the Director General a report in the approved form as it relates to the test but does not disclose the name or address of the patient if the medical condition is also a Category 5 medical condition (s 16(1)).

Pathologists are required to provide notification by code consisting of the two initials of the patient's surname, date of birth, sex, the name of doctor or name of laboratory making the report, and, in the case of laboratories, the name and address of the doctor, clinic or blood bank requesting and the probable mode of disease transmission.

A medical practitioner is prohibited from stating the name or address of the patient in a s 14 notification, or, except as prescribed, in a written or oral request for a test to find out if the patient suffers from a Category 5 medical condition. Penalty: 50 penalty units (s 17(1)). The prescribed exception is where the patient is a patient within the meaning of the Public Hospitals Act 1929 or the Private Hospitals and Day Procedure Centres Act 1988 (Reg 7(1)).

The chief executive officer of a hospital is required to provide the Director General with information about people with notifiable diseases who are or have been patients in the hospital in accordance with the 'Doctor/Hospital E Form' published by the Department of Health (s 69 and Reg 81(b)).

The Director General may, by written notice, require a named person to undergo a particular medical examination by a medical practitioner chosen by that person if the Director General believes on reasonable grounds that the person is suffering from a Category 5 Medical condition (s 22) . . .

An authorised medical practitioner may make a written public health order if satisfied on reasonable grounds that a person is suffering from a Category 5 medical condition and the person is behaving in such a way that is endangering, or is likely to endanger, the health of the public because that person is suffering from that medical condition (s 23(1)).

A public health order must specify the name of the person to whom it applies, the circumstances purporting to justify it, and state that, unless the order is earlier varied as to its duration or is earlier revoked, it expires a specified number of days (not exceeding 28) after its service on the person (s 23(2)).

A public health order must require the person to whom it applies to do any one or more of the following:

(a) refrain from specified conduct;
(b) undergo specified treatment;
(c) undergo counselling by a specified person or by one or more persons belonging to a specified class of persons;
(d) submit to the supervision of a specified person or one or more persons belonging to a specified class of persons;
(e) undergo specified treatment and be detained at a specified place while undergoing the treatment;
(f) (for Category 5 medical conditions) be detained at a specified place where the order is in force (s 23(3)).

The order may include ancillary or consequential provisions to the matters it contains (s 23(4)), including provisions relating to security and public health (s 27). A public health order does not take effect until it is served personally on the person to whom it applies (s 24(5)).

A public health order that relates to a Category 5 medical condition ceases to have any effect if:

(a) the person subject to the order is not, within three business days after service on the person of the order, also served with a copy of an application made to a Local Court [Note: in this Act, references to the Local Court or District Court have been replaced with the Tribunal. The Tribunal means the Administrative Decisions Tribunal, which was established by the Administrative Decisions Tribunal Act 1997] for confirmation of the order; or

(b) such an application is made and the Local Court revokes the order; or

(c) the order expires before it is confirmed or revoked by a Local Court; or

(d) the order expires before or after an application to continue the order is made to the District Court under s 26 (s 24(1)).

Local Court confirmation

The Local Court to which application is made for confirmation of a public order based on a Category 5 medical condition is, as soon as practicable, to inquire into the circumstances surrounding the making of the order and, if satisfied that the making of the order was justified, is to confirm the order or vary the order and confirm it as varied, or if not so satisfied, is to revoke the order (s 25(1) and (2)). The Local Court may vary the order only by adding a requirement that could have been included in the order when made, or by substituting any such requirement for any one or more of them already included (s 25(2)).

A Local Court may, from time to time, adjourn an inquiry under this section for not more than seven days (s 25(4)). A Local Court may obtain the assistance of any person having medical or other qualifications relevant to the subject matter and take into account a certificate given by such a person.

An authorised medical practitioner may, before the expiry of a public health order that is based on a Category 5 medical condition and has been confirmed by a Local Court, apply to the District Court for continuation of the order (s 26(1)). An application for continuation of a public health order may be made under this section only if the applicant is satisfied, on reasonable grounds, that the person to whom the order relates would, if not subject to such an order, continue to endanger the health of the public as a consequence of the Category 5 medical condition (s 26(2)).

If continuation of a public health order is applied for under this section and the person subject to the order notifies the District Court that continuation of the order is not opposed, the court may, without inquiry, continue the order for a period not exceeding six months (s 26(3)). Unless the order is continued under subsection (3), the District Court is to make such inquiries as it thinks fit in relation to the application and may continue the order, with or without variation, for a period not exceeding six months, refuse to continue the order; or revoke the order (s 26(4)). The District Court may vary the order only by omitting a requirement included in the order; adding a requirement that could have been included in the order when made; or substituting any such requirement for any one or more of them already included in the order (s 26(5)). For the purposes of an inquiry under this section, the District Court may obtain the assistance of any person having medical or other qualifications relevant to the subject matter of the inquiry, and take into account a certificate given by such a person.

Representation

A party to proceedings before a court may be represented by a barrister or solicitor or, with the leave of the court, by a person other than a barrister or solicitor (s 39).

Cancellation of orders

If an authorised medical practitioner considers that the person to whom a public health order applies is no longer endangering, or likely to endanger, the health of the public, the medical practitioner is to revoke the order and immediately give written notice of the revocation to the person to whom the order applied and to the appropriate court (s 31).

Contravention of orders

A certificate by an authorised medical practitioner to the effect that a named person is contravening a public health order is sufficient ground for the issue to a police officer of a warrant to apprehend the person and detain the person in custody pending an inquiry under s 30 (s 29(1)). A police officer who is provided with such a certificate is, as soon as practicable, to obtain a warrant, apprehend the named person and detain the person in custody pending an inquiry under s 30 (s 29(2)). Section 27 applies in relation to detention following apprehension under this section in the same way as it would apply if the certificate that led to the apprehension had been a public health order (s 29(3)). If a person alleged to have contravened a public health order is apprehended and brought before the appropriate court or appears voluntarily before the appropriate court, the court is to inquire into the allegation (s 30(1)). If, after inquiry, the appropriate court is not satisfied that the person has contravened a public health order, it is to order that the person be discharged (s 30(2)). If, after inquiry, the appropriate court is satisfied that a person has contravened a public health order, it may confirm the public health order or:

(a) vary the public health order by adding a requirement, direction or other provision that could have been included in the order when made; or
(b) vary the public health order by substituting any such requirement, direction or other provision for any one or more of them already included in the order; or
(c) caution the person and take no further action in the matter (s 30(3)).

A person may be dealt with under this section in respect of an alleged contravention of a public health order whether or not the person has been charged under s 28 for an offence in relation to the same contravention (s 30(4)).

Penalty for contravention of a public health order

If the person to whom a public health order applies contravenes the order, the person is guilty of an offence. The maximum penalty is 50 penalty units and/or imprisonment for six months. Proceedings for an offence under this section may be brought only by the Director General or a police officer.

Prosecution for an offence under this section does not preclude action under s 30 in respect of the contravention on which the prosecution is based (s 28).

Escapees

If a person detained under a public health order or following apprehension under s 29 escapes from a place of detention, he or she may be apprehended at any time by the person for the time being in charge of the place from which the person escaped, an authorised medical practitioner, a police officer, or any person assisting the above. On being apprehended, the escapee must be returned to the place from which he or she escaped (s 33).

It is an offence for a person to, without lawful authority, release, or attempt to release a person detained under a public health order or following detention under s 29 or 33, or a person being conveyed to a place at which he or she is to be so detained (s 34(1)). It is a defence to a prosecution under this section or a prosecution for the aiding, abetting, counselling or procuring the escape of a person detained under a public health order or following apprehension under s 29 or 33, if it is proved that the action of the defendant did not endanger the health of the public and that the defendant knew this to be so.

An appeal lies to the District Court (s 41).

Closure of courts and orders restricting publication

The court in which proceedings have been instituted or are being heard may make orders having the effect of prohibiting or restricting the publication of matters relating to the proceedings or to a person in respect of whom the proceedings have been instituted (s 35(1)). The orders that a court may make under this section include orders prohibiting or restricting publication of any one or more of the following:

(a) any report that relates to the proceedings;
(b) the identity of the person in respect of whom the proceedings have been instituted;

(c) any information from which the identity of that person could be deduced;
(d) any information from which could be deduced the identity of a person in respect of whom a public health order is, or at any time was, sought or made, whether or not in the proceedings (s 35(2)).

An order under this section may be made by the court of its own motion or on the application of a party to the proceedings (s 35(3)). If an application under this section is made by a party to the proceedings, the onus is on the other party to show cause why the application should be refused (s 35(4)). A person who contravenes an order under this section (whether aware of the order or not) is guilty of an offence.

Medical records

A person to whom a public health order applies, or the authorised agent of such a person, is, unless the appropriate court otherwise directs, entitled to inspect, and make copies of, medical records relating to the person that are kept by another person. If the medical records are not kept in a readable form, the person in charge of the records is to provide a readable copy of them (s 36).

Queensland

Health Act 1937

'Human immunodeficiency virus infection' was declared to be a 'notifiable disease' for the purposes of the Health Act 1937 by a notice published in the *Government Gazette* on 4 June 1988.

Notification

A medical practitioner who, upon examining or treating a patient, believes the patient is suffering from a notifiable disease or has symptoms of a kind notified by the Chief Health Officer [Note: in this Act, references to the Chief Executive Health Officer have been replaced with chief executive] as indicating a notifiable disease must, as soon as is practicable after forming that belief, give notice thereof to the Chief Health Officer (s 32A(1)).

If the patient is examined or treated in a public hospital the medical practitioner shall, as soon as practicable after forming the belief, also give notice to the medical superintendent of the hospital of that belief and the medical superintendent has a duty to notify the Chief Health Officer of that belief (s 32A(2)).

The notice must state the nature of the disease or the nature of the symptoms, the date of onset of the disease or symptoms and the date on which the medical practitioner formed the belief required to be notified, and the name, sex, address, age, occupation, and ethnic origin of the patient (s 32A(3)).

The person in charge of a place in which a pathological examination is carried out which indicates that a person is suffering from a notifiable disease must, as soon as practicable, notify the Chief Health Officer (s 32A(4)).

The notice must specify the nature of the disease and the results of the examination, the name and sex and, if the information is readily ascertainable, the address, age and occupation of the person from whom the specimens were taken and the name of the referring medical practitioner (s 32A(5)).

Where notice is required to be given under s 32A of the name and address of a person, it is sufficient to comply with that requirement to supply a reference to a code from which that name and address can be provided by the person giving the notice, if required to do so by the Chief Health Officer (s 32A(8)).

Testing, treatment and isolation

Persons may be detained where they are suspected by a medical practitioner of having a notifiable disease and they refuse testing, examination or treatment or where they are already in a hospital and do not have proper accommodation to go to on leaving hospital (s 37).

The Chief Health Officer may, with the approval of the Minister, establish and maintain any place for the temporary isolation and treatment of any person the Health Officer believes is suffering from a notifiable disease (s 35).

Detention for failing to submit to medical examination or treatment

If a person suspected by a medical practitioner to be suffering from or to have been exposed to a notifiable disease:

(a) fails or refuses to enter or remain in a hospital or temporary isolation place; or
(b) refuses to submit to any reasonable examination, test or treatment in respect of that notifiable disease;

a justice (of the peace) may, upon the application of the Chief Health Officer, and upon the production of a certificate of the medical practitioner certifying as to his or her suspicion, order that the person be removed to a public hospital or temporary isolation place specified in the order (s 36(1)).

The order is to be directed to all members of the police force and sufficiently authorises a member of the force to take the subject of the order to the place specified in it. The order also authorises the person in charge of the hospital or place to detain the person (s 36(2)).

The Chief Health Officer may order a person so detained to be transferred to another hospital or isolation place (s 36(3)).

A person admitted to a public hospital or temporary isolation place under the order must remain there for such period as, in the opinion of the Chief Health Officer, is necessary for the person's proper isolation and treatment or, as the case may be, for determining whether the person is suffering from a notifiable disease (s 36(4)).

Where a person is detained in a public hospital or temporary isolation place, the person in charge of the public hospital or temporary isolation place or anyone acting at his or her direction may exercise such force as may be reasonably necessary for the purpose of:

(a) detaining the person in the public hospital or place;
(b) isolating and treating the person in respect of a notifiable disease; or
(c) performing any examination or test to determine whether the person is suffering from a notifiable disease (s 36(5)).

A person in respect of whom an order has been made who:

(a) restricts or obstructs any person in the execution of an order;
(b) fails to remain in the public hospital or temporary isolation place until the Chief Health Officer approves discharge; or
(c) assaults, resists or obstructs any person in the exercise of any power conferred by s 36, commits an offence.

Penalty: 20 penalty units (s 36(6)).

Detention of people without proper accommodation

A stipendiary magistrate may, upon proper cause shown to him or her, make an order directing the detention in a public hospital of any person suspected to be suffering from any notifiable disease who is then in a hospital and would not on leaving the hospital be provided with lodging or accommodation in which proper precautions could be taken to prevent the spreading of the disease (s 37).

Any such order may be limited to some specific time, but the magistrate may extend the time as often as may appear to be necessary (s 37). A member of the police force or any other officer of the public hospital in which a person is being detained pursuant to any such order may take all necessary measures and do all necessary acts to enforce the order (s 37).

Other duties and powers

Where the Chief Health Officer suspects that a person is suffering from a notifiable disease, any officer may require the person to provide:

(a) his or her name and address;
(b) the name and address or whereabouts of any person who may have communicated the disease to him or her or to whom he or she may have communicated the disease;
(c) information concerning the circumstances in which he may have

been exposed to the disease or may have exposed others to the disease.

Penalty for failure to provide such information as required: 20 penalty units (s 32B).

A local authority may require the cleansing and disinfection of premises or the destruction of buildings and articles (ss 38 and 39).

The Governor in Council may make orders regarding withholding children from school in cases where they are suffering from a specific disease (s 47(1)).

Whenever any notifiable disease occurs or is suspected to have occurred amongst children attending any school, any medical officer of health, or any medical practitioner, registered nurse, or other officer authorised in writing for the purpose by the Chief Health Officer, may enter any house and examine all or any of the persons or children found in or residing at such house for the purpose of ascertaining whether such person or children are infected by or carriers of such notifiable disease, and all persons concerned shall permit such examination (s 47(3)).

South Australia

Public and Environmental Health Act 1987

'Human Immunodeficiency Virus' is both a notifiable disease and a controlled notifiable disease for the purposes of the Act.

Notification

Upon becoming aware that a person is suffering from a notifiable disease or has died from a notifiable disease, a medical practitioner must report the existence of the disease to the South Australian Health Commission and furnish the Commission with such information as is required (s 30(1)).

Testing, treatment and isolation

Where the Commission has reasonable grounds to suspect that a person is or may be suffering from a controlled notifiable disease, it may give notice in writing requiring a person to present for a medical examination (s 31(1)).

If a person fails to comply with the notice, a magistrate may issue a warrant for the apprehension and examination of the person, who may be detained for up to 48 hours for the purpose of the examination (s 31(2)–(4)).

If the examination discloses that the person is not suffering from the disease, the person is entitled to reasonable compensation for the expenses incurred in attending the examination (s 31(5)).

Where a medical practitioner has certified that a person is suffering from a controlled notifiable disease and the Commission is of the opinion that in the interests of public health a person should be kept in quarantine, a magistrate may, on the application of the Commission, issue a warrant for the person's detention (s 32(1)). In an emergency, the warrant may be issued by telephone (s 32(2)).

The person detained must be given a notice setting out the reason for the detention (s 32(3)).

A person may not be detained for more than 72 hours unless, after considering any representations made by or on behalf of the person under detention, a magistrate extends the period of detention (s 32(4)). However, the period of detention may not be extended beyond six months unless the extension is authorised by a Supreme Court judge (s 32(6)).

The detainee must be examined by a medical practitioner at intervals not exceeding four weeks or such shorter period as determined by a magistrate or judge, but these examinations must not proceed if the person objects to being examined (s 32(7)).

The Commission may give written directions to a person who has been certified by a medical practitioner as suffering from a controlled notifiable disease if the Commission is of the opinion that the person should take or refrain from action to prevent the spread of infection. These may include a direction that the person reside at a specified place; place himself or herself under the supervision of a staff member of the Commission or a medical practitioner and obey that person's directions; submit to a medical examination at such intervals as required; refrain from performing specified work.

The Commission may also give any other directions as to the person's conduct or supervision that it considers should apply in order to prevent the spread of infection (s 33(1) and (2)).

A person so directed may apply to a magistrate for a review of the direction (s 33(3)).

A person who fails to comply with a direction risks a $5,000 penalty, and the person may be made the subject of a warrant under which he or she may be apprehended and brought before a magistrate who may give further directions and issue a warrant for the person's quarantine (s 33(5)).

An appeal from the magistrate's decision lies to a single judge of the Supreme Court (s 34).

The Commission may impose areas of quarantine and restrict movement into and out of any premises or place where there is a danger to public health from the possible spread of a controlled notifiable disease. A $5,000 penalty is imposed on persons who disobey the Commission's directions in this regard.

Other duties and powers

The Commission is required to provide each local council with a monthly report on the occurrence of notifiable diseases in its area and problems caused by the diseases.

The local council is required to take such action as is reasonably open to it to assist in preventing the spread of a disease which constitutes a threat to public health (s 36(9)).

Where there is a danger to public health from the possible spread of a controlled notifiable disease, the Commission or an officer authorised by the Commission may give directions and take such action as may be appropriate to avert the danger. This action may include directions as to disinfection of premises and things, destruction of articles, seizure of things, imposition of quarantine, and restrictions on people's movements (s 36(1) and (2)). A $5,000 penalty is imposed for failure to comply with such directions without reasonable excuse (s 36(3)).

A person exercising power under this provision may enter premises at any reasonable time, but must not break into premises unless authorised by warrant (s 36(7)).

Authorised officers are empowered to enter and inspect premises (after giving reasonable notice to the occupier), to inspect vehicles, to make inquiries and inspections with respect to things or persons found in such premises or vehicles, to remove articles that may constitute evidence of the commission of an offence, to take visual or aural recordings, to carry out tests and to require a person to answer questions and produce documents (s 38).

Failure to comply with an officer's directions or refusing to answer questions fully and truthfully is an offence, carrying a penalty of $2,500 (s 38(4)). The privilege against self-incrimination is preserved (s 38(5)).

Victoria

Health Act 1958

Health (Infectious Diseases) Act 1991

Health (Infectious Diseases) Regulations 1990

Under the Health (Infectious Diseases) Regulations 1990, 'Acquired Immunodeficiency Syndrome', 'HIV types I and II' and 'HTLV type I and all other forms' are declared to be 'infectious diseases' for the purposes of the Health Act 1958. 'Acquired Immunodeficiency Syndrome' is also declared to be a 'notifiable disease'.

The following principles are to be applied when determining the application of the provisions in the Act dealing with the management and control of infectious diseases:

(a) The spread of infectious diseases should be prevented or limited without imposing unnecessary restrictions on personal liberty or privacy;

(b) A person at risk of contracting or being infected with an infectious disease must take all reasonable precautions to avoid contracting or being infected with the disease;
(c) A person who suspects that he or she has an infectious disease must ascertain:

   (i) whether he or she is infected; and
   (ii) what precautions should be taken to prevent others being infected;

(d) A person with an infectious disease must take necessary measures to ensure that others are not unknowingly placed at risk of becoming infected;
(e) A person with an infectious disease or at risk of contracting or being infected with an infectious disease has a right:

   (i) to be protected from unlawful discrimination;
   (ii) to have his or her privacy respected;
   (iii) to receive information about the medical and social consequences of the disease and any proposed treatment; and
   (iv) to have access to available and appropriate treatments;

   so long as those rights do not infringe on the wellbeing of others (s 119).

Notification

A medical practitioner who becomes aware that a person the practitioner is attending shows evidence of, has died with, or is a carrier of a notifiable disease must notify the Chief General Manager (Reg 7). The regulations prescribe a form for AIDS notifications that is different from that to be used for other notifiable diseases. The form requires the patient's initials to be provided but not the name.

A person in charge of a prescribed place in which the testing of blood for HIV is carried out must keep a written record with the prescribed particulars for each prescribed period containing as far as is possible the following information:

(a) the number of tests carried out on human blood for HIV;
(b) the number of persons in respect of whom tests have been carried out who fall into each prescribed category;
(c) the number of persons newly diagnosed as being infected with HIV who fall into each particular prescribed category;
(d) the age, sex, and particular prescribed category of each newly diagnosed person;
(e) the date the specimen was taken from a newly diagnosed person (s 130(2)).

[Note: sub-ss (c)–(e) have been replaced with a single sub-s (c) which states 'any information relating to each newly diagnosed person required by the regulations'.]

The person in charge of a prescribed place must send a copy of the record to the Chief General Manager [Note: in this Act, references to the Chief General Manager have been replaced with the Secretary] at the end of each prescribed period (s 130(3)).

A medical practitioner must, when requesting a test for HIV, give the information that is required by the laboratory for the purposes of maintaining its records (s 130(4)).

In complying with these duties, the medical practitioner is prohibited from supplying particulars by which a person may be identified (s 130(5)).

The Chief General Manager and person in charge of a prescribed place must ensure that information is not kept which will identify any person whose blood is tested (s 130(6)).

A medical practitioner must, when requested in writing by the Chief General Manager, provide information (other than particulars by which a patient may be identified) as to the age, sex and particular prescribed category of any patient of that medical practitioner who has been newly diagnosed as HIV infected (s 130(7)).

General penalty for subsections (2)–(7): 10 penalty units.

Testing, treatment and isolation

If the Chief General Manager reasonably believes that:

(a) a person has an infectious disease or has been exposed to an infectious disease in circumstances where a person is reasonably likely to contract the disease; and
(b) if infected with that infectious disease, the person is likely to transmit that disease; and
(c) there is a serious risk to public health,

the Chief General Manager may make an order in writing stating why it is believed the person has an infected disease that is likely to be transmitted, and requiring the person to be examined and tested for the disease (s 121(1)).

If the person has been examined and tested for an infectious disease and the results of the test are positive, the Chief General Manager may make an order in writing requiring that the person undergo counselling about that disease, if counselling is appropriate having regard to the nature of the disease (s 121(2)).

If the Chief General Manager is satisfied that:

(a) a person has an infectious disease or has been exposed to an infectious disease in circumstances where a person is reasonably likely to contract the disease; and
(b) if infected with that infectious disease the person is likely to transmit that disease; and

(c) there is a serious risk to public health; and
(d) if counselling is appropriate having regard to the nature of the disease, the person has been counselling (sic) but without success in achieving appropriate and responsible behaviour change,

the Chief General Manager may make an order in writing imposing restrictions on the person's behaviour or movements (s 121(3)).

If subsection (3) applies but:

(a) the Chief General Manager considers that an order referred to in subsection (3) is inappropriate, having regard to the nature of the infectious disease; or
(b) the person who is the subject of the order fails to comply with the restrictions imposed by an order under that subsection;

the Chief General Manager may make an order requiring that the person be isolated and detained at the place, for the period and in the manner stated in the order (s 121(4)).

If an order is made under subsection (1) but the person refuses to undergo a test for an infectious disease, the Chief General Manager may make an interim order for the isolation and detention of the person for a period not exceeding 72 hours for the purpose of examining the person and testing for that disease and may renew the order for a further period or further periods not exceeding 72 hours (s 121(5)).

An order must name the infectious disease, identify the person believed to be infected, and, if applicable, name the counsellor, state the period for which the person is to be isolated, the type of examination, testing or counselling required, or state the type of restrictions imposed (s 121(6)).

The order may be made subject to conditions and may be varied or revoked by the Chief General Manager (s 121(7)).

The Chief General Manager must review an isolation order at intervals not exceeding 28 days and may renew the order for a further period or periods not exceeding 28 days.

The order lapses if the test carried out on the person shows that he or she is not infected with the infectious disease named in the order and no test shows that the person is or may be infected with that infectious disease (s 121(9)).

A penalty of 50 penalty units is imposed for failing to comply with the order (s 121(10)).

The Chief General Manager may authorise a medical officer of the Department to carry out an isolation order (s 121(11)).

If, to enforce the order, the medical officer finds that it is necessary to arrest the person to whom the order relates, the medical officer may obtain the assistance of any member of the police force to do so (s 121(12)).

For the purposes of arresting a person under subsection (12), the medical officer may with any assistance that is required:

(a) enter any premises; and
(b) use any force that may reasonably be necessary (s 121(13)).

The medical officer who has arrested a person under subsection (12) must take that person to the place stated in the order (s 121(14)).

A person who acts in reliance on an authorisation of the Chief General Manager under subsection (11) is not liable to any civil or criminal action for so acting, whether or not there was any defect in the authorisation (s 121(15)).

A person to whom a restriction order, isolation order or interim isolation order under s 121 relates may at any time but not more than:

(a) in the case of an interim isolation order, once during the period of the order; or
(b) in the case of any other order, once during a period of 28 days;

apply to the Chief General Manager for a review of the order (s 122(1)).

The Chief General Manager must review the order and revoke, vary or confirm the order within the period of five days after receiving the application for review (s 122(2)).

A person may appeal to the Supreme Court against an order made by the Chief General Manager (s 122(3)).

An order against which an appeal has been lodged remains in force despite the lodging of the appeal (s 122(4)).

The court must hear and determine an appeal against an order urgently (s 122(5)).

When determining an appeal, the court must consider the following matters:

(a) the method by which the disease is transmitted;
(b) the seriousness of the risk of other people being infected;
(c) the past behaviour and likely conduct of the person to whom the order relates;
(d) the extent of the restrictions imposed on the person to whom the order relates (s 122(6)).

Upon determining an appeal against an order, the Supreme Court may make an order in substitution for the order made by the Chief General Manager, and has the same powers as the Chief General Manager to fix the terms and conditions of the order (s 122(7)).

If an appeal against an order has been determined but there has been a change in circumstances, the person to whom the order relates may apply to the Chief General Manager under subsection (1) for a review of the order (s 122(8)).

Examining and testing after incidents involving care givers or custodians

'Specified infectious disease' means HIV; any form of hepatitis which may be transmitted by blood or body fluid; or an infectious disease so declared by the regulations (s 3).

'Care giver or custodian' means:

(a) a legally qualified medical practitioner or registered dentist or registered nurse; or
(b) an ambulance officer; or
(c) in relation to a person taken into legal or protective custody, any legal custodian of that person; or
(d) a person who works in a prescribed field of health, welfare or custodial care (s 118).

If the Chief General Manager reasonably believes that:

(a) an incident has occurred, while a care giver or custodian is acting in that capacity, in which, if any of those involved were infected by a specified disease, the disease could have been transmitted to any of the other people involved; and
(b) any of those people to whom the disease could have been transmitted has been counselled by a medical practitioner about the risk of transmission of the disease in the particular circumstances and about the medical and social consequences of being infected with the disease and has consented to be tested for that disease; and
(c) any of those persons who, if he or she had the disease, could have transmitted it:

    (i) has been offered counselling, irrespective of whether the offer was accepted; and
    (ii) has refused to be tested for the disease; and

(d) the making of the order is necessary in the interest of rapid diagnosis and treatment for any of those involved,

the Chief General Manager may make an order under subsection (2) (s 120A(1)).

An order referred to in subsection (1) must:

(a) be in writing;
(b) give the details of the incident which led to its making;
(c) name the person to whom it applies;
(d) name the disease for which the person must be tested, which must be a disease for which another person has agreed to be tested under subsection (1)(b);
(e) require the person named in the order to be tested for that disease;
(f) state where and when (or, in the case of a series of tests, the period within which) the tests must be undertaken;
(g) state the type of testing required (s 120A(2)).

An order must not be made under this section if more than three months has passed since the happening of the incident which would enable it to be made (s 120A(3)). The order may be made subject to conditions and may be varied or revoked by the Chief General Manager. A penalty of 50 units is imposed for failing to comply with the order (s 120A(4)).

The Chief General Manager may alternatively authorise the testing of a previously stored sample of the person's blood in some circumstances (s 120B). No action lies against a pathologist or medical practitioner who conducts such a test (s 120C(1)). The test results must be reported without delay to the Chief General Manager, who must give notice of them to the appropriate person mentioned in s 120A(1)(b)) and to the person tested (s 120C(3) and (4)).

When advising a person mentioned in s 120A(1)(b) of the results of such a test, the Chief General Manager must not include information that would identify the person tested (s 120D(1)). A person mentioned in s 120A(1)(b) who receives notice of the results of such a test on another person must not disclose, communicate, or make a record of, anything in those results that would identify that other person. Penalty: 50 penalty units.

Quarantine orders

The Governor in Council may proclaim an emergency for the purpose of stopping, limiting or preventing the spread of an infectious disease (s 123).

During a state of emergency, the Chief General Manager may make orders that persons of a specified class be prevented from entering or leaving a proclaimed area, that persons of a specified class be arrested without warrant and detained in a proclaimed area, and that land, buildings or things be seized and destroyed, disinfected or used in preventing the spread of infection (s 124).

A proclamation may be revoked by further proclamation of the Governor in Council or by a resolution of either House of Parliament. Provision is made for the recalling of Parliament by petition if Parliament is not sitting at the time the proclamation is published (s 123(3) and (4)).

Other duties and powers

The Chief General Manager may require a medical practitioner to carry out an autopsy if it is reasonably believed that an infectious disease caused or contributed to a person's death, provided that the coroner does not have jurisdiction over the body (s 126).

Medical practitioners are prohibited from carrying out or authorising the carrying out of a test for HIV on a person who requests it unless the person has been given information about the medical and social consequences of being tested and of the possible results of the test (s 127(1)). This requirement does not apply to the authorising or carrying out of a test for HIV by a pathologist if the pathologist authorises or carries out the test on the authority of another medical practitioner (s 121(7A)).

If the results of the test are positive, the person must not be advised of this except by a medical practitioner or a person of a prescribed class who must also give the person tested information about the medical and social consequences of being infected with the virus and guidelines on ways to prevent the transmission of the virus to others (s 127(2)). Penalty: 10 penalty units.

A person who, in the course of providing a service, acquires information that a person has been or is required to be tested for HIV or is infected with HIV, must take all reasonable steps to develop and implement systems to protect the privacy of that person. Penalty: 50 penalty units (s 128).

If a pathologist gives information to the Chief General Manager about an infectious disease, an action does not lie against that pathologist for giving that information or because the information is given without the consent of the person to whom it relates or the person for whom it was prepared (s 137(4)).

Contact tracing

If the Chief General Manager believes that an outbreak of infectious disease may occur, or has occurred, the Chief General Manager may direct any person who has been or who may have been in contact with a person who is infected with or is a carrier of the disease to give such information about the contact to the Chief General Manager as is considered necessary to trace the source or prevent the spread of the infectious disease (Reg 14(1)(c)).

Western Australia

Health Act 1911

Infectious Diseases (Inspection of Persons) Regulations

Health – Dangerous Infectious Diseases Order 1991

Health – Infectious Diseases Order 1991

In 1983, AIDS was declared to be an infectious disease and a dangerous infectious disease for the purposes of the Health Act 1911. AIDS-related complex, lymphadenopathy syndrome, and HTLV 111 infection were declared to be infectious diseases and dangerous infectious diseases in 1985. In 1991, these declarations were replaced by declarations that HIV infection and AIDS are infectious diseases and dangerous infectious diseases under the Health Act.

Notification

A medical practitioner attending a patient who is found to be suffering from an infectious disease or from any sickness the symptoms of which raise a reasonable suspicion that it may be an infectious disease must, upon becoming aware of the nature of the disease, give notice thereof to the occupier of the house where the person is found, the local authority and the Commissioner for Public Health (s 276(1)(c)). [Note: in this Act, references to the Commissioner for Public Health have been replaced with Executive Director, Public Health.]

The occupier of a house in which a person is found to be suffering from an infectious disease, or from a sickness the symptoms of which raise a reasonable suspicion that it may be an infectious disease, must notify the local authority of that finding (s 276(1)(a)).

Hospitals are deemed to be houses for the purposes of s 276(1) (s 276(5)).

If, in the opinion of the Commissioner, any place in Western Australia is affected by a dangerous infectious disease, the Commissioner may require all medical practitioners, deputy registrars, schoolteachers and members of the police force residing in such place to report the occurrence by telegraph or letter to the Commissioner and the local authority (s 287(1)).

No medical practitioner shall be liable in any proceedings for any misstatement made in good faith in a notification of an infectious disease if he or she promptly notifies the local authorities of any change in the diagnosis (s 289).

Local authorities must report at least once in every month to the Commissioner regarding the existence of any infectious disease in the district.

Testing, treatment and isolation

The Regulations provide that any health official who suspects on reasonable grounds that a person may be suffering from an infectious disease or may be a medium for the transmission of an infectious disease may examine that person. The person is required to permit the removal of such specimens as are considered necessary for a proper examination. The health official is empowered to enter upon any land or into any house and may remove the person to any other place where the examination may be more conveniently made.

The Health Act provides that the Commissioner may, with the Minister's authorisation, order any person whom he or she believes on reasonable grounds, or suspects, is suffering from or harbouring the organisms of a dangerous infectious disease to submit to a medical examination as specified, and to permit the taking of medical samples. If the person is under 18, the order is to be served on the person's parents or guardians who are required to take all action necessary to ensure that the order is obeyed (s 251(5)).

The Commissioner, if authorised by the Minister, may order places and things to be isolated, quarantined and disinfected (s 251(6)); persons to be prohibited from leaving a place of quarantine until they have been examined and found to be free from dangerous infectious diseases (s 251(8)).

Any public health official or the Commissioner may by warrant require any police officer or health surveyor to apprehend any person who has been ordered to be quarantined or isolated and has failed to obey the order, and to convey the person to the place of quarantine or isolation (s 253). A medical officer of health may order any person who is suffering from an infectious disease to be removed to a hospital if the officer thinks it expedient to do so in the interests of public health (s 263(1)); or if the officer is satisfied that the patient is without proper accommodation or is living in a house where the person cannot be effectively isolated so as to prevent the risk of the infection spreading to other persons living in the house (s 263(2)).

Other duties and powers

The Commissioner may also direct a postmortem examination of a person who has died, or is supposed to have died, from a dangerous infectious disease, and may give directions as to the disposal of the body (s 251(17a)).

The local authority may cleanse or disinfect premises and disinfect or destroy articles to prevent infectious disease (ss 260 and 261).

It is an offence for a person affected with an infectious disease to wilfully expose himself or herself in any public place without taking proper precautions against spreading infection, or to enter a public vehicle without notifying the owner, conductor or driver that he or she is so infected (s 264).

A person in charge of any infected person also commits an offence if he or she allows the person to do anything in breach of this provision (s 264(1)(c)).

Every owner, driver or conductor of a public vehicle must cause the vehicle to be disinfected if it has, to his or her knowledge, been used to convey a person with an infectious disease (s 265).

It is an offence where a person:

(a) sells, gives, lends, transmits or exposes any things which have been exposed to infection from an infectious disease, unless they have first been effectively disinfected, or proper precautions have been taken against spreading the infection;
(b) lets a house or room to be shared or occupied in common by or with a person suffering from an infectious disease;
(c) lets a house or room in which there is, or has been, any person suffering from an infectious disease, unless the premises have been disinfected to the satisfaction of a medical officer of health or a health surveyor as certified by a certificate under the officer's hand;
(d) when letting premises, conceals the fact that a person suffering from

a dangerous infectious disease has been living there within the previous six weeks (s 267).

The provision of accommodation to a hotel guest or lodger in a common lodging house is deemed to fall within s 267(b)–(d).

It is an offence for a person to cease occupation of premises in which a person affected with an infectious disease has resided within six weeks previously without having the house disinfected to the satisfaction of a medical officer or without first giving to the owner and to the local authority notice of the previous existence of the disease. The person ceasing occupation also commits an offence by knowingly making a false answer to a question, asked by the owner or person negotiating for the hire of the premises, as to the fact of there being a person suffering from an infectious disease previously in occupation (s 268).

Where an infectious disease occurs in a house in which a child attending a school resides, the occupier of the house and the parent or guardian of the child shall immediately give notice in writing to the head teacher of the child's school of the occurrence of the disease (s 276(3)).

The local authority must give immediate notice to the head teacher of a school of any case of infectious disease reported to the local authority contracted by a child who has attended that school (s 276(6)).

It is an offence for the occupier of a factory or contractor to allow the cleaning, repair, or manufacture of clothes in a dwelling-house, or building occupied therewith, while an inmate of the dwelling-house is suffering from an infectious disease (s 279).

It is an offence for a person knowingly or negligently to send to school a child who has been suffering from a dangerous infectious disease within the past three months, or who has been resident in a house in which such disease has existed within the past six weeks, without a certificate from a medical practitioner that the child is free from disease and infection and unless the clothes of the child have been properly disinfected (s 285).

Public Health Act 1997

In the Australian Capital Territory, the Public Health Act 1928 has been repealed and replaced by the Public Health Act 1997.

Part III of the Public Health Act states that the Minister may declare an activity that may result in the transmission of disease, or that may otherwise adversely affect the health of individuals in the context of the wider health of the community, to be a public health risk activity (s 18(1)).

A declaration under this section indicates whether the declared activity or procedure is a licensable or a non-licensable activity or procedure, as the case may be.

Information regarding activity and procedural licenses are contained in divisions 2 and 3 of Part III.

Part V of the Act provides for inspection and analysis.

Where an authorised officer has reasonable grounds for believing that it is necessary to do so, he or she may, using such reasonable force and assistance as is necessary, enter a place (s 76). Items in the place may be seized, and if an authorised officer believes on reasonable grounds a thing is contaminated and its continued use would give rise to a serious public health risk, he or she may destroy it (s 92).

Notification

Part VI of the Act provides for notifiable conditions and public health hazards. The principles of Part VI are to be construed in accordance with the following principles:

(a) the investigation of notifiable conditions, and any actions taken as a consequence, shall be carried out in order to minimise the adverse public health effects of such conditions;

(b) a person who engages in activities that are known to carry a potential risk of exposure to a transmissible notifiable condition, and any person responsible for the care, support or education of such a person, has the following responsibilities:

   (i) to take all reasonable precautions to avoid the contracting of the condition by the person who engages in such activities;

   (ii) if there are reasonable grounds for believing that the person who engages in such activities has been exposed to the condition – to ascertain whether the condition has been contracted, and what precautions should reasonably be taken to avoid exposing others to the condition;

   (iii) if there are reasonable grounds for believing that the person who engages in such activities has contracted, or is likely to have contracted, the condition – to comply with preventative measures or treatment that will minimise the risk to others of exposure to the condition;

   (iv) if there are reasonable grounds for believing that the person who engages in such activities has contracted, or is likely to have contracted, the condition – to take reasonable measures to ensure that others are not unknowingly placed at risk through any action or inaction of the person or any person responsible for the care, support or education of the person;

(c) a person who has, or may have, a notifiable condition, or who engages in activities that are known to carry a potential risk of exposure to a notifiable condition, shall be accorded the following rights, to the extent that their exercise does not conflict with the requirements of this Part and does not infringe unduly on the wellbeing of others:

   (i) the right to privacy;

(ii) the right to receive all reasonably available information about the medical and social consequences of the condition and any proposed treatment.

Division 2 of Part VI of the Act provides for notification of notifiable conditions.

If a medical practitioner has reasonable grounds for believing that his or her patient has or may have a notifiable condition, the practitioner shall as soon as practicable, notify the Chief Health Officer of any of his or her patients who the practitioner has reasonable grounds for believing to have a notifiable condition. Penalty for non-compliance, 5 penalty units (s 102(4)).

A medical practitioner shall, as soon as practicable, notify the Chief Health Officer of any deceased person who was a patient of the practitioner immediately before death, or who was examined by the practitioner after death, if the practitioner has reasonable grounds for believing that the person had, or may have had, a notifiable condition at the time of death. Penalty: 5 penalty units (s 102(5)).

Persons in charge of a hospital (s 104), pathologists (s 103) and other responsible persons (s 105) are also required to notify the Chief Health Officer under certain circumstances, with penalties provided for non-compliance.

Northern Territory

Notifiable Diseases Act 1981

On 21 July 1983, 'acquired immune deficiency syndrome' was declared to be a notifiable disease for the purposes of the Notifiable Diseases Act. However, this declaration was revoked on 13 January 1988 and replaced by a declaration that 'human immune deficiency virus (HIV) infection groups 1–4' were to be notifiable diseases under the Act. AIDS was added to Schedule 3 of the Act by the Notifiable Diseases Amendment Act 1985, which came into operation on 30 October 1985.

An 'infected person' is a person who is suffering from a notifiable disease, who is a carrier of a notifiable disease or a person from whom a notifiable disease may be contracted (s 5).

A 'suspect person' is a person who is suspected of being an infected person, or a person who has or may have been exposed to an infected person or to goods which are known or suspected to be infected or a source of infection (s 5).

Notification

A medical practitioner who diagnoses that a person is an infected person or considers that a person is a suspect person is required to give notification of this in a manner approved by the Chief Medical Officer. [Note: in this Act, references to the Chief Medical Officer have been replaced by

Chief Health Officer.] The practice in the Northern Territory is for notification to be given by code.

An infected person or a suspect person must supply to a medical practitioner or medical officer the names and addresses of possible contacts (s 9).

Medical practitioners must notify a medical officer of the death of an infected or suspect person (s 15).

Testing, isolation and treatment

A medical officer may, by notice in writing personally served on an infected person or suspect person, direct the person to carry out measures which the medical officer believes necessary for the treatment of, or to prevent the spread or possible spread of, the relevant notifiable disease (s 11). A person served with a notice under s 11 may appeal to a magistrate [Note: in this Act, references to a magistrate have been replaced by the local court] against the notice or a direction contained in the notice (s 12).

Where a person is served with a notice under s 11 and the person fails to comply with the notice, the Chief Medical Officer may make such orders as he or she thinks fit, including an order that the person be removed to and detained at a hospital or other place until a medical officer authorises the release of the person on the grounds that the person is not an infected person or is no longer a suspect person (s 13).

The Chief Medical Officer may require a specified person or class of persons to attend medical examinations and to answer questions to determine whether the person or any member of the class is an infected or suspect person (s 14).

The Administrator or Minister may declare an area to be an isolation area (s 17).

In relation to an isolation area, the Chief Medical Officer may prohibit the movement of a person or classes of persons; prohibit the movement of goods; require persons or classes of persons to submit to medical examinations, answer questions and submit to medical treatment; authorise the destruction, disposal or treatment of goods, buildings or other things known or suspected to be infected or a source of infection (s 18).

A medical officer or authorised person may ask questions of persons who are, or are believed to have been, located within an isolation area while a s 17 declaration is in force, or within 14 days prior to such a declaration, to ascertain the identity of the person and his or her contacts, whether the person has been in an isolation area, whether the person is an infected person or suspect person, and the details of goods with which a person has had contact (s 19).

A person who is suspected of having left an isolation place in contravention of a s 18 order may be arrested without warrant, placed in isolation, and submitted to a medical examination and treatment (s 20).

Other duties and powers

A person who has reasonable grounds to believe that he or she may be an infected person or a suspect person must consult a medical practitioner at the first reasonable opportunity (s 7).

Infected persons must provide a medical practitioner, medical officer or other authorised person with the names and addresses of all persons from whom the notifiable disease may have been contracted. A suspect person must provide the names and addresses of all persons with whom he or she has been in contact during a period of time specified by the medical practitioner, medical officer or authorised person (s 9).

A medical practitioner who diagnoses that a person is an infected person or who considers a person to be a suspect person must advise the person, or, in the case of a child [Note: when the child has attained the age of 16 advising the parents or guardian of the child is at the medical practitioner's discretion: s 10(c)], the child's parents or guardian, of the nature of the disease, measures to prevent the spread of the disease and the treatment required (s 10).

A medical officer may, by notice in writing, direct an infected or suspect person to carry out measures believed necessary for the treatment of, or prevention of the spread of, a notifiable disease (s 11).

A person may appeal to a magistrate against a direction contained in the notice (s 12).

The Chief Medical Officer may make such oral or written orders as he or she thinks fit in relation to a person who fails to comply with a s 11 notice, including an order that the person's residence, workplace or educational institution be closed or disinfected, that any possibly contaminated articles be destroyed or disinfected, or that a person be placed under detention until a medical officer authorises release on the grounds that the person is not an infected person or is no longer a suspect person (s 13).

A medical officer may give such orders as are thought fit in relation to the disposal of the body of a deceased person who, at the time of death, was an infected person or a suspect person (s 15).

A person who contravenes or fails to comply with a provision of, or an order under, this Act or the Regulations for which a penalty is not provided by a provision of this Act or the Regulations other than this section, is punishable upon conviction by a fine of $1,000 or imprisonment for six months (s 38(2)).

A prosecution for an offence against a provision, or an order under this Act or the Regulations shall not be commenced unless approved by the Chief Medical Officer (s 38(3)).

Note also that some States of Australia make those who deliberately infect others with HIV guilty of an offence.

New South Wales

Public Health Act 1991

Infectious diseases appear in Schedule 1 to the Public Health Act 1991. The Public Health (Scheduled Medical Conditions) Regulation 1991 provides that AIDS is a Category 2 condition (to be notified by medical practitioners) and human immunodeficiency virus (HIV) infection is a Category 3 condition (to be notified by laboratories). AIDS is also listed in Schedule 3 as a notifiable disease. Both AIDS and HIV infection appear in Category 5 of Schedule 1.

A person who knows that he or she suffers from a sexually transmissible medical condition is guilty of an offence if he or she has sexual intercourse with another person unless, before the intercourse takes place, the other person:

(a) has been informed of the risk of contracting the condition from the person with whom intercourse is proposed, and
(b) has voluntarily agreed to accept the risk.

Penalty: 50 penalty units ($5,000) (s 13(1)).

An owner or occupier of a building or place who knowingly permits another person to have sexual intercourse at the building or place for the purpose of prostitution and, in doing so, commits an offence under s 13(1), commits an offence (s 13(2)). For the purposes of this section, a person is not to be presumed incapable of having sexual intercourse if the only ground for the presumption is the age of the person (s 13(3)).

'Sexual intercourse' means sexual connection by the introduction into the vagina, anus or mouth of a person of any part of the penis of another person, or cunnilingus (s 13(4)).

A person who suffers from a Category 2, Category 3, Category 4 or Category 5 medical condition, is in a public place or other place of public resort (including public transport) and fails to take reasonable precautions against spreading the medical condition is guilty of an offence (s 11(1)). It is a defence if, at the time of the commission of the alleged offence, the person concerned was ignorant of the existence of the medical condition on which the prosecution is based (s 11(2)).

These offences are summary and can be heard only by a magistrate (s 79(1)). Proceedings for a summary offence must be commenced within six months from the time the alleged offence occurred (s 56 Justices Act 1902). A conviction, sentence or order other than a public health order can be appealed.

Queensland

Health Act 1937

'Human immunodeficiency virus infection' was declared to be a 'notifiable disease' and a 'controlled notifiable disease' for the purposes of the Health Act 1937 by a notice published in the Government Gazette on 4 June 1988.

Any person who knowingly infects another person with a controlled notifiable disease commits an offence against this Act unless at the time the disease was transmitted to that other person, that other person:

(a) was the spouse or de facto spouse of the first-mentioned person;
(b) knew that the first-mentioned person was infected with the controlled notifiable disease; and
(c) voluntarily accepted the risk of being infected.

Penalty: 200 penalty units or two years' imprisonment or both (s 48(3)). [Note: s 48 now states: 'A person must not deliberately or recklessly put someone at risk of infection (sub-s (2)) or infect someone else (sub-s (3)) with a controlled notifiable disease. A person does not commit an offence against sub-s (2) if, when the other person was put at risk of infection from the disease, the other person knew the person was infected with the disease and voluntarily accepted the risk (sub-s (5)).']

All proceedings in relation to controlled notifiable diseases must be heard in camera (s 48(7)).

All offences against the provisions of the Act, and all penalties, forfeitures, costs and expenses, unless otherwise stated, are to be prosecuted under the Justices Act 1886 (s 176).

Unless otherwise stated, proceedings for an offence against the Act may be a summary manner within time limited by the Justices Act 1886 or within six months after the Chief Health Officer or the Local Authority first became aware of the offence, whichever is the later (s 177).

South Australia

Public and Environmental Health Act 1987

Criminal Law Consolidation Act 1935

Human immunodeficiency virus is both a notifiable disease and a controlled notifiable disease for the purposes of the Act.

A person infected with a controlled notifiable disease shall take all reasonable measures to prevent transmission of the disease to others. Penalty: $10,000 (s 37(1)). Offences against the Act are summary offences (s 45(1)). Proceedings for an offence against this Act cannot be commenced except upon the complaint of:

an authorised officer;

a member of the staff of the Commission;

the chief executive officer of a local council;

a member of the police force; or

a person acting on the written authority of the Minister (s 45(2)).

Proceedings with respect to an offence under this Act must be commenced within one year after the date on which the offence is alleged to have been committed (s 45(3)).

Victoria

Health Act 1958

Health (Infectious Diseases) Regulations 1990

Under the Health (Infectious Diseases) Regulations 1990, 'Acquired Immunodeficiency Syndrome', 'HIV types I and II' and 'HTLV type I and all other forms' are declared to be 'infectious diseases' for the purposes of the Health Act 1958. 'Acquired Immunodeficiency Syndrome' is also declared to be a 'notifiable disease'.

A person must not knowingly or recklessly infect another person with an infectious disease. Penalty: 200 penalty units. It is a defence to prove that the person infected with the infectious disease knew of and voluntarily accepted the risk of being infected with that infectious disease (s 120).

Unless otherwise expressly provided, all complaints of and information for offences under this Act may be heard in a summary way before a magistrate (s 444). There is a right of appeal to the County Court (s 445).

Where an offence is punishable by summary conviction, an information must be laid within 12 months from the time when the matter of such information arose (s 26(4) Magistrates Courts Act 1989). [Note: s 26(4) has been repealed.]

Western Australia

Health Act 1911

Health – Dangerous Infectious Diseases Order 1991

Health – Infectious Diseases Order 1991

In 1983, AIDS was declared to be an infectious disease and a dangerous infectious disease for the purposes of the Health Act 1911. AIDS-related complex, lymphadenopathy syndrome, and HTLV III infection were declared to be infectious diseases and dangerous infectious diseases in 1985. In 1991, these declarations were replaced when AIDS and HIV infection were declared to be infectious diseases and dangerous infectious diseases.

Any person who:

(a) while affected with any infectious disease, wilfully exposes himself in any public house, or in any public place, or public vehicle without proper precautions against spreading the infection; or

(b) while affected as aforesaid, enters any public vehicle, without previously notifying to the owner, conductor, or driver thereof that he is so affected; or
(c) being in charge of any person so affected, so exposes such person or allows him to do anything in breach of this section,
commits an offence (s 264(1)).

It is an offence where a person:

(a) sells, gives, lends, transmits or exposes any things which have been exposed to infection from an infectious disease, unless they have first been effectively disinfected, or proper precautions have been taken against spreading the infection;
(b) lets a house or room to be shared or occupied in common by or with a person suffering from an infectious disease;
(c) lets a house or room in which there is, or has been, any person suffering from an infectious disease, unless the premises have been disinfected to the satisfaction of a medical officer of health or a health surveyor as certified by a certificate under the officer's hand;
(d) when letting premises, conceals the fact that a person suffering from a dangerous infectious disease has been living there within the previous six weeks (s 267).

The provision of accommodation to a hotel guest or lodger in a common house is deemed to fall within s 267(b)–(d) . . .

It is an offence for the occupier of a factory or contractor to allow the cleaning, repair, or manufacture of clothes in a dwelling-house, or building occupied therewith, while an inmate of the dwelling-house is suffering from an infectious disease (s 279).

It is an offence for a person knowingly or negligently to send to school a child who has been suffering from a dangerous infectious disease within the past three months, or who has been resident in a house in which such disease has existed within the past six weeks, without a certificate from a medical practitioner that the child is free from disease and infection and unless the clothes of the child have been properly disinfected (s 285).

Proceedings may be brought by the local authority (ie, the relevant municipality) or by the 'health surveyor' of the local authority (s 358). The offences are to be prosecuted summarily before two or more justices (s 362).

Australian Capital Territory

Public Health Act 1928

Public Health (Infectious and Notifiable Diseases) Regulations 1983

On 30 September 1983, an amendment to the Public Health (Infectious and Notifiable Diseases) Regulations declared 'Acquired Immunodeficiency Syndrome' to be a 'notifiable disease'. While HIV infection is classified as neither an infectious nor a notifiable disease in the ACT, persons with HIV infection may be deemed to be 'suffering from AIDS'. Where the organism presumed to cause an infectious or notifiable disease is found to be present in a person, that person is deemed to be suffering from that disease (Reg 3(3)). (It has been noted that the common tests for HIV do not detect the presence in the body of the virus, but identify the presence of the antibodies to the virus.)

Although AIDS is a notifiable but not an infectious disease under the Act, the definition of 'contact' includes people who, in the opinion of the Medical Officer of Health, may have been exposed to or been a source of an infectious or a notifiable disease. The regulations noted below also apply to people suffering from infectious diseases.

Any person who knows that he or she is a contact must not wilfully go into a house or place to which the public have resort, or any public vehicle, without taking proper precautions against spreading the infection (Reg 13).

A person who is in charge of a contact is prohibited from allowing the person under his or her control from breaching Reg 13 (Reg 14). A person in charge of a vehicle in which a person known or believed to be a contact has been conveyed must disinfect the vehicle if required to do so by the Medical Officer of Health (Reg 20).

A person who contravenes or fails to comply with a provision of these Regulations or the terms of a notice, requisition, instruction, direction or order given under these Regulations is guilty of an offence and, on conviction, is punishable by a fine not exceeding:

(a) in the case of a continuing offence – the aggregate of $500 and an amount, not exceeding $1,000, calculated at the rate of $50 for every day during which the offence continues; and
(b) in any other case – $500 (Reg 23).

The above laws have been the subject of some scrutiny and concern in the literature, see generally Godwin, J, 'Detention of people with HIV/AIDS' (1989) September National AIDS Bulletin 30; Hamblin, J, 'Health care: rights and responsibilities' (1992) May Law Society Journal 66; Lansdell, GT, 'AIDS, the law and civil liberties' (1991) 154 Medical Journal of Australia 61; Donovan, R, 'The plaguing of a faggot, the leperising of a whore: criminally cultured AIDS bodies, and "carrier" laws', in Bessant, J, Carrington, K and Cook, S, *Cultures of Crime and Violence*, 1995, Melbourne: La Trobe University Press.

Note that in Tasmania a different solution to the 'AIDS' problem has been adopted. Rather than including AIDS as a notifiable disease within the Public Health Acts, the Tasmanian Legislature passed, in 1993, the HIV/AIDS Preventive Measures Act. Any person in that State may request an AIDS test and must give consent before the test is administered. Note that consent in this context is defined to mean 'consent given without any force, fraud or threat and with knowledge and understanding of the medical and social consequences of the matter to which the consent relates'. Patients may, under the Act, be required to undergo HIV testing before surgical procedures; though if they refuse consent it is not clear whether they may be forced to do so.

A patient's HIV status is the subject of strict confidentiality protection in Tasmania.

PART III: A NATIONAL STRATEGY ON AIDS?

1998 CCH *Australia Medical Law Reporter* [22–550]

The Federal Government published its first National HIV/AIDS strategy in August 1989 to provide a framework for an integrated response to the HIV epidemic and a plan for action across a range of policy and programme activities. The main themes of the first strategy were prevention, education, and high quality health care. The second strategy, published in October 1993, continued these themes and fine-tuned the first Strategy in recognition of advances made in biomedical and social research and in epidemiology. During the first two strategies, Australia was one of the few countries where the incidence of HIV infection declined . . .

The third strategy (December 1996–1999) built on the second strategy to provide a framework for an integrated response to the HIV epidemic in the context of sexual health and related communicable diseases in Australia . . . The five priority areas to guide implementation of the third strategy are education and prevention, treatment and care, research, international assistance and co-operation and legal and ethical matters.

For up to date information on the National HIV/AIDS Strategy, see:

http://www.health.gov.au

The current National HIV/AIDS Strategy builds on an important foundation established under previous HIV/AIDS Strategies – the partnership between and with affected communities, governments at all levels, and medical, scientific and health care professionals . . . The Strategy expresses a commitment by the nation to the pursuit of two goals, namely:

- to eliminate the transmission of HIV; and
- to minimise the personal and social impacts of HIV infection.

7

TRANSPLANTS

Transplants are often thought of as a medical miracle. The ability of a person to give life by donating part of himself or herself to others is quite extraordinary. Small pause though gives rises to several questions. In the chapter on criminal law aspects of treatment, we saw that a person, in giving consent to treatment being performed on him or her, is consenting to what otherwise would be a battery. Public interest favours this as being one of a number of lawful exceptions. But if the removal of an organ is not to benefit the person making the donation (or worse still, where the donation of an organ might place the donor at some risk to his or her health); would public policy still favour the operation being lawful?

Following the Australian Law Reform Commission Model Legislation on Transplants in 1977, transplants in Australia are now regulated by a virtually uniform set of statutes in each State. The relevant statutes are the Human Tissue Act 1983 (NSW), the Human Tissue Act 1982 (Vic), the Transplantation and Anatomy Act 1979 (Qld), the Transplantation and Anatomy Act 1983 (SA), the Human Tissue and Transplant Act 1982 (WA), the Human Tissue Act 1985 (Tas), the Human Tissue Transplant Act 1978 (NT), the Transplantation and Anatomy Act 1978 (ACT). The provisions of this act will be examined in due course. Firstly, some of the policy issues will be canvassed.

Transplants are traditionally divided into two categories:

1 *Inter-vivos* (ie, from one live person to another);
2 Cadaveric (ie, the removal of an organ or tissue from a person after that person has died for transplantation into a living person).

In addition, it is common to distinguish between a transplant of:

1 Regenerative tissue (ie, tissue which, even if removed, will 'grow back');
2 Non-regenerative tissue (ie, tissue which, once removed, will not 'grow back').

The use of foetal tissue in transplants is beyond the scope of this work.

PART I: TRANSPLANTS IN AUSTRALIA

National Health and Medical Research Council, *An Australian Code of Practice for Transplantation of Cadaveric Organs and Tissues*, 1991, Canberra: AGPS, pp 1–3

Introduction

Organ transplantation is a valuable therapeutic measure and one which is accepted as a welcome alternative to severe debility or handicap or to premature death. Corneal, renal, bone marrow, bone, liver, heart, heart-lung and pancreas transplantations are well established procedures in Australia. In the future, however, therapeutic gain or even survival for those with severe organic disease will depend increasingly on the availability of organ donors and the retrieval of any organs suitable for transplantation.

Treatment of corneal blindness by corneal transplantation was first undertaken in Australia in 1948. Since that time several thousand grafts have been performed, most of which have resulted in significant long-term improvement of vision. However, at present, patients not infrequently are required to wait months, and sometimes years, before a donor cornea becomes available. The pattern of anterior chamber disease is changing and improved surgical techniques involving corneal transplantation are available to treat the disease. Consequently, the need for donor corneas is even more urgent.

Treatment of patients with terminal renal failure by dialysis and transplantation has been available in Australia since the early 1960s and now some 5,000 patients are supported by dialysis or kidney transplantation, some of whom also have pancreas transplants because of diabetes associated with the original renal failure. The number of patients supported by dialysis or kidney transplants increases by 10% to 16% each year. In terms of economy and personal health, renal transplantation when suitable is usually the preferred therapy but, unfortunately, some patients after starting dialysis must wait for periods of two to three years before a kidney becomes available.

Heart, heart-lung transplants and transplants of heart valves are being carried out in several Australian centres, with a five-year actuarial survival of better than 80% for the heart transplant recipients. Transplantation of heart valves increasingly is becoming a preferred procedure for those with some major valvular disorders of the heart.

Liver transplantation in Australia commenced early in 1985 and is now well established in several States. The overall one-year patient actuarial survival figure of 72% is similar to that of established overseas units. A procedure by which adult donor livers may be reduced to a size suitable for infants has meant that the lives of many children have been saved; prior to the development of this procedure, approximately one-third of children accepted for a liver transplant died while waiting for a suitable donor to be identified.

Bone autografts taken from an individual patient for use elsewhere in the same patient has been a common practice for many years. The use of massive allografts taken from deceased donor subjects for resurfacing procedures in joints, for limb salvage rather than amputation following surgery for bone tumours, and for revision total joint surgery has been available in Australia since 1986.

One of the reasons for the shortage of donors and consequent delays in offering lifesaving procedures to those in need of organ transplantation is the lack of awareness on the part of both the public and the medical profession of the extent of the shortage of donors, of the high degree of success which now results from organ transplantation, and of the benefit it brings to patients. It is estimated that, of those involved in traffic accidents and who die in hospital, at least 8% would be suitable organ donors and many more would be suitable corneal donors; at present less than 3% of those who die from road accidents become organ donors.

In recent years, educational and promotional programmes have encouraged organ donation to the extent that medical staff increasingly are being approached by relatives who enquire whether organs from dying persons can be used for transplantation; despite these efforts the number of suitable organs offered for transplant remains well below the number required. Consequently, these programmes will need to be maintained, and also reviewed regularly to assess their effectiveness, if the community at large is to appreciate fully the extent to which organ transplantation influences the quality of life and even survival for those in need of it.

Factors contributing to the lack of donor referrals are varied and involve medical and general communities alike. One important reason is actual or perceived difficulty in approaching the relatives of a potential organ donor.

Members of some families identify themselves as prospective donors but, as distressed next of kin, can easily overlook the issue of organ donation in the face of a sudden death within the family. This oversight seldom indicates that they are unwilling or unprepared to consider the option. An Australian survey suggests that the majority of the population involved wish to be consulted and by being approached gain some degree of comfort that can help compensate them for their sudden loss. Experience has shown that when relatives are approached with sensitivity, organ donation is viewed by many of them as the one positive aspect of the death of their relative.

It should not be assumed, therefore, that the next of kin are too distressed to be approached, or that the idea of organ donation would be inappropriate due to religious or cultural beliefs. All major religions regard organ donation as a gift of life and there are no objections by any religious group to the receiving of a transplant.

While the important decision is the responsibility of the most senior available next of kin, it is also appropriate for other members of the family to consider whether or not donation of organs is to be made. If members of the family are given an opportunity to discuss their position, free of any pressure to provide consent, they are more likely to be confident that the decision made is the right one. A decision about organ donation is obviously made easier if the wishes of the patient are known or the issues had been discussed.

The staff who have been responsible for the care of the potential donor, and who have established a relationship with the family, can play an important role in confirming that there is no objection to organ donation. This requires an acceptance that, even if all attempts to save the life of their relative have been unsuccessful, other lives can be enriched and indeed saved by their gift.

Many hospitals have formulated their own policies for approaching relatives; the procedures involved should be as flexible as possible in recognition of the fact that each situation is different. The whole process of organ and tissue transplantation is a complex and busy one. Nevertheless, the dignity of the setting in which patients and their families are placed during this process must be recognised and maintained by all those actively engaged in clinical management . . .

PART II: *INTER VIVOS* TRANSPLANTS

The situation of transplants at common law is aptly summarised by Dworkin.

Dworkin, G, 'The law relating to organ transplantation in England' (1970) 33 Modern Law Review 353

The first heart transplant at the end of 1967 fired the imagination of the world. It also proved to be the signal for medical teams in many countries to perform heart transplants, lung transplants, liver transplants and also to step up the rate of kidney transplants. The term 'spare-part surgery' became part of popular language. Today doubts are still being expressed as to whether or not there has been a false start. The countries in which these pioneer operations are occurring have been caught unawares and the medical, legal, ethical and social issues are still being debated.

This is a new area of medical endeavour; its consequences are still so speculative that nobody can claim an Olympian detachment from them. Those who work outside the field do not yet know enough about it to form rational and objective conclusions. Paradoxically, those who work in the thick of it . . . know too much and are too committed to their own projects to offer impartial counsel to the public, who are the ultimate judges of the value of spare-part surgery. (Longmore, D, *Spare Part Surgery*, 1968, at 169, Aldus, New York.)

. . . surgical operations were lawful if four conditions were satisfied:

(i) The patient must give a full, free and informed consent. The importance of consent cannot be overemphasised. American and Canadian courts have examined the nature of legal consent in surgical cases to a far greater degree than courts in England. It is clear that, in any common law jurisdiction, the general principle is that a patient should be informed of all the material facts relating to the operation which would enable a reasonable person to weigh up the risks and benefits and arrive at a rational decision whether or not to undergo the operation. Also, there should be no unfair pressure upon the patient which induces him to give his consent in spite of all the risks.

(ii) The operation must be therapeutic: it must be expressly for the patient's benefit. The major distinguishing feature between surgical operations and unlawful mutilation is, of course, that all surgical operations are allegedly in the medical interests of the patient. Coke refers to a case in 1603 where 'a young and lustie rogue prevailed upon a friend to cut off his left hand, so that he might be better able to beg'. Both were found guilty of the crime of maim; today, they would also be criminally liable. In the criminal codes of some countries, the provisions concerning surgical operations expressly state that they must be for the patient's benefit; in other countries this, until recently, has been accepted as being obvious.

(iii) There must be lawful justification. This is a relatively unexplored and open-ended requirement. Ethical and social questions are more relevant here and the courts may occasionally use this rubric to extend the law to meet new circumstances. Most surgical operations are lawful. The most obvious example of an unlawful operation is that of abortion because, apart from those cases where abortion is permissible under the [English Abortion Act], abortions are statutory criminal offences, whether performed by doctors or unqualified persons . . .

(iv) Generally, the operation must be performed by a person with appropriate medical skills. This is a requirement which does not raise any problems in the context of the discussion in this article.

It has been suggested, convincingly, that it is time that the law's attitude towards surgery became more realistic:

An operation should be treated as a positive, beneficent, admirable action from the outset, not as a lawful infliction of harm. It is a cure, and only where essential elements are lacking in a situation does it become wrongful. After all, we do not construe marital, or nowadays even extramarital, intercourse as rape licensed by virtue of consent and perhaps registration (Daube, D, *Ethics in Medical Progress*, 1966, p 193) . . .

Is it lawful to remove a kidney from a live donor?

The legality of live donor transplants turns upon whether or not the first three conditions for lawful surgical operations are satisfied.

First, is the operation therapeutic? There is no doubt that the purpose of a kidney transplant is to benefit the donee. It seems equally clear that to take a kidney from a living donor can rarely be of any benefit to him. It is arguable that the donor who is left with one healthy kidney may be in no worse position than the patient with two, since after a time the remaining kidney apparently does the work of two. Indeed, it may be that life insurance companies would accept an otherwise healthy donor as a normal risk. The difficulty, however, arises should anything happen to the solitary kidney: a kidney illness to a person with only one kidney is generally far more serious than to a person with two. A kidney transplant, then, in most cases can be of no therapeutic value to the donor.

Secondly, is there lawful justification for the surgical procedure? It has been suggested that the removal of a kidney from a healthy donor is not a maiming in the accepted sense because it is no great disability in most cases to lose one kidney. One calculation suggests that the total risk involved to the donor is 0.12%, divided into an immediate risk of 0.05% as a post-operative accidental risk, and 0.07% as the risk of any kind of accident occurring later to affect the remaining kidney. Whether or not this can be said to be a maiming, it is most certainly the infliction of bodily harm which is capable of being more than transient or trifling.

Arguments, of varying force, can be put forward to support the view that such transplants are lawfully justified. Thus, the courts have by implication recognised the legality of some kinds of homografts; for example, the practice of taking blood from donors for the purposes of blood transfusions is incapable, without more, of being legally challenged today. The position of a blood donor and a kidney donor, although in some ways similar in kind, is, however, clearly different in degree. It is difficult to categorise the blood transfusion procedure as the infliction of bodily harm of more than a trifling or transient nature.

Perhaps a closer, though by no means close, analogy is that of skin grafting. In an American case, *Bonner v Moran* ((1941) 126 F (2d) 121), a court held a surgeon liable for trespass when a 15 year old boy consented to skin grafts being taken from his body for the benefit of his badly burned cousin. The basis of the decision was that the boy was not old enough to give his consent, and his parents should have done so for him. By implication, it can be argued that the court would have allowed a non-therapeutic skin graft had the proper consent been obtained.

Another argument is that the courts should treat a volunteer in this situation in the same favourable way as rescuers. A volunteer who risks his life or exposes himself to injury, for example, in rescuing a person from a fire, is not condemned for his actions if he has acted reasonably, nor are they regarded as unlawful; instead, he may be entitled to recover damages for any injury he suffers from the person whose negligence created the dangerous situation. The courts treat rescuers favourably: 'danger invites rescue' is now an accepted phrase. If this is so, the law should look favourably on him as he is a volunteer donor so that the act would not be categorised as unlawful.

These are merely some arguments which a willing court might use if it was prepared to restate the existing law to meet new medical trends. Speaking extra-judicially, Edmund Davies LJ has said that he would:

> be surprised if a surgeon were successfully sued for trespass to the person or convicted of causing bodily harm to one of full age and intelligence who freely consented to act as donor – always provided that the operation did not present unreasonable risk to the donor's life or health. That proviso is essential. A man may declare himself ready to die for another, but the surgeon must not take him at his word ((1969) Proceedings of the Royal Society of Medicine 633, at 634).

Until this issue is judicially or legislatively resolved, however, it is arguable in legal theory that the taking of a kidney from a healthy donor is normally an unlawful operation.

Thirdly, is there an informed voluntary consent? Even if the courts were to decide that live donor transplants were, within limits, lawfully justified, problems could arise in connection with the donor's consent to the removal of a kidney. In addition to all the strict requirements that the donor must be fully informed of all the relevant facts and risks, so that he can make up his own mind, difficulties may arise in those situations where the donor and donee are related. The relationship between donor and donee may be, for example, that of twins or parent and child: in these family situations the social and psychological pressures upon a person who knows that his failure to give consent will result in the death of the sick person must be very strong indeed. It may often be difficult to decide whether a consent in this situation is truly voluntary. It is true that where doctors are in doubt whether the donor's consent is in fact voluntary they may solve the problem (for the donor, at least, and his family, though not for the potential donee) by saying that the donor is medically unsuitable. Although the medical prospects are better where the blood relationship is closest, the chances of a truly voluntary consent are greater where the relationship is distant or non-existent . . .

In legal theory then, the transplantation of kidneys or other organs from live, healthy donors could be attacked as being unlawful operations although the question is not free from all doubt. Medical practice has, by and large, progressed in this field without too much attention to the niceties of the law. But can surgeons ignore the strict legal position, confident that no legal proceedings will be taken against them unless they have been negligent? It may be true that the chances of criminal proceedings being brought against a surgeon are slight, but they cannot be ruled out entirely. If the donor dies during the operation or immediately afterwards there is, technically, a risk of a manslaughter charge. Similarly, it may be unwise to assume that a donor is unlikely to bring civil proceedings against the medical authorities, merely because he appears to have given his voluntary consent. If the health of the donor suffers, at the time of the operation or afterwards, he may feel aggrieved and take proceedings; if the donor dies, leaving dependents, financial factors may encourage litigation . . .

PART III: CAN A PERSON BE SAID TO OWN HIS OR HER BODILY PARTS?

We are all familiar with the proposition that, generally speaking, the owner of property is free to alienate (that is, sell or give away) his or her own property. It is also common for people to, for example, sell their hair for use in such things as wigs. Is it possible, then, that a person could sell (or give away) his or her own body parts? Putting the question another way, does the law recognise property in human body parts?

The negative answer to this question is based largely on the vagaries of English legal history. Until an Act known as the Judicature Acts, there were a number of different courts, each exercising their own (sometimes conflicting) legal jurisdictions. One of this set of courts was known as the Ecclesiastical Court (or the Church's Court). After someone's death, his soul was said to proceed to the next world and was thus properly the province of the Ecclesiastical Courts. The Common Law and Equitable Courts (the precursor to the modern courts) had no jurisdiction over the body after death. From this, the common law rule developed that the common law recognised no rights in human body parts. This common law was 'imported' to Australia by the Australian Courts Act 1828.

The history of this rule is analysed in some depth by Matthews, P, 'Whose body? People as property' (1983) 36 Current Legal Problems 193, pp 208–14. The rule's modern application is explored by Griggs in the extract reproduced below.

Griggs, L, 'The ownership of excised body parts: does an individual have the right to sell?' (1994) 1 Journal of Law and Medicine 223

Introduction

Medical biotechnology has created a use and a demand for human tissue that was unforeseeable 20 years ago. Today the heart, liver, kidney, cornea, hormone-producing glands, ears, skin, bone and blood are all capable of transplantation. However, the demand for these body parts far exceeds the supply. There are approximately 2,000 people waiting for kidney transplants and the average waiting time is about three years. Some 20% of patients awaiting heart-lung transplants die because organs are not available. One possible solution to overcome this imbalance would be to recognise a property interest (that is, ownership by the individual) in body parts. It is an issue that has become extremely important in North America and will assume greater importance throughout the world as medical advances allow for greater uses to be made of spare body parts.

Are body parts susceptible to a common law notion of ownership?

The common law idea of ownership is different from the Roman notion of ownership. The latter accepted that a person exercised '*dominium*' over an item to which they were entitled. Any person entitled to *dominium* could claim from another person by an action called *vindicatio*. This required the person to show that the thing was his or hers and there was no necessity to name a defendant. The owner was the person who claimed a thing by this action. Possession, on the other hand, was really a matter of fact. By contrast, the common law systems have all drawn a crucial distinction between ownership and possession. Possession may be considered to be nine-tenths of the law but it would, in most situations, be regarded as something less than ownership. For example, if a car is lent for a specific purpose, the bailee (the person in possession) is not entitled to sell or give the car away. The owner, by comparison, has something larger, a greater bundle of rights that he or she can exercise. Ownership in this sense is the largest bundle of rights known to property law. It allows the person the fullest enjoyment of the property and the ability to use, manage and freely alienate that thing.

There is no doubt that an individual possesses, uses and manages their body parts. For example, an individual can waste and/or destroy their lungs or liver by tobacco consumption or excessive drinking. In addition, a person can remain the owner of their body parts indefinitely. But does the individual have the right to the capital of the part and the incident of transmissibility? In essence, can a person claim full common law ownership (as distinct from possession) of their organs and sell them? This is an issue that arose directly in the United States decision of *Moore v Regents of University of California* (793 P (2d) 479 (Cal 1990)).

Moore v Regents of University of California

In 1976 Moore had his spleen removed as part of his treatment for leukaemia. During the period from 1976 to 1983, Moore had samples of his blood, bone marrow and other substances taken, allegedly as part of his treatment. These samples were used to further the biotechnological research of Moore's physician, Dr David Golde. During one visit, Moore was requested to alter his admission form to read that he would consent to research on the excised body parts. Moore consulted a solicitor who discovered that Dr Golde and his research assistant, Shirley Quan, had established and patented the Mo-Cell Line, the potential profits of which were estimated to be nearly US$3 billion. Moore brought 13 causes of action against the hospital and Golde and Quan.

Both the Californian Court of Appeal and the Supreme Court recognised that patients should have some rights over the fate of their body tissues. The majority of the Court of Appeal protected that interest by finding property rights in body parts, so any use of those parts by researchers without the consent of the patient was conversion. The majority of the Supreme Court rejected that analysis, concluding that there was no precedent for finding property rights in the human body and that policy did not support the extension of property law to recognise the human body. Instead, the majority found that patients' rights are best protected by imposing fiduciary obligations on surgeons towards patients. The result is that surgically removed tissues cannot be used without the patient's consent.

While this decision ultimately rejected the notion of property (and thus ownership) in the human body, the current state of the law in Australia is not as precise.

Property rights in the human body

The general common law rule is that there is no property in a dead body. The rule was recognised in decisions such as *Haynes's Case* (1614) 12 Co Rep 113 and *Exelby v Handyside* (1749) 2 East PC 652. Another source of the 'no property' rule was the writings of Coke who considered that 'cadaver' was an acronym for '*caro data vermibus*' (Latin for 'flesh given to the worms').

In Australia, the issue is complicated by the High Court decision in *Doodeward v Spence* (1908) 6 CLR 406. This case considered the ownership of a stillborn child. The plaintiff was a showman who exhibited the child, the infant having two heads. Upon prosecution for indecent exhibition of a corpse, the defendant police officer took the child and upon the plaintiff claiming the return of the exhibit, the police only gave back the bottle and preserving fluid. The plaintiff brought an action in detinue. The High Court, by a majority of two to one, ruled that the plaintiff was entitled to the return of the exhibit. In the majority, Griffith CJ stated:

> I do not know of any definition of property which is not wide enough to include such a right of permanent possession. By whatever name the right is called, I think it exists, and that, so far as it constitutes property, a human body, or a portion of a human body, is capable by law of becoming the subject of property. It is not necessary to give an exhaustive enumeration of the circumstances under which such a right may be acquired, but I entertain no doubt that, when a person has by the lawful exercise of work or skill so dealt with a human body or part of a human body in his lawful possession that it has acquired some attributes differentiating it from a mere corpse awaiting burial, he acquires a right to retain possession of it, at least as against any person not entitled to have it delivered to him for the purpose of burial (at 414).

In dissent, Higgins J adopted the rule that there was no property in a human body, whereas Barton J, the other majority judge, was only prepared to make an exception to the general rule in the case of the stillborn infant. His Honour considered that the general rule applied to an unburied corpse and that in this case the stillborn infant could not be said to be awaiting burial. Barton J stated:

> It has never existed independently of the physical attachment to the mother. It was never alive in the ordinary sense of human life. It has never drawn the breath of life so as to have expired, for it was stillborn. It has been preserved in a jar or bottle with spirits since the day of its birth, now 40 years ago. Add to these facts that it is an aberration of nature, having two heads. Can such a thing be, without shock to the mind, associated with the notion of the process that we know as a Christian burial? . . . Do not all these considerations lead us to doubt whether such a thing as a deadborn foetal monster, preserved in spirits as a curiosity during four decades, can now be regarded as a corpse awaiting burial, the thing which judges have discussed in decisions and lawyers in textbooks? (at 416).

According to Matthews:

> On the question of property in unburied corpses, we have the ratio of a dissenting judge and the *obiter* of one majority judge, against the ratio of the other majority judge. It is therefore not easy to assess the significance in precedent terms ... of *Doodeward v Spence* (Matthews, above, at 214).

It was accepted in the decision of *Rank Hovis McDougall's Application* (1974) 46 Australian Official Journal of Patents, Trade Marks and Designs 3915 that property rights could exist in living things. In that case, a patent was successfully obtained for the process of isolating a micro-organism and the variations induced in that organism. The Patent Act 1990 (Cth) also recognises that a micro-organism can be patented. It should be noted, however, that s 18(2) of that Act states: 'Human beings, and the biological processes for their generation, are not patentable inventions.' The United States Supreme Court, in *Diamond v Chakrabarty* (1980) 447 US 303, has also accepted that an invention may be the subject of patent protection even though it consists of living matter. The common law has also accepted in times past that the human body can be the subject of ownership.

Due to the decision of *Doodeward v Spence*, it is difficult to provide a general principle that accurately summarises the law in Australia. What can be said is that there is no clear statement that a person can exercise ownership over their body or body parts.

Examples where property rights in body parts have been accepted

Courts and legislatures have accepted that renewable body parts can be the subject of ownership. The sale of blood in American jurisdictions, the recognition of property in hair, urine and bone marrow, and the existence of sperm banks all indicate that the individual can exercise proprietary rights over the human body. However, the same recognition of non-renewable body parts has not been made. It does not appear that the legislatures of the States and Territories have altered the commonly accepted position that there is no property in a human body . . .

Arguments for and against property rights in body parts

A number of arguments can be raised against the sale of body parts. The obvious contentions are that human body parts are not tradeable commodities, that transacting in human flesh takes us back to the days of slavery, and that disadvantaged members of society will be 'further victimised by being forced to sell their organs for needed funds'. On this last point, allegations have been made that South American children have been adopted by European couples, but then murdered and their kidneys, testicles and hearts sold for between A$40,000 and $100,000. 'It was [also] reported in the London *Daily Telegraph* that in Hong Kong one could purchase kidneys obtained from felons executed in Canton in the People's Republic of China for $11,000.' There have also been documented cases of 'outright theft of organs'. Further, it is argued that the supply of diseased and unhealthy organs will increase and that the already high cost of medical care will rise.

Conversely, it could be argued that the finding of proprietary rights in an individual is consistent with:

> . . . protecting the integrity of individuals and extends rather than reduces individual rights. The law already gives individuals powerful rights to determine what is done to their bodies while they are intact and supports this by sanctioning the killing of another to protect oneself. It is anomalous to give this level of protection to the intact body and yet give the source of a detached part no rights whatsoever (Huynen, S, 'Biotechnology – a challenge for Hippocrates' (1991) 6 Auckland University Law Review 534, at 539).

How can the supply of transplantable organs be increased?

Various measures have been recommended to increase the supply of body parts. Australia, instead of opting for a system whereby people elect to be organ donors, could make it mandatory that people donate unless they choose not to. However, one method that would give recognition to the interest of the individual in their own body and provide for an immediate cash benefit is to develop 'some form of futures market in cadaver organs'. This would involve people receiving a cash benefit today in return for the right to remove their organs on death.

This would allow the decision to donate to be made rationally at a non-stressful time by the donor, who is also able to enjoy the reward. The scheme could be entered into by potential donors for life, or on an annual basis with the option to contract out at renewal.

Conclusion

The demand for organs available for transplantation can only increase as medical advances allow greater opportunities for this type of surgery.

However, the idea that these body parts can be recognised as property is fraught with difficulties.

> The notion of property becomes more sophisticated and involved with power and politics as things serve purposes other than to provide for the enjoyment of their owner . . . If there are ready alternatives for the thing then others will not want it and exclusion is pointless. There is thus a sense in which property is a factor of scarcity. (Bradbook, AJ, MacCallum, SV and Moore, AP, *Australian Real Property Law*, 1991, Sydney: Lawbook Co, at 18–19.)

There is no doubt that the supply of transplantable body parts is scarce and as medical technology continues unabated the demand for hearts, livers, kidneys and other transplantable organs will increase. The need for greater organ donation will become correspondingly greater. 'Although the point might rarely arise in practice, it would seem absurd that these valuable objects (for they are, when severed, nothing more) should continue to be treated as *res nullius*.'

The 'no property' rule was adopted in an era that could not foresee the possibilities brought to us by medical science. It is time that the right of an individual to claim and retain ownership (and thus property) in their own body is recognised. 'If a flourishing "spare part" market should arise, then it is up to Parliament to regulate it.'

PART IV: TRANSPLANT LEGISLATION

The common law as to transplants has been extensively modified in Australia by statutes. The relevant statutes are summarised in the extract below.

CCH *Australian Health and Medical Law Reporter*, paras 19–030–19–240

Trading in tissue

All jurisdictions prohibit 'trading in tissue'. This means making contracts or arrangements by which, in return for some sort of remuneration, a person agrees to:

- sell or supply tissue, or the right to take it, from their own or another person's body;
- sell the right to a postmortem or anatomical examination of their own or another person's body.

The buyer of such tissue or rights is also covered by the section. Furthermore, advertising for the sale or purchase of such tissue or rights is prohibited. Any such contracts or arrangements are void, ie of no effect, and legally unenforceable.

The prohibition does not extend to the following situations:

- the tissue has been treated or processed and the sale or supply is made so that it can be used by a medical practitioner for therapeutic, medical or scientific purposes;
- necessary expenses involved in the removal of tissue under the legislation are reimbursed;
- ministerial authorisation has been obtained.

LEGISLATION

NSW Human Tissue Act 1983 (s 32)
Vic Human Tissue Act 1982 (ss 38–40)
Qld Transplantation and Anatomy Act 1979 (ss 40–44)
SA Transplantation and Anatomy Act 1983 (s 35)
WA Human Tissue and Transplant Act 1982 (ss 29–30)
Tas Human Tissue Act 1985 (s 27)
ACT Transplantation and Anatomy Act 1978 (s 44)

Definitions

With minor variations, the following definitions apply for the purposes of the legislation.

Child

A person who has not attained 18 years of age and (except in Western Australia and Queensland) is unmarried.

Regenerative tissue

Tissue which, after injury or removal, is replaced in the body of a living person by natural processes.

Next of kin

Means 'senior available next of kin'.

Senior available next of kin

1 In connection with a deceased child means (in the following order):

- a parent;
- a brother or sister 18 years of age or over; or
- a person who was a guardian of a child immediately before death.

2 In connection with a deceased adult means (in the following order):

- a person who was a spouse of the deceased immediately before death;
- a son or daughter 18 years of age or over;
  a parent of the deceased; or

- a brother or sister of the deceased who is 18 years of age or older.

Note that the classes of kin are in hierarchical order so that when there are members of more than one class available, consents must be sought from the given by a member of the most closely related class.

Some jurisdictions have special provision for the inclusion of adoptive parents/children or persons of the half-blood in these classes.

Tissue

Includes an organ or part of a human body and a substance extracted from, or from a part of, the human body. It includes ova, semen and foetal tissue except where these are specifically excluded. Blood is excluded from the sections on tissue generally and considered separately.

Transplantation

Is deemed in most of the legislation to include the transplantation of any part of tissue or substance obtained from it.

Designated officer

In most of the jurisdictions, a designated officer is the medical practitioner who has the relevant duties under the Acts. Each jurisdiction provides for the appointment, removal, etc of these officers. In Queensland, Tasmania and the Northern Territory, the duties are discharged by persons variously described, eg 'person in charge of the hospital' (NT). The statutes provide also for their appointment, removal, etc. New South Wales has provision for a designated specialist who has responsibilities under the death definition provisions.

LEGISLATION

NSW Human Tissue Act 1983 (ss 4; 5)
Vic Human Tissue Act 1982
Qld Transplantation and Anatomy Act 1979 (ss 4; 6)
SA Transplantation and Anatomy Act 1983 (ss 5; 6)
WA Human Tissue and Transplant Act 1982 (ss 3; 4)
Tas Human Tissue Act 1985 (ss 3; 4)
NT Human Tissue Transplant Act (ss 4; 5)
ACT Transplantation and Anatomy Act 1978 (ss 4; 5)

Donation of tissue by living persons

Scope of discussion

In this section of the commentary, blood, ova, semen/spermatozoa and foetal tissue are excluded from consideration.

Adults

Regenerative tissue

Typically, a living adult of sound mind, following medical advice which explains the nature and effect of the removal, may give his or her written consent to the removal of specified tissue. In most jurisdictions, the terms of the consent must be stated, ie which tissue is to be removed and for which of the purposes permitted under the statutes.

In some jurisdictions, this consent must be signed in the presence of the medical practitioner who furnished the advice.

In South Australia and Western Australia, it is expressly stated that family members and/or friends must be absent when the consent is signed.

All jurisdictions except South Australia and Western Australia require an accompanying certificate to be given by the designated officer or medical practitioner present when the consent was given.

This certificate, with slight variations, must typically state:

- the terms of the consent;
- that the requisite medical advice was duly furnished;
- that the consent was given in the presence of the certifier;
- that the donor is an adult of sound mind; and
- that the donor's consent was freely given.

Non-regenerative tissue

The terms and conditions under which a living adult of sound mind may consent to the removal of non-regenerative tissue are the same as for regenerative tissue (see above). However, this may only be for the purpose of transplantation into the body of another living person. Furthermore, the tissue removal may only take place 24 hours or longer after the consent was signed. This allows the donor a 'cooling-off period'. The accompanying medical certificate (where required) must additionally specify the time at which the consent was given.

All tissue donated is tested for HIV antibodies. Donors must also make a declaration that to their knowledge they are not HIV positive.

LEGISLATION

NSW Human Tissue Act 1983 (ss 6–9)
Vic Human Tissue Act 1982 (ss 5–12)
Qld Transplantation and Anatomy Act 1979 (ss 8–12)
SA Transplantation and Anatomy Act 1983 (ss 7–10)
WA Human Tissue and Transplant Act 1982 ss (6–10)
Tas Human Tissue Act 1985 (ss 6–10)
NT Human Tissue Transplant Act 1978 (ss 6–10)
ACT Transplantation and Anatomy Act 1978 (ss 6–10)

Children

Note that some jurisdictions (ie Victoria, Queensland, Western Australia and the Australian Capital Territory) state that any reference to 'parents' in these sections is not to be read as including a reference to the guardian of a child or to another person standing *in loco* to a child.

Regenerative tissue

All jurisdictions (except the Northern Territory) provide for the removal of regenerative tissue from children. However, this must only be for the purpose of transplantation into the body of a parent or sibling. In Western Australia, Tasmania and the Australian Capital Territory, this is extended to include transplantation into the body of a relative.

Consent may be given in writing by a parent of the child, following medical advice as to the nature and effect of the removal, which must be furnished to, and understood by, both parent and child.

In all jurisdictions except South Australia and Western Australia, an accompanying certificate must be provided by a designated officer or medical practitioner which typically must restate the terms of the consent and:

- that the requisite medical advice was duly furnished;
- the consent was given in his or her presence;
- the parent was of sound mind and freely gave the consent;
- that the child understood the nature and effect of the tissue removal and transplantation;
- the child was in agreement with the proposed procedure.

In Queensland, a cooling-off period of 24 hours is additionally required.

In South Australia, the tissue removal must be approved by a ministerial committee.

Only Victoria and Queensland make provision for removal of regenerative tissue from a child who does not, due to his or her age, understand what is going on. These States provide that the relevant designated officer or medical practitioner additionally certify that they are of the opinion that the proposed recipient family member is in danger of dying without the transplant. In Queensland, there is the added proviso, which must also be certified, that the risk to the donor child is minimal.

Non-regenerative tissue

The Australian Capital Territory is the only jurisdiction which makes provision for the removal of non-regenerative tissue from a child. All other jurisdictions forbid it, expressly or impliedly.

In the Australian Capital Territory, the tissue removal may only take place when a family member is in danger of dying without a transplant and both parents of the child consent to the procedure. These two requirements must be incorporated into a certificate given by the relevant medical practitioner, which also contains the other declarations noted above. The matter must then be referred to a ministerial committee for decision. Where only one parent is available, the matter may still be referred to the committee.

LEGISLATION

NSW Human Tissue Act 1983 (ss 6; 10–11)
Vic Human Tissue Act 1982 (ss 5; 13–17)
Qld Transplantation and Anatomy Act 1979 (ss 12A–12E)
SA Transplantation and Anatomy Act 1983 (s 7; 11–14)
Tas Human Tissue Act 1985 (ss 5; 10–13)
ACT Transplantation and Anatomy Ordinance 1978 (ss 6; 11–14)

Revocation of consents or agreements

All the legislation provides that any of the consents or agreements mentioned in the preceding discussion may be revoked at any time, orally or in writing. Such revocation is conclusive.

In New South Wales, Victoria and the Northern Territory, more complex provisions require that certain persons, eg the medical practitioners attending the donor (in or out of hospital), nurses or nurses' aids, to whom the donor has indicated his or her revocation, must inform the designated officer or equivalent. The designated officer or equivalent must then make enquiries as to whether anyone is proposing to remove tissue and inform them that consent has been withdrawn. They must also return the consent and accompanying certificate to the potential donor.

In Victoria the revocation must be recorded and the record retained for three years.

LEGISLATION

NSW Human Tissue Act 1983 (ss 12–15)
Vic Human Tissue Act 1982 (ss 10; 11; 16)
Qld Transplantation and Anatomy Act 1979 (ss 13–15)
SA Transplantation and Anatomy Act 1983 (ss 15–17)
WA Human Tissue and Transplant Act 1982 (ss 15–17)
Tas Human Tissue Act 1985 (ss 14–17)
NT Human Tissue Transplant Act (ss 11–13)
ACT Transplantation and Anatomy Act 1978 (ss 15–19)

Effect of consents or agreements

All jurisdictions provide that the appropriate consents, agreements and certificates are 'sufficient authority' for the removal of the specified tissue for the specified purpose. (The consent of the recipient will have been obtained under the usual procedures for surgery.) However, the tissue removal must not be performed by the medical practitioner who gave the certificate.

This 'sufficient authority' means that the medical practitioner who performs the removal will have a statutory defence to any action for trespass by the donor and the procedure will be lawful.

Lack of sufficient authority will render the practitioner criminally liable.

All jurisdictions except South Australia and Western Australia expressly indicate situations where consents and certificates are not sufficient authority. Essentially, this occurs where the medical practitioner proposing to remove tissue knows or has reasonable grounds for suspecting that:

- consent has been revoked;
- a relevant certificate contains statements which are false or misleading (in a material particular – NSW);
- a child donor is no longer in agreement with the proposed procedure.

LEGISLATION

NSW Human Tissue Act 1983 (ss 12–15)
Vic Human Tissue Act 1982 (ss 10; 11; 16)
Qld Transplantation and Anatomy Act 1979 (ss 13–15)
SA Transplantation and Anatomy Act 1983 (ss 15–17)
WA Human Tissue and Transplant Act 1982 (ss 15–17)
Tas Human Tissue Act 1985 (ss 14–17)
NT Human Tissue Transplant Act (ss 11–13)
ACT Transplantation and Anatomy Act 1978 (ss 15–19)

Removal of tissue after death

Definition of death

In all jurisdictions except Western Australia there is now a statutory definition of death which states that death has occurred when there is:

- irreversible cessation of all brain function; or
- irreversible cessation of blood circulation.

In all jurisdictions except Western Australia and Queensland this definition applies for the purposes of the whole law of the jurisdiction.

In Queensland, it applies only for the purposes of the Transplantation and Anatomy Act. Note, however, that cessation of brain function is the test where life support systems are in use.

In Western Australia, although there is no statutory definition, for the purposes of human tissue removal, the Act provides that tissue shall not be removed until two medical practitioners have certified that all brain function has irreversibly ceased.

Coroners' consents

It is important to note that under no circumstances can the tissue removal go ahead without the consent of the coroner where he or she would have jurisdiction under the various Coroners Acts or, in the Northern Territory and Australian Capital Territory, where there is no death certificate.

All jurisdictions confirm that the coroner may make conditions on his or her consent and that the consent may be oral and confirmed later in writing.

Where a donor is unconscious and/or on life support systems

Tissue may be removed after death for the purposes specified by the legislation.

When a potential donor is unconscious before death, the designated officer (or equivalent) may make enquiries as to whether the person had ever expressed a consent or objection to organ donation during his or her lifetime. Any election is conclusive. If no election can be ascertained, then the senior available next of kin may be asked if he or she objects (see 19–050). His or her indication may be acted on unless the donor recovers consciousness.

If after reasonable enquiries the existence or whereabouts of the senior available next of kin cannot be ascertained, then the designated officer (or equivalent) may authorise tissue removal.

Effect of authorisations

When authorisations have been obtained under the requirements of the legislation, they constitute sufficient authority for the tissue removal to proceed, with the provisos that:

- the removal may not be carried out by the medical practitioner who gave the authorisation nor a medical practitioner who carried out the examination referred to above;
- the removal must proceed under the terms of the consent or authorisation.

LEGISLATION

NSW Human Tissue Act 1983 (ss 22–27; 33)
Vic Human Tissue Act 1982 (ss 25–27; 41)
Qld Transplantation and Anatomy Act 1979 (ss 22–25; 45)
SA Transplantation and Anatomy Act 1983 (ss 21–24; Death Definition Act 1983, s 2)
WA Human Tissue and Transplant Act 1982 (ss 22–24)
Tas Human Tissue Act 1985 (ss 23–26; 27A)
NT Human Tissue Transplant Act (ss 17–23)
ACT Transplantation and Anatomy Act 1978 (ss 26–31; 45)

Transplantation of cornea

The surgical technique to transplant cornea from a deceased person into a living person with cataracts has been available much longer than those transplantation techniques which require long courses of immunosuppressive therapy in order to be successful. By comparison, corneal transplantation carries with it fewer risks than kidney or heart transplantation. However, in order to be suitable for transplantation, the cornea must be removed from the deceased within six hours of death. A Doctor has not always been available within this time limit, meaning that tissue that could have been used is lost. New South Wales, Victoria, South Australia and Western Australia have taken action to rectify this situation by providing legislation to allow suitably trained authorised personnel, other than medical practitioners, to remove the cornea so that it may be prepared for transplantation into a living person. This legislation does not affect the need for a medical practitioner to certify death, or the need to obtain consent from relatives to obtain the tissues for transplantation purposes.

LEGISLATION

NSW Human Tissue Act 1983 (s 27(A))
Vic Human Tissue Act 1982 (s 25(b))
SA Transplantation and Anatomy Act 1983 (s 24(1)(b))
WA Human Tissue and Transplant Act 1982 (s 24(1)(b)(c))

Tasmania

Donors must make a declaration relating to their medical suitability for donation. A person who has undergone HIV testing in accordance with the HIV/AIDS Preventive Measures Act 1993 is not liable in any civil or criminal proceedings if he or she believes on reasonable grounds that the result of the test was negative.

Northern Territory

A declaration from the donor must be obtained in the prescribed form.

Australian Capital Territory

The Australian Red Cross Society, hospital or medical practitioner is protected from liability if the Society obtains from the donor a declaration in a form approved by the Minister and a blood sample is tested and the result is negative.

For a more detailed discussion of the limitation of liability for the inadvertent transmission of HIV/AIDS.

LEGISLATION

NSW Human Tissue Act 1983 (Part IIIA)
Vic Health (Infectious Diseases) Regulations 1990 (Schedule 6)
Qld Transplantation and Anatomy Act 1979 (s 48A)
SA Blood Contaminants Act 1985 (ss 4; 5)
WA Blood and Tissue (Transmissible Disease) Regulations 1985 (Regs 5(1); 6(1); 9(1); 10(1))
Tas Blood Transfusion (Limitation of Liability) Act 1986 (ss 4; 5); HIV/AIDS Preventive Measures Act 1993 (s 8(3))
NT Notifiable Diseases Act 1981 (s 26A(2)(a); Schedule 6)
ACT Blood Donation (Acquired Immune Deficiency Syndrome) Act 1985 (ss 4; 5)

Use of bodies for teaching purposes

Legislation in some jurisdictions (Vic, SA, Qld, Tas, ACT) specifically regulates donations of tissue for anatomical purposes and schools of anatomy. In Western Australia, the valid authorisation of a postmortem examination is sufficient authority for the use of the body for teaching purposes.

The legislation in each State and the Australian Capital Territory provides for schools of anatomy to be established/authorised by the Minister (or Governor-in-Council, Qld). The Minister can make regulations for the control of the schools and these regulations typically closely regulate such things as:

- the way in which the body is transported to the school;
- the conditions under which examinations, teaching and study are to be carried out;
- the furnishing of return, etc by the person in charge;
- precautions to be taken with regard to receipt, custody and subsequent burial or cremation of bodies;
- appointment of Government inspectors and inspection of schools.

Adults

All jurisdiction provides that adults of sound mind may consent to removal of blood from their body. The removal must be for transfusion or the use of the blood (or any of its constituents) for other therapeutic medical or scientific purposes. The consent may be oral or written and constitutes 'sufficient authority' for the blood removal.

Authorised premises for blood removal

Some jurisdictions (Vic, Tas, NT, ACT) prescribe the places (eg, hospital, Red Cross premises) where the blood removal is to be carried out. However, most jurisdictions have further special public health requirements which must be observed when blood is removed from a person. In New South Wales, any private organisation can establish a commercial blood bank provided that its services meet the same high standards as the Red Cross blood bank under terms specified in the Human Tissue Act 1983. In order to carry on a business of supplying blood, blood products (or semen) an authorisation must be obtained from the Director General of the Department of Health. The Director General may impose conditions or restrictions when issuing the authorisation. These conditions may be subsequently varied or the authorisation may be revoked if the organisation has failed to comply with a condition of the authorisation. The legislation provides for the appointment of inspectors who have powers of entry, inspection and seizure of suspected contaminated goods.

Children: parental consent

All jurisdictions except the Northern Territory make provision for the parent of a child to consent to the removal of blood from a child for the purposes stated above. Some jurisdictions also allow a guardian to so consent.

The parental consent only constitutes sufficient authority when medical advice is of the opinion that the blood removal will not be prejudicial to the health of the child and the child is in agreement with the procedure. However, most jurisdictions now have further special public health requirements which must be observed.

Special provisions concerning blood donations

All jurisdictions now have various Acts and Regulations concerning blood donation and the transmission of HIV.

Blood transfusions to children without parental consent

Legislation in each State or Territory provides for blood transfusions and other medical treatment to children without parental consent in emergency situations, either by specific provisions dealing with blood transfusions or under general consent in emergency situations.

LEGISLATION

NSW Children (Care and Protection) Act 1987 (s 20A); Human Tissue Act 1983 (Part IIIB)
Vic Human Tissue Act 1982 (ss 20–24)
Qld Transplantation and Anatomy Act 1979 (s 20)
SA Transplantation and Anatomy Act 1983 (ss 18; 19); Consent to Medical Treatment and Palliative Care Act 1995 (s 13(5))
WA Human Tissue and Transplant Act 1982 (ss 18–21)

Tas Human Tissue Act 1985 (ss 18–21)
NT Human Tissue Transplant Act 1978 (ss 14; 15)
ACT Transplantation and Anatomy Act 1978 (ss 20–23)

Declarations concerning HIV/AIDS

As an additional safeguard against HIV infection, all donors are required to make a declaration about their sexual contacts and self-administration of intravenous drugs since the emergence of the epidemic.

New South Wales

Before blood or tissue can be received for transfusion or transplantation, a certificate must be signed by the donor as to his or her medical suitability as a donor. A penalty is imposed if a person knowingly signs a false or misleading statement.

Victoria

Statements must be obtained from donors by the Red Cross Society or its agent, voluntary workers or a hospital verifying the medical suitability of the donor. Donors making false statements concerning material particulars are liable to a penalty or imprisonment and are also exposed to possible civil liability.

Queensland

It is an offence to knowingly give false or misleading information in regard to body tissue to be used for transplant or transfusion.

South Australia

Donors of blood or semen must provide declaration as to their suitability as donors. The liability of donors, the Red Cross Society, hospitals and persons administering blood transfusions is limited providing that declarations have been sought and obtained from donors.

Western Australia

Donors of blood and other tissue are required to make a declaration as to their medical suitability for donation.

The conditions under which removal of a body to a school of anatomy may be authorised and the effect of such authorisations mirror the conditions for postmortem examinations.

In Queensland, the positive consent of the deceased must, however, be in writing attested to by two witnesses. The purposes are expressed to be for anatomical examination and for study and teaching.

LEGISLATION

Vic	Human Tissue Act 1982 (ss 28–37)
Qld	Transplantation and Anatomy Act 1979 (ss 31–39)
SA	Transplantation and Anatomy Act 1983 (ss 29–34)
WA	Human Tissue and Transplant Act 1982 (s 28)
Tas	Anatomy Act 1964 (ss 3–9; 12–20)
ACT	Transplantation and Anatomy Act 1978 (ss 36–43)

In 1990, the National Health and Medical Research Council produced *An Australian Code of Practice for Transplantation of Cadaveric Organs and Tissues.* Much of the Code is a restatement of the law on the topic of transplants. Note the practical advice extracted below.

National Health and Medical Research Council, *An Australian Code of Practice for Transplantation of Cadaveric Organs and Tissues*, 1991, Canberra: AGPS

Choice

Patients who may become suitable organ donors after death are those who have suffered severe and irreversible brain damage; such patients will be dependent on artificial ventilation or expected shortly to become so. Other donors may be suitable for tissues such as blood vessels, bone, corneas, heart valves and skin.

Patients who are unsuitable as donors are:

patients with malignant disease, excluding those with primary brain tumours and those with low-grade localised tumours of skin;

patients with any known disease of the donor organ;

patients with systemic or severe localised infection;

groups at high risk of being infected with or carriers of HIV or hepatitis B virus.

In general, patients over the age of 65 years are not ideally suitable as organ donors. However, the specific requirements and constraints in relation to the selection of donors for different categories of transplantation are a matter for the relevant transplant group of donors.

It may not be easy to determine whether a patient would be a suitable donor should he or she die. In general, patients who have had a sudden irreversible arrest of cardiorespiratory function (for example, myocardial infarction), and those in the so-called 'brought in dead' category, are unlikely to be suitable as donors other than for tissues listed . . . above. Prolonged circulatory arrest is not a contra-indication to collection of corneal donor material, so that most persons who die in traffic accidents could be suitable donors. If there are any doubts about the suitability of patients in these categories, hospital staff should contact the transplant co-ordinator or experienced members of transplant teams.

When a hospital has in its care a potential organ donor the local transplant co-ordinator should be approached as soon as possible, and it should be made clear whether or not authorisation for the removal of organs has been given.

Approach to relatives

If it is known at the death of the patient, without having to ask relatives, that the deceased had consented to act as a donor (for example, if a patient carries a signed donor card or has otherwise recorded his or her wish to be considered an organ donor), there is no legal requirement in any State or Territory to establish lack of objection on the part of relatives. However, the possibility of organ donation should be discussed with the family in all cases.

If a relative objects despite the known request of the deceased patient, the hospital may, in all States and Territories, legally ignore the relatives. However, in practice the wishes of the next of kin, who usually will uphold the known request of the patient, are respected.

If it is not known at death whether the deceased had consented or objected to act as a donor, the hospital is legally responsible to make all reasonable enquiries as to the existence of relatives, and seek the views of the most senior next of kin, if removal of organs or tissues is proposed or intended.

In circumstances where a hospital has legal power to take organs or tissues from a deceased patient without reference to relatives, for example, when it is understood that a patient has no relatives or none are known to be available, every reasonable effort should still be made by the designated officer to locate the next of kin as required under the relevant legislation. If this cannot be achieved after reasonable effort, the designated officer may give the necessary authority for removal of organs.

A hospital involved in organ or tissue transplantation should decide as a policy matter what procedure it should adopt for dealing with relatives of deceased patients. The hospital must at the same time ensure that the law of the relevant State or Territory is observed.

Australian experience has shown that the transplant co-ordinator is often the most appropriate person to approach the relatives. However, there may be occasions when the person best qualified to assume this responsibility is the doctor in charge of the patient or another senior person with experience in carrying out personal interviews of a sensitive nature. In some circumstances, a social worker, nurse, chaplain or the family doctor may be the appropriate person. Any approach should be made with proper sensitivity and a feeling for the distress of the relatives. Their views should be sought wherever possible at a personal interview but there may be occasions when the only practical means of discussing the matter is by telephone. Experience shows that donor families appreciate receiving an account of the way in which the donation process operates.

Effective liaison within and between hospitals is essential if the needs of different potential recipients are to be met. Consequently, it would be appropriate for the person designated to approach relatives for permission to remove organs to seek approval to remove corneal and other tissues as part of the request.

Relatives should not normally be approached until it becomes obvious that death of the patient is inevitable, although sometimes relatives may approach hospital staff and suggest some time in advance that the patient's organs might be used for transplantation after his or her death. Relatives may also offer to consent to the removal of an organ from patients who have died but whose organs are not suitable for transplantation; in such cases reference can also be made with appropriate sensitivity to the need for tissues such as blood vessels, bone, corneas, heart valves and skin.

It is in the interest of each hospital to keep a written record of its approaches to relatives whether or not there is a legal requirement to obtain in writing any consent, non-objection or objection given or made by a relative or person approached.

It is inadvisable to remove organs from a dead minor without the consent of the family, even if the minor had requested the removal.

It has been found in practice that relatives, on an initial approach, may refuse permission but may change their minds later after they have thought and felt their way through the idea. It should be remembered that where permission is given by relatives, this constitutes not only a gift of the deceased, but their gift in part as well.

The need for bereavement counselling is emphasised and should be considered. Appropriate arrangements for support, if necessary over a period of time, should be made where possible as there is good evidence of increased morbidity and mortality in the year following unresolved grief.

There should be no contact between the recipient and the family of the donor although, as a matter of courtesy and in recognition of the significance of the donation, the family of the donor may be informed about the outcome in general terms . . .

8

COMPLAINTS

In the earlier part of this book, we discussed the circumstances in which a health care practitioner might fall below the standard expected of him or her, giving rise in the patient to a right to sue for damages. But what is the situation where, though the patient is dissatisfied, the conduct of the health care practitioner does not amount to negligence, battery or breach of contract? Or in circumstances where, although the patient wants to bring the health care practitioner's conduct to the attention of relevant authorities, the patient does not want to pursue a claim for damages?

Both of these scenarios are dealt with in complaints procedures. There are, of course, informal complaints such as that made directly to the practitioner concerned. Similarly, in respect of health care practitioners working in the public sector, the Ombudsman may conduct an investigation and make recommendations. Other than this procedure, though, patients may, in some States, make a complaint under a Health Care Complaints Statute.

PART I: COMPLAINTS SCHEMES

The background to the complaints statutes is summarised by Buetow.

Buetow, S, 'Formal complaints and disciplinary proceedings involving medical practitioners' (1995) 14 Medicine and Law, pp 559–61

> Aggrieved patients and other participants in different health systems often have a variety of procedures available to them for complaining formally about the professional conduct of medical practitioners and for having comments recorded, investigated and resolved. These procedures include administrative complaints, disciplinary proceedings, legal action and alternative dispute resolution options such as mediation, conciliation, independent expert appraisal and arbitration.
>
> Administrative complaints and disciplinary proceedings involving medical practitioners have been increasing over the past decade in countries such as the United Kingdom. In the absence of any salient diminution of standards or increase in misconduct by medical practitioners, the rise represents a growing preference by aggrieved patients for complaint mechanisms conflict resolution.

As a corollary of increased recognition of patient rights and provider accountability, complaints have been encouraged and patients, in general, seem to have become better informed than they once were about matters such as where to complain. Complaints mechanisms are a means of avoiding some of the litigious claims for compensation for injury resulting from medical care. The incidence of tort action has itself been increasing, especially in the United States, though also, for example, in the United Kingdom. Suits for civil damages often involve extensive delays and are frequently expensive and stressful. The findings of these litigation cases are often unpredictable, with few patients receiving compensation. Reconciliation in the doctor-patient relationship is unlikely.

The increases in administrative complaints and disciplinary proceedings have probably helped to slow the growth in tort actions. This is suggested, in New South Wales, for example, by the little overlap between complainants and those who sue, and by disciplinary cases being rarely subject to civil claims for compensation . . . Alternative dispute resolution procedures also have their advocates. Because of their non-adversarial character, these procedures may quickly reach, at low cost, agreements mutually acceptable to the participants in the dispute. This can help to protect the doctor-patient relationship. However these procedures, which have themselves been criticised, complement rather than replace the other options.

It is against this background that numbers of formal complaints have increased and may rise still further. In a national survey in Denmark, formal complaints were the tip of the iceberg of conflicts arising between patients and physicians. Complaints were made about just 11.7% of the 240 cases of reported patient dissatisfaction, only 14.9% of all the dissatisfied patients attributing their decision not to complain to their dissatisfaction being too slight. More frequent explanations for not complaining were that this option was perceived to be futile or too troublesome.

Administrative complaints are themselves not immune to criticism. In the United Kingdom, for example, the array of complaints procedures can be bewildering and hospital procedures for examining clinical practices and the treatment of complaints have been stated to lack rigour and be over defensive. In Australia, resort to the tort system by aggrieved patients is sometimes encouraged by the lack of openness of preventive and disciplinary processes. Nevertheless, few studies have examined the character and extent of patient complaints about alleged physician negligence or how the health authorities handle such cases from a disciplinary point of view. In Australia, such examinations have been limited to some consumer groups undertaking comparisons of the different complaints bodies that operate in the States and recommending improvements.

The 1993–98 Medicare Agreements between the Commonwealth and all the States have provided for some consistency of approach across Australia. Building on proposals contained in a national health strategy, the

> agreements have provided for the establishment by each State of an independent complaints body with powers to investigate, conciliate and adjudicate on the complaints it receives.
>
> In 1984, New South Wales became the first Australian State to set up a formal mechanism to investigate health consumer complaints. More recently, this State has legislated for, and instituted, new complaints mechanisms and disciplinary procedures to protect patient rights and regulate the conduct of the State's medical profession. Of the six Australian States, only New South Wales, Victoria and Queensland, plus the Australian Capital Territory, currently have a formal complaints body with a statutory basis. Moreover, New South Wales has long been active in enacting legislation to protect the health interests of its population, including consumers and providers of health services. A New South Wales Medical Board was established in 1810, becoming the second medical board (professional accrediting body for the medical profession) in the world, the Tasmanian Medical Board being the first . . .

Buetow refers to the establishment in 1984 of a formal mechanism to investigate complaints in New South Wales. This mechanism, the Complaints Unit, was an internal unit of the health department, established without public debate. Buetow notes that it lacked clear procedures and statutory authority to access records. A Royal Commission into the practices of the Chelmsford Hospital in New South Wales recommended that the unit be made separate from the health department. This was done by the Health Complaints Act of 1993.

What follows are some comments made by Buetow on the New South Wales scheme. Next there are some general comments about schemes in the other States followed by an extract from the Review of Professional Indemnity Arrangements for Health Care Professionals Interim Report entitled *Compensation and Professional Indemnity in Health Care*, 1994, AGPS, Canberra, which covers in some detail, the operation of the various schemes.

New South Wales

Buetow (above) at pp 562–63:

> [The Act established two bodies.] The first of these was the Health Care Complaints Commission. It replaced the Complaints Unit and was empowered by legislation to provide an independent mechanism for receiving and dealing with health care complaints including the initiation of disciplinary action against medical practitioners. The second statutory body was the Health Conciliation Registry which assumed responsibility for administering the conciliation of complaints referred to it by the commission.
>
> In response to consumer concerns about accountability, the new Act further provided for the establishment of a parliamentary joint committee to monitor and review the performance by the commission of its

statutory responsibilities. Evidence is taken in public except where it is deemed to relate to a confidential matter.

The Commission has itself been committed to accountability and the public interest though consumer representatives have expressed concern that the public interest is defined by professional standards rather that the interests of consumers. The act provided for the continuation of the Consumer Advisory Committee which had worked with the Complaints Unit since 1988 to represent consumer interests. There is still no formal mechanism of assessing consumer satisfaction with the complaints procedures though complainants dissatisfied with the handling of their complaints can seek a review of the investigation process.

Under the Health Complaints Act, any person is entitled to make a complaint free of expense about the professional conduct of a medical practitioner. To be acted on the allegations must be made in writing. The Commission is required to assist complainants lodge their complaints if asked to do so. The grounds for complaints are a criminal conviction, lack of competence, impairment, bad character, unsatisfactory professional conduct and professional misconduct.

A complaint can be made against a medical practitioner regardless of whether he or she is currently registered as such. Since early 1994, a national compendium of medical registers has operated to provide a system of mutual recognition of medical registration across State borders. The Commission and Medical Board are required to notify each other about any complaint received about a registered medical practitioner.

The person against whom the complaint has been made must be notified of the complaint as soon as practicable and always within 60 days of its receipt. Within this period, a preliminary assessment of the complaint must be made.

The Commission and Medical Board are required to consult over the appropriate course of action to take, including referral for investigation or conciliation. Investigation of complaints must take place if the commission or medical board considers this necessary. Before referral for investigation can take place, the complainant must verify the complaint by statutory declaration. The complaint must be investigated if, for example, it provides grounds for disciplinary action. The commission can initiate its own investigations into matters of public concern.

Investigations are to determine the appropriate action to be taken in respect of the complaint. To undertake an investigation, the commission, which may seek expert advice on the subject of the complaint, has powers of entry, search and seizure. If needed, a search warrant can be obtained. Obstruction of the investigation is an offence.

The Commission will prosecute complaints that are substantiated. Its inability to support individuals seeking civil damages has been criticised for denying an accessible alternative to litigation. However, recent research shows that the desire to receive financial compensation is

> less important as a reason for civil suits than is wanting to prevent recurrence of similar incidents and finding out what happened and why.

Note that under the New South Wales Act, a complaint may be dealt with via two means. Complaints which raise concerns of professional misconduct or safety are dealt with by way of investigation. Complaints not concerning these matters may be referred to a body called the Health Conciliation Registry for conciliation. This is a process of discussion and negotiation in the hope that a settlement may be reached. This process is voluntary and confidentiality is assured under the Act.

As Buetow notes, the Commission cannot order damages. It may, however, recommend changes in clinical practice or refer complaints to any registration board.

Victoria

The operation of the relevant schemes for making health care complaints is similar in Victoria and Queensland. In Victoria, the relevant legislation is the Health Services (Conciliation and Review) Act 1987. The Act establishes two bodies: the Health Services Commissioner and the Health Services Council. Complaints may be made by 'a user' (a patient) or a user's representative, that a health care provider has acted unreasonably in: refusing health care, in the manner in which health care is provided, in restricting the user's access to health care records or in disclosing them to others. Complaint may also be made that a health care institution acted unreasonably by failing to investigate a complaint.

Complaints may only be considered within 12 months of the alleged incident (unless the Commissioner determines otherwise). The Commissioner may refer a complaint for conciliation, may investigate the allegations himself or may refer matters to a registration board 'or to a person, organisation or agency'. These steps may only be taken if the Commissioner is satisfied that 'all reasonable steps' have been taken by the user to resolve the matter with the health care provider.

Queensland

The Health Rights Commission Act 1991 established the Health Rights Commission. The Act also establishes a Health Rights Commissioner and a Health Rights Advisory Council. The grounds under which a complaint may be made to the Commission are broadly the same as in Victoria. The complaint may be made by 'the user', the Minister of Health or 'any other person' where the Commissioner thinks it in the public interest to hear from that person. The same requirement as found in Victoria, that the user must have tried to resolve the matter with the practitioner first, also applies in Queensland, except where it is not practicable to do so. A similar one year time limit for complaints operates in Queensland. Complaints can either be dealt with via conciliation or investigation.

A point of departure for the Queensland Act is the requirement that the Commissioner draft, within three years, a Code of Health Rights and Responsibilities.

Linden-Laufer, S, 'A code of health rights and responsibilities: the adequacy of existing recognition and protection' (1993) 1 Journal of Law and Medicine 168

Rights

. . . Today, with the availability of more information, the public are becoming better educated. In the context of health care, people are challenging the accuracy of many long-held assumptions regarding the medical and health care community. The position of health care professionals on the 'professional pedestal' is no longer secure and today they are treated in much the same way as any other provider of goods or services.

The initial consumer movement of the 1970s was largely paternalistic in approach, with most legislation aiming to protect individuals and to provide remedies for injuries incurred. Consumerism today has taken on a different perspective, giving more recognition to concepts of individual responsibility and autonomy. This approach is reflected in many contemporary laws and regulations which tend to emphasise interests of autonomy and seek to ensure a more equal relationship between consumer and supplier. Nowhere is this more evident than in the health care arena, where the law has well and truly moved beyond simply providing protections and mechanisms of redress to giving legal recognition to the somewhat illusory concept of 'rights'.

This change in focus is especially evident in Queensland, with the passage of the Health Rights Commission Act 1991 (Qld) (the Act). In addition to setting up the Health Rights Commission as an independent body to provide for the investigation, review and conciliation of health service complaints, the Act contemplates the development of a formal Code of Health Rights and Responsibilities.

In order to understand the full implications of a formal Code of Health Rights and Responsibilities, it is appropriate first to consider the notion of rights. What does it mean to say someone has 'a right'? What is meant when one says that someone is entitled to something?

Section 3(1) of the Act defines 'health rights' as 'the rights of an individual relating to the provision of a health service', a definition that does not really take the concept very far other than placing it in the context of health services. The term 'rights' becomes all the more difficult because it can be understood at a number of different levels, depending upon the way in which the term 'rights' is actually used . . .

In analysing the meaning of 'rights', it is useful to refer to a model of rights developed by a well-known American jurist, Hohfeld. The 'Hohfeld model' of rights is a useful scheme with which to consider the implications of a Code of Health Rights and Responsibilities.

Hohfeld pointed out that the term 'rights' is apt to mislead, largely because it is used in so many different ways, both in common English usage and more importantly, in legal usage. The *Macquarie Dictionary* defines the term 'right', *inter alia*, as follows:

> . . . in accordance with what is just or good . . . in conformity with fact, reason, or some standard or principle; correct . . . correct in judgment, opinion, or action . . . a just claim or title, whether legal, prescriptive, or moral . . . that which is due to anyone by just claim . . . that which is ethically good and proper and in conformity with the moral law . . . to do justice to.

This definition clearly recognises a correlation between 'rights' and 'morality' or ethical values. If there is such a relationship between 'rights' and the ethical or moral concerns of society, then those 'rights' that do exist will need to be constantly assessed to ensure that they continue to reflect the values held by society.

The legal usage of the term 'rights' is even more variable. Essentially, Hohfeld identified four different legal uses of the term, namely:

(i) claim rights (which according to Hohfeld are true rights);
(ii) powers;
(iii) immunities; and
(iv) liberties (or, as Hohfeld calls them, 'privileges').

The difference in effect between these different uses of the term 'rights' lies in their implication for the legal relationship existing between parties.

(i) Claim rights

As a true right, a claim right implies a reciprocal duty or obligation on another identifiable person. Such rights may exist voluntarily, for example, by way of contract between parties, in which case they will be limited to the specific parties to that contract. Claim rights may also be imposed by legislation or common law, in which case they will have a wider impact.

Claim rights pervade the health care arena. For example, under the Medicare system in Australia, a person who presents at the accident and emergency unit of a public hospital has an enforceable right against an identifiable person or institution to be treated. That person or institution has a positive co-relative obligation to provide that individual with the necessary services. Similarly, under freedom of information legislation, an individual citizen has the right to access their medical records in a public institution, and that institution has a positive legal duty to provide them with access.

Likewise, at common law, reference may be made to the recent High Court decision in *Rogers v Whitaker*. By recognising the existence of an enforceable duty on the part of a medical practitioner to provide a patient with information concerning the risks involved in treatment provided by the medical practitioner (at least those risks that are 'material' in the circumstances), the High Court, in effect, gave clear legal assistance to the 'right' of a patient to be so informed. It is, however, in the context of so-called 'claim rights' that most misunderstanding and confusion exist. For example, those groups that advocate 'active' euthanasia would argue that individuals have a 'right to die'. Despite the use of 'rights' language, this is not a true claim right. If it were so, it would, in the Hohfeld sense, mean that there was a reciprocal duty or obligation on the part of a medical practitioner to accede to a patient's request for a fatal injection. Clearly, this is not the case in Australia, despite the position adopted by medical practitioners in some other countries, for example, the Netherlands, where many doctors openly give their patients the fatal injection upon request, in the belief that it is their duty or obligation.

(ii) Liberties

In many respects, the so-called 'right to die' fits better at the other end of the spectrum, as a mere 'liberty right'. Liberty rights do not entail any duty owed by another. They are often referred to as 'freedoms', indicating that there is some recognition or respect by the law for individual freedoms, such as the freedom of choice or perhaps even the broader notion of patient autonomy. In this way, the law does not impose any duty on the individual, the holder of the liberty right, which would otherwise interfere with that person's freedom to choose. In other words, 'liberties' constitute the very minimum form of protection afforded by the law in that it will not interfere with an individual's 'right' to choose. The fundamental right to autonomy is thus a liberty right in the sense that the law recognises a freedom to determine what is done to one's own body.

So, too, the 'right to die' (a specific exercise of the broader autonomy principle) is a liberty right, in that the criminal law today has removed suicide as an offence. It is not a claim right in the strong positive sense described above as there is no requirement, obligation or duty imposed on another person to assist a person to die.

However, the distinction at either end of the spectrum between 'claim rights' and mere 'liberties' is not always clear. This is because often, liberties may actually be surrounded by a perimeter of claim rights. The 'right to die' provides a good example. Through the common law on consent and more specifically refusal of consent or indeed even stronger statements by specific legislation . . . the so-called 'right to die' becomes a limited claim right in that the law provides a patient with some protection by imposing an obligation on others not to exercise their liberty rights in a way which interferes with that of the patient. Specifically, under the Victorian legislation, a medical practitioner commits a statutory offence of medical trespass if he treats a patient contrary to directions contained in a duly executed refusal of treatment certificate.

In this way, many of the 'rights' that people assert often contain liberty as well as a claim right component, and the claim right component can be either positive or negative.

(iii) Powers

Liberty rights can, and often do, become what Hohfeld refers to as powers, largely as the result of specific legislation. Hohfeld's definition of a 'power' refers to the ability to alter legal rights and duties, or legal relations in general. Powers differ from claim rights in that there is no co-relative duty imposed on another person. A good example is provided by the specific provisions that exist in most jurisdictions in Australia enabling a medical superintendent of a hospital to stand in the shoes of a parent vis-à-vis providing consent to a necessary blood transfusion for a minor. This power directly alters the legal 'rights' and relations between parent and child regarding the ability of a parent to consent to medical treatment in respect of the child.

(iv) Immunities

Finally, by his definition of 'immunities', Hohfeld appears to contemplate the situation that exists in the United States of America where there is a formal Bill of Rights, setting out a number of constitutionally guaranteed interests, for example, the freedom of speech or the right to privacy which has been utilised in both abortion and euthanasia debates. Such constitutional 'rights' cannot be readily abrogated by legislatures. In other words, the State or Government of the day cannot intervene in certain circumstances by denying individuals any freedom or liberty rights that are recognised in the Bill of Rights.

In Australia, despite much debate over the years and, indeed, more recently in Queensland, there is no equivalent Bill of Rights under the Australian Constitution. Thus, in Australia, the so-called 'right of freedom of speech' is more likely to be classified as a liberty right rather than an immunity. This is clearly an area where a formal Code of Health Rights and Responsibilities has enormous potential to alter the status of existing 'rights'.

Immunity rights can also exist outside the traditional State/citizen model. An example is provided by the High Court decision in *Re Marion*, concerning the ability of a parent to consent to the sterilisation of their intellectually impaired child. As a result of that decision, a child has, in effect, an immunity right as against the parent, in that there is imposed on the parent a disability to consent to the sterilisation of the child. That is, the parent cannot interfere with the child's liberty rights, in this case the right to autonomy and more specifically, the right to procreate.

Of course, the Hohfeld model of rights does not, itself, provide a precise mode of classification. As demonstrated above, many so-called 'rights' themselves often straddle two or more classifications. For example, anti-discrimination legislation, in one sense, creates a positive duty on the part of a medical practitioner to treat an HIV positive patient, and in this respect could be regarded as creating a claim right: that is, a right to be treated without discrimination. In another sense, this right to treatment could also be classified as a mere power, in that it imposes a liability on the part of the medical practitioner if he or she refuses to provide treatment. Despite problems in precise definition, the Hohfeld model does highlight just how difficult, indeterminate, illusory and indeed often contradictory the concept of 'rights' actually is. Nevertheless, in spite of the lack of clear division among the different types of 'rights', it is important that some formal consideration be given to these problems of definition . . .

These distinctions and problems of definition are vital in the context of determining the specific content of a Code of Health Rights and Responsibilities, and, perhaps even more importantly, deciding how such a Code is to be promulgated and enforced. Depending upon the mode in which a Code is implemented and the 'rights' that it contains, some 'rights', especially those that may currently be mere liberty rights, will take on a different legal status. If, for example, a Code is promulgated by way of legislation, it may, in effect, create new claim rights.

Rights and responsibilities

When one talks about rights, in whatever sense, it is obvious that it is not all one-sided. Some balance is required. This is reflected in the Act by the very title of the Code which refers to 'rights' as well as 'responsibilities'.

The Macquarie Dictionary defines 'responsible' as, *inter alia*:

> . . . answerable or accountable, as for something within one's power, control, or management . . . having a capacity for moral decisions and therefore accountable.

In this way, the use of the word 'responsibilities', in its ordinary, common language meaning, stands as a clear acknowledgment of the need for accountability. It recognises the existence of an obligation, both morally and perhaps even legally.

This reference to 'responsibilities', and its specific recognition and contemplation in a Code of Health Rights and Responsibilities presents as a double-edged sword. On the one hand, the reference to both 'rights' and 'responsibilities' contemplates a co-relative obligation, albeit perhaps only morally, on the other party to the relationship to be responsible for ensuring that the respective rights contained in the Code are recognised. So, for example, when one talks of the right of a patient to be informed of material risks inherent in medical treatment, this places an obligation squarely on the health care professional to provide the patient with the relevant information. This view of responsibilities is specifically recognised by the Act itself. Section 3(1) of the Act defines 'health responsibilities' as 'the responsibilities of a provider in relation to the provision of a health service'.

However, the reference to both 'rights' and 'responsibilities' also implies that the person claiming the right may themselves bear some responsibility. Nowhere is this more evident than in the context of deciding upon treatment, where the need for joint responsibility is a vital part of the decision-making process. Thus, the patient, once informed, carries the burden of responsibility for that information, as in the case of a heavy smoker, who, having been fully informed of the risks of smoking whilst taking a contraceptive pill, is ultimately accountable for the consequences of choosing to pursue that form of contraception. Similarly, one could argue, a patient bears the burden of responsibility for providing the health care professional with information that may impact upon treatment, especially if asked a specific question by the health care professional: as, for example, where a medical practitioner asks a patient about other medication currently being taken.

Interestingly, the Consumers' Health Forum of Australia, when advocating a formal Charter of Health Rights, recognised the role of patient responsibility in such a Charter, but left it to another day to consider its full implications. Does this perhaps imply that the burden of responsibility is something that patients may not be willing to assume, at least not in all cases? In this respect, perhaps Dostoyevsky's Grand Inquisitor in *The Brothers Karamazov* may have been correct in predicting that patients may not wish to assume the responsibility engendered by what he referred to as 'that terrible gift of freedom'.

This leads on to the next issue. Having canvassed briefly what is meant by the concepts of 'rights' and 'responsibilities', it is necessary to consider the intended role or effect of a formal Code of Health Rights and Responsibilities. The problem is perhaps best summed up by a cartoon from the Consumers' Health Forum of Australia depicting the need for an umbrella Code to provide health consumers with the necessary protections that are currently lacking.

One could ask: Is there really a need for an umbrella? Are consumers 'out in the rain', so to speak and, if they are, what form should the umbrella, or Code, take? These are but some of the many difficult questions involved in formulating a Code of Health Rights and Responsibilities. The consultative process in Queensland over the next year will hopefully provide some direction.

The issues raised by the analogy to an umbrella are obvious. Many of the so-called 'rights' to be contained in a Code of Health Rights and Responsibilities are already recognised in one form or another by our legal system, if not through common law actions such as negligence and trespass to the person, then through specific legislative provisions – for example, anti-discrimination legislation or freedom of information legislation.

The real question to be asked is whether any of the existing recognitions and protections afforded in law are sufficient. Is there still room for additional protection by way of an 'umbrella' Code? More importantly, what form should that protection take? Should it, for example, have a separate legislative base?

Organisations like the Consumers' Health Forum of Australia have been advocating an 'umbrella' Code for some years now. The reasons given, apart from the obvious ones of clarity and comprehensiveness, are that existing recognition or protection of 'rights', where they do exist in law, are often unclear, uncertain and inconsistent. On this point, most lawyers would concede that, at least in the case of those rights having their base in common law, there is some substance to such claims. The common law is, of course, slow to develop and keep abreast of changes, largely because it is case driven. For example, it was not until two recent High Court decisions that two important 'rights' issues were to some degree resolved.

In *Re Marion*, the High Court drew together considerable differences of opinion between divisions in the Family Court of Australia on the ability of parents to consent to the sterilisation of their intellectually impaired child. More recently, *Rogers v Whitaker* seems to have clarified the position for all States and Territories in Australia on the matter of informing patients of material risks inherent in medical treatment.

Another problem with the common law is that cases which concern such important and difficult 'rights' issues also involve complex policy considerations, a task that many would argue is better left to Parliament, the duly elected representative of the people, than to judges. This, itself, highlights the concern that issues of 'rights' and 'responsibilities', intertwined as they are with difficult questions of morality, are perhaps best dealt with after a process of public consultation.

Even where specific legislation does exist, advocates of a formal Code of Rights argue that there is considerable variation in the degree of protection afforded between the various States and Territories in Australia. For example, only Victoria, South Australia, Northern Territory and more recently the Australian Capital Territory have specific legislation recognising, in part, the right of a patient to refuse certain medical treatment in circumstances where the patient is no longer capable of expressing that wish.

The arguments against the formulation of a Code of Health Rights and Responsibilities are equally numerous. Many would argue that it is the flexible nature of the common law that enables it to adapt to changes in society. In this way, a formal Code of Health Rights and Responsibilities has inherent limitations. At best, a Code can only attempt to identify the basic principles and rights and as such, will only ever result in a 'normative' statement of principles. A formal Code of Health Rights and Responsibilities would itself, necessarily, be lacking in specifics.

The principles, rights and responsibilities contained in a Code are often written in vague terms, leaving it to others such as the courts, to imply the necessary qualifications. On the other hand, if a Code is expressed in specific terms, spelling out the exact parameters of the rights protected, there may be problems in rigidity. In particular, the Code and the protections it contains may be inadequate in dealing with unforeseen or new social situations, especially if one accepts the correlation between 'rights' and general notions of morality. The more specific and detailed the approach in formulating a Code of Health Rights and Responsibilities, the more likely that the document itself will inhibit the development and recognition afforded to future rights and freedoms, something the common law has always prided itself on doing well. This particular concern may well add further weight to the view that a Code of Health Rights and Responsibilities can, and indeed should, only contain a Statement of fundamental, universal and enduring rights, rather than those of particular relevance to contemporary society.

Once attention is focused on the content of the Code, problems exist both in identifying those rights to be contained in the Code, but equally, and conversely, those rights which might be omitted. A fundamental defect often identified with a written Code of Rights is that many 'rights' may ultimately be excluded from the formal document and may, over time, gradually become of decreasing value to society.

There are, of course, some solutions to the problem. Greater flexibility in interpretation can be achieved by adopting a general objects clause or preamble. This itself would assist in further development of rights at common law. Equally, promulgation of the Code as an ordinary Act of Parliament, rather than one having a formal constitutional base, would allow for greater flexibility and ability to amend.

There are many other important issues that should be addressed in the process of formulating a Code of Health Rights and Responsibilities. For example, in determining the content of the Code, should the rights specifically identified be recognised as 'absolute' rights, or should there be provision for restrictions in those circumstances where individual rights may need to be balanced against the broader interests of society?

Related to issues concerning the content of a Code, one may well ask a more fundamental question: what is the purpose of formulating a Code of Health Rights and Responsibilities? Is it simply to provide a universal statement of fundamental principles to guide Government in the formulation of policy and ultimately, legislation? Alternatively, should the Code be enforceable and, if so, against whom (for example, Government and other individuals) and by what means (for example, by legal action through the courts, or some other independent tribunal)? If a Code of Health Rights and Responsibilities fails to provide any specific remedy for a violation of the rights it recognises, then one must seriously question whether there is indeed a need for such an 'umbrella'. It has been said that 'a right without a sanction to enforce it is but the expression of a pious hope'. The rationale for having a Code of Health Rights and

Responsibilities that is ultimately unenforceable may be related solely to its role as a moral educator and potential standard setter.

On the other hand, some would argue, especially in the event of a statutory basis for the Code, that there will be a concomitant increase in litigation. This would result in more so-called 'defensive' medicine. More people, it is argued, would resort to the legal system for the purpose of asserting their 'rights'. The desirability or otherwise of this prospect is largely a matter for individual determination. It is, nevertheless, an important issue that must be addressed, and public input is required. Regardless of the various arguments for and against the development of a formal Code, at least in Queensland, there is a specific legislative commitment to the formulation of a Code of Health Rights and Responsibilities.

The development of a Code of Health Rights and Responsibilities for Queensland

Section 37(1) of the Act states:

> Within three years after the commencement of this Act, the Commissioner is to develop a Code of Health Rights and Responsibilities for the consideration of the Minister.

The process of developing the Code is also spelt out in the Act. Section 38 states:

> In developing the Code of Health Rights and Responsibilities, the Commissioner is to:
>
> (a) consult with the Council [that is, the Health Rights Advisory Council of Queensland]; and
> (b) invite submissions from and consult with interested persons and bodies to the extent necessary to ensure that a wide range of views is available in the development of the Code.

That process is well and truly under way. Preliminary Discussion Papers were released in August 1993 inviting interested parties to make submissions to the Health Rights Commissioner. This stage of consultation sought submissions on fundamental issues such as the sorts of rights to be included in a formal Code, what rights are currently denied in practice and the means by which existing rights can best be guaranteed. In this respect, the initial phase of public consultation focused on the principles to be taken into account in formulating the Code, as well as its scope and content. The closing date for submissions in this phase was 15 December 1993. The responses are now being analysed and used to develop a first draft of the Code. This draft Code will be made available for further public discussion and debate early in 1994. The aim is to meet the deadline set out in the Act, and have a draft Code of Health Rights and Responsibilities presented to the Minister by 1995.

As for the principles to be contained in the Code, the Act itself provides direction. Whilst giving some scope to the Health Rights Commissioner to make independent recommendations as to the content of the Code, s 39(2) and specifically s 39(3) identify the relevant principles that must be considered in determining the content of the Code. The initial Discussion Paper released by the Health Rights Commission in August 1993 included both the principles set out in the Act as well as those principles developed by the Commissioner from those specified in the Act.

Principles to be reflected in the Code

Section 39(2)(a) states:

> In developing the content of the Code, the Commissioner:
>
> (a) may have regard to all matters relevant to the provision and use of health services.

One of the principles identified by the Commissioner as relevant under this section is that every person is entitled to treatment and health services of high quality given as promptly as circumstances permit. This principle encompasses three different ideas:

(i) the right to treatment;
(ii) the right to high-quality care; and
(iii) the right to access timely and appropriate care.

(i) The right to treatment, including the right to obtain a second opinion

Under the Medicare system in Australia, this general human right of access to health care facilities is already recognised. The entitlement is, however, limited to public health services. It does not encompass any right to private health services. Indeed, this limitation has been recognised by many professional associations which make it clear that, except in cases of emergency, there is no obligation on the part of private health care providers to treat.

Examples of existing statutory recognition of this right to treatment are numerous. Section 1.6(a) of the Health Services Act 1991 (Qld), has as its stated objective:

> to ensure that the health and wellbeing of all Queenslanders is promoted, maintained and improved according to principles of social justice and equity.

At the federal level, the Human Rights and Equal Opportunity Act 1986 (Cth), Schedule 5, provides Australian residents with the means of implementing rights recognised under various United Nations treaties to which Australia is a signatory. For example, the Declaration of the Rights of Disabled Persons (1971) guarantees disabled citizens the right to medical, psychological and/or functional treatment, including medical and social rehabilitation, AIDS counselling, training and education.

Further recognition of this right to treatment is reflected in many professional codes of conduct. The Australian Medical Association's Code of Ethics (1992) states that a medical practitioner has a 'responsibility not to deny treatment to any patient on basis of colour, race, religion, political beliefs or nature of illness'. A medical practitioner could only refuse to treat in non-emergency situations and then only after giving the patient adequate notice. Equally, this could only be done where alternative care is reasonably available.

The real problem in formally recognising the right to treatment in a Code of Health Rights and Responsibilities is one of balance. Is the right to treatment absolute? To what extent is or should the consumer's right to treatment be balanced against a health provider's legitimate right to refuse to treat? Should the Code go so far as to specify situations in which a provider is obliged to treat? More particularly, should there be provision for the 'good Samaritan' situation: that is, should a Code recognise a positive duty on the part of a health professional to treat in an emergency? Such an absolute right to treatment or, more importantly, responsibility on the part of a health care professional to treat, would be inconsistent with existing legal provisions. At common law, there is no general positive duty to go to the assistance of another person, there being no general liability for omissions.

(ii) The right to high-quality care

No doubt providers, consumers and governments expect high quality health services and this is reflected in various mechanisms already in place to ensure that certain standards are maintained. Most professional codes reflect this need to maintain high standards. Further recognition at the government level is demonstrated by the National Mental Health Policy 1991, Australian Health Minister's Conference, which states, *inter alia*, that a health consumer has a 'right to timely and high-quality mental health care'. This concern with the quality of health care services is also seen in many statutes. For example, under s 3.18(2)(a) of the Health Services Act 1991 (Qld), affirms, as part of the function of a Regional Health Authority:

> . . . that health services in the region are of a high quality, delivered equitably and under regular evaluation and review.

The Pharmacy Board of Queensland has recently promulgated a statutory Code of Professional Conduct of Pharmacists under s 27 of the Pharmacy Act 1976 (Qld). Part of this Code of Professional Conduct requires a pharmacist to 'keep abreast of the progress of pharmaceutical knowledge to maintain the highest standards of professional competence'.

Perhaps one of the biggest challenges in drafting a Code of Health Rights and Responsibilities is determining whether and, if so, how, one can guarantee the delivery of a certain quality of care. There are a number of alternatives that may be considered, for example, provision for re-accreditation of all health care providers, and required participation in quality development activities and ongoing continuing education.

(iii) The right to access timely and appropriate care

This principle raises an important and somewhat political contemporary question, that is, the equity of access to health care services according to need. With increased demand to the wide range of treatments and services now available, there is increasing pressure on the health system. This has resulted in obvious shortages and the current problem of 'waiting lists'. Such issues force a consideration of a more difficult task, that is, evolving some ethical basis for allocating scarce health resources.

Again, there is already clear and wide acknowledgment of this principle in many professional codes and administrative policy statements of governments. Further recognition exists in many legislative provisions, such as the Disability Services Act 1992 (Qld), which recognises the need to plan, develop and co-ordinate disability programmes and services; and the recent Medicare Agreements Act, which contains the following:

> Principle 2: Access to public hospital services is to be on the basis of clinical need.
>
> Principle 3: To the maximum practicable extent, a State will ensure the provision of public hospital services equitably to all eligible persons, regardless of their geographical location.

This question of resource allocation is exceedingly difficult. In the context of a Code of Health Rights and Responsibilities, there are additional matters to consider – for example, whether the Code should promote the right of consumers to participate directly in these allocation questions, as was the case in Oregon, in the United States, where a list of priority services was created with direct public participation, even though the scheme was never implemented.

The Act itself identifies other specific principles that are to be reflected in the Code.

Section 39(3)(a) and (b) requires the Health Rights Commissioner to have regard to the following:

(a) that an individual should be entitled to participate effectively in decisions about the individual's health; and
(b) that an individual should be entitled to take an active role in the individual's health care.

Essentially these provisions recognise the basic principle of autonomy, the 'right' of a patient to participate in the decision-making process and notions of freedom and choice in the provision of health care. These essentially constitute the 'liberty rights' defined by Hohfeld. Most of these 'rights' are again already recognised, in one form or another, in professional codes of conduct, institutional handbooks, guidelines and protocols. In some cases the common law may elevate these liberty rights into claim rights, as in the context of consent, by way of an action in negligence and the imposition of a duty to inform of risks, as well as an action in trespass, protecting against non-consensual treatment. Further protection is afforded by State and Territories Fair Trading Acts and the Trade Practices Act 1974 (Cth), which provides for an action for misleading and deceptive conduct. Specific legislation, such as the Medicare Agreements Act 1993 (Cth), enables people to choose between being a private or public patient in a public hospital, as well as calling on State and Territory governments to provide information to users about available hospital services. Other legislative provisions address more specialised cases such as where patients have a disability or are unable to consent due to some other impairment. The Intellectually Disabled Citizens Act 1985 (Qld) enables the legal friend to give valid consent on behalf of such persons, but only after ensuring that the patient participates to the extent that is possible in light of his or her impairment. Similarly, the recent Disability Services Act 1992 (Qld) recognises these same rights in the context of the provision of services for people with disabilities.

The problem in formulating a Code of Health Rights and Responsibilities is that, whilst there is recognition already for these principles, there is, nevertheless, considerable doubt as to the extent to which they are being followed and adopted in practice. This specific concern again impacts upon issues involving the mode by which the Code is to be promulgated. Here again, the Code has enormous potential to affect the availability and adequacy of existing remedies. Section 39(3)(c) states:

> . . . that an individual should be entitled to be provided with health services in a considerate way that takes into account the individual's background, needs and wishes.

This is a clear statement recognising basic liberty rights, or freedoms, as opposed to true claim rights. What is contemplated by this provision are such things as the right of a patient to be treated with consideration, dignity, understanding and courtesy. Reference to these principles further highlights concerns regarding the mode in which the Code of Health Rights and Responsibilities is to be promulgated: if by way of legislation, these 'freedoms' might ultimately be elevated into powers or even true claim rights, thereby altering their legal status.

Another principle identified by the Health Rights Commissioner under this section of the Act is the concern that a person receiving a health service should not be abused or exploited sexually, physically or emotionally by the provider of the service. Again, this is something that is already widely recognised in many professional codes of conduct and institutional handbooks and policies. It is also an area where there are numerous existing legal protections, for example, an action for assault or unlawful detention, both of which are criminal offences under the Criminal Code (Qld). Similarly, there are many civil actions available at common law including an action for false imprisonment and a complaint of sexual harassment under Commonwealth, State and Territory legislation. There is a further offence of ill-treatment, wilful neglect or molesting a patient under most Mental Health Acts. And, of course, there is the ultimate sanction of professional disciplinary proceedings.

The requirement in the Act that the Code of Health Rights and Responsibilities specifically reflects this principle again forces a further consideration of the adequacy of existing laws and mechanisms to discipline health care providers. One particular issue for consideration in formulating the Code is whether it should not only contain statements about freedom from such abuse, but go further and provide additional protection for more vulnerable health service consumers, such as women or the elderly.

Section 39(3)(d) states:

> . . . that an individual who:
>
> (i) provides a health service; or
> (ii) provides care for another individual receiving a health service;
>
> should be given consideration and recognition for the contribution the individual makes to health care.

This statement recognises the other side of the 'rights' equation, namely the notion of 'responsibilities'. It confirms that health consumers have rights but so too do they have co-relative responsibilities.

Recognition of these co-relative responsibilities on the part of health consumers currently exists in many professional codes and institutional handbooks. Particular emphasis is placed on notions of consideration (as per s 39(3)(c) above), participation and forthrightness, especially in the context of information disclosure. Specifically, such provisions impose responsibility on the patient to follow instructions of the provider. More importantly, patients are seen as being accountable for their own decisions. From a legal perspective, of some concern in the development of the Code is an assessment of the sufficiency of existing protection given to providers. Indeed, this may well have been the impetus for including this principle specifically in the Act.

Section 39(3)(e) states:

> . . . that the-confidentiality of information about an individual's health should be preserved.

The 'right' to confidentiality and privacy is again a 'right' currently recognised by the law in various forms: for example, by professional codes of conduct; institution/health department guidelines, protocols and policies; accreditation guidelines, largely focusing on the systems in place in institutions to ensure the confidential storage of and access to files; common law actions of contract, equity or tort; and specific legislation.

Of particular concern in this context is the need to strike an appropriate balance between the individual right to confidentiality and privacy versus a third party's right to know, a problem of special significance in the context of HIV/AIDS.

Section 39(3)(f) states:

> . . . that an individual should be entitled to reasonable access to records concerning the individual's health.

Again, there is some specific recognition already afforded by legislation. Most States and Territories now have freedom of information legislation guaranteeing a patient the right to access their records in most circumstances. One limitation, however, to existing 'rights' is that they exist only in the public sector. In the private sector there is still a gap, although most private institutions appear to have their own internal policy encouraging ready access, as is the policy, for example, of the Queensland Health Department.

In developing a Code of Health Rights and Responsibilities, specific consideration may well be given to this gap, and whether a similar right of access should be recognised in the private sector. Indeed, recent reports indicate a similar approach being advocated by the Federal Privacy Commissioner.

Section 39(3)(g) states:

> . . . that an individual should be entitled to reasonable access to procedures for the redress of grievances with respect to the provision of health services.

This right is well recognised in most jurisdictions throughout Australia by the establishment of alternative complaint-handling bodies . . .

It should, however, be noted that recognition of this principle is not necessarily limited to the provision of legal mechanisms for redress. One important question for future consideration concerns the use of patient advocates. Should a Code of Health Rights and Responsibilities contain specific recognition of a right to access advocacy services? This is already recognised under the Disability Services Act 1992 (Qld), which acknowledges the need for access to advocacy services to enable those with a disability to participate adequately in decision-making. One issue that needs to be considered in the development of a Code of Health Rights and Responsibilities is whether this principle should be recognised as a specific right.

Conclusion

These are but some of the interesting challenges ahead in Queensland. Regardless of the precise form in which the Code is ultimately modelled, the task of formulating a Code of Health Rights and Responsibilities, by its very process, will generate discussion, debate and awareness of this important aspect of the health care relationship, namely the rights, duties and needs of both parties to the relationship: the patient/user and health care professional/the institution. Formal recognition of 'rights' and 'responsibilities' in whatever form can and will legitimise claims.

From another perspective, however, there is no doubt that a Code enshrining certain fundamental principles can only ever constitute half of the ultimate task. A Code of Health Rights and Responsibilities can never be expected to work like a magic wand. The mere formulation of a Code will not provide a panacea. Little will ultimately be achieved unless both parties to the health care relationship are provided with the necessary means and opportunities to facilitate the two-way process of interaction and communication that is at the very heart of most of the fundamental principles required to be reflected in the Code.

Australian Capital Territory

The Health Complaints Act 1993 makes provision, like the relevant Queensland legislation, for the formation of a Code of Health Rights and Responsibilities. The Act is similar, in its definitions of and handling of complaints to the Queensland and Victorian statutes, except that there is a two-year period within which a complaint needs to be made. The Act establishes the Commissioner for Health Complaints and a Health Rights Advisory Council.

South Australia

There is no independent complaints mechanism in South Australia. There is an Advice and Complaints Office as a part of the Health Commission in that State. The Supported Residential Facilities Act 1992 allows residents of a 'residential facility' to make complaints to the licensing authority who may investigate the claim 'and take such action as they think fit'.

Tasmania

In Tasmania the relevant Act is the Health Complaints Act 1995. That Act establishes a Health Complaints Commissioner (who, historically, has been the Ombudsman of the State of Tasmania). The Commissioner has power to investigate or conciliate health complaints.

Northern Territory

The position is similar in the Northern Territory where a Commissioner for Health and Community Services Complaints was established pursuant to the Health and Community Services Complaints Act 1998.

Western Australia

The relevant Act in Western Australia is the Health Services (Conciliation and Review) Act 1995. That Act established an Office of Health Review which has the power to investigate or refer to conciliation complaints about health services.

Review of professional indemnity arrangements for health care professionals, *Compensation and Professional Indemnity in Health Care*, 1994, Canberra: AGPS, pp 176–87

A Commonwealth discussion paper argues that a complaints body requires powers of investigation, conciliation and adjudication, and that the complaints body should have powers of search and entry of premises, powers to compel parties to attend hearings and produce documents and evidence. A summary of four of the State complaints mechanisms with a statutory basis follows. The Professional Indemnity Review (PIR) notes that in all four cases described, the intention appears to be to resolve the grievance as informally as possible, especially where a breakdown in communication between the health care professional and the patient has occurred, and to use powers conferred by legislation only where necessary, for example, where there may have been a breach of professional standards or professional misconduct.

Victoria

The purposes of the Health Services (Conciliation and Review) Act 1987 (Victoria) are to: provide an independent, accessible review mechanism for users of health services; provide a means for reviewing and improving the quality of health service provision; and set out the functions and powers of the Health Services Commissioner. The Act also provides for the establishment of a Health Services Review Council.

The Commissioner has a range of functions relating to investigation of complaints about health services; suggesting ways of removing and minimising the causes of complaints; conciliating between users and providers where a complaint has been made; recording and publishing information about complaints; and education, training and awareness regarding complaints and the procedures under the Act.

The functions of the Health Services Review Council include advising the Minister for Health on the health complaints system and the operations of the Commissioner; advising the Minister and the Commissioner on issues referred to it by the Commissioner; and, with the Minister's approval, referring matters relating to health service complaints to the Commissioner for inquiry. The Review Council consists of nine persons appointed by the Minister. Three persons represent the interests of providers and three persons represent the interests of users. The other three persons appointed have no affiliation with any professional association for users or providers or any association which represents, advocates for or advises providers or users.

If a registration board investigates or deals with a complaint concerning the provision of a health service by a provider, the board must report to the Commissioner. Before a board deals with any of the matters about which a complaint may be made under the Act, the board must give a copy of the complaint to the Commissioner. The board and the Commissioner may agree that the complaint is suitable for conciliation under the Act. If the board and the Commissioner do not agree the complaint is suitable for conciliation, the board may continue dealing with the complaint. Before accepting or referring to an authority other than a registration board, the Commissioner must give a copy of the complaint to the appropriate registration board. Where the Commissioner gives a copy of a complaint to a registration board, it must not be taken as a complaint to, or a referral of the complaint to, the board. Nor must the information provided be used by the board as the basis for any investigation, inquiry into, or other action relating to, the complaint, unless the complaint is referred to the board under Section 19(6) of the Act. Under Section 19(6), if a complaint relates to a registered provider the Commissioner must refer the complaint to the appropriate registration board if the Commissioner, after consultation, considers the board has the power to resolve or deal with the matter and the matter is not suitable for conciliation under the Act.

The grounds for complaint include that a provider acted unreasonably: by not providing a health service; in the manner of providing a health service; in providing a health service; by denying or restricting the user's access to records relating to the user; or in disclosing the user's health records. A complaint may be made that a public or private health institution acted unreasonably by not properly investigating, or not taking proper action upon a complaint, made to the institution by the user about a provider's action of the kind mentioned above. A complaint may be made that a provider acted unreasonably in any of the ways above by not following the guiding principles set out in the Preamble to the Act.

Complaints may be made by a user; a representative chosen by the user; in certain circumstances, by a user's representative recognised by the Commissioner but not chosen by the user; and a provider complaining on behalf of a user about any of the matters noted in the previous paragraph, where the provider satisfies the Commissioner that, because of the user's state of health or general situation, it would be difficult or impossible for the user to make a complaint.

Complaints may be made orally or in writing. Oral complaints may be required to be confirmed in writing, and further information may be required within a time specified by the Commissioner. A person who complains must give her or his name and such other personal identity information as the Commissioner may require. In certain circumstances, the Commissioner may keep the complainant's identity confidential. A complainant may withdraw a complaint at any time by notifying the Commissioner and the Commissioner must then stop dealing with the complaint.

The Commissioner must reject a complaint if, in the Commissioner's opinion, it is frivolous, vexatious or trivial or does not warrant investigation. If an issue raised in a complaint has been dealt with by a court, the Administrative Appeals tribunal, an industrial relations tribunal or a registration board, the Commissioner must reject the complaint to the extent to which it relates to the issue, unless the Commissioner deems it relates to matters not raised before the court, Tribunal, industrial tribunal or board. The Commissioner must reject a complaint about an incident which occurred more than 12 months before the complaint is made if there is no good reason shown for the delay. The Commissioner may reject a complaint if the complainant, when requested, does not confirm the complaint in writing; give more information about the complaint within the specified time; or give the Commissioner more personal identity information. A complaint must not be referred for conciliation or investigation unless the Commissioner is satisfied that the user, or someone acting on the user's behalf, has taken all reasonable steps to resolve the matter with the provider. Where a complaint, in the Commissioner's opinion, raises issues which require investigation by another person, organisation or agency, the Commissioner may refer the complaint as appropriate.

The Commissioner must decide within 28 days of receiving a complaint to accept it; reject it; or to refer it. In deciding, the Commissioner may make such inquiries as considered appropriate, but the Commissioner must not exercise the power to compel persons to answer questions or produce documents or to enter premises. If a complaint is accepted in whole or in part, and the Commissioner considers it suitable for conciliation, it must be referred for conciliation without delay. There are a number of circumstances where the Commissioner must stop dealing with an issue raised in a complaint, for example, if it becomes the subject of legal proceedings. The Commissioner must provide written notice to the complainant and provider within 14 days of ceasing to deal with a complaint.

Conciliators may be appointed under the Act to encourage the settlement of complaints by arranging for informal discussions between the parties; helping to conduct those discussions; and, if possible, assisting the parties to reach agreement. Generally, neither the complainant nor the provider may be represented by another person during conciliation. Evidence of anything said or admitted during conciliation is not admissible in proceedings before a court or tribunal and cannot be used by the Commissioner as grounds for exercising a power of investigation or inquiry. The conciliator must report to the Commissioner on progress and results of the conciliation process. The report must include details of any agreement reached. If no agreement has been reached, the conciliator may recommend that the Commissioner should, or should not, investigate the matter, or the conciliator may make no recommendation. On the same day, the conciliator makes a report to the Commissioner, a copy must be given to the complainant and the provider.

If the Commissioner considers that a complaint relating to a registered provider which has been referred for conciliation cannot be resolved through the conciliation process and that the provider's registration board has powers to resolve or deal with the matter, the Commissioner must refer the complaint to the board without delay. If a conciliator recommends against investigation of a complaint, the Commissioner must not investigate it, refer it again for conciliation or deal with it in any way authorised by the Act. If the conciliator makes no recommendation about a complaint, or recommends investigation, the Commissioner may investigate it; refer it again for conciliation; or deal with it in any way authorised by the Act.

Within 14 days of starting an investigation into a complaint, the Commissioner must give written notice of the investigation to the provider. The Commissioner has powers to compel attendance and call for evidence and documents in the investigation of a complaint. The Commissioner may apply for a warrant to enter and inspect premises and to inspect or take copies or extracts of documents. The Commissioner must give written notice within 14 days of deciding whether a complaint is justified to the user and the provider, including the reasons for the decision and any action the Commissioner considers ought to be taken to remedy the complaint. Generally, within 45 days after receiving a notice, a provider must report in writing to the Commissioner about action taken on the complaint. Penalties apply for non-compliance.

New South Wales

In 1984, New South Wales was the first State to establish a health consumer complaints mechanism. It was originally an administratively established investigative body connected to the New South Wales Health Department. It provides investigative services for the health care disciplinary boards in New South Wales. Following the Chelmsford Royal Commission, which recommended that it have a statutory basis and that it be independent of the Health Departments legislation was prepared to do this. Following a period of intense controversy and criticism from consumers, a revised Bill was introduced and passed in November 1993. The Health Complaints Act 1993 (NSW) establishes two statutory bodies:

> the Health Care Complaints Commission to receive and deal with complaints (the Health Complaints Unit); and
>
> the Health Conciliation Registry to administer the conciliation of complaints referred to it by the Commission.

A Parliamentary Joint Committee, to be known as the Committee on the Health Care Complaints Commission, is also provided for, to monitor and review the exercise by the Commission of its functions. This Committee was included in response to consumer concerns about the Commission's lack of accountability under the draft Bill.

The Commission must notify the appropriate authority of complaints notified to it about health practitioners registered by the authority. Before taking action on a complaint, the Commission and the registration authority must consult. If either the Commission or the Registry thinks it should be investigated, then the Commission will investigate a complaint. If neither determines it should be investigated, but if either or both believe it should be conciliated and the parties to the complaint consent, it must be referred for conciliation to the Registry. The registration authority is prevented from taking action concerning a complaint while the Commission is investigating it, or the Registry is conciliating it – except where necessary to protect the life or health of any person. The Commission is required to supply information concerning handling of complaints to registration authorities on request.

A complaint may be made about the professional conduct of a health practitioner, a health service which affects the clinical management or care of an individual, and a complaint may be made against a health service provider, even where not qualified or entitled to provide the service concerned. Health service providers include those providing alternative health services as well as the range of allopathic or traditional health services.

Any person may make a complaint. It can be made by lodging it in writing and staff of the Commission have a duty to assist a person make a complaint if assistance is requested. An assessment is made within 60 days of receipt or, where further particulars are called for, 60 days from the date specified for the particulars to be supplied to determine whether it should be investigated, conciliated, referred to the Director General of the Department of Health, referred to another person or body, or declined to be entertained.

A complaint must be investigated if the appropriate registration authority is of the opinion it should be, or if it appears to raise a public health or safety issue; raises a significant question as to the appropriate care or treatment of a client by a health service provider; provides grounds for disciplinary action against a health practitioner, or involves gross negligence on the part of a health practitioner. The complaint must be verified by statutory declaration before investigation. Investigations by the Commission are for the purpose of obtaining information concerning the matter complained of and to determine what action should be taken. The Commission may obtain an expert report; authorise officers to apply for a search warrant; or exercise powers of entry, search and seizure where the warrant is obtained.

Following assessment, the Commission may discontinue dealing with the complaint where it is frivolous, vexatious or not made in good faith; the subject is trivial; it is under investigation by some other competent person or body, or has been or is the subject of legal proceedings; it misses issues that require investigation by another person or body; there is an alternative means of dealing with it and the complainant has no sufficient reason for not pursuing the alternative means; the complaint relates to a matter which occurred more than five years before the complaint was made and the complainant has no sufficient reason for the delay; the complainant has failed to provide further particulars within the time specified by the Commission; or the complaint falls within Commonwealth responsibilities. On completion of an investigation into a health organisation, the Commission must do one or more of the following: terminate the matter; make recommendations or comments to the health organisation on the subject of the complaint (if this happens, a report must be made to the Director General and the report must include the reasons for the conclusions and the reasons for any action recommended). On completion of an investigation into a health practitioner, the Commission must prosecute, intervene in any proceedings that may be undertaken before a disciplinary body, refer the matter to an appropriate authority, if any, make comments to the health practitioner, terminate the matter or refer it to the Director of Public Prosecutions. The Commission must review a decision after assessment if requested to do so by the complainant.

The Commission may refer a complaint for conciliation where the appropriate registration authority is of the opinion it should be so referred, or, following the assessment, the complaint is not required to be investigated and the parties to the complaint consent to conciliation. The Health Conciliation Registry can only receive matters via the Commission.

On referral, the Registry must appoint a conciliator. The process is voluntary. The role of the conciliator is to conciliate by bringing the parties together for discussion, negotiation and settlement of the complaint; undertake any activity for the purpose of promoting that discussion, negotiation and settlement; and assist the parties to reach agreement.

No legal representation is permitted. An agent may appear for a party if the Registry is convinced it will facilitate the matter and the agent is able to represent the party effectively. The process is confidential. Nothing said nor any documents prepared for the conciliation process are admissible in any proceedings before a court, tribunal or body. However, source documents and documents which have not been created especially for the purposes of conciliation are not subject to this limitation. The conciliation process is terminated where either party terminates the process; the parties reach agreement; the conciliator terminates the process after concluding it is unlikely the parties will reach agreement; or a significant issue of public health or safety has been raised.

The legislation amends the Ombudsman Act 1974 to prevent the Ombudsman from investigating the conduct of a conciliator in relation to the conciliation of a complaint. It also amends the Freedom of Information Act 1989 to exempt the complaint handling, investigating and reporting functions of the Commission in relation to a complaint that is in the course of being dealt with by the Commission, and the conciliation functions of the Registry.

The PIR is aware of criticisms of the first draft of the New South Wales legislation. It was said that under the Bill the complaints commissioner: would not be independent of the Minister; would have absolute power in investigating a complaint and in assessing if disciplinary action should be taken; have discretion to ignore a complaint, with no independent review if a complaint is not acted upon; and have discretion to screen complaints and determine if they need investigation or conciliation via referral to the conciliation registry. The revised Bill appears to address many of these concerns, though it appears there is still some disquiet.

The PIR is particularly aware of consumer concerns about the complaints process raised in connection with the administration of deep-sleep therapy (DST) and with electro-convulsive therapy (ECT) at the Chelmsford Hospital in New South Wales in the 1970s. A Royal Commission found that there was no support for the use of DST, it was extremely dangerous, therapeutically ineffective and had been carried out at Chelmsford without adequate facilities, staff and equipment to deal with risks. As a result 24 patients died between 1963–79.

Three doctors who administered DST and ECT at Chelmsford had proceedings initiated against them before the Medical Tribunal in 1985–86 and in 1991 by the New South Wales Department of Health. However, in both cases, the doctors were able to obtain a permanent stay of proceedings. The complaints were said to be an abuse of the right to lodge a complaint because of the long delay since the alleged misconduct in the administration of DST. This case underlines the need for patients' grievances to be investigated and acted upon without undue delay by the appropriate complaints or disciplinary body. The conclusions of these cases have also left consumers with great dissatisfaction about the capacity of the disciplinary system to effectively deal with even the clearest breaches of standards of care. Similar outcomes on criminal cases have equally angered consumers in New South Wales.

Queensland

The Health Rights Commission Act 1991 (Qld) establishes the Health Rights Commission, comprising the Health Rights Commissioner and officers of the Commission. The Act also establishes the Health Rights Advisory Council. The Health Rights Commissioner is appointed by the Governor in Council. The Governor in Council determines the terms and conditions of appointment, and the Governor may remove or suspend a Commissioner under certain circumstances. The Commissioner is to act independently, impartially and in the public interest in performing the functions set out in the Act. The Commissioner's functions include suggesting ways of improving health services and increasing and preserving health rights; receiving, resolving and assessing health complaints; conciliating or investigating health service complaints; providing advice and reports to the Minister and to registration boards; and providing advice to the Health Rights Advisory Council.

The Health Rights Advisory Council consists of six members appointed by the Minister. Two members represent the interests of providers and two represent the interests of users. The functions of the Council include advising the Minister on the redress of grievances relating to health services; educating, advising and informing providers and users; and the operation of the Commission. The Council advises the Commissioner on the redress of health service complaints and refers matters relating to complaints to the Commissioner for advice.

If the Commissioner considers a complaint against a registered provider is not suitable for conciliation and should be investigated, and the relevant registration board has adequate functions and powers of investigation, the Commissioner may refer the complaint to the registration board, after consultation with the board. The Commissioner need not take further action on a complaint referred to a board.

A registration board receiving a complaint from the Commissioner is to perform its functions, investigate the complaint and report to the Commissioner on its findings and action taken or proposed. If a registration board receives a complaint covered by the Act, it must refer the complaint to the Commissioner and take no further action on it unless the Commissioner refers it back to the board under the Act. The Act provides for the Commissioner to receive information, comment and make recommendations about a complaint from a board, and the Commissioner may request a board to provide reasonable information. The board must comply with the Commissioner's request. The Commissioner must inform a relevant registration board of a decision to investigate or conciliate a complaint within 14 days of the decision. The board may request information on the progress and results of a Commissioner's investigation, and the commissioner must comply with the request. Where a Commissioner's report recommends that the board take action as set out in the report, the board is to report to the Commissioner on progress and results of action so taken. The Commissioner may intervene at any time in a disciplinary proceeding before a registration board in relation to a health service complaint about a registered provider and, on intervention, the Commissioner becomes a party to the proceeding.

A health service complaint may be made by the user, under certain circumstances, by persons acting on a user's behalf; the Minister; and any other person where the Commissioner considers that the public interest requires that such a person be permitted to make a complaint. The Legal Friend of an assisted citizen for the purpose of the Intellectually Disabled Citizens Act 1985 may make a health service complaint on behalf of the assisted citizen. Complaints may be made orally, either in person or by distance communication, or in writing. Generally, the Commissioner will fix a time by which an oral complaint is to be confirmed in writing. The complaint must reveal the complainant's name and address, and other personal identity information the Commissioner reasonably requires. In certain circumstances, the Commissioner may keep information confidential and may accept an anonymous health service complaint in the public interest. An oath or affidavit may be required by the Commissioner to verify a complaint.

A complaint may be made that a provider acted unreasonably: by not providing a health service; in the way of providing a health service; in providing a health service; by denying or restricting a user's access to records relating to the user; or in disclosing information about a user. A complaint may be made that a public or private body that provides a health service acted unreasonably by not properly investigating, or not taking proper action, in relation to a complaint made to the body by the user about a provider's action of kind mentioned in the Act.

Within 28 days of receiving a complaint, the Commissioner is to decide whether to accept it for assessment, or take no further action on it. Within 14 days of the decision, the Commissioner must notify the complainant with reasons for the decision if no further action is to be taken. No further action may be taken if the complaint is considered frivolous, vexatious or trivial; is misconceived or lacking in substance; or has been adequately dealt with by the Commission or another public authority. The Commissioner may decide not to take action in certain other circumstances, including where the matter of complaint arose more than one year before the complaint was made to the Commissioner, or the complainant was aware of the complaint more than one year before making the complaint to the Commissioner.

Where an assessment is to be made, the Commissioner notifies the provider also and invites submissions before the assessment is made. Before accepting a complaint for action, the Commissioner must be satisfied that the complainant has taken reasonable steps, and has been given reasonable opportunity, to resolve the complaint with the provider, or be satisfied that this is not practicable. Generally, the Commissioner gives notice to the complainant and the provider of the decision following assessment. In accepting a complaint, the Commissioner may decide to conciliate the complaint; investigate it; or refer it to a registration board.

The Commissioner may appoint conciliators. A conciliator's function is to encourage the settlement of the complaint. Any matters of public interest are to be drawn to the attention of the conciliator by the Commissioner before the conciliation begins, and at the start of the conciliation, these matters are drawn to the parties' attention by the conciliator. The conciliator must report to the Commissioner on any matters of public interest raised by the complaint, unless previously identified by the Commissioner. The conciliator reports to the Commissioner as the Commissioner requests and must do so at the conclusion of conciliation. If agreement has not been reached, the Commissioner may investigate the complaint; refer it to a registration board; decide not to take further action; or further conciliate the complaint. Parties reaching agreement may enter into a contract in settlement of the complaint. Anything said or admitted during conciliation cannot be used as evidence in a court or tribunal and cannot be used by the Commissioner as grounds for an investigation or inquiry.

In investigating a complaint, the Commissioner has power to require a person to provide specified information; attend and answer questions; and produce a specified record in the person's possession. Penalties are available for non-compliance. In certain circumstances, entry and search may be effected by authorised persons and evidence may be seized. The Commissioner may refer matters raised by, or in the course of, investigations to a person or body which has a function or power under an act of the Commonwealth or State to investigate the matter. Where the Commissioner refers a complaint and requests reports on progress or results of the person or body's investigations, the request must be complied with. The Commissioner's powers of investigation are not affected by such a referral.

At any time the Commissioner may make a report in relation to an investigation. Reports may be given to the complainant; the provider; an employer of the provider; a registration board; a professional association; the Minister; or any person or body that has a function or power to take action on matters raised in the report. The report may contain, as the Commissioner considers appropriate, information; comment; opinion; and recommendations for action. Comments adverse to a person or body identifiable from the report must not be included unless the person or body has been given an opportunity to make submissions on the adverse comment and to give the Commissioner a written statement in relation to the comment. If a statement is provided, and the Commissioner is requested to include it in the report, the Commissioner must include it, or a fair summary, in the report.

Australian Capital Territory

The Health Complaints Act 1993 (ACT) was passed in December 1993. It establishes the Health Complaints Unit and a Health Rights Advisory Council. The Act provides for the Executive to appoint a Commissioner for Health Complaints. The instrument of appointment may specify terms and conditions related to the Commissioner's appointment and, under certain conditions, the Executive may terminate the appointment of a Commissioner for Health Complaints. Except as provided for by the Act, the Commissioner for Health Complaints is not subject to the direction of any other person in relation to the performance of a function under the Act. The Act provides for the Minister to direct the Commissioner to enquire into, and report on, a specified matter relating to the provision of a health service and to participate in a proceeding under the Health Professions Boards Procedures Act 1981.

The Commissioner's functions include receiving and resolving health service complaints; enabling users of health services to contribute to the review and improvement of health services; and providing education and advice in relation to health rights and responsibilities.

The Health Rights Advisory Council's functions include advising the Minister and the Commissioner in relation to the redress of grievances relating to health services or their provision; and referring to the Commissioner any matter that may be properly dealt with by the Commissioner under the Act. The Council is to consist of five members appointed by the Minister for a term of not more than three years. Two members are to represent the interests of users and two are to represent the interests of providers.

If a health profession board receives a complaint which appears to be covered by the Act, the board must notify the Commissioner and provide relevant information in its possession. If the Commissioner so requests, the complaint must be referred to the Commissioner. A board which has referred a complaint to the Commissioner, must not take any action on it, unless it is referred back to the board or a report on the complaint from the Commissioner is given to the board. Where the Commissioner refers a complaint to the board, the board must notify the Commissioner in writing of whether it intends to conduct a proceeding and whether it has taken, or intends to take, any other action in relation to the complaint and, if so, details of that action. The Commissioner may be a party to any proceeding.

The grounds for complaint include that a provider acted unreasonably by not providing health services; the provision of the service, or part thereof, was unnecessary; a provider acted unreasonably in providing the service; the provider failed to act with due skill; a provider failed to treat the user in a considerate way; and a provider failed to respect the user's privacy or dignity. Grounds for complaint cover situations where a user was not provided with relevant information relating to informed choice; about sources of further advice or education; about treatment and services received; or any prognosis that it would be reasonable to be provided with. Complaints may be made that a provider acted unreasonably by denying or restricting a user's access to records; not making information available about the user's condition that the provider was able to make available; in disclosing information about the user; or by not taking proper action in relation to a complaint made to her or him by the user.

Complaints may be made by the user, or where the user has attained 18 years, by a person appointed by the user to make a complaint on the user's behalf; where the user has not attained 18 years, by a parent or guardian; the donee of a power of attorney; by a person who has the care of the affairs of a user under any other law or order of a court; a person approved by the Commissioner, if it is difficult or impossible for the user to make a complaint; and in certain circumstances, by the provider of another health service. Generally, a complaint is to be in writing, signed by the complainant, disclosing the complainant's name and address. The Commissioner may require the complainant to provide further information or documents, or verify information by statutory declaration. A complainant may withdraw a complaint at any time by written notification.

The Commissioner must assess a complaint received and, if it is not to be referred to another body, then the Commissioner may refer the complaint to a conciliator for conciliation, investigation, or no further action.

The Commissioner must not refer a complaint for conciliation if it appears to indicate the existence of a significant issue of public safety or public interest; or a significant question as to the practice of a provider; or Section 27 would prevent the Commissioner from disclosing to the provider information that would enable the user to be identified. Section 27 of the Act deals with the circumstances under which confidentiality of details about the user and the complaint must be preserved by the Commissioner.

The Commissioner must take no further action on a complaint where satisfied that the complainant or the matter complained of are not covered under the Act; the user became aware of the circumstances giving rise to the complaint more than 24 months before the complaint was made; reasonable steps have not been taken by the complainant to resolve the grievance with the provider; all the issues involved in the complaint have been adjudicated upon by a court, tribunal, board or other person or body established by law; a court has commenced a hearing that relates to the subject matter of the complaint; the complainant has been given reasonable information/explanations and there would be no benefit in entertaining the complaint further; the complaint lacks substance; the complaint is frivolous, vexatious or was not made in good faith . . .

The Commissioner may appoint conciliators whose function is to encourage a settlement of a health service complaint. A complainant or provider shall not be represented by another person in the conciliation process unless the Commissioner is satisfied that such representation is likely to assist substantially in resolving the complaint. A conciliator shall report on progress with conciliation when requested to do so by the Commissioner, or when the conciliator is satisfied that agreement has been reached by the complainant and the provider, or when satisfied that it is not possible for agreement to be reached on all or some of the issues. Any agreement reached in the conciliation process may be put in a form that is binding on both parties.

In investigating a complaint, the Commissioner may require a person to appear and/or produce documents and/or answer questions; and take possession of, and retain for a period not exceeding two months, documents or records. There are penalties for refusing to be sworn or make an affirmation, answer a question, provide information, or produce a document or record.

The Commissioner must prepare a report of findings and conclusions at the completion of an investigation, and may do so during the course of an investigation. A copy must be given to the complainant, and may be given to the Minister, or a provider mentioned in the report, or certain other persons or bodies.

If, after investigating, the Commissioner views the complaint as justified, but it appears incapable of resolution, the Commissioner may give the provider a notice and advise the complainant of the notice. A notice must set out any action the Commissioner considers the provider ought

> to take in order to remedy each unresolved grievance disclosed by the complainant, among other things. A provider receiving a notice has 45 days to inform the Commissioner in writing of action taken to remedy the grievances. There is a penalty for non-compliance.
>
> Amendments to the Ombudsman Act 1989 ensure that the Ombudsman has no jurisdiction over the Commissioner or staff of the Health Complaints Unit and that the Ombudsman does not have jurisdiction to investigate actions, and/or decisions, of the Commissioner or staff of the Health Complaints Unit. The Ombudsman must refer a complaint to the Commissioner if the Ombudsman determines it is within the Commissioner's jurisdiction . . .

The Commonwealth Attorney General's Department *Justice Statement*, 1995, Canberra: AGPS supports the development of standards for consumer dispute schemes which cover:

- independence and impartiality;
- accessibility and timeliness;
- efficiency and effectiveness;
- openness and accountability;
- consumer participation;
- data collection and reporting requirements.

How well do the existing complaints schemes reflect the above standards?

PART II: DISCIPLINARY PROCEEDINGS

Strictly speaking, disciplinary proceedings are not really a patient complaint procedure. This is because, as Wallace points out (below), the purpose of the proceedings are different. They are not instituted to punish an offending health care practitioner (unlike criminal proceedings), nor to recompense the patient who has suffered harm (unlike a tortious action). Rather, their purpose is the maintenance of standards within the relevant profession.

Given the plethora of registration bodies concerned in health care (and the fact that Australia has six States and two Territories, each of which has their own registering and disciplinary authorities!) it is not possible, in a work of this kind, to canvass disciplinary proceedings in any detail. Readers interested in this area of the law are referred to the *Australian Health and Medical Law Reporter* published by CCH. For the moment, some general comments will be offered.

The first thing to note is that, even within the same profession, there are great differences between States as to what matters may lead a person to be dealt with by a disciplinary body. Most States provide for a person to be disciplined if he or she is practising while suffering from ill health which affects his or her ability to practise or if he or she is practising while suffering from an addiction to alcohol or drugs. Most jurisdictions also recognise the offence of professional misconduct. Beyond that, there is little in common.

Wallace provides a very good summary of reported and unreported cases as to what amounts to misconduct.

Wallace, M, *Health Care and the Law*, 2nd edn, 1995, Sydney: Lawbook Co, pp 289–97

***Ex parte Meehan; Re Medical Practitioners Act* [1965] NSWR 30**

A doctor carried out major elective surgery without the presence of another practitioner to assist with surgical procedures or to administer anaesthetics. No harm occurred to the patients, but his behaviour was found to be misconduct and he was suspended for 12 months. He appealed to the New South Wales Court of Appeal.

The Court of Appeal decided that the doctor had been ill-advised, neither reckless nor indifferent to the patient's welfare. It agreed that this was, however, misconduct:

> . . . the only generalisation as to the meaning . . . of 'infamous conduct in any professional respect' [the wording of the relevant legislation] which can be attempted as capable of application to the varying situations which may arise, is that it refers to conduct which, being sufficiently related to the pursuit of the profession, is such as would reasonably incur the strong reprobation of professional brethren of good repute and competence.

The court reduced the suspension to a reprimand, because it was convinced the doctor would not repeat the conduct.

***Heathcote v New South Wales Nurses Board*, unreported, 12 April 1991, District Court of NSW**

On the night of 24 June 1987, at 2.10 am, a patient was brought to Wilcannia Hospital by his relatives. He was described as being 'in the dings', a colloquial term meaning suffering from alcohol withdrawal. He was hallucinating, but he had no signs of tremor, vomiting, sweating, or feeling hot or cold, nor was he complaining of any head or chest pain. The charge nurse, Nurse Heathcote, decided he was not seriously ill. She checked his history and found he had previously been admitted for alcohol withdrawal.

The patient, confused and vague, wandered around the premises and disappeared temporarily, returning with wood to boil the billy for tea. Nurse Heathcote had rung the police because she feared for the patient's wellbeing when he disappeared. He disappeared a second time, and so Nurse Heathcote rang the Director of Nursing at her home and told her about her concerns for the patient's safety. The Director of Nursing agreed with her contacting the police.

The police arrived soon after with the patient in their 'paddy wagon', and in their presence Nurse Heathcote rang the medical officer of the Royal Flying Doctor Service at Broken Hill and discussed the situation with him. She stated her concern that she could not ensure the safety of the patient in his present condition, as she had no adequate means of restraining him. She explained his condition and suggested he remain in police custody overnight. The doctor agreed, saying that the only other thing she should do 'before he heads off to the police station is just do his sugar . . . And wish him well as he goes away'.

After a blood sugar test, which was normal, was carried out, Nurse Heathcote arranged with the police that they should let her know how the patient settled at the Police Station. She undertook to call in at 8.30 in the morning to take his blood pressure. At 3 am, the police reported that the patient was 'sleeping', but at 8.30 am, when she called at the Station, they informed her that he was dead, having hung himself.

Subsequently, a complaint was made to the NSW Nurses Registration Board under s 19 of the Nurses Registration Act 1953 which was then in force. Nurse Heathcote was found guilty of misconduct by the Board, which suspended her registration for one year. She appealed to the District Court as provided by the former Act.

The District Court overturned the finding of the Board, thus exonerating the nurse's care of the patient. Ward J in his judgment stated that conduct cannot always be assessed in abstract terms and by consideration of textbook or teaching utterances. It must be considered in the light of the circumstances existing at the time, including available facilities, misunderstandings, and 'aberrant human behaviour'. He went on to say that the question to which the Board must address itself is, 'does the conduct of the nurse incur the strong reprobation of professional peers of good repute and competence?'

The court held that Nurse Heathcote did make a proper systematic assessment within the limits of what was available to her in terms of co-operation by the patient, the amount of time available to her, and within the scale of priorities she faced at the time. She was trying, by observation, to find the cause of the patient's condition and was faced with some difficulty as he was 'wandering uncontrollably'. She did make and record adequate observations under the circumstances. She was faced with a novel situation, did not know what to do, and sought assistance from the Director of Nursing and the doctor.

The court further held that Nurse Heathcote did read the history and inform the doctor of it. No further information had been sought by the doctor. Also, there was strong argument before the court that medical diagnosis is not part of a nurse's practice. Nurse Heathcote did state her opinion that the patient was 'in the dings', and the doctor did not indicate that he did not understand that expression. However, the doctor was not entitled to rely on her diagnosis. One witness did suggest that Nurse Heathcote should have insisted on either the doctor coming to see the patient or his being sent to another hospital with better facilities. The court nevertheless decided that 'It is not sufficient for some peers merely to express criticisms of judgments when other judgments are properly open in the circumstances' and relied on the fact that 'there was a strong body of opinion that none of her conduct was such as to incur the strong reprobation of her professional peers of good repute and competence'.

Ward J went on to say Nurse Heathcote did not have a duty to determine the suitability of the police custody and noted that she did ask the police to report to her, and arranged to check on the patient in the morning. Finally, he held that there was no obligation to consider alternative treatment, as the doctor had directed she 'only' take patient's blood pressure and 'wish him well as he goes away'.

It would appear that there can be problems when disciplinary provisions are very general and quite vague. They depend on past court decisions, and therefore do not give clear directions to nurses. They do not consider the particular nature of the nurse's role, and the fact that nurses, unlike other professionals, may be employees of hospitals, working under the direction of doctors, as well as exercising their own judgment in some matters, and thus may face a conflict of responsibilities. However, Ward J pointed out at p 21 of the decision, it is also necessary to take account of the fact that:

> . . . conduct cannot be always assessed in the abstract. It must be evaluated in the light of the exigencies existing due to factors which often include aberrant human behaviour, insufficient facilities, misunderstandings due to language use. It is important the court directs its attention in relation to consideration of professional misconduct to the question – does the conduct of the nurse incur strong reprobation of professional peers of good repute and competence? – and that it recognises that what may appear initially to be misconduct will not necessarily be deemed so, if it is considered to be acceptable by a reputable minority view. The test is not met merely by finding contentious areas of criticism, often founded on abstract conceptions without consideration of existing unusual circumstances.

One must distinguish between conduct, which may be improper and reprehensible in a general sense, and that which is improper and reprehensible in a professional sense.

Hoile v Medical Board of South Australia **(1960) 104 CLR 157**

A doctor had formed and pursued a sexual relationship with a nurse in the hospital. He was the medical superintendent of the hospital, and sexual activity occurred on hospital premises while the woman was on duty and on at least one occasion she was the only nurse on duty. This was held by the Medical Board to be misconduct. The doctor appealed to the High Court.

The court held:

> [Not all] departures on the part of a medical practitioner from the standards of moral conduct amount to misconduct in a professional respect. But if his professional relationships are the occasion or source of the misconduct and it is sufficiently serious it may be deemed by the Medical Board to be infamous conduct in a professional respect.

In this case the activity was held to be professional misconduct for:

> However much the general moral aspect of the matter may be emphasised as going to the relationship between man and woman, it remains true that the place was the hospital, the woman was a nurse, the man a doctor and moreover superintendent of the hospital.

A recent case which set out some general guidelines regarding the nature of misconduct is *Pillai v Messiter (No 2)* (1989) 16 NSWLR 197. In that case, the court (*per* Kirby P) made the following points:

> The purpose of discipline is protection of the public from not only 'delinquents and wrongdoers within professions' but also 'seriously incompetent professional people' who are 'ignorant of basic rules or indifferent as to rudimentary professional requirements'.
>
> Something more than professional incompetence or deficiencies in practice is required:
>
> It includes a deliberate departure from accepted standards or such serious negligence as, although not deliberate, to portray indifference and an abuse of the privileges which accompany registration as a medical practitioner.

The court also considered the effect of removal of the appellant from the register, considering whether this would achieve the objective of protecting the public. It decided it would not, as the event was an isolated, unintended error, which could not have been prevented by removal of the doctor from registration. Also, others had failed to notice the mistake, making the punishment of one person inappropriate.

Versteegh v Nurses Board of South Australia, Supreme Court of South Australia, 4 December 1992 (*Australian Health and Medical Law Reporter*, para 77–064)

A registered nurse was found guilty of professional misconduct under s 41 of the Nurses Act 1984. She was reprimanded by the registration board, and certain conditions placed on her right to provide nursing care. The Board had referred to its own guidelines, the policy of the nursing home where she worked, legislation on drugs and the International Council of Nursing Code of Ethics. The nurse faced charges in relation to:

(a) drugs (failing to give residents drugs as prescribed, failing to check, count and record as required by law, discarding a bottle that contained methadone tablets, and failing to record administration of drugs);
(b) breach of confidentiality (requesting a medical practitioner other than the resident's own practitioner to review the resident's leg ulcer without seeking the resident's consent or authority from her doctor);
(c) unsatisfactory nursing care (not permitting a patient with multiple

sclerosis to be seated when being washed, causing pain and suffering).

The nurse appealed to the Supreme Court arguing, among other things, that she had not fallen short of the required standard. She argued that in respect of (a), she had rather made a simple mistake in some circumstances, and in others had failed to make necessary entries because she had been very busy. In respect of (b), she argued that she had only been trying to act in the patient's best interests, and in respect of (c), she had acted in the most suitable way in the circumstances.

The court held that the failure to give drugs when they were prescribed and to make accurate records of drug administration was likely to compromise the care of the residents significantly. It noted the importance of checking drugs to ensure none are missing . . . It also found that the nurse had breached confidentiality by calling in another doctor. She could not say she was acting in the resident's interest, it concluded, for if she was, she would have discussed the matter with the resident's practitioner (and, one might add, the resident) first. Finally, conduct with the resident suffering from multiple sclerosis could not be excused on the basis that she had acted according to her own judgment (as presumably her judgment should have led her to treat the resident differently). The court held that 'unprofessional conduct' has a broader meaning than common law negligence and is not limited to 'disgraceful or dishonourable' conduct. Rather, it is conduct which falls short of that followed and approved of by other members of the nursing profession.

Two cases which involved what was considered misconduct, but which attracted different responses by the respective Medical Boards give insight into the legal approach to the intention of the practitioner involved.

Ex parte Fitzgerald; Re New South Wales Medical Board (1945) 46 SR (NSW) 111

A practitioner issued a certificate under the Lunacy Act 1898 (NSW) in circumstances the board found to be 'gravely and inexcusably wrong'. He had not examined the person for whom the certificate was written. The doctor was suspended for 12 months. He appealed to the Supreme Court.

The court, while accepting the gravity of the behaviour, nevertheless allowed the doctor to retain his practising certificate. Jordan CJ said that this case was exceptional, and indicated that the court would consider the general depravity or lack of scruple on the part of the doctor; or the likelihood of repetition of the behaviour.

Stevenson v Medical Board of Victoria, unreported, Supreme Court of Victoria, 27 June 1986

A doctor dealing with home births diagnosed pre-eclampsia but 'deliberately prescribed a course of treatment which he knew was unorthodox and contrary to long-accepted medical opinion and practice, and he thereby, and knowingly, put at serious risk both the mother and the foetus'.

The court found against the doctor because he acted on beliefs which had no reasonable scientific foundation, which had been given no scientific credence, and which, the court held, he must have known were likely to endanger the mother and child irrespective of the correctness of beliefs. One should not act on beliefs which have no established scientific foundation, and are not accepted by one's profession, and would put another person in danger, even if one believes one is right.

Cranley v Medical Board of Western Australia, Supreme Court of Western Australia, 21 December 1990 (*Australian Health and Medical Law Reporter*, para 77–036)

A doctor had been charged with infamous behaviour in a professional respect under the Medical Act 1984. He had adopted the 'harm reduction' approach to drug addiction. This involved prescribing for known drug addicts doses of intravenous Valium for self-administration, oral Doloxene and Valium, and oral Rohypnol and Valium. The doctor prescribed these drugs because, under the circumstances, the physical and social harm resulting from this approach to treatment of the patients justified the risk of abuse. He argued that the addicts were 'needle-fixated', that Schedule 4 drugs were less harmful than Schedule 8 drugs, and that the substitution of these drugs could lead to a cure. The Board rejected this approach and opted instead to rule that on the basis that (1) the treatment was not orthodox treatment and (2) by regulation the prescription of the drugs should have been authorised by the Health Department the doctor was guilty of the charge. The doctor appealed to the Supreme Court.

The Supreme Court, in relation to (1), accepted evidence that although the doctor's treatment was unorthodox, there was a 'respectable' body of medical opinion which recognised the potential therapeutic value of the 'harm reduction' approach It would not be appropriate to find someone who did not follow the orthodox approach guilty of misconduct on that basis alone. There might be a fine line between harm reduction strategy and misconduct, but it would be unsafe to find misconduct on the basis of particular doctors disagreeing with his judgment. In relation to (2), the court held that although the doctor should have notified the Health Department, his failure to do so did not in the circumstances constitute misconduct . . .

In most States, conviction for a serious criminal offence can render a person subject to disciplinary procedures. The seriousness of the offence in some cases is defined by the penalty it attracts; there being no specific definition in others. Criminal conviction itself need not lead to disqualification from practising.

Skinner v Beaumont [1974] 2 NSWLR 106

The doctor in this case had been convicted of conspiring to unlawfully procure two miscarriages. He had referred them to an unregistered practitioner. He was duly removed from the medical register. He appealed against that removal on the grounds that it was not in the public interest for disqualification for this type of offence.

Hutley J of the Supreme Court held (at 109):

> The deliberate defiance, even with good motives, of a legal and professional responsibility, cannot in my opinion be excused, otherwise the distribution of drugs to alleviate the cravings of addicts would be an exculpatory circumstance.

However, he considered the doctor's good reputation and the fact that the occasion would not arise again (due to change in the law which made abortion more widely available). This fact, the judge said, was critical to his decision. He also considered the welfare of the public, declaring that it would be deprived of a good practitioner.

Contrast this case with the following one:

Basser v Medical Board of Victoria [1981] VR 953

A doctor provided prescriptions to patients for toxic drugs improperly and unreasonably, without proper medical grounds and in greater than reasonable doses. He neither examined the patients adequately nor supervised their use of the medication. His name was removed from the register. He appealed from this decision to the Supreme Court.

The court treated his behaviour as very serious, here invoking such descriptions as reckless indifference and gross negligence. Although they did not consider the criminality or otherwise of his actions. The court said:

> It should not be accepted that the concept of moral turpitude was an additional ingredient in every charge of infamous conduct. If a sense of reckless indifference or gross negligence were proven against a medical practitioner in any respect, right-thinking colleagues of the person charged would inevitably regard such conduct as reprehensible, disgraceful, shameful or dishonourable.

In the third edition of her work (2001) Wallace (at 432–436) additionally refers to the following examples of conduct which might amount to unprofessional conduct or misconduct:

- Provision of drugs to Addicts of Cash and Other Services (*Kirumba v Walton* 4th Oct 1990, CA (NSW));

- Intimate Relations with Clients or Past Clients (*Childs v Walton* 13 November 1990, CA (NSW); *Jacobsen v Nurses Tribunal and Anor* 3 October 1997, SC NSW);
- Failure to Properly Assess and Treat Injuries to a Child (*Medical Board of South Australia v Christpoulos* (2000) SADC 47).

Wallace correctly cautions '. . . what constitutes conduct that is considered grave enough for disciplinary action depends so heavily on circumstances and perceived standards of professional conduct' (at 432).

Given that disciplinary proceedings are regarded as being civil proceedings, it is possible for a practitioner to be the subject of both a criminal prosecution and punishment, as well as a disciplinary body hearing and punishment. This might occur, for example, where a medical practitioner was accused of committing an indecent assault on a patient. The application of this idea has been explored in the New Zealand context by Andrew Alston. See Alston, A, 'When a medical practitioner's conduct is subject to both criminal and professional disciplinary proceedings', in Pietrovicz, R, Volume III, 1994, *ALTA Conference Proceedings* 1149.

INDEX

For Product Safety Concerns and Information please contact our EU representative GPSR@taylorandfrancis.com
Taylor & Francis Verlag GmbH, Kaufingerstraße 24, 80331 München, Germany

www.ingramcontent.com/pod-product-compliance
Lightning Source LLC
LaVergne TN
LVHW020950300926
849160LV00007B/99